NORTH CAROLINA TROOPS
1861-1865
A ROSTER

Richmond June 1st 1862

Dear Father

I reached Richmond Wednesday evening and met a man who said he could give us a house if we had provision so he [took our] baggage to the house of me [several] of [our] company in Richmond Lieut Northington was [here] and I went to him and he sent several of [the] men to the Regiment with us I reached the place [Saturday] evening. Our Boys was in the fight [the yankees got our] wounded in which number was [Bob] Wood Tom Warren and another man [out of] our company We had others wounded but [they] made their escape 2 Oun[r] boys lost their [clothing and everything] [?] [with] out anything except what they have got on we are in the woods and havent got a tent in the Regiment we had the hardest rain I ever saw the night I reached here I made a shelter with my blanket and slept on the ground. Brother is not very well but he stood picket the night it rained so hard he staid with me last night he will stay with me all the time. We have bin under marching orders two day we are about twelve miles from Richmond I heard heavy cannonading yesterday and this morning below Richmond Brother will send for the recruits and the men that ran away all the men we save at Weldon ran away. There are thirty of our men on the sick list some are sick and some are not we sent all of our sick to Petersburg. I am not well but I will try to stay with the company. Direct your letter to Richmond care of Col. Wade 12. Reg N.C. State troops my love to all write soon to your son

J. B. Brickell

Letter from Private James B. Brickell, Company G, Twelfth Regiment N.C. Troops, to his father, June 1, 1862, following the battle of Seven Pines, Virginia, May 31, 1862. The letter is among the James B. Brickell Papers in the Division of Archives and History of the North Carolina Department of Cultural Resources, Raleigh.

North Carolina Troops
1861-1865
A Roster

COMPILED BY
WEYMOUTH T. JORDAN, JR.

UNIT HISTORIES BY
LOUIS H. MANARIN

VOL. V
INFANTRY

11th-15th
REGIMENTS

RALEIGH, NORTH CAROLINA

DIVISION OF ARCHIVES AND HISTORY

1975

©1975 by North Carolina Division of Archives and History
Printed and Bound by
The North Carolina State University Print Shop, Raleigh
and
The G & K Typesetting Service, Greensboro

PREFACE

This volume is the fifth in a projected series of thirteen volumes of a roster of North Carolinians who served in the Confederate and Union forces in the Civil War. Begun in February, 1961, the project to compile such a roster was an outgrowth of the work of the North Carolina Confederate Centennial Commission under the direction of its chairman, the late Colonel Hugh Dortch, and its executive secretary, Mr. Norman C. Larson. Dr. Louis H. Manarin, the editor of the first three volumes, was first a member of the Confederate Centennial Commission staff. At the termination of that commission in June, 1965, the Roster Project was transferred to the State Department of Archives and History (which, under state government reorganization, became the Division of Archives and History of the State Department of Cultural Resources). Dr. Manarin remained at the head of the project through January, 1970, when he resigned to become state archivist of Virginia. Dr. Manarin was succeeded by Mr. Weymouth T. Jordan, Jr., in the post of editor of the North Carolina Roster Project, but he has continued his services to his native state as the author of the unit histories which appear in this volume.

To both Mr. Jordan and Dr. Manarin and to Secretary Grace J. Rohrer of the Department of Cultural Resources; Dr. Robert E. Stipe, director of the Division of Archives and History; Mrs. Memory F. Mitchell, chief of the Historical Publications Section; and the staff of the Roster Project, I wish to express my appreciation for their efforts in making possible this memorial to those from our state who fought and died for North Carolina.

JAMES E. HOLSHOUSER, JR.

December 31, 1974

Governor of North Carolina

CONTENTS

INTRODUCTION

Information relative to the raising of military units in North Carolina, the size of those units, the manner in which they were designated, and the treatment in this series of Militia, Home Guard, Sharpshooter, and other miscellaneous units has been presented in the introductions to Volumes I - III and will not be repeated here. Readers seeking explanations of those points are referred to the volumes cited.

The principal source of information for the individual service records contained in this volume is the compiled military service records on file in Record Group 109 in the National Archives, Washington, D. C., and available on microfilm at the Division of Archives and History in Raleigh. Record Group 109 consists of individual service record envelopes for each soldier in which are filed data cards containing information abstracted from primary Civil War records. The envelopes are filed numerically by unit and then alphabetically by surname. Primary records from which information contained in the data cards was abstracted include company muster rolls, payrolls, rosters, appointment books, hospital registers, prison registers and rolls, parole rolls, inspection reports, and other records containing service record information. Some envelopes also contain primary documents such as enlistment and discharge papers, vouchers, and requisitions relating to the soldier's service. In addition to the foregoing primary sources, the Roll of Honor, compiled by the state adjutant general during the war, was loaned to federal authorities in Washington at the time Record Group 109 was compiled, and the information contained in the Roll was incorporated into the record group.

A second National Archives source utilized in this volume was the Papers of and Relating to Military and Civilian Personnel, 1861-1865. Those records consist of cards and manuscripts collected and compiled for Record Group 109 but, for various reasons, not filed in envelopes for individual soldiers.

Material obtained from the National Archives was supplemented by information contained in the records of the North Carolina State Archives. These included the records of the adjutant general and the registrar of commissions, muster rolls for periods not covered by muster rolls on file at the National Archives, bounty rolls, private letters and diaries, and state pension applications filed by Confederate veterans and their widows. Information relative to Confederate service was abstracted from membership applications, Cross of Honor certificates, and Cross of Military Service certificates in the possession of the North Carolina Division of the United Daughters of the Confederacy. Information was also abstracted from Confederate gravestone records compiled by the same organization. Also utilized were the published registers of Hollywood Cemetery, Richmond, Virginia; Stonewall Cemetery, Winchester, Virginia; the cemeteries at Sharpsburg, Maryland, and Gettysburg, Pennsylvania; and unpublished registers of Northern cemeteries compiled by the Office of the Quartermaster General, United States Army, in 1912 and 1914.

Because of the shortcomings of the *Roster of North Carolina Troops in the War Between the States,* edited by John W. Moore (Raleigh: [State of North Carolina], 4 volumes, 1882), hereinafter cited as Moore's *Roster,* that source and local rosters compiled from it were not used. However, in some instances, published and unpublished local rosters not based on Moore's *Roster* were utilized. The names of individual soldiers, together with any service record information available, were abstracted from *Histories of the Several Regiments and Battalions from North Carolina in the Great War, 1861-'65* (Raleigh and Goldsboro: State of North Carolina, 5 volumes, 1901), by Walter Clark, hereinafter cited as Clark's *Regiments,* and information from other relevant histories, published and unpublished, was also abstracted for use in this volume. Additional material was found in other manuscript repositories in North Carolina and several neighboring states, and correspondence was received from all over the country from interested individuals who supplied information about North Carolina soldiers. A final source, which has remained almost untouched because of lack of time and staff, is contemporary newspapers published in the state.

Information abstracted from the foregoing sources was arranged and consolidated for each member of each unit for which a roster appears in this volume. The method adopted for listing individual unit members is as follows:

Field and Staff: By rank and date of appointment, *e.g.*
                    Colonels, Lieutenant Colonels, Majors,
                    Adjutants, and staff members
Band: Alphabetically
Companies: 1. Officers
                       A. Captains: Chronologically by date of appointment
                       B. Lieutenants: Alphabetically
                    2. Enlisted men: Noncommissioned officers and Privates are listed alphabetically, regardless of rank. The "rank of final date" is cited after the soldier's name; promotions and demotions are reported in the service record. First Sergeants are listed as such, but Sergeants of other grades and Corporals of all grades are listed simply as Sergeants and Corporals.

Personal names are spelled as they were spelled in primary records, the only exceptions being when a signature was available or when the soldier's descendants provided information concerning his name. A number of oddities and corruptions have undoubtedly resulted, and the index has been extensively cross-referenced to assist the researcher in locating names that may appear in corrupted form.

In composing the service records in this volume, the editor has cited as the enlistment date for each soldier the date of enlistment that was recorded for him on the earliest surviving muster roll of the company in which he served. The place of enlistment was derived from the same source. Actually, there were at least four dates on which a soldier might be reported to have entered service: the date he enrolled for service, the date he enlisted, the date his unit was mustered into state service, and the date his unit was mustered into Confederate service. The *place* of enlistment might be the county where he enrolled for service, the town or county where he joined the unit to which he was assigned, or the camp of instruction to which he was assigned. No standard procedure was followed by company clerks in citing either the date or the place a soldier enlisted, and individual clerks would sometimes alter their previous procedure. However, if volunteers or conscripts reported to the company in a group they were usually mustered in as follows: date of enlistment recorded as the date they reported to their local recruiting or conscription officer for duty; place of enlistment recorded as either the camp of instruction to which the group was sent or the county in which the recruit volunteered or was conscripted. If volunteers or conscripts reported individually, the company clerk usually recorded the date and place of enlistment as the date and place the soldier joined the company. As the war progressed, and particularly in 1864-1865, the latter method came into general use.

In composing a service record for each soldier the editor has adhered to the following rules: All references to counties are as of 1861-1865 boundaries. In instances where primary records indicate that an individual was born in a county which had not been formed at the time of the individual's birth, an asterisk appears after the county (*e.g.*, Born in Alamance County*), and the assumption can probably be made that the individual in question was born at a locality that later became part of the county cited. All references to cities and towns are as of their 1861-1865 designation; however, in instances where the place name has been changed the 1861-1865 designation is followed by the current designation in parentheses—*e.g.*, Smithville (Southport). Place names of North Carolina counties, cities, towns, etc., are not followed by reference to the state except for clarity (*e.g.*, Greensboro; but Washington, North Carolina). Place names for counties and localities in other states are followed by the name of the state only on the first occasion they are mentioned in a service record. In a few cases it proved impossible to ascertain the state in which a hamlet or geographical feature was located, either because no such place name could be located at all or because two or more places with the same name were located in two or more states and no evidence was available as to which of the places was the one intended. Such place names appear in quotation marks in this volume (*e.g.*, "Table Knob," or "Warrenton"). Quotation marks are also used in cases where a battle and a date cited in primary records are contradictory (*e.g.*, Killed at "Sharpsburg, Maryland, July 3, 1863.") West Virginia place names are cited as being in West Virginia only if the reference is on or subsequent to June 20, 1863, the date West Virginia was admitted to the Union. If the citation is prior to that date, the locality is listed as being in Virginia; hence, some place names may be listed as being in West Virginia in one service record but as being in Virginia in a second one (*e.g.,* Martinsburg).

The phrase "on or about" is used when a historical event such as a battle is cited in primary records as having taken place on a date that only approximates the date on which the event actually occurred (*e.g.,* Wounded at Gettysburg, Pennsylvania, on or about July 5, 1863.) This phrase is also used when an event which is not a verified or verifiable historical fact is cited in primary records as having occurred on two or more dates which are more or less consecutive, the date cited being the one which seems most probably correct on the basis of available evidence (*e.g.,* Died at Raleigh on or about April 8, 1864.) In instances where there is no reason to favor one such date as being more probably correct than another, hyphenated dates are given if the dates are more or less consecutive (*e.g.,* Died at Raleigh, April 2-8, 1864.) When such dates are not more or less consecutive they are cited individually (*e.g.,* Died at Raleigh, April 2 or June 5, 1864.) Hyphenated dates preceded by the word "in" indicate a single event that happened during the period in question (*e.g.,* Hospitalized at Goldsboro in July-August, 1863), but dates preceded by the word "during" indicate a condition that prevailed *throughout* the period in question (*e.g.,* Hospitalized at Goldsboro during July-August, 1863.) Again, this system was found necessary because in many instances the exact date of an event could not be determined.

The phrase "present or accounted for" is used to indicate that a soldier was either present for duty or absent for reasons other than desertion or extended absence without leave (*i.e.,* sixty days or more). Desertion and absence without leave were apparently considered synonymous terms by many company clerks; hence, a soldier who absented himself without authorization but returned of his own accord sixty days later might be listed as a deserter in the records of one company, while a man who absented himself from another company for the same period and under the same circumstances might merely be listed as absent without leave. The editor has judged it best not to standardize these terms, however inequitable the prevailing system may now seem, and references to desertion or absence without leave are, in the overwhelming majority of cases, direct quotations from primary sources. Because of space limitations, no reference whatever is made to unauthorized absences of less than sixty days.

When the word "reported" appears at the beginning of a sentence and is not followed by a reference to the source of the report, company records of one kind or another are the source that should be inferred. In some instances, failure to keep this point in mind may result in confusion (*e.g.,* Reported captured at Sharpsburg, Maryland, September 17, 1862; however, records of the Federal Provost Marshal do not substantiate that report.)

During the fourteen years since the inception of the roster project rules of capitalization, punctuation, and style have changed considerably. For example, it is no longer considered good form to capitalize an individual's title or rank unless it appears before his name. However, except in those few instances where a new system provided greater clarity or seemed distinctly advantageous, systems employed in earlier volumes have been retained. One particularly noticeable punctuation oddity that perhaps should be mentioned involves the use in the possessive case of singular nouns ending in "s." Personal names are rendered "s's" (*e.g.,* Jones's men), but, on the theory that the historic spelling of a place name cannot be altered by a change in rules of modern punctuation, place names ending in the possessive are rendered without the final "s" (*e.g.,* Gaines' Mill, Virginia). The reader will also note some deviation from contemporary rules relating to the hyphenization of words at the end of lines. Because of the exteme brevity of the lines-of-print in this volume, such deviations were unavoidable.

In compiling a roster of the 11th Regiment N.C. Troops (1st Regiment N.C. Volunteers), it was found that many soldiers who served in that regiment served previously in the 1st Regiment N.C. Infantry (6 months, 1861)—for which a roster was published in Volume III of this series—and enlisted in the 11th Regiment after the 1st Infantry was disbanded. In most cases, men who served together in a given company of the 1st Infantry later enlisted in a given company of the 11th Regiment; *e.g.,* former members of Company D, 1st Infantry generally enlisted in Company G, 11th Regiment. Primary records of the 11th Regiment contain citations establishing previous service in the 1st Infantry for some of these men; however, for many of them the only evidence that they served in both regiments is that their names are found, often in forms that are not precisely identical, in the records of both regiments. The editor has deemed it injudicious to assume in all cases that such parallelism establishes previous service in the 1st Infantry, especially when an undistinctive name is involved. Therefore, no statement of previous service in the 1st Infantry has been made in service records of members of the 11th Regiment unless a positive statement to that effect was found in primary records or unless the following conditions were met: (1) the name of a soldier who served in a given company of the 11th Regiment was found in the records of a company of the 1st Infantry in which other members of that company of the 11th Regiment are known to have served; (2) the soldier's name was relatively distinctive and (except for minor differences in spelling or instances where initials are given instead of names) was the same in the records of both regiments; (3) the soldier's county of birth and residence (if cited) were identical in the records of both regiments; (4) the age of the soldier, if cited in the records of both regiments, was not contradictory (a time lag, as well as an error factor of two years, was allowed for). A certain degree of flexibility has been employed in observing these rules, but, generally speaking, unless the foregoing conditions prevailed, a soldier listed in the 11th Regiment was not cited as having served previously in the 1st Infantry. In cases where the above criteria were substantially but inconclusively met, service records are followed by a statement in brackets to the effect that the soldier in question *may* have served previously in a certain company of the 1st Infantry.

The problem of cross-referencing service records of soldiers who served in two or more units is not limited to men who served in the 1st Infantry and 11th Regiment but is sufficiently chronic to merit further discussion at this point. A specific case may serve best to illustrate the difficulties involved and the precautions that should be taken by users of *North Carolina Troops*. Private William T. Wood originally enlisted in Company A, 17th Regiment N.C. Troops (2nd Organization). In November, 1862, he was transferred to Company B, 8th Regiment N.C. State Troops. His service record in the roster for Company A, 17th Regiment should therefore conclude with a statement that he was transferred to Company B, 8th Regiment in November, 1862, and his service record in the roster for Company B, 8th Regiment should begin with a statement that he served previously in Company A, 17th Regiment and was transferred to the 8th Regiment in November, 1862. Unfortunately, as often happens in the case of transferees, there was no record in the files of the 8th Regiment of Private Wood's previous service in the 17th Regiment, and the roster for the 8th Regiment was already in print when his previous service in the 17th Regiment was discovered in the records of the latter unit; hence, the appropriate cross-reference in the roster of the 8th Regiment was omitted. In an attempt to circumvent cross-referencing problems of the foregoing type, an effort has been made to locate additional records for soldiers whose careers either begin abruptly in mid-war or terminate inexplicably; however, for a variety of technical reasons that was not always possible. Therefore, until a revised edition of *North Carolina Troops* is published at some uncertain but probably far distant date, reference should be made to the index of each volume in this series (or to the master index that will be published at its conclusion) whenever the service record of a soldier begins or terminates in a manner that does not preclude the possibility of previous or later service in another unit.

I would like to express my sincere appreciation to those persons who have contributed to the publication of this volume:

—Mr. C. F. W. Coker, former chief of the Archives and Records Section of this department; Dr. Thornton W. Mitchell, current chief of the Archives and Records Section; and Mrs. Memory F. Mitchell, chief of the Historical Publications Section, provided valuable support, guidance, and counsel.

—Miss Marie D. Moore, historical publications editor with the Historical Publications Section, read the unit histories in manuscript and advised the editor in matters of style, syntax, grammar, and punctuation.

—Mr. Ersell C. Liles, senior editorial assistant of the roster project (October, 1971-May, 1972), abstracted the service records upon which the entire roster of the 12th Regiment N.C. Troops (2nd Regiment N.C. Volunteers) is based.

—Miss Dianne G. Massey, editorial assistant of the roster project (June, 1969-December, 1973, and June-August, 1974), made many important contributions through her attention to accuracy, consistency, and detail.

—Miss Margaret S. Odell, editorial assistant of the roster project (January-May, 1974), and Miss Eleanor E. Hill, who now serves in that capacity, assisted with the proofreading and were distinguished for the accuracy and volume of their work.

—Mrs. Rose P. Ennemoser, secretary of the roster project since March, 1973, typed the entire manuscript for this volume, compiled the index, and performed all of her secretarial and clerical duties with exceptional reliability, accuracy, patience, and good humor.

—Mr. James Walker of the staff of the National Archives and Records Service provided valuable guidance and assistance during the course of a research visit by the editor to that institution.

—Mr. S. H. Harrington of Erwin, North Carolina, provided information concerning the local designations of several companies for which rosters are published in this volume.

Weymouth T. Jordan, Jr.
Editor

December 31, 1974

NORTH CAROLINA TROOPS

1861-1865

A ROSTER

11th REGIMENT N. C. TROOPS

(1st REGIMENT N. C. VOLUNTEERS)

This regiment was the successor of the 1st Regiment N.C. Infantry (6 months, 1861), which had been mustered in for six months' service on May 13, 1861, as the 1st Regiment of North Carolina Volunteers. By Special Orders No. 222, Adjutant and Inspector General's Office, Richmond, dated November 14, 1861, the volunteer regiments from North Carolina were redesignated from 1 through 14 to 11 through 24. This was done to clear up the confusion resulting from the fact that the State Troops regiments had been numbered 1 through 10. Under Special Orders No. 222, the 1st Regiment of North Carolina Volunteers, which had been called the Bethel Regiment because of its action at Big Bethel on June 10, 1861, was to be redesignated the 11th Regiment N.C. Troops (1st Regiment N.C. Volunteers); however, the regiment was mustered out of service the day before the order was issued. Since the 1st Regiment of North Carolina Volunteers was no longer in service, there was, for the time being, no unit designated 11th Regiment N.C. Troops (1st Regiment N.C. Volunteers).

It was not until March, 1862, that a regiment was organized to fill the vacancy. It was recognized as the successor of the 1st Regiment of North Carolina Volunteers, known as the Bethel Regiment, and was to be composed of men who had served in the original regiment. Although many of the men from the original six months' regiment enlisted in the new regiment, many had already enlisted in other units, and two companies from the old regiment joined other regiments prior to the formation of the new regiment. When this regiment was organized at Camp Mangum, near Raleigh, on March 31, 1862, it was recognized as the successor to the 1st Regiment of North Carolina Volunteers and was designated the 11th Regiment N.C. Troops (1st Regiment N.C. Volunteers). At the same time it adopted the appellation of Bethel Regiment. To avoid confusion, the 1st Regiment of North Carolina Volunteers was later officially referred to as the 1st Regiment N.C. Infantry (6 months, 1861). In reality, the 1st Regiment of North Carolina Volunteers, later referred to as the 1st Regiment N.C. Infantry (6 months, 1861), and the 11th Regiment N.C. Troops (1st Regiment N.C. Volunteers) were two distinct regiments. The first was known as the Bethel Regiment because it fought at Big Bethel. The second adopted the name of Bethel Regiment because it was considered as the successor to the first and because it contained men who had served in the original regiment.

The 11th Regiment N.C. Troops (1st Regiment N.C. Volunteers) remained at Camp Mangum until early May, 1862, when it was ordered to Wilmington. There the regiment was assigned to the garrison and went into camp at Camp Davis, Topsail Sound. In June the regiment moved to Camp Lamb, near Wilmington. There it remained until August when it returned to Camp Davis. During the month of August, Companies I and K were stationed at Fowler's Point. While in the Wilmington area the regiment spent most of its time drilling and adapting to routine camp life.

On October 5, 1862, the regiment was transferred to the Blackwater River line in Virginia. While stationed at Camp Wilson, near Franklin, Virginia, detachments from the regiment patrolled the river. The regiment was ordered to Kinston on December 13 to join the force resisting a Federal force advancing from New Bern under General John G. Foster. Arriving the night of December 14, the regiment joined the Confederate troops under General N. G. Evans who, following the loss of Kinston that day, had prepared a line of battle about two miles east of the town. The next day, December 15, he ordered his command to retire toward Goldsboro. As the troops withdrew, General Evans placed this regiment, together with some artillery and infantry, under the command of General B. H. Robertson, who was ordered to defend the Neuse River crossing at White Hall (Seven Springs). On December 16, General Foster arrived at White Hall, eighteen miles southeast of Goldsboro. There he found the bridge burned and General Robertson's forces posted on the opposite bank of the river. After making a strong feint as if he intended to rebuild the bridge, General Foster retired his command toward Goldsboro. General Robertson reported the action as follows (*O.R., S.I., Vol. XVIII, pp. 121-122*):

About 9 a.m. on the 16th a brisk picket skirmish commenced. I visited the bridge, and after giving the necessary instructions went back to order up the Thirty-first North Carolina Regiment, Col. [John V.] Jordan, which had arrived during the night, and which I placed in position as much sheltered as circumstances would permit. I then posted the artillery as well as the nature of the ground would admit and ordered both shell and solid shot to be fired. For some time previous the enemy had been firing from 12 to 18 pounders, some of immense caliber. Owing to a range of hills on the White Hall side the enemy had the advantage of position. The point occupied by his troops being narrow, not more than one regiment at a time could advantageously engage him. I therefore held [Colonel Collett] Leventhorpe, [Colonel D. D.] Ferebee, and [General N. G.] Evans in reserve, leaving the artillery, Thirty-first Regiment and two picket companies in front. The cannonading from the enemy's batteries became so terrific that the Thirty-first Regiment withdrew from their position without instructions but in good order. I immediately ordered Colonel Leventhorpe forward [with the 11th Regiment N.C. Troops (1st Regiment N.C. Volunteers)]. The alacrity with which the order was obeyed by his men gave ample proof of their gallant bearing, which they so nobly sustained during the entire fight, which raged with intensity for several hours after they became engaged. No veteran soldiers ever fought better or inflicted more terrible loss upon an enemy considering the numbers engaged. It was with difficulty they could be withdrawn from the field. Three times did they drive the Yankee cannoneers from their guns and as often prevent their infantry regiments from forming line in their front. In spite of the four hostile regiments whose standards waved from the opposite bank did these brave men continue to hold their ground, and finally drove the enemy in confusion from the field. More than 100 of their dead and wounded were left upon the river bank. The conduct of this regiment reflects the greatest credit upon its accomplished and dauntless commander.

Colonel Ferebee, of the Fifty-ninth Regiment, displayed the most signal coolness and courage. For several hours, with 18 men of the picket guard belonging to the Eleventh Regiment, he fought the enemy at close quarters, notwithstanding his own command was not in action.

A report of casualties at White Hall noted that the regiment lost 7 killed and 20 wounded.

The next day, December 17, the regiment was ordered to Goldsboro, where it arrived after the fighting. After destroying the railroad bridge below Goldsboro on December 17, General Foster retired with his command to New Bern. General Evans's troops reoccupied Kinston on December 22, and that night the regiment was ordered to Weldon. There it went into camp at Camp Robinson, where it was assigned to General James Johnston Pettigrew's brigade. In addition to this regiment, Pettigrew's brigade consisted of the 26th Regiment N.C. Troops, 44th Regiment N.C. Troops, 47th Regiment N.C. Troops, and the 52nd Regiment N.C. Troops. Although the head-quarters of the brigade was at Petersburg, Virginia, regiments were detached to protect the railroad from Petersburg to Magnolia, North Carolina. This regiment was detached from the brigade in January, 1863, and stationed at Greenville, where it undertook to protect the area from enemy raiding parties and collected commissary supplies.

In March, 1863, Pettigrew's brigade took part in General D. H. Hill's unsuccessful campaign to capture New Bern and Washington, North Carolina. General Hill planned a three-pronged attack on New Bern. One force was to move on New Bern while two flanking columns were to cut off the town and silence supporting batteries. Pettigrew's brigade was to move from Magnolia to shell Fort Anderson on the Neuse River. On March 13 the force in the center captured the Federal entrenchments at Deep Gully, about eight miles from New Bern. Pettigrew started his bombardment the next day but found his artillery was worthless. He decided not to attack the fort. The third column failed to accomplish its objective also, and General Hill was forced to abandon the attempt to capture New Bern. He then turned to Washington and laid siege to the town on March 30. While the town was under siege Pettigrew's brigade was engaged at Blount's Creek on April 11 and turned back a Federal relief column. The movement of Federal reinforcements up the Pamlico River to Washington on April 13 forced General Hill to abandon the siege on April 15.

Following the unsuccessful campaign, the regiments of the brigade were again detached, and toward the end of April the regiment moved by way of Hookerton to Kinston to meet a Federal demonstration. On May 1, 1863, Pettigrew's brigade

boarded the railroad cars at Kinston under orders to move to Richmond, Virginia. Upon arriving at Richmond, a portion of the brigade was ordered to Hanover Junction, and detachments were sent to protect the railroad and the bridges over the North Anna and South Anna rivers against a Federal cavalry raid. After the threat passed, the brigade was consolidated at Hanover Junction. From there the brigade moved up to Hamilton's Crossing, near Fredericksburg, Virginia, early in June. There the brigade was assigned to General Henry Heth's division, General A. P. Hill's corps, Army of Northern Virginia.

General Lee put his army in motion toward the Shenandoah Valley on June 4 to begin the campaign that would end at Gettysburg, Pennsylvania. General Richard Ewell's corps moved first and was followed by General James Longstreet's corps. General Hill's corps remained at Fredericksburg to watch the Federal forces opposite the town. Ewell's corps moved into the valley and encountered the Federals at Winchester on June 13. General Longstreet's corps occupied Culpeper Court House. On June 13 the Federal forces at Fredericksburg began moving north, and Hill's corps moved up the Rappahannock River to follow the army. Just prior to the move, the 44th Regiment N.C. Troops was detached from Pettigrew's brigade; it remained at Hanover Junction and vicinity throughout the Gettysburg campaign. General Ewell's corps marched into Pennsylvania on June 22, and on June 24 Lee ordered Longstreet and Hill to follow. By June 27 Hill's corps was encamped near Chambersburg, Pennsylvania. On June 29 Hill was ordered to move to Cashtown, and Longstreet was directed to follow the next day. General Ewell's corps had proceeded eastward to Carlisle and was ordered to rejoin the army at Cashtown or Gettysburg as circumstances might require.

General Heth's division reached Cashtown on June 29, and the next morning Pettigrew's brigade was sent to procure supplies at Gettysburg. General Pettigrew found the town occupied by the enemy and withdrew to Cashtown. General Hill arrived at Cashtown with General W. Dorsey Pender's division during the evening of June 30 and decided to advance with Heth's and Pender's divisions the next morning. As Heth's division advanced, Pettigrew's brigade was held in reserve. After the first encounter with the enemy, Pettigrew's brigade was put in the center of Heth's line with General J. M. Brocken-brough's brigade on the left and General James J. Archer's brigade on the right. The order to advance came, and the whole line moved to encounter the enemy. As Heth's division became engaged, General Ewell's corps came in from Carlisle to strike the enemy on his right flank. After driving the enemy from three lines, Heth's division was relieved by Pender's division, and the attack continued until the Federals retired through Gettysburg to Cemetery Heights just south of the town. Major [John T.] Jones of the 26th Regiment N.C. Troops reported the activities of Pettigrew's brigade on July 1, 1863 (*O.R.*, S.I., Vol. XXVII, pt. 2, pp. 642-643):

Early on the morning of July 1, we moved down the pike toward Gettysburg. When within about 2½ miles of the town, we deployed to the left of the pike, but soon crossed over to the right, other regiments of the division having been engaged for some time. We took up our position in rear of our batteries after we moved to the right. After remaining in this position about half an hour, exposed to a random fire from the enemy's guns, losing probably a dozen men killed and wounded, we received orders to advance. We moved forward about half a mile, and halted in a skirt of woods.

The following is the position of the regiments in the brigade: On the right, the Fifty-second North Carolina, next the Forty-seventh North Carolina, then the Eleventh North Carolina, and on the left the Twenty-sixth. In our front was a wheat-field about a fourth of a mile wide; then came a branch, with thick underbrush and briars skirting the banks. Beyond this was again an open field, with the exception of a wooded hill directly in front of the Twenty-sixth Regiment, about covering its front.

Skirmishers being thrown out, we remained in line of battle until 2 p.m., when orders to advance were received. The brigade moved forward in beautiful style, at quick time, just with the brigade on our left, commanded by Colonel [J. M.] Brockenbrough. When nearing the branch referred to, the enemy poured a galling fire into the left of the brigade from the opposite bank, where they had massed in heavy force while we were in line of battle in the woods. The Forty-seventh and Fifty-second, although exposed to a hot fire from artillery and infantry, lost but few in comparison with the Eleventh and Twenty-sixth. On went the command across the branch and up the opposite slope, driving the enemy at the point of the bayonet back upon their second line. This second line was encountered by our left (the Twenty-sixth), while the other regiments were exposed to a heavy shelling. The enemy's single line in the field was engaged principally with the right of the Eleventh and Forty-seventh. The enemy did not perceive the Fifty-second, which flanked their left, until they discovered themselves by a raking and destructive fire into their ranks, by which they were broken. On this second line, the fighting was terrible—our men advancing, the enemy stubbornly resisting, until the two lines were pouring volleys into each other at a distance not greater than 20 paces. At last the enemy were compelled to give way. They again made a stand in the woods, and the third time they were driven from their position, losing a stand of colors, which was taken by the Twenty-sixth; but, owing to some carelessness, they were left behind, and were picked up by some one else.

While the Twenty-sixth was thus engaged, the rest of the line, having cleared the field and being exposed to a heavy fire from the enemy's batteries, were ordered to fall back, which they did in perfect order. The Twenty-sixth, not receiving the order, were now engaged in collecting ammunition from the enemy's dead, being entirely out themselves. Just as they were ready to advance again, General Pender's division passed over them. They followed on, and assisted in driving the enemy from the heights on the edge of the town. They then halted. That night the brigade bivouacked in the woods they had occupied previous to making the charge.

The brigade remained in position in the woods throughout the day of July 2 and was not engaged. During the evening of July 2 the brigade moved with the division about a mile to the right and went into position behind the batteries facing Cemetery Hill. Heth's division was directed to form on the left of General George Pickett's division in the assault on the Federal center on July 3. Major Jones reported the attack as follows (*O.R.*, S.I., Vol. XXVII, pt. 2, pp. 643-644):

We remained here [in rear of the batteries] until about 12 o'clock on the 3d, when our batteries opened upon the enemy's position. About 2 o'clock we were ordered to advance. It was an open field in front, about three-quarters of a mile in width. In moving off, there was some confusion in the line, owing to the fact that it had been ordered to close in on the right on Pickett's division, while that command gave way to the left. This was soon corrected, and the advance was made in perfect order. When about half across the intervening space, the enemy opened on us a most destructive fire of grape and canister. When within about 250 or 300 yards of the stone wall behind which the enemy was posted, we were met with a perfect hail-storm of lead from their small-arms. The brigade dashed on, and many had reached the wall, when we received a deadly volley from the left. The whole line on the left had given way, and we were being rapidly flanked. With our thinned ranks and in such a position, it would have been folly to stand, and against such odds. We therefore fell back to our original position in rear of the batteries. After this day's fight, but one field officer was left in the brigade. Regiments that went in with colonels came out commanded by lieutenants.

Following the failure of the assault, Lee held his army ready to repulse an expected attack. On the night of July 4 the army took up line of march for Hagerstown and arrived there on July 7. There a defensive line was established to hold the enemy while preparations were made to cross the Potomac. On July 13 the army began moving to cross the river, and Hill's corps was designated rear guard. As the army crossed, the rear guard retired under pressure from the enemy. Major Jones reported (*O.R.*, S.I., Vol. XXVII, pt. 2, p. 644):

After traveling all night in mud and rain, about 8 o'clock on the morning of the 14th we took position in a wheat-field as a portion of the rear guard, while the rest of the troops crossed the river at the pontoon bridge (about 1½ miles) at Falling Waters. The men stacked arms, and most of them were asleep, feeling perfectly secure, as our cavalry were out in front. We had been here probably two hours when the enemy's cavalry dashed in upon us, causing some confusion, as the men were just aroused from sleep. Soon as they saw what was the matter, they seized their guns, and soon made way with the cavalry; all but 3 of them were killed or wounded. General Pettigrew was here mortally wounded. He had received a severe contusion on the hand on the 3d, but would not report off duty. I was informed of his condition, and that

I was senior officer of the brigade, subject to the orders of Lieutenant-Colonel [S. G.] Shepard, commanding General Archer's brigade.

Soon after this, I received orders to fall back gradually to the river. I did so, fighting the enemy, who had now brought up an infantry force, all the way. In this I lost a few men killed and several taken prisoners, most of whom gave out from exhaustion. I could have saved most of those lost by a more hasty retreat along the road, but in that event would have left a brigade on my left completely in the hands of the enemy.

We crossed the pontoon about 12 m., just as the bridge was being cut loose. The brigade was marched next day to Bunker Hill, where it remained until I was relieved from command by the arrival of Lieutenant-Colonel [W. J.] Martin, of the Eleventh.

Thus ended Lee's invasion of Pennsylvania. During the Gettysburg campaign the regiment lost 50 killed and 159 wounded.

Lee moved his army east of the Blue Ridge Mountains when the Federal army crossed into Virginia. By August 4 the Army of Northern Virginia occupied the Rapidan River line, and the Federal army occupied the Rappahannock River line. About this time the 44th Regiment N.C. Troops rejoined the brigade, and Colonel Thomas C. Singletary of that regiment assumed command of the brigade. He remained in command until Colonel W. W. Kirkland was appointed brigadier general and assigned to command the brigade, and Pettigrew's brigade became Kirkland's brigade, Heth's division, A. P. Hill's corps.

On October 10 Lee's army moved to strike the right flank of the Federal army. The move compelled the Federal commander, General George Meade, to order his army to retire toward Centreville. As the rear guard of Meade's army was passing through Bristoe Station, General A. P. Hill's corps, with Heth's division in front, came on the field. Without waiting for the rest of the army to come up or to reconnoiter, General Hill ordered an attack. General Kirkland's brigade was placed on the left of the road with this regiment on the extreme left of the line. General John R. Cooke's North Carolina brigade was put on the right of the road. The brigades advanced to the attack down an open hill toward the Federal troops entrenched behind a railroad embankment. As soon as the brigades entered the open area the Federal infantry and artillery opened fire. Cooke's brigade was caught in the open and was forced to retire with heavy casualties. Kirkland's brigade continued to advance, and this regiment succeeded in driving the Federals from one point on the railroad. With both flanks exposed and no reinforcements in sight, the brigade was ordered to retire. It did so under heavy fire. Some of the men refused to cross the open field and were captured. During the engagement this regiment lost 4 killed, 11 wounded, and 43 missing. General Kirkland was wounded during the attack and Colonel Singletary assumed command of the brigade.

No further attempts were made to attack the enemy, and during the night the Federal rear guard continued its retreat to Centreville. Lee decided not to follow the Federal army and ordered his army to retire to the Rappahannock. After the battle at Rappahannock Bridge, Lee moved his army back to the Rapidan River line. General Meade began moving his army on November 26 to cross the Rapidan below Lee's position. Lee ordered his army to intercept the Federal army. Upon finding the Federals advancing toward him, Lee retired to Mine Run and entrenched, whereupon Meade moved up and entrenched. Lee, receiving reports that the Federal flank was exposed,. determined to attack on the morning of December 2, but when the troops moved out they found that the Federal army had retired. A pursuit was undertaken, but Meade recrossed the Rapidan unmolested. Lee then ordered his troops back, and the army went into winter quarters. This regiment spent the winter of 1863-1864 in camp with the brigade near Orange Court House.

On the morning of May 4, 1864, while the Federal army under General U. S. Grant was moving across the lower Rapidan, Kirkland's brigade was near Orange Court House. When information was received that Grant was crossing, Lee ordered Ewell's corps to move on the left on the Orange Turnpike and Hill's corps to move in the center on the Plank Road. Longstreet's corps at Gordonsville was ordered to move up on Hill's right. On the morning of May 5, with Kirkland's brigade in the lead, Hill's column encountered Federal cavalry near Parker's Store and succeeded in forcing it back. The crossroads at Parker's Store was then occupied by the Confederates. Immediately north on the Orange Turnpike, Ewell encountered the enemy in corps strength. Hill ordered Heth's division to deploy in line of battle across the Plank Road. Kirkland's brigade was held in reserve on the road behind Cooke's brigade while the remaining two brigades of the division were on either side of Cooke's line. Elements of the Federal II Corps attacked Heth's line around four o'clock. During the attack Kirkland's brigade was sent to the relief of Cooke's hard-pressed men. The line held under repeated assaults, and Kirkland's brigade charged over the Confederate line. Efforts to dislodge the enemy failed, whereupon the brigade retired to the Confederate line. Heth's division was holding off seven enemy brigades, and more were advancing. Wilcox's division was ordered to the support of Heth, and the four brigades from that division arrived in time to stabilize the line.

On the morning of May 6, at 5:00 **A.M.,** Federal columns struck Hill's line in front and on the left flank. Heth's division was on the left of the road. The attack was so swift that units were overrun. Kirkland's brigade managed to fall back and rallied to support Cooke's brigade, which had been in reserve. Other units joined in support of Cooke's position, but Federal pressure forced them to retire. Only the timely arrival of Longstreet's corps prevented the collapse of Lee's right. Longstreet's fresh troops blunted the Federal attack and drove it back. Hill's troops regrouped and were ordered to close the gap between Ewell's right and Longstreet's left. Kirkland's brigade went into position on the extreme right of the gap and was on the immediate left of Longstreet's line. The battle continued throughout the day on Longstreet's front, and night brought an end to the fighting.

Late in the evening of May 7 orders came to close

on the right. Grant was heading toward Spotsylvania Court House, and Lee was moving to intercept him. Throughout the night of May 7-8 the Confederates moved to the right. The race for the courthouse was won by the Confederates on the morning of May 8. When the rest of the army came up a strong defensive line was constructed. Hill's corps was positioned on the right of the line with Ewell's corps in the center and Longstreet's corps on the left. Heth's division formed the right of the Confederate line. On May 10 Heth's division was pulled out of the line and moved to the left where, on the Shady Grove road, it turned back a Federal reconnaissance force. On the morning of May 11, the division was moved back to Spotsylvania Court House on the right of the line. Early the next morning the Federals launched a sudden attack on a salient, known as the Mule Shoe, in the Confederate center. Reinforcements were thrown in to check the Federal advance, and after heavy fighting the Confederates held until a new line to the rear of the apex of the salient was completed. The regiments of Kirkland's brigade were detached to support various artillery positions around the courthouse and were not directly involved in the fighting at the Mule Shoe.

After several unsuccessful attempts against the Confederate line, General Grant moved his army eastward. Lee moved his army to block Grant at the North Anna River, where Lee set up a strong defensive position with Hill's corps on the left. Wilcox's division of Hill's corps engaged the enemy on May 23, but Heth's division was not directly engaged. Grant withdrew during the night of May 26-27 and crossed the Pamunkey River, again sidestepping to the Confederate right. Ewell's corps, now commanded by General Jubal Early, marched some twenty-four miles on May 27 and entrenched between Beaver Dam Creek and Pole Green Church. Longstreet's corps came up on Early's right and Hill's corps extended along the left of Early's line. On May 30, under orders from General Lee, Early moved to attack the Federal left at Bethesda Church. The attack failed to turn the Federal left but revealed that the enemy was moving to the Confederate right. On the afternoon of June 1 Cooke's and Kirkland's brigades repulsed an attack launched to conceal the Federal shift.

The two armies began to concentrate at Cold Harbor, and on June 1 a spirited engagement occurred. On June 2 Hill was ordered to leave Heth's division on the left to support Early's corps and to move his other two divisions to the Confederate right. While Hill moved to anchor the right, Heth's division joined Early's two divisions in striking the Federal right flank and in driving them from their first line of entrenchments. General Kirkland was seriously wounded during the charge, and Colonel George H. Faribault of the 47th Regiment N. C. Troops assumed command of the brigade. Darkness halted the action. The next day Grant launched an unsuccessful general assault against the six-mile-long Confederate line. One point of concentration was against the Confederate left in an attempt to flank the position and get in the rear of the main line. At least three attacks were launched against Heth's division. Each was repulsed. Late in the day Heth was ordered to move to the right and join Hill's corps at Turkey Hill. Early on the morning of June

4 Heth moved and joined the other divisions of the corps.

When Grant moved south of the Chickahominy Lee followed, and Hill's corps made contact near Riddell's Shop on June 13. A defensive line was established, but no general engagement followed. Grant then crossed the James River and moved on Petersburg. Hill's corps remained north of the James until ordered to move to Petersburg on June 17. When it arrived on June 18 it went into position on the extreme right of the Petersburg line and extended the line beyond the Weldon Railroad. Heth's division began entrenching and remained in the line until ordered to the north side of the James River on July 28 to confront a Federal feint. On July 30 the Federal mine was exploded at Petersburg, and the attack was turned back. The feint north of the James was withdrawn, and Heth's division returned to the Petersburg line on August 2. Following this move, Heth's men enjoyed three weeks of comparative quiet. It was at this time that Colonel William MacRae of the 15th Regiment N.C. Troops (5th Regiment N.C. Volunteers) was appointed temporary brigadier general, to rank from June 22, 1864, and placed in command of Kirkland's brigade. MacRae was promoted to brigadier general on November 4, 1864. Thus Kirkland's brigade became known as MacRae's brigade and served as such for the remainder of the war.

On August 18 the Federals took possession of the Weldon Railroad at Globe Tavern, and all efforts by troops under Hill failed to dislodge them. MacRae's brigade was not engaged in the action. South of Globe Tavern another Federal force occupied the railroad at Reams' Station. Moving around the enemy position at Globe Tavern, Hill ordered MacRae's brigade, six other brigades of his corps, and two divisions of cavalry to attack the Federal position at Reams' Station. The troops moved on the afternoon of August 24 and arrived before Reams' Station the next morning. An assault by two brigades was repulsed, but a stronger attack on the Federal right in which MacRae's brigade took part succeeded in breaking through the Federal line. Some 2,000 men and nine pieces of artillery were captured as the Federals were driven back in disorder. The Confederate infantry returned to Petersburg that night.

Heth's division did not see action in the field again until September 30 when it was engaged at Jones' Farm. Grant moved to extend his line to tie in with the position at Globe Tavern. Each side advanced to the attack, and, although initially successful, the Confederates could not prevent the Federals from establishing their line. On October 27 a Federal force moved to gain possession of the high ground north of Hatcher's Run in the vicinity of Burgess' Mill. General Hill concentrated Heth's and Mahone's divisions and General Wade Hampton's cavalry force to oppose the advance. Mahone was sent to strike the Federal right, Hampton moved to attack his left, and Heth held him in front. The attack on the Federal right failed, but the simultaneous attack on the left was pressed vigorously until dark. The next day the Federal force withdrew and returned to its former position. On October 29 MacRae's brigade returned to its camp near the Hart house and went into winter quarters.

Early in February, 1865, General Grant ordered a move on the left of his line to secure a position on the Boydton Plank Road at Hatcher's Run. Hill's troops were engaged on February 5 but met with little success. Upon securing the position on Hatcher's Run, Grant planned his next move. It began on March 29 and terminated with the routing of a Confederate force at Five Forks on April 1. This victory opened the way for an advance on the Confederate line at Petersburg in flank and rear. On April 2 the Federals launched a general attack against the line. The 11th Regiment N.C. Troops (1st Regiment N.C. Volunteers) and the 26th Regiment N.C. Troops were the only two regiments of MacRae's brigade in the trenches. The rest of the brigade was on the right. The Federals broke through on the left of these two regiments, turned to the left, and swept down the trenches. MacRae's men fell back to the next line. That night Lee decided to evacuate the Petersburg line, and his army pulled out of the trenches to take up the march to Amelia Court House.

Lee's army concentrated at Amelia Court House on April 4-5 and continued the retreat on April 6. At Sayler's Creek on April 6 the Confederates failed to hold the advancing Federals and sustained heavy losses. The remnants of two corps were defeated and captured. Lee's army moved through Farmville on April 7, and on April 8 MacRae's brigade formed the rear guard of the army. Lee surrendered his army at Appomattox Court House on April 9, 1865. When the army was paroled on April 12, only seventy-four men of the regiment were present.

FIELD AND STAFF

COLONELS

LEVENTHORPE, COLLETT
Previously served as Colonel of the 34th Regiment N.C. Troops. Transferred to this regiment on or about March 31, 1862. Present or accounted for until wounded in the left arm at Gettysburg, Pennsylvania, July 1-3, 1863. Captured at or near Gettysburg on or about July 5, 1863. Hospitalized at various Federal hospitals until confined at Fort McHenry, Maryland, Septeber 28, 1863. Transferred to Point Lookout, Maryland, January 23, 1864. Paroled at Point Lookout and transferred for exchange on or about March 10, 1864. Resigned April 27, 1864, by reason of wounds received at Gettysburg.

MARTIN, WILLIAM JOSEPH
Previously served as Captain of Company G, 28th Regiment N. C. Troops. Appointed Major to rank from April 28, 1862, and transferred to this regiment. Promoted to Lieutenant Colonel to rank from May 6, 1862. Present or accounted for until

wounded in the head and left arm at Bristoe Station, Virginia, October 14, 1863. Returned to duty at an unspecified date and was promoted to Colonel on April 27, 1864. Present or accounted for until wounded in the left thigh at Jones' Farm, Virginia, September 30, 1864. Reported absent wounded through February, 1865. Paroled at Appomattox Court House, Virginia, April 9, 1865.

LIEUTENANT COLONELS

OWENS, WILLIAM A.
Previously served as Major of the 34th Regiment N.C. Troops. Promoted to Lieutenant Colonel on March 31, 1862, and transferred to this regiment. Present or accounted for until promoted to Colonel on May 6, 1862, and transferred to the 53rd Regiment N. C. Troops.

BIRD, FRANCIS W.
Previously served as Captain of Company C of this regiment. Promoted to Major on or about December 3, 1863, to rank from July 1, 1863, and transferred to the Field and Staff. Promoted to Lieutenant Colonel on April 27, 1864. Present or accounted for until wounded at Reams' Station, Virginia, August 25, 1864. Died August 26, 1864.

MAJORS

ELIASON, WILLIAM ADLAI
Previously served as Assistant Quartermaster (Captain) of the 7th Regiment N.C. State Troops. Appointed Major of this regiment to rank from March 31, 1862; however, he declined the appointment. Later served as Lieutenant Colonel of the 49th Regiment N.C. Troops.

ROSS, EGBERT A.
Previously served as Captain of Company A of this regiment. Appointed Major to rank from May 6, 1862, and transferred to the Field and Staff. Present or accounted for until killed at Gettysburg, Pennsylvania, July 1, 1863.

ADJUTANTS

LUCAS, HENDERSON C.
Previously served as 1st Sergeant of Company G, 34th Regiment N. C. Troops. Appointed Adjutant (1st Lieutenant) of this regiment on or about July 11, 1862, to rank from June 1, 1862. Present or accounted for until wounded at Gettysburg, Pennsylvania, July 1-3, 1863. Died at Martinsburg, West Virginia, on or about July 25, 1863, of wounds.

MARTIN, EDWARD A.
Previously served as 1st Sergeant of Company K of this regiment. Appointed Adjutant (1st Lieutenant) on September 3, 1863, to rank from August 18, 1863, and transferred to the Field and Staff. Present or accounted for until wounded at Hatcher's Run, Virginia, February 5, 1865. Reported absent wounded through February, 1865.

ASSISTANT QUARTERMASTER

TATE, JOHN M.

Previously served as 2nd Lieutenant in Company D of this regiment. Appointed Assistant Quartermaster (1st Lieutenant) to rank from April 22, 1862, and transferred to the Field and Staff. Promoted to Assistant Quartermaster (Captain) on July 10, 1862, to rank from May 5, 1862. Present or accounted for until transferred to an unspecified post at Charlotte on July 8, 1864. Later served as Quartermaster (Captain) of Wilcox's division.

ASSISTANT COMMISSARIES OF SUBSISTENCE

LOWRIE, PATRICK JOHNSON

Previously served as 1st Lieutenant in Company H of this regiment. Appointed Assistant Commissary of Subsistence (Captain) on July 11, 1862, to rank from June 1, 1862, and transferred to the Field and Staff. Died at Wilmington on July 12, 1862, of disease.

SUMMEY, JOHN S. E.

Resided in Buncombe County and enlisted at age 45. Appointed Assistant Commissary of Subsistence (Captain) on October 7, 1862, to rank from July 24, 1862. Transferred to an unspecified post at Asheville when his position was abolished on May 29, 1863.

SURGEONS

WILSON, JOHN, Jr.

Resided in Caswell County and enlisted at age 35. Appointed Surgeon to rank from March 25, 1862, or June 30, 1862. Present or accounted for until ordered to report to Raleigh on November 28, 1864. Later served as Surgeon of the military prison hospital at Salisbury.

FUQUA, WILLIAM M.

Appointed Surgeon of this regiment on or about November 29, 1864. Present or accounted for through February, 1865.

ASSISTANT SURGEON

McCOMBS, JAMES PARKS

Resided in Mecklenburg County and enlisted at age 25. Appointed Assistant Surgeon on September 26, 1862, to rank from April 5, 1862, or June 25, 1862. Present or accounted for until captured at Gettysburg, Pennsylvania, July 5, 1863. Confined at various localities until confined at Fort McHenry, Maryland, August 10, 1863. Exchanged on or about November 21, 1863. Present or accounted for until paroled at Appomattox Court House, Virginia, April 9, 1865.

CHAPLAINS

RIDLEY, J. S.

Appointed Chaplain of this regiment of April 30, 1862. No further records.

KNAPP, THEODORE JUDSON

Served as 1st Lieutenant in Company F of this regiment. Appointed Chaplain of this regiment in October, 1862; however, regimental records do not indicate that he accepted the appointment or served in that capacity. No further records.

SMITH, ARISTIDES S.

Resided in Virginia. Appointed Chaplain of this regiment of November 17, 1862, to rank from July 20, 1862. Present or accounted for until he resigned on January 4, 1864, by reason of his age and "rheumatism." Age given on letter of resignation as 54. Resignation accepted January 20, 1864.

ENSIGN

RAYNER, JAMES T.

Previously served as Sergeant in Company C of this regiment. Appointed Ensign (1st Lieutenant) on August 16, 1864, and transferred to the Field and Staff. Present or accounted for until captured on the Appomattox River, Virginia, April 3, 1865. Confined at Old Capitol Prison, Washington, D.C., until transferred to Johnson's Island, Ohio, April 21, 1865. Released at Johnson's Island on June 19, 1865, after taking the Oath of Allegiance.

SERGEANTS MAJOR

McCORKLE, JAMES G.

Previously served as 1st Sergeant of Company A of this regiment. Appointed Sergeant Major in April, 1862, and transferred to the Field and Staff. Present or accounted for until captured at Gettysburg, Pennsylvania, July 3, 1863. Confined at Fort Delaware, Delaware, until exchanged on July 31, 1863. Rejoined the regiment on October 25, 1863. Present or accounted for until appointed 2nd Lieutenant on or about November 26, 1863, and transferred to Company D of this regiment.

RHODES, ROBERT H.

Previously served as Private in Company C of this regiment. Appointed Sergeant Major in September-October, 1864, and transferred to the Field and Staff. Present or accounted for until captured at Petersburg, Virginia, April 2, 1865. Confined at Fort Delaware, Delaware, until released on or about May 3, 1865, after taking the Oath of Allegiance.

QUARTERMASTER SERGEANTS

FINGER, SIDNEY M.

Previously served as Corporal in Company I of this regiment. Promoted to Quartermaster Sergeant in July, 1862, and transferred to the Field and Staff. Present or accounted for until appointed Assistant Quartermaster (Captain) of the Eighth Congressional District of North Carolina to rank from June 16, 1863.

SIMS, JAMES MONROE

Previously served as Sergeant in Company A of this regiment. Promoted to Quartermaster Sergeant on November 1, 1863, and transferred to the Field and Staff. Present or accounted for until captured at Petersburg, Virginia, April 3, 1865. Confined at Hart's Island, New York Harbor, until released on June 23, 1865, after taking the Oath of Allegiance.

COMMISSARY SERGEANTS

LOWRIE, JAMES B.
Previously served as Private in Company H of this regiment. Promoted to Commissary Sergeant on May 8, 1862, and transferred to the Field and Staff. Present or accounted for until reduced to ranks on or about August 9, 1862, and transferred back to Company H.

DICKERSON, WILLIAM T.
Previously served as Sergeant in Company K of this regiment. Promoted to Commissary Sergeant on August 9, 1862, and transferred to the Field and Staff. Present or accounted for until appointed 2nd Lieutenant to rank from July 30, 1863, and transferred back to Company K.

ORDNANCE SERGEANTS

WILLIAMS, JAMES W.
Previously served as Private in Company G of this regiment. Promoted to Ordnance Sergeant on May 1, 1862, and transferred to the Field and Staff. Present or accounted for until appointed 2nd Lieutenant to rank from September 10, 1862, and transferred back to Company G.

MOTZ, GEORGE
Previously served as Private in Company I of this regiment. Promoted to Ordnance Sergeant on November 3, 1862, and transferred to the Field and Staff. Present or accounted for until reduced to the rank of Sergeant in September-October, 1863, and transferred back to Company I.

MARDRE, WILLIAM B.
Previously served as Private in Company C of this regiment. Promoted to Ordnance Sergeant in September-October, 1863, and transferred to the Field and Staff. Present or accounted for until paroled at Appomattox Court House, Virginia, April 9, 1865.

HOSPITAL STEWARD

WILSON, WILLIAM M.
Previously served as Private in Company A of this regiment. Promoted to Hospital Steward in May-June, 1864, and transferred to the Field and Staff. Present or accounted for until paroled at Appomattox Court House, Virginia, April 9, 1865.

BAND

CLINE, WILLIAM A., Musician
Previously served as Musician in Company I of this regiment. Transferred to the regimental band in February, 1865. Paroled at Appomattox Court House, Virginia, April 9, 1865.

COON, ADOLPHUS S., Musician
Previously served as Musician in Company I of this regiment. Transferred to the regimental band in February, 1865. Paroled at Appomattox Court House, Virginia, April 9, 1865.

CROWELL, ELIAS M., Musician
Previously served as Private in Company H of this regiment. Promoted to Musician in July-August, 1864, and was transferred to the regimental band prior to November 1, 1864. Present or accounted for until captured at Petersburg, Virginia, April 2, 1865. Confined at Point Lookout, Maryland, until released on June 26, 1865, after taking the Oath of Allegiance.

DAVIS, JAMES T., Musician
Previously served as Private in Company G of this regiment. Promoted to Musician (Drummer) in September-October, 1864, and transferred to the regimental band. Present or accounted for until paroled at Appomattox Court House, Virginia, April 9, 1865.

GIBSON, JAMES A., Musician
Previously served as Private in Company A of this regiment. Promoted to Musician in September-October, 1864, and transferred to the regimental band. Present or accounted for until he deserted to the enemy on or about April 9, 1865. Released on or about April 12, 1865, after taking the Oath of Allegiance.

GOODSON, JOHN L., Musician
Previously served as Private in Company K of this regiment. Promoted to Musician in September-October, 1864, and transferred to the regimental band. Present or accounted for until he deserted to the enemy on or about March 14, 1865. Released on or about March 18, 1865, after taking the Oath of Allegiance.

HICKS, JOSEPH S., Musician
Previously served as Private in Company D of this regiment. Promoted to Musician and transferred to the regimental band in September-October, 1864. Present or accounted for until captured at Petersburg, Virginia, April 3, 1865. Confined at Point Lookout, Maryland, until released on June 27, 1865, after taking the Oath of Allegiance.

McCONNELL, JAMES H., Musician
Previously served as Private in Company H of this regiment. Present or accounted for until appointed Musician in September-October, 1864, and transferred to the regimental band. Present or accounted for through February, 1865.

MARTIN, WILLIAM E., Musician
Previously served as Musician in Company I of this regiment. Transferred to the regimental band in September-October, 1864. Present or accounted for until hospitalized at Charlotte on January 17, 1865, with "hepatitis." Died in hospital at Charlotte in February, 1865.

MORRISON, WILLIAM T., Musician
Previously served as Private in Company H of this regiment. Promoted to Musician in September-October, 1864, and transferred to the regimental band. Paroled at Salisbury on May 26, 1865.

MOTZ, CHARLES, Musician
Previously served in Company I of this regiment. Transferred to the regimental band in September-October, 1864, while a prisoner of war in confinement at Point Lookout, Maryland. Paroled at Point Lookout and transferred for exchange on

or about February 18, 1865. Reported present with a detachment of paroled and exchanged prisoners at Camp Lee, near Richmond, Virginia, February 27, 1865.

SEAGLE, MONROE, Musician
Previously served in Company I of this regiment. Transferred to the regimental band in September-October, 1864. Present or accounted for through February, 1865.

TODD, ELISHA, Chief Musician
Previously served in Company C of this regiment. Transferred to the regimental band in September-October, 1864. Present or accounted for until captured at Petersburg, Virginia, April 3, 1865. Confined at Point Lookout, Maryland, until released on June 21, 1865, after taking the Oath of Allegiance.

TODD, NEHEMIAH J., Musician
Previously served in Company C of this regiment. Transferred to the regimental band in September-October, 1864. Present or accounted for until captured in hospital at Richmond, Virginia, April 3, 1865. Died in hospital at Richmond on April 21, 1865, of "typhoid fever."

WINGATE, CHARLES C., Musician
Previously served as Private in Company A of this regiment. Promoted to Musician in September-October, 1864, and transferred to the regimental band. Present or accounted for until captured at or near Petersburg, Virginia, April 2, 1865. Confined at Fort Delaware, Delaware, until released on June 19, 1865, after taking the Oath of Allegiance.

COMPANY A

This company was composed primarily of men from Mecklenburg and Gaston counties and began organizing at Charlotte on or about February 1, 1862. On March 31, 1862, it was mustered in as Company A of this regiment. After that date the company functioned as a part of the regiment, and its history for the war period is recorded as a part of the regimental history.

The information contained in the following roster of the company was compiled principally from company muster rolls for May, 1862, through February, 1865. No company muster rolls were found for the period prior to May, 1862, or for the period after February, 1865. In addition to the company muster rolls, Roll of Honor records, receipt rolls, hospital records, prisoner of war records, and other primary records, supplemented by state pension applications, United Daughters of the Confederacy records, and postwar rosters and histories, all provided useful information.

OFFICERS
CAPTAINS

ROSS, EGBERT A.
Previously served as Captain of Company C, 1st Regiment N.C. Infantry (6 months, 1861). Appointed Captain of this company on February 1, 1862. Present or accounted for until appointed Major to rank from May 6, 1862, and transferred to the Field and Staff of this regiment.

HAND, WILLIAM L.
Resided in Mecklenburg or Gaston counties and enlisted at age 20. Appointed 1st Lieutenant to rank from January 14, 1862, and promoted to Captain to rank from May 6, 1862. Present or accounted for until captured at Gettysburg, Pennsylvania, July 3, 1863. Confined at Fort Delaware, Delaware, until transferred to Johnson's Island, Ohio, July 18, 1863. Paroled at Johnson's Island on March 14, 1865. Received at Cox's Wharf, James River, Virginia, March 22, 1865, for exchange.

LIEUTENANTS

ALEXANDER, CHARLES W., 1st Lieutenant
Previously served as 3rd Lieutenant in Company C, 1st Regiment N.C. Infantry (6 months, 1861). Appointed 2nd Lieutenant in this company to rank from February 1, 1862, and promoted to 1st Lieutenant to rank from May 6, 1862. Present or accounted for until retired to the Invalid Corps on or about July 15, 1864, by reason of "extensive exotosis of upper and internal portion of left femur." Paroled at Charlotte on May 16, 1865.

ALEXANDER, RICHARD B., 3rd Lieutenant
Resided in Mecklenburg County where he enlisted at age 22, February 1, 1862, for the war. Mustered in as Sergeant and promoted to 1st Sergeant in May-June, 1863. Present or accounted for until wounded in the left shoulder at Gettysburg, Pennsylvania, July 1-3, 1863. Rejoined the company in September-October, 1863, and was promoted to 3rd Lieutenant on October 11, 1864. Present or accounted for until captured at Hatcher's Run, Virginia, April 2, 1865. Confined at Old Capitol Prison, Washington, D.C., until transferred to Johnson's Island, Ohio, April 9, 1865. Released at Johnson's Island on June 17, 1865, after taking the Oath of Allegiance.

HAND, ROBERT H., 2nd Lieutenant
Previously served as Private in Company C, 1st Regiment N.C. Infantry (6 months, 1861). Appointed 2nd Lieutenant in this company to rank from March 31, 1862. Present or accounted for until wounded in the back at Gettysburg, Pennsylvania, July 1, 1863. Captured at or near Greencastle, Pennsylvania, July 5, 1863. Hospitalized at Chambersburg, Pennsylvania, and was confined at Fort Delaware, Delaware, September 2-4, 1863. Transferred to Johnson's Island, Ohio, September 16, 1863. Paroled at Johnson's Island on March 14, 1865, and was received at Cox's Wharf, James River, Virginia, March 22, 1865, for exchange.

MONTGOMERY, JAMES H., 3rd Lieutenant
Resided in Mecklenburg County where he enlisted at age 26, February 1, 1862, for the war. Mustered in as Private. Present or accounted for until wounded and captured at Gettysburg, Pennsyl-

vania, July 3, 1863. Hospitalized at Chester, Pennsylvania. Exchanged prior to August 22, 1863. Rejoined the company prior to November 1, 1863, and was promoted to 3rd Lieutenant in July-August, 1864. Present or accounted for until wounded in the leg at Reams' Station, Virginia, on or about August 25, 1864. Leg amputated. Died in hospital at Richmond, Virginia, September 9, 1864, of wounds.

TAYLOR, WILLIAM B., 2nd Lieutenant
Previously served as Corporal in Company C, 1st Regiment N.C. Infantry (6 months, 1861). Enlisted in this company on February 1, 1862, for the war. Mustered in as Sergeant and was appointed 3rd Lieutenant to rank from June 2, 1862. Present or accounted for until hospitalized at Charlotte on June 30, 1864, with a gunshot wound; however, place and date wounded not reported. Promoted to 2nd Lieutenant in July-August, 1864. Returned to duty on September 5, 1864, and present or accounted for until paroled at Appomattox Court House, Virginia, April 9, 1865.

NONCOMMISSIONED OFFICERS AND PRIVATES

ALEXANDER, J. N., Corporal
Resided in Mecklenburg County where he enlisted at age 28, February 1, 1862, for the war. Mustered in as Private and promoted to Corporal in July-August, 1864. Present or accounted for until reported absent wounded in September-October, 1864; however, place and date wounded not reported. Rejoined the company in January-February, 1865, and present or accounted for until paroled at Appomattox Court House, Virginia, April 9, 1865.

ALEXANDER, JOHN G., Private
Previously served in Company C, 1st Regiment N.C. Infantry (6 months, 1861). Enlisted in this company on February 1, 1862. Present or accounted for until killed at Reams' Station, Virginia, August 25, 1864.

ALEXANDER, M. A., Private
Resided in Mecklenburg County where he enlisted at age 23, February 1, 1862, for the war. Present or accounted for until wounded and captured at Gettysburg, Pennsylvania, July 3, 1863. Confined at Fort Delaware, Delaware, until transferred to Point Lookout, Maryland, where he arrived October 22, 1863. Hospitalized at Point Lookout prior to November 1, 1863. No further records.

ALEXANDER, M. R., Private
Previously served in Company C, 1st Regiment N.C. Infantry (6 months, 1861). Enlisted in this company on February 1, 1862, for the war. Present or accounted for until wounded in the right shoulder at Gettysburg, Pennsylvania, July 1-3, 1863. Rejoined the company in September-October, 1863. Present or accounted for until reported absent wounded in September-October, 1864; however, place and date wounded not reported. Rejoined the company in November-December, 1864, and present or accounted for until captured near Petersburg, Virginia, March 25, 1865.

Confined at Point Lookout, Maryland, until released on June 23, 1865, after taking the Oath of Allegiance.

ALEXANDER, MILTON Mc., Private
Resided in Mecklenburg County where he enlisted at age 27, February 1, 1862, for the war. Present or accounted for until reported captured at Gettysburg, Pennsylvania, July 3, 1863; however, records of the Federal Provost Marshal do not substantiate that report. Roll of Honor indicates he was wounded at Gettysburg. No further records.

ALEXANDER, ROBERT C., Private
Resided in Mecklenburg County where he enlisted at age 18, February 1, 1862, for the war. Present or accounted for until captured at Gettysburg, Pennsylvania, July 3, 1863. Confined at Fort Delaware, Delaware, until released on June 19, 1865, after taking the Oath of Allegiance.

ALEXANDER, WILLIAM R., _____
Records of Company E, 1st Regiment N.C. Infantry (6 months, 1861), indicate that he served in this regiment; however, records of this regiment do not indicate that he served herein. [May have served later as Captain of Company I, 60th Regiment N.C. Troops.]

ALEXANDER, WILLIAM S., Private
Previously served in Company E, 1st Regiment N.C. Infantry (6 months, 1861). Enlisted in this company on February 13, 1864. Present or accounted for until captured at or near Petersburg, Virginia, April 2, 1865. Confined at Fort Delaware, Delaware, until released on June 19, 1865, after taking the Oath of Allegiance.

ALLEN, CYRUS A., Private
Resided in Mecklenburg County where he enlisted at age 19, March 1, 1863, for the war. Present or accounted for until wounded and captured at Gettysburg, Pennsylvania, July 3, 1863. Confined at Fort Delaware, Delaware, until transferred to hospital at Chester, Pennsylvania, July 19, 1863. Paroled at Chester and transferred for exchange on or about August 20, 1863. Returned to duty on November 3, 1863, and present or accounted for until captured at or near Petersburg, Virginia, April 2, 1865. Confined at Fort Delaware until released on June 19, 1865, after taking the Oath of Allegiance.

ALLEN, H. W., Private
Resided in Mecklenburg County where he enlisted at age 24, May 3, 1862, for the war. Present or accounted for until wounded in the right arm and captured at Gettysburg, Pennsylvania, July 1-5, 1863. Hospitalized at Gettysburg until transferred to Davids Island, New York Harbor, July 17-24, 1863. Paroled at Davids Island and transferred to City Point, Virginia, where he was received September 16, 1863, for exchange. Reported absent wounded or absent on detached service until he rejoined the company in November-December, 1864. Present or accounted for until retired to the Invalid Corps on February 10, 1865.

ALLEN, J. C., Private
Enlisted in Mecklenburg County on May 3, 1862,

for the war. Present or accounted for until discharged in July, 1862, by reason of disability.

AUTEN, P. S., Private
Resided in Mecklenburg County where he enlisted at age 26, July 7, 1862, for the war. Present or accounted for until wounded and captured at Gettysburg, Pennsylvania, July 3, 1863. Died at or near Gettysburg on August 1, 1863.

BARNETT, E. L. S., Private
Resided in Mecklenburg County where he enlisted at age 23, February 1, 1862, for the war. Present or accounted for until discharged on or about January 19, 1863. Reason discharged not reported.

BARNETTE, JAMES F., Private
Resided in Mecklenburg County where he enlisted at age 18, February 1, 1862, for the war. Present or accounted for until transferred to Company C, 37th Regiment N.C. Troops, January 1, 1864.

BARNETTE, JOHN L., Private
Born in Mecklenburg County where he resided prior to enlisting in Mecklenburg County at age 19, February 1, 1862, for the war. Present or accounted for until wounded at Gettysburg, Pennsylvania, July 1, 1863. Died on or about July 5, 1863, of wounds.

BIGHAM, J. H., Private
Born in Bertie or Mecklenburg counties and resided in Mecklenburg County where he enlisted at age 18, December 27, 1862, for the war. Present or accounted for until he died in hospital at Gordonsville, Virginia, November 19, 1863, of "pneumonia."

BIGHAM, JAMES W., Corporal
Resided in Mecklenburg County and was by occupation a farmer prior to enlisting in Mecklenburg County at age 27, July 7, 1862, for the war. Mustered in as Private. Present or accounted for until wounded in the arm at Gettysburg, Pennsylvania, July 1-3, 1863. Rejoined the company prior to October 28, 1863. Promoted to Corporal in November-December, 1864. Present or accounted for until paroled at Appomattox Court House, Virginia, April 9, 1865.

BIGHAM, JOHN R., Private
Resided in Mecklenburg County where he enlisted at age 19, February 1, 1862, for the war. Present or accounted for until wounded in the thigh and right buttock and captured at Gettysburg, Pennsylvania, on or about July 3, 1863. Hospitalized at various Federal hospitals until admitted to hospital at Point Lookout, Maryland, April 26, 1864. Died at Point Lookout on or about August 28, 1864. Cause of death not reported.

BLACK, EZEKIEL, Private
Resided in Mecklenburg County where he enlisted on October 29, 1864, for the war. Present or accounted for until captured at or near Petersburg, Virginia, April 2, 1865. Confined at Fort Delaware, Delaware, until released on June 19, 1865, after taking the Oath of Allegiance.

BLACK, JAMES M., Private
Resided in Mecklenburg County where he enlisted at age 28, February 1, 1862, for the war. Present

or accounted for until captured at Petersburg, Virginia, April 3, 1865. Confined at Hart's Island, New York Harbor, until released on June 18, 1865, after taking the Oath of Allegiance.

BLACK, THOMAS JEFFERSON, Private
Resided in Mecklenburg County where he enlisted at age 18, April 20, 1862, for the war. Present or accounted for until captured on the South Side Railroad, near Petersburg, Virginia, April 2, 1865. Confined at Hart's Island, New York Harbor, until released on June 18, 1865, after taking the Oath of Allegiance.

BLAKELEY, MONROE, Private
Resided in Mecklenburg County where he enlisted at age 20, February 1, 1862, for the war. Present or accounted for until he died in Mecklenburg County on or about April 18, 1862. Cause of death not reported.

BLAKELY, J. J., Private
Resided in Mecklenburg County where he enlisted at age 18, March 1, 1863, for the war. Present or accounted for until captured at Falling Waters, Maryland, July 14, 1863. Confined at Old Capitol Prison, Washington, D.C., until transferred to Point Lookout, Maryland, on or about August 9, 1863. Died at Point Lookout on or about April 1, 1865, of "pneumonia."

BRIGMAN, C. C., Private
Resided in Mecklenburg County where he enlisted at age 26, February 1, 1862, for the war. Present or accounted for until reported absent wounded in November-December, 1862; however, place and date wounded not reported. Rejoined the company in March-April, 1863, and present or accounted for until he died "at home" in Mecklenburg County in November-December, 1863, of disease. Roll of Honor indicates that he was wounded at an unspecified date at Franklin, Virginia.

BROWN, WILLIAM J., Sergeant
Previously served as Private in Company C, 1st Regiment N.C. Infantry (6 months, 1861). Enlisted in this company on February 1, 1862, for the war. Mustered in as Private and promoted to Corporal on June 2, 1862. Promoted to Sergeant on June 15, 1863. Present or accounted for until wounded and captured at Gettysburg, Pennsylvania, July 1-5, 1863. Hospitalized at Gettysburg until transferred to Davids Island, New York Harbor, July 17-24, 1863. Paroled at Davids Island and transferred to City Point, Virginia, where he was received August 28, 1863, for exchange. Returned to duty on November 2, 1863, and present or accounted for until wounded at Spotsylvania Court House, Virginia, May 10, 1864. Reported absent wounded through February, 1865.

BYRUM, JAMES, Private
Resided in Mecklenburg County where he enlisted at age 47, February 1, 1862, for the war. Present or accounted for until hospitalized at Wilmington on or about August 6, 1862, with typhoid fever. Died in hospital at Wilmington on August 8, 1862.

CAMPBELL, WILLIAM H., Private
Resided in Mecklenburg County where he enlisted at age 20, May 3, 1862, for the war. Present or

accounted for until he died in hospital at Wilmington on July 24, 1862. Cause of death not reported.

CHESHIER, MILTON E., Private
Resided in Mecklenburg County where he enlisted at age 23, February 1, 1862, for the war. Present or accounted for until hospitalized at Wilmington on June 6, 1862, with a gunshot wound; however, place and date wounded not reported. Rejoined the company in July-August, 1862, and present or accounted for until he died in hospital at Richmond, Virginia, January 19, 1865. Cause of death not reported.

COCHRANE, JOHN F., Corporal
Resided in Mecklenburg County where he enlisted at age 26, February 1, 1862, for the war. Mustered in as Private. Present or accounted for until captured at Bristoe Station, Virginia, October 14, 1863. Confined at Old Capitol Prison, Washington, D.C., until transferred to Point Lookout, Maryland, October 27, 1863. Paroled at Point Lookout and transferred to City Point, Virginia, March 16, 1864, for exchange. Rejoined the company prior to September 1, 1864, and was promoted to Corporal in March-April, 1865. Present or accounted for until captured at or near Petersburg, Virginia, April 2, 1865. Reported in confinement at Fort Delaware, Delaware, April 4, 1865. No further records.

CREASEMON, JOSEPH, Private
Resided in Gaston County and enlisted in Mecklenburg County at age 17, February 1, 1862, for the war. Present or accounted for until he died at Raleigh on April 20, 1862, of disease.

DARNELL, J. J., Private
Resided in Mecklenburg County where he enlisted at age 28, March 1, 1863, for the war. Present or accounted for until wounded at Gettysburg, Pennsylvania, July 1-3, 1863. Company muster rolls indicate that he was captured at Gettysburg; however, records of the Federal Provost Marshal do not substantiate that report. Returned to duty on November 18, 1863, and present or accounted for until he died "at home" on September 23, 1864, of disease.

DEATON, JAMES C., Private
Born in Mecklenburg County where he resided as a farmer prior to enlisting in Mecklenburg County at age 29, February 1, 1862, for the war. Present or accounted for until discharged on November 13, 1862, by reason of "hemiplegia." Paroled at Charlotte on May 13, 1865.

DUCKWORTH, HENRY DUVAL, Corporal
Resided in Mecklenburg County where he enlisted at age 18, February 1, 1862, for the war. Mustered in as Private and promoted to Corporal in January-February, 1865. Present or accounted for until captured at or near Petersburg, Virginia, April 2, 1865. Confined at Fort Delaware, Delaware, until released on June 19, 1865, after taking the Oath of Allegiance.

DUCKWORTH, J. A., Private
Enlisted in Mecklenburg County on April 22, 1864, for the war. Present or accounted for

through March 28, 1865.

DULIN, DANIEL, Private
Born in Mecklenburg County where he resided as a farmer prior to enlisting in Mecklenburg County at age 21, April 20, 1862, for the war. Present or accounted for until wounded in the left hip and captured at Gettysburg, Pennsylvania, July 1-4, 1863. Reported in hospital at Davids Island, New York Harbor, on or about July 24, 1863. Exchanged prior to January 1, 1864, and was retired to the Invalid Corps on April 1, 1864, by reason of wounds received at Gettysburg.

EARNHEARDT, J. H., Private
Resided in Mecklenburg County where he enlisted at age 22, February 1, 1862, for the war. Present or accounted for until killed at Gettysburg, Pennsylvania, July 1, 1863.

EARNHEARDT, J. M., Sergeant
Previously served as Private in Company C, 1st Regiment N.C. Infantry (6 months, 1861). Enlisted in this company on February 1, 1862, for the war. Mustered in as Private. Present or accounted for until wounded in the right side at Gettysburg, Pennsylvania, July 3, 1863. Rejoined the company prior to September 1, 1863, and was promoted to Corporal in January-February, 1864. Promoted to Sergeant in September-October, 1864. Present or accounted for until captured at or near Petersburg, Virginia, April 2, 1865. Reported in confinement at Fort Delaware, Delaware, April 4, 1865. Final disposition not reported; however, North Carolina pension records indicate that he survived the war.

EARNHEARDT, S. O., Private
Resided in Mecklenburg County where he enlisted at age 40, April 1, 1863, for the war. Present or accounted for until captured at Falling Waters, Maryland, July 14, 1863. Confined at Point Lookout, Maryland, where he died on or about April 15, 1864, of "chro[nic] diarrhoea."

ELLIOTT, WILLIAM A., Private
Born in Mecklenburg County where he resided prior to enlisting in Mecklenburg County at age 21, July 7, 1862, for the war. Present or accounted for until killed at Gettysburg, Pennsylvania, July 1, 1863.

ELMS, JOHN P., 1st Sergeant
Previously served as Sergeant in Company C, 1st Regiment N.C. Infantry (6 months, 1861). Enlisted in this company on May 15, 1862, for the war. Promoted to 1st Sergeant from an unspecified rank on June 2, 1862. Present or accounted for until appointed 3rd Lieutenant on or about July 16, 1863, and transferred to Company I, 37th Regiment N.C. Troops.

ERNHARDT, WILLIAM C., Private
Resided in Mecklenburg County where he enlisted at age 35, April 1, 1863, for the war. Present or accounted for until captured at Gettysburg, Pennsylvania, on or about July 3, 1863. Confined at Fort Delaware, Delaware, until transferred to Point Lookout, Maryland, on or about October 15, 1863. Died in hospital at Point Lookout on October 23, 1863, of "chr[onic] diarrhoea."

EWING, GEORGE R., Private

Resided in Mecklenburg County where he enlisted at age 20, February 1, 1862, for the war. Present or accounted for until wounded and captured at Gettysburg, Pennsylvania, July 1-4, 1863. Hospitalized at Davids Island, New York Harbor, until paroled and transferred to City Point, Virginia, where he was received August 28, 1863, for exchange. Returned to duty on November 11, 1863, and present or accounted for until hospitalized at Richmond, Virginia, October 2, 1864, with a gunshot wound of the left hip. Place and date wounded not reported. Reported absent wounded until he was reported absent without leave in January-February, 1865. Paroled at Charlotte on May 15, 1865.

EWING, WILLIAM E., Private

Born in Mecklenburg County where he resided as a farmer prior to enlisting in Mecklenburg County at age 25, July 7, 1862, for the war. Present or accounted for until wounded and captured at Gettysburg, Pennsylvania, July 1-5, 1863. Hospitalized at various Federal hospitals until paroled and transferred to City Point, Virginia, where he was received August 24, 1863, for exchange. Rejoined the company in January-February, 1864, and present or accounted for until paroled at Charlotte on May 20, 1865.

FARTHING, PAUL, Sergeant

Place and date of enlistment not reported. Died at Camp Chase, Ohio, or at Camp Dennison, Ohio, April 11, 1865. Place and date captured and cause of death not reported.

FARTHING, R. P., Private

Place and date of enlistment not reported. Died at Camp Chase, Ohio, or at Camp Dennison, Ohio, April 24, 1865. Place and date captured and cause of death not reported.

FISHER, J. W., Private

Resided in Gaston County and enlisted in Mecklenburg County at age 22, February 1, 1862, for the war. Present or accounted for until captured near Petersburg, Virginia, March 25, 1865. Confined at Point Lookout, Maryland, until released on June 26, 1865, after taking the Oath of Allegiance.

FLOW, R. H., Private

Resided in Mecklenburg County where he enlisted at age 21, February 1, 1862, for the war. Present or accounted for until reported absent wounded in November-December, 1864; however, place and date wounded not reported. Reported absent wounded through February, 1865. Paroled at Charlotte on May 18, 1865. [May have served previously in Company C, 1st Regiment N.C. Infantry (6 months, 1861).]

FORD, WILLIAM C., Private

Resided in Mecklenburg County where he enlisted at age 33, April 20, 1862, for the war. Present or accounted for through February, 1865.

FRAZIER, I. S. A., Private

Resided in Mecklenburg County where he enlisted at age 20, February 1, 1862, for the war. Present

or accounted for until wounded at Franklin, Virginia, in November, 1862. Rejoined the company in January-February, 1864, and present or accounted for until retired to the Invalid Corps on November 17, 1864. Captured in hospital at Richmond, Virginia, April 3, 1865, and paroled on April 23, 1865. [May have served previously in Company C, 1st Regiment N.C. Infantry (6 months, 1861).]

GALLOWAY, JAMES S., Private

Previously served in Company C, 1st Regiment N.C. Infantry (6 months, 1861). Enlisted in this company on February 1, 1862, for the war. Present or accounted for until wounded in the breast at Gettysburg, Pennsylvania, July 1, 1863. Died in hospital at Richmond, Virginia, July 21, 1863, of wounds received at Gettysburg.

GARRISON, J. S., Private

Born in Mecklenburg County where he resided prior to enlisting in Mecklenburg County at age 18, December 29, 1862, for the war. Present or accounted for until killed at Gettysburg, Pennsylvania, July 3, 1863.

GIBSON, JAMES A., Private

Previously served in Company C, 1st Regiment N.C. Infantry (6 months, 1861). Enlisted in this company on February 1, 1862, for the war. Present or accounted for until promoted to Musician in September-October, 1864, and transferred to the regimental band.

GLENN, DAVID P., Private

Previously served in Company C, 1st Regiment N.C. Infantry (6 months, 1861). Enlisted in this company of February 1, 1862, for the war. Present or accounted for until wounded in the right arm at Gettysburg, Pennsylvania, July 1-3, 1863. Right arm amputated. Reported absent wounded until discharged on or about February 9, 1864.

GLENN, FRANK C., Private

Resided in Mecklenburg County where he enlisted at age 27, May 3, 1862, for the war. Present or accounted for through February, 1865. Paroled at Charlotte on May 3, 1865.

GLOVER, JOSHUA, Private

Resided in Mecklenburg County where he enlisted at age 37, March 1, 1863, for the war. Present or accounted for until wounded in the left thigh and captured at Gettysburg, Pennsylvania, July 1-3, 1863. Hospitalized at Gettysburg and at Baltimore, Maryland, until paroled at Baltimore on November 12, 1863, and transferred to City Point, Virginia, where he was received November 17, 1863, for exchange. Rejoined the company in May-June, 1864, and present or accounted for through February, 1865.

GOODRUM, C. H., Private

Enlisted in Mecklenburg County on February 25, 1864, for the war. Present or accounted for until he died in hospital at Lynchburg, Virginia, on or about July 16, 1864. Cause of death not reported.

GOODRUM, WILLIAM J., Private

Resided in Mecklenburg County where he enlisted at age 18, March 1, 1863, for the war. Present or accounted for until wounded in the abdomen and captured at Gettysburg, Pennsylvania, July 1-3, 1863. Died in hospital at Chester, Pennsylvania, July 18, 1863, of wounds.

GRAY, WALTER W., Private
Resided in Mecklenburg County where he enlisted at age 20, February 1, 1862, for the war. Present or accounted for through February, 1865. Paroled at Charlotte on May 20, 1865.

GRIBBLE, ROBERT J., Sergeant
Resided in Mecklenburg County where he enlisted at age 21, February 1, 1862, for the war. Mustered in as Corporal. Present or accounted for until hospitalized at Richmond, Virginia, October 2, 1864, with a gunshot wound of the left ankle; however, place and date wounded not reported. Returned to duty on December 3, 1864, and was promoted to Sergeant in January-February, 1865. Present or accounted for until captured at or near Petersburg, Virginia, April 2, 1865. Confined at Fort Delaware, Delaware, until released on June 19, 1865, after taking the Oath of Allegiance. [May have served previously in Company C, 1st Regiment N.C. Infantry (6 months, 1861).]

GROVES, ROBERT A., Private
Resided in Gaston County and enlisted in Mecklenburg County at age 22, February 1, 1862, for the war. Present or accounted for until captured at Falling Waters, Maryland, July 14, 1863. Confined at Baltimore, Maryland, until transferred to Point Lookout, Maryland, August 21, 1863. Paroled at Point Lookout on March 17, 1864, and transferred to City Point, Virginia, for exchange. Rejoined the company prior to July 1, 1864, and present or accounted for until captured at or near Petersburg, Virginia, April 2, 1865. Confined at Point Lookout until released on June 27, 1865, after taking the Oath of Allegiance.

HAND, ANDREW J., Private
Previously served in Company K, 1st Regiment N.C. Infantry (6 months, 1861). Enlisted in this company on February 1, 1862, for the war. Present or accounted for until captured at Gettysburg, Pennsylvania, July 1-5, 1863. Hospitalized at Gettysburg with an unspecified illness and was transferred to Davids Island, New York Harbor, July 17-24, 1863. Paroled at Davids Island on August 24, 1863, and transferred to City Point, Virginia, for exchange. Returned to duty on November 2, 1863, and present or accounted for until captured near Petersburg, Virginia, October 27, 1864. Confined at Point Lookout, Maryland, until paroled on or about February 13, 1865, and transferred for exchange. Reported present with a detachment of paroled and exchanged prisoners at Camp Lee, near Richmond, Virginia, February 17, 1865.

HARRIS, N. O., Private
Resided in Mecklenburg County where he enlisted at age 23, May 3, 1862, for the war. Present or accounted for until hospitalized at Richmond, Virginia, July 15, 1863, with a shell wound of the right shoulder; however, place and date wounded not reported. Rejoined the company in September-October, 1863, and present or accounted for until

captured near Petersburg, Virginia, March 25, 1865. Confined at Point Lookout, Maryland, until released on June 27, 1865, after taking the Oath of Allegiance.

HARRIS, W. C., Private
Previously served in Company C, 1st Regiment N.C. Infantry (6 months, 1861). Enlisted in this company on May 3, 1862, for the war. Present or accounted for until captured at or near Petersburg, Virginia, April 2, 1865. Confined at Fort Delaware, Delaware, until released on June 19, 1865, after taking the Oath of Allegiance.

HENDERSON, ISAAC SEBRING, Private
Resided in Mecklenburg County where he enlisted at age 20, February 1, 1862, for the war. Present or accounted for through February, 1865.

HENDERSON, THOMAS M., Private
Resided in Mecklenburg County where he enlisted at age 22, February 1, 1862, for the war. Present or accounted for until captured at Falling Waters, Maryland, July 14, 1863. Confined at Old Capitol Prison, Washington, D.C., until transferred to Point Lookout, Maryland, August 8, 1863. Died at Point Lookout on February 9, 1864. Cause of death not reported.

HERRING, G. T., Private
Previously served in Company C, 1st Regiment N.C. Infantry (6 months, 1861). Enlisted in this company on February 1, 1862, for the war. Present or accounted for until wounded at Gettysburg, Pennsylvania, July 1-3, 1863. Rejoined the company in January-February, 1864, and present or accounted for until paroled at Appomattox Court House, Virginia, April 9, 1865.

HERRON, J. M., Private
Enlisted at Camp Holmes on November 12, 1864, for the war. Present or accounted for through February, 1865.

HILL, HENRY H., Corporal
Previously served as Private in Company C, 1st Regiment N.C. Infantry (6 months, 1861). Enlisted in this company on February 1, 1862, for the war. Mustered in as Private. Present or accounted for until hospitalized at Richmond, Virginia, October 2, 1864, with a gunshot wound of the left side of the head; however, place and date wounded not reported. Rejoined the company in January-February, 1865, and was promoted to Corporal. Present or accounted for until captured at or near Petersburg, Virginia, April 2, 1865. Confined at Fort Delaware, Delaware, until released on June 19, 1865, after taking the Oath of Allegiance.

HILL, MILAS, Private
Resided in Mecklenburg County where he enlisted at age 34, July 7, 1862, for the war. Present or accounted for until captured in hospital at Richmond, Virginia, April 3, 1865. Confined at Libby Prison, Richmond, until transferred to Newport News, Virginia, April 23, 1865. Released at Newport News on June 30, 1865, after taking the Oath of Allegiance.

HILL, MILTON, Private
Resided in Mecklenburg County where he enlisted

at age 30, February 1, 1862, for the war. Present or accounted for until reported captured at Gettysburg, Pennsylvania, July 5, 1863; however, records of the Federal Provost Marshal do not substantiate that report. Company muster rolls indicate he was a prisoner until he was exchanged in May-June, 1864. Rejoined the company prior to September 1, 1864, and present or accounted for until captured in hospital at Richmond, Virginia, April 3, 1865. Turned over to the Federal Provost Marshal on or about April 22, 1865. Final disposition not reported.

HOBBS, F., Private
Resided in Mecklenburg County where he enlisted at age 17, May 15, 1862, for the war. Present or accounted for until wounded at Gettysburg, Pennsylvania, July 1-3, 1863. Rejoined the company in September-October, 1863, and present or accounted for until captured at or near Petersburg, Virginia, April 2, 1865. Confined at Point Lookout, Maryland, until released on June 27, 1865, after taking the Oath of Allegiance.

HOLMES, THOMAS L., Private
Previously served in Company C, 1st Regiment N.C. Infantry (6 months, 1861). Enlisted in this company on February 1, 1862, for the war. Present or accounted for until wounded in the left hip at Jones' Farm, Virginia, September 30, 1864. Died in hospital at Richmond, Virginia, October 25, 1864, of wounds.

HOVIS, MONROE, Private
Resided in Gaston County and enlisted in Mecklenburg County at age 23, February 1, 1862, for the war. Present or accounted for until wounded in the left shoulder at Spotsylvania Court House, Virginia, May 12, 1864. Rejoined the company in July-August, 1864, and present or accounted for until paroled at Appomattox Court House, Virginia, April 9, 1865.

HOWARD, THOMAS M., Private
Previously served in Company C, 1st Regiment N.C. Infantry (6 months, 1861). Enlisted in this company on May 15, 1862, for the war. Present or accounted for until hospitalized at Richmond, Virginia, May 24, 1864, with a gunshot wound; however, place and date wounded not reported. Rejoined the company in July-August, 1864, and present or accounted for until captured at or near Petersburg, Virginia, April 2, 1865. Confined at Fort Delaware, Delaware, until released on June 19, 1865, after taking the Oath of Allegiance.

HUNTER, A. J., Private
Enlisted in Mecklenburg County on June 11, 1864, for the war. Present or accounted for until promoted to Sergeant and transferred to Company E of this regiment on or about October 15, 1864.

HUNTER, DAVID PARKS, Private
Resided in Mecklenburg County where he enlisted at age 20, February 1, 1862, for the war. Present or accounted for until captured in hospital at Gettysburg, Pennsylvania, July 5, 1863. Hospitalized at Gettysburg until transferred to hospital at Davids Island, New York Harbor, July 17-24, 1863. Paroled at Davids Island and transferred to

City Point, Virginia, where he was received September 8, 1863, for exchange. Rejoined the company in March-April, 1864, and present or accounted for until captured at or near Petersburg, Virginia, April 2, 1865. Confined at Fort Delaware, Delaware, until released on June 19, 1865, after taking the Oath of Allegiance.

HUNTER, MADISON, Private
Resided in Mecklenburg County where he enlisted at age 18, February 1, 1862, for the war. Present or accounted for through February, 1865; however, he was reported absent on duty as a pioneer during much of that period. Paroled at Appomattox Court House, Virginia, April 9, 1865.

HUNTER, THOMAS H., Private
Resided in Mecklenburg County where he enlisted at age 18, February 1, 1862, for the war. Present or accounted for until he died on or about August 25, 1864, of disease. Place of death not reported.

HUTCHISON, JAMES H., Private
Resided in Mecklenburg County where he enlisted at age 24, February 1, 1862, for the war. Present or accounted for until wounded at Gettysburg, Pennsylvania, July 1, 1863. Died on or about July 5, 1863.

HUTSPETH, LEWIS, Private
Resided in Mecklenburg County where he enlisted at age 22, February 1, 1862, for the war. Present or accounted for until hospitalized at Wilmington on July 22, 1862, with pneumonia. Died in hospital at Wilmington on July 31, 1862.

ICEHOWER, WILLIAM S., Corporal
Previously served as Private in Company C, 1st Regiment N.C. Infantry (6 months, 1861). Enlisted in this company on February 1, 1862, for the war. Mustered in as Corporal. Present or accounted for until wounded and captured at Gettysburg, Pennsylvania, July 1-5, 1863. Hospitalized at Gettysburg until transferred to Davids Island, New York Harbor, July 17-24, 1863. Paroled at Davids Island and transferred to City Point, Virginia, where he was received September 16, 1863, for exchange. Rejoined the company in January-April, 1864, and present or accounted for until killed at Cold Harbor, Virginia, June 2, 1864.

JENKINS, DAVID, Private
Resided in Gaston County and enlisted in Mecklenburg County at age 20, February 1, 1862, for the war. Present or accounted for until wounded in the right thigh and captured at Gettysburg, Pennsylvania, July 1-3, 1863. Hospitalized at Gettysburg and at Chester, Pennsylvania, until transferred to Point Lookout, Maryland, October 2, 1863. Confined at Point Lookout until paroled on February 18, 1865, and transferred to Boulware's and Cox's Wharf, James River, Virginia, for exchange. Reported present with a detachment of paroled and exchanged prisoners at Camp Lee, near Richmond, Virginia, February 28, 1865.

JENKINS, JACOB, Private
Resided in Gaston County and enlisted in Mecklenburg County at age 22, July 7, 1862, for the war. Present or accounted for until captured at Falling

Waters, Maryland, July 14, 1863. Confined at Point Lookout, Maryland, until paroled and transferred to City Point, Virginia, March 16, 1864, for exchange. Rejoined the company in May-June, 1864, and present or accounted for through February, 1865.

JOHNSON, THOMAS NEAL, Private
Previously served in Company C, 1st Regiment N.C. Infantry (6 months, 1861). Enlisted in this company on April 1, 1862, for the war. Present or accounted for until wounded and captured at Gettysburg, Pennsylvania, July 1-5, 1863. Confined at Fort Delaware, Delaware, until transferred to Point Lookout, Maryland, October 15-18, 1863. Paroled at Point Lookout and transferred for exchange on or about February 13, 1865. Reported present with a detachment of paroled and exchanged prisoners at Camp Lee, near Richmond, Virginia, February 18, 1865.

JOHNSTON, ALFRED, Private
Born in Yadkin County* and resided in Mecklenburg County where he was by occupation a mail carrier prior to enlisting in Mecklenburg County at age 20, February 1, 1862, for the war. Present or accounted for until discharged on September 2, 1863, by reason of "phthisis pulmonalis."

KENNEDY, WILLIAM, Private
Previously served in Company C, 1st Regiment N.C. Infantry (6 months, 1861). Enlisted in this company on February 1, 1862, for the war. Present or accounted for until reported absent on wounded furlough on company muster rolls dated May-December, 1864. Place and date wounded not reported. Reported absent on detached service on company muster roll dated January-February, 1865. Paroled at Appomattox Court House, Virginia, April 9, 1865.

KERNS, JOHN DIXON, Private
Resided in Mecklenburg County where he enlisted at age 26, February 1, 1862, for the war. Present or accounted for until wounded and captured at or near Petersburg, Virginia, April 2, 1865. Confined at Fort Delaware, Delaware, April 4, 1865. Final disposition not reported; however, North Carolina pension records indicate that he survived the war.

KERNS, THOMAS J., Private
Place and date of enlistment not reported. Captured at or near Petersburg, Virginia, April 2, 1865, and confined at Fort Delaware, Delaware, April 4, 1865. No further records.

KING, CAMPBELL C., Private
Resided in Mecklenburg County where he enlisted at age 25, May 3, 1862, for the war. Present or accounted for until captured at Bristoe Station, Virginia, October 14, 1863. Confined at Old Capitol Prison, Washington, D.C., until transferred to Point Lookout, Maryland, October 27, 1863. Paroled at Point Lookout on March 3, 1864, and transferred to City Point, Virginia, for exchange. Present or accounted for until hospitalized at Raleigh on June 19, 1864, with a gunshot wound; however, place and date wounded not reported. Rejoined the company in November-December, 1864, and present or accounted for until captured

at or near Petersburg, Virginia, April 2, 1865. Confined at Fort Delaware, Delaware, until released on June 19, 1865, after taking the Oath of Allegiance.

KING, JOHN A., Private
Resided in Mecklenburg County where he enlisted at age 24, May 3, 1862, for the war. Present or accounted for through February, 1865.

KINNEY, BENJAMIN, Private
Resided in Mecklenburg County where he enlisted at age 40, December 29, 1862, for the war. Present or accounted for through February, 1865.

KNIPPER, THOMAS, Private
Resided in Mecklenburg County where he enlisted at age 26, February 1, 1862, for the war. Present or accounted for until captured at or near Petersburg, Virginia, April 2, 1865. Confined at Fort Delaware, Delaware, until released on June 19, 1865, after taking the Oath of Allegiance.

LEWIS, EMANUEL, Sergeant
Resided in Gaston County and enlisted in Mecklenburg County at age 19, February 1, 1862, for the war. Mustered in as Private and promoted to Corporal on June 15, 1863. Present or accounted for until wounded in the left hand at Wilderness, Virginia, May 5, 1864. Reported absent wounded through October, 1864. Promoted to Sergeant in November-December, 1864, but was retired prior to March 1, 1865.

McCALL, J. A., Private
Enlisted in Mecklenburg County on February 29, 1864, for the war. Present or accounted for through February, 1865.

McCONNEL, JOHN F., Private
Enlisted in Mecklenburg County on February 1, 1862, for the war. Present or accounted for until wounded and captured at Gettysburg, Pennsylvania, July 1-5, 1863. Died in hospital at Gettysburg of wounds. Date of death not reported.

McCONNEL, JOHN H., Private
Resided in Mecklenburg County where he enlisted at age 19, February 1, 1862, for the war. Present or accounted for until wounded at Gettysburg, Pennsylvania, July 1-3, 1863. Returned to duty prior to September 1, 1863, and present or accounted for until captured at or near Petersburg, Virginia, April 2, 1865. Confined at Fort Delaware, Delaware, until released on June 19, 1865, after taking the Oath of Allegiance.

McCONNEL, THOMAS Y., Private
Resided in Mecklenburg County where he enlisted at age 18, February 1, 1862, for the war. Present or accounted for through February, 1865.

McCORKLE, JAMES G., 1st Sergeant
Previously served as Sergeant in Company C, 1st Regiment N.C. Infantry (6 months, 1861). Enlisted in this company on February 1, 1862, for the war. Mustered in as 1st Sergeant. Present or accounted for until appointed Sergeant Major in April, 1862, and transferred to the Field and Staff of this regiment.

McELROY, SAMUEL J., Sergeant
Previously served as Private in Company C, 1st

Regiment N.C. Infantry (6 months, 1861). Enlisted in this company on February 1, 1862, for the war. Mustered in as Sergeant. Present or accounted for until wounded and captured at Gettysburg, Pennsylvania, July 1-5, 1863. Hospitalized at Davids Island, New York Harbor, until paroled and transferred to City Point, Virginia, where he was received September 16, 1863, for exchange. Rejoined the company in March-April, 1864, and present or accounted for until hospitalized at Richmond, Virginia, on or about October 2, 1864, with a gunshot wound of the right side of the face. Place and date wounded not reported. Rejoined the company in January-February, 1865, and present or accounted for through February, 1865.

McGINN, ROBERT F., Private
Resided in Mecklenburg County where he enlisted at age 30, May 15, 1862, for the war. Present or accounted for until captured at Falling Waters, Maryland, July 14, 1863. Confined at Baltimore, Maryland, until transferred to Point Lookout, Maryland, where he arrived August 17, 1863. Died at Point Lookout on February 2, 1864. Cause of death not reported.

McGINNIS, SIDNEY A., Private
Resided in Mecklenburg County where he enlisted at age 27, March 1, 1863, for the war. Present or accounted for until wounded and captured at Gettysburg, Pennsylvania, July 3, 1863. Confined at Fort Delaware, Delaware, until transferred to Point Lookout, Maryland, October 15-18, 1863. Died at Point Lookout on February 15, 1864. Cause of death not reported.

McWHIRTER, JAMES, Private
Resided in Mecklenburg County where he enlisted at age 18, October 3, 1863, for the war. Present or accounted for until he died in hospital at Gordonsville, Virginia, January 31, 1864, of "febris cont. com."

McWHIRTER, JOHN, Private
Resided in Mecklenburg County where he enlisted at age 20, February 1, 1862, for the war. Present or accounted for through June, 1863. Company records indicate he was wounded and captured at Gettysburg, Pennsylvania, July 3, 1863; however, records of the Federal Provost Marshal do not substantiate that report. No further records.

MONTEITH, H. L. D., Private
Resided in Mecklenburg County where he enlisted at age 20, February 1, 1862, for the war. Present or accounted for until captured near Petersburg, Virginia, March 25, 1865. Confined at Point Lookout, Maryland, until released on June 29, 1865, after taking the Oath of Allegiance.

MONTEITH, MOSES O., Private
Previously served in Company C, 1st Regiment N.C. Infantry (6 months, 1861). Enlisted in this company on July 7, 1862, for the war. Present or accounted for through April, 1864. Company records indicate he was wounded and "left on [the] battle field" at Wilderness, Virginia, May 5, 1864. Records of the Federal Provost Marshal do not indicate that he was captured. No further records.

MONTEITH, R. J., Private
Previously served in Company C, 1st Regiment N.C. Infantry (6 months, 1861). Enlisted in this company on February 1, 1862, for the war. Present or accounted for until paroled at Appomattox Court House, Virginia, April 9, 1865.

NEAL, G. A., Private
Resided in Mecklenburg County where he enlisted at age 18, February 1, 1862, for the war. Present or accounted for until wounded in the left thigh and/or left shoulder and captured at Gettysburg, Pennsylvania, July 1-3, 1863. Date exchanged not reported; however, he was hospitalized at Raleigh on September 29, 1864, with "amputation of left arm." Furloughed for sixty days on October 7, 1864. No further records.

NEILY, THOMAS W., 1st Sergeant
Previously served as Private in Company C, 1st Regiment N.C. Infantry (6 months, 1861). Enlisted in this company on February 1, 1862, for the war. Mustered in as Corporal and promoted to Sergeant on June 2, 1862. Present or accounted for until wounded at Gettysburg, Pennsylvania, July 1-3, 1863. Returned to duty on December 17, 1863, and present or accounted for until hospitalized at Charlotte on October 24, 1864, with a gunshot wound of the left thigh. Place and date wounded not reported. Promoted to 1st Sergeant in November-December, 1864, and was present or accounted for through February, 1865. Paroled at Appomattox Court House, Virginia, April 9, 1865.

NEWELL, A. H., Private
Born in Mecklenburg County where he resided prior to enlisting in Mecklenburg County at age 19, February 1, 1862, for the war. Present or accounted for until hospitalized at Richmond, Virginia, July 15, 1863, with a contusion of the left shoulder; however, place and date injured not reported. Rejoined the company prior to September 1, 1863, and present or accounted for until he died on August 27, 1864, of disease. Place of death not reported.

NORMENT, ISAAC, Private
Previously served in Company C, 1st Regiment N.C. Infantry (6 months, 1861). Enlisted in this company on May 15, 1862, for the war. Present or accounted for until wounded at Gettysburg, Pennsylvania, July 1, 1863. Returned to duty prior to September 1, 1863, and present or accounted for until captured at Petersburg, Virginia, April 3, 1865. Confined at Hart's Island, New York Harbor, until released on June 14, 1865, after taking the Oath of Allegiance.

NORMENT, JOHN, Private
Previously served in Company C, 1st Regiment N.C. Infantry (6 months, 1861). Enlisted in this company of February 1, 1862, for the war. Present or accounted for through February, 1865.

ORMAN, J. E., Private
Born in Mecklenburg County where he resided as a farmer prior to enlisting in Mecklenburg County at age 17, February 1, 1862, for the war. Present or accounted for until paroled at Appomattox Court House, Virginia, April 9, 1865.

ORR, JAMES F., Private
Resided in Mecklenburg County where he enlisted at age 39, February 1, 1862, for the war. Present or accounted for until captured near Petersburg, Virginia, October 25-27, 1864. Confined at Point Lookout, Maryland, until paroled and transferred for exchange on January 17, 1865. Rejoined the company prior to April 3, 1865, when he was captured at Petersburg. Confined at Hart's Island, New York Harbor, until released on June 19, 1865, after taking the Oath of Allegiance. [May have served previously in Company C, 1st Regiment N.C. Infantry (6 months, 1861).]

ORR, N. C. H., Private
Previously served in Company C, 1st Regiment N.C. Infantry (6 months, 1861). Enlisted in this company on February 1, 1862, for the war. Present or accounted for until captured at Bristoe Station, Virginia, October 14, 1863. Confined at Old Capitol Prison, Washington, D. C., until transferred to Point Lookout, Maryland, October 27, 1863. Died at Point Lookout on September 30, 1864. Cause of death not reported.

PAYSOUR, C., Private
Resided in Gaston County and enlisted in Mecklenburg County at age 33, March 1, 1863, for the war. Present or accounted for until wounded and captured at Gettysburg, Pennsylvania, July 1-3, 1863. Hospitalized at Gettysburg until transferred to Davids Island, New York Harbor, July 17-24, 1863. Paroled at Davids Island until transferred to City Point, Virginia, where he was received August 28, 1863, for exchange. Returned to duty on November 3, 1863, and present or accounted for until captured near Petersburg, Virginia, March 25, 1865. Confined at Point Lookout, Maryland, until released on June 16, 1865, after taking the Oath of Allegiance.

PETTIS, STEPHEN J., Private
Resided in Mecklenburg County. Place and date of enlistment not reported. Captured at or near Petersburg, Virginia, April 2, 1865, and confined at Fort Delaware, Delaware, until released on or about June 19, 1865, after taking the Oath of Allegiance.

PETTUS, H. M., Private
Resided in Gaston County and enlisted in Mecklenburg County at age 23, May 15, 1862, for the war. Present or accounted for until paroled at Appomattox Court House, Virginia, April 9, 1865. [May have served previously in Company C, 1st Regiment N.C. Infantry (6 months, 1861).]

PETTUS, JOHN W., Private
Previously served in Company C, 37th Regiment N.C. Troops. Transferred to this company in January-February, 1864. Present or accounted for until reported absent wounded in May-June, 1864; however, place and date wounded not reported. Reported absent wounded or absent on furlough through February, 1865. Rejoined the company prior to April 2, 1865, when he was captured at or near Petersburg, Virginia. Confined at Fort Delaware, Delaware, until released on June 19, 1865, after taking the Oath of Allegiance.

PEYSOUR, S. P., Private
Resided in Gaston County and enlisted in Mecklenburg County on November 7, 1864, for the war. Present or accounted for until captured at or near Petersburg, Virginia, April 2, 1865. Confined at Fort Delaware, Delaware, until released on June 19, 1865, after taking the Oath of Allegiance.

POWELL, DANIEL, Private
Resided in Gaston County and enlisted in Mecklenburg County at age 27, April 20, 1862, for the war. Present or accounted for until killed at Gettysburg, Pennsylvania, July 1, 1863.

PRIM, THOMAS A., Private
Resided in Mecklenburg County where he enlisted at age 18, March 1, 1863, for the war. Present or accounted for until wounded at Gettysburg, Pennsylvania, July 1, 1863. Died of wounds. Place and date of death not reported.

QUERY, R. L., Private
Resided in Mecklenburg County where he enlisted at age 21, February 1, 1862, for the war. Present or accounted for until captured at or near Petersburg, Virginia, April 2, 1865. Confined at Fort Delaware, Delaware, until released on June 19, 1865, after taking the Oath of Allegiance.

QUERY, S. F., Private
Resided in Mecklenburg County where he enlisted at age 21, February 1, 1862, for the war. Present or accounted for until hospitalized at Charlotte on January 13, 1865, with a gunshot wound of the "lower left extremities." Place and date wounded not reported. Captured in hospital at Charlotte at an unspecified date and was paroled on or about May 15, 1865.

RABORN, M. D., Private
Resided in Mecklenburg County where he enlisted at age 18, May 3, 1862, for the war. Present or accounted for through June, 1863. Reported absent without leave from July-August, 1863, until he returned to duty on November 19, 1863. Present or accounted for through February, 1865.

RATCHFORD, E. C., Private
Resided in Gaston County and enlisted in Mecklenburg County at age 27, April 20, 1862, for the war. Present or accounted for until he died in hospital at Weldon on January 21, 1863, of "erysipelas."

ROBERTS, PEYTON, Private
Born in Mecklenburg County where he resided as a farmer prior to enlisting in Mecklenburg County at age 20, February 1, 1862, for the war. Present or accounted for until wounded in the right foot and captured at Gettysburg, Pennsylvania, July 1-5, 1863. Hospitalized at Gettysburg until transferred to Davids Island, New York Harbor, July 17-24, 1863. Paroled at Davids Island and transferred to City Point, Virginia, where he was received September 8, 1863, for exchange. Reported absent wounded until discharged on February 17, 1865, by reason of wounds received at Gettysburg.

ROSS, ROBERT A., Private
Resided in Mecklenburg County where he enlisted at age 41, February 1, 1862, for the war. Present

or accounted for until transferred to Company H of this regiment on July 11, 1862.

RUDDOCK, B. M., Private
Resided in Mecklenburg County where he enlisted at age 18, February 1, 1862, for the war. Present or accounted for until reported absent wounded in September-October, 1864; however, place and date wounded not reported. Rejoined the company in January-February, 1865, and present or accounted for through February, 1865.

RUDDOCK, B. W., Private
Resided in Mecklenburg County where he enlisted at age 16, February 1, 1862, for the war. Present or accounted for until hospitalized at Richmond, Virginia, October 31, 1864, with a gunshot wound of the right leg; however, place and date wounded not reported. Reported absent wounded through February, 1865.

RUDDOCK, THEO C., Private
Previously served as Private in Company C, 1st Regiment N.C. Infantry (6 months, 1861). Enlisted in this company on February 1, 1862, for the war. Mustered in as Corporal. Present or accounted for until captured at Falling Waters, Maryland, July 14, 1863. Confined at Baltimore, Maryland, and at Point Lookout, Maryland. Promoted to Sergeant in January-February, 1864, while a prisoner of war. Paroled at Point Lookout on March 3, 1864, and transferred to City Point, Virginia, for exchange. Reduced to ranks in September-October, 1864. Captured near Petersburg, Virginia, October 27, 1864, and confined at Point Lookout until released on June 3, 1865, after taking the Oath of Allegiance.

SIMPSON, JOHN W., Private
Resided in Mecklenburg County where he enlisted at age 18, March 1, 1863, for the war. Present or accounted for through April 11, 1865; however, he was reported absent sick during much of that period.

SIMPSON, ROBERT F., Private
Previously served in Company C, 1st Regiment N.C. Infantry (6 months, 1861). Enlisted in this company on February 1, 1862, for the war. Present or accounted for until wounded and captured at Gettysburg, Pennsylvania, July 3-5, 1863. Hospitalized at various Federal hospitals until confined at Point Lookout, Maryland, October 15-18, 1863. Confined at Point Lookout until paroled and transferred for exchange of February 13, 1865. Reported present with a detachment of paroled and exchanged prisoners at Camp Lee, near Richmond, Virginia, February 17, 1865.

SIMS, JAMES MONROE, Sergeant
Previously served as Private in Company C, 1st Regiment N.C. Infantry (6 months, 1861). Enlisted in this company on February 1, 1862, for the war. Mustered in as Sergeant. Present or accounted for until captured at Falling Waters, Maryland, July 14, 1863. Confined at Baltimore, Maryland, until paroled and transferred to City Point, Virginia, August 23, 1863, for exchange. Returned to duty on October 30, 1863. Promoted to Quartermaster Sergeant on November 1, 1863, and transferred to

the Field and Staff of this regiment.

SMITH, JOHN S., Private
Resided in Mecklenburg County where he enlisted at age 36, March 1, 1863, for the war. Present or accounted for until wounded in the head and captured at Gettysburg, Pennsylvania, July 3, 1863. Died at Gettysburg on July 15, 1863, of wounds.

STOWE, J. C., Private
Resided in Gaston County and was by occupation a farmer prior to enlisting in Mecklenburg County at age 25, April 20, 1862, for the war. Present or accounted for until wounded at Jones' Farm, Virginia, September 30, 1864. Hospitalized at Richmond, Virginia, where he died November 2, 1864, of wounds.

STOWE, J. M., Private
Previously served in Company C, 1st Regiment N.C. Infantry (6 months, 1861). Enlisted in this company on February 1, 1862, for the war. Present or accounted for until wounded in the left thigh and captured at Gettysburg, Pennsylvania, July 1-5, 1863. Hospitalized at various Federal hospitals until paroled and transferred to City Point, Virginia, where he was received November 17, 1863, for exchange. Reported absent wounded through February, 1865. Paroled at Charlotte on May 12, 1865.

TAYLOR, H. S., Private
Resided in Mecklenburg County where he enlisted at age 22, February 1, 1862, for the war. Present or accounted for until captured near Petersburg, Virginia, October 27, 1864. Confined at Point Lookout, Maryland, until released on June 3, 1865, after taking the Oath of Allegiance.

TAYLOR, J. Q., Private
Enlisted in Mecklenburg County on January 27, 1864, for the war. Present or accounted for until he "died of wounds done by himself" on October 24, 1864. Place of death not reported.

TAYLOR, R. C. C., Private
Resided in Mecklenburg County where he enlisted at age 19, February 1, 1862, for the war. Present or accounted for until captured at or near Petersburg, Virginia, April 2, 1865. Confined at Fort Delaware, Delaware, until released on June 19, 1865, after taking the Oath of Allegiance.

THOMASSON, J. B., Private
Resided in Mecklenburg County and enlisted on October 29, 1864, for the war. Present or accounted for until captured at or near Petersburg, Virginia, April 2, 1865. Confined at Fort Delaware, Delaware, until released on June 19, 1865, after taking the Oath of Allegiance.

THOMPSON, J. B., Private
Resided in Mecklenburg County and enlisted at age 30, February 1, 1862, for the war. Present or accounted for until discharged in May, 1862, by reason of disability.

WALLACE, W. A. W., Private
Resided in Mecklenburg County where he enlisted at age 19, February 1, 1862, for the war. Present or accounted for until captured at Falling Waters,

Maryland, July 14, 1863. Confined at Baltimore, Maryland, and at Point Lookout, Maryland, until paroled and transferred to City Point, Virginia, March 16, 1864, for exchange. Rejoined the company in May-June, 1864, and present or accounted for until captured at or near Petersburg, Virginia, April 2, 1865. Confined at Point Lookout until released on June 21, 1865, after taking the Oath of Allegiance. Roll of Honor indicates he was wounded at Gettysburg, Pennsylvania.

WEST, J. L., Private
Born in Gaston County* where he resided as a farmer prior to enlisting in Mecklenburg County at age 27, May 15, 1862, for the war. Present or accounted for until discharged on May 28, 1863, by reason of lung disease.

WHITERS, B. A., Private
Resided in Mecklenburg County where he enlisted at age 26, February 1, 1862, for the war. Present or accounted for until reported absent wounded in September-October, 1864. Place and date wounded not reported. Reported absent wounded through February, 1865.

WILLIAMS, S. H., Private
Resided in Gaston County and enlisted in Mecklenburg County at age 29, February 1, 1862, for the war. Present or accounted for through February, 1865. Paroled at Charlotte on May 12, 1865.

WILSON, WILLIAM M., Private
Resided in Mecklenburg County where he enlisted at age 20, April 1, 1863, for the war. Present or accounted for until captured at or near Chambersburg, Pennsylvania, July 3-4, 1863. Confined at various Federal prisons until paroled at Point Lookout, Maryland, May 3, 1864, and transferred for exchange. Promoted to Hospital Steward in May-June, 1864, and transferred to the Field and Staff of this regiment.

WINGATE, ANGUS, Private
Previously served in Company K, 1st Regiment N.C. Infantry (6 months, 1861). Enlisted in this company on February 1, 1862, for the war. Present or accounted for until killed at Gettysburg, Pennsylvania, July 3, 1863.

WINGATE, CHARLES C., Private
Previously served in Company C, 1st Regiment N.C. Infantry (6 months, 1861). Enlisted in this company on February 1, 1862, for the war. Present or accounted for until appointed Musician in September-October, 1864, and transferred to the regimental band.

WINGATE, MURCHISON, Private
Previously served in Company K, 1st Regiment N.C. Infantry (6 months, 1861). Enlisted in this company on February 1, 1862, for the war. Present or accounted for until captured at or near Petersburg, Virginia, April 2, 1865. Confined at Fort Delaware, Delaware, until released on June 19, 1865, after taking the Oath of Allegiance.

WRIGHT, TAYLOR, Private
Resided in Gaston County and enlisted in Mecklenburg County at age 18, March 1, 1863, for

the war. Present or accounted for until wounded in the back and captured at Gettysburg, Pennsylvania, July 3-5, 1863. Confined at Fort Delaware, Delaware, until exchanged on July 31, 1863. Returned to duty on November 9, 1863, and present or accounted for until reported absent wounded in September-October, 1864. Place and date wounded not reported. Rejoined the company in November-December, 1864, and present or accounted for through February, 1865.

COMPANY B

This company was composed primarily of men from Burke, Wilkes, and Caldwell counties and began organizing on or about December 20, 1861. On March 31, 1862, it was mustered in as Company B of this regiment. After that date the company functioned as a part of the regiment, and its history for the war period is recorded as a part of the regimental history.

The information contained in the following roster of the company was compiled principally from company muster rolls for May, 1862, through February, 1865. No company muster rolls were found for the period prior to May, 1862, or for the period after February, 1865. In addition to the company muster rolls, Roll of Honor records, receipt rolls, hospital records, prisoner of war records, and other primary records, supplemented by state pension applications, United Daughters of the Confederacy records, and postwar rosters and histories, all provided useful information.

OFFICERS

CAPTAINS

ARMFIELD, MARK D.
Previously served as 2nd Lieutenant in Company G, 1st Regiment N.C. Infantry (6 months, 1861). Appointed Captain of this company to rank from December 3, 1861. Present or accounted for until captured at Gettysburg, Pennsylvania, July 3-4, 1863. Confined at Fort McHenry, Maryland, and at Fort Delaware, Delaware, until transferred to Johnson's Island, Ohio, July 18, 1863. Died at Johnson's Island on December 3, 1863, of "general debility."

PARKS, THOMAS R.
Previously served as Sergeant in Company G, 1st Regiment N.C. Infantry (6 months, 1861). Appointed 1st Lieutenant in this company to rank from February 15, 1862. Present or accounted for until captured at Falling Waters, Maryland, July 14, 1863. Confined at Baltimore, Maryland, and at Point Lookout, Maryland. Promoted to Captain on December 3, 1863, while a prisoner of war. Paroled at Point Lookout on March 3, 1864, and transferred for exchange. Rejoined the company in May-June, 1864, and present or accounted for until paroled at Appomattox Court House, Virginia, April 9, 1865.

LIEUTENANTS

DORSEY, ELISHA WESLEY, 1st Lieutenant
Resided in Burke County and enlisted at age 26. Appointed 3rd Lieutenant to rank from February 15, 1862. Present or accounted for until wounded in the right leg and captured at Gettysburg, Pennsylvania, July 1-5, 1863. Right leg amputated. Hospitalized at various Federal hospitals. Promoted to 1st Lieutenant in December, 1863, while a prisoner of war. Paroled and exchanged in December, 1864. Captured in hospital at Richmond, Virginia, April 3, 1865, and paroled on April 27, 1865.

WALKER, ELISHA FLETCHER, 3rd Lieutenant
Resided in Burke County where he enlisted at age 28, February 1, 1862, for the war. Mustered in as Private. Present or accounted for until wounded in the shoulder and side at Gettysburg, Pennsylvania, July 1-3, 1863. Rejoined the company in September-October, 1863, and was appointed 3rd Lieutenant on February 15, 1864. Present or accounted for until captured near Petersburg, Virginia, October 27, 1864. Confined at Old Capitol Prison, Washington, D.C., until transferred to Fort Delaware, Delaware, December 16, 1864. Released at Fort Delaware on June 17, 1865, after taking the Oath of Allegiance. North Carolina pension records indicate he was wounded in the leg at Wilderness, Virginia.

WARLICK, JOHN L., 2nd Lieutenant
Previously served as Corporal in Company G, 1st Regiment N.C. Infantry (6 months, 1861). Enlisted in this company on May 15, 1862, with the rank of Private. Promoted to Corporal on August 19, 1862, and promoted to Sergeant in November-December, 1862. Present or accounted for until wounded and captured at Gettysburg, Pennsylvania, July 1-4, 1863. Hospitalized at Gettysburg until transferred to Davids Island, New York Harbor, July 17-24, 1863. Paroled at Davids Island on August 24, 1863, and transferred for exchange. Promoted to 1st Sergeant in November-December, 1863, and appointed 2nd Lieutenant to rank from February 15, 1864. Rejoined the company in March-April, 1864, and present or accounted for until paroled at Farmville, Virginia, April 11-21, 1865.

WARLICK, PORTLAND A., 2nd Lieutenant
Previously served as Private in Company G, 1st Regiment N.C. Infantry (6 months, 1861). Appointed 2nd Lieutenant in this company to rank from February 15, 1862. Present or accounted for until wounded in the left arm at Gettysburg, Pennsylvania, July 3, 1863. Reported absent wounded or absent sick until he died in hospital at Richmond, Virginia, December 28, 1863, of "typhoid pneumonia."

NONCOMMISSIONED OFFICERS AND PRIVATES

ANDREWS, GEORGE W., Private
Resided in Wilkes County where he enlisted at age 28, February 1, 1862, for the war. Present or accounted for until wounded in the left leg and captured at Gettysburg, Pennsylvania, July 1-5, 1863. Hospitalized at Gettysburg until transferred to Davids Island, New York Harbor, July 17-24, 1863. Paroled at Davids Island and transferred to City Point, Virginia, where he was received October 28, 1863, for exchange. Reported absent wounded through February, 1865.

ANDREWS, JAMES, Private
Resided in Wilkes County where he enlisted at age 18, February 11, 1863, for the war. Present or accounted for until wounded in the left leg at Gettysburg, Pennsylvania, July 3, 1863. Captured at Falling Waters, Maryland, July 14, 1863. Confined at Fort McHenry, Maryland, and at Point Lookout, Maryland, until paroled and transferred on March 16, 1864, for exchange. Rejoined the company in July-August, 1864, and present or accounted for until captured at or near Petersburg, Virginia, April 2, 1865. Confined at Point Lookout until released on June 23, 1865, after taking the Oath of Allegiance.

ANDREWS, WILLIAM, Private
Resided in Wilkes County where he enlisted at age 27, February 1, 1862, for the war. Present or accounted for through February, 1865.

ANTHONY, J. J., Private
Resided in Burke County where he enlisted at age 37, February 1, 1862, for the war. Present or accounted for until hospitalized at Wilmington on or about July 6, 1862, with a gunshot wound; however, place and date wounded not reported. Returned to duty July 22, 1862, and present or accounted for until he died in hospital at Richmond, Virginia, June 13, 1863, of "febris typhoides."

ANTHONY, P. B., Private
Resided in Burke County where he enlisted at age 28, February 1, 1862, for the war. Present or accounted for until wounded at Gettysburg, Pennsylvania, July 1-3, 1863. Died in hospital at Harrisonburg, Virginia, July 18, 1863, or wounds and/or "febris typhoides." [May have served previously in Company G, 1st Regiment N.C. Infantry (6 months, 1861).]

BAKER, M., Private
Enlisted in Burke County on February 15, 1862, for the war. Company muster roll dated July-August, 1862, indicates that he "enlisted & after-[wards] he joined another company in Caldwell County." No further records.

BEACH, J., Private
Enlisted in Burke County on February 1, 1862, for the war. Company muster roll dated July-August, 1862, states that he "belonged to another com-[pany] & [was] never sworn in."

BOWMAN, JACOB, Private
Resided in Caldwell County where he enlisted at age 30, February 1, 1862, for the war. Present or accounted for until captured at Falling Waters, Maryland, July 14, 1863. Confined at Baltimore, Maryland, and at Point Lookout, Maryland, until paroled on March 3, 1864, and transferred for exchange. Deserted on or about May 2, 1864.

BOWMAN, SAMUEL, Private
Previously served in Company F, 41st Regiment N.C. Troops (3rd Regiment N.C. Cavalry). Transferred to this company on December 5, 1864. Present or accounted for until captured at or near Petersburg, Virginia, April 2, 1865. Confined at Point Lookout, Maryland, until released on June 23, 1865, after taking the Oath of Allegiance.

BRANCH, A. C., Private
Resided in Burke County where he enlisted at age 20, January 15, 1862, for the war. Present or accounted for until wounded and captured at Gettysburg, Pennsylvania, July 3, 1863. Confined at Fort Delaware, Delaware, until transferred to Point Lookout, Maryland, October 15-18, 1863. Confined at Point Lookout until paroled and transferred for exchange on or about February 13, 1865. Paroled at Morganton on May 16, 1865.

BRANCH, GREEN A., _____
Place and date of enlistment not reported. Company muster roll dated January-February, 1865, states that he died on February 19, 1865. Place and cause of death not reported.

BRANCH, M., Private
Resided in Burke County where he enlisted at age 25, February 1, 1862, for the war. Present or accounted for until wounded in the left knee and captured at Gettysburg, Pennsylvania, July 1-4, 1863. Hospitalized at Gettysburg until transferred to Davids Island, New York Harbor, July 17-24, 1863. Transferred to Fort Wood, Bedloe's Island, New York Harbor, on or about October 24, 1863, and transferred to Point Lookout, Maryland, January 10, 1864. Paroled at Point Lookout and transferred on May 16, 1864, for exchange. Rejoined the company prior to July 1, 1864, and present or accounted for until captured at or near Petersburg, Virginia, April 2, 1865. Confined at Hart's Island, New York Harbor, until released on June 19, 1865, after taking the Oath of Allegiance.

BRANCH, REUBEN, Private
Previously served in Company G, 1st Regiment N.C. Infantry (6 months, 1861). Enlisted in this company on January 15, 1862, for the war. Present or accounted for until captured at or near Petersburg, Virginia, April 2, 1865. Confined at Point Lookout, Maryland, until released on June 23, 1865, after taking the Oath of Allegiance.

BREWER, WILLIAM, Private
Resided in McDowell County and enlisted in Burke County at age 20, February 9, 1863, for the war. Present or accounted for until captured at Falling Waters, Maryland, July 14, 1863. Took the Oath of Allegiance in August, 1863.

BRISTOL, E. B., 1st Sergeant
Resided in Burke County where he enlisted at age 21, February 15, 1862, for the war. Mustered in as 1st Sergeant. Present or accounted for until killed at White Hall on December 16, 1862. [May have served previously in Company G, 1st Regiment N.C. Infantry (6 months, 1861).]

BRISTOL, LAMBERT AUGUSTUS, Private
Resided in Burke County where he enlisted at age 16, February 1, 1862, for the war. Present or

accounted for until discharged on April 1, 1864. Reason discharged not reported.

BUTLER, JOHN, Private
Resided in Rutherford County and enlisted in Burke County on November 16, 1863, for the war. Present or accounted for until captured at or near Petersburg, Virginia, April 2, 1865. Confined at Point Lookout, Maryland, until released on June 23, 1865, after taking the Oath of Allegiance.

CANNON, JAMES, Private
Resided in Caldwell County where he enlisted at age 22, February 1, 1862, for the war. Present or accounted for until reported absent wounded in July-August, 1864; however, place and date wounded not reported. Reported absent wounded through February, 1865.

CARLTON, R. W., Corporal
Previously served as Private in Company G, 1st Regiment N.C. Infantry (6 months, 1861). Enlisted in this company on December 20, 1861, for the war. Mustered in as Corporal. Present or accounted for until wounded and captured at Gettysburg, Pennsylvania, July 1-5, 1863. Confined at Fort Delaware, Delaware, where he died September 16, 1863, of "chronic diarrhoea."

CARROLL, JOHN, Private
Previously served in Company E, 1st Regiment N.C. Infantry (6 months, 1861). [Name listed in Volume III of this series as John H. Cordell.] Enlisted in this company on January 15, 1862, for the war. Mustered in as Musician but reduced to ranks in September-October, 1862. Present or accounted for until wounded at White Hall on December 16, 1862. Reported absent wounded through February, 1865. Paroled at Morganton on May 16, 1865.

CARSWELL, NATHAN, Private
Resided in Burke County where he enlisted at age 28, February 11, 1863, for the war. Present or accounted for until he deserted on August 5, 1863.

CARSWELL, R. R., Private
Resided in Burke County where he enlisted at age 30, February 11, 1863, for the war. Present or accounted for until wounded and captured at Gettysburg, Pennsylvania, July 1-4, 1863. Hospitalized at Gettysburg until transferred to Davids Island, New York Harbor, July 17-24, 1863. Paroled at Davids Island on August 24, 1863, and transferred for exchange. Reported absent wounded until reported absent without leave on November 1, 1863. Company muster roll dated March-April, 1864, states he was "in the woods as a deserter." Company records do not indicate that he returned to duty; however, he was paroled at Morganton on May 16, 1865.

CARSWELL, THOMAS H., Private
Resided in Burke County where he enlisted at age 26, February 11, 1863, for the war. Present or accounted for until he deserted on June 22, 1863. Returned to duty on August 29, 1863, and present or accounted for until he deserted to the enemy on or about March 29, 1865. Paroled on or about May 23, 1865.

CAUSBY, D. A., Private
Resided in Burke County where he enlisted at age

38, January 15, 1862, for the war. Present or accounted for until captured at Falling Waters, Maryland, July 14, 1863. Confined at Baltimore, Maryland, until transferred to Point Lookout, Maryland, on or about August 21, 1863. Died in hospital at Point Lookout on March 10, 1864, of "chro[nic] diarrhoea."

CHAPMAN, WILLIAM, Private
Resided in Burke County where he enlisted at age 26, February 11, 1863, for the war. Present or accounted for until he deserted on or about June 22, 1863. Company records do not indicate that he returned to duty; however, North Carolina pension records indicate that he was mortally wounded in North Carolina in March, 1865.

CHESTER, J. M., Private
Resided in Burke County and enlisted at Camp Vance on May 23, 1864, for the war. Present or accounted for until captured at or near Petersburg, Virginia, April 2, 1865. Confined at Point Lookout, Maryland, until released on June 24, 1865, after taking the Oath of Allegiance.

CLARK, JOHN M., Private
Resided in Burke County where he enlisted at age 25, January 15, 1862, for the war. Present or accounted for until captured at Falling Waters, Maryland, July 14, 1863. Confined at Baltimore, Maryland, and at Point Lookout, Maryland, until released on January 21, 1864, after taking the Oath of Allegiance and joining the U.S. service. Reportedly assigned to the 1st Regiment U.S. Volunteer Infantry; however, records of that unit do not indicate that he served therein. No further records.

CLARKE, B. B., Private
Resided in Burke County where he enlisted at age 20, January 15, 1862, for the war. Present or accounted for until reported absent without leave from August 25, 1863, through October, 1863. Rejoined the company in November-December, 1863, and present or accounted for until reported absent without leave from November-December, 1864, through February, 1865.

CLAUNTZ, JONES, Private
Enlisted in Burke County on October 20, 1864, for the war. Present or accounted for until captured in hospital at Richmond, Virginia, April 3, 1865. Confined at Libby Prison, Richmond, until transferred to Newport News, Virginia, April 24, 1865. Hospitalized at Newport News on May 23, 1865, with "debilitas" and died June 14, 1865.

COFFEY, JOHN C., Private
Enlisted in Burke County on May 23, 1864, for the war. Present or accounted for through February, 1865.

COLEMAN, C. A., Private
Resided in Burke County where he enlisted on January 7, 1865, for the war. Present or accounted for until captured at or near Petersburg, Virginia, April 2, 1865. Confined at Point Lookout, Maryland, until released on June 17, 1865, after taking the Oath of Allegiance.

COOK, DAVID, Private
Resided in Burke County where he enlisted at age

28, March 5, 1863, for the war. Deserted April 29, 1863. Died in hospital at Richmond, Virginia, February 6, 1864, of "typhoid pneumonia."

COOK, JOHN, Private
Resided in Burke County where he enlisted at age 20, May 5, 1862, for the war. Present or accounted for until wounded and captured at Gettysburg, Pennsylvania, July 1-3, 1863. Confined at Fort Delaware, Delaware, until transferred to Point Lookout, Maryland, October 15-18, 1863. Confined at Point Lookout until paroled on February 18, 1865, and transferred for exchange. Rejoined the company prior to April 2, 1865, when he was captured at or near Petersburg, Virginia. Confined at Point Lookout until released on June 26, 1865, after taking the Oath of Allegiance.

COOK, THOMAS, Private
Resided in Burke County where he enlisted at age 22, February 1, 1862, for the war. Present or accounted for until he deserted on April 29, 1863. Returned to duty on August 29, 1863. Present or accounted for until captured at Bristoe Station, Virginia, October 14, 1863. Confined at Old Capitol Prison, Washington, D.C., until transferred to Point Lookout, Maryland, February 3, 1864. Released at Point Lookout on February 19, 1864, after taking the Oath of Allegiance and joining the U.S. Army. Assigned to Company E, 1st Regiment U.S.Volunteer Infantry.

COOPER, WILLIAM E., Private
Previously served in Company F, 41st Regiment N.C. Troops (3rd Regiment N.C. Cavalry). Transferred to this company on December 5, 1864. Present or accounted for until captured at or near Petersburg, Virginia, April 2, 1865. Confined at Point Lookout, Maryland, until released on June 24, 1865, after taking the Oath of Allegiance.

COURTNEY, JAMES, Private
Resided in Caldwell County and was by occupation a farmer prior to enlisting in Caldwell County at age 35, February 1, 1862, for the war. Present or accounted for until captured at Falling Waters, Maryland, July 14, 1863. Confined at Baltimore, Maryland, and at Point Lookout, Maryland, until paroled on March 9, 1864, and transferred for exchange. Rejoined the company in May-June, 1864, and present or accounted for until discharged on February 3, 1865. Reason discharged not reported.

CRAWLEY, J. W., Corporal
Resided in Burke County where he enlisted at age 21, January 15, 1862, for the war. Mustered in as Private. Present or accounted for until captured at Falling Waters, Maryland, July 14, 1863. Confined at Baltimore, Maryland, until paroled and transferred to City Point, Virginia, where he was received August 24, 1863, for exchange. Rejoined the company in November-December, 1863, and present or accounted for until hospitalized at Danville, Virginia, on or about May 18, 1864, with a gunshot wound of the neck. Place and date wounded not reported. Rejoined the company in July-August, 1864, and was promoted to Corporal on August 29, 1864. Present or accounted for until

captured near Petersburg, Virginia, October 27, 1864. Confined at Point Lookout, Maryland, until released on June 3, 1865, after taking the Oath of Allegiance.

CROUCH, ELIPHUS, Private
Resided in Burke County where he enlisted at age 22, January 15, 1862, for the war. Present or accounted for until captured at or near Petersburg, Virginia, April 2, 1865. Confined at Point Lookout, Maryland, until released on June 24, 1865, after taking the Oath of Allegiance.

CROUTCH, PEYTON, Private
Previously served in Company G, 1st Regiment N.C. Infantry (6 months, 1861). Enlisted in this company on January 15, 1862, for the war. Present or accounted for until he died in hospital at Staunton, Virginia, August 1, 1863, of "pneumonia."

CRUMP, E. M., Private
Enlisted in Caldwell County on February 1, 1862, for the war. Reported absent without leave in May-June, 1862. Company muster roll dated July-August, 1862, states that he joined another company in Caldwell County. No further records.

DALE, DAVID, Private
Resided in Burke County where he enlisted at age 28, February 1, 1862, for the war. Present or accounted for until discharged on June 23, 1862, by reason of "disability."

DAVIS, B. L., Private
Resided in McDowell County where he enlisted at age 18, February 1, 1862, for the war. Present or accounted for until captured at Falling Waters, Maryland, July 14, 1863. Confined at Old Capitol Prison, Washington, D.C., until transferred to Point Lookout, Maryland, August 8, 1863. Paroled at Point Lookout and transferred to Venus Point, Savannah River, Georgia, November 15, 1864. Rejoined the company in January-February, 1865, and present or accounted for until captured at or near Petersburg, Virginia, April 2, 1865. Confined at Point Lookout until released on June 26, 1865, after taking the Oath of Allegiance. Roll of Honor indicates he was wounded at Gettysburg, Pennsylvania.

DAY, SAMUEL M., Private
Resided in Caldwell County where he enlisted at age 38, February 1, 1862, for the war. Present or accounted for until captured at Gettysburg, Pennsylvania, July 1-5, 1863. Confined at Fort Delaware, Delaware, until transferred to Point Lookout, Maryland, October 15-18, 1863. Confined at Point Lookout until paroled on February 18, 1865, and transferred for exchange. Reported present with a detachment of paroled and exchanged prisoners at Camp Lee, near Richmond, Virginia, February 28, 1865.

DORSEY, THOMAS A., Private
Previously served in Company G, 1st Regiment N.C. Infantry (6 months, 1861). Enlisted in this company on February 1, 1862, for the war. Present or accounted for until wounded and captured at Gettysburg, Pennsylvania, July 1-5, 1863. Hospitalized at Gettysburg and at Baltimore, Maryland,

until paroled on November 12, 1863. Rejoined the company in January-February, 1864, and was promoted to Corporal February 15, 1864. Reduced to ranks August 29, 1864. Present or accounted for until he was reported transferred to the 41st Regiment N.C. Troops (3rd Regiment N.C. Cavalry) on December 7, 1864; however, records of that regiment do not indicate that he served therein.

DUCKWORTH, J. N., Private
Born in Burke County where he resided as a farmer prior to enlisting in Burke County at age 16, February 1, 1862, for the war. Present or accounted for until wounded and captured at Gettysburg, Pennsylvania, July 1-5, 1863. Hospitalized at Gettysburg until transferred to Davids Island, New York Harbor, July 17-24, 1863. Paroled at Davids Island and transferred for exchange on or about September 27, 1863. Rejoined the company in January-February, 1864, and present or accounted for until discharged on February 3, 1865, by reason of "the expiration of his enlistment."

DUCKWORTH, WALTER, Private
Resided in Burke County and was by occupation a farmer prior to enlisting in Burke County at age 30, February 1, 1862, for the war. Present or accounted for until killed at White Hall on December 16, 1862.

DUCKWORTH, WILLIAM, Private
Resided in Burke County where he enlisted at age 34, December 15, 1862, for the war. Present or accounted for until killed at Gettysburg, Pennsylvania, July 1, 1863.

DUVAL, JOHN M., 1st Sergeant
Previously served as Private in Company G, 1st Regiment N.C. Infantry (6 months, 1861). Enlisted in this company on December 20, 1861, for the war. Mustered in as Sergeant. Present or accounted for until wounded at Gettysburg, Pennsylvania, July 1, 1863. Captured at Hagerstown, Maryland, at an unspecified date and died at Hagerstown in August, 1863, of wounds. Company records indicate he was promoted to 1st Sergeant in September-October, 1863. No further records.

EATON, J. H., Private
Previously served in Company G, 9th Regiment N.C. State Troops (1st Regiment N.C. Cavalry). Transferred to this company on December 5, 1864. Present or accounted for through February, 1865.

ELLIOTT, HIRAM C., Private
Resided in Burke County where he enlisted at age 35, February 26, 1863, for the war. Present or accounted for until paroled at Appomattox Court House, Virginia, April 9, 1865.

ERNEST, HAMILTON, Private
Born in Burke County where he resided as a farmer prior to enlisting in Burke County at age 23, February 1, 1862, for the war. Present or accounted for until discharged on August 19, 1862, by reason of "frequent paraxems of nervous depression" and an injury to the left side of the chest "received while wrestling with a man who fell on him."

ERWIN, GEORGE PHIFER, 1st Sergeant

Resided in Burke County where he enlisted at age 21, December 20, 1861, for the war. Mustered in as Sergeant and promoted to 1st Sergeant on December 20, 1862. Present or accounted for until appointed Assistant Quartermaster and transferred to the 60th Regiment N.C. Troops on or about May 13, 1861.

FERREE, THOMAS C., Sergeant

Resided in Burke County where he enlisted at age 24, February 1, 1862, for the war. Mustered in as Private and promoted to Sergeant on September 1, 1863. Present or accounted for until he died in hospital at Richmond, Virginia, October 29, 1864, of "diarrhoea chronica."

FINCANNON, JOHN, Private

Resided in Burke County where he enlisted at age 30, February 1, 1862, for the war. Present or accounted for until wounded at Gettysburg, Pennsylvania, July 1-3, 1863. Returned to duty prior to September 1, 1863, and present or accounted for until he died on August 18, 1864. Place and cause of death not reported.

FOX, WILLIAM J., Private

Resided in Burke County where he enlisted at age 28, February 1, 1862, for the war. Present or accounted for until transferred to Company F, 41st Regiment N.C. Troops (3rd Regiment N.C. Cavalry), December 7, 1864.

GALLOWAY, H. H., Sergeant

Previously served as Private in Company G, 1st Regiment N.C. Infantry (6 months, 1861). Enlisted in this company on December 20, 1861, for the war. Mustered in as Corporal. Present or accounted for until captured at Falling Waters, Maryland, July 14, 1863. Confined at Baltimore, Maryland, and at Point Lookout, Maryland. Promoted to Sergeant in November-December, 1863, while a prisoner of war. Paroled at Point Lookout on March 3, 1864, and transferred for exchange. Rejoined the company in May-June, 1864, and present or accounted for until captured at or near Petersburg, Virginia, April 2, 1865. Confined at Point Lookout until released on June 28, 1865, after taking the Oath of Allegiance.

GARRISON, L. D., Private

Resided in Burke County where he enlisted on October 23, 1864, for the war. Present or accounted for until he deserted to the enemy on or about March 29, 1865. Took the Oath of Allegiance at Washington, D.C., April 4, 1865.

GILBERT, JOHNSON, Private

Resided in Caldwell County where he enlisted at age 40, February 1, 1862, for the war. Present or accounted for until hospitalized at Richmond, Virginia, December 9, 1864, with a gunshot wound of the right foot; however, place and date wounded not reported. Reported absent wounded through February, 1865.

GRIFFIN, DAVID, Private

Resided in Burke County where he enlisted at age 30, February 1, 1862, for the war. Present or accounted for until captured at Falling Waters, Maryland, July 14, 1863. Confined at Baltimore, Maryland, and at Point Lookout, Maryland, until paroled at Point Lookout on February 18, 1865, and transferred for exchange. Reported present with a detachment of paroled and exchanged prisoners at Camp Lee, near Richmond, Virginia, February 28, 1865.

GRIFFIN, JAMES, Private

Resided in Burke County where he enlisted at age 28, February 1, 1862, for the war. Present or accounted for until captured at Falling Waters, Maryland, July 14, 1863. Took the Oath of Allegiance in August, 1863, and joined the U.S.Army. Assigned to Company H, 3rd Regiment Maryland Cavalry.

GRIFFIN, WILLIAM L., Private

Resided in Burke County where he enlisted at age 26, February 1, 1862, for the war. Present or accounted for until captured near Petersburg, Virginia, October 27, 1864. Confined at Point Lookout, Maryland, until paroled on or about March 28, 1865, and transferred for exchange.

GURLEY, WILLIAM A., Private

Born in Burke County and resided in Rowan County where he was by occupation a farmer prior to enlisting in Burke County on February 1, 1862, for the war. "Never sworn in" as a member of this company and enlisted in Company B, 46th Regiment N.C. Troops, March 1, 1862.

HARBISON, TOLBERT, Private

Resided in Burke County where he enlisted at age 20, February 1, 1862, for the war. Present or accounted for until he died at Wilmington on June 13, 1862, of disease.

HARBISON, W. T., Private

Resided in Burke County where he enlisted at age 18, February 1, 1862, for the war. Present or accounted for until wounded in the right leg at or near Cold Harbor, Virginia, June 2, 1864. Right leg amputated. Reported absent wounded through February, 1865.

HARRIS, L. B., Private

Resided in Burke County where he enlisted at age 17, February 1, 1862, for the war. Present or accounted for until captured at Falling Waters, Maryland, July 14, 1863. Confined at Baltimore, Maryland, and at Point Lookout, Maryland, until paroled on March 3, 1864, and transferred for exchange. Rejoined the company in May-June, 1864, and present or accounted for until wounded at or near Burgess' Mill, Virginia, October 27, 1864. Returned to duty on November 10, 1864, and present or accounted for until captured at or near Petersburg, Virginia, April 2, 1865. Confined at Point Lookout until released on June 27, 1865, after taking the Oath of Allegiance.

HAWKS, REUBEN, Private

Born in Warren County and resided in Burke County where he was by occupation a farmer prior to enlisting in Burke County at age 45, February 1, 1862, for the war. Present or accounted for until discharged on April 24, 1864, by reason of "chronic rheumatism."

HENNESSA, R. J., Sergeant

Resided in Burke County where he enlisted at age 20, December 20, 1861, for the war. Mustered in as Corporal. Present or accounted for until captured at Gettysburg, Pennsylvania, July 3, 1863. Confined at Fort Delaware, Delaware, until transferred to Point Lookout, Maryland, October 15-18, 1863. Exchanged at an unspecified date in February-April, 1864. Promoted to Sergeant on February 15, 1864. Present or accounted for until paroled at Appomattox Court House, Virginia, April 9, 1865. [May have served previously in Company G, 1st Regiment N.C. Infantry (6 months, 1861).]

JOHNSON, DAVID, Private

Enlisted in Burke County on January 25, 1864, for the war. Present or accounted for until he died in hospital at Richmond, Virginia, July 6, 1864, of "typhoid fever."

JOHNSON, JOHN, Private

Resided in Burke County where he enlisted at age 26, March 5, 1863, for the war. Deserted April 29, 1863.

JOHNSON, SOLOMON, Private

Resided in Burke County where he enlisted at age 30, March 5, 1863, for the war. Deserted April 29, 1863, but was apprehended and returned on December 1, 1863. Reported absent sick until he died in hospital at Charlottesville, Virginia, March 5, 1864, of "typhoid fever."

JUSTICE, SAMUEL, Private

Resided in Burke County where he enlisted at age 45, February 1, 1862, for the war. Present or accounted for until he died in hospital at Richmond, Virginia, May 22, 1864, of "diarrhoea chron[ic]."

JUSTIS, A. P., Private

Resided in Burke County where he enlisted at age 30, February 1, 1862, for the war. Present or accounted for until he died in hospital at Wilmington on July 15, 1862. Cause of death not reported.

KELLER, DAVID, Private

Resided in Caldwell County where he enlisted at age 26, February 1, 1862, for the war. Present or accounted for until he died near Wilmington on June 11, 1862, of "diarrhoea and measles."

KELLER, GEORGE, Private

Resided in Caldwell County where he enlisted at age 35, February 1, 1862, for the war. Present or accounted for until wounded at or near Burgess' Mill, Virginia, on or about October 27, 1864. Died October 28, 1864, of wounds.

KELLER, JOHN J., Private

Resided in Caldwell County where he enlisted at age 18, February 11, 1863, for the war. Present or accounted for until wounded and captured at Gettysburg, Pennsylvania, July 1-5, 1863. Confined at Fort Delaware, Delaware, until transferred to Point Lookout, Maryland, October 15-18, 1863. Died at Point Lookout on December 21, 1863. Cause of death not reported.

KINCAID, ROBERT, Private

Enlisted in Caldwell County at age 45, August 1, 1864, for the war. Present or accounted for until paroled at Appomattox Court House, Virginia, April 9, 1865. Died in hospital at Washington, D.C., May 3, 1865, of "diarrhoea chronic."

KINCAID, WILLIAM, Private

Resided in Burke County and enlisted in Caldwell County on November 2, 1864, for the war. Present or accounted for until captured at or near Petersburg, Virginia, April 2, 1865. Confined at Point Lookout, Maryland, until released on June 28, 1865, after taking the Oath of Allegiance.

KINSTON, M., Private

Place and date of enlistment not reported. Died at Point Lookout, Maryland, April 23, 1865. Place and date captured and cause of death not reported.

LAND, JOHN, Private

Resided in Alexander County and enlisted in Wilkes County on November 15, 1864, for the war. Present or accounted for until captured in hospital at Richmond, Virginia, April 3, 1865. Confined at Libby Prison, Richmond, until transferred to Newport News, Virginia, April 23, 1865. Released at Newport News on July 3, 1865, after taking the Oath of Allegiance. Died in hospital at Richmond on July 9, 1865. Cause of death not reported.

LANDIS, J. N., Private

Resided in McDowell County where he enlisted at age 35, February 1, 1862, for the war. Present or accounted for until hospitalized at Farmville, Virginia, on or about April 7, 1865, with a gunshot wound of both eyes. Place and date wounded not reported. Paroled at Farmville, April 11-21, 1865.

LANDIS, W. T., Private

Resided in Burke County and enlisted in McDowell County at age 24, February 1, 1862, for the war. Present or accounted for until wounded in the left leg at Gettysburg, Pennsylvania, July 1, 1863. Reported absent wounded or absent on detached service through February, 1865.

LANE, T. H., Private

Born in Burke County and was by occupation a farmer prior to enlisting in Burke County at age 21, February 1, 1862, for the war. Present or accounted for until discharged on September 22, 1862, by reason of "chronic contraction of the finger & thumb or the right hand with complete loss of power." Died prior to September 25, 1863. Place and cause of death not reported.

LEDFORD, WILLIAM, Private

Enlisted in Burke County on January 25, 1864, for the war. Present or accounted for through February, 1865; however, he was reported absent sick during most of that period.

LIVINGSTON, JORDAN, Private

Resided in Wilkes County where he enlisted at age 21, February 1, 1862, for the war. Present or accounted for until wounded at Gettysburg, Pennsylvania, July 1, 1863. Reported absent at home or absent on detached service until he rejoined the company in September-October, 1864. Present or accounted for until captured in hospital at

Richmond, Virginia, April 3, 1865. No further records.

LIVINGSTON, LARKIN, Private
Resided in Wilkes County where he enlisted at age 18, February 1, 1862, for the war. Present or accounted for until captured at Bristoe Station, Virginia, October 14, 1863. Confined at Old Capitol Prison, Washington, D.C., until transferred to Point Lookout, Maryland, October 27, 1863. Paroled at Point Lookout and transferred for exchange on or about March 3, 1864. Present or accounted for until hospitalized at Petersburg, Virginia, June 23, 1864, with a gunshot wound of the left arm; however, place and date wounded not reported. Returned to duty on September 20, 1864, and present or accounted for until paroled at Appomattox Court House, Virginia, April 9, 1865.

LONDON, JAMES WILBURN, Sergeant
Previously served in Company G, 1st Regiment N.C. Infantry (6 months, 1861). Enlisted in this company on February 1, 1862, for the war. Mustered in as Private and promoted to Sergeant on November 1, 1864. Present or accounted for until wounded in the left arm at or near Burgess' Mill, Virginia, February 5, 1865. Left arm amputated. Furloughed from hospital at Richmond, Virginia, March 2, 1865.

LOUDERMILK, GEORGE, Private
Resided in Burke County where he enlisted at age 34, February 1, 1862, for the war. Present or accounted for until hospitalized at Richmond, Virginia, May 19, 1864, with a gunshot wound; however, place and date wounded not reported. Rejoined the company in September-October, 1864, and present or accounted for until captured at or near Petersburg, Virginia, April 2, 1865. Confined at Point Lookout, Maryland, until released on June 28, 1865, after taking the Oath of Allegiance.

LOVEN, GEORGE A., Private
Resided in Burke County where he enlisted at age 24, November 10, 1862, for the war. Present or accounted for until wounded at White Hall on December 16, 1862. Reported absent wounded through February, 1865.

McCALL, W. W., Private
Born in Caldwell County* where he resided as a farmer prior to enlisting in Caldwell County at age 41, February 1, 1862, for the war. Present or accounted for until discharged on March 8, 1864, by reason of "chronic debility & emaciation proceeding from hepatic disease of long standing."

MACE, WILLIAM H., Private
Previously served in Company G, 1st Regiment N.C. Infantry (6 months, 1861). Enlisted in this company on February 1, 1862, for the war. Present or accounted for until transferred to Company D of this regiment on April 18, 1862.

McGIMSEY, W. W., Sergeant
Resided in Burke County where he enlisted at age 27, December 20, 1861, for the war. Mustered in as Sergeant. Present or accounted for until wounded at Gettysburg, Pennsylvania, July 1, 1863. Rejoined the company in January-February, 1864, and present

or accounted for until paroled at Appomattox Court House, Virginia, April 9, 1865.

McNEALY, HARVEY, Private
Enlisted in Burke County on February 1, 1862, for the war. Company muster roll dated May-June, 1862, states he was absent without leave. Company muster roll dated July-August, 1862, states he was "not sworn in." No further records.

MICHAUX, JOHN P., 1st Sergeant
Previously served as Private in Company G, 1st Regiment N.C. Infantry (6 months, 1861). Enlisted in this company on December 20, 1861, for the war. Mustered in as Sergeant. Present or accounted for until captured at Falling Waters, Maryland, July 14, 1863. Confined at Baltimore, Maryland, and at Point Lookout, Maryland. Promoted to 1st Sergeant on February 15, 1864, while a prisoner of war. Paroled at Point Lookout on or about March 3, 1864, and transferred for exchange. Rejoined the company in May-June, 1864, and present or accounted for until February, 1865.

MILLER, JOHN M., 1st Sergeant
Resided in Watauga County. Place and date of enlistment not reported. Captured at Boone on March 28, 1865. Confined at various localities until confined at Louisville, Kentucky, May 15, 1865. Released on June 16, 1865, after taking the Oath of Allegiance. [May have served previously in Company G, 1st Regiment N.C. Infantry (6 months, 1861).]

MINCEY, KINCHEN, Private
Resided in Burke County where he enlisted at age 30, February 11, 1863, for the war. Present or accounted for until he deserted on September 23, 1863. Returned to duty on January 27, 1864. Present or accounted for until captured near Petersburg, Virginia, October 27, 1864. Confined at Point Lookout, Maryland, where he died April 23, 1865, of "chronic dysentery."

MOODY, DAVID E., Private
Born in Burke County where he resided as a farmer prior to enlisting in Burke County at age 45, February 1, 1862, for the war. Present or accounted for until he deserted on May 15, 1862. "Brought back" on August 13, 1862, and present or accounted for until discharged on April 10, 1863, by reason of old age, general debility, and rheumatism. Records of the Federal Provost Marshal indicate he died at Camp Chase, Ohio, or at Camp Dennison, Ohio, May 31, 1865. Place and date captured and cause of death not reported.

MOORE, JOSEPH A., Private
Resided in McDowell County and enlisted in Burke County at age 21, February 1, 1862, for the war. Present or accounted for until transferred to Company F, 41st Regiment N.C. Troops (3rd Regiment N.C. Cavalry), December 7, 1864.

MOORE, THOMAS B., Private
Resided in Burke County where he enlisted at age 21, February 1, 1862, for the war. Mustered in as Corporal but reduced to ranks in July-August, 1862. Present or accounted for until wounded at Gettysburg, Pennsylvania, July 1, 1863. Captured at Gettysburg or at Martinsburg, West Virginia, in

July, 1863. Hospitalized at Baltimore, Maryland, until paroled and transferred for exchange on or about November 17, 1863. Rejoined the company in May-June, 1864, and present or accounted for until killed at New Market, Virginia July 30, 1864. [May have served previously in Company G, 1st Regiment N.C. Infantry (6 months, 1861).]

MORGAN, A. A., Private
Born in Burke County where he resided as a farmer prior to enlisting in Burke County at age 25, February 1, 1862, for the war. Present or accounted for until wounded in the right arm and captured at Gettysburg, Pennsylvania, July 1-5, 1863. Right arm amputated. Hospitalized at Gettysburg until transferred to hospital at Baltimore, Maryland, on or about October 1, 1863. Paroled and transferred for exchange on or about November 12, 1863. Reported absent wounded until he was discharged on April 1, 1864, by reason of amputation.

MORGAN, JOHN, Private
Resided in Burke County where he enlisted at age 16, February 1, 1862, for the war. Died at Camp Davis, near Wilmington, June 18, 1862, of disease.

MORGAN, P. W., Private
Resided in Burke County where he enlisted at age 28, February 1, 1862, for the war. Present or accounted for until captured at Falling Waters, Maryland, July 14, 1863. Took the Oath of Allegiance in August, 1863.

MORRISON, A. H., Private
Resided in Burke County where he enlisted at age 18, February 1, 1862, for the war. Present or accounted for until wounded at White Hall on December 16, 1862. Rejoined the company in March-April, 1863, and present or accounted for until killed at Gettysburg, Pennsylvania, July 1, 1863.

MOSES, S. A., Private
Resided in Burke County where he enlisted at age 28, February 1, 1862, for the war. Present or accounted for until captured at or near Petersburg, Virginia, April 2, 1865. Confined at Point Lookout, Maryland, until released on June 29, 1865, after taking the Oath of Allegiance.

MULL, HENRY, Private
Resided in Burke County where he enlisted at age 20, February 1, 1862, for the war. Present or accounted for until he deserted on June 22, 1863. Apprehended and returned to the company on or about October 8, 1863. Captured by the enemy at Bristoe Station, Virginia, October 14, 1863. Confined at Old Capitol Prison, Washington, D.C., until transferred to Point Lookout, Maryland, October 27, 1863. Released at Point Lookout on January 25, 1864, after taking the Oath of Allegiance and joining the U.S. service. Assigned to Company C, 1st Regiment U.S. Volunteer Infantry.

PARKS, AUSTIN L., Private
Previously served in Company F, 41st Regiment N.C. Troops (3rd Regiment N.C. Cavalry). Transferred to this company on February 9, 1864. Present or accounted for until captured at or near

Petersburg, Virginia, April 2, 1865. Confined at Point Lookout, Maryland, where he died April 15, 1865, of "pneumonia."

PARKS, H. H., Corporal
Enlisted in Burke County on April 29, 1862, for the war. Mustered in as Private and promoted to Corporal in November-December, 1862. Present or accounted for until reported missing and "supposed killed" at Gettysburg, Pennsylvania, July 3, 1863. [May have served previously in Company G, 1st Regiment N.C. Infantry (6 months, 1861).] No further records.

PARKS, J. P., Corporal
Resided in Burke County where he enlisted at age 18, November 10, 1862, for the war. Mustered in as Private. Present or accounted for until captured at Falling Waters, Maryland, July 14, 1863. Confined at Baltimore, Maryland, and at Point Lookout, Maryland, until paroled on March 3, 1864, and transferred for exchange. Rejoined the company in May-June, 1864, and was promoted to Corporal in November-December, 1864. Present or accounted for until captured at or near Petersburg, Virginia, April 2, 1865. Confined at Point Lookout until released on June 16, 1865, after taking the Oath of Allegiance.

PATTON, GEORGE, Private
Resided in Burke County and enlisted in McDowell County at age 15, February 1, 1862, for the war. Present or accounted for until he died at Camp Mangum, near Raleigh, April 8, 1862, of "typhoid fever."

PATTON, J. S., Private
Enlisted in Burke County on December 20, 1862, for the war. Present or accounted for through December, 1862. No further records.

PATTON, JOHN, Private
Resided in Burke County and enlisted in McDowell County at age 18, February 1, 1862, for the war. Present or accounted for until he died at Camp Mangum, near Raleigh, April 9, 1862, of "typhoid fever."

PATTON, W. S., Private
Resided in Burke County where he enlisted at age 18, February 1, 1862, for the war. Present or accounted for until captured at Bristoe Station, Virginia, October 14, 1863. Confined at Point Lookout, Maryland, until paroled and transferred to Venus Point, Savannah River, Georgia, where he was received November 15, 1864, for exchange. Rejoined the company prior to January 1, 1865, and present or accounted for until captured at or near Petersburg, Virginia, April 2, 1865. Confined at Point Lookout until released on June 16, 1865, after taking the Oath of Allegiance.

PEARSON, JAMES A., Private
Previously served in Company G, 1st Regiment N.C. Infantry (6 months, 1861). Enlisted in this company on February 1, 1862; however, he was apparently never sworn in as a company member. Enlisted in Company B, 46th Regiment N.C. Troops, February 24, 1862.

PEARSON, MICHAEL, Private
Born in Burke County where he resided as a

farmer prior to enlisting in Burke County at age 45, February 1, 1862, for the war. Present or accounted for until wounded at Gettysburg, Pennsylvania, July 1-3, 1863. Returned to duty in November-December, 1863. Present or accounted for through January, 1865; however, he was reported absent sick during much of that period. Discharged on February 3, 1865. Reason discharged not reported. [May have served previously in Company G, 1st Regiment N.C. Infantry (6 months, 1861).]

PEARSON, THOMAS A., Private
Resided in Burke County where he enlisted at age 28, February 1, 1862, for the war. Present or accounted for until reported absent wounded in July-August, 1864; however, place and date wounded not reported. Returned to duty on January 7, 1865, and present or accounted for until captured at or near Petersburg, Virginia, April 2, 1865. Confined at Point Lookout, Maryland, until released on June 16, 1865, after taking the Oath of Allegiance. [May have served previously in Company G, 1st Regiment N.C. Infantry (6 months, 1861).]

PENDLEY, ADOLPHUS, Private
Resided in Burke County where he enlisted on October 23, 1864, for the war. Present or accounted for until captured at or near Petersburg, Virginia, April 2, 1865. Confined at Point Lookout, Maryland, until released on June 16, 1865, after taking the Oath of Allegiance.

PERRY, ALFRED, Private
Resided in Burke County where he enlisted at age 35, February 1, 1862, for the war. Present or accounted for until captured at Falling Waters, Maryland, July 14, 1863. Confined at Old Capitol Prison, Washington, D.C., until transferred to Point Lookout, Maryland, August 8, 1863. Paroled at Point Lookout and transferred to Venus Point, Savannah River, Georgia, where he was received November 15, 1864, for exchange. Present or accounted for through February, 1865.

PHILLIPS, C. S., Private
Resided in Burke County where he enlisted at age 16, February 1, 1862, for the war. Present or accounted for until paroled at Appomattox Court House, Virginia, April 9, 1865.

PHILLIPS, ELIJAH, Private
Resided in Burke County where he enlisted at age 42, February 1, 1862, for the war. Present or accounted for until he died in hospital at Richmond, Virginia, September 5, 1864. Cause of death not reported.

PUCKET, E. W., Private
Resided in Burke County where he enlisted at age 18, February 1, 1862, for the war. Present or accounted for until wounded and captured at Gettysburg, Pennsylvania, July 3, 1863. Confined at Fort McHenry, Maryland, until transferred to Fort Delaware, Delaware, July 7-12, 1863. Died at Fort Delaware on July 23, 1864, of "typhoid fever" or "chron[ic] diarrhoea."

PUETT, JOHN WESLEY, Private
Resided in Burke County where he enlisted at age 17, February 1, 1862, for the war. Present or accounted for until he died in hospital at Wilmington on June 25, 1862, of disease.

SHELTON, JAMES, Private
Resided in Surry County where he enlisted on January 24, 1864, for the war. Present or accounted for until reported absent wounded in September-October, 1864; however, place and date wounded not reported. Returned to duty on December 1, 1864. Present or accounted for until captured near Petersburg, Virginia, March 25, 1865. Confined at Point Lookout, Maryland, until released on June 20, 1865, after taking the Oath of Allegiance.

SHORT, DANIEL, Private
Enlisted in Burke County on November 16, 1863, for the war. Present or accounted for until he deserted on January 5, 1864. Rejoined the company in May-June, 1864, and present or accounted for until captured near Petersburg, Virginia, October 27, 1864. Confined at Point Lookout, Maryland, until paroled on January 17, 1865, and transferred for exchange. Reported present with a detachment of paroled and exchanged prisoners at Camp Lee, near Richmond, Virginia, January 26, 1865.

SHORT, W. W., Private
Resided in Burke County where he enlisted at age 37, February 1, 1862, for the war. Present or accounted for until he died in hospital at Wilmington on July 21, 1862, of "febris remitt[ent]."

SHUFFLER, HARVEY, Private
Resided in Burke County where he enlisted at age 22, February 1, 1862, for the war. Present or accounted for until wounded at White Hall on December 16, 1862. Rejoined the company in January-February, 1863, and present or accounted for until killed at Williamsport, Maryland, July 7, 1863.

SHUFFLER, JOHN, Private
Resided in Burke County where he enlisted at age 30, February 1, 1862, for the war. Present or accounted for until wounded in the foot and right leg at Bristoe Station, Virginia, on or about October 14, 1863. Reported absent on detached service until he returned to duty on December 1, 1864. Present or accounted for until captured at Hatcher's Run, Virginia, April 2, 1865. Confined at Point Lookout, Maryland, until released on June 20, 1865, after taking the Oath of Allegiance.

SHUFFLER, SIDNEY S., Private
Resided in Burke County where he enlisted at age 18, February 1, 1862, for the war. Present or accounted for until captured at Falling Waters, Maryland, July 14, 1863. Confined at Point Lookout, Maryland, until paroled and transferred to City Point, Virginia, March 16, 1864, for exchange. Rejoined the company in May-June, 1864, and present or accounted for until captured near Petersburg, Virginia, October 27, 1864. Confined at Point Lookout until released on June 20, 1865, after taking the Oath of Allegiance.

SHUFFLER, WILLIAM, Private
Resided in Burke County where he enlisted at age 27, February 1, 1862, for the war. Present or accounted for until wounded at White Hall on December 16, 1862. Rejoined the company in March-April, 1863, and present or accounted for until captured at Falling Waters, Maryland, July 14, 1863. Confined at Baltimore, Maryland, and at Point Lookout, Maryland, until paroled and transferred for exchange on March 16, 1864. Rejoined the company in May-June, 1864, and present or accounted for until captured at or near Petersburg, Virginia, April 2, 1865. Confined at Point Lookout until released on June 20, 1865, after taking the Oath of Allegiance.

SIMS, SAMUEL, Private
Resided in Burke County where he enlisted at age 30, February 1, 1862, for the war. Present or accounted for until he deserted on June 22, 1863. Returned from desertion March 10, 1864. Court-martialed and sentenced to five years at hard labor. No further records.

SINGLETON, J. V., Private
Resided in Burke County where he enlisted at age 27, February 1, 1862, for the war. Present or accounted for until paroled at Appomattox Court House, Virginia, April 9, 1865.

SINGLETON, LUCIUS W., Corporal
Born in Burke County where he resided as a farmer prior to enlisting in Burke County at age 17, February 1, 1862, for the war. Mustered in as Private. Present or accounted for until wounded in the left arm at Gettysburg, Pennsylvania, July 1-3, 1863. Rejoined the company in January-February, 1864, and was promoted to Corporal on February 15, 1864. Present or accounted for until captured at Petersburg, Virginia, April 3, 1865. Confined at Hart's Island, New York Harbor, until released on or about June 19, 1865, after taking the Oath of Allegiance.

SINGLETON, M. D., Private
Resided in Burke County where he enlisted at age 21, February 1, 1862, for the war. Present or accounted for until he died on March 1, 1864. Place and cause of death not reported. [May have served previously in Company G, 1st Regiment N.C. Infantry (6 months, 1861).]

SINGLETON, R. W., Private
Enlisted in Burke County on October 5, 1864, for the war. Present or accounted for until captured at Hatcher's Run, Virginia, April 2, 1865. Confined at Point Lookout, Maryland, until released on June 4, 1865, after taking the Oath of Allegiance.

SINGLETON, S. S., Private
Resided in Burke County where he enlisted at age 22, February 1, 1862, for the war. Present or accounted for until captured at Falling Waters, Maryland, July 14, 1863. Confined at Baltimore, Maryland, and at Point Lookout, Maryland, until paroled and transferred for exchange on March 16, 1864. Rejoined the company in May-June, 1864, and present or accounted for until paroled at Lynchburg, Virginia, April 15, 1865.

SLOAN, JOHN, Private
Resided in Burke County where he enlisted on October 20, 1864, for the war. Present or accounted for until captured at Hatcher's Run, Virginia, March 29, 1865. Confined at Point Lookout, Maryland, until released on June 20, 1865, after taking the Oath of Allegiance.

SMITH, ALEXANDER, Private
Resided in Burke County and enlisted at age 20, March 5, 1863, for the war. Present or accounted for until he deserted near Culpeper, Virginia, June 22, 1863.

SMITH, ALVA, Private
Resided in Burke County where he enlisted at age 21, February 1, 1862, for the war. Present or accounted for until captured at Falling Waters, Maryland, July 14, 1863. Confined at Baltimore, Maryland, and at Point Lookout, Maryland, until paroled and transferred for exchange on March 16, 1864. Rejoined the company in May-June, 1864, and present or accounted for until wounded in the right knee at Petersburg, Virginia, in June-October, 1864. Reported absent wounded until retired to the Invalid Corps on December 22, 1864.

SMITH, ANDERSON, Private
Resided in Burke County where he enlisted at age 25, February 1, 1862, for the war. Present or accounted for until reported "missing on [the] march" in May-June, 1864. Court-martialed on or about June 22, 1864. Present or accounted for until reported absent without leave in January-February, 1865. Rejoined the company prior to April 2, 1865, when he was captured at or near Petersburg, Virginia. Confined at Point Lookout, Maryland, until released on June 20, 1865, after taking the Oath of Allegiance.

SMITH, E. C., Private
Resided in Burke County where he enlisted on January 7, 1865, for the war. Present or accounted for until captured at Hatcher's Run, Virginia, April 2, 1865. Confined at Point Lookout, Maryland, until released on June 20, 1865, after taking the Oath of Allegiance.

SMITH, HENRY, Private
Resided in Burke County where he enlisted at age 18, February 13, 1863, for the war. Present or accounted for until captured at Falling Waters, Maryland, July 14, 1863. Confined at Baltimore, Maryland, and at Point Lookout, Maryland, until paroled and transferred for exchange on March 16, 1864. Rejoined the company in July-August, 1864, and present or accounted for until wounded in the left eye at Petersburg, Virginia, October 2, 1864. Returned to duty on January 20, 1865, and present or accounted for until captured at or near Petersburg, April 2, 1865. Confined at Point Lookout until released on June 20, 1865, after taking the Oath of Allegiance.

SMITH, J. C., Private
Resided in Burke County where he enlisted at age 25, February 1, 1862, for the war. Present or accounted for until captured at Falling Waters, Maryland, July 14, 1863. Confined at Baltimore,

Maryland, and at Point Lookout, Maryland, until paroled and transferred for exchange on March 16, 1864. Rejoined the company in May-June, 1864, and present or accounted for through February, 1865. Paroled at Morganton on May 16, 1865.

SMITH, THOMAS, Private
Resided in Burke County where he enlisted at age 26, April 10, 1862, for the war. Present or accounted for until he deserted near Culpeper, Virginia, June 22, 1863.

SMITH, WILLIAM A., Private
Resided in Burke County where he enlisted at age 28, February 1, 1862, for the war. Present or accounted for until wounded and captured at Gettysburg, Pennsylvania, July 1-3, 1863. Hospitalized at Gettysburg until transferred to Davids Island, New York Harbor, on or about July 17, 1863. Died in hospital at Davids Island on October 1, 1863, of wounds.

STACY, GEORGE L., Private
Previously served in Company G, 1st Regiment N.C. Infantry (6 months, 1861). Enlisted in this company on February 1, 1862, for the war. Present or accounted for until captured at Gettysburg, Pennsylvania, July 1-4, 1863. Confined at Fort Delaware, Delaware, until transferred to Fort Mifflin, Pennsylvania, on or about November 30, 1863. Took the Oath of Allegiance at Fort Mifflin or deserted from Fort Mifflin on May 16, 1864. No further records.

STILL, J. D., Private
Place and date of enlistment not reported. Paroled at Charlotte on May 16, 1865.

SUDDERTH, ROBERT WINSLOW, Private
Previously served in Company F, 41st Regiment N.C. Troops (3rd Regiment N.C. Cavalry). Transferred to this company on December 5, 1864. Present or accounted for until captured at or near Petersburg, Virginia, April 2, 1865. Confined at Point Lookout, Maryland, until released on June 20, 1865, after taking the Oath of Allegiance.

SWINK, ARCHIBALD, Private
Resided in Burke County where he enlisted at age 26, February 13, 1863, for the war. Present or accounted for until captured at or near Petersburg, Virginia, October 27, 1864. Confined at Point Lookout, Maryland, until released on June 20, 1865, after taking the Oath of Allegiance.

TEEM, J. P., Private
Resided in Burke County where he enlisted at age 18, April 1, 1862, for the war. Present or accounted for until captured at Gettysburg, Pennsylvania, July 1-4, 1863. Confined at Fort Delaware, Delaware, until transferred to Point Lookout, Maryland, October 15-18, 1863. Confined at Point Lookout until paroled and transferred for exchange on or about February 10, 1865. Reported in hospital at Richmond, Virginia, February 15, 1865. Paroled at Salisbury on May 25, 1865.

TEEM, WILLIAM C., Private
Resided in Burke County where he enlisted on August 31, 1863, for the war. Present or accounted

for until reported absent wounded in September-October, 1864; however, place and date wounded not reported. Rejoined the company in November-December, 1864, and present or accounted for until captured at or near Petersburg, Virginia, April 2, 1865. Confined at Point Lookout, Maryland, until released on June 21, 1865, after taking the Oath of Allegiance.

WAKEFIELD, S. D., Private
Previously served in Company G, 1st Regiment N.C. Infantry (6 months, 1861). Enlisted in this company on February 1, 1862, for the war. Present or accounted for until wounded and captured at Gettysburg, Pennsylvania, July 1-3, 1863. Confined at Fort Delaware, Delaware, where he died on September 10, 1863, of "chronic diarrhoea."

WALKER, J. R., Private
Resided in Rutherford County where he enlisted on October 1, 1863, for the war. Present or accounted for until captured at or near Petersburg, Virginia, October 27, 1864. Confined at Point Lookout, Maryland, until released on May 14, 1865, after taking the Oath of Allegiance.

WALKER, JOSEPH, Private
Resided in Burke County where he enlisted at age 30, February 28, 1863, for the war. Present or accounted for until captured at or near Petersburg, Virginia, April 2, 1865. Confined at Point Lookout, Maryland, until released on June 21, 1865, after taking the Oath of Allegiance.

WARLICK, A. P., Corporal
Resided in Burke County where he enlisted at age 19, April 29, 1862, for the war. Mustered in as Private. Present or accounted for until wounded at Gettysburg, Pennsylvania, July 1-3, 1863. Returned to duty prior to September 1, 1863, and was promoted to Corporal on November 1, 1863. Present or accounted for until hospitalized at Richmond, Virginia, June 16, 1864, with a gunshot wound and diarrhoea; however, place and date wounded not reported. Died June 30, 1864, of "diarrhoea ch[ronic]."

WARLICK, D. LOGAN, Private
Resided in Burke County where he enlisted at age 40, November 1, 1863, for the war. Present or accounted for until killed at Spotsylvania Court House, Virginia, May 12, 1864.

WARLICK, W. J., Private
Enlisted in Burke County on April 15, 1864, for the war. Present or accounted for through February, 1865.

WATTS, HOSEA, Private
Resided in Burke County where he enlisted at age 30, March 5, 1863, for the war. Present or accounted for until he deserted on April 29, 1863.

WATTS, JOHN, Private
Enlisted in Burke County on November 20, 1864, for the war. Present or accounted for until captured at Hatcher's Run, Virginia, April 2, 1865. Confined at Point Lookout, Maryland, where he died April 21, 1865, of "inf of the lungs."

WEST, J. P., _____
Place and date of enlistment not reported. Died at

Richmond, Virginia, on or about August 28, 1865. Cause of death not reported.

WILKINS, T. B., _____
Place and date of enlistment not reported. Died at Richmond, Virginia, on or about September 18, 1864. Cause of death not reported.

WILLIAMS, J. B., Private
Resided in Burke County where he enlisted at age 20, February 1, 1862, for the war. Present or accounted for until wounded in the left foot at Gettysburg, Pennsylvania, July 1, 1863. Reported absent wounded until he rejoined the company in January-February, 1864. Present or accounted for until captured near Petersburg, Virginia, October 27, 1864. Confined at Point Lookout, Maryland, until released on June 21, 1865, after taking the Oath of Allegiance.

WILLIAMS, JOHN AMBROSE, Private
Resided in Burke County where he enlisted at age 26, February 1, 1862, for the war. Present or accounted for until he died in hospital at Raleigh on April 20, 1862, of "pneumonia."

WILLIAMS, MARK, Private
Enlisted in Burke County on October 5, 1864, for the war. Present or accounted for through December, 1864.

WILLIAMS, R. G., Private
Resided in Burke County where he enlisted at age 22, February 1, 1862, for the war. Present or accounted for until hospitalized at Farmville, Virginia, May 10-11, 1864, with a gunshot wound; however, place and date wounded not reported. Rejoined the company in September-October, 1864, and present or accounted for until captured near Petersburg, Virginia, March 25, 1865. Confined at Point Lookout, Maryland, until released on June 17, 1865, after taking the Oath of Allegiance.

YORK, WILLIAM, Private
Resided in Burke County where he enlisted at age 38, March 5, 1863, for the war. Present or accounted for until he deserted on April 29, 1863.

COMPANY C

This company was composed primarily of men from Bertie County and began organizing at Windsor on or about January 23, 1862. On March 31, 1862, it was mustered in as Company C of this regiment. After that date the company functioned as a part of the regiment, and its history for the war period is recorded as a part of the regimental history.

The information contained in the following roster of the company was compiled principally from company muster rolls for May, 1862, through February, 1865. No company muster rolls were found for the period prior to May, 1862, or for the period after February, 1865. In addition to the company muster rolls, Roll of Honor records, receipt rolls, hospital records, prisoner of war records, and other primary records, supplemented by state pension applications, United Daughters of the Confederacy records, and postwar rosters and histories, all provided useful information.

OFFICERS
CAPTAINS

BIRD, FRANCIS W.
Previously served as 2nd Lieutenant in Company L, 1st Regiment N.C. Infantry (6 months, 1861). Appointed Captain of this company to rank from January 22, 1862. Present or accounted for until promoted to Major on or about December 3, 1863, to rank from July 1, 1863, and transferred to the Field and Staff of this regiment.

OUTLAW, EDWARD RALPH
Previously served as Corporal in Company L, 1st Regiment N.C. Infantry (6 months, 1861). Appointed 2nd Lieutenant in this company to rank from January 22, 1862. Promoted to 1st Lieutenant on July 1, 1863, and was promoted to Captain in January-February, 1864. Present or accounted for until paroled at Appomattox Court House, Virginia, April 9, 1865.

LIEUTENANTS

COOPER, THOMAS W., 1st Lieutenant
Previously served as Corporal in Company L, 1st Regiment N.C. Infantry (6 months, 1861). Appointed 1st Lieutenant in this company to rank from January 22, 1862. Present or accounted for until killed at Gettysburg, Pennsylvania, July 1, 1863.

CRAIGE, CLINGMAN, 2nd Lieutenant
Previously served as Private in Company L, 1st Regiment N.C. Infantry (6 months, 1861). Enlisted in this company on January 23, 1862, for the war. Mustered in as 1st Sergeant. Present or accounted for until wounded and captured at or near Hagerstown, Maryland, July 7-13, 1863. Appointed 2nd Lieutenant to rank from July 30, 1863, while a prisoner of war. Died August 15 or September 15, 1863, of wounds. Place of death not reported.

RHODES, EDWARD A., 2nd Lieutenant
Born in Texas and resided in Bertie County prior to enlisting at age 20. Appointed 2nd Lieutenant to rank from January 22, 1862. Present or accounted for until killed at Gettysburg, Pennsylvania, July 1, 1863.

TODD, WILLIAM H., 1st Lieutenant
Previously served as Private in Company L, 1st Regiment N.C. Infantry (6 months, 1861). Enlisted in this company on January 23, 1862, for the war. Mustered in as Corporal and promoted to Sergeant on December 29, 1862. Present or accounted for until hospitalized at Richmond, Virginia, July 20, 1863, with a gunshot wound of the left thigh; however, place and date wounded not reported. Rejoined the company prior to September 1, 1863, and was promoted to 1st Lieutenant in January-February, 1864. Present or accounted for until wounded in the right buttock at Reams' Station, Virginia, August 25, 1864. Rejoined the company in September-October, 1864, and present or accounted for through February, 1865.

WINSTON, PATRICK H., 2nd Lieutenant
Previously served as Sergeant Major of the 32nd Regiment N.C. Troops. Transferred to this company

on February 27, 1864, upon appointment as 2nd Lieutenant to rank from January 25, 1864. Present or accounted for until captured at or near Burgess' Mill, Virginia, October 27, 1864. Confined at Old Capitol Prison, Washington, D.C., until transferred to Fort Delaware, Delaware, December 16, 1864. Released at Fort Delaware on May 30, 1865, after taking the Oath of Allegiance.

NONCOMMISSIONED OFFICERS AND PRIVATES

ADAMS, JAMES H., Sergeant
Resided in Bertie County where he enlisted at age 20, January 23, 1862, for the war. Mustered in as Corporal. Present or accounted for until hospitalized at Richmond, Virginia, July 16, 1863, with a gunshot wound of the left hand; however, place and date wounded not reported. Rejoined the company prior to September 1, 1863, and was promoted to Sergeant prior to November 1, 1863. Present or accounted for until he died in hospital at Lynchburg, Virginia, January 24, 1864, of "variola."

ALEXANDER, THOMAS B., Private
Resided in Bertie County and enlisted at age 30, January 23, 1862, for the war. Transferred to Company B, 3rd Battalion N.C. Light Artillery on January 28, 1862.

BAKER, GILBERT, Private
Born in Bertie County where he resided as a farmer prior to enlisting in Bertie County at age 18, January 23, 1862, for the war. Present or accounted for until discharged on August 17, 1862, by reason of "chronic rheumatism."

BAZEMORE, ARMSTEAD L., Sergeant
Born in Bertie County where he resided as a farmer prior to enlisting in Bertie County at age 20, January 23, 1862, for the war. Mustered in as Private and promoted to Sergeant on October 1, 1864. Present or accounted for through February, 1865; however, he was reported absent sick during much of that period.

BAZEMORE, HENRY, Private
Resided in Bertie County where he enlisted at age 34, January 23, 1862, for the war. Present or accounted for until wounded at White Hall on December 16, 1862. Returned to duty on December 1, 1863, and present or accounted for until captured at or near Petersburg, Virginia, April 2, 1865. Confined at Point Lookout, Maryland, until released on June 23, 1865, after taking the Oath of Allegiance.

BAZEMORE, WILLIAM H., Private
Resided in Bertie County where he enlisted at age 25, January 23, 1862, for the war. Present or accounted for until wounded in the left hand at White Hall on December 16, 1862. Rejoined the company in January-February, 1863, and present or accounted for until he deserted to the enemy on or about March 6, 1865. Took the Oath of Allegiance on or about March 10, 1865.

BAZEMORE, WILLIAM J., Private
Resided in Bertie County where he enlisted at age 27, January 23, 1862, for the war. Present or accounted for until he died in hospital at Weldon on February 10, 1863, of disease.

BLACKSTONE, WILLIAM R., Private
Previously served in Company F, 1st Regiment N.C. State Troops. Enlisted in this company on January 23, 1862, for the war. Present or accounted for until reported absent without leave from January 23, 1863, through August, 1863. Rejoined the company in September-October, 1863, and present or accounted for until reported absent without leave from November 17, 1863, until February 24, 1864. Present or accounted for until paroled at Appomattox Court House, Virginia, April 9, 1865.

BOWERS, J. A., Private
Place and date of enlistment not reported. Died in hospital at Point Lookout, Maryland, May 5, 1865, of "pneumonia." Place and date captured not reported.

BRITTON, DANIEL W., Sergeant
Resided in Bertie County where he enlisted at age 18, January 23, 1862, for the war. Mustered in as Corporal and promoted to Sergeant in January-February, 1863. Present or accounted for until transferred to Company G, 32nd Regiment N.C. Troops, March 18, 1864.

BROGDEN, WILLIAM G., Private
Resided in Bertie County where he enlisted at age 17, May 7, 1862, for the war. Present or accounted for until hospitalized at Richmond, Virginia, May 16, 1864, with a gunshot wound; however, place and date wounded not reported. Returned to duty August 15, 1864, and present or accounted for until wounded in the left hip and/or eye and captured at or near Petersburg, Virginia, April 2, 1865. Hospitalized at Old Capitol Prison, Washington, D.C., where he died June 2, 1865, of wounds.

BURDEN, JAMES M., Corporal
Previously served as Private in Company L, 1st Regiment N.C. Infantry (6 months, 1861). Enlisted in this company on January 23, 1862, for the war. Mustered in as Private and promoted to Corporal on February 15, 1864. Present or accounted for until hospitalized at Danville, Virginia, June 4, 1864, with a gunshot wound of the hip or left hand; however, place and date wounded not reported. Rejoined the company in November-December, 1864, and present or accounted for until captured at Burkeville, Virginia, April 6, 1865. Confined at Point Lookout, Maryland, until released on June 23, 1865, after taking the Oath of Allegiance.

BUTLER, JOHN, Private
Resided in Bertie County where he enlisted at age 29, January 23, 1862, for the war. Present or accounted for until he deserted on January 15, 1863.

BUTLER, LEVIN E., Private
Previously served in Company L, 1st Regiment N.C. Infantry (6 months, 1861). Enlisted in this company on January 23, 1862, for the war. Present or accounted for until captured at Bristoe Station, Virginia, October 14, 1863. Confined at Old Capitol Prison, Washington, D.C., until transferred to Point Lookout, Maryland, October 27, 1863. Paroled and transferred for exchange on September 18, 1864. Present or accounted for through February, 1865.

BUTLER, THADDEUS W., Private

Enlisted in Company B, 3rd Battalion N.C. Light Artillery in January, 1862; however, he was transferred to this unit before being mustered in to the 3rd Battalion N.C. Light Artillery. Present or accounted for until he deserted on August 26, 1863.

BUTLER, WILLIAM H., Corporal

Previously served as Private in Company L, 1st Regiment N.C. Infantry (6 months, 1861). Enlisted in this company on January 23, 1862, for the war. Mustered in as Private and promoted to Musician August 19, 1862. Promoted to Corporal on February 15, 1864. Present or accounted for until reported absent wounded in September-October, 1864; however, place and date wounded not reported. Rejoined the company in November-December, 1864, and present or accounted for through February, 1865.

BYRUM, JESSE B., Private

Resided in Bertie County where he enlisted at age 26, January 23, 1862, for the war. Present or accounted for until captured at Falling Waters, Maryland, July 14, 1863. Confined at Baltimore, Maryland, and at Point Lookout, Maryland, until paroled on March 3, 1864, and transferred for exchange. Rejoined the company in May-June, 1864, and present or accounted for until captured at or near Petersburg, Virginia, April 2, 1865. Confined at Point Lookout until released on June 23, 1865, after taking the Oath of Allegiance.

BYRUM, REUBEN L., Private

Resided in Bertie County where he enlisted at age 22, January 23, 1862, for the war. Present or accounted for until captured at Falling Waters, Maryland, July 14, 1863. Confined at Baltimore, Maryland, and at Point Lookout, Maryland, until paroled on March 3, 1864, and transferred for exchange. Rejoined the company in May-June, 1864, and present or accounted for until captured at or near Petersburg, Virginia, April 2, 1865. Confined at Point Lookout until released on June 23, 1865, after taking the Oath of Allegiance.

CALE, THOMAS F., Private

Resided in Bertie County where he enlisted at age 18, January 23, 1862, for the war. Present or accounted for until he deserted on October 20, 1864.

CALE, WILLIAM H., Private

Enlisted in Company B, 3rd Battalion N.C. Light Artillery in January, 1862; however, he was transferred to this unit before being mustered in to the 3rd Battalion N.C. Light Artillery. Present or accounted for until he deserted to the enemy on or about September 1, 1862.

CARPENTER, LEVI, Private

Place and date of enlistment not reported. Died at Camp Douglas, Illinois, December 12, 1864. Place and date captured and cause of death not reported.

CARTER, BENJAMIN, Private

Resided in Bertie County where he enlisted at age 22, May 7, 1862, for the war. Present or accounted for until killed at Gettysburg, Pennsylvania, July 1-3, 1863.

CARTER, JOSEPH B., 1st Sergeant

Previously served as Private in Company L, 1st

Regiment N.C. Infantry (6 months, 1861). Enlisted in this company on January 23, 1862, for the war. Mustered in as Corporal and promoted to Sergeant on September 1, 1863. Promoted to 1st Sergeant on February 15, 1864. Present or accounted for until killed at Reams' Station, Virginia, August 25, 1864.

CASPER, GEORGE M., Private

Resided in Bertie County where he enlisted at age 36, May 15, 1862, for the war. Present or accounted for until he deserted on October 24, 1864.

CASPER, JAMES H., Private

Resided in Bertie County where he enlisted at age 21, January 23, 1862, for the war. Present or accounted for until captured at Falling Waters, Maryland, July 14, 1863. Confined at Old Capitol Prison, Washington, D.C., until transferred to Point Lookout, Maryland, August 8, 1863. Released at Point Lookout on January 26, 1864, after joining the U.S. Army. Assigned to Company D, 1st Regiment U.S. Volunteer Infantry.

CASPER, JOSEPH W., Private

Enlisted in Bertie County at age 20, January 23, 1862, for the war. Present or accounted for until killed at Gettysburg, Pennsylvania, July 1-3, 1863.

CASPER, JUSTIN, Private

Resided in Bertie County where he enlisted at age 18, January 23, 1862, for the war. Present or accounted for until he died in hospital at Raleigh on or about May 21, 1862, of disease.

CASPER, THOMAS, Private

Previously served in Company G, 32nd Regiment N.C. Troops. Transferred to this company on March 18, 1864. Present or accounted for until he deserted on October 24, 1864.

CASPER, WILLIAM J., Private

Resided in Bertie County where he enlisted at age 26, January 23, 1862, for the war. Present or accounted for until he deserted on October 24, 1864.

CASTELLAW, JAMES C., Private

Resided in Bertie County where he enlisted at age 36, January 23, 1862, for the war. Present or accounted for until he died at Camp Mangum on March 23, 1862, of disease.

COOPER, ASA, Private

Resided in Bertie County and enlisted in New Hanover County on May 15, 1862, for the war. Present or accounted for through February, 1865.

COPELAND, WILLIAM D., Private

Resided in Bertie County where he enlisted at age 21, April 22, 1862, for the war. Present or accounted for until he died in hospital at Wilmington on May 10, 1862, of disease.

CORPREW, JONATHAN, Private

Resided in Bertie County where he enlisted at age 20, January 23, 1862, for the war. Present or accounted for until wounded at White Hall on December 16, 1862. Returned to duty prior to January 1, 1863, and present or accounted for until wounded at Gettysburg, Pennsylvania, July 1-3, 1863. Returned to duty prior to September 1, 1863, and present or accounted for until he deserted on October 24, 1864.

CULLIFER, JOHN C., Private

Enlisted in Company B, 3rd Battalion N.C. Light Artillery in January, 1862; however, he was transferred to this unit prior to being mustered in to the 3rd Battalion N.C. Light Artillery. Present or accounted for until he deserted on January 10, 1864.

CULLIPHER, SIMON, Private

Born in Bertie County where he resided prior to enlisting in Bertie County at age 48, May 7, 1862, for the war. Present or accounted for until he died in hospital at Richmond, Virginia, January 7, 1864, of "smallpox" or "erysipelas."

CULLIPHER, WILLIAM T., Private

Resided in Bertie County where he enlisted at age 19, January 23, 1862, for the war. Present or accounted for until he deserted on or about December 31, 1862.

DAVIS, ALFRED, Private

Resided in Bertie County where he enlisted at age 23, January 23, 1862, for the war. Present or accounted for until he died at Wilmington on July 29, 1862, of disease.

DAVIS, ALLEN, Private

Resided in Bertie County where he enlisted at age 24, January 23, 1862, for the war. Present or accounted for until wounded in the arm at or near Spotsylvania Court House, Virginia, on or about May 18, 1864. Reported absent wounded through February, 1865. Paroled at Appomattox Court House, Virginia, April 9, 1865.

DAVIS, AUGUSTUS, Private

Resided in Bertie County where he enlisted at age 22, January 23, 1862, for the war. Present or accounted for until reported absent wounded in July-August, 1862; however, place and date wounded not reported. Rejoined the company in September-October, 1862, and present or accounted for until hospitalized at Richmond, Virginia, August 29, 1863, with a gunshot wound. Place and date wounded not reported. Returned to duty on December 1, 1863, and present or accounted for until he deserted on November 7, 1864.

DAVIS, EDWARD, Private

Resided in Bertie County where he enlisted at age 23, January 23, 1862, for the war. Present or accounted for until he died in hospital at Weldon on October 20, 1863, of "ulcers."

DAVIS, JOHN, Private

Resided in Bertie County and enlisted in New Hanover County at age 36, May 17, 1862, for the war. Present or accounted for until captured at or near Burgess' Mill, Virginia, October 27, 1864. Confined at Point Lookout, Maryland, until paroled and transferred for exchange on March 28, 1865.

EVANS, AARON J., Private

Resided in Bertie County where he enlisted at age 19, January 23, 1862, for the war. Present or accounted for until captured at Bristoe Station, Virginia, October 14, 1863. Confined at Old Capitol Prison, Washington, D.C., until released on December 17, 1863, after taking the Oath of Allegiance.

FLOYD, JAMES R., Sergeant

Resided in Bertie County where he enlisted at age 18, January 23, 1862, for the war. Mustered in as Private. Present or accounted for until wounded and captured at Gettysburg, Pennsylvania, July 1-3, 1863. Hospitalized at Gettysburg until transferred to Davids Island, New York Harbor, July 17-24, 1863. Exchanged on or about September 8, 1863, and rejoined the company in November-December, 1863. Promoted to Corporal in March-April, 1864, and promoted to Sergeant on October 1, 1864. Present or accounted for through February, 1865.

FLOYD, JOHN G., 1st Sergeant

Resided in Bertie County where he enlisted at age 20, January 23, 1862, for the war. Mustered in as Private and promoted to Corporal on December 29, 1862. Promoted to Sergeant on February 15, 1864, and promoted to 1st Sergeant on October 1, 1864. Present or accounted for until captured at or near Burgess' Mill, Virginia, October 27, 1864. Confined at Point Lookout, Maryland, until paroled and transferred for exchange on March 28, 1865.

FREEMAN, JACOB W., Private

Resided in Bertie County where he enlisted at age 33, January 23, 1862, for the war. Present or accounted for until reported absent on sick furlough in Bertie County on August 14, 1863. Reported absent without leave on October 19, 1863, and was killed in Bertie County on June 26, 1864.

GARNER, ELIAS, Private

Enlisted in Wake County on April 26, 1864, for the war. Present or accounted for until he deserted on July 1, 1864.

GILLAM, FRANCIS, Sergeant

Resided in Bertie County where he enlisted at age 22, January 23, 1862, for the war. Mustered in as Sergeant. Present or accounted for through October, 1862. Roll of Honor indicates he was promoted to Assistant Surgeon. No further records.

GILLIAM, JOHN H., Private

Previously served in Company L, 1st Regiment N.C. Infantry (6 months, 1861). Enlisted in this company on January 23, 1862, as a substitute. Present or accounted for until discharged on or about April 9, 1864, by reason of "his age and a general failure of health." Discharge papers give his age as 56.

GOFF, THOMAS G., Private

Born in Bertie County where he resided as a farmer prior to enlisting in Bertie County at age 21, January 23, 1862, for the war. Transferred to Company B, 3rd Battalion N.C. Light Artillery, on or about January 28, 1862.

GREGORY, JOHN T., Private

Born in Bertie County where he resided prior to enlisting in Bertie County at age 20, January 23, 1862, for the war. Present or accounted for until captured at Gettysburg, Pennsylvania, July 3, 1863. Confined at Fort Delaware, Delaware, until transferred to Point Lookout, Maryland, October 15-18, 1863. Died at Point Lookout on or about February 10, 1864, of "smallpox."

GREGORY, LEMUEL D., Private

Resided in Bertie County where he enlisted at age 19, January 23, 1862, for the war. Present or accounted for until hospitalized at Wilmington on or about August 12, 1862, with "febris typhoid." Died in hospital at Wilmington on August 23, 1862.

GREGORY, WILLIAM L., Private
Resided in Bertie County where he enlisted at age 25, January 23, 1862, for the war. Present or accounted for until his foot was "shot off" at Gettysburg, Pennsylvania, July 1-3, 1863. Captured at Gettysburg or at Williamsport, Maryland, at an unspecified date. Died of wounds. Place and date of death not reported.

HARGROVES, ISRAEL, Private
Born in Chatham County and was by occupation a farmer prior to enlisting in Wake County at age 41, April 24, 1864, for the war. Present or accounted for until reported "missing in action on May 5, 1864. Reported "in arrest" on company muster rolls dated July-October, 1864. Rejoined the company in November-December, 1864, but was discharged on March 9, 1865. Reason discharged reported on discharge papers as follows: "He is at times perfectly insane. He preaches when under these fits, both night and day, to imaginary audiences. . . ."

HARGROVES, RICHARD, Private
Resided in Chatham County and enlisted on or about April 24, 1864, for the war. Reported missing in action on May 5, 1864. Reported absent "in arrest" on company muster rolls dated July-October, 1864. Died in hospital at Richmond, Virginia, October 26, 1864, of "anasarca."

HARMON, JAMES F., Private
Resided in Bertie County where he enlisted on November 24, 1863, for the war. Present or accounted for until captured at or near Burgess' Mill, Virginia, October 27, 1864. Confined at Point Lookout, Maryland, until released on June 13, 1865, after taking the Oath of Allegiance.

HARRELL, GEORGE B., Corporal
Previously served as Private in Company L, 1st Regiment N.C. Infantry (6 months, 1861). Enlisted in this company on January 23, 1862, for the war. Mustered in as Private and promoted to Corporal on October 1, 1864. Present or accounted for until captured at or near Petersburg, Virginia, April 2, 1865. Confined at Point Lookout, Maryland, until released on June 27, 1865, after taking the Oath of Allegiance.

HAWKS, JAMES W., Private
Previously served in Company E, 9th Regiment N.C. State Troops (1st Regiment N.C. Cavalry). Transferred to this company on December 6, 1864. Present or accounted for until captured at Dinwiddie Court House, Virginia, March 29, 1865. Confined at Point Lookout, Maryland, until released on June 13, 1865, after taking the Oath of Allegiance.

HOGGARD, WILLIAM, Private
Resided in Bertie County where he enlisted at age 28, January 23, 1862, for the war. Present or accounted for until hospitalized at Wilmington on or about July 12, 1862, with "gonorrhea." Died August 10, 1862.

HOGGARD, WILLIAM M., Sergeant
Resided in Bertie County where he enlisted at age 40, January 23, 1862, for the war. Mustered in as Sergeant. Present or accounted for until he died at

Weldon on January 18, 1863, of "erysepilas."

HOLDER, THOMAS, Private
Resided in Bertie County where he enlisted at age 18, January 23, 1862, for the war. Present or accounted for until wounded and captured at Gettysburg, Pennsylvania, July 1-3, 1863. Died of wounds. Place and date of death not reported.

HUGHES, HENRY, Private
Resided in Bertie County where he enlisted at age 50, January 23, 1862, for the war. Present or accounted for until he deserted "from the guard house at Camp Davis" on September 24, 1862. Deserted to the enemy on or about March 13, 1864, and took the Oath of Amnesty at Fort Monroe, Virginia, March 20, 1864.

JACKSON, JOSEPH C., Private
Resided in Bertie County where he enlisted at age 29, January 23, 1862, for the war. Present or accounted for until captured at Falling Waters, Maryland, July 14, 1863. Confined at Baltimore, Maryland, and at Point Lookout, Maryland, until transferred to Elmira, New York, where he arrived August 18, 1864. Died at Elmira on November 12, 1864, of "hospital gangrene."

JENKINS, DOCTRINE, Private
Resided in Bertie County where he enlisted at age 23, January 23, 1862, for the war. Present or accounted for until he died in hospital at Raleigh on April 20, 1862, of "pneumonia and rubeola."

JERNIGAN, SAMUEL, Private
Resided in Bertie County where he enlisted at age 21, January 23, 1862, for the war. Present or accounted for until he died at Camp Mangum on April 26, 1862, of disease.

JONES, WILEY, Private
Enlisted in Wake County on April 26, 1864, for the war. Present or accounted for until he deserted on October 24, 1864.

KING, JOSEPH, Private
Resided in Bertie County and enlisted in New Hanover County at age 19, May 17, 1862, for the war. Present or accounted for until captured at Gettysburg, Pennsylvania, July 1-3, 1863. Confined at various camps until confined at Fort Delaware, Delaware, on or about October 28, 1863. Released at Fort Delaware on June 19, 1865, after taking the Oath of Allegiance.

KUTER, JAMES L., Private
Resided in Bertie County where he enlisted at age 24, January 23, 1862, for the war. Present or accounted for until he deserted on December 31, 1862.

LEGGETT, WILLIAM, Private
Resided in Bertie County where he enlisted at age 19, January 23, 1862, for the war. Present or accounted for until he deserted to the enemy on or about March 6, 1865.

LONGEE, AUGUSTUS H., Private
Enlisted in Wake County on April 16, 1864, for the war. Present or accounted for until captured at Wilderness, Virginia, May 5-6, 1864. Confined at Point Lookout, Maryland, until released on May 17, 1864, after joining the U.S. Army. Assigned to

Company H, 1st Regiment U.S. Volunteer Infantry.

LUCUS, AUGUSTUS G., Private
Enlisted in Wake County on April 26, 1864, for the war. Present or accounted for until he was "lost on [the] march" from Spotsylvania Court House, Virginia, in May-June, 1864. Company muster rolls dated July-October, 1864, indicate he was a prisoner of war; however, records of the Federal Provost Marshal do not substantiate that report. Company muster rolls dated November, 1864-February, 1865, indicate that he deserted on December 1, 1864.

MARDRE, WILLIAM B., Private
Previously served in Company L, 1st Regiment N.C. Infantry (6 months, 1861). Enlisted in this company on or about July 7, 1862, for the war. Present or accounted for until appointed Ordnance Sergeant in September-October, 1863, and transferred to the Field and Staff of this regiment.

MITCHELL, JAMES E., Private
Resided in Bertie County where he enlisted at age 17, April 22, 1862, for the war. Present or accounted for until captured at Bristoe Station, Virginia, October 14, 1863. Confined at Old Capitol Prison, Washington, D.C., until transferred to Point Lookout, Maryland, October 27, 1863. Paroled at Point Lookout on March 3, 1864, and transferred for exchange. Rejoined the company in May-June, 1864, and present or accounted for until captured on the South Side Railroad, near Petersburg, Virginia, April 1, 1865. Confined at Hart's Island, New York Harbor, until released on June 17, 1865, after taking the Oath of Allegiance.

MITCHELL, JEREMIAH P., Private
Previously served in Company L, 1st Regiment N.C. Infantry (6 months, 1861). Enlisted in this company on January 23, 1862, for the war. Present or accounted for until killed at Gettysburg, Pennsylvania, July 1, 1863.

MIZELL, JOHN N., Private
Resided in Bertie County where he enlisted at age 17, April 22, 1862, for the war. Present or accounted for until he died at Wilmington on July 25, 1862, of "febris typhoid."

MORRIS, WILLIAM D., Private
Resided in Bertie County where he enlisted at age 43, January 23, 1862, for the war. Present or accounted for through April, 1863.

MYERS, NATHAN, Private
Previously served in Company L, 1st Regiment N.C. Infantry (6 months, 1861). Enlisted in this company on April 22, 1862, for the war. Present or accounted for until hospitalized at Danville, Virginia, on or about May 18, 1864, with a gunshot wound of the hand; however, place and date wounded not reported. Returned to duty on or about May 29, 1864, and present or accounted for until captured at Harper's Farm, Virginia, April 6, 1865. Confined at Point Lookout, Maryland, until released on June 29, 1865, after taking the Oath of Allegiance.

MYERS, THOMAS L., Private
Previously served in Company L, 1st Regiment N.C. Infantry (6 months, 1861). Enlisted in this company on April 22, 1862, for the war. Present or accounted

for until he died at Camp Mangum on May 5, 1862, of disease.

OWENS, RICHARD, Corporal
Previously served in Company L, 1st Regiment N.C. Infantry (6 months, 1861). Enlisted in this company on January 23, 1862, for the war. Mustered in as Private and promoted to Corporal in September-October, 1863. Present or accounted for until he deserted to the enemy at Plymouth on or about February 17, 1864. Took the Oath of Allegiance at Fort Monroe, Virginia, February 24, 1864.

PARKER, CULLEN, Private
Resided in Bertie County where he enlisted at age 20, January 23, 1862, for the war. Present or accounted for until he died in Bertie County on December 16, 1862, of disease.

PARKER, JAMES B., Private
Enlisted in Bertie County on February 15, 1864, for the war. Present or accounted for until paroled at Appomattox Court House, Virginia, April 9, 1865.

PARKER, JOHN H., Private
Resided in Bertie County where he enlisted at age 20, January 23, 1862, for the war. Present or accounted for until captured at Falling Waters, Maryland, July 14, 1863. Confined at Baltimore, Maryland, until transferred to Point Lookout, Maryland, August 16, 1863. Released at Point Lookout on February 25, 1864, after joining the U.S. Army. Assigned to Company F, 1st Regiment U.S. Volunteer Infantry.

PARKER, THOMAS H., Private
Previously served in Company L, 1st Regiment N.C. Infantry (6 months, 1861). Enlisted in this company on January 23, 1862, for the war. Present or accounted for until hospitalized at Richmond, Virginia, October 2, 1864, with a gunshot wound of the left hand; however, place and date wounded not reported. Rejoined the company in November-December, 1864, and present or accounted for until captured at Amelia Court House, Virginia, April 6, 1865. Confined at Point Lookout, Maryland, until released on June 16, 1865, after taking the Oath of Allegiance.

PARKER, WILLIAM G., Sergeant
Born in Bertie County where he resided prior to enlisting in Bertie County at age 42, January 23, 1862, for the war. Mustered in as Private and promoted to Sergeant in January-February, 1863. Present or accounted for until wounded at Gettysburg, Pennsylvania, July 1, 1863. Died at Winchester, Virginia, on or about July 20, 1863, of wounds.

PEELE, THOMAS H., Private
Previously served in Company L, 1st Regiment N.C. Infantry (6 months, 1861). Enlisted in this company on April 22, 1862, for the war. Present or accounted for until killed at Gettysburg, Pennsylvania, July 1-3, 1863.

PHELPS, THOMAS, Private
Born in Bertie County where he resided as a farmer prior to enlisting in Bertie County at age 42, January 23, 1862, for the war. Present or accounted for until discharged on April 24, 1864. Reason discharged reported as follows: "He was in the early part of his life a very intemperate man, which has caused him

to decline very rapidly in his old age. . . . [He is] afflicted constantly with rheumatism. . . ."

PHELPS, W. J., Private
Place and date of enlistment not reported. Discharged at Camp Mangum on April 22, 1862, by reason of disability.

PIERCE, JAMES H., Private
Born in Bertie County where he resided prior to enlisting in Bertie County at age 22, January 23, 1862, for the war. Present or accounted for until killed at Gettysburg, Pennsylvania, July 1, 1863.

POWELL, WILLIAM A., Private
Enlisted in Wake County on September 17, 1864, for the war. Present or accounted for through February, 1865.

POWELL, WILLIAM W., Sergeant
Previously served as Private in Company L, 1st Regiment N.C. Infantry (6 months, 1861). Enlisted in this company on January 23, 1862, for the war. Mustered in as Private and promoted to Corporal in January-February, 1863. Present or accounted for until wounded and captured at Gettysburg, Pennsylvania, July 1-5, 1863. Hospitalized at Gettysburg until transferred to hospital at Davids Island, New York Harbor, July 17-24, 1863. Paroled at Davids Island and transferred for exchange on or about September 16, 1863. Promoted to Sergeant on February 15, 1864, and returned to duty on February 27, 1864. Present or accounted for until captured at or near Petersburg, Virginia, April 2, 1865. Confined at Point Lookout, Maryland, until released on June 17, 1865, after taking the Oath of Allegiance.

POWERS, JESSE A., Private
Enlisted in Wake County on April 26, 1864, for the war. Present or accounted for through February, 1865. Captured at Petersburg, Virginia, at an unspecified date. Confined at Point Lookout, Maryland, until released on June 30, 1865.

PRITCHARD, ANDREW J., Private
Resided in Bertie County where he enlisted at age 19, January 23, 1862, for the war. Present or accounted for until wounded in the right arm, right knee, right thigh, and right hip at Gettysburg, Pennsylvania, July 1, 1863. Returned to duty on May 9, 1864, and present or accounted for until captured in hospital at Richmond, Virginia, April 3, 1865. Confined at Libby Prison, Richmond, until transferred to Newport News, Virginia, April 23, 1865. Released at Newport News on June 14, 1865, after taking the Oath of Allegiance.

PRITCHARD, JAMES W., Private
Enlisted in Bertie County on January 23, 1865, for the war. Present or accounted for through February, 1865.

PRITCHARD, JOSEPH J., Private
Resided in Bertie County where he enlisted at age 20, January 23, 1862, for the war. Present or accounted for until he deserted on January 28, 1864.

RAWLS, JAMES R., Corporal
Previously served as Private in Company L, 1st Regiment N.C. Infantry (6 months, 1861). Enlisted in this company on January 23, 1862, for the war.

Mustered in as Private. Present or accounted for until captured at Bristoe Station, Virginia, October 14, 1863. Confined at Old Capitol Prison, Washington, D.C., until transferred to Point Lookout, Maryland, October 27, 1863. Paroled at Point Lookout and transferred for exchange on or about March 3, 1864. Returned to duty on May 9, 1864, and was promoted to Corporal on October 1, 1864. Present or accounted for until he deserted on October 11, 1864.

RAYNER, JAMES T., Sergeant
Previously served as Private in Company L, 1st Regiment N.C. Infantry (6 months, 1861). Enlisted in this company on January 23, 1862, for the war. Mustered in as Sergeant. Present or accounted for until wounded in the left leg and captured at Gettysburg, Pennsylvania, July 1-5, 1863. Hospitalized at various Federal hospitals until paroled at Baltimore, Maryland, September 25, 1863, and transferred for exchange. Rejoined the company in July-August, 1864. Promoted to Ensign (1st Lieutenant) on August 16, 1864, and transferred to the Field and Staff of this regiment.

RHODES, ROBERT H., Private
Previously served in Company A, 63rd Regiment N.C. Troops (5th Regiment N.C. Cavalry). Transferred to this company on February 9, 1864, with the rank of Private. Present or accounted for until appointed Sergeant Major of this regiment and transferred to the Field and Staff in September-October, 1864.

RICE, NAPOLEON B., Private
Previously served in Company L, 1st Regiment N.C. Infantry (6 months, 1861). Enlisted in this company on January 23, 1862, for the war. Present or accounted for until wounded at Gettysburg, Pennsylvania, July 1-3, 1863. Died at Winchester, Virginia, July 17, 1863, of wounds.

SERLYN, ANTHONY, Private
Born in Holland and resided in Bertie County where he was by occupation a miller prior to enlisting in New Hanover County at age 51, May 17, 1862, for the war as a substitute. Present or accounted for until discharged on April 9, 1864, by reason of "his age & . . . chronic rheumatism."

SIMMONS, WILLIAM H., Private
Resided in Bertie County where he enlisted at age 26, January 23, 1862, for the war. Present or accounted for until discharged on or about June 2, 1862, by reason of disability.

SKILES, HENRY, Private
Previously served in Company L, 1st Regiment N.C. Infantry (6 months, 1861). Enlisted in this company on May 17, 1862, for the war. Present or accounted for until he deserted on October 24, 1864.

SKILES, JAMES W., Private
Born in Bertie County where he resided as a farmer prior to enlisting in New Hanover County at age 30, May 17, 1862, for the war as a substitute. Present or accounted for until he deserted on January 15, 1863. Went over to the enemy at Plymouth on or about October 22, 1863, and joined the U.S. service. Assigned to Company B, 2nd Regiment N.C. Infantry (U.S.), October 23, 1863.

SKILES, ROBERT M., Private
Resided in Bertie County where he enlisted at age 32, January 23, 1862, for the war. Present or accounted for until captured at Falling Waters, Maryland, July 14, 1863. Confined at Baltimore, Maryland, and at Point Lookout, Maryland, until paroled and transferred for exchange on or about May 3, 1864. Returned to duty on June 18, 1864, and present or accounted for until he deserted to the enemy on or about February 12, 1865.

SMITH, DAVID H., Private
Resided in Gaston County. Place and date of enlistment not reported. Captured at Hatcher's Run, Virginia, April 2, 1865. Confined at Old Capitol Prison, Washington, D.C., until transferred to Elmira, New York, May 1, 1865. Released at Elmira on June 23, 1865, after taking the Oath of Allegiance.

SMITWICK, A., Private
Enlisted on May 17, 1862, for the war. Discharged May 29, 1862, by reason of disability.

STEALY, LAFAYETTE, Private
Resided in Bertie County and enlisted at age 20, January 23, 1862, for the war. Transferred to Company B, 3rd Battalion N.C. Light Artillery, January 28, 1862.

STEWART, THADDEUS C., Private
Resided in Bertie County and was by occupation a farmer prior to enlisting in Bertie County at age 18, January 23, 1862, for the war. Present or accounted for until he died at Raleigh on March 23, 1862, of "brain fever."

STOKES, GASTON, Private
Enlisted in Wake County on September 17, 1864, for the war. Present or accounted for until hospitalized at Farmville, Virginia, on or about April 8, 1865, with a gunshot wound of the left shoulder; however, place and date wounded not reported. Paroled at Farmville, April 11-21, 1865.

STONE, DAVID G., Private
Born in Bertie County where he resided prior to enlisting in Bertie County at age 21, January 23, 1862, for the war. Present or accounted for until killed at Gettysburg, Pennsylvania, July 1, 1863.

STONE, JOHN, Private
Resided in Bertie County where he enlisted at age 16, May 7, 1862, for the war as a substitute. Present or accounted for until captured at Bristoe Station, Virginia, October 14, 1863. Confined at Old Capitol Prison, Washington, D.C., until transferred to Point Lookout, Maryland, October 27, 1863. Released at Point Lookout on February 25, 1864, after taking the Oath of Allegiance and joining the U.S. Army. Assigned to Company F, 1st Regiment U.S. Volunteer Infantry.

TAYLOR, WILLIAM H., Private
Resided in Bertie County and was by occupation a farmer prior to enlisting in Bertie County at age 25, April 22, 1862, for the war. Present or accounted for until he died at Franklin Depot, Virginia, November 21, 1862, of "pneumonia."

THATCH, STEPHEN, Private
Resided in Bertie County where he enlisted at age 26, January 23, 1862, for the war. Present or accounted for until captured near Plymouth on or about January 27, 1864. Confined at Point Lookout, Maryland, where he died on March 5, 1865, of "chronic diarrhoea."

THOMAS, JOSEPH T., Private
Previously served in Company L, 1st Regiment N.C. Infantry (6 months, 1861). Enlisted in this company on May 3, 1862, for the war. Present or accounted for until discharged on August 17, 1862, by reason of heart disease.

THOMPSON, DAVID, Sergeant
Previously served as Private in Company L, 1st Regiment N.C. Infantry (6 months, 1861). Enlisted in this company on January 23, 1862, for the war. Mustered in as Sergeant. Present or accounted for until he deserted to the enemy on January 19, 1863.

TODD, AUGUSTUS, Private
Resided in Bertie County where he enlisted at age 31, January 23, 1862, for the war. Present or accounted for until he deserted on January 19, 1863.

TODD, ELISHA, Chief Musician
Resided in Bertie County where he enlisted at age 20, January 23, 1862, for the war. Mustered in as Private and appointed Chief Musician in March-April, 1864. Present or accounted for until transferred to the regimental band in September-October, 1864.

TODD, LEWIS, Sergeant
Resided in Bertie County where he enlisted at age 33, May 3, 1862, for the war. Mustered in as Private and promoted to Corporal in September-October, 1863. Promoted to Sergeant in March-April, 1864. Present or accounted for until captured at Amelia Court House, Virginia, April 3, 1865. Confined at Point Lookout, Maryland, until released on June 21, 1865, after taking the Oath of Allegiance.

TODD, NEHEMIAH J., Musician
Enlisted in Bertie County on November 24, 1863, for the war. Mustered in as Private and promoted to Musician in March-April, 1864. Present or accounted for until transferred to the regimental band in September-October, 1864.

TRUMBULL, JOHN D., Private
Resided in Bertie County where he enlisted at age 22, January 23, 1862, for the war. Present or accounted for until he deserted on November 14, 1862.

WARD, WARREN J., Private
Resided in Bertie County where he enlisted at age 17, January 23, 1862, for the war. Present or accounted for until he deserted on January 15, 1863. Deserted to the enemy at Plymouth on or about March 13, 1864. Confined at Fort Monroe, Virginia, until released on March 24, 1864, after taking the Oath of Amnesty.

WARD, WHITMEL T., Private
Resided in Bertie County where he enlisted at age 43, April 22, 1862, for the war. Present or accounted for until discharged on or about September 1, 1862, after being "rejected by [the] Surgeon."

WARD, WILLIAM C., Private
Enlisted in Bertie County on February 15, 1864, for

the war. Present or accounted for until captured at
or near Burgess' Mill, Virginia, October 27, 1864.
Confined at Point Lookout, Maryland, where he died
on March 18, 1865, of "pneumonia."

WARD, WILLIAM T., 1st Sergeant
Resided in Bertie County where he enlisted at age
21, January 23, 1862, for the war. Mustered in as
Private and promoted to 1st Sergeant on September
1, 1863. Present or accounted for until he deserted
while on sick furlough in Bertie County on January
5, 1864.

WHITE, RIDDICK, Private
Resided in Bertie County where he enlisted at age
18, January 23, 1862, for the war. Present or
accounted for until he died in hospital at
Wilmington on or about August 20, 1862, of
continued fever.

WILLIAMS, JAMES H., Private
Resided in Bertie County where he enlisted at age
18, January 23, 1862, for the war. Present or
accounted for until wounded and captured at
Gettysburg, Pennsylvania, July 1-3, 1863. Died of
wounds. Place and date of death not reported.

WILLIAMS, OLIVER M., Private
Resided in Orange County and enlisted in Wake
County on September 17, 1864, for the war. Present
or accounted for until captured at or near
Petersburg, Virginia, April 2, 1865. Confined at
Point Lookout, Maryland, until released on June 21,
1865, after taking the Oath of Allegiance.

WILLIAMS, WILLIAM, Private
Resided in Bertie County where he enlisted at age
22, January 23, 1862, for the war. Present or
accounted for until he deserted on January 15, 1863.
Deserted to the enemy at Plymouth on or about
March 13, 1864. Confined at Fort Monroe, Virginia,
until released on March 24, 1864, after taking the
Oath of Amnesty.

WILLIAMSON, HENRY C., Private
Enlisted in Wake County on April 26, 1864, for the
war. Present or accounted for until he deserted on
July 1, 1864.

WRIGHT, JOHN, Private
Enlisted in Wake County on April 26, 1864, for the
war. Present or accounted for until he deserted on
September 20, 1864.

COMPANY D

This company was composed primarily of men from
Burke County and began organizing at Morganton in
February, 1862. On March 31, 1862, it was mustered
in as Company D of this regiment. After that date the
company functioned as a part of the regiment, and its
history for the war period is recorded as a part of the
regimental history.

The information contained in the following roster of
the company was compiled principally from company
muster rolls for May, 1862, through February, 1865.
No company muster rolls were found for the period
prior to May, 1862, or for the period after February,
1865. In addition to the company muster rolls, Roll of

Honor records, receipt rolls, hospital records, prisoner
of war records, and other primary records, supplemented by state pension applications, United Daughters
of the Confederacy records, and postwar rosters and
histories, all provided useful information.

OFFICERS
CAPTAINS

BROWN, CALVIN S.
Previously served as 1st Lieutenant in Company G,
1st Regiment N.C. Infantry (6 months, 1861). Appointed Captain of this company to rank from February 4, 1862. Present or accounted for until he
resigned on January 7, 1864, by reason of
"sunstroke."

KINCAID, W. J.
Previously served as 1st Sergeant in Company G, 1st
Regiment N.C. Infantry (6 months, 1861). Appointed 1st Lieutenant in this company to rank from
February 14, 1862. Present or accounted for until
wounded and captured at Gettysburg, Pennsylvania,
July 1-5, 1863. Confined at various Federal prisons
until confined at Johnson's Island, Ohio, October 31,
1863. Promoted to Captain on January 7, 1864,
while a prisoner of war. Confined at Johnson's Island
until transferred to Point Lookout, Maryland, March
21, 1865. Transferred to Fort Delaware, Delaware,
where he arrived April 28, 1865. Released at Fort
Delaware on June 12, 1865, after taking the Oath of
Allegiance.

LIEUTENANTS

ELIAS, LOUIS, 1st Lieutenant
Resided in Burke County where he enlisted at age
17, February 5, 1862, for the war. Mustered in as 1st
Sergeant and appointed 2nd Lieutenant to rank from
April 22, 1862. Promoted to 1st Lieutenant on
January 7, 1864. Present or accounted for through
February, 1865. Paroled at Statesville on May 19,
1865.

KINCAID, GEORGE W., 3rd Lieutenant
Resided in Burke County where he enlisted at age
23, February 15, 1862, for the war. Mustered in as
Sergeant and appointed 3rd Lieutenant to rank from
May 24, 1862. Present or accounted for until killed
at Gettysburg, Pennsylvania, July 3, 1863.

McCORKLE, JAMES G., 2nd Lieutenant
Previously served as Sergeant Major of this regiment.
Appointed 2nd Lieutenant on November 26, 1863,
and transferred to this company. Present or
accounted for until captured at or near Burgess'
Mill, Virginia, October 27, 1864. Confined at Old
Capitol Prison, Washington, D.C., until transferred
to Fort Delaware, Delaware, December 16, 1864.
Released at Fort Delaware on June 17, 1865, after
taking the Oath of Allegiance.

TATE, JOHN M., 2nd Lieutenant
Resided in Mecklenburg or Burke counties and
enlisted at age 32. Appointed 2nd Lieutenant on
February 14, 1862. Present or accounted for until
appointed Assistant Quartermaster (1st Lieutenant)
to rank from April 22, 1862, and transferred to the
Field and Staff of this regiment.

NONCOMMISSIONED OFFICERS AND PRIVATES

ABEE, A. J., Private
Enlisted in Burke County on September 10, 1864, for the war. Present or accounted for until captured at or near Burgess' Mill, Virginia, October 27, 1864. Confined at Point Lookout, Maryland, until paroled and transferred for exchange on or about February 10, 1865.

ALBRIGHT, WILLIAM S., Private
Enlisted in Burke County on June 27, 1864, for the war. Present or accounted for until wounded in the head near Petersburg, Virginia, October 1, 1864. Died in hospital at Richmond, Virginia, October 4, 1864, of wounds.

ALLEY, A. J., Private
Place and date of enlistment not reported. Hospitalized at Richmond, Virginia, February 15, 1865. No further records.

BAKER, LUCIUS, Private
Resided in Burke County where he enlisted at age 22, March 1, 1862, for the war. Present or accounted for until wounded in the left hip at Bristoe Station, Virginia, October 14, 1863. Reported absent wounded through February, 1865.

BEACH, J. C., Private
Resided in Burke County where he enlisted at age 16, April 12, 1862, for the war. Present or accounted for until he died in hospital at Wilmington on July 29, 1862. Cause of death not reported.

BENFIELD, MARTIN, Private
Enlisted in Burke County on February 23, 1864, for the war. Present or accounted for through February, 1865. Paroled at Salisbury on May 25, 1865.

BENFIELD, T. W., Private
Resided in Burke County where he enlisted at age 25, April 18, 1862, for the war. Present or accounted for until hospitalized at Richmond, Virginia, July 20, 1863, with a gunshot wound of the thigh; however, place and date wounded not reported. Rejoined the company in November-December, 1863, and present or accounted for until reported absent wounded in July-August, 1864. Place and date wounded not reported. Died in hospital at Richmond on September 19, 1864, of wounds. [May have served previously in Company G, 1st Regiment N.C. Infantry (6 months, 1861).]

BINGHAM, R. W., Private
Resided in Burke County where he enlisted at age 25, March 11, 1862, for the war. Present or accounted for until captured at Bristoe Station, Virginia, October 14, 1863. Confined at Old Capitol Prison, Washington, D.C., until transferred to Point Lookout, Maryland, October 27, 1863. Hospitalized at Point Lookout on August 8, 1864, with diarrhoea and died on or about August 12, 1864.

BLACK, CLINTON M., Private
Enlisted in Burke County on November 18, 1864, for the war. Present or accounted for through February, 1865. Paroled at Salisbury on May 25, 1865.

BLACK, S. J., Sergeant
Resided in Burke County where he enlisted at age 40, February 22, 1862, for the war. Mustered in as Sergeant. Present or accounted for until captured at Falling Waters, Maryland, July 14, 1863. Confined at Baltimore, Maryland, and at Point Lookout, Maryland, until paroled on March 3, 1864, and transferred for exchange. Returned to duty May 26, 1864, and present or accounted for through February, 1865. [May have served previously in Company G, 1st Regiment N.C. Infantry (6 months, 1861).]

BLAIN, WILLIAM M., Private
Resided in Virginia and enlisted in Burke County at age 34, February 4, 1862, for the war. Present or accounted for until he died in hospital near Petersburg, Virginia, October 3, 1864, of wounds. Place and date wounded not reported. [May have served previously in Company E, 1st Regiment N.C. Infantry (6 months, 1861).]

BLUE, DAVID, Private
Resided in Burke County where he enlisted at age 23, February 18, 1862, for the war. Present or accounted for until captured at Falling Waters, Maryland, July 14, 1863. Confined at Baltimore, Maryland, and at Point Lookout, Maryland, until paroled and transferred for exchange on or about March 3, 1864. Returned to duty on May 20, 1864, and present or accounted for through February, 1865.

BRITTAIN, J. T., Private
Resided in Burke County where he enlisted at age 18, April 10, 1862, for the war. Present or accounted for until captured at Falling Waters, Maryland, July 14, 1863. Confined at Old Capitol Prison, Washington, D.C., and at Point Lookout, Maryland, until paroled and transferred for exchange on or about March 3, 1864. Returned to duty on May 20, 1864, and present or accounted for until transferred to Company F, 41st Regiment N.C. Troops (3rd Regiment N.C. Cavalry), December 8, 1864.

BRITTAIN, O. J., 1st Sergeant
Previously served as Private in Company G, 1st Regiment N.C. Infantry (6 months, 1861). Enlisted in this company on February 8, 1862, for the war. Mustered in as Sergeant and promoted to 1st Sergeant on April 22, 1862. Present or accounted for until captured at Falling Waters, Maryland, July 14, 1863. Confined at Baltimore, Maryland, and at Point Lookout, Maryland, until paroled and transferred for exchange on or about March 3, 1864. Rejoined the company in May-June, 1864, and present or accounted for until transferred to Company F, 41st Regiment N.C. Troops (3rd Regiment N.C. Cavalry), December 8, 1864.

BRITTAIN, SAMUEL, Private
Resided in Burke County where he enlisted at age 21, February 14, 1862, for the war. Present or accounted for until paroled at Appomattox Court House, Virginia, April 9, 1865. Paroled again at Morganton on May 27, 1865.

BUTLER, ERWIN, Private
Enlisted in Burke County at age 30, February 28, 1863, for the war. Deserted June 18, 1863, but rejoined the company on September 20, 1864. Present or accounted for until paroled at Appomat-

tox Court House, Virginia, April 9, 1865. North Carolina pension records indicate he was wounded in the left arm in Burke County in August, 1863.

BUTLER, JOHN M., Private
Resided in Burke County where he enlisted at age 17, February 15, 1862, for the war. Present or accounted for until wounded in the right thigh and captured at Appomattox Court House, Virginia, April 9, 1865. Hospitalized at various Federal hospitals until admitted to hospital at Washington, D.C., May 2, 1865. Released June 14, 1865.

BUTLER, THOMAS P., Private
Enlisted in Burke County on February 16, 1864, for the war. Present or accounted for until he died in hospital at Richmond, Virginia, July 14, 1864. Cause of death not reported.

BUTLER, W. H., Sergeant
Resided in Burke County where he enlisted at age 37, February 26, 1863, for the war. Mustered in as Private and promoted to Corporal on September 1, 1863. Promoted to Sergeant on December 8, 1864. Present or accounted for until paroled at Appomattox Court House, Virginia, April 9, 1865. Roll of Honor indicates that he was wounded but does not give place and date.

CAUSBY, GEORGE, Private
Resided in Burke County where he enlisted at age 18, February 24, 1862, for the war. Present or accounted for until reported absent wounded in November-December, 1862; however, place and date wounded not reported. Rejoined the company in January-February, 1863, and present or accounted for until captured at or near Gettysburg, Pennsylvania, July 3-6, 1863. Confined at Fort Delaware, Delaware, and at Point Lookout, Maryland, until paroled and transferred for exchange on or about March 3, 1864. Returned to duty on May 20, 1864, and present or accounted for until captured at or near Petersburg, Virginia, April 2, 1865. Confined at Point Lookout until released on June 26, 1865, after taking the Oath of Allegiance.

CAUSBY, JOHN N., Corporal
Resided in Burke County where he enlisted at age 22, February 22, 1862, for the war. Mustered in as Corporal. Present or accounted for until he died in hospital at Wilmington on June 8, 1862, of disease.

CAUSBY, WILLIAM, Private
Resided in Burke County where he enlisted at age 16, March 12, 1862, for the war. Present or accounted for until wounded at Gettysburg, Pennsylvania, July 1-3, 1863. Rejoined the company prior to September 1, 1863, and present or accounted for until reported absent wounded in July-August, 1864. Place and date wounded not reported. Rejoined the company in September-October, 1864, and present or accounted for until paroled at Appomattox Court House, Virginia, April 9, 1865.

CHRISENBERY, THOMAS C., Private
Resided in Burke County where he enlisted at age 30, January 31, 1863, for the war. Present or accounted for until killed at Gettysburg, Pennsylvania, July 1, 1863.

CLARK, BENJAMIN, Private
Resided in Burke County where he enlisted at age 37, March 11, 1862, for the war. Present or accounted for through October, 1863. Company muster roll dated November-December, 1863, states he was a former prisoner who was paroled on or about December 10, 1863; however, place and date captured not reported. Records of the Federal Provost Marshal do not substantiate the report of his capture. Present or accounted for from January-February, 1864, until captured in hospital at Richmond, Virginia, April 3, 1865. Confined at Libby Prison, Richmond, until transferred to Newport News, Virginia, April 23, 1865. Released at Newport News on June 30, 1865, after taking the Oath of Allegiance.

CLARK, BENJAMIN A., Musician
Resided in Burke County and was by occupation a farmer prior to enlisting in Burke County at age 28, February 10, 1862, for the war. Mustered in as Musician (Drummer). Present or accounted for until hospitalized at Wilmington on June 23, 1862, with typhoid fever. Died June 27, 1862.

CLARK, J. C., Private
Enlisted in Burke County on June 10, 1864, for the war. Present or accounted for until he died in hospital at Richmond, Virginia, March 13, 1865, of "diarrhoea ch[ronic]."

CLARK, MICHAEL, Private
Resided in Burke County where he enlisted at age 30, March 17, 1862, for the war. Present or accounted for until wounded and captured at Gettysburg, Pennsylvania, July 1-5, 1863. Hospitalized at Gettysburg until transferred to Davids Island, New York Harbor, July 17-24, 1863. Exchanged on or about August 31, 1863. Rejoined the company in March-April, 1864, and present or accounted for until paroled at Appomattox Court House, Virginia, April 9, 1865.

CLAY, J. M., Sergeant
Resided in Burke County where he enlisted at age 22, February 27, 1862, for the war. Mustered in as Private and promoted to Corporal on May 24, 1862. Promoted to Sergeant on April 15, 1863. Present or accounted for until he "lost an eye" and was captured at Gettysburg, Pennsylvania, July 3, 1863. Hospitalized at various Federal hospitals until transferred for exchange on or about August 31, 1863. Rejoined the company in January-February, 1864, and present or accounted for through February, 1865.

CLAY, JAMES HERVEY, Private
Previously served in Company F, 41st Regiment N.C. Troops (3rd Regiment N.C. Cavalry). Transferred to this company in November-December, 1864. Present or accounted for until paroled at Appomattox Court House, Virginia, April 9, 1865.

CODY, W. A., Private
Resided in Burke County where he enlisted at age 30, March 24, 1862, for the war. Deserted April 24, 1862.

COOK, JOHN D., Private
Born in Burke County where he resided prior to enlisting in Burke County at age 22, February 15, 1863, for the war. Present or accounted for until hospitalized at Richmond, Virginia, July 15, 1863,

with a gunshot wound of the left cheek; however, place and date wounded not reported. Returned to duty on August 4, 1863, and present or accounted for until reported absent wounded on company muster roll dated November-December, 1863. Place and date wounded not reported. Died in hospital at Richmond on or about February 1, 1864. Company muster roll dated March-April, 1864, and Roll of Honor indicate that he deserted prior to his death. No further records.

DONALDSON, S. L., Corporal

Enlisted in Burke County on June 14, 1864, for the war. Mustered in as Private and promoted to Corporal on December 8, 1864. Present or accounted for through February, 1865.

EARNHART, WILLIAM, Private

Born in Surry County and resided in Burke County where he was by occupation a farmer prior to enlisting in Burke County at age 47, February 22, 1862, for the war. Present or accounted for until discharged on May 5, 1862, by reason of "bronchitis."

FAIR, HEZEKIAH, Private

Resided in Burke County where he enlisted at age 28, May 1, 1862, for the war. Present or accounted for until captured at Falling Waters, Maryland, July 14, 1863. Confined at various Federal prisons until confined at Point Lookout, Maryland, August 23, 1863. Paroled at Point Lookout at an unspecified date and transferred for exchange. Received at Cox's Landing, James River, Virginia, February 14-15, 1865, for exchange.

FARR, HENRY, Private

Resided in Burke County where he enlisted at age 22, May 1, 1862, for the war. Present or accounted for until captured at or near Burgess' Mill, Virginia, October 27, 1864. Confined at Point Lookout, Maryland, where he died April 18, 1865, of "chronic diarrhoea & scurvy."

GILES, ALEXANDER, Private

Resided in Bertie County where he enlisted at age 22, May 1, 1862, for the war. Present or accounted for until captured at or near Appomattox Court House, Virginia, April 5, 1865. Confined at Point Lookout, Maryland, until released on June 3, 1865, after taking the Oath of Allegiance.

GILES, S. L., Private

Resided in Burke County where he enlisted at age 37, February 22, 1862, for the war. Present or accounted for until wounded in the right leg at Gettysburg, Pennsylvania, July 1-3, 1863. Reported absent wounded or absent on detail through February, 1865. Paroled at Greensboro on May 1, 1865.

GILES, W. W., Private

Born in Burke County where he resided prior to enlisting in Burke County at age 28, May 1, 1862, for the war. Present or accounted for until captured at or near Gettysburg, Pennsylvania, July 3-6, 1863. Confined at Fort Delaware, Delaware, until transferred to Point Lookout, Maryland, October 15-18, 1863. Died at Point Lookout on or about November 27, 1863, of "chronic diarrhoea."

GOOD, GEORGE, Private

Resided in Burke County where he enlisted at age 38, February 22, 1862, for the war. Present or accounted for through February, 1865. Paroled at Morganton on May 13, 1865. [May have served previously in Company G, 1st Regiment N.C. Infantry (6 months, 1861).]

GRIFFIN, EDMUND, Private

Resided in Caldwell County. Place and date of enlistment not reported. Captured near Petersburg, Virginia, March 25, 1865, and confined at Point Lookout, Maryland, until released on June 27, 1865, after taking the Oath of Allegiance.

HALL, ALEX., Private

Place and date of enlistment not reported. Died at Elmira, New York, April 2, 1865. Place and date captured and cause of death not reported.

HAWKINS, W. P., Private

Resided in Burke County where he enlisted on March 22, 1864, for the war. Present or accounted for until hospitalized at Danville, Virginia, June 29, 1864, with a gunshot wound of the left leg; however, place and date wounded not reported. Returned to duty July 8, 1864, and present or accounted for until captured at or near Petersburg, Virginia, April 2, 1865. Confined at Point Lookout, Maryland, until released on June 13, 1865, after taking the Oath of Allegiance.

HENNESSEE, EMANUEL A., Corporal

Resided in Burke County where he enlisted at age 30, March 1, 1862, for the war. Mustered in as Private and promoted to Corporal in September-October, 1863. Present or accounted for until wounded in the forehead on the Weldon Railroad on November 2, 1864. Retired to the Invalid Corps on January 5, 1865. North Carolina pension records indicate that his wounds resulted in paralysis of the right arm and leg and loss of power of speech.

HENNESSEE, P. W., Private

Resided in Burke County where he enlisted at age 24, February 4, 1862, for the war. Mustered in as Sergeant but was reduced to ranks on April 15, 1863. Present or accounted for until captured at Gettysburg, Pennsylvania, July 3, 1863. Confined at Fort Delaware, Delaware, until exchanged on July 31, 1863. Returned to duty on November 21, 1863, and present or accounted for until captured at or near Petersburg, Virginia, April 2, 1865. Confined at Point Lookout, Maryland, until released on June 27, 1865, after taking the Oath of Allegiance.

HENSON, ADAM, Private

Resided in Burke County where he enlisted at age 22, February 18, 1862, for the war. Present or accounted for until he was listed as a deserter on August 3, 1863. Returned to duty on December 1, 1864, and was acquitted by a general court-martial. Present or accounted for through February, 1865.

HERN, W. R., Private

Born in Fairfield District, South Carolina, and resided in Burke County where he was by occupation a tailor prior to enlisting in Burke County at age 48, February 22, 1862, for the war. Present or accounted for until discharged on February 22, 1865, by reason of "expiration of term of service" and because he was "over [the] conscript age."

HICKS, JOSEPH S., Private
Resided in Burke County where he enlisted at age 32, February 15, 1862, for the war. Present or accounted for until promoted to Musician and transferred to the regimental band in September-October, 1864. [May have served previously in Company G, 1st Regiment N.C. Infantry (6 months, 1861).]

HICKS, RUFUS, Private
Resided in Burke County where he enlisted at age 28, September 14, 1862, for the war. Present or accounted for until captured at the North Anna River, Virginia, February 24, 1864. Confined at Point Lookout, Maryland, until paroled and transferred for exchange on or about March 17, 1865. [May have served previously in Company G, 1st Regiment N.C. Infantry (6 months, 1861).]

HINSON, JOHN A., Private
Place and date of enlistment not reported. Captured at Gettysburg, Pennsylvania, July 3-5, 1863, and confined at Fort Delaware, Delaware. Released on or about September 22, 1863, after joining the U.S. Army. Reportedly assigned to Company E, 3rd Regiment Maryland Cavalry; however, records of that unit do not indicate that he served therein. No further records.

HOOD, J. C., Private
Resided in Burke County where he enlisted at age 19, March 1, 1862, for the war. Present or accounted for until he died in hospital at Wilmington on July 30, 1862. Cause of death not reported.

HUFFMAN, ABRAM, Private
Resided in Burke County where he enlisted at age 35, February 28, 1863, for the war. Present or accounted for until captured at Falling Waters, Maryland, July 14, 1863. Confined at Baltimore, Maryland, and at Point Lookout, Maryland, until paroled and transferred for exchange on or about March 3, 1864. Rejoined the company in July-August, 1864, and present or accounted for until killed at Jones' Farm, Virginia, September 30, 1864.

JENKINS, HIRAM, Private
Enlisted in Burke County on July 9, 1864, for the war. Present or accounted for through February, 1865.

JOHNSON, DANIEL L., Private
Resided in Bertie County where he enlisted at age 19, February 14, 1862, for the war. Present or accounted for until hospitalized at Danville, Virginia, on or about June 16, 1864, with a gunshot wound of the hand; however, place and date wounded not reported. Rejoined the company in September-October, 1864, and present or accounted for until he deserted to the enemy on or about March 21, 1865. Took the Oath of Allegiance on or about March 29, 1865.

JOHNSON, J. W., Private
Resided in Burke County where he enlisted at age 28, March 1, 1862, for the war. Present or accounted for until captured at Falling Waters, Maryland, July 14, 1863. Confined at Baltimore,

Maryland, until transferred to Point Lookout, Maryland, where he arrived September 16, 1863. Confined at Point Lookout until paroled and transferred for exchange on or about February 10, 1865. Reported present with a detachment of paroled and exchanged prisoners at Camp Lee, near Richmond, Virginia, February 17, 1865.

JOHNSON, ROBERT N., Private
Resided in Burke County where he enlisted at age 20, February 22, 1862, for the war. Present or accounted for until captured at or near Burgess' Mill, Virginia, October 27, 1864. Confined at Point Lookout, Maryland, until released on June 12, 1865, after taking the Oath of Allegiance.

JORDAN, N. W., Sergeant
Resided in Burke or Hertford counties prior to enlisting in Burke County at age 25, February 14, 1862, for the war. Mustered in as Private and promoted to Corporal on October 20, 1862. Promoted to Sergeant on November 10, 1864. Present or accounted for until captured at or near Petersburg, Virginia, April 2, 1865. Confined at Point Lookout, Maryland, until released on June 28, 1865, after taking the Oath of Allegiance.

KEITH, JOHN C., Private
Resided in Burke County where he enlisted at age 19, February 18, 1862, for the war. Present or accounted for until wounded by the "accidental discharge of his gun" in November-December, 1862. Died in hospital at Goldsboro on January 14, 1863, of wounds.

KINCAID, J. W., Private
Resided in Burke County where he enlisted at age 30, March 12, 1862, for the war. Present or accounted for until killed at Gettysburg, Pennsylvania, July 1, 1863.

KINCAID, W. W., Private
Resided in Burke County where he enlisted at age 32, February 12, 1862, for the war. Present or accounted for until he deserted at Winchester, Virginia, July 16, 1863. Rejoined the company on December 10, 1863, and present or accounted for until captured at Spotsylvania Court House, Virginia, in May, 1864. Confined at Old Capitol Prison, Washington, D. C., until transferred to Fort Delaware, Delaware, June 15, 1864. Died at Fort Delaware on April 26, 1865, of "anemia" or "debility."

KINNEY, A. D., Private
Place and date of enlistment not reported. Captured at Mechanicsville, Virginia, May 30, 1864, and confined at Point Lookout, Maryland, until transferred to Elmira, New York, July 8, 1864. Released at Elmira on June 30, 1865.

LANE, JOHN E., Sergeant
Previously served as Private in Company G, 1st Regiment N.C. Infantry (6 months, 1861). Enlisted in this company on February 15, 1862, for the war. Mustered in as Corporal and promoted to Sergeant on May 24, 1862. Present or accounted for until killed at Wilderness, Virginia, May 5, 1864.

LANE, SAMUEL, Private
Resided in Burke County where he enlisted at age 50, February 22, 1862, for the war. Present or

accounted for through July, 1863. Company muster roll dated July-August, 1863, states he deserted on August 2, 1863. Killed near Madison Court House, Virginia, August 10, 1863.

LARGENT, JOHN P., Corporal

Previously served in Company E, 16th Regiment N.C. Troops (6th Regiment N.C. Volunteers). Enlisted in this company on May 1, 1862, for the war. Mustered in as Private. Present or accounted for until wounded and captured at Gettysburg, Pennsylvania, July 1-5, 1863. Hospitalized at Davids Island, New York Harbor, until paroled and transferred for exchange on or about September 8, 1863. Rejoined the company in March-April, 1864, and was promoted to Corporal on December 8, 1864. Present or accounted for until he deserted to the enemy on or about March 21, 1865. Took the Oath of Allegiance on March 29, 1865.

LAWMON, W. L., Private

Resided in Burke County where he enlisted on September 6, 1864, for the war. Present or accounted for until captured at or near Petersburg, Virginia, April 2, 1865. Confined at Point Lookout, Maryland, until released on June 28, 1865, after taking the Oath of Allegiance.

LOUDON, THOMAS, Private

Resided in Burke County where he enlisted at age 26, May 1, 1862, for the war. Died in hospital at Wilmington on or about July 11, 1862, of "continued fever."

MACE, ABRAHAM, Private

Resided in Burke County where he enlisted at age 18, February 28, 1863, for the war. Present or accounted for until captured at Falling Waters, Maryland, July 14, 1863. Confined at Old Capitol Prison, Washington, D.C., until transferred to Point Lookout, Maryland, on or about July 31, 1863. Transferred to Elmira, New York, August 16, 1864, and died at Elmira on September 16, 1864, of "typhoid pneumonia."

MACE, WILLIAM H., Private

Previously served in Company B of this regiment. Transferred to this company on April 18, 1862, with the rank of Private. Promoted to Corporal in March-April, 1863. Present or accounted for until wounded at Gettysburg, Pennsylvania, July 1-3, 1863. Deserted August 2, 1863, and was reduced to ranks in September-October, 1863. Returned to duty on October 9, 1863, and was captured at Bristoe Station, Virginia, October 14, 1863. Confined at Old Capitol Prison, Washington, D.C., until transferred to Point Lookout, Maryland, October 27, 1863. Released at Point Lookout on January 21, 1864, after taking the Oath of Allegiance and joining the U.S. Army. Assigned to Company A, 1st Regiment U.S. Volunteer Infantry.

McKESSON, JAMES C., Private

Previously served in Company G, 1st Regiment N.C. Infantry (6 months, 1861). Enlisted in this company on May 1, 1862, for the war. Present or accounted for until wounded and captured at Gettysburg, Pennsylvania, July 3-4, 1863. Confined at Fort Delaware, Delaware, until transferred to Point Lookout, Maryland, October 18, 1863. Exchanged prior to November 1, 1863, and was reported absent without

leave on company muster rolls dated January-April, 1864. Returned to duty in May-June, 1864, and present or accounted for through February, 1865. Paroled at Morganton on May 14, 1865.

McMILLON, PLEASANT, Private

Enlisted in Burke County on July 9, 1864, for the war. Present or accounted for until captured at or near Petersburg, Virginia, April 2, 1865. Confined at Point Lookout, Maryland, where he died June 23, 1865, of "pneumonia."

MARTIN, JOSEPH, Private

Enlisted in Burke County on September 6, 1864, for the war. Present or accounted for until captured at or near Burgess' Mill, Virginia, October 27, 1864. Confined at Point Lookout, Maryland, until paroled and transferred for exchange on or about February 10, 1865. Hospitalized at Richmond, Virginia, February 15, 1865.

MELTON, E. A., Private

Previously served in Company G, 1st Regiment N.C. Infantry (6 months, 1861). Enlisted in this company on February 10, 1862, for the war. Present or accounted for until captured at Gettysburg, Pennsylvania, July 3, 1863. Confined at Fort Delaware, Delaware, until hospitalized at Chester, Pennsylvania, July 19, 1863, with pleurisy. Transferred to City Point, Virginia, August 17, 1863, for exchange. Rejoined the company in September-October, 1863, and present or accounted for until hospitalized at Richmond, Virginia, May 7, 1864, with a gunshot wound of the right thigh. Place and date wounded not reported. Rejoined the company in July-August, 1864, and present or accounted for until captured while on picket duty on October 3, 1864. Confined at Point Lookout, Maryland, until released on June 29, 1865, after taking the Oath of Allegiance.

MELTON, W. H. A., Private

Resided in Burke County where he enlisted at age 24, April 7, 1862, for the war. Present or accounted for until wounded at White Hall on December 16, 1862. Returned to duty prior to January 1, 1863, and present or accounted for until he died in hospital at Lynchburg, Virginia, May 8, 1864, of "pneumonia."

MILLER, JACKSON, Private

Resided in Burke County where he enlisted at age 22, February 12, 1862, for the war. Present or accounted for until wounded in the right thigh and captured at Gettysburg, Pennsylvania, July 1-5, 1863. Hospitalized at Gettysburg until transferred to Davids Island, New York Harbor, July 17-24, 1863. Transferred to Bedloe's Island, New York Harbor, in October, 1863, and was transferred to Point Lookout, Maryland, on or about January 10, 1864. Paroled at Point Lookout and transferred for exchange on or about March 6, 1864. Returned to duty in July-August, 1864, and present or accounted for until captured near Petersburg, Virginia, March 25, 1865. Confined at Point Lookout until released on June 29, 1865, after taking the Oath of Allegiance.

MILLER, MARSHALL, Private

Resided in Burke County where he enlisted at age 28, February 12, 1862, for the war. Present or accounted for until captured at Falling Waters, Maryland, July 14, 1863. Confined at Baltimore, Maryland, and at Point Lookout, Maryland, until paroled and transferred for exchange on or about March 3, 1864. Rejoined the company in May-June, 1864, and present or accounted for until he died in hospital at Richmond, Virginia, October 8, 1864, of a gunshot wound. Place and date wounded not reported.

MITCHELL, JACKSON, Private
Resided in Burke County and enlisted at age 28, January 1, 1863, for the war. Deserted June 18, 1863.

MITCHELL, JOHN, Private
Enlisted in Burke County on January 1, 1863, for the war. Present or accounted for until he deserted on June 17, 1863. Returned from desertion on August 30, 1863, and present or accounted for until captured at or near Petersburg, Virginia, April 2, 1865. Confined at Point Lookout, Maryland, until released on June 6, 1865, after taking the Oath of Allegiance.

MOREFIELD, JOHN, Private
Enlisted in Burke County on March 25, 1864, for the war. Present or accounted for until mortally wounded at Reams' Station, Virginia, August 25, 1864. Died the same day.

MOSTELLER, ISAIAH, Private
Resided in Burke County where he enlisted at age 38, February 26, 1863, for the war. Present or accounted for until reported absent wounded in May-June, 1864; however, place and date wounded not reported. Rejoined the company in July-August, 1864, and present or accounted for until captured near Petersburg, Virginia, March 25, 1865. Confined at Point Lookout, Maryland, until released on June 29, 1865, after taking the Oath of Allegiance. North Carolina pension records indicate he was wounded in the left arm at an unspecified date.

MOSTELLER, JOHN, Private
Resided in Burke County where he enlisted on November 11, 1864, for the war. Present or accounted for until captured at or near Petersburg, Virginia, April 2, 1865. Confined at Point Lookout, Maryland, until released on June 15, 1865, after taking the Oath of Allegiance.

PEARSON, JOHN, Private
Previously served in Company G, 1st Regiment N.C. Infantry (6 months, 1861). Enlisted in this company on February 8, 1862, for the war. Present or accounted for until wounded at Gettysburg, Pennsylvania, July 1-3, 1863. Returned to duty prior to September 1, 1863, and present or accounted for until captured at or near Petersburg, Virginia, April 2, 1865. Confined at Point Lookout, Maryland, until released on June 16, 1865, after taking the Oath of Allegiance.

PEARSON, ROBERT G., Private
Resided in Burke County where he enlisted at age 38, January 1, 1863, for the war. Present or accounted for until captured near Petersburg, Virginia, March 25, 1865. Confined at Point Lookout, Maryland, until released on June 16, 1865, after taking the Oath of Allegiance.

POINDEXTER, D. A., Private
Born in Surry County and was by occupation a farmer prior to enlisting in Surry County on July 9, 1864, for the war. Present or accounted for until discharged on October 8, 1864, by reason of "deformity of spine." Discharge papers give his age as 30.

POTEET, JOHN, Private
Resided in Burke County where he enlisted at age 37, January 1, 1863, for the war. Present or accounted for until captured at Falling Waters, Maryland, July 14, 1863. Confined at Baltimore, Maryland, and at Point Lookout, Maryland, until paroled and transferred for exchange on or about March 3, 1864. Rejoined the company in May-June, 1864, and present or accounted for until transferred to Company F, 41st Regiment N.C. Troops (3rd Regiment N.C. Cavalry), December 8, 1864.

POTEET, SAMUEL, Private
Resided in Burke County where he enlisted at age 25, February 22, 1862, for the war. Present or accounted for until he died "at home" on October 14, 1863. Cause of death not reported.

POWELL, JOSEPH H., Private
Resided in Burke County where he enlisted on February 16, 1864, for the war. Present or accounted for until captured at or near Petersburg, Virginia, April 2, 1865. Confined at Point Lookout, Maryland, until released on June 16, 1865, after taking the Oath of Allegiance.

POWELL, KEMP W., Private
Resided in Burke County where he enlisted at age 25, February 18, 1862, for the war. Present or accounted for until hospitalized at Wilmington on or about June 24, 1862, with remittent fever. Died at Wilmington on July 9, 1862.

POWELL, MOSES, Private
Resided in Burke County where he enlisted at age 18, February 21, 1862, for the war. Present or accounted for through February, 1865.

POWELL, WILLIAM P., Private
Resided in Burke County where he enlisted at age 15, April 12, 1862, for the war. Present or accounted for until captured at Bristoe Station, Virginia, October 14, 1863. Confined at Old Capitol Prison, Washington, D.C., and at Point Lookout, Maryland, until paroled and transferred for exchange on or about March 3, 1864. Returned to duty on May 20, 1864, and present or accounted for until captured at or near Petersburg, Virginia, April 2, 1865. Confined at Point Lookout until released on June 16, 1865, after taking the Oath of Allegiance.

PRUETT, RANSOM, Private
Resided in Burke County where he enlisted at age 40, February 28, 1863, for the war. Present or accounted for until he deserted on June 18, 1863. Returned to duty on December 10, 1863, but died "in camp" on December 16, 1863. Cause of death not reported.

RAMSEY, JONAS, Private
Resided in Burke County where he enlisted at age 27, February 14, 1863, for the war. Present or accounted for until he deserted on June 17, 1863.

ROSS, S. A., Private
Enlisted in Burke County on January 18, 1864, for the war. Present or accounted for until he died in hospital at Richmond, Virginia, August 7, 1864. Cause of death not reported.

RUDISILL, ABSALOM, Private
Enlisted in Burke County on March 3, 1864, for the war. Present or accounted for until hospitalized at Charlottesville, Virginia, May 7, 1864, with a gunshot wound of the right hand; however, place and date wounded not reported. Rejoined the company in July-August, 1864, and present or accounted for until captured at or near Burgess' Mill, Virginia, October 27, 1864. Confined at Point Lookout, Maryland, until exchanged on February 10, 1865.

SAULMAN, JAMES W., Private
Resided in Burke County where he enlisted at age 22, February 10, 1862, for the war. Present or accounted for until captured at Petersburg, Virginia, April 3, 1865. Confined at Hart's Island, New York Harbor, until released on June 19, 1865, after taking the Oath of Allegiance.

SAULMAN, JOHN M., Private
Resided in Burke County where he enlisted at age 18, February 10, 1862, for the war. Present or accounted for until wounded in the right ankle at Gettysburg, Pennsylvania, July 1, 1863. Reported absent wounded through February, 1865.

SETTLEMIRE, DAVID, Private
Resided in Burke County where he enlisted at age 38, February 28, 1863, for the war. Present or accounted for until wounded in the stomach at Gettysburg, Pennsylvania, July 1-3, 1863. Reported absent wounded or absent sick through February, 1865.

SIMPSON, JOHN E., Corporal
Previously served as Private in Company G, 1st Regiment N.C. Infantry (6 months, 1861). Enlisted in this company on March 27, 1862, for the war. Mustered in as Private and promoted to Corporal on June 8, 1862. Present or accounted for until captured at Gettysburg, Pennsylvania, July 3-4, 1863. Confined at Fort Delaware, Delaware, and at Point Lookout, Maryland, until paroled and transferred for exchange on February 13, 1865. Reported present with a detachment of paroled and exchanged prisoners at Camp Lee, near Richmond, Virginia, February 17, 1865. Paroled at Morganton on May 15, 1865.

SIMPSON, THOMAS A., Private
Resided in Burke County where he enlisted on February 23, 1864, for the war. Present or accounted for until captured at or near Petersburg, Virginia, April 2, 1865. Confined at Point Lookout, Maryland, until released on June 20, 1865, after taking the Oath of Allegiance.

SPAIN, H. P., Private
Previously served in Company H of this regiment. Transferred to this company on April 2, 1864. Present or accounted for until reported absent wounded in May-June, 1864; however, place and date wounded not reported. Reported absent wounded through February, 1865.

STARNEY, JOSHUA, Private
Enlisted in Burke County on September 15, 1864, for the war. Present or accounted for until he deserted at an unspecified date. Apprehended and was "shot for desertion" on December 4, 1864.

SUDDERTH, E. M., Private
Resided in Burke County where he enlisted at age 37, March 4, 1862, for the war. Present or accounted for until killed at Gettysburg, Pennsylvania, July 3, 1863.

SUMMERS, PERRY, Private
Resided in Burke County where he enlisted at age 18, February 8, 1862, for the war. Present or accounted for until wounded in the breast at Gettysburg, Pennsylvania, July 1-3, 1863. Rejoined the company in September-October, 1863, and present or accounted for until mortally wounded at Bristoe Station, Virginia, October 14, 1863. Died October 15, 1863.

TATE, H. A., Private
Previously served in Company C, 1st Regiment N.C. Infantry (6 months, 1861). Enlisted in this company on February 14, 1862, for the war. Mustered in as Corporal and promoted to Sergeant on April 22, 1862. Reduced to ranks on October 20, 1862. Present or accounted for until wounded in the right thigh and captured at Gettysburg, Pennsylvania, July 3, 1863. Right leg amputated. Hospitalized at Gettysburg where he died August 25, 1863, after undergoing a second amputation.

TAYLOR, CHARLES, Private
Resided in Burke County where he enlisted at age 28, March 12, 1862, for the war. Present or accounted for until wounded at Gettysburg, Pennsylvania, July 1-3, 1863. Reported captured at Falling Waters, Maryland, July 14, 1863; however, records of the Federal Provost Marshal do not substantiate that report. Reported absent sick until he died "at home" on December 1, 1863. Cause of death not reported.

TAYLOR, GEORGE W., Private
Resided in Burke County where he enlisted at age 47, March 10, 1862, for the war. Present or accounted for until he deserted on August 2, 1863. Died in hospital at Richmond, Virginia, December 26, 1863, of "pneumonia typhoid."

TAYLOR, JOEL, Private
Born in Burke County where he resided as a farmer prior to enlisting in Burke County at age 16, April 12, 1862, for the war. Present or accounted for until discharged on July 4, 1862, by reason of "phthisis."

TODD, R. L., Private
Resided in Burke County where he enlisted at age 18, February 25, 1862, for the war. Present or accounted for until wounded and captured at Gettysburg, Pennsylvania, July 1-3, 1863. Died July 26, 1863. Place and cause of death not reported.

UPTON, DAN H., Private
Enlisted in Burke County on September 15, 1864, for the war. Present or accounted for until wounded in the left hand near Petersburg, Virginia, October 1, 1864. Reported absent wounded through February, 1865.

WADKINS, J. B., Private
Resided in Burke County where he enlisted at age 32, March 10, 1862, for the war. Present or accounted for until wounded in the left leg and/or right ankle at Gettysburg, Pennsylvania, July 1, 1863. Reported absent wounded or absent on detail through February, 1865. Paroled at Appomattox Court House, Virginia, April 9, 1865.

WALLS, M. LAFAYETTE, Private
Resided in Burke County where he enlisted at age 33, March 8, 1862, for the war. Present or accounted for until reported absent wounded in November-December, 1862; however, place and date wounded not reported. Rejoined the company in January-February, 1863, and present or accounted for until killed at Gettysburg, Pennsylvania, July 1, 1863.

WHISENHUNT, ALEXANDER, Private
Resided in Burke County where he enlisted at age 22, February 15, 1862, for the war. Present or accounted for until he died at Raleigh on April 14, 1862, of "pneumonia."

WHISENHUNT, B. R., Private
Resided in Burke County where he enlisted at age 30, February 22, 1862, for the war. Present or accounted for until captured at Falling Waters, Maryland, July 14, 1863. Confined at Baltimore, Maryland, and at Point Lookout, Maryland, until paroled and transferred for exchange on or about March 3, 1864. Rejoined the company in May-June, 1864, and present or accounted for until captured at or near Petersburg, Virginia, April 2, 1865. Confined at Point Lookout until released on June 21, 1865, after taking the Oath of Allegiance.

WHISENHUNT, JAMES, Private
Resided in Burke County where he enlisted at age 18, February 12, 1862, for the war. Present or accounted for until he died in hospital at Camp Mangum, near Raleigh, April 22, 1862, of disease.

WHISENHUNT, STANHOPE, Private
Resided in Burke County where he enlisted at age 32, February 12, 1862, for the war. Present or accounted for until he died at Camp Mangum, near Raleigh, April 18, 1862, of disease.

WHISENHUNT, WILBURN, Private
Resided in Burke County where he enlisted at age 26, February 12, 1862, for the war. Present or accounted for until he died in hospital at Raleigh on or about June 6, 1863, of "anemia."

WILLIAMS, BAIRD, Private
Enlisted in Burke County on February 23, 1864, for the war. Present or accounted for until he died in hospital at Richmond, Virginia, December 25, 1864. Cause of death not reported.

WILLIAMS, E. H., Private
Resided in Burke County where he enlisted at age 26, February 8, 1862, for the war. Present or accounted for until wounded and captured at Gettysburg, Pennsylvania, July 1-5, 1863. Hospitalized at Gettysburg until transferred to Davids Island, New York Harbor, July 17-24, 1863. Paroled at Davids Island on August 24, 1863, and transferred for exchange. Rejoined the company in January-

February, 1864, and present or accounted for through February, 1865. Paroled at Salisbury on May 25, 1865.

WILLIAMS, J. A., Private
Resided in Burke County where he enlisted at age 35, February 13, 1862, for the war. Present or accounted for until he deserted on November 13, 1863. Apprehended at an unspecified date and was court-martialed. Confined at Richmond, Virginia, "with ball and chain." Died in hospital at Castle Thunder Prison, Richmond, July 26, 1864. Cause of death not reported.

WILLIAMS, J. L., Private
Born in Burke County where he resided as a farmer prior to enlisting in Burke County at age 27, February 19, 1862, for the war. Present or accounted for until discharged on July 4, 1862, by reason of "inability and bronchitis following measles with a tendency to dropsy."

WILLIAMS, JOHN, Private
Resided in Burke County where he enlisted at age 28, March 18, 1862, for the war. Present or accounted for until captured at or near Petersburg, Virginia, April 2, 1865. Confined at Point Lookout, Maryland, until released on June 21, 1865, after taking the Oath of Allegiance.

WILLIAMS, JOSEPH, Private
Resided in Burke County where he enlisted at age 25, March 12, 1862, for the war. Present or accounted for until he died "at home" on September 23, 1863. Cause of death not reported.

WILLIAMS, MARCUS, Private
Born in Burke County where he was by occupation a farmer prior to enlisting in Burke County at age 33, February 25, 1863, for the war. Present or accounted for until discharged on September 14, 1863, by reason of "anemia and ascites."

WILLIAMS, MOLTON, Private
Resided in Burke County where he enlisted at age 23, February 15, 1862, for the war. Present or accounted for until captured at Falling Waters, Maryland, July 14, 1863. Confined at Baltimore, Maryland, and at Point Lookout, Maryland, until paroled and transferred for exchange on or about March 3, 1864. Rejoined the company in May-June, 1864, and present or accounted for until captured near Petersburg, Virginia, March 25, 1865. Confined at Point Lookout until released on June 21, 1865, after taking the Oath of Allegiance. [May have served previously in Company G, 1st Regiment N.C. Infantry (6 months, 1861).]

WILLIAMS, W. A., Private
Resided in Burke County where he enlisted on March 12, 1864, for the war. Present or accounted for until captured in hospital at Richmond, Virginia, April 3, 1865. Confined at Libby Prison, Richmond, and was transferred to Newport News, Virginia, April 23, 1865. Released at Newport News on June 30, 1865, after taking the Oath of Allegiance.

WILLIAMS, W. M., Private
Resided in Burke County where he enlisted at age 20, April 17, 1862, for the war. Present or accounted for until hospitalized at Richmond, Virginia, September 7, 1863, with a gunshot wound; however,

place and date wounded not reported. Returned to duty on October 7, 1863, and present or accounted for through February, 1865. Paroled at Morganton on May 16, 1865.

WILLIAMS, WILLIAM H., Private
Resided in Burke County where he enlisted at age 24, February 10, 1862, for the war. Present or accounted for until wounded and captured at or near Gettysburg, Pennsylvania, July 1-6, 1863. Reported in a Federal hospital at Winchester, Virginia, July 30, 1863. Exchanged in November-December, 1863, and rejoined the company in January-February, 1864. Present or accounted for through February, 1865. Paroled at Salisbury on May 25, 1865. [May have served previously in Company G, 1st Regiment N.C. Infantry (6 months, 1861).]

WINTERS, MOULTON, Corporal
Previously served as Private in Company G, 1st Regiment N.C. Infantry (6 months, 1861). Enlisted in this company on February 10, 1862, for the war. Mustered in as Corporal. Present or accounted for until killed at Gettysburg, Pennsylvania, July 1, 1863.

WOMACK, WILLIAM T., 1st Sergeant
Resided in Burke County where he enlisted at age 30, February 10, 1862, for the war. Mustered in as Private and promoted to Corporal on April 22, 1862. Promoted to Sergeant on October 20, 1862, and promoted to 1st Sergeant on December 8, 1864. Present or accounted for until paroled at Appomattox Court House, Virginia, April 9, 1865.

WOOD, WILLIAM, Private
Resided in Burke County where he enlisted at age 18, March 1, 1862, for the war. Present or accounted for until wounded and captured at Gettysburg, Pennsylvania, July 1-4, 1863. Hospitalized at Gettysburg until transferred to Davids Island, New York Harbor, July 17-24, 1863. Died in hospital at Davids Island on September 5, 1863, of wounds.

COMPANY E

This company was composed primarily of men from Mecklenburg and Iredell counties and began organizing at Charlotte and at Statesville in February, 1862. On March 31, 1862, it was mustered in as Company E of this regiment. After that date the company functioned as a part of the regiment, and its history for the war period is recorded as a part of the regimental history.

The information contained in the following roster of the company was compiled principally from company muster rolls for May, 1862, through February, 1865. No company muster rolls were found for the period prior to May, 1862, or for the period after February, 1865. In addition to the company muster rolls, Roll of Honor records, receipt rolls, hospital records, prisoner of war records, and other primary records, supplemented by state pension applications, United Daughters of the Confederacy records, and postwar rosters and histories, all provided useful information.

OFFICERS
CAPTAINS

NICHOLS, JOHN S. A.
Resided in Mecklenburg County and enlisted at age 28. Appointed Captain to rank from February 12, 1862. Present or accounted for until he died at Wilmington on July 11, 1862. Cause of death not reported.

KERR, WILLIAM J.
Previously served as Private in Company B, 1st Regiment N.C. Infantry (6 months, 1861). Appointed 1st Lieutenant in this company to rank from March 20, 1862, and was promoted to Captain to rank from July 12, 1862. Present or accounted for until wounded in the left leg on July 23, 1864. Battle in which wounded not reported. Rejoined the company in November-December, 1864, and present or accounted for until he resigned on March 16, 1865, while under charges of "drunkenness" and "absence without leave."

LIEUTENANTS

ALEXANDER, JAMES FRANCIS, 2nd Lieutenant
Resided in Mecklenburg County where he enlisted at age 26, February 24, 1862, for the war. Mustered in as Sergeant but was reduced to ranks in November-December, 1862. Promoted to Sergeant on July 8, 1863, and was appointed 2nd Lieutenant to rank from December 14, 1863. Present or accounted for until captured at Hatcher's Run, Virginia, April 2, 1865. Confined at Old Capitol Prison, Washington, D.C., until transferred to Johnson's Island, Ohio, April 9, 1865. Released at Johnson's Island on June 17, 1865, after taking the Oath of Allegiance.

CLANTON, JOHN BEATTY, 1st Lieutenant
Resided in Mecklenburg County and enlisted at age 32. Appointed 2nd Lieutenant to rank from March 20, 1862, and promoted to 1st Lieutenant to rank from July 11, 1862. Present or accounted for until wounded and captured at Gettysburg, Pennsylvania, July 1-3, 1863. Hospitalized at Gettysburg where he died on July 27, 1863, of wounds.

GRIER, PAUL BARRINGER, 2nd Lieutenant
Appointed 2nd Lieutenant in this company to rank from August 29, 1863. Killed at Bristoe Station, Virginia, October 14, 1863.

MEANS, WILLIAM N. M., 2nd Lieutenant
Previously served as Private in Company B, 1st Regiment N.C. Infantry (6 months, 1861). Appointed 3rd Lieutenant in this company to rank from March 20, 1862, and was promoted to 2nd Lieutenant on July 12, 1862. Present or accounted for until killed at White Hall on December 16, 1862.

ROZZELL, WILLIAM F., 2nd Lieutenant
Previously served as Private in Company B, 1st Regiment N.C. Infantry (6 months, 1861). Enlisted in this company on May 24, 1862, for the war. Mustered in as 1st Sergeant and elected 3rd Lieutenant on July 12, 1862. Promoted to 2nd Lieutenant on January 22, 1863. Present or accounted for until wounded and captured at Gettysburg, Pennsylvania, July 1-3, 1863. Died in hospital at Gettysburg on or about July 10, 1863, of wounds.

TURNER, WILLIAM S., 1st Lieutenant
Resided in Mecklenburg County where he enlisted at age 24, March 12, 1862, for the war. Mustered in as Sergeant and appointed 3rd Lieutenant to rank from January 22, 1863. Promoted to 1st Lieutenant to rank from July 27, 1863. Present or accounted for until captured at Petersburg, Virginia, October 27, 1864. Confined at Old Capitol Prison, Washington, D.C., until transferred to Fort Delaware, Delaware, December 16, 1864. Died at Fort Delaware on June 2, 1865, of "inf of lungs."

NONCOMMISSIONED OFFICERS AND PRIVATES

ABERNATHY, ENOCH K., Private
Born in Catawba County* and resided in Mecklenburg County where he was by occupation a farmer prior to enlisting in Mecklenburg County on February 15, 1862, for the war. Present or accounted for until discharged on November 10, 1864, by reason of "infirmity of age & chronic orchitis." Discharge papers give his age as 54.

ADAMS, G. HANNIBAL A., Private
Previously served in Company C, 41st Regiment N.C. Troops (3rd Regiment N.C. Cavalry). Transferred to this company on December 1, 1864. Present or accounted for until captured near Petersburg, Virginia, March 25, 1865. Confined at Point Lookout, Maryland, until released on June 22, 1865, after taking the Oath of Allegiance.

ALEXANDER, PETER, Private
Born in Kershaw District, South Carolina, and resided in Mecklenburg County where he was by occupation a farmer prior to enlisting in Mecklenburg County on February 22, 1862, for the war. Present or accounted for until discharged on December 16, 1863, by reason of "chronic rheumatism." Discharge papers give his age as 60.

ALLEN, FULTON, Private
Enlisted at Camp Holmes on September 15, 1864, for the war. Present or accounted for until hospitalized at Richmond, Virginia, October 2, 1864, with a gunshot wound of the left foot; however, place and date wounded not reported. Left foot amputated. Reported absent wounded until he was discharged in January-February, 1865.

ASHLEY, MOSES, Private
Enlisted at Camp Holmes on October 1, 1864, for the war. Present or accounted for through February, 1865. Paroled at Charlotte on May 27, 1865.

AUTON, SAMUEL W., Private
Resided in Mecklenburg County where he enlisted at age 24, March 8, 1862, for the war. Present or accounted for until captured at or near Petersburg, Virginia, April 2, 1865. Confined at Fort Delaware, Delaware, until released on June 19, 1865, after taking the Oath of Allegiance.

BAKER, AARON W., Private
Enlisted in Mecklenburg County on April 19, 1864, for the war. Present or accounted for through February, 1865.

BAKER, JOEL M., Private
Resided in Mecklenburg County where he enlisted at age 18, March 11, 1862, for the war. Present or accounted for through February, 1865; however, he

was reported absent sick during much of that period. Paroled at Charlotte on May 12, 1865.

BAKER, WILLIAM M., Private
Previously served in Company C, 41st Regiment N.C. Troops (3rd Regiment N.C. Cavalry). Transferred to this company in November-December, 1864. Present or accounted for until captured at or near Petersburg, Virginia, April 2, 1865. Confined at Hart's Island, New York Harbor, until released on June 20, 1865, after taking the Oath of Allegiance.

BALLARD, BENJAMIN H., Private
Enlisted at Camp Holmes on October 1, 1864, for the war. Present or accounted for until he deserted to the enemy on or about March 13, 1865. Took the Oath of Allegiance on or about March 18, 1865.

BASS, BURTON, Private
Resided in Iredell County where he enlisted at age 23, February 26, 1862, for the war. Present or accounted for until captured near Petersburg, Virginia, October 27, 1864. Confined at Point Lookout, Maryland, where he died on March 10, 1865, of "chronic diarrhoea."

BASS, JAMES A., Private
Born in Iredell County where he resided prior to enlisting in Iredell County at age 28, February 26, 1862, for the war. Present or accounted for until wounded at Gettysburg, Pennsylvania, July 1, 1863. Reported absent wounded until discharged on November 10, 1864, by reason of "exostosis of left tibia."

BEAL, CHARLES, Private
Enlisted at Camp Holmes on October 1, 1864, for the war. Present or accounted for until captured near Petersburg, Virginia, October 27, 1864. Confined at Point Lookout, Maryland, where he died January 2, 1865, of "peritonitis."

BEAL, JOHN, Private
Enlisted at Camp Holmes on October 1, 1864, for the war. Present or accounted for until captured near Petersburg, Virginia, October 27, 1864. Confined at Point Lookout, Maryland, where he died March 9, 1865, of "catarrh."

BEATY, JOHN W., Private
Resided in Mecklenburg County where he enlisted at age 43, March 26, 1862, for the war. Present or accounted for until captured near Petersburg, Virginia, October 27, 1864. Confined at Point Lookout, Maryland, until paroled and transferred for exchange on March 28, 1865.

BELK, WILLIAM A., Private
Resided in Mecklenburg County where he enlisted at age 19, March 3, 1862, for the war. Present or accounted for until captured at Bristoe Station, Virginia, October 14, 1863. Confined at Old Capitol Prison, Washington, D.C., until transferred to Point Lookout, Maryland, October 27, 1863. Released at Point Lookout on January 25, 1864, after joining the U.S. Navy.

BIRD, WILLIAM L., Private
Resided in Mecklenburg County where he enlisted at age 25, March 8, 1862, for the war. Present or accounted for until wounded at White Hall on December 16, 1862. Rejoined the company in January-February, 1863, and present or accounted for until wounded in the right leg and captured at Gettysburg, Pennsylvania, July 1-4, 1863. Hospitalized at Gettysburg until transferred to Davids Island,

New York Harbor, July 17-24, 1863. Paroled at Davids Island and transferred for exchange on or about October 22, 1863. Rejoined the company in March-April, 1864, and present or accounted for until captured at or near Petersburg, Virginia, April 2, 1865. Confined at Fort Delaware, Delaware, until released on June 19, 1865, after taking the Oath of Allegiance.

BRADLEY, JOHN LAWSON, Private
Resided in Iredell County where he enlisted at age 22, February 26, 1862, for the war. Present or accounted for until captured at Gettysburg, Pennsylvania, July 1-5, 1863. Confined at Fort Delaware, Delaware, until transferred to Point Lookout, Maryland, October 15-18, 1863. Confined at Point Lookout until exchanged on or about February 10, 1865. Reported present with a detachment of paroled and exchanged prisoners at Camp Lee, near Richmond, Virginia, February 17, 1865.

BRADSHAW, JOHN F., Private
Resided in Lincoln County and enlisted at Camp Holmes on October 1, 1864, for the war. Present or accounted for until captured near Petersburg, Virginia, March 25, 1865. Confined at Point Lookout, Maryland, until released on June 23, 1865, after taking the Oath of Allegiance.

BRENER, JOSEPH, Private
Enlisted in Mecklenburg County on May 17, 1862, for the war. "Never reported himself to the company."

BRIMER, JOHN, Private
Resided in Mecklenburg County where he enlisted at age 26, April 7, 1862, for the war. Present or accounted for until wounded in the leg at Gettysburg, Pennsylvania, July 1, 1863. Reported absent wounded or absent on detail through February, 1865.

CAMPBELL, JOHN W., Private
Enlisted at Camp Holmes on October 1, 1864, for the war. Wounded in the right arm near Petersburg, Virginia, October 27, 1864. Reported absent wounded through February, 1865.

CAMPBELL, MILTON, Private
Born in Lincoln County and was by occupation a farmer prior to enlisting at Camp Holmes at age 30, October 25, 1864, for the war. Present or accounted for until discharged on November 19, 1864, by reason of "want of physical vigor & development."

CARMACK, JOHN, Private
Resided in Mecklenburg County where he enlisted at age 35, February 28, 1862, for the war. Mustered in as Private and promoted to Sergeant on September 3, 1862. Reduced to ranks in September-October, 1864. Present or accounted for until he deserted to the enemy on or about March 13, 1865. Took the Oath of Allegiance on or about March 18, 1865.

CATHEY, WILLIAM C., Corporal
Resided in Mecklenburg County where he enlisted at age 26, March 12, 1862, for the war. Mustered in as Private and promoted to Corporal on January 22, 1863. Present or accounted for until wounded in the left arm and captured at Gettysburg, Pennsylvania, July 1-5, 1863. Left arm amputated. Hospitalized at Gettysburg until transferred to Davids Island, New York Harbor, July 17-24, 1863. Exchanged on or about September 27, 1863. Reported absent wound-

ed until retired to the Invalid Corps on December 15, 1864.

CHRISTY, JAMES F., Private
Resided in Iredell County where he enlisted at age 25, April 19, 1862, for the war. Present or accounted for until wounded in the right leg at Gettysburg, Pennsylvania, July 1, 1863. Reported absent wounded until he died "at home" on September 4, 1863, of wounds.

CLARK, JAMES A., Private
Resided in Mecklenburg County where he enlisted at age 38, April 1, 1863, for the war. Present or accounted for until killed at Gettysburg, Pennsylvania, July 1, 1863.

CLEMMENS, ROBERT R., Private
Enlisted at Camp Holmes on September 15, 1864, for the war. Present or accounted for until hospitalized at Farmville, Virginia, on or about April 1, 1865. Paroled at Lynchburg, Virginia, April 15, 1865.

CULBERSON, JOHN W., Private
Enlisted at Camp Holmes on October 1, 1864, for the war. Captured near Petersburg, Virginia, October 27, 1864, and confined at Point Lookout, Maryland. Paroled and transferred for exchange on or about February 18, 1865. Died in hospital at Richmond, Virginia, March 4, 1865, of "chron[ic] diarrhoea."

DENTON, JOHN H., Private
Previously served in Company C, 41st Regiment N.C. Troops (3rd Regiment N.C. Cavalry). Transferred to this company in November-December, 1864, and present or accounted for through February, 1865.

DIXON, WILLIAM W., Private
Resided in Mecklenburg County where he enlisted at age 43, March 6, 1863, for the war. Present or accounted for until wounded at Gettysburg, Pennsylvania, July 2, 1863. Died prior to September 1, 1863, of wounds. Place and exact date of death not reported.

EDWARDS, MARSHALL, Private
Enlisted at Camp Holmes on September 15, 1864, for the war. Captured near Petersburg, Virginia, October 27, 1864. Confined at Point Lookout, Maryland, where he died December 18, 1864, of "acute dysentery."

EDWARDS, SHEPHERD, Private
Resided in Anson County and enlisted at Camp Holmes on September 15, 1864, for the war. Present or accounted for until captured at or near Petersburg, Virginia, April 2, 1865. Confined at Fort Delaware, Delaware, until released on June 19, 1865, after taking the Oath of Allegiance.

ELLER, ALEXANDER, Private
Born in Iredell County where he resided as a farmer prior to enlisting in Iredell County at age 42, March 1, 1862, for the war. Present or accounted for until he deserted on June 17, 1863. Returned to duty on October 11, 1863, and present or accounted for until discharged on July 16, 1864, by reason of "oedema of the lower extremities & [he] is generally unfit for active field service."

ELLER, SAMUEL W., Private
Resided in Iredell County and enlisted in Wake County at age 20, April 23, 1862, for the war. Present or accounted for until he deserted to the

enemy at Rapidan Station, Virginia, September 14, 1863. Confined at Old Capitol Prison, Washington, D.C., until released on or about March 14, 1864, after taking the Oath of Allegiance.

ELLWOOD, JOHN J., Private
Enlisted in Mecklenburg County on February 19, 1864, for the war. Deserted March 22, 1864.

ERWIN, JOSEPH J., Private
Born in Iredell County and was by occupation a farmer prior to enlisting at Orange Court House, Virginia, at age 18, December 25, 1863, for the war. Present or accounted for until discharged on April 21, 1864, by reason of "general debility with abdominal dropsy & disease of hip."

FINGER, JOHN, Private
Resided in Mecklenburg County where he enlisted at age 36, March 12, 1862, for the war. Present or accounted for until wounded in the neck at Gettysburg, Pennsylvania, July 1-3, 1863. Rejoined the company prior to September 1, 1863, and was wounded and captured at Bristoe Station, Virginia, October 14, 1863. Confined at Old Capitol Prison, Washington, D.C., until transferred to Point Lookout, Maryland, October 27, 1863. Released at Point Lookout on January 22, 1864, after taking the Oath of Allegiance and joining the U.S. Navy. [May have served previously in Company B, 1st Regiment N.C. Infantry (6 months, 1861).]

GARRISON, ALFRED, Private
Enlisted at Camp Holmes on October 1, 1864, for the war. Present or accounted for until captured near Petersburg, Virginia, October 27, 1864. Confined at Point Lookout, Maryland, where he died on March 26, 1865, of "erysipelas."

GOODMAN, JOHN E., Sergeant
Resided in Iredell County where he enlisted at age 33, February 26, 1862, for the war. Mustered in as Corporal and promoted to Sergeant on July 12, 1862. Present or accounted for until killed at Gettysburg, Pennsylvania, July 1, 1863.

GRIER, THOMAS H., Private
Resided in Mecklenburg County where he enlisted at age 22, February 24, 1862, for the war. Present or accounted for until discharged on August 2, 1862, by reason of disability.

GRIFFIN, GEORGE, Private
Resided in Mecklenburg County where he enlisted at age 18, March 4, 1862, for the war. Present or accounted for until he died at Camp Davis, near Wilmington, on or about May 18, 1862, of disease.

HARRIS, CHARLES C., Private
Resided in Mecklenburg County. Company records give his enlistment date as September 16, 1861; however, he was not listed on the rolls of this company until November-December, 1864. Present or accounted for until captured at or near Petersburg, Virginia, April 2, 1865. Confined at Fort Delaware, Delaware, until released on June 19, 1865, after taking the Oath of Allegiance.

HARTGROVE, RICHARD D. S., Private
Resided in Mecklenburg County where he enlisted at age 23, February 27, 1862, for the war. Present or accounted for until wounded at White Hall on December 16, 1862. Rejoined the company in January-February, 1863, and present or accounted for until wounded in the thigh at Gettysburg, Pennsylvania, July 1-3, 1863. Rejoined the company in

May-June, 1864, and present or accounted for until captured near Petersburg, Virginia, October 27, 1864. Confined at Point Lookout, Maryland, where he died March 19, 1865, of "pneumonia."

HARTGROVE, WILLIAM W., Sergeant
Resided in Mecklenburg County where he enlisted at age 32, March 10, 1862, for the war. Mustered in as Private. Present or accounted for until wounded at White Hall on December 16, 1862. Promoted to Corporal on January 22, 1863, and rejoined the company prior to May 1, 1863. Present or accounted for until wounded in the left thigh at Gettysburg, Pennsylvania, July 1, 1863. Returned to duty on November 18, 1863, and present or accounted for through April, 1864. Reported absent wounded from May-June, 1864, through October, 1864; however, place and date wounded not reported. Promoted to Sergeant in September-October, 1864, and rejoined the company in November-December, 1864. Present or accounted for until paroled at Appomattox Court House, Virginia, April 9, 1865.

HARTLINE, ADAMS, Private
Enlisted at Camp Holmes on October 27, 1864, for the war. Present or accounted for until paroled at Appomattox Court House, Virginia, April 9, 1865.

HARTLINE, ANDREW, Private
Resided in Iredell County and enlisted at Camp Holmes on October 27, 1864, for the war. Present or accounted for until captured at or near Petersburg, Virginia, April 2, 1865. Confined at Point Lookout, Maryland, until released on June 27, 1865, after taking the Oath of Allegiance.

HARTLINE, DAVID L., Private
Resided in Iredell County where he enlisted at age 27, February 26, 1862, for the war. Present or accounted for until wounded in the right foot at Gettysburg, Pennsylvania, July 1-3, 1863. Rejoined the company prior to September 1, 1863, and present or accounted for until reported absent wounded in May-June, 1864. Returned to duty in September-October, 1864, and present or accounted for until paroled at Appomattox Court House, Virginia, April 9, 1865.

HARTLINE, GEORGE H., Private
Resided in Iredell County where he enlisted at age 32, March 15, 1862, for the war. Present or accounted for until he died in hospital at Wilmington on August 10, 1862. Cause of death not reported.

HARTLINE, PAUL, Private
Resided in Iredell County where he enlisted at age 40, February 26, 1862, for the war. Present or accounted for until wounded at White Hall on December 16, 1862. Rejoined the company in January-February, 1863, and present or accounted for until captured at or near Petersburg, Virginia, April 2, 1865. Confined at Point Lookout, Maryland, until released on June 27, 1865, after taking the Oath of Allegiance.

HELMS, EZEKIEL T., Private
Resided in Mecklenburg County where he enlisted at age 28, March 12, 1863, for the war. Present or accounted for until killed at Gettysburg, Pennsylvania, July 1, 1863.

HILL, JAMES W., Private
Resided in Mecklenburg County where he enlisted at age 35, March 4, 1862, for the war. Present or accounted for until wounded in the "femerus" and

captured at Gettysburg, Pennsylvania, July 1-6, 1863. Hospitalized at various Federal hospitals until paroled at Davids Island, New York Harbor, August 24, 1863, and transferred for exchange. Rejoined the company in January-February, 1864, and present or accounted for until killed at or near Reams' Station, Virginia, on or about August 26, 1864.

HIPP, STEPHEN, Private
Enlisted in Mecklenburg County on April 19, 186[2], for the war. Present or accounted for until discharged on August 2, 1862, by reason of disability.

HODGES, GREEN, Private
Enlisted at Camp Holmes on October 1, 1864, for the war. Present or accounted for through October, 1864.

HOLDSCLAW, ROBERT H., Private
Previously served in Company K, 63rd Regiment N.C. Troops (5th Regiment N.C. Cavalry). Transferred to this company in November-December, 1864. Present or accounted for through February, 1865.

HOLLINGSWORTH, JOHN BRYAN, Corporal
Resided in Mecklenburg County where he enlisted at age 23, February 24, 1862, for the war. Mustered in as Private and promoted to Corporal in September-October, 1864. Present or accounted for until captured at or near Petersburg, Virginia, April 2, 1865. Confined at Fort Delaware, Delaware, until released on June 19, 1865, after taking the Oath of Allegiance.

HOLTON, HARRISON, Private
Enlisted in Mecklenburg County on March 16, 1864, for the war. Present or accounted for until paroled at Appomattox Court House, Virginia, April 9, 1865.

HUNTER, A. J., Sergeant
Previously served as Private in Company A of this regiment. Transferred to this company on or about October 15, 1864, upon promotion to Sergeant. Present or accounted for through February, 1865.

JAMISON, JAMES W., Corporal
Resided in Mecklenburg County where he enlisted at age 25, March 7, 1863, for the war. Mustered in as Private and promoted to Corporal in September-October, 1864. Present or accounted for until captured near Petersburg, Virginia, October 27, 1864. Confined at Point Lookout, Maryland, where he died on March 7, 1865, of "inflammation of the lungs."

JAMISON, JONES W., Private
Resided in Mecklenburg County where he enlisted at age 20, February 28, 1863, for the war. Present or accounted for until captured at Falling Waters, Maryland, July 14, 1863. Confined at Baltimore, Maryland, and at Point Lookout, Maryland, until paroled and transferred for exchange on or about March 3, 1864. Rejoined the company in May-June, 1864, and present or accounted for until captured near Petersburg, Virginia, October 27, 1864. Confined at Point Lookout until paroled and transferred for exchange on March 28, 1865.

JAMISON, THOMAS J., Corporal
Resided in Mecklenburg County where he enlisted at age 35, March 12, 1862, for the war. Mustered in as Private. Present or accounted for until wounded at White Hall on December 16, 1862. Rejoined the

company in January-February, 1863, and present or accounted for until wounded at Gettysburg, Pennsylvania, July 1-3, 1863. Rejoined the company prior to September 1, 1863, and was promoted to Corporal on December 18, 1864. Present or accounted for until captured at or near Petersburg, Virginia, April 2, 1865. Confined at Hart's Island, New York Harbor, until released on June 17, 1865, after taking the Oath of Allegiance.

JOHNSTON, J. W., Corporal
Company records indicate he enlisted on March 3, 1862, for the war; however he was not listed on the rolls of this company until January-February, 1865. The company muster roll of that date indicates he was captured on October 27, 1864; however, records of the Federal Provost Marshal do not substantiate that report. No further records.

JOHNSTON, JAMES C., Private
Enlisted at Camp Holmes on September 20, 1864, for the war. Present or accounted for through October, 1864.

KING, ARGUILE, Private
Born in Mecklenburg County where he resided as a farmer prior to enlisting in Mecklenburg County at age 56, April 19, 1862, for the war. Present or accounted for until discharged on April 1, 1864, by reason of "chronic rheumatism & the natural infirmity of age."

KING, H., Private
Place and date of enlistment not reported. Died at Point Lookout, Maryland, January 27, 1865. Place and date captured and cause of death not reported.

KISTLER, PAUL H., Private
Resided in Mecklenburg County and enlisted at Camp Holmes at age 20, May 9, 1862, for the war. Present or accounted for until discharged on March 23, 1863, by reason of "being a minor."

KYLES, FIELDING, Private
Resided in Iredell County and was by occupation a farmer prior to enlisting in Iredell County at age 42, February 26, 1862, for the war. Present or accounted for until captured near Petersburg, Virginia, October 27, 1864. Confined at Point Lookout, Maryland, until released on June 28, 1865, after taking the Oath of Allegiance.

KYLES, JOHN, Private
Resided in Iredell County and enlisted at Camp Holmes on October 27, 1864, for the war. Present or accounted for until captured near Petersburg, Virginia, March 25, 1865. Confined at Point Lookout, Maryland, until released on June 28, 1865, after taking the Oath of Allegiance.

KYLES, WILLIAM, Private
Resided in Iredell County where he enlisted at age 38, February 26, 1862, for the war. Present or accounted for until he died in hospital at Danville, Virginia, October 28, 1864, of "diarrhoea chronic."

LAMBERT, JONATHAN M., Private
Resided in Iredell County where he enlisted at age 18, March 1, 1862, for the war. Present or accounted for until he died in hospital at Richmond, Virginia, February 14, 1864, of disease.

LAMBERT, WILLIAM T., Private
Resided in Iredell County and enlisted at Camp Holmes on November 18, 1864, for the war. Present or accounted for until captured at or near Petersburg, Virginia, April 2, 1865. Confined at Fort Delaware, Delaware, until released on June 19, 1865, after taking the Oath of Allegiance.

LAWSON, HUDSON, Private
Enlisted at Camp Holmes on September 15, 1864, for the war. Present or accounted for until he died in hospital at Richmond, Virginia, January 26, 1865, of "diarrhoea."

LEDWELL, DAVID D., Private
Enlisted at Camp Holmes on September 1, 1864, for the war. Present or accounted for through February, 1865. Paroled at Charlotte on May 16, 1865.

LEWIS, LINDSAY, Private
Resided in Mecklenburg County where he enlisted at age 23, February 24, 1862, for the war. Present or accounted for until wounded in the right foot at Gettysburg, Pennsylvania, July 1, 1863. Reported absent wounded until detailed as a Provost Guard on December 16, 1863. Reported absent on detail through February, 1865. Paroled at Gordonsville, Virginia, May 22, 1865.

LIMEBARGER, MANASSAS, Private
Enlisted at Camp Holmes on September 1, 1864, for the war. Present or accounted for until captured near Petersburg, Virginia, on or about September 30, 1864. Confined at Point Lookout, Maryland, until paroled and transferred for exchange on or about February 10, 1865. Reported in hospital at Richmond, Virginia, February 16, 1865.

LOFTIN, MARTIN, Private
Enlisted at Camp Holmes on October 1, 1864, for the war. Present or accounted for until captured near Petersburg, Virginia, October 27, 1864. Confined at Point Lookout, Maryland, where he died February 12, 1865, of "typhoid fever."

McCORKLE, HUGH P., Private
Resided in Mecklenburg County where he enlisted at age 35, March 3, 1862, for the war. Present or accounted for until captured at Falling Waters, Maryland, July 14, 1863. Confined at Baltimore, Maryland, and at Point Lookout, Maryland, until paroled and transferred for exchange on or about March 16, 1864. Rejoined the company in July-August, 1864, and present or accounted for until captured at or near Petersburg, Virginia, April 2, 1865. Confined at Point Lookout until released on June 29, 1865, after taking the Oath of Allegiance.

McDONALD, DAVID W., 1st Sergeant
Previously served as Private in Company C, 1st Regiment N.C. Infantry (6 months, 1861). Enlisted in this company on March 12, 1862, for the war. Mustered in as Sergeant and promoted to 1st Sergeant on July 12, 1862. Present or accounted for until wounded at Gettysburg, Pennsylvania, July 1, 1863. Rejoined the company in September-October, 1863, and present or accounted for until killed at Jones' Farm, Virginia, September 30, 1864.

McDONALD, JOHN H., 1st Sergeant
Previously served as Private in Company C, 1st Regiment N.C. Infantry (6 months, 1861). Enlisted in this company on March 12, 1862, for the war. Mustered in as Corporal and promoted to Sergeant in July-August, 1864. Promoted to 1st Sergeant on October 1, 1864. Present or accounted for until paroled at Appomattox Court House, Virginia, April 9, 1865.

McLELLAND, WILLIAM, Private
Previously served in Company B, 1st Regiment N.C. Infantry (6 months, 1861). Enlisted in this company on May 5, 1862, for the war. Present or accounted for until captured at Gettysburg, Pennsylvania, on or about July 5, 1863. Confined at Baltimore, Maryland, and at Point Lookout, Maryland, until paroled and transferred for exchange on or about March 3, 1864. Rejoined the company in May-June, 1864, and present or accounted for until paroled at Appomattox Court House, Virginia, April 9, 1865.

McLURE, CYRUS A., Private
Resided in Mecklenburg County where he enlisted at age 28, March 12, 1862, for the war. Present or accounted for until wounded in the left index finger and captured either at Gettysburg, Pennsylvania, July 3, 1863, or at Falling Waters, Maryland, July 14, 1863. Finger amputated. Hospitalized at Baltimore, Maryland, where he was paroled and transferred for exchange on or about September 25, 1863. Rejoined the company in March-April, 1864, and present or accounted for until captured near Petersburg, Virginia, October 27, 1864. Confined at Point Lookout, Maryland, until exchanged on February 10, 1865. Reported in hospital at Richmond, Virginia, February 16, 1865.

McLURE, JAMES D., Private
Resided in Mecklenburg County where he enlisted at age 25, March 12, 1862, for the war. Present or accounted for until hospitalized at Wilmington on or about August 7, 1862, with continued fever. Died August 10, 1862.

McQUAY, JAMES, Private
Resided in Mecklenburg County where he enlisted at age 35, April 30, 1862, for the war. Present or accounted for until killed at Gettysburg, Pennsylvania, July 3, 1863.

McQUAY, JOHN B., Private
North Carolina pension records indicate that he enlisted on or about February 10, 1865, for the war. No further records.

McQUAY, SEABORN, Private
Resided in Mecklenburg County where he enlisted at age 28, March 10, 1862, for the war. Present or accounted for until he died at Wilmington in June, 1862, of disease.

McQUAY, WILLIAM H., Private
Resided in Mecklenburg County where he enlisted at age 20, March 10, 1862, for the war. Present or accounted for until wounded and captured at Gettysburg, Pennsylvania, July 1, 1863. Died at Gettysburg on July 7, 1863, of wounds.

MADDOX, GEORGE W., Private
Enlisted at Camp Holmes on September 1, 1864, for the war. Present or accounted for through February, 1865. Company muster roll dated January-February,

1865, states he was captured October 27, 1864; however, records of the Federal Provost Marshal do not substantiate that report.

MARTIN, W. H., Private
Place and date of enlistment not reported. Deserted to the enemy on or about March 8, 1865. Took the Oath of Allegiance on or about March 10, 1865.

MARTIN, WILLIAM, Private
Resided in Mecklenburg County where he enlisted at age 19, March 5, 1862, for the war. Present or accounted for until wounded at Gettysburg, Pennsylvania, July 1, 1863. Rejoined the company in September-October, 1863, and present or accounted for through February, 1865.

MATHESON, JOHN S., Private
Enlistment date reported as August 12, 1862; however, he was not listed on the rolls of this company until November-December, 1864. Present or accounted for until he deserted to the enemy on or about March 9, 1865. Took the Oath of Allegiance on or about March 13, 1865.

MEANS, JOHN S., Private
Enlisted on March 24, 1864, for the war. Present or accounted for through October, 1864.

MEANS, JOHN S., Corporal
Resided in Mecklenburg County where he enlisted at age 22, March 5, 1862, for the war. Mustered in as Corporal. Present or accounted for until he died at Wilmington on August 22, 1862, of "fever."

MILLER, JOHN F., Private
Resided in Mecklenburg County where he enlisted at age 30, February 13, 1862, for the war. Present or accounted for until he deserted on October 8, 1862.

MITSCHKA, JOHN, Private
Resided in Mecklenburg County or in New York City and enlisted in Mecklenburg County at age 40, February 19, 1862, for the war. Present or accounted for until captured at Gettysburg, Pennsylvania, July 2, 1863. Took the Oath of Allegiance at Fort Delaware, Delaware, in May, 1865.

MUNDAY, OSBORNE M., Private
Previously served in Company K, 63rd Regiment N.C. Troops (5th Regiment N.C. Cavalry). Transferred to this company in November-December, 1864. Present or accounted for until he deserted to the enemy on or about March 9, 1865. Took the Oath of Allegiance on or about March 13, 1865.

MURDOCK, WILLIAM D., Private
Resided in Iredell County where he enlisted at age 27, April 19, 1862, for the war. Present or accounted for until hospitalized at Richmond, Virginia, July 11, 1863, with a gunshot wound of the right foot; however, place and date wounded not reported. Reported absent sick until he was listed as a deserter in September-October, 1864.

NARRON, JOHN G., Private
Enlisted at Camp Holmes on September 15, 1864, for the war. Present or accounted for until captured near Petersburg, Virginia, October 27, 1864. Confined at Point Lookout, Maryland, where he died November 23, 1864, of "strangulated inguinal hernia."

NEEL, GEORGE A., Private
Resided in Mecklenburg County and was by occupation a farmer prior to enlisting in Mecklenburg County at age 18, February 1, 1863, for the war. Present or accounted for until wounded in the left arm and captured at Gettysburg, Pennsylvania, July 1-5, 1863. Left arm amputated. Hospitalized at Gettysburg until transferred to Davids Island, New York Harbor, July 17-24, 1863. Paroled at Davids Island and transferred for exchange on or about September 16, 1863. Discharged on or about February 17, 1864, by reason of disability.

NISBET, JOHN G., Private
Resided in Mecklenburg County where he enlisted at age 46, February 14, 1862, for the war. Present or accounted for until he died "at home" on June 30, 1862, of disease.

NULL, JOHN S., Private
Previously served in Company K, 63rd Regiment N.C. Troops (5th Regiment N.C. Cavalry). Transferred to this company in November-December, 1864. Present or accounted for until he deserted on March 9, 1865. Took the Oath of Allegiance on or about March 13, 1865.

OSTWALT, FRANCIS L., Private
Resided in Iredell County where he enlisted at age 38, February 26, 1862, for the war. Present or accounted for until captured at Gettysburg, Pennsylvania, July 3, 1863. Confined at Fort Delaware, Delaware, until transferred to Point Lookout, Maryland, October 15-18, 1863. Admitted to the smallpox hospital at Point Lookout on November 21, 1863, and died December 30, 1863.

PINNIX, JOHN A., Private
Enlisted at Camp Holmes on September 15, 1864, for the war. Present or accounted for until paroled at Appomattox Court House, Virginia, April 9, 1865.

PINNIX, JOSEPH W., Private
Enlisted at Camp Holmes on September 15, 1864, for the war. Present or accounted for until wounded in the left knee at or near Petersburg, Virginia, April 2, 1865. Hospitalized at various localities until admitted to a Federal hospital at Fort Monroe, Virginia, April 13, 1865. Discharged from hospital on July 9, 1865, after taking the Oath of Allegiance. Hospital records give his age as 20.

POOL, GEORGE S., Private
Resided in Mecklenburg County and was by occupation a teamster prior to enlisting in Mecklenburg County at age 33, March 14, 1862, for the war. Present or accounted for until wounded in the left hip at Spotsylvania Court House, Virginia, May 10, 1864. Reported absent wounded through February, 1865. Admitted to hospital at Charlotte on March 17, 1865, with a gunshot wound of the "lower right extremities"; however, place and date wounded not reported. Paroled at Charlotte on May 15, 1865.

PRIEST, NEAL, Private
Enlisted at Camp Holmes on October 1, 1864, for the war. Present or accounted for through October, 1864.

PUCKETT, JULIUS J., Sergeant
Resided in Mecklenburg County where he enlisted at age 28, March 12, 1862, for the war. Mustered in as Private and promoted to Corporal in August, 1862. Present or accounted for until wounded in the right leg at Gettysburg, Pennsylvania, July 1, 1863. Returned to duty on December 3, 1863, and was promoted to Sergeant in October, 1864. Present or accounted for until captured near Petersburg, Virginia, October 27, 1864. Confined at Point Lookout, Maryland, until released on June 16, 1865, after taking the Oath of Allegiance.

PUCKETT, WILLIAM C., Private
Resided in Mecklenburg County where he enlisted at age 24, March 10, 1862, for the war. Present or accounted for until wounded in the left thigh at Gettysburg, Pennsylvania, July 1, 1863. Rejoined the company in November-December, 1863, and present or accounted for until paroled at Appomattox Court House, Virginia, April 9, 1865.

RHYNE, DAVID, Private
Resided in Gaston County and enlisted at Camp Holmes on September 1, 1864, for the war. Present or accounted for until captured near Petersburg, Virginia, October 27, 1864. Confined at Point Lookout, Maryland, until released on June 19, 1865, after taking the Oath of Allegiance.

RICHEY, MOSES S.,_____
North Carolina pension records indicate he enlisted on October 23, 1864, for the war. No further records.

RICHEY, WILLIAM F., Private
Resided in Iredell County where he enlisted at age 35, April 19, 1863, for the war. Present or accounted for until wounded and captured at Gettysburg, Pennsylvania, July 1-3, 1863. Died in hospital at Gettysburg, July 6-9, 1863.

RIED, JAMES C., Private
Resided in Mecklenburg County where he enlisted on February 19, 1864, for the war. Present or accounted for until captured near Petersburg, Virginia, October 27, 1864. Confined at Point Lookout, Maryland, until paroled and transferred for exchange on January 17, 1865. Rejoined the company prior to April 2, 1865, when he was captured at "Cox Road." Confined at Hart's Island, New York Harbor, until released on June 17, 1865, after taking the Oath of Allegiance.

RIEVS, WILLIAM R., Private
Resided in Mecklenburg County where he enlisted at age 26, March 12, 1862, for the war. Present or accounted for until wounded at Gettysburg, Pennsylvania, July 1, 1863. Returned to duty on October 25, 1863, and present or accounted for until reported absent wounded in July-August, 1864. Place and date wounded not reported. Returned to duty in September-October, 1864, and present or accounted for until captured near Petersburg, Virginia, February 5, 1865. Confined at Point Lookout, Maryland, until released on June 30, 1865, after taking the Oath of Allegiance.

ROZZELL, JAMES T., Sergeant
Previously served as Private in Company B, 1st Regiment N.C. Infantry (6 months, 1861). Enlisted

in this company on May 9, 1862, for the war. Mustered in as Private and promoted to Corporal on July 12, 1862. Promoted to Sergeant on January 22, 1863. Present or accounted for until mortally wounded at Wilderness, Virginia, May 5, 1864. Place and date of death not reported.

SHERRILL, WILBURN AUGUSTUS, Private
Resided in Iredell County where he enlisted at age 32, March 1, 1862, for the war. Present or accounted for until discharged on or about October 25, 1862, by reason of disability.

SMITH, DAVID J., Private
Resided in Mecklenburg County where he enlisted at age 23, February 27, 1862, for the war. Present or accounted for until wounded in the neck near Petersburg, Virginia, March 27, 1865. Hospitalized at Richmond, Virginia, until transferred to Farmville, Virginia, April 1, 1865. Paroled at Farmville, April 11-21, 1865.

SPRINKLE, I., Private
Place and date of enlistment not reported. Paroled at Appomattox Court House, Virginia, April 9, 1865.

STINSON, JOHN B., Private
Resided in Mecklenburg County where he enlisted at age 36, March 1, 1862, for the war. Discharged June 20, 1862. Reason discharged not reported.

STONE, ALEXANDER, Private
Resided in Mecklenburg County where he enlisted at age 30, February 19, 1862, for the war. Present or accounted for until captured at or near Gettysburg, Pennsylvania, July 4, 1863. Confined at Fort Delaware, Delaware, until transferred to Point Lookout, Maryland, October 15-18, 1863. Hospitalized at Point Lookout on October 26, 1863, with acute diarrhoea. Died in hospital at Point Lookout on January 28, 1864.

TURNER, JOHN W., Private
Enlisted at Camp Holmes on September 15, 1864, for the war. Present or accounted for through March 16, 1865. Paroled at Salisbury on May 18, 1865, and took the Oath of Allegiance at Salisbury on June 12, 1865.

WALKER, BENJAMIN H., Private
Resided in Mecklenburg County where he enlisted at age 35, February 22, 1862, for the war. Present or accounted for until killed at White Hall on December 16, 1862.

WALKER, J. H., Private
Enlisted in Mecklenburg County in March, 1862, for the war. Died at Camp Mangum on or about March 6, 1862, of disease.

WALKER, JAMES H., Corporal
Resided in Mecklenburg County where he enlisted at age 33, May 9, 1862, for the war. Mustered in as Private and promoted to Corporal in September-October, 1864. Present or accounted for until captured near Petersburg, Virginia, October 27, 1864. Confined at Point Lookout, Maryland, until released on June 22, 1865, after taking the Oath of Allegiance.

WALKER, JOHN H., Private
Resided in Mecklenburg County where he enlisted at

age 18, March 12, 1862, for the war. Present or accounted for until captured at or near Petersburg, Virginia, April 2, 1865. Confined at Fort Delaware, Delaware, until released on June 19, 1865, after taking the Oath of Allegiance.

WALKER, LANDSEY L., Private
Resided in Caswell County and enlisted at Camp Holmes on September 15, 1864, for the war. Present or accounted for until captured at Petersburg, Virginia, April 3, 1865. Confined at Hart's Island, New York Harbor, until released on or about June 19, 1865, after taking the Oath of Allegiance.

WALKER, LEVI A., Private
Resided in Mecklenburg County where he enlisted at age 32, March 8, 1862, for the war. Present or accounted for until wounded and captured at Gettysburg, Pennsylvania, July 1-4, 1863. Hospitalized at Gettysburg until transferred to Davids Island, New York Harbor, July 17-24, 1863. Paroled at Davids Island and transferred for exchange on or about September 16, 1863. Rejoined the company in January-February, 1864, and present or accounted for until killed at Spotsylvania Court House, Virginia, May 11, 1864.

WILLIAMSON, EDWARD Y., Private
Resided in Mecklenburg County where he enlisted at age 20, February 24, 1862, for the war. Present or accounted for until captured at Gettysburg, Pennsylvania, July 3, 1863. Confined at Fort Delaware, Delaware, where he died August 20, 1863, of "cerebretis."

WILSON, JOHN R., Private
Enlisted in Mecklenburg County on April 9, 1864, for the war. Present or accounted for through February, 1865.

WILSON, ROBERT LEROY, Sergeant
Resided in Mecklenburg County where he enlisted at age 30, March 4, 1862, for the war. Mustered in as Corporal and promoted to Sergeant on January 22, 1863. Present or accounted for until captured near Petersburg, Virginia, October 27, 1864. Confined at Point Lookout, Maryland, where he died April 10, 1865. Cause of death not reported.

WINGATE, JAMES, Private
Resided in Mecklenburg County where he enlisted at age 36, March 14, 1862, for the war. Present or accounted for until wounded and captured at Gettysburg, Pennsylvania, July 1-4, 1863. Confined at various Federal hospitals until confined at Fort Delaware, Delaware, July 24, 1863. Transferred to Point Lookout, Maryland, October 15-18, 1863. Hospitalized at Point Lookout on November 3, 1863, with "scorbutis & diarrhoea" and died December 29, 1863.

WINGATE, THOMAS, Private
Resided in Mecklenburg County where he enlisted at age 32, March 14, 1862, for the war. Present or accounted for until wounded at Gettysburg, Pennsylvania, July 1, 1863. Reported absent wounded until he was listed as a deserter on December 4, 1863. Returned to duty on May 3, 1864, and present or accounted for until captured near Petersburg, Virginia, October 27, 1864. Confined at Point Lookout, Maryland, until exchanged on January 17, 1865.

Reported present with a detachment of paroled and exchanged prisoners at Camp Lee, near Richmond, Virginia, January 26, 1865.

WOODWARD, JAMES, Private
Place and date of enlistment not reported. Paroled at Salisbury on May 16, 1865.

YAUNTS, REUBIN C., Private
Resided in Mecklenburg County where he enlisted at age 28, February 14, 1862, for the war. Present or accounted for until court-martialed on or about June 21, 1862, and "confined at Guard Tent to wear ball & chain for six months." Reason he was court-martialed not reported. Returned to duty in November-December, 1862, and present or accounted for until killed at Gettysburg, Pennsylvania, July 1, 1863.

YORK, GEORGE W., Private
Resided in Stanly County and enlisted at Camp Holmes on September 1, 1864, for the war. Present or accounted for until captured near Petersburg, Virginia, October 27, 1864. Confined at Point Lookout, Maryland, until released on June 22, 1865, after taking the Oath of Allegiance.

COMPANY F

This company was composed primarily of men from Chowan, Hertford, and Perquimans counties and began organizing at Edenton and at Winton on or about February 15, 1862. On March 31, 1862, it was mustered in as Company F of this regiment. After that date the company functioned as a part of the regiment, and its history for the war period is recorded as a part of the regimental history.

The information contained in the following roster of the company was compiled principally from company muster rolls for May, 1862, through February, 1865. No company muster rolls were found for the period prior to May, 1862, or for the period after February, 1865. In addition to the company muster rolls, Roll of Honor records, receipt rolls, hospital records, prisoner or war records, and other primary records, supplemented by state pension applications, United Daughters of the Confederacy records, and postwar rosters and histories, all provided useful information.

OFFICERS
CAPTAIN

SMALL, EDWARD A.
Previously served as 2nd Lieutenant in Company M, 1st Regiment N.C. Infantry (6 months, 1861). Appointed Captain of this company to rank from February 15, 1862. Present or accounted for until captured at Gettysburg, Pennsylvania, July 3, 1863. Confined at Fort Delaware, Delaware, until transferred to Johnson's Island, Ohio, July 18, 1863. Paroled at Johnson's Island on or about March 14, 1865, and transferred for exchange. Company records do not indicate whether he returned to duty; however, he took the Oath of Allegiance at Norfolk, Virginia, June 3, 1865.

LIEUTENANTS

HOSKINS, BLAKE B., 3rd Lieutenant

Previously served as Sergeant in Company A, 1st Regiment N.C. State Troops. Appointed 3rd Lieutenant in this company to rank from April 7, 1862. Present or accounted for until wounded and captured at Gettysburg, Pennsylvania, July 1-3, 1863. Died at Gettysburg on July 9, 1863, of wounds.

KNAPP, THEODORE JUDSON, 1st Lieutenant

Previously served as Private in Company M, 1st Regiment N.C. Infantry (6 months, 1861). Appointed 1st Lieutenant in this company to rank from February 15, 1862. Present or accounted for until appointed Chaplain of this regiment in October, 1862; however, regimental records do not indicate that he accepted the appointment or served in that capacity. Resigned October 16, 1862, by reason of poor health.

REA, WILLIAM D., 2nd Lieutenant

Previously served as Private in Company M, 1st Regiment N.C. Infantry (6 months, 1861). Enlisted in this company on February 15, 1862, for the war. Mustered in as Sergeant and was appointed 2nd Lieutenant to rank from November 25, 1862. Present or accounted for until wounded in the left hip and right foot at Gettysburg, Pennsylvania, July 1-3, 1863. Returned to duty in September-October, 1863, and present or accounted for until wounded in the jaw at or near Petersburg, Virginia, on or about August 21, 1864. Retired to the Invalid Corps on February 1, 1865, by reason of disability.

ROBERTS, STEPHEN W., 1st Lieutenant

Previously served as Private in Company M, 1st Regiment N.C. Infantry (6 months, 1861). Appointed 2nd Lieutenant in this company to rank from February 15, 1862, and promoted to 1st Lieutenant on September 25, 1862. Present or accounted for until wounded in the shoulder at Gettysburg, Pennsylvania, July 1-3, 1863. Returned to duty prior to September 1, 1863, and present or accounted for until wounded in the left leg at Wilderness, Virginia, May 5, 1864. Reported absent sick until he returned to duty on March 7, 1865. No further records.

NONCOMMISSIONED OFFICERS AND PRIVATES

ASHLEY, BENBURY, Private

Resided in Chowan County where he enlisted at age 46, February 15, 1862, for the war. Present or accounted for until discharged on April 3, 1862, by reason of disability.

ASKEW, BRYANT, Private

Resided in Hertford County where he enlisted at age 18, February 15, 1862, for the war. Present or accounted for until captured at or near Petersburg, Virginia, April 2, 1865. Confined at Fort Delaware, Delaware, until released on June 19, 1865, after taking the Oath of Allegiance.

ASKEW, ENOS, Private

Resided in Hertford County where he enlisted at age 28, February 15, 1862, for the war. Present or accounted for until he died in Hertford County on April 24, 1862, of disease.

ASKEW, JOSHUA, Private

Resided in Hertford County where he enlisted at age 23, February 15, 1862, for the war. Present or accounted for until captured by the enemy in March-April, 1865. Confined at Hart's Island, New York Harbor, April 11, 1865. Released at Hart's Island on June 19, 1865, after taking the Oath of Allegiance.

ASKEW, MILES, Private

Resided in Chowan County where he enlisted at age 17, February 15, 1862, for the war. Present or accounted for until wounded in the head and captured at Gettysburg, Pennsylvania, July 1-3, 1863. Hospitalized at various Federal hospitals until paroled at Baltimore, Maryland, September 25, 1863, and transferred for exchange. Returned to duty in March-April, 1864, and present or accounted for until wounded at Reams' Station, Virginia, August 25, 1864. Reported absent wounded through February, 1865.

BACKUS, THOMAS, Private

Resided in Chowan County where he enlisted at age 46, February 15, 1862, for the war. Present or accounted for until he died in hospital at Danville, Virginia, June 27, 1863, of "meningitis" or "brain fever."

BAGLEY, THOMAS C., Private

Previously served in Company I, 17th Regiment N.C. Troops (1st Organization). Transferred to this company on or about January 19, 1863. Present or accounted for until captured at Falling Waters, Maryland, July 14, 1863. Confined at Old Capitol Prison, Washington, D.C., until transferred to Point Lookout, Maryland, August 8, 1863. Took the Oath of Allegiance in the winter of 1863-1864 and was released.

BAILEY, RICHARD, Private

Resided in Perquimans County where he enlisted at age 29, April 28, 1862, for the war. Present or accounted for until transferred to the C.S. Navy on April 1, 1864.

BATEMAN, T. C., Private

Resided in Chowan County where he enlisted at age 18, February 15, 1862, for the war. Present or accounted for until captured at Falling Waters, Maryland, July 14, 1863. Confined at Old Capitol Prison, Washington, D.C., until transferred to Point Lookout, Maryland, August 8, 1863. Released at Point Lookout on February 1, 1864, after taking the Oath of Allegiance and joining the U.S. Army. Assigned to Company A, 1st Regiment U.S. Volunteer Infantry.

BATES, F. W., Private

Resided in Chowan County and enlisted in Hertford or Perquimans counties at age 33, February 15, 1862, for the war. Mustered in as Private and promoted to Corporal in April, 1862. Reduced to ranks in November, 1862. Present or accounted for until wounded and captured at Gettysburg, Pennsylvania, July 1-3, 1863. Confined at Davids Island, New York Harbor, on or about July 17, 1863. Released after taking the Oath of Allegiance in the winter of 1863-1864.

BENBURY, WILLIAM E., Sergeant
Resided in Chowan County where he enlisted at age 20, February 15, 1862, for the war. Mustered in as Private and promoted to Corporal in November, 1862. Present or accounted for until wounded in the arm at Gettysburg, Pennsylvania, July 1-3, 1863. Returned to duty in November-December, 1863, and was promoted to Sergeant on December 7, 1864. Present or accounted for until wounded in the left thigh and right shoulder and captured at or near Petersburg, Virginia, April 2, 1865. Hospitalized at Washington, D.C., until released on June 12, 1865, after taking the Oath of Allegiance.

BOGUE, JESSE, Private
Resided in Perquimans County and enlisted in Chowan County at age 32, February 15, 1862, for the war. Present or accounted for until hospitalized at Richmond, Virginia, January 30, 1864, with a gunshot wound of the right arm; however, place and date wounded not reported. Returned to duty in March-April, 1864, and present or accounted for until paroled at Appomattox Court House, Virginia, April 9, 1865.

BOYCE, KENNY, Private
Resided in Chowan County where he enlisted at age 18, February 15, 1862, for the war. Present or accounted for until he died in hospital at Raleigh on April 3, 1862, of "typhoid fever."

BRATTEN, WILLIAM J., Private
Resided in Perquimans County and enlisted in Chowan County at age 33, February 15, 1862, for the war as a substitute. Present or accounted for until captured at Bristoe Station, Virginia, October 14, 1863. Confined at Old Capitol Prison, Washington, D.C., until transferred to Point Lookout, Maryland, October 27, 1863. Confined at Point Lookout until paroled and transferred for exchange on or about February 24, 1865.

BRIDGES, ROSWALD DANIEL, Private
Resided in Hertford County where he enlisted at age 32, February 15, 1862, for the war. Present or accounted for until wounded in the right thigh at or near Jones' Farm, Virginia, on or about October 1, 1864. Hospitalized at Richmond, Virginia. Returned to duty prior to March 1, 1865, and present or accounted for until captured at or near Petersburg, Virginia, April 2, 1865. Confined at Point Lookout, Maryland, until released on June 23, 1865, after taking the Oath of Allegiance.

BRIGGS, ANDREW, Private
Resided in Chowan County where he enlisted at age 18, February 15, 1862, for the war. Present or accounted for until captured near Petersburg, Virginia, October 27, 1864. Confined at Point Lookout, Maryland, until released on June 23, 1865, after taking the Oath of Allegiance.

BRIGGS, JAMES, Private
Resided in Chowan County where he enlisted at age 19, February 15, 1862, for the war. Present or accounted for until captured at Bristoe Station, Virginia, October 14, 1863. Confined at Old Capitol Prison, Washington, D.C., until transferred to Point Lookout, Maryland, October 27, 1863. Released at Point Lookout on October 17, 1864, after joining the

U.S. Army. Assigned to Company C, 4th Regiment U.S. Volunteer Infantry.

BRISCOE, ROBERT, Corporal
Resided in Hertford County where he enlisted at age 42, February 15, 1862, for the war. Mustered in as Corporal. Present or accounted for until wounded in the leg and captured at Gettysburg, Pennsylvania, July 3, 1863. Hospitalized at Chester, Pennsylvania, where he died on August 10, 1863, of "exhaustion following gunshot wound."

BYRUM, A. J., Private
Resided in Chowan County where he enlisted at age 21, February 15, 1862, for the war. Present or accounted for until wounded in the left leg at Gettysburg, Pennsylvania, July 3, 1863. Left leg amputated. Reported absent wounded through May 27, 1864. No further records.

BYRUM, GEORGE F., Private
Resided in Chowan County where he enlisted at age 19, February 15, 1862, for the war. Present or accounted for until he deserted at Franklin, Virginia, in October, 1862.

BYRUM, ISAAC, Private
Previously served in Company M, 1st Regiment N.C. Infantry (6 months, 1861). Enlisted in this company on February 15, 1862, for the war. Present or accounted for until wounded in the left leg and captured at Gettysburg, Pennsylvania, July 3-5, 1863. Left leg amputated. Hospitalized at various Federal hospitals until confined at Point Lookout, Maryland, October 2, 1863. Paroled at Point Lookout and transferred for exchange on March 17, 1864. Reported absent wounded until retired to the Invalid Corps on June 2, 1864.

CONNER, J. R., Private
Resided in Bertie County and enlisted in Hertford County at age 18, April 7, 1862, for the war. Present or accounted for until wounded in the thigh and captured at Gettysburg, Pennsylvania, July 1-5, 1863. Hospitalized at Gettysburg until transferred to Davids Island, New York Harbor, July 17-24, 1863. Paroled and transferred for exchange on or about September 16, 1863. Deserted in November, 1863, while absent or furlough. [May have served previously in Company L, 1st Regiment N.C. Infantry (6 months, 1861).]

COPELAND, TIMOTHY, Private
Resided in Chowan County where he enlisted at age 43, February 15, 1862, for the war. Present or accounted for until he died in Chowan County on July 24, 1864. Cause of death not reported.

CREECY, HENRY L., Private
Resided in Perquimans County and enlisted in Chowan County at age 20, February 15, 1862, for the war. Present or accounted for until captured at Bristoe Station, Virginia, October 14, 1863. Confined at Old Capitol Prison, Washington, D.C., until transferred to Point Lookout, Maryland, October 27, 1863. Confined at Point Lookout until paroled and transferred for exchange on or about February 24, 1865.

CREECY, JAMES E., Corporal
Resided in Perquimans County and enlisted in

Chowan County at age 23, February 15, 1862, for the war. Mustered in as Corporal. Present or accounted for until captured at Falling Waters, Maryland, July 14, 1863. Confined at Old Capitol Prison, Washington, D.C., until transferred to Point Lookout, Maryland, August 8, 1863. Died at Point Lookout on February 15, 1864. Cause of death not reported.

DAIL, JOSEPH, Private
Resided at Portsmouth, Virginia, and enlisted at Orange Court House, Virginia, January 25, 1864, for the war. Present or accounted for until captured at or near Petersburg, Virginia, April 2, 1865. Confined at Point Lookout, Maryland, until released on June 12, 1865, after taking the Oath of Allegiance.

DAIL, JOSHUA, Private
Resided in Perquimans County where he enlisted at age 22, April 14, 1862, for the war. Died at Camp Holmes, Virginia, May 13, 1862, of "measles."

DAVENPORT, C. G., 1st Sergeant
Resided in Chowan County where he enlisted at age 31, February 15, 1862, for the war. Mustered in as Sergeant and promoted to 1st Sergeant on December 8, 1864. Present or accounted for through February, 1865.

DAVIDSON, LOUIS, Private
Resided in Hertford County where he enlisted at age 40, April 12, 1862, for the war. Present or accounted for until wounded and captured at Gettysburg, Pennsylvania, July 1-3, 1863. Hospitalized at Gettysburg until transferred to Davids Island, New York Harbor, on or about July 17, 1863. Died in hospital at Davids Island on July 27, 1863, of wounds.

DEANS, WILLIAM D., Private
Born in Chowan County and was by occupation a farmer prior to enlisting in Chowan County on February 15, 1862, for the war. Present or accounted for until discharged on October 3, 1862, by reason of being physically "unfit for duty."

ELLIOTT, CHARLES W., Private
Resided in Chowan County where he enlisted at age 22, February 15, 1862, for the war. Present or accounted for until he died at Camp Mangum on April 13, 1862, of disease. [May have served previously in Company M, 1st Regiment N.C. Infantry (6 months, 1861).]

FARMER, JOSEPH J., Private
Resided in Hertford County where he enlisted at age 22, April 20, 1862, for the war. Present or accounted for until captured at Bristoe Station, Virginia, October 14, 1863. Confined at Point Lookout, Maryland, until released on January 23, 1864, after taking the Oath of Allegiance and joining the U.S. Army. Assigned to Company F, 1st Regiment U.S. Volunteer Infantry. [May have served previously in Company L, 1st Regiment N.C. Infantry (6 months, 1861).]

FLEETWOOD, JOSEPH, Private
Resided in Perquimans County and enlisted in Chowan County at age 33, April 19, 1862, for the war. Discharged May 1, 1862, by reason of disability.

FLOYD, HENRY, Private
Resided in Hertford County where he enlisted at age 31, February 15, 1862, for the war. Present or accounted for until captured at Gettysburg, Pennsylvania, July 3, 1863. Confined at Fort Delaware, Delaware, where he died October 6, 1863. Cause of death not reported.

FOREHAND, ADAM, Private
Resided in Chowan County where he enlisted at age 22, February 15, 1862, for the war. Present or accounted for until captured at Falling Waters, Maryland, July 14, 1863. Confined at Baltimore, Maryland, and at Point Lookout, Maryland, until paroled and transferred for exchange on or about May 3, 1864. Returned to duty in July-August, 1864, and present or accounted for until captured near Petersburg, Virginia, October 27, 1864. Confined at Point Lookout until released on June 27, 1865, after taking the Oath of Allegiance.

GARRETT, STEPHEN, Private
Resided in Chowan County where he enlisted at age 39, February 15, 1862, for the war. Present or accounted for until captured at Bristoe Station, Virginia, October 14, 1863. Confined at Old Capitol Prison, Washington, D.C., until transferred to Point Lookout, Maryland, October 27, 1863. Died in hospital at Point Lookout on November 6, 1863, of "chronic diarrhoea."

GATLING, WILLIAM J., Private
Resided in Hertford County where he enlisted at age 34, February 15, 1862, for the war. Present or accounted for until discharged on August 4, 1862, by reason of disability.

GOODWIN, AMARIAH, Private
Resided in Perquimans or Chowan counties prior to enlisting in Perquimans County at age 26, April 26, 1862, for the war. Present or accounted for until he deserted to the enemy at Petersburg, Virginia, July 19, 1864. Confined at Fort Monroe, Virginia, until released on September 8, 1864, after taking the Oath of Amnesty.

GOODWIN, B. F., Private
Resided in Chowan County where he enlisted at age 23, February 15, 1862, for the war. Present or accounted for until captured at Falling Waters, Maryland, July 14, 1863. Confined at Old Capitol Prison, Washington, D.C., until transferred to Point Lookout, Maryland, August 8, 1863. Died at Point Lookout on January 6, 1864. Cause of death not reported.

GOODWIN, ELI, Private
Resided in Chowan County where he enlisted at age 22, February 15, 1862, for the war. Present or accounted for until he died at Weldon on January 19, 1863. Cause of death not reported.

GREEN, SAMUEL, Private
Resided in Hertford County where he enlisted at age 24, February 15, 1862, for the war. Present or accounted for until he died in hospital at Raleigh on March 16, 1862, of "meningitis."

GRIFFIN, JOSHUA, Private
Resided in Chowan County where he enlisted at age 16, April 19, 1862, for the war. Present or accounted

for until he deserted to the enemy on February 23, 1865. Released at Washington, D.C., on or about February 27, 1865, after taking the Oath of Allegiance.

HARRIS, THOMAS C., Corporal
Resided in Perquimans County where he enlisted at age 29, April 28, 1862, for the war. Mustered in as Private. Present or accounted for until wounded in the left side and captured at Gettysburg, Pennsylvania, July 3, 1863. Hospitalized at Gettysburg and at Baltimore, Maryland, until paroled at Baltimore on August 23, 1863, and transferred for exchange. Returned to duty in November-December, 1863, and was promoted to Corporal in January-February, 1864. Present or accounted for until captured near Petersburg, Virginia, October 27, 1864. Confined at Point Lookout, Maryland, where he died January 2, 1865, of "hepatitis."

HASKETT, THOMAS T., Private
Resided in Perquimans County where he enlisted at age 23, April 28, 1862, for the war. Present or accounted for until wounded in the left leg and captured at Gettysburg, Pennsylvania, July 3, 1863. Hospitalized at Baltimore, Maryland, until paroled and transferred for exchange on or about September 25, 1863. Retired to the Invalid Corps on April 1, 1864, by reason of wounds received at Gettysburg.

HEDRICKS, THOMAS, Private
Resided in Chowan County where he enlisted at age 54, February 15, 1862, for the war. Present or accounted for until transferred to the C.S. Navy on April 1, 1864.

HENDRIX, NATHAN, Private
Resided in Perquimans County and enlisted in Chowan County at age 20, April 19, 1862, for the war. Present or accounted for until October 29, 1863, when he was reported absent without leave. Listed as a deserter in July-August, 1864.

HUDSON, JOHN W., Private
Resided in Chowan County where he enlisted at age 43, February 15, 1862, for the war. Present or accounted for until he died in hospital at Franklin, Virginia, October 29, 1862, of "pneumonia."

JONES, THEOPHILUS, Private
Resided in Perquimans County and enlisted in Chowan County at age 44, February 15, 1862, for the war. Present or accounted for until wounded and captured at Gettysburg, Pennsylvania, July 3, 1863. Confined at Fort Delaware, Delaware, until released on June 7, 1865, after taking the Oath of Allegiance. [May have served previously in Company M, 1st Regiment N.C. Infantry (6 months, 1861).]

JORDAN, HANCE, Private
Resided in Chowan County where he enlisted at age 27, April 11, 1862, for the war. Present or accounted for until reported missing at Wilderness, Virginia, May 6, 1864. Company muster roll dated November-December, 1864, indicates that he had "returned to his home in the enemy's lines" and had "failed to report to his command since." No further records.

JORDAN, N. C., Private
Resided in Chowan County where he enlisted at age 28, February 15, 1862, for the war. Present or

accounted for until wounded at Gettysburg, Pennsylvania, July 1, 1863. Died at Gettysburg on July 3, 1863, of wounds.

JORDAN, ROBERT S., Corporal
Resided in Perquimans County where he enlisted at age 21, April 28, 1862, for the war. Mustered in as Private and promoted to Corporal on December 7, 1864. Present or accounted for until captured at or near Petersburg, Virginia, April 2, 1865. Confined at Point Lookout, Maryland, until released on June 28, 1865, after taking the Oath of Allegiance.

LANE, CALEB, Private
Resided in Perquimans County where he enlisted at age 23, April 26, 1862, for the war. Present or accounted for until he was reported captured at Gettysburg, Pennsylvania, July 3, 1863; however, records of the Federal Provost Marshal do not substantiate that report. No further records.

LANE, WILLIAM, Private
Resided in Perquimans County where he enlisted at age 22, April 28, 1862, for the war. Present or accounted for until captured at Gettysburg, Pennsylvania, July 3, 1863. Confined at Fort Delaware, Delaware, until transferred to Point Lookout, Maryland, October 15-18, 1863. Died at Point Lookout on October 15, 1864, of "acute diarrhoea."

LASSITER, GEORGE W., Private
Resided in Chowan County where he enlisted at age 20, February 15, 1862, for the war. Present or accounted for until captured at or near Petersburg, Virginia, April 2, 1865. Confined at Fort Delaware, Delaware, until released on June 19, 1865, after taking the Oath of Allegiance.

LEARY, QUINTON L., Private
Resided in Chowan County and enlisted in Hertford County at age 18, April 12, 1862, for the war. Present or accounted for until discharged on August 16, 1862, by reason of disability. [May have served previously in Company A, 1st Regiment N.C. State Troops.]

LEARY, WILLIAM H., Private
Previously served in Company M, 1st Regiment N.C. Infantry (6 months, 1861). Enlisted in this company on February 15, 1862, for the war. Mustered in as Corporal but was reduced to ranks on June 15, 1864. Present or accounted for until captured at Petersburg, Virginia, April 3, 1865. Confined at Hart's Island, New York Harbor, until released on June 14, 1865, after taking the Oath of Allegiance.

LONG, JOHN, Private
Born in Perquimans County where he resided as a farmer prior to enlisting in Perquimans County at age 28, February 15, 1862, for the war. Present or accounted for until wounded in the elbow at or near Petersburg, Virginia, on or about August 21, 1864. Reported absent wounded until retired to the Invalid Corps on or about February 21, 1865.

LONG, JOSEPH S., Corporal
Resided in Perquimans County where he enlisted at age 20, April 28, 1862, for the war. Mustered in as Private. Present or accounted for until wounded in the left thigh and arm and captured at Gettysburg, Pennsylvania, July 3, 1863. Hospitalized at various

Federal hospitals until confined at Point Lookout, Maryland, October 4, 1863. Paroled at Point Lookout and transferred for exchange on or about March 16, 1864. Returned to duty in May-June, 1864, and was promoted to Corporal on June 15, 1864. Present or accounted for until paroled at Burkeville Junction, Virginia, April 14-17, 1865.

LONG, RICHARD, Private
Resided in Perquimans County where he enlisted at age 28, April 17, 1862, for the war. Present or accounted for until discharged on August 13, 1862, by reason of disability.

McDOWELL, GEORGE B., 1st Sergeant
Resided in Chowan County where he enlisted at age 32, February 15, 1862, for the war. Mustered in as Ordnance Sergeant. Present or accounted for until wounded in the hip and foot at Gettysburg, Pennsylvania, July 1-3, 1863. Returned to duty prior to September 1, 1863, and was promoted to 1st Sergeant in January-February, 1864. Present or accounted for until he was reported transferred to the 47th Regiment N.C. Troops in July-August, 1864; however, records of the 47th Regiment N.C. Troops do not indicate that he served therein. No further records.

MANSFIELD, CALVIN, Private
Resided in Perquimans County where he enlisted at age 22, April 28, 1862, for the war. Present or accounted for until reported "in confinement" from November-December, 1862, until February 28, 1863. Present or accounted for until captured at Falling Waters, Maryland, July 14, 1863. Confined at Baltimore, Maryland, and at Point Lookout, Maryland, until paroled and transferred for exchange on or about March 3, 1864. Reported absent without leave on June 9, 1864. Never rejoined the company. No further records.

MARDRE, NATHANIEL, Sergeant
Previously served as Private in Company M, 1st Regiment N.C. Infantry (6 months, 1861). Enlisted in this company on February 15, 1862, for the war. Mustered in as Sergeant. Present or accounted for until captured at Falling Waters, Maryland, July 14, 1863. Paroled at Baltimore, Maryland, August 23, 1863. Returned to duty in November-December, 1863, and present or accounted for until wounded at Wilderness, Virginia, May 5, 1864. Returned to duty in July-August, 1864. Present or accounted for until reported absent wounded in January-February, 1865; however, place and date wounded not reported. No further records.

MILLER, JAMES, Private
Resided in Chowan County where he enlisted at age 18, February 15, 1862, for the war. Present or accounted for until wounded in the arm at Wilderness, Virginia, May 5, 1864. Returned to duty in July-August, 1864, and present or accounted for until captured at Petersburg, Virginia, April 3, 1865. Confined at Hart's Island, New York Harbor, until released on June 19, 1865, after taking the Oath of Allegiance.

MODLIN, ELISHA, Private
Previously served in Company M, 1st Regiment N.C. Infantry (6 months, 1861). Enlisted in this company on February 15, 1862, for the war. Present or accounted for through February, 1865.

MOORE, LEVI, Private
Resided in Perquimans County where he enlisted at age 18, April 26, 1862, for the war. Present or accounted for until he died in hospital at Wilmington on June 16, 1862, of disease.

MUNDS, THOMAS, Private
Born in Chowan County where he resided as a farmer prior to enlisting in Chowan County at age 20, February 15, 1862, for the war. Present or accounted for until hospitalized at Charlottesville, Virginia, January 12, 1864, with a gunshot wound; however, place and date wounded not reported. Returned to duty in March-April, 1864, and present or accounted for until captured at or near Petersburg, Virginia, April 2, 1865. Confined at Point Lookout, Maryland, until released on June 15, 1865, after taking the Oath of Allegiance.

NIXON, THOMAS W., Private
Resided in Washington County and enlisted in Chowan County at age 24, April 12, 1862, for the war. Present or accounted for until he deserted at Smithville on November 26, 1862.

NOWELL, JACOB, Private
Resided in Hertford County where he enlisted at age 27, February 15, 1863, for the war. Present or accounted for until captured at or near Hazel Run, Virginia, on or about July 28, 1863. Confined at Point Lookout, Maryland, where he took the Oath of Allegiance and joined the U.S. Army on February 2, 1864. Assigned to Company B, 1st Regiment U.S. Volunteer Infantry.

PARRISH, STEPHEN, Private
Previously served in Company M, 1st Regiment N.C. Infantry (6 months, 1861). Enlisted in this company on February 15, 1862, for the war. Present or accounted for until wounded at or near Jones' Farm, Virginia, on or about October 1, 1864. Reported absent wounded through February, 1865.

PARRISH, WILLIAM E., Private
Resided in Chowan County where he enlisted at age 21, February 15, 1862, for the war. Present or accounted for until wounded in the left thigh at Gettysburg, Pennsylvania, July 1, 1863. Returned to duty in September-October, 1863, and present or accounted for until he died in hospital at Greensboro on August 27, 1864, of "collitis ac[u]t[e]."

PEIRCE, JOB, Private
Resided in Hertford County where he enlisted at age 23, April 7, 1862, for the war. Present or accounted for until captured near Petersburg, Virginia, October 27, 1864. Confined at Point Lookout, Maryland, until released on June 16, 1865, after taking the Oath of Allegiance.

PEIRCE, RICHARD, Private
Enlisted in Hertford County on April 14, 1862, for the war. Present or accounted for until transferred to another unit on September 13, 1862. Unit to which transferred not reported.

PERRY, TIMOTHY, Private
Resided in Chowan County where he enlisted at age 26, February 15, 1862, for the war. Present or

accounted for until he died in hospital at Richmond, Virginia, on or about September 10, 1864, of "debilitas."

POTTER, JOHN, Private
Resided in Perquimans County where he enlisted at age 27, April 28, 1862, for the war. Present or accounted for until reported "in confinement" from November-December, 1862, until February 28, 1863. Present or accounted for until captured at Bristoe Station, Virginia, October 14, 1863. Confined at Old Captiol Prison, Washington, D.C., until transferred to Point Lookout, Maryland, October 27, 1863. Released at Point Lookout on January 25, 1864, after taking the Oath of Allegiance and joining the U.S. service. Unit to which assigned not reported; however, he may have served in the navy. No further records.

POTTER, SAMUEL, Private
Resided in Perquimans County where he enlisted at age 19, February 15, 1862, for the war. Present or accounted for until captured at Bristoe Station, Virginia, October 14, 1863. Confined at Old Capitol Prison, Washington, D.C., until transferred to Point Lookout, Maryland, October 27, 1863. Paroled and transferred for exchange on or about March 16, 1864. Returned to duty in May-June, 1864, and present or accounted for until paroled at Burkeville Junction, Virginia, April 14-17, 1865.

POWELL, WILLIAM H., Private
Resided in Perquimans County where he enlisted at age 22, April 14, 1862, for the war. Present or accounted for until hospitalized at Wilmington on or about July 17, 1862, with "febris typhoid." Died August 7, 1862.

PROCTOR, JOHN R., Private
Resided in Perquimans County and enlisted in Chowan County at age 18, April 17, 1862, for the war. Present or accounted for until wounded and captured at Gettysburg, Pennsylvania, July 1, 1863. Reported in hospital at Hagerstown, Maryland, in August, 1863. Died of wounds while a prisoner of war; however, place and date of death not reported.

ROBINSON, HENRY D., Private
Resided in Hertford County where he enlisted at age 18, April 19, 1862, for the war. Present or accounted for until hospitalized at Wilmington on or about June 16, 1862, with "typhoid fever." Died July 6, 1862.

ROBINSON, JOHN, Private
Born in Hertford County where he resided as a farmer prior to enlisting in Hertford County at age 48, April 16, 1862, for the war. Present or accounted for until discharged on July 20, 1862, by reason of disability.

ROUNTREE, NOAH, Private
Resided in Gates County and enlisted in Chowan County at age 31, April 17, 1862, for the war. Present or accounted for until killed at White Hall on December 16, 1862.

RUSSELL, WILLIAM D., Private
Resided in Gates County and enlisted in Chowan County at age 23, April 17, 1862, for the war. Never reported for duty and was dropped from the rolls as

a deserter in May-June, 1863.

SAUNDERS, GEORGE R., Private
Resided in Perquimans County and enlisted in Chowan County at age 18, May 15, 1862, for the war. Present or accounted for through October, 1862. Reported absent sick from November-December, 1862, until January-February, 1864, when he was listed as a deserter.

SAUNDERS, WILLIAM F., Private
Resided in Hertford County where he enlisted at age 18, February 15, 1862, for the war. Present or accounted for until captured at Petersburg, Virginia, April 3, 1865. Confined at Hart's Island, New York Harbor, until released on June 19, 1865, after taking the Oath of Allegiance.

SIMPSON, FREDERICK, Private
Resided in Chowan County where he enlisted at age 21, February 15, 1862, for the war. Present or accounted for until captured near Petersburg, Virginia, March 25, 1865. Confined at Point Lookout, Maryland, until released on June 19, 1865, after taking the Oath of Allegiance.

SMALL, THOMAS M., Sergeant
Resided in Chowan County where he enlisted at age 24, April 18, 1862, for the war. Mustered in as Sergeant. Present or accounted for until wounded at or near Petersburg, Virginia, August 21, 1864. Reported absent wounded through February, 1865.

SMITH, CHARLTON, Private
Resided in Perquimans County where he enlisted at age 34, April 28, 1862, for the war. Present or accounted for until reported captured at Gettysburg, Pennsylvania, July 3, 1863; however, records of the Federal Provost Marshal do not substantiate that report. No further records.

SMITH, JAMES J., Private
Born in Perquimans County where he resided as a farmer prior to enlisting in Chowan County at age 21, April 19, 1862, for the war. Present or accounted for until paroled at Farmville, Virginia, April 11-21, 1865.

SMITH, WILLIAM J., Private
Resided in Chowan County where he enlisted at age 26, February 15, 1862, for the war. Present or accounted for until killed at Gettysburg, Pennsylvania, July 3, 1863.

STEARNS, DAVID M., Private
Resided in Chowan County where he enlisted at age 19, February 15, 1862, for the war. Present or accounted for until captured at Bristoe Station, Virginia, October 14, 1863. Confined at Old Capitol Prison, Washington, D.C., until transferred to Point Lookout, Maryland, October 27, 1863. Released at Point Lookout on February 1, 1864, after taking the Oath of Allegiance and joining the U.S. Army. Assigned to Company E, 1st Regiment U.S. Volunteer Infantry.

STEARNS, JAMES W., Private
Resided in Chowan County where he enlisted at age 34, February 15, 1862, for the war. Present or accounted for until he deserted at Petersburg, Virginia, July 19, 1864.

STEARNS, JOHN, Private

Resided in Chowan County where he enlisted at age 29, February 15, 1862, for the war. Present or accounted for until he deserted at Franklin, Virginia, in October, 1862.

SUTTON, S. S., Private

Resided in Chowan County where he enlisted at age 34, February 15, 1862, for the war. Present or accounted for until hospitalized at Richmond, Virginia, July 20, 1863, with a gunshot wound of the left arm; however, place and date wounded not reported. Returned to duty prior to September 1, 1863, and present or accounted for until captured at Bristoe Station, Virginia, October 14, 1863. Confined at Old Capitol Prison, Washington, D.C., until transferred to Point Lookout, Maryland, October 27, 1863. Paroled at Point Lookout and transferred for exchange on or about March 3, 1864. Returned to duty in May-June, 1864, and present or accounted for until wounded at or near Burgess' Mill, Virginia, October 27, 1864. Reported absent wounded through February, 1865.

SWAIN, JAMES W., Private

Born in Washington County and resided in Perquimans County where he was by occupation a farmer prior to enlisting in Chowan County at age 47, February 15, 1862, for the war. Present or accounted for until wounded in the left ankle at Bristoe Station, Virginia, October 14, 1863. Discharged April 21, 1864, by reason of wounds received at Bristoe Station.

TAYLOR, JOSEPH W., Private

Resided in Hertford County where he enlisted at age 17, April 7, 1862, for the war. Present or accounted for until captured at Gettysburg, Pennsylvania, July 3-4, 1863. Confined at Fort Delaware, Delaware, until transferred to Point Lookout, Maryland, October 15-18, 1863. Paroled at Point Lookout and transferred for exchange on or about May 3, 1864. Returned to duty prior to July 1, 1864, and present or accounted for until wounded at or near Jones' Farm, Virginia, on or about October 1, 1864. Reported absent wounded through February, 1865.

THATCH, HENRY C., Private

Resided in Perquimans County where he enlisted at age 24, April 28, 1862, for the war. Present or accounted for until reported captured at Gettysburg, Pennsylvania, July 3, 1863; however, records of the Federal Provost Marshal do not substantiate that report. No further records.

TROTMAN, JOSEPH W., Sergeant

Resided in Perquimans County where he enlisted at age 28, February 15, 1862, for the war. Mustered in as Sergeant but was reduced to ranks on April 18, 1862. Promoted to Sergeant in November-December, 1862. Present or accounted for until captured at Gettysburg, Pennsylvania, July 3, 1863. Confined at Point Lookout, Maryland, until paroled and transferred for exchange on or about March 16, 1864. Returned to duty in May-June, 1864, and present or accounted for until wounded at or near Petersburg, Virginia, August 22, 1864. Reported absent wounded through February, 1865.

WARD, AARON, Private

Previously served in Company M, 1st Regiment N.C. Infantry (6 months, 1861). Enlisted in this company on February 15, 1862, for the war. Present or accounted for until captured near Petersburg, Virginia, March 25, 1865. Confined at Point Lookout, Maryland, until released on June 21, 1865, after taking the Oath of Allegiance.

WARD, ANDERSON S., Private

Born in Chowan County where he resided as a farmer prior to enlisting in Chowan County at age 19, February 15, 1862, for the war. Present or accounted for until captured at Petersburg, Virginia, April 3, 1865. Confined at Hart's Island, New York Harbor, until released on June 19, 1865, after taking the Oath of Allegiance.

WELCH, WILLIAM B., Private

Resided in Chowan County where he enlisted at age 21, February 15, 1862, for the war. Present or accounted for until he died in hospital at Petersburg, Virginia, October 21, 1862, of "erysipelas."

WELCH, WILLIAM G., Private

Resided in Perquimans County where he enlisted at age 50, February 15, 1862, for the war. Present or accounted for until he died in hospital at Richmond, Virginia, on or about June 7, 1864, of "dysentery acute."

WHEDBEE, GEORGE W., Private

Resided in Perquimans County where he enlisted at age 19, April 26, 1862, for the war. Present or accounted for until wounded and captured at Gettysburg, Pennsylvania, July 1-4, 1863. Hospitalized at Gettysburg until transferred to Davids Island, New York Harbor, July 17-24, 1863. Paroled at Davids Island and transferred to City Point, Virginia, where he was received September 16, 1863, for exchange. Returned to duty in March-April, 1864, and present or accounted for until he deserted at Petersburg, Virginia, July 19, 1864.

WHITE, ISAAC N., Corporal

Resided in Perquimans County where he enlisted at age 19, February 15, 1862, for the war. Mustered in as Private. Present or accounted for until wounded and captured at Gettysburg, Pennsylvania, July 3, 1863. Confined at Fort Delaware, Delaware, until exchanged on July 31, 1863. Returned to duty in November-December, 1863, and was promoted to Corporal in January-February, 1864. Present or accounted for until captured at or near Petersburg, Virginia, April 2, 1865. Confined at Point Lookout, Maryland, until released on June 21, 1865, after taking the Oath of Allegiance.

WHITE, JAMES, Private

Resided in Perquimans County and enlisted in Chowan County at age 20, April 19, 1862, for the war. Present or accounted for until wounded in the lung and captured at Gettysburg, Pennsylvania, July 3, 1863. Died in hospital at Baltimore, Maryland, July 16, 1863, of wounds.

WHITE, JAMES B., Private

Resided in Hertford or Bertie counties and enlisted in Hertford County at age 32, April 19, 1862, for the war. Present or accounted for until wounded in the right arm at Gettysburg, Pennsylvania, July 1-3,

1863. Returned to duty in January-February, 1864, and present or accounted for until captured at or near Petersburg, Virginia, April 2, 1865. Confined at Point Lookout, Maryland, until released on June 21, 1865, after taking the Oath of Allegiance.

WHITE, ROBERT, Private
Previously served in Company M, 1st Regiment N.C. Infantry (6 months, 1861). Enlisted in this company on February 15, 1862, for the war. Present or accounted for until captured at Falling Waters, Maryland, July 14, 1863. Confined at Old Capitol Prison, Washington, D.C., until transferred to Point Lookout, Maryland, on or about August 23, 1863. Transferred to Elmira, New York, August 18, 1864. Paroled at Elmira on March 10, 1865, and transferred to Boulware's Wharf, James River, Virginia, where he received March 15, 1865, for exchange.

WILLIAMS, JAMES, Private
Resided in Chowan County where he enlisted at age 18, February 15, 1862, for the war. Reported absent without leave on May 1, 1862, and was listed as a deserter in May-June, 1863. [May have served previously in Company M, 1st Regiment N.C. Infantry (6 months, 1861).]

WINGATE, JOSEPH W., Private
Resided in Perquimans County where he enlisted at age 20, April 26, 1862, for the war. Present or accounted for until hospitalized at Richmond, Virginia, January 30, 1864, with a gunshot wound of the left arm; however, place and date wounded not reported. Retired April 8, 1864.

COMPANY G

This company was composed primarily of men from Orange and Chatham counties and began organizing at Chapel Hill on or about February 26, 1862. On March 31, 1862, it was mustered in as Company G of this regiment. After that date the company functioned as a part of the regiment, and its history for the war period is recorded as a part of the regimental history.

The information contained in the following roster of the company was compiled principally from company muster rolls for May, 1862, through February, 1865. No company muster rolls were found for the period prior to May, 1862, or for the period after February, 1865. In addition to the company muster rolls, Roll of Honor records, receipt rolls, hospital records, prisoner of war records, and other primary records, supplemented by state pension applications, United Daughters of the Confederacy records, and postwar rosters and histories, all provided useful information.

OFFICERS

CAPTAINS

JENNINGS, JAMES R.
Previously served as 1st Lieutenant in Company D, 1st Regiment N.C. Infantry (6 months, 1861). Appointed Captain of this company to rank from February 6, 1862. Present or accounted for until he died at Camp Davis, near Wilmington, September

16, 1862, of "yellow fever."

FREELAND, JOHN FLETCHER
Previously served as Sergeant in Company D, 1st Regiment N.C. Infantry (6 months, 1861). Appointed 1st Lieutenant in this company to rank from February 6, 1862, and was promoted to Captain to rank from September 16, 1862. Present or accounted for until paroled at Appomattox Court House, Virginia, April 9, 1865.

LIEUTENANTS

McDADE, JOHN H., 1st Lieutenant
Previously served as Private in Company D, 1st Regiment N.C. Infantry (6 months, 1861). Appointed 2nd Lieutenant in this company to rank from February 6, 1862, and was promoted to 1st Lieutenant to rank from September 16, 1862. Present or accounted for until killed at Gettysburg, Pennsylvania, July 1, 1863.

NORWOOD, THOMAS FLETCHER, 2nd Lieutenant
Resided in Chatham County and enlisted at age 21. Appointed 2nd Lieutenant to rank from February 6, 1862. Present or accounted for until he resigned on August 7, 1862, by reason of "very feeble" health.

TENNEY, NATHANIEL B., 2nd Lieutenant
Resided in Orange County where he enlisted at age 26, February 26, 1862, for the war. Mustered in as 1st Sergeant and appointed 2nd Lieutenant to rank from September 17, 1862. Present or accounted for until killed at Gettysburg, Pennsylvania, July 1, 1863.

WADDELL, DUNCAN C., 1st Lieutenant
Resided in Chatham County and enlisted in Orange County at age 18, February 15, 1863, for the war. Mustered in as Private. Present or accounted for until wounded and captured at Gettysburg, Pennsylvania, July 1-5, 1863. Confined at Fort McHenry, Maryland, and at Fort Delaware, Delaware, until exchanged at an unspecified date. Appointed 1st Lieutenant to rank from July 30, 1863, "for gallant conduct on the field at Gettysburg." Returned to duty in November-December, 1863, and present or accounted for until hospitalized at Petersburg, Virginia, August 26, 1864, with a gunshot wound of the right lung. Place and date wounded not reported. Reported absent wounded or absent on detached service through March, 1865.

WHITAKER, JAMES RUFFIN, 2nd Lieutenant
Resided in Orange County where he enlisted at age 24, February 26, 1862, for the war. Mustered in as Corporal and promoted to Sergeant in September-October, 1862. Appointed 2nd Lieutenant to rank from July 30, 1863. Present or accounted for until captured at Hatcher's Run, Virginia, April 2, 1865. Confined at Old Capitol Prison, Washington, D.C., until transferred to Johnson's Island, Ohio, April 9, 1865. Released at Johnson's Island on June 20, 1865, after taking the Oath of Allegiance. [May have served previously in Company D, 1st Regiment N.C. Infantry (6 months, 1861).]

WHITTED, WILLIAM GRAHAM, 3rd Lieutenant
Previously served as Private in Company D, 1st Regiment N.C. Infantry (6 months, 1861). Enlisted

in this company on February 26, 1862, for the war. Mustered in as Sergeant. Present or accounted for until captured at Falling Waters, Maryland, July 14, 1863. Confined at Baltimore, Maryland, and at Point Lookout, Maryland, until paroled and transferred for exchange on or about March 3, 1864. Returned to duty in May-June, 1864, and was appointed 3rd Lieutenant on October 11, 1864. Present or accounted for until wounded in the thigh at Hatcher's Run, Virginia, February 5, 1865. Reported absent wounded until furloughed for sixty days on or about March 14, 1865.

WILLIAMS, JAMES W., 2nd Lieutenant
Previously served as Sergeant in Company D, 1st Regiment N.C. Infantry (6 months, 1861). Enlisted in this company on or about February 26, 1862, for the war. Mustered in as Private. Present or accounted for until promoted to Ordnance Sergeant on May 1, 1862, and transferred to the Field and Staff of this regiment. Transferred back to this company upon appointment as 2nd Lieutenant to rank from September 10, 1862. Present or accounted for until killed at Gettysburg, Pennsylvania, July 1, 1863.

NONCOMMISSIONED OFFICERS AND PRIVATES

ALLEN, RUFFIN, Private
Resided in Orange County where he enlisted at age 33, February 1, 1863, for the war. Present or accounted for until captured at Bristoe Station, Virginia, October 14, 1863. Confined at Old Capitol Prison, Washington, D.C., until transferred to Point Lookout, Maryland, October 27, 1863. Died at Point Lookout on September 3, 1864. Cause of death not reported.

ANDREWS, GEORGE, Private
Enlisted in Davie County. Enlistment date given as April 23, 1861; however, he was not listed on the rolls of this company until November-December, 1864. Present or accounted for through February, 1865. No further records.

ANDREWS, WESLEY, Private
Resided in Orange County where he enlisted at age 30, February 1, 1863, for the war. Present or accounted for until wounded and captured at Gettysburg, Pennsylvania, July 1-3, 1863. Died at Gettysburg on or about July 10, 1863, of wounds.

AVERETT, D. T., Private
Previously served in Company B, 9th Regiment N.C. State Troops (1st Regiment N.C. Cavalry). Transferred to this company in November-December, 1864. Present or accounted for until captured at or near Petersburg, Virginia, April 2, 1865. Confined at Fort Delaware, Delaware, until released on June 19, 1865, after taking the Oath of Allegiance.

BARTS, ALLEN, Private
Enlisted in Wake County on August 18, 1864, for the war. Present or accounted for through April 10, 1865.

BENNETT, H. M., Private
Enlisted in Wake County on August 15, 1864, for the

war. Present or accounted for through February, 1865.

BLACKWOOD, EDMOND, Private
Enlisted at Camp Hill on April 10, 1864, for the war. Present or accounted for until wounded at or near Spotsylvania Court House, Virginia, on or about May 10, 1864. Returned to duty in September-October, 1864, and present or accounted for until he deserted to the enemy on or about March 3, 1865. Released on or about March 7, 1865, after taking the Oath of Allegiance.

BLACKWOOD, PHILO, Private
Previously served in Company D, 1st Regiment N.C. Infantry (6 months, 1861). Enlisted in this company on February 26, 1862, for the war. Present or accounted for until wounded at Gettysburg, Pennsylvania, July 1, 1863. Returned to duty in September-October, 1863, and present or accounted for through February, 1865.

BLACKWOOD, ROBERT, Private
Resided in Orange County and enlisted at age 30, February 26, 1862, for the war. No further records.

BOOKER, J. C., Private
Enlisted in Orange County on August 15, 1864, for the war. Present or accounted for through February, 1865.

BOON, JAMES H., Private
Enlisted in Wake County on September 28, 1864, for the war. Present or accounted for until captured at or near Petersburg, Virginia, April 2, 1865. Confined at Point Lookout, Maryland, until released on June 3, 1865, after taking the Oath of Allegiance.

BROCKWELL, A. J., Private
Resided in Orange County where he enlisted at age 37, February 1, 1863, for the war. Present or accounted for until captured at or near Petersburg, Virginia, April 2, 1865. Confined at Fort Delaware, Delaware, until released on June 19, 1865, after taking the Oath of Allegiance.

BROCKWELL, ANDERSON, Private
Born in Orange County where he resided as a farmer prior to enlisting in Orange County at age 52, February 26, 1862, for the war. Present or accounted for until discharged on September 16, 1863, by reason of injuries of the spine and pelvic viscera received in a railroad accident.

BURCH, DUDLEY Y., Private
Resided in Orange County where he enlisted at age 30, February 26, 1862, for the war. Present or accounted for until wounded in the head and captured near Petersburg, Virginia, March 25, 1865. Confined at Point Lookout, Maryland, until released on June 23, 1865, after taking the Oath of Allegiance.

BURGESS, HENRY T., Private
Resided in Orange County and was by occupation a farmer prior to enlisting in Orange County at age 19, February 26, 1862, for the war. Present or accounted for until he died at home in Orange County on July 16, 1862. Cause of death not reported.

BURGESS, WASHINGTON, Private
Resided in Orange County where he enlisted at age

24, February 26, 1862, for the war. Present or accounted for until captured at or near Petersburg, Virginia, April 2, 1865. Confined at Fort Delaware, Delaware, until released on June 19, 1865, after taking the Oath of Allegiance.

CAMPBELL, ROBERT, Private

Resided in Orange County where he enlisted at age 19, February 26, 1862, for the war. Present or accounted for through August, 1864. Company muster rolls dated September, 1864-February, 1865, indicate that he was a prisoner of war; however, records of the Federal Provost Marshal do not substantiate that report. [May have served previously in Company D, 1st Regiment N.C. Infantry (6 months, 1861).] No further records.

CANADY, GIDEON, Private

Born in Wake County and resided in Orange County where he was by occupation a farmer prior to enlisting in Orange County at age 48, February 26, 1862, for the war. Present or accounted for until discharged on September 12, 1863, by reason of "chronic lameness caused probably by rheumatism."

CANADY, RUFFIN, Private

Enlisted in Wake County on or about July 17, 1864, for the war. Present or accounted for through February, 1865.

CATES, JOHN W., Private

Resided in Orange County where he enlisted at age 19, February 26, 1862, for the war. Present or accounted for until hospitalized at Richmond, Virginia, August 16, 1864, with a gunshot wound of the right shoulder; however, place and date wounded not reported. Returned to duty in September-October, 1864, and present or accounted for until he deserted to the enemy on or about March 20, 1865. Released on or about March 25, 1865, after taking the Oath of Allegiance.

CATES, STEPHEN P., Private

Resided in Orange County and enlisted at age 26, February 26, 1862, for the war. No further records.

CATES, THOMAS, Private

Enlisted in Wake County on October 19, 1864, for the war. Present or accounted for until he deserted to the enemy on or about March 20, 1865. Released on or about March 25, 1865, after taking the Oath of Allegiance.

CATES, WILLIAM, Private

Resided in Orange County where he enlisted at age 28, February 26, 1862, for the war. Reported absent without leave in May-June, 1862, and was reported "in confinement" in July-August, 1862. Deserted on November 3, 1862. Died in hospital at Raleigh on January 28, 1863, of "feb[ris] typhoides."

CATES, WILLIAM B., Private

Resided in Orange County where he enlisted at age 27, February 26, 1862, for the war. Present or accounted for until he died at Raleigh on January 27, 1863. Cause of death not reported.

CHEEK, JOHN A., Private

Resided in Orange County where he enlisted at age 30, February 26, 1862, for the war. Present or accounted for until captured at Falling Waters, Maryland, July 14, 1863. Confined at Baltimore,

Maryland, and at Point Lookout, Maryland, until paroled and transferred for exchange on or about March 3, 1864. Returned to duty in May-June, 1864, and present or accounted for until he deserted to the enemy on or about March 7, 1865. Released on or about March 7, 1865, after taking the Oath of Allegiance.

CHEEK, NATHANIEL J., Sergeant

Resided in Orange County where he enlisted at age 26, February 26, 1862, for the war. Mustered in as Private and promoted to Corporal in November-December, 1863. Promoted to Sergeant on October 11, 1864. Present or accounted for until captured at or near Petersburg, Virginia, April 2, 1865. Confined at Fort Delaware, Delaware, until released on June 19, 1865, after taking the Oath of Allegiance.

CHEEK, THOMAS F., Private

Enlisted in Orange County on September 28, 1863, for the war. Present or accounted for until captured near Petersburg, Virginia, October 27, 1864. Confined at Point Lookout, Maryland, until paroled and transferred for exchange on March 17, 1865. Received at Boulware's Wharf, James River, Virginia, March 19, 1865, for exchange.

CHEEK, VIRGIL C., Sergeant

Resided in Orange County where he enlisted at age 18, February 1, 1863, for the war. Mustered in as Private and promoted to Corporal on October 11, 1864. Promoted to Sergeant in March-April, 1865. Present or accounted for until captured at or near Petersburg, Virginia, April 2, 1865. Confined at Fort Delaware, Delaware, until released on June 19, 1865, after taking the Oath of Allegiance.

CHISENHALL, SAMUEL, Private

Resided in Orange County where he enlisted at age 20, February 26, 1862, for the war. Present or accounted for until captured at or near Petersburg, Virginia, April 2, 1865. Confined at Point Lookout, Maryland, where he died May 8, 1865, of "pneumonia." [May have served previously in Company D, 1st Regiment N.C. Infantry (6 months, 1861).]

CLEMENTS, GEORGE R., Private

Enlisted in Orange County on March 20, 1864, for the war. Present or accounted for until he deserted to the enemy on or about March 20, 1865. Released on or about March 25, 1865, after taking the Oath of Allegiance.

CLEMENTS, JAMES H., Private

Previously served in Company D, 1st Regiment N.C. Infantry (6 months, 1861). Enlisted in this company on February 26, 1862, for the war. Present or accounted for until captured near Petersburg, Virginia, October 27, 1864. Confined at Point Lookout, Maryland, until paroled and transferred for exchange on March 17, 1865. Company records do not indicate whether he returned to duty; however, he was paroled at Raleigh on May 11, 1865.

CLEMENTS, JOHN R., Sergeant

Previously served as Private in Company D, 1st Regiment N.C. Infantry (6 months, 1861). Enlisted in this company on February 26, 1862, for the war. Mustered in as Private and promoted to Sergeant in July-August, 1863. Present or accounted for until hospitalized at Richmond, Virginia, July 15, 1863, with a contusion of the right hip; however, place and date injured not reported. Returned to duty prior to September 1, 1863. Present or accounted for until hospitalized at Danville, Virginia, on or about May 18, 1864, with a gunshot wound of the hand; however, place and date wounded not reported. Returned to duty in September-October, 1864, and present or accounted for until he deserted to the enemy on or about March 2, 1865. Released on or about March 6, 1865, after taking the Oath of Allegiance.

CLEMENTS, WILLIAM G., Private

Resided in Orange County where he enlisted at age 18, February 26, 1862, for the war. Present or accounted for until hospitalized at Danville, Virginia, on or about June 16, 1864, with a gunshot wound of the finger; however, place and date wounded not reported. Returned to duty in September-October, 1864, and present or accounted for until captured at or near Petersburg, Virginia, April 2, 1865. Confined at Point Lookout, Maryland, until released on June 26, 1865, after taking the Oath of Allegiance.

COLE, GEORGE, Private

Resided in Orange County where he enlisted at age 20, February 26, 1862, for the war. Present or accounted for until hospitalized at Wilmington on or about July 5, 1862, with "febris typhoid." Died at Wilmington on July 12, 1862. [May have served previously in Company D, 1st Regiment N.C. Infantry (6 months, 1861).]

COUCH, WILLIAM H., Corporal

Previously served as Private in Company D, 1st Regiment N.C. Infantry (6 months, 1861). Enlistment date in this company reported as July 15, 1862; however, he was not listed in the records of this company until May-June, 1864. Mustered in as Corporal. Present or accounted for until captured near Petersburg, Virginia, October 27, 1864. Confined at Point Lookout, Maryland, where he died April 24, 1865, of "chronic diarrhoea."

CRAIG, JOHN W., Private

Enlisted in Orange County. Enlistment date reported as July 15, 1862; however, he was not listed in the records of this company until May-June, 1864. Present or accounted for until he died on February 20, 1865. Place and cause of death not reported.

CRUMPLER, H. C., Private

Enlisted in Orange County on August 11, 1864, for the war. Present or accounted for until transferred to Barringer's cavalry brigade on December 6, 1864. Regiment to which transferred not reported.

DANIEL, ALGERNON, Private

Born in Orange County where he resided as a farmer prior to enlisting in Orange County at age 18, February 26, 1862, for the war. Present or accounted for until wounded in both hips and captured at Gettysburg, Pennsylvania, July 1-4, 1863. Hospitalized at Gettysburg until transferred to Davids Island, New York Harbor, July 17-24, 1863. Transferred to Fort Delaware, Delaware, April 19, 1864. Exchanged on September 18, 1864. Reported absent wounded until retired on or about February 17, 1865, by reason of wounds received at Gettysburg.

DANIEL, ALVIS, Private

Born in Chatham County and was by occupation a cabinetmaker prior to enlisting in Orange County at age 27, February 26, 1862, for the war. Present or accounted for until discharged on June 22, 1863, by reason of "chronic diarrhoea with debility."

DANIEL, ROBERT, Private

Resided in Orange County where he enlisted at age 24, February 26, 1862, for the war. Present or accounted for until captured at Falling Waters, Maryland, July 14, 1863. Confined at Old Capitol Prison, Washington, D.C., until transferred to Point Lookout, Maryland, August 8, 1863. Transferred to Elmira, New York, August 16, 1864. Paroled at Elmira and transferred for exchange on or about February 20, 1865. Furloughed from hospital at Richmond, Virginia, March 6, 1865.

DAVIS, BENJAMIN, Private

Resided in Orange County where he enlisted at age 49, February 26, 1862, for the war. Present or accounted for until paroled at Raleigh on April 22, 1865.

DAVIS, DEMARCUS, Private

Born in Orange County where he resided as a farmer prior to enlisting in Orange County at age 29, February 26, 1862, for the war. Present or accounted for until discharged on March 15, 1864, by reason of "paralysis."

DAVIS, DUNCAN, Private

Resided in Orange County where he enlisted on December 15, 1863, for the war. Present or accounted for until captured near Petersburg, Virginia, October 27, 1864. Confined at Point Lookout, Maryland, until released on June 12, 1865, after taking the Oath of Allegiance.

DAVIS, FENDALL, Private

Resided in Orange County where he enlisted at age 18, May 3, 1862, for the war. Present or accounted for until wounded in the right hip at Gettysburg, Pennsylvania, July 1, 1863. Returned to duty prior to September 1, 1863, and present or accounted for until he deserted to the enemy on or about March 3, 1865. Released on or about March 7, 1865, after taking the Oath of Allegiance.

DAVIS, HENRY A., Private

Resided in Orange County where he enlisted at age 18, February 26, 1862, for the war. Present or accounted for until captured at Bristoe Station, Virginia, October 14, 1863. Confined at Old Capitol Prison, Washington, D.C., until transferred to Point Lookout, Maryland, October 27, 1863. Paroled at Point Lookout and transferred for exchange on or about May 3, 1864. Returned to duty in July-August, 1864, and present or accounted for until captured at or near Petersburg, Virginia, April 2, 1865. Confined at Fort Delaware, Delaware, until released on June 19, 1865, after taking the Oath of Allegiance.

DAVIS, JAMES T., Private

Resided in Orange County where he enlisted at age 18, February 26, 1862, for the war. Present or accounted for until promoted to Musician (Drummer) in September-October, 1864, and transferred to the regimental band.

DAVIS, THOMAS C., 1st Sergeant
Resided in Orange County where he enlisted at age 24, February 26, 1862, for the war. Mustered in as Sergeant and was promoted to 1st Sergeant in July-August, 1863. Present or accounted for until wounded in the right ankle and captured at Gettysburg, Pennsylvania, July 1-4, 1863. Hospitalized at Gettysburg until transferred to Davids Island, New York Harbor, July 17-24, 1863. Paroled and exchanged on or about September 8, 1863. Returned to duty in January-February, 1864, and present or accounted for until hospitalized at Richmond, Virginia, June 2, 1864, with a gunshot wound. Place and date wounded not reported. Returned to duty in July-August, 1864, and present or accounted for until captured at or near Petersburg, Virginia, April 2, 1865. Confined at Fort Delaware, Delaware, until released on June 8, 1865. [May have served previously in Company D, 1st Regiment N.C. Infantry (6 months, 1861).]

DOUGLASS, ASHLEY, Private
Born in Orange County and resided in Chatham County where he was by occupation a farmer prior to enlisting in Orange County at age 49, February 26, 1862, for the war. Present or accounted for until discharged on September 2, 1862, by reason of an injury of the "left lower maxillary bone."

DURHAM, WILLIAM S., Private
Previously served in Company D, 1st Regiment N.C. Infantry (6 months, 1861). Enlisted in this company on February 26, 1862, for the war. Mustered in as Corporal but was reduced to ranks in May-June, 1863. Present or accounted for until wounded at Gettysburg, Pennsylvania, July 1, 1863. Died July 3, 1863, of wounds.

EDWARDS, CORNELIUS, Private
Resided in Orange County where he enlisted at age 26, February 26, 1862, for the war. Present or accounted for until wounded at Gettysburg, Pennsylvania, July 1, 1863. Died at Williamsport, Maryland, July 6, 1863, of wounds.

FERRELL, LUICO, Corporal
Enlisted in Orange County on July 15, 1862, for the war. Mustered in as Private and promoted to Corporal on October 11, 1864. Present or accounted for until reported wounded and in hospital in September-October, 1864; however, place and date wounded not reported. Died on November 27, 1864. Place and cause of death not reported.

FLINTOFF, WILLIAM D., Private
Resided in Orange County where he enlisted at age 18, February 26, 1862, for the war. Present or accounted for until wounded at Gettysburg, Pennsylvania, July 1-3, 1863. Returned to duty in January-February, 1864. Present or accounted for until hospitalized at Richmond, Virginia, October 2, 1864, with a gunshot wound of the right side; however, place and date wounded not reported. Died in hospital at Richmond on November 9, 1864, of wounds.

FOWLER, WASHINGTON, Private
Resided in Orange County where he enlisted at age 29, September 6, 1862, for the war. Present or accounted for until paroled at Appomattox Court

House, Virginia, April 9, 1865.

FRANKLIN, WILLIAM R., Private
Resided in Orange County where he enlisted at age 38, February 26, 1862, for the war. Present or accounted for through February, 1865.

GARRATT, ESAU, Private
Resided in Orange County where he enlisted at age 19, February 26, 1862, for the war. Present or accounted for until wounded in the lung and captured at Gettysburg, Pennsylvania, July 1-3, 1863. Hospitalized at Hagerstown, Maryland, where he died July 11, 1863.

GARRETT, WOODSTON, Private
Resided in Orange County where he enlisted at age 21, February 26, 1862, for the war. Present or accounted for until captured near Petersburg, Virginia, October 27, 1864. Confined at Point Lookout, Maryland, until paroled and transferred for exchange on or about February 10, 1865. Company records do not indicate whether he returned to duty; however, he was paroled at Greensboro on May 20, 1865.

GATTIS, JAMES B., Private
Resided in Orange County where he enlisted. Enlistment date given as October 26, 1863; however, he was not listed on the rolls of this company until May-June, 1864. Present or accounted for until captured at or near Petersburg, Virginia, April 2, 1865. Confined at Point Lookout, Maryland, until released on June 27, 1865, after taking the Oath of Allegiance.

GATTIS, JAMES K., Private
Resided in Orange County where he enlisted at age 52, May 3, 1862, for the war. Present or accounted for until he died at Chapel Hill on February 8, 1864. Cause of death not reported.

GATTIS, JOHN T., Private
Enlisted in Orange County on April 11, 1864, for the war. Present or accounted for until wounded at Hatcher's Run, Virginia, on or about February 9, 1865. North Carolina pension records indicate that he survived the war.

GEORGE, DAVID, Private
Resided in Columbus County. Place and date of enlistment not reported. Took the Oath of Allegiance at Point Lookout, Maryland, June 27, 1865. Place and date captured not reported.

GRAVES, C. J. C., Private
Resided in Wake County. Place and date of enlistment not reported. Deserted to the enemy on or about March 14, 1865. Released on or about March 18, 1865, after taking the Oath of Allegiance.

HARWOOD, WESLEY J., Sergeant
Previously served as Private in Company D, 1st Regiment N.C. Infantry (6 months, 1861). Enlisted in this company on February 26, 1862, for the war. Mustered in as Corporal and promoted to Sergeant on October 11, 1864. Present or accounted for until paroled at Appomattox Court House, Virginia, April 9, 1865.

HATHCOCK, CARNEY, Private
Resided in Chatham County and enlisted in Orange County at age 20, February 26, 1862, for the war.

Present or accounted for until hospitalized at Wilmington on or about July 16, 1862, with "febris typhoides." Died at Wilmington on July 21, 1862.

HATHCOCK, FRANKLIN, Private

Enlisted in Orange County on February 26, 1862, for the war. Present or accounted for until he deserted at Orange Court House, Virginia, July 21, 1863. Returned to duty on December 1, 1863, and present or accounted for until reported absent without leave on company muster roll dated January-February, 1865.

HESTER, JOHN W., Private

Resided in Orange County where he enlisted at age 24, February 26, 1862, for the war. Present or accounted for until captured at or near Petersburg, Virginia, April 2, 1865. Confined at Fort Delaware, Delaware, until released on June 19, 1865, after taking the Oath of Allegiance. [May have served previously in Company D, 1st Regiment N.C. Infantry (6 months, 1861).]

HOLLOWAY, WILLIAM H., Private

Enlisted in Orange County on August 13, 1864, for the war. Present or accounted for until transferred to Company E, 47th Regiment N.C. Troops, February 1, 1865.

HUNTER, ANDERSON, Private

Resided in Orange County where he enlisted at age 23, February 1, 1863, for the war. Present or accounted for until captured at or near Petersburg, Virginia, April 2, 1865. Confined at Fort Delaware, Delaware, until released on June 19, 1865, after taking the Oath of Allegiance.

HUSKEY, WILLIAM, Private

Resided in Orange County where he enlisted at age 24, February 26, 1862, for the war. Present or accounted for until he deserted to the enemy on October 20, 1864. Confined at Camp Hamilton, Virginia, until released on November 16, 1864, after taking the Oath of Amnesty. [May have served previously in Company D, 1st Regiment N.C. Infantry (6 months, 1861).]

IVEY, EDWARD, Private

Resided in Orange County where he enlisted at age 51, February 26, 1862, for the war. Present or accounted for until hospitalized at Richmond, Virginia, on or about April 11, 1864, with a wound; however, place and date wounded not reported. Retired to the Invalid Corps on or about April 20, 1864.

IVEY, THOMAS, Private

Resided in Orange County where he enlisted at age 40, February 26, 1862, for the war. Present or accounted for until discharged at Camp Mangum on May 9, 1862. Reason discharged not reported.

IVEY, WILLIAM G., Corporal

Resided in Orange County where he enlisted at age 23, February 26, 1862, for the war. Mustered in as Corporal. Present or accounted for until wounded and captured at Gettysburg, Pennsylvania, July 1-3, 1863. Hospitalized at Gettysburg until transferred to Davids Island, New York Harbor, on or about July 23, 1863. Died at Davids Island on August 8, 1863, of wounds.

JOLLY, WILLIAM, Private

Resided in Orange County where he enlisted at age 23, February 26, 1862, for the war. Present or accounted for until captured at Falling Waters, Maryland, July 14, 1863. Confined at Old Capitol Prison, Washington, D.C., until transferred to Point Lookout, Maryland, August 8, 1863. Transferred to Elmira, New York, August 16, 1864. Paroled at Elmira on October 11, 1864, and transferred to Venus Point, Savannah River, Georgia, for exchange. Company muster rolls indicate he died on November 10, 1864; however, records of the Federal Provost Marshal indicate he was received for exchange at Venus Point on November 15, 1864. No further records.

KING, BAXTER, Private

Previously served in Company D, 1st Regiment N.C. Infantry (6 months, 1861). Enlisted in this company on February 26, 1862, for the war. Present or accounted for until wounded in the hip at Gettysburg, Pennsylvania, July 1-3, 1863. Returned to duty in November-December, 1863, and present or accounted for until captured near Petersburg, Virginia, March 25, 1865. Confined at Point Lookout, Maryland, until released on June 28, 1865, after taking the Oath of Allegiance.

KING, BELLFIELD, Private

Resided in Orange or Chatham counties prior to enlisting in Orange County at age 20, May 3, 1862, for the war. Present or accounted for until captured at or near Petersburg, Virginia, on or about April 2, 1865. Confined at Fort Delaware, Delaware, until released on June 19, 1865, after taking the Oath of Allegiance.

KING, JAMES, Private

Enlisted in Wake County on October 26, 1864, for the war. Present or accounted for until captured at or near Petersburg, Virginia, April 2, 1865. Confined at Point Lookout, Maryland, until released on June 28, 1865, after taking the Oath of Allegiance.

KING, JOHN, Private

Resided in Orange County where he enlisted at age 39, February 26, 1862, for the war. Present or accounted for until captured at or near Petersburg, Virginia, April 2, 1865. Confined at Fort Delaware, Delaware, until released on June 19, 1865, after taking the Oath of Allegiance.

KING, RUFUS, Private

Resided in Orange County where he enlisted at age 20, February 26, 1862, for the war. Present or accounted for until captured at Falling Waters, Maryland, July 14, 1863. Confined at Old Capitol Prison, Washington, D. C., until transferred to Point Lookout, Maryland, August 8, 1863. Paroled at Point Lookout and transferred to Venus Point, Savannah River, Georgia, where he was received on November 15, 1864, for exchange. Returned to duty in January-February, 1865, and present or accounted for until he deserted to the enemy on or about March 20, 1865. Released on or about March 25, 1865, after taking the Oath of Allegiance.

KING, W. D., Private

Resided in Wake County and enlisted on August 15,

1864, for the war. Present or accounted for until captured at or near Petersburg, Virginia, April 2, 1865. Confined at Fort Delaware, Delaware, until released on June 19, 1865, after taking the Oath of Allegiance.

KING, WHITFIELD, Private
Born in Orange County and resided in Chatham County where he was by occupation a farmer prior to enlisting in Orange County at age 18, May 3, 1862, for the war. Died at Camp Davis, near Wilmington, on or about June 10, 1862, of "measles."

KING, WILLIAM H., Private
Resided in Orange County where he enlisted at age 24, February 1, 1863, for the war. Present or accounted for until captured near Petersburg, Virginia, June 14, 1864. Confined at Point Lookout, Maryland, until paroled and transferred to Venus Point, Savannah River, Georgia, where he was received November 15, 1864, for exchange. Reported absent without leave on company muster roll dated January-February, 1865.

KING, WILLIS, Private
Enlisted in Orange County on December 1, 1863, for the war. Present or accounted for through February, 1865; however, he was reported absent sick during most of that period.

LEWTER, CHARLES M., Corporal
Enlisted in Orange County. Enlistment date reported as July 15, 1862; however, he was not listed on the rolls of this company until May-June, 1864. Promoted to Corporal on October 11, 1864. Present or accounted for until captured near Petersburg, Virginia, October 27, 1864. Confined at Point Lookout, Maryland, until paroled and transferred to Boulware's Wharf, James River, Virginia, where he was received March 30, 1865, for exchange.

LLOYD, JOHN W., Private
Resided in Chatham County and enlisted in Orange County at age 18, February 26, 1862, for the war. Died in hospital at Raleigh on April 5, 1862, of "int[ermittent] fever and meningitis."

LLOYD, THADEUS, Private
Resided in Orange County where he enlisted at age 23, February 26, 1862, for the war. Present or accounted for until wounded at Gettysburg, Pennsylvania, July 1-3, 1863. Returned to duty prior to September 1, 1863, and present or accounted for until he deserted to the enemy in March-April, 1865. Released on or about May 29, 1865, after taking the Oath of Allegiance.

LLOYD, WILLIAM, Private
Enlisted in Orange County. Enlistment date reported as July 15, 1862; however, he was not listed on the rolls of this company until May-June, 1864. Present or accounted for until captured near Petersburg, Virginia, October 27, 1864. Confined at Point Lookout, Maryland, until released on June 12, 1865, after taking the Oath of Allegiance.

McDADE, HENRY L., Private
Resided in Orange County where he enlisted at age 24, February 26, 1862, for the war. Mustered in as Sergeant. Present or accounted for until captured at

Martinsburg, West Virginia, July 23, 1863. Confined at Baltimore, Maryland, and at Fort McHenry, Maryland, until transferred to Point Lookout, Maryland, November 1, 1863. Reduced to ranks on October 11, 1864, while a prisoner of war. Paroled at Point Lookout and transferred to Cox's Landing, James River, Virginia, February 14-15, 1865, for exchange. Paroled at Appomattox Court House, Virginia, April 9, 1865.

MANGUM, W. C., Private
Enlisted in Granville County. Enlistment date reported as August 28, 1863; however, he was not listed on the rolls of this company until November-December, 1864. Present or accounted for until paroled at Appomattox Court House, Virginia, April 9, 1865.

MANN, CASWELL S., Private
Previously served in Company E, 63rd Regiment N.C. Troops (5th Regiment N.C. Cavalry). Transferred to this company in September-December, 1864. Present or accounted for until captured in hospital at Richmond, Virginia, April 3, 1865. Confined at Libby Prison, Richmond, until transferred to Newport News, Virginia, April 23, 1865. Released at Newport News on July 3, 1865, after taking the Oath of Allegiance.

MANN, WILLIAM S., Private
Previously served in Company E, 63rd Regiment N.C. Troops (5th Regiment N.C. Cavalry). Transferred to this company on February 16, 1865. Deserted to the enemy on or about March 14, 1865. Released on or about March 18, 1865, after taking the Oath of Allegiance.

MARCOM, HENDERSON, Private
Resided in Orange County where he enlisted at age 35, February 26, 1862, for the war. Present or accounted for until he deserted on or about October 10, 1863.

MERRITT, JAMES Y., Private
Enlisted in Orange County on April 2, 1864, for the war. Present or accounted for until reported absent without leave on company muster roll dated September-October, 1864. Returned to duty on December 12, 1864, and present or accounted for until he deserted to the enemy on or about March 14, 1865. Released on or about March 18, 1865, after taking the Oath of Allegiance.

MINCEY, JOHN, Private
Resided in Orange County and enlisted at age 20, February 26, 1862, for the war. Present or accounted for until wounded in the left foot at Gettysburg, Pennsylvania, July 3, 1863. Returned to duty in January-February, 1864, and present or accounted for until captured at or near Petersburg, Virginia, April 2, 1865. Confined at Point Lookout, Maryland, until released on June 15, 1865, after taking the Oath of Allegiance.

NEVILL, JOHN S., Private
Resided in Chatham County and enlisted in Orange County on February 26, 1862, for the war. Present or accounted for until discharged on July 21, 1862. Reason discharged not reported.

NEVILLE, JOHN, Private
Resided in Orange County and enlisted at Camp

Davis at age 32, August 29, 1862, for the war. Present or accounted for until captured near Petersburg, Virginia, October 27, 1864. Confined at Point Lookout, Maryland, until released on June 29, 1865, after taking the Oath of Allegiance.

NORWOOD, DAVID J., Corporal
Resided in Chatham County and enlisted in Orange County at age 20, February 26, 1862, for the war. Mustered in as Private and promoted to Corporal in September-October, 1862. Present or accounted for until captured at Gettysburg, Pennsylvania, July 3, 1863. Confined at Fort Delaware, Delaware, where he died September 14, 1863, of "inf[ection] of lungs."

NUTT, E. D., Private
Enlisted in Wake County on October 19, 1864, for the war. Present or accounted for until he deserted to the enemy on or about March 3, 1865. Released on or about March 7, 1865, after taking the Oath of Allegiance.

PEARSON, EDWARD, Private
Resided in Chatham County and was by occupation a farmer prior to enlisting in Orange County at age 20, February 26, 1862, for the war. Present or accounted for until he died at Wilmington on July 19, 1862, of "fever."

PEARSON, FORREST, Private
Resided in Chatham County and enlisted in Orange County at age 18, February 26, 1862, for the war. Present or accounted for until he died at Camp Mangum, near Raleigh, April 6, 1862, of disease.

PEARSON, HENRY C., Private
Resided in Chatham County and enlisted in Orange County at age 35, February 26, 1862, for the war. Present or accounted for until he deserted to the enemy on or about March 14, 1865. Released on or about March 18, 1865, after taking the Oath of Allegiance.

PENDERGRASS, C. H., Private
Resided in Orange County where he enlisted at age 19, February 1, 1863, for the war. Present or accounted for until wounded in the right shoulder at Gettysburg, Pennsylvania, July 1-3, 1863. Returned to duty prior to September 1, 1863, and present or accounted for until captured near Petersburg, Virginia, October 27, 1864. Confined at Point Lookout, Maryland, until released on June 15, 1865, after taking the Oath of Allegiance.

PENDERGRASS, GEORGE, Private
Resided in Orange County where he enlisted at age 20, February 26, 1862, for the war. Present or accounted for until captured at Bristoe Station, Virginia, October 14, 1863. Confined at Old Capitol Prison, Washington, D. C., until transferred to Point Lookout, Maryland, October 27, 1863. Paroled and transferred to Boulware's Wharf, James River, Virginia, where he was received March 16, 1865, for exchange.

PENDERGRASS, GEORGE W., Private
Born in Orange County where he resided as a farmer prior to enlisting in Orange County at age 36, May 9, 1862, for the war. Present or accounted for until discharged on September 27, 1863, by reason of "chronic rheumatism."

PENDERGRASS, JAMES A., Private
Resided in Orange County where he enlisted at age 25, February 26, 1862, for the war. Present or accounted for through February, 1865.

PENDERGRASS, JAMES M., Private
Resided in Orange County where he enlisted at age 32, August 29, 1862, for the war. Present or accounted for until he died in hospital at Richmond, Virginia, October 4, 1864, of "febris typhoides."

PENDERGRASS, JOHN L., Private
Resided in Orange County where he enlisted at age 29, February 26, 1862, for the war. Present or accounted for until captured at Gettysburg, Pennsylvania, July 1-5, 1863. Confined at Davids Island, New York Harbor, July 17-24, 1863. Paroled and transferred for exchange on or about September 16, 1863. Returned to duty in January-February, 1864. Present or accounted for until reported absent wounded during September-December, 1864; however, place and date wounded not reported. Reported absent on detached service in January-February, 1865.

PENDERGRASS, THOMPSON, Private
Resided in Orange County where he enlisted at age 40, February 26, 1862, for the war. Present or accounted for until discharged on July 19, 1862. Reason discharged not reported.

PENDERGRASS, WILLIAM, Private
Resided in Orange County where he enlisted at age 26, April 10, 1862, for the war. Present or accounted for until killed at Gettysburg, Pennsylvania, July 1, 1863.

PENDERGRASS, WILLIAM H., Private
Resided in Orange County where he enlisted at age 20, December 20, 1862, for the war. Present or accounted for through February, 1865.

PENDIGRANT, ALVIS, Private
Resided in Orange County. Place and date of enlistment not reported. Captured at or near Petersburg, Virginia, April 2, 1865, and confined at Fort Delaware, Delaware, until released on June 19, 1865, after taking the Oath of Allegiance. [May have served previously in Company D, 1st Regiment N.C. Infantry (6 months, 1861).]

PENN, J. W., Private
Place and date of enlistment not reported. Captured in hospital at Petersburg, Virginia, April 3, 1865. No further records.

PETTY, HENRY, Private
Resided in Chatham County and enlisted in Orange County at age 19, February 26, 1862, for the war. Present or accounted for until captured at Bristoe Station, Virginia, October 14, 1863. Confined at Old Capitol Prison, Washington, D. C., until transferred to Point Lookout, Maryland, October 27, 1863. Paroled at Point Lookout and transferred to Venus Point, Savannah River, Georgia, where he was received November 15, 1864, for exchange. Returned to duty in January-February, 1865, and present or accounted for until captured at or near Petersburg, Virginia, April 2, 1865. Confined at Fort Delaware, Delaware, until released on June 19, 1865, after taking the Oath of Allegiance.

PETTY, JOHN W., Private
Previously served in Company D, 1st Regiment N. C. Infantry (6 months, 1861). Enlisted in this company on February 26, 1862, for the war. Present or accounted for until he died in hospital at Richmond, Virginia, November 29, 1863, of "meningitis."

POTTS, JOHN W., Private
Enlisted in Orange County on September 28, 1863, for the war. Present or accounted for until captured near Petersburg, Virginia, October 27, 1864. Confined at Point Lookout, Maryland, until paroled and transferred for exchange on or about February 18, 1865. Died in hospital at Richmond, Virginia, February 23, 1865, of "apoplexy."

REEVES, EDWARD, Private
Resided in Orange County where he enlisted at age 31, February 26, 1862, for the war. Present or accounted for until captured at Falling Waters, Maryland, July 14, 1863. Confined at Old Capitol Prison, Washington, D. C., until transferred to Point Lookout, Maryland, August 8, 1863. Transferred to Elmira, New York, August 16, 1864. Died at Elmira on September 24, 1864, of "chronic diarrhoea."

RIGGSBEE, HAWKINS, Private
Resided in Orange County where he enlisted on February 1, 1863, for the war. Present or accounted for until captured at or near Petersburg, Virginia, April 2, 1865. Confined at Fort Delaware, Delaware, until released on June 19, 1865, after taking the Oath of Allegiance.

RODGERS, W. T., Private
Resided in Wake County and enlisted in Orange County on August 18, 1864, for the war. Present or accounted for until captured near Petersburg, Virginia, October 27, 1864. Confined at Point Lookout, Maryland, until released on June 17, 1865, after taking the Oath of Allegiance.

ROLLINS, THOMAS B., Private
Previously served as 3rd Lieutenant in Company G, 63rd Regiment N.C. Troops (5th Regiment N.C. Cavalry). Enlisted in this company on August 13, 1864, for the war. Present or accounted for until transferred to Barringer's Cavalry Brigade on December 6, 1864. Regiment to which transferred not reported.

SARTAIN, ZERA, Private
Resided in Orange County and enlisted at age 22, February 26, 1862, for the war. Present or accounted for until discharged at Camp Mangum, near Raleigh, May 9, 1862. Reason discharged not reported.

SEAGRAVES, CHARLES J., Private
Previously served in Company E, 63rd Regiment N.C. Troops (5th Regiment N.C. Cavalry). Transferred to this company in November-December, 1864, and present or accounted for until captured in hospital at Richmond, Virginia, April 13, 1865. Transferred to the Federal Provost Marshal on April 14, 1865. No further records.

SLEDGE, WILLIAM P., Private
Previously served in Company G, 41st Regiment N.C. Troops (3rd Regiment N.C. Cavalry). Transferred to this company in November-December, 1864, and present or accounted for until captured at

or near Petersburg, Virginia, April 2, 1865. Confined at Fort Delaware, Delaware, until released on June 19, 1865, after taking the Oath of Allegiance.

SMITH, CARNEY, Corporal
Resided in Chatham County and enlisted in Orange County at age 24, February 26, 1862, for the war. Mustered in as Private and promoted to Corporal in March-April, 1865. Present or accounted for until captured at or near Petersburg, Virginia, April 2, 1865. Confined at Fort Delaware, Delaware, until released on June 19, 1865, after taking the Oath of Allegiance.

SMITH, JOHN M., Sergeant
Resided in Orange County where he enlisted at age 25, February 1, 1863, for the war. Mustered in as Private. Present or accounted for until hospitalized at Richmond, Virginia, June 19, 1864, with a gunshot wound; however, place and date wounded not reported. Returned to duty in September-October, 1864, and was promoted to Corporal on November 1, 1864. Promoted to Sergeant in March-April, 1865. Present or accounted for until captured at or near Petersburg, Virginia, April 2, 1865. Confined at Point Lookout, Maryland, until released on June 19, 1865, after taking the Oath of Allegiance.

SNIPES, JETER J., Corporal
Resided in Orange County where he enlisted at age 20, on or about May 3, 1862, for the war. Mustered in as Private and promoted to Corporal in May-July, 1863. Present or accounted for until wounded in the left lung and captured at Gettysburg, Pennsylvania, July 1-3, 1863. Hospitalized at Gettysburg until transferred to Chester, Pennsylvania, on or about July 17, 1863. Died in hospital at Chester on July 19, 1863, of wounds.

SPARROW, GEORGE W., Private
Previously served in Company D, 1st Regiment N. C. Infantry (6 months, 1861). Enlisted in this company on February 26, 1862, for the war. Present or accounted for until he deserted to the enemy on or about March 14, 1865. Released on or about March 18, 1865, after taking the Oath of Allegiance.

SPARROW, HILLORY, Private
Enlisted in Wake County on October 19, 1864, for the war. Present or accounted for until wounded in the hip at Hatcher's Run, Virginia, February 5, 1865. Furloughed on March 14, 1865, but deserted to the enemy the same day. Released on or about March 18, 1865, after taking the Oath of Allegiance.

SPARROW, HOUSTON, Private
Resided in Orange County where he enlisted at age 22, February 26, 1862, for the war. Present or accounted for until he deserted to the enemy on or about March 3, 1865. Released on or about March 7, 1865, after taking the Oath of Allegiance.

SPARROW, HUTSON, Private
Enlisted in Wake County on October 19, 1864, for the war. Present or accounted for through December, 1864. Reported absent wounded in January-February, 1865; however, place and date wounded not reported. No further records.

SPARROW, VAN B., Private
Resided in Orange County where he enlisted at age

28, February 26, 1862, for the war. Present or accounted for until wounded at Gettysburg, Pennsylvania, July 1, 1863. Returned to duty on August 8, 1863, and present or accounted for until captured at Bristoe Station, Virginia, October 14, 1863. Confined at Old Capitol Prison, Washington, D. C., until transferred to Point Lookout, Maryland, October 27, 1863. Exchanged on March 3, 1864. Returned to duty in May-June, 1864, and present or accounted for through February, 1865.

SPARROW, WILLIAM T., Private
Resided in Orange County where he enlisted at age 20, February 26, 1862, for the war. Present or accounted for until captured at Falling Waters, Maryland, July 14, 1863. Confined at Baltimore, Maryland, and at Point Lookout, Maryland, until paroled and transferred for exchange on or about March 3, 1864. Returned to duty in May-June, 1864, and present or accounted for until he deserted to the enemy on or about March 14, 1865. Released on or about March 18, 1865, after taking the Oath of Allegiance.

STEPHENS, T. GASTON, Private
Enlisted in Wake County on September 26, 1864, for the war. Present or accounted for until transferred to Company I, 41st Regiment N. C. Troops (3rd Regiment N. C. Cavalry), December 6, 1864.

STRAIN, JAMES A., Private
Resided in Orange County where he enlisted at age 22, February 26, 1862, for the war. Present or accounted for until captured near Petersburg, Virginia, October 27, 1864. Confined at Point Lookout, Maryland, where he died March 29, 1865, of "chronic diarrhoea."

STRAIN, THOMAS, Private
Resided in Orange County where he was by occupation a farmer prior to enlisting in Orange County at age 26, March 1, 1863, for the war. Present or accounted for until wounded in the left shoulder at Gettysburg, Pennsylvania, July 1, 1863. Returned to duty in January-February, 1864, and present or accounted for until captured near Petersburg, Virginia, October 27, 1864. Confined at Point Lookout, Maryland, until released on June 19, 1865, after taking the Oath of Allegiance.

STUBBLEFIELD, W. W., Private
Place and date of enlistment not reported. Captured in hospital at Richmond, Virginia, April 3, 1865, and transferred to the Federal Provost Marshal on April 14, 1865. No further records.

SUGG, WILLIAM MADISON, Sergeant
Previously served as Private in Company D, 1st Regiment N. C. Infantry (6 months, 1861). Enlisted in this company on September 10, 1862, for the war. Mustered in as Private. Present or accounted for until captured at Gettysburg, Pennsylvania, July 3, 1863. Confined at Fort Delaware, Delaware, until transferred to Point Lookout, Maryland, October 15-18, 1863. Date exchanged not reported. Promoted to Corporal in March-April, 1864, and returned to duty in May-June, 1864. Promoted to Sergeant on October 11, 1864. Present or accounted for until he deserted to the enemy on March 3, 1865. Released on or about March 7, 1865, after taking the Oath of

Allegiance.

SUITT, BENTLY, Private
Resided in Orange County where he enlisted at age 22, February 26, 1862, for the war. Present or accounted for until wounded at Gettysburg, Pennsylvania, July 1, 1863. Returned to duty in September-October, 1863, and present or accounted for through December, 1864. Reported absent without leave in January-February, 1865. No further records.

TENNEY, WILLIAM C., Private
Previously served in Company D, 1st Regiment N.C. Infantry (6 months, 1861). Enlisted in this company on February 1, 1863, for the war. Present or accounted for through June, 1863. Captured at Gettysburg, Pennsylvania, July 4, 1863, or "voluntarily surrendered" at Carlisle, Pennsylvania, August 1, 1863. Confined at Fort Delaware, Delaware, until released on May 31, 1865, after taking the Oath of Allegiance.

THOMPSON, JAMES J., Private
Born in Wake County and resided in Orange County where he was by occupation a farmer prior to enlisting in Orange County at age 25, February 26, 1862, for the war. Present or accounted for through February, 1865; however, he was absent sick or absent on detail during most of that period.

THRIFT, PINKNEY, Private
Previously served in Company D, 1st Regiment N. C. Infantry (6 months, 1861). Enlisted in this company on February 26, 1862, for the war. Present or accounted for until captured near Petersburg, Virginia, October 27, 1864. Confined at Point Lookout, Maryland, until released on May 15, 1865, after taking the Oath of Allegiance.

THRIFT, WILLIAM, Private
Resided in Chatham County and enlisted in Orange County at age 22, February 26, 1862, for the war. Present or accounted for until captured at Gettysburg, Pennsylvania, July 1-3, 1863. Confined at Fort Delaware, Delaware, until released on June 19, 1865, after taking the Oath of Allegiance.

TILLEY, JOHN, Private
Enlisted in Orange County on August 15, 1864, for the war. Present or accounted for until paroled at Greensboro on or about April 28, 1865.

TILLY, WILLIAM A., Private
Resided in Orange County where he enlisted on February 26, 1862, for the war. Mustered in as Private and promoted to Sergeant in July-August, 1863. Present or accounted for until wounded in the right leg at or near Mine Run, Virginia, November 27, 1863. Reported absent wounded until retired to the Invalid Corps on September 17, 1864. Reduced to ranks on October 11, 1864.

TRIPP, JERRY, Private
Resided in Chatham County and enlisted in Orange County at age 20, February 26, 1862, for the war. Present or accounted for until wounded in the breast and left shoulder at Gettysburg, Pennsylvania, July 1, 1863. Returned to duty in November-December, 1863, and present or accounted for until he deserted to the enemy on or about March 14, 1865. Released on or about March 18, 1865, after taking the Oath of Allegiance.

TRIPP, WILLIAM, Private
Resided in Chatham County and enlisted in Wake County on October 28, 1864, for the war. Present or accounted for until captured at or near Petersburg, Virginia, April 2, 1865. Confined at Fort Delaware, Delaware, until released on June 19, 1865, after taking the Oath of Allegiance.

TURNER, RICHARD, Private
Resided in Orange County where he enlisted at age 28, February 1, 1863, for the war. Present or accounted for until he died at Richmond, Virginia, on or about May 20, 1863, of disease.

VANN, LEMUEL D., Private
Previously served in Company D, 1st Regiment N. C. Infantry (6 months, 1861). Enlisted in this company on February 26, 1862, for the war. Present or accounted for until he deserted on July 21, 1863. Returned to duty on November 10, 1863. Present or accounted for until he deserted to the enemy on or about March 3, 1865. Released on or about March 7, 1865, after taking the Oath of Allegiance.

WALTERS, GEORGE F., Private
Resided in Orange County where he enlisted at age 18, April 25, 1863, for the war. Present or accounted for through February, 1865.

WALTERS, J. F., Private
Place and date of enlistment not reported. Deserted to the enemy on or about March 3, 1865. Released on or about March 7, 1865, after taking the Oath of Allegiance.

WALTERS, SIDNEY, Private
Resided in Orange County where he enlisted on February 22, 1865, for the war. Present or accounted for until captured at or near Petersburg, Virginia, April 2, 1865. Confined at Point Lookout, Maryland, until released on June 21, 1865, after taking the Oath of Allegiance.

WATSON, JONES M., Private
Previously served in Company D, 1st Regiment N. C. Infantry (6 months, 1861). Enlisted in this company on February 26, 1862, for the war. Mustered in as Sergeant and promoted to 1st Sergeant in September-October, 1862. Appointed 3rd Lieutenant to rank from July 30, 1863. Cashiered on September 5, 1864. Reason cashiered not reported. Enlisted in Company I, 41st Regiment N.C. Troops (3rd Regiment N.C. Cavalry), October 16, 1864.

WEATHERS, RICHARD, Private
Enlisted in Wake County on September 26, 1864, for the war. Present or accounted for until transferred to Barringer's cavalry brigade on December 6, 1864. Regiment to which transferred not reported.

WHITAKER, THOMAS J., Private
Resided in Orange County where he enlisted at age 18, February 26, 1862, for the war. Present or accounted for until captured at Falling Waters, Maryland, July 14, 1863. Confined at Old Capitol Prison, Washington, D. C., and at Baltimore, Maryland, until transferred to Point Lookout, Maryland, on or about August 23, 1863. Paroled and transferred for exchange on or about March 3, 1864. Returned to duty in May-June, 1864, and present or accounted for until he died in hospital at Richmond,

Virginia, October 10, 1864, of "diarr[hoea] chron[ic]."

WILLIAMS, FORREST, Private
Resided in Chatham County and enlisted in Orange County at age 22, February 26, 1862, for the war. Present or accounted for until he died "at home" on October 14, 1864. Cause of death not reported.

WILLIAMS, JOHNSON, Private
Resided in Chatham County and enlisted in Wake County on October 28, 1864, for the war. Present or accounted for until captured at or near Petersburg, Virginia, April 2, 1865. Confined at Fort Delaware, Delaware, until released on June 19, 1865, after taking the Oath of Allegiance.

WILLIAMS, NORRIS, Private
Resided in Chatham County and enlisted in Orange County at age 20, February 26, 1862, for the war. Present or accounted for until captured at or near Petersburg, Virginia, April 2, 1865. Confined at Fort Delaware, Delaware, until released on June 19, 1865, after taking the Oath of Allegiance.

WILLIAMS, SAMUEL, Private
Resided in Chatham County and enlisted in Orange County at age 18, February 26, 1862, for the war. Present or accounted for until wounded at Gettysburg, Pennsylvania, July 1, 1863. Reported absent wounded until retired to the Invalid Corps on August 16, 1864.

COMPANY H

This company was composed primarily of men from Mecklenburg County and began organizing at Charlotte on or about March 10, 1862. On March 31, 1862, it was mustered in as Company H of this regiment. After that date the company functioned as a part of the regiment, and its history for the war period is recorded as a part of the regimental history.

The information contained in the following roster of the company was compiled principally from company muster rolls for May, 1862, through February, 1865. No company muster rolls were found for the period prior to May, 1862, or for the period after February, 1865. In addition to the company muster rolls, Roll of Honor records, receipt rolls, hospital records, prisoner of war records, and other primary records, supplemented by state pension applications, United Daughters of the Confederacy records, and postwar rosters and histories, all provided useful information.

OFFICERS
CAPTAIN

GRIER, WILLIAM LOWNDES
Previously served as 3rd Lieutenant in Company G, 15th Regiment Mississippi Infantry. Appointed Captain of this company to rank from March 10, 1862. Present or accounted for through February, 1865.

LIEUTENANTS

BOYCE, CHARLES B., 1st Lieutenant

Resided in Mecklenburg County and enlisted at age 25. Appointed 2nd Lieutenant to rank from March 10, 1862, and was promoted to 1st Lieutenant prior to July 1, 1862. Present or accounted for until he died in Mecklenburg County on August 9, 1862. Cause of death not reported.

KNOX, JOHN H., 2nd Lieutenant

Resided in Mecklenburg County where he enlisted at age 24, March 14, 1862, for the war. Mustered in as Sergeant and appointed 2nd Lieutenant to rank from August 16, 1862. Present or accounted for until wounded in the left wrist at Gettysburg, Pennsylvania, July 1, 1863. Returned to duty in September-October, 1863, and present or accounted for until wounded at Wilderness, Virginia, May 5, 1864. Died in hospital at Staunton, Virginia, May 29, 1864, of wounds. [May have served previously in Company C, 1st Regiment N. C. Infantry (6 months, 1861).]

LOWRIE, JAMES B., 1st Lieutenant

Resided in Mecklenburg County where he enlisted at age 24, May 1, 1862, for the war. Mustered in as Private. Promoted to Commissary Sergeant on May 8, 1862, and transferred to the Field and Staff of this regiment. Reduced to ranks on or about August 9, 1862, and transferred back to this company. Appointed 1st Lieutenant to rank from October 23, 1862. Present or accounted for until killed at Gettysburg, Pennsylvania, July 1, 1863. [May have served previously in Company B, 1st Regiment N. C. Infantry (6 months, 1861).]

LOWRIE, PATRICK JOHNSON, 1st Lieutenant

Resided in Mecklenburg County and enlisted at age 30. Appointed 1st Lieutenant to rank from March 14, 1862. Present or accounted for until appointed Assistant Commissary of Subsistence (Captain) on July 11, 1862, to rank from June 1, 1862, and transferred to the Field and Staff of this regiment.

LOWRIE, ROBERT B., 1st Lieutenant

Previously served in Company C, 10th Regiment N.C. State Troops (1st Regiment N.C. Artillery). Transferred to this company on June 13, 1862, with the rank of Private. Appointed 1st Lieutenant to rank from July 30, 1863. Present or accounted for until paroled at Appomattox Court House, Virginia, April 9, 1865.

SAVILLE, JAMES M., 2nd Lieutenant

Previously served as Private in Company C, 1st Regiment N. C. Infantry (6 months, 1861). Enlisted in this company on March 14, 1862, for the war. Mustered in as 1st Sergeant and appointed 2nd Lieutenant to rank from May 26, 1862. Present or accounted for until wounded at Gettysburg, Pennsylvania, July 1-3, 1863. Returned to duty prior to September 1, 1863, and present or accounted for until wounded in the left shoulder at Jones' Farm, Virginia, September 30, 1864. Reported absent wounded through February, 1865. Captured at or near Hatcher's Run, Virginia, March 25, 1865, and confined at Old Capitol Prison, Washington, D. C., until transferred to Johnson's Island, Ohio, April 9, 1865. Released at Johnson's Island on June 17, 1865, after taking the Oath of Allegiance.

NONCOMMISSIONED OFFICERS AND PRIVATES

ABBERNATHEY, L. D., Private

Enlisted in Mecklenburg County on March 14, 1862, for the war. Never reported to the company and was listed as a deserter.

ABBERNATHY, EZEKIEL, Private

Resided in Mecklenburg County and enlisted at age 35, March 14, 1862, for the war. Present or accounted for until he died at home in Mecklenburg County on June 25, 1863, of disease.

ALEXANDER, JOHN A., Private

Resided in Mecklenburg County where he enlisted at age 18, March 24, 1863, for the war. Present or accounted for until wounded at Wilderness, Virginia, May 5, 1864. Died in hospital at Staunton, Virginia, June 2, 1864, of wounds.

ANDREWS, E. M., Private

Enlisted in Wake County on December 2, 1864, for the war. Present or accounted for until paroled at Appomattox Court House, Virginia, April 9, 1865.

ASHLEY, LEE T., Private

Resided in Mecklenburg County and was by occupation a farmer prior to enlisting in Mecklenburg County at age 27, April 20, 1862, for the war. Present or accounted for until he died at home in Mecklenburg County on or about November 15, 1862, of disease.

ASHLEY, WILLIAM, Private

Enlisted in Mecklenburg County on February 1, 1864, for the war. Present or accounted for until captured near Petersburg, Virginia, October 27, 1864. Confined at Point Lookout, Maryland, until released on June 3, 1865, after taking the Oath of Allegiance. Medical records give his age as 19.

BAILEY, WILLIAM, Private

Enlisted at Camp Stokes on December 3, 1864, for the war. Present or accounted for until paroled at Lynchburg, Virginia, April 15, 1865.

BELK, WILLIAM, Private

Resided in Rowan County and enlisted at Camp Holmes on September 3, 1864, for the war. Present or accounted for until captured at or near Petersburg, Virginia, April 2, 1865. Confined at Point Lookout, Maryland, until released on June 24, 1865, after taking the Oath of Allegiance.

BELL, C. E., Corporal

Resided in Mecklenburg County and enlisted at age 31, March 14, 1862, for the war. Mustered in as Corporal. No further records.

BIGGART, JAMES, Private

Resided in Mecklenburg County where he enlisted at age 58, April 15, 1862, for the war. Present or accounted for through February, 1865; however, he was absent on detail during most of that period. Paroled at Charlotte in May, 1865.

BLACK, JOHN B., Private

Resided in Mecklenburg County where he enlisted at age 34, March 14, 1862, for the war. Present or accounted for until discharged on August 4, 1862, by reason of disability.

BLAIR, STEPHEN W., Private
Resided in Mecklenburg County where he enlisted at age 18, March 14, 1862, for the war. Present or accounted for until paroled at Appomattox Court House, Virginia, April 9, 1865.

BLANKENSHIP, J. N., Private
Resided in Mecklenburg County where he enlisted at age 27, May 1, 1862, for the war. Present or accounted for until discharged at Camp Davis on June 15, 1862. Reason discharged not reported.

BLANKENSHIP, STEPHEN PETTUS, 1st Sergeant
Resided in Mecklenburg County where he enlisted at age 27, May 1, 1862, for the war. Mustered in as Private and promoted to Corporal in July-August, 1862. Promoted to Sergeant on April 30, 1863, and promoted to 1st Sergeant on April 2, 1864. Present or accounted for until captured near Petersburg, Virginia, October 27, 1864. Confined at Point Lookout, Maryland, until paroled and transferred to Boulware's Wharf, James River, Virginia, where he was received March 30, 1865, for exchange. Paroled at Salisbury on May 25, 1865.

BLANKENSHIP, T. G., Private
Born in Alexander County* and resided in Iredell County where he was by occupation a farmer prior to enlisting at Camp Vance at age 45, October 1, 1863, for the war. Present or accounted for until discharged on September 22, 1864, by reason of "anasarca produced by cardiac obstruction and old unreduced dislocation of ankle."

BOYCE, HUGH, Private
Resided in Mecklenburg County where he enlisted at age 30, March 14, 1862, for the war. Discharged in April, 1862. Reason discharged not reported.

BOYD, DAVID, Private
Enlisted in Mecklenburg County. Enlistment date reported as August 5, 1862; however, he was not listed on the rolls of this company until January-February, 1865. Captured at or near Petersburg, Virginia, April 2, 1865, and confined at Point Lookout, Maryland, until released on June 6, 1865, after taking the Oath of Allegiance.

BOYD, J. J., Private
Resided in Mecklenburg County where he enlisted. Enlistment date reported as January 5, 1862; however, he was not listed on the rolls of this company until November-December, 1864. Present or accounted for until captured at or near Petersburg, Virginia, April 2, 1865. Confined at Point Lookout, Maryland, where he died on April 29, 1865, of "infection of lungs."

BOYD, JESSE A., Private
Previously served in Company H, 18th Regiment South Carolina Infantry. Transferred to this company on November 15, 1864. Present or accounted for until captured at or near Petersburg, Virginia, April 2, 1865. Confined at Point Lookout, Maryland, where he died April 29, 1865, of "pneumonia."

BROWER, A. M., Private
Resided in Randolph County and enlisted at Camp Holmes on September 12, 1864, for the war. Present or accounted for until captured at or near Petersburg, Virginia, April 2, 1865. Confined at Point

Lookout, Maryland, until released on June 23, 1865, after taking the Oath of Allegiance.

BROWN, JAMES WILLIAM, Private
Resided in Mecklenburg County where he enlisted at age 24, March 14, 1862, for the war. Mustered in as Private and promoted to Corporal on May 1, 1862. Reduced to ranks prior to September 1, 1862. Present or accounted for until transferred to Company B, 13th Regiment N. C. Troops (3rd Regiment N. C. Volunteers), September 4, 1863, in exchange for Private James H. McConnell.

BRYANT, SIDNEY A., Private
Resided in Mecklenburg County where he enlisted at age 23, March 14, 1862, for the war. Present or accounted for until captured near Petersburg, Virginia, October 27, 1864. Confined at Point Lookout, Maryland, until released on June 23, 1865, after taking the Oath of Allegiance.

BURNS, H. F., Private
Enlisted in Mecklenburg County on January 1, 1864, for the war. Present or accounted for until he died at Lynchburg, Virginia, May 16, 1864. Cause of death not reported.

BURNS, ROBERT, Private
Resided in South Carolina and enlisted in Mecklenburg County at age 27, March 14, 1862, for the war. Present or accounted for until transferred to Company E, 17th Regiment South Carolina Infantry, August 8, 1864.

CALDWELL, J. S. P., Sergeant
Resided in Mecklenburg County where he enlisted at age 27, March 14, 1862, for the war. Mustered in as Sergeant. Present or accounted for until captured at Falling Waters, Maryland, July 14, 1863. Confined at Old Capitol Prison, Washington, D. C., until transferred to Point Lookout, Maryland, August 8, 1863. Paroled and transferred to Venus Point, Savannah River, Georgia, where he was received November 15, 1864, for exchange. Returned to duty prior to January 1, 1865, and present or accounted for until captured at or near Petersburg, Virginia, April 2, 1865. Confined at Point Lookout until released on June 3, 1865, after taking the Oath of Allegiance. [May have served previously in Company C, 1st Regiment N. C. Infantry (6 months, 1861).]

CAMPBELL, JOHN C., Corporal
Resided in Mecklenburg County where he enlisted at age 26, May 1, 1862, for the war. Mustered in as Private and promoted to Corporal on August 15, 1862. Present or accounted for until transferred to Company E, 17th Regiment South Carolina Infantry, August 8, 1864.

CAMPBELL, THOMAS J., Corporal
Resided in Mecklenburg County where he enlisted at age 22, March 14, 1862, for the war. Mustered in as Corporal. Present or accounted for until killed at Gettysburg, Pennsylvania, July 1, 1863. [May have served previously in Company C, 1st Regiment N. C. Infantry (6 months, 1861).]

CAROTHERS, JAMES, Private
Enlisted in Wake County on April 20, 1864, for the war. Present or accounted for until he died in hospital at Richmond, Virginia, June 10, 1864. Cause of death not reported.

CAROTHERS, JAMES A., Private
Resided in Mecklenburg County where he enlisted at age 34, March 14, 1862, for the war. Present or accounted for until wounded at Spotsylvania Court House, Virginia, in May, 1864. Returned to duty in September-October, 1864, and present or accounted for until captured at or near Petersburg, Virginia, April 2, 1865. Confined at Point Lookout, Maryland, until released on June 8, 1865, after taking the Oath of Allegiance.

CAROTHERS, JOHN D., Private
Resided in Mecklenburg County where he enlisted at age 36, April 14, 1863, for the war. Present or accounted for until he died in hospital at Mount Jackson, Virginia, August 2, 1863, of disease.

CARPENTER, JOSEPH C., Private
Resided in Gaston County and enlisted at Camp Holmes on September 17, 1864, for the war. Present or accounted for until captured near Petersburg, Virginia, March 25, 1865. Confined at Point Lookout, Maryland, until released on June 22, 1865, after taking the Oath of Allegiance.

CARPENTER, WILLIAM B., Private
Enlisted at Camp Holmes on September 17, 1864, for the war. Present or accounted for until captured near Petersburg, Virginia, October 27, 1864. Confined at Point Lookout, Maryland, until transferred to Boulware's Wharf, James River, Virginia, where he was received March 30, 1865, for exchange.

CARTER, R. J., Private
Enlisted at Camp Holmes on September 21, 1864, for the war. Present or accounted for until transferred to Barringer's cavalry brigade on December 8, 1864. Regiment to which transferred not reported.

CHRISTENBERY, C. E., Private
Resided in Mecklenburg County where he enlisted at age 31, May 1, 1862, for the war. Present or accounted for until he died in hospital at Goldsboro on May 10, 1863, of "pleuritis."

CLARK, PATRICK M., Private
Resided in Mecklenburg County where he enlisted at age 34, March 14, 1862, for the war. Mustered in as Sergeant. Present or accounted for until wounded at White Hall on December 16, 1862. Returned to duty in January-February, 1863, and present or accounted for until wounded at Gettysburg, Pennsylvania, July 1, 1863. Returned to duty in November-December, 1863. Reduced to ranks in November-December, 1864. Present or accounted for until captured at or near Petersburg, Virginia, April 2, 1865. Confined at Point Lookout, Maryland, until released on June 26, 1865, after taking the Oath of Allegiance.

CLARK, W. A., Private
Resided in Mecklenburg County where he enlisted at age 19, April 15, 1862, for the war. Present or accounted for until he died at Charlotte on October 20, 1862. Cause of death not reported.

COBB, C. R., Private
Resided in Catawba County and enlisted in Wake County on April 20, 1864, for the war. Present or accounted for until captured at or near Petersburg, Virginia, April 2, 1865. Confined at Point Lookout, Maryland, until released on June 24, 1865, after taking the Oath of Allegiance.

COBB, CHARLES E., Private
Resided in Mecklenburg County where he enlisted at age 17, March 14, 1862, for the war. Present or accounted for until discharged on October 30, 1862. Reason discharged not reported.

COFFEY, BENJAMIN MORROW, Private
Resided in Mecklenburg County where he enlisted at age 19, March 14, 1862, for the war. Present or accounted for until wounded in the left leg and blinded in the right eye at Gettysburg, Pennsylvania, July 1, 1863. Captured at Winchester, Virginia, July 30, 1863. Exchanged at an unspecified date and reported absent wounded through June, 1864. North Carolina pension records indicate that he survived the war.

COLEMAN, H. G., Private
Enlisted at Camp Holmes on September 21, 1864, for the war. Present or accounted for until transferred to Barringer's cavalry brigade on December 8, 1864. Regiment to which transferred not reported.

COOPER, JAMES M., Private
Resided in Mecklenburg County where he enlisted at age 32, March 14, 1862, for the war. Present or accounted for until captured at Falling Waters, Maryland, July 14, 1863. Confined at Old Capitol Prison, Washington, D. C., until transferred to Point Lookout, Maryland, August 8, 1863. Paroled and transferred to Boulware's Wharf, James River, Virginia, where he was received March 16, 1865, for exchange. Company records do not indicate whether he returned to duty; however, he was paroled at Charlotte on May 12, 1865.

COX, ELI, Private
Resided in Gaston County and enlisted at Camp Stokes on November 3, 1864, for the war. Present or accounted for until captured at or near Petersburg, Virginia, April 2, 1865. Confined at Point Lookout, Maryland, until released on June 24, 1865, after taking the Oath of Allegiance.

CROWELL, ELIAS M., Private
Previously served as 2nd Lieutenant in Company I, 37th Regiment N. C. Troops. Enlisted as a Private in this company on June 1, 1862, for the war. Present or accounted for until promoted to Musician in July-August, 1864. Transferred to the regimental band prior to November 1, 1864.

DEGGERHART, J. L., Private
Resided in Mecklenburg County and enlisted at Camp Vance at age 18, November 21, 1863, for the war. Present or accounted for until captured near Petersburg, Virginia, October 27, 1864. Confined at Point Lookout, Maryland, until paroled and transferred to Boulware's Wharf, James River, Virginia, where he was received March 30, 1865, for exchange. Company records do not indicate whether he returned to duty; however, he was paroled at Salisbury on May 27, 1865.

DEGGERHEART, L. D., Private
Enlisted in Mecklenburg County on March 10, 1862, for the war. Discharged May 1, 1862. Reason discharged not reported.

DIXON, HUGH M., Private
Resided in Mecklenburg County where he enlisted at age 19, March 14, 1862, for the war. Present or

accounted for until he died "at home" on January 6, 1863. Cause of death not reported.

DOLLIHITE, W. H., Private
Resided in Stokes County and enlisted in Mecklenburg County at age 35, January 21, 1863, for the war. Present or accounted for until he died in hospital at Goldsboro on February 15, 1863, of "typhoid fever."

DREWEY, A. G., Private
Resided in Mecklenburg County where he enlisted at age 25, March 25, 1862, for the war. Present or accounted for through January 3, 1865; however, he was reported absent sick during most of that period.

DUCKWORTH, J. A., Private
Resided in Mecklenburg County and enlisted in Wake County on April 26, 1864, for the war. Present or accounted for until captured at or near Petersburg, Virginia, April 2, 1865. Confined at Fort Delaware, Delaware, until released on June 19, 1865, after taking the Oath of Allegiance.

EARNHART, GEORGE, Private
Resided in Rowan County and enlisted at Camp Holmes on September 3, 1864, for the war. Present or accounted for until captured at or near Petersburg, Virginia, April 2, 1865. Confined at Point Lookout, Maryland, until released on June 12, 1865, after taking the Oath of Allegiance.

EDWARDS, JAMES M., Private
Enlisted in Wake County on April 26, 1864, for the war. Present or accounted for until captured near Petersburg, Virginia, October 27, 1864. Confined at Point Lookout, Maryland, where he died April 15, 1865, of "chronic diarrhoea & scurvy." Medical records give his age as 24.

ELLIS, DANIEL, Private
Resided in Cumberland County and enlisted at Camp Holmes on September 10, 1864, for the war. Present or accounted for until captured near Petersburg, Virginia, October 27, 1864. Confined at Point Lookout, Maryland, until released on June 26, 1865, after taking the Oath of Allegiance.

ELMS, JAMES A., Private
Enlisted in Mecklenburg County on May 1, 1862, for the war. Present or accounted for until he died at Camp Davis on June 20, 1862, of disease.

ETTERS, JAMES H., Private
Resided in Mecklenburg County where he enlisted at age 36, March 10, 1862, for the war. Present or accounted for until he died "at home" on July 15, 1863. Cause of death not reported.

FINGER, H. F., Private
Enlisted in Wake County on April 5, 1864, for the war. Present or accounted for until he died in hospital at Richmond, Virginia, June 24, 1864, of "febris typh[oid]."

FITE, W. J., Private
Resided in Gaston County and enlisted at Camp Holmes on November 3, 1864, for the war. Present or accounted for until captured at or near Petersburg, Virginia, April 2, 1865. Confined at Point Lookout, Maryland, until released on June 26, 1865, after taking the Oath of Allegiance.

GREER, EDWARD, Private
Resided in Mecklenburg County where he enlisted at age 17, May 1, 1862, for the war. Present or accounted for until discharged in November, 1862. Reason discharged not reported.

GREER, Z. B., Private
Resided in Mecklenburg County where he enlisted at age 19, March 10, 1862, for the war. Present or accounted for until he died in hospital at Wilmington on September 1, 1862, of "typhoid fever."

HALL, N. C., Private
Enlisted in Wake County on April 20, 1864, for the war. Present or accounted for until wounded at Cold Harbor, Virginia, June 2, 1864. Reported absent wounded or absent sick through February, 1865.

HALL, R. B., Private
Resided in Mecklenburg County and enlisted in Wake County on April 20, 1864, for the war. Present or accounted for until wounded in the left hand at Cold Harbor, Virginia, June 2, 1864. Returned to duty in November-December, 1864, and present or accounted for until he deserted to the enemy on February 6, 1865. Released on or about February 9, 1865, after taking the Oath of Amnesty.

HAMEL, A. R., Private
Resided in Mecklenburg County where he enlisted at age 33, October 27, 1862, for the war. Present or accounted for until wounded and captured at Gettysburg, Pennsylvania, July 3, 1863. Confined at Davids Island, New York Harbor, where he died on August 28, 1863, of wounds and/or "chro[nic] diarrhoea."

HANNA, JOHN N., Sergeant
Resided in Mecklenburg County where he enlisted at age 30, May 1, 1862, for the war. Mustered in as Private and promoted to Corporal on April 1, 1864. Promoted to Sergeant in September-December, 1864. Present or accounted for until captured near Petersburg, Virginia, October 27, 1864. Confined at Point Lookout, Maryland, until paroled and transferred to Boulware's Wharf, James River, Virginia, where he was received March 30, 1865, for exchange.

HARGET, ALEY, Private
Resided in Mecklenburg County where he enlisted at age 30, May 1, 1862, for the war. Present or accounted for until he died "at home" on February 10, 1864. Cause of death not reported.

HARMON, LEVI, Private
Resided in Mecklenburg County and enlisted in Gaston County at age 22, March 14, 1862, for the war. Present or accounted for until captured near Petersburg, Virginia, October 27, 1864. Confined at Point Lookout, Maryland, until paroled and transferred to Boulware's Wharf, James River, Virginia, where he was received March 30, 1865, for exchange.

HARRIS, FRANCIS CALHOUN, 1st Sergeant
Resided in South Carolina and enlisted in Mecklenburg County at age 24, March 14, 1862, for the war. Mustered in as Private and promoted to 1st Sergeant on June 6, 1862. Present or accounted for until wounded in the left arm and captured at Gettysburg, Pennsylvania, July 1-4, 1863. Left arm amputated. Hospitalized at Gettysburg until transferred to Davids

Island, New York Harbor, July 17-24, 1863. Paroled and transferred for exchange on or about September 8, 1863. Reported absent wounded until discharged on March 14, 1864.

HARRIS, JAMES H., Private
Resided in Mecklenburg County where he enlisted at age 36, March 17, 1862, for the war. Present or accounted for through December, 1864; however, he was reported absent sick or absent without leave during most of that period. Discharged on January 8, 1865. Reason discharged not reported.

HARRIS, JOHN C., Private
Resided in Mecklenburg County where he enlisted at age 33, March 17, 1862, for the war. Mustered in as Private and promoted to Corporal on December 1, 1862. Present or accounted for until reported absent without leave on company muster roll dated January-February, 1863. Returned to duty in March-April, 1863, and was reduced to ranks on April 30, 1863. Reported absent without leave on company muster rolls dated May-August, 1863. Returned to duty in September-October, 1863, and present or accounted for until transferred to Company E, 17th Regiment South Carolina Infantry, August 8, 1864.

HARRIS, R. H., Private
Resided in Mecklenburg County and enlisted at age 27, March 14, 1862, for the war. Discharged in May, 1862. Reason discharged not reported.

HAYES, JESSE B., Private
Resided in Mecklenburg County where he enlisted at age 28, March 15, 1862, for the war. Present or accounted for until captured near Petersburg, Virginia, October 27, 1864. Confined at Point Lookout, Maryland, until released on June 3, 1865, after taking the Oath of Allegiance.

HENDERSON, WRIGHT R., Private
Previously served in Company B, 41st Regiment N.C. Troops (3rd Regiment N.C. Cavalry). Transferred to this company in November-December, 1864, and present or accounted for until he deserted to the enemy on March 6, 1865. Released on or about March 10, 1865, after taking the Oath of Allegiance.

HENRY, B. G., Private
Born in Mecklenburg County and was by occupation a farmer prior to enlisting in Wake County at age 22, April 20, 1864, for the war. Present or accounted for until wounded in the left forearm at Cold Harbor, Virginia, June 2, 1864. Retired on February 17, 1865, by reason of wounds.

HENRY, T. B., Private
Enlisted in Wake County on April 20, 1864, for the war. Present or accounted for until wounded at Cold Harbor, Virginia, June 2, 1864. Rejoined the company prior to October 27, 1864, when he was wounded near Petersburg, Virginia. Returned to duty in January-February, 1865, and present or accounted for until in hospital at Richmond, Virginia, April 3, 1865. "Escaped from hospital" on May 6, 1865.

HERRON, JOHN WILLIAM, Private
Resided in Mecklenburg County where he enlisted at age 28, May 1, 1862, for the war. Present or accounted for until discharged on August 4, 1862. Reason discharged not reported.

HILL, CORNELIUS H., Corporal
Resided in Wake County where he enlisted at age 22, May 1, 1862, for the war. Mustered in as Private and promoted to Corporal on May 1, 1862. Present or accounted for until discharged on October 18, 1862. Reason discharged not reported.

HINNANT, HENRY, Private
Resided in Johnston County and enlisted at Camp Holmes on July 23, 1863, for the war. Present or accounted for until wounded in the right hand at Jones' Farm, Virginia, September 30, 1864. Reported absent wounded through February, 1865. Paroled at Goldsboro on May 9, 1865.

HOFFMAN, MILES, Private
Resided in Gaston County and enlisted at Camp Holmes on September 10, 1864, for the war. Present or accounted for until captured at or near Petersburg, Virginia, April 2, 1865. Confined at Point Lookout, Maryland, until released on June 21, 1865, after taking the Oath of Allegiance.

HOLLAND, ROBERT, Private
Enlisted at Camp Holmes on September 8, 1864, for the war. Present or accounted for until paroled at Appomattox Court House, Virginia, April 9, 1865.

HOOVER, S. L., Private
Resided in Mecklenburg County where he enlisted at age 30, May 1, 1862, for the war. Present or accounted for until captured near Petersburg, Virginia, October 27, 1864. Confined at Point Lookout, Maryland, until paroled and transferred for exchange on or about February 18, 1865. Reported present with a detachment of paroled and exchanged prisoners at Camp Lee, near Richmond, Virginia, February 28, 1865.

HOTCHKISS, SETH AUGUSTUS, Private
Resided in Mecklenburg County where he enlisted at age 20, March 14, 1862, for the war. Mustered in as Corporal and promoted to Sergeant on August 15, 1862. Reduced to ranks on March 28, 1863. Present or accounted for until captured at Gettysburg, Pennsylvania, July 4-5, 1863. Confined at Fort McHenry, Maryland, until transferred to Fort Delaware, Delaware, in July, 1863. Released at Fort Delaware in 1865 after taking the Oath of Allegiance.

HOVIS, MOSES, Private
Resided in Gaston County and enlisted in Wake County on April 5, 1864, for the war. Present or accounted for until captured at or near Petersburg, Virginia, April 2, 1865. Confined at Point Lookout, Maryland, until released on June 13, 1865, after taking the Oath of Allegiance.

HUDSPETH, GEORGE, Private
Resided in Lincoln County and enlisted in Wake County on April 5, 1864, for the war. Present or accounted for until wounded at Wilderness, Virginia, May 5, 1864. Returned to duty in September-October, 1864, and present or accounted for until captured at or near Petersburg, Virginia, April 2, 1865. Confined at Point Lookout, Maryland, until released on June 27, 1865, after taking the Oath of Allegiance.

HUMPHREYS, DAVID, Private
Born in Mecklenburg County and was by occupation

a farmer prior to enlisting in Wake County at age 18, April 20, 1864, for the war. Present or accounted for until discharged on July 16, 1864, by reason of "chronic rheumatism."

HUMPHREYS, J. L., Private
Resided in Mecklenburg County and enlisted at age 36, March 14, 1862, for the war. Present or accounted for until wounded at Reams' Station, Virginia, August 25, 1864. Returned to duty in November-December, 1864, and present or accounted for until paroled at Appomattox Court House, Virginia, April 9, 1865.

HUMPHREYS, THOMAS L., Corporal
Resided in Mecklenburg County where he enlisted at age 30, May 1, 1862, for the war. Mustered in as Private and promoted to Corporal in March-April, 1865. Present or accounted for until captured at or near Petersburg, Virginia, April 2, 1865. Confined at Point Lookout, Maryland, until released on June 27, 1865, after taking the Oath of Allegiance.

INGLE, PETER, Private
Resided in Mecklenburg County where he enlisted at age 31, March 15, 1862, for the war. Present or accounted for until wounded at Gettysburg, Pennsylvania, July 1-3, 1863. Returned to duty prior to September 1, 1863, and present or accounted for until captured near Petersburg, Virginia, October 27, 1864. Confined at Point Lookout, Maryland, until paroled and transferred to Boulware's Wharf, James River, Virginia, where he was received March 30, 1865, for exchange.

JOHNSON, J. W., Private
Enlisted at Camp Vance. Enlistment date reported as December 15, 1863; however, he was not listed on the rolls of this company until May-June, 1864. Present or accounted for through February, 1865. [May have served previously in Company C, 1st Regiment N. C. Infantry (6 months, 1861).]

KEENER, PETER, Private
Enlisted at Camp Holmes on September 17, 1864, for the war. Present or accounted for until paroled at Appomattox Court House, Virginia, April 9, 1865.

KERR, RUFUS D., Private
Resided in Mecklenburg County where he enlisted at age 18, March 19, 1862, for the war. Present or accounted for until he died in hospital at Wilmington on July 12, 1862, of disease.

KEY, ABEL, Private
Resided in Mecklenburg County where he enlisted at age 35, March 15, 1862, for the war. Present or accounted for until wounded at Gettysburg, Pennsylvania, July 1, 1863. Returned to duty in November-December, 1863, and present or accounted for until he died on December 15, 1864. Place and cause of death not reported.

KILPATRICK, WILLIAM F., Corporal
Previously served in Company I, 9th Regiment N. C. State Troops (1st Regiment N. C. Cavalry). Transferred to this company on December 6, 1864, and was promoted to Corporal in December, 1864. Present or accounted for until captured at or near Petersburg, Virginia, April 2, 1865. Confined at Point Lookout, Maryland, until released on June 8,

1865, after taking the Oath of Allegiance.

KNOX, WILLIAM H., Private
Resided in Mecklenburg County where he enlisted at age 22, March 19, 1862, for the war. Present or accounted for until captured at Falling Waters, Maryland, July 14, 1863. Confined at Baltimore, Maryland, and at Point Lookout, Maryland, until paroled and transferred for exchange on or about March 3, 1864. Returned to duty in May-June, 1864, and present or accounted for until captured near Petersburg, Virginia, March 25, 1865. Confined at Point Lookout until released on June 28, 1865, after taking the Oath of Allegiance.

McCONNELL, JAMES H., Musician
Previously served as Musician in Company B, 13th Regiment N. C. Troops (3rd Regiment N. C. Volunteers). Transferred to this company with the rank of Private on September 4, 1863, in exchange for Private James William Brown. Appointed Musician in September-October, 1864, and transferred to the regimental band.

McMILLAN, JAMES E., Sergeant
Resided in Mecklenburg County where he enlisted at age 34, March 14, 1862, for the war. Mustered in as Private and promoted to Corporal on August 1, 1863. Promoted to Sergeant on December 15, 1863. Present or accounted for until wounded at Wilderness, Virginia, May 5, 1864. Died in hospital at Lynchburg, Virginia, June 25, 1864, of wounds.

McQUAIGE, JAMES W., Private
Resided in Mecklenburg County where he enlisted at age 30, May 1, 1862, for the war. Present or accounted for until captured near Petersburg, Virginia, October 27, 1864. Confined at Point Lookout, Maryland, until paroled and transferred to Cox's Landing, James River, Virginia, where he was received February 14-15, 1865, for exchange.

McQUAIGE, W. D., Private
Enlisted in Mecklenburg County on May 1, 1862, for the war. Reported absent without leave from July-August, 1862, through December, 1862, and was discharged "by Civil Authority" in January-February, 1863.

MADDEN, JAMES P., Private
Resided in Mecklenburg County where he enlisted at age 24, March 15, 1862, for the war. Present or accounted for until he died in hospital at Charlottesville, Virginia, January 20, 1864, of "diarrh[oea] chro[nic]."

MARSHALL, JOHN, Private
Previously served in Company B, 41st Regiment N.C. Troops (3rd Regiment N.C. Cavalry). Transferred to this company in November-December, 1864. Deserted to the enemy on or about December 16, 1864. Released on or about December 20, 1864, after taking the Oath of Allegiance.

MARSHBURN, JAMES NELSON, Private
Previously served in Company B, 41st Regiment N.C. Troops (3rd Regiment N.C. Cavalry). Transferred to this company in November-December, 1864. Present or accounted for until wounded in the right leg at Hatcher's Run, Virginia, February 5, 1865. Right leg amputated. Reported absent wounded through

March 21, 1865. North Carolina pension records indicate that he survived the war.

MERRITT, SAMUEL N., Private
Enlisted in Mecklenburg County on May 1, 1862, for the war. Discharged August 12, 1862. Reason discharged not reported.

MINCEY, WILEY, Private
Resided in Mecklenburg County where he enlisted at age 20, March 14, 1862, for the war. Present or accounted for until captured at Falling Waters, Maryland, July 14, 1863. Confined at Point Lookout, Maryland, until paroled and transferred for exchange on or about March 3, 1864. Returned to duty in May-June, 1864, and present or accounted for until captured at or near Petersburg, Virginia, April 2, 1865. Confined at Point Lookout until released on June 29, 1865, after taking the Oath of Allegiance.

MORRISON, S. C., Private
Company muster roll dated November-December, 1862, indicates he enlisted in Mecklenburg County᾽ for the war. No further records.

MORRISON, WILLIAM T., Musician
Previously served in Company F, 15th Regiment Mississippi Infantry. Transferred to this company on November 1, 1862, with the rank of Private. Present or accounted for until captured at Gettysburg, Pennsylvania, July 3, 1863. Confined at Fort Delaware, Delaware, until exchanged on July 31, 1863. Present or accounted for until promoted to Musician in September-October, 1864, and transferred to the regimental band.

NEELY, JOHN J., Sergeant
Born in Mecklenburg County where he resided as a farmer prior to enlisting in Mecklenburg County at age 20, April 17, 1862, for the war. Mustered in as Private and promoted to Corporal on August 8, 1864. Promoted to Sergeant in November-December, 1864. Present or accounted for until captured at or near Petersburg, Virginia, April 2, 1865. Confined at Point Lookout, Maryland, until released on June 29, 1865, after taking the Oath of Allegiance.

NEWMAN, ELIAS, Private
Place and date of enlistment not reported. Captured at or near Petersburg, Virginia, April 2, 1865, and confined at Point Lookout, Maryland, until released on June 29, 1865.

PAGE, D. J., Private
Enlisted at Camp Holmes on September 8, 1864, for the war. Present or accounted for until transferred to Barringer's cavalry brigade on December 8, 1864. Regiment to which transferred not reported.

PARKS, THOMAS B., Private
Enlisted at Camp Holmes on September 8, 1864, for the war. Present or accounted for until transferred to Company I, 19th Regiment N. C. Troops (2nd Regiment N. C. Cavalry), December 8, 1864.

PEPPER, JOHN, Private
Enlisted at Camp Holmes on September 8, 1864, for the war. Present or accounted for until wounded at Hatcher's Run, Virginia, February 5, 1865. No further records.

PORTER, R. C., Private
Resided in Mecklenburg County where he enlisted at age 17, March 2, 1863, for the war. Present or accounted for until wounded in the right thigh and captured at Gettysburg, Pennsylvania, July 1-5, 1863. Hospitalized at Gettysburg until transferred to Davids Island, New York Harbor, July 17-24, 1863. Paroled at Davids Island and transferred for exchange on or about September 16, 1863. Returned to duty in January-February, 1864, and present or accounted for until he deserted to the enemy on or about March 22, 1865. Released on or about March 29, 1865, after taking the Oath of Allegiance.

PRICE, J. A., Private
Enlisted at Camp Holmes on September 8, 1864, for the war. Present or accounted for until he died in hospital at Richmond, Virginia, February 20, 1865. Cause of death not reported.

REID, W. M., Corporal
Resided in Mecklenburg County where he enlisted at age 28, May 1, 1862, for the war. Mustered in as Private and promoted to Corporal on August 8, 1864. Present or accounted for through January 8, 1865.

RHINE, A. M., Private
Enlisted at Camp Holmes on September 17, 1864, for the war. Present or accounted for until captured at or near Petersburg, Virginia, April 2, 1865. Confined at Point Lookout, Maryland, until released on June 6, 1865, after taking the Oath of Allegiance.

RICE, J. S., Private
Enlisted at Camp Vance. Enlistment date reported as October 23, 1863; however, he was not listed on the rolls of this company until May-June, 1864. Present or accounted for through February, 1865.

ROCHELLE, THOMAS B., Private
Previously served in Company B, 41st Regiment N.C. Troops (3rd Regiment N.C. Cavalry). Transferred to this company in November-December, 1864. Present or accounted for until captured at or near Petersburg, Virginia, April 2, 1865. Confined at Point Lookout, Maryland, until released on June 19, 1865, after taking the Oath of Allegiance.

ROSS, ROBERT A., Private
Previously served in Company A of this regiment. Transferred to this company on July 11, 1862. Present or accounted for until he died "at home" on January 24, 1863, of pneumonia.

RUSSELL, JOHN C., Private
Resided in Mecklenburg County where he enlisted at age 22, March 21, 1862, for the war. Present or accounted for until captured at or near Gettysburg, Pennsylvania, on or about July 3, 1863. Confined at Fort Delaware, Delaware, until paroled and transferred for exchange on September 30, 1864. Reported absent without leave from November-December, 1864, through February, 1865.

SANDERS, JACOB, Private
Enlisted at Camp Holmes on September 3, 1864, for the war. Present or accounted for until paroled at Appomattox Court House, Virginia, April 9, 1865.

SAVILLE, ROBERT D., Sergeant
Resided in Mecklenburg County where he enlisted at

age 24, March 14, 1862, for the war. Mustered in as Sergeant. Present or accounted for until wounded at Gettysburg, Pennsylvania, July 1-3, 1863. Reported absent wounded until discharged on December 15, 1863. Reason discharged not reported.

SCOTT, RAYFORD S., Private
Previously served in Company B, 41st Regiment N.C. Troops (3rd Regiment N.C. Cavalry). Transferred to this company in November-December, 1864. Present or accounted for until captured at Hatcher's Run, Virginia, March 29, 1865. Confined at Point Lookout, Maryland, where he died on May 23, 1865, of "erysipelas."

SLOOP, ALEXANDER, Private
Resided in Mecklenburg County where he enlisted at age 47, March 10, 1862, for the war. Present or accounted for until captured at Gettysburg, Pennsylvania, July 4-5, 1863. Confined at Fort Delaware, Delaware, until transferred to Point Lookout, Maryland, October 15-18, 1863. Paroled and transferred for exchange on September 18, 1864. Hospitalized at Richmond, Virginia, September 21, 1864. No further records.

SMITH, ABB J., Private
Born in Mecklenburg County where he resided as a farmer prior to enlisting in Mecklenburg County at age 21, April 15, 1862, for the war. Present or accounted for until discharged on August 28, 1863, by reason of "valvular disease of the heart."

SMITH, JAMES W., Private
Resided in Mecklenburg County where he enlisted at age 27, March 18, 1862, for the war. Present or accounted for until reported missing in action at Bristoe Station, Virginia, October 14, 1863. Returned to duty in November-December, 1863, and present or accounted for until wounded at Wilderness, Virginia, May 5, 1864. Returned to duty in July-August, 1864, and present or accounted for until captured near Petersburg, Virginia, October 27, 1864. Confined at Point Lookout, Maryland, until released on June 20, 1865, after taking the Oath of Allegiance.

SMITH, JOHN T., Sergeant
Born in York District, South Carolina, and resided in Mecklenburg County where he was by occupation a farmer prior to enlisting in Mecklenburg County at age 24, March 12, 1862, for the war. Mustered in as Private and promoted to Corporal on April 30, 1863. Promoted to Sergeant on April 2, 1864. Present or accounted for until paroled at Appomattox Court House, Virginia, April 9, 1865.

SMITH, THOMAS J., Private
Resided in Mecklenburg County where he enlisted at age 19, March 15, 1862, for the war. Present or accounted for until captured at Falling Waters, Maryland, July 14, 1863. Confined at Old Capitol Prison, Washington, D. C., until transferred to Point Lookout, Maryland, August 8, 1863. Company muster roll dated January-February, 1864, states that he died at Point Lookout at an unspecified date; however, records of the Federal Provost Marshal do not substantiate that report. No further records.

SNEAD, FRANKLIN, Private
Enlisted in Wake County on April 5, 1864, for the war. Reported absent without leave on company muster roll dated September-October, 1864, but returned to duty on December 1, 1864. Present or accounted for until captured at or near Petersburg, Virginia, April 2, 1865. Confined at Point Lookout, Maryland, until released on June 20, 1865, after taking the Oath of Allegiance.

SNIDER, J. A., Private
Resided in Mecklenburg County where he enlisted at age 37, January 21, 1863, for the war. Present or accounted for until killed at Gettysburg, Pennsylvania, July 3, 1863.

SPAIN, H. P., Private
Enlisted on February 10, 1864, for the war. Present or accounted for until transferred to Company D of this regiment on April 2, 1864.

SQUIRES, J. A., Private
Resided in Mecklenburg County and enlisted at Camp Holmes on September 3, 1864, for the war. Present or accounted for until captured near Petersburg, Virginia, October 27, 1864. Confined at Point Lookout, Maryland, until released on June 19, 1865, after taking the Oath of Allegiance.

STANFORD, J. L., Private
Resided in Mecklenburg County where he enlisted on February 1, 1864, for the war. Present or accounted for until wounded at Wilderness, Virginia, May 5, 1864. Returned to duty on December 1, 1864, and present or accounted for until captured at or near Petersburg, Virginia, April 2, 1865. Confined at Point Lookout, Maryland, until released on June 14, 1865, after taking the Oath of Allegiance.

SUMMERON, GEORGE, Private
Resided in Lincoln County and enlisted at Camp Holmes on September 17, 1864, for the war. Present or accounted for until wounded in the left leg and captured near Petersburg, Virginia, October 27, 1864. Hospitalized at Washington, D. C. Hospital records give his age as 44. Transferred to Old Capitol Prison, Washington, April 17, 1865. Transferred to Elmira, New York, May 11, 1865. Released at Elmira on June 12, 1865, after taking the Oath of Allegiance.

SUMMY, J. B., Private
Resided in Gaston County and enlisted at Camp Holmes on September 17, 1864, for the war. Present or accounted for until captured at or near Petersburg, Virginia, April 2, 1865. Confined at Point Lookout, Maryland, until released on June 20, 1865, after taking the Oath of Allegiance.

TAGGERT, J. C., Private
Resided in Iredell County and enlisted at Camp Vance on October 1, 1863, for the war. Present or accounted for until wounded in the right breast at Cold Harbor, Virginia, June 1, 1864. Reported absent without leave from September-October, 1864, through December, 1864, but returned to duty in January, 1865. Captured at or near Petersburg, Virginia, April 2, 1865, and confined at Point Lookout, Maryland, until released on June 21, 1865, after taking the Oath of Allegiance.

THROWER, ALEX, Corporal
Resided in Mecklenburg County where he enlisted at age 18, April 10, 1862, for the war. Mustered in as

Private and promoted to Corporal on April 30, 1863. Present or accounted for until wounded at Wilderness, Virginia, May 5, 1864. Returned to duty prior to August 21, 1864, when he was wounded at or near Petersburg, Virginia. Reported absent wounded through February, 1865.

THROWER, JEFF T., Private
Resided in Mecklenburg County where he enlisted at age 20, May 1, 1862, for the war. Present or accounted for until wounded at White Hall on December 16, 1862. Returned to duty in July-August, 1863, and present or accounted for until captured at Bristoe Station, Virginia, October 14, 1863. Confined at Old Capitol Prison, Washington, D. C., until transferred to Point Lookout, Maryland, October 27, 1863. Paroled and transferred for exchange on March 16, 1864. Returned to duty in May-June, 1864, and present or accounted for until wounded at Jones' Farm, Virginia, September 30, 1864. Reported absent wounded through December, 1864.

TREDENICK, RICHARD, Private
Enlisted in Mecklenburg County on May 1, 1862, for the war. Reported absent without leave through December, 1862. No further records.

TURBEFIELD, JAMES, Private
Enlisted at Camp Holmes on November 3, 1864, for the war. Present or accounted for until he deserted to the enemy on or about February 15, 1865. Released on or about February 20, 1865, after taking the Oath of Allegiance.

WALLER, P. L., Private
Enlisted at Camp Holmes on September 3, 1864, for the war. Present or accounted for until wounded at or near Petersburg, Virginia, October 27, 1864. Reported absent wounded through February, 1865.

WARREN, THOMAS M., Private
Enlisted at Camp Holmes on September 10, 1864, for the war. Present or accounted for until captured near Petersburg, Virginia, October 27, 1864. Confined at Point Lookout, Maryland, until paroled and transferred for exchange on or about February 13, 1865. Reported present with a detachment of paroled and exchanged prisoners at Camp Lee, near Richmond, Virginia, February 18, 1865.

WATERS, ALLEN, Private
Previously served in Company H, 41st Regiment N.C. Troops (3rd Regiment N.C. Cavalry). Transferred to this company in November-December, 1864, and present or accounted for through February, 1865.

WATT, C. B., Sergeant
Previously served in Company B, 4th Regiment South Carolina Cavalry. Transferred to this company on April 13, 1863, with the rank of Private. Promoted to Corporal on April 1, 1864, and promoted to Sergeant in March-April, 1865. Present or accounted for until captured near Petersburg, Virginia, March 25, 1865. Confined at Point Lookout, Maryland, until released on June 21, 1865, after taking the Oath of Allegiance.

WILKERSON, JAMES F., Private
Enlisted at Camp Holmes on September 10, 1864, for the war. Present or accounted for until transfer-

red to Barringer's cavalry brigade on December 8, 1864. Regiment to which transferred not reported.

WILKERSON, JOHN, Private
Enlisted in Mecklenburg County on April 1, 1864, for the war. Present or accounted for through February, 1865.

WILKERSON, WILLIAM H., Private
Resided in Mecklenburg County where he enlisted at age 20, March 10, 1862, for the war. Present or accounted for until wounded in the head at Cold Harbor, Virginia, June 1, 1864. Reported absent wounded through February, 1865.

WILLSON, W. H., Private
Place and date of enlistment not reported. Paroled at Appomattox Court House, Virginia, April 9, 1865.

WILSON, J. F., Private
Enlisted at Camp Holmes on September 8, 1864, for the war. Present or accounted for through October, 1864.

WINGATE, R. J., Private
Resided in Mecklenburg County where he enlisted at age 19, March 10, 1862, for the war. Present or accounted for until wounded in the thigh at Wilderness, Virginia, May 5, 1864. Reported absent on detached service or absent without leave until he was reported "in arrest" in January-February, 1865. No further records.

WOMBLE, J. M., Private
Enlisted at Camp Holmes on September 10, 1864, for the war. Present or accounted for until he deserted on December 25, 1864.

WOOTEN, BRYANT H., Private
Previously served in Company I, 9th Regiment N. C. State Troops (1st Regiment N. C. Cavalry). Transferred to this company on December 6, 1864, but deserted to the enemy on or about December 18, 1864. Released on or about December 20, 1864, after taking the Oath of Allegiance.

YOUNG, JAMES H., Private
Resided in Mecklenburg County where he enlisted at age 19, March 12, 1862, for the war. Present or accounted for until he died in hospital at Petersburg, Virginia, November 21, 1862. Cause of death not reported.

COMPANY I

This company was composed primarily of men from Lincoln and Gaston counties and began organizing at Lincolnton on or about March 9, 1862. On March 31, 1862, it was mustered in as Company I of this regiment. After that date the company functioned as a part of the regiment, and its history for the war period is recorded as a part of the regimental history.

The information contained in the following roster of the company was compiled principally from company muster rolls for May, 1862, through February, 1865. No company muster rolls were found for the period prior to May, 1862, or for the period after February, 1865. In addition to the company muster rolls, Roll of Honor records, receipt rolls, hospital records, prisoner of war records, and other primary records, supplemented by state pension applications, United Daughters of the Confederacy records, and postwar rosters and histories, all provided useful information.

OFFICERS
CAPTAIN

HAYNES, ALBERT SIDNEY
Previously served as 3rd Lieutenant in Company K, 1st Regiment N. C. Infantry (6 months, 1861). Appointed Captain of this company to rank from February 12, 1862. Present or accounted for until wounded and captured at Gettysburg, Pennsylvania, July 1-5, 1863. Hospitalized at Gettysburg until transferred to Davids Island, New York Harbor, July 17-24, 1863. Transferred to Fort Wood, Bedloe's Island, New York Harbor, on or about October 24, 1863, and was transferred to Johnson's Island, Ohio, where he arrived October 31, 1863. Transferred to Point Lookout, Maryland, March 14, 1865, and was transferred to Cox's Wharf, James River, Virginia, March 22, 1865, for exchange.

LIEUTENANTS

COON, DAVID A., 1st Lieutenant
Previously served as Sergeant in Company K, 1st Regiment N. C. Infantry (6 months, 1861). Appointed 1st Lieutenant in this company to rank from February 12, 1862. Present or accounted for until wounded in the right foot and both eyes and captured at Gettysburg, Pennsylvania, July 3, 1863. Hospitalized at Gettysburg and at Baltimore, Maryland, until confined at Fort McHenry, Maryland, January 29, 1864. Transferred to Fort Delaware, Delaware, June 15, 1864. Released at Fort Delaware on June 12, 1865, after taking the Oath of Allegiance.

HOYLE, LEMUEL J., 2nd Lieutenant
Previously served as Sergeant in Company K, 1st Regiment N. C. Infantry (6 months, 1861). Appointed 2nd Lieutenant in this company to rank from March 12, 1862. Present or accounted for until wounded at Gettysburg, Pennsylvania, July 3, 1863. Returned to duty prior to September 1, 1863, and present or accounted for through April 2, 1865.

RAMSEUR, OLIVER A., 2nd Lieutenant
Previously served as Private in Company K, 1st Regiment N. C. Infantry (6 months, 1861). Appointed 2nd Lieutenant in this company to rank from March 12, 1862. Present or accounted for until wounded and captured at Gettysburg, Pennsylvania, July 3-4, 1863. Confined at Fort McHenry, Maryland, and at Fort Delaware, Delaware, until transferred to Johnson's Island, Ohio, July 18, 1863. Paroled at Johnson's Island and transferred for exchange on March 14, 1865

NONCOMMISSIONED OFFICERS AND PRIVATES

ABERNATHY, WILLIAM A., Private
Previously served in Company K, 1st Regiment N. C. Infantry (6 months, 1861). Enlisted in this company on March 12, 1862, for the war. Present or accounted for until wounded in the mouth and captured at Gettysburg, Pennsylvania, July 3, 1863. Confined at Fort Delaware, Delaware, until transferred to Point Lookout, Maryland, October 15-18, 1863. Paroled at Point Lookout and transferred for exchange on March 17, 1864. Reported absent sick until he died "at home" on January 2, 1865, of disease.

ABERNETHY, JAMES A., Private
Resided in Lincoln County where he enlisted at age 18, March 22, 1862, for the war. Present or accounted for until wounded in the left hand at Gettysburg, Pennsylvania, July 1, 1863. Discharged December 15, 1863, by reason of wounds received at Gettysburg.

ABERNETHY, JAMES BERTRAM, Private
Enlisted in Lincoln County on October 19, 1864, for the war. Present or accounted for until wounded in the left hand; however, place and date wounded not reported. Retired to the Invalid Corps on December 15, 1864. Age given on hospital record as 20.

ADERHOLDT, JOHN ABRAM FRANKLIN, Corporal
Born in Gaston County* where he resided prior to enlisting in Lincoln County at age 23, May 8, 1862, for the war. Mustered in as Private and promoted to Corporal on November 1, 1863. Present or accounted for until wounded in the arm at Petersburg, Virginia, in 1865. Paroled at Appomattox Court House, Virginia, April 9, 1865.

ALLRAN, JACOB, Private
Born in Lincoln County where he resided prior to enlisting in Lincoln County at age 34, March 15, 1862, for the war. Present or accounted for until wounded at Gettysburg, Pennsylvania, July 1, 1863. Returned to duty prior to November 1, 1863, and present or accounted for until he died in hospital at Lynchburg, Virginia, May 25, 1864, of "pneumonia."

ALLRAN, JOHN P., Private
Born in Burke County and resided in Lincoln County where he enlisted at age 28, March 15, 1862, for the war. Present or accounted for until he died at Wilmington on or about July 2, 1862. Cause of death not reported.

AVERY, ABSALOM, Private
Resided in Lincoln County where he enlisted at age 33, May 8, 1862, for the war. Present or accounted for until wounded at Gettysburg, Pennsylvania, July 1, 1863. Returned to duty prior to September 1, 1863, and present or accounted for until captured at or near Burgess' Mill, Virginia, October 27, 1864. Confined at Point Lookout, Maryland, until paroled and transferred for exchange on or about February 10, 1865. Reported in hospital at Richmond, Virginia, February 24, 1865.

BALLARD, THOMAS J., Private
Previously served in Company K, 1st Regiment N. C. Infantry (6 months, 1861). Enlisted in this company on March 15, 1862, for the war. Present or accounted for until he died at Goldsboro on December 26, 1862. Cause of death not reported.

BELL, MARTIN, Private
Resided in Gaston County and enlisted in Lincoln County at age 17, March 9, 1862, for the war. Present or accounted for until transferred to Company H, 49th Regiment N. C. Troops, May 1, 1862.

BELL, ROBERT M., 1st Sergeant
Resided in Lincoln County where he enlisted at age 28, March 17, 1862, for the war. Mustered in as 1st Sergeant. Present or accounted for until wounded at Gettysburg, Pennsylvania, July 3, 1863. Returned to duty in January-February, 1864, and present or accounted for until wounded near Petersburg, Virginia, August 21, 1864. Died in hospital at Richmond, Virginia, September 1, 1864, of wounds.

BISANER, JACOB H., Sergeant
Resided in Lincoln County where he enlisted at age 18, March 11, 1862, for the war. Mustered in as Private. Present or accounted for until wounded in the left side and captured at Gettysburg, Pennsylvania, July 1-5, 1863. Hospitalized at Gettysburg until transferred to Davids Island, New York Harbor, July 17-24, 1863. Paroled and transferred for exchange on or about September 8, 1863. Returned to duty on February 23, 1864, and was promoted to Sergeant on August 31, 1864. Present or accounted for until captured at Petersburg, Virginia, April 3, 1865. Confined at Hart's Island, New York Harbor, until released on June 19, 1865, after taking the Oath of Allegiance.

BLACKBURN, A. LAFAYETTE, Private
Resided in Lincoln County where he enlisted at age 20, March 11, 1862, for the war. Present or accounted for until wounded and captured at Gettysburg, Pennsylvania, July 1-5, 1863. Hospitalized at Gettysburg until transferred to Davids Island, New York Harbor, July 17-24, 1863. Paroled and transferred for exchange on or about October 28, 1863. Returned to duty on February 23, 1864, and present or accounted for until wounded in the left leg at or near Jones' Farm, Virginia, on or about September 30, 1864. Died in hospital at Richmond, Virginia, October 30, 1864, of wounds.

BOLICK, B. SIDNEY, Private
Resided in Lincoln County where he enlisted at age 20, March 17, 1862, for the war. Present or accounted for until wounded and captured at Gettysburg, Pennsylvania, July 3, 1863. Confined at Fort Delaware, Delaware, until transferred to Point Lookout, Maryland, October 15-18, 1863. Died at Point Lookout in October, 1863, of disease.

BOYLES, ALEXANDER, Private
Resided in Lincoln County where he enlisted on May 8, 1862, for the war. Present or accounted for until he died at Goldsboro on December 10, 1862, of disease.

BOYLES, FRANK J., Private
Resided in Lincoln County where he enlisted on April 2, 1862, for the war. Present or accounted for until he died in hospital at Raleigh on January 20, 1863, of "pneumonia."

BOYLES, JOHN, Private
Resided in Lincoln County where he enlisted on May 8, 1862, for the war. Present or accounted for until wounded and captured at Gettysburg, Pennsylvania, July 1, 1863. Died in hospital at Chambersburg, Pennsylvania, August 10, 1863, of wounds.

BOYLES, JOSEPH, Private
Resided in Lincoln County where he enlisted on July 15, 1862, for the war. Present or accounted for until wounded in the right arm and captured at or near Falling Waters, Maryland, on or about July 14, 1863. Confined at Baltimore, Maryland, and at Point Lookout, Maryland, until paroled and transferred for exchange on or about March 3, 1864. Returned to duty in July-August, 1864, and present or accounted for until captured at or near Burgess' Mill, Virginia, October 27, 1864. Confined at Point Lookout until paroled and transferred to Boulware's Wharf, James River, Virginia, where he was received March 30, 1865, for exchange.

BOYLES, WILLIAM S., Private
Resided in Lincoln County where he enlisted at age 19, March 28, 1862, for the war. Present or accounted for until he deserted to the enemy on October 7, 1864. Released on or about October 12, 1864, after taking the Oath of Allegiance.

BROWN, JOHN A., Private
Resided in Gaston County and was by occupation a farmer prior to enlisting in Lincoln County at age 23, March 15, 1862, for the war. Present or accounted for until he died at Wilmington on August 20, 1862, of "fever."

BYNUM, BENJAMIN S., Private
Enlisted at Camp Vance on October 17, 1863, for the war. Present or accounted for until he died in hospital at Richmond, Virginia, October 31, 1864, of "diarrhoea chron[ic]."

CAMPBELL, A. LORENZO, Private
Resided in Lincoln County where he enlisted at age 18, May 13, 1863, for the war. Present or accounted for until captured at Chester Gap, Virginia, July 21, 1863. Hospitalized at Washington, D. C., July 30, 1863, with "pneumonia" and died August 5, 1863.

CARPENTER, ALBERT, Private
Resided in Lincoln County and was by occupation a farmer prior to enlisting in Lincoln County at age 18, March 21, 1862, for the war. Present or accounted for until hospitalized at Wilmington on or about July 14, 1862, with "febris typhoides." Died July 17, 1862.

CARPENTER, DAVID, Private
Resided in Lincoln County where he enlisted on March 26, 1862, for the war. Present or accounted for until wounded and captured at Gettysburg, Pennsylvania, July 1-5, 1863. Confined at Fort McHenry, Maryland, until transferred to Fort Delaware, Delaware, on or about July 30, 1863. Transferred to Point Lookout, Maryland, October 15-18, 1863. Died at Point Lookout on March 19, 1864. Cause of death not reported.

CARPENTER, HENRY, Private
Resided in Lincoln County where he enlisted on March 26, 1863, for the war. Present or accounted for until wounded in the left hip and captured at Gettysburg, Pennsylvania, July 1-3, 1863. Hospitalized at Baltimore, Maryland, where he died on or about July 31, 1863, of wounds. Hospital records give his age as 40.

CARPENTER, HENRY S., Private
Resided in Gaston County where he enlisted at age 23, March 21, 1862, for the war. Present or accounted for until captured at or near Burgess' Mill, Virginia, October 27, 1864. Confined at Point Lookout, Maryland, until paroled and transferred to Boulware's Wharf, James River, Virginia, where he was received March 30, 1865, for exchange.

CARPENTER, JACOB J., Private
Resided in Gaston County and enlisted in Lincoln County at age 24, March 13, 1862, for the war. Present or accounted for until wounded and captured at Gettysburg, Pennsylvania, July 1-3, 1863. Died July 21, 1863, of wounds. Place of death not reported.

CARPENTER, JOSEPH, Private
Resided in Gaston County and enlisted in Lincoln County at age 23, March 9, 1862, for the war. Present or accounted for until he died at Wilmington on September 21, 1862, of "fever."

CARPENTER, MICHAEL, Private
Resided in Lincoln County where he enlisted at age 18, March 15, 1862, for the war. Present or accounted for until wounded in the leg at Bristoe Station, Virginia, October 14, 1863. Returned to duty in March, 1864, and present or accounted for until captured near Petersburg, Virginia, March 25, 1865. Confined at Point Lookout, Maryland, until released on June 26, 1865, after taking the Oath of Allegiance.

CARPENTER, WILLIAM FRANK, Private
Resided in Lincoln County where he enlisted at age 32, March 21, 1862, for the war. Present or accounted for until wounded and captured at Gettysburg, Pennsylvania, July 1-5, 1863. Hospitalized at various Federal hospitals until paroled at Baltimore, Maryland, August 23, 1863, and transferred for exchange. Returned to duty in November-December, 1863, and present or accounted for until captured at or near Burgess' Mill, Virginia, October 27, 1864. Confined at Point Lookout, Maryland, until paroled and transferred to Boulware's Wharf, James River, Virginia, where he was received March 30, 1865, for exchange.

CATHEY, ROBERT A., Corporal
Resided in Lincoln County where he enlisted at age 25, March 21, 1862, for the war. Mustered in as Private and promoted to Corporal on May 1, 1862. Present or accounted for until killed at Gettysburg, Pennsylvania, July 3, 1863.

CLANTON, WILLIAM L., Private
Resided in Iredell County and enlisted at Camp Vance on October 17, 1863, for the war. Present or accounted for until captured at or near Petersburg, Virginia, April 2, 1865. Confined at Point Lookout, Maryland, until released on June 24, 1865, after taking the Oath of Allegiance.

CLARK, JAMES M., Private
Resided in Lincoln County where he enlisted at age 31, March 21, 1862, for the war. Present or accounted for until captured at Chambersburg, Pennsylvania, or at Greencastle, Pennsylvania, July 3-5, 1863. Confined at various localities until transferred to Fort Delaware, Delaware, where he arrived August 19, 1863. Transferred to Point Lookout, Maryland, October 15-18, 1863. Paroled at Point Lookout on February 18, 1865, and transferred for exchange. Reported present with a detachment of paroled and exchanged prisoners at Camp Lee, near Richmond, Virginia, February 27, 1865.

CLINE, WILLIAM A., Musician
Resided in Lincoln County where he enlisted at age 30, September 8, 1862, for the war. Mustered in as Musician. Present or accounted for until captured at or near Gettysburg, Pennsylvania, July 3-5, 1863. Confined at Fort Delaware, Delaware, until transferred to Point Lookout, Maryland, October 15-18, 1863. Paroled at Point Lookout and transferred for exchange on or about February 13, 1865. Transferred to the regimental band in February, 1865.

CODY, ABSALOM G., Private
Resided in Lincoln County where he enlisted at age 17, March 23, 1863, for the war. Present or accounted for until killed at Gettysburg, Pennsylvania, July 1, 1863.

CODY, JAMES, Private
Previously served in Company K, 1st Regiment N. C. Infantry (6 months, 1861). Enlisted in this company on March 9, 1862, for the war. Present or accounted for until reported absent wounded in May-June, 1864; however, place and date wounded not reported. Returned to duty in September-October, 1864, and present or accounted for until paroled at Appomattox Court House, Virginia, April 9, 1865.

CODY, JOHN, Private
Enlisted in Lincoln County on February 8, 1864, for the war. Present or accounted for until hospitalized at Charlotte on September 9, 1864, with a gunshot wound of the left eye; however, place and date wounded not reported. Returned to duty on September 14, 1864, and present or accounted for until paroled at Appomattox Court House, Virginia, April 9, 1865.

COON, ADOLPHUS S., Musician
Resided in Lincoln County where he enlisted at age 19, March 14, 1862, for the war. Mustered in as Private and promoted to Musician in September-October, 1862. Present or accounted for until captured at or near Gettysburg, Pennsylvania, July 3-5, 1863. Confined at Fort Delaware, Delaware, until transferred to Point Lookout, Maryland, October 15-18, 1863. Paroled at Point Lookout and transferred for exchange on or about February 18, 1865. Transferred to the regimental band in February, 1865.

CORNWELL, SIDNEY, Private
Resided in Lincoln County where he enlisted at age 18, March 13, 1862, for the war. Present or accounted for until wounded at Gettysburg, Pennsylvania, July 3, 1863. Returned to duty in November-December, 1863, and present or accounted for until

killed near Petersburg, Virginia, October 1, 1864.

COX, HENRY V., Private

Resided in Lincoln County where he enlisted at age 45, March 15, 1862, for the war. Present or accounted for through February, 1865; however, he was reported absent sick during much of that period. Paroled at Appomattox Court House, Virginia, April 9, 1865.

CRAFT, MICHAEL J., Private

Resided in Gaston County and enlisted in Lincoln County at age 27, March 15, 1862, for the war. Present or accounted for until wounded at White Hall on December 16, 1862. Returned to duty in March-April, 1863. Present or accounted for until hospitalized at Danville, Virginia, on or about June 16, 1864, with a gunshot wound of the arm; however, place and date wounded not reported. Returned to duty in November-December, 1864, and present or accounted for through February, 1865.

CRYTS, HENRY JACKSON, Private

Resided in Gaston County and enlisted in Lincoln County at age 30, March 15, 1862, for the war. Present or accounted for until he died "at home" on September 23, 1863. Cause of death not reported.

CULBERT, DANIEL, Private

Resided in Lincoln County. Place and date of enlistment not reported. Captured at Hatcher's Run, Virginia, April 2, 1865, and confined at Point Lookout, Maryland, until released on June 24, 1865, after taking the Oath of Allegiance.

DAVIS, SAMUEL, Private

Resided in Lincoln County where he enlisted on March 23, 1862, for the war. Present or accounted for until wounded at Gettysburg, Pennsylvania, July 1, 1863. Returned to duty in September-October, 1863, and present or accounted for through February, 1865.

DELLINGER, FRED WASHINGTON, Private

Resided in Lincoln County where he enlisted at age 18, March 15, 1862, for the war. Present or accounted for until wounded and captured at or near Gettysburg, Pennsylvania, July 4-14, 1863. Hospitalized at Gettysburg and at Davids Island, New York Harbor, until paroled and transferred for exchange on or about September 8, 1863. Returned to duty on February 23, 1864. Present or accounted for until hospitalized at Farmville, Virginia, May 11, 1864, with a gunshot wound of the right breast; however, place and date wounded not reported. Returned to duty in September-October, 1864, and present or accounted for until transferred to Company E, 34th Regiment N. C. Troops, February 1, 1865.

DELLINGER, JOHN F., Private

Resided in Lincoln County and was by occupation a farmer prior to enlisting in Lincoln County at age 19, March 9, 1862, for the war. Present or accounted for until killed at White Hall on December 16, 1862.

DELLINGER, P. FRANK, Private

Resided in Lincoln County where he enlisted at age 18, March 9, 1862, for the war. Present or accounted for until killed at Gettysburg, Pennsylvania, July 3, 1863.

DELLINGER PHILIP, Private

Resided in Lincoln County where he enlisted at age 22, March 11, 1862, for the war. Present or accounted for until wounded and captured at Gettysburg, Pennsylvania, July 1-5, 1863. Hospitalized at Gettysburg until transferred to Davids Island, New York Harbor, July 17-24, 1863. Paroled and transferred for exchange on or about September 8, 1863. Returned to duty on February 23, 1864, and present or accounted for until wounded in the right leg at Wilderness, Virginia, on or about May 5, 1864. Right leg amputated. Retired to the Invalid Corps on November 15, 1864.

EVANS, JOHN R., Private

Enlisted in Lincoln County on February 13, 1864, for the war. Present or accounted for until paroled at Appomattox Court House, Virginia, April 9, 1865.

FINGER, D. CALVIN, Sergeant

Resided in Lincoln County where he enlisted at age 27, March 11, 1862, for the war. Mustered in as Sergeant. Present or accounted for through February, 1865; however, he was reported absent sick or absent on detail during most of that period.

FINGER, ROBERT P., Private

Resided in Lincoln County where he enlisted at age 20, March 11, 1862, for the war. Present or accounted for until killed at Gettysburg, Pennsylvania, July 3, 1863.

FINGER, SIDNEY M., Corporal

Resided in Lincoln County where he enlisted at age 24, March 22, 1862, for the war. Mustered in as Corporal. Present or accounted for until promoted to Quartermaster Sergeant in July, 1862, and transferred to the Field and Staff of this regiment.

GAULT, ALBERT R. F., Private

Enlisted in Lincoln County on August 15, 1864, for the war. Present or accounted for until captured at or near Burgess' Mill, Virginia, October 27, 1864. Confined at Point Lookout, Maryland, until paroled and transferred for exchange on or about February 18, 1865. Paroled at Appomattox Court House, Virginia, April 9, 1865.

GAULT, JAMES, Private

Resided in Lincoln County where he enlisted at age 17, March 15, 1862, for the war. Present or accounted for until killed at White Hall on December 16, 1862.

GILBERT, J. FRANK, Private

Resided in Lincoln County where he enlisted at age 33, March 15, 1862, for the war. Present or accounted for until he died at Wilmington on October 23, 1862, of "yellow fever."

GILBERT, MARCUS, Private

Born in Lincoln County where he resided prior to enlisting in Lincoln County at age 39, March 3, 1863, for the war. Present or accounted for until he died in hospital at Gordonsville, Virginia, September 17, 1863, of "febris typhoides."

GLASSCOCK, SPENCER S., Private

Born in Mecklenburg County, Virginia, and resided in Gaston County where he was by occupation a shoemaker prior to enlisting in Lincoln County at age 48, March 15, 1862, for the war. Present or accounted for until discharged on October 23, 1862, by reason of "age & chronic rheumatism."

GLASSCOCK, STANHOPE A., Private
Resided in Cleveland County and enlisted in Lincoln County at age 23, March 28, 1862, for the war. Present or accounted for until wounded and captured at Gettysburg, Pennsylvania, July 3, 1863. Died in hospital at Gettysburg on July 19, 1863, of wounds.

GLENN, DAVID M., Private
Resided in Lincoln or Gaston counties and enlisted in Lincoln County at age 17, March 13, 1862, for the war. Present or accounted for until wounded at Gettysburg, Pennsylvania, July 1, 1863. Returned to duty prior to September 1, 1863, and present or accounted for until wounded at Wilderness, Virginia, May 4-5, 1864. Returned to duty in July-August, 1864, and present or accounted for until captured at Southerland Station, Virginia, April 2, 1865. Confined at Hart's Island, New York Harbor, until released on June 19, 1865, after taking the Oath of Allegiance.

GLENN, ROBERT JASPER, Private
Resided in Gaston County and enlisted in Lincoln County at age 19, March 13, 1862, for the war. Present or accounted for until wounded at Reams' Station, Virginia, on or about August 25, 1864. Returned to duty in September-October, 1864, and present or accounted for until captured at Petersburg, Virginia, April 3, 1865. Confined at Hart's Island, New York Harbor, until released on June 17, 1865, after taking the Oath of Allegiance.

HAFNER, ADOLPHUS J., Private
Resided in Lincoln County where he enlisted at age 16, March 15, 1862, for the war. Present or accounted for until killed at Gettysburg, Pennsylvania, July 3, 1863.

HAFNER, DANIEL M., Private
Resided in Lincoln County where he enlisted at age 27, March 15, 1862, for the war. Present or accounted for until he died at home in Lincoln County on August 21, 1862, of "fever."

HAFNER, GEORGE HENRY, Private
Enlisted in Lincoln County on May 8, 1862, for the war. Present or accounted for until hospitalized at Wilmington on or about July 6, 1862, with a gunshot wound; however, place and date wounded not reported. Returned to duty on July 20, 1862. Present or accounted for until hospitalized at Farmville, Virginia, July 11, 1863, with a gunshot wound of the left arm; however, place and date wounded not reported. Returned to duty in November-December, 1863, and present or accounted for through February, 1865.

HAFNER, HOSEA, Private
Resided in Lincoln County where he enlisted at age 16, March 15, 1862, for the war. Present or accounted for until wounded at Gettysburg, Pennsylvania, July 1-3, 1863. Returned to duty prior to September 1, 1863, and present or accounted for until captured at Richmond, Virginia, April 3, 1865. Confined at Libby Prison, Richmond, until transferred to Newport News, Virginia, April 23, 1865. Transferred to Fort Monroe, Virginia, on or about

June 15, 1865, and was released on June 20, 1865, after taking the Oath of Allegiance.

HAFNER, JACOB L., Private
Resided in Lincoln County where he enlisted at age 17, March 15, 1862, for the war. Present or accounted for until wounded in the left arm and captured at Gettysburg, Pennsylvania, July 1-4, 1863. Arm amputated. Hospitalized at Gettysburg and at Davids Island, New York Harbor, until paroled and transferred for exchange on or about September 8, 1863. Reported absent wounded until discharged on March 14, 1864.

HAFNER, JOHN, Private
Resided in Lincoln County where he enlisted at age 19, March 15, 1862, for the war. Present or accounted for until killed at Gettysburg, Pennsylvania, July 1, 1863.

HAFNER, JULIUS A., Private
Resided in Lincoln County where he enlisted at age 29, March 19, 1862, for the war. Present or accounted for until wounded at Spotsylvania Court House, Virginia, in May, 1864. Returned to duty in July-August, 1864, and present or accounted for until captured near Petersburg, Virginia, March 25, 1865. Confined at Point Lookout, Maryland, until released on June 27, 1865, after taking the Oath of Allegiance.

HAFNER, MICHAEL, Private
Resided in Lincoln County where he enlisted at age 37, March 15, 1862, for the war. Present or accounted for until he died at Wilmington on August 12, 1862. Cause of death not reported.

HALLMAN, ABEL, Private
Resided in Lincoln County where he enlisted at age 30, March 17, 1862, for the war. Present or accounted for until captured at or near Petersburg, Virginia, April 2, 1865. Confined at Point Lookout, Maryland, until released on June 27, 1865, after taking the Oath of Allegiance.

HALLMAN, ANDREW, Private
Resided in Lincoln County where he enlisted at age 32, March 19, 1862, for the war. Present or accounted for through February, 1865; however, he was reported absent sick during much of that period.

HALLMAN, MICHAEL, Private
Resided in Lincoln County where he enlisted at age 23, March 17, 1862, for the war. Present or accounted for until discharged on January 27, 1863, by reason of "rheumatism."

HARRELSON, JAMES FRANKLIN, Corporal
Resided in Gaston County and enlisted in Lincoln County at age 41, March 15, 1862, for the war. Mustered in as Corporal. Present or accounted for until reported absent wounded in May-June, 1864; however, place and date wounded not reported. Reported absent wounded or absent on detail through February, 1865. Present or accounted for until captured at or near Richmond, Virginia, April 3, 1865. Paroled on April 20, 1865.

HARVEY, NELSON, Private
Resided in Gaston County and enlisted in Lincoln County at age 44, March 15, 1862, for the war. Present or accounted for until discharged on June 6,

1862, by reason of disability.

HAUN, CHRISTY S., Private
Resided in Lincoln County where he enlisted at age 18, March 13, 1862, for the war. Present or accounted for until wounded at Gettysburg, Pennsylvania, July 3, 1863. Reported absent wounded or absent on detail through February, 1865.

HAYNES, ANDREW R., Sergeant
Born in Lincoln County where he resided prior to enlisting in Lincoln County at age 22, March 11, 1862, for the war. Mustered in as Sergeant. Present or accounted for until killed at Gettysburg, Pennsylvania, July 3, 1863.

HAYNES, DANIEL A., Private
Resided in Lincoln County where he enlisted at age 47, March 15, 1862, for the war. Present or accounted for until paroled at Appomattox Court House, Virginia, April 9, 1865.

HAYNES, DANIEL H., Private
Resided in Lincoln County where he enlisted on April 24, 1862, for the war. Present or accounted for until killed at Gettysburg, Pennsylvania, July 1, 1863.

HAYNES, JOHN F., Private
Previously served in Company K, 1st Regiment N. C. Infantry (6 months, 1861). Enlisted in this company on April 24, 1862, for the war. Present or accounted for until captured at or near Gettysburg, Pennsylvania, July 3-5, 1863. Confined at Fort Delaware, Delaware, until transferred to Point Lookout, Maryland, October 15-18, 1863. Confined at Point Lookout until paroled and transferred for exchange on or about February 13, 1865. Reported present with a detachment of paroled and exchanged prisoners at Camp Lee, near Richmond, Virginia, February 18, 1865.

HAYNES, R. WORKMAN, Private
Resided in Lincoln County where he enlisted at age 20, March 9, 1862, for the war. Died at Camp Mangum, near Raleigh, May 1, 1862, of "measles."

HAYNES, RYANN WORKMAN, Private
Resided in Gaston County and enlisted in Lincoln County on February 19, 1864, for the war. Present or accounted for until reported absent wounded in May-June, 1864; however, place and date wounded not reported. Returned to duty in November-December, 1864, and present or accounted for until captured at or near Petersburg, Virginia, April 2, 1865. Confined at Point Lookout, Maryland, until released on June 13, 1865, after taking the Oath of Allegiance.

HILL, WILLIAM L. G., Private
Resided in Lincoln County and enlisted at Camp Holmes on October 28, 1864, for the war. Present or accounted for until captured at or near Petersburg, Virginia, April 2, 1865. Confined at Point Lookout, Maryland, until released on June 13, 1865, after taking the Oath of Allegiance.

HOOVER, DANIEL RUFUS, Private
Enlisted in Lincoln County at age 17, May 8, 1862, for the war. Present or accounted for until wounded at Gettysburg, Pennsylvania, July 3, 1863. Reported absent wounded or absent on detail until he returned

to duty in March-April, 1864. Present or accounted for until retired to the Invalid Corps on December 15, 1864, by reason of "disability from wounds."

HOOVER, DAVID M., Private
Resided in Lincoln County where he enlisted at age 20, March 15, 1862, for the war. Present or accounted for until wounded at White Hall on December 16, 1862. Returned to duty in March-April, 1863, and present or accounted for until killed at Gettysburg, Pennsylvania, July 1, 1863.

HOUSER, HENRY, Private
Resided in Lincoln County where he enlisted at age 22, March 17, 1862, for the war. Present or accounted for until wounded and captured at Gettysburg, Pennsylvania, July 1-5, 1863. Hospitalized at various Federal hospitals until paroled at Baltimore, Maryland, August 23, 1863, and transferred for exchange. Returned to duty in November-December, 1863. Present or accounted for until hospitalized at Richmond, Virginia, June 6, 1864, with a gunshot wound; however, place and date wounded not reported. Reported absent wounded through February, 1865.

HOVIS, B. MONROE, Private
Resided in Lincoln County where he enlisted on April 25, 1862, for the war. Present or accounted for until captured at Gettysburg, Pennsylvania, July 3, 1863. Confined at Fort Delaware, Delaware, until transferred to Point Lookout, Maryland, October 15-18, 1863. Died at Point Lookout on or about May 8, 1864, of disease.

HOVIS, LABAN L., Corporal
Previously served as Private in Company K, 1st Regiment N. C. Infantry (6 months, 1861). Enlisted in this company on March 14, 1862, for the war. Mustered in as Corporal. Present or accounted for until wounded in the jaw and captured at Gettysburg, Pennsylvania, July 1-5, 1863. Hospitalized at Gettysburg until transferred to Davids Island, New York Harbor, July 17-24, 1863. Paroled at Davids Island and transferred to City Point, Virginia, where he was received September 16, 1863, for exchange. Returned to duty on February 23, 1864, and present or accounted for until captured at or near Petersburg, Virginia, April 2, 1865. Confined at Point Lookout, Maryland, until released on June 27, 1865, after taking the Oath of Allegiance.

HUBBARD, CHARLES, Private
Resided in Lincoln County where he enlisted at age 27, March 15, 1862, for the war. Present or accounted for until captured at Bristoe Station, Virginia, October 14, 1863. Confined at Point Lookout, Maryland, until paroled and transferred for exchange on or about February 24, 1865.

HUBBARD, DANIEL, Private
Resided in Lincoln County where he enlisted on March 23, 1863, for the war. Present or accounted for until he deserted on July 22, 1863. Returned to duty on November 19, 1863, and present or accounted for until captured at or near Petersburg, Virginia, April 2, 1865. Confined at Point Lookout, Maryland. Final disposition not reported.

HUBBARD, DAVID, Private
Resided in Lincoln County where he enlisted on

March 15, 1862, for the war. Present or accounted for until wounded at Gettysburg, Pennsylvania, July 1, 1863. Reported absent wounded or absent on detail through June, 1864. Rejoined the company prior to August 25, 1864, when he was wounded in the left leg at Reams' Station, Virginia. Left leg amputated. Reported absent wounded through February, 1865.

HUBBARD, MATTHEW, Private

Born in Lincoln County where he resided as a farmer prior to enlisting in Lincoln County at age 64, March 15, 1862, for the war. Present or accounted for until discharged on or about January 14, 1863, by reason of "the natural infirmities of age."

HUDSPETH, JOHN T., Private

Resided in Lincoln County where he enlisted at age 31, March 15, 1862, for the war. Present or accounted for until hospitalized at Danville, Virginia, on or about June 16, 1864, with a gunshot wound of the finger; however, place and date wounded not reported. Returned to duty in November-December, 1864, and present or accounted for until paroled at Appomattox Court House, Virginia, April 9, 1865.

HUSS, JACOB, Private

Resided in Lincoln County where he enlisted at age 23, March 9, 1862, for the war. Present or accounted for until killed at Bristoe Station, Virginia, October 14, 1863.

HUSS, JOHN, Private

Resided in Lincoln County where he enlisted at age 20, March 9, 1862, for the war. Present or accounted for until captured at Falling Waters, Maryland, July 14, 1863. Confined at Baltimore, Maryland, and at Point Lookout, Maryland, until paroled and transferred for exchange on or about March 3, 1864. Returned to duty in September-October, 1864, and present or accounted for until captured at or near Petersburg, Virginia, April 2, 1865. Confined at Point Lookout until released on June 27, 1865, after taking the Oath of Allegiance.

JETTON, TAYLOR B., Private

Resided in Lincoln County where he enlisted at age 15, July 10, 1862, for the war. Present or accounted for until captured at Falling Waters, Maryland, July 14, 1863. Confined at Old Capitol Prison, Washington, D. C., until transferred to Point Lookout, Maryland, August 9, 1863. Paroled at Point Lookout and transferred for exchange on or about May 3, 1864. Returned to duty in July-August, 1864, and present or accounted for until captured at or near Petersburg, Virginia, April 2, 1865. Confined at Point Lookout until released on June 14, 1865, after taking the Oath of Allegiance.

JETTON, WILLIAM H., Sergeant

Previously served as Private in Company K, 1st Regiment N. C. Infantry (6 months, 1861). Enlisted in this company on March 11, 1862, for the war. Mustered in as Sergeant. Present or accounted for until killed at Gettysburg, Pennsylvania, July 3, 1863.

JOHNSON, ELI, Private

Resided in Lincoln or Catawba counties and enlisted in Lincoln County at age 24, March 15, 1862, for the war. Present or accounted for until reported absent wounded in September-October, 1864; however, place and date wounded not reported. Reported in hospital at Richmond, Virginia, December 9, 1864, with a gunshot wound of the left leg. Returned to duty prior to January 1, 1865, and present or accounted for until captured at or near Petersburg, Virginia, April 2, 1865. Confined at Point Lookout, Maryland, until released on June 28, 1865, after taking the Oath of Allegiance.

JOHNSON, HARVEY M., Private

Resided in Catawba County and enlisted in Lincoln County on August 15, 1864, for the war. Present or accounted for until captured at or near Petersburg, Virginia, April 2, 1865. Confined at Point Lookout, Maryland, until released on June 14, 1865, after taking the Oath of Allegiance.

JOHNSON, LEONIDAS, Private

Born in Lincoln County where he resided as a salesman prior to enlisting in Halifax County at age 25, January 2, 1863, for the war. Present or accounted for until wounded in the jaw at Gettysburg, Pennsylvania, July 3, 1863. Returned to duty in January-February, 1864, and present or accounted for through February, 1865.

JOHNSON, ROBERT, Private

Resided in Lincoln County where he enlisted on March 3, 1863, for the war. Present or accounted for until captured at or near Chester Gap, Virginia, July 21, 1863. Confined at Old Capitol Prison, Washington, D. C. Died in hospital at Washington on August 25, 1863, of "chronic diarrhoea." Hospital records give his age as 20.

KEEVER, GEORGE P., Private

Resided in Lincoln County where he enlisted at age 18, March 15, 1862, for the war. Present or accounted for until wounded and captured at Gettysburg, Pennsylvania, July 1, 1863. Died at Gettysburg on July 7, 1863, of wounds.

KINCAID, CEPHAS G., Private

Resided in Lincoln County where he enlisted at age 18, July 4, 1863, for the war. Present or accounted for until captured at or near Burgess' Mill, Virginia, October 27, 1864. Confined at Point Lookout, Maryland, until paroled and transferred to Boulware's Wharf, James River, Virginia, where he was received March 30, 1865, for exchange.

KISER, HENRY, Private

Enlisted in Lincoln County on February 19, 1864, for the war. Present or accounted for until killed near Petersburg, Virginia, August 21, 1864.

KISER, HIRAM ABRAM, Private

Resided in Lincoln County where he enlisted at age 26, March 21, 1862, for the war. Present or accounted for until wounded in the head at Gettysburg, Pennsylvania, July 1, 1863. Returned to duty in January-February, 1864, and present or accounted for through February, 1865.

KISER, JACOB, Private

Resided in Lincoln County where he enlisted at age 37, March 15, 1862, for the war. Present or accounted for until he deserted on July 22, 1863. Returned to duty on November 12, 1863, and present or accounted for until transferred to Barringer's cavalry brigade on December 7, 1864. Regiment to which transferred not reported.

KISER, JOHN A., Private
Resided in Lincoln County where he enlisted at age 30, March 15, 1862, for the war. Present or accounted for until wounded at Bristoe Station, Virginia, October 14, 1863. Died in hospital at Richmond, Virginia, November 14, 1863, of wounds.

LENHARDT, CAMERON L., Private
Previously served in Company K, 1st Regiment N. C. Infantry (6 months, 1861). Enlisted in this company on March 9, 1862, for the war. Present or accounted for until wounded in the left shoulder and captured at Gettysburg, Pennsylvania, July 3, 1863. Died July 30, 1863, of wounds. Place of death not reported.

LEONHARDT, JACOB M., Private
Resided in Lincoln County where he enlisted on March 9, 1863, for the war. Present or accounted for until killed at Gettysburg, Pennsylvania, July 3, 1863.

LEONHARDT, JOSEPH M., Private
Resided in Lincoln County where he enlisted at age 28, March 11, 1862, for the war. Present or accounted for until wounded at Gettysburg, Pennsylvania, July 1, 1863. Returned to duty prior to September 1, 1863, and present or accounted for until wounded at Bristoe Station, Virginia, October 14, 1863. Returned to duty in January-February, 1864. Present or accounted for until reported absent wounded in May-June, 1864; however, place and date wounded not reported. Returned to duty in November-December, 1864, and present or accounted for until paroled at Appomattox Court House, Virginia, April 9, 1865.

McCOY, WILLIAM H., Private
Resided in Lincoln County where he enlisted at age 17, May 23, 1862, for the war. Present or accounted for until paroled at Appomattox Court House, Virginia, April 9, 1865.

MARTIN, WILLIAM E., Musician
Previously served in Company K, 1st Regiment N.C. Infantry (6 months, 1861). Enlisted in this company on April 25, 1862, for the war. Mustered in as Private and promoted to Musician in September-October, 1862. Present or accounted for until transferred to the regimental band in September-October, 1864.

MILLER, JACOB A., Sergeant
Resided in Lincoln County where he enlisted at age 27, May 8, 1862, for the war. Mustered in as Private and promoted to Sergeant on November 1, 1863. Present or accounted for until wounded in the groin and captured at or near Burkeville Junction, Virginia, April 2, 1865. Hospitalized at various Federal hospitals until released on or about June 12, 1865, after taking the Oath of Allegiance.

MOONEY, McCAMERON, Private
Resided in Lincoln or Gaston counties and enlisted in Lincoln County at age 18, March 15, 1862, for the war. Present or accounted for until captured at or near Burgess Mill, Virginia, October 27, 1864. Confined at Point Lookout, Maryland, until released on June 29, 1865, after taking the Oath of Allegiance.

MOTZ, CHARLES, Musician
Resided in Lincoln County and enlisted at Camp Mangum at age 18, May 3, 1862, for the war. Mustered in as Private and promoted to Musician in September-October, 1862. Present or accounted for until captured at or near Gettysburg, Pennsylvania, July 3-5, 1863. Confined at Fort Delaware, Delaware, until confined at Point Lookout, Maryland, October 15-18, 1863. Transferred from this company to the regimental band in September-October, 1864, while a prisoner of war.

MOTZ, GEORGE, Sergeant
Previously served as Private in Company K, 1st Regiment N.C. Infantry (6 months, 1861). Enlisted in this company on or about May 13, 1862, for the war. Mustered in as Private. Present or accounted for until promoted to Ordnance Sergeant on November 3, 1862, and transferred to the Field and Staff of this regiment. Reduced to the rank of Sergeant in September-October, 1863, and transferred back to this company. Present or accounted for until captured at Farmville, Virginia, April 6, 1865. Confined at Point Lookout, Maryland, until released on June 29, 1865, after taking the Oath of Allegiance.

MULLIN, ALFRED E., Private
Resided in Lincoln County and enlisted at Camp Wilson, Virginia, November 13, 1862, for the war. Present or accounted for until captured at Bristoe Station, Virginia, October 14, 1863. Confined at Old Capitol Prison, Washington, D.C., until transferred to Point Lookout, Maryland, October 27, 1863. Confined at Point Lookout until paroled and transferred for exchange on or about February 13, 1865. Paroled at Appomattox Court House, Virginia, April 9, 1865.

NANCE, WILLIAM W., Private
Enlisted at Camp Vance on October 17, 1863, for the war. Present or accounted for until he died in hospital at Gordonsville, Virginia, January 19, 1864, of "diarrhoea chr[onic]."

OAKS, JOHN, Private
Resided in Lincoln County where he enlisted on March 23, 1863, for the war. Present or accounted for until wounded in the head and captured at or near Gettysburg, Pennsylvania, July 1-5, 1863. Confined at Fort Delaware, Delaware, until transferred to Point Lookout, Maryland, October 15-18, 1863. Confined at Point Lookout until paroled and transferred for exchange on or about February 13, 1865. Rejoined the company prior to April 2, 1865, when he was captured at or near Petersburg, Virginia. Confined at Hart's Island, New York Harbor, until released on June 17, 1865, after taking the Oath of Allegiance.

PAGE, LEMUEL, Private
Born in Greenville District, South Carolina, and resided in Lincoln County where he was by occupation a farmer prior to enlisting in Lincoln County at age 49, March 15, 1862, for the war. Present or accounted for until discharged on October 23, 1862, by reason of "palsy & general debility & age."

PARKER, ASA, Private

Resided in Lincoln or Cleveland counties and enlisted in Lincoln County at age 20, March 15, 1862, for the war. Present or accounted for until captured at or near Petersburg, Virginia, April 5, 1865. Confined at Hart's Island, New York Harbor, until released on June 19, 1865, after taking the Oath of Allegiance.

POOL, ALBERT J., Private

Resided in Lincoln County or at Yorkville, South Carolina, and enlisted in Lincoln County at age 20, March 12, 1862, for the war. Present or accounted for until wounded at Gettysburg, Pennsylvania, July 1, 1863. Returned to duty in January-February, 1864, and present or accounted for until captured at or near Hanover Junction, Virginia, May 24, 1864. Confined at Point Lookout, Maryland, until transferred to Elmira, New York, July 9, 1864. Released at Elmira on May 19, 1865, after taking the Oath of Allegiance.

QUICKEL, LEVI H., Private

Resided in Lincoln County where he enlisted at age 18, August 20, 1863, for the war. Present or accounted for until captured at or near Petersburg, Virginia, April 2, 1865. Confined at Point Lookout, Maryland, until released on June 17, 1865, after taking the Oath of Allegiance.

RAMSEUR, JOHN F., 1st Sergeant

Resided in Lincoln County where he enlisted at age 23, March 21, 1862, for the war. Mustered in as Private and promoted to Sergeant on November 1, 1863. Promoted to 1st Sergeant on August 31, 1864. Present or accounted for until captured at or near Petersburg, Virginia, April 2, 1865. Confined at Point Lookout, Maryland, until released on June 17, 1865, after taking the Oath of Allegiance.

RAMSEUR, JOHN M., Private

Resided in Lincoln County where he enlisted at age 18, August 20, 1863, for the war. Present or accounted for until captured at Bristoe Station, Virginia, October 14, 1863. Confined at Old Capitol Prison, Washington, D.C., until transferred to Point Lookout, Maryland, October 27, 1863. Confined at Point Lookout until paroled and transferred to Boulware's Wharf, James River, Virginia, where he was received March 16, 1865, for exchange.

RAMSEUR, THEODORE J., Private

Previously served in Company K, 1st Regiment N.C. Infantry (6 months, 1861). Enlisted in this company on March 21, 1862, for the war. Present or accounted for until wounded in the leg at Cold Harbor, Virginia, June 1, 1864. Leg amputated. Retired to the Invalid Corps on December 1, 1864.

RAMSEUR, WALTER G., Sergeant

Previously served as Private in Company K, 1st Regiment N.C. Infantry (6 months, 1861). Enlisted in this company on March 21, 1862, for the war. Mustered in as Sergeant. Present or accounted for until wounded in the back at Bristoe Station, Virginia, October 14, 1863. Died in hospital at Richmond, Virginia, October 27, 1863, of wounds.

RAMSEY, R. NELSON, Private

Born in Lincoln County where he resided prior to enlisting in Lincoln County at age 19, March 12,

1862, for the war. Present or accounted for until killed at Gettysburg, Pennsylvania, July 1, 1863.

REEP, THOMAS, Private

Resided in Lincoln County where he enlisted at age 21, March 15, 1862, for the war. Present or accounted for until he died "at home" in December, 1864, of "chronic diarrhoea."

REINHARDT, CHARLES, Private

Resided in Lincoln County where he enlisted on September 23, 1863, for the war. Present or accounted for until he died in hospital at Liberty, Virginia, June 29, 1864, of "pleuritis."

REINHARDT, ROBERT P., Private

Born in Catawba County* where he resided as a farmer prior to enlisting in Lincoln County on January 5, 1863, for the war. Present or accounted for until wounded in the left arm at Gettysburg, Pennsylvania, July 1, 1863. Reported absent wounded until he was retired on or about March 8, 1865, by reason of "necrosis of left arm." Retirement papers give his age as 24.

RHODES, JACOB H., Sergeant

Resided in Lincoln County where he enlisted at age 28, May 8, 1862, for the war. Mustered in as Private and promoted to Sergeant on November 1, 1863. Present or accounted for until captured at or near Petersburg, Virginia, April 2, 1865. Confined at Point Lookout, Maryland, until released on June 17, 1865, after taking the Oath of Allegiance.

RICHEY, JOSEPH C., Private

Resided in Lincoln County where he enlisted at age 35, March 15, 1862, for the war. Present or accounted for until wounded at Gettysburg, Pennsylvania, July 1, 1863. Returned to duty in November-December, 1863, and present or accounted for until killed at Wilderness, Virginia, May 5, 1864.

RINCIK, DANIEL, Private

Resided in Catawba County and enlisted in Lincoln County at age 28, March 21, 1862, for the war. Present or accounted for until captured at Falling Waters, Maryland, July 14, 1863. Confined at Baltimore, Maryland, and at Point Lookout, Maryland, until paroled and transferred for exchange on or about March 16, 1864. Returned to duty in May-June, 1864, and present or accounted for through February, 1865.

RINCK, ANDREW, Private

Enlisted at Camp Vance on October 17, 1863, for the war. Present or accounted for until wounded in the throat and right shoulder and captured at or near Petersburg, Virginia, April 2, 1865. Died in hospital at Fort Monroe, Virginia, April 13, 1865, of wounds. Hospital records give his age as 42.

RINCK, NOAH, Private

Born in Catawba County* where he resided as a farmer prior to enlisting in Lincoln County at age 41, March 21, 1862, for the war. Present or accounted for until discharged on March 18, 1864, by reason of "paraplegia."

ROSEMAN, ROBERT M., Private

Enlisted in Lincoln County on April 20, 1864, for the war. Wounded in the ankle near Richmond, Virginia, prior to July 1, 1864. Reported absent wounded or absent on detail through February, 1865. Paroled at Greensboro on May 1, 1865.

SEAGLE, ANDREW, Private
Resided in Lincoln County where he enlisted at age 31, March 21, 1862, for the war. Present or accounted for until captured at Reams' Station, Virginia, on or about August 22, 1864. Confined at Point Lookout, Maryland, until released on May 13, 1865, after taking the Oath of Allegiance.

SEAGLE, MONROE, Musician
Resided in Lincoln County where he enlisted at age 27, May 8, 1862, for the war. Mustered in as Private and promoted to Musician in September-October, 1862. Present or accounted for until transferred to the regimental band in September-October, 1864.

SEAGLER, ALFRED A., Private
Resided in Lincoln County where he enlisted at age 45, March 15, 1862, for the war. Present or accounted for until killed at Gettysburg, Pennsylvania, July 1, 1863.

SHERRILL, WILLIAM A., Private
Previously served in Company K, 1st Regiment N.C. Infantry (6 months, 1861). Enlisted in this company on March 17, 1862, for the war. Present or accounted for until reported absent wounded in May-June, 1864; however, place and date wounded not reported. Returned to duty in July-August, 1864, and present or accounted for until captured near Petersburg, Virginia, on or about February 5, 1865. Confined at Point Lookout, Maryland, until released on June 20, 1865, after taking the Oath of Allegiance.

SHRUM, J. FRANKLIN, Private
Resided in Lincoln County where he enlisted at age 26, March 17, 1862, for the war. Present or accounted for until he died in hospital at Petersburg, Virginia, December 15, 1862, of "pneumonia."

SHUFORD, NOAH, Private
Resided in Lincoln County where he enlisted at age 37, March 23, 1863, for the war. Present or accounted for until wounded in the left leg at Gettysburg, Pennsylvania, July 1, 1863. Reported absent wounded through February, 1865.

SHUFORD, SIDNEY, Private
Resided in Lincoln County where he enlisted at age 34, May 8, 1862, for the war. Present or accounted for until captured at or near Petersburg, Virginia, April 2, 1865. Confined at Point Lookout, Maryland, until released on June 19, 1865, after taking the Oath of Allegiance.

SHULL, ANTHONY, Private
Resided in Gaston County and enlisted in Lincoln County at age 28, March 15, 1862, for the war. Present or accounted for until wounded at White Hall on December 16, 1862. Returned to duty prior to January 1, 1863, and present or accounted for until captured at Falling Waters, Maryland, July 14, 1863. Confined at Old Capitol Prison, Washington, D.C., until transferred to Point Lookout, Maryland, August 8, 1863. Transferred to Elmira, New York, August 16, 1864, and died at Elmira on October 7, 1864, of "chronic diarrhoea."

SIGMON, ELIJAH, Private
Resided in Lincoln County where he enlisted on

March 26, 1863, for the war. Present or accounted for until wounded and captured at Gettysburg, Pennsylvania, July 1, 1863. Hospitalized at Gettysburg until transferred to Fort McHenry, Maryland, July 19, 1863. Transferred to Fort Delaware, Delaware, on or about July 30, 1863, and was transferred to Point Lookout, Maryland, October 15-18, 1863. Died at Point Lookout on November 26, 1863, of disease.

SIGMON, NOAH, Private
Resided in Lincoln County where he enlisted on March 26, 1863, for the war. Present or accounted for until killed at Bristoe Station, Virginia, October 14, 1863.

SMITH, DAVID G., Private
Resided in Lincoln County where he enlisted on March 26, 1863, for the war. Present or accounted for until he was "left sick in hospital" and/or was wounded and captured at Gettysburg, Pennsylvania, July 1-3, 1863. Died either at Baltimore, Maryland, July 19, 1863, of wounds or at Chambersburg, Pennsylvania, July 20, 1863, of "typhoid fever."

SMITH, JOHN J., Private
Resided in Lincoln County where he enlisted on March 26, 1863, for the war. Present or accounted for until reported absent wounded in July-August, 1864; however, place and date wounded not reported. Reported absent wounded through February, 1865. Company records indicate that his leg was amputated as a result of wounds.

SPEAGLE, AARON, Private
Resided in Catawba County and enlisted in Lincoln County on April 8, 1863, for the war. Present or accounted for until wounded at Gettysburg, Pennsylvania, July 1, 1863. Returned to duty prior to September 1, 1863, and present or accounted for until he died in hospital at Richmond, Virginia, on or about October 7, 1864, of "febris typh[oid]."

SPEAGLE, CAIN, Private
Enlisted at Camp Holmes on August 19, 1864, for the war. Present or accounted for until captured at or near Burgess' Mill, Virginia, October 27, 1864. Confined at Point Lookout, Maryland, where he died January 25, 1865, of "chronic diarrhoea."

SPEAGLE, L. MONROE, Private
Resided in Catawba County and enlisted in Lincoln County at age 18, March 3, 1863, for the war. Present or accounted for until killed at Gettysburg, Pennsylvania, July 1, 1863.

SPEAGLE, WILLIAM P., Private
Resided in Catawba County and enlisted in Lincoln County at age 18, March 15, 1862, for the war. Present or accounted for until wounded in the right shoulder at Gettysburg, Pennsylvania, July 1, 1863. Reported absent wounded or absent on detail through February, 1865. Captured in hospital at Richmond, Virginia, April 3, 1865, and paroled at Richmond on or about April 22, 1865.

STROUP, DANIEL S., Private
Resided in Gaston County and enlisted in Lincoln County at age 19, March 15, 1862, for the war. Present or accounted for until wounded and captured at Gettysburg, Pennsylvania, July 3, 1863. Confined at Fort Delaware, Delaware, until transfer-

red to Point Lookout, Maryland, October 15-18, 1863. Confined at Point Lookout until paroled and transferred to Venus Point, Savannah River, Georgia, where he was received November 15, 1864, for exchange. Returned to duty in January-February, 1865, and present or accounted for until captured at or near Petersburg, Virginia, April 2, 1865. Confined at Point Lookout until released on June 20, 1865, after taking the Oath of Allegiance.

STRUTT, PINKNEY S., Private
Resided in Lincoln County where he enlisted at age 19, March 15, 1862, for the war. Present or accounted for until wounded and captured at Gettysburg, Pennsylvania, July 1, 1863. Hospitalized at Gettysburg until transferred to Davids Island, New York Harbor, July 17-24, 1863. Died in hospital at Davids Island on August 18, 1863, of "pyaemia."

SULLIVAN, C. COATSWORTH, Private
Resided in Lincoln County where he enlisted at age 25, March 9, 1862, for the war. Present or accounted for until wounded in the left leg and captured at Petersburg, Virginia, on or about March 30, 1865. Confined at Point Lookout, Maryland, until released on June 26, 1865, after taking the Oath of Allegiance.

SUMMEROW, PETER J., Private
Resided in Lincoln County where he enlisted at age 18, May 8, 1862, for the war. Present or accounted for until captured at or near Petersburg, Virginia, April 2, 1865. Confined at Point Lookout, Maryland, until released on June 20, 1865, after taking the Oath of Allegiance.

TALLANT, AARON, Private
Resided in Catawba County and enlisted in Lincoln County on April 8, 1863, for the war. Present or accounted for until wounded at Gettysburg, Pennsylvania, July 1, 1863. Returned to duty on January 6, 1864, when he was detailed for light duty. Rejoined the company in November-December, 1864, and present or accounted for through February, 1865.

TOTHEROW, GEORGE, Private
Resided in Lincoln County where he enlisted at age 20, March 9, 1862, for the war. Present or accounted for until discharged on December 22, 1862, by reason of disability.

WACASTER, ABRAHAM, Private
Resided in Lincoln County where he enlisted at age 51, March 19, 1862, for the war. Present or accounted for through October, 1864; however, he was reported absent sick or absent on detail during most of that period. Died "at home" on December 14, 1864, of disease.

WACASTER, ADOLPHUS, Private
Previously served in Company K, 1st Regiment N.C. Infantry (6 months, 1861). Enlisted in this company on March 15, 1862, for the war. Present or accounted for until wounded and captured at Gettysburg, Pennsylvania, July 1, 1863. Hospitalized at various Federal hospitals until paroled and transferred for exchange on or about August 22, 1863. Returned to duty in November-December, 1863. Present or accounted for until reported captured at Wilderness, Virginia, May 5, 1864; however, records of the Federal Provost Marshal do not substantiate that report. No further records.

WARLICK, JOHN C., Private
Resided in Lincoln County where he enlisted at age 21, May 8, 1862, for the war. Present or accounted for until wounded in the right breast and left leg at Gettysburg, Pennsylvania, July 3, 1863. Returned to duty in September-October, 1863, and present or accounted for until wounded in the left arm at Reams' Station, Virginia, on or about August 21, 1864. Returned to duty in November-December, 1864, and present or accounted for until captured at or near Petersburg, Virginia, April 2, 1865. Confined at Point Lookout, Maryland, until released on June 3, 1865, after taking the Oath of Allegiance.

WATTS, JAMES I., Private
Born in Burke County and resided in Gaston County prior to enlisting in Lincoln County at age 38, March 15, 1862, for the war. Present or accounted for until hospitalized at Wilmington on or about June 25, 1862, with "febris typhoid." Died at Wilmington on July 3, 1862.

WEAVER, PHILIP C., Private
Resided in Lincoln County and enlisted in Wayne County on December 20, 1862, for the war. Present or accounted for until wounded at Bristoe Station, Virginia, October 14, 1863. Returned to duty in January-February, 1864, and present or accounted for until captured at or near Burgess' Mill, Virginia, October 27, 1864. Confined at Point Lookout, Maryland, until released on June 4, 1865, after taking the Oath of Allegiance.

WELLS, OLIVER, Corporal
Previously served as Private in Company K, 1st Regiment N.C. Infantry (6 months, 1861). Enlisted in this company on March 9, 1862, for the war. Mustered in as Corporal. Present or accounted for until wounded at Gettysburg, Pennsylvania, July 1-3, 1863. Returned to duty prior to September 1, 1863, and present or accounted for until captured at Bristoe Station, Virginia, October 14, 1863. Confined at Old Capitol Prison, Washington, D.C., until transferred to Point Lookout, Maryland, October 24, 1863. Paroled at Point Lookout and transferred for exchange on or about February 24, 1865.

WILSON, HARRISON S., Private
Resided in Lincoln County where he enlisted on September 20, 1864, for the war. Present or accounted for until captured at or near Petersburg, Virginia, April 2, 1865. Confined at Point Lookout, Maryland, until released on June 30, 1865, after taking the Oath of Allegiance.

WISE, ZENAS, Private
Resided in Lincoln County where he enlisted at age 25, March 21, 1862, for the war. Present or accounted for until paroled at Appomattox Court House, Virginia, April 9, 1865.

WOOD, JOHN H., Private
Resided in Lincoln County where he enlisted at age 25, March 17, 1862, for the war. Present or accounted for until he died in hospital at Wilmington on or about September 1, 1862, of "typhoid fever."

WOOD, PERRY, Private
Resided in Lincoln County where he enlisted at age 20, March 17, 1862, for the war. Present or accounted for until wounded in the left hand at Gettysburg, Pennsylvania, July 3, 1863. Returned to duty prior to September 1, 1863, and present or accounted for until captured at or near Burgess' Mill, Virginia, October 27, 1864. Confined at Point Lookout, Maryland, where he died May 19, 1865. Cause of death not reported.

WYONT, DAVID, Private
Resided in Lincoln County where he enlisted on March 23, 1863, for the war. Present or accounted for until wounded at Gettysburg, Pennsylvania, July 1-3, 1863. Returned to duty prior to September 1, 1863, and present or accounted for until captured at or near Burgess' Mill, Virginia, October 27, 1864. Confined at Point Lookout, Maryland, until released on June 22, 1865, after taking the Oath of Allegiance.

YODER, DAVID, Private
Resided in Lincoln County where he enlisted at age 18, March 3, 1863, for the war. Present or accounted for until captured at Bristoe Station, Virginia, October 14, 1863. Confined at Old Capitol Prison, Washington, D.C., until transferred to Point Lookout, Maryland, October 27, 1863. Confined at Point Lookout until paroled and transferred to Boulware's Wharf, James River, Virginia, where he was received March 16, 1865, for exchange.

COMPANY K

This company was composed primarily of men from Buncombe County and began organizing at Swannanoa on or about March 1, 1862. On March 31, 1862, it was mustered in as Company K of this regiment. After that date the company functioned as a part of the regiment, and its history for the war period is recorded as a part of the regimental history.

The information contained in the following roster of the company was compiled principally from company muster rolls for May, 1862, through February, 1865. No company muster rolls were found for the period prior to May, 1862, or for the period after February, 1865. In addition to the company muster rolls, Roll of Honor records, receipt rolls, hospital records, prisoner of war records, and other primary records, supplemented by state pension applications, United Daughters of the Confederacy records, and postwar rosters and histories, all provided useful information.

OFFICERS

CAPTAIN

YOUNG, JAMES MADISON
Previously served as Sergeant in Company E, 1st Regiment N.C. Infantry (6 months, 1861). Appointed Captain of this company to rank from March 1, 1862. Present or accounted for until hospitalized at Richmond, Virginia, August 29, 1864, with a gunshot wound of the head; however, place and date wounded not reported. Returned to duty in Septem-

ber-October, 1864, and present or accounted for until paroled at Appomattox Court House, Virginia, April 9, 1865.

LIEUTENANTS

BOYD, BENJAMIN F., 2nd Lieutenant
Resided in Georgia. Appointed 3rd Lieutenant in this company to rank from August 18, 1863. Promoted to 2nd Lieutenant on November 1, 1863. Present or accounted for until reported as a prisoner of war from September-October, 1863, through December, 1864; however, records of the Federal Provost Marshal do not substantiate that report. Company muster roll dated January-February, 1865, states that he was a paroled prisoner. Paroled at Charlotte on May 11, 1865.

BURGIN, JOHN A., 1st Lieutenant
Previously served as Private in Company E, 1st Regiment N.C. Infantry (6 months, 1861). Appointed 2nd Lieutenant in this company to rank from March 1, 1862, and was promoted to 1st Lieutenant on September 1, 1862. Present or accounted for until killed at Gettysburg, Pennsylvania, July 3, 1863.

BURGIN, JOHN W., 1st Lieutenant
Previously served as Private in Company E, 1st Regiment N.C. Infantry (6 months, 1861). Appointed 3rd Lieutenant in this company to rank from March 1, 1862, and promoted to 2nd Lieutenant on November 1, 1862. Promoted to 1st Lieutenant on July 1, 1863. Present or accounted for until killed at Gettysburg, Pennsylvania, July 3, 1863.

COLEMAN, ROBERT L., 1st Lieutenant
Previously served as Private in Company E, 1st Regiment N.C. Infantry (6 months, 1861). Appointed 1st Lieutenant in this company to rank from March 1, 1862. Present or accounted for until appointed Assistant Commissary of Subsistence and transferred to the 60th Regiment N.C. Troops on or about September 1, 1862.

DICKERSON, WILLIAM T., 1st Lieutenant
Previously served as Private in Company E, 1st Regiment N.C. Infantry (6 months, 1861). Enlisted in this company on or about April 29, 1862, for the war. Mustered in as Sergeant. Promoted to Commissary Sergeant and transferred to the Field and Staff of this regiment on August 9, 1862. Appointed 2nd Lieutenant to rank from July 30, 1863, and transferred back to this company. Promoted to 1st Lieutenant on November 1, 1863. Present or accounted for until captured at or near Burgess' Mill, Virginia, October 27, 1864. Confined at Old Capitol Prison, Washington, D.C., until transferred to Fort Delaware, Delaware, December 16, 1864. Paroled at Fort Delaware and transferred for exchange on March 7, 1865.

GASH, LUCIUS W., 3rd Lieutenant
Resided in Buncombe County and enlisted in Wake County at age 17, April 20, 1862, for the war. Mustered in as Private and promoted to Corporal on July 1, 1862. Present or accounted for until wounded in the foot at Gettysburg, Pennsylvania, July 1, 1863. Returned to duty in September-October, 1863, and was promoted to Sergeant prior to November 1, 1863. Appointed 3rd Lieutenant to rank from Janu-

ary 27, 1864. Present or accounted for until wounded at Spotsylvania Court House, Virginia, May 12, 1864. Died at Spotsylvania Court House on May 14, 1864.

YOUNG, SAMUEL M., 3rd Lieutenant

Resided in Buncombe County where he enlisted at age 24, March 1, 1862, for the war. Mustered in as Private and promoted to Sergeant on August 9, 1862. Appointed 3rd Lieutenant to rank from November 10, 1862. Present or accounted for until wounded and captured at Gettysburg, Pennsylvania, July 1, 1863. Died in hospital at Gettysburg on July 7, 1863, of wounds.

NONCOMMISSIONED OFFICERS AND PRIVATES

ADAMS, BIARD, Private

Resided in Buncombe County where he enlisted at age 52, April 7, 1862, for the war. Present or accounted for until he died in hospital at Weldon on February 24, 1863, of "erysipelas."

ALLISON, THOMAS J., Private

Previously served in Company E, 1st Regiment N. C. Infantry (6 months, 1861). Enlisted in this company on March 1, 1862, for the war. Present or accounted for until he deserted on August 20, 1863. Returned to duty on October 24, 1863, and present or accounted for until he deserted to the enemy on or about March 14, 1865. Released on or about March 18, 1865, after taking the Oath of Allegiance.

ANDERSON, WILLIAM W., Sergeant

Previously served as Private in Company E, 1st Regiment N. C. Infantry (6 months, 1861). Enlisted in this company on March 1, 1862, for the war. Mustered in as Corporal and promoted to Sergeant on November 10, 1862. Present or accounted for until killed at Gettysburg, Pennsylvania, July 1, 1863.

ATKIN, THOMAS S., Sergeant

Resided in Buncombe County where he enlisted at age 18, March 1, 1863, for the war. Mustered in as Private and promoted to Corporal on September 1, 1863. Promoted to Sergeant in September-October, 1864. Present or accounted for until captured at or near Burgess' Mill, Virginia, October 27, 1864. Confined at Point Lookout, Maryland, where he died January 8, 1865, of "chronic diarrhoea." Roll of Honor indicates he was wounded at Big Creek Gap, Tennessee, March 4, 1862.

BAKER, JOSEPH H., Private

Resided in Buncombe County where he enlisted at age 18, March 1, 1862, for the war. Present or accounted for until he died "at home" on or about December 20, 1862, of "fever."

BALL, JEREMIAH C., Private

Resided in Buncombe County where he enlisted at age 21, April 29, 1862, for the war. Present or accounted for until reported absent without leave on November 20, 1863. Reported absent without leave until he was listed as a deserter on March 19, 1864.

BARTLETT, JACOB S., 1st Sergeant

Previously served as Private in Company E, 1st Regiment N. C. Infantry (6 months, 1861). Enlisted in

this company on March 1, 1862, for the war. Mustered in as Private and promoted to Corporal on November 10, 1862. Promoted to Sergeant in January-February, 1864, and promoted to 1st Sergeant on September 1, 1864. Present or accounted for until paroled at Appomattox Court House, Virginia, April 9, 1865.

BARTLETT, JAMES P., Private

Resided in Buncombe County where he enlisted at age 38, April 27, 1863, for the war. Present or accounted for until captured at or near Gettysburg, Pennsylvania, July 3, 1863. Confined at Fort Delaware, Delaware, until transferred to Point Lookout, Maryland, October 15-18, 1863. Died at Point Lookout on January 1, 1864. Cause of death not reported.

BARTLETT, JOHN H., Private

Resided in Buncombe County where he enlisted at age 40, April 27, 1863, for the war. Present or accounted for until reported missing at Wilderness, Virginia, May 5, 1864. No further records.

BELL, GEORGE H., Private

Resided in Buncombe County where he enlisted at age 18, March 1, 1863, for the war. Present or accounted for until wounded near Spotsylvania Court House, Virginia, in May, 1864. Reported absent wounded through February, 1865. Roll of Honor indicates he was also wounded at Blount's Creek on April 18, 1863.

BELL, JAMES A., Private

Resided in Buncombe County where he enlisted at age 18, March 1, 1863, for the war. Present or accounted for until wounded and captured at Gettysburg, Pennsylvania, July 1-3, 1863. Died in hospital at Gettysburg on July 10, 1863, of wounds.

BIRD, GEORGE P., Corporal

Resided in Buncombe County where he enlisted at age 18, March 1, 1862, for the war. Mustered in as Private and promoted to Corporal on April 11, 1864. Present or accounted for until wounded at Wilderness, Virginia, May 5, 1864. Died in hospital at Gordonsville, Virginia, May 16, 1864, of wounds.

BIRD, T. J., Private

Resided in Buncombe County where he enlisted on November 3, 1864, for the war. Present or accounted for until captured at or near Petersburg, Virginia, April 2, 1865. Confined at Point Lookout, Maryland, until released on June 23, 1865, after taking the Oath of Allegiance.

BIRD, WILSON R., Private

Resided in Buncombe County where he enlisted at age 18, September 14, 1863, for the war. Present or accounted for until captured at Petersburg, Virginia, April 3, 1865. Confined at Point Lookout, Maryland, until released on June 3, 1865, after taking the Oath of Allegiance.

BLACK, PATRICK, Private

Born in Buncombe County where he resided as a farmer prior to enlisting in Buncombe County at age 57, March 1, 1862, for the war. Present or accounted for until discharged on October 17, 1864, by reason of "a want of physical vigor and endurance in consequence of his advanced years." Roll of Honor indicates he was wounded at Blount's Creek on April

18, 1863.

BRITTAIN, WILLIAM T., Private
Previously served in Company G, 9th Regiment N.C. State Troops (1st Regiment N.C. Cavalry). Transferred to this company on November 24, 1863. Present or accounted for until captured at Wilderness, Virginia, May 5, 1864. Confined at Point Lookout, Maryland, until released on June 20, 1864, after joining the U. S. Army. Assigned to Company D, 1st Regiment U. S. Volunteer Infantry.

BROWN, THOMAS KIVEL, Sergeant
Resided in Buncombe County where he enlisted at age 18, March 1, 1862, for the war. Mustered in as Private and promoted to Corporal on September 1, 1863. Promoted to Sergeant in September-October, 1864. Present or accounted for through February, 1865.

BURGIN, BENJAMIN J., Corporal
Previously served as Private in Company E, 1st Regiment N. C. Infantry (6 months, 1861). Enlisted in this company on March 1, 1862, for the war. Mustered in as Private and promoted to Corporal in September-October, 1864. Present or accounted for until captured at or near Burgess' Mill, Virginia, October 27, 1864. Confined at Point Lookout, Maryland, until paroled and transferred to Boulware's Wharf, James River, Virginia, where he was received March 30, 1865, for exchange.

BURNETT, THOMAS W., Private
Resided in Buncombe County where he enlisted at age 17, March 1, 1862, for the war. Present or accounted for until wounded in the left arm at Gettysburg, Pennsylvania, July 1, 1863. Reported absent wounded until retired to the Invalid Corps on May 12, 1864.

BURNETT, WILLIAM A., Private
Resided in Buncombe County where he enlisted at age 26, March 1, 1862, for the war. Present or accounted for until he deserted on July 26, 1863. Deserted to the enemy on or about June 30, 1864. Released on or about July 1, 1864, after taking the Oath of Allegiance.

BURNS, ELISHA P., Private
Resided in Buncombe County where he enlisted at age 20, March 1, 1862, for the war. Present or accounted for until he deserted on August 20, 1863. Returned to duty on November 10, 1863. Hospitalized at Charlottesville, Virginia, December 25, 1863, with acute diarrhoea and typhoid fever. Died in hospital at Charlottesville on January 20, 1864, of "pneumonia."

BURNS, JOHN J., Private
Resided in Buncombe County where he enlisted at age 22, March 1, 1862, for the war. Present or accounted for until wounded at White Hall on December 16, 1862. Returned to duty in January-February, 1863, and present or accounted for until captured at Gettysburg, Pennsylvania, July 1-5, 1863. Confined at Fort Delaware, Delaware, where he died March 3, 1865, of "inf[lammation]of brain."

CLAYTON, WILLIAM L., Private
Resided in Buncombe County and enlisted at Camp Vance on April 9, 1864, for the war. Present or

accounted for until captured at or near Petersburg, Virginia, April 2, 1865. Confined at Point Lookout, Maryland, until released on June 26, 1865, after taking the Oath of Allegiance.

CORDELL, DAVID L., Private
Resided in Buncombe County and was by occupation a farmer prior to enlisting in Buncombe County on March 1, 1862, for the war. Present or accounted for until reported absent wounded in May-June, 1863; however, place and date wounded not reported. Returned to duty in November-December, 1863, and present or accounted for until captured at or near Burgess' Mill, Virginia, October 27, 1864. Confined at Point Lookout, Maryland, until released on or about May 13, 1865, after taking the Oath of Allegiance.

CORDELL, JAMES M., Private
Resided in Buncombe County where he enlisted on April 27, 1863, for the war. Present or accounted for until captured at or near Gettysburg, Pennsylvania, on or about July 3, 1863. Confined at Fort Delaware, Delaware, until paroled for exchange on or about July 30, 1863. Died in camp near Orange Court House, Virginia, January 18, 1864, of "consumption."

CORDELL, JOHN H., Private
Previously served in Company E, 1st Regiment N. C. Infantry (6 months, 1861). Enlisted in this company on March 1, 1862, for the war. Present or accounted for until he deserted on August 20, 1863. Returned to duty on October 24, 1863, and present or accounted for until he deserted on August 22, 1864. Returned to duty and was wounded in battle prior to November 1, 1864; however, place and date wounded not reported. Reported absent wounded until he returned to duty in January-February, 1865. Present or accounted for until captured at or near Petersburg, Virginia, April 2, 1865. Confined at Point Lookout, Maryland, until released on June 26, 1865, after taking the Oath of Allegiance.

CORDELL, JOSEPH H., Private
Resided in Buncombe County where he enlisted on March 1, 1862, for the war. Present or accounted for until he deserted on August 20, 1863. Returned to duty on October 24, 1863, and present or accounted for until he deserted on June 30, 1864.

CREASMAN, ABRAHAM, Jr., Private
Resided in Buncombe County where he enlisted on April 15, 1862, for the war. Present or accounted for through February, 1865.

CREASMAN, ABRAHAM, Sr., Private
Resided in Buncombe County where he enlisted on April 27, 1863, for the war. Present or accounted for until captured at or near Burgess' Mill, Virginia, October 27, 1864. Confined at Point Lookout, Maryland, until paroled and transferred to Boulware's Wharf, James River, Virginia, March 30, 1865, for exchange. Paroled at Appomattox Court House, Virginia, April 9, 1865.

CREASMAN, JACOB, Private
Resided in Buncombe County where he enlisted on September 14, 1863, for the war. Present or accounted for until captured in hospital at Richmond, Virginia, April 3, 1865. Confined at Point Lookout,

Maryland, on or about May 2, 1865. Released at Point Lookout on June 26, 1865, after taking the Oath of Allegiance.

CREASMAN, JOSEPH H., Private
Resided in Buncombe County where he enlisted on April 27, 1863, for the war. Present or accounted for until killed at Gettysburg, Pennsylvania, July 1, 1863.

CREASMAN, WILLIAM J., Private
Resided in Buncombe County where he enlisted on March 1, 1862, for the war. Present or accounted for until he deserted to the enemy on or about June 30, 1864. Took the Oath of Allegiance at Knoxville, Tennessee, July 1, 1864; however, company muster rolls indicate that he returned to duty in September-October, 1864. Present or accounted for until furloughed for sixty days from hospital at Richmond, Virginia, February 24, 1865.

CREASMAN, WILLIAM L., Private
Resided in Buncombe County where he enlisted on March 1, 1862, for the war. Present or accounted for until he deserted on July 26, 1863. Deserted to the enemy prior to July 1, 1864, when he took the Oath of Allegiance at Knoxville, Tennessee.

CROOK, JASPER A., Corporal
Resided in Buncombe County where he enlisted on March 1, 1862, for the war. Mustered in as Private and promoted to Corporal in September-October, 1864. Present or accounted for through February, 1865.

CROW, JOSEPH W., Private
Resided in Buncombe County where he enlisted on March 1, 1862, for the war. Present or accounted for until reported absent wounded in May-June, 1864; however, place and date wounded not reported. Returned to duty in July-August, 1864, and present or accounted for until paroled at Farmville, Virginia, April 11-21, 1865.

CROW, LEVI, Private
Resided in Buncombe County where he enlisted on April 15, 1862, for the war. Present or accounted for through February, 1865.

DARNOLD, JAMES C., Private
Resided in Buncombe County and enlisted in New Hanover County on August 19, 1862, for the war. Present or accounted for until wounded and captured at Gettysburg, Pennsylvania, July 1, 1863. Hospitalized at Gettysburg until transferred to Davids Island, New York Harbor, where he arrived July 19, 1863. Died at Davids Island on or about July 29, 1863, of wounds. [May have served previously in Company E, 1st Regiment N. C. Infantry (6 months, 1861).]

DAVIDSON, JOHN M., Sergeant
Resided in Buncombe County where he enlisted at age 18, March 1, 1862, for the war. Mustered in as Private and promoted to Corporal on November 10, 1862. Promoted to Sergeant in September-October, 1863. Present or accounted for until captured at Bristoe Station, Virginia, October 14, 1863. Confined at Old Capitol Prison, Washington, D. C., until transferred to Point Lookout, Maryland, October 27, 1863. Confined at Point Lookout until re-

leased on June 26, 1865, after taking the Oath of Allegiance.

DAVIS, F. M., Private
Resided in Buncombe County where he enlisted on September 14, 1863, for the war. Present or accounted for through February, 1865.

DEGGERHEART, J. V., Private
Resided in Mecklenburg County where he enlisted at age 19, March 10, 1862, for the war. Present or accounted for until captured at Burgess' Mill, Virginia, October 27, 1864. Confined at Point Lookout, Maryland, where he died January 31, 1865, of "acute dysentery."

DICKERSON, J. R., Private
Previously served in Company G, 9th Regiment N.C. State Troops (1st Regiment N.C. Cavalry). Transferred to this company in November-December, 1864. Present or accounted for until paroled at Appomattox Court House, Virginia, April 9, 1865.

DISHMAN, WILLIAM, Private
Enlisted in Iredell County on November 15, 1864, for the war. Present or accounted for until he deserted to the enemy on or about March 9, 1865. Released on or about March 13, 1865, after taking the Oath of Allegiance.

EVERETT, JAMES H., Private
Previously served in Company B, 9th Regiment N.C. State Troops (1st Regiment N.C. Cavalry). Transferred to this company subsequent to December 31, 1864, but prior to March 1, 1865. Deserted to the enemy on or about March 9, 1865, and was released on or about March 13, 1865, after taking the Oath of Allegiance.

GLENDOWN, JOSEPH B., Private
Resided in Buncombe County where he enlisted at age 19, March 1, 1862, for the war. Present or accounted for until killed at High Point on January 3, 1864, "by Railway Car."

GOODSON, HENRY, Private
Resided in Buncombe County where he enlisted on September 14, 1863, for the war. Present or accounted for through February, 1865.

GOODSON, JOHN L., Musician
Resided in Buncombe County where he enlisted at age 19, March 1, 1862, for the war. Mustered in as Private and promoted to Musician in November-December, 1862. Reduced to ranks in November-December, 1863, but was again promoted to Musician in September-October, 1864. Present or accounted for until transferred to the regimental band in September-October, 1864.

GOODSON, THOMAS, Private
Resided in Buncombe County where he enlisted on March 1, 1862, for the war. Present or accounted for until captured at Falling Waters, Maryland, July 14, 1863. Confined at Baltimore, Maryland, until transferred to Point Lookout, Maryland, August 17, 1863. Transferred to Elmira, New York, August 18, 1864. Paroled at Elmira on October 11, 1864, and transferred for exchange; however, he died at Fort Monroe, Virginia, on or about November 1, 1864. Cause of death not reported.

GUDGER, JOHN P., Private
Resided in Buncombe County where he enlisted at age 36, March 1, 1862, for the war. Present or accounted for until wounded at White Hall on December 16, 1862. Returned to duty prior to January 1, 1863, and present or accounted for until he died "at home" on October 29, 1863. Cause of death not reported.

HALL, JOHN P., Private
Resided in Buncombe County where he enlisted at age 23, March 1, 1862, for the war. Present or accounted for until captured at Falling Waters, Maryland, July 14, 1863. Confined at Baltimore, Maryland, and at Point Lookout, Maryland, until paroled and transferred for exchange on or about March 3, 1864. Failed to rejoin the company and was listed as a deserter on June 1, 1864. Returned to duty on January 1, 1865, and present or accounted for until paroled at Appomattox Court House, Virginia, April 9, 1865.

HARRIS, ABEL F., Sergeant
Resided in Buncombe County where he enlisted at age 28, March 1, 1862, for the war. Mustered in as Sergeant. Present or accounted for until he died at Petersburg, Virginia, October 24, 1862, of "contin-[ued] fever."

HARRIS, THOMAS L., Private
Resided in Buncombe County where he enlisted at age 26, March 1, 1862, for the war. Present or accounted for until captured at Gettysburg, Pennsylvania, July 3, 1863. Confined at Fort Delaware, Delaware, until transferred to Point Lookout, Maryland, October 15-18, 1863. Paroled and transferred for exchange on or about May 3, 1864. Returned to duty in July-August, 1864, and present or accounted for until he deserted to the enemy on or about March 9, 1865. Released on or about March 13, 1865, after taking the Oath of Allegiance.

HENDERSON, EZEKIEL, Private
Resided in Buncombe County where he enlisted at age 30, April 27, 1863, for the war. Present or accounted for until wounded and captured at Gettysburg, Pennsylvania, July 1-5, 1863. Hospitalized at Gettysburg until transferred to Davids Island, New York Harbor, July 17-24, 1863. Paroled and transferred for exchange on or about September 8, 1863. Failed to rejoin the company and was listed as a deserter on March 19, 1864. Returned to duty in July-August, 1864, and present or accounted for until wounded in the left thigh and captured at or near Burgess' Mill, Virginia, October 27, 1864. Hospitalized at Baltimore, Maryland, until transferred to Point Lookout, Maryland, on or about January 28, 1865. Died at Point Lookout on April 28, 1865, of "chronic diarrhoea." [May have served previously in Company E, 1st Regiment N. C. Infantry (6 months, 1861).]

HOWARD, ANDERSON Z., Private
Previously served in Company E, 1st Regiment N. C. Infantry (6 months, 1861). Enlisted in this company on March 1, 1862, for the war. Present or accounted for until he died in hospital at Charlottesville, Virginia, January 29, 1864, of "typhoid fever."

JOHNSTON, JOHN FRANKLIN, Private
Enlisted at Camp Vance on April 4, 1864, for the war. Present or accounted for until reported absent wounded in July-August, 1864; however, place and date wounded not reported. Died in hospital at Richmond, Virginia, September 26, 1864, of "gangrene."

JUSTICE, EPHRAIM, Private
Resided in McDowell County where he enlisted at age 43, October 9, 1863, for the war. Present or accounted for through February, 1865.

JUSTICE, FOSTER M., Private
Resided in Buncombe or Duplin counties and enlisted in Buncombe County at age 28, April 15, 1862, for the war. Present or accounted for until captured at Bristoe Station, Virginia, October 14, 1863. Confined at Old Capitol Prison, Washington, D. C., until released on or about December 13, 1863, after taking the Oath of Allegiance.

KELLEY, J. J., Private
Previously served in Company A, 19th Regiment N.C. Troops (2nd Regiment N.C. Cavalry). Transferred to this company on November 13, 1864; however, the transfer order was revoked on March 16, 1865, and he returned to Company A, 19th Regiment N.C. Troops.

KELLY, ALFRED B., Private
Resided in McDowell County where he enlisted at age 22, April 15, 1862, for the war. Present or accounted for until he deserted on December 23, 1862. Returned to duty on December 10, 1863, and was court-martialed. Reported in confinement until he died in hospital at Salisbury on or about December 20, 1864, of "pneumonia."

KELLY, PATRICK, Private
Resided in McDowell County and enlisted in Buncombe County on April 15, 1862, for the war. Present or accounted for until transferred to the C.S. Navy on April 1, 1864.

KYLES, JAMES, Private
Enlisted in Buncombe County on April 27, 1863, for the war. Present or accounted for until captured at Falling Waters, Maryland, July 14, 1863. Confined at Baltimore, Maryland, until transferred to Point Lookout, Maryland, August 17, 1863. Transferred to Elmira, New York, August 16, 1864. Died at Elmira on November 20, 1864, of "chronic diarrhoea."

LINDSAY, ANDREW JACKSON, Corporal
Previously served as Private in Company E, 1st Regiment N. C. Infantry (6 months, 1861). Enlisted in this company on November 3, 1864, for the war. Mustered in as Private and promoted to Corporal on January 1, 1865. Present or accounted for until captured at or near Petersburg, Virginia, April 2, 1865. Confined at Point Lookout, Maryland, until released on June 29, 1865, after taking the Oath of Allegiance.

LUTHER, W. A., Private
Previously served in Company G, 9th Regiment N.C. State Troops (1st Regiment N.C. Cavalry). Transferred to this company in November-December, 1864. Present or accounted for until paroled at Appomattox Court House, Virginia, April 9, 1865.

McCLURE, OTTWAY B., Private

Resided in Buncombe County where he enlisted on March 1, 1864, for the war. Present or accounted for until wounded at or near Cold Harbor, Virginia, on or about June 1, 1864. Returned to duty in September-October, 1864, and present or accounted for until captured at or near Petersburg, Virginia, April 2, 1865. Confined at Point Lookout, Maryland, until released on June 15, 1865, after taking the Oath of Allegiance.

McKEE, WILLIAM H., Private

Resided in Buncombe County where he enlisted on March 1, 1862, for the war. Mustered in as Corporal but was reduced to ranks in September-October, 1863. Present or accounted for until he deserted on August 20, 1863. Returned to duty on October 24, 1863, and present or accounted for until he deserted on June 30, 1864. Reported "absent in arrest" in July-August, 1864, but returned to duty prior to October 27, 1864, when he was captured at or near Burgess' Mill, Virginia. Confined at Point Lookout, Maryland, until paroled and transferred to Boulware's Wharf, James River, Virginia, where he was received March 30, 1865, for exchange.

McREED, WILLIAM, Private

Resided in Buncombe County where he enlisted at age 18, April 27, 1863, for the war. Present or accounted for until wounded at Gettysburg, Pennsylvania, July 1, 1863. Died on or about July 15, 1863, of wounds. Place of death not reported.

MARTIN, EDWARD A., 1st Sergeant

Previously served in Company G, 28th Regiment N.C. Troops. Transferred to this company on August 1, 1863, with the rank of Private. Promoted to 1st Sergeant prior to September 3, 1863, when he was appointed Adjutant (1st Lieutenant) to rank from August 18, 1863, and transferred to the Field and Staff of this regiment.

MASON, ELIAS P., Private

Born in Lincoln County and resided in McDowell County where he was by occupation a farmer prior to enlisting in Buncombe County at age 30, March 1, 1862, for the war. Present or accounted for through February, 1865; however, he was reported absent sick during much of that period. Discharged on or about March 14, 1865, by reason of "organic disease of the heart producing ascites."

MILLER, DAVID U., Private

Resided in Buncombe County and enlisted in New Hanover County at age 23, September 17, 1862, for the war. Present or accounted for until he deserted on August 20, 1863. Returned to duty on October 24, 1863, and present or accounted for until he deserted to the enemy on or about March 14, 1865. Released on or about March 18, 1865, after taking the Oath of Allegiance.

MILLER, GABRIEL P., Private

Resided in Buncombe County where he enlisted at age 37, April 27, 1863, for the war. Present or accounted for until he deserted on August 20, 1863. Returned to duty on October 24, 1863, and present or accounted for until he died on February 26, 1865. Place and cause of death not reported.

MILLER, JAMES M., Private

Enlisted at Camp Vance on April 4, 1864, for the war. Present or accounted for until wounded at Hatcher's Run, Virginia, February 5, 1865. Died at Richmond, Virginia, February 7, 1865, of wounds.

MILLER, JOSEPH A., Private

Enlisted in Buncombe County on March 1, 1864, for the war. Present or accounted for until captured at or near Burgess' Mill, Virginia, October 27, 1864. Confined at Point Lookout, Maryland, until released on June 3, 1865, after taking the Oath of Allegiance.

MILLER, WILLIAM A. P., Private

Born in Buncombe County and was by occupation a farmer prior to enlisting in Buncombe County on November 1, 1863, for the war. Present or accounted for through February, 1865. A company record dated February 22, 1865, gives his age as 19.

MORRIS, ARCHIBALD G., Private

Enlisted in Buncombe County at age 16, March 1, 1862, for the war. Present or accounted for until he died in hospital at Raleigh on May 2, 1862, of "pneumonia and typhoid fever."

MORRIS, CHARLES, Private

Resided in Buncombe County where he enlisted at age 35, March 1, 1862, for the war. Present or accounted for until wounded in the head and left arm at White Hall on December 16, 1862. Returned to duty prior to January 1, 1863, and present or accounted for until captured at Falling Waters, Maryland, July 14, 1863. Confined at Old Capitol Prison, Washington, D. C., until transferred to Point Lookout, Maryland, on or about July 31, 1863. Transferred to Elmira, New York, August 16, 1864. Paroled at Elmira on March 10, 1865, and transferred to Boulware's Wharf, James River, Virginia, where he was received March 15, 1865, for exchange.

MORRIS, CORNELIUS, Private

Resided in Buncombe County where he enlisted at age 33, March 1, 1862, for the war. Present or accounted for until wounded at White Hall on December 16, 1862. Returned to duty prior to January 1, 1863, and present or accounted for until wounded in the right elbow and captured at Falling Waters, Maryland, July 14, 1863. Confined at Baltimore, Maryland, until transferred to Point Lookout, Maryland, on or about August 16, 1863. Died at Point Lookout on December 10, 1863, of "diarrhoea and catarrh."

MORRIS, MONROE, Private

Resided in Buncombe County and enlisted at Franklin, Virginia, at age 27, October 27, 1862, for the war. Present or accounted for until captured at or near Gettysburg, Pennsylvania, on or about July 3, 1863. Confined at Fort Delaware, Delaware, until transferred to Point Lookout, Maryland, October 15-18, 1863. Died at Point Lookout on February 2, 1864. Cause of death not reported.

MORRIS, ZEBIDEE W., Private

Resided in Buncombe County where he enlisted at age 40, April 27, 1863, for the war. Present or accounted for until hospitalized at Richmond, Virginia, on or about October 20, 1863, with a gunshot wound of the left ankle. Date of wound reported as

August 12, 1863. Returned to duty in January-February, 1864, and present or accounted for until wounded in the right arm at or near Petersburg, Virginia, August 21, 1864. Right arm amputated. Reported absent wounded through February, 1865.

MORRISON, WILLIAM V., Private

Resided in Buncombe County where he enlisted at age 18, March 1, 1863, for the war. Present or accounted for until killed at Gettysburg, Pennsylvania, July 1, 1863.

NEIGHBOUR, FERDINAND, Private

Resided in Buncombe County where he enlisted on April 27, 1863, for the war. Present or accounted for until captured at Gettysburg, Pennsylvania, July 1-5, 1863. Confined at Baltimore, Maryland, and at Point Lookout, Maryland, until paroled and transferred for exchange on or about March 16, 1864. Returned to duty in May-June, 1864, and present or accounted for until he deserted to the enemy on or about December 27, 1864. Released on or about December 29, 1864, after taking the Oath of Amnesty.

NOAH, ELI, Private

Enlistment date reported as December 23, 1861; however, he was not listed on the rolls of this company until November-December, 1864. Present or accounted for until he deserted to the enemy on or about March 20, 1865. Released on or about March 25, 1865, after taking the Oath of Allegiance.

PATTON, CALVIN, Private

Born in Buncombe County and was by occupation a farmer prior to enlisting at Camp Vance at age 44, April 15, 1864, for the war. Present or accounted for until discharged on August 1, 1864, by reason of "paralysis affecting his right shoulder and arm [and] . . . dropsy in the legs. . . ."

PATTON, GEORGE A., Private

Resided in Buncombe County where he enlisted at age 19, March 1, 1862, for the war. Present or accounted for until wounded in the left leg and right ankle at Wilderness, Virginia, May 5, 1864. Returned to duty in September-October, 1864, and present or accounted for until captured at or near Petersburg, Virginia, April 2, 1865. Confined at Point Lookout, Maryland, until released on June 17, 1865, after taking the Oath of Allegiance.

PATTON, JAMES L. M., Private

Resided in Buncombe County where he enlisted at age 18, March 1, 1863, for the war. Present or accounted for until captured at or near Petersburg, Virginia, April 2, 1865. Confined at Point Lookout, Maryland, until released on June 17, 1865, after taking the Oath of Allegiance.

PATTON, JOHN MERRILL, Sergeant

Resided in Buncombe County and enlisted on March 1, 1862, for the war. Mustered in as Corporal and promoted to Sergeant on November 10, 1862. Present or accounted for until wounded and captured at Gettysburg, Pennsylvania, July 1-5, 1863. Hospitalized at Gettysburg until transferred to Davids Island, New York Harbor, July 17-24, 1863. Paroled at Davids Island and transferred for exchange on or about September 16, 1863. Returned to duty in March-April, 1864, and present or accounted for

until appointed 2nd Lieutenant to rank from March 12, 1864, and transferred to Company C, 69th Regiment N. C. Troops (7th Regiment N. C. Cavalry), July 31, 1864.

PATTON, ROBERT CROCKET, Private

Resided in Buncombe County where he enlisted at age 30, March 1, 1862, for the war. Present or accounted for until discharged on or about June 3, 1862, by reason of disability.

PICKENS, GEORGE ANDREW, Sergeant

Resided in Buncombe County where he enlisted at age 18, December 20, 1862, for the war. Mustered in as Private and promoted to Corporal on April 11, 1864. Present or accounted for until wounded in the shoulder at Wilderness, Virginia, May 5, 1864. Returned to duty in September-October, 1864, and was promoted to Sergeant on January 1, 1865. Present or accounted for until captured at or near Petersburg, Virginia, April 2, 1865. Confined at Point Lookout, Maryland, until released on June 17, 1865, after taking the Oath of Allegiance.

PITTMAN, JOHN M., Private

Resided in Buncombe County and was by occupation a farmer prior to enlisting in Buncombe County at age 30, March 1, 1862, for the war. Present or accounted for until wounded in the shoulder at Gettysburg, Pennsylvania, July 1-3, 1863. Reported absent wounded until November 20, 1863, when he was reported absent without leave. Listed as a deserter on March 19, 1864. Deserted to the enemy on or about June 30, 1864, and was released on or about July 1, 1864, after taking the Oath of Allegiance.

POORE, WILLIAM H., Private

Resided in Buncombe County where he enlisted at age 22, March 1, 1862, for the war. Present or accounted for until captured at Falling Waters, Maryland, July 14, 1863. Confined at Baltimore, Maryland, and at Point Lookout, Maryland, until paroled and transferred for exchange on or about March 3, 1864. Failed to rejoin the company and was listed as a deserter on May 1, 1864. Returned to duty on January 1, 1865, and present or accounted for through March 16, 1865.

POWERS, JAMES R., Private

Resided in Buncombe County where he enlisted at age 22, March 1, 1862, for the war. Present or accounted for until captured at Falling Waters, Maryland, July 14, 1863. Confined at Old Capitol Prison, Washington, D. C., until transferred to Point Lookout, Maryland, August 8, 1863. Transferred to Elmira, New York, August 16, 1864. Paroled at Elmira on March 10, 1865, and transferred to Boulware's Wharf, James River, Virginia, where he was received March 15, 1865, for exchange.

PROPST, L. H., Private

Enlisted in Catawba County on October 28, 1864, for the war. Present or accounted for through February, 1865.

ROBERTS, MARTIN P., Private

Previously served in Company E, 1st Regiment N. C. Infantry (6 months, 1861). Enlisted in this company on June 3, 1863, for the war. Present or accounted for until captured at Falling Waters, Maryland, July 14, 1863. Confined at Baltimore, Maryland, and at

Point Lookout, Maryland, until transferred to Johnson's Island, Ohio, October 20, 1863. Released at Johnson's Island on May 12, 1865, after taking the Oath of Allegiance.

SHOPE, THOMAS J., Private

Resided in Buncombe County where he enlisted on February 1, 1864, for the war. Present or accounted for until captured at or near Petersburg, Virginia, April 2, 1865. Confined at Point Lookout, Maryland, until released on June 20, 1865, after taking the Oath of Allegiance.

SHROATE, ALFRED M., Private

Resided in Buncombe County where he enlisted on September 14, 1863, for the war. Present or accounted for until hospitalized at Richmond, Virginia, March 30, 1864, with "chronic diarrhoea." Died in hospital at Richmond on April 28, 1864, of "debilitas."

SMITH, ALFRED B., Private

Previously served in Company E, 1st Regiment N. C. Infantry (6 months, 1861). Enlisted in this company on March 1, 1862, for the war. Present or accounted for until wounded in the face and neck and captured at Gettysburg, Pennsylvania, July 1-5, 1863. Exchanged prior to July 15, 1863, when he was hospitalized at Richmond, Virginia. Reported absent wounded until retired to the Invalid Corps on April 11, 1864.

SMITH, JOHN B., Private

Previously served in Company E, 1st Regiment N. C. Infantry (6 months, 1861). Enlisted in this company on March 1, 1862, for the war. Present or accounted for until he died at Petersburg, Virginia, December 16, 1862, of "pneumonia."

SMITH, RICHARD, Private

Resided in Buncombe County where he enlisted at age 25, March 1, 1862, for the war. Present or accounted for until he deserted on June 30, 1864. Returned to duty in September-October, 1864, when he was reported absent wounded. Place and date wounded not reported. Returned to duty on November 26, 1864, and present or accounted for until captured at Richmond, Virginia, April 3, 1865. Confined at Libby Prison, Richmond, until transferred to Newport News, Virginia, April 23, 1865. Released at Newport News on June 30, 1865, after taking the Oath of Allegiance.

SMITH, THOMAS, Private

Resided in Buncombe County where he enlisted at age 20, March 1, 1862, for the war. Present or accounted for until he died at Wilson on September 24, 1862, of "febris typhoides." [May have served previously in Company E, 1st Regiment N.C. Infantry (6 months, 1861).]

SMITH, WILLIAM E., Private

Resided in Buncombe County where he enlisted on March 1, 1863, for the war. Present or accounted for until he deserted on August 20, 1863. Returned to duty on October 24, 1863, and present or accounted for until reported absent wounded in May-June, 1864. Place and date wounded not reported. Returned to duty in September-October, 1864, and present or accounted for until he deserted to the enemy on or about March 14, 1865. May have served pre-

viously in Company E, 1st Regiment N.C. Infantry (6 months, 1861).]

SPAKE, CHRISTOPHER, Private

Resided in Gaston County and enlisted on November 4, 1864, for the war. Present or accounted for until captured near Petersburg, Virginia, March 25, 1865. Confined at Point Lookout, Maryland, until released on June 20, 1865, after taking the Oath of Allegiance.

STEPP, J. M., Private

Resided in Buncombe County where he enlisted on November 3, 1864, for the war. Present or accounted for until captured at or near Petersburg, Virginia, April 2, 1865. Confined at Point Lookout, Maryland, until released on June 20, 1865, after taking the Oath of Allegiance.

STROUP, S. F., Private

Enlisted in Buncombe County on January 1, 1865, for the war. Present or accounted for until captured at or near Petersburg, Virginia, April 2, 1865. Confined at Point Lookout, Maryland, until released on June 30, 1865, after taking the Oath of Allegiance.

STROUP, WILLIAM J., Private

Resided in Buncombe County where he enlisted at age 26, March 1, 1862, for the war. Present or accounted for until killed at Gettysburg, Pennsylvania, July 3, 1863.

SUTTLES, JOHN, Private

Resided in Buncombe County where he enlisted at age 22, March 1, 1862, for the war. Present or accounted for until he deserted on August 20, 1863. Returned to duty on December 1, 1863, and present or accounted for until he deserted on June 30, 1864.

TRANTHAM, JOHN, Private

Resided in Buncombe County where he enlisted at age 18, March 1, 1862, for the war. Present or accounted for until captured at Bristoe Station, Virginia, October 14, 1863. Confined at Old Capitol Prison, Washington, D.C., until transferred to Point Lookout, Maryland, October 27, 1863. Paroled at Point Lookout and transferred for exchange on January 17, 1865. Reported present with a detachment of paroled and exchanged prisoners at Camp Lee, near Richmond, Virginia, January 26, 1865.

TRANTHAM, JOSEPH, Private

Resided in Buncombe County where he enlisted at age 20, March 1, 1862, for the war. Present or accounted for until captured at Bristoe Station, Virginia, October 14, 1863. Confined at Old Capitol Prison, Washington, D.C., until transferred to Point Lookout, Maryland, October 27, 1863. Confined at Point Lookout until released on or about June 21, 1865, after taking the Oath of Allegiance.

TRIPLETT, JAMES H., 1st Sergeant

Previously served as Private in Company E, 1st Regiment N.C. Infantry (6 months, 1861). Enlisted in this company on May 1, 1862, for the war. Mustered in as Sergeant and promoted to 1st Sergeant on August 9, 1862. Present or accounted for until killed at Gettysburg, Pennsylvania, July 1, 1863.

WATKINS, JESSE M., Private

Resided in Buncombe County where he enlisted on March 1, 1862, for the war. Present or accounted for until he deserted on August 20, 1863. Returned to duty on October 24, 1863, and present or accounted for until captured at Spotsylvania Court House, Virginia, on or about May 8, 1864. Confined at Point Lookout, Maryland, until transferred to Elmira, New York, July 25, 1864. Released at Elmira on July 11, 1865, after taking the Oath of Allegiance. Records of the Federal Provost Marshal give his age as 32.

WATKINS, MINIARD E., Private
Resided in Buncombe County and enlisted at Franklin, Virginia, October 27, 1862, for the war. Present or accounted for until captured at Falling Waters, Maryland, July 14, 1863. Confined at Baltimore, Maryland, until transferred to Point Lookout, Maryland, on or about August 16, 1863. Died in hospital at Point Lookout on November 28, 1863, of "diarrhoea chronic."

WATKINS, URIAH PRESTON, Private
Resided in Buncombe County and enlisted at Camp Davis on May 15, 1862, for the war. Present or accounted for until he deserted on December 23, 1862. Arrested and brought back to camp on January 4, 1863. Present or accounted for until captured at Falling Waters, Maryland, July 14, 1863. Confined at Baltimore, Maryland, until transferred to Point Lookout, Maryland, on or about August 16, 1863. Transferred to Elmira, New York, July 25, 1864. Paroled at Elmira and transferred to Venus Point, Savannah River, Georgia, on or about October 29, 1864, for exchange. Company muster roll dated January-February, 1865, states he was absent without leave.

WEST, JOHN, 1st Sergeant
Resided in Buncombe County where he enlisted at age 44, March 1, 1862, for the war. Mustered in as Sergeant and promoted to 1st Sergeant on April 11, 1864. Present or accounted for until wounded at Spotsylvania Court House, Virginia, May 10, 1864. Died May 11, 1864, of wounds.

WEST, JOHN P., Corporal
Resided in Buncombe County where he enlisted at age 18, March 1, 1862, for the war. Mustered in as Private and promoted to Corporal in September-October, 1864. Present or accounted for until hospitalized at Richmond, Virginia, February 10, 1865, with a gunshot wound of the right leg; however, place and date wounded not reported. Right leg amputated. Died in hospital at Richmond on April 27, 1865, of "hemorrhage."

WEST, W. R., Private
Enlisted at Camp Vance on May 23, 1864, for the war. Present or accounted for until he deserted on June 30, 1864. [May have served previously in Company E, 1st Regiment N.C. Infantry (6 months, 1861).]

WEST, WILLIAM RILEY, 1st Sergeant
Resided in Buncombe County where he enlisted on March 1, 1862, for the war. Mustered in as Sergeant. Present or accounted for until wounded in the head at Gettysburg, Pennsylvania, July 1, 1863. Promoted to 1st Sergeant on September 1, 1863. Reported absent wounded until retired to the Invalid Corps on April 11, 1864. [May have served previously in Com-

pany E, 1st Regiment N.C. Infantry (6 months, 1861).]

WHITE, WILLIAM H., Private
Resided in Buncombe County where he enlisted on March 1, 1862, for the war. Present or accounted for until he died in hospital at Richmond, Virginia, July 30, 1864, of disease.

WILLIAMS, HENRY L., Private
Resided in Buncombe County where he enlisted on March 1, 1862, for the war. Present or accounted for until wounded at White Hall on December 16, 1862. Returned to duty in July-August, 1863, and present or accounted for until wounded at Spotsylvania Court House, Virginia, May 10, 1864. Reported absent wounded until retired to the Invalid Corps on October 26, 1864.

WILLIAMS, RICHARD M., Private
Previously served in Company E, 1st Regiment N.C. Infantry (6 months, 1861). Enlisted in this company on April 15, 1862, for the war. Present or accounted for until he deserted to the enemy on or about March 14, 1865. Released on or about March 18, 1865, after taking the Oath of Allegiance.

WILSON, JOHN W., Private
Resided in Buncombe County where he enlisted at age 43, March 1, 1862, for the war. Present or accounted for until wounded at Gettysburg, Pennsylvania, July 1-3, 1863. Returned to duty prior to September 1, 1863, and present or accounted for through February, 1865. [May have served previously in Company E, 1st Regiment N.C. Infantry (6 months, 1861).

WORLEY, GEORGE WILLIAM, Sergeant
Previously served as Private in Company E, 1st Regiment N.C. Infantry (6 months, 1861). Enlisted in this company on March 1, 1862, for the war. Mustered in as Private and promoted to Corporal in September-October, 1863. Promoted to Sergeant on April 11, 1864. Present or accounted for until captured near Petersburg, Virginia, October 27, 1864. Confined at Point Lookout, Maryland, until paroled and transferred for exchange on or about February 13, 1865. Reported present with a detachment of paroled and exchanged prisoners at Camp Lee, near Richmond, Virginia, February 17, 1865.

WRIGHT, ALEXANDER S., Private
Resided in Buncombe County where he enlisted at age 20, March 1, 1862, for the war. Present or accounted for until he died at Camp Mangum, near Raleigh, on or about April 27, 1862, of "measles."

YOUNG, MARCUS A., Private
Resided in Buncombe County where he enlisted at age 17, March 1, 1862, for the war. Present or accounted for until wounded and captured at Gettysburg, Pennsylvania, July 1-5, 1863. Hospitalized at various Federal hospitals until paroled and transferred for exchange on or about September 17, 1863. Returned to duty in March-April, 1864, and present or accounted for until wounded at Wilderness, Virginia, May 5, 1864. Returned to duty in September-October, 1864, and present or accounted for until paroled at Appomattox Court House, Virginia, April 9, 1865.

MISCELLANEOUS

The following list of names was compiled from primary records which indicate that these men served in the 11th Regiment N.C. Troops (1st Regiment N.C. Volunteers) but do not indicate the company to which they belonged.

BAUM, A., _____
Place and date of enlistment not reported. Died at Richmond, Virginia, on or about April 25, 1865. Cause of death not reported.

BOWDEN, LOUIS T., Private
Records of Company F, 63rd Regiment N.C. Troops (5th Regiment N.C. Cavalry) indicate that he transferred to that unit from this regiment on March 15, 1864; however, records of this regiment do not indicate that he served herein.

COLE, ELISHA, Private
Resided in Orange County. Place and date of enlist-ment not reported. Captured at Appomattox Court House, Virginia, on or about April 9, 1865, and took the Oath of Allegiance at Petersburg, Virginia, May 27, 1865.

SMITH, L. J., Private
Resided in Wilkes County. Place and date of enlist-ment not reported. Captured at Richmond, Virginia, April 3, 1865. Confined at Newport News, Virginia, until released on June 14, 1865, after taking the Oath of Allegiance.

WILKINSON, J. M., Private
Place and date of enlistment not reported. Deserted to the enemy on or about March 22, 1865, and was released on or about March 29, 1865, after taking the Oath of Allegiance.

WILKINSON, J. T., 2nd Lieutenant
Place and date of enlistment not reported. Surrendered at Plymouth on March 29, 1865, and took the Oath of Allegiance the same day.

12th REGIMENT N. C. TROOPS

(2nd Regiment N. C. Volunteers)

This regiment was organized for twelve months' service at the camp of instruction near Garysburg on May 15, 1861, and was designated the 2nd Regiment North Carolina Infantry (Volunteers). A total of twelve companies, most of which had been in various camps of instruction from late April, 1861, were assigned to the regiment at Garysburg. The companies were designated by various letters prior to being assigned specific letters from A to M. Eventually the regiment was reduced to the normal regimental complement of ten companies.

The regiment was mustered into Confederate States service on May 18, 1861, and left Garysburg by rail for Richmond on May 22, 1861. It remained at Richmond until May 25, 1861, when it was ordered to proceed by rail to Norfolk, Virginia, for service under General Benjamin Huger. The regiment arrived at Norfolk at 3:00 A.M., Monday, May 27, and encamped at Camp Carolina, Ward's farm, near the old fairgrounds. There the regiment remained until moved some seven miles to Camp Fisher, near Sewell's Point. Two additional companies, designated Companies N and O, were assigned to the regiment while it was at Sewell's Point. In October, 1861, the regiment was reduced to ten companies when Companies L, M, N, and O were transferred out of the regiment. They became Companies A, B, C, and D of the 1st Battalion N.C. Infantry, which was later raised to a regiment and designated the 32nd Regiment N.C. Troops.

In November, 1861, the regiment moved to Camp Arrington, Sewell's Point, and went into winter quarters. On November 14 the regiment was redesignated the 12th Regiment N.C. Troops (2nd Regiment N.C. Volunteers). Of the ten companies in the regiment, two had been enlisted for six months' service. After serving for that period, Company C was mustered out on November 18, 1861, and Company D was mustered out on December 14, 1861. Many of the men of Company C reenlisted in Company A, 43rd Regiment N.C. Troops, while the men of Company D reenlisted in Company A, 46th Regiment N.C. Troops and Company B, 50th Regiment N.C. Troops. With the mustering out of Companies C and D, the regiment was reduced to eight companies, which were redesignated A through H. Captain Shugan Snow's company was assigned to the regiment after being mustered in in February, 1862, and became Company I. In March, 1862, Captain Robert W. Alston's company was mustered in and assigned to the regiment as Company K.

Under the conscript act of April 16, 1862, all twelve months' regiments were required to reorganize and reenlist for three years or the duration of the war. This regiment held elections and reorganized on May 1, 1862. Later that month Captain John Drake's company was assigned to the regiment and designated 2nd Company H. The company remained with the regiment until July 22, 1862, when it was transferred to the 32nd Regiment N.C. Troops and became 2nd Company H of that regiment.

While at Sewell's Point the regiment was attached to General William Mahone's brigade. When Norfolk was evacuated in early May, 1862, Mahone's brigade retired to Petersburg, where the regiment was detached and ordered to join General L. O'B. Branch's brigade at Gordonsville. After the regiment joined that command, Branch was ordered to move his brigade to Ashland. There it did picket duty watching the right flank of the Federal army in front of Richmond and the Federal force at Fredericksburg.

On May 27 Branch's force was engaged at Peake's Crossing, near Hanover Court House. During the battle this regiment was ordered to the Confederate left where it had a sharp skirmish with the enemy. Before he committed all his troops, Branch received word that the Federals were moving on his flanks. He then ordered his men to disengage and retire to Ashland. During the battle the regiment lost 7 killed and 20 wounded.

Shortly after Branch's command reached Ashland, the regiment was ordered to rejoin Mahone's brigade in front of Richmond. On June 17 the regiment was transferred from Mahone's brigade and assigned to General Samuel Garland's brigade. In addition to this regiment, Garland's brigade consisted of the 5th Regiment N.C. State Troops, 13th Regiment N.C. Troops (3rd Regiment N.C. Volunteers), 20th Regiment N.C. Troops (10th Regiment N.C. Volunteers), and 23rd Regiment N.C. Troops (13th Regiment N.C. Volunteers). Garland's brigade was assigned to General D. H. Hill's division.

On June 25, during the action at King's School House, Garland's brigade moved up the Williamsburg road to support the Confederates under General Benjamin Huger. The brigade occupied rifle pits in rear of the action and was exposed to artillery fire during the entire afternoon. After dark the brigade retired to its old camp.

At about 2:00 A.M. on the morning of June 26 the brigade moved to the Chickahominy Bridge on the Mechanicsville Turnpike to join the troops concentrating under General Robert E. Lee for an attack on the Federal right at Mechanicsville. At 4:00 P.M. General Roswell S. Ripley's brigade, D.H. Hill's division, crossed the bridge to aid General A.P. Hill's troops engaged at Mechanicsville. The remainder of the division followed but did not take an active part in the day's action. That night General D. H. Hill received orders to cooperate with General T.J. Jackson on the Cold Harbor road. General Jackson's troops were on the Confederate left. At daylight General Hill found his route blocked and sent Garland's and G. B. Anderson's brigades to the left to turn the enemy's position. The Federals abandoned their defenses when the two brigades began to move on their flank and rear, and Hill's whole division moved toward Cold Harbor.

In the meantime, General Jackson had been forced to change his route and was proceeding on a road that would bring his troops behind and to the right of D.H. Hill's division. Hill advanced his troops to Cold Harbor and then deployed them along the edge of Powhite Swamp. To his right, Jackson's men came into position, and on their right the troops of A. P. Hill's and James Longstreet's divisions were engaging the enemy at Gaines' Mill. Jackson's and D. H. Hill's troops were ordered forward to the support of Longstreet and

A. P. Hill. Garland's brigade was on the extreme left of the Confederate line. As Anderson's brigade on Garland's right met the enemy on the edge of the swamp, Garland's brigade moved to attack. After a short but bloody contest the woods were cleared of the enemy. A general attack was ordered, and the Federals, under pressure from the front and threatened by possible attack on their right, withdrew. Night brought an end to the contest, and the Federals made good their escape.

From Gaines' Mill the Confederate left wing, under command of General Jackson, moved to cross the Chickahominy at Grapevine Bridge, which had been destroyed by the enemy in his retreat. There the troops went into bivouac while the bridge was being rebuilt, June 28-29. On June 30 the troops advanced across the bridge and marched to White Oak Bridge, which the Federals had also destroyed. There a strong enemy force kept the Confederates from rebuilding the bridge and thus held Jackson's men at bay while the battle of Frayser's Farm was raging. Following the battle the bridge was rebuilt, and Jackson's men joined forces with the right wing of the army and moved to meet the enemy at Malvern Hill. General D. H. Hill's division was placed in the Confederate center. Late on the afternoon of July 1 a general assault was launched on the enemy positions at Malvern Hill. Hill's division advanced across an open field with the enemy batteries some 700 to 800 yards distant. Garland's brigade advanced until forced to halt and take cover about halfway to the objective. As support was not forthcoming, the brigade retired. During the night the Federals retired to Harrison's Landing. The battle of Malvern Hill was the last engagement of the Seven Days' battles around Richmond, June 25-July 1, 1862. This regiment was actively engaged at Gaines' Mill, June 27, and Malvern Hill, July 1, and lost 51 killed, 160 wounded, and 1 missing.

The brigade remained in bivouac near Malvern Hill until marched back to its original camp near Richmond on July 9-10. D. H. Hill's division was left in front of Richmond to watch the Federal army at Harrison's Landing while Jackson and then Longstreet moved to confront General John Pope's Federal force in middle Virginia. In mid-August, General Garland's brigade was moved to Hanover Junction with two other brigades of the division. On August 26 the brigades at Hanover Junction marched to join the remainder of the division at Orange Court House. The entire division moved to join the Army of Northern Virginia on August 28. It reached the army at Chantilly, September 2, 1862, after the second battle of Manassas, and crossed into Maryland on September 4-5.

Upon reaching Frederick, Maryland, the army halted, and General Lee determined to send Jackson to capture Harpers Ferry while Longstreet advanced to Hagerstown. On September 10 D. H. Hill's division moved out of Frederick as the rear guard of Longstreet's column. Mounting pressure from the advancing Federals, plus the necessity of protecting Jackson at Harpers Ferry, resulted in the deployment of Hill's division along the South Mountain gaps below Boonsboro on September 13. Hill stationed Garland's brigade at Fox's Gap, where the brigade came under heavy fire during the engagement on September 14. The regiment was sent forward to reinforce the 5th Regiment N.C.

State Troops, which was under heavy pressure. Unfortunately, the regiment was without regimental officers, and the senior captain failed to coordinate the advance of the regiment. The result was disastrous. As they came under fire the men began to scatter. Some advanced to support the 5th Regiment N.C. State Troops, some retired from the field, and some moved to the flanks and joined other units for the remainder of the fight. The commanding officer of the 13th Regiment N.C. Troops (3rd Regiment N.C. Volunteers) reported that "we were joined by a small party of the Twelfth North Carolina Regiment early in the morning, who continued with us throughout the day and rendered us very efficient aid." (*O.R.*, S.I., Vol. XIX, pt. 1, p. 1047)

During the engagement on September 14 General Garland was mortally wounded, and Colonel McRae of the 5th Regiment N.C. State Troops assumed command of the brigade. Reinforced, the brigade held until the next day when it was withdrawn under general orders to concentrate at Sharpsburg. Upon arriving at Antietam Creek on September 15, the brigade went into position on the heights east of the creek. Later D.H. Hill's troops were moved into position, between the troops of Jackson on the left and Longstreet on the right, on the Confederate line in front of Sharpsburg.

On the morning of September 17 the Confederate left was vigorously assaulted, and Garland's brigade, still under Colonel McRae, and two other brigades of Hill's division (Colquitt's and Ripley's) were ordered to support Jackson's right. Colonel McRae reported (*O.R.*, S.I., Vol. XIX, pt. 1, p. 1043):

> The brigade was moved from its position, on the Hagerstown road, to the support of Colquitt's, which was then about engaging [*sic*] the enemy on our left front. This was about 10 o'clock. We moved by the left flank, until we reached a point near the woods, when line of battle was formed and the advance begun. Some confusion ensued, from conflicting orders. When the brigade crossed the fence, it was halted and formed and again advanced. Coming in sight of the enemy, the firing was commenced steadily and with good will, and from an excellent position, but, unaccountably to me, an order was given to cease fire — that General Ripley's brigade was in front. This produced great confusion, and in the midst of it a force of the enemy appearing on the right, it commenced to break, and a general panic ensued. It was in vain that the field and most of the company officers exerted themselves to rally it. The troops left the field in confusion, the field officers, company officers, and myself bringing up the rear. Subsequently several portions of the brigade, under Colonel [Alfred] Iverson, Captain [T. M.] Garrett, and others, were rallied and brought into action, rendering useful service.

Even though the line was under severe pressure, the Confederate left held with the aid of reinforcements. The main Federal attack then shifted to the Confederate center which also held until the battle shifted to the Confederate right. Although severely crippled, the Confederate line held during the battle of September 17. On more than one occasion during that day, reinforcements arrived just in time to blunt Federal assault columns. The next day the two opposing armies rested on the field, and during the night of September 18 the Army of Northern Virginia retired across the Potomac

River and went into camp. Regimental losses for the brigade were not reported, but during the Maryland campaign the brigade lost 40 killed, 210 wounded, and 187 missing.

The Army of Northern Virginia remained in the Shenandoah Valley until the Army of the Potomac crossed the Potomac River east of the Blue Ridge. By use of his cavalry, Lee sought to discover the enemy's intentions. On October 28, 1862, Longstreet's corps moved east of the mountains to Culpeper Court House while Jackson's corps moved closer to Winchester. D.H. Hill's division was posted at the forks of the Shenandoah River to guard the mountain passes. During October the 13th Regiment N.C. Troops (3rd Regiment N.C. Volunteers) was transferred out of the brigade. On November 6 Colonel Alfred Iverson, 20th Regiment N.C. Troops (10th Regiment N.C. Volunteers) was promoted to brigadier general and assigned to command Garland's brigade, which then became known as Iverson's brigade.

When the enemy's intention was discerned, Lee moved Longstreet to Culpeper Court House and ordered Jackson to prepare to move. Hill's division was pulled back and sent to Strasburg. From there the division took up the line of march to Gordonsville on November 21, and from Gordonsville it marched to Fredericksburg. On December 3 Hill's division was sent to Port Royal, below Fredericksburg, to prevent any crossing of the Rappahannock River at or near that point. It remained there until December 12, when it was ordered to Fredericksburg. Upon arriving at the latter place on the morning of December 13, it was assigned to the third defensive line. During the battle of that day the division was subjected to heavy artillery fire but saw little action. After the battle it was advanced to the second line, where it remained throughout the next day. On December 15 it went into the first line, where it remained for two days. While on the field the regiment was never actually engaged but lost five men wounded from the artillery fire.

Following the battle the regiment went into winter quarters near Fredericksburg. There it spent the winter of 1862-1863 on picket duty on the Rappahannock River. In January, 1863, General D. H. Hill was ordered to report to the Adjutant and Inspector General in Richmond for reassignment. His division was assigned to General Edward Johnson, who was absent wounded. The senior brigadier, Robert E. Rodes, assumed command until General Johnson returned to active duty, and the division remained in General Jackson's corps. On April 29, 1863, it received orders to march to Hamilton's Crossing, below Fredericksburg. There it was placed in position on the right of the forces in the Fredericksburg entrenchments and extended the line to Massaponax Creek. During April 29-30 the division was subjected to occasional shelling, but no general action occurred. Concluding that the enemy activity at Massaponax Creek was a feint, Lee ordered the division moved up to Hamilton's Crossing during the evening of April 30.

General Hooker's Federal army had, in the meantime, moved up the left bank of the Rappahannock to cross over behind the Confederates at Fredericksburg. General Lee now shifted a portion of his army to oppose this threat, and on May 1 Jackson's corps moved down the Orange and Fredericksburg Plank Road in the direction of Chancellorsville. Johnson's division, under General Rodes, was in the advance, with General Ramseur's brigade in front and Iverson's brigade just behind. To Jackson's right, Major General Richard H. Anderson's division engaged the enemy. About three miles from Chancellorsville, Iverson's brigade was moved forward by the right flank in line of battle parallel to the road. Finding the enemy retiring, the brigade was ordered to hold its position. At sundown the brigade was ordered to withdraw and move in the direction of Chancellorsville. It camped about one mile from the town that night.

Immediately after daylight on the morning of May 2 the brigade was ordered to relieve General Ramseur's brigade in front and to the right of the road leading into Chancellorsville. About 10:00 A.M. Iverson was instructed to rejoin the division. The brigade followed General Trimble's division as Jackson moved his men to flank the Federal position at Chancellorsville. After hard marching, Jackson's corps succeeded in reaching a point about four miles west of Chancellorsville on the exposed right flank of Hooker's army.

As the troops came up, Jackson ordered that they be deployed in three lines for the attack. Four brigades of the division were placed in the first of the three lines of battle. Iverson's brigade was placed on the left of the first line. The attack began about 5:15 P.M. General Iverson reported the battle as follows (O.R., S.I., Vol. XXV, pt. 1, pp. 984-985):

Advancing through the dense and tangled undergrowth in the following order—Fifth North Carolina on the right, connecting with Rodes' Brigade; Twelfth North Carolina next, then the Twentieth North Carolina, and on the left the Twenty-third North Carolina, moving by the flank—the skirmishers soon engaged, and the whole pressed hotly and quickly to the attack. The enemy seemed to be completely taken by surprise, and made no organized resistance. At several points regiments appeared, but were quickly dispersed. Their line of intrenchments were taken by my brigade completely in rear, and the enemy broke and streamed over the hills toward Chancellorsville. The second line, commanded by Brigadier-General [Raleigh E.] Colston, closed in with us at this point, and caused great confusion, the two lines rushing forward pell-mell upon the enemy, and becoming mingled in almost inextricable confusion, no officer being able to tell what men he commanded. A battery played upon us until we approached very close, and then retired, leaving one gun on the ground passed over by the Fifth North Carolina.

The gallant and lamented Maj. D[avid] P[inkney] Rowe, commanding the Twelfth North Carolina, fell, mortally wounded, in the first of the fight, a noble sacrifice to his country's cause.

The whole affair from the moment of attack was a wild scene of triumph on our part. Hungry men seized provisions as they passed the camps of the enemy, and rushed forward, eating, shouting, and firing. A force of the enemy's cavalry advanced to charge, but were sent fleeing to the rear, the Yankee officers leading their men in retreat. The enemy were driven over a mile before a halt was ordered, and night was falling upon us.

After much labor the brigade—divided in many portions by the celerity of the movement and the confusion caused by the second line closing up with us—was collected together and moved to the rear, to take post in the third line of battle for the following morning.

During the night of May 2-3 efforts were made to re-organize Jackson's troops into three lines so that the attack could be renewed on the morning of May 3. General Iverson assigned Lieutenant Colonel Robert D. Johnston of the 23rd Regiment N.C. Troops (13th Regiment N.C. Volunteers) to command the 12th Regiment N.C. Troops (2nd Regiment N.C. Volunteers) after Major Rowe's death. When he assumed command, Lieutenant Colonel Johnston reported that the regiment numbered 200 enlisted men and 25 officers.

The attack was renewed early on May 3. About 6:00 A.M. the brigade advanced with the whole line. Lieutenant Colonel Johnston reported the regiment's movements as the battle progressed to the final Confederate victory (O.R., S.I., Vol, XXV, pt. 1, p. 990):

We were ordered forward immediately, and advanced for a mile through an almost impenetrable thicket of pines and over marshes until we came upon the barricade constructed by the enemy, where I discovered that the Fifth North Carolina had become separated from the brigade in the tangled wilderness through which we had passed. It being utterly impossible to hear any commands, I had advanced but a few hundred yards beyond the barricade when a battery of the enemy opened upon me with canister, enfilading my whole command, and a force of infantry also appeared upon my left flank. I immediately dispatched Adjt. J[ohn] T[illery] Gregory with this information to General Iverson, and moved my regiment by the right flank until I closed up on the brigade, and, having deployed a company as skirmishers upon my left, I moved forward but a short distance when I came upon the enemy in heavy force in my front. A severe fight ensued of half hour or more duration, and the enemy were gradually falling back before us, closely followed, when the skirmishers upon my left flank were driven in, and volley after volley was poured into my flank ere I could give the command to fall back. And it is with pride and gratification that I can say, though the whole command was under a withering cross-fire for a few moments, yet not a man gave way until I had given the order.

Our loss was severe at this place, and the enemy were so close that some few were captured in the retreat.

The line was again reformed, irrespective of regiments, at the barricade, and General Iverson having placed some troops in position to protect our left, the whole line advanced a second time, and came [upon] the right flank of a heavy line of infantry moving toward the Plank road. When within easy range, we delivered a scathing fire into their flank—with greater effect, from the number of their dead, than upon any other part of the field that came under my observation. The enemy retreated in great confusion, and I ordered the whole line forward. We had advanced but a short distance when the troops protecting our left flank became hotly engaged, and were retiring stubbornly before an immensely superior force. This compelled our line to fall back a few hundred yards, where the line was again reformed, and halted until ordered by (I think) both Generals Pender and Thomas to fall back to the Plank road. After two or three hours' rest, we were moved down the Plank road, and took position near the brick house, under a heavy fire from the enemy's batteries.

While the regiment was engaged as Johnston reported, General Lee had driven the enemy and effected a junction with the right of Jackson's corps, now under command of General J.E.B. Stuart. The entire Confederate line converged on Chancellorsville and forced the Federals to retire. Once Chancellorsville was occupied, Hill's division was ordered to entrench along the Plank Road. It occupied this position until Hooker's army recrossed the Rappahannock and Lee moved his army back to Fredericksburg. On May 6 Iverson's brigade encamped at its old camp near Fredericksburg. During the Chancellorsville campaign the regiment lost 12 killed, 96 wounded, and 11 missing or captured.

Following the Chancellorsville campaign and the death of Jackson, the Army of Northern Virginia was divided into three corps. Iverson's brigade was assigned to Major General Robert E. Rodes's division, Lieutenant General Richard S. Ewell's 2nd Corps. The brigade composition remained the same. The division left camp on June 3 and reached just beyond Culpeper Court House on June 7. Ewell's corps, with Rodes's division leading, was on the march to Pennsylvania. From Culpeper Court House the division moved to Brandy Station to assist the cavalry on June 9 but arrived after the battle was over. It then resumed its march toward the Shenandoah Valley. Rodes's division received orders on June 12 to proceed to Cedarville by way of Chester Gap in advance of the other two divisions of the corps. At Cedarville, Rodes received orders to move on to Berryville and Martinsburg and into Maryland, while the other two divisions of the corps moved on Winchester. Berryville was occupied on June 13, after its defenders made good their escape. On June 14, Rodes's division deployed before the defenses of Martinsburg. Fearing the defenders might escape, Rodes ordered a charge. The Confederates drove the enemy at almost a run for two miles beyond the town. However, the enemy infantry escaped by taking the Shepherdstown road while the Confederates concentrated on the Federal cavalry and artillery on the Williamsport road. On June 15 Rodes heard of the victory at Winchester and moved his men to Williamsport. The division remained at Williamsport until the balance of the corps moved up. On June 19 Rodes's division was put in motion and marched to Hagerstown, where it remained two days. The division resumed its march on June 22, crossed into Pennsylvania, and bivouacked at Greencastle. The next day the division moved toward Chambersburg and passed through that town on June 24. There Major General Edward Johnson's division joined Rodes's, and together they moved to Carlisle, arriving there on June 27.

On the night of June 30 Rodes's division was at Heidlersburg, where General Ewell received orders to proceed to Cashtown or Gettysburg, as circumstances might dictate. Rodes's division moved on the morning of July 1 for Cashtown. While en route, word came that A. P. Hill's corps was moving on Gettysburg, and General Ewell directed Rodes to proceed toward Gettysburg. When Rodes's division arrived on the field, A. P. Hill's men were already engaged. Rodes moved his division into position on Hill's left, placing four brigades on the line and one in reserve. Iverson's brigade was on the right center of Rodes's line. The timely arrival of Major General Jubal Early's division, on the left of Rodes, combined with the assaults launched from Hill's and Rodes's lines, drove the enemy through the town of Gettysburg. General Iverson reported the activities of his brigade on that and succeeding days at Gettysburg as follows (*O.R.*, S.I., Vol. XXVII, pt. 2, pp. 578-580):

[M]y brigade, being in the advance of Maj. Gen. R. E. Rodes' division, was ordered by him to form line of battle and advance toward the firing at Gettysburg. This advance brought my brigade across a wooded height overlooking the plain and the town of Gettysburg.

. . . .

Learning that the Alabama brigade, on my left, was moving, I advanced at once, and soon came in contact with the enemy, strongly posted in woods and behind a concealed stone wall. My brigade advanced to within 100 yards, and a most desperate fight took place. I observed a gap on my left, but presumed that it would soon be filled by the advancing Alabama brigade, under Colonel [E. A.] O'Neal. Brigadier-General [Junius] Daniel came up to my position, and I asked him for immediate support, as I was attacking a strong position. He promised to send me a large regiment, which I informed him would be enough, as the Third Alabama Regiment was then moving down on my right, and I then supposed was sent to my support. At the same time, I pointed out to General Daniel a large force of the enemy who were about to outflank my right, and asked him to take care of them. He moved past my position, and engaged the enemy some distance to my right, but the regiment he had promised me, and which I had asked him to forward to the position at which I stood, and where I was being pressed most heavily, did not report to me at all.

I again sent Capt. D.P. Halsey, assistant adjutant-general, to ask General Daniel for aid, who informs me [*sic*] that he met his staff officer, and was told that one regiment had been sent, and no more could be spared. I then found that this regiment had formed on the right of the Third Alabama, which was on my right, and could not be used in time to save my brigade, for Colonel O'Neal's (Alabama) brigade had in the meantime advanced on my left, and been almost instantaneously driven back, upon which the enemy, being relieved from pressure, charged in overwhelming force upon and captured nearly all that were left unhurt in three regiments of my brigade.

When I saw white handkerchiefs raised, and my line of battle still lying down in position, I characterized the surrender as disgraceful; but when I found afterward that 500 of my men were left lying dead and wounded on a line as straight as a dress parade, I exonerated, with one or two disgraceful individual exceptions, the survivors, and claim for the brigade that they nobly fought and died without a man running to the rear. No greater gallantry and heroism has been displayed during this war.

I endeavored, during the confusion among the enemy incident to the charge and capture of my men, to make a charge with my remaining regiment and the Third Alabama, but in the noise and excitement I presume my voice could not be heard.

The fighting here ceased on my part, the Twelfth North Carolina still retaining its position until, Brigadier-General Ramseur coming up, I pointed out the position of the enemy to him, and as soon as I observed his troops about to flank the enemy, I advanced the Twelfth North Carolina

and fragments of the other regiments (which Capt. D. P. Halsey had already prepared for a forward movement) into the woods overlooking the town, and took possession of them.

Going out to the front to stop General Ramseur's men from firing into mine, who were in their front, I observed that the enemy were retreating along the railroad, and immediately hastened the Twelfth North Carolina forward to cut them off. The Fifty-third North Carolina Regiment, of General Daniel's brigade, joined in the pursuit, and the Twelfth and Fifty-third North Carolina were the first to reach the railroad along which the enemy were retreating. Numberless prisoners were cut off by us, but I would not permit my men to take them to the rear, as I considered them safe.

Arriving in the town, and having but very few troops left, I informed General Ramseur that I would attach them to his brigade, and act in concert with him, and we formed on the street facing the heights beyond Gettysburg occupied by the enemy, where we remained till the night of July 2, when I was informed by General Ramseur that a night attack was ordered upon the position of the enemy to the right of the town. I had received no instructions, and perceiving that General Ramseur was acquainted with the intentions of the major-general commanding the division, I raised no question of rank, but conformed the movements of my brigade to that of Brigadier-General Ramseur, advanced with him, got under the fire of the enemy's skirmishers and artillery without returning the fire, and perceiving, as I believe every one did, that we were advancing to certain destruction, when other parts of the line fell back, I also gave the order to retreat, and formed in the road, in which we maintained a position during that night and the whole of July 3, while the fight of that day was progressing, and from which we fell back about 3 **A.M.** of July 4 to the ridge near the theological seminary.

From this position, I was moved about 2 **P.M.** [the] same day, to escort the wagon train on the Fairfield road.

On the night of July 4-5 the division began to move toward Hagerstown by way of Fairfield. On the morning of July 6 it became the rear guard of the army and was engaged in several brief skirmishes that day. At Hagerstown, on July 6, Iverson's brigade successfully repulsed an enemy cavalry charge, drove the enemy through Hagerstown, and marched to within two miles of Williamsport that night. Entering Williamsport on July 7, Iverson assumed the duties of provost marshal and used his brigade for several days as guards. On the night of July 14 the division recrossed the Potomac and marched to near Darkesville. During the Gettysburg campaign the regiment lost 10 killed and 46 wounded.

When the Federal army began crossing the Potomac River east of the Blue Ridge, General Lee had to move his army east of the mountains to interpose it between the enemy and Richmond. By August 1, 1863, the Army of Northern Virginia was encamped near Orange Court House, with the Army of the Potomac at Warrenton. By August 4 Lee withdrew his army to the Rapidan River line. On September 8 Brigadier General Robert D. Johnston was assigned to command Iverson's brigade which then became Johnston's brigade. The composition of the brigade did not change, and it remained in Rodes's division. In October Lee attempt-

ed to turn the flank of the Federal army. The movement maneuvered the Federal commander into falling
back, and on October 14 the Federal rear guard was
intercepted at Bristoe Station. Failure to coordinate
the attack resulted in heavy casualties to troops of
A.P. Hill's corps and in the escape of the Federal rear
guard. The regiment took part in the movement with
the brigade and division, but Ewell's corps was not
engaged at Bristoe Station. However, this regiment,
with two other regiments from the brigade, was engaged in a skirmish at Raccoon Ford and Stevensburg on
October 11 while supporting General Fitzhugh Lee's
cavalry and lost 3 killed and 11 wounded.

With the escape of the Federal army to Centreville,
Lee retired to the upper Rappahannock River. Rodes's
division was positioned opposite Kelly's Ford, guarding
Wheatley's Ford, three quarters of a mile above, and
Steven's Ford, one and a quarter miles below Kelly's
Ford. Thus the division had a two-mile front. The
Federal army followed the Confederates and launched
an attack at Kelly's Ford on November 7. Rodes's division was subjected to artillery fire but, except for the
units at Kelly's Ford, was not engaged. Johnston's brigade lost 3 wounded and 2 missing. That night Rodes
moved his division, under orders, to Pony Mountain.

Lee withdrew his army south across the upper Rapidan River toward Orange Court House, where the
army went into camp. Johnston's brigade encamped
near Morton's Ford, and companies from the regiment
went on picket duty at various fords on the river. On
November 26 the Federal army crossed the lower Rapidan and turned west to face Lee's army. Lee thought
the Federal army was moving south to a position between the Confederate army and Richmond. He put his
army in motion to strike the Federal army on its flank.
The activities of Johnston's brigade in the move and the
resulting Mine Run campaign were described in Johnston's report as follows (O.R., S.I., Vol. XXIX, pt. 1,
pp. 893-894):

At an early hour on the morning of the 27th,
this brigade, with the division, moved down the
river about 4 miles and formed in line of battle on
the left of the road leading to Zoar Church. After
a short delay, we were moved by the right flank,
turning to the left at Zoar Church on the road
that leads into the Orange and Fredericksburg
pike at Locust Grove Tavern. We came into the
enemy's immediate front at Grassy Branch, where,
by direction of the major-general commanding
[Rodes], I formed my brigade in line in the woods
on the west bank of the run, with General Daniel
on my right. Skirmishers were thrown forward,
and were engaged continuously throughout the
day.

My brigade occupying the left of the division,
and being unable to find out where General Edward Johnson's division was, I directed Colonel [T.
F.] Toon, commanding the Twentieth North
Carolina Regiment, on the left of the brigade, to
throw forward two companies to protect my left
flank; but fortunately the enemy did not discover
and take advantage of the gap thus left between
the two divisions. Very soon after dark the whole
command was withdrawn behind Mine Run and
bivouacked on the pike (Orange and Fredericksburg) near where it crossed the run.

Early on the morning of November 28, under
the direction of the major-general commanding, I

placed my troops in line on the left of the division,
connecting with General Edward Johnson's right.
The Twenty-third North Carolina Regiment, Lieutenant-Colonel [W. W.] Davis commanding, was
placed in position in the rifle-pits about 400 yards
in advance of the main line. Our position was
strengthened by heavy earth-works and abatis. The
enemy pursued with alacrity, and the skirmishing
began early in the morning and was continued
throughout the 28th and the following day, a large
amount of ammunition being expended without
any result. Some half dozen of the enemy were
killed and wounded by my skirmishers.

On the morning of December 2, the enemy's
skirmishers retired from our front. . . .

Thus ended the Mine Run campaign, during which
the regiment lost one man wounded. Both armies went
into winter quarters, and Johnston's brigade returned
to Morton's Ford. This regiment built winter quarters
near Orange Court House, where it remained until
moved to Taylorsville, Hanover County, February 4,
1864. Upon arriving at the latter place on February 5,
the regiment again went into winter quarters. There it
remained for the rest of the winter.

On the morning of May 4, 1864, while the Federal
army under General U. S. Grant was moving across the
lower Rapidan, Johnston's brigade was at Hanover
Junction. Ordered up, the brigade arrived on the field
of battle at the Wilderness early on the morning of
May 6. The two armies had been heavily engaged on
the previous day, and the action now continued. General Ewell, corps commander, assigned Johnston's brigade to support General John B. Gordon's brigade of
Early's division on the Confederate left. Gordon was
preparing to assault the Federal right, and with Johnston's brigade as support the attack was launched. After routing the right of the Federal line, darkness
brought an end to the fighting and to the battle.

Late in the evening of May 7 orders came to close on
the right, and throughout the night of May 7-8 the
troops moved in that direction. On the march, orders
were received assigning General Early to command
General A. P. Hill's corps. Early's division was placed
under General John B. Gordon, and Johnston's brigade
was transferred from Rodes's division to Gordon's
(Early's old) division. General Gordon reported the
movement of his division and the action at Spotsylvania
Court House as follows (O.R., S.I., Vol. XXXVI, pt.
1, pp. 1078-1079):

BATTLE OF MAY 10 AT SPOTSYLVANIA

The march to Spotsylvania Court-House was
begun by my brigade, with Early's division, on the
night of the 7th. On the morning of the 8th I was
placed in command of this division, consisting of
three brigades— [John] Pegram's (Virginia), Johnston's (North Carolina), and Gordon's (Georgia)—
and on the afternoon of the same day reached
Spotsylvania Court-House. On the afternoon of the
10th I received orders to move my division rapidly
from the left of our lines to the support of Rodes'
division, now being heavily assaulted by the enemy. When my division reached this position the
enemy had carried the portion of work held by
[George P.] Doles' brigade, Rodes' division, and
had reached a point more than 100 yards in rear
of the line. My leading brigade (Johnston's North
Carolina) was immediately formed, by direction of
Lieutenant-General Ewell, across the head of the

enemy's column and ordered to charge. In the mean time Gordon's brigade was also formed and ordered forward. The enemy was driven back with considerable loss, and our lines re-established. The loss in these two brigades was light.

BATTLE OF MAY 12

Orders from Lieutenant-General Ewell directed that I should use my division as a support to either Johnson's or Rodes' division, or to both, as circumstances should require. I had, therefore, placed my largest brigade (Gordon's, now Evans') in rear of Rodes' right and Johnson's left, and directly in front of the McCool house. The other two brigades were held in reserve near the Harris house. During the night of the 11th I received information from Major-General Johnson that the enemy was massing in his front, and under the general instructions I had received from corps headquarters I sent another brigade (Pegram's) to report to him. At the earliest dawn I heard musketry in the direction of the Salient, held by Jones' brigade, of Johnson's division, and at once ordered my other brigade (Johnston's) to move toward the firing. The situation at this time was as follows: Evans' brigade was in position immediately in rear of the left of Johnson's division and Rodes' right. Pegram's brigade was placed by General Johnson in the trenches near his left and to the left of the Salient, and Johnston's brigade was moving from the Harris house toward the Salient. The check given by Jones' brigade to the enemy's assaulting column was so slight that no time was afforded for bringing into position the supporting force. No information was brought to me of the success of the enemy, and in the early dawn and dense fog I was unable to learn anything of the situation until Johnston's brigade met in the woodland between the McCool house and the Salient with the head of the enemy's column.

Brigadier-General Johnston was wounded, and his brigade was soon overpowered and driven back. I at once discovered that the situation was critical, and ordered Colonel [Clement A.] Evans to move his brigade at a double-quick from its position near the trenches to the McCool house, and sent a staff officer to ascertain the position of Pegram's brigade, and, if possible, to withdraw it to the same point. This was promptly done. The fog was so dense that I could not ascertain the progress of the enemy, except by the sound of his musketry and the direction from which his balls came. At this point (the McCool house) I ordered Colonel Evans to send in three of his regiments to ascertain the enemy's position and check his advance until the other troops could be gotten into line. The attacking column, it was ascertained, had advanced considerably to the right of this point, and the temporary check given by these regiments afforded only time enough for moving the remainder of Evans' and Pegram's brigades farther around to the right. A line was soon formed near the Harris house, and these two brigades ordered to attack. They charged with the greatest spirit, driving the enemy with heavy loss from nearly the whole of the captured works from the left of [Cadmus M.] Wilcox's division to the Salient on General Johnson's line, and fully one-fourth of a mile beyond. Several of the lost guns were recaptured by the Thirteenth Virginia Regiment, of Pegram's brigade, and brought back to the branch near the McCool house. Unfortunately, the artillery officer to whom these guns were reported failed to find them and bring them off.

The enemy still held a portion of the line to the left of the Salient, and during the night of the 12th the troops were withdrawn to a new line in rear of the Harris house.

As Johnston's brigade moved forward under orders of General Gordon, it met the full force of the Federal column which had just broken through the line at the salient. The men of the brigade made a valiant stand, but the overpowering force of the Federal column forced them to retire. Over two-thirds of the regiment were left dead and wounded on the field; however, the survivors, together with those of other regiments in the brigade, joined the reinforcements that came up and drove the enemy back to the original line of the salient.

After several unsuccessful attempts against the Confederate line, General Grant began to move his army eastward. The increased Federal activity to the east led Lee to order the 2nd Corps to reconnoiter to find out what was going on. Ewell's corps moved out of the entrenchments and engaged the rear elements of the Federal army on May 19. An unsuccessful attack was made, and the reinforced Federal rear guard forced the Confederates on the defensive. Ewell's men held the Federals back and took advantage of night to break off the engagement and retire. Although unsuccessful in the attack, the move disclosed the enemy's movement, and Lee moved his army accordingly.

On May 20 General Early returned to command his division, and General Gordon was assigned to command another division. From May 20 to 27 the brigade was in Early's division, Ewell's corps. However, because of General Ewell's absence due to illness, General Early was assigned to temporary command of the 2nd Corps, and General Stephen D. Ramseur was assigned to command Early's old division. This change in command was carried out in official orders on June 4, 1864.

On May 22 Ewell's corps arrived at Hanover Junction with Longstreet's corps. Hill's corps arrived on the morning of May 23. From there the Army of Northern Virginia moved to the North Anna, where it blocked the Federal army once again. At North Anna, May 24-25, Ewell's corps, now commanded by General Early, was on the Confederate right and was not engaged. Grant withdrew during the night of May 26-27 and crossed the Pamunkey River, again sidestepping to the Confederate right. Early's corps marched some twenty-four miles on May 27 and entrenched between Beaver Dam Creek and Pole Green Church. Longstreet's corps came up on Early's right, and Hill's corps extended along the left of Early's line. On May 30, under orders from General Lee, Early moved to attack the Federal left at Bethesda Church. The attack failed to turn the Federal left but did reveal that the enemy was moving to the Confederate right.

The two armies began to concentrate at Cold Harbor, and on June 1 a spirited engagement occurred. Again Lee moved to his right, and the new alignment left Early's corps on the Confederate left. Early was ordered to move out on June 2 to strike the Federal right. The attack met with partial success until Federal reinforcements arrived to drive it back. During the battle of Cold Harbor, June 3, 1864, Early's corps was under attack by General A. E. Burnside's IX Corps and a part of General G. K. Warren's V Corps. The Confederate line held against heavy Federal attack columns, and Grant ordered his army to disengage.

Following the battle the armies remained in position observing and skirmishing until June 12, when Grant began moving his army to cross the James River. General Early's corps was withdrawn from the line on June 11 and was ordered to Lynchburg on June 12 to defend the city against an anticipated attack by troops under General David Hunter. Early was directed to remain in the Shenandoah Valley after striking Hunter's force.

General Early's troops began arriving at Lynchburg on June 17. By the next day, Early's entire command was there. Hunter retired after a brief skirmish, and, following an unsuccessful attempt to overtake the retreating Federals, Early proceeded into the Shenandoah Valley. Still in Johnston's brigade, Ramseur's division, this regiment took part in Early's Valley campaign of 1864. On July 6 Early's command crossed into Maryland and advanced on Washington, D.C. At the battle of Monocacy River, July 9, Ramseur's division demonstrated in front while Gordon's division moved across the Monocacy on the enemy's flank. Driving the Federals, Early's troops moved on to Washington, where they arrived July 11. Finding the defenses heavily manned on the morning of July 12, Early called off a planned assault, and on the night of July 12 the Confederates began to retire toward Virginia. Back in the Shenandoah Valley, Early's force was engaged at Stephenson's Depot, where Ramseur's men were driven in disorder, July 20, and at Kernstown, July 24, before moving to Martinsburg.

Early in August, 1864, the Federals began concentrating a large force under General Phil Sheridan at Harpers Ferry. On August 10 Early began a series of maneuvers to create the impression of a larger force than he had. His men were northeast of Winchester when Sheridan began to move. On September 19 contact was made, and Early concentrated his army to receive the attack. The Confederates were making a determined defense east of Winchester when the left of the line came under heavy attack and the whole line began to retire. During the initial stages of the battle General Robert E. Rodes was killed as he deployed his division between Gordon's and Ramseur's divisions. These three divisions held the main line against repeated assaults, and only when the left appeared to be turned did they begin to retire to a defensive line close to the town. Again the Federals assaulted the front and left of the line. Word of a Federal column turning the right caused Early to issue orders for a general withdrawal; however, upon finding that the troops moving on the right were his own men adjusting the alignment of the line, Early tried to counter the order. It was too late. The troops continued to the rear through Winchester and rallied south of the town. From there they continued to retreat to Fisher's Hill near Strasburg.

At Fisher's Hill, General Ramseur was placed in command of Rodes's division, and General John Pegram was assigned to command Ramseur's old division. Sheridan struck Early's left and center at Fisher's Hill on September 22 and forced a general retreat. Early regrouped at Waynesboro on September 28. There he received reinforcements and again began to move down the valley. On October 7 his troops occupied New Market. Moving to Fisher's Hill on October 12-13, Early found the enemy on the north bank of Cedar Creek. On October 19 Early launched a surprise attack on the

Federal camp. The attack was initially successful, and the Confederates succeeded in driving the Federals from two defensive lines. Early delayed the attack on the third line and assumed the defensive. Rallying his troops, Sheridan launched a devastating counterattack and routed Early's army. In this battle the three divisions of the 2nd Corps were commanded by General Gordon. While attempting to rally the men, General Ramseur was mortally wounded and captured. The 2nd Corps regrouped at New Market after the Cedar Creek disaster and went into camp. There the 1st Battalion N.C. Sharpshooters was assigned to Johnston's brigade, Pegram's division. With the exception of minor skirmishing and the repulse of a Federal cavalry force on November 22, the army remained inactive.

No reports of casualties for the engagements from May through October, 1864, were found for individual battles, but the reports on some of the company muster rolls reveal the extent to which the regiment was engaged. Company C started the campaign in May with 35 men on the roll. Of these, 12 were killed between May and October. The clerk for Company F reported that of the 32 men present for duty on May 1, 1864, 4 had been killed and 15 wounded by October 31, 1864. Of the 27 men present in Company I on May 1, 4 were killed and 17 were wounded between May 1 and October 31. Company K suffered even greater casualties: Of the 36 men present on May 1, 3 were killed, 23 were wounded, and 1 was captured during the six months of fighting. The rest of the company clerks did not report the casualties suffered by their companies.

The activities of the regiment in November and December, 1864, were reported by the clerk of 2nd Company D on the muster roll for November-December, 1864, dated January 3, 1865:

> Since the last record of events, made the 31st October, 1864, this company has been in no engagement with the enemy. It marched from New Market on the 10th Nov., 1864, and goes beyond Woodstock. On the 11th it goes in two miles of Newtown — and returns to Strasburg on the 12th — On the 13th it reached Edenburg on its return & on the 14th it resumes old camp at New Market. On the 18th it moved camp and went into quarters at Lacey's Springs. On Dec. 6th order to move camp — reached Waynesboro — distance of 40 ms. — on 7th — arrived in Petersburg on the 11th — occupied the winter quarters of Finnegan's Brig. until the 13th — when we were marched down to our present position — on the extreme right of General Lee's army, where we have erected comfortable quarters.

Early in December, 1864, the 2nd Corps was ordered to return to Richmond. Gordon's and Pegram's divisions moved on December 6 by way of Staunton, where they took the trains for Petersburg. Upon arriving in Petersburg the divisions were sent into the defensive lines near Hatcher's Run. There the regiment went into winter quarters. Early in February, 1865, the brigade was engaged at Hatcher's Run in an unsuccessful attempt to prevent the Federal army from extending its line. During the battle General Pegram was killed, and General James A. Walker was assigned to command Pegram's division. After the battle the regiment was detailed to guard the crossings of the Roanoke River to prevent the passage of deserters from the army. The regiment was then ordered back to Petersburg to take part in the attack on Fort Stedman and arrived in the city on the night of March 24. There it joined the brigade in preparation for the assault. Although initially successful, the attack on March 25 was turned back by the concentrated firepower and manpower of the Federal army. The brigade then went back into the lines south of the city.

On April 1, 1865, a Federal force under General Sheridan defeated a Confederate force at Five Forks on the extreme right of Lee's line. This victory opened the right flank of the line and provided the Federals an avenue of advance to the rear of the Petersburg line. On April 2 a general assault was launched against the line in front of Petersburg. The line was breached after heavy fighting, and the Confederates were forced to fall back. The brigade was engaged in the fighting and succeeded in driving some of the Federals out of the trenches; however, conditions along the line and the defeat at Five Forks made retreat necessary, and it began the night of April 2-3. Gordon's corps acted as rear guard as the army moved to Amelia Court House. It camped five miles east of the town on April 4 while the army awaited the collection of supplies. The next day the retreat resumed and continued through the night of April 5-6. As the rear guard, Gordon's men were subjected to attacks by Federal cavalry and infantry. At a crossing of Sayler's Creek, on April 6, Gordon's men made a stand and repulsed the attack on their front. To the south of Gordon's position the Confederates under Generals Ewell and Anderson were severely defeated and captured. The Federals then moved on Gordon's right. The pressure forced the line to break in confusion, but Gordon rallied the survivors west of the creek and rejoined the army. At Farmville, on April 7, the men of Gordon's corps went to the relief of General Mahone's division. The Federals were held, and the army continued the retreat.

On the night of April 7-8 Gordon's corps moved to the advance of the army. His lead elements reached Appomattox Court House in the late afternoon of April 8 and halted. Later that evening they found the Federal cavalry in their front. It was decided that an attack should be made the next morning to cut through the enemy. Gordon's men moved into position west of the town during the night with Johnston's brigade on the left of the Lynchburg road. At 5:00 A.M. the advance began and drove the Federal cavalry from the crossroads. The Confederates then took up a defensive position and came under attack by Federal infantry and cavalry. Gordon held his line until word came of the truce. A cease-fire was arranged, and Gordon began to withdraw. The Army of Northern Virginia was surrendered on that date, April 9, and on April 12, 139 men of the 12th Regiment N.C. Troops (2nd Regiment N.C. Volunteers) were paroled.

FIELD AND STAFF

COLONELS

WILLIAMS, SOLOMON
Resided in Nash County where he was by occupation a "soldier" prior to enlisting in Wake County at age 25. Appointed Colonel to rank from May 14, 1861.

Present or accounted for until transferred to the Field and Staff of the 19th Regiment N. C. Troops (2nd Regiment N. C. Cavalry) upon appointment as Colonel of that regiment on June 6, 1862.

WADE, BENJAMIN O.
Previously served as Captain of Company F of this regiment. Transferred to the Field and Staff upon appointment as Lieutenant Colonel on May 1, 1862. Promoted to Colonel on or about June 6, 1862. Present or accounted for until he resigned on or about December 30, 1862. Reason he resigned not reported.

COLEMAN, HENRY EATON
Previously served as Captain of Company B of this regiment and as Aide-de-Camp (Lieutenant Colonel) on the staff of Brigadier General Alfred Iverson. Appointed Colonel of this regiment on August 11, 1863, to rank from May 4, 1863. Present or accounted for until wounded at Spotsylvania Court House, Virginia, May 12, 1864. Reported absent wounded through December, 1864.

LIEUTENANT COLONELS

CANTWELL, EDWARD
Resided in Wake or New Hanover counties and was by occupation a lawyer prior to enlisting at age 36. Appointed Lieutenant Colonel to rank from May 14, 1861, but was defeated for reelection when the regiment was reorganized on May 1, 1862. Later served as Aide-de-Camp to Brigadier General Thomas Lanier Clingman and as Lieutenant Colonel of the 59th Regiment N. C. Troops (4th Regiment N. C. Cavalry).

JONES, THOMAS L.
Previously served as Captain of 2nd Company C of this regiment. Promoted to Major on May 1, 1862, and transferred to the Field and Staff. Promoted to Lieutenant Colonel on May 24, 1862. Present or accounted for until he resigned on October 11, 1862, by reason of disability. Resignation accepted on or about October 20, 1862.

JOHNSTON, ROBERT D.
Served as Lieutenant Colonel of the 23rd Regiment N. C. Troops (13th Regiment N. C. Volunteers). Placed in temporary command of this regiment at the battle of Chancellorsville, Virginia, May 3, 1863, after Major David Pinkney Rowe was wounded the previous day.

DAVIS, WILLIAM S.
Previously served as Captain of 2nd Company C of this regiment. Promoted to Lieutenant Colonel on May 24, 1863, and transferred to the Field and Staff. Present or accounted for until wounded in the left arm at Cedar Creek, Virginia, October 19, 1864. Left arm amputated. Reported absent wounded until he resigned on February 10, 1865, by reason of disability.

MAJORS

BURTON, AUGUSTUS W.
Previously served as Captain of Company E of this regiment. Elected Major on May 14, 1861, and transferred to the Field and Staff. Present or accounted for until he was defeated for reelection

when the regiment was reorganized on May 1, 1862.

ROWE, DAVID PINKNEY

Previously served as Captain of Company A of this regiment. Promoted to Major on or about July 1, 1862, and transferred to the Field and Staff. Present or accounted for until mortally wounded at Chancellorsville, Virginia, May 2, 1863. Died May 3, 1863.

ALSTON, ROBERT W.

Previously served as Captain of Company K of this regiment. Promoted to Major on or about May 24, 1863, and transferred to the Field and Staff. Present or accounted for until wounded in the mouth and jaw at Cedar Creek, Virginia, October 19, 1864. Reported absent wounded through February 27, 1865, but returned to duty prior to March 25, 1865, when he was wounded at Fort Stedman, Virginia. Paroled at Richmond, Virginia, on or about April 17, 1865.

ADJUTANTS

PEGRAM, JOHN C.

Resided in Virginia and was by occupation an engineer prior to enlisting at Richmond, Virginia, at age 22. Appointed Adjutant (1st Lieutenant) on or about May 14, 1861. Present or accounted for until he resigned on or about May 1, 1862. Appointed Adjutant (1st Lieutenant) of the 19th Regiment N. C. Troops (2nd Regiment N. C. Cavalry) on or about June 6, 1862.

BUNN, ELIAS

Previously served as Private in 1st Company H of this regiment. Appointed Adjutant on or about May 1, 1862, and transferred to the Field and Staff. Mortally wounded at Hanover Court House, Virginia, May 27, 1862. Place and date of death not reported.

FOOTE, THOMAS J.

Previously served as Sergeant Major of this regiment. Appointed Adjutant (Major) on June 6, 1862, to rank from May 1, 1862. Present or accounted for until wounded at Gaines' Mill, Virginia, June 27, 1862. Died on or about July 1, 1862, of wounds. Place of death not reported.

GREGORY, JOHN TILLERY

Previously served as 2nd Lieutenant in Company G of this regiment. Appointed Adjutant (2nd Lieutenant) on July 1, 1862, and transferred to the Field and Staff. Present or accounted for until captured near Spotsylvania Court House, Virginia, May 12, 1864. Confined at Point Lookout, Maryland, until transferred to Fort Delaware, Delaware, June 23, 1864. Released at Fort Delaware on June 7, 1865, after taking the Oath of Allegiance.

COLLINS, BENJAMIN M.

Previously served as 1st Lieutenant in 2nd Company C of this regiment. Appointed Acting Adjutant (1st Lieutenant) on May 12, 1864, and transferred to the Field and Staff. Present or accounted for until paroled at Appomattox Court House, Virginia, April 9, 1865.

ASSISTANT QUARTERMASTERS

ALSTON, WILLIAM T.

Previously served as 2nd Lieutenant in 2nd Company C of this regiment. Appointed Assistant Quartermaster (Captain) on May 14, 1861, and transferred to the Field and Staff. Present or accounted for until he resigned on or about May 13, 1862, by reason of "spinal irritation and partial paralysis of the inferior extremities."

POWELL, BENJAMIN FRANKLIN

Previously served as Quartermaster Sergeant of this regiment. Appointed Assistant Quartermaster (Captain) on June 28, 1862, to rank from May 8, 1862. Present or accounted for until he resigned on October 21, 1863. Reason he resigned not reported. Resignation accepted November 11, 1863.

NORTHINGTON, JOHN S.

Previously served as 1st Lieutenant in Company G of this regiment. Appointed Assistant Quartermaster (Captain) on December 3, 1863, to rank from November 11, 1863, and transferred to the Field and Staff. Present or accounted for until transferred on or about September 15, 1864, upon appointment as Assistant to the Quartermaster of "Johnston's Brigade."

ASSISTANT COMMISSARIES OF SUBSISTENCE

ARRINGTON, W. T.

Was by occupation a farmer prior to enlisting in Nash County at age 42. Appointed Assistant Commissary of Subsistence on May 14, 1861. Resigned September 1, 1861. Reason he resigned not reported.

WILLIAMS, SAMUEL T.

Previously served as Corporal in 2nd Company D of this regiment. Appointed Assistant Commissary of Subsistence (Captain) on October 31, 1861, and transferred to the Field and Staff. Present or accounted for until he was transferred back to 2nd Company D on or about July 3, 1863, after the position of Assistant Commissary of Subsistence was abolished.

SURGEONS

JOHNSON, JAMES

Resided in Northampton County and was by occupation a surgeon prior to enlisting in Wake County at age 44. Appointed Surgeon on or about May 14, 1861. Present or accounted for until he resigned on or about December 1, 1861. Reason he resigned not reported.

HALL, JAMES K.

Resided in Mecklenburg County. Appointed Surgeon on or about July 29, 1861. Present or accounted for until appointed Surgeon of the 22nd Regiment N. C. Troops (12th Regiment N. C. Volunteers) on or about November 19, 1861.

PEETE, RICHARD S. FENNEL

Born in Mecklenburg County, Virginia, and resided in Warren County prior to enlisting at age 33. Appointed Surgeon on or about May 23, 1862. Present or accounted for until he resigned on March 25, 1864, by reason of disability.

LAWSON, JOHN W.

Resided in Virginia. Appointed Surgeon on March 18, 1864, and was assigned to this regiment on April 9, 1864. Present or accounted for until captured at Winchester, Virginia, September 19, 1864. Confined at Baltimore, Maryland, and at Fort Monroe, Virginia. Records of the Federal Provost Marshal give his age as 25. Exchanged on or about January 6, 1865. Rejoined the company at an unspecified date and was present or accounted for until paroled at Appomattox Court House, Virginia, April 9, 1865.

ASSISTANT SURGEONS

YOUNG, PETER WESLEY

Resided in Granville County and was by occupation a surgeon prior to enlisting in Wake County at age 31. Appointed Assistant Surgeon on or about May 11, 1861. Present or accounted for until promoted to Surgeon to rank from October 8, 1861, or January 6, 1862, and transferred to the 38th Regiment N. C. Troops.

MILLER, JOHN FULLENWIDER

Previously served as Private in Company E of this regiment. Appointed Assistant Surgeon on May 18, 1861, and transferred to the Field and Staff. Present or accounted for until promoted to Surgeon on May 17, 1862, and transferred to the 38th Regiment N.C. Troops.

CHEEK, BENJAMIN A.

Appointed Assistant Surgeon on July 1, 1861. Present or accounted for until appointed Assistant Surgeon of the 22nd Regiment N. C. Troops (12th Regiment N. C. Volunteers) on or about November 19, 1861.

HOLT, PLEASANT A.

Resided in Alamance County or in Florida and enlisted at age 45. Appointed Assistant Surgeon on August 1, 1861. Present or accounted for until promoted to Surgeon (Major) either on August 6, 1861, to rank from May 16, 1861, or on July 24, 1861, and transferred to the 6th Regiment N. C. State Troops.

ALSTON, SOLOMON W.

Previously served as Private in 2nd Company C of this regiment. Appointed Assistant Surgeon to rank from November 1, 1861, and transferred to the Field and Staff. Present or accounted for until he died on July 10, 1862, of "fever." Place of death not reported.

COKE, GEORGE H.

Appointed Assistant Surgeon on November 2, 1861. Resigned December 18, 1861. Reason he resigned not reported.

MARSTON, WILLIAM WHITFIELD

Resided in Virginia and enlisted at age 26. Appointed Assistant Surgeon (Major) on July 22, 1861. Present or accounted for until captured at or near Sharpsburg, Maryland, on or about September 17, 1862. Confined at Fort McHenry, Maryland, until paroled and transferred to Aiken's Landing, James River, Virginia, where he was received October 19, 1862, for exchange. Declared exchanged at Aiken's Landing on November 10, 1862. Present or accounted for until he was relieved from duty with this regiment on April 29, 1864, and ordered to report to the Surgeon General's office for reassignment.

COOK, JOSEPH H.

Appointed Assistant Surgeon on October 14, 1862, to rank from August 31, 1862. No further records.

PENNEY, GEORGE A.

Appointed Assistant Surgeon on April 15, 1864. Field and Staff muster roll dated April 30-October 31, 1864, indicates that he was a prisoner of war; however, records of the Federal Provost Marshal do not substantiate that report. Field and Staff muster roll dated November-December, 1864, states that he was present. Paroled at Appomattox Court House, Virginia, April 9, 1865.

CHAPLAINS

FITZGERALD, FREDERICK

Was by occupation a preacher prior to enlisting in Wake County at age 35. Appointed Chaplain (Major) on or about June 1, 1861. Present or accounted for until he resigned on December 18, 1861. Reason he resigned not reported.

LONG, B. F.

Appointed Chaplain (Major) on July 21, 1862, to rank from July 9, 1862. Present or accounted for until he resigned on November 10, 1862, by reason of ill health. Resignation accepted November 12, 1862.

SERGEANTS MAJOR

FOOTE, THOMAS J.

Previously served as Private in 2nd Company C of this regiment. Promoted to Sergeant Major on June 15, 1861, and transferred to the Field and Staff. Present or accounted for until appointed Adjutant (Major) of this regiment on June 6, 1862, to rank from May 1, 1862.

COOK, JOHN THOMAS

Previously served as Private in Company F of this regiment. Appointed Sergeant Major in October, 1862, and transferred to the Field and Staff. Present or accounted for until wounded in the leg at Chancellorsville, Virginia, May 2, 1863. Died in June, 1863, of wounds. Place of death not reported.

BATTLE, DOSSEY

Previously served as Sergeant in 1st Company H of this regiment. Promoted to Sergeant Major in March, 1863, and transferred to the Field and Staff. Present or accounted for until wounded at Chancellorsville, Virginia, May 2, 1863. Returned to duty prior to July 1, 1863, and present or accounted for until appointed 2nd Lieutenant on or about August 6, 1863, and transferred to Company A, 7th Regiment N. C. State Troops.

ROBARDS, WILLIAM J.

Previously served as Sergeant in 2nd Company D of this regiment. Promoted to Sergeant Major on June 25, 1863, and transferred to the Field and Staff. Wounded at Gettysburg, Pennsylvania, July 1, 1863. Reported absent wounded through August, 1863. Date he returned to duty not reported; however, he was appointed 2nd Lieutenant on December 5, 1863, and transferred to Company A, 7th Regiment N. C. State Troops.

BARKLEY, WILLIAM D.

Previously served as 1st Sergeant of Company G of this regiment. Promoted to Sergeant Major in March-April, 1864, and transferred to the Field and Staff. Present or accounted for until captured at Sayler's Creek, Virginia, April 6, 1865. Confined at

Old Capitol Prison, Washington, D. C., until transferred to Johnson's Island, Ohio, April 17, 1865. Released at Johnson's Island on June 18, 1865, after taking the Oath of Allegiance.

QUARTERMASTER SERGEANTS

POWELL, BENJAMIN FRANKLIN
Previously served as Private in 2nd Company C of this regiment. Promoted to Quartermaster Sergeant on June 1, 1861, and transferred to the Field and Staff. Present or accounted for until appointed Assistant Quartermaster (Captain) of this regiment on June 28, 1862, to rank from May 8, 1862.

ARRINGTON, SAMUEL PETER
Previously served as Private in 2nd Company C of this regiment. Promoted to Quartermaster Sergeant on May 8, 1862, and transferred to the Field and Staff. Present or accounted for until paroled at Appomattox Court House, Virginia, April 9, 1865.

COMMISSARY SERGEANT

BULLOCK, RICHARD A.
Previously served as Private in Company B of this regiment. Promoted to Commissary Sergeant on November 24, 1861, and transferred to the Field and Staff at an unspecified date prior to November 1, 1862. Present or accounted for until paroled at Appomattox Court House, Virginia, April 9, 1865.

ORDNANCE SERGEANT

DEAL, JACOB AUGUSTUS
Previously served as Sergeant in Company E of this regiment. Promoted to Ordnance Sergeant on May 7, 1862, and transferred to the Field and Staff. Present or accounted for until paroled at Appomattox Court House, Virginia, April 9, 1865.

DRILLMASTERS

BROWN, G. W.
Was by occupation a "cadet" prior to enlisting at Richmond, Virginia, at age 20, on or about June 30, 1861. No further records.

CHRISTIAN, N. H.
Was by occupation a "cadet" prior to enlisting at Richmond, Virginia, at age 18, on or about June 30, 1861. No further records.

COLEMAN, NATHANIEL R.
Was by occupation a "cadet" prior to enlisting at Richmond, Virginia, at age 14, on or about June 30, 1861. Later served in the 24th Regiment N. C. Troops (14th Regiment N. C. Volunteers).

HARDY, T. A.
Was by occupation a farmer prior to enlisting at Norfolk, Virginia, at age 23, on or about June 30, 1861. No further records.

HASKINS, C. T.
Was by occupation a "cadet" prior to enlisting at Richmond, Virginia, at age 19, on or about June 30, 1861. No further records.

MASI, FREDERICK
Was by occupation a "cadet" prior to enlisting at Richmond, Virginia, at age 18, on or about June 30, 1861. No further records.

SEGAR, J.
Was by occupation a "cadet" prior to enlisting at Richmond, Virginia, at age 20, on or about June 30, 1861. No further records.

SMITH, J. M.
Was by occupation a "cadet" prior to enlisting at Richmond, Virginia, at age 17, on or about June 30, 1861. No further records.

WARING, M. M.
Was by occupation a "cadet" prior to enlisting at Richmond, Virginia, at age 18, on or about June 30, 1861. Present or accounted for through July 17, 1861. No further records.

MUSICIAN

WRIGHT, ABNER B., Musician
Previously served in Company E of this regiment. Transferred to the Field and Staff in January-February, 1864. Transferred back to Company E in May-October, 1864.

COMPANY A

This company, known as the "Catawba Rifles," was raised in Catawba County and enlisted at Newton on April 27, 1861. It tendered its service to the state and was ordered to Garysburg, where it was assigned to this regiment. The company was mustered in as Captain John Ray's Company and was designated Company K and Company G before it was designated Company A. After it was mustered into the regiment the company functioned as a part of the regiment, and its history for the war period is recorded as a part of the regimental history.

The information contained in the following roster of the company was compiled principally from company muster rolls for April 27, 1861-February, 1862; July-October, 1862; January-August, 1863; and November, 1863-December, 1864. No company muster rolls were found for March-June, 1862; November-December, 1862; September-October, 1863; or for the period after December, 1864. In addition to the company muster rolls, Roll of Honor records, receipt rolls, hospital records, prisoner of war records, and other primary records, supplemented by state pension applications, United Daughters of the Confederacy records, and postwar rosters and histories, all provided useful information.

OFFICERS

CAPTAINS

RAY, JOHN
Resided in Catawba County and was by occupation a merchant prior to enlisting in Catawba County at age 37. Elected Captain on May 12, 1861, to rank from April 27, 1861. Present or accounted for until appointed Captain of Company F, 32nd Regiment N. C. Troops, September 14, 1861.

ROWE, DAVID PINKNEY
Resided in Catawba County and was by occupation a carpenter prior to enlisting in Catawba County at age 25. Appointed 3rd Lieutenant to rank from April 27, 1861, and promoted to 2nd Lieutenant on

May 12, 1861. Promoted to Captain to rank from September 16, 1861. Present or accounted for until wounded at Gaines' Mill, Virginia, June 27, 1862. Promoted to Major on or about July 1, 1862, and transferred to the Field and Staff of this regiment.

WILFONG, YANCY M.

Resided in Catawba County and was by occupation a farmer prior to enlisting in Catawba County at age 21. Appointed 3rd Lieutenant to rank from April 27, 1861, and was promoted to 1st Lieutenant to rank from September 16, 1861. Promoted to Captain on June 3, 1862. Present or accounted for until killed at Spotsylvania Court House, Virginia, May 12, 1864.

JOHNSTON, JOSEPH FORNEY

Previously served as Aide-de-Camp (1st Lieutenant) on the staff of Brigadier General Robert D. Johnston. Appointed Captain of this company subsequent to December 22, 1864. Paroled at Charlotte on May 13, 1865.

LIEUTENANTS

BRADBURN, THOMAS W., 2nd Lieutenant

Resided in Catawba County where he enlisted at age 41, April 27, 1861. Mustered in as Private and promoted to 3rd Lieutenant on September 16, 1861. Promoted to 2nd Lieutenant in February-April, 1862. Defeated for reelection when the company was reorganized on May 1, 1862. Roll of Honor indicates that he died. Place, date, and cause of death not reported.

BROWN, JAMES M., 2nd Lieutenant

Resided in Catawba County and was by occupation a teacher prior to enlisting in Catawba County at age 22, April 27, 1861. Mustered in as Private and promoted to Sergeant on September 16, 1861. Appointed 2nd Lieutenant to rank from May 1, 1862. Present of accounted for until wounded in the left knee at Malvern Hill, Virginia, July 1, 1862. Reported absent wounded until he resigned on April 9, 1863. Resignation accepted April 18, 1863.

DEAL, MARCUS SYLVANUS, 1st Lieutenant

Resided in Catawba County and was by occupation a teacher prior to enlisting in Catawba County at age 21, April 27, 1861. Mustered in as Private and promoted to Corporal on November 1, 1861. Appointed 2nd Lieutenant on April 15, 1862. Promoted to 1st Lieutenant on May 16, 1864. Present or accounted for until captured at Fisher's Hill, Virginia, September 22, 1864. Confined at Fort Delaware, Delaware, until released on June 17, 1865, after taking the Oath of Allegiance.

RUDISILL, HENRY PHILIP, 2nd Lieutenant

Resided in Catawba County and was by occupation a carpenter prior to enlisting in Catawba County at age 18, April 27, 1861. Mustered in as Corporal and promoted to Sergeant in February-October, 1862. Present or accounted for until wounded in the right hand at or near Gaines' Mill, Virginia, on or about June 27, 1862. Returned to duty prior to November 1, 1862, and was promoted to 1st Sergeant in November, 1862-February, 1863. Elected 2nd Lieutenant on April 25, 1863. Present or accounted for until wounded in the left arm and captured at Winchester, Virginia, September 19, 1864. Left arm

amputated. Hospitalized at Baltimore, Maryland, until transferred to Point Lookout, Maryland. Paroled and transferred to Venus Point, Savannah River, Georgia, where he was received November 15, 1864, for exchange. Reported absent wounded until he resigned on February 3, 1865, by reason of disability from wounds.

SHERRILL, URIAH FRANK, 1st Lieutenant

Resided in Catawba County and was by occupation a merchant prior to enlisting in Catawba County at age 27. Elected 1st Lieutenant on May 12, 1861. Died at or near Norfolk, Virginia, July 23, 1861, of "fever."

YOUNT, MILES A., 1st Lieutenant

Resided in Catawba County and was by occupation a carpenter prior to enlisting in Catawba County at age 26, April 27, 1861. Mustered in as 1st Sergeant and was appointed 2nd Lieutenant to rank from September 16, 1861. Promoted to 1st Lieutenant on June 3, 1862. Present or accounted for until wounded and captured at or near Sharpsburg, Maryland, on or about September 17, 1862. Confined at Fort McHenry, Maryland, and at Fort Monroe, Virginia, until received at Aiken's Landing, James River, Virginia, October 19, 1862, for exchange. Declared exchanged at Aiken's Landing on November 10, 1862. Present or accounted for until hospitalized at Richmond, Virginia, February 17, 1864, with a gunshot wound of the left side; however, place and date wounded not reported. Retired to the Invalid Corps on May 16, 1864.

NONCOMMISSIONED OFFICERS AND PRIVATES

ABERNATHY, JOHN R., Private

Resided in Catawba County and was by occupation a farmer prior to enlisting in Catawba County at age 23, April 27, 1861, for one year. Mustered in as Sergeant but was reduced to ranks in March-October, 1862. Present or accounted for until wounded at or near Gaines' Mill, Virginia, on or about June 27, 1862. Reported absent wounded until transferred to Company B, 19th Regiment N. C. Troops (2nd Regiment N. C. Cavalry) on June 11, 1863.

ABERNATHY, PATRICK, Private

Resided in Catawba County and was by occupation a "smith" prior to enlisting in Catawba County at age 22, April 27, 1861. Present or accounted for until transferred to Company F, 32nd Regiment N. C. Troops, September 14, 1861.

ARNDT, JOHN MARVIN, Private

Born in Catawba County where he resided as a farmer prior to enlisting in Catawba County at age 19, April 27, 1861. Present or accounted for until wounded in the right leg at Cold Harbor, Virginia, June 1, 1864. Right leg amputated. Reported absent wounded until discharged on February 3, 1865, by reason of disability.

BAILEY, GEORGE, Private

Resided in Catawba County and was by occupation a tanner prior to enlisting in Catawba County at age 23, April 27, 1861. Present or accounted for until transferred to Company F, 32nd Regiment N. C. Troops, on or about September 14, 1861.

BAILEY, JOHN, Private
Resided in Catawba County and was by occupation a laborer prior to enlisting in Catawba County at age 28, April 27, 1861. Present or accounted for until transferred to Company F, 32nd Regiment N. C. Troops, September 14, 1861.

BARRINGER, ALFRED M., Private
Resided in Catawba County and was by occupation a carpenter prior to enlisting in Catawba County at age 21, April 27, 1861. Present or accounted for until wounded at Malvern Hill, Virginia, July 1, 1862. Died at Richmond, Virginia, July 6, 1862, of wounds.

BEARD, W. F., Private
Place and date of enlistment not reported. Paroled at Salisbury on May 2, 1865.

BOLCH, SALATHIEL A., Private
Resided in Catawba County and was by occupation a laborer or farmer prior to enlisting in Catawba County at age 18, April 27, 1861. Present or accounted for until wounded at Malvern Hill, Virginia, July 1, 1862. Returned to duty prior to November 1, 1862, and present or accounted for until captured at or near Strasburg, Virginia, on or about October 20, 1864. Confined at Point Lookout, Maryland, until released on May 12, 1865, after taking the Oath of Allegiance.

BOST, ELIAS G., Sergeant
Born in Catawba County* where he resided as a carpenter or farmer prior to enlisting in Catawba County at age 23, April 27, 1861. Mustered in as Private and promoted to Corporal on September 16, 1861. Promoted to Sergeant on August 1, 1863. Present or accounted for until reported absent wounded from January-February, 1864, through December, 1864. Place and date wounded not reported. Paroled at Appomattox Court House, Virginia, April 9, 1865.

BOST, HARVEY, Private
Born in Catawba County* where he resided as a carpenter prior to enlisting in Catawba County at age 26, October 16, 1861. Present or accounted for until wounded in the left arm at Chancellorsville, Virginia, May 1-3, 1863. Left arm amputated. Reported absent wounded until discharged on January 27, 1864, by reason of disability.

BOST, NOAH A., Private
Resided in Catawba County and was by occupation a laborer prior to enlisting in Catawba County at age 22, April 27, 1861. Present or accounted for until killed at Malvern Hill, Virginia, July 1, 1862.

BOST, ROBERT A., Private
Resided in Catawba County and was by occupation a farmer prior to enlisting in Catawba County at age 27, April 27, 1861. Present or accounted for until transferred to Company K, 46th Regiment N. C. Troops, June 8, 1862.

BOWMAN, ELKANA L., Private
Resided in Catawba County and was by occupation a carpenter prior to enlisting in Catawba County at age 26, April 27, 1861. Present or accounted for through June, 1863. Not listed in the records of this company after June, 1863. No further records.

BOWMAN, J. A., Private
Enlisted in Catawba County on April 1, 1862. Present or accounted for until killed at or near Wilderness, Virginia, on or about May 6, 1864.

BOWMAN, LANSON, Private
Resided in Catawba County where he enlisted at age 23, April 27, 1861. Present or accounted for until killed at Gettysburg, Pennsylvania, July 1, 1863.

BOWMAN, NOAH, Private
Resided in Catawba or Alexander counties and was by occupation a farmer prior to enlisting in Catawba County at age 19, April 27, 1861. Present or accounted for until he deserted on April 28, 1863. Apprehended at an unspecified date and was confined at Castle Thunder Prison, Richmond, Virginia. Escaped at an unspecified date but was recaptured on October 7, 1863. Confined again at Castle Thunder but escaped on or about December 1, 1863, and deserted to the enemy. Confined at Old Capitol Prison, Washington, D. C., until released on or about March 15, 1864, after taking the Oath of Amnesty.

BOWMAN, POLYCARP C., Private
Resided in Catawba County where he enlisted at age 19, April 1, 1862. Present or accounted for until hospitalized at Danville, Virginia, May 18, 1864, with a gunshot wound of the head; however, place and date wounded not reported. Returned to duty prior to November 1, 1864, and present or accounted for until paroled at Appomattox Court House, Virginia, April 9, 1865.

BOWMAN, Q. E., Private
Resided in Catawba County where he enlisted at age 26, April 27, 1861. Present or accounted for until hospitalized at Richmond, Virginia, May 18, 1864, with a gunshot wound; however, place and date wounded not reported. Returned to duty prior to October 19, 1864, when he was wounded in the left foot and captured at Cedar Creek, Virginia. Hospitalized at Baltimore, Maryland, until exchanged on or about October 29, 1864. Reported absent wounded until paroled at Charlotte in May, 1865.

BOWMAN, WILLIAM, Private
Resided in Catawba County where he enlisted at age 18, April 1, 1862. Present or accounted for until killed at Spotsylvania Court House, Virginia, May 12, 1864.

BOWMAN, WILSON, Private
Resided in Catawba County where he enlisted at age 26, April 1, 1862. Present or accounted for until he deserted on August 11, 1863. Reported under arrest on company muster roll dated November-December, 1863, and was court-martialed on or about February 12, 1864. Reported absent sick through December, 1864. Paroled at Richmond, Virginia, on or about April 21, 1865.

BRADBURN, JAMES M., Private
Resided in Catawba County where he enlisted at age 23, April 27, 1861. Present or accounted for until transferred to Company F, 32nd Regiment N. C. Troops, September 14, 1861.

BRADBURN, MUNROE J., Private
Was by occupation a laborer prior to enlisting in Ca-

tawba County at age 23, April 27, 1861. Present or accounted for through July 1, 1861. No further records.

BROWN, CALVIN N., Private
Resided in Catawba County where he enlisted at age 26, April 1, 1862. Present or accounted for until hospitalized at Richmond, Virginia, September 27, 1862, with a wound of the foot; however, place and date wounded not reported. Returned to duty prior to March 1, 1863. Present or accounted for until hospitalized at Richmond on May 6, 1863, with a gunshot wound of the right finger; however, place and date wounded not reported. Returned to duty in March-April, 1864, and present or accounted for until captured at Spotsylvania Court House, Virginia, May 12, 1864. Confined at Point Lookout, Maryland, until transferred to Elmira, New York, August 10, 1864. Released at Elmira on June 12, 1865, after taking the Oath of Allegiance.

BROWN, JAMES, Private
Resided in Catawba County and enlisted at age 18, April 1, 1862. Present or accounted for until wounded in the thigh at Hanover Court House, Virginia, May 27, 1862. Died in hospital at Richmond, Virginia, June 6, 1862, of wounds.

BROWN, SAMUEL, Private
Resided in Catawba County and was by occupation a laborer prior to enlisting in Catawba County at age 19, April 27, 1861. Present or accounted for until he deserted in September-October, 1861.

BUMGARNER, T. H., Private
Resided in Catawba County where he enlisted at age 22, April 1, 1862. Present or accounted for until captured in hospital at Richmond, Virginia, April 3, 1865. Paroled on April 20, 1865.

BURNS, WILLIAM, Private
Resided in Catawba County where he enlisted at age 18, September 1, 1862, for the war. Present or accounted for until killed at Chancellorsville, Virginia, May 3, 1863.

CLINE, ELI P. R., Private
Resided in Catawba County and was by occupation a tanner prior to enlisting in Catawba County at age 25, April 27, 1861. Present or accounted for until discharged on August 16, 1863. Reason discharged not reported.

CLINE, HENRY L., Private
Resided in Catawba County and was by occupation a carpenter prior to enlisting in Catawba County at age 19, April 27, 1861. Present or accounted for until he died on or about September 6, 1861. Place and cause of death not reported.

CLINE, JONATHAN, Private
Resided in Catawba County where he enlisted at age 23, April 1, 1862. Present or accounted for until killed at Spotsylvania Court House, Virginia, May 19, 1864.

CLINE, PERRY R., Private
Resided in Catawba County and was by occupation a wheelwright prior to enlisting in Catawba County at age 18, April 27, 1861. Present or accounted for until wounded at Malvern Hill, Virginia, July 1, 1862. Returned to duty prior to November 1, 1862,

and present or accounted for until he deserted on August 3, 1863. Apprehended at an unspecified date and was court-martialed on or about December 26, 1863. Returned to duty on or about April 27, 1864, and present or accounted for until captured at Washington, D. C., on or about July 13, 1864. Confined at Old Capitol Prison, Washington, until transferred to Elmira, New York, July 23, 1864. Paroled at Elmira on March 14, 1865, and transferred to Boulware's Wharf, James River, Virginia, where he was received on or about March 18, 1865, for exchange.

CLINE, WILLIAM H., Private
Resided in Catawba County and was by occupation a farmer prior to enlisting in Catawba County at age 20, April 27, 1861. Present or accounted for until wounded at Malvern Hill, Virginia, July 1, 1862. Returned to duty prior to November 1, 1862, and present or accounted for through April, 1864. Company muster rolls dated May-December, 1864, state that he was a prisoner of war; however, records of the Federal Provost Marshal do not substantiate that report. No further records.

CLONINGER, ELCANAH, Private
Born in Catawba County* where he resided as a farmer prior to enlisting in Catawba County at age 37, April 1, 1862. Present or accounted for until wounded in the right arm at Malvern Hill, Virginia, July 1, 1862. Right arm amputated. Reported absent wounded until discharged on February 1, 1864, by reason of disability. Took the Oath of Allegiance at Salisbury on June 6, 1865.

COFFEY, A., Private
Resided in Caldwell County prior to enlisting at Camp Vance on May 25, 1864, for the war. Present or accounted for until captured near Petersburg, Virginia, March 25, 1865. Confined at Point Lookout, Maryland, until released on June 24, 1865, after taking the Oath of Allegiance.

CONRAD, DANIEL E., Private
Resided in Catawba County where he enlisted at age 18, April 27, 1861. Present or accounted for until transferred to Company F, 32nd Regiment N. C. Troops, September 14, 1861.

CONRAD, JOHN T., Private
Enlisted in Catawba County at age 19, April 27, 1861. Present or accounted for until transferred to Company F, 32nd Regiment N. C. Troops, September 14, 1861.

CORPENNING, ALBERT, Private
Resided in Catawba County where he enlisted at age 37, March 14, 1863, for the war. Present or accounted for until wounded in the head at Chancellorsville, Virginia, May 2, 1863. Returned to duty in November-December, 1863. Present or accounted for until hospitalized at Richmond, Virginia, May 19, 1864, with a gunshot wound of the left thigh; however, place and date wounded not reported. Returned to duty in November-December, 1864, and present or accounted for until captured at or near High Bridge, Virginia, on or about April 6, 1865. Confined at Point Lookout, Maryland, until released on June 26, 1865, after taking the Oath of Allegiance.

COX, GEORGE M., Private
Place and date of enlistment not reported. Captured at Petersburg, Virginia, April 2, 1865, and confined at Point Lookout, Maryland, until released on June 24, 1865, after taking the Oath of Allegiance.

DALY, ABRAHAM, Private
Resided in Catawba County and was by occupation a laborer prior to enlisting in Catawba County at age 18, April 27, 1861. Present or accounted for until transferred to Company F, 32nd Regiment N. C. Troops, September 14, 1861.

DEAL, E. D., Private
Resided in Catawba County where he enlisted on April 1, 1862. Present or accounted for until wounded in the left leg at Chancellorsville, Virginia, May 2, 1863. Returned to duty in November-December, 1863, and present or accounted for until captured at Spotsylvania Court House, Virginia, May 12, 1864. Confined at Point Lookout, Maryland, until transferred to Elmira, New York, August 10, 1864. Released at Elmira on June 30, 1865, after taking the Oath of Allegiance.

DEAL, ELCANAH, Private
Resided in Catawba County where he enlisted at age 33, April 1, 1862. Present or accounted for through December, 1864; however, he was reported absent sick or absent on light duty during most of that period. Died "at home" in 1865 of disease. Exact date of death not reported.

DEAL, GOVAN, Private
Resided in Catawba County where he enlisted at age 22, April 1, 1862. Present or accounted for until he died at Richmond, Virginia, on July 16, 1862, or August 15, 1862, of "typhoid fever."

DEAL, HENRY J., Private
Resided in Catawba County and was by occupation a farmer prior to enlisting in Catawba County at age 21, April 27, 1861. Present or accounted for until killed at Chancellorsville, Virginia, May 3, 1863.

DEAL, M. M., Private
Enlisted in Catawba County on November 1, 1863, for the war. Present or accounted for until captured near Spotsylvania Court House, Virginia, May 12, 1864. Confined at Point Lookout, Maryland, until transferred to Elmira, New York, August 10, 1864. Died at Elmira on April 20, 1865, of "pneumonia."

DEITZE, JACOB, Private
Resided in Catawba County where he enlisted at age 21, April 1, 1862. Present or accounted for until he was "killed by accident" at Shepherdstown, Virginia, September 20, 1862.

DELLINGER, JOHN H., Private
Resided in Catawba County and was by occupation a farmer prior to enlisting in Catawba County at age 21, April 27, 1861. Present or accounted for until transferred to Company F, 32nd Regiment N. C. Troops, September 14, 1861.

DIXON, JACOB A., Private
Resided in Catawba County and was by occupation a laborer prior to enlisting in Catawba County at age 23, April 27, 1861. Present or accounted for until killed at Spotsylvania Court House, Virginia, May 12, 1864.

DUNLAP, J. H., Private
Place and date of enlistment not reported. Reported on duty as a provost guard at Jamestown in April, 1865. No further records.

EATON, JAMES A., Private
Resided in Catawba or Gaston counties and was by occupation a cabinetmaker prior to enlisting in Catawba County at age 19, April 27, 1861. Present or accounted for until transferred to Company F, 32nd Regiment N. C. Troops, September 14, 1861.

EPPS, JOHN A., Private
Resided in Catawba County and was by occupation a farmer prior to enlisting in Catawba County at age 21, April 27, 1861. Present or accounted for until wounded at Malvern Hill, Virginia, July 1, 1862. Returned to duty in November, 1862-February, 1863, and present or accounted for until wounded in the arm and shoulder at Chancellorsville, Virginia, May 2, 1863. Returned to duty prior to July 1, 1863, and present or accounted for until paroled at Appomattox Court House, Virginia, April 9, 1865.

FINGER, DANIEL, Private
Resided in Catawba County and was by occupation a laborer prior to enlisting in Catawba County at age 17, April 27, 1861. Present or accounted for until wounded at Malvern Hill, Virginia, July 1, 1862. Discharged July 6, 1862, by reason of being under age.

FOX, GEORGE, Private
Resided in Catawba County where he enlisted at age 17, April 1, 1862. Present or accounted for until wounded at Malvern Hill, Virginia, July 1, 1862. Returned to duty in November, 1862-February, 1863, and present or accounted for until wounded in the face at Chancellorsville, Virginia, May 3, 1863. Returned to duty prior to July 1, 1863, and present or accounted for until captured at Fort Stedman, Virginia, March 25, 1865. Confined at Point Lookout, Maryland, March 27, 1865. No further records.

FRY, JOSEPH N., Private
Previously served in Company E, McRae's Battalion N. C. Cavalry. Transferred to this company in May-October, 1864, and present or accounted for until transferred back to Company E, McRae's Battalion N. C. Cavalry, on or about March 8, 1865.

FRY, MILES, Private
Resided in Catawba County where he enlisted at age 18, April 1, 1862. Present or accounted for until wounded in the leg at Chancellorsville, Virginia, May 3, 1863. Returned to duty prior to July 1, 1863, and present or accounted for until killed at or near Warrenton, Virginia, on or about October 14, 1863.

FRY, W. W., Private
Resided in Alexander County and enlisted in Catawba County at age 17, November 1, 1863, for the war. Present or accounted for until wounded at Petersburg, Virginia, on or about April 2, 1865. Captured in hospital at Richmond, Virginia, April 3, 1865, and transferred to Point Lookout, Maryland, May 9, 1865. Released at Point Lookout on June 26, 1865, after taking the Oath of Allegiance.

GAULTNEY, GEORGE R., Private
Was by occupation a merchant prior to enlisting in

Catawba County on June 15, 1861. Present or accounted for through July 1, 1861. Roll of Honor indicates he was discharged. Date and reason discharged not reported.

HALMAN, DANIEL E., Private
Resided in Catawba County where he enlisted at age 19, July 17, 1861. Present or accounted for through November, 1862. Company muster rolls indicate that he died at Hanover Junction, Virginia, on or about December 18, 1862; however, Roll of Honor indicates he died in the smallpox camp near Fredericksburg, Virginia, in December, 1862.

HARWELL, CAMA, Private
Resided in Catawba County and was by occupation a farmer prior to enlisting in Catawba County at age 21, April 27, 1861. Present or accounted for until wounded at or near Gaines' Mill, Virginia, on or about June 27, 1862. Returned to duty prior to November 1, 1862, and present or accounted for until wounded in the right thigh at Chancellorsville, Virginia, May 2-3, 1863. Returned to duty prior to July 1, 1863, and present or accounted for until wounded in both thighs and captured at Spotsylvania Court House, Virginia, May 12, 1864. Hospitalized at various Federal hospitals until confined at Old Capitol Prison, Washington, D. C., August 17, 1864. Transferred to Elmira, New York, August 28, 1864, and was released at Elmira on June 16, 1865, after taking the Oath of Allegiance.

HAWN, ELISHA L., Private
Resided in Catawba County and was by occupation a carpenter prior to enlisting in Catawba County at age 22, April 27, 1861. Present or accounted for until paroled at Appomattox Court House, Virginia, April 9, 1865.

HEDRICK, SIDNEY, Private
Resided in Catawba County where he enlisted at age 23, April 1, 1862. Present or accounted for until reported as a prisoner of war from July, 1862, through November, 1862. Place and date captured not reported. Returned to duty prior to March 1, 1863, and present or accounted for through December, 1864.

HEDRICK, WILLIAM F., Private
Resided in Catawba County where he enlisted at age 21, April 1, 1862. Present or accounted for until reported missing at Chancellorsville, Virginia, May 3, 1863. Returned to duty prior to July 1, 1863, and present or accounted for until wounded in the left thigh and captured at Cedar Creek, Virginia, October 19, 1864. Confined at Baltimore, Maryland, until paroled and transferred to Venus Point, Savannah River, Georgia, where he was received November 15, 1864, for exchange. Paroled at Appomattox Court House, Virginia, April 9, 1865.

HEFNER, LEWIS S., Private
Resided in Catawba County and was by occupation a carpenter prior to enlisting in Catawba County at age 20, April 27, 1861. Present or accounted for through December, 1864.

HERMAN, E. L., Private
Enlisted in Catawba County on April 1, 1862. Present or accounted for until discharged on January 27, 1863. Reason discharged not reported. North

Carolina pension records indicate he was wounded near Richmond, Virginia, in July, 1862.

HERMAN, J. C., Private
Enlisted in Catawba County on May 21, 1864, for the war. Present or accounted for until paroled at Appomattox Court House, Virginia, April 9, 1865.

HEVNER, WALTER, Musician
Enlisted in Catawba County on August 13, 1861. Mustered in as Musician. Present or accounted for until discharged on September 1, 1861. Reason discharged not reported.

HOKE, BARTLET E., Private
Resided in Catawba County where he enlisted at age 34, July 17, 1861. Mustered in as Private and promoted to Corporal in February-October, 1862. Present or accounted for until he deserted on August 3, 1863. Apprehended at an unspecified date and court-martialed on or about December 26, 1863. Reduced to ranks on January 10, 1864. Reported in confinement at Castle Thunder Prison, Richmond, Virginia, July 4, 1864. Died in hospital at Richmond on July 15, 1864, of "dysenteria."

HOKE, JOHN D., Private
Born in Catawba County where he resided as a farmer prior to enlisting in Catawba County at age 24, April 27, 1861. Present or accounted for until transferred to Company F, 38th Regiment N. C. Troops, June 1, 1862, in exchange for Private John Q. Warren.

HOKE, JULIUS B., Private
Resided in Catawba County and was by occupation a farmer prior to enlisting in Catawba County at age 17, April 27, 1861. Present or accounted for until paroled at Appomattox Court House, Virginia, April 9, 1865. North Carolina pension records indicate that his left foot was amputated and his right leg was crushed as a result of a train accident in April, 1865.

HOKE, P. C., Private
Enlisted in Catawba County on May 21, 1864, for the war. Mustered in as Corporal and reduced to ranks on August 17, 1864. Present or accounted for until paroled at Appomattox Court House, Virginia, April 9, 1865.

HOLLER, ISRAEL J., Private
Enlisted in Catawba County on May 25, 1864, for the war. Present or accounted for until captured at Winchester, Virginia, September 19, 1864. Confined at Harpers Ferry, West Virginia, until transferred to Point Lookout, Maryland, where he arrived September 26, 1864. Paroled at Point Lookout and transferred to Boulware's Wharf, James River, Virginia, where he was received March 18, 1865, for exchange.

HOOVER, ADOLPHUS A., Sergeant
Born in Catawba County* where he resided as a farmer prior to enlisting in Catawba County at age 23, April 27, 1861. Mustered in as Private and promoted to Corporal in August-December, 1863. Promoted to Sergeant in February-April, 1864. Present or accounted for until wounded in the left arm at Spotsylvania Court House, Virginia, May 12, 1864. Left arm amputated. Reported absent wounded until retired on November 26, 1864, by reason of disability.

HOOVER, DAVID B., Private
Born in Catawba County* where he resided as a blacksmith prior to enlisting in Catawba County at age 22, April 27, 1861. Present or accounted for until wounded at Malvern Hill, Virginia, July 1, 1862. Returned to duty prior to November 1, 1862, and present or accounted for until killed at Chancellorsville, Virginia, May 3, 1863. Nominated for the Badge of Distinction for gallantry at Chancellorsville.

HOWARD, LEVI M., Private
Resided in Catawba or Burke counties and was by occupation a farmer prior to enlisting in Catawba County at age 22, April 27, 1861. Present or accounted for until transferred to Company F, 32nd Regiment N. C. Troops, September 14, 1861.

HOWARD, NELSON, Private
Resided in Catawba County and was by occupation a farmer prior to enlisting in Catawba County at age 19, April 27, 1861. Present or accounted for until transferred to Company F, 32nd Regiment N. C. Troops, September 14, 1861.

HUFFMAN, W. L., Private
Place and date of enlistment not reported. Paroled at Appomattox Court House, Virginia, April 9, 1865.

HUFFMAN, WILLIAM F., Private
Resided in Catawba County where he enlisted at age 18, July 17, 1861. Present or accounted for until wounded in the leg at Chancellorsville, Virginia, May 2, 1863. Returned to duty prior to July 1, 1863, and present or accounted for through December, 1864.

HUNSUCKER, NELSON W., Private
Resided in Catawba County and was by occupation a mason prior to enlisting in Catawba County at age 25, April 27, 1861. Present or accounted for until transferred to Company F, 32nd Regiment N. C. Troops, September 14, 1861.

HUNSUCKER, S. PHILO, Private
Resided in Catawba County where he enlisted at age 33, October 16, 1861. Present or accounted for until wounded at Gettysburg, Pennsylvania, July 1, 1863. Returned to duty prior to September 1, 1863, and present or accounted for until captured at Kelly's Ford, Virginia, on or about November 8, 1863. Confined at Old Capitol Prison, Washington, D. C., until transferred to Fort Delaware, Delaware, June 15, 1864. Died at Fort Delaware on March 8, 1865, of "ch[ronic] diarrhoea."

INGOLD, ALBRIGHT A., Corporal
Resided in Catawba County and was by occupation a farmer prior to enlisting in Catawba County at age 19, April 27, 1861. Mustered in as Private and promoted to Corporal on September 16, 1861. Present or accounted for until he died at Richmond, Virginia, in August, 1862. Cause of death not reported.

INGOLD, LUTHER, Private
Resided in Catawba County where he enlisted at age 24, April 1, 1862. Present or accounted for until captured at Fort Stedman, Virginia, March 25, 1865. Confined at Point Lookout, Maryland, until released on June 28, 1865, after taking the Oath of Allegiance.

ISENHOWER, H. G., Private
Enlisted at Camp Vance on April 1, 1864, for the war. Present or accounted for until captured at or near Sayler's Creek, Virginia, April 6, 1865. Confined at Point Lookout, Maryland, until released on June 3, 1865, after taking the Oath of Allegiance.

KALE, EPHRAIM P., Private
Resided in Catawba County and was by occupation a farmer prior to enlisting in Catawba County at age 24, April 27, 1861. Present or accounted for until transferred to Company F, 32nd Regiment N. C. Troops, September 14, 1861.

KALE, HENDERSON L., Private
Born in Catawba County* where he resided as a merchant or millwright prior to enlisting in Catawba County at age 44, April 27, 1861. Present or accounted for until transferred to Company F, 32nd Regiment N. C. Troops, September 14, 1861.

KALE, PALSER, Jr., Private
Born in Catawba County* where he resided as a merchant or millwright prior to enlisting in Catawba County at age 29, April 27, 1861. Present or accounted for until transferred to Company F, 32nd Regiment N.C. Troops, September 14, 1861.

KILLIAN, WILLIAM S., Private
Resided in Catawba County and was by occupation a farmer prior to enlisting in Catawba County at age 18, April 27, 1861. Present or accounted for until he deserted on August 3, 1863. Apprehended at an unspecified date and was court-martialed on or about December 26, 1863. Returned to duty in November-December, 1863, and present or accounted for until captured at Winchester, Virginia, September 19, 1864. Confined at Point Lookout, Maryland, until paroled and transferred to Venus Point, Savannah River, Georgia, where he was received November 15, 1864, for exchange. Returned to duty at an unspecified date and was captured at or near Sayler's Creek, Virginia, April 6, 1865. Confined at Point Lookout until released on June 19, 1865, after taking the Oath of Allegiance.

LAFONE, NOAH E., Private
Resided in Catawba County where he enlisted at age 18, April 1, 1862. Present or accounted for until paroled at Appomattox Court House, Virginia, April 9, 1865.

LAYFONG, YODAM T., Private
Was by occupation a carpenter prior to enlisting in Catawba County at age 22, April 27, 1861. Present or accounted for until paroled at Appomattox Court House, Virginia, April 9, 1865.

LEFFON, TIMOTHY, Private
Resided in Catawba County where he enlisted at age 18, April 1, 1862. Present or accounted for until reported absent wounded in May-October, 1864; however, place and date wounded not reported. Reported absent wounded through December, 1864, but returned to duty prior to April 9, 1865, when he was paroled at Appomattox Court House, Virginia.

LONG, WILLIAM ALEXANDER, Private
Resided in Catawba County and was by occupation a farmer prior to enlisting in Catawba County at age

21, April 27, 1861. Present or accounted for until transferred to Company F, 32nd Regiment N. C. Troops, September 14, 1861.

LORETZ, DANIEL PINCKNEY, Private
Resided in Catawba County where he was by occupation a farmer prior to enlisting in Catawba County at age 19, April 27, 1861. Present or accounted for until transferred to Company F, 32nd Regiment N.C. Troops, September 14, 1861.

LOWRANCE, BARTLET A., Corporal
Resided in Catawba County and was by occupation a farmer prior to enlisting in Catawba County at age 19, April 27, 1861. Mustered in as Private. Present or accounted for until wounded and captured at Gettysburg, Pennsylvania, July 1-4, 1863. Hospitalized at Davids Island, New York Harbor, July 17-24, 1863. Paroled at Davids Island on or about August 24, 1863, and transferred to City Point, Virginia, where he was received August 28, 1863, for exchange. Returned to duty in November-December, 1863, and present or accounted for until promoted to Corporal on January 2, 1865. Paroled at Appomattox Court House, Virginia, April 9, 1865.

LOWRANCE, WILLIAM E., Corporal
Resided in Catawba County and was by occupation a teacher prior to enlisting in Catawba County at age 23, April 27, 1861. Mustered in as Corporal. Present or accounted for until transferred to Company F, 32nd Regiment N. C. Troops, September 14, 1861.

McNEILL, THOMAS J., Private
Resided in Catawba County and was by occupation a farmer prior to enlisting in Catawba County at age 20, April 27, 1861. Present or accounted for until transferred to Company F, 32nd Regiment N. C. Troops on or about September 14, 1861.

MATHIS, JOHN, Private
Born in Catawba County where he resided as a farmer prior to enlisting in Catawba County at age 16, April 1, 1862. Present or accounted for until discharged on September 23, 1862, by reason of being under age.

MEGEE, JONAS M., Corporal
Resided in Catawba County and was by occupation a carpenter prior to enlisting in Catawba County at age 19, April 27, 1861. Mustered in as Private. Present or accounted for until captured at Sharpsburg, Maryland, September 17, 1862. Confined at Fort McHenry, Maryland, and at Fort Monroe, Virginia, until transferred to Aiken's Landing, James River, Virginia, where he was received October 19, 1862, for exchange. Declared exchanged at Aiken's Landing on November 10, 1862. Returned to duty in November, 1862-February, 1863, and was promoted to Corporal on May 1, 1863. Present or accounted for until wounded in the right arm at Gettysburg, Pennsylvania, July 1-3, 1863. Captured at or near Gettysburg on or about July 4, 1863. Hospitalized at various Federal hospitals until paroled on November 12, 1863, and transferred for exchange. Hospitalized at Richmond, Virginia, November 16, 1863. Reported absent wounded until discharged on April 5, 1864, by reason of wounds received at Gettysburg.

MICHAEL, HENRY, Private
Resided in Catawba County and was by occupation a carpenter prior to enlisting in Catawba County at age 29, April 27, 1861. Present or accounted for until he died at Petersburg, Virginia, July 13, 1862. Cause of death not reported.

MICHAEL, PETER, Private
Resided in Catawba County where he enlisted at age 37, March 14, 1863, for the war. Present or accounted for until reported as a prisoner of war on company muster roll dated May 1-October 31, 1864; however, records of the Federal Provost Marshal do not substantiate that report. Reported absent sick on company muster roll dated November-December, 1864. Paroled at Appomattox Court House, Virginia, April 9, 1865.

MILLER, ANDREW, Private
Resided in Catawba County and was by occupation a shoemaker prior to enlisting in Catawba County at age 21, April 27, 1861. Present or accounted for until transferred to Company F, 32nd Regiment N.C. Troops, September 14, 1861.

MILLER, J. F., Private
Resided in Catawba County where he enlisted at age 28, April 1, 1862. Present or accounted for until wounded at Gaines' Mill, Virginia, June 27, 1862. Returned to duty prior to November 1, 1862, and present or accounted for through December, 1864. Took the Oath of Allegiance at Statesville on May 27, 1865.

MITCHELL, D. L., Private
Resided in Catawba County where he enlisted at age 24, April 1, 1862. Present or accounted for until he deserted on May 1, 1863. Apprehended at an unspecified date and was court-martialed on or about December 26, 1863. Reported in confinement until he was released on or about December 1, 1864. No further records.

MIZE, GEORGE WASHINGTON L., Private
Resided in Catawba County and was by occupation a blacksmith prior to enlisting in Catawba County at age 19, April 27, 1861. Present or accounted for until transferred to Company F, 32nd Regiment N.C. Troops, September 14, 1861.

MOORE, W. N., Private
Resided in Catawba or Gaston counties and enlisted in Catawba County at age 21, April 27, 1861. Present or accounted for until transferred to Company F, 32nd Regiment N. C. Troops, on or about September 14, 1861.

MOORE, WILLIAM, Private
Resided in Catawba County and was by occupation a farmer prior to enlisting in Catawba County at age 21, April 27, 1861. Present or accounted for until wounded at Sharpsburg, Maryland, September 17, 1862. Returned to duty in November, 1862-February, 1863, and present or accounted for until captured at or near Chancellorsville, Virginia, May 3, 1863. Exchanged on or about May 13, 1863. Present or accounted for until captured at or near Stephenson's Depot, Virginia, on or about July 20, 1864. Confined at Wheeling, West Virginia, until transferred to Camp Chase, Ohio, July 27, 1864. Paroled at Camp Chase and transferred to Boul-

ware's and Cox's Wharf,¹ James River, Virginia, where he was received March 10-12, 1865, for exchange. Paroled at Newton on April 19, 1865.

MOOSE, DANIEL, Private
Resided in Catawba County and was by occupation a carpenter prior to enlisting in Catawba County at age 19, April 27, 1861. Present or accounted for until wounded at Chancellorsville, Virginia, May 1-3, 1863. Returned to duty prior to July 1, 1863, and present or accounted for until hospitalized at Charlotte on October 28, 1864, with a gunshot wound of the right hand. Place and date wounded not reported. Returned to duty on November 19, 1864, and present or accounted for through December, 1864.

MOOSE, ELCANAH A., Private
Resided in Catawba County and was by occupation a carpenter prior to enlisting in Catawba County at age 18, April 27, 1861. Present or accounted for until wounded in the head at Chancellorsville, Virginia, May 2, 1863. Returned to duty prior to July 1, 1863, and present or accounted for until captured near Washington, D. C., July 14, 1864. Confined at Old Capitol Prison, Washington, until transferred to Elmira, New York, July 23, 1864. Paroled at Elmira on or about February 9, 1865, and transferred to Boulware's and Cox's Wharf, James River, Virginia, where he was received February 20-21, 1865, for exchange. Reported present with a detachment of paroled and exchanged prisoners at Camp Lee, near Richmond, Virginia, February 28, 1865.

MOOSE, JULIUS, Private
Born in Catawba County and resided in Catawba or Alexander counties where he was by occupation a farmer or laborer prior to enlisting in Catawba County at age 17, April 27, 1861. Present or accounted for until transferred to Company F, 32nd Regiment N. C. Troops, September 14, 1861.

MURPHY, WILLIAM F., Private
Born in Catawba County* where he resided as a farmer prior to enlisting in Catawba County at age 22, April 27, 1861. Present or accounted for until wounded in the left arm and left leg and captured at Gettysburg, Pennsylvania, July 1-3, 1863. Hospitalized at various Federal hospitals until exchanged on or about August 24, 1863. Reported absent sick or absent on detached service through December, 1864. Paroled at Greensboro on May 5, 1865.

PERRY, JOHN, Musician
Born at Petersburg, Virginia, and resided in Virginia where he was by occupation a student prior to enlisting at Norfolk, Virginia, at age 12, May 27, 1861. Mustered in as Musician (Drummer). Present or accounted for until discharged on or about July 12, 1862, by reason of being under age.

POOL, JOHN H., Private
Resided in Catawba County and was by occupation a cabinetmaker prior to enlisting in Catawba County at age 19, April 27, 1861. Present or accounted for until transferred to Company F, 23rd Regiment N.C. Troops (13th Regiment N.C. Volunteers) on or about March 1, 1862.

POPE, ELKANAH L., Private
Resided in Catawba County and was by occupation a

farmer prior to enlisting in Catawba County at age 30, April 27, 1861. Present or accounted for until discharged on July 15, 1862. Reason discharged not reported.

POPE, JOHN, Private
Resided in Catawba County and was by occupation a laborer prior to enlisting in Catawba County at age 20, April 27, 1861. Present or accounted for until transferred to Company F, 32nd Regiment N. C. Troops, September 14, 1861.

PROPST, NOAH L., Corporal
Resided in Catawba County and was by occupation a farmer prior to enlisting in Catawba County at age 20, April 27, 1861. Mustered in as Private and promoted to Corporal in February-April, 1864. Present or accounted for until paroled at Appomattox Court House, Virginia, April 9, 1865.

REINHARDT, ROBERT P., Private
Resided in Catawba County and was by occupation a carpenter prior to enlisting in Catawba County at age 20, April 27, 1861. Present or accounted for until discharged on or about March 1, 1862, after providing a substitute in Company E of this regiment.

RITZELL, A. A., Private
Resided in Catawba County where he enlisted at age 31, April 27, 1862. Present or accounted for through December, 1864.

RITZELL, HENRY J., Private
Born in Catawba County* where he resided as a farmer prior to enlisting in Catawba County at age 20, April 27, 1861. Present or accounted for until captured at South Mountain, Maryland, on or about September 15, 1862. Confined at Fort Delaware, Delaware, until transferred to Aiken's Landing, James River, Virginia, October 2, 1862, for exchange. Declared exchanged at Aiken's Landing on November 10, 1862. Returned to duty prior to March 1, 1863, and present or accounted for until wounded in the left leg at or near Stephenson's Depot, Virginia, July 20, 1864. Left leg amputated. Reported absent wounded until retired on February 3, 1865, by reason of disability.

ROBB, GEORGE W., Private
Resided in Catawba County and was by occupation a farmer prior to enlisting in Catawba County at age 19, April 27, 1861. Present or accounted for until wounded in the leg and groin at Chancellorsville, Virginia, May 2, 1863. Returned to duty in September-December, 1863, and present or accounted for until wounded in the leg at Fisher's Hill, Virginia, September 22, 1864. Leg amputated. Company muster rolls dated May 1-December, 1864, indicate that he was a prisoner of war; however, records of the Federal Provost Marshal do not substantiate that report. No further records.

ROBINSON, ADAM P., Private
Resided in Catawba County where he enlisted at age 18, October 16, 1861. Present or accounted for until he died in hospital at Lynchburg, Virginia, August 24, 1862, of "diarrhoea chron[ic]."

ROBINSON, GEORGE W., Private
Resided in Catawba County and was by occupation a

merchant prior to enlisting in Catawba County at age 27, April 27, 1861. Present or accounted for until he died in hospital at Richmond, Virginia, September 7, 1862, of "febris typhoides."

ROBINSON, JAMES FERDINAND, Private
Resided in Catawba County and was by occupation a farmer prior to enlisting in Catawba County at age 18, May 22, 1861. Present or accounted for until killed at Spotsylvania Court House, Virginia, May 12, 1864.

ROWE, D. LAFAYETTE, Private
Resided in Catawba County where he enlisted at age 21, August 13, 1861. Present or accounted for until wounded in the breast at Gettysburg, Pennsylvania, July 1-3, 1863. Returned to duty in November-December, 1863, and present or accounted for until hospitalized at Charlottesville, Virginia, September 24, 1864, with a gunshot wound of the left leg. Place and date wounded not reported. Reported absent wounded through December, 1864.

ROWE, NOAH J., Private
Resided in Catawba County where he enlisted at age 35, October 16, 1861. Present or accounted for until wounded in the arm at Chancellorsville, Virginia, May 2, 1863. Returned to duty in September-December, 1863, and present or accounted for until captured at Spotsylvania Court House, Virginia, May 12, 1864. Confined at Point Lookout, Maryland, until transferred to Elmira, New York, August 10, 1864. Released at Elmira on June 27, 1865, after taking the Oath of Allegiance.

ROWE, SIDNEY H., Corporal
Previously served in Company F, 23rd Regiment N.C. Troops (13th Regiment N.C. Volunteers). Transferred to this company on June 6, 1861, with the rank of Private. Promoted to Corporal in March-April, 1864. Present or accounted for until captured at Spotsylvania Court House, Virginia, May 12, 1864. Confined at Point Lookout, Maryland, until transferred to Elmira, New York, August 10, 1864. Died at Elmira on December 20, 1864, of "pneumonia."

SAPAUGH, JOHN, Corporal
Resided in Catawba County and was by occupation a farmer prior to enlisting in Catawba County at age 22, April 27, 1861. Mustered in as Private and promoted to Corporal in March-April, 1864. Present or accounted for until killed at the Monocacy River, Maryland, July 9, 1864. Roll of Honor indicates that he was wounded at Malvern Hill, Virginia.

SESSIELL, ALBERT, Private
Enlisted in Catawba County on April 1, 1862. Company muster roll dated July 1-October 31, 1862, indicates that he was a prisoner of war; however, records of the Federal Provost Marshal do not substantiate that report. No further records.

SETTLEMYER, ALLEN M., Private
Enlisted in Catawba County on January 1, 1864, for the war. Present or accounted for through December, 1864. North Carolina pension records indicate he was wounded near Appomattox, Virginia, in April, 1865.

SETTLEMYRE, DANIEL S., Private
Resided in Catawba County where he was by occupa-tion a carpenter prior to enlisting in Catawba County at age 23, April 27, 1861. Present or accounted for until captured at Hanover Court House, Virginia, May 27, 1862. Confined at Fort Monroe, Virginia. Exchanged at Aiken's Landing, James River, Virginia, August 5, 1862. Rejoined the company in November, 1862-February, 1863, and present or accounted for until captured at Spotsylvania Court House, Virginia, May 12, 1864. Confined at Point Lookout, Maryland, until transferred to Elmira, New York, August 10, 1864. Released at Elmira on May 13, 1865, after taking the Oath of Allegiance.

SETTLEMYRE, JOHN P., Private
Resided in Catawba County and was by occupation a carpenter prior to enlisting in Catawba County at age 22, April 27, 1861. Present or accounted for until captured at Fredericksburg, Virginia, May 3, 1863. Exchanged on or about May 13, 1863. Present or accounted for until he deserted on August 23, 1863. Returned to duty at an unspecified date and was court-martialed on or about December 26, 1863. Reported absent sick until discharged on April 15, 1864, by reason of disability.

SETZER, DAVID, Private
Resided in Catawba County and was by occupation a farmer prior to enlisting in Catawba County at age 23, April 27, 1861. Present or accounted for until he was reported absent without leave in May-June, 1863. Returned to duty on January 1, 1864, and present or accounted for until killed at Spotsylvania Court House, Virginia, May 12, 1864.

SETZER, J. NOAH, Private
Resided in Catawba County and was by occupation a farmer prior to enlisting in Catawba County at age 22, April 27, 1861. Present or accounted for until paroled at Appomattox Court House, Virginia, April 9, 1865.

SETZER, JACOB, Private
Resided in Catawba County and was by occupation a farmer prior to enlisting in Catawba County at age 34, April 1, 1862. Present or accounted for until captured at Warrenton, Virginia, September 29, 1862. Paroled and exchanged at an unspecified date and returned to duty in November, 1862-February, 1863. Present or accounted for until captured at Petersburg, Virginia, March 25, 1865. Confined at Point Lookout, Maryland, until released on May 14, 1865, after taking the Oath of Allegiance.

SETZER, MARCUS, Private
Previously served in Company F, 38th Regiment N.C. Troops. Transferred to this company on June 10, 1862, in exchange for Private Albert L. Sigman. Present or accounted for until wounded in the leg at Chancellorsville, Virginia, May 3, 1863. Returned to duty prior to July 1, 1863, and present or accounted for until paroled at Appomattox Court House, Virginia, April 9, 1865.

SHERRILL, JAMES ALBERT, Private
Resided in Catawba County where he was by occupa-tion a merchant prior to enlisting in Catawba County at age 17, April 27, 1861. Present or accounted for until killed at South Mountain, Maryland, September 14, 1862.

SHERRILL, JOHN A. L., Private
Resided in Catawba County where he was by occupation a farmer prior to enlisting in Catawba County at age 25, April 27, 1861. Mustered in as Sergeant and promoted to 1st Sergeant in November-December, 1861. Present or accounted for until wounded at Hanover Court House, Virginia, May 27, 1862. Returned to duty prior to November 1, 1862, and was appointed 3rd Lieutenant prior to March 1, 1863. "Failed to pass the board" and was reduced to ranks in February-April, 1863. Present or accounted for until paroled at Appomattox Court House, Virginia, April 9, 1865.

SHERRILL, MILES OSBORNE, 1st Sergeant
Born in Catawba County where he resided as a merchant or farmer prior to enlisting in Catawba County at age 19, April 27, 1861. Mustered in as Corporal and was reduced to ranks in November-December, 1861. Promoted to Sergeant in February-October, 1862, and was promoted to 1st Sergeant on May 1, 1863. Present or accounted for until wounded in the right leg and captured at Spotsylvania Court House, Virginia, May 9, 1864. Right leg amputated. Hospitalized at various Federal hospitals until confined at Old Capitol Prison, Washington, D. C., October 25, 1864. Transferred to Elmira, New York, December 16, 1864. Paroled at Elmira on February 9, 1865, and transferred for exchange. Received at Boulware's and Cox's Wharf, James River, Virginia, February 20-21, 1865, for exchange.

SHERRILL, THOMAS, Private
Resided in Catawba County and was by occupation a merchant prior to enlisting in Catawba County at age 18, April 27, 1861. Present or accounted for until transferred to Company F, 32nd Regiment N.C. Troops, September 14, 1861.

SHERRILL, WILLIAM P., Private
Resided in Catawba County and was by occupation a merchant prior to enlisting in Catawba County at age 25, April 27, 1861. Present or accounted for until transferred to Company F, 32nd Regiment N.C. Troops, September 14, 1861.

SHOOK, J. CALVIN, Corporal
Resided in Catawba County where he enlisted at age 22, April 1, 1862. Mustered in as Private and promoted to Corporal on July 1, 1864. Present or accounted for until captured near Petersburg, Virginia, March 25, 1865. Confined at Point Lookout, Maryland, until released on June 20, 1865, after taking the Oath of Allegiance.

SHOOK, JOHN, Private
Enlisted in Catawba County on April 1, 1862. Died in hospital at Richmond, Virginia, August 7, 1862, of "continued fever."

SHOOK, TOBIAS, Private
Resided in Catawba County and was by occupation a carpenter prior to enlisting in Catawba County at age 21, April 27, 1861. Present or accounted for through December, 1864.

SHURRILL, J. A., Private
Resided in Catawba County and enlisted at age 32, April 27, 1861. Roll of Honor indicates that he was discharged. Date and reason discharged not reported.

SIGMAN, ALBERT L., Private
Born in Catawba County* where he resided as a farmer prior to enlisting in Catawba County at age 25, April 27, 1861. Present or accounted for until transferred to Company F, 38th Regiment N. C. Troops, June 10, 1862, in exchange for Private Marcus Setzer.

SIGMAN, JOHN C., Private
Born in Catawba County where he resided as a farmer prior to enlisting in Catawba County at age 18, April 27, 1861. Present or accounted for until transferred to Company F, 32nd Regiment N. C. Troops, September 14, 1861.

SIGMAN, JULIUS E., Private
Resided in Catawba County and was by occupation a farmer prior to enlisting in Catawba County at age 19, April 27, 1861. Present or accounted for until transferred to Company F, 32nd Regiment N. C. Troops, September 14, 1861.

SIGMAN, MARCUS L., Private
Resided in Catawba County and was by occupation a farmer prior to enlisting in Catawba County at age 24, April 27, 1861. Present or accounted for until reported absent without leave on company muster roll dated July 1-October 31, 1862. Returned to duty prior to March 1, 1863, and present or accounted for until wounded in the side at Chancellorsville, Virginia, May 3, 1863. Returned to duty prior to July 1, 1863, and present or accounted for until captured in hospital at Richmond, Virginia, April 3, 1865. Confined at Libby Prison, Richmond, until transferred to Newport News, Virginia, April 23, 1865. Released at Newport News on June 30, 1865, after taking the Oath of Allegiance.

SIGMAN, NEWTON, Private
Resided in Catawba County where he enlisted at age 22, October 16, 1861. Present or accounted for until wounded at Malvern Hill, Virginia, on or about July 1, 1862. Returned to duty prior to February 1, 1863, and present or accounted for until wounded in the leg at Chancellorsville, Virginia, May 2, 1863. Returned to duty prior to July 1, 1863, and present or accounted for until captured at Harper's Farm, Virginia, April 6, 1865. Confined at City Point, Virginia, until transferred to Point Lookout, Maryland, where he took the Oath of Allegiance on June 19, 1865.

SIGMAN, WESLEY, Private
Resided in Catawba County and was by occupation a farmer prior to enlisting in Catawba County at age 21, April 27, 1861. Present or accounted for until reported absent wounded on company muster rolls dated May-August, 1863; however, place and date wounded not reported. Roll of Honor indicates that he deserted on April 27, 1863. No further records.

SIGMON, ALFRED, Private
Resided in Catawba County where he enlisted at age 19, April 1, 1862. Present or accounted for until wounded in the back and captured at South Mountain, Maryland, on or about September 14, 1862. Paroled on or about September 24, 1862, and returned to duty in November, 1862-February, 1863. Present or accounted for until captured at Fisher's Hill, Virginia, on or about September 22, 1864.

Confined at Harpers Ferry, West Virginia, until transferred to Point Lookout, Maryland, October 13, 1864. Transferred to Venus Point, Savannah River, Georgia, where he was received November 15, 1864, for exchange. Reported absent sick through December, 1864. Paroled at Greensboro on or about April 28, 1865.

SIGMON, CALVIN T., Private
Resided in Catawba County where he enlisted at age 24, October 16, 1861. Present or accounted for until wounded in the shoulder at Chancellorsville, Virginia, May 2, 1863. Returned to duty in January-February, 1864, and present or accounted for until paroled at Appomattox Court House, Virginia, April 9, 1865.

SIGMON, JETHRO, Private
Resided in Catawba County where he enlisted at age 37, March 14, 1863, for the war. Present or accounted for until he died in hospital at Richmond, Virginia, on or about June 12, 1864, of wounds. Place and date wounded not reported.

SIGMON, MARCUS, Private
Resided in Catawba County where he enlisted at age 20, April 1, 1862. Present or accounted for until hospitalized at Richmond, Virginia, March 26, 1865, with a gunshot wound of the left leg; however, place and date wounded not reported. No further records.

SIGMON, RILEY SYLVANUS, Private
Resided in Catawba County and was by occupation a farmer prior to enlisting in Catawba County at age 18, April 27, 1861. Present or accounted for until he died at Richmond, Virginia, September 4, 1862, of "typhoid fever."

SIGMON, W. R., Private
Resided in Catawba County where he enlisted at age 45, April 1, 1862. Present or accounted for until paroled at Appomattox Court House, Virginia, April 9, 1865.

SIGMON, WILLIAM, Private
Enlisted in Catawba County on April 1, 1862. Present or accounted for through December 12, 1863; however, he was reported absent sick during most of that period. No further records.

SIPE, JACOB, Private
Resided in Catawba County where he enlisted at age 18, April 1, 1862. Present or accounted for until hospitalized at Culpeper, Virginia, September 27, 1862, with a shell wound; however, place and date wounded not reported. Returned to duty prior to November 1, 1862. Present or accounted for until reported as a prisoner of war on company muster rolls dated May 1-December, 1864; however, records of the Federal Provost Marshal do not substantiate that report. No further records.

SIPE, NOAH, Private
Resided in Catawba County prior to enlisting at Camp Vance on November 1, 1863, for the war. Present or accounted for until captured at High Bridge, Virginia, April 6, 1865. Confined at Point Lookout, Maryland, until released on June 19, 1865, after taking the Oath of Allegiance.

SMITH, JULIUS A., Private
Resided in Catawba County and was by occupation a farmer prior to enlisting in Catawba County at age 20, April 27, 1861. Present or accounted for until transferred to Company F, 32nd Regiment N. C. Troops, September 14, 1861.

SMITH, PETER F., Corporal
Resided in Catawba County and was by occupation a teacher prior to enlisting in Catawba County at age 26, April 27, 1861. Mustered in as Corporal. Present or accounted for until transferred to Company F, 32nd Regiment N. C. Troops, September 14, 1861.

SMYER, GEORGE S., Sergeant
Resided in Catawba County and was by occupation a student prior to enlisting in Catawba County at age 21, April 27, 1861. Mustered in as Private and promoted to Sergeant in February-October, 1862. Present or accounted for until wounded at Malvern Hill, Virginia, July 1, 1862. Returned to duty prior to November 1, 1862, and present or accounted for until killed at Hagerstown, Maryland, July 6, 1863.

SMYER, L. Q., Private
Resided in Catawba County where he enlisted at age 37, March 14, 1863, for the war. Present or accounted for through December, 1864.

SMYER, SILAS, Sergeant
Resided in Catawba County and was by occupation a farmer prior to enlisting in Catawba County at age 25, April 27, 1861. Mustered in as Private and promoted to Corporal on September 1, 1862. Promoted to Sergeant in March-April, 1864. Present or accounted for until wounded in the left thigh and left hand and captured at Winchester, Virginia, September 19, 1864. Hospitalized at various Federal hospitals until confined at Point Lookout, Maryland, October 18, 1864. Paroled and transferred to Venus Point, Savannah River, Georgia, where he was received November 15, 1864, for exchange. Reported absent wounded through December, 1864, but returned to duty prior to March 25, 1865, when he was captured at Fort Stedman, Virginia. Confined at Old Capitol Prison, Washington, D. C., until transferred to Elmira, New York, May 1, 1865. Released at Elmira on July 7, 1865, after taking the Oath of Allegiance.

TRAVIS, NELSON, Private
Resided in Catawba County and was by occupation a farmer prior to enlisting in Catawba County at age 21, April 27, 1861. Present or accounted for until wounded in the hand at Chancellorsville, Virginia, May 2, 1863. Returned to duty prior to July 1, 1863, and present or accounted for until hospitalized at Richmond, Virginia, March 26, 1865, with a gunshot wound of the right foot. Place and date wounded not reported. Took the Oath of Allegiance on July 5, 1865.

TURBYFIELD, THOMAS A., Private
Born in Iredell County and resided in Catawba County where he was by occupation a farmer prior to enlisting in Catawba County at age 21, April 27, 1861. Present or accounted for until killed at Chancellorsville, Virginia, on or about May 3, 1863.

TURBYFIELD, W. O., Private
Resided in Catawba County where he enlisted at age 24, November 22, 1861. Present or accounted for

until he died in camp near Fredericksburg, Virginia, April 17, 1863, of "chronic diarrhoea."

TURNER, JOHN, Private

Resided in Catawba County and was by occupation a farmer prior to enlisting in Catawba County at age 17, June 15, 1861. Present or accounted for until transferred to Company E, 32nd Regiment N. C. Troops, November 1, 1861.

TURNER, JOSEPHUS, Private

Resided in Catawba County and was by occupation a merchant prior to enlisting in Catawba County at age 21, June 15, 1861. Present or accounted for through February, 1862. Roll of Honor indicates he was discharged. Date and reason discharged not reported.

VAN GARDNER, T. H., Private

Place and date of enlistment not reported. Records of the Federal Provost Marshal indicate he was captured at or near Richmond, Virginia, April 3, 1865, and was paroled on April 18, 1865.

WARREN, JOHN Q., Private

Previously served in Company F, 38th Regiment N.C. Troops. Transferred to this company on June 1, 1862, in exchange for Private John D. Hoke. Present or accounted for until hospitalized at Petersburg, Virginia, August 5, 1863, with a gunshot wound of the right thigh; however, place and date wounded not reported. Returned to duty prior to January 1, 1864, and present or accounted for until captured near Washington, D.C., July 14, 1864. Confined at Old Capitol Prison, Washington, until transferred to Elmira, New York, July 23, 1864. Released at Elmira on July 7, 1865, after taking the Oath of Allegiance.

WEBB, C. A., Private

Resided in Catawba County prior to enlisting at Camp Vance on October 12, 1863, for the war. Mustered in as Private and promoted to Corporal on November 11, 1863. Reduced to ranks prior to May 1, 1864. Present or accounted for until captured at Harper's Farm, Virginia, April 6, 1865. Confined at Point Lookout, Maryland, until released on June 22, 1865, after taking the Oath of Allegiance.

WEBB, CURTIS, Private

Resided in Catawba County and was by occupation a farmer prior to enlisting in Catawba County at age 16, April 27, 1861. Present or accounted for through February, 1862. Roll of Honor indicates he was discharged at an unspecified date by reason of being under age.

WHITE, WILSON, Private

Resided in Catawba County and was by occupation a farmer prior to enlisting in Catawba County at age 19, April 27, 1861. Present or accounted for until paroled at Appomattox Court House, Virginia, April 9, 1865.

WHITENER, LEROY R., Sergeant

Born in Catawba County* where he resided as a carpenter prior to enlisting in Catawba County at age 23, April 27, 1861. Mustered in as Private and promoted to Sergeant on May 1, 1863. Present or accounted for until wounded in the right leg and captured at Gettysburg, Pennsylvania, July 1-4, 1863.

Hospitalized at Gettysburg until transferred to Davids Island, New York Harbor, July 17-24, 1863. Paroled at Davids Island and transferred to City Point, Virginia, where he was received August 28, 1863, for exchange. Rejoined the company prior to January 1, 1864, and present or accounted for until paroled at Appomattox Court House, Virginia, April 9, 1865.

WHITENER, PETER WILFONG, Private

Resided in Catawba County and was by occupation a carpenter prior to enlisting in Catawba County at age 21, April 27, 1861. Present or accounted for until wounded in the side and captured at Chancellorsville, Virginia, May 3, 1863. Exchanged on or about May 13, 1863. Returned to duty prior to July 1, 1863, when he was wounded in the left thigh and captured at Gettysburg, Pennsylvania. Left leg amputated. Hospitalized at Gettysburg and at Baltimore, Maryland, until paroled and transferred to City Point, Virginia, where he was received November 17, 1863, for exchange. Reported absent wounded until he was retired on June 9, 1864, by reason of disability.

WILFONG, GEORGE M., Private

Resided in Catawba County and was by occupation a merchant prior to enlisting in Catawba County at age 27, April 27, 1861. Mustered in as Sergeant but was reduced to ranks in March-October, 1862. Present or accounted for until paroled at Appomattox Court House, Virginia, April 9, 1865.

WILFONG, SIDNEY THEODORE, Sergeant

Born in Catawba County where he resided as a tanner prior to enlisting in Catawba County at age 17, April 27, 1861. Mustered in as Private. Present or accounted for until wounded in the left thigh at Gaines' Mill, Virginia, June 27, 1862. Returned to duty prior to November 1, 1862, and was promoted to Sergeant in November, 1862-February, 1863. Present or accounted for until wounded in the right arm and captured at Chancellorsville, Virginia, May 3, 1863. Hospitalized at Washington, D. C., where his right arm was amputated. Paroled at Washington and transferred for exchange on or about June 25, 1863. Reported absent wounded until discharged on or about January 29, 1864, by reason of disability.

WILKERSON, JACOB M., Private

Born in Catawba County where he resided as a farmer prior to enlisting in Catawba County at age 19, July 17, 1861. Present or accounted for until wounded at Malvern Hill, Virginia, July 1, 1862. Returned to duty in May-June, 1863, but was furloughed in July-August, 1863, by reason of disability. Reported absent on light duty at Gordonsville, Virginia, from November-December, 1863, through April, 1864. Returned to duty prior to September 19, 1864, when he was captured at Winchester, Virginia. Confined at Harpers Ferry, West Virginia, until transferred to Point Lookout, Maryland, where he arrived September 26, 1864. Paroled at Point Lookout and transferred to Boulware's Wharf, James River, Virginia, where he was received March 18, 1865, for exchange.

WILKERSON, JOHN F., Private

Born in Catawba County where he resided as a farmer prior to enlisting in Catawba County at age

18, August 14, 1863, for the war. Present or accounted for until paroled at Appomattox Court House, Virginia, April 9, 1865.

WILKERSON, RUFUS, Private
Resided in Catawba County where he enlisted at age 18, April 1, 1862. Present or accounted for until wounded at Malvern Hill, Virginia, July 1, 1862. Reported absent wounded through April, 1863, and reported absent on detached service from May-June, 1863, through August, 1863. Returned to duty prior to January 1, 1864, and present or accounted for until captured near Petersburg, Virginia, March 25, 1865. Confined at Point Lookout, Maryland, until released on June 21, 1865, after taking the Oath of Allegiance.

WILSON, DANIEL C., Private
Resided in Catawba County and was by occupation a farmer prior to enlisting in Catawba County at age 19, April 27, 1861. Present or accounted for until transferred to Company E, 32nd Regiment N. C. Troops, September 14, 1861.

WILSON, JOSEPH HENRY, Private
Resided in Catawba County and was by occupation a railroad conductor prior to enlisting in Catawba County at age 27, April 27, 1861. Present or accounted for until wounded at Malvern Hill, Virginia, July 1, 1862. Died at home in Catawba County on or about October 13, 1862, of wounds.

YOUNT, ELCANAH, Private
Resided in Catawba County where he enlisted at age 38, March 14, 1863, for the war. Present or accounted for through April, 1863. Company muster rolls dated May-December, 1863, indicate that he was captured on July 1, 1863; however, records of the Federal Provost Marshal do not substantiate that report. Company muster roll dated January-February, 1864, indicates he was absent on furlough. Returned to duty in March-April, 1864, and present or accounted for until hospitalized at Charlottesville, Virginia, June 16, 1864, with "debilitas." Died in hospital at Charlottesville on July 2, 1864.

YOUNT, JOHN HOSEA, Private
Resided in Catawba County and was by occupation a carpenter prior to enlisting in Catawba County at age 29, April 27, 1861. Present or accounted for until captured at Petersburg, Virginia, March 25, 1865. Confined at Point Lookout, Maryland, until released on June 3, 1865, after taking the Oath of Allegiance.

YOUNT, SIDNEY LEANDER, Sergeant
Born in Catawba County* where he resided as a farmer prior to enlisting in Catawba County at age 20, April 27, 1861. Mustered in as Private and promoted to Sergeant in March-October, 1862. Present or accounted for until wounded at Malvern Hill, Virginia, July 1, 1862. Returned to duty prior to November 1, 1862, and present or accounted for until wounded in the left arm at Chancellorsville, Virginia, May 3, 1863. Left arm amputated. Reported absent wounded until discharged on or about January 29, 1864, by reason of disability.

COMPANY B

This company, known as the "Townsville Guards," was raised in Granville County and enlisted at Townsville on April 26, 1861. It tendered its service to the state and was ordered to Garysburg, where it was assigned to this regiment. The company was mustered in as Captain Henry Eaton Coleman's Company and was designated Company D, Company F, and Company G of this regiment before it was designated Company B. After it was mustered into the regiment the company functioned as a part of the regiment, and its history for the war period is recorded as a part of the regimental history.

The information contained in the following roster of the company was compiled principally from company muster rolls for April 26, 1861-February, 1862; October-November 1, 1862; January-August, 1863; and November, 1863-December, 1864. No company muster rolls were found for March-September, 1862; November 2, 1862-December 31, 1862; September-October, 1863; or for the period after December, 1864. In addition to the company muster rolls, Roll of Honor records, receipt rolls, hospital records, prisoner of war records, and other primary records, supplemented by state pension applications, United Daughters of the Confederacy records, and postwar rosters and histories, all provided useful information.

OFFICERS
CAPTAINS

COLEMAN, HENRY EATON
Resided in Granville County and was by occupation a farmer prior to enlisting in Granville County at age 24. Appointed Captain to rank from April 26, 1861. Present or accounted for until he was defeated for reelection when the regiment was reorganized on May 1, 1862. Later served as Colonel of this regiment.

TAYLOR, JOHN T.
Resided in Granville County and was by occupation a farmer prior to enlisting in Granville County at age 27. Appointed 1st Lieutenant to rank from April 26, 1861, and was elected Captain on May 1, 1862. Present or accounted for until killed at Gaines' Mill, Virginia, June 27, 1862.

TAYLOR, MASSILON F.
Resided in Granville County and was by occupation a student prior to enlisting in Granville County at age 20, April 26, 1861. Mustered in as 1st Sergeant and elected 1st Lieutenant to rank from May 1, 1862. Promoted to Captain on June 27, 1862. Present or accounted for until wounded at Hagerstown, Maryland, July 6, 1863. Died July 13, 1863, of wounds. Place of death not reported.

HUNT, JAMES M. B.
Resided in Granville County and was by occupation a student prior to enlisting in Granville County at age 19, April 26, 1861. Mustered in as Sergeant and elected 2nd Lieutenant to rank from May 1, 1862. Promoted to 1st Lieutenant on June 27, 1862. Present or accounted for until wounded at Gettysburg, Pennsylvania, July 1-3, 1863. Promoted to

Captain on July 13, 1863. Returned to duty in January-February, 1864, and present or accounted for until captured at Cedar Creek, Virginia, October 19, 1864. Confined at Fort Delaware, Delaware, until released on June 17, 1865, after taking the Oath of Allegiance.

LIEUTENANTS

HENDERSON, ARCHIBALD ERSKIN, "Lieutenant"
Resided in Granville County prior to enlisting at Camp Carolina, Virginia, at age 18, June 1, 1861. Mustered in as Private and promoted to 1st Sergeant on May 1, 1862. Promoted to "Lieutenant" on September 28, 1864. Present or accounted for until wounded in the right leg at Hatcher's Run, Virginia, February 6, 1865. Right leg amputated. Reported absent wounded through March 31, 1865.

MORROW, THOMAS HUNTER, 3rd Lieutenant
Resided in Granville County and was by occupation a farmer prior to enlisting in Granville County at age 23. Appointed 3rd Lieutenant on April 26, 1861. Present or accounted for until he was defeated for reelection when the regiment was reorganized on May 1, 1862.

PASCHALL, BENJAMIN I., 1st Lieutenant
Resided in Granville County and was by occupation a teacher prior to enlisting in Granville County at age 25, April 26, 1861. Mustered in as Corporal and appointed 3rd Lieutenant on May 1, 1862. Promoted to 2nd Lieutenant to rank from June 27, 1862, and promoted to 1st Lieutenant on June 13, 1863. Present or accounted for until captured at Sayler's Creek, Virginia, April 6, 1865. Confined at Old Capitol Prison, Washington, D. C., until transferred to Johnson's Island, Ohio, April 17, 1865. Released at Johnson's Island on June 11, 1865, after taking the Oath of Allegiance.

SNEED, WILLIAM M., Jr., 2nd Lieutenant
Resided in Granville County and was by occupation a student prior to enlisting in Granville County at age 18, April 26, 1861. Mustered in as Private and appointed 3rd Lieutenant on November 14, 1862. Promoted to 2nd Lieutenant on July 13, 1863. Present or accounted for until captured at Spotsylvania Court House, Virginia, May 12, 1864. Confined at Point Lookout, Maryland, until transferred to Fort Delaware, Delaware, June 23, 1864. Released at Fort Delaware on June 16, 1865, after taking the Oath of Allegiance.

TOWNES, WILLIAM HUNT, 2nd Lieutenant
Resided in Granville County and was by occupation a farmer prior to enlisting in Granville County at age 27. Appointed 2nd Lieutenant on April 26, 1861. Present or accounted for until he was defeated for reelection when the regiment was reorganized on May 1, 1862. Later served as 1st Lieutenant in Company D, 55th Regiment N. C. Troops.

NONCOMMISSIONED OFFICERS AND PRIVATES

ALSTON, JOSEPH ROBERT, Private
Resided in Granville County and was by occupation

a farmer prior to enlisting in Granville County at age 23, June 1, 1861. Present or accounted for until wounded in the hand, foot, left shoulder and left arm and captured at Gettysburg, Pennsylvania, July 1, 1863. Hospitalized at Gettysburg until transferred to hospital at Baltimore, Maryland, September 14, 1863. Paroled at Baltimore and transferred for exchange on or about September 25, 1863. Reported absent wounded until retired to the Invalid Corps on July 26, 1864.

ANDERSON, H. B., Private
Place and date of enlistment not reported. Captured at Frederick City, Maryland, October 1, 1862. Died at Fort Delaware, Delaware, October 8, 1862. Cause of death not reported.

ANDREWS, JOHN W., Private
Resided in Granville County and enlisted at Camp Carolina, Virginia, at age 26, July 1, 1861. Present or accounted for until hospitalized at Richmond, Virginia, June 30, 1862, with a gunshot wound; however, place and date wounded not reported. Returned to duty prior to November 2, 1862, and present or accounted for until captured at Spotsylvania Court House, Virginia, May 18, 1864. Confined at Point Lookout, Maryland, until transferred to Elmira, New York, July 3, 1864. Paroled at Elmira on February 9, 1865, and transferred to Boulware's and Cox's Wharf, James River, Virginia, where he was received February 20-21, 1865, for exchange. Reported present with a detachment of paroled and exchanged prisoners at Camp Lee, near Richmond, February 28, 1865.

ANDREWS, THOMAS W., Private
Resided in Granville County and was by occupation a farmer prior to enlisting in Granville County at age 19, April 26, 1861. Present or accounted for until captured at or near Boonsboro, Maryland, on or about September 15, 1862. Confined at Fort Delaware, Delaware, until transferred to Aiken's Landing, James River, Virginia, October 2, 1862, for exchange. Declared exchanged at Aiken's Landing on November 10, 1862. Present or accounted for until wounded in the thigh and captured at Gettysburg, Pennsylvania, July 1-4, 1863. Hospitalized at Gettysburg until transferred to Davids Island, New York Harbor, July 17-24, 1863. Paroled at Davids Island and transferred to City Point, Virginia, where he was received September 8, 1863, for exchange. Returned to duty in February-April, 1864, and present or accounted for until captured at Spotsylvania Court House, Virginia, May 18-20, 1864. Confined at Point Lookout, Maryland, until transferred to Elmira, New York, July 3, 1864. Paroled at Elmira on March 10, 1865, and transferred to Boulware's Wharf, James River, Virginia, where he was received March 15, 1865, for exchange. Paroled at Appomattox Court House, Virginia, April 9, 1865.

AUSTIN, J., Private
Place and date of enlistment not reported. Hospitalized at Richmond, Virginia, March 22, 1865, and furloughed for thirty days on March 28, 1865.

BALL, WILLIAM, Private
Resided in Granville County and was by occupation

a mason prior to enlisting in Granville County at age 28, April 26, 1861. Present or accounted for until wounded at Malvern Hill, Virginia, July 1, 1862. Reported absent wounded until reported absent without leave on January 16, 1863. Reported absent without leave until February 21, 1864, when he returned to duty. Present or accounted for until paroled at Burkeville Junction, Virginia, April 14-17, 1865.

BARNES, JAMES B., Private
Resided in Granville County and was by occupation a farmer prior to enlisting in Granville County at age 30, April 26, 1861. Present or accounted for until paroled at Farmville, Virginia, April 11-21, 1865.

BELL, JOHN A., Private
Resided in Granville County and was by occupation a hotelkeeper prior to enlisting in Granville County at age 25, April 26, 1861. Mustered in as Corporal but reduced to ranks in February-October, 1862. Present or accounted for until captured at South Mountain, Maryland, September 14, 1862. Confined at Fort Delaware, Delaware, until transferred to Aiken's Landing, James River, Virginia, October 2, 1862, for exchange. Declared exchanged at Aiken's Landing on November 10, 1862. Listed as a deserter on November 14, 1862. Roll of Honor indicates that he deserted to the enemy, "being a Yankee by birth."

BENNET, JOSEPH E., Sergeant
Resided in Granville County and was by occupation a farmer prior to enlisting in Granville County at age 18, April 26, 1861. Mustered in as Private and promoted to Corporal on May 1, 1862. Promoted to Sergeant in May-September, 1864. Present or accounted for until captured at Port Republic, Virginia, on or about September 27, 1864. Confined at Harpers Ferry, West Virginia, until transferred to Point Lookout, Maryland, October 10, 1864. Paroled at Point Lookout and transferred to Cox's Landing, James River, Virginia, where he was received February 14-15, 1865, for exchange. Returned to duty prior to April 3, 1865, when he was hospitalized at Danville, Virginia, with a gunshot wound of the lip and nose. Place and date wounded not reported. Furloughed for thirty days on April 9, 1865.

BENNETT, EDWARD J., Private
Resided in Granville County and enlisted at Fredericksburg, Virginia, at age 18, March 8, 1863, for the war. Present or accounted for through December, 1864.

BRAME, TIGNAL H., Sergeant
Resided in Granville County where he was by occupation a teacher prior to enlisting in Granville County at age 30, April 26, 1861. Mustered in as Sergeant. Present or accounted for until appointed Assistant Commissary of Subsistence (Captain) on or about February 1, 1862, and transferred to the 54th Regiment N. C. Troops.

BRAME, WILLIAM HENRY, Private
Resided in Granville County and was by occupation a farmer prior to enlisting in Granville County at age 21, April 26, 1861. Present or accounted for through February 11, 1865.

BRIM, W. H., Private
Place and date of enlistment not reported. Paroled at Appomattox Court House, Virginia, April 9, 1865.

BUCHANNON, MICAJAH T., Private
Resided in Warren County and was by occupation a farmer prior to enlisting in Granville County at age 19, April 26, 1861. Present or accounted for until wounded in the leg at Malvern Hill, Virginia, July 1, 1862. Returned to duty in May-June, 1863, and present or accounted for until hospitalized at Richmond, Virginia, September 16, 1863, with a fractured arm. Place and date injured not reported. Returned to duty on December 2, 1863, and present or accounted for until captured at Spotsylvania Court House, Virginia, May 20, 1864. Confined at Point Lookout, Maryland, until transferred to Elmira, New York, July 3, 1864. Released at Elmira on June 30, 1865, after taking the Oath of Allegiance.

BULLOCK, GEORGE BURNS, Sergeant
Born in Warren County and resided in Warren or Granville counties where he was by occupation a farmer or student prior to enlisting in Granville County at age 22, April 26, 1861. Mustered in as Sergeant. Present or accounted for until appointed 2nd Lieutenant in November, 1862, and transferred to Company I, 23rd Regiment N. C. Troops (13th Regiment N. C. Volunteers).

BULLOCK, RICHARD A., Private
Resided in Granville County and was by occupation a farmer prior to enlisting in Granville County at age 20, April 26, 1861. Mustered in as Private and promoted to Commissary Sergeant on November 24, 1861. Transferred to the Field and Staff of this regiment at an unspecified date prior to November 1, 1862.

BURROUGHS, CHARLES G., Private
Resided in Granville County and was by occupation a farmer prior to enlisting in Granville County at age 21, April 26, 1861. Present or accounted for through December, 1864.

BURROUGHS, WILLIAM LUTHER, Private
Born in Granville County where he resided as a clerk prior to enlisting in Granville County at age 24, April 26, 1861. Present or accounted for through December, 1864.

BUTLER, EDWARD G., Sergeant
Born in Virginia and resided in Granville County where he was by occupation a student of divinity prior to enlisting in Granville County at age 20, April 26, 1861. Mustered in as Private. Present or accounted for until captured at Malvern Hill, Virginia, July 1, 1862. Confined at Fort Columbus, New York Harbor, and at Fort Delaware, Delaware, until exchanged at Aiken's Landing, James River, Virginia, August 5, 1862. Returned to duty prior to November 1, 1862, and was promoted to Sergeant in November, 1862-February, 1863. Present or accounted for until captured at Sayler's Creek, Virginia, on or about April 6, 1865. Confined at Old Capitol Prison, Washington, D. C., until transferred to Johnson's Island, Ohio, April 21, 1865. Released at Johnson's Island on June 18, 1865, after taking the Oath of Allegiance. Records of the Federal Provost Marshal for 1865 give his rank as 3rd Lieutenant; however, company records and other sources do not substantiate that report.

BYRON, LEWIS T., Private
Resided in Granville County and was by occupation a farmer prior to enlisting in Granville County at age 21, April 26, 1861. Present or accounted for until he died in hospital at Richmond, Virginia, on or about August 31, 1862, of "contin[ued] fever."

CLACK, ALFRED S., Private
Resided in Granville County and was by occupation a farmer prior to enlisting in Granville County at age 23, April 26, 1861. Present or accounted for until discharged on September 18, 1861. Reason discharged not reported.

COBBLE, B., Private
Place and date of enlistment not reported. Paroled at Salisbury on May 3, 1865.

COLLINS, JESSE M., Private
Resided in Granville County and was by occupation a laborer prior to enlisting in Granville County at age 23, April 26, 1861. Present or accounted for until wounded in the right lung and captured at Gettysburg, Pennsylvania, July 1-3, 1863. Hospitalized at Gettysburg until transferred to Davids Island, New York Harbor, at an unspecified date. Paroled at Davids Island on August 24, 1863, and transferred to City Point, Virginia, for exchange. Reported absent wounded until reported absent without leave on October 20, 1863. Returned to duty in January-February, 1864, and present or accounted for until hospitalized at Danville, Virginia, June 4, 1864, with a gunshot wound of the jaw. Place and date wounded not reported. Reported absent wounded until he returned to duty in November-December, 1864. Present or accounted for through January 28, 1865.

COOK, BENJAMIN S., Private
Resided in Virginia and was by occupation a blacksmith prior to enlisting in Granville County at age 21, April 26, 1861. Present or accounted for until captured at or near Boonsboro, Maryland, on or about September 15, 1862. Confined at Fort Delaware, Delaware, until transferred to Aiken's Landing, James River, Virginia, October 2, 1862, for exchange. Declared exchanged at Aiken's Landing on November 10, 1862. Present or accounted for until transferred to 2nd Company G, 14th Regiment Virginia Infantry, March 5, 1863.

COOK, J. H., Private
Enlisted in Wake County on October 5, 1864, for the war. Present or accounted for until paroled at Appomattox Court House, Virginia, April 9, 1865.

COOK, JOHN S., Private
Enlisted in Wake County on October 5, 1864, for the war. Present or accounted for through October, 1864.

CURRIN, CHARLES F., Private
Resided in Granville County and enlisted in Alexander County at age 19, March 13, 1864, for the war. Present or accounted for until wounded in the left leg and captured at Cedar Creek, Virginia, October 19, 1864. Hospitalized at Baltimore, Maryland, until transferred to Point Lookout, Maryland, November 22, 1864. Released at Point Lookout on or about June 26, 1865, after taking the Oath of Allegiance.

CURRIN, FLEMING, Private
Enlisted in Alexander County on March 13, 1864, for the war. Present or accounted for until wounded at Spotsylvania Court House, Virginia, May 12, 1864. Died May 22, 1864, of wounds. Place of death not reported.

CURRIN, JAMES, Private
Enlisted in Wayne County on August 31, 1864, for the war. Present or accounted for until captured at Cedar Creek, Virginia, October 19, 1864. Confined at Point Lookout, Maryland, until paroled and transferred to Cox's Landing, James River, Virginia, where he was received February 14-15, 1865, for exchange. Reported present with a detachment of paroled and exchanged prisoners at Camp Lee, near Richmond, Virginia, February 18, 1865.

CURRIN, JOHN P., Private
Resided in Granville County and was by occupation a farmer prior to enlisting in Granville County at age 19, April 26, 1861. Present or accounted for through December, 1864.

CURRIN, SAMUEL J., Private
Resided in Granville County and was by occupation a farmer prior to enlisting in Granville County at age 24, April 26, 1861. Present or accounted for until hospitalized at Richmond, Virginia, July 6, 1862, with a gunshot wound of the foot; however, place and date wounded not reported. Discharged in July, 1862, after furnishing Private William Dail as a substitute.

DAIL, WILLIAM, Private
Resided in Virginia prior to enlisting at Richmond, Virginia, at age 36, July 20, 1862, for the war as a substitute for Private Samuel J. Currin. Deserted on or about August 1, 1862.

DANIEL, JOHN W., Private
Enlisted in Alexander County on March 14, 1864, for the war. Present or accounted for until wounded and captured at or near Spotsylvania Court House, Virginia, May 9-10, 1864. Confined at Fort Delaware, Delaware, until paroled and transferred to Varina, Virginia, where he was received September 22, 1864, for exchange. Hospitalized at Richmond, Virginia, September 22, 1864, and was furloughed on October 1, 1864. Reported absent without leave on December 5, 1864. No further records.

DIXON, GEORGE, Private
Resided in Virginia where he enlisted at age 36, August 15, 1862, for the war. Present or accounted for until he deserted on September 12, 1862.

DUPEE, JOHN B., Private
Resided in Granville County and was by occupation a farmer prior to enlisting in Granville County at age 24, April 26, 1861. Present or accounted for until reported absent and in the insane asylum at Raleigh on company muster rolls dated November, 1861-February, 1862. Roll of Honor indicates that he was discharged. Date and reason discharged not reported.

DUTY, GEORGE W., Private
Resided in Granville County and was by occupation a farmer prior to enlisting in Granville County at age 18, April 26, 1861. Present or accounted for until

killed at Gettysburg, Pennsylvania, July 1, 1863. Roll of Honor states that he was "a good and faithful soldier."

DUTY, JOSEPH F., Private
Resided in Granville County and was by occupation a farmer prior to enlisting in Granville County at age 23, April 26, 1861. Present or accounted for until killed at Malvern Hill, Virginia, July 1, 1862.

EAKES, JOHN S., Private
Enlisted in Alexander County on April 24, 1864, for the war. Present or accounted for until paroled at Appomattox Court House, Virginia, April 9, 1865.

EAKES, WILLIAM S., Sergeant
Resided in Granville County and was by occupation a farmer prior to enlisting in Granville County at age 23, April 26, 1861. Mustered in as Private and promoted to Sergeant on November 7, 1862. Present or accounted for until at or near Gettysburg, Pennsylvania, July 1, 1863. Returned to duty prior to September 1, 1863, and present or accounted for until wounded in the foot at Cedar Creek, Virginia, October 19, 1864. Returned to duty December 28, 1864.

ELAM, J. D., Private
Enlisted at Spotsylvania Court House, Virginia, May 15, 1864, for the war. Present or accounted for through December, 1864.

ELLINGTON, BYRD, Private
Resided in Virginia prior to enlisting at Camp Carolina, Virginia, at age 24, July 1, 1861. Present or accounted for until captured at Spotsylvania Court House, Virginia, May 19-20, 1864. Confined at Point Lookout, Maryland, until transferred to Elmira, New York, July 3, 1864. Released at Elmira on June 30, 1865, after taking the Oath of Allegiance.

ELLIS, ROBERT M., Sergeant
Resided in Granville County and was by occupation a farmer prior to enlisting in Granville County at age 21, April 26, 1861. Mustered in as Private and promoted to Sergeant in February-September, 1862. Present or accounted for through November 1, 1862. Roll of Honor indicates he was discharged after providing a substitute. Date discharged not reported.

FLARTY, THOMAS, Private
Resided in Virginia prior to enlisting at Ashby's Gap, Virginia, at age 46, October 31, 1862, for the war as a substitute for Private James E. Townes. Deserted on or about November 9, 1862.

FORREST, JAMES, Private
Resided in Granville County and was by occupation a farmer prior to enlisting in Granville County at age 25, April 26, 1861. Present or accounted for until discharged in October, 1862, by reason of being a foreigner. Later served in Company D, 48th Regiment N.C. Troops.

FRAZIER, JOHN W., Corporal
Resided in Granville County and was by occupation a farmer prior to enlisting in Granville County at age 22, April 26, 1861. Mustered in as Private. Present or accounted for until wounded at or near Gaines' Mill, Virginia, on or about June 27, 1862. Returned to duty prior to March 1, 1863, and was promoted to Corporal on May 1, 1864. Present or accounted for

until wounded at Spotsylvania Court House, Virginia, May 12, 1864. Died in hospital at Richmond, Virginia, on or about May 30, 1864, of wounds.

GODFREY, ALLISON, Musician
Enlisted at Camp Carolina at age 12 in June, 1861. Mustered in as Musician (Bugler). Present or accounted for through June 30, 1861. No further records.

GORDON, FRANK, Private
Resided in Virginia and enlisted at Richmond, Virginia, at age 16, July 20, 1862, for the war as a substitute. Present or accounted for until wounded at Spotsylvania Court House, Virginia, May 12, 1864. Rejoined the company prior to November 1, 1864, and present or accounted for until paroled at Appomattox Court House, Virginia, April 9, 1865.

GORDON, HENRY H., Private
Resided in Granville County and was by occupation a farmer prior to enlisting in Granville County at age 22, April 26, 1861. Present or accounted for until wounded at Mount Jackson, Virginia, September 23, 1864. Reported absent wounded through October, 1864, and reported absent without leave in November-December, 1864.

GORDON, JAMES HENRY, Private
Resided in Granville County and was by occupation a farmer prior to enlisting in Granville County at age 20, April 26, 1861. Present or accounted for until paroled at Appomattox Court House, Virginia, April 9, 1865.

GORDON, JAMES R., Private
Resided in Granville County and was by occupation a farmer prior to enlisting in Granville County at age 39, April 26, 1861. Present or accounted for until discharged on July 26, 1862, by reason of being over age.

GORDON, THOMAS, Private
Resided in Granville County and was by occupation a farmer prior to enlisting in Granville County at age 19, April 26, 1861. Present or accounted for until reported missing at South Mountain, Maryland, on or about September 14, 1862. No further records.

GREGORY, WILLIAM H., Private
Resided in Granville County and was by occupation a farmer prior to enlisting in Wake County at age 18, May 5, 1861. Present or accounted for until discharged on May 5, 1862. Reason discharged not reported.

GRIFFIN, NELSON, Private
Was by occupation a student prior to enlisting in Granville County at age 20, April 26, 1861. Discharged May 1, 1861. Reason discharged not reported.

GRISHAM, JAMES A., Private
Resided in Granville County and enlisted at Camp Carolina, Virginia, at age 25, July 1, 1861. Present or accounted for until captured at Spotsylvania Court House, Virginia, May 12, 1864. Confined at Point Lookout, Maryland, until transferred to Elmira, New York, August 10, 1864. Released at Elmira on June 23, 1865, after taking the Oath of Allegiance.

HAGOOD, WILLIAM R., Private
Resided in Granville County and was by occupation a farmer prior to enlisting in Granville County at age 30, April 26, 1861. Present or accounted for through February, 1862. Roll of Honor indicates he was discharged after furnishing a substitute. Date discharged not reported.

HALL, JOHN T., Private
Resided in Granville County and was by occupation a farmer prior to enlisting in Granville County at age 18, April 26, 1861. Present or accounted for until reported absent without leave from August 1, 1863, until February 20, 1864. Present or accounted for through December, 1864.

HARRIS, GEORGE B., Private
Was by occupation a lawyer prior to enlisting in Granville County at age 23, April 30, 1861. Company muster roll dated July-August, 1861, states he was discharged August 30, 1861, and was deceased. No further records.

HARRIS, JAMES N., Private
Resided in Granville County and was by occupation a farmer prior to enlisting in Granville County at age 25, April 26, 1861. Present or accounted for until wounded in the left thigh at Gaines' Mill, Virginia, June 27, 1862. Returned to duty prior to November 2, 1862, and present or accounted for until wounded in the arm at or near Morton's Ford, Virginia, October 11, 1863. Returned to duty in January-February, 1864, and present or accounted for until paroled at Appomattox Court House, Virginia, April 9, 1865.

HEPPER, T. W., Private
Place and date of enlistment not reported. Captured at Winchester, Virginia, September 19, 1864. Confined at Point Lookout, Maryland. No further records.

HESTER, JOHN HENRY, Private
Resided in Granville County and was by occupation a carpenter prior to enlisting in Granville County at age 25, April 26, 1861. Present or accounted for until wounded in the leg at Malvern Hill, Virginia, July 1, 1862. Returned to duty prior to March 1, 1863, and present or accounted for until hospitalized at Richmond, Virginia, May 6, 1864, with a gunshot wound of the left knee. Place and date wounded not reported. Reported absent wounded until he returned to duty on March 2, 1865.

HODGE, JAMES BOYD, Private
Born in Burke County and resided in Granville County where he was by occupation a miller or farmer prior to enlisting in Granville County at age 27, April 26, 1861. Present or accounted for until discharged on October 20, 1862, by reason of "syphilis."

HOLLOWAY, WILLIAM S., Sergeant
Resided in Granville County and was by occupation a farmer prior to enlisting in Granville County at age 20, April 26, 1861. Mustered in as Corporal and promoted to Sergeant in February-October, 1862. Hospitalized at Richmond, Virginia, June 28, 1862, with a gunshot wound; however, place and date wounded not reported. Medical records indicate that he died in hospital at Richmond on July 29, 1862; however, company muster roll dated October 1-November 1, 1862, states he was discharged on or about August 15, 1862, after providing a substitute.

HUNT, J. W., Private
Previously served in Company K, 6th Regiment N.C. State Troops. Transferred to this company on November 15, 1864, in exchange for Private William C. Overby. Present or accounted for until paroled at Appomattox Court House, Virginia, April 9, 1865.

HUNT, RICHARD B., Private
Resided in Granville County prior to enlisting at Gordonsville, Virginia, at age 30, May 1, 1862. Present or accounted for until hospitalized at Richmond, Virginia, June 3, 1864, with a gunshot wound; however, place and date wounded not reported. Returned to duty on June 7, 1864, and present or accounted for through December, 1864.

HUNT, WILLIAM P., Corporal
Resided in Granville County and was by occupation a farmer prior to enlisting in Granville County at age 18, April 26, 1861. Mustered in as Private and promoted to Corporal in February-October, 1862. Present or accounted for until wounded and captured at or near South Mountain, Maryland, on or about September 14, 1862. Died in hospital at Frederick, Maryland, September 26, 1862, of wounds.

HUTCHINS, R. P., Private
Enlisted in Wake County on October 5, 1864, for the war. Present or accounted for until paroled at Greensboro on May 19, 1865.

JENKINS, ROBERT ALEXANDER, Private
Resided in Granville County and was by occupation a tobacconist prior to enlisting in Granville County at age 23, April 26, 1861. Present or accounted for through February, 1862. Roll of Honor states he was discharged after furnishing Private Fred Snyder as a substitute. Date discharged not reported.

JOHNSON, JAMES, Sergeant
Previously served as Sergeant in Company M, 6th Regiment Alabama Infantry. Transferred to this company on November 8, 1861. Present or accounted for through February, 1862. No further records.

JONES, JAMES A., Private
Resided in Granville County and was by occupation a shoemaker prior to enlisting in Granville County at age 36, April 26, 1861. Present or accounted for until he was listed as a deserter on August 18, 1862. Returned to duty in December, 1862-February, 1863, and present or accounted for until wounded in the left arm and captured at Gettysburg, Pennsylvania, July 1-3, 1863. Left arm amputated. Hospitalized at Gettysburg until transferred to Davids Island, New York Harbor, July 17-24, 1863. Paroled at Davids Island and transferred to City Point, Virginia, where he was received September 8, 1863, for exchange. Reported absent wounded until he was retired on August 31, 1864, by reason of disability.

JONES, REUBEN, Private
Resided in Granville County and was by occupation a shoemaker prior to enlisting in Granville County at age 22, April 26, 1861. Present or accounted for until he died at Camp Carolina, near Norfolk, Virginia, October 18, 1861, of "typhoid fever."

JONES, W. P., Private

Enlisted at New Market, Virginia, October 19, 1864, for the war. Present or accounted for through December, 1864.

JONES, WILLIAM, Private

Resided in Granville County and was by occupation a farmer prior to enlisting in Granville County at age 21, April 26, 1861. Present or accounted for until captured at Spotsylvania Court House, Virginia, May 19-20, 1864. Confined at Point Lookout, Maryland, until transferred to Elmira, New York, on or about July 6, 1864. Paroled at Elmira and transferred to Venus Point, Savannah River, Georgia, where he was received November 15, 1864, for exchange. Reported absent without leave on December 5, 1864, but rejoined the company prior to April 14-17, 1865, when he was paroled at Burkeville Junction, Virginia.

KEETON, JOHN EDWARD, Private

Born in Lunenburg County, Virginia, and resided in Granville County where he was by occupation a dry goods clerk prior to enlisting in Granville County at age 26, April 26, 1861. Present or accounted for until discharged on February 25, 1862, by reason of "phthisis pulmonalis."

KELLY, JOHN J., Private

Resided in Granville County and was by occupation a watchman prior to enlisting in Granville County at age 22, April 26, 1861. Present or accounted for until discharged on November 22, 1861. Reason discharged not reported.

KITTRELL, HENRY CLAY, Private

Resided in Granville County and was by occupation a farmer prior to enlisting in Granville County at age 18, April 26, 1861. Present or accounted for until captured at South Mountain, Maryland, September 14, 1862. Confined at Fort Delaware, Delaware, until transferred to Aiken's Landing, James River, Virginia, October 2, 1862, for exchange. Declared exchanged at Aiken's Landing on November 10, 1862. Discharged in December, 1862, after providing a substitute.

KNOTT, BEVERLY F., Private

Enlisted in Alexander County on March 14, 1864, for the war. Present or accounted for until he died at Lacey's Springs, Virginia, on or about November 25, 1864, of disease.

KNOTT, GEORGE F., Private

Resided in Granville County and was by occupation a farmer prior to enlisting in Granville County at age 26, April 26, 1861. Present or accounted for until wounded at Gaines' Mill, Virginia, June 27, 1862. Rejoined the company prior to November 2, 1862, and present or accounted for until captured at or near Sayler's Creek, Virginia, April 6, 1865. Confined at Point Lookout, Maryland, until released on June 28, 1865, after taking the Oath of Allegiance.

KNOTT, JAMES W., Private

Resided in Granville County prior to enlisting at Camp Ruffin at age 29, November 26, 1861. Present or accounted for until wounded in the left thigh and captured at South Mountain, Maryland, on or about September 14, 1862. Hospitalized at Frederick, Maryland, and was received at City Point, Virginia, January 26, 1863, for exchange. Failed to rejoin the

company and was reported absent without leave on July 1, 1863. Returned to duty in September-December, 1863, and present or accounted for until paroled at Appomattox Court House, Virginia, April 9, 1865.

KNOTT, JOHN HENRY, Private

Resided in Granville County and was by occupation a farmer prior to enlisting in Granville County at age 22, April 26, 1861. Present or accounted for until wounded in the head at Chancellorsville, Virginia, May 2, 1863. Returned to duty prior to July 1-3, 1863, when he was wounded in the left foot at Gettysburg, Pennsylvania. Returned to duty in September-December, 1863, and present or accounted for until captured at Spotsylvania Court House, Virginia, May 12, 1864. Confined at Point Lookout, Maryland, until transferred to Elmira, New York, August 10, 1864. Died at Elmira on May 26, 1865, of "erysipelas."

KNOTT, WILLIAM H., Private

Resided in Granville County and was by occupation a farmer prior to enlisting in Granville County at age 24, April 26, 1861. Present or accounted for until he died in hospital at Petersburg, Virginia, June 7, 1862, of "acute diarrhoea."

LLOYD, DAVID, Private

Born in Granville County where he resided as a farmer prior to enlisting in Granville County at age 47, April 26, 1861. Present or accounted for until discharged on February 7, 1862, by reason of an "old luxation of the shoulder joint."

LOWERY, JAMES MUNROE, Private

Resided in Granville County and was by occupation a drummer prior to enlisting in Granville County at age 13, April 26, 1861. Present or accounted for until discharged on July 26, 1862, by reason of being under age.

LOWERY, WILLIAM A., Private

Born in Virginia and resided in Granville County where he was by occupation a shoemaker or farmer prior to enlisting in Granville County at age 35, April 26, 1861. Present or accounted for until he died in hospital at Richmond, Virginia, August 6, 1862, of "diphtheria."

LOYD, R. A., Private

Enlisted at Bunker Hill, West Virginia, August 1, 1864, for the war. Present or accounted for until wounded at Cedar Creek, Virginia, October 19, 1864. Reported absent wounded through December, 1864.

McCARTY, WILLIAM, Private

Resided in Virginia and enlisted at age 46, November 22, 1862, for the war as a substitute. Deserted November 29, 1862.

MARROW, JAMES A., Private

Resided in Granville County and was by occupation a farmer prior to enlisting in Granville County at age 19, April 26, 1861. Present or accounted for until discharged on or about August 18, 1862, after providing a substitute.

MATTHEWS, WILLIAM, Private

Resided in Granville County and was by occupation a farmer prior to enlisting in Granville County at age

19, April 26, 1861. Present or accounted for until he died in hospital at Richmond, Virginia, June 27, 1862, of "congestion of brain."

MORGAN, JOHN C., Private

Enlisted in Alexander County on March 16, 1864, for the war. Present or accounted for until killed at Spotsylvania Court House, Virginia, on or about May 10, 1864.

MUNN, WHEELER, Private

Resided in Granville County prior to enlisting at Camp Carolina, Virginia, at age 23, July 1, 1861. Present or accounted for until wounded in the right thigh at Brandy Station, Virginia, October 11, 1863. Returned to duty in January-April, 1864, and present or accounted for through December, 1864.

MUNN, WILLIAM H., Private

Resided in Granville County prior to enlisting at Camp Carolina, Virginia, at age 25, July 1, 1861. Present or accounted for until he was reported absent without leave for three months on company muster roll dated November-December, 1863. Returned to duty in January-February, 1864, and present or accounted for through December, 1864.

MURPHY, JOHN, Private

Resided in Virginia and enlisted at age 46, December 7, 1862, for the war as a substitute. Deserted the same day.

NEAL, WILLIAM W., Private

Resided in Warren County prior to enlisting at Camp Carolina, Virginia, at age 30, July 1, 1861. Present or accounted for through February, 1862. Roll of Honor states he was killed at Norfolk, Virginia, "by a member of the company." Date of death not reported.

NEWMAN, AMASA J., Private

Resided in Warren County prior to enlisting at Camp Carolina, Virginia, at age 35, July 1, 1861. Present or accounted for until killed at Spotsylvania Court House, Virginia, May 19, 1864.

NEWMAN, LEWIS H., Private

Resided in Granville County and was by occupation a teacher prior to enlisting in Granville County at age 22, April 26, 1861. Present or accounted for until reported absent without leave on company muster roll dated November-December, 1864. No further records.

NEWTON, B. D., Private

Enlisted in Alexander County on March 15, 1864, for the war. Present or accounted for until wounded in the right knee and captured at Cedar Creek, Virginia, October 19, 1864. Hospitalized at Baltimore, Maryland, where he died November 18, 1864, of "gangrene" and "exhaustion."

NORWOOD, MARION, Private

Resided in Virginia and enlisted at age 17, May 7, 1862, for the war as a substitute. Discharged at an unspecified date by reason of disability.

OVERBY, CAIN, Private

Resided in Granville County prior to enlisting at Fredericksburg, Virginia, at age 22, March 8, 1863, for the war. Present or accounted for through December, 1864.

OVERBY, JAMES T., Private

Resided in Granville County and was by occupation a clerk prior to enlisting at Camp Carolina, Virginia, at age 25, June 24, 1861. Present or accounted for until he was reportedly transferred to the 50th Regiment N.C. Troops in May, 1862; however, records of that unit do not indicate that he served therein. No further records.

OVERBY, LARKIN W., Private

Resided in Granville County and was by occupation a farmer prior to enlisting in Granville County at age 23, April 26, 1861. Present or accounted for until paroled at Appomattox Court House, Virginia, April 9, 1865.

OVERBY, WILLIAM C., Private

Resided in Granville County and was by occupation a farmer prior to enlisting in Granville County at age 28, April 26, 1861. Present or accounted for until wounded in the left side and captured at Gettysburg, Pennsylvania, July 1-4, 1863. Hospitalized at Gettysburg until transferred to Davids Island, New York Harbor, July 17-24, 1863. Paroled at Davids Island and transferred to City Point, Virginia, where he was received September 16, 1863, for exchange. Reported absent wounded or absent on detail until he rejoined the company on October 1, 1864. Present or accounted for until transferred to Company K, 6th Regiment N.C. State Troops on November 15, 1864, in exchange for Private J. W. Hunt.

PARRISH, WILLIAM Y., Private

Resided in Granville County and was by occupation a farmer prior to enlisting in Granville County at age 22, April 26, 1861. Present or accounted for until he died on September 23, 1862, of "typhoid fever." Place of death not reported.

PASCHALL, JOHN WILLIAM N., Private

Resided in Warren County and was by occupation a grocery clerk prior to enlisting in Granville County at age 18, April 26, 1861. Present or accounted for through December, 1864.

PASCHALL, ROBERT H. M., Sergeant

Resided in Granville County and was by occupation a grocer prior to enlisting in Granville County at age 27, April 26, 1861. Mustered in as Private and promoted to Sergeant in February-October, 1862. Present or accounted for until wounded at Hanover Court House, Virginia, May 27, 1862. Returned to duty prior to November 2, 1862, and present or accounted for until wounded in the leg and elbow at Gettysburg, Pennsylvania, July 1-3, 1863. Returned to duty in November-December, 1863, and present or accounted for until wounded at Cedar Creek, Virginia, October 19, 1864. Returned to duty prior to November 1, 1864, and present or accounted for until paroled at Appomattox Court House, Virginia, April 9, 1865.

PENDLETON, D. C., Private

Place and date of enlistment not reported. Paroled at Salisbury on May 3, 1865.

PERRY, EDWARD, Private

Resided in Virginia prior to enlisting at Fredericksburg, Virginia, at age 46, December 7, 1862, for the war. Present or accounted for until he died in hospital at Guinea Station, Virginia, on or about January

2, 1863, of disease.

PHIPPS, JOSEPH L., Corporal
Resided in Virginia and was by occupation a painter prior to enlisting in Granville County at age 20, April 26, 1861. Mustered in as Private. Present or accounted for until wounded in the left thigh at Gaines' Mill, Virginia, June 27, 1862. Returned to duty prior to November 2, 1862, and was promoted to Corporal on September 1, 1864. Present or accounted for until paroled at Appomattox Court House, Virginia, April 9, 1865.

PHYSIOC, JAMES E., Private
Resided in Granville County and was by occupation a tailor prior to enlisting in Granville County at age 25, April 26, 1861. Present or accounted for until wounded at Gaines' Mill, Virginia, June 27, 1862. Returned to duty prior to November 2, 1862, and present or accounted for through December, 1864.

REEKES, THOMAS E., Private
Resided in Granville County and was by occupation a saddler prior to enlisting in Granville County at age 48, April 26, 1861. Present or accounted for until discharged on July 26, 1862, by reason of being over age.

RILEY, JAMES, Private
Resided in Virginia and enlisted at Fredericksburg, Virginia, at age 46, December 7, 1862, for the war as a substitute. Deserted the same day. Company muster roll dated January-February, 1863, states that he "escaped from arrest while under sentence of death."

ROBERTSON, LEN H., Private
Resided in Granville County and was by occupation a carpenter prior to enlisting in Granville County at age 40, April 26, 1861. Present or accounted for through February, 1862. Roll of Honor indicates that he deserted. Date of desertion not reported.

ROBERTSON, THOMAS, Private
Resided in Granville County and was by occupation a farmer prior to enlisting in Granville County at age 23, April 26, 1861. Present or accounted for until he deserted at Harpers Ferry, West Virginia, July 4, 1864. Confined at Old Capitol Prison, Washington, D.C., until transferred to Elmira, New York, August 12, 1864. Released at Elmira on May 19, 1865, after taking the Oath of Allegiance.

ROWLAND, THAD P., Private
Enlisted in Wake County on August 12, 1864, for the war. Present or accounted for through December, 1864.

ROYSTER, WILLIAM DAVID, Private
Resided in Granville County and was by occupation a student prior to enlisting in Granville County at age 19, April 26, 1861. Present or accounted for until wounded in the left arm and captured at Monocacy, Maryland, July 9, 1864. Hospitalized at Frederick, Maryland, until transferred to hospital at Baltimore, Maryland, July 30, 1864. Confined at Fort McHenry, Maryland, October 19, 1864, and was transferred to Point Lookout, Maryland, October 26, 1864. Paroled at Point Lookout and transferred to Venus Point, Savannah River, Georgia, where he was received November 15, 1864, for exchange. Compa-

ny muster roll dated November-December, 1864, states he was absent without leave.

RUSSELL, ROBERT G., Private
Resided in Granville County and was by occupation a student prior to enlisting in Granville County at age 19, April 26, 1861. Present or accounted for until appointed Sergeant Major of the 54th Regiment N.C. Troops, May 10, 1862.

SATTERWHITE, DAVID W., Private
Resided in Virginia and enlisted in Granville County at age 23, May 1, 1862, for the war. Present or accounted for through November 1, 1862. No further records.

SATTERWHITE, JAMES E., Private
Resided in Granville County and was by occupation a farmer prior to enlisting in Granville County at age 19, April 26, 1861. Present or accounted for until captured at or near Front Royal, Virginia, on or about July 23, 1863. Confined at Old Capitol Prison, Washington, D.C., until confined at Point Lookout, Maryland, August 23, 1863. Paroled at Point Lookout on February 18, 1865, and transferred to Boulware's and Cox's Wharf, James River, Virginia, where he was received February 20-21, 1865, for exchange. Reported present with a detachment of paroled and exchanged prisoners at Camp Lee, near Richmond, Virginia, February 28, 1865.

SATTERWHITE, ROBERT M., Private
Resided in Granville County and was by occupation a farmer prior to enlisting in Granville County at age 20, April 26, 1861. Present or accounted for until discharged in January-February, 1862, by reason of disability.

SATTERWHITE, WILLIAM L., Private
Resided in Granville County and was by occupation a farmer prior to enlisting in Granville County at age 40, April 26, 1861. Present or accounted for until discharged on June 25, 1861. Reason discharged not reported.

SMADER, FREDERICK, Private
Resided in Virginia and enlisted at age 46, June 10, 1862, for the war as a substitute. Deserted the same day.

SNYDER, FRED, Private
Enlisted in Richmond, Virginia, in June, 1862, for the war as a substitute for Private Robert Alexander Jenkins. Deserted in June, 1862.

STRUM, JOHN J., Private
Resided in Granville County and was by occupation a farmer prior to enlisting in Granville County at age 20, April 26, 1861. Present or accounted for until killed at South Mountain, Maryland, September 14, 1862.

TAYLOR, ROBERT HENRY, Private
Resided in Granville County and was by occupation a farmer prior to enlisting in Granville County at age 19, April 26, 1861. Present or accounted for until he was killed "by the explosion of a shell" at Norfolk, Virginia, January 31, 1862.

TAYLOR, THOMAS W., Private
Born in Granville County where he resided as a student prior to enlisting at Richmond, Virginia, at age 19, May 29, 1862, for the war. Present or ac-

counted for until wounded in the left leg at Gaines' Mill, Virginia, June 27, 1862. Reported absent wounded until discharged on December 14, 1863, by reason of wounds received at Gaines' Mill.

THOMASON, WILLIAM J., Private
Born in Granville County where he resided as a painter prior to enlisting in Granville County at age 24, April 26, 1861. Present or accounted for until discharged on February 25, 1862, by reason of "rheumatism."

TOWNES, JAMES E., Private
Resided in Granville County and was by occupation a student prior to enlisting in Granville County at age 20, April 26, 1861. Mustered in as Sergeant but was reduced to the rank of Corporal in July-August, 1861. Reduced to ranks in March-October, 1862. Present or accounted for until discharged on or about October 31, 1862, after providing Private Thomas Flarty as a substitute. Later served in Company A, 3rd Regiment Virginia Cavalry.

TUCKER, CHARLES A., Private
Resided in Granville County prior to enlisting at Camp Carolina, Virginia, at age 18, July 1, 1861. Present or accounted for until killed on August 20, 1864. Battle in which killed not reported.

VINES, C. W., Private
Enlisted in Alexander County on March 5, 1864, for the war. Deserted April 6, 1864.

WADE, MOSES T., Private
Resided in Granville County and was by occupation a farmer prior to enlisting in Granville County at age 19, April 26, 1861. Present or accounted for until captured at or near Falling Waters, Maryland, on or about July 14, 1863. Confined at Old Capitol Prison, Washington, D.C., until transferred to Point Lookout, Maryland, August 23, 1863. Confined at Point Lookout until transferred to Elmira, New York, August 18, 1864. Transferred to Boulware's Wharf, James River, Virginia, where he was received March 15, 1865, for exchange.

WATKINS, AUGUSTUS ALSTON, Private
Resided in Warren County and enlisted at Camp Carolina, Virginia, at age 22, July 1, 1861. Present or accounted for until wounded in the right leg and captured at Gettysburg, Pennsylvania, July 1-3, 1863. Hospitalized at Gettysburg until transferred to Davids Island, New York Harbor, July 17-24, 1863. Paroled at Davids Island and transferred to City Point, Virginia, where he was received August 28, 1863, for exchange. Reported absent without leave on October 20, 1863, but returned to duty in January-February, 1864. Present or accounted for until paroled at Appomattox Court House, Virginia, April 9, 1865.

WIER, WILLIAM THOMAS, Corporal
Resided in Granville County and was by occupation a carpenter prior to enlisting in Granville County at age 27, April 26, 1861. Mustered in as Private and promoted to Corporal on May 1, 1862. Present or accounted for until paroled at Appomattox Court House, Virginia, April 9, 1865.

WILKERSON, BENTLEY, Private
Born in Virginia and resided in Granville County where he was by occupation a farmer prior to enlisting in Granville County at age 25, April 26, 1861.

Present or accounted for until wounded in the lungs and captured at Hanover Court House, Virginia, May 27, 1862. Reported in hospital at Gaines' Mill, Virginia, June 5, 1862. Records of the Federal Provost Marshal do not indicate his subsequent disposition; however, Roll of Honor indicates he was killed in the battle at Hanover Court House.

WILLIAMS, JAMES F., Private
Resided in Warren County and was by occupation a farmer prior to enlisting in Granville County at age 22, April 26, 1861. Present or accounted for until wounded at Gaines' Mill, Virginia, June 27, 1862. Returned to duty in March-April, 1863, and was killed at Chancellorsville, Virginia, May 1-2, 1863.

WILSON, ISAAC H., Private
Resided in Granville County and was by occupation a farmer prior to enlisting in Granville County at age 20, April 26, 1861. Present or accounted for until he died in hospital at Camp Carolina, near Norfolk, Virginia, September 23, 1861, of "pneumonia."

WILSON, JAMES HENRY, Private
Resided in Granville County prior to enlisting at Camp Carolina, Virginia, at age 28, July 1, 1861. Present or accounted for until hospitalized at Richmond, Virginia, July 4, 1862, with a gunshot wound of the head. Place and date wounded not reported. Died in hospital at Richmond on August 6, 1862.

WILSON, JOHN, Private
Resided in Granville County and was by occupation an overseer prior to enlisting in Granville County at age 26, April 26, 1861. Present or accounted for until wounded in the face and captured at Gettysburg, Pennsylvania, July 1-3, 1863. Hospitalized at Gettysburg, where he died on or about July 12, 1863, of "hemorrhage from carotid."

WILSON, MARION McD., Corporal
Resided in Granville County and was by occupation a farmer prior to enlisting in Granville County at age 19, April 26, 1861. Mustered in as Private and promoted to Corporal in March-October, 1862. Present or accounted for until wounded in the left side at Gaines' Mill, Virginia, June 27, 1862. Returned to duty prior to November 2, 1862. Discharged at an unspecified date after providing a substitute.

WILSON, ROBERT STEPHEN, Private
Resided in Granville County and was by occupation a farmer prior to enlisting in Granville County at age 25, April 26, 1861. Present or accounted for until captured at or near Front Royal, Virginia, July 23, 1863. Confined at Baltimore, Maryland, until transferred to Point Lookout, Maryland, where he arrived on August 23, 1863. Confined at Point Lookout until paroled and transferred to Venus Point, Savannah River, Georgia, where he was received November 15, 1864, for exchange.

WILSON, WILLIAM FRANK, Private
Resided in Granville County and was by occupation an overseer prior to enlisting in Granville County at age 30, April 26, 1861. Present or accounted for until wounded at Gaines' Mill, Virginia, June 27, 1862. Died in hospital at Richmond, Virginia, July 12, 1862, of wounds.

WRENN, LAFAYETTE, Private
Enlisted in Alexander County at age 17, May 1, 1864, for the war. Wounded in the left thigh and captured at Spotsylvania Court House, Virginia, May 9, 1864. Hospitalized at various Federal hospitals until confined at Old Capitol Prison, Washington, D.C., August 11, 1864. Transferred to Elmira, New York, where he arrived on August 29, 1864. Paroled at Elmira and transferred to Venus Point, Savannah River, Georgia, where he was received November 15, 1864, for exchange.

YANCEY, BEVERLY W., Private
Resided in Granville County and was by occupation a farmer prior to enlisting in Granville County at age 20, April 26, 1861. Present or accounted for until killed at Gaines' Mill, Virginia, June 27, 1862. Roll of Honor indicates that he was "a brave and worthy man."

YANCEY, JAMES E. R., Private
Resided in Granville County and was by occupation a farmer prior to enlisting in Granville County at age 19, April 26, 1861. Present or accounted for until paroled at Appomattox Court House, Virginia, April 9, 1865.

YANCEY, WILLIAM DANIEL, Private
Resided in Granville County and was by occupation a farmer prior to enlisting in Granville County at age 17, April 26, 1861. Present or accounted for until wounded in the head at Malvern Hill, Virginia, July 1, 1862. Returned to duty in January-February, 1864, but was retired to the Invalid Corps on October 24, 1864, by reason of wounds received at Malvern Hill.

YANCY, C., Private
Place and date of enlistment not reported. Paroled at Appomattox Court House, Virginia, April 9, 1865.

1st COMPANY C

This company, known as the "Duplin Rifles," was raised in Duplin County and enlisted at Kenansville for six months' service on April 15, 1861. It tendered its service to the state and was ordered to Garysburg, where it was assigned to this regiment. The company was mustered in as Captain Thomas S. Kenan's Company of Light Infantry and was designated Company C. On November 18, 1861, the company was mustered out after six months' service. Since the company was the first company to serve as Company C of this regiment, it was later referred to as 1st Company C.

The information contained in the following roster of the company was compiled principally from company muster rolls for April 15 through November 18, 1861. In addition to the company muster rolls, Roll of Honor records, receipt rolls, hospital records, prisoner of war records, and other primary records, supplemented by state pension applications, United Daughters of the Confederacy records, and postwar rosters and histories, all provided useful information.

OFFICERS
CAPTAIN

KENAN, THOMAS S.
Born in Duplin County where he resided as a lawyer prior to enlisting in Duplin County at age 23, April 15, 1861, for six months. Appointed Captain to rank from April 22, 1861. Present or accounted for until the company was disbanded on November 18, 1861. Later served as Captain of Company A, 43rd Regiment N.C. Troops.

LIEUTENANTS

ALLEN, WILLIAM A., 2nd Lieutenant
Born in Wake County and resided in Duplin County where he was by occupation a lawyer prior to enlisting in Duplin County at age 35, April 15, 1861, for six months. Appointed 2nd Lieutenant to rank from April 22, 1861. Present or accounted for until the company was disbanded on November 18, 1861. Later served as Captain of Company C, 51st Regiment N.C. Troops.

HINSON, JOHN W., 2nd Lieutenant
Born in Wayne County and resided in Duplin County where he was by occupation a merchant prior to enlisting in Duplin County at age 28, April 15, 1861, for six months. Appointed 2nd Lieutenant to rank from April 22, 1861. Present or accounted for until the company was disbanded on November 18, 1861. Later served as 2nd Lieutenant in Company A, 43rd Regiment N.C. Troops.

WATSON, THOMAS S., 1st Lieutenant
Resided in Duplin County and was by occupation a merchant prior to enlisting in Duplin County at age 35, April 15, 1861, for six months. Appointed 1st Lieutenant to rank from April 22, 1861. Present or accounted for until the company was disbanded on November 18, 1861.

NONCOMMISSIONED OFFICERS AND PRIVATES

BAMBERGER, HERMAN, Private
Resided in Duplin County and was by occupation a merchant prior to enlisting in Duplin County at age 23, April 15, 1861, for six months. Present or accounted for until the company was disbanded on November 18, 1861.

BARDEN, JOHN L., Private
Resided in Duplin County and was by occupation a merchant prior to enlisting in Duplin County at age 21, April 15, 1861, for six months. Present or accounted for until transferred to Captain William C. Howard's Cavalry Company (N.C. Local Defense Troops), November 1, 1861.

BARDEN, ROBERT W., Private
Resided in Duplin County and was by occupation a farmer prior to enlisting in Duplin County at age 20, April 15, 1861, for six months. Present or accounted for until the company was disbanded on November 18, 1861. Later served in Company A, 43rd Regiment N.C. Troops.

BASS, WILLIAM H., Private
Born in Duplin County where he resided as a farmer

prior to enlisting in Duplin County at age 22, April 15, 1861, for six months. Present or accounted for until the company was disbanded on November 18, 1861. Later served in Company A, 43rd Regiment N.C. Troops.

BEST, JAMES WRIGHT, Sr., Private
Enlisted at Camp Carolina, Virginia, August 1, 1861, for six months. Present or accounted for until the company was disbanded on November 18, 1861. Later served in Company A, 38th Regiment N. C. Troops.

BLACKBURN, JOHN W., Private
Resided in Duplin County and was by occupation a mechanic prior to enlisting in Duplin County at age 18, April 15, 1861, for six months. Present or accounted for until the company was disbanded on November 18, 1861.

BOSTICK, DAVID R., Private
Born in Duplin County where he resided as a farmer prior to enlisting in Duplin County at age 22, April 15, 1861, for six months. Present or accounted for until the company was disbanded on November 18, 1861. Later served in Company D, 13th Battalion N.C. Infantry.

BOSTICK, THOMAS J., Corporal
Born in Duplin County where he resided as a clerk prior to enlisting in Duplin County at age 20, April 15, 1861, for six months. Mustered in as Corporal. Present or accounted for until the company was disbanded on November 18, 1861. Later served as 2nd Lieutenant in Company A, 43rd Regiment N. C. Troops.

BOWDEN, WILLIAM B., Private
Resided in Duplin County and was by occupation a clerk prior to enlisting in Duplin County at age 26, April 15, 1861, for six months. Present or accounted for until the company was disbanded on November 18, 1861. Later served in Company B, 13th Battalion N. C. Infantry.

BOYETT, JONAS, Private
Resided in Duplin County and was by occupation a mechanic prior to enlisting in Duplin County at age 26, April 15, 1861, for six months. Present or accounted for until the company was disbanded on November 18, 1861. Later served in Company A, 40th Regiment N. C. Troops (3rd Regiment N. C. Artillery).

BRADSHAW, DAVID W., Private
Born in Duplin County where he resided as a farmer or laborer prior to enlisting in Duplin County at age 18, April 15, 1861, for six months. Present or accounted for until the company was disbanded on November 18, 1861. Later served in Company A, 43rd Regiment N. C. Troops.

BRINSON, ISAAC T., Private
Resided in Duplin County and was by occupation a laborer prior to enlisting in Duplin County at age 22, April 15, 1861, for six months. Present or accounted for until he died on October 20, 1861. Place and cause of death not reported.

BRINSON, JOHN, Private
Born in Duplin County where he resided as a farmer or laborer prior to enlisting in Duplin County at age

20, April 15, 1861, for six months. Present or accounted for until the company was disbanded on November 18, 1861. Later served in Company D, 13th Battalion N. C. Infantry.

BRINSON, WILLIAM N., Private
Born in Duplin County where he resided as a farmer or laborer prior to enlisting in Duplin County at age 24, April 15, 1861, for six months. Present or accounted for until the company was disbanded on November 18, 1861. Later served in Company A, 43rd Regiment N. C. Troops.

BROWN, BRYANT, Private
Resided in Duplin County and was by occupation a farmer prior to enlisting in Duplin County at age 22, April 15, 1861, for six months. Present or accounted for until the company was disbanded on November 18, 1861. Later served in Company B, 1st Battalion N. C. Heavy Artillery.

BROWN, HEZEKIAH, Private
Born in Duplin County where he resided as a merchant prior to enlisting in Wake County on April 22, 1861, for six months. Present or accounted for until the company was disbanded on November 18, 1861. Later served in Company A, 43rd Regiment N. C. Troops.

BROWN, ISAAC, Private
Born in Duplin County where he resided as a student prior to enlisting at Camp Carolina, Virginia, July 5, 1861, for six months. Present or accounted for until the company was disbanded on November 18, 1861. Later served in Company A, 43rd Regiment N. C. Troops.

BROWN, JOHN W., Private
Born in Duplin County where he resided as a farmer or student prior to enlisting in Duplin County at age 24, April 15, 1861, for six months. Present or accounted for until the company was disbanded on November 18, 1861. Later served in Company A, 43rd Regiment N. C. Troops.

BROWN, MIKE, Private
Resided in Duplin County and was by occupation a laborer prior to enlisting in Duplin County at age 30, April 15, 1861, for six months. Present or accounted for until the company was disbanded on November 18, 1861.

BRYAN, THOMAS K., Private
Resided in Duplin County and was by occupation a merchant prior to enlisting in Duplin County at age 31, April 15, 1861, for six months. Present or accounted for until the company was disbanded on November 18, 1861.

CAFFREY, THOMAS, Private
Born in County Cavan, Ireland, and resided in Duplin County where he was by occupation a laborer prior to enlisting in Duplin County at age 30, April 15, 1861, for six months. Present or accounted for until the company was disbanded on November 18, 1861. Later served in Company A, 43rd Regiment N. C. Troops.

CARR, J. J., Private
Resided in Duplin County and enlisted at age 21, April 22, 1861, for six months. No further records.

CARR, JAMES O., Private
Born in Duplin County where he resided as a student or farmer prior to enlisting in Duplin County at age 22, April 15, 1861, for six months. Present or accounted for until the company was disbanded on November 18, 1861. Later served in Company A, 43rd Regiment N. C. Troops.

CARR, JOSEPH H., Private
Resided in Duplin County and was by occupation a farmer prior to enlisting in Duplin County at age 30, April 15, 1861, for six months. Present or accounted for until the company was disbanded on November 18, 1861. Later served in Company A, 43rd Regiment N. C. Troops.

CARR, JOSEPH J., Private
Born in Duplin County where he resided as a farmer or student prior to enlisting in Duplin County at age 21, April 15, 1861, for six months. Present or accounted for until the company was disbanded on November 18, 1861. Later served in Company A, 43rd Regiment N. C. Troops.

CARR, ROBERT B., 1st Sergeant
Born in Duplin County where he resided as a farmer prior to enlisting in Duplin County at age 33, April 15, 1861, for six months. Mustered in as 1st Sergeant. Present or accounted for until the company was disbanded on November 18, 1861. Later served as 1st Lieutenant in Company A, 43rd Regiment N.C. Troops.

CARROLL, LUTHER RICE, Color Sergeant
Resided in Duplin County and was by occupation a farmer prior to enlisting in Duplin County at age 23, April 15, 1861, for six months. Mustered in as Color Sergeant. Present or accounted for until the company was disbanded on November 18, 1861.

COLE, ROBERT N., Private
Resided in Duplin County and was by occupation a farmer prior to enlisting in Duplin County at age 21, April 15, 1861, for six months. Present or accounted for until the company was disbanded on November 18, 1861. Later served in Company B, 41st Regiment N. C. Troops (3rd Regiment N. C. Cavalry).

DAVIS, THOMAS E., Private
Born in Duplin County where he resided as a farmer prior to enlisting in Duplin County at age 24, April 15, 1861, for six months. Present or accounted for until the company was disbanded on November 18, 1861. Later served in Company A, 43rd Regiment N. C. Troops.

DOBSON, THOMAS GARRISON, Private
Resided in Duplin County and was by occupation a farmer prior to enlisting in Duplin County at age 23, April 15, 1861, for six months. Present or accounted for until the company was disbanded on November 18, 1861. Later served in Company B, 41st Regiment N. C. Troops (3rd Regiment N. C. Cavalry).

EVANS, MAC H., Private
Resided in Duplin County and was by occupation a farmer prior to enlisting in Duplin County at age 23, April 15, 1861, for six months. Present or accounted for until he died on October 12, 1861. Place and cause of death not reported.

FARRIOR, STEPHEN DECATUR, Corporal
Born in Duplin County where he resided as a merchant or farmer prior to enlisting in Duplin County at age 24, April 15, 1861, for six months. Mustered in as Corporal. Present or accounted for until the company was disbanded on November 18, 1861. Later served as 3rd Lieutenant in Company A, 43rd Regiment N. C. Troops.

FORLAW, ROBERT H., Corporal
Born in Duplin County where he resided as a mechanic prior to enlisting in Duplin County at age 31, April 15, 1861, for six months. Mustered in as Corporal. Present or accounted for until the company was disbanded on November 18, 1861. Later served in Company A, 43rd Regiment N. C. Troops.

FREDERICK, SIMON P., Private
Born in Duplin County where he resided as a student or "drillmaster" prior to enlisting in Duplin County at age 21, April 15, 1861, for six months. Present or accounted for until the company was disbanded on November 18, 1861. Later served in Company B, 51st Regiment N. C. Troops.

GAVIN, WILLIAM C., Private
Resided in Duplin County and was by occupation a laborer prior to enlisting in Duplin County at age 28, April 15, 1861, for six months. Present or accounted for until the company was disbanded on November 18, 1861. Later served in Company B, 3rd Regiment N. C. State Troops.

GRADY, LOUIS D. H., Private
Resided in Duplin County and was by occupation a student prior to enlisting in Duplin County at age 18, April 15, 1861, for six months. Present or accounted for until the company was disbanded on November 18, 1861. Later served in 1st Company I, 36th Regiment N. C. Troops (2nd Regiment N. C. Artillery).

GRADY, WILLIAM H., Private
Born in Duplin County where he resided as a student or farmer prior to enlisting in Duplin County at age 18, April 15, 1861, for six months. Present or accounted for until the company was disbanded on November 18, 1861. Later served in Company A, 43rd Regiment N. C. Troops.

GRAY, JAMES M., Private
Resided in Duplin County and was by occupation a laborer prior to enlisting in Duplin County at age 26, April 15, 1861, for six months. Present or accounted for until the company was disbanded on November 18, 1861.

GRISSOM, CHARLES, Private
Resided in Duplin County and was by occupation a mechanic prior to enlisting in Duplin County at age 22, April 15, 1861, for six months. Present or accounted for until the company was disbanded on November 18, 1861. Later served in Company B, 41st Regiment N. C. Troops (3rd Regiment N. C. Cavalry).

GUY, ALEXANDER G., Private
Born in Duplin County where he resided as a farmer prior to enlisting in Duplin County at age 26, April 15, 1861, for six months. Present or accounted for until the company was disbanded on November 18,

1861. Later served in Company A, 43rd Regiment N. C. Troops.

GUY, JOHN J., Private
Born in Duplin County where he resided as a mechanic or carpenter prior to enlisting in Duplin County at age 23, April 15, 1861, for six months. Present or accounted for until the company was disbanded on November 18, 1861. Later served in Company D, 13th Battalion N. C. Troops.

GUY, OWEN, Private
Enlisted at Camp Carolina, Virginia, August 1, 1861, for six months. Present or accounted for until the company was disbanded on November 18, 1861. Later served in Company B, 3rd Regiment N. C. State Troops.

HALL, BENJAMIN F., Private
Born in Duplin County where he resided as a student prior to enlisting in Duplin County at age 19, April 15, 1861, for six months. Present or accounted for until the company was disbanded on November 18, 1861. Later served in Company A, 43rd Regiment N. C. Troops.

HALL, EDWARD J., Private
Born in Duplin County where he resided as a merchant or clerk prior to enlisting in Duplin County at age 29, April 15, 1861, for six months. Present or accounted for until the company was disbanded on November 18, 1861. Later served in Company D, 13th Battalion N. C. Infantry.

HALL, JEREMIAH P., Private
Born in Duplin County where he resided as a clerk or farmer prior to enlisting in Duplin County at age 27, April 15, 1861, for six months. Present or accounted for until the company was disbanded on November 18, 1861. Later served in Company D, 13th Battalion N.C. Infantry.

HAWES, REUBEN J. T., Private
Born in Duplin County where he resided as a farmer prior to enlisting in Duplin County at age 25, April 15, 1861, for six months. Present or accounted for until the company was disbanded on November 18, 1861. Later served in Company D, 13th Battalion N.C. Infantry.

HERRING, OWEN F., Sergeant
Resided in Duplin County and was by occupation a student prior to enlisting in Duplin County at age 18, April 15, 1861, for six months. Mustered in as Sergeant. Present or accounted for until the company was disbanded on November 18, 1861.

HERRING, THOMAS JAMES, Private
Born in Sampson County and resided in Duplin County where he was by occupation a student or farmer prior to enlisting in Duplin County at age 19, April 15, 1861, for six months. Present or accounted for until the company was disbanded on November 18, 1861. Later served as Captain of Company B, 51st Regiment N. C. Troops.

HOUSTON, HIRAM V., Private
Born in Duplin County where he resided as a student prior to enlisting in Duplin County at age 19, April 15, 1861, for six months. Present or accounted for until the company was disbanded on November 18, 1861. Later served as 1st Lieutenant in Company C,

51st Regiment N. C. Troops.

HOUSTON, ROBERT B., Private
Resided in Duplin County and was by occupation a lawyer prior to enlisting in Duplin County at age 27, April 15, 1861, for six months. Present or accounted for until the company was disbanded on November 18, 1861. Later served in Company B, 3rd Regiment N. C. State Troops.

HUSSEY, JOHN E., Corporal
Born in Duplin County where he resided as a grocer prior to enlisting in Duplin County at age 28, April 15, 1861, for six months. Mustered in as Corporal. Present or accounted for until the company was disbanded on November 18, 1861. Later served in Company D, 13th Battalion N. C. Infantry.

JERNIGAN, GEORGE W., Private
Born in Duplin County and was by occupation a farmer prior to enlisting in Duplin County at age 20, April 15, 1861, for six months. Present or accounted for until the company was disbanded on November 18, 1861. Later served in Company E, 20th Regiment N.C. Troops (10th Regiment N.C. Volunteers).

JONES, GEORGE W., Private
Born in Duplin County where he resided as a farmer prior to enlisting in Duplin County at age 22, April 15, 1861, for six months. Present or accounted for until the company was disbanded on November 18, 1861. Later served in Company A, 43rd Regiment N. C. Troops.

KELLY, THOMAS J., Private
Resided in Duplin County and was by occupation a physician prior to enlisting in Duplin County at age 23, April 15, 1861, for six months. Present or accounted for until the company was disbanded on November 18, 1861. Later served as 2nd Lieutenant in Company B, 3rd Regiment N. C. State Troops.

KENAN, JAMES G., Private
Born in Duplin County where he resided as a medical student prior to enlisting in Duplin County at age 21, April 15, 1861, for six months. Present or accounted for until the company was disbanded on November 18, 1861. Later served as Captain of Company A, 43rd Regiment N. C. Troops.

KING, FRANCIS M., Musician
Enlisted in Wake County on April 22, 1861, for six months. Mustered in as Musician (Drummer). Company muster roll dated September-October, 1861, indicates that he was discharged. Reason discharged not reported.

LANIER, DAVID J., Private
Resided in Duplin County and was by occupation a farmer prior to enlisting in Duplin County at age 27, April 15, 1861, for six months. Present or accounted for until the company was disbanded on November 18, 1861. Later served in Company B, 41st Regiment N. C. Troops (3rd Regiment N. C. Cavalry).

McGEE, JAMES W., Private
Resided in Duplin County and was by occupation a physician prior to enlisting in Duplin County at age 22, April 15, 1861, for six months. Present or accounted for until the company was disbanded on November 18, 1861. Later served in Company C, 51st Regiment N. C. Troops.

MAREDDY, BRYANT B., Private

Resided in Duplin County and was by occupation a farmer prior to enlisting in Duplin County at age 19, April 15, 1861, for six months. Present or accounted for until the company was disbanded on November 18, 1861.

MATHIS, KEDAR L., Private

Born in Duplin County where he resided as a farmer prior to enlisting in Duplin County at age 26, April 15, 1861, for six months. Present or accounted for until the company was disbanded on November 18, 1861. Later served in Company A, 43rd Regiment N. C. Troops.

MIDDLETON, ISAAC J., Private

Resided in Duplin County and was by occupation a mechanic prior to enlisting in Duplin County at age 23, April 15, 1861, for six months. Present or accounted for until the company was disbanded on November 18, 1861. Later served in Company B, 3rd Regiment N. C. State Troops.

MILLER, RICHARD E., Private

Resided in Duplin County and was by occupation a farmer prior to enlisting in Duplin County at age 23, April 15, 1861, for six months. Present or accounted for until the company was disbanded on November 18, 1861.

MILLER, STEPHEN H., Private

Born in Duplin County where he resided as a student prior to enlisting in Duplin County at age 19, April 15, 1861, for six months. Present or accounted for until the company was disbanded on November 18, 1861. Later served in Company A, 43rd Regiment N. C. Troops.

OUTLAW, WILLIAM H., Private

Resided in Duplin County and was by occupation a student prior to enlisting in Duplin County at age 22, April 15, 1861, for six months. Present or accounted for until the company was disbanded on November 18, 1861. Later served in Company B, 3rd Regiment N. C. State Troops.

PERNELL, MILES, Private

Resided in Duplin County and was by occupation a mechanic prior to enlisting in Duplin County at age 27, April 15, 1861, for six months. Present or accounted for until the company was disbanded on November 18, 1861. Later served in Company B, 3rd Regiment N. C. State Troops.

PITMAN, JOHN A., Private

Resided in Duplin County and was by occupation a laborer prior to enlisting in Duplin County at age 22, April 15, 1861, for six months. Present or accounted for until the company was disbanded on November 18, 1861.

POWELL, DAVID R., Private

Resided in Duplin County and was by occupation a student prior to enlisting in Duplin County at age 18, April 15, 1861, for six months. Present or accounted for until the company was disbanded on November 18, 1861. Later served in Company A, 43rd Regiment N. C. Troops.

PRIDGEN, S. LAFAYETTE, Private

Resided in Duplin County and was by occupation a farmer prior to enlisting in Duplin County at age

24, April 15, 1861, for six months. Present or accounted for until the company was disbanded on November 18, 1861.

QUIN, WILLIAM F., Private

Resided in Duplin County and was by occupation a laborer prior to enlisting in Duplin County at age 25, April 15, 1861, for six months. Present or accounted for until the company was disbanded on November 18, 1861. [May have served later in Company B, 41st Regiment N. C. Troops (3rd Regiment N. C. Cavalry).]

RICH, LEWIS J., Private

Resided in Duplin County and was by occupation a farmer prior to enlisting in Duplin County at age 22, April 15, 1861, for six months. Present or accounted for until the company was disbanded on November 18, 1861. Later served in Company A, 43rd Regiment N. C. Troops.

RICH, PINKNEY, Private

Resided in Duplin County and was by occupation a farmer prior to enlisting in Duplin County at age 18, April 15, 1861, for six months. Present or accounted for until the company was disbanded on November 18, 1861.

RILEY, JOHN G., Private

Resided in Duplin County and was by occupation a laborer prior to enlisting in Duplin County at age 23, April 15, 1861, for six months. Present or accounted for until the company was disbanded on November 18, 1861.

SANDLIN, HIRAM L., Private

Born in Duplin County where he resided as a farmer prior to enlisting in Duplin County at age 23, April 15, 1861, for six months. Present or accounted for until the company was disbanded on November 18, 1861. Later served in Company B, 51st Regiment N.C. Troops.

SANDLIN, JESSE, Private

Born in Duplin County where he resided as a farmer prior to enlisting at age 20, April 22, 1861, for six months. There are no further records relating to his service with this company; however, he later served in Company A, 38th Regiment N. C. Troops.

SHAW, LEWIS J., Private

Resided in Duplin County and was by occupation a student prior to enlisting in Duplin County at age 19, April 15, 1861, for six months. Present or accounted for until the company was disbanded on November 18, 1861. Later served in Company B, 3rd Regiment N. C. State Troops.

SIMMONS, FRANCIS A., Private

Resided in Duplin County and was by occupation a farmer prior to enlisting in Duplin County at age 32, April 15, 1861, for six months. Present or accounted for until the company was disbanded on November 18, 1861. Later served in Company A, 43rd Regiment N. C. Troops.

SLOAN, WILLIAM H., Private

Resided in Duplin County and was by occupation a merchant prior to enlisting in Duplin County at age 20, April 15, 1861, for six months. Present or accounted for until the company was disbanded on November 18, 1861. Later served in Company C,

59th Regiment N. C. Troops (4th Regiment N. C. Cavalry).

SMITH, DAVID J., Private
Born in Sampson County and resided in Duplin County where he was by occupation a student or farmer prior to enlisting in Duplin County at age 23, April 15, 1861, for six months. Present or accounted for until the company was disbanded on November 18, 1861. Later served in Company B, 51st Regiment N. C. Troops.

SMITH, JACOB J., Private
Resided in Duplin County and was by occupation a student prior to enlisting in Duplin County at age 19, April 15, 1861, for six months. Present or accounted for until the company was disbanded on November 18, 1861.

SMITH, JESSE THOMAS, Private
Born in Sampson County and resided in Duplin County where he was by occupation a clerk or student prior to enlisting in Duplin County at age 24, April 15, 1861, for six months. Present or accounted for until the company was disbanded on November 18, 1861. Later served in Company B, 51st Regiment N. C. Troops.

SMITH, WILLIAM, Private
Resided in Duplin County and was by occupation a student prior to enlisting in Duplin County at age 21, April 15, 1861, for six months. Present or accounted for until discharged in September-October, 1861. Reason discharged not reported.

SOUTHERLAND, COLUMBUS C., Private
Resided in Duplin County and was by occupation a student prior to enlisting in Duplin County at age 18, April 15, 1861, for six months. Present or accounted for until he died on October 2, 1861. Place and cause of death not reported.

SOUTHERLAND, EDWARD, Private
Born in Duplin County where he resided as a merchant or student prior to enlisting in Duplin County at age 25, April 15, 1861, for six months. Present or accounted for until the company was disbanded on November 18, 1861. Later served as 2nd Lieutenant in Company D, 13th Battalion N. C. Infantry.

SOUTHERLAND, GEORGE N., Private
Born in Duplin County where he resided as a student or farmer prior to enlisting in Duplin County at age 19, April 15, 1861, for six months. Present or accounted for until the company was disbanded on November 18, 1861. Later served in Company B, 41st Regiment N. C. Troops (3rd Regiment N. C. Cavalry).

SOUTHERLAND, WILLIAM J., Private
Born in Duplin County where he resided as a student or farmer prior to enlisting in Duplin County at age 20, April 15, 1861, for six months. Present or accounted for until the company was disbanded on November 18, 1861. Later served in Company D, 13th Battalion N. C. Infantry.

STANFORD, GEORGE W., Private
Born in Duplin County where he resided as a student prior to enlisting in Duplin County at age 18, April 15, 1861, for six months. Present or accounted for until the company was disbanded on November 18,

1861. Later served in Company C, 51st Regiment N.C. Troops.

STANFORD, SAMUEL M., Sergeant
Born in Duplin County where he resided as a lawyer prior to enlisting in Duplin County at age 23, April 15, 1861, for six months. Mustered in as Sergeant. Present or accounted for until the company was disbanded on November 18, 1861. Later served as Captain of Company C, 51st Regiment N.C. Troops.

STRICKLAND, JOHN W., Private
Resided in Duplin County and was by occupation a farmer prior to enlisting in Duplin County at age 23, April 15, 1861, for six months. Present or accounted for until the company was disbanded on November 18, 1861. Later served in Company B, 1st Battalion N. C. Heavy Artillery.

SULLIVAN, ANDREW M., Private
Born in Duplin County where he resided as a student prior to enlisting in Duplin County at age 18, April 15, 1861, for six months. Present or accounted for until the company was disbanded on November 18, 1861. Later served as 2nd Lieutenant in Company C, 51st Regiment N. C. Troops.

TAYLOR, J. J., Private
Resided in Duplin County and enlisted at age 19, April 22, 1861, for six months. No further records.

TEACHEY, ROBERT, Private
Resided in Duplin County and was by occupation a mechanic prior to enlisting in Duplin County at age 22, April 15, 1861, for six months. Present or accounted for until the company was disbanded on November 18, 1861. Later served in Company A, 40th Regiment N. C. Troops (3rd Regiment N. C. Artillery).

THOMAS, DANIEL F., Private
Born in Duplin County where he resided as a farmer prior to enlisting at Camp Carolina, Virginia, August 1, 1861, for six months. Present or accounted for until the company was disbanded on November 18, 1861. Later served in Company A, 38th Regiment N. C. Troops.

THOMAS, LEWIS, Private
Resided in Duplin County and was by occupation a mechanic prior to enlisting in Duplin County at age 27, April 15, 1861, for six months. Present or accounted for until the company was disbanded on November 18, 1861.

TUCKER, OWEN, Private
Resided in Duplin County and was by occupation a mechanic prior to enlisting in Duplin County at age 20, April 15, 1861, for six months. Present or accounted for until the company was disbanded on November 18, 1861. Later served in Company E, 30th Regiment N. C. Troops.

TURNER, DAVID W., Private
Resided in Duplin County and was by occupation a mechanic prior to enlisting in Duplin County at age 23, April 15, 1861, for six months. Present or accounted for until the company was disbanded on November 18, 1861. Later served in Company B, 41st Regiment N. C. Troops (3rd Regiment N. C. Cavalry).

TURNER, JAMES B., Private

Born in Duplin County where he resided as a farmer prior to enlisting at Camp Carolina, Virginia, August 1, 1861, for six months. Present or accounted for until the company was disbanded on November 18, 1861. Later served in Company A, 43rd Regiment N. C. Troops.

TURNER, JOHN W., Private

Born in Duplin County where he resided as a farmer prior to enlisting at Camp Carolina, Virginia, August 1, 1861, for six months. Present or accounted for until the company was disbanded on November 18, 1861. Later served in Company D, 13th Battalion N.C. Infantry.

WALLACE, JOHN P., Private

Born in County Sligo, Ireland, and resided in Duplin County where he was by occupation a bootmaker or mechanic prior to enlisting in Duplin County at age 23, April 15, 1861, for six months. Present or accounted for until the company was disbanded on November 18, 1861. Later served in Company D, 13th Battalion N. C. Infantry.

WATSON, EDWARD L., Private

Born in Sampson County where he resided as a mechanic prior to enlisting in Duplin County at age 28, April 15, 1861, for six months. Present or accounted for until the company was disbanded on November 18, 1861. Later served as Captain of Company C, 51st Regiment N. C. Troops.

WILLIAMS, DAVID, Private

Resided in Duplin County and was by occupation a clerk prior to enlisting in Duplin County at age 20, April 15, 1861, for six months. Present or accounted for until the company was disbanded on November 18, 1861.

WILLIAMS, ROBERT K., Private

Born in Sampson County and resided in Duplin County where he was by occupation a mechanic or trader prior to enlisting in Duplin County at age 26, April 15, 1861, for six months. Present or accounted for until the company was disbanded on November 18, 1861. Later served in Company B, 51st Regiment N. C. Troops.

WILLIAMSON, JESSE R., Sergeant

Born in Sampson County and resided in Duplin County where he was by occupation a carpenter or mechanic prior to enlisting in Duplin County at age 25, April 15, 1861, for six months. Mustered in as Sergeant. Present or accounted for until the company was disbanded on November 18, 1861. Later served in Company B, 51st Regiment N. C. Troops.

WILLIAMSON, OBEDIAH H., Private

Resided in Duplin County and was by occupation a student prior to enlisting in Duplin County at age 19, April 15, 1861, for six months. Present or accounted for until the company was disbanded on November 18, 1861.

WOODARD, JAMES F., Private

Resided in Duplin County and was by occupation a mechanic prior to enlisting in Duplin County at age 25, April 15, 1861, for six months. Present or accounted for until the company was disbanded on November 18, 1861.

2nd COMPANY C

This company, known as the "Warren Rifles," was raised in Warren County and enlisted at Warrenton on May 2, 1861. It tendered its service to the state and was ordered to Garysburg, where it was assigned to this regiment. The company was mustered in as Captain Thomas L. Jones's Light Infantry Company and was designated Company E, Company G, Company H, and Company I before it was designated Company C. Since it was the second company to be designated Company C, it was officially referred to as 2nd Company C. After the company was mustered into the regiment it functioned as a part of the regiment, and its history for the war period is recorded as a part of the regimental history.

The information contained in the following roster of the company was compiled principally from company muster rolls for May 4, 1861-February, 1862; June 30-November 1, 1862; January-August, 1863; and November, 1863-December, 1864. No company muster rolls were found for March 1-June 29, 1862; November 2-December 31, 1862; September-October, 1863; or for the period after December, 1864. In addition to the company muster rolls, Roll of Honor records, receipt rolls, hospital records, prisoner of war records, and other primary records, supplemented by state pension applications, United Daughters of the Confederacy records, and postwar rosters and histories, all provided useful information.

OFFICERS

CAPTAINS

JONES, THOMAS L.

Resided in Warren County and was by occupation a medical student prior to enlisting in Warren County at age 21. Appointed Captain on May 4, 1861. Present or accounted for until promoted to Major on May 1, 1862, and transferred to the Field and Staff of this regiment.

DAVIS, WILLIAM S.

Resided in Warren County and was by occupation a student prior to enlisting in Warren County at age 21. Appointed 1st Lieutenant to rank from April 30, 1861, and promoted to Captain on May 1, 1862. Present or accounted for until promoted to Lieutenant Colonel on May 24, 1863, and transferred to the Field and Staff of this regiment.

PLUMMER, KEMP

Resided in Warren County and was by occupation a farmer prior to enlisting in Warren County at age 28, May 4, 1861. Mustered in as Sergeant and was promoted to 1st Sergeant on May 15, 1861. Elected 1st Lieutenant to rank from May 1, 1862. Present or accounted for until wounded in the hand at Chancellorsville, Virginia, May 2, 1863. Promoted to Captain on May 24, 1863, and returned to duty prior to July 1, 1863. Present or accounted for until wounded at Fort Stedman, Virginia, March 25, 1865. Returned to duty prior to April 2, 1865, when he was wounded at Petersburg, Virginia. Reported in hospital at Farmville, Virginia, April 6, 1865, and was transferred to Kittrell's Springs the same day. No further records.

LIEUTENANTS

ALSTON, WILLIAM T., 2nd Lieutenant
Resided in Warren County and was by occupation a merchant prior to enlisting in Halifax County at age 32. Appointed 2nd Lieutenant on or about May 4, 1861. Appointed Assistant Quartermaster (Captain) on May 14, 1861, and transferred to the Field and Staff of this regiment.

COLLINS, BENJAMIN M., 1st Lieutenant
Resided in Warren County and was by occupation a student prior to enlisting in Warren County at age 20, May 4, 1861. Mustered in as Corporal and appointed 2nd Lieutenant to rank from May 1, 1862. Present or accounted for until wounded at South Mountain, Maryland, September 14, 1862. Returned to duty prior to March 1, 1863, and was promoted to 1st Lieutenant on or about May 1, 1863. Present or accounted for until wounded "in three places" at Gettysburg, Pennsylvania, July 1, 1863. Returned to duty in January-February, 1864, and present or accounted for until appointed Acting Adjutant on May 12, 1864, and transferred to the Field and Staff of this regiment.

FLEMING, WILLIAM B., 2nd Lieutenant
Resided in Warren County and was by occupation a clerk prior to enlisting in Warren County at age 18, May 4, 1861. Mustered in as Private and promoted to Corporal in February-June, 1862. Present or accounted for until wounded at Malvern Hill, Virginia, July 1, 1862. Returned to duty prior to December 1, 1862, and was promoted to Sergeant in February-March, 1863. Present or accounted for until wounded and captured at Chancellorsville, Virginia, May 3, 1863. Exchanged on or about May 13, 1863, and rejoined the company prior to July 1, 1863. Present or accounted for until wounded in the leg at Morton's Ford, Virginia, October 11, 1863. Returned to duty prior to January 1, 1864, and was promoted to 1st Sergeant on March 20, 1864. Present or accounted for until wounded in the arm and back at Spotsylvania Court House, Virginia, May 12, 1864. Returned to duty prior to November 1, 1864, and was appointed 2nd Lieutenant on November 4, 1864. Present or accounted for until paroled at Appomattox Court House, Virginia, April 9, 1865.

MAYFIELD, JOHN W., 3rd Lieutenant
Resided in Warren County and was by occupation a farmer prior to enlisting in Warren County at age 27, May 4, 1861. Mustered in as Sergeant and was appointed 3rd Lieutenant to rank from May 1, 1862. Present or accounted for until he died at home in Warren County on or about June 15, 1862, of disease.

SOUTHERLAND, JAMES, 2nd Lieutenant
Resided in Warren County and was by occupation a farmer prior to enlisting in Warren County at age 21, May 4, 1861. Mustered in as 1st Sergeant and was appointed 2nd Lieutenant on May 15, 1861. Present or accounted for until defeated for reelection when the regiment was reorganized on May 1, 1862.

TWITTY, ROBERT CHEEK, 2nd Lieutenant
Resided in Warren County and was by occupation a farmer prior to enlisting in Warren County at age 23. Appointed 2nd Lieutenant to rank from May 4, 1861. Present or accounted for until he was defeated for reelection when the regiment was reorganized on May 1, 1862. Later served in Company E, 9th Regiment N. C. State Troops (1st Regiment N. C. Cavalry).

WARD, MEDICUS M., 2nd Lieutenant
Resided in Warren County and was by occupation a merchant prior to enlisting in Warren County at age 23, May 4, 1861. Mustered in as Private and promoted to 1st Sergeant on May 1, 1862. Present or accounted for until wounded at Gaines' Mill, Virginia, June 27, 1862. Returned to duty prior to November 2, 1862, and was elected 2nd Lieutenant on November 6, 1862. Present or accounted for until killed at Winchester, Virginia, September 19, 1864.

NONCOMMISSIONED OFFICERS AND PRIVATES

ADCOCK, E. G., Private
Resided in Warren County and was by occupation a farmer prior to enlisting in Warren County at age 18, May 4, 1861. Present or accounted for until wounded at Gaines' Mill, Virginia, June 27, 1862. Returned to duty prior to November 2, 1862, and present or accounted for until wounded in the hand at Chancellorsville, Virginia, May 3, 1863. Returned to duty prior to July 1, 1863, and present or accounted for until wounded in the arm and right lung and captured at Spotsylvania Court House, Virginia, May 19, 1864. Died in hospital at Washington, D.C., May 30, 1864, of wounds.

ADCOCK, JAMES E. D., Private
Resided in Warren County and was by occupation a farmer prior to enlisting in Warren County at age 18, May 4, 1861. Present or accounted for until he died in hospital at Richmond, Virginia, July 1, 1862, of disease.

ALLEY, ROBERT S., Private
Resided in Warren County and was by occupation a mechanic prior to enlisting in Warren County at age 23, May 4, 1861. Present or accounted for until he died in hospital at Richmond, Virginia, on or about June 26, 1862, of disease.

ALSTON, EDWARD, Private
Resided in Warren County and enlisted at Camp Carolina, Virginia, at age 27, June 25, 1861. Present or accounted for until transferred to Company I of this regiment upon appointment as 2nd Lieutenant to rank from February 16, 1862.

ALSTON, PHILEMON G., Private
Resided in Warren County and was by occupation a farmer prior to enlisting in Warren County at age 18, May 4, 1861. Present or accounted for until transferred to Company K of this regiment on May 1, 1862.

ALSTON, PHILL, Private
Resided in Warren County where he enlisted at age 23, July 15, 1861. Present or accounted for through February, 1862. No further records.

ALSTON, SAMUEL T., Private
Resided in Warren County and was by occupation a

farmer prior to enlisting in Warren County at age 28, May 4, 1861. Present or accounted for until transferred to Company K of this regiment upon appointment as 3rd Lieutenant to rank from March 25, 1862.

ALSTON, SOLOMON W., Private
Resided in Warren County and was by occupation a doctor prior to enlisting in Warren County at age 22, May 4, 1861. Mustered in as Private. Present or accounted for until appointed Assistant Surgeon to rank from November 1, 1861, and transferred to the Field and Staff of this regiment.

ARMSTRONG, JOSHUA, Private
Born in Baltimore County, Maryland, and resided in Warren County where he was by occupation a wheelwright prior to enlisting in Warren County at age 20, May 4, 1861. Present or accounted for until discharged on or about August 7, 1862, by reason of being "a citizen of Maryland."

ARMSTRONG, THOMAS, Private
Resided in Warren County or at Norfolk, Virginia, and enlisted at Camp Ruffin at age 17, October 30, 1861. Present or accounted for until wounded at Gettysburg, Pennsylvania, July 1, 1863. Returned to duty in September-December, 1863, and present or accounted for until wounded in the thorax and captured at Spotsylvania Court House, Virginia, May 12, 1864. Hospitalized at Washington, D.C., where he died on May 20, 1864, of wounds.

ARRINGTON, SAMUEL PETER, Private
Resided in Warren County and was by occupation a merchant prior to enlisting in Warren County at age 21, May 4, 1861. Mustered in as Corporal but was reduced to ranks prior to November 1, 1861. Present or accounted for until promoted to Quartermaster Sergeant on May 8, 1862, and transferred to the Field and Staff of this regiment.

BALTHROP, WILLIAM R., Private
Resided in Warren County and was by occupation a clerk prior to enlisting in Warren County at age 24, May 4, 1861. Present or accounted for until he died in hospital at Richmond, Virginia, on or about August 3, 1862, of "disease" or "the effects of a slight wound on the top of the head received in one of the battles around Richmond."

BOBBITT, HARVEY, Private
Resided in Warren County and enlisted at Richmond, Virginia, at age 46, June 10, 1862, for the war. Present or accounted for until wounded at Malvern Hill, Virginia, July 1, 1862. Reported absent without leave on January 10, 1863, and was listed as a deserter prior to August 16, 1863, when he returned to duty. Present or accounted for until captured at Cedar Creek, Virginia, October 19, 1864. Confined at Point Lookout, Maryland, until paroled and transferred to Boulware's Wharf, James River, Virginia, on or about January 21, 1865, for exchange. Reported present with a detachment or paroled and exchanged prisoners at Camp Lee, near Richmond, January 26, 1865.

BOLCH, JACOB, Private
Enlisted in Wake County on September 30, 1864, for the war. Present or accounted for through December, 1864.

BOWDEN, WILLIAM H., Private
Resided in Warren County and was by occupation a student prior to enlisting in Warren County at age 19, May 4, 1861. Present or accounted for until wounded at Fisher's Hill, Virginia, September 22, 1864. Returned to duty in November-December, 1864, and present or accounted for until paroled at Appomattox Court House, Virginia, April 9, 1865.

BUGG, WILLIAM P., Private
Born in Montgomery, Alabama, and resided in Warren County where he was by occupation a clerk or salesman prior to enlisting in Warren County at age 22, May 4, 1861. Present or accounted for until wounded in the left elbow at Hanover Court House, Virginia, May 27, 1862. Discharged at Richmond, Virginia, August 26, 1862, by reason of wounds received at Hanover Court House.

BURNEY, JOHN R., Private
Resided in Warren County and was by occupation a farmer prior to enlisting in Warren County at age 25, May 4, 1861. Present or accounted for through March 1, 1862. No further records.

BURROUGHS, JOHN HENRY, Private
Enlisted in Warren County. Date of enlistment not reported. Hospitalized at Richmond, Virginia, March 26, 1865, with a gunshot wound of the left thigh. Place and date wounded not reported. Captured in hospital at Richmond on April 3, 1865, and was paroled on April 25, 1865.

BURWELL, WILLIAM HENRY, Private
Resided in Warren County and was by occupation a farmer prior to enlisting in Warren County at age 24, May 4, 1861. Present or accounted for through February, 1862. There is no further record of his service with this company; however, records of the U.D.C. indicate that he survived the war.

BYRUM, JOHN R., Private
Born in Warren County and was by occupation a farmer prior to enlisting in Wake County on August 11, 1864, for the war. Present or accounted for until wounded in the left arm and captured at Winchester, Virginia, September 19, 1864. Left arm amputated. Hospitalized at Baltimore, Maryland, until confined at Point Lookout, Maryland, October 29, 1864. Paroled and transferred to Venus Point, Savannah River, Georgia, where he was received on or about November 15, 1864, for exchange. Retired to the Invalid Corps on or about February 21, 1865. Retirement records give his age as 19.

CARROLL, JAMES R., Sergeant
Resided in Warren County and was by occupation a farmer prior to enlisting in Warren County at age 31, May 4, 1861. Mustered in as Private and promoted to Sergeant on November 1, 1862. Present or accounted for through November 1, 1862. No further records. [May have served later in the Signal Corps.]

CHEATHAM, BENJAMIN F., Private
Resided in Warren County and was by occupation a merchant prior to enlisting in Warren County at age 27, May 4, 1861. Present or accounted for through February, 1862. No further records.

CLARK, JAMES, Private
Enlisted at Taylorsville, Virginia, April 1, 1864, for the war. Present or accounted for until paroled at Lynchburg, Virginia, on or about April 13, 1865.

CLARKE, GEORGE C., Private
Resided in Warren County and was by occupation a farmer prior to enlisting in Warren County at age 19, May 4, 1861. Present or accounted for until paroled at Appomattox Court House, Virginia, April 9, 1865.

CLARKE, PATRICK H., Private
Resided in Warren County and was by occupation a farmer prior to enlisting in Warren County at age 21, May 4, 1861. Present or accounted for until wounded at Malvern Hill, Virginia, July 1, 1862. Returned to duty prior to March 1, 1863, and present or accounted for until killed at Spotsylvania Court House, Virginia, May 12, 1864.

COLLINS, JAMES S., Private
Resided in Warren County and was by occupation a student prior to enlisting in Warren County at age 18, May 4, 1861. Present or accounted for until killed at Malvern Hill, Virginia, July 1, 1862.

CONNER, W. W., Private
Resided in Warren County and enlisted at Norfolk, Virginia, at age 23, May 1, 1862, for the war. Present or accounted for until captured at Hanover Court House, Virginia, May 27, 1862. Reported in confinement at Fort Columbus, New York Harbor, June 4, 1862, and was exchanged at Aiken's Landing, James River, Virginia, August 5, 1862. Returned to duty prior to November 2, 1862, and present or accounted for through December, 1864.

COTTLE, T., Private
Resided in Duplin County prior to enlisting in Wake County on May 15, 1864, for the war. Present or accounted for until captured at or near Bermuda Hundred, Virginia, on or about April 3, 1865. Confined at Hart's Island, New York Harbor, April 11, 1865. Took the Oath of Allegiance at Hart's Island on June 14, 1865, but was hospitalized at Davids Island, New York Harbor, July 1, 1865. Hospitalized at New York City on August 16, 1865, and was transferred to Wilmington on August 19, 1865. No further records.

CUNINGHAM, M., Private
Resided in New Hanover County and enlisted at age 46, December 6, 1862, for the war as a substitute. Deserted December 12, 1862.

CURL, WILLIAM M., Private
Born in Warren County where he resided as a farmer prior to enlisting at Norfolk, Virginia, at age 19, May 1, 1862, for the war. Present or accounted for until wounded in the left wrist at or near Winchester, Virginia, on or about September 19, 1864. Retired from service on or about December 27, 1864, by reason of "complete anchylosis of the [wrist] joint."

CURTIS, ROBERT H., Corporal
Resided in Warren County and was by occupation a clerk prior to enlisting in Warren County at age 20, May 4, 1861. Mustered in as Private. Present or accounted for until wounded at Gaines' Mill, Virginia, June 27, 1862. Returned to duty prior to Novem-

ber 2, 1862, and present or accounted for until wounded in the arm at Chancellorsville, Virginia, May 3, 1863. Returned to duty prior to July 1-3, 1863, when he was wounded at Gettysburg, Pennsylvania. Returned to duty prior to September 1, 1863, and was promoted to Corporal on November 1, 1863. Present or accounted for until killed at Spotsylvania Court House, Virginia, May 12, 1864.

CURTIS, WILLIAM E., Private
Resided in Warren County and was by occupation a farmer prior to enlisting in Warren County at age 21, May 4, 1861. Present or accounted for until killed at Malvern Hill, Virginia, July 1, 1862.

DANIEL, ERASMUS A., Private
Resided in Halifax County and was by occupation a farmer prior to enlisting in Warren County at age 26, May 4, 1861. Present or accounted for until appointed Assistant Commissary of Subsistence and transferred to the 14th Regiment N.C. Troops (4th Regiment N.C. Volunteers) on or about June 3, 1861.

DANIEL, JAMES J., Private
Resided in Warren County and was by occupation a farmer prior to enlisting in Warren County at age 19, May 4, 1861. Present or accounted for until captured by the enemy at an unspecified date while in hospital at Paris, Virginia. Paroled November 5, 1862. Present or accounted for until hospitalized at Richmond, Virginia, April 18, 1864, with bronchitis. No further records.

DANIEL, JOHN W., Private
Resided in Warren County prior to enlisting at Camp Arrington, Virginia, at age 20, March 5, 1862. Present or accounted for through December, 1864; however, he was reported absent on detail or absent sick during most of that period. Captured in hospital at Richmond, Virginia, April 3, 1865, and was transferred to Newport News, Virginia, April 23, 1865. Released on June 30, 1865, after taking the Oath of Allegiance.

DANIEL, WILLIAM D., Private
Resided in Halifax County and enlisted at Camp Carolina, Virginia, at age 19, August 20, 1861. Present or accounted for until appointed Sergeant Major on January 24, 1863, and transferred to the Field and Staff of the 2nd Battalion N.C. Infantry.

DARNELL, WILLIAM, Private
Resided in Warren County and enlisted at age 24, May 1, 1862, for the war. Present or accounted for until killed at Gaines' Mill, Virginia, June 27, 1862.

DAVIS, J. E., Private
Place and date of enlistment not reported. Captured at Petersburg, Virginia, April 3, 1865, and confined at Hart's Island, New York Harbor, until released on June 19, 1865.

DAVIS, JOSHUA E., Private
Resided in Warren County and was by occupation a farmer prior to enlisting in Warren County at age 26, May 4, 1861. Present or accounted for until wounded at Spotsylvania Court House, Virginia, May 19, 1864. Died June 15, 1864, of wounds. Place of death not reported.

DAVIS, RICHARD A., Private
Resided in Warren County and was by occupation a farmer prior to enlisting in Warren County at age 29, May 4, 1861. Present or accounted for through December, 1864.

DAVIS, THOMAS, Private
Resided in Virginia and enlisted at age 46, February 15, 1863, for the war as a substitute. Deserted February 16, 1863.

DAVIS, WILLIAM E., 1st Sergeant
Resided in Warren County and enlisted at Norfolk, Virginia, at age 18, March 5, 1862. Mustered in as Private and promoted to Sergeant on August 15, 1864. Promoted to 1st Sergeant on November 4, 1864. Present or accounted for until paroled at Appomattox Court House, Virginia, April 9, 1865.

DOWLING, DAVID T., Private
Resided in Warren County and was by occupation a farmer prior to enlisting at Norfolk, Virginia, at age 18, June 15, 1861. Present or accounted for until captured at Spotsylvania Court House, Virginia, May 19-20, 1864. Confined at Point Lookout, Maryland, until transferred to Elmira, New York, July 3, 1864. Paroled at Elmira and transferred to James River, Virginia, March 2, 1865, for exchange. Hospitalized at Richmond, Virginia, March 6, 1865, and was furloughed for thirty days on March 28, 1865.

DOWLING, WILLIAM, Private
Resided in Warren County where he enlisted at age 42, August 24, 1863, for the war. Present or accounted for until killed at Spotsylvania Court House, Virginia, on or about May 19, 1864.

DRAKE, JOHN O., Sergeant
Resided in Warren County and was by occupation a clerk prior to enlisting at Norfolk, Virginia, at age 23, June 1, 1861. Mustered in as Private and promoted to Sergeant in February-June, 1862. Present or accounted for until paroled at Appomattox Court House, Virginia, April 9, 1865.

DRAKE, JOSEPH EDWIN, Sergeant
Resided in Warren County and was by occupation a farmer prior to enlisting in Warren County at age 26, May 4, 1861. Mustered in as Private and promoted to Sergeant in February-June, 1862. Wounded at Gaines' Mill, Virginia, June 27, 1862. Returned to duty prior to November 2, 1862, and present or accounted for until wounded in the thigh at Chancellorsville, Virginia, May 2, 1863. Returned to duty prior to July 1, 1863, but was discharged on August 3, 1863, after providing a substitute.

DUKE, HENLEY T., Private
Resided in Warren County and was by occupation a farmer prior to enlisting in Warren County at age 29, May 4, 1861. Present or accounted for until hospitalized at Richmond, Virginia, July 5, 1862, with a gunshot wound; however, place and date wounded not reported. Returned to duty prior to September 14, 1862, when he was wounded at South Mountain, Maryland. Returned to duty prior to November 2, 1862. Present or accounted for until hospitalized at Richmond on February 19, 1865, with a gunshot wound of the right leg; however, place and date wounded not reported. Reported in hospital at Richmond on March 10, 1865. No further records.

DUKE, SIMON, Private
Enlisted in Wake County on August 11, 1864, for the war. Present or accounted for until paroled at Appomattox Court House, Virginia, April 9, 1865.

DUNCAN, GORDON C., Private
Resided in Warren County and was by occupation a farmer prior to enlisting in Warren County at age 27, May 4, 1861. Present or accounted for until he broke his right leg in a fall from a mule at Winchester, Virginia, September 19, 1864, and was captured. Hospitalized at Baltimore, Maryland, until confined at Fort McHenry, Maryland, November 19, 1864. Transferred to Point Lookout, Maryland, January 2, 1865. Paroled and transferred to Cox's Landing, James River, Virginia, on or about February 14, 1865. Reported present with a detachment of paroled and exchanged prisoners at Camp Lee, near Richmond, Virginia, February 18, 1865.

ELLINGTON, WILLIAM, Private
Resided in Warren County and was by occupation a farmer prior to enlisting in Warren County at age 22, May 4, 1861. Present or accounted for until killed at Gaines' Mill, Virginia, June 27, 1862.

EVANS, WILLIAM J., Private
Born in Warren County where he resided as a carpenter or mechanic prior to enlisting in Warren County at age 19, May 4, 1861. Present or accounted for until discharged on or about January 28, 1864, by reason of "ulcer of the right leg."

FAIN, JOHN D., Private
Resided in Granville County and was by occupation a farmer prior to enlisting at Richmond, Virginia, at age 20, June 1, 1861. Present or accounted for until hospitalized at Richmond on June 28, 1862, with a gunshot wound; however, place and date wounded not reported. Returned to duty prior to November 2, 1862, and present or accounted for until appointed 2nd Lieutenant in Company C, 33rd Regiment N.C. Troops and transferred on or about November 23, 1863.

FALKENER, ALEXANDER B., Private
Resided in Warren County and was by occupation a farmer prior to enlisting in Warren County at age 26, May 4, 1861. Present or accounted for through April, 1864. Detailed as a Provost Guard at Raleigh on or about May 1, 1864, by reason of wounds; however, place and date wounded not reported. Reported absent on detail through March 14, 1865.

FELTS, NATHANIEL G., Private
Resided in Warren County and was by occupation a farmer prior to enlisting in Warren County at age 26, May 4, 1861. Present or accounted for until captured at Spotsylvania Court House, Virginia, May 12, 1864. Confined at Point Lookout, Maryland, until transferred to Elmira, New York, August 10, 1864. Died at Elmira on September 9, 1864, of "diphtheria."

FELTS, ROBERT B., Private
Resided in Warren County and was by occupation a farmer prior to enlisting in Warren County at age 22, May 4, 1861. Present or accounted for until he died in hospital at Richmond, Virginia, September 9, 1862, of "int[ermittent] fever."

FISHER, JOHN W., Private

Resided in Warren County prior to enlisting at Gordonsville, Virginia, at age 43, May 11, 1862, for the war as a substitute. Present or accounted for until captured at South Mountain, Maryland, September 14, 1862. Confined at Fort Delaware, Delaware, until transferred to Aiken's Landing, James River, Virginia, October 2, 1862, for exchange. Declared exchanged at Aiken's Landing on November 10, 1862. Present or accounted for until wounded at Gettysburg, Pennsylvania, July 1, 1863. Returned to duty in January-February, 1864. Reported on detail from March-April, 1864, through December, 1864. No further records.

FITTS, FRANCIS MICHAEL, Private

Previously served in Company G, 4th Regiment Alabama Infantry. Transferred to this company in January-February, 1863. Transferred to Company B, 30th Regiment N.C. Troops, March 24, 1863, in exchange for Private Wyatt A. Floyd.

FLEMING, GEORGE M., Private

Born in Warren County where he resided as a farmer prior to enlisting in Warren County at age 19, May 4, 1861. Present or accounted for until killed at Malvern Hill, Virginia, July 1, 1862.

FLEMING, PATRICK H., Private

Resided in Warren County and was by occupation a farmer prior to enlisting at Norfolk, Virginia, at age 21, June 15, 1861. Present or accounted for until he died in hospital at Petersburg, Virginia, June 10, 1862, of "chronic diarrhoea."

FLEMING, SOLOMON, Private

Resided in Warren County and was by occupation a farmer prior to enlisting in Warren County at age 22, May 4, 1861. Present or accounted for through December, 1864; however, he was reported absent on detail during much of that period. Captured in hospital at Richmond, Virginia, April 3, 1865, and was paroled at Richmond on April 17, 1865.

FLOYD, WYATT A., Private

Previously served in Company B, 30th Regiment N.C. Troops. Transferred to this company on March 24, 1863, in exchange for Private Frank M. Fitts. Present or accounted for until wounded at Spotsylvania Court House, Virginia, May 19, 1864. Died May 25, 1864, of wounds. Place of death not reported.

FOOTE, THOMAS J., Private

Resided in Warren County and enlisted in Halifax County at age 23, May 14, 1861. Present or accounted for until appointed Sergeant Major on June 15, 1861, and transferred to the Field and Staff of this regiment.

FYE, JONAS, Private

Enlisted in Wake County on September 30, 1864, for the war. Present or accounted for through December, 1864.

GREEN, WILLIAM P., Private

Resided in Warren County and was by occupation a clerk prior to enlisting in Warren County at age 29, May 4, 1861. Present or accounted for until killed at Malvern Hill, Virginia, July 1, 1862.

GUTHRIE, JOHN J., Private

Enlisted at Camp Carolina, Virginia, August 30, 1861. Company muster roll dated September-October, 1861, states he was promoted on September 1, 1861. No further records.

HAGOOD, LEMUEL P., Private

Resided in Warren County and was by occupation a farmer prior to enlisting in Halifax County at age 28, June 23, 1861. Present or accounted for until he died at Ridgeway on or about June 24, 1862, of disease.

HARRIS, ALEXANDER A., Private

Resided in Warren County and was by occupation a farmer prior to enlisting in Warren County at age 19, May 4, 1861. Present or accounted for until wounded in the hand at Chancellorsville, Virginia, May 2, 1863. Returned to duty prior to July 1, 1863, and present or accounted for until captured at Spotsylvania Court House, Virginia, May 19-20, 1864. Confined at Point Lookout, Maryland, until transferred to Elmira, New York, July 3, 1864. Released at Elmira on June 30, 1865, after taking the Oath of Allegiance.

HARRIS, G. B., Private

Enlisted at Taylorsville, Virginia, April 20, 1864, for the war. Wounded at Spotsylvania Court House, Virginia, May 10, 1864, and died in hospital at Richmond, Virginia, June 3, 1864, of wounds.

HARRIS, RICHARD J., Private

Resided in Warren County and was by occupation a farmer prior to enlisting in Warren County at age 27, May 4, 1861. Present or accounted for through February, 1862. No further records.

HARRIS, SAMUEL C., Private

Resided in Warren County and was by occupation a farmer prior to enlisting in Warren County at age 23, May 4, 1861. Present or accounted for until hospitalized at Farmville, Virginia, June 3, 1864, with a gunshot wound of the head; however, place and date wounded not reported. Returned to duty June 20, 1864, and present or accounted for until captured at Cedar Creek, Virginia, October 19, 1864. Confined at Point Lookout, Maryland, until paroled and transferred to Aiken's Landing, James River, Virginia, where he was received March 30, 1865, for exchange.

HARRIS, T., Private

Enlisted in Wake County on August 14, 1864, for the war. Present or accounted for until paroled at Appomattox Court House, Virginia, April 9, 1865.

HARRIS, W. H., Private

Resided in Warren County and enlisted at age 21, May 4, 1861. Died in camp at Norfolk, Virginia, in July, 1861. Cause of death not reported.

HARRIS, WILLIAM, Private

Was by occupation a farmer prior to enlisting in Warren County at age 23, May 4, 1861. Died September 11, 1861. Place and cause of death not reported.

HAWKS, THOMAS J., Private

Resided in Warren County and was by occupation a farmer prior to enlisting in Warren County at age 21, May 4, 1861. Present or accounted for until

wounded at Malvern Hill, Virginia, July 1, 1862.
Died July 3, 1862, of wounds. Place of death not reported.

HENDERSON, RICHARD B., Private
Resided in Granville County and was by occupation
a farmer prior to enlisting in Warren County at age
28, May 4, 1861. Present or accounted for through
February, 1862. No further records.

HENDRICK, W. D., Private
Resided in Warren County and enlisted in Wake
County on October 3, 1863, for the war. Present or
accounted for until captured at Sayler's Creek, Virginia, April 6, 1865. Confined at Point Lookout,
Maryland, until released on June 13, 1865, after
taking the Oath of Allegiance.

HICKS, JOHN W., Private
Previously served in Company F, 8th Regiment N.C.
State Troops. Transferred to this company on May
1, 1862. Present or accounted for until he died "at
home" on or about July 30, 1863, of disease.

HICKS, WILOUGHBY H., Private
Resided in Warren County and was by occupation a
farmer prior to enlisting in Warren County at age
20, May 4, 1861. Present or accounted for until
killed at Chancellorsville, Virginia, May 2, 1863.

HILLIARD, JOHN, Corporal
Resided in Warren County and enlisted at Norfolk,
Virginia, at age 28, May 1, 1862, for the war. Mustered in as Private and promoted to Corporal on
December 1, 1864. Present or accounted for until
paroled at Appomattox Court House, Virginia, April
9, 1865.

HILLIARD, THOMAS, Private
Resided in Warren County and enlisted at Richmond, Virginia, at age 27, June 1, 1862, for the
war. Present or accounted for until wounded at
Gaines' Mill, Virginia, June 27, 1862. Returned to
duty at an unspecified date prior to May 1, 1863,
and present or accounted for until captured at Spotsylvania Court House, Virginia, May 12, 1864. Confined at Point Lookout, Maryland, until transferred
to Elmira, New York, August 10, 1864. Released at
Elmira on June 23, 1865, after taking the Oath of
Allegiance.

HILLIARD, THOMAS D., Private
Enlisted at Clarksville on March 3, 1864, for the
war. Killed at Spotsylvania Court House, Virginia,
May 19, 1864.

HILLIARD, WILLIAM A., Private
Resided in Warren County and was by occupation a
farmer prior to enlisting at Norfolk, Virginia, at age
23, June 15, 1861. Present or accounted for until he
died in camp at Norfolk in January, 1862. Cause of
death not reported.

HUMPHREYS, J. T., Private
Enlisted in Alexander County on March 20, 1864,
for the war. Present or accounted for until wounded
in the face at Spotsylvania Court House, Virginia,
May 19, 1864. Reported absent wounded until he
was retired on or about February 14, 1865, by reason
of permanent disability. Paroled at Lynchburg, Virginia, April 15, 1865.

JONES, JOHN T., Corporal
Was by occupation a farmer prior to enlisting in
Warren County at age 19, May 4, 1861. Mustered in
as Corporal. Present or accounted for through February, 1862. No further records.

JONES, JOSEPH BLOOMFIELD, Corporal
Resided in Warren County and was by occupation a
farmer prior to enlisting in Warren County at age
24, May 4, 1861. Mustered in as Corporal. Present
or accounted for until transferred to Company F, 8th
Regiment N.C. State Troops, May 4, 1862.

KEARNEY, JOSEPH C., Private
Resided in Warren County and was by occupation a
student prior to enlisting in Warren County at age
18, May 4, 1861. Present or accounted for until he
died in hospital at Farmville, Virginia, August 3,
1862, of "feb[ris] typh[oid]."

KEHR, WILLIAM, Musician
Enlisted at Camp Carolina, Virginia, August 30,
1861. Mustered in as Musician (Bugler). Present or
accounted for until discharged on January 1, 1862.
Reason discharged not reported.

KEY, G., Private
Enlisted in Wake County on September 30, 1864, for
the war. Present or accounted for through December, 1864.

KIMBALL, BARTHOLOMEW, Private
Resided in Warren County and enlisted in Wake
County on August 11, 1864, for the war. Present or
accounted for until captured near Petersburg, Virginia, March 25, 1865. Confined at Point Lookout,
Maryland, until released on June 14, 1865, after
taking the Oath of Allegiance.

KING, ANTHONY C., Private
Resided in Warren County and was by occupation a
farmer prior to enlisting in Warren County at age
21, May 4, 1861. Present or accounted for until
killed at Gaines' Mill, Virginia, June 27, 1862.

KING, HENRY D., Corporal
Resided in Warren County and was by occupation a
farmer prior to enlisting in Warren County at age
15, May 4, 1861. Mustered in as Private. Present or
accounted for until wounded in the hand at Chancellorsville, Virginia, May 3, 1863. Returned to duty
prior to July 1, 1863, and present or accounted for
until promoted to Corporal on September 12, 1864.
Wounded in the right leg and captured at Cedar
Creek, Virginia, October 19, 1864. Right leg amputated. Died in hospital at Winchester, Virginia, October 28, 1864, of "tetanus."

LAMBERT, LEWIS F., Private
Resided in Warren County and enlisted at Norfolk,
Virginia, at age 25, May 1, 1862, for the war. Pres-
ent or accounted for until wounded in the breast at
Chancellorsville, Virginia, May 2, 1863. Returned to
duty prior to July 1-3, 1863, when he was wounded
at Gettysburg, Pennsylvania. Died in hospital at
Staunton, Virginia, July 23, 1863, of wounds.

LAUGHTER, MITCHELL, Private
Resided in Warren County and was by occupation a
farmer prior to enlisting in Warren County at age
50, May 4, 1861. Present or accounted for until discharged in January, 1862. Reason discharged not
reported.

LEVISTER, T. P., Private
Previously served in Company F of this regiment. Transferred to this company on October 18, 1864. Present or accounted for until wounded in the face and/or neck and captured at Petersburg, Virginia, January 27, 1865. Hospitalized at various Federal hospitals until confined at Point Lookout, Maryland, February 11, 1865. Released on June 3, 1865, after taking the Oath of Allegiance.

LITTLE, LEWIS, Private
Enlisted in Wake County on September 30, 1864, for the war. Present or accounted for until paroled at Appomattox Court House, Virginia, April 9, 1865.

LOYD, JAMES A., Private
Was by occupation a mechanic prior to enlisting in Warren County at age 24, May 4, 1861. Present or accounted for until discharged "by sentence of Gen[era]l Court Martial" on December 1, 1861.

MABRY, L., Private
Resided in Warren County and enlisted at age 17, May 1, 1862, for the war. Died at Lynchburg, Virginia, in July, 1862, of disease.

McCAFFERTY, OWEN, Private
Resided in Warren County and enlisted at Orange Court House, Virginia, at age 47, August 3, 1863, for the war as a substitute. Present or accounted for until captured at Fisher's Hill, Virginia, September 22, 1864. Confined at Point Lookout, Maryland, until released on March 3, 1865, after taking the Oath of Allegiance.

MAYFIELD, JAMES H., Sergeant
Resided in Warren County prior to enlisting at Camp Ruffin, Virginia, at age 29, October 16, 1861. Mustered in as Private and promoted to Sergeant on May 1, 1862. Present or accounted for until discharged on August 1, 1862, after providing Private Peter Smith as a substitute.

MITCHELL, PETER, Sergeant
Resided in Warren County and was by occupation a farmer prior to enlisting in Warren County at age 29, May 4, 1861. Mustered in as Sergeant. Present or accounted for through February, 1862. No further records.

MOSS, IRA J., Private
Resided in Warren County and enlisted at Norfolk, Virginia, at age 27, March 5, 1862. Present or accounted for until wounded in the hand at Chancellorsville, Virginia, May 3, 1863. Returned to duty at an unspecified date and was detailed for hospital duty in November-December, 1863. Rejoined the company in April-October, 1864, and present or accounted for until paroled at Appomattox Court House, Virginia, April 9, 1865.

MOSS, J. E., Private
Enlisted in Wake County on May 21, 1864, for the war. Present or accounted for until paroled at Appomattox Court House, Virginia, April 9, 1865.

MOSS, RICHARD, Private
Resided in Warren County and enlisted at Norfolk, Virginia, at age 17. Enlistment date reported as May 1, 1862; however, he was not listed on the rolls of this company until January-February, 1863. Present or accounted for until captured at Martinsburg,

West Virginia, July 29, 1863. Confined at Fort McHenry, Maryland, until transferred to City Point, Virginia, March 16, 1864, for exchange. Rejoined the company prior to November 1, 1864, and present or accounted for until paroled at Appomattox Court House, Virginia, April 9, 1865. Roll of Honor indicates he was wounded at South Mountain, Maryland, September 14, 1862.

MOSS, WILLIAMS, Private
Resided in Warren County and was by occupation a farmer prior to enlisting at Norfolk, Virginia, at age 18, June 25, 1861. Present or accounted for until wounded in the breast at Gettysburg, Pennsylvania, July 1, 1863. Returned to duty in September-December, 1863. Present or accounted for until hospitalized at Richmond, Virginia, May 19, 1864, with a gunshot wound of the right side; however, place and date wounded not reported. Returned to duty prior to October 19, 1864, when he was killed at Cedar Creek, Virginia.

MYRICK, G. W., Private
Enlisted in Wake County on August 11, 1864, for the war. Present or accounted for through December, 1864.

NEWELL, LEMUEL A., Private
Born in Warren County where he resided as a farmer prior to enlisting in Warren County at age 29, May 4, 1861. Present or accounted for through May, 1862. Discharge papers indicate he was discharged on June 12, 1862, by reason of "an organic lesion of the brain" caused by a previous concussion; however, company records indicate he was wounded at Malvern Hill, Virginia, July 1, 1862. No further records.

NEWELL, SAMUEL T., Private
Resided in Warren County and was by occupation a farmer prior to enlisting in Warren County at age 25, May 4, 1861. Present or accounted for through February, 1862. No further records.

NEWMAN, W. A., Private
Enlisted at Taylorsville, Virginia, May 1, 1864, for the war. Present or accounted for until wounded at Spotsylvania Court House, Virginia, May 10, 1864. Reported absent wounded or absent in hospital through December, 1864. No further records.

PALMER, HORACE, Corporal
Resided in Warren County and was by occupation a farmer prior to enlisting in Warren County at age 27, May 4, 1861. Mustered in as Private and promoted to Corporal in March-October, 1862. Present or accounted for until wounded at Malvern Hill, Virginia, July 1, 1862. Reported absent wounded or absent on detail through January 17, 1865.

PALMER, PAUL, Private
Resided in Warren County and was by occupation a farmer prior to enlisting in Warren County at age 28, May 4, 1861. Present or accounted for through February, 1862. A regimental return dated October, 1862, states he was recommended for discharge and sent home to Warren County. No further records.

PALMER, WILLIAM HENDRICK, Private
Resided in Warren County and enlisted in Wake County at age 18, October 10, 1862, for the war. Present or accounted for until wounded in the head

at Winchester, Virginia, September 19, 1864. Wounds resulted in loss of sight in his left eye. Reported absent wounded through December, 1864, but was paroled at Appomattox Court House, Virginia, April 9, 1865.

PASCHALL, RICHARD H., Private

Born in Warren County where he resided as a farmer prior to enlisting in Warren County at age 33, May 4, 1861. Present or accounted for until wounded at Malvern Hill, Virginia, July 1, 1862. Returned to duty prior to November 2, 1862, and present or accounted for until paroled at Appomattox Court House, Virginia, April 9, 1865.

PEARCY, JOSHUA, Private

Resided in Warren County and enlisted in Wake County at age 25, October 1, 1862, for the war. Present or accounted for until he died at Lynchburg, Virginia, July 26, 1864, of disease.

PEARCY, WILLIAM, Private

Resided in Warren County and was by occupation a farmer prior to enlisting in Warren County at age 18, May 4, 1861. Present or accounted for until killed at Hagerstown, Maryland, July 6, 1863. Roll of Honor indicates that he was awarded a medal for gallantry.

PICKFORD, THOMAS J., Private

Resided in Warren County and was by occupation a medical student prior to enlisting in Warren County at age 23, May 4, 1861. Mustered in as Sergeant but was reduced to ranks in February-October, 1862. Present or accounted for until transferred to Company K of this regiment on February 1, 1863.

PITCHFORD, JAMES ALSTON, Private

Born in Warren County where he resided as a farmer prior to enlisting in Warren County at age 27, May 4, 1861. Present or accounted for until discharged on or about January 31, 1862, by reason of "rheumatism."

PLUMMER, AUSTIN, Private

Resided in Warren County and was by occupation a farmer prior to enlisting in Warren County at age 25, May 4, 1861. Present or accounted for through November 1, 1862. No further records.

POWELL, BENJAMIN FRANKLIN, Private

Resided in Warren County and was by occupation a merchant prior to enlisting in Halifax County at age 39, May 14, 1861. Mustered in as Private. Present or accounted for until promoted to Quartermaster Sergeant on June 1, 1861, and transferred to the Field and Staff of this regiment.

PROPST, JOHN, Private

Enlisted in Wake County on September 30, 1864, for the war. Present or accounted for through December, 1864.

QUINCEY, GEORGE R., Private

Resided in Warren County and enlisted at Norfolk, Virginia, at age 16, June 1, 1861. Present or accounted for until discharged on or about October 15, 1862, by reason of being under age.

REGAN, THOMAS T., Private

Resided in Warren County and was by occupation a farmer prior to enlisting in Halifax County at age 19, May 26, 1861. Present or accounted for until killed at Malvern Hill, Virginia, July 1, 1862.

RENN, JOSEPH J., Private

Resided in Warren County and was by occupation a student prior to enlisting in Warren County at age 22, May 4, 1861. Present or accounted for until wounded in the back and captured at Spotsylvania Court House, Virginia, May 12, 1864. Confined at Old Capitol Prison, Washington, D.C., June 1, 1864, and transferred to Elmira, New York, July 23, 1864. Released at Elmira on June 19, 1865, after taking the Oath of Allegiance.

ROACH, JOHN, Private

Resided in Virginia and enlisted at age 47, December 6, 1862, for the war as a substitute. Deserted December 11, 1862.

ROBERTSON, BENJAMIN P., Private

Resided in Warren County and was by occupation a farmer prior to enlisting in Warren County at age 19, May 4, 1861. Present or accounted for until wounded in the head and captured at Hanover Court House, Virginia, May 27, 1862. Blinded in the left eye as a result of wounds. Confined at Fort Monroe, Virginia. Exchanged at an unspecified date. Reported absent wounded or absent on detail from November-December, 1863, through December, 1864.

ROBERTSON, THOMAS, Private

Resided in Warren County and was by occupation a farmer prior to enlisting in Warren County at age 20, May 4, 1861. Present or accounted for until wounded in the abdomen and captured at Hanover Court House, Virginia, May 27, 1862. Exchanged prior to June 4, 1862, when he died at "Gaines." Cause of death not reported.

ROBINSON, WILLIAM A., Private

Resided in Warren County and was by occupation a farmer prior to enlisting in Warren County at age 30, May 4, 1861. Present or accounted for through February, 1862. Discharged at an unspecified date after providing Private George Williams as a substitute.

RODWELL, THOMAS D., Private

Resided in Warren County and enlisted at Camp Carolina, Virginia, at age 37, July 2, 1861. Present or accounted for until discharged on or about July 16, 1862, by reason of being over age.

ROSE, LEWIS D., Private

Resided in Warren County and enlisted in Wake County at age 20, October 1, 1862, for the war. Present or accounted for until paroled at Appomattox Court House, Virginia, April 9, 1865.

ROSE, W. A., Private

Place and date of enlistment not reported. Captured at White Oak Road, Virginia, on or about April 2, 1865. Confined at Old Capitol Prison, Washington, D.C., until released on June 6, 1865, after taking the Oath of Allegiance.

RUDD, THOMAS H., Private

Resided in Warren County and was by occupation a farmer prior to enlisting in Warren County at age 23, May 4, 1861. Present or accounted for until hospitalized at Richmond, Virginia, July 24, 1862, with "diarrhoea." Died in hospital at Richmond on August 17, 1862.

RUSSELL, EDWIN H., 1st Sergeant

Resided in Warren County and was by occupation a student prior to enlisting in Warren County at age 19, May 4, 1861. Mustered in as Private and promoted to Sergeant on May 1, 1862. Promoted to 1st Sergeant on November 1, 1862. Present or accounted for until wounded in the hip at Chancellorsville, Virginia, May 3, 1863. Returned to duty in September-December, 1863, and present or accounted for through February, 1864. No further records.

RUSSELL, JAMES H., Private

Resided in Warren County and was by occupation a farmer prior to enlisting in Warren County at age 23, May 4, 1861. Present or accounted for until hospitalized at Richmond, Virginia, June 28, 1862, with a gunshot wound; however, place and date wounded not reported. Returned to duty prior to November 2, 1862. Present or accounted for until hospitalized at Richmond on February 8, 1865, with a gunshot wound of the scalp; however, place and date wounded not reported. Furloughed for sixty days on March 16, 1865.

SAVAGE, WILLIAM, Private

Born in Kentucky and resided in Warren County prior to enlisting in Wake County at age 30, October 1, 1862, for the war. Present or accounted for until captured at Gettysburg, Pennsylvania, July 4, 1863. Confined at Fort Delaware, Delaware, until released on or about September 22, 1863, after joining the U.S. service. Assigned to duty with the 3rd Maryland Cavalry. Clark's *Regiments* indicates that he distinguished himself at Chancellorsville, Virginia, May 1-3, 1863, when he "captured a colonel and ten men."

SCOGGIN, JAMES H., Private

Resided in Virginia and enlisted at Richmond, Virginia, at age 18, June 1, 1861. Present or accounted for until paroled at Appomattox Court House, Virginia, April 9, 1865.

SETSER, H. F., Private

Enlisted in Wake County on September 30, 1864, for the war. Present or accounted for through December, 1864.

SHEARIN, JAMES O., Private

Resided in Warren County and was by occupation a mechanic prior to enlisting in Warren County at age 21, May 4, 1861. Present or accounted for until killed at Hanover Court House, Virginia, May 27, 1862.

SHEARIN, PETER D., Private

Resided in Warren County and was by occupation a student prior to enlisting in Warren County at age 20, May 4, 1861. Present or accounted for until promoted to Corporal and transferred to Company I of this regiment in March, 1862.

SHEARIN, WILLIAM H., Private

Resided in Warren County and was by occupation a farmer prior to enlisting in Warren County at age 20, May 4, 1861. Present or accounted for until he died at Fredericksburg, Virginia, March 3, 1863, of disease.

SIGMAN, AMON, Private

Enlisted in Wake County on September 30, 1864, for the war. Present or accounted for through December, 1864.

SIGMAN, Q. G., Private

Enlisted in Wake County on September 30, 1864, for the war. Present or accounted for until paroled at Appomattox Court House, Virginia, April 9, 1865.

SMITH, JOHN L., Private

Resided in Warren County and was by occupation a farmer prior to enlisting in Warren County at age 21, May 4, 1861. Present or accounted for until wounded in the foot at Chancellorsville, Virginia, on or about May 4, 1863. Foot amputated. Died in July, 1863, of wounds. Place of death not reported.

SMITH, JOHN TYLER, Corporal

Resided in Warren County and was by occupation a farmer prior to enlisting in Warren County at age 20, May 4, 1861. Mustered in as Private and promoted to Corporal on May 1, 1862. Present or accounted for until wounded at Malvern Hill, Virginia, July 1, 1862. Returned to duty prior to September 14, 1862, when he was wounded at South Mountain, Maryland. Returned to duty at an unspecified date prior to November-December, 1863, when he was detailed in the Quartermaster Department at Raleigh. Reported absent on detail through December, 1864. Paroled at Goldsboro on May 8, 1865.

SMITH, NATHANIEL, Private

Resided in Warren County and enlisted in Wake County at age 23, October 1, 1862, for the war. Present or accounted for until captured near Petersburg, Virginia, March 25, 1865. Confined at Point Lookout, Maryland, until released on June 20, 1865, after taking the Oath of Allegiance.

SMITH, PETER, Private

Resided in Montgomery County prior to enlisting at Richmond, Virginia, at age 16, August 1, 1862, for the war as a substitute for Sergeant James H. Mayfield. Captured at South Mountain, Maryland, on or about September 15, 1862. Confined at Fort Delaware, Delaware, until paroled and transferred to Aiken's Landing, James River, Virginia, October 2, 1862, for exchange. Declared exchanged at Aiken's Landing on November 10, 1862. Failed to rejoin the company and was listed as a deserter on December 4, 1862.

SMITHWICK, JAMES ROBERT, Corporal

Resided in Warren County and was by occupation a farmer prior to enlisting in Warren County at age 37, May 4, 1861. Mustered in as Private and promoted to Corporal on June 20, 1861. Present or accounted for until discharged on July 11, 1862, by reason of being over age.

SPRUILL, CHARLES W., Private

Resided in Warren County and was by occupation a sawyer prior to enlisting in Warren County at age 23, May 4, 1861. Present or accounted for through February, 1862. No further records.

STAINBACK, THOMAS E., Private

Resided in Warren County and was by occupation a student prior to enlisting in Warren County at age 20, May 4, 1861. Present or accounted for until wounded at Gaines' Mill, Virginia, June 27, 1862. Died June 28, 1862, of wounds.

STALLINGS, OCTAVIUS, Private

Resided in Virginia and enlisted in Warren County at age 20, May 4, 1861. Present or accounted for until captured at Spotsylvania Court House, Virginia, May 19-20, 1864. Confined at Point Lookout, Maryland, until transferred to Elmira, New York, July 3, 1864. Died at Elmira on November 26, 1864, of "pneumonia."

STALLINGS, SOLOMON P., Private

Resided in Warren County where he enlisted at age 29, May 4, 1861. Present or accounted for until wounded in the leg at Chancellorsville, Virginia, May 2, 1863. Returned to duty prior to July 1, 1863. Present or accounted for until hospitalized at Richmond, Virginia, on or about July 14, 1864, with a gunshot wound of the left leg; however, place and date wounded not reported. Returned to duty prior to November 1, 1864, and present or accounted for until captured at Petersburg, Virginia, April 3, 1865. Confined at Hart's Island, New York Harbor, until released on June 17, 1865, after taking the Oath of Allegiance.

STEED, JAMES H., Private

Resided in Warren County where he enlisted at age 28, May 4, 1861. Present or accounted for until killed at Malvern Hill, Virginia, July 1, 1862.

STEVENSON, JOHN D., Private

Resided in Warren County and was by occupation a mechanic prior to enlisting in Warren County at age 25, May 4, 1861. Present or accounted for through December, 1864; however, he was absent on detail during most of that period. Captured in hospital at Richmond, Virginia, April 3, 1865, and was paroled at Richmond on April 18, 1865.

TUCKER, WILLIAM J., Private

Resided in Warren County where he enlisted at age 18, May 4, 1861. Present or accounted for until he died in hospital at Richmond, Virginia, September 4, 1862, of "diphtheria."

TUNSTALL, NATHANIEL, Private

Resided in Warren County and was by occupation a merchant prior to enlisting in Warren County at age 22, May 4, 1861. Present or accounted for until wounded at Gaines' Mill, Virginia, June 27, 1862. Returned to duty prior to November 2, 1862, and present or accounted for until he died in hospital at Danville, Virginia, August 5, 1863, of "chronic diarrhoea."

TWISDALE, PLEASANT A., Private

Resided in Warren County and was by occupation a mechanic prior to enlisting in Warren County at age 21, May 4, 1861. Present or accounted for until killed at Malvern Hill, Virginia, July 1, 1862.

TWITTY, HENRY FITTS, Private

Resided in Warren County where he enlisted at age 40, August 24, 1863, for the war. Present or accounted for until wounded near Morton's Ford, Virginia, October 11, 1863. Returned to duty in January-February, 1864, and present or accounted for until wounded in the right arm at Spotsylvania Court House, Virginia, May 9, 1864. Returned to duty prior to November 1, 1864, and present or accounted for through December, 1864.

TWITTY, JOHN ELDREDGE, Sergeant

Resided in Warren County and was by occupation a farmer prior to enlisting in Warren County at age 23, May 4, 1861. Mustered in as Private. Present or accounted for until wounded at Malvern Hill, Virginia, July 1, 1862. Returned to duty prior to November 1, 1862, when he was promoted to Corporal. Promoted to Sergeant in November-December, 1863. Present or accounted for until wounded in the sternum and right lung and captured at Spotsylvania Court House, Virginia, May 12, 1864. Hospitalized at Washington, D.C., where he died on May 21, 1864, of wounds.

VAN LANDINGHAM, RICHARD P., Sergeant

Enlisted in Warren County. Enlistment date reported as March 7, 1862; however, he was not carried on the rolls of this company until January-February, 1863. Mustered in as Private. Promoted to Corporal on August 15, 1864, and promoted to Sergeant on November 4, 1864. Present or accounted for until paroled at Appomattox Court House, Virginia, April 9, 1865.

WALKER, J. T., Private

Enlisted at Taylorsville, Virginia, February 20, 1864, for the war. Present or accounted for until paroled at Appomattox Court House, Virginia, April 9, 1865.

WARD, SAMUEL ALSTON, Corporal

Resided in Warren County and was by occupation a clerk prior to enlisting at Norfolk, Virginia, at age 19, June 25, 1861. Mustered in as Private and promoted to Corporal on February 20, 1863. Present or accounted for until killed at Chancellorsville, Virginia, May 3, 1863. Nominated for the Badge of Distinction for gallantry at Chancellorsville.

WATKINS, JOHN C., Private

Resided in Warren County and was by occupation a clerk prior to enlisting in Warren County at age 19, May 4, 1861. Present or accounted for through February, 1862. Discharged at an unspecified date. Reason discharged not reported.

WATKINS, PLUMMER G., Private

Resided in Warren County and was by occupation a farmer prior to enlisting in Warren County at age 23, May 4, 1861. Present or accounted for until killed at Gaines' Mill, Virginia, June 27, 1862.

WATKINS, T. M., Private

Resided in Warren County and enlisted at Norfolk, Virginia, at age 25, March 5, 1862. Present or accounted for through December, 1863. No further records.

WATKINS, WILLIAM R., Private

Resided in Warren County and was by occupation a clerk prior to enlisting in Warren County at age 20, May 4, 1861. Present or accounted for until wounded in the right leg at Malvern Hill, Virginia, July 1, 1862. Died in hospital at Richmond, Virginia, August 12, 1862, of wounds and/or disease.

WATSON, JAMES T., Private

Resided in Warren County and was by occupation a farmer prior to enlisting in Warren County at age 29, May 4, 1861. Present or accounted for until he died in hospital at Richmond, Virginia, on or about May 13, 1863, of disease.

WHITE, THOMAS E., Private

Resided in Warren County and was by occupation a teacher prior to enlisting in Warren County at age 21, May 4, 1861. Present or accounted for until discharged on January 30, 1862. Reason discharged not reported. Reenlisted in the company on May 6, 1863. Present or accounted for through December, 1864; however, he was reported absent on detail during most of that period.

WILLIAMS, GEORGE, Private

Resided in Maryland prior to enlisting at age 35, June 8, 1863, for the war as a substitute for Private William A. Robinson. Deserted the same day.

WILLIAMS, HARRY GUSTON, Private

Born in Warren County where he resided prior to enlisting at Camp Carolina, Virginia, at age 20, July 15, 1861. Present or accounted for until killed at Malvern Hill, Virginia, July 1, 1862, "while gallantly bearing the colors of his regiment in [the] face of the enemy."

WILLIAMS, JOHN T., Private

Resided in Warren County or at Petersburg, Virginia, and enlisted in Wake County at age 25, October 1, 1862, for the war. Present or accounted for until wounded in the leg at Chancellorsville, Virginia, May 3, 1863. Returned to duty prior to July 1-3, 1863, when he was wounded in the left knee at Gettysburg, Pennsylvania. Captured at Gettysburg or at Greencastle, Pennsylvania, July 4-5, 1863. Confined at Fort Delaware, Delaware, until transferred to Johnson's Island, Ohio, November 23, 1863. Transferred to Point Lookout, Maryland, March 21, 1865. Released at Point Lookout on June 22, 1865, after taking the Oath of Allegiance.

WILLIAMS, ROBERT G., Private

Resided in Warren County and was by occupation a farmer prior to enlisting in Warren County at age 19, May 4, 1861. Present or accounted for until wounded near Morton's Ford, Virginia, October 11, 1863. Returned to duty prior to January 1, 1864, and present or accounted for until captured at Fisher's Hill, Virginia, September 22, 1864. Confined at Point Lookout, Maryland, until paroled and transferred to Boulware's Wharf, James River, Virginia, where he was received March 19, 1865, for exchange.

WILLIAMS, ROBERT L., Private

Resided in Warren or Franklin counties prior to enlisting at Camp Carolina, Virginia, at age 17, July 15, 1861. Present or accounted for until appointed 2nd Lieutenant to rank from March 25, 1862, and transferred to Company K of this regiment.

1st COMPANY D

This company, known as the "Lumberton Guards," was raised in Robeson County and enlisted at Lumberton for six months' service on April 24, 1861. It tendered its service to the state and was ordered to Garysburg, where it was assigned to this regiment. The company was mustered in as Captain Richard M. Norment's Company and was designated Company E before it was designated Company D. On December 16, 1861, the company was mustered out after six months'

service. Since the company was the first company to serve as Company D of this regiment, it was later referred to as 1st Company D.

The information contained in the following roster of the company was compiled principally from company muster rolls for April 24 through December 16, 1861. In addition to the company muster rolls, Roll of Honor records, receipt rolls, hospital records, prisoner of war records, and other primary records, supplemented by state pension applications, United Daughters of the Confederacy records, and postwar rosters and histories, all provided useful information.

OFFICERS

CAPTAIN

NORMENT, RICHARD M.

Born in Mecklenburg County and resided in Robeson County where he was by occupation a physician prior to enlisting in Robeson County at age 32. Appointed Captain to rank from April 24, 1861. Present or accounted for until the company was disbanded on December 16, 1861. Later served as Captain of Company A, 46th Regiment N.C. Troops.

LIEUTENANTS

McKINNEY, HENRY R., 2nd Lieutenant

Born at Elmira, New York, and resided in Robeson County where he was by occupation a carpenter or mechanic prior to enlisting in Robeson County at age 23, April 24, 1861. Appointed 2nd Lieutenant to rank from April 24, 1861. Present or accounted for until the company was disbanded on December 16, 1861. Later served as Captain of Company A, 46th Regiment N.C. Troops.

NORMENT, OWEN CLINTON, 1st Lieutenant

Born in Robeson County where he resided as a clerk or carpenter prior to enlisting in Robeson County at age 27, April 24, 1861. Appointed 1st Lieutenant to rank from April 24, 1861. Present or accounted for until the company was disbanded on December 16, 1861. Later served as 2nd Lieutenant in Company D, 18th Regiment N.C. Troops (8th Regiment N.C. Volunteers).

OATES, THOMAS J., 3rd Lieutenant

Resided in Robeson County and was by occupation a telegraph operator prior to enlisting in Robeson County at age 20. Appointed 3rd Lieutenant to rank from April 24, 1861. Present or accounted for until the company was disbanded on December 16, 1861.

NONCOMMISSIONED OFFICERS AND PRIVATES

ATKINSON, ATLAS, Corporal

Born in Robeson County where he resided as a farmer prior to enlisting in Robeson County at age 22, April 24, 1861, for six months. Mustered in as Corporal. Present or accounted for until the company was disbanded on December 16, 1861. Later served as 1st Lieutenant in Company B, 50th Regiment N.C. Troops.

ATKINSON, BRIGHT, Corporal

Resided in Robeson County and was by occupation a

farmer prior to enlisting in Robeson County at age 26, April 24, 1861, for six months. Mustered in as Corporal. Present or accounted for until the company was disbanded on December 16, 1861. Later served as Sergeant in Company B, 50th Regiment N.C. Troops.

ATKINSON, E. C., Sergeant

Born in Robeson County where he resided as farmer prior to enlisting in Robeson County at age 24, April 24, 1861, for six months. Mustered in as Sergeant. Present or accounted for until the company was disbanded on December 16, 1861. Later served as Captain of Company B, 50th Regiment N.C. Troops.

BAGGET, CORNELIUS, Private

Resided in Robeson County and was by occupation a farmer prior to enlisting in Robeson County at age 25, April 24, 1861, for six months. Present or accounted for until the company was disbanded on December 16, 1861.

BAGGETT, BARTON, Private

Resided in Robeson County and was by occupation a farmer prior to enlisting in Robeson County at age 23, April 24, 1861, for six months. Present or accounted for until the company was disbanded on December 16, 1861. Later served in Company F, 31st Regiment N.C. Troops.

BARNES, JOHN C., Private

Resided in Robeson County and was by occupation a farmer prior to enlisting in Robeson County at age 21, April 24, 1861, for six months. Present or accounted for until the company was disbanded on December 16, 1861. Later served in Company F, 31st Regiment N.C. Troops.

BAXLEY, STEPHEN, Private

Born in Robeson County where he resided as a farmer or laborer prior to enlisting in Robeson County at age 21, April 24, 1861, for six months. Present or accounted for until the company was disbanded on December 16, 1861. Later served in Company A, 46th Regiment N.C. Troops.

BLEDSOE, EDWARD, Private

Resided in Robeson County and was by occupation a saddler prior to enlisting in Robeson County at age 18, April 24, 1861, for six months. Present or accounted for until discharged on or about September 21, 1861, by reason of disability.

BOON, SAMPSON, Private

Resided in Robeson County and was by occupation a carpenter prior to enlisting in Robeson County at age 21, April 24, 1861, for six months. Present or accounted for until the company was disbanded on December 16, 1861. [May have served later in Company G, 51st Regiment N.C. Troops.]

BOON, STEPHEN, Private

Resided in Robeson County and was by occupation a carpenter prior to enlisting in Robeson County at age 24, April 24, 1861, for six months. Present or accounted for until the company was disbanded on December 16, 1861. [May have served later in Company A, 30th Regiment N.C. Troops.]

BRIGMAN, NOAH, Private

Born in Marion District, South Carolina, and was by occupation a farmer. Place and date of enlistment not reported. Later served in Company D, 18th Regiment N.C. Troops (8th Regiment N.C. Volunteers). No further records.

BRITT, ALEXANDER, Jr., Private

Born in Robeson County where he resided as a farmer prior to enlisting in Robeson County at age 16, April 24, 1861, for six months. Present or accounted for until the company was disbanded on December 16, 1861. Later served in Company B, 50th Regiment N.C. Troops.

BRITT, ALEXANDER, Sr., Private

Born in Robeson County where he resided as a farmer prior to enlisting in Robeson County at age 31, April 24, 1861, for six months. Present or accounted for until the company was disbanded on December 16, 1861. Later served in Company B, 50th Regiment N.C. Troops.

BRITT, ALVA G., Private

Born in Robeson County where he resided as a farmer prior to enlisting in Robeson County at age 18, April 24, 1861, for six months. Present or accounted for until the company was disbanded on December 16, 1861. Later served in Company B, 50th Regiment N.C. Troops.

BRITT, ARICK, Private

Resided in Robeson County and was by occupation a laborer prior to enlisting in Robeson County at age 18, April 24, 1861, for six months. Present or accounted for until the company was disbanded on December 16, 1861. Later served in Company A, 5th Regiment N.C. State Troops.

BRITT, HENRY L., Private

Born in Robeson County where he resided as a farmer prior to enlisting in Robeson County at age 26, April 24, 1861, for six months. Present or accounted for until the company was disbanded on December 16, 1861. Later served in Company B, 50th Regiment N.C. Troops.

BRITT, JAMES E., Private

Born in Robeson County where he resided as a farmer prior to enlisting in Robeson County at age 28, April 24, 1861, for six months. Present or accounted for until the company was disbanded on December 16, 1861. Later served in Company B, 50th Regiment N.C. Troops.

BRITT, JOHN G., Private

Resided in Robeson County and was by occupation a farmer prior to enlisting in Robeson County at age 22, April 24, 1861, for six months. Present or accounted for until the company was disbanded on December 16, 1861. [May have served later in Company E, 51st Regiment N.C. Troops.]

BULLARD, B. A., Private

Name appears on an undated list of the members of this company. Place and date of enlistment not reported. No further records.

BULLARD, ELSEPH, _____

Name appears on an undated list of the members of this company. Place and date of enlistment not reported. Later served in Company A, 46th Regiment N.C. Troops. No further records.

BULLOCK, ALEX, _____

Name appears on an undated list of the members of

this company. Place and date of enlistment not reported. No further records.

BULLOCK, ATLAS, Private
Resided in Robeson County and was by occupation a farmer prior to enlisting in Robeson County at age 23, April 24, 1861, for six months. Present or accounted for until the company was disbanded on December 16, 1861. Later served in Company E, 51st Regiment N.C. Troops.

BULLOCK, CHARLES BAKER, Private
Resided in Robeson County and was by occupation a farmer prior to enlisting in Robeson County at age 20, April 24, 1861, for six months. Present or accounted for until the company was disbanded on December 16, 1861. Later served in Company F, 51st Regiment N. C. Troops.

BULLOCK, JOSEPH H., Private
Resided in Robeson County and was by occupation a farmer prior to enlisting in Robeson County at age 19, April 24, 1861, for six months. Present or accounted for until the company was disbanded on December 16, 1861. Later served in Company E, 51st Regiment N. C. Troops.

BULLOCK, WILLIAM A., Private
Resided in Robeson County and was by occupation a farmer prior to enlisting in Robeson County at age 21, April 24, 1861, for six months. Present or accounted for until the company was disbanded on December 16, 1861. Later served as 2nd Lieutenant in Company E, 51st Regiment N. C. Troops.

BULLOCK, WILLIAM P., Private
Resided in Robeson County and was by occupation a farmer prior to enlisting in Robeson County at age 22, April 24, 1861, for six months. Present or accounted for until the company was disbanded on December 16, 1861.

CARTER, THOMAS, Private
Resided in Robeson County and was by occupation a laborer prior to enlisting in Robeson County at age 22, April 24, 1861, for six months. Present or accounted for until the company was disbanded on December 16, 1861.

CHAVIS, BETHEL J., Private
Resided in Robeson County and was by occupation a laborer prior to enlisting in Robeson County at age 20, April 24, 1861, for six months. Present or accounted for until the company was disbanded on December 16, 1861.

COLLINS, RANDALL P., Sergeant
Born in Robeson County where he resided as a farmer prior to enlisting in Robeson County at age 18, April 24, 1861, for six months. Mustered in as Corporal and promoted to Sergeant in August-September, 1861. Present or accounted for until the company was disbanded on December 16, 1861. Later served as 2nd Lieutenant in Company B, 50th Regiment N. C. Troops.

DAVIS, CALVIN, Private
Resided in Robeson County and was by occupation a laborer prior to enlisting in Robeson County at age 22, April 24, 1861, for six months. Present or accounted for until the company was disbanded on December 16, 1861. Later served in Company F, 3rd

Regiment N. C. State Troops.

DAVIS, WASHINGTON W., Private
Resided in Robeson County and was by occupation a merchant prior to enlisting in Robeson County at age 24, April 24, 1861, for six months. Mustered in as Sergeant but was reduced to ranks in August-September, 1861. Present or accounted for until the company was disbanded on December 16, 1861.

DILLIARD, JOHN H., Private
Resided in Robeson County and was by occupation a laborer prior to enlisting in Robeson County at age 19, April 24, 1861, for six months. Present or accounted for until the company was disbanded on December 16, 1861.

FLOYD, FAULKNER J., Private
Resided in Robeson County and was by occupation a farmer prior to enlisting in Robeson County at age 16, April 24, 1861, for six months. Present or accounted for until the company was disbanded on December 16, 1861. Later served in Company F, 51st Regiment N. C. Troops.

FREEMAN, JOSEPH H., Corporal
Born in Robeson County where he resided as a farmer prior to enlisting in Robeson County at age 20, April 24, 1861, for six months. Mustered in as Private and promoted to Corporal in August-September, 1861. Present or accounted for until the company was disbanded on December 16, 1861. Later served as 2nd Lieutenant in Company A, 46th Regiment N. C. Troops.

FULMORE, ANDREW C., Private
Resided in Robeson County and was by occupation a farmer prior to enlisting in Robeson County at age 17, April 24, 1861, for six months. Present or accounted for until the company was disbanded on December 16, 1861. Later served as 1st Lieutenant in Company F, 51st Regiment N. C. Troops.

GREEN, HARVEY, _____
Name appears on an undated list of the members of this company. Place and date of enlistment not reported. No further records.

GREEN, HENRY, Private
Resided in Robeson County and was by occupation a laborer prior to enlisting in Robeson County at age 28, April 24, 1861, for six months. Present or accounted for until the company was disbanded on December 16, 1861.

GRIFFIN, SILAS, Private
Resided in Robeson County and was by occupation a farmer prior to enlisting in Robeson County at age 24, April 24, 1861, for six months. Present or accounted for until the company was disbanded on December 16, 1861. Later served in Company E, 40th Regiment N. C. Troops (3rd Regiment N. C. Artillery).

GRIMSLEY, TRAVIS L., Private
Born in Robeson County where he resided as a farmer prior to enlisting in Robeson County at age 20, April 24, 1861, for six months. Present or accounted for until the company was disbanded on December 16, 1861. Later served in Company B, 50th Regiment N. C. Troops.

HAMMOND, HAYNES L., Private

Resided in Robeson County and was by occupation a laborer prior to enlisting in Robeson County at age 19, April 24, 1861, for six months. Present or accounted for until the company was disbanded on December 16, 1861. Later served in Company D, 26th Regiment South Carolina Infantry.

HAMMOND, STEPHEN, Private

Resided in Robeson County and was by occupation a laborer prior to enlisting in Robeson County at age 30, April 24, 1861, for six months. Present or accounted for until the company was disbanded on December 16, 1861. Later served in Company D, 26th Regiment South Carolina Infantry.

HAMMOND, STRATFORD, Sergeant

Born in Robeson County where he resided as a farmer or laborer prior to enlisting in Robeson County at age 20, April 24, 1861, for six months. Mustered in as Private and promoted to Sergeant in September-October, 1861. Present or accounted for until the company was disbanded on December 16, 1861. Later served in Company A, 46th Regiment N.C. Troops.

HARTMAN, JACOB W., Private

Resided in Robeson County and was by occupation a clerk prior to enlisting in Robeson County at age 20, April 24, 1861, for six months. Present or accounted for until the company was disbanded on December 16, 1861. Later served as 2nd Lieutenant in Company F, 51st Regiment N. C. Troops.

HEATHCOCK, WILLIAM H., Private

Resided in Robeson County and was by occupation a carpenter prior to enlisting in Robeson County at age 24, April 24, 1861, for six months. Present or accounted for until the company was disbanded on December 16, 1861.

HESTERS, JOHN T., Private

Resided in Robeson County and was by occupation a laborer prior to enlisting in Robeson County at age 18, April 24, 1861, for six months. Present or accounted for until the company was disbanded on December 16, 1861. Later served in Company F, 31st Regiment N. C. Troops.

HILL, WILLIAM, _____

Born in Robeson County. Place and date of enlistment nor reported. Died at Wilmington on December 1, 1861. Cause of death not reported.

HILL, WILLIAM M., Private

Born in Robeson County where he resided as a farmer prior to enlisting in Robeson County at age 21, April 24, 1861, for six months. Present or accounted for until the company was disbanded on December 16, 1861. Later served in Company B, 50th Regiment N. C. Troops.

HOWELL, JOHN J., Private

Resided in Robeson County and was by occupation a farmer prior to enlisting in Robeson County at age 22, April 24, 1861, for six months. Present or accounted for until the company was disbanded on December 16, 1861. Later served in Company A, 46th Regiment N. C. Troops.

IVEY, BENJAMIN W., Private

Born in Robeson County where he resided as a farm-er or laborer prior to enlisting in Robeson County at age 22, April 24, 1861, for six months. Present or accounted for until the company was disbanded on December 16, 1861. Later served in Company A, 5th Regiment N. C. State Troops.

IVEY, OLIVER McKAY, Private

Born in Robeson County where he resided as a farmer prior to enlisting in Robeson County at age 23, April 24, 1861, for six months. Present or accounted for until the company was disbanded on December 16, 1861. Later served in Company B, 50th Regiment N. C. Troops.

JENKINS, CORNELIUS, Private

Born in Robeson County where he resided as a farmer prior to enlisting in Robeson County at age 28, April 24, 1861, for six months. Present or accounted for until discharged on July 13, 1861, by reason of "inability to perform military duty."

JONES, RICHARD R., Private

Born in Robeson County and was by occupation a merchant or clerk prior to enlisting at Camp Carolina, Virginia, at age 19, June 24, 1861, for six months. Present or accounted for until the company was disbanded on December 16, 1861. Later served in Company A, 46th Regiment N. C. Troops.

KINLAW, PINKNEY J., _____

Born in Robeson County where he resided as a laborer. Place and date of enlistment not reported. Later served in Company A, 31st Regiment N. C. Troops. No further records.

LAMB, ALEXANDER, Private

Born in Robeson County where he resided as a farmer or laborer prior to enlisting in Robeson County at age 30, April 24, 1861, for six months. Present or accounted for until the company was disbanded on December 16, 1861. Later served in Company B, 50th Regiment N. C. Troops.

LAMB, BARNABAS, Private

Born in Robeson County where he resided as a farmer or laborer prior to enlisting in Robeson County at age 26, April 24, 1861, for six months. Present or accounted for until the company was disbanded on December 16, 1861. Later served in Company B, 50th Regiment N. C. Troops.

LEVINER, HARRIS, Private

Resided in Robeson County and was by occupation a laborer prior to enlisting in Robeson County at age 24, April 24, 1861, for six months. Present or accounted for until the company was disbanded on December 16, 1861.

LEWIS, COUNSIL, Private

Resided in Robeson County and was by occupation a farmer prior to enlisting in Robeson County at age 20, April 24, 1861, for six months. Present or accounted for until the company was disbanded on December 16, 1861. Later served in Company F, 31st Regiment N. C. Troops.

LEWIS, WARREN A., Private

Born in Robeson County where he resided as a farmer prior to enlisting in Robeson County at age 18, April 24, 1861, for six months. Present or accounted for until the company was disbanded on December 16, 1861. Later served in Company B, 50th Regiment N. C. Troops.

McKENLAW, D. C., _____
Name appears on an undated list of the members of this company. Place and date of enlistment not reported. No further records. [May have served later in Company G, 24th Regiment N. C. Troops (14th Regiment N. C. Volunteers).]

McLAUGHLIN, JOHN W., Private
Resided in Robeson County and was by occupation a laborer prior to enlisting in Robeson County at age 23, April 24, 1861, for six months. Present or accounted for until the company was disbanded on December 16, 1861.

McLEAN, WESTON G., Private
Born in Robeson County where he resided as a farmer prior to enlisting in Robeson County at age 22, April 24, 1861, for six months. Present or accounted for until the company was disbanded on December 16, 1861. Later served in Company E, 51st Regiment N. C. Troops.

McMILLAN, WILLIAM J., Private
Resided in Robeson County and was by occupation a farmer prior to enlisting in Robeson County at age 21, April 24, 1861, for six months. Present or accounted for until the company was disbanded on December 16, 1861. Later served in Company D, 51st Regiment N. C. Troops.

MEARS, DWIGHT H., Private
Born in Robeson County where he resided as a farmer prior to enlisting in Robeson County at age 18, April 24, 1861, for six months. Present or accounted for until the company was disbanded on December 16, 1861. Later served in Company A, 46th Regiment N. C. Troops.

MEARS, JOHN C., Private
Born in Robeson County where he resided as a farmer prior to enlisting in Robeson County at age 20, April 24, 1861, for six months. Present or accounted for until the company was disbanded on December 16, 1861. Later served in Company A, 46th Regiment N. C. Troops.

MERCER, JOHN P., Private
Born in Robeson County where he resided as a farmer prior to enlisting in Robeson County at age 22, April 24, 1861, for six months. Present or accounted for until the company was disbanded on December 16, 1861. Later served in Company D, 51st Regiment N. C. Troops.

MOORE, OWEN C., Private
Resided in Robeson County and was by occupation a painter prior to enlisting in Robeson County at age 24, April 24, 1861, for six months. Present or accounted for until the company was disbanded on December 16, 1861. [May have served later in 2nd Company B, 36th Regiment N. C. Troops (2nd Regiment N. C. Artillery).]

MOORE, WILLIAM P., Private
Born in Robeson County where he resided as a painter or mail carrier prior to enlisting in Robeson County at age 26, April 24, 1861, for six months. Present or accounted for until the company was disbanded on December 16, 1861. Later served in Company A, 46th Regiment N. C. Troops.

MUNN, OLLIN, 1st Sergeant
Born in Bladen County and was by occupation a farmer. Place and date of enlistment not reported. Promotion record not reported. Later served in Company B, 18th Regiment N.C. Troops (8th Regiment N.C. Volunteers). No further records.

NORTON, JOSHUA, _____
Name appears on an undated list of the members of this company. Place and date of enlistment not reported. No further records.

PARHAM, WILLIAM HENRY, Private
Born in Robeson County where he resided as a laborer prior to enlisting in Robeson County at age 21, April 24, 1861, for six months. Present or accounted for until the company was disbanded on December 16, 1861. Later served in Company D, 51st Regiment N. C. Troops.

PARKER, BENJAMIN T., Private
Resided in Robeson County and enlisted at Camp Carolina, Virginia, July 1, 1861, for six months. Present or accounted for until the company was disbanded on December 16, 1861. Later served in Company C, 30th Regiment N.C. Troops.

PEBERTH, WILLIAM T., Musician
Enlisted at Camp Carolina, Virginia, July 1, 1861, for six months. Mustered in as Musician. Present or accounted for until discharged on November 16, 1861. Reason discharged not reported.

PETERSON, JOHN, Private
Resided in Robeson County and was by occupation a farmer prior to enlisting in Robeson County at age 21, April 24, 1861, for six months. Present or accounted for until the company was disbanded on December 16, 1861. Later served in Company E, 51st Regiment N.C. Troops.

PHILLIPS, LEVI L., Private
Born in Robeson County where he resided as a clerk prior to enlisting in Robeson County at age 18, April 24, 1861, for six months. Present or accounted for until the company was disbanded on December 16, 1861. Later served in Company A, 46th Regiment N.C. Troops.

PITMAN, JAMES P., Corporal
Resided in Robeson County and was by occupation a farmer prior to enlisting in Robeson County at age 22, April 24, 1861, for six months. Mustered in as Corporal. Present or accounted for until the company was disbanded on December 16, 1861. Later served as 1st Lieutenant in Company E, 51st Regiment N. C. Troops.

PITMAN, RANDOLPH, Private
Born in Robeson County where he resided as a carpenter or farmer prior to enlisting in Robeson County at age 22, April 24, 1861, for six months. Present or accounted for until the company was disbanded on December 16, 1861. Later served in Company E, 51st Regiment N. C. Troops.

PITMAN, RANSOM, Private
Resided in Robeson County and was by occupation an artificer prior to enlisting in Robeson County at age 25, April 24, 1861, for six months. Present or accounted for until the company was disbanded on December 16, 1861.

PITTMAN, HARRISON M., Private

Resided in Robeson County and was by occupation a farmer prior to enlisting in Robeson County at age 20, April 24, 1861, for six months. Present or accounted for until the company was disbanded on December 16, 1861.

POUNDS, JACOB A., Private

Resided in Robeson County and was by occupation a laborer prior to enlisting in Robeson County at age 21, April 24, 1861, for six months. Present or accounted for until the company was disbanded on December 16, 1861. [May have served later in 3rd Company G, 36th Regiment N. C. Troops (2nd Regiment N. C. Artillery).]

RAIBAN, ARMAN, Private

Born in Brunswick County and resided in Robeson County where he was by occupation a laborer prior to enlisting in Robeson County at age 21, April 24, 1861, for six months. Present or accounted for until discharged on or about June 16, 1861, by reason of "inability to perform military duty." [May have served later in Company C, 1st Battalion N.C. Heavy Artillery.]

REGAN, JAMES W., Private

Resided in Robeson County and was by occupation a farmer prior to enlisting in Robeson County at age 20, April 24, 1861, for six months. Not carried on the rolls of this company after July 1, 1861. Later served in Company G, 24th Regiment N. C. Troops (14th Regiment N. C. Volunteers).

SCOTT, JOHN P., Private

Born in Robeson County where he resided as a farmer prior to enlisting in Robeson County at age 32, April 24, 1861, for six months. Present or accounted for until the company was disbanded on December 16, 1861. Later served in Company A, 46th Regiment N. C. Troops.

SMITH, GEORGE A., Private

Born in Robeson County where he resided as a clerk or farmer prior to enlisting in Robeson County at age 18, April 24, 1861, for six months. Present or accounted for until the company was disbanded on December 16, 1861. Later served in Company E, 51st Regiment N. C. Troops.

SMITH, JAMES P., Corporal

Born in Robeson County where he resided as a farmer prior to enlisting in Robeson County at age 20, April 24, 1861, for six months. Mustered in as Private and promoted to Corporal at an unspecified date. Present or accounted for until the company was disbanded on December 16, 1861. Later served in Company E, 51st Regiment N. C. Troops.

SMITH, REUBEN, Private

Resided in Robeson County and was by occupation a farmer prior to enlisting in Robeson County at age 28, April 24, 1861, for six months. Present or accounted for until the company was disbanded on December 16, 1861. Later served in Company C, 30th Regiment N.C. Troops.

SMITH, THOMAS R., Private

Resided in Robeson County and was by occupation a farmer prior to enlisting in Robeson County at age 23, April 24, 1861, for six months. Present or accounted for until the company was disbanded on

December 16, 1861. Later served in Company A, 46th Regiment N. C. Troops.

SPEIGHTS, WILLIAM N., Private

Enlisted in Robeson County on April 24, 1861, for six months. Present or accounted for until the company was disbanded on December 16, 1861. Later served in Company G, 24th Regiment N. C. Troops (14th Regiment N. C. Volunteers).

STEGALL, ISAAC H., Private

Resided in Robeson County and was by occupation a painter prior to enlisting in Robeson County at age 22, April 24, 1861, for six months. Present or accounted for until the company was disbanded on December 16, 1861.

STEPHENS, JOEL L., Private

Resided in Robeson County and was by occupation a farmer prior to enlisting in Robeson County at age 21, April 24, 1861, for six months. Present or accounted for until the company was disbanded on December 16, 1861.

SUTTON, WADE H., Private

Born in Robeson County where he resided as a farmer prior to enlisting in Robeson County at age 23, April 24, 1861, for six months. Present or accounted for until the company was disbanded on December 16, 1861. Later served in Company A, 46th Regiment N. C. Troops.

THOMPSON, GILES W., Private

Born in Robeson County where he resided as a farmer prior to enlisting in Robeson County at age 20, April 24, 1861, for six months. Present or accounted for until the company was disbanded on December 16, 1861. Later served as 1st Lieutenant in Company E, 51st Regiment N.C. Troops.

THOMPSON, STEPHEN A., Sergeant

Resided in Robeson County and was by occupation a farmer prior to enlisting in Robeson County at age 19, April 24, 1861, for six months. Mustered in as Sergeant. Present or accounted for until the company was disbanded on December 16, 1861. Later served in Company D, 18th Regiment N. C. Troops (8th Regiment N. C. Volunteers).

WALTER, JEREMIAH D., Private

Resided in Robeson County and was by occupation a farmer prior to enlisting in Robeson County at age 23, April 24, 1861, for six months. Present or accounted for until the company was disbanded on December 16, 1861. Later served in Company C, 56th Regiment N.C. Troops.

WARWICK, ARCHIBALD R., Private

Born in Robeson County where he resided as a farmer prior to enlisting in Robeson County at age 25, April 24, 1861, for six months. Present or accounted for until the company was disbanded on December 16, 1861. Later served in Company A, 46th Regiment N. C. Troops.

WARWICK, BRIGHT B., Private

Resided in Robeson County and was by occupation a farmer prior to enlisting in Robeson County at age 21, April 24, 1861, for six months. Present or accounted for until he died in hospital near Norfolk, Virginia, September 28, 1861, of "typhoid pneumonia."

WARWICK, JOSEPH, Private

Born in Robeson County where he resided as a farmer prior to enlisting in Robeson County at age 28, April 24, 1861, for six months. Present or accounted for until the company was disbanded on December 16, 1861. Later served in Company A, 46th Regiment N. C. Troops.

WILSON, ALEXANDER, Private

Resided in Robeson County and was by occupation a laborer prior to enlisting in Robeson County at age 21, April 24, 1861, for six months. Present or accounted for until he died at Camp Carolina, Virginia, August 10, 1861, of "typhoid fever."

WISHART, FRANCIS MARION, 1st Sergeant

Born in Robeson County where he resided as a merchant or clerk prior to enlisting in Robeson County at age 22, April 24, 1861, for six months. Mustered in as Sergeant and promoted to 1st Sergeant in July-August, 1861. Present or accounted for until the company was disbanded on December 16, 1861. Later served as 1st Lieutenant in Company A, 46th Regiment N. C. Troops.

WOOD, ALEXANDER, Private

Resided in Robeson County and was by occupation a plasterer prior to enlisting in Robeson County at age 19, April 24, 1861, for six months. Present or accounted for until the company was disbanded on December 16, 1861.

WOOD, EDWARD, Private

Resided in Robeson County and was by occupation a laborer prior to enlisting in Robeson County at age 22, April 24, 1861, for six months. Present or accounted for until the company was disbanded on December 16, 1861.

2nd COMPANY D

This company, known as the "Granville Greys," was raised in Granville County and enlisted at Oxford on April 22, 1861. It tendered its service to the state and was ordered to Garysburg, where it was assigned to this regiment. The company was mustered in as Captain George Wortham's Company and was designated Company B before it was designated Company D. Since it was the second company to serve as Company D, it was officially referred to as 2nd Company D. After it was mustered into the regiment the company functioned as a part of the regiment, and its history for the war period is recorded as a part of the regimental history.

The information contained in the following roster of the company was compiled principally from company muster rolls for April 22, 1861-February, 1862; June 30-October 31, 1862; January-August, 1863; and November, 1863-December, 1864. No company muster rolls were found for March 1-June 29, 1862; November-December, 1862; September-October, 1863; or for the period after December, 1864. In addition to the company muster rolls, Roll of Honor records, receipt rolls, hospital records, prisoner of war records, and other primary records, supplemented by state pension applications, United Daughters of the Confederacy records, and postwar rosters and histories, all provided useful information.

OFFICERS

CAPTAINS

WORTHAM, GEORGE

Resided in Granville County and was by occupation a lawyer prior to enlisting in Granville County at age 38. Appointed Captain on or about April 22, 1861. Present or accounted for until promoted to Major on April 15, 1862, and transferred to the 50th Regiment N. C. Troops.

LANDIS, AUGUSTUS, Jr.

Born in Granville County where he resided as a merchant prior to enlisting in Granville County at age 27, April 22, 1861. Mustered in as Orderly Sergeant and was elected 1st Lieutenant to rank from April 22, 1861. Promoted to Captain on May 1, 1862. Present or accounted for until wounded "above the knee joint" at Gaines' Mill, Virginia, June 27, 1862. Reported absent wounded or absent on detail until he resigned on October 9, 1863, by reason of disability from wounds. Resignation accepted October 28, 1863.

SPENCER, ALEXANDER F., Captain

Resided in Granville County and was by occupation a mason prior to enlisting in Granville County at age 32, April 22, 1861. Mustered in as Private and promoted to Corporal on June 25, 1861. Promoted to Sergeant on January 8, 1862, and was elected 2nd Lieutenant to rank from May 1, 1862. Promoted to Captain on October 28, 1863. Present or accounted for until wounded at Cedar Creek, Virginia, October 19, 1864. Reported absent wounded through December, 1864.

LIEUTENANTS

CANNADY, W. E., 1st Lieutenant

Appointed 1st Lieutenant on or about April 22, 1861. Resigned May 28, 1861. Reason he resigned not reported. No further records.

GRIFFIN, GOLD M., 2nd Lieutenant

Resided in Tennessee or in Granville County and was by occupation a "gentleman" prior to enlisting in Granville County at age 26, April 22, 1861. Mustered in as Private and elected 2nd Lieutenant to rank from May 1, 1862. Present or accounted for until hospitalized at Culpeper, Virginia, September 26, 1862, with a gunshot wound; however, place and date wounded not reported. Resigned March 4, 1863. Later served as Private in Company C, 32nd Regiment N. C. Troops.

HESTER, JOHN C., 1st Lieutenant

Resided in Granville County and was by occupation a druggist prior to enlisting in Granville County at age 26. Appointed 3rd Lieutenant to rank from April 22, 1861, and was promoted to 1st Lieutenant to rank from May 1, 1862. Present or accounted for until wounded in the leg at Chancellorsville, Virginia, May 3, 1863. Returned to duty prior to July 1, 1863, and present or accounted for until he resigned on October 28, 1863, by reason of having been "elected to the position of clerk of several courts in Granville County."

HUNTER, JOHN BEVERLY, 2nd Lieutenant

Resided in Granville County and was by occupation

a farmer prior to enlisting in Granville County at age 27. Appointed 2nd Lieutenant to rank from April 22, 1861. Present or accounted for until he resigned on January 1, 1862. Reason he resigned not reported.

SMITH, MAURICE THOMAS, 2nd Lieutenant
Born in Granville County where he resided as a farmer prior to enlisting in Granville County at age 26, April 22, 1861. Mustered in as 1st Sergeant and appointed 2nd Lieutenant to rank from January, 1862. Present or accounted for until he was defeated for reelection when the regiment was reorganized on May 1, 1862. Later served as Captain of Company K, 55th Regiment N. C. Troops.

NONCOMMISSIONED OFFICERS
AND PRIVATES

ADAMS, REUBEN, Private
Resided in Union County and enlisted in Burke County at age 26, February 28, 1863, for the war. Present or accounted for until discharged on April 30, 1863, by reason of disability.

ALLEN, GARLAND E. H., Private
Resided in Granville County and was by occupation a "printer's d[evil]" prior to enlisting in Granville County at age 16, April 22, 1861. Present or accounted for until wounded at Malvern Hill, Virginia, July 1, 1862. Reported absent wounded through October, 1862. Discharged at an unspecified date. No further records.

ALLEN, ROBERT L., Private
Resided in Warren County and was by occupation a farmer prior to enlisting in Granville County at age 22, April 22, 1861. Present or accounted for until wounded at Malvern Hill, Virginia, July 1, 1862. Returned to duty in March-April, 1863, and present or accounted for until wounded in the leg at Chancellorsville, Virginia, May 2-3, 1863. Returned to duty prior to July 1-4, 1863, when he was captured at Gettysburg, Pennsylvania. Hospitalized at Gettysburg with an unspecified disability and was transferred to Davids Island, New York Harbor, July 17-24, 1863. Paroled at Davids Island and transferred to City Point, Virginia, where he was received September 8, 1863, for exchange. Returned to duty in January-February, 1864, and was present or accounted for until killed at Spotsylvania Court House, Virginia, May 12, 1864.

BARKER, D. T., Private
Enlisted in Wake County on February 3, 1864, for the war. Present or accounted for until paroled at Appomattox Court House, Virginia, April 9, 1865.

BARNES, GEORGE W., 1st Sergeant
Resided in Granville County and was by occupation a clerk prior to enlisting in Granville County at age 19, April 22, 1861. Mustered in as Private and promoted to Sergeant on November 1, 1862. Promoted to 1st Sergeant in January-February, 1863. Present or accounted for until wounded in the right shoulder and/or wrist at Spotsylvania Court House, Virginia, May 12, 1864. Returned to duty prior to September 19, 1864, when he was captured at Winchester, Virginia. Confined at Point Lookout, Maryland, until

paroled and transferred to Boulware's Wharf, James River, Virginia, where he was received March 18, 1865, for exchange.

BARNETT, JOSEPH, Private
Born in Granville County where he resided as a farmer prior to enlisting in Granville County at age 22, April 22, 1861. Present or accounted for until wounded at Gaines' Mill, Virginia, June 27, 1862. Died at Richmond, Virginia, on or about July 6, 1862, of wounds.

BATTLE, DOSSEY, Private
Born in Edgecombe County and resided in Edgecombe or Nash counties prior to enlisting at Norfolk, Virginia, at age 20, August 15, 1861. Mustered in as Private. Present or accounted for until transferred to 1st Company H of this regiment on January 4, 1863.

BATTLE, JUNIUS C., Private
Born in Orange County where he resided as a teacher prior to enlisting in Granville County at age 18, April 22, 1861. Mustered in as Corporal but was reduced to ranks in February-June, 1862. Present or accounted for until wounded at South Mountain, Maryland, September, 14, 1862. Died at Middleton, Maryland, on or about October 1, 1862, of wounds.

BEASLEY, FLEMING S., Private
Born in Granville County where he resided as a clerk prior to enlisting in Granville County at age 20, April 22, 1861. Present or accounted for until killed at Malvern Hill, Virginia, July 1, 1862.

BELL, LUTHER R., Private
Born in Camden County and resided in Granville County where he was by occupation a student prior to enlisting in Granville County at age 18, May 5, 1861. Present or accounted for until killed at Malvern Hill, Virginia, July 1, 1862.

BENNETT, WILLIAM, Private
Resided in Kentucky and enlisted at Bunker Hill, Virginia, at age 26, October 17, 1862, for the war as a substitute. Present or accounted for through August, 1863. Company muster rolls dated November, 1863-December, 1864, indicate that he was a prisoner of war; however, records of the Federal Provost Marshal do not substantiate that report.

BLALOCK, MILLINGTON, Sergeant
Resided in Granville County and was by occupation a student prior to enlisting in Granville County at age 18, May 5, 1861. Mustered in as Private and promoted to Sergeant in November, 1862-February, 1863. Present or accounted for until captured at Chancellorsville, Virginia, May 3, 1863. Exchanged at City Point, Virginia, on or about May 13, 1863. Rejoined the company prior to July 1, 1863, and present or accounted for until captured at High Bridge, Virginia, April 6, 1865. Confined at Point Lookout, Maryland, until released on June 23, 1865, after taking the Oath of Allegiance.

BLOUNT, JOHN, Private
Born in Union County* where he resided as a farmer prior to enlisting in Union County at age 23, March 23, 1863, for the war. Present or accounted for until wounded in the foot at Chancellorsville, Virginia, May 2, 1863. Reported absent without leave on August 23, 1863, but returned to duty in January-February, 1864. Discharged on or about March 15,

1864, by reason of disability.

BROCIUS, WILLIAM K., Private
Resided in Granville County and was by occupation a mail contractor prior to enlisting in Granville County at age 29, April 22, 1861. Present or accounted for until discharged on May 7, 1862, by reason of being a mail contractor.

BRODIE, E. G., Private
Resided in Granville County and was by occupation a student prior to enlisting in Granville County at age 17, May 17, 1861. Present or accounted for until appointed Ordnance Sergeant and transferred to Company K, 54th Regiment N. C. Troops, May 7, 1862.

BROWN, JAMES, Private
Resided in Virginia and enlisted at Gordonsville, Virginia, at age 35, November 26, 1862, for the war as a substitute. Present or accounted for through March, 1864. Company muster rolls dated April 30-December, 1864, indicate that he was a prisoner of war; however, records of the Federal Provost Marshal do not substantiate that report. No further records.

BURCHETT, C. R., Private
Enlisted in Wake County on August 25, 1864, for the war. Present or accounted for through December, 1864.

CALAHAN, JOHN, Private
Resided in Virginia and enlisted at age 23, November 20, 1862, for the war as a substitute. Deserted November 28, 1862.

CANNADAY, JOHN, Sr., Private
Was by occupation a farmer prior to enlisting at Norfolk, Virginia, at age 23, July 10, 1861. Present or accounted for until furloughed from hospital at Richmond, Virginia, August 5, 1862. No further records.

CANNADAY, JOHN P., Private
Resided in Granville County and was by occupation a farmer prior to enlisting in Wake County at age 18, April 30, 1861. Present or accounted for until he was reported transferred to the 23rd Regiment N. C. Troops (13th Regiment N. C. Volunteers), August 1, 1862; however, records of the 23rd Regiment do not indicate that he served therein. No further records.

CANNADY, JOHN F., Private
Resided in Granville County and enlisted at Norfolk, Virginia, at age 24, July 12, 1861. Present or accounted for until discharged on or about November 20, 1862, after providing a substitute. Later served in Company G, 63rd Regiment N. C. Troops (5th Regiment N. C. Cavalry).

CARPENTER, J. M., Private
Resided in Cleveland County where he enlisted at age 28, February 26, 1863, for the war. Present or accounted for until wounded by a "falling . . . limb" at Chancellorsville, Virginia, May 2, 1863. Returned to duty prior to July 1, 1863, when he was wounded in the "right ring finger" at Gettysburg, Pennsylvania. Finger amputated. Captured at Gettysburg or at Chambersburg, Pennsylvania, July 1-5, 1863. Hospitalized at various Federal hospitals until transferred to City Point, Virginia, where he was received August 24, 1863, for exchange. Reported absent

without leave from September 20, 1863, until he returned to duty in March-April, 1864. Captured at Spotsylvania Court House, Virginia, May 12, 1864. Confined at Point Lookout, Maryland, until transferred to Elmira, New York, August 10, 1864. Paroled at Elmira and transferred to Venus Point, Savannah River, Georgia, where he was received November 15, 1864, for exchange.

CARPENTER, PETER H., Private
Resided in Cleveland County where he enlisted at age 26, February 26, 1863, for the war. Present or accounted for until captured near Spotsylvania Court House, Virginia, May 12, 1864. Confined at Point Lookout, Maryland, until transferred to Elmira, New York, August 10, 1864. Died at Elmira on March 3, 1865, of "typhoid fever."

CASE, J. J., Private
Enlisted in Wake County on September 22, 1864, for the war. Present or accounted for through December, 1864.

CASH, THOMAS J., Private
Previously served in Company E, 23rd Regiment N.C. Troops (13th Regiment N.C. Volunteers). Transferred to this company on June 1, 1862. Killed at Gaines' Mill, Virginia, June 27, 1862.

CHANDLER, SEYMOUR, Private
Resided in Granville County and was by occupation a farmer prior to enlisting in Wake County at age 21, April 30, 1861. Present or accounted for until wounded at Gaines' Mill, Virginia, June 27, 1862. Returned to duty in November, 1862-February, 1863, and present or accounted for until captured at Winchester, Virginia, July 20, 1864. Confined at Camp Chase, Ohio, until transferred to Boulware's and Cox's Wharf, James River, Virginia, where he was received on or about March 10, 1865, for exchange.

CLEMENTS, AMOS GOOCH, Private
Born in Granville County where he resided prior to enlisting at Norfolk, Virginia, at age 20, March 4, 1862. Present or accounted for until captured at Gettysburg, Pennsylvania, July 3-4, 1863. Confined at Fort Delaware, Delaware, until transferred to Point Lookout, Maryland, October 18, 1863. Confined at Point Lookout until paroled and transferred to Boulware's and Cox's Wharf, James River, Virginia, where he was received February 20-21, 1865, for exchange. Reported present with a detachment of paroled and exchanged prisoners at Camp Lee, near Richmond, Virginia, February 28, 1865.

COLE, R. L., Private
Resided in Georgia and enlisted at Winchester, Virginia, at age 46, September 11, 1862, for the war as a substitute. Sent to hospital on September 12, 1862, and never returned. Listed as a deserter in November-December, 1864.

CREWS, THOMAS J., Private
Resided in Granville County and was by occupation a surveyor prior to enlisting in Granville County at age 22, April 22, 1861. Mustered in as Sergeant but was reduced to ranks in March-August, 1862. Discharged on August 19, 1862, after providing a substitute.

CRITCHER, JOSEPH, Private
Born in Granville County where he resided as a farmer prior to enlisting in Granville County at age 22, April 22, 1861. Present or accounted for until discharged on December 11, 1861, by reason of disability.

CRITCHER, WILLIAM H., Private
Born in Granville County where he resided as a druggist prior to enlisting in Granville County at age 19, April 22, 1861. Present or accounted for until hospitalized at Richmond, Virginia, June 22, 1862, with "fever." Died in hospital at Richmond on June 29, 1862.

CRUDUP, JOSIAH, Private
Resided in Granville County where he enlisted at age 21, April 22, 1861. Present or accounted for until he died on October 18, 1861, of disease. Place of death not reported.

CULBRETH, JOHN J., Corporal
Resided in Florida and was by occupation a clerk prior to enlisting in Wake County at age 25, April 30, 1861. Mustered in as Private and promoted to Corporal in March-October, 1862. Present or accounted for until captured at South Mountain, Maryland, September 14, 1862. Paroled on or about October 4, 1862. Returned to duty prior to March 1, 1863, and present or accounted for until transferred to Company D, 2nd Battalion Florida Infantry on or about November 25, 1863.

DANIEL, GEORGE B., Private
Was by occupation a farmer prior to enlisting in Granville County at age 25, April 22, 1861. Present or accounted for until "discharged by promotion" on October 12, 1861. [May have served later as Captain of Company F, 17th Regiment N. C. Troops (2nd Organization).]

DAVIS, JAMES R., Private
Resided in Granville County and was by occupation a farmer prior to enlisting in Granville County at age 22, April 22, 1861. Present or accounted for until discharged on December 31, 1861, by reason of disability.

DAWS, H. A., Private
Enlisted in Wake County on July 4, 1864, for the war. Present or accounted for until wounded in the right thigh in action between Petersburg, Virginia, and Farmville, Virginia, March 29-April 9, 1865. Captured by Federal forces and was hospitalized at City Point, Virginia, where he died on April 24, 1865.

DORSEY, HOWARD, Private
Enlisted in Granville County on February 1, 1864, for the war. Present or accounted for until captured at Winchester, Virginia, September 19, 1864. Confined at Point Lookout, Maryland, until paroled and transferred to Cox's Landing, James River, Virginia, where he was received February 14-15, 1865, for exchange. Reported present with a detachment of paroled and exchanged prisoners at Camp Lee, near Richmond, Virginia, February 18, 1865.

DURHAM, JAMES Private
Born in Warren County where he resided as a teacher prior to enlisting at Camp Carolina, Virginia, at age 28, July 1, 1861. Present or accounted

for until discharged on or about February 22, 1862, by reason of disability.

EDMONDS, NATHANIEL, Private
Born in Halifax County, Virginia, and resided in Granville County where he was by occupation a farmer prior to enlisting in Granville County on April 26, 1861. Present or accounted for until discharged on or about February 22, 1862, by reason of "rheumatism." Company records report his age as 29; however, discharge records give his age as 48. No further records.

ELIXSON, JAMES W., Private
Resided in Granville County and was by occupation a farmer prior to enlisting in Wake County at age 26, May 5, 1861. Present or accounted for until he died on or about August 30, 1861, of disease. Place of death not reported.

FLANAGAN, MICHAEL C., Private
Resided in Virginia and enlisted at Guinea Station, Virginia, at age 46, December 31, 1862, for the war as a substitute. Present or accounted for until he deserted to the enemy on or about May 4, 1863. Took the Oath of Amnesty the same day.

GODFREY, WILLIAM R., Private
Resided in Union County where he enlisted at age 21, March 23, 1863, for the war. Present or accounted for until wounded in the head at Chancellorsville, Virginia, May 2, 1863. Reported absent wounded until reported absent without leave on August 23, 1863. Reported absent without leave until he was detailed at Charlotte on October 11, 1864. No further records.

GOOCH, G., Private
Enlisted in Wake County on June 1, 1864, for the war. Present or accounted for until wounded at Cedar Creek, Virginia, October 19, 1864. Reported absent wounded through December, 1864.

GREGORY, CHARLES, Private
Resided in Granville County and was by occupation a farmer prior to enlisting in Wake County at age 30, May 5, 1861. Present or accounted for until hospitalized at Richmond, Virginia, June 27, 1862, with a gunshot wound; however, place and date wounded not reported. Discharged on or about September 11, 1862, after providing a substitute.

GREGORY, FRANCIS R., Private
Resided in Granville County and was by occupation a physician prior to enlisting in Granville County at age 23, April 22, 1861. Present or accounted for until discharged on June 1, 1862. Reason discharged not reported.

GREGORY, H., Private
Enlisted in Wake County on March 27, 1864, for the war. Present or accounted for through December, 1864.

GREGORY, HERBERT, Private
Resided in Granville County and was by occupation a farmer prior to enlisting in Granville County at age 25, April 30, 1861. Mustered in as Sergeant but was reduced to ranks in March-October, 1862. Present or accounted for until he was reported transferred to the 23rd Regiment N.C. Troops (13th Regiment N.C. Volunteers) on July 6, 1862; however, records

of the 23rd Regiment do not indicate that he served therein. No further records.

GRIFFIN, BENJAMIN, Private
Enlisted in Nash County on March 1, 1862. Present or accounted for through June, 1862. No further records.

HANCOCK, THOMAS C., Private
Born in Granville County where he resided as a physician prior to enlisting at Norfolk, Virginia, at age 22, August 9, 1861. Present or accounted for until he died at Gordonsville, Virginia, on or about May 15, 1862, of disease.

HARGROVE, J. H., Private
Resided in Granville County and was by occupation a farmer prior to enlisting in Wake County at age 20, April 30, 1861. Present or accounted for until wounded in the left knee and captured at Sharpsburg, Maryland, September 17, 1862. Left leg amputated. Died in hospital at Frederick, Maryland, October 10, 1862, of wounds.

HART, HENRY, Private
Resided in Granville County and enlisted at age 18, April 22, 1861. Discharged in June, 1862, by reason of disability.

HART, RICHARD A., Private
Born in Edgecombe County and resided in Granville County where he was by occupation a farmer or merchant prior to enlisting in Wake County at age 22, April 30, 1861. Present or accounted for until wounded in the right leg at Chancellorsville, Virginia, May 2, 1863. Right leg amputated. Reported absent wounded until he was retired on or about April 5, 1864, by reason of disability.

HART, THOMAS C., Corporal
Resided in Granville or Warren counties and was by occupation a student prior to enlisting in Granville County at age 19, April 22, 1861. Mustered in as Private and promoted to Corporal in November, 1862-February, 1863. Present or accounted for until hospitalized at Richmond, Virginia, May 18, 1864, with a gunshot wound of the arm and shoulder; however, place and date wounded not reported. Reported absent wounded until November-December, 1864, when he was reported absent without leave. Returned to duty prior to April 6, 1865, when he was captured at Sayler's Creek, Virginia. Confined at Point Lookout, Maryland, until released on June 28, 1865, after taking the Oath of Allegiance.

HART, WILLIAM H., Private
Was by occupation a farmer prior to enlisting in Granville County at age 20, April 30, 1861. Not listed on the rolls of this company after June 30, 1861. No further records.

HAYES, JOSEPH S., Private
Resided in Granville County and was by occupation a farmer prior to enlisting in Granville County at age 18, April 22, 1861. Present or accounted for until wounded at Gettysburg, Pennsylvania, July 1, 1863. Returned to duty prior to September 1, 1863. Killed in battle near Warrenton, Virginia, October 14, 1863.

HENDERSON, A. B., Private
Place and date of enlistment not reported. Paroled

at Greensboro on May 12, 1865.

HOBGOOD, J. L., Private
Resided in Granville County and enlisted at Norfolk, Virginia, at age 21, March 4, 1862. Present or accounted for until wounded in the leg at Chancellorsville, Virginia, May 2, 1863. Reported absent wounded or absent on detail through December, 1864.

HOBGOOD, R. H., Private
Resided in Granville County and enlisted at Norfolk, Virginia, at age 18, May 6, 1862, for the war. Present or accounted for until wounded in the shoulder at Chancellorsville, Virginia, May 3, 1863. Died in hospital at Richmond, Virginia, June 5, 1863, of wounds and "typhoid fever."

HOBGOOD, SHELTON, Corporal
Born in Granville County where he resided as a farmer prior to enlisting in Granville County at age 23, April 22, 1861. Mustered in as Private and promoted to Corporal in November, 1862-February, 1863. Present or accounted for until killed at Fredericksburg, Virginia, January 5, 1863, "by [the] accidental falling of a tree."

HOLLOWAY, WILLIAM T., Private
Resided in Granville County and was by occupation a saddler prior to enlisting in Granville County at age 20, April 22, 1861. Present or accounted for until wounded in battle near Richmond, Virginia, in June-July, 1862. Died at Richmond in August, 1862, of wounds.

HUNT, G., Private
Enlisted in Wake County on June 16, 1864, for the war. Present or accounted for through December, 1864.

JONES, RICHARD B., Private
Born in Granville County where he resided as a shoemaker prior to enlisting in Granville County at age 18, April 22, 1861. Present or accounted for until hospitalized at Richmond, Virginia, June 30, 1862, with a gunshot wound; however, place and date wounded not reported. Died in hospital at Richmond on July 6, 1862, of wounds.

KANUP, A. L., Private
Enlisted in Wake County on September 8, 1864, for the war. Present or accounted for until paroled at Appomattox Court House, Virginia, April 9, 1865.

KINGSBURY, CHARLES F., Private
Resided in Granville County and was by occupation a tobacconist prior to enlisting in Granville County at age 22, April 22, 1861. Present or accounted for until hospitalized at Richmond, Virginia, June 28, 1862, with a gunshot wound; however, place and date wounded not reported. Discharged from service on or about July 6, 1862, after providing a substitute.

KITCHIN, WILLIAM HODGE, Private
Resided in Halifax County and was by occupation a student prior to enlisting at Norfolk, Virginia, at age 26, June 11, 1861. Present or accounted for until transferred to Company G of this regiment in March-October, 1862.

KITTRELL, EGBERT P., Private
Resided in Granville County and was by occupation

a farmer prior to enlisting in Granville County at age 20, April 30, 1861. Present or accounted for until captured at Cedar Creek, Virginia, October 19, 1864. Confined at Point Lookout, Maryland, until paroled and transferred to Boulware's Wharf, James River, Virginia, where he was received March 30, 1865, for exchange.

LAEL, CALVIN, Private
Enlisted at Hanover Junction, Virginia, February 14, 1864, for the war. Present or accounted for until wounded in the left leg and captured at Spotsylvania Court House, Virginia, May 9, 1864. Hospitalized at Washington, D.C., until transferred to Elmira, New York, July 23, 1864. Released at Elmira on June 27, 1865, after taking the Oath of Allegiance.

LANDIS, GEORGE W., Private
Resided in Granville County and was by occupation a clerk prior to enlisting in Granville County at age 20, April 22, 1861. Present or accounted for until wounded at Gettysburg, Pennsylvania, July 1, 1863. Transferred to Company E, 54th Regiment N.C. Troops, August 20, 1863.

LANKFORD, THOMAS A., Sergeant
Resided in Granville County and was by occupation a clerk prior to enlisting in Granville County at age 21, April 22, 1861. Mustered in as Private and promoted to Sergeant on August 1, 1862. Present or accounted for until wounded in the left lung and captured at Gettysburg, Pennsylvania, July 1, 1863. Hospitalized at Gettysburg until transferred to Davids Island, New York Harbor, July 17-24, 1863. Paroled and transferred to City Point, Virginia, where he was received on or about September 8, 1863, for exchange. Returned to duty in March-April, 1864, and was detailed in the Quartermaster Department at Raleigh. Reported absent on detail through February 12, 1865.

McBANE, D., Private
Enlisted in Wake County on September 22, 1864, for the war. Present or accounted for until listed as a deserter in November-December, 1864.

McCADDEN, HENRY C., Private
Resided in Virginia and was by occupation a saddler prior to enlisting in Wake County at age 22, April 30, 1861. Present or accounted for until discharged on December 31, 1862, after providing a substitute.

McCANN, FELIX, Private
Born in Philadelphia, Pennsylvania, and resided in Pennsylvania where he was by occupation a jeweler prior to enlisting in Granville County at age 19, April 22, 1861. Present or accounted for until killed at Gaines' Mill, Virginia, June 27, 1862.

McCLANAHAN, THOMAS W., Private
Born in Granville County where he resided as a farmer prior to enlisting in Granville County at age 25, April 22, 1861. Present or accounted for until discharged on or about January 25, 1862, by reason of "phthisis pulmonalis."

McGHEE, JOHN C., Private
Resided in Virginia and was by occupation a teacher prior to enlisting in Granville County at age 22, April 22, 1861. Present or accounted for until wounded at Malvern Hill, Virginia, July 1, 1862. Reported absent wounded until reported absent

without leave on May 7, 1863. Reported absent without leave through April, 1864. No further records.

MACON, JAMES H., Sergeant
Resided in Granville County and was by occupation a clerk prior to enlisting in Granville County at age 24, April 22, 1861. Mustered in as Private and promoted to Sergeant in March-October, 1862. Present or accounted for until killed near Warrenton, Virginia, October 14, 1863.

MALLORY, J. R., Private
Place and date of enlistment not reported. Paroled at Appomattox Court House, Virginia, April 9, 1865.

MALLORY, JAMES S., Private
Born in Granville County where he resided as a farmer prior to enlisting in Granville County at age 22, April 22, 1861. Present or accounted for until he died on November 29, 1862, of disease. Place of death not reported.

MALLORY, S. C., Private
Resided in Granville County where he enlisted at age 17, March 4, 1862. Present or accounted for until wounded at Gettysburg, Pennsylvania, July 1, 1863. Returned to duty prior to September 1, 1863, and present or accounted for until paroled at Appomattox Court House, Virginia, April 9, 1865.

MALLORY, WILLIAM C., Private
Resided in Granville County and was by occupation a teacher prior to enlisting in Granville County at age 24, April 22, 1861. Mustered in as Sergeant but was reduced to ranks in March-October, 1862. Present or accounted for until captured at Gettysburg, Pennsylvania, July 1-4, 1863. Confined at Davids Island, New York Harbor, July 17-24, 1863. Paroled and transferred to City Point, Virginia, where he was received September 8, 1863, for exchange. Returned to duty in January-February, 1864, and present or accounted for until paroled at Appomattox Court House, Virginia, April 9, 1865.

MEADOWS, JOHN STEVEN, Private
Resided in Granville County and enlisted at Norfolk, Virginia, at age 24, August 1, 1861. Present or accounted for until captured at or near South Mountain, Maryland, on or about September 14, 1862. Confined at Fort Delaware, Delaware, until paroled and transferred to Aiken's Landing, James River, Virginia, October 2, 1862, for exchange. Declared exchanged at Aiken's Landing on November 10, 1862. Returned to duty prior to March 1, 1863, and present or accounted for until wounded in the arm and captured at Gettysburg, Pennsylvania, July 1-5, 1863. Arm amputated. Hospitalized at Davids Island, New York Harbor, July 17-24, 1863. Paroled and transferred to City Point, Virginia, where he was received September 8, 1863, for exchange. Reported absent wounded through February, 1864. No further records.

MEADOWS, L. P., Private
Resided in Granville County and was by occupation an artist prior to enlisting in Wake County at age 19, April 30, 1861. Present or accounted for until wounded and captured at Gettysburg, Pennsylvania, July 1-4, 1863. Confined at Fort Delaware, Delaware, until transferred to Point Lookout, Maryland, Octo-

ber 18, 1863. Confined at Point Lookout until paroled and transferred to Venus Point, Savannah River, Georgia, where he was received on November 15, 1864, for exchange. Died prior to January 1, 1865. Place and cause of death not reported.

MEADOWS, THOMAS P., Private
Resided in Granville County and was by occupation a farmer prior to enlisting in Wake County at age 24, April 30, 1861. Present or accounted for until killed at Gettysburg, Pennsylvania, July 1, 1863.

MILLER, M. V., Private
Enlisted at Morton's Ford, Virginia, November 25, 1863, for the war. Present or accounted for through December, 1864.

MINOR, A. G., Private
Resided in Granville County and was by occupation a farmer prior to enlisting in Wake County at age 19, April 30, 1861. Present or accounted for until he died in hospital at Richmond, Virginia, December 15, 1862, of dysentery.

MINOR, JAMES H., Sergeant
Resided in Granville County and was by occupation a clerk prior to enlisting in Wake County at age 21, May 1, 1861. Mustered in as Private and promoted to Sergeant in March-July, 1862. Present or accounted for until wounded near Richmond, Virginia, in June-July, 1862. Battle in which wounded not reported. Died July 31, 1862, of wounds. Place of death not reported.

MINOR, RICHARD VAN BUREN, Private
Resided in Granville County and was by occupation a farmer prior to enlisting in Wake County at age 20, April 30, 1861. Present or accounted for until appointed 2nd Lieutenant on September 25, 1862, and transferred to Company E, 23rd Regiment N.C. Troops (13th Regiment N.C. Volunteers).

MINOR, THOMAS J., Corporal
Born in Granville County where he resided as a farmer prior to enlisting in Granville County at age 22, April 22, 1861. Mustered in as Private and promoted to Corporal on May 14, 1861. Present or accounted for until killed at Sharpsburg, Maryland, September 17, 1862.

MITCHELL, ROBERT, Corporal
Resided in Granville County and was by occupation a student prior to enlisting in Wake County at age 18, April 30, 1861. Mustered in as Private and promoted to Corporal on August 1, 1862. Present or accounted for until wounded in the hip at Chancellorsville, Virginia, May 2, 1863. Returned to duty prior to July 1, 1863, and present or accounted for until killed at Spotsylvania Court House, Virginia, May 9, 1864.

MIZE, ROBERT L., Private
Born in Granville County where he resided as a farmer prior to enlisting in Wake County at age 21, April 30, 1861. Present or accounted for until wounded in battle near Richmond, Virginia, in June-July, 1862. Died at Richmond on or about July 6, 1862, of wounds.

MONROE, _____, Cook
Enlisted at Richmond, Virginia, August 1, 1862. Not listed on the rolls of this company after October 31,

1862. No further records.

MOORE, GEORGE D., Private
Was by occupation a farmer prior to enlisting at Norfolk, Virginia, at age 21, July 16, 1861. No further records.

MOORE, H. D. E., Private
Resided in Virginia and enlisted at Norfolk, Virginia, at age 18, July 12, 1861. Present or accounted for until discharged on or about August 11, 1862. Reason discharged not reported.

MOORE, JOHN W., Private
Resided in Virginia and was by occupation a farmer prior to enlisting in Wake County at age 23, April 30, 1861. Present or accounted for until discharged on May 9, 1862, by reason of disability.

MOSS, EDWARD T., Private
Resided in Virginia and was by occupation a farmer prior to enlisting in Wake County at age 22, April 30, 1861. Present or accounted for until wounded in the right hand at Gaines' Mill, Virginia, June 27, 1862. Reported absent wounded until detailed as Assistant Enrolling Officer of the Fifth Congressional District of North Carolina in May-June, 1863. Reported absent on detail as an enrolling officer through December, 1864.

MURRAY, W. J., Private
Enlisted in Wake County on September 22, 1864, for the war. Present or accounted for until paroled at Appomattox Court House, Virginia, April 9, 1865.

NUTT, WILLIAM HENRY, Musician
Resided in Duplin County and enlisted at Richmond, Virginia, at age 15, May 25, 1861. Mustered in as Musician (Drummer). Present or accounted for until transferred to Company B, 50th Regiment N.C. Troops, May 6, 1862.

PARHAM, JOSIAH, Private
Resided in Granville County and was by occupation a peddler prior to enlisting in Granville County at age 24, April 30, 1861. Present or accounted for until he died in hospital at Richmond, Virginia, December 27, 1862, of "pneumonia."

PARHAM, THOMAS BUCKNER, Private
Was by occupation a clerk prior to enlisting in Granville County at age 20, April 22, 1861. Present or accounted for until transferred to Company K, 54th Regiment N.C. Troops, June 3, 1862.

PASCHALL, LUNSFORD A., Corporal
Born in Granville County where he resided as a merchant or clerk prior to enlisting in Granville County at age 24, April 22, 1861. Mustered in as Private and promoted to Corporal on January 8, 1862. Present or accounted for until appointed 1st Lieutenant on or about May 16, 1862, and transferred to Company E, 54th Regiment N.C. Troops.

PASCHALL, R. S., Private
Resided in Florida and was by occupation a farmer prior to enlisting in Wake County at age 22, April 30, 1861. Present or accounted for until discharged on December 11, 1861, by reason of disability.

PASCHALL, WILLIAM H., Private
Resided in Granville County and was by occupation a turkey hunter prior to enlisting in Granville County at age 43, April 22, 1861. Present or accounted for

until discharged on May 6, 1862. Reason discharged not reported.

PATTON, G., Private
Enlisted in Wake County on September 22, 1864, for the war. Present or accounted for through December, 1864.

PHELPS, HENRY, Private
Resided in Virginia prior to enlisting at Frederick City, Maryland, at age 45, September 8, 1862, for the war as a substitute. Deserted to the enemy or was captured at South Mountain, Maryland, September 14, 1862. Confined at Fort Delaware, Delaware, until paroled and transferred to Aiken's Landing, James River, Virginia, October 2, 1862, for exchange. Declared exchanged at Aiken's Landing on November 10, 1862. No further records.

PHILPOTT, SOLOMON H., Private
Resided in Granville County and was by occupation a farmer prior to enlisting at Norfolk, Virginia, at age 23, June 17, 1861. Present or accounted for until hospitalized at Richmond, Virginia, May 19, 1864, with a gunshot wound of the right ankle; however, place and date wounded not reported. Returned to duty prior to September 19, 1864, when he was killed at Winchester, Virginia. Roll of Honor indicates he was wounded at an unspecified date in battle near Richmond and states that he "died with his face to the foe, manly battling for his country's independence."

POOL, S. P., Private
Resided in Pasquotank County and was by occupation a student prior to enlisting at Norfolk, Virginia, at age 23, May 25, 1861. Present or accounted for until discharged on September 8, 1862, after providing a substitute.

PROPST, J. H., Private
Enlisted in Wake County on June 17, 1864, for the war. Present or accounted for through December, 1864.

RANEY, C. W., Sergeant
Resided in Granville County and was by occupation a farmer prior to enlisting in Granville County at age 22, April 30, 1861. Mustered in as Private and promoted to Sergeant in March-October, 1862. Discharged October 17, 1862, after providing a substitute.

RANEY, GEORGE, Private
Born in Granville County where he resided as a farmer prior to enlisting at Norfolk, Virginia, at age 19, July 10, 1861. Present or accounted for until he died on July 3, 1862, of disease. Place of death not reported.

RICHARDSON, GEORGE, Cook
Enlisted at Richmond, Virginia, August 23, 1862, for the war. Not listed on the rolls of this company after August 31, 1862. No further records.

ROBARDS, J. W., Private
Resided in Granville County and was by occupation a student prior to enlisting in Granville County at age 21, April 30, 1861. Present or accounted for through December, 1864; however, he was reported absent on detail as a clerk during much of that period. Paroled at Appomattox Court House, Virginia, April 9, 1865.

ROBARDS, WILLIAM J., Sergeant
Resided in Granville County and was by occupation a student prior to enlisting in Granville County at age 22, April 22, 1861. Mustered in as Private and promoted to Sergeant in November, 1862-February, 1863. Present or accounted for until appointed Sergeant Major on June 25, 1863, and transferred to the Field and Staff of this regiment.

ROWLAND, A. W., 1st Sergeant
Resided in Granville County and was by occupation a clerk prior to enlisting in Granville County at age 19, April 22, 1861. Mustered in as Private and promoted to Corporal on May 5, 1861. Promoted to 1st Sergeant in March-October, 1862. Present or accounted for until hospitalized at Richmond, Virginia, July 2, 1862, with a gunshot wound; however, place and date wounded not reported. Returned to duty prior to September 14, 1862, when he was captured at South Mountain, Maryland. Confined at Fort Delaware, Delaware, until paroled and transferred to Aiken's Landing, James River, Virginia, October 2, 1862, for exchange. Declared exchanged at Aiken's Landing on November 10, 1862. Discharged November 26, 1862, after providing a substitute.

ROWLAND, T. J., Private
Enlisted at Norfolk, Virginia, at age 17, May 6, 1862, for the war. Present or accounted for until wounded in the neck at Morton's Ford, Virginia, October 11, 1863. Died October 12, 1863, of wounds.

ROYSTER, GEORGE W., Private
Previously served in Company K, 55th Regiment N. C. Troops. Transferred to this company on October 16, 1862. Present or accounted for until wounded in the head at Chancellorsville, Virginia, May 3, 1863. Returned to duty prior to July 1, 1863. Present or accounted for until reported absent wounded on company muster roll dated April 30-October 31, 1864; however, place and date wounded not reported. Retired to the Invalid Corps on December 21, 1864, by reason of "t[otal] d[isability]."

ROYSTER, JAMES, Private
Resided in Granville County and was by occupation a farmer prior to enlisting in Granville County at age 28, April 30, 1861. Present or accounted for until wounded at South Mountain, Maryland, September 14, 1862. Returned to duty in March-April, 1863, and present or accounted for until wounded at Gettysburg, Pennsylvania, July 3, 1863. Returned to duty prior to January 1, 1864. Present or accounted for until hospitalized at Winchester, Virginia, July 30, 1864, with a gunshot wound of the thigh; however, place and date wounded not reported. Returned to duty prior to November 1, 1864, and present or accounted for through December, 1864.

ROYSTER, THOMAS D., Private
Resided in Granville County and was by occupation a farmer prior to enlisting in Wake County at age 28, April 30, 1861. Present or accounted for until paroled at Appomattox Court House, Virginia, April 9, 1865.

RUSSELL, WILLIAM H., Private
Born in Granville County where he resided as a farmer prior to enlisting in Granville County at age

2nd Co. D, 12th Regiment N. C. Troops

20, April 30, 1861. Present or accounted for until transferred to Company E, 23rd Regiment N.C. Troops (13th Regiment N.C.Volunteers), on or about June 1, 1862.

SATTERWHITE, JAMES A., Private
Born in Granville County where he resided as a farmer prior to enlisting in Granville County at age 26, April 22, 1861. Present or accounted for until discharged on July 30, 1862, by reason of "incipient tuberculosis of the left lung." Roll of Honor indicates that he served also on the staff of Brigadier General Lawrence O'B. Branch.

SHANKS, WILLIAM B., Private
Born in Mecklenburg County and resided in Granville County where he was by occupation a farmer prior to enlisting in Granville County at age 18, April 30, 1861. Present or accounted for until wounded in the "bowels" and captured at Sharpsburg, Maryland, September 17, 1862. Died of wounds. Place and date of death not reported.

SIGMAN, BARNETT, Private
Resided in Cleveland County where he enlisted at age 48, February 26, 1863, for the war. Present or accounted for until wounded at Gettysburg, Pennsylvania, July 1, 1863. Returned to duty in September-December, 1863, and present or accounted for until wounded in both thighs at Spotsylvania Court House, Virginia, May 12, 1864. Reported absent wounded through December, 1864.

SKINNER, WILLIAM H., Private
Resided in Granville County and enlisted at age 18, October 20, 1862, for the war. Discharged at an unspecified date by reason of disability.

SMITH, BALTHROP, Private
Resided in Granville County and was by occupation a tailor prior to enlisting in Granville County at age 18, April 22, 1861. Present or accounted for until wounded in the shoulder at Gettysburg, Pennsylvania, July 1, 1863. Returned to duty prior to September 1, 1863, and present or accounted for until captured at or near Winchester, Virginia, July 20, 1864. Confined at Camp Chase, Ohio, until released on June 10, 1865, after taking the Oath of Allegiance.

SMITH, JOHN, Private
Born in Granville County where he resided as a carpenter or miller prior to enlisting in Granville County at age 34, April 22, 1861. Present or accounted for until discharged at Richmond, Virginia, July 16, 1862, by reason of being over age.

SMITH, JOHN, Musician
Enlisted at Norfolk, Virginia, January 8, 1862. Mustered in as Musician. Present or accounted for through February, 1862. No further records.

SMITH, THOMAS M., Sergeant
Resided in Granville County and enlisted at age 27, April 22, 1861. Mustered in as Sergeant. No further records.

SMITHWICK, JAMES R., Corporal
Resided in Warren County and was by occupation a farmer prior to enlisting in Warren County at age 37, May 4, 1861. Mustered in as Private and promoted to Corporal on June 20, 1861. Present or accounted for until discharged on July 11, 1862, by

reason of being over age.

STONE, D. B., Private
Previously served in Company E, 23rd Regiment N.C. Troops (13th Regiment N.C. Volunteers). Transferred to this company on or about August 6, 1862. Present or accounted for until wounded in the side and captured at Gettysburg, Pennsylvania, July 1, 1863. Hospitalized at Gettysburg until transferred to Davids Island, New York Harbor, July 17-24, 1863. Paroled at Davids Island and transferred to City Point, Virginia, where he was received September 8, 1863, for exchange. Returned to duty in January-February, 1864. Present or accounted for until hospitalized at Danville, Virginia, April 3, 1865, with a gunshot wound of the scalp; however, place and date wounded not reported. Furloughed for thirty days on April 9, 1865.

STONE, ROBERT F., Private
Previously served in Captain Cooper's Company, Virginia Light Artillery. Transferred to this company on or about February 10, 1864. Present or accounted for until reported absent wounded on company muster roll dated April 30-October 31, 1864; however, place and date wounded not reported. Hospital records indicate he was wounded in the thigh and was permanently disabled.

STONE, THOMAS W., Corporal
Resided in Granville County and was by occupation a saddler prior to enlisting in Granville County at age 24, April 30, 1861. Mustered in as Private. Present or accounted for until wounded at Fredericksburg, Virginia, December 13, 1862. Returned to duty in March-April, 1863, and was wounded in the leg at Chancellorsville, Virginia, May 3, 1863. Nominated for the Badge of Distinction for gallantry at Chancellorsville. Promoted to Corporal in May-June, 1863. Returned to duty prior to July 1, 1863, and was captured at or near Gettysburg, Pennsylvania, on or about July 1-3, 1863. Exchanged prior to August 31, 1863. Present or accounted for until wounded in the left shoulder at Spotsylvania Court House, Virginia, May 12, 1864. Reported absent wounded until discharged on or about January 27, 1865, by reason of wounds received at Spotsylvania Court House.

STOVALL, WILKINS, Private
Born in Granville County where he resided as a farmer prior to enlisting in Granville County at age 25, April 30, 1861. Present or accounted for until appointed 3rd Lieutenant on or about May 6, 1862, and transferred to Company K, 55th Regiment N.C Troops.

SWIFT, GEORGE W., Private
Was by occupation a farmer prior to enlisting in Granville County at age 20, April 30, 1861. Present or accounted for until he "disappeared mysteriously" on February 18, 1862.

TAMONI, PHILIP, Private
Born in Switzerland and resided in Virginia prior to enlisting at Richmond, Virginia, at age 35, July 5, 1862, for the war as a substitute. Present or accounted for until wounded and captured at Gettysburg, Pennsylvania, July 1-5, 1863. Confined at Fort Delaware, Delaware, through September 5, 1863.

Released at an unspecified date after joining the U.S. service. Assigned to Company D, 3rd Regiment Maryland Cavalry.

TAYLOR, JAMES H., Private
Resided in Granville County and was by occupation a farmer prior to enlisting in Granville County at age 22, April 22, 1861. Present or accounted for until reported transferred to the 54th Regiment N.C. Troops at an unspecified date; however, records of the 54th Regiment do not indicate that he served therein. No further records.

TERRY, J. C., Private
Enlisted in Wake County on July 4, 1864, for the war. Present or accounted for until paroled at Appomattox Court House, Virginia, April 9, 1865.

TERRY, STEPHEN D., Private
Resided in Granville County and was by occupation a farmer prior to enlisting in Granville County at age 22, May 7, 1861. Present or accounted for until hospitalized at Richmond, Virginia, April 2, 1864, with "variola." Died at Richmond on or about April 15, 1864.

THARINGTON, W. W., Private
Enlisted in Wake County on August 25, 1864, for the war. Captured at Fisher's Hill, Virginia, September 22, 1864, and confined at Point Lookout, Maryland, until paroled and transferred to Boulware's and Cox's Wharf, James River, Virginia, where he was received February 20-21, 1865, for exchange. Reported present with a detachment of paroled and exchanged prisoners at Camp Lee, near Richmond, Virginia, February 28, 1865.

THOMAS, ROBERT, Private
Born in Granville County where he resided as a medical student prior to enlisting in Granville County at age 20, April 22, 1861. Present or accounted for through August, 1864; however, he was reported absent on various medical details during most of that period.

THOMPSON, JOSEPH, Private
Enlisted in Wake County on September 22, 1864, for the war. Present or accounted for until he was listed as a deserter on company muster roll dated November-December, 1864.

THORP, PETERSON, Jr., Private
Resided in Granville County and was by occupation a farmer prior to enlisting in Granville County at age 22, April 22, 1861. Present or accounted for until transferred to Company K, 55th Regiment N.C. Troops, August 4, 1862.

TUNSTALL, R. A., Private
Enlisted in Wake County on October 1, 1864, for the war. Present or accounted for through October, 1864, but deserted prior to January 1, 1865.

VAUGHN, ALEXANDER, Private
Was by occupation a farmer prior to enlisting in Granville County at age 20, April 30, 1861. Not listed on the rolls of this company after June 30, 1861. No further records.

VAUGHN, ANDREW, Private
Born in Granville County or in Mecklenburg County, Virginia, and resided in Granville County prior to enlisting in Wake County at age 20, May 5, 1861.

Present or accounted for until he died in hospital at Richmond, Virginia, on or about June 17, 1862, of disease.

WATSON, JOHN G., Private
Resided in Granville County where he enlisted at age 26, April 30, 1861. Present or accounted for until he died in hospital at Lynchburg, Virginia, January 15, 1863, of disease.

WEAVER, GEORGE W., Private
Resided in Granville County and was by occupation a farmer prior to enlisting in Granville County at age 25, April 22, 1861. Present or accounted for through December, 1864; however, he was reported absent on detail in the Pioneer Corps during much of that period.

WEBB, WILLIAM H., Jr., Private
Resided in Granville County and was by occupation a farmer prior to enlisting at Norfolk, Virginia, at age 20, May 30, 1861. Present or accounted for until appointed 2nd Lieutenant and transferred to Company K, 55th Regiment N.C. Troops on or about May 6, 1862.

WEBB, WILLIAM P., Private
Resided in Granville County and was by occupation a farmer prior to enlisting in Granville County at age 23, April 30, 1861. Present or accounted for until he died on November 1, 1861, of disease. Place of death not reported.

WHISNANT, JOHN, Private
Resided in Cleveland County and enlisted in Burke County at age 26, February 28, 1863, for the war. Present or accounted for until discharged on April 30, 1863, by reason of disability.

WIGGINS, JAMES, Private
Born in Granville County where he resided as a clerk prior to enlisting in Granville County at age 17, May 17, 1861. Present or accounted for until discharged on or about December 11, 1861, by reason of disability.

WIGGINS, JOSEPH, Private
Resided in Granville County and was by occupation a clerk prior to enlisting in Granville County at age 19, April 22, 1861. Present or accounted for until he was reported transferred to Company K, 44th Regiment N.C. Troops in June, 1862; however, records of the 44th Regiment do not indicate that he served therein. No further records.

WILKERSON, JAMES, Corporal
Born in Granville County and was by occupation a farmer prior to enlisting in Granville County at age 22, April 22, 1861. Mustered in as Private and promoted to Corporal in March-July, 1862. Present or accounted for until he died on July 31, 1862, of disease. Place of death not reported.

WILLIAMS, CHARLES HENRY, Sergeant
Resided in Granville County and was by occupation a clerk prior to enlisting in Granville County at age 22, April 22, 1861. Mustered in as Private and promoted to Sergeant in January-April, 1865. Present or accounted for until paroled at Appomattox Court House, Virginia, April 9, 1865.

WILLIAMS, JOHN, Private
Resided in Virginia and enlisted at Richmond, Vir-

ginia, at age 45, August 19, 1862, for the war as a substitute. Deserted the same day.

WILLIAMS, PLUMMER H., Private
Resided in Granville County and was by occupation a farmer prior to enlisting in Granville County at age 21, April 30, 1861. Present or accounted for until he died at Guinea Station, Virginia, May 7, 1863, of disease.

WILLIAMS, ROBERT, Private
Enlisted in Wake County on July 4, 1864, for the war. Present or accounted for through December, 1864.

WILLIAMS, ROBERT A., Private
Resided in Granville County and enlisted at Norfolk, Virginia, at age 25, March 4, 1862. Present or accounted for until wounded in the left hand and/or left arm at Williamsport, Maryland, July 9, 1863. Reported absent wounded until he was detailed for "conscript duty" in March-April, 1864. Reported absent on detail through January 18, 1865.

WILLIAMS, SAMUEL T., Corporal
Resided in Granville County and was by occupation an editor prior to enlisting in Granville County at age 23, May 14, 1861. Mustered in as Private and was promoted to Corporal prior to October 31, 1861, when he was appointed Assistant Commissary of Subsistence (Captain) and transferred to the Field and Staff of this regiment. Rejoined the company in July-August, 1863, with the rank of Private after the position of Assistant Commissary of Subsistence was abolished. Present or accounted for through December, 1864.

WILSON, WILLIAM R., Private
Resided in Granville County and was by occupation a physician prior to enlisting in Granville County at age 23, April 30, 1861. Present or accounted for until appointed Assistant Surgeon on or about August 1, 1861, and transferred to the 24th Regiment N.C.Troops (14th Regiment N.C.Volunteers).

WOOD, RICHARD S., Private
Was by occupation a farmer prior to enlisting in Granville County at age 33, May 7, 1861. Present or accounted for until discharged on January 25, 1862. Reason discharged not reported.

YANCEY, P. H., Private
Resided in Granville County and enlisted at age 20, April 22, 1861. Company records indicate that he was transferred to the 23rd Regiment N.C.Troops (13th Regiment N.C.Volunteers) at an unspecified date; however, records of the 23rd Regiment do not substantiate that report. No further records.

YANCEY, S. P., Private
Enlisted at Richmond, Virginia, July 6, 1862, for the war. Present or accounted for until wounded in the right arm and captured at Gettysburg, Pennsylvania, July 1-3, 1863. Right arm amputated. Died in hospital at Gettysburg on July 26, 1863, of "pyemia."

YORK, JASPER E., Private
Enlisted in Granville County on February 1, 1864, for the war. Present or accounted for until hospitalized at Richmond, Virginia, April 17, 1864, with a gunshot wound of the right ankle. Date of wound given as March 22, 1864. Reported absent wounded

until he returned to duty on November 29, 1864. Present or accounted for through December, 1864.

YORK, JOHN W., Private
Resided in Granville County and was by occupation a farmer prior to enlisting at Norfolk, Virginia, at age 21, June 17, 1861. Present or accounted for through December, 1864; however, he was reported absent on detail during most of that period. Captured in hospital at Richmond, Virginia, April 3, 1865. Paroled at Richmond on April 17, 1865.

YOUNG, WILLIAM H., Corporal
Resided in Granville County and was by occupation a lawyer prior to enlisting in Granville County at age 24, April 22, 1861. Mustered in as Private and promoted to Corporal prior to June 7, 1861, when he was transferred to the C. S. Navy.

COMPANY E

This company, known as the "Cleveland Guards," was raised in Cleveland County and enlisted at Shelby on April 22, 1861. It tendered its service to the state and was ordered to Garysburg, where it was assigned to this regiment. The company was mustered in as Captain Augustus W. Burton's Company and was designated Company D, Company H, and Company I, before it was designated Company E. After it was mustered into the regiment the company functioned as a part of the regiment, and its history for the war period is recorded as a part of the regimental history.

The information contained in the following roster of the company was compiled principally from company muster rolls for April 22, 1861-February, 1862; April 30-October 31, 1862; and December 31, 1862-December, 1864. No company muster rolls were found for March 1-April 29, 1862; November 1-December 30, 1862; or for the period after December, 1864. In addition to the company muster rolls, Roll of Honor records, receipt rolls, hospital records, prisoner of war records, and other primary records, supplemented by state pension applications, United Daughters of the Confederacy records, and postwar rosters and histories, all provided useful information.

OFFICERS
CAPTAINS

BURTON, AUGUSTUS W.
Resided in Cleveland County and was by occupation a lawyer prior to enlisting in Cleveland County at age 32. Appointed Captain on April 23, 1861. Elected Major on May 14, 1861, and transferred to the Field and Staff of this regiment.

FULTON, JEROME B.
Resided in Cleveland County and was by occupation a clerk prior to enlisting in Cleveland County at age 30, April 22, 1861. Mustered in as Corporal and was elected Captain on May 20, 1861. Present or accounted for until he was defeated for reelection when the regiment was reorganized on May 1, 1862.

JENKINS, JESSE
Resided in Cleveland County and was by occupation

a merchant prior to enlisting in Cleveland County at age 29. Appointed 2nd Lieutenant to rank from April 22, 1861, and was promoted to Captain on May 1, 1862. Present or accounted for until wounded in the right thigh at Gaines' Mill, Virginia, June 27, 1862. Returned to duty prior to November 1, 1862, but resigned on or about November 19, 1862, by reason of wounds received at Gaines' Mill.

GIDNEY, JOHN W.

Resided in Cleveland County and was by occupation a lawyer prior to enlisting in Cleveland County at age 22, May 16, 1861. Mustered in as Private and was elected 1st Lieutenant to rank from May 1, 1862. Promoted to Captain on November 19, 1862. Present or accounted for until he resigned on September 20, 1864, by reason of having been elected to the House of Commons of the North Carolina General Assembly. Resignation accepted October 27, 1864.

DURHAM, PLATO

Resided in Rutherford or Cleveland counties and was by occupation a law student prior to enlisting in Cleveland County at age 21, June 18, 1861. Mustered in as Private and was elected 3rd Lieutenant to rank from November 1, 1862. Promoted to 1st Lieutenant on November 19, 1862, and was promoted to Captain on October 27, 1864. Present or accounted for until paroled at Appomattox Court House, Virginia, April 9, 1865.

LIEUTENANTS

DURHAM, CICERO A., 1st Lieutenant

Resided in Cleveland County and was by occupation a cadet prior to enlisting in Cleveland County at age 17. Appointed 1st Lieutenant to rank from April 22, 1861. Present or accounted for until he was defeated for reelection when the regiment was reorganized on May 1, 1862. Later served as Adjutant of the 49th Regiment N.C. Troops.

HARDIN, IRVIN J., 2nd Lieutenant

Born in Cleveland County* where he resided as a farmer prior to enlisting in Cleveland County at age 23, April 22, 1861. Mustered in as Private and appointed 2nd Lieutenant to rank from May 1, 1862. Present or accounted for until he died in hospital at Richmond, Virginia, August 12, 1862, of "typhoid fever."

HOKE, PHILOW PETER, 2nd Lieutenant

Resided in Cleveland County and was by occupation a saddler prior to enlisting in Cleveland County at age 33. Appointed 2nd Lieutenant to rank from April 22, 1861. Present or accounted for until he was defeated for reelection when the regiment was reorganized on May 1, 1862.

LOGAN, BENJAMIN F., 1st Lieutenant

Resided in Cleveland County and was by occupation a clerk prior to enlisting in Cleveland County at age 19, April 22, 1861. Mustered in as Private and promoted to Corporal on August 31, 1861. Promoted to 1st Sergeant on May 1, 1862, and was elected 3rd Lieutenant on January 13, 1863. Promoted to 1st Lieutenant on October 27, 1864. Present or accounted for until paroled at Appomattox Court House, Virginia, April 9, 1865.

MILLER, DAVID M., 2nd Lieutenant

Born in Cleveland County where he resided as a clerk prior to enlisting in Cleveland County at age 20, April 22, 1861. Mustered in as Corporal and promoted to Sergeant on October 10, 1861. Appointed 2nd Lieutenant to rank from May 1, 1862. Present or accounted for until killed at Malvern Hill, Virginia, July 1, 1862.

NONCOMMISSIONED OFFICERS AND PRIVATES

ADAMS, ROBERT L., Private

Resided in Cleveland County and was by occupation a wheelwright prior to enlisting in Cleveland County at age 33, April 22, 1861. Present or accounted for until killed at Gettysburg, Pennsylvania, July 1, 1863.

BARRY, ROBERT S., Private

Born in Lancaster District, South Carolina, and resided in Cleveland County where he was by occupation a harness maker prior to enlisting in Cleveland County at age 34, April 22, 1861. Present or accounted for until hospitalized at Richmond, Virginia, July 2, 1862, with a gunshot wound; however, place and date wounded not reported. Discharged on or about July 21, 1862, by reason of being over age.

BEAM, A. R., Private

Resided in Cleveland County where he enlisted at age 23, April 22, 1861. Discharged on May 15, 1861, by reason of disability.

BEAM, J. C., Private

Resided in Cleveland County where he enlisted at age 18, April 22, 1861. Discharged on May 15, 1861, by reason of disability.

BEAM, JOHN M., Private

Resided in Cleveland County and was by occupation a farmer prior to enlisting in Cleveland County at age 26, April 22, 1861. Present or accounted for until he died in hospital at Richmond, Virginia, on October 4, 1863, of "typhoid fever."

BIGGERS, ZIMRI P., Private

Resided in Cleveland County and was by occupation a carpenter prior to enlisting in Cleveland County at age 26, April 22, 1861. Present or accounted for until discharged on March 23, 1863, by reason of disability. North Carolina pension records indicate that he lost his sight in one eye as a result of wounds received at Bunker Hill, Virginia, in January, 1863.

BLACKWELL, EDWARD W., Private

Born in Prince George County, Virginia, and resided in Cleveland County where he was by occupation a tailor prior to enlisting in Cleveland County at age 35, April 22, 1861. Present or accounted for until discharged on or about July 21, 1862, by reason of being over age.

BLANTON, CHARLES P., Private

Born in Cleveland County* where he resided as a farmer prior to enlisting in Cleveland County at age 21, August 12, 1861. Present or accounted for until he died in hospital at Richmond, Virginia, June 14, 1862, of "feb[ris] typh[oid]."

BLANTON, JOHN BROADUS, Private
Resided in Cleveland County where he enlisted at age 23, August 12, 1861. Present or accounted for until wounded in the left thigh and captured at Gettysburg, Pennsylvania, July 1-4, 1863. Hospitalized at Gettysburg until transferred to Davids Island, New York Harbor, July 17-24, 1863. Paroled at Davids Island and transferred to City Point, Virginia, where he was received September 8, 1863, for exchange. Returned to duty in January-February, 1864, and present or accounted for until wounded at Cedar Creek, Virginia, October 19, 1864. Reported absent wounded through December, 1864.

BLANTON, WILLIAM A., Private
Born in Cleveland County* where he resided as a farmer prior to enlisting in Cleveland County at age 21, June 23, 1861. Present or accounted for until he died at Lynchburg, Virginia, July 3, 1862, of "typhoid fever."

BLANTON, WILLIAM C., Private
Born in Cleveland County* where he resided as a farmer prior to enlisting in Cleveland County at age 21, April 22, 1861. Present or accounted for until killed at Hanover Court House, Virginia, May 27, 1862.

BOSTICK, W. H., Private
Enlisted in Cleveland County on August 22, 1864, for the war. Present or accounted for until paroled at Appomattox Court House, Virginia, April 9, 1865.

BRIDGES, SAMUEL J., Private
Born in Cleveland County* where he resided as a farmer prior to enlisting in Cleveland County at age 30, August 12, 1861. Present or accounted for until he died in hospital at Staunton, Virginia, October 14, 1864, of "chronic diarrhoea."

BRIDGES, ZACHARIAH, Private
Resided in Cleveland County where he enlisted at age 22, July 29, 1861. Present or accounted for through December, 1864.

BROCK, HENRY N., Private
Resided in Union District, South Carolina, and enlisted in Catawba County on May 1, 1864, for the war. Present or accounted for until hospitalized at Danville, Virginia, May 18, 1864, with a gunshot wound of the shoulder; however, place and date wounded not reported. Returned to duty prior to September 1, 1864, and present or accounted for until captured near Petersburg, Virginia, March 25, 1865. Confined at Point Lookout, Maryland, until released on June 24, 1865, after taking the Oath of Allegiance.

BROOKES, DAVID M., Private
Resided in Cleveland County and was by occupation a farmer prior to enlisting in Cleveland County at age 23, April 22, 1861. Present or accounted for until hospitalized at Richmond, Virginia, July 2, 1862, with a gunshot wound; however, place and date wounded not reported. Returned to duty July 7, 1862, and present or accounted for until captured at Spotsylvania Court House, Virginia, May 12, 1864. Confined at Point Lookout, Maryland, until transferred to Elmira, New York, August 10, 1864. Paroled at Elmira and transferred to James

River, Virginia, February 20, 1865, for exchange. No further records.

BROWN, ROBERT G., Sergeant
Resided in Cleveland County and was by occupation a farmer prior to enlisting in Cleveland County at age 21, April 22, 1861. Mustered in as Private and promoted to Sergeant on January 14, 1863. Present or accounted for until wounded at Winchester, Virginia, September 19, 1864. Returned to duty prior to January 1, 1865, and present or accounted for until paroled at Appomattox Court House, Virginia, April 9, 1865.

CABANESS, NAPOLEON B., Private
Born in Cleveland County where he resided as a farmer prior to enlisting in Cleveland County at age 20, April 22, 1861. Present or accounted for until he died in hospital at Richmond, Virginia, July 7, 1862, of "typhoid fever."

CABANISS, JAMES P., Private
Born in Cleveland County* where he resided as a farmer prior to enlisting in Cleveland County at age 22, April 22, 1861. Mustered in as Private and promoted to Corporal on October 10, 1861. Reduced to ranks on August 15, 1863. Present or accounted for through December, 1864.

CHANDLER, W. M. L., Private
Enlisted in Wake County at age 18, March 14, 1864, for the war. Present or accounted for until hospitalized at Richmond, Virginia, May 17, 1864, with a gunshot wound of the thigh; however, place and date wounded not reported. Died in hospital at Staunton, Virginia, on or about November 13, 1864, of disease.

CHAPMAN, WILLIAM L., 1st Sergeant
Resided in Cleveland County and was by occupation a farmer prior to enlisting in Cleveland County at age 23, April 22, 1861. Mustered in as Private and promoted to Corporal on January 1, 1863. Promoted to 1st Sergeant on May 2, 1863. Present or accounted for until wounded in the leg at Chancellorsville, Virginia, May 3, 1863. Returned to duty prior to July 1, 1863. Present or accounted for until reported absent wounded on company muster roll dated May 1-August 31, 1864; however, place and date wounded not reported. Reported absent wounded through December, 1864. Hospitalized at Charlotte on January 17, 1865, with a gunshot wound of the "upper left extremities." Place and date wounded not reported. Returned to duty February 9, 1865.

CLINE, AMBROSE, Private
Resided in Cleveland County where he enlisted at age 22, August 5, 1861. Present or accounted for until wounded in the hand at Chancellorsville, Virginia, May 2, 1863. Returned to duty prior to July 1, 1863, and present or accounted for until wounded in the elbow and captured at Winchester, Virginia, September 19, 1864. Arm amputated. Died in hospital at Winchester on October 14, 1864, of "pyaemia."

CLINE, LABIN WILSON, Private
Enlisted in Catawba County at age 17, March 10, 1864, for the war. Present or accounted for until reported absent wounded on company muster roll dated May 1-August 31, 1864; however, battle in

which wounded not reported. Reported absent wounded through December, 1864. North Carolina pension records indicate he was wounded in July, 1864. Other records indicate he was wounded at Spotsylvania Court House, Virginia; at Strasburg, Virginia; and at Appomattox Court House, Virginia.

COLLINS, JOHN M., Private
Previously served in Company E, 34th Regiment N.C.Troops. Transferred to this company on April 16, 1863, in exchange for Private Devany Putman. Present or accounted for until wounded in the thigh and captured at Gettysburg, Pennsylvania, July 1-3, 1863. Hospitalized at Gettysburg until confined at Fort Delaware, Delaware, on or about July 12, 1863. Exchanged on or about July 31, 1863. Rejoined the company prior to January 15, 1864, and present or accounted for through December, 1864.

CONNER, JAMES B., Private
Born in Cleveland County where he resided as a farmer prior to enlisting in Cleveland County at age 20, August 12, 1861. Present or accounted for until he died in hospital at Richmond, Virginia, on or about July 6, 1862, of "fever."

CONNER, PHILLIP H., Private
Enlisted in Cleveland County at age 18, February 27, 1864, for the war. Present or accounted for until captured at Spotsylvania Court House, Virginia, May 12, 1864. Confined at Point Lookout, Maryland, until transferred to Elmira, New York, August 10, 1864. Paroled at Elmira and transferred to James River, Virginia, March 2, 1865, for exchange. Hospitalized at Richmond, Virginia, March 9, 1865. North Carolina pension records indicate that he survived the war.

CORNWALL, FRANKLIN M., Private
Resided in Cleveland County and was by occupation a farmer prior to enlisting in Cleveland County at age 21, May 16, 1861. Present or accounted for until killed at Spotsylvania Court House, Virginia, May 13, 1864.

CORNWELL, AMOS H., Private
Enlisted in Cleveland County at age 18, February 3, 1864, for the war. Present or accounted for until captured at Cedar Creek, Virginia, October 19, 1864. Confined at Point Lookout, Maryland, until paroled and transferred to Boulware's and Cox's Wharf, James River, Virginia, February 20-21, 1865, for exchange. Reported present with a detachment of paroled and exchanged prisoners at Camp Lee, near Richmond, February 23, 1865.

CORNWELL, JAMES J., Private
Resided in Cleveland County where he enlisted at age 24, August 12, 1861. Present or accounted for until wounded at Gaines' Mill, Virginia, June 27, 1862. Returned to duty prior to July 1, 1862, and present or accounted for until wounded in the shoulder at Chancellorsville, Virginia, May 2, 1863. Returned to duty prior to July 1, 1863, and present or accounted for until wounded in the right side of the chest and captured at Spotsylvania Court House, Virginia, May 12, 1864. Hospitalized at Washington, D.C., and was confined at Old Capitol Prison, Washington, August 23, 1864. Transferred to Elmira, New York, August 28, 1864. Released at Elmira on June 19, 1865, after taking the Oath of Allegiance.

COSTNER, JAMES, Private
Resided in Cleveland County and was by occupation a farmer prior to enlisting in Cleveland County at age 21, April 22, 1861. Present or accounted for until wounded at Gaines' Mill, Virginia, June 27, 1862. Hospitalized at Richmond, Virginia, where he died on or about September 25, 1862, of "jaundice fol[lowing] wounds."

CRITES, WILLIAM C., Private
Previously served in Company E, 34th Regiment N.C.Troops. Transferred to this company on June 8, 1863, in exchange for Private Andrew C. Fulenwider. Present or accounted for until wounded in the back at Morton's Ford, Virginia, October 11, 1863. Returned to duty prior to January 15, 1864, and present or accounted for until captured at Winchester, Virginia, July 20, 1864. Confined at Camp Chase, Ohio, until released on or about May 8, 1865, after taking the Oath of Allegiance.

CROWDER, SIDNEY A., Private
Resided in Cleveland County and was by occupation a tailor prior to enlisting in Cleveland County at age 22, April 22, 1861. Present or accounted for until killed at Chancellorsville, Virginia, May 1, 1863.

DALTON, JOHN W., Private
Resided in Cleveland County and was by occupation a farmer prior to enlisting in Cleveland County at age 23, April 22, 1861. Present or accounted for until discharged on May 14, 1862, by reason of disability.

DAVIS, J. E., Private
Previously served in Company F of this regiment. Transferred to this company on November 1, 1864. Present or accounted for until paroled at Appomattox Court House, Virginia, April 9, 1865.

DEAL, JACOB AUGUSTUS, Sergeant
Resided in Cleveland County where he enlisted at age 23, April 22, 1861. Mustered in as Private and promoted to Sergeant in March-April, 1862. Promoted to Ordnance Sergeant on May 7, 1862, and transferred to the Field and Staff of this regiment.

DELLINGER, MOSES P., Sergeant
Resided in Cleveland County and was by occupation a carpenter prior to enlisting in Cleveland County at age 27, April 22, 1861. Mustered in as Private and promoted to Corporal on July 1, 1862. Present or accounted for until reported in confinement at Fort Delaware, Delaware, October 2, 1862; however, place and date captured not reported. Transferred to Aiken's Landing, James River, Virginia, October 2, 1862, for exchange. Declared exchanged at Aiken's Landing on November 10, 1862. Promoted to Sergeant on January 1, 1863. Present or accounted for until captured at Chancellorsville, Virginia, May 3, 1863. Exchanged on May 10, 1863. Present or accounted for until wounded at Morton's Ford, Virginia, October 11, 1863. Reported absent wounded or absent on detail through December, 1864.

DELLINGER, PETER, Private
Resided in Gaston County and enlisted in Cleveland County at age 36, March 15, 1863, for the war. Present or accounted for until hospitalized at Charlottesville, Virginia, September 1, 1864, "while convalescing from typhoid fever." Died at Charlottesville

on September 19, 1864, of "measles."

DELLINGER, WILLIAM, Private
Resided in Cleveland County and was by occupation a carpenter prior to enlisting in Cleveland County at age 25, May 23, 1861. Present or accounted for until captured at or near Williamsport, Maryland, on or about September 17, 1862. Exchanged at Aiken's Landing, James River, Virginia, on or about October 6, 1862. Present or accounted for through December, 1864.

DOGGETT, JAMES R. R., Private
Born in Cleveland County where he resided as a farmer prior to enlisting in Cleveland County at age 18, August 12, 1861. Present or accounted for until he died in hospital at Richmond, Virginia, July 10, 1862, of "typhoid fever."

DOGGETT, MINOR W., Sergeant
Born in Cleveland County* where he resided as a farmer prior to enlisting in Cleveland County at age 21, April 22, 1861. Mustered in as Corporal and promoted to Sergeant on October 10, 1861. Present or accounted for until hospitalized at Richmond, Virginia, June 29, 1862, with a gunshot wound of the left hand; however, place and date wounded not reported. Returned to duty prior to November 1, 1862, but was discharged on or about December 8, 1862, by reason of disability from wounds.

DORITY, MARCUS A., Private
Resided in Cleveland County and was by occupation a farmer prior to enlisting in Cleveland County at age 24, April 22, 1861. Present or accounted for until reported absent wounded on company muster roll dated April 30-October 31, 1864; however, place and date wounded not reported. Reported absent wounded through December, 1864. Captured at Petersburg, Virginia, March 25, 1865, and confined at Point Lookout, Maryland, until released on June 26, 1865, after taking the Oath of Allegiance.

DURHAM, BENJAMIN H., Private
Born in Cleveland County where he resided as a farmer prior to enlisting in Cleveland County at age 17, April 22, 1861. Present or accounted for until he died at Fort Nelson, Virginia, or at Portsmouth, Virginia, August 12, 1861, of disease.

DURHAM, CHARLES C., Private
Resided in Cleveland County and was by occupation a farmer prior to enlisting in Cleveland County at age 47, April 22, 1861. Present or accounted for until discharged on May 3, 1862, by reason of being over age.

DURHAM, CHARLES J., Private
Resided in Cleveland County where he enlisted at age 24, May 1, 1862, for the war. Present or accounted for until wounded at Gettysburg, Pennsylvania, July 1, 1863. Died July 13, 1863, of wounds. Place of death not reported.

DURHAM, COLUMBUS, Private
Resided in Rutherford County and was by occupation a farmer prior to enlisting in Cleveland County at age 17, April 22, 1861. Present or accounted for until wounded in the hand at Chancellorsville, Virginia, May 2, 1863. Returned to duty prior to July 1, 1863. Present or accounted for until hospitalized at Richmond, Virginia, February 10, 1865, with a gunshot wound of the left leg; however, place and date wounded not reported. Returned to duty on February 17, 1865, and present or accounted for until paroled at Appomattox Court House, Virginia, April 9, 1865.

DURHAM, LEMUEL N., Private
Resided in Cleveland County and was by occupation a dentist prior to enlisting in Cleveland County at age 29, April 22, 1861. Mustered in as Corporal but was reduced to ranks on April 30, 1862. Present or accounted for until discharged on May 7, 1862, by reason of disability.

DURHAM, RICHARD JOHN, Private
Resided in Cleveland County and was by occupation a farmer prior to enlisting in Cleveland County at age 16, April 22, 1861. Present or accounted for until discharged on May 3, 1862, by reason of being under age.

DURHAM, SEATON G., Private
Born in Cleveland County* where he resided as a merchant prior to enlisting in Cleveland County at age 23, April 22, 1861. Present or accounted for until killed at Gaines' Mill, Virginia, June 27, 1862.

DURHAM, SEPIO E., Private
Resided in Rutherford County and was by occupation a farmer prior to enlisting in Cleveland County at age 19, April 22, 1861. Present or accounted for until he died in hospital at Portsmouth, Virginia, October 22, 1861, of disease.

ELMORE, JAMES, Private
Resided in Cleveland County and was by occupation a farmer prior to enlisting in Cleveland County at age 23, April 22, 1861. Present or accounted for until September-October, 1863, when he was reported "under arrest" charged with "misbehaviour before the enemy." Court-martialed on or about December 26, 1863, but returned to duty in January-February, 1864. Present or accounted for until captured near Petersburg, Virginia, March 25, 1865. Confined at Point Lookout, Maryland, until released on June 11, 1865, after taking the Oath of Allegiance.

ESKRIDGE, GARDNER M., Private
Born in Cleveland County* where he resided as a farmer prior to enlisting in Cleveland County at age 23, August 12, 1861. Present or accounted for until hospitalized at Richmond, Virginia, June 28, 1862, with "rubeola." Died in hospital at Richmond on July 7, 1862, of "fever."

ESKRIDGE, JOHN H., Private
Born in Cleveland County* where he resided as a farmer prior to enlisting in Cleveland County at age 23, April 22, 1861. Present or accounted for until he died in hospital at Richmond, Virginia, July 10, 1862, of "typhoid fever."

ESKRIDGE, JOHN J. G., Private
Resided in Cleveland County and was by occupation a farmer prior to enlisting in Cleveland County at age 20, April 22, 1861. Present or accounted for until he died in hospital at Richmond, Virginia, August 1, 1862, of "typhoid fever."

ESKRIDGE, M., Private
Enlisted in Cleveland County at age 17, on or about April 22, 1861. No further records.

ESKRIDGE, WILLIAM HARRISON H., Private
Resided in Cleveland County and was by occupation a farmer prior to enlisting in Cleveland County at age 21, May 16, 1861. Present or accounted for until wounded in the right arm and captured at Fisher's Hill, Virginia, September 22, 1864. Right arm amputated. Hospitalized at various Federal hospitals until confined at Fort McHenry, Maryland, December 9, 1864. Transferred to Point Lookout, Maryland, January 2, 1865. Released at Point Lookout on June 3, 1865, after taking the Oath of Allegiance.

FRIDDLE, THOMAS A., Private
Enlisted in Burke County at age 18, February 19, 1864, for the war. Present or accounted for until paroled at Appomattox Court House, Virginia, April 9, 1865.

FROMBARGER, DAVID, Private
Resided in Cleveland County where he enlisted at age 36, April 22, 1861. Present or accounted for until discharged on June 14, 1861, by reason of disability.

FULENWIDER, ANDREW C., Private
Resided in Cleveland County and was by occupation a clerk prior to enlisting in Cleveland County at age 35, May 15, 1861. Present or accounted for until transferred to Company E, 34th Regiment N.C. Troops, June 8, 1863, in exchange for Private William C. Crites.

FULTON, JEREMIAH W., Sergeant
Resided in Cleveland County and was by occupation a clerk prior to enlisting in Cleveland County at age 20, April 22, 1861. Mustered in as Sergeant. Present or accounted for until discharged on or about June 15, 1862, after furnishing Private Squire S. Simmons as a substitute.

GIDNEY, JONATHAN C., Private
Resided in Cleveland County and was by occupation a doctor prior to enlisting in Cleveland County at age 25, May 16, 1861. Present or accounted for until hospitalized at Richmond, Virginia, May 19, 1864, with a gunshot wound of the right foot; however, place and date wounded not reported. Reported absent wounded or absent on detached service through December, 1864.

GILBERT, W. W., Private
Resided in Cleveland County where he enlisted at age 23, April 22, 1861. Present or accounted for until discharged on May 15, 1861, by reason of disability.

GILLESPIE, WILLIAM F., Private
Born in Cleveland County where he resided as a farmer prior to enlisting in Cleveland County at age 17, May 16, 1861. Present or accounted for until discharged on October 2, 1862, by reason of being under age.

GLASSCOCK, THOMAS J., Private
Resided in Cleveland County where he enlisted at age 23, August 31, 1861. Present or accounted for until he was "shock[ed] by the explosion of a shell" at Chancellorsville, Virginia, May 2, 1863. Returned

to duty prior to July 1, 1863, and present or accounted for until captured at Winchester, Virginia, September 19, 1864. Confined at Point Lookout, Maryland, until paroled and transferred to Venus Point, Savannah River, Georgia, where he was received November 15, 1864, for exchange.

GOLD, MARION B., Private
Resided in Cleveland County and was by occupation a farmer prior to enlisting in Cleveland County at age 18, April 22, 1861. Present or accounted for until wounded at Malvern Hill, Virginia, July 1, 1862. Died at Richmond, Virginia, on or about July 4, 1862, of wounds.

GOLD, WILLIAM C., Private
Resided in Cleveland County where he enlisted at age 21, August 31, 1861. Present or accounted for until he died in hospital at Richmond, Virginia, July 16, 1862, of "rubeola."

GOLD, WILLIAMSON FORTUNE, Corporal
Resided in Cleveland County and was by occupation a farmer prior to enlisting in Cleveland County at age 24, May 16, 1861. Mustered in as Private and promoted to Corporal in August, 1863. Present or accounted for until captured at Fisher's Hill, Virginia, September 22, 1864. Confined at Point Lookout, Maryland, until paroled and transferred to Cox's Landing, James River, Virginia, where he was received February 14-15, 1865, for exchange.

GOODE, D. P., Private
Previously served in Company D, 2nd Regiment N.C. Junior Reserves. Transferred to this company on May 20, 1864. Present or accounted for until wounded in the left leg at Petersburg, Virginia, March 25, 1865. Left leg amputated. Captured in hospital at Richmond, Virginia, April 3, 1865. Confined at Point Lookout, Maryland, May 12, 1865. Released at Point Lookout on June 26, 1865, after taking the Oath of Allegiance.

GOODE, THOMAS FRANKLIN, Private
Born in Cleveland County where he resided as a farmer prior to enlisting in Cleveland County at age 19, May 16, 1861. Present or accounted for until paroled at Farmville, Virginia, April 15, 1865.

GREEN, PETER, Private
Resided in Cleveland County and was by occupation a lawyer prior to enlisting in Cleveland County at age 23, April 22, 1861. Present or accounted for until discharged in May, 1861, by reason of disability.

GREEN, SAMUEL J., Private
Resided in Cleveland County and was by occupation a farmer prior to enlisting in Cleveland County at age 19, April 22, 1861. Mustered in as Private and promoted to Corporal in May-June, 1862. Reduced to ranks on July 1, 1862. Present or accounted for until captured at Williamsport, Maryland, September 15, 1862. Confined at Fort Delaware, Delaware, until transferred to Aiken's Landing, James River, Virginia, October 2, 1862, for exchange. Declared exchanged at Aiken's Landing on November 10, 1862. Discharged on December 1, 1862, after providing Private Absalom Spangler as a substitute.

GREEN, THOMAS F., Private
Resided in Cleveland County and was by occupation

a farmer prior to enlisting in Cleveland County at age 18, April 22, 1861. Present · or accounted for until transferred to Company H, 28th Regiment N.C. Troops, April 2, 1863.

GREEN, W. H., Private
Enlisted in Cleveland County on August 22, 1864, for the war. Present or accounted for until captured at Winchester, Virginia, September 19, 1864. Confined at Baltimore, Maryland. Records of the Federal Provost Marshal give his age as 42. Transferred to James River, Virginia, in February, 1865, for exchange. Hospitalized at Richmond, Virginia, February 25, 1865, and was furloughed for thirty days on March 6, 1865.

GRIGG, LEROY R., Private
Resided in Cleveland County and was by occupation a farmer prior to enlisting in Cleveland County at age 21, April 22, 1861. Present or accounted for until discharged on May 3, 1862, by reason of disability.

HALLMAN, EPHRAIM, Private
Resided in Cleveland County and was by occupation a carpenter prior to enlisting in Cleveland County on April 22, 1861. Present or accounted for until discharged in May, 1861, by reason of disability.

HALLMAN, HOSEA, Private
Resided in Cleveland County where he enlisted on April 22, 1861. Present or accounted for until discharged in June, 1861, by reason of disability.

HALLMAN, VARDRA, Private
Resided in Cleveland County where he enlisted at age 22, April 22, 1861. Present or accounted for until captured at Woodstock, Virginia, October 20, 1864. Confined at Point Lookout, Maryland, until released on May 12, 1865.

HAMRICK, DAVID, Private
Resided in Cleveland County where he enlisted at age 31, July 29, 1861. Present or accounted for until killed at Chancellorsville, Virginia, on or about May 2, 1863.

HAMRICK, ELIJAH, Private
Born in Cleveland County* where he resided as a farmer prior to enlisting in Cleveland County at age 33, April 22, 1861. Present or accounted for until wounded in the side at Chancellorsville, Virginia, May 2, 1863. Returned to duty prior to September 1, 1863, and present or accounted for until paroled at Appomattox Court House, Virginia, April 9, 1865.

HAMRICK, JAMES M., Private
Previously served in Company H, 28th Regiment N.C. Troops. Transferred to this company on April 24, 1863. Present or accounted for until paroled at Appomattox Court House, Virginia, April 9, 1865.

HAMRICK, LEANDER A., Private
Resided in Cleveland County and was by occupation a farmer prior to enlisting in Cleveland County at age 19, April 22, 1861. Present or accounted for until wounded at Gaines' Mill, Virginia, June 27, 1862. Returned to duty on July 7, 1862, and present or accounted for until he died in hospital at Richmond, Virginia, January 4, 1863, of "febris typhoides."

HARDIN, A. C., Private
Enlisted in Cleveland County at age 18, March 31, 1864, for the war. Present or accounted for until he died on July 5, 1864, of disease. Place of death not reported.

HARDIN, CRAYTON, Private
Resided in Cleveland County and was by occupation a laborer prior to enlisting in Cleveland County at age 20, June 18, 1861. Present or accounted for until reported transferred to Company H, 28th Regiment N.C.Troops, April 24, 1863; however, records of the 28th Regiment do not indicate that he served therein. No further records.

HARDIN, JAMES POLK, Private
Born in Cleveland County where he resided as a student prior to enlisting in Cleveland County at age 17, April 22, 1861. Present or accounted for until discharged on or about July 12, 1862, by reason of being under age.

HARMON, PETER B., Private
Resided in Cleveland County and was by occupation a farmer prior to enlisting in Cleveland County at age 23, April 22, 1861. Present or accounted for until paroled at Appomattox Court House, Virginia, April 9, 1865.

HARMON, QUINCY JEFFERSON, Corporal
Born in Cleveland County* where he resided as a farmer prior to enlisting in Cleveland County at age 27, April 22, 1861. Mustered in as Private and promoted to Corporal on May 1, 1862. Present or accounted for until wounded at Gaines' Mill, Virginia, June 27, 1862. Died June 28, 1862, of wounds. Place of death not reported.

HARRELLSON, JOHN J., Private
Born in Lincoln County and resided in Cleveland County where he was by occupation a carpenter prior to enlisting in Cleveland County at age 34, April 22, 1861. Present or accounted for until discharged on or about July 21, 1862, by reason of being over age.

HAWKINS, ASBURY D., Private
Enlisted in Cleveland County at age 32, June 26, 1861. Discharged at Camp Carolina, Virginia, July 1, 1861. Reason discharged not reported.

HAWKINS, JAMES B., Private
Resided in Cleveland County where he enlisted at age 24, July 29, 1861. Present or accounted for until discharged on May 3, 1862, by reason of disability.

HEATHER, WILLIAM, Private
Place and date of enlistment not reported. Captured in hospital at Petersburg, Virginia, April 3, 1865, and was paroled on April 28, 1865.

HENDRICK, THOMAS W., Private
Born in Cleveland County where he resided as a farmer prior to enlisting in Cleveland County at age 18, April 22, 1861. Present or accounted for until killed at Malvern Hill, Virginia, July 1, 1862.

HICKS, JAMES B., Private
Resided in Cleveland County and was by occupation a cabinetmaker prior to enlisting in Cleveland County at age 34, April 22, 1861. Present or accounted for until he died in hospital at Richmond, Virginia, June 17, 1862, of "fever."

HILL, JOSEPH W., Private
Resided in Cleveland County and was by occupation a farmer prior to enlisting in Cleveland County at age 19, April 22, 1861. Present or accounted for until he died in hospital at Portsmouth, Virginia, October 15, 1861, of "fever."

HILL, W. R., Private
Enlisted in Cleveland County on June 1, 1864, for the war. Present or accounted for until paroled at Appomattox Court House, Virginia, April 9, 1865.

HOEY, JOHN E., Sergeant
Resided in Cleveland County and was by occupation a teacher prior to enlisting in Cleveland County at age 26, April 22, 1861. Mustered in as Sergeant. Present or accounted for until discharged in October, 1861. Reason discharged not reported. Later served as Adjutant of the 29th Regiment N.C. Troops.

HOKE, FREDERICK L., Private
Born in Lincoln County and resided in Cleveland County where he was by occupation a tanner or farmer prior to enlisting in Cleveland County at age 40, April 22, 1861. Present or accounted for until discharged on or about July 21, 1862, by reason of being over age.

HOPPER, SAMUEL L., Sergeant
Resided in Cleveland County and was by occupation a clerk prior to enlisting in Cleveland County at age 21, April 22, 1861. Mustered in as Private and promoted to Corporal in January-February, 1862. Promoted to Sergeant on January 1, 1863. Present or accounted for through February 25, 1865.

HORN, W. W., Private
Resided in Cleveland County where he enlisted at age 17, April 12, 1864, for the war. Present or accounted for until captured near Spotsylvania Court House, Virginia, May 12, 1864. Confined at Point Lookout, Maryland, until transferred to Elmira, New York, August 10, 1864. Paroled at Elmira and transferred to Venus Point, Savannah River, Georgia, where he was received November 15, 1864, for exchange. Rejoined the company at an unspecified date. Wounded in the left wrist and captured at Appomattox Court House, Virginia, April 9, 1865. Hospitalized at various Federal hospitals until hospitalized at Washington, D.C., May 2, 1865. Released on or about June 14, 1865, after taking the Oath of Allegiance.

HOWELL, EZEKIEL H., Private
Resided in Cleveland or Lincoln counties and was by occupation a carpenter prior to enlisting in Cleveland County at age 22, April 22, 1861. Present or accounted for until captured at Spotsylvania Court House, Virginia, May 12, 1864. Confined at Point Lookout, Maryland, until transferred to Elmira, New York, August 10, 1864. Released at Elmira on June 23, 1865, after taking the Oath of Allegiance.

HUFFMAN, ALFRED, Private
Enlisted in Catawba County at age 47, April 12, 1864, for the war. Present or accounted for until paroled at Appomattox Court House, Virginia, April 9, 1865.

HUGHES, ANDREW J., Private
Resided in Cleveland County and was by occupation a farmer prior to enlisting in Cleveland County at age 23, April 22, 1861. Present or accounted for until captured at Hanover Court House, Virginia, May 27, 1862. Confined at Fort Monroe, Virginia, and at Fort Columbus, New York Harbor. Exchanged at Aiken's Landing, James River, Virginia, August 5, 1862. Returned to duty prior to March 6, 1863, and present or accounted for until wounded near Morton's Ford, Virginia, October 11, 1863. Returned to duty prior to November 1, 1863, and present or accounted for until wounded in the right shoulder at Spotsylvania Court House, Virginia, May 12, 1864. Reported absent wounded through October, 1864, and was reported absent on detail in November-December, 1864. Paroled at Charlotte on May 3, 1865.

INGOLD, FRANCIS F., Private
Enlisted in Catawba County at age 17, April 28, 1864, for the war. Present or accounted for until mortally wounded at Spotsylvania Court House, Virginia, May 9, 1864.

IRBY, JOSEPH K., Sr., Private
Born in Lincoln County and resided in Cleveland County where he was by occupation a brickmason prior to enlisting in Cleveland County at age 53, April 22, 1861. Present or accounted for until discharged on or about June 17, 1862, by reason of being over age.

IRVIN, AUSTIN, Private
Born in Cleveland County where he resided as a student prior to enlisting in Cleveland County at age 16, April 22, 1861. Present or accounted for until discharged on or about July 12, 1862, by reason of being under age.

JARRETT, M. W., Private
Previously served in Company G of this regiment. Transferred to this company on December 6, 1864. Present or accounted for through December, 1864.

JOLLEY, CRAWFORD D. D., Private
Resided in Cleveland County and was by occupation a farmer prior to enlisting in Cleveland County at age 21, April 22, 1861. Present or accounted for until wounded at Chancellorsville, Virginia, May 3, 1863. Returned to duty prior to July 1, 1863, and present or accounted for until wounded in the left shoulder at Spotsylvania Court House, Virginia, May 12, 1864. Returned to duty prior to September 1, 1864, and present or accounted for until paroled at Appomattox Court House, Virginia, April 9, 1865.

JOLLEY, STANFORD W., Private
Previously served in Company D, 16th Regiment N.C. Troops (6th Regiment N.C. Volunteers). Transferred to this company on or about June 25, 1861. Present or accounted for until wounded in the left arm and left knee at Chancellorsville, Virginia, May 3, 1863. Died in hospital at Richmond, Virginia, June 16, 1863, following an amputation.

JONES, ASBURY N., Private
Resided in Cleveland County where he enlisted at age 20, July 29, 1861. Present or accounted for until wounded in the breast and/or hip at Malvern Hill, Virginia, July 1, 1862. Died in Cleveland County on

August 8, 1862, of wounds.

JONES, EDMUND A., Private
Resided in Cleveland County and was by occupation a farmer prior to enlisting in Cleveland County at age 22, April 22, 1861. Present or accounted for until hospitalized at Richmond, Virginia, July 4, 1862, with a gunshot wound of the left breast; however, place and date wounded not reported. Returned to duty at an unspecified date and was present or accounted for until wounded in the hand at Chancellorsville, Virginia, May 2, 1863. Returned to duty prior to July 1, 1863, and present or accounted for until paroled at Appomattox Court House, Virginia, April 9, 1865.

JONES, HARPER F., Private
Born in Guilford County and resided in Cleveland County where he was by occupation a harness maker prior to enlisting in Cleveland County at age 36, April 22, 1861. Present or accounted for until wounded in the thigh or left knee and captured at Spotsylvania Court House, Virginia, May 12, 1864. Hospitalized at various Federal hospitals until confined at Old Capitol Prison, Washington, D.C., September 7, 1864. Transferred to Fort Delaware, Delaware, September 19, 1864. Paroled and transferred to Aiken's Landing, James River, Virginia, September 30, 1864, for exchange. Present or accounted for through January 27, 1865.

JONES, JAMES C., Private
Resided in Cleveland County where he enlisted at age 18, April 28, 1862. Present or accounted for until wounded in the face and neck at Gaines' Mill, Virginia, June 27, 1862. Hospitalized at Richmond, Virginia, where he died on July 14, 1862, of wounds.

LACKEY, EDWARD J., Private
Born in Cleveland County* where he resided prior to enlisting in Cleveland County at age 24, October 6, 1861. Present or accounted for until wounded in the side at Chancellorsville, Virginia, May 2, 1863. Died at Chancellorsville on May 8, 1863, of wounds.

LAYTON, WILLIAM P., Private
Resided in Cleveland County and was by occupation a carriage maker prior to enlisting in Cleveland County at age 19, April 22, 1861. Present or accounted for until killed at Gettysburg, Pennsylvania, July 1, 1863.

LOGAN, JOHN P., Private
Previously served in 2nd Company E, 5th Regiment South Carolina Infantry. Transferred to this company in January-April, 1863. Present or accounted for until reported absent wounded on company muster roll dated April 30-October 31, 1864; however, place and date wounded not reported. Returned to duty in November-December, 1864, and present or accounted for through December, 1864.

LOGAN, LEONIDAS M., Private
Born in Cleveland County where he resided as a clerk prior to enlisting in Cleveland County at age 18, May 1, 1862, for the war. Present or accounted for until wounded in the right cheek at Malvern Hill, Virginia, July 1, 1862. Returned to duty at an unspecified date prior to March 6, 1863. Present or accounted for until captured near Spotsylvania Court House, Virginia, May 10, 1864. Confined at Point Lookout, Maryland, until transferred to Elmira, New York, August 10, 1864. Released at Elmira on June 16, 1865, after taking the Oath of Allegiance.

LONDON, MONROE, Private
Born in Cleveland County where he resided as a farmer prior to enlisting in Cleveland County at age 18, August 31, 1861. Present or accounted for until killed at Malvern Hill, Virginia, July 1, 1862.

McAFEE, AUGUST A., Private
Resided in Cleveland County where he enlisted on April 22, 1861. Rejected by the mustering officer by reason of general disability. Later served in Company G, 49th Regiment N.C. Troops.

McGINNESS, LARKIN, Private
Born in Cleveland County* where he resided as a farmer prior to enlisting in Cleveland County at age 22, July 29, 1861. Present or accounted for until killed at Gaines' Mill, Virginia, June 27, 1862.

McMULLIN, J. W., Private
Place and date of enlistment not reported. Captured at Harper's Farm, Virginia, April 6, 1865, and confined at Point Lookout, Maryland, until released on June 29, 1865.

McMURRAY, J. M., Private
Resided in Cleveland County where he enlisted on August 22, 1864, for the war. Present or accounted for through December, 1864. Captured by the enemy at an unspecified place and date. Confined at Point Lookout, Maryland, until released on June 29, 1865, after taking the Oath of Allegiance.

McSWAIN, THOMAS, Private
Resided in Cleveland County where he enlisted on August 9, 1864, for the war. Present or accounted for until captured at Amelia Court House, Virginia, April 6, 1865. Confined at Point Lookout, Maryland, until released on June 29, 1865, after taking the Oath of Allegiance.

McSWAIN, WILLIAM M., Private
Resided in Cleveland County and was by occupation a farmer prior to enlisting in Cleveland County at age 35, April 22, 1861. Present or accounted for until discharged on May 3, 1862, by reason of being over age.

MARTIN, W. A. G., Private
Previously served in Company D, 2nd Regiment N.C. Junior Reserves. Transferred to this company on or about May 20, 1864. Present or accounted for until paroled at Appomattox Court House, Virginia, April 9, 1865.

MILLER, ABEL P., Private
Resided in Catawba County where he enlisted at age 18, March 28, 1864, for the war. Present or accounted for until paroled at Appomattox Court House, Virginia, April 9, 1865.

MILLER, G. P., Private
Place and date of enlistment not reported. Paroled at Appomattox Court House, Virginia, April 9, 1865.

MILLER, JOHN FULLENWIDER, Private
Resided in Cleveland County and was by occupation a surgeon prior to enlisting in Cleveland County at

age 30, April 22, 1861. Present or accounted for until appointed Assistant Surgeon and transferred to the Field and Staff of this regiment on May 18, 1861.

MILLER, JONES M., Private

Resided in Catawba County where he enlisted at age 17, March 5, 1864, for the war. Present or accounted for until transferred to Company H, 28th Regiment N.C Troops prior to May 1, 1864.

MILLER, ROBERT, Private

Resided in Catawba County where he enlisted at age 17, April 12, 1864, for the war. Present or accounted for until captured at Harper's Farm, Virginia, April 6, 1865. Confined at Point Lookout, Maryland, until released on June 15, 1865, after taking the Oath of Allegiance.

MOOSE, GEORGE R., Private

Enlisted in Catawba County at age 17, March 10, 1864, for the war. Present or accounted for until paroled at Appomattox Court House, Virginia, April 9, 1865.

MOSS, ARCHIBALD, Private

Enlisted in Cleveland County at age 16, March 12, 1864, for the war. Present or accounted for through October, 1864, but was reported "under arrest" in November-December, 1864. Court-martial records dated January 9, 1865, state that he was charged with attempting to disable himself for military duty by shooting himself in the fingers of the left hand at Spotsylvania Court House, Virginia, May 10, 1864. Private Moss pleaded not guilty to the charges and the outcome of the case is not reported. No further records.

NEAL, JOHN H., Private

Resided in Cleveland County where he enlisted at age 17, July 29, 1861. Present or accounted for until paroled at Appomattox Court House, Virginia, April 9, 1865.

NOWEL, JOHN P., Private

Resided in Cleveland County and was by occupation a tailor prior to enlisting in Cleveland County at age 39, April 22, 1861. Present or accounted for until he was furloughed for seven days in June, 1861. Never rejoined the company. No further records.

OATES, ADDISON T., Private

Resided in Cleveland County and was by occupation a farmer prior to enlisting in Cleveland County at age 18, April 1, 1863, for the war. Present or accounted for until wounded in the thigh and/or left arm at Chancellorsville, Virginia, May 3, 1863. Returned to duty in September-October, 1863, and present or accounted for until paroled at Appomattox Court House, Virginia, April 9, 1865.

OATES, JOHN C., Corporal

Resided in Cleveland County and was by occupation a farmer prior to enlisting in Cleveland County at age 18, April 22, 1861. Mustered in as Private and promoted to Corporal in September-October, 1863. Present or accounted for through February 7, 1865.

OATES, WILLIAM R., Private

Resided in Cleveland County and was by occupation a farmer prior to enlisting in Cleveland County at age 20, April 22, 1861. Present or accounted for

until paroled at Appomattox Court House, Virginia, April 9, 1865.

OSBORNE, JAMES E., Private

Resided in Cleveland County and was by occupation a doctor prior to enlisting in Cleveland County at age 40, April 22, 1861. Present or accounted for until appointed Assistant Surgeon at an unspecified date. Unit to which assigned not reported.

OWENS, TOLIVER C., Private

Born in Cleveland County* where he resided as a cabinetmaker prior to enlisting on April 22, 1861. Present or accounted for until wounded in the left shoulder at Gaines' Mill, Virginia, June 27, 1862. Discharged in July, 1862, by reason of being over age. A company record dated July 1, 1862, gives his age as 36.

POSTON, SAMUEL, Private

Previously served in an unspecified company of this regiment. Transferred to this company on October 28, 1864. Present or accounted for until paroled at Appomattox Court House, Virginia, April 9, 1865. [For additional information see the miscellaneous section for this regiment.]

PUTMAN, DEVANY, Private

Resided in Cleveland County and was by occupation a laborer prior to enlisting in Cleveland County at age 26, June 9, 1861. Present or accounted for until transferred to Company E, 34th Regiment N.C. Troops, April 16, 1863, in exchange for Private John M. Collins.

QUINN, ANONYMOUS W., Private

Resided in Cleveland County and was by occupation a tailor prior to enlisting in Cleveland County at age 33, April 22, 1861. Mustered in as Sergeant and promoted to 1st Sergeant on August 22, 1861. Reduced to ranks in March-October, 1862. Present or accounted for until captured near Rockville, Maryland, July 13, 1864. Confined at Old Capitol Prison, Washington, D.C., until transferred to Elmira, New York, on or about July 25, 1864. Paroled at Elmira on or about February 20, 1865, and transferred to James River, Virginia, for exchange.

REDMOND, ALBERT J., Private

Resided in Cleveland County and was by occupation a clerk prior to enlisting in Cleveland County at age 21, May 22, 1861. Mustered in as Private and promoted to Sergeant on May 1, 1862. Reduced to ranks on December 23, 1862. Present or accounted for until captured at Hagerstown, Maryland, July 5, 1863. Confined at Fort Delaware, Delaware, until transferred to Point Lookout, Maryland, October 15-18, 1863. Transferred to Elmira, New York, on or about August 14, 1864. Paroled at Elmira and transferred to James River, Virginia, February 20, 1865, for exchange.

RUNNIONS, TIMOTHY J., Private

Born in Cleveland County where he resided as a farmer prior to enlisting in Cleveland County at age 20, May 22, 1861. Present or accounted for until killed at Gaines' Mill, Virginia, June 27, 1862.

SCOTT, THOMAS C., Private

Born in London, England, and resided in Cleveland County where he was by occupation a printer prior to enlisting in Cleveland County at age 17, July 29, 1861. Present or accounted for until discharged on October 2, 1862, by reason of being under age.

SCRUGGS, JESSE M., Private
Resided in Cleveland County where he enlisted at age 40, May 16, 1861. Present or accounted for until reported absent without leave in July-August, 1863. Reported absent without leave until he was captured by the Home Guard on or about February 17, 1864. Discharged March 18, 1864. Reason discharged not reported.

SCRUGGS, TOLIVER D., Private
Born in Rutherford County and resided in Cleveland County where he was by occupation a farmer prior to enlisting in Cleveland County at age 22, May 16, 1861. Present or accounted for until discharged on or about March 25, 1864, by reason of "chronic rheumatism."

SIMMONS, LEANDER J., Private
Resided in Cleveland County where he enlisted at age 18, August 12, 1861. Present or accounted for until mortally wounded at Charles Town, West Virginia, August 22, 1861.

SIMMONS, SQUIRE S., Private
Born in Cleveland County* where he resided as a farmer prior to enlisting in Cleveland County at age 42, June 15, 1862, for the war as a substitute for Sergeant Jeremiah W. Fulton. Killed at Malvern Hill, Virginia, July 1, 1862.

SMITH, WILLIAM W., Musician
Enlisted at Taylorsville, Virginia, at age 12, March 21, 1864, for the war. Mustered in as Musician. Present or accounted for through December, 1864.

SPANGLER, ABSALOM, Private
Resided in Cleveland County where he enlisted on December 1, 1862, for the war as a substitute for Private Samuel J. Green. Present or accounted for through April 8, 1865.

SPANGLER, WILLIAM N., Private
Resided in Cleveland County where he enlisted at age 19, May 16, 1861. Present or accounted for until hospitalized at Danville, Virginia, July 2, 1862, with a gunshot wound; however, place and date wounded not reported. Returned to duty prior to November 1, 1862, and present or accounted for until wounded in the "leg below the knee" and in the right thigh at Chancellorsville, Virginia, May 2, 1863. Reported absent wounded through August, 1863. Returned to duty prior to January 15, 1864, and present or accounted for until captured at Spotsylvania Court House, Virginia, May 12, 1864. Confined at Old Capitol Prison, Washington, D.C., until transferred to Fort Delaware, Delaware, June 15, 1864. Released at Fort Delaware on June 19, 1865, after taking the Oath of Allegiance.

STARK, RICHARD, Private
Resided in Virginia and enlisted at Norfolk, Virginia, at age 13, May 7, 1862, for the war. Present or accounted for until discharged on May 13, 1863, under the provisions of the Conscript Act.

SWRONCE, GEORGE, Private
Enlisted in Catawba County at age 18, March 13, 1864, for the war. Present or accounted for until

wounded in the left knee and thigh and captured at Sayler's Creek, Virginia, April 6, 1865. Hospitalized at various Federal hospitals until hospitalized at Washington, D.C., April 19, 1865. Released on August 25, 1865, after taking the Oath of Allegiance.

TIDWELL, WILLIAM T. A., Private
Born in Lancaster District, South Carolina, and resided in Cleveland County where he was by occupation a laborer or farmer prior to enlisting in Cleveland County at age 36, April 22, 1861. Present or accounted for until discharged on or about July 21, 1862, by reason of being over age. Later served in Company F, 49th Regiment N.C. Troops.

TOMS, JAMES MADISON, Private
Resided in Cleveland County and was by occupation a student prior to enlisting in Cleveland County at age 19, April 22, 1861. Present or accounted for until discharged on August 7, 1862, after furnishing Private Isham White as a substitute.

TOWRY, JOHN H., Private
Previously served in Company F of this regiment. Transferred to this company on November 1, 1864. Present or accounted for until paroled at Appomattox Court House, Virginia, April 9, 1865.

TUCKER, WILLIAM MARCUS, Private
Resided in Cleveland County and was by occupation a farmer prior to enlisting in Cleveland County at age 22, April 22, 1861. Present or accounted for until captured at Harper's Farm, Virginia, April 6, 1865. Confined at Point Lookout, Maryland, until released on June 21, 1865, after taking the Oath of Allegiance.

WARLICK, DANIEL, Private
Resided in Cleveland County and was by occupation a blacksmith prior to enlisting in Cleveland County at age 23, April 22, 1861. Present or accounted for until wounded in the left thigh and captured at Cedar Creek, Virginia, October 19, 1864. Hospitalized at Baltimore, Maryland, until confined at Point Lookout, Maryland, October 29, 1864. Paroled at Point Lookout and transferred to Venus Point, Savannah River, Georgia, where he was received November 15, 1864, for exchange.

WARLICK, WILLIAM A., Private
Resided in Cleveland County and was by occupation a farmer prior to enlisting in Cleveland County at age 26, April 22, 1861. Present or accounted for until discharged on or about September 16, 1863, by reason of "general & nervous debility."

WASHBURN, THOMAS J., Private
Resided in Cleveland County and was by occupation a farmer prior to enlisting in Cleveland County at age 27, April 22, 1861. Present or accounted for until paroled at Appomattox Court House, Virginia, April 9, 1865.

WATTS, JAMES, Private
Resided in Cleveland County and was by occupation a farmer prior to enlisting in Cleveland County at age 39, May 16, 1861. Present or accounted for until he died at Camp Carolina, Virginia, July 31, 1861, of disease.

WEATHERS, ALBERT Y., Private
Born in Cleveland County where he resided as a

farmer prior to enlisting in Cleveland County at age 20, May 16, 1861. Present or accounted for until killed at Gaines' Mill, Virginia, June 27, 1862.

WEATHERS, RUFUS P., Private
Resided in Cleveland County where he enlisted at age 18, August 12, 1861. Present or accounted for through April, 1864. Captured by the enemy at an unspecified date prior to October 24, 1864, when he was hospitalized at Baltimore, Maryland, with an unspecified complaint. Died in hospital at Baltimore on October 26, 1864. Cause of death not reported. Company muster roll dated April 30-October 31, 1864, states that he was absent wounded. No further records.

WEEB, P. B., Private
Enlisted in Cleveland County at age 18, March 31, 1864, for the war. Present or accounted for until paroled at Appomattox Court House, Virginia, April 9, 1865.

WEBER, JOHN S., Sergeant
Born at Spartanburg, South Carolina, and resided in Cleveland County where he was by occupation a student or farmer prior to enlisting in Cleveland County at age 19, April 22, 1861. Mustered in as Private and promoted to Sergeant on November 1, 1864. Present or accounted for through February 27, 1865.

WELLS, JOHN K., Jr., Private
Born in Cleveland County where he resided as a student prior to enlisting in Cleveland County at age 18, March 12, 1863, for the war. Present or accounted for until wounded in the thigh at Chancellorsville, Virginia, May 2, 1863. Returned to duty prior to September 1, 1863, and present or accounted for until paroled at Appomattox Court House, Virginia, April 9, 1865.

WELLS, LEWIS M., 1st Sergeant
Resided in Cleveland County and was by occupation a farmer prior to enlisting in Cleveland County at age 21, April 22, 1861. Mustered in as Private and promoted to Sergeant on May 2, 1862. Promoted to 1st Sergeant on January 14, 1863. Present or accounted for until killed at Chancellorsville, Virginia, May 2, 1863. Nominated for the Badge of Distinction for gallantry at Chancellorsville.

WHISNANT, DAVID D., Corporal
Resided in Cleveland County and was by occupation a farmer prior to enlisting in Cleveland County at age 20, April 22, 1861. Mustered in as Private and promoted to Corporal on January 1, 1863. Present or accounted for until wounded in the arm at Chancellorsville, Virginia, May 3, 1863. Returned to duty prior to July 1, 1863, when he was wounded at Gettysburg, Pennsylvania. Reported absent wounded through August, 1863, but returned to duty prior to January 15, 1864. Present or accounted for until paroled at Appomattox Court House, Virginia, April 9, 1865.

WHISNANT, E. M., Private
Enlisted in Cleveland County for the war. Place and date of enlistment not reported. First listed on a company muster roll dated April 30-October 31, 1864. Wounded in the left leg and captured at

Cedar Creek, Virginia, October 19, 1864. Left leg amputated. Hospitalized at Baltimore, Maryland. Hospital records give his age as 37. Confined at Point Lookout, Maryland, October 29, 1864. Paroled and transferred to Venus Point, Savannah River, Georgia, where he was received November 15, 1864, for exchange.

WHITE, ISHAM, Private
Resided in Cleveland County where he enlisted at age 52, August 7, 1862, for the war as a substitute for Private James Madison Toms. Present or accounted for until he died in hospital at Richmond, Virginia, January 17, 1864, of "diarrhoea chron[ic]."

WILKINS, DRURY S., Private
Born in York District, South Carolina, and resided in Cleveland County where he was by occupation a farmer prior to enlisting in Cleveland County at age 32, April 22, 1861. Present or accounted for until paroled at Newton on or about April 19, 1865. North Carolina pension records indicate he was wounded in the hip at Spotsylvania Court House, Virginia, in May, 1864.

WILLIS, JOSEPH J., Private
Born in Cleveland County* where he resided as a farmer prior to enlisting in Cleveland County at age 23, August 5, 1861. Present or accounted for until wounded at Malvern Hill, Virginia, July 1, 1862. Died in hospital at Richmond, Virginia, on or about July 3, 1862, of wounds.

WILSON, POLK, Private
Enlisted in Catawba County at age 17, March 5, 1864, for the war. Present or accounted for until reported transferred to the 28th Regiment N.C. Troops prior to May 1, 1864. Records of the 28th Regiment do not indicate that he served therein; however, he may have served in Company H of that regiment under the name of David P. Wilson. No further records.

WILSON, WILLIAM M., Private
Born in Catawba County* and resided in Catawba or Cleveland counties where he was by occupation a farmer or tanner prior to enlisting in Cleveland County at age 25, April 22, 1861. Present or accounted for until captured at Wilderness, Virginia, May 6, 1864. Confined at Point Lookout, Maryland, until transferred to Elmira, New York, August 10, 1864. Released at Elmira on June 21, 1865, after taking the Oath of Allegiance.

WRAY, JAMES ALEXANDER, Private
Resided in Cleveland County and was by occupation a doctor prior to enlisting in Cleveland County at age 26, April 22, 1861. Present or accounted for until discharged on May 3, 1862, by reason of disability.

WRAY, SAMUEL L., Private
Resided in Cleveland County and was by occupation a merchant prior to enlisting in Cleveland County at age 21, April 22, 1861. Mustered in as Corporal but was reduced to ranks in March-June, 1862. Present or accounted for through April, 1864, but was reported absent without leave on company muster rolls dated April 30-December, 1864. No further records.

WRIGHT, ABNER B., Musician
Previously served in Company H, 28th Regiment

N.C. Troops. Transferred to this company on April 24, 1863, with the rank of Private. Promoted to Musician on April 27, 1863. Present or accounted for until transferred to the Field and Staff of this regiment in January-February, 1864. Transferred back to this company in May-October, 1864, and present or accounted for until paroled at Appomattox Court House, Virginia, April 9, 1865.

WRIGHT, GEORGE H., Private
Born in Cleveland County* where he resided as a farmer prior to enlisting in Cleveland County at age 24, April 22, 1861. Present or accounted for until wounded in the right leg at Chancellorsville, Virginia, May 2, 1863. Reported absent wounded through August, 1863, but returned to duty prior to March 1, 1864. Present or accounted for until wounded in the right shoulder at Spotsylvania Court House, Virginia, May 12, 1864. Reported absent wounded until he was retired from service on or about February 21, 1865, by reason of wounds received at Spotsylvania Court House.

WRIGHT, WILLIAM J., Private
Born in Cleveland County where he resided as a farmer prior to enlisting in Cleveland County at age 19, June 18, 1861. Present or accounted for until he died "at home" in Cleveland County on or about August 4, 1862, of "fever."

WRIGHT, WILLIAM W., 1st Sergeant
Resided in Cleveland County and was by occupation a farmer prior to enlisting in Cleveland County at age 50, April 22, 1861. Mustered in as 1st Sergeant. Present or accounted for until appointed Captain of Company H, 28th Regiment N.C. Troops, August 22, 1861.

WYCKOFF, J. L., Private
Resided in Catawba County and enlisted at West Point, Georgia, at age 17, March 29, 1864, for the war. Present or accounted for until hospitalized at Richmond, Virginia, May 16, 1864, with a gunshot wound; however, place and date wounded not reported. Returned to duty in November-December, 1864, and present or accounted for until captured at Richmond on April 6, 1865. Confined at Point Lookout, Maryland, until released on June 16, 1865, after taking the Oath of Allegiance.

YOUNT, DANIEL P., Private
Previously served in Company C, 28th Regiment N.C. Troops. Enlisted in this company on or about October 24, 1864. Present or accounted for until paroled at Appomattox Court House, Virginia, April 9, 1865.

YOUNT, DAVID, Private
Previously served in Company C, 28th Regiment N.C. Troops. Enlisted in this company on or about October 24, 1864. Present or accounted for until captured at Petersburg, Virginia, April 2, 1865. Confined at Point Lookout, Maryland, until released on June 22, 1865, after taking the Oath of Allegiance.

COMPANY F

This company, known as the "Warren Guards," was raised in Warren County and enlisted at Warrenton on April 18, 1861. It tendered its service to the state and was ordered to Garysburg, where it was assigned to this regiment. The company was mustered in as Captain Benjamin O. Wade's Company and was designated Company A before it was designated Company F. After it was mustered into the regiment the company functioned as a part of the regiment, and its history for the war period is recorded as a part of the regimental history.

The information contained in the following roster of the company was compiled principally from company muster rolls for April 18, 1861-February 28, 1862; September 30-October 31, 1862; January-August, 1863; and November, 1863-December, 1864. No company muster rolls were found for March 1-September 29, 1862; November-December, 1862; September-October, 1863; or for the period after December, 1864. In addition to the company muster rolls, Roll of Honor records, receipt rolls, hospital records, prisoner of war records, and other primary records, supplemented by state pension applications, United Daughters of the Confederacy records, and postwar rosters and histories, all provided useful information.

OFFICERS

CAPTAINS

WADE, BENJAMIN O.
Resided in Warren County and was by occupation a druggist prior to enlisting in Warren County at age 22. Appointed Captain on April 18, 1861. Present or accounted for until promoted to Lieutenant Colonel on May 1, 1862, and transferred to the Field and Staff of this regiment.

HARMON, NATHANIEL C.
Resided in Warren County and was by occupation a tinsmith prior to enlisting in Warren County at age 25. Appointed 3rd Lieutenant to rank from April 22, 1861, and was elected 1st Lieutenant on May 1, 1862. Promoted to Captain on May 4, 1862. Present or accounted for until he resigned on September 9, 1863, by reason of "tuberculosis." Resignation accepted October 24, 1863.

TURNBULL, JOHN R.
Resided in Warren County and was by occupation a merchant prior to enlisting in Warren County at age 20, April 18, 1861. Mustered in as Private and appointed 2nd Lieutenant on May 1, 1862. Promoted to 1st Lieutenant to rank from May 3, 1862. Present or accounted for until wounded at South Mountain, Maryland, September 14, 1862. Returned to duty in March-April, 1863, and was promoted to Captain on October 24, 1863. Present or accounted for until wounded at Spotsylvania Court House, Virginia, in May, 1864. Returned to duty prior to November 1, 1864, and present or accounted for until wounded and captured at Fort Stedman, Virginia, March 25, 1865. Confined at Old Capitol Prison, Washington, D.C., until transferred to Fort Delaware, Delaware, March 30, 1865. Released at Fort Delaware on June 7, 1865, after taking the Oath of Allegiance.

LIEUTENANTS

BENNETT, ISHAM H., 2nd Lieutenant

Resided in Warren County and was by occupation a farmer prior to enlisting in Warren County at age 35. Appointed 3rd Lieutenant on April 18, 1861, and promoted to 2nd Lieutenant in July-August, 1861. Present or accounted for until he was defeated for reelection when the regiment was reorganized on May 1, 1862.

JOHNSON, WILLIAM E., 2nd Lieutenant

Resided in Warren County and was by occupation a salesman prior to enlisting in Warren County at age 23, April 18, 1861. Mustered in as Private and promoted to Sergeant in March-October, 1862. Appointed 2nd Lieutenant to rank from November 1, 1862. Present or accounted for until wounded in the head at Chancellorsville, Virginia, May 2, 1863. Died May 3, 1863, of wounds.

MONTGOMERY, WALTER ALEXANDER, 2nd Lieutenant

Previously served in Company E, 9th Regiment N.C. State Troops (1st Regiment N.C. Cavalry). Enlisted in this company on August 21, 1861. Mustered in as Private and promoted to Sergeant in November-December, 1862. Present or accounted for until wounded in the side at Chancellorsville, Virginia, May 1-3, 1863. Returned to duty on June 3, 1863, and was wounded at Gettysburg, Pennsylvania, July 1, 1863. Returned to duty prior to September 1, 1863, and was appointed 2nd Lieutenant on November 8, 1864. Present or accounted for until paroled at Appomattox Court House, Virginia, April 9, 1865.

MOSELEY, NATHAN S., 1st Lieutenant

Resided in Warren County and was by occupation a merchant prior to enlisting in Warren County at age 21, April 18, 1861. Mustered in as 1st Sergeant and was elected 3rd Lieutenant to rank from May 1, 1862. Promoted to 2nd Lieutenant on May 4, 1862. Mentioned in dispatches for gallantry at Chancellorsville, Virginia, where he commanded the regimental sharpshooters, May 1-3, 1863. Present or accounted for until wounded in the neck at Gettysburg, Pennsylvania, July 1-3, 1863. Rejoined the company in September-December, 1863, and was promoted to 1st Lieutenant on October 24, 1863. Present or accounted for until wounded in both thighs and captured at Spotsylvania Court House, Virginia, on or about May 12, 1864. Hospitalized at Fredericksburg, Virginia, and at Washington, D.C., until confined at Old Capitol Prison, Washington, July 14, 1864. Transferred to Fort Delaware, Delaware, July 22, 1864, and was transferred to Hilton Head, South Carolina, August 20, 1864. Confined at Fort Pulaski, Georgia, October 20, 1864, but was transferred back to Hilton Head on November 19, 1864. Transferred back to Fort Delaware where he was confined on May 12, 1865. Released on June 7, 1865, after taking the Oath of Allegiance.

SEPARK, JOSEPH H., 1st Lieutenant

Resided in Warren County and was by occupation a molder prior to enlisting in Warren County at age 29. Appointed 1st Lieutenant on April 18, 1861. Present or accounted for until he was defeated for reelection when the regiment was reorganized on May 1, 1862.

NONCOMMISSIONED OFFICERS AND PRIVATES

AIKEN, WILLIAM D., Private

Was by occupation a farmer prior to enlisting in Northampton County at age 22, May 17, 1861. Not listed on the rolls of this company after June 30, 1861. No further records.

ALLEN, AUSTIN, Private

Resided in Warren County where he enlisted at age 18, February 20, 1863, for the war. Present or accounted for until wounded at Gettysburg, Pennsylvania, July 1, 1863. Returned to duty in September-December, 1863, and present or accounted for until paroled at Appomattox Court House, Virginia, April 9, 1865.

ALLEN, DANIEL, Private

Resided in Warren County and was by occupation a farmer prior to enlisting in Warren County at age 20, April 29, 1861. Present or accounted for until wounded at "Malve[rn Hill, Virginia, July 1, 1862]." Returned to duty prior to March 1, 1863, and present or accounted for until wounded in the spine and captured at Gettysburg, Pennsylvania, July 1, 1863. Died in hospital at Gettysburg on July 16, 1863, of wounds.

ALLEN, HUGH J., Corporal

Resided in Warren County where he enlisted at age 18, August 19, 1861. Mustered in as Private and promoted to Corporal in November, 1862-February, 1863. Present or accounted for until wounded in the head at Chancellorsville, Virginia, May 3, 1863. Died the same day.

ALLEN, JACOB STINER, Private

Born in Warren County where he resided as a carpenter prior to enlisting in Warren County at age 21, April 18, 1861. Present or accounted for until captured at Spotsylvania Court House, Virginia, May 12, 1864. Confined at Point Lookout, Maryland, until transferred to Elmira, New York, August 10, 1864. Paroled at Elmira and transferred to Cox's Landing, James River, Virginia, where he was received February 14-15, 1865, for exchange.

ALLEN, PETER H., Corporal

Born in Warren County where he resided as a teacher prior to enlisting in Warren County at age 21, May 30, 1861. Mustered in as Private and promoted to Corporal in March-October, 1862. Present or accounted for until wounded in the sternum at Morton's Ford, Virginia, October 11, 1863. Returned to duty prior to January 1, 1864, and present or accounted for until wounded in the chest at Spotsylvania Court House, Virginia, May 19, 1864. Reported absent wounded until retired to the Invalid Corps on March 21, 1865.

ALLEN, TURNER, Private

Resided in Warren County and was by occupation a teacher prior to enlisting in Warren County at age 25, April 29, 1861. Present or accounted for until killed at Malvern Hill, Virginia, July 1, 1862.

ANGERMAN, WILLIAM H., Private
Born at Petersburg, Virginia, and resided in Warren or Orange counties where he was by occupation a salesman or clerk prior to enlisting in Warren County at age 19, April 18, 1861. Present or accounted for until transferred to Company G, 28th Regiment N.C. Troops, March 4, 1863.

BAKER, JOHN, Private
Resided in Warren County and was by occupation a farmer prior to enlisting in Warren County at age 26, April 29, 1861. Present or accounted for until he died at Danville, Virginia, September 5, 1862, of "febris typhoides."

BARTLETT, LEONIDAS J., Private
Resided in Warren County and was by occupation a painter prior to enlisting in Warren County at age 23, May 5, 1861. Present or accounted for until mortally wounded at Malvern Hill, Virginia, July 1, 1862. Place and date of death not reported.

BELLAMY, THOMAS M., Private
Resided in Warren County and was by occupation an artist or medical student prior to enlisting in Warren County at age 28, April 18, 1861. Mustered in as Sergeant but was reduced to ranks in March-October, 1862. Present or accounted for through March, 1865; however, he was reported absent on hospital duty during most of that period. Captured in hospital at Richmond, Virginia, April 3, 1865, and was paroled at Richmond on April 20, 1865.

BOBBITT, JAMES M., Private
Resided in Warren County where he enlisted on February 8, 1864, for the war. Present or accounted for until wounded in the arm at or near Spotsylvania Court House, Virginia, on or about May 10, 1864. Reported absent wounded or absent sick through December, 1864. Paroled at Appomattox Court House, Virginia, April 9, 1865.

BOBBITT, PLUMMER A., 1st Sergeant
Resided in Warren County where he enlisted at age 18, July 16, 1862, for the war. Mustered in as Private. Present or accounted for until wounded in both thighs and captured at Gettysburg, Pennsylvania, July 1-4, 1863. Hospitalized at Davids Island, New York Harbor, until paroled and transferred to City Point, Virginia, where he was received August 28, 1863, for exchange. Returned to duty prior to January 1, 1864, and was promoted to Corporal in January-February, 1864. Promoted to 1st Sergeant in November-December, 1864. Present or accounted for until paroled at Appomattox Court House, Virginia, April 9, 1865.

BOBBITT, WILLIAM H., Jr., Private
Was by occupation a coach maker prior to enlisting in Warren County at age 19, April 18, 1861. Present or accounted for until paroled at Appomattox Court House, Virginia, April 9, 1865.

BOBBITT, WILLIAM HENRY, Sr., Private
Resided in Warren County and was by occupation a farmer prior to enlisting in Warren County at age 19, April 29, 1861. Present or accounted for until transferred to Company F, 8th Regiment N.C. State Troops, March 30, 1863.

BOTTOM, JAMES A., Private
Resided in Warren County and was by occupation a carpenter prior to enlisting in Warren County at age 24, April 18, 1861. Present or accounted for until wounded in the right hand at Chancellorsville, Virginia, May 2, 1863. Reported absent wounded, absent without leave, or absent on duty as a nurse through December, 1864. Paroled at Greensboro on or about April 28, 1865.

BRANNAN, DENNIS, Private
Resided in Warren County and enlisted at Paris, Virginia, at age 28, November 1, 1862, for the war as a substitute for Private Michael Collins. Deserted November 25, 1862.

BROOKS, SILAS, Private
Born in Mecklenburg County, Virginia, and resided in Warren County where he was by occupation a farmer prior to enlisting in Warren County at age 18, April 29, 1861. Present or accounted for until discharged on or about October 11, 1862, by reason of "phthisis pulmonalis." Died prior to August 29, 1864. Place, cause, and exact date of death not reported.

BROWN, CHARLES Z., Private
Resided in Warren County and was by occupation a farmer prior to enlisting in Warren County at age 31, April 18, 1861. Present or accounted for through February 25, 1865.

CANNON, WILLIAM H., Private
Resided in Warren County and was by occupation a barkeeper prior to enlisting in Warren County at age 25, April 29, 1861. Present or accounted for through December, 1864.

CAPPS, WILLIAM H., Private
Resided in Warren County and was by occupation a farmer prior to enlisting in Warren County at age 19, April 29, 1861. Present or accounted for until he died in hospital at Richmond, Virginia, February 6, 1863, of "pneumonia."

CHEEK, THOMAS, Private
Enlisted in Warren County at age 17, May 18, 1861. Present or accounted for until killed at Gaines' Mill, Virginia, June 27, 1862.

CHEEK, WILLIAM R., Private
Resided in Warren County and was by occupation a farmer prior to enlisting in Warren County at age 17, May 18, 1861. Present or accounted for until discharged in June, 1862, after providing a substitute. Reenlisted in the company on February 2, 1864, and present or accounted for until paroled at Appomattox Court House, Virginia, April 9, 1865.

COLLINS, MICHAEL, Private
Resided in Warren County and was by occupation a farmer prior to enlisting in Warren County at age 23, April 18, 1861. Present or accounted for until discharged in November, 1862, after providing Private Dennis Brannan as a substitute.

COOK, JOHN THOMAS, Private
Resided in Warren County where he enlisted at age 24, August 2, 1861. Mustered in as Private. Present or accounted for until wounded at Gaines' Mill, Virginia, June 27, 1862. Company records do not indicate whether he returned to duty; however, he was

appointed Sergeant Major in October, 1862, and transferred to the Field and Staff of this regiment.

COTTRELL, THOMAS H., Private
Resided in Warren County and was by occupation a farmer prior to enlisting in Warren County at age 19, April 18, 1861. Present or accounted for until reported absent wounded in May-August, 1864; however, place and date wounded not reported. Returned to duty in November-December, 1864, but was retired to the Invalid Corps on January 13, 1865, by reason of "t[otal] d[isability]."

CROWDER, BARTLETT, Private
Resided in Warren County and was by occupation a shoemaker prior to enlisting in Warren County at age 30, April 18, 1861. Present or accounted for until discharged on May 17, 1862, by reason of being a "nonconscript."

DARNELL, WILLIAM E., Private
Resided in Warren County and was by occupation a carpenter prior to enlisting in Warren County at age 23, April 18, 1861. Present or accounted for until captured at Wilderness, Virginia, May 6, 1864. Confined at Point Lookout, Maryland, where he died on August 7, 1864. Cause of death not reported.

DAVIS, GEORGE W., Sergeant
Resided in Warren County and was by occupation a merchant prior to enlisting in Warren County at age 25, April 18, 1861. Mustered in as Sergeant. Present or accounted for until captured at Spotsylvania Court House, Virginia, May 12, 1864. Confined at Point Lookout, Maryland, until transferred to Elmira, New York, August 10, 1864. Released at Elmira on June 19, 1865, after taking the Oath of Allegiance.

DAVIS, J. E., Private
Enlisted in Cleveland County on October 23, 1864, for the war. Present or accounted for until transferred to Company E of this regiment on November 1, 1864.

DAVIS, JAMES A., Private
Resided in Warren County and was by occupation a farmer prior to enlisting in Warren County at age 28, April 18, 1861. Present or accounted for until wounded at Morton's Ford, Virginia, October 11, 1863. Returned to duty in January-February, 1864, and present or accounted for through December, 1864. Captured at an unspecified date subsequent to December 31, 1864, and was confined at Hart's Island, New York Harbor, until released on June 20, 1865, after taking the Oath of Allegiance.

DAVIS, RICHARD B., Private
Resided in Warren County and was by occupation a farmer prior to enlisting in Warren County at age 23, April 18, 1861. Mustered in as Corporal but was reduced to ranks in March-October, 1862. Present or accounted for until wounded at Malvern Hill, Virginia, July 1, 1862. Reported absent wounded until discharged on April 22, 1863, by reason of wounds.

DAVIS, THOMAS E., Private
Resided in Warren County where he enlisted at age 18, May 1, 1862, for the war. Present or accounted for until hospitalized at Charlottesville, Virginia, October 15, 1863, with a gunshot wound; however,

place and date wounded not reported. Returned to duty November 30, 1863, and present or accounted for until killed at Cedar Creek, Virginia, October 19, 1864.

DAVIS, WILLIAM W., Private
Resided in Warren County where he enlisted at age 17, May 1, 1862, for the war. Present or accounted for until he died at Richmond, Virginia, on or about August 16, 1862, of disease.

DORSAY, A. S., Private
Enlisted in Wake County on August 11, 1864, for the war. Present or accounted for until paroled at Appomattox Court House, Virginia, April 9, 1865.

DOWTIN, SAMUEL W., Private
Resided in Warren County and was by occupation a farmer prior to enlisting in Warren County at age 23, May 20, 1861. Present or accounted for through December, 1864; however, he was reported absent sick or absent on detached service during most of that period.

DRAPER, JEREMIAH, Corporal
Resided in Warren County and was by occupation a cabinetmaker prior to enlisting in Warren County at age 27, April 29, 1861. Mustered in as Private. Present or accounted for until wounded in the back at Chancellorsville, Virginia, May 3, 1863. Nominated for the Badge of Distinction for gallantry at Chancellorsville. Returned to duty prior to July 1, 1863, and was promoted to Corporal in July-August, 1863. Present or accounted for until wounded and captured at Cedar Creek, Virginia, October 19, 1864. Confined at Point Lookout, Maryland, until paroled and transferred to Venus Point, Savannah River, Georgia, where he was received November 15, 1864, for exchange. Reported absent wounded through December, 1864. Returned to duty at an unspecified date. Hospitalized at Petersburg, Virginia, March 25, 1865, with a gunshot wound of the left arm and/or left lung. Place and date wounded not reported. Captured in hospital at Petersburg on April 3, 1865. Records of the United Daughters of the Confederacy indicate that he survived the war.

DUKE, GEORGE MARK, Corporal
Born in Warren County where he resided as a farmer prior to enlisting in Warren County at age 16, April 29, 1861. Mustered in as Private. Present or accounted for until discharged on July 29, 1862, by reason of being under age. Reenlisted in the company on August 10, 1862. Present or accounted for until wounded in the thigh at or near Spotsylvania Court House, Virginia, on or about May 9, 1864. Returned to duty prior to September 1, 1864, and was promoted to Corporal in November-December, 1864. Present or accounted for until paroled at Appomattox Court House, Virginia, April 9, 1865.

DUKE, JOSEPH H., Private
Resided in Warren County where he enlisted at age 18, February 20, 1863, for the war. Present or accounted for until wounded at Winchester, Virginia, September 19, 1864. Returned to duty in November-December, 1864, and present or accounted for until paroled at Appomattox Court House, Virginia, April 9, 1865.

DUKE, MATTHEW, Private
Resided in Warren County where he enlisted at age 42, August 10, 1863, for the war. Present or accounted for through December, 1864; however, he was reported absent sick during most of that period.

DUKE, MYRICK D., Private
Resided in Warren County and was by occupation a farmer prior to enlisting in Warren County at age 19, April 29, 1861. Present or accounted for until wounded in the left shoulder at Chancellorsville, Virginia, May 3, 1863. Returned to duty in November-December, 1863, and present or accounted for until killed at Spotsylvania Court House, Virginia, May 12, 1864.

EDWARDS, ROBERT V., Private
Resided in Warren or Franklin counties and was by occupation a millwright prior to enlisting in Warren County at age 24, April 19, 1861. Present or accounted for through December, 1864; however, he was reported absent sick or absent on hospital detail during most of that period. Captured at Petersburg, Virginia, April 3, 1865, and confined at Hart's Island, New York Harbor, until released on June 20, 1865, after taking the Oath of Allegiance.

EGERTON, WILLIAM H., Private
Resided in Warren County and was by occupation a farmer prior to enlisting in Warren County at age 31, April 29, 1861. Present or accounted for until killed at Gaines' Mill, Virginia, June 27, 1862.

ELLIOTT, WILLIAM J., Private
Resided in McDowell County. Place and date of enlistment not reported. Deserted to the enemy prior to April 20, 1865, when he took the Oath of Allegiance at Louisville, Kentucky.

EVANS, JOHN L., Private
Resided in Warren County where he enlisted at age 40, April 20, 1863, for the war. Present or accounted for until discharged in June, 1863, by reason of disability. Reenlisted in the company on September 8, 1863, and was detailed for hospital duty. Discharged on March 24, 1864, by reason of disability.

EVANS, R., Private
Place and date of enlistment not reported; however, he was first listed on the rolls of this company in November-December, 1864. Hospitalized at Petersburg, Virginia, January 15, 1865, with "febris cont. simplex, erysipilas idiopathic sup" and died February 11, 1865.

FALKENER, HENRY L., Corporal
Resided in Warren County and was by occupation a farmer prior to enlisting in Warren County at age 20, April 18, 1861. Mustered in as Private and promoted to Corporal in January-February, 1862. Present or accounted for until transferred to the Quartermaster Department in May, 1862. Later served in Company G, 41st Regiment N.C. Troops (3rd Regiment N.C. Cavalry).

FARRAR, ALEXANDER J., Private
Resided in Warren County and was by occupation a clerk prior to enlisting at age 19, April 18, 1861. Present or accounted for until transferred to Company F, 14th Regiment Virginia Infantry in May, 1861.

FARRIS, DAVID F., Private
Resided in Warren County and was by occupation a tailor prior to enlisting in Warren County at age 19, April 18, 1861. Present or accounted for until he deserted on or about February 7, 1862. Returned to duty in March-April, 1863, and present or accounted for until transferred to Company G, 18th Regiment Virginia Infantry on or about December 12, 1864.

FITTS, HENRY, Private
Resided in Warren County and was by occupation a farmer prior to enlisting in Warren County at age 28, April 18, 1861. Present or accounted for until hospitalized at Richmond, Virginia, June 28, 1862, with a gunshot wound; however, place and date wounded not reported. Reported absent wounded or absent sick until he died at Staunton, Virginia, on or about November 10, 1862, of disease.

FITTS, JAMES H., Private
Resided in Warren County and was by occupation a farmer prior to enlisting in Warren County at age 24, April 18, 1861. Present or accounted for until he died at Petersburg, Virginia, June 14, 1861, of disease.

FITTS, JAMES M., Private
Resided in Warren County and was by occupation a farmer prior to enlisting at age 16, May 18, 1861. Present or accounted for until discharged on May 17, 1862, by reason of being under age.

FLANIGAN, WILLIAM R., Private
Resided in Warren County and was by occupation a farmer prior to enlisting in Warren County at age 19, April 29, 1861. Present or accounted for until discharged in November, 1862, after providing Private B. F. Jones as a substitute.

FLEMING, RICHARD D., 1st Sergeant
Resided in Warren County and was by occupation a dentist prior to enlisting in Warren County at age 26, April 18, 1861. Mustered in as Private and promoted to 1st Sergeant in March-October, 1862. Present or accounted for until discharged on August 8, 1862, after providing Private Jacob Hart as a substitute.

FLEMING, THOMAS B., Private
Born in Warren County where he resided as a farmer prior to enlisting in Warren County at age 34, May 2, 1861. Present or accounted for until discharged on August 2, 1862, by reason of being over age. Reenlisted in the company on July 9, 1864, and present or accounted for until wounded in the right side of the chest and captured at Sayler's Creek, Virginia, April 6, 1865. Hospitalized at various Federal hospitals until confined at Fort McHenry, Maryland, May 9, 1865. Released on June 9, 1865, after taking the Oath of Allegiance.

FLOYD, CHARLES F., Private
Resided in Warren County and was by occupation a farmer prior to enlisting in Warren County at age 20, April 29, 1861. Present or accounted for until wounded in the left ankle and captured at Gettysburg, Pennsylvania, July 1-4, 1863. Confined at Fort Delaware, Delaware, until transferred to Point Lookout, Maryland, on or about October 15, 1863. Died in hospital at Point Lookout on October 18, 1863, of "chr[onic] diarrhoea."

FOOTE, JAMES S., Sergeant

Resided in Warren County and was by occupation a teacher prior to enlisting in Warren County at age 21, April 18, 1861. Mustered in as Private and promoted to Sergeant at an unspecified date. Company records indicate that he was transferred to the 1st Regiment North Carolina "Regulars" on July 1, 1861; however, records of that unit do not indicate that he served therein. Later served as 2nd Lieutenant in Company B, 30th Regiment N.C. Troops.

GILLILAND, JAMES R., Private

Resided in Warren County and was by occupation a farmer prior to enlisting in Warren County at age 22, April 29, 1861. Present or accounted for until wounded at Winchester, Virginia, September 19, 1864. Returned to duty in November-December, 1864, and present or accounted for until paroled at Appomattox Court House, Virginia, April 9, 1865.

GOODLOE, LEWIS D., Private

Resided in Warren County and was by occupation a bookkeeper prior to enlisting in Warren County at age 23, April 18, 1861. Present or accounted for until appointed 2nd Lieutenant and transferred to Company I, 35th Regiment N.C. Troops, February 13, 1863.

GOODWIN, THOMAS, Private

Resided in Warren County and was by occupation a tailor prior to enlisting in Warren County at age 30, May 18, 1861. Present or accounted for until killed at Gaines' Mill, Virginia, June 27, 1862.

GREEN, AUSTIN W., Private

Resided in Warren County and was by occupation a farmer prior to enlisting in Warren County at age 21, April 18, 1861. Mustered in as Corporal. Present or accounted for until wounded at Malvern Hill, Virginia, July 1, 1862. Reported absent wounded through August, 1862, and was reduced to ranks prior to September 1, 1862. Appointed Adjutant (1st Lieutenant) on September 1, 1862, and transferred to the Field and Staff of the 2nd Battalion N.C. Infantry.

GREEN, PLUMMER W., Private

Resided in Warren County and was by occupation a farmer prior to enlisting in Warren County at age 28, April 18, 1861. Present or accounted for until wounded at Malvern Hill, Virginia, July 1, 1862. Returned to duty prior to November 1, 1862, and present or accounted for until discharged on January 8, 1863, after providing Private Michael O'Neill as a substitute.

GREEN, WHARTON J., Private

Resided in Warren County and was by occupation a farmer prior to enlisting in Warren County at age 30, April 18, 1861. Present or accounted for until discharged on June 18, 1861, upon appointment as Colonel in Wise's Legion. Later served as Lieutenant Colonel of the 2nd Battalion of N.C. Infantry.

HARPER, GEORGE W., Private

Born in Franklin County and resided in Warren County where he was by occupation a wheelwright or coach maker prior to enlisting in Warren County at age 33, April 29, 1861. Present or accounted for until discharged on or about July 15, 1862, by reason of being over age.

HARRIS, JEREMIAH B., Corporal

Resided in Warren County and was by occupation a painter prior to enlisting in Warren County at age 21, May 3, 1861. Mustered in as Private and promoted to Corporal in March-October, 1862. Present or accounted for until wounded in the right thigh at Gettysburg, Pennsylvania, July 1, 1863. Returned to duty in November-December, 1863. Present or accounted for until wounded and captured at Cedar Creek, Virginia, October 19, 1864. Died at Strasburg, Virginia, October 30, 1864, of wounds.

HARRIS, JOHN P., Private

Born in Warren County where he resided as a shoemaker prior to enlisting in Warren County at age 44, May 18, 1861. Present or accounted for until discharged on or about June 22, 1862, by reason of disability.

HART, JACOB, Private

Enlisted in Wake County at age 28, August 9, 1862, for the war as a substitute for 1st Sergeant Richard D. Fleming. Deserted the same day.

HAWKS, N., Private

Resided in Warren County and enlisted in Wake County on May 21, 1864, for the war. Present or accounted for until captured near Petersburg, Virginia, March 25, 1865. Confined at Point Lookout, Maryland, until released on June 27, 1865, after taking the Oath of Allegiance.

HICKS, WILLIAM L., Sergeant

Resided in Warren County and was by occupation a farmer prior to enlisting in Warren County at age 21, April 29, 1861. Mustered in as Private and promoted to Corporal in March-October, 1862. Present or accounted for until wounded at Gaines' Mill, Virginia, June 27, 1862. Returned to duty prior to November 1, 1862, and was promoted to Sergeant in November, 1862-February, 1863. Present or accounted for until wounded in both legs at Winchester, Virginia, September 19, 1864. Reported absent wounded through December, 1864. No further records.

HOLT, HENRY CLAY, Private

Resided in Warren County and was by occupation a carpenter prior to enlisting in Warren County at age 18, May 3, 1861. Present or accounted for until he died at Richmond, Virginia, on or about June 23, 1862, of disease.

HUBBARD, JOHN G., Private

Born in Mecklenburg County, Virginia, and resided in Warren County where he was by occupation a postmaster prior to enlisting in Warren County at age 34, April 18, 1861. Present or accounted for until discharged on or about July 29, 1862, by reason of being over age.

HUNDLEY, JOHN A., Private

Resided in Warren County where he enlisted at age 33, July 26, 1861. Present or accounted for until captured near Hanover Court House, Virginia, May 28, 1862. Confined at Fort Monroe, Virginia, until transferred to Fort Delaware, Delaware, June 29, 1862. Exchanged at Aiken's Landing, James River, Virginia, August 5, 1862. Rejoined the company prior to November 1, 1862, and present or accounted for until captured near Petersburg, Virginia, March 25, 1865. Confined at Point Lookout, Maryland, until released on June 27, 1865, after taking the Oath of Allegiance.

HUNDLEY, WILLIAM B., Private
Born in Warren County where he resided as a salesman prior to enlisting in Warren County at age 22, April 18, 1861. Present or accounted for until wounded in the knee at Gaines' Mill, Virginia, June 27, 1862. Reported absent wounded until discharged on or about May 19, 1863, by reason of wounds received at Gaines' Mill.

HUNTER, SAMUEL W., Private
Resided in Warren County and was by occupation a salesman prior to enlisting in Warren County at age 46, April 18, 1861. Present or accounted for until discharged on May 17, 1862, by reason of being over age.

JONES, B. F., Private
Enlisted at Port Royal, Virginia, at age 46, December 4, 1862, for the war as a substitute for Private William R. Flanigan. Deserted December 5, 1862.

JONES, EDWARD, Private
Resided in Warren County and was by occupation a farmer prior to enlisting in Warren County at age 28, April 18, 1861. Present or accounted for until he died in Warren County on or about August 16, 1862, of disease.

JONES, JAMES W., Private
Resided in Warren County where he enlisted at age 26, September 8, 1861. Present or accounted for until killed at Malvern Hill, Virginia, July 1, 1862.

JONES, STEPHEN W., Private
Born in Norfolk County, Virginia, and resided in Warren County where he was by occupation a deputy sheriff or student prior to enlisting in Warren County at age 18, April 18, 1861. Present or accounted for until transferred to Company C, 46th Regiment N.C. Troops, on or about February 19, 1862, upon appointment as 1st Lieutenant.

KEHR, CHARLES H., Private
Enlisted in Warren County on July 20, 1861. Present or accounted for through December, 1861. No further records.

KING, A., Private
Enlisted in Wake County on May 25, 1864, for the war. Present or accounted for through March 8, 1865.

KING, E., Private
Enlisted in Wake County on August 15, 1864, for the war. Present or accounted for through December, 1864.

KING, T., Private
Enlisted in Wake County on May 25, 1864, for the war. Present or accounted for through October, 1864.

LANCASTER, WILLIAM L., Private
Resided in Warren County and was by occupation a farmer prior to enlisting in Warren County at age 20, April 18, 1861. Present or accounted for until he died in hospital at Richmond, Virginia, June 25,

1862, of disease.

LEVISTER, T. P., Private
Enlisted in Wake County on August 18, 1864, for the war. Present or accounted for until transferred to 2nd Company C of this regiment on October 18, 1864.

LOWERY, ALBERT P., Private
Resided in Granville County or in Richmond, Virginia, and was by occupation a farmer prior to enlisting in Granville County at age 19, April 26, 1861. Present or accounted for until captured at Spotsylvania Court House, Virginia, May 19-20, 1864. Confined at Point Lookout, Maryland, until transferred to Elmira, New York, July 3, 1864. Released at Elmira on or about June 6, 1865, after taking the Oath of Allegiance.

MABRY, CHARLES R., Private
Resided in Warren County and was by occupation a farmer prior to enlisting in Warren County at age 19, April 18, 1861. Present or accounted for until paroled at Appomattox Court House, Virginia, April 9, 1865.

MABRY, JOHN, Private
Enlisted in Wake County on May 21, 1864, for the war. Present or accounted for until paroled at Appomattox Court House, Virginia, April 9, 1865.

McDOUGALD, MALCOM, _____
Place and date of enlistment not reported. Transferred to Company C, 9th Regiment N.C. State Troops (1st Regiment N.C. Cavalry), August 20, 1861.

McDOWELL, W., Private
Resided in Wake County where he enlisted on September 1, 1864, for the war. Present or accounted for until captured at Sayler's Creek, Virginia, April 6, 1865. Confined at Point Lookout, Maryland, until released on June 15, 1865, after taking the Oath of Allegiance.

McLEAN, NATHANIEL, Private
Resided in Warren County and was by occupation a lawyer prior to enlisting in Warren County at age 34, April 29, 1861. Present or accounted for until discharged on or about October 2, 1862, by reason of being over age.

MARLOW, GEORGE, Private
Enlisted in Warren County on April 13, 1864, for the war. Present or accounted for until hospitalized at Farmville, Virginia, March 1, 1865, with a gunshot wound of the left leg; however, place and date wounded not reported. Died in hospital at Farmville on April 4, 1865. Cause of death not reported.

MARLOW, JAMES V., Private
Resided in Warren County and was by occupation a farmer prior to enlisting in Warren County at age 22, April 18, 1861. Present or accounted for until captured at Fisher's Hill, Virginia, September 22, 1864. Hospitalized at Baltimore, Maryland, with "debility" until confined at Point Lookout, Maryland, October 26, 1864. Paroled at Point Lookout and transferred to Venus Point, Savannah River, Georgia, where he was received November 15, 1864, for exchange. Returned to duty at an unspecified date subsequent to December 31, 1864, and was captured at Sayler's Creek, Virginia, April 6, 1865. Con-

fined at Point Lookout until released on June 15, 1865, after taking the Oath of Allegiance.

MILLER, JOHN E., Private

Born in Pittsylvania County, Virginia, and resided in Warren County where he was by occupation a teacher prior to enlisting in Warren County at age 23, May 18, 1861. Present or accounted for until wounded in the forearm and knee at Gaines' Mill, Virginia, June 27, 1862. Reported absent wounded until discharged on September 25, 1862, by reason of wounds received at Gaines' Mill.

MILLS, GEORGE V., Private

Resided in Warren County and was by occupation a cabinetmaker prior to enlisting in Warren County at age 19, May 3, 1861. Present or accounted for until he died in hospital at Richmond, Virginia, June 15, 1862, of "febris typhoides."

MONTGOMERY, ROBERT C., Private

Resided in Warren County where he enlisted at age 17, June 1, 1861. Present or accounted for until wounded in the left arm at Gaines' Mill, Virginia, June 27, 1862. Present or accounted for through October, 1862, but was discharged at an unspecified date by reason of wounds received at Gaines' Mill. Reenlisted in the company on February 8, 1864, and present or accounted for until wounded in the left foot at Spotsylvania Court House, Virginia, May 12, 1864. Returned to duty prior to September 1, 1864, and present or accounted for until paroled at Appomattox Court House, Virginia, April 9, 1865.

NEWELL, L. A., Private

Enlisted in Wake County on August 4, 1864, for the war. Present or accounted for until paroled at Burkeville Junction, Virginia, April 14-17, 1865.

NEWMAN, M. T., Private

Enlisted in Wake County on August 11, 1864, for the war. Present or accounted for through December, 1864.

NEWMAN, MACON G., Private

Resided in Warren County and was by occupation a farmer prior to enlisting in Warren County at age 35, May 18, 1861. Present or accounted for until discharged on May 17, 1862, by reason of being over age.

NICHOLSON, BENJAMIN M., Private

Resided in Warren County and was by occupation a farmer prior to enlisting in Warren County at age 18, April 29, 1861. Present or accounted for until transferred to Company C, 46th Regiment N.C. Troops, May 1, 1862.

OBERNDORFER, HENRY, Private

Born in Wintzburg, Bavaria, and resided in Warren County where he was by occupation a salesman prior to enlisting in Warren County at age 17, April 18, 1861. Present or accounted for until discharged on or about July 12, 1862, by reason of being a foreigner.

O'NEILL, MICHAEL, Private

Enlisted at Fredericksburg, Virginia, at age 47, January 8, 1863, for the war as a substitute for Private Plummer W. Green. Deserted on January 10, 1863.

PARRISH, EDWARD P., Private

Resided in Warren County and was by occupation a

"daguerrean artist" prior to enlisting in Warren County at age 21, April 18, 1861. Mustered in as Corporal but was reduced to ranks in January-February, 1862. Present or accounted for until wounded in the right breast at Cedar Creek, Virginia, October 19, 1864. Reported absent wounded through December, 1864. Paroled at Appomattox Court House, Virginia, April 9, 1865.

PATTERSON, HENRY, Private

Resided in Warren County and was by occupation a carpenter prior to enlisting in Warren County at age 21, May 1, 1861. Present or accounted for until paroled at Richmond, Virginia, April 18, 1865.

PEGRAM, JOHN L., Private

Resided in Warren County and was by occupation a farmer prior to enlisting in Warren County at age 20, April 29, 1861. Present or accounted for until he died in hospital at Richmond, Virginia, July 3, 1862, of disease.

PERKINSON, WILLIAM F., Sergeant

Resided in Warren County and was by occupation a farmer prior to enlisting in Warren County at age 24, April 29, 1861. Mustered in as Private and promoted to Sergeant in March-October, 1862. Present or accounted for until he died in hospital at Richmond, Virginia, August 9, 1862, of "diarrhoea."

PHILLIPS, WILLIAM R., Private

Was by occupation a mail agent prior to enlisting in Warren County at age 26, April 18, 1861. No further records.

PIERCE, RICHARD, Private

Resided in Wake County and enlisted on July 9, 1864, for the war. Present or accounted for through December, 1864.

PIERCE, ROBERT, Private

Enlisted in Wake County on July 9, 1864, for the war. Present or accounted for through December, 1864.

PITCHER, ADOLPHUS R., 1st Sergeant

Born in Guernsey, England, and resided in Warren County where he was by occupation a printer prior to enlisting in Warren County at age 24, April 29, 1861. Mustered in as Private and promoted to 1st Sergeant in November, 1862-February, 1863. Present or accounted for until killed at Winchester, Virginia, on or about July 21, 1864.

PITCHFORD, STERLING T., Private

Resided in Warren County and was by occupation a farmer prior to enlisting in Warren County at age 20, April 18, 1861. Present or accounted for until killed at Gaines' Mill, Virginia, June 27, 1862.

PLUMMER, ALFRED A., Private

Born in Warren County where he resided as a farmer prior to enlisting in Warren County at age 23, April 18, 1861. Present or accounted for until discharged on March 1, 1862, by reason of "a disease of the bladder." Later served in Company G, 41st Regiment N.C. Troops (3rd Regiment N.C. Cavalry).

PLUMMER, WALTER G., Private

Resided in Warren County and was by occupation a farmer prior to enlisting in Warren County at age 18, May 18, 1861. Present or accounted for until paroled at Richmond, Virginia, April 18, 1865; however, he was reported absent sick or absent on detached service during most of that period.

POWELL, WILLIAM B., Private
Resided in Warren County and was by occupation a farmer prior to enlisting in Warren County at age 28, April 29, 1861. Present or accounted for until hospitalized at Richmond, Virginia, June 28, 1862, with a gunshot wound; however, place and date wounded not reported. Reported absent without leave on September 25, 1862. Enlisted in Company B, 12th Battalion N.C. Cavalry, November 15, 1862.

QUALLS, HENRY S., Private
Resided in Warren or Halifax counties and was by occupation a farmer prior to enlisting in Warren County at age 24, April 29, 1861. Present or accounted for until wounded in the left thigh and captured at Petersburg, Virginia, March 25, 1865. Hospitalized at Washington, D.C., until released on or about June 12, 1865, after taking the Oath of Allegiance.

QUALLS, JAMES, Private
Resided in Warren or Halifax counties and was by occupation a farmer prior to enlisting in Warren County at age 21, April 29, 1861. Present or accounted for until wounded in the leg at Petersburg, Virginia, March 25, 1865. Captured in hospital at Richmond, Virginia, April 3, 1865. Transferred to Libby Prison, Richmond, at an unspecified date and was transferred to Newport News, Virginia, April 23, 1865. Released on June 3, 1865, after taking the Oath of Allegiance.

REAVIS, JAMES R., Private
Resided in Warren County and was by occupation a farmer prior to enlisting in Warren County at age 22, April 29, 1861. Present or accounted for until he was "killed accidentally" at Spotsylvania Court House, Virginia, May 11, 1864.

RICE, JAMES T., Private
Resided in Warren County and was by occupation a salesman prior to enlisting in Warren County at age 17, April 29, 1861. Present or accounted for until hospitalized at Richmond, Virginia, June 28, 1862, with a gunshot wound; however, place and date wounded not reported. Returned to duty prior to November 1, 1862. Present or accounted for until hospitalized at Danville, Virginia, May 18, 1864, with a gunshot wound; however, place and date wounded not reported. Reported absent wounded or absent sick until he returned to duty on January 30, 1865. Paroled at Farmville, Virginia, April 11-21, 1865.

RIGGAN, JOHN H., Private
Resided in Warren County where he enlisted at age 36, July 25, 1861. Present or accounted for until discharged in March-December, 1862, by reason of disability.

ROBERTSON, JEFFERSON H., Private
Resided in Warren County where he enlisted at age 32, February 20, 1863, for the war. Present or accounted for through December, 1864; however, he was reported absent sick or absent on hospital duty during most of that period.

RONALDS, HUGH, Private
Was by occupation a salesman prior to enlisting in Warren County at age 27, April 18, 1861. Present or accounted for until discharged on January 1, 1862, by reason of "sickness."

RUDD, ALEXANDER B., Private
Resided in Warren County and was by occupation a farmer prior to enlisting in Warren County at age 20, April 29, 1861. Present or accounted for until he died in hospital at Richmond, Virginia, on or about June 30, 1862, of "fever" and/or "pneumonia."

SCHMIDT, KARL, Private
Enlisted in Warren County on July 28, 1861. Present or accounted for until discharged on January 1, 1862. Reason discharged not reported.

SHADRICK, J., Private
Enlisted in Wake County. Date of enlistment not reported; however, he was first listed on the rolls of this company in November-December, 1864. Present or accounted for through December, 1864.

SHROYER, EDWARD, Private
Resided in Warren County where he enlisted at age 30, October 3, 1861. Present or accounted for until reported absent without leave on July 1, 1862. Reported absent without leave through October 31, 1862, but returned to duty prior to March 1, 1863. Present or accounted for until hospitalized at Richmond, Virginia, May 17, 1864, with a gunshot wound; however, place and date wounded not reported. Reported absent wounded, absent sick, or absent on detail until captured in hospital at Richmond on April 3, 1865. Paroled at Richmond on April 24, 1865.

SKINNER, WILLIAM L., Private
Resided in Warren County and was by occupation a student or farmer prior to enlisting in Warren County at age 25, April 18, 1861. Present or accounted for until transferred to Company K, 14th Regiment N.C. Troops (4th Regiment N.C. Volunteers), June 28, 1861.

SOMERVILLE, JAMES B., Private
Previously served as Sergeant in Company B, 12th Regiment Virginia Infantry. Transferred to this company in March, 1864, with the rank of Private. Apparently he served in the company only a few days as he was appointed 3rd Lieutenant on March 17, 1864, and transferred to Company B, 37th Regiment N.C. Troops.

SPRUILL, PETER E., Private
Resided in Warren County and was by occupation a lawyer prior to enlisting in Warren County at age 25, April 18, 1861. Mustered in as Sergeant but was reduced to ranks in March-June, 1862. Present or accounted for until hospitalized at Richmond, Virginia, June 14, 1862, with "chronic diarrhoea." Died at Richmond on June 25, 1862.

TERRELL, JAMES M., Private
Resided in Warren County where he enlisted at age 20, August 1, 1861. Present or accounted for until captured at Gettysburg, Pennsylvania, or at Hagerstown, Maryland, July 1-5, 1863. Confined at Fort Delaware, Delaware, until transferred to Point Lookout, Maryland, October 18, 1863. Died in hospital at

Point Lookout on November 26, 1863, of "typhoid fever."

TERRELL, JOHN W., Corporal

Resided in Warren County where he enlisted at age 23, May 1, 1862, for the war. Mustered in as Private. Present or accounted for until wounded at Gaines' Mill, Virginia, June 27, 1862. Returned to duty prior to November 1, 1862, and was promoted to Corporal in November-December, 1864. Present or accounted for through December, 1864.

THORNTON, ROBERT BOYD, Private

Resided in Warren County and was by occupation a farmer prior to enlisting in Warren County at age 21, April 29, 1861. Present or accounted for until wounded in the arm at Chancellorsville, Virginia, May 3, 1863. Returned to duty prior to July 1-5, 1863, when he was wounded in the left leg and captured at Gettysburg, Pennsylvania. Left leg amputated. Hospitalized at Gettysburg until transferred to hospital at Baltimore, Maryland, September 10, 1863. Paroled at Baltimore and transferred to City Point, Virginia, where he was received on September 27, 1863, for exchange. Reported absent wounded until discharged on April 7, 1864, by reason of disability.

TOWRY, JOHN H., Private

Enlisted in Cleveland County on October 25, 1864, for the war. Transferred to Company E of this regiment on November 1, 1864.

TUCKER, FRANCIS J., Private

Resided in Warren County and was by occupation a teacher prior to enlisting in Warren County at age 23, May 18, 1861. Present or accounted for through August, 1863. Company muster roll dated November-December, 1863, states he was wounded at Warrenton, Virginia. Returned to duty in March-April, 1864, and present or accounted for until he deserted from hospital at Richmond, Virginia, March 11, 1865.

TUCKER, GEORGE W. S., Private

Resided in Warren County and was by occupation a farmer prior to enlisting in Warren County at age 19, May 18, 1861. Present or accounted for until captured at Spotsylvania Court House, Virginia, May 12-20, 1864. Confined at Point Lookout, Maryland, until transferred to Elmira, New York, July 3, 1864. Paroled at Elmira and transferred to James River, Virginia, February 20, 1865, for exchange.

TUCKER, R. Y., Private

Resided in Warren County where he enlisted on April 12, 1864, for the war. Present or accounted for until captured at Sayler's Creek, Virginia, April 6, 1865. Confined at Point Lookout, Maryland, until released on June 21, 1865, after taking the Oath of Allegiance.

VAUGHAN, F. C., Private

Place and date of enlistment not reported. Hospitalized at Richmond, Virginia, March 26, 1865, with a contusion of the right foot. Place and date injured not reported. Captured in hospital at Richmond on April 3, 1865, and was paroled on May 9, 1865.

VAUGHAN, W. T., Private

Enlisted in Wake County on May 21, 1864, for the war. Present or accounted for through December, 1864.

WALKER, WILLIAM, Private

Enlisted in Wake County on July 25, 1864, for the war. Present or accounted for until paroled at Burkeville Junction, Virginia, April 14-17, 1865.

WARD, JOSEPH R. D., Private

Resided in Warren County and was by occupation a carpenter prior to enlisting in Warren County at age 22, April 29, 1861. Present or accounted for until wounded in the leg at Malvern Hill, Virginia, July 1, 1862. Died in hospital at Richmond, Virginia, July 12, 1862, of wounds.

WHITE, THOMAS H., Sergeant

Resided in Warren County and was by occupation a merchant prior to enlisting in Warren County at age 25, April 29, 1861. Mustered in as Private and promoted to Sergeant in March-October, 1862. Present or accounted for until wounded in the lung and captured at Gettysburg, Pennsylvania, July 1-4, 1863. Hospitalized at Gettysburg until transferred to Davids Island, New York Harbor, July 17-24, 1863. Paroled at Davids Island and transferred to City Point, Virginia, where he was received August 28, 1863, for exchange. Reported absent wounded or absent on light duty through December, 1864.

WHITE, WILLIAM HOWERTON, Private

Resided in Warren County and was by occupation a farmer prior to enlisting in Warren County at age 18, April 19, 1861. Present or accounted for until captured at Gettysburg, Pennsylvania, on or about July 4, 1863. Confined at Fort Delaware, Delaware, until transferred to Point Lookout, Maryland, October 18, 1863. Confined at Point Lookout until paroled and transferred to Cox's Landing, James River, Virginia, where he was received February 14-15, 1865, for exchange.

WHITE, WILLIAM JONES, Private

Born in Warren County where he resided as a student prior to enlisting in Warren County at age 18, April 18, 1861. Present or accounted for until transferred to Company E, 9th Regiment N.C. State Troops (1st Regiment N.C. Cavalry), August 19, 1861.

WIGGINS, ROBERT H., Private

Born in Greensville County, Virginia, and resided in Warren County where he was by occupation a wheelwright prior to enlisting in Warren County at age 33, April 29, 1861. Present or accounted for until discharged on or about July 29, 1862, by reason of being over age. Reenlisted in the company on April 12, 1864, and present or accounted for until paroled at Appomattox Court House, Virginia, April 9, 1865.

WILLIAMS, THOMAS H., Corporal

Resided in Warren County and was by occupation a salesman prior to enlisting in Warren County at age 20, April 29, 1861. Mustered in as Corporal. Present or accounted for until transferred to Company G, 43rd Regiment N.C. Troops, May 10, 1862.

WILLIAMS, THOMAS H., Private

Resided in Warren County and was by occupation a wheelwright prior to enlisting in Warren County at age 24, April 29, 1861. Present or accounted for until he died at Fisher's Hill, Virginia, on or about October 17, 1864, of "congestion of the stomach."

WILLIAMS, WALLACE W., Private
Resided in Warren County and was by occupation a salesman prior to enlisting in Warren County at age 19, April 18, 1861. Present or accounted for through December, 1864.

WOMBLE, WILLIAM D., Private
Resided in Warren County and was by occupation a farmer prior to enlisting in Warren County at age 23, May 28, 1861. Present or accounted for until killed at Gaines' Mill, Virginia, June 27, 1862.

WOOTTEN, DANIEL T., Private
Resided in Prince Edward County, Virginia, or in Warren County and was by occupation a carpenter prior to enlisting in Warren County at age 18, April 18, 1861. Present or accounted for until wounded in the left thigh and captured at Gettysburg, Pennsylvania, July 1-4, 1863. Hospitalized at Gettysburg until transferred to Davids Island, New York Harbor, July 17-24, 1863. Paroled and transferred to City Point, Virginia, where he was received September 8, 1863, for exchange. Returned to duty in January-February, 1864, and present or accounted for until captured at Spotsylvania Court House, Virginia, May 12, 1864. Confined at Point Lookout, Maryland, until transferred to Elmira, New York, August 10, 1864. Released at Elmira on June 21, 1865, after taking the Oath of Allegiance.

YANCEY, GEORGE H., Private
Resided in Warren County and was by occupation a farmer prior to enlisting in Warren County at age 19, April 29, 1861. Present or accounted for until transferred to the Field and Staff, 9th Regiment N.C. State Troops (1st Regiment N.C. Cavalry) on or about October 1, 1861, upon appointment as Commissary Sergeant.

COMPANY G

This company, known as the "Halifax Light Infantry," was raised in Halifax County and enlisted at Halifax on April 25, 1861. It tendered its service to the state and was ordered to Garysburg, where it was assigned to this regiment. The company was mustered in as Captain James H. Whitaker's Company and was designated Company C, Company E, and Company F before it was designated Company G. After it was mustered into the regiment the company functioned as a part of the regiment, and its history for the war period is recorded as a part of the regimental history.

The information contained in the following roster of the company was compiled principally from company muster rolls for April 25, 1861-February 28, 1862; June 30-October 31, 1862; February 1-August 31, 1863; and November, 1863-December, 1864. No company muster rolls were found for March 1-June 29, 1862; November, 1862-January, 1863; September-October, 1863; or for the period after December, 1864. In addition to the company muster rolls, Roll of Honor records, receipt rolls, hospital records, prisoner of war records, and other primary records, supplemented by state pension applications, United Daughters of the Confederacy records, and postwar rosters and histories, all provided useful information.

OFFICERS
CAPTAINS

WHITAKER, JAMES H.
Resided in Halifax County and was by occupation a clerk prior to enlisting in Halifax County at age 28. Appointed Captain to rank from April 25, 1861. Present or accounted for until he was defeated for reelection when the regiment was reorganized on May 1, 1862.

BRICKELL, STERLING H.
Resided in Halifax County and was by occupation a lawyer prior to enlisting in Halifax County at age 23, April 25, 1861. Mustered in as Sergeant and was elected Captain on May 1, 1862. Present or accounted for until wounded in the left hip and right forearm at Chancellorsville, Virginia, May 2-3, 1863. Reported absent wounded or absent on detail until he rejoined the company in January-February, 1864. Present or accounted for until he resigned on March 7, 1864, by reason of wounds received at Chancellorsville and "a tubercular condition of the lungs." Resignation accepted April 12, 1864.

TORMEY, JOHN
Resided in Halifax County and was by occupation a salesman prior to enlisting in Halifax County at age 26, April 25, 1861. Mustered in as 1st Sergeant and appointed 3rd Lieutenant on February 24, 1863. Present or accounted for until wounded at Hagerstown, Maryland, July 6, 1863. Returned to duty in September-December, 1863, and was promoted to 1st Lieutenant on November 11, 1863. Promoted to Captain on April 12, 1864. Present or accounted for until captured at or near Winchester, Virginia, July 20, 1864. Confined at Wheeling, West Virginia, until transferred to Camp Chase, Ohio, July 27, 1864. Paroled and transferred to Boulware's and Cox's Wharf, James River, Virginia, where he was received March 10-12, 1865, for exchange.

LIEUTENANTS

ANTHONY, WHITMEL HILL, 1st Lieutenant
Previously served with the "Palmetto Guard" at Charleston, South Carolina. Appointed 1st Lieutenant in this company to rank from April 25, 1861. Present or accounted for until he was defeated for reelection when the regiment was reorganized on May 1, 1862. Later served as Captain of Company B, 9th Regiment N.C. State Troops (1st Regiment N.C. Cavalry).

DANIEL, THOMAS W., 2nd Lieutenant
Resided in Halifax County and was by occupation a salesman prior to enlisting in Halifax County at age 21, April 25, 1861. Mustered in as Private and promoted to 3rd Lieutenant to rank from May 1, 1862. Promoted to 2nd Lieutenant on July 1, 1862. Present or accounted for until killed at Chancellorsville, Vir-

ginia, May 1-3, 1863.

GARY, WILLIAM CRAWFORD, 2nd Lieutenant
Resided in Halifax County and was by occupation a druggist prior to enlisting in Halifax County at age 26. Appointed 2nd Lieutenant to rank from April 25, 1861. Present or accounted for until he died "at home" on or about February 5, 1862, of disease.

GREGORY, JOHN TILLERY, 2nd Lieutenant
Born in Northampton County and resided in Halifax County where he was by occupation a merchant prior to enlisting in Halifax County at age 29, April 25, 1861. Mustered in as Private and was promoted to Sergeant in October-November, 1861. Appointed 2nd Lieutenant to rank from May 1, 1862. Present or accounted for until appointed Adjutant (2nd Lieutenant) on July 1, 1862, and transferred to the Field and Staff of this regiment.

NORTHINGTON, JOHN S., 1st Lieutenant
Resided in Halifax County and was by occupation a merchant prior to enlisting in Halifax County at age 25. Appointed 3rd Lieutenant to rank from April 25, 1861, and was promoted to 2nd Lieutenant in February, 1862. Elected 1st Lieutenant on May 1, 1862. Present or accounted for until appointed Assistant Quartermaster (Captain) on December 3, 1863, to rank from November 11, 1863, and transferred to the Field and Staff of this regiment.

SNOW, JOHN A., 1st Lieutenant
Resided in Halifax County and was by occupation a farmer prior to enlisting in Halifax County at age 25, April 25, 1861. Mustered in as Corporal and was promoted to Sergeant on May 1, 1862. Present or accounted for until wounded in the hand at Chancellorsville, Virginia, May 2, 1863. Returned to duty in July-August, 1863, and promoted to 1st Lieutenant on May 1, 1864. Present and accounted for until hospitalized at Charlottesville, Virginia, October 24, 1864, with a gunshot wound of the right thigh; however, place and date wounded not reported. Returned to duty in January-April, 1865, and was wounded in the left arm at Petersburg, Virginia, April 2, 1865. Left arm amputated. Captured in hospital at Richmond, Virginia, April 3, 1865, and was transferred to the Federal Provost Marshal on April 28, 1865. North Carolina pension records indicate that he survived the war.

TILLERY, HENRY LEE, 3rd Lieutenant
Resided in Halifax or Nash counties and was by occupation a farmer prior to enlisting in Halifax County at age 22, April 25, 1861. Mustered in as Corporal and was promoted to 3rd Lieutenant to rank from February 15, 1862. Present or accounted for until he was defeated for reelection when the regiment was reorganized on May 1, 1862.

NONCOMMISSIONED OFFICERS AND PRIVATES

ALLEN, WILLIAM G., Private
Resided in Halifax County and was by occupation a farmer prior to enlisting in Halifax County at age 19, April 25, 1861. Present or accounted for until captured at Petersburg, Virginia, April 3, 1865.

Confined at Hart's Island, New York Harbor, until released on June 17, 1865, after taking the Oath of Allegiance.

ANDERSON, JAMES WEIR, Private
Resided in Halifax County and was by occupation a salesman prior to enlisting in Halifax County at age 22, April 25, 1861. Present or accounted for until killed at Gaines' Mill, Virginia, June 27, 1862.

ANDLETON, NICHOLAS, Private
Resided in Halifax County where he enlisted at age 21, April 25, 1861. Present or accounted for until paroled at Appomattox Court House, Virginia, April 9, 1865.

ANDLETON, RICHARD, Private
Resided in Halifax County where he enlisted on April 25, 1861. Present or accounted for until wounded at Malvern Hill, Virginia, July 1, 1862. Reported absent wounded through October, 1862. Not listed again on company records until he was reported as present in March-April, 1864. Present or accounted for until captured at Winchester, Virginia, September 19, 1864. Confined at Point Lookout, Maryland, until released on May 12, 1865.

ANTHONY, JOHN, Corporal
Resided in Halifax County and enlisted at Norfolk, Virginia, at age 26, July 8, 1861. Mustered in as Private and promoted to Corporal on May 1, 1862. Present or accounted for until killed at Malvern Hill, Virginia, July 1, 1862.

ANTHONY, PEYTON T., Private
Resided in Halifax County and was by occupation a farmer prior to enlisting in Halifax County at age 18, April 25, 1861. Present or accounted for until transferred to Company H, 13th Regiment Virginia Cavalry, February 10, 1862.

ARRINGTON, WILLIAM B., Private
Born in Nash County where he resided as a farmer prior to enlisting in Halifax County at age 28, April 25, 1861. Present or accounted for until discharged on or about February 3, 1862, by reason of "angina pectoris."

AYCOCK, WILLIAM C., Private
Resided in Halifax County and was by occupation a mechanic prior to enlisting in Halifax County at age 28, May 16, 1861. Present or accounted for until wounded in the back at Malvern Hill, Virginia, July 1, 1862. Died in hospital at Richmond, Virginia, prior to July 17, 1862, of wounds and "dysentery."

BARCLIFT, WILLIAM S., Private
Resided in Halifax County and was by occupation a farmer prior to enlisting in Halifax County at age 28, April 25, 1861. Present or accounted for until he was transferred "to conscript duty" on July 1, 1863. No further records.

BARFIELD, JOHN W., Private
Resided in Halifax County and was by occupation a salesman prior to enlisting in Halifax County at age 18, May 16, 1861. Present or accounted for until he died at Guinea Station, Virginia, February 13, 1863, of disease.

BARKLEY, C. R., Private
Resided in Nash County and enlisted at Rapidan, Virginia, at age 29, May 16, 1862, for the war. Pres-

ent or accounted for until wounded and captured at South Mountain, Maryland, or at Sharpsburg, Maryland, September 14-17, 1862. Hospitalized at Frederick, Maryland, where he died September 30, 1862, of wounds and/or "febris typhoides."

BARKLEY, J. R., Private
Enlisted in Wake County on May 19, 1864, for the war. Present or accounted for through December, 1864.

BARKLEY, JOSEPH Y., Private
Resided in Halifax County and was by occupation a salesman prior to enlisting in Halifax County at age 23, April 25, 1861. Present or accounted for until he died in hospital at Richmond, Virginia, May 31, 1863, of "pneumonia."

BARKLEY, WILLIAM D., 1st Sergeant
Resided in Halifax County and was by occupation a salesman prior to enlisting in Halifax County at age 25, April 25, 1861. Mustered in as Corporal and promoted to Sergeant in July-October, 1862. Promoted to 1st Sergeant on February 24, 1863. Present or accounted for until appointed Sergeant Major in March-April, 1864, and transferred to the Field and Staff of this regiment.

BARNES, GEORGE L., Private
Resided in Halifax County and enlisted at Richmond, Virginia, at age 21, May 30, 1862, for the war. Present or accounted for until wounded in the right shoulder at Malvern Hill, Virginia, July 1, 1862. Reported absent wounded through October, 1862, but returned to duty prior to March 2, 1863. Present or accounted for until paroled at Appomattox Court House, Virginia, April 9, 1865.

BATTS, JOHN W., Private
Resided in Halifax County and was by occupation a farmer prior to enlisting in Halifax County at age 24, May 16, 1861. Present or accounted for until killed at Malvern Hill, Virginia, July 1, 1862.

BELL, WILLIAM T., Private
Resided in Northampton County and was by occupation a farmer prior to enlisting in Halifax County at age 22, April 25, 1861. Mustered in as Private. Present or accounted for until appointed 3rd Lieutenant and transferred to Company C, 32nd Regiment N.C. Troops, on or about July 29, 1861.

BOLICK, S. B., Private
Resided in Catawba County and enlisted in Wake County on October 6, 1864, for the war. Present or accounted for until captured at Sayler's Creek, Virginia, April 6, 1865. Confined at Point Lookout, Maryland, until released on June 23, 1865, after taking the Oath of Allegiance.

BOND, WILLIAM R., Private
Born in Halifax County where he resided as a farmer or student prior to enlisting in Halifax County at age 22, May 16, 1861. Present or accounted for until appointed 3rd Lieutenant and transferred to Company F, 43rd Regiment N.C. Troops, on or about February 27, 1862.

BOONE, A. N., Private
Enlisted at Norfolk, Virginia, August 22, 1861. Present or accounted for through February, 1862.

BOONE, G. A., Private
Resided in Northampton County and enlisted at age 22, June 1, 1861. Present or accounted for until killed at Malvern Hill, Virginia, July 1, 1862.

BOWERS, ROBERT D., Private
Resided in Halifax County and was by occupation a tailor prior to enlisting in Halifax County at age 35, April 25, 1861. Present or accounted for until discharged on May 16, 1862, by reason of being over age.

BOYD, ROBERT J., Private
Resided in Halifax County and was by occupation a farmer prior to enlisting in Halifax County at age 20, April 25, 1861. Present or accounted for until discharged on or about October 20, 1861. Reason discharged not reported.

BRACKETT, ELIJAH, Private
Resided in Cleveland County and enlisted in Wake County at age 27, February 26, 1863, for the war. Present or accounted for until discharged on May 10, 1863, by reason of disability.

BRANCH, GEORGE A., Private
Resided in Halifax County and enlisted at Richmond, Virginia, at age 33, May 30, 1862, for the war. Present or accounted for through December, 1864; however, he was absent on detail during much of that period.

BRANCH, WILLIAM H., Private
Resided in Halifax County and was by occupation a farmer prior to enlisting in Halifax County at age 25, April 25, 1861. Present or accounted for until wounded at Gaines' Mill, Virginia, June 27, 1862. Reported absent wounded through October, 1862, but returned to duty prior to May 3, 1863, when he was captured at Chancellorsville, Virginia. Exchanged at City Point, Virginia, May 13, 1863. Present or accounted for until hospitalized at Farmville, Virginia, June 2, 1864; however, place and date wounded not reported. Returned to duty on June 20, 1864, and was captured near Washington, D.C., July 13, 1864. Confined at Old Capitol Prison, Washington, until transferred to Elmira, New York, July 23, 1864. Paroled at Elmira and transferred to Boulware's and Cox's Wharf, James River, Virginia, where he was received February 20-21, 1865, for exchange. Reported present with a detachment of paroled and exchanged prisoners at Camp Lee, near Richmond, Virginia, February 28, 1865.

BRICKELL, JAMES B., Private
Resided in Halifax County and enlisted at Richmond, Virginia, at age 20, May 30, 1862, for the war. Present or accounted for until wounded in the left leg and captured at South Mountain, Maryland, on or about September 14, 1862. Hospitalized at Frederick, Maryland, and at Baltimore, Maryland, until paroled and transferred to City Point, Virginia, where he was received February 18, 1863, for exchange. Reported absent wounded until detailed for light duty on September 10, 1863. Reported absent on detail through February 20, 1865.

BRINKLEY, ROBERT, Sergeant
Resided in Halifax County and was by occupation a farmer prior to enlisting in Halifax County at age

33, April 25, 1861. Mustered in as Private and promoted to Corporal in March-October, 1862. Present or accounted for until wounded at Gaines' Mill, Virginia, June 27, 1862, or at Malvern Hill, Virginia, July 1, 1862. Promoted to Sergeant in November, 1862-February, 1863, but was reported absent wounded until he returned to duty in November-December, 1863. Present or accounted for through February 20, 1865; however, he was reported absent on light duty during most of that period.

CARTER, WILLIAM WADE, Private
Resided in Halifax County and was by occupation a merchant prior to enlisting at Camp Carolina, Virginia, at age 38, July 8, 1861. Present or accounted for until wounded at Gaines' Mill, Virginia, June 27, 1862, or at Malvern Hill, Virginia, July 1, 1862. Reported absent wounded through December, 1863. No further records.

CHESANNA, ALEXANDER, Private
Resided in Halifax County and was by occupation a salesman prior to enlisting in Halifax County at age 33, May 16, 1861. Present or accounted for until discharged on May 16, 1862, under the provisions of the Conscript Act.

CHRISTIE, HENRY B., Private
Resided in Halifax County and was by occupation a farmer prior to enlisting in Halifax County at age 22, May 16, 1861. Present or accounted for until wounded in the right arm at Gaines' Mill, Virginia, June 27, 1862. Reported absent wounded until discharged on September 6, 1863, by reason of wounds received at Gaines' Mill.

COGGINS, M. L., Private
Place and date of enlistment not reported. Reported in confinement in a Federal prison at Knoxville, Tennessee, April 12, 1865. Transferred to Chattanooga, Tennessee, April 14, 1865. No further records.

COLLINS, B. F., Private
Born in Franklin County and resided in Halifax County where he was by occupation a salesman prior to enlisting in Halifax County at age 17, April 25, 1861. Present or accounted for until discharged on July 15, 1862, by reason of being under age. North Carolina pension records indicate he was wounded at Bentonville, March 19-20, 1865. [May have served later in Company A, 40th Regiment N.C. Troops (3rd Regiment N.C. Artillery).]

COLTER, DAVIDSON M., Private
Resided in Catawba County. Place and date of enlistment not reported; however, he was first listed in the records of this company on January 12, 1865. Captured at Petersburg, Virginia, March 25, 1865, and confined at Point Lookout, Maryland, until released on June 26, 1865, after taking the Oath of Allegiance.

CONTE, FRANCIS, Private
Born in Italy where he resided as a salesman prior to enlisting in Halifax County at age 23, April 25, 1861. Present or accounted for until captured at Hanover Court House, Virginia, May 27, 1862. Confined at Fort Columbus, New York Harbor, until exchanged at Aiken's Landing, James River, Virginia, August 5, 1862. Rejoined the company prior to

September 14, 1862, when he was captured at South Mountain, Maryland. Confined at Fort Delaware, Delaware, until transferred to Aiken's Landing on October 2, 1862, for exchange. Discharged on November 7, 1862, by reason of being an Italian citizen.

DAY, DAVID H., Private
Resided in Halifax County and was by occupation a farmer prior to enlisting in Halifax County at age 27, April 25, 1861. Present or accounted for until discharged on June 1, 1861. Reason discharged not reported.

DAY, ROBERT J., Private
Resided in Halifax County and was by occupation a farmer prior to enlisting in Halifax County at age 20, April 25, 1861. Present or accounted for until hospitalized at Culpeper, Virginia, September 26, 1862, with a gunshot wound; however, place and date wounded not reported. Returned to duty in November, 1862-February, 1863, and present or accounted for until reported absent without leave on company muster rolls dated April 30-December, 1864. No further records.

DAY, WILLIAM H., Private
Resided in Halifax County and was by occupation a merchant prior to enlisting at Camp Carolina, Virginia, at age 17, July 9, 1861. Present or accounted for until appointed 2nd Lieutenant to rank from April 20, 1862, and transferred to Company K, 1st Regiment N.C. State Troops.

DEVINEY, ROBERT, Private
Resided in Cleveland County and enlisted in Wake County at age 28, February 26, 1863, for the war. Present or accounted for until captured at Spotsylvania Court House, Virginia, May 12, 1864. Confined at Point Lookout, Maryland, until transferred to Elmira, New York, August 10, 1864. Died at Elmira on December 4, 1864, of "pneumonia."

DICKINS, WILLIAM H., Private
Resided in Halifax County and was by occupation a farmer prior to enlisting in Halifax County at age 21, May 16, 1861. Present or accounted for until captured at Sayler's Creek, Virginia, April 6, 1865. Confined at Point Lookout, Maryland, until released on June 3, 1865, after taking the Oath of Allegiance.

DREW, LEWIS W., Color Corporal
Resided in Northampton County and was by occupation a farmer prior to enlisting in Halifax County at age 27, April 25, 1861. Mustered in as Private and promoted to Color Corporal in March-October, 1862. Present or accounted for until wounded at Malvern Hill, Virginia, July 1, 1862. Reported absent wounded through October, 1862, but returned to duty prior to March 1, 1863. Transferred to Company H, 19th Regiment N.C. Troops (2nd Regiment N.C. Cavalry), March 7, 1863.

DRINAN, GEORGE D., Musician
Resided in Virginia and enlisted at Norfolk, Virginia, at age 16, June 4, 1861. Mustered in as Musician. Present or accounted for until discharged on August 1, 1863, by reason of being under age.

EDMONDSON, WILLIAM H., Corporal
Resided in Halifax County and was by occupation a

doctor prior to enlisting in Halifax County at age 23, May 16, 1861. Mustered in as Private and promoted to Corporal in March-October, 1862. Present or accounted for until appointed Assistant Surgeon and transferred to the 52nd Regiment Virginia Infantry, February 1, 1863.

EMRY, THOMAS LEYBURN, Private
Previously served in 1st Company B, 6th Regiment South Carolina Infantry. Transferred to this company on August 9, 1861. Present or accounted for until hospitalized at Charlottesville, Virginia, December 20, 1862, with "laceration wounds." Place and date wounded not reported. Returned to duty on or about February 3, 1863, and present or accounted for until appointed 2nd Lieutenant and transferred to "conscript duty" on September 2, 1863.

FENNER, OWEN, Private
Resided in Halifax County and was by occupation a blacksmith prior to enlisting in Halifax County at age 22, May 16, 1861. Present or accounted for until wounded in the hand at Gaines' Mill, Virginia, June 27, 1862, or at Malvern Hill, Virginia, July 1, 1862. Died in hospital at Richmond, Virginia, October 25, 1862, of "wounds" and/or "double pneumonia."

FERRALL, FRANCIS B., Private
Resided in Halifax County and was by occupation a merchant prior to enlisting at Camp Carolina, Virginia, at age 19, July 9, 1861. Present or accounted for until discharged on August 1, 1862, after providing a substitute.

FINGER, A. W., Private
Enlisted in Wake County on October 6, 1864, for the war. Present or accounted for until paroled at Burkeville Junction, Virginia, April 14-17, 1865.

FORT, W. E., Color Corporal
Born at Baltimore, Maryland, and resided in Maryland prior to enlisting at Bunker Hill, Virginia, at age 21, September 25, 1862, for the war. Mustered in as Color Corporal. Present or accounted for until killed at Chancellorsville, Virginia, May 1-3, 1863.

GLASGOW, W. H., Private
Enlisted in Halifax County on January 8, 1864, for the war. Present or accounted for until hospitalized at Richmond, Virginia, May 19, 1864, with a gunshot wound of the left breast; however, place and date wounded not reported. Returned to duty on July 2, 1864, and present or accounted for until captured at Petersburg, Virginia, February 6, 1865. Confined at Point Lookout, Maryland, until released on May 12, 1865.

GREGORY, CASPER W., Color Corporal
Born in Halifax County where he resided as a farmer prior to enlisting in Halifax County at age 24, May 16, 1861. Mustered in as Private and promoted to Color Corporal in November, 1862-February, 1863. Present or accounted for until wounded in the lung and left shoulder at Gettysburg, Pennsylvania, July 1, 1863. Reported absent wounded until retired to the Invalid Corps on April 6, 1864, by reason of wounds received at Gettysburg.

GREGORY, LAWRANCE B., Private
Resided in Halifax County and was by occupation a farmer prior to enlisting in Halifax County at age

16, April 25, 1861. Present or accounted for until transferred to Company B, 30th Regiment N.C. Troops, December 19, 1861.

HERBERT, EDWARD, Private
Resided in Halifax County and was by occupation a salesman prior to enlisting in Halifax County at age 20, May 16, 1861. Present or accounted for until discharged on or about July 20, 1862, by reason of disability.

HERBERT, JOHN H., Private
Resided in Halifax County and enlisted at Norfolk, Virginia, at age 23, August 12, 1861. Present or accounted for until captured near Petersburg, Virginia, March 25, 1865. Confined at Point Lookout, Maryland, until released on June 3, 1865, after taking the Oath of Allegiance.

HOLT, JOHN A., Private
Resided in Halifax County and was by occupation a farmer prior to enlisting in Halifax County at age 18, May 16, 1861. Present or accounted for until wounded in the left leg at Chancellorsville, Virginia, May 2-3, 1863. Left leg amputated. Reported absent wounded through December, 1864. Paroled at Greensboro at an unspecified date in 1865.

HOWELL, PETER C., 1st Sergeant
Born in Buckingham County, Virginia, and resided in Halifax County where he was by occupation a mechanic prior to enlisting in Halifax County at age 28, April 25, 1861. Mustered in as Private and promoted to Corporal in November, 1862-February, 1863. Promoted to Sergeant on April 5, 1863, and promoted to 1st Sergeant on April 20, 1864. Present or accounted for until wounded in the left arm at Spotsylvania Court House, Virginia, May 19, 1864. Left arm amputated. Reported absent wounded until he was retired on or about February 3, 1865, by reason of disability.

HUFFSTETLER, J. H., Private
Resided in Gaston County and enlisted in Wake County at age 29, February 26, 1863, for the war. Present or accounted for until he died in hospital at Richmond, Virginia, June 17, 1864, of "anasarca."

HUGHES, W. G., Private
Resided in Randolph County and enlisted in Wake County at age 26, February 26, 1863, for the war. Present or accounted for until captured at Petersburg, Virginia, April 2, 1865. Confined at Point Lookout, Maryland, until released on June 27, 1865, after taking the Oath of Allegiance.

HUX, JESSE E., Private
Resided in Halifax County and was by occupation a farmer prior to enlisting in Halifax County at age 22, May 16, 1861. Present or accounted for through April, 1863. Nominated for the Badge of Distinction for gallantry at Chancellorsville, Virginia, May 1-3, 1863. Present or accounted for until wounded in the left thigh at Spotsylvania Court House, Virginia, May 16, 1864. Reported absent wounded through December, 1864.

HUX, WILLIAM H., Corporal
Resided in Halifax County and was by occupation a farmer prior to enlisting in Halifax County at age 18, May 16, 1861. Mustered in as Private and pro-

moted to Corporal in March-October, 1864. Present or accounted for until hospitalized at Charlottesville, Virginia, September 26, 1864, with a gunshot wound of the neck. North Carolina pension records indicate he was wounded at Mount Jackson, Virginia. Returned to duty in November-December, 1864, and present or accounted for until captured at Petersburg, Virginia, April 3, 1865. Confined at Hart's Island, New York Harbor, until released on June 17, 1865, after taking the Oath of Allegiance.

INGRAM, JOHN W., Private
Resided in Northampton County and was by occupation a farmer prior to enlisting in Halifax County at age 24, April 25, 1861. Present or accounted for until he deserted on or about August 10, 1863.

INGRAM, JOSEPH M., Private
Resided in Halifax County and was by occupation a farmer prior to enlisting in Halifax County at age 27, April 25, 1861. Present or accounted for until he was reported captured by the enemy on May 12, 1864; however, records of the Federal Provost Marshal do not substantiate that report. No further records.

INGRAM, MOSES L., Private
Resided in Northampton County and was by occupation a merchant prior to enlisting at Camp Carolina, Virginia, at age 26, July 9, 1861. Present or accounted for until he died on August 1, 1862, of disease. Place of death not reported.

INGRAM, SIMEON W., Private
Born in Northampton County where he resided as a farmer or mechanic prior to enlisting in Halifax County at age 29, April 25, 1861. Present or accounted for until discharged on February 8, 1863, by reason of disability.

IVEY, JOHN H., Private
Resided in Halifax County and was by occupation a lawyer prior to enlisting in Halifax County at age 26, May 16, 1861. Present or accounted for until he died on February 8, 1862, of disease. Place of death not reported.

IVEY, RICHARD B., Private
Resided in Halifax County and was by occupation a farmer prior to enlisting in Halifax County at age 18, April 25, 1861. Present or accounted for through December, 1864.

JARRETT, M. W., Private
Enlisted in Catawba County on October 24, 1864, for the war. Present or accounted for until transferred to Company E of this regiment on December 6, 1864.

JOHNSON, W. GASTON, Private
Enlisted in Wake County on October 6, 1864, for the war. Present or accounted for until captured at Petersburg, Virginia, March 25, 1865. Confined at Point Lookout, Maryland, until released on June 4, 1865, after taking the Oath of Allegiance.

JUDKINS, J. N., Private
Born in Surry County, Virginia, and resided in Halifax County where he was by occupation a clerk prior to enlisting at Norfolk, Virginia, at age 30, September 1, 1861. Present or accounted for until discharged on or about August 5, 1862, by reason of dis-

ability.

KEARNEY, JOHN, Private
Resided in Virginia and enlisted at Fredericksburg, Virginia, at age 45, December 2, 1862, for the war. Present or accounted for until wounded in the leg at Chancellorsville, Virginia, May 1-2, 1863. Leg amputated. Reported absent wounded until retired to the Invalid Corps on November 30, 1864. Deserted from hospital at Richmond, Virginia, February 1, 1865, and was reported in confinement in a Federal prison at Richmond on April 10, 1865.

KEETER, GEORGE, Private
Born in Halifax County where he resided as a farmer prior to enlisting on or about March 4, 1862. Present or accounted for until discharged on or about June 23, 1862, by reason of disability. Discharge papers give his age as 23.

KINLEY, WILLIAM, Private
Resided in Lincoln County and enlisted in Wake County at age 38, February 26, 1863, for the war. Present or accounted for until captured at or near Cedar Creek, Virginia, October 19, 1864. Confined at Point Lookout, Maryland, where he died on May 7, 1865, of "scurvy."

KITCHIN, WILLIAM HODGE, Private
Previously served in 2nd Company D of this regiment. Transferred to this company in March-October, 1862. Company muster roll dated June 30-October 31, 1862, states that he was present. Present or accounted for until appointed 2nd Lieutenant on January 15, 1863, and transferred to Company I of this regiment.

LEWIS, STERLING, Private
Resided in Halifax County and enlisted at Richmond, Virginia, at age 24, May 30, 1862, for the war. Present or accounted for until captured at Petersburg, Virginia, April 3, 1865. Confined at Hart's Island, New York Harbor, until released on June 17, 1865, after taking the Oath of Allegiance.

LINEBARGER, WILLIAM ALEXANDER, Private
Enlisted in Wake County on October 6, 1864, for the war. Present or accounted for until transferred to Company D, 28th Regiment N.C. Troops, February 8, 1865.

MABRY, ROBERT G., Private
Resided in Halifax County and was by occupation a farmer prior to enlisting in Halifax County at age 19, April 25, 1861. Present or accounted for until wounded in the foot at Gaines' Mill, Virginia, June 27, 1862. Reported absent wounded until discharged on or about January 31, 1863, by reason of wounds received at Gaines' Mill.

McGILL, JOHN, Private
Resided in Halifax County and enlisted in Wake County at age 34, March 1, 1863, for the war. Present or accounted for until captured at Cedar Creek, Virginia, October 19, 1864. Confined at Point Lookout, Maryland, until paroled and transferred to Boulware's Wharf, James River, Virginia, where he was received March 30, 1865, for exchange.

McNEAL, JAMES, Private
Enlisted in Wake County on April 5, 1864, for the

war. Captured at Spotsylvania Court House, Virginia, May 12-20, 1864. Confined at Point Lookout, Maryland, until transferred to Elmira, New York, July 3, 1864. Paroled at Elmira and transferred to James River, Virginia, March 2, 1865, for exchange. Reported in hospital at Richmond, Virginia, March 10, 1865.

MALONE, RICHARD T., Private
Was by occupation a mechanic prior to enlisting in Halifax County at age 36, May 16, 1861. Deserted August 5, 1861.

MARSHALL, JAMES T., Private
Resided in Halifax County and was by occupation a tailor prior to enlisting in Halifax County at age 19, April 25, 1861. Present or accounted for until killed at South Mountain, Maryland, September 14, 1862.

MERRITT, GEORGE B., Private
Resided in Halifax County and was by occupation a saddler prior to enlisting in Halifax County at age 20, April 25, 1861. Present or accounted for until he died in hospital at Richmond, Virginia, July 24, 1862, of "fever cont[inued] & typhoid."

MILES, JAMES W., Private
Resided in Halifax or Northampton counties and was by occupation a farmer prior to enlisting in Halifax County at age 21, April 25, 1861. Present or accounted for until transferred to Company D, 32nd Regiment N.C. Troops, September 10, 1861.

MILLER, GEORGE A., Private
Resided in Virginia and enlisted at age 48, August 1, 1862, for the war as a substitute. Present or accounted for until killed at South Mountain, Maryland, or at Sharpsburg, Maryland, September 14-17, 1862.

MILLICAN, DAVID A., Corporal
Resided in Halifax County and was by occupation a farmer prior to enlisting at Camp Carolina, Virginia, at age 19, June 27, 1861. Mustered in as Private and promoted to Corporal on April 1, 1863. Present or accounted for until wounded at Gettysburg, Pennsylvania, July 1-3, 1863. Returned to duty prior to September 1, 1863, and present or accounted for through April, 1864. No further records.

MINDEE, D. W., Private
Resided in Halifax County. Place and date of enlistment not reported. Captured at Petersburg, Virginia, April 2, 1865, and confined at Hart's Island, New York Harbor, until released on June 17, 1865, after taking the Oath of Allegiance.

MITCHELL, W. P., Private
Resided in Halifax County and enlisted at Norfolk, Virginia, at age 28, August 15, 1861. Present or accounted for until wounded at Gaines' Mill, Virginia, June 27, 1862. Reported absent wounded or absent on detail until February 25, 1864, when he was reported absent without leave. Reported absent without leave through April, 1864. Returned to duty prior to November 1, 1864, when he was detailed at Weldon. Reported absent on detail through December, 1864.

MORE, GEORGE, _____
Born in England and resided in South Carolina. Place and date of enlistment not reported. Deserted to the enemy on or about February 18, 1865. Transferred from Hilton Head, South Carolina, to New York City on or about March 22, 1865. No further records.

MORRIS, JOHN W., Private
Resided in Union County and enlisted in Wake County at age 23, February 26, 1863, for the war. Present or accounted for until reported absent without leave on July 4, 1863. Reported absent without leave through February, 1864. Returned to duty in March-September, 1864, and was confined at Castle Thunder Prison, Richmond, Virginia, September 16, 1864. Reported on hospital duty at Lynchburg, Virginia, in November-December, 1864. No further records.

MURPHY, JAMES, Private
Previously served in Company D, 28th Regiment N.C. Troops. Transferred to this company on February 8, 1865. Captured at Petersburg, Virginia, March 25, 1865, and confined at Point Lookout, Maryland, until released on June 29, 1865, after taking the Oath of Allegiance.

MYERS, MARCUS, Private
Born in Germany and resided in Halifax County where he was by occupation a merchant prior to enlisting in Halifax County at age 25, April 25, 1861. Present or accounted for until discharged on or about April 29, 1863, by reason of "chronic diarrhoea, hectic fever, and severe cough arising from tubercular disease."

NEVILL, THOMAS W., Private
Resided in Halifax County and was by occupation a farmer prior to enlisting in Halifax County at age 30, May 16, 1861. Present or accounted for until captured at South Mountain, Maryland, September 14, 1862. Confined at Fort Delaware, Delaware, until transferred to Aiken's Landing, James River, Virginia, October 2, 1862, for exchange. Declared exchanged at Aiken's Landing on November 10, 1862. Returned to duty prior to March 1, 1863, and present or accounted for until wounded in the abdomen at Chancellorsville, Virginia, May 2, 1863. Returned to duty prior to July 1, 1863, and present or accounted for through December, 1864.

NEVILLE, RICHARD H., Private
Resided in Halifax County and was by occupation a farmer prior to enlisting in Halifax County at age 26, April 25, 1861. Present or accounted for until captured at South Mountain, Maryland, September 14, 1862. Exchanged on or about October 2, 1862, and present or accounted for until captured near Washington, D. C., July 12, 1864. Confined at Old Capitol Prison, Washington, until transferred to Elmira, New York, July 23, 1864. Died at Elmira on March 19, 1865, of "pneumonia."

NORFLEET, JOHN, Private
Resided in Halifax County and was by occupation a farmer prior to enlisting in Halifax County at age 18, May 16, 1861. Present or accounted for until wounded in the left shoulder at Malvern Hill, Virginia, July 1, 1862. Reported absent wounded through October, 1862, but returned to duty prior to March 2, 1863. Reported absent on light duty from May-June, 1863, through December, 1864. Paroled at Lynchburg, Virginia, in April, 1865.

NORTHINGTON, GEORGE W., 1st Sergeant
Resided in Halifax County and was by occupation a salesman prior to enlisting in Halifax County at age 18, May 16, 1861. Mustered in as Private and promoted to Corporal on April 1, 1863. Promoted to Sergeant on June 1, 1863, and promoted to 1st Sergeant in May-October, 1864. Company muster rolls dated April 30-December, 1864, indicate that he was absent wounded; however, place and date wounded not reported. Paroled at Appomattox Court House, Virginia, April 9, 1865.

OUSBY, WILLIAM C., Sergeant
Born in Halifax County where he resided as a farmer prior to enlisting in Halifax County at age 28, April 25, 1861. Mustered in as Sergeant. Present or accounted for until appointed 1st Lieutenant and transferred to Company F, 43rd Regiment N.C. Troops, on or about February 14, 1862.

OWENS, N. B., Private
Resided in Halifax County and enlisted at age 20, October 12, 1862, for the war. Died in hospital at Richmond, Virginia, December 19, 1862, of "febris typhoides."

PAIR, J. L., Private
Resided in Halifax County and enlisted at Norfolk, Virginia, at age 25, April 25, 1862, for the war. Present or accounted for until wounded at Gaines' Mill, Virginia, June 27, 1862. Returned to duty in May-June, 1863, and present or accounted for until captured at Spotsylvania Court House, Virginia, May 12, 1864. Confined at Point Lookout, Maryland, until transferred to Elmira, New York, August 10, 1864. Released at Elmira on June 11, 1865, after taking the Oath of Allegiance.

PARKER, F. R., Private
Born in Halifax County where he resided as a constable prior to enlisting in Halifax County at age 22, April 25, 1861. Present or accounted for until transferred to Company I of this regiment on March 30, 1862.

PITTARD, CONFUCIUS, Private
Born in Warren County and was by occupation a farmer prior to enlisting in Halifax County at age 23, April 25, 1861. Present or accounted for until discharged on or about July 25, 1862, by reason of disability.

PONTON, HENRY D., Private
Resided in Halifax County and was by occupation a farmer prior to enlisting in Halifax County at age 20, April 25, 1861. Present or accounted for until discharged on or about December 24, 1862, after providing a substitute.

PONTON, JOHN H., Private
Resided in Halifax County and was by occupation a farmer prior to enlisting in Halifax County at age 33, April 25, 1861. Present or accounted for through February, 1862. Discharged at an unspecified date by reason of being a Justice of the Peace.

PORTER, JOSEPH W., Private
Resided in Halifax County and was by occupation a farmer prior to enlisting in Halifax County at age 19, May 16, 1861. Present or accounted for until killed at Cold Harbor, Virginia, June 3, 1864.

PRITCHARD, JEREMIAH O., Private
Resided in Halifax County and was by occupation a farmer prior to enlisting in Halifax County at age 28, May 16, 1861. Present or accounted for until he died in the "naval hospital" on December 23, 1861, of disease.

RICHARDS, BENJAMIN W., Private
Resided in Halifax County and was by occupation a salesman prior to enlisting in Halifax County at age 18, April 25, 1861. Present or accounted for until killed at Gaines' Mill, Virginia, June 27, 1862.

RICHARDS, WILLIAM H., Private
Resided in Halifax County and was by occupation a farmer prior to enlisting in Halifax County at age 25, April 25, 1861. Present or accounted for until wounded at Gaines' Mill, Virginia, June 27, 1862. Hospitalized at Charlottesville, Virginia, October 16, 1862, with a contusion of the heel; however, records do not indicate whether this was the wound he received at Gaines' Mill. Returned to duty prior to March 2, 1863, and present or accounted for until killed at Spotsylvania Court House, Virginia, May 12, 1864.

ROBERTSON, JOHN T., Private
Resided in Halifax County and was by occupation a farmer prior to enlisting in Halifax County at age 22, April 25, 1861. Present or accounted for until wounded in the leg at Gaines' Mill, Virginia, June 27, 1862. Returned to duty prior to November 1, 1862, and present or accounted for until he deserted on September 14, 1863. Not listed again on the rolls of this company until November-December, 1864, when he was reported as present.

ROGGERS, ROBERT CALVIN, Private
Resided in Halifax County and was by occupation a farmer prior to enlisting in Halifax County at age 22, May 16, 1861. Present or accounted for until hospitalized at Charlottesville, Virginia, May 17, 1864, with a gunshot wound of the left leg; however, place and date wounded not reported. Returned to duty prior to September 19, 1864, when he was wounded in the leg and captured at Winchester, Virginia. Hospitalized at Baltimore, Maryland, October 29, 1864, and was transferred to Point Lookout, Maryland, November 22, 1864. Paroled at Point Lookout and transferred to Cox's Landing, James River, Virginia, where he was received February 14-15, 1865, for exchange. Hospitalized at Richmond, Virginia, until furloughed for sixty days on February 24, 1865.

ROOK, WILLIAM B., Private
Resided in Northampton County and was by occupation a farmer prior to enlisting in Halifax County at age 19, April 25, 1861. Present or accounted for until wounded in the shoulder at Chancellorsville, Virginia, May 2, 1863. Reported absent wounded until he was listed as a deserter on October 1, 1863.

RUSSELL, THOMAS B., Private
Resided in Halifax County and was by occupation a salesman prior to enlisting in Halifax County at age 22, April 25, 1861. Present and accounted for until killed at Gaines' Mill, Virginia, June 27, 1862.

SHEARIN, D. A., Private
Resided in Halifax County and enlisted at age 36,

April 25, 1861. Killed October 1, 1861, in a railroad accident. Place of death not reported.

SHEARIN, ELISHA DAVID, Private

Enlisted in Halifax County at age 44, May 16, 1861. Present or accounted for until killed in a railroad accident near Suffolk, Virginia, on or about October 1, 1861.

SHERRAN, ABNER, Private

Resided in Halifax County and was by occupation a farmer prior to enlisting in Halifax County at age 22, May 16, 1861. Present or accounted for until killed at Chancellorsville, Virginia, May 1-3, 1863.

SHERRAN, ALPHEUS F., Private

Born in Halifax County where he resided as a farmer prior to enlisting in Halifax County at age 18, May 16, 1861. Present or accounted for until wounded in the shoulder at Gaines' Mill, Virginia, June 27, 1862. Reported absent wounded until he returned to duty in January-February, 1864. Discharged on or about March 6, 1864, by reason of disability.

SHERRAN, CRAWFORD, Private

Born in Halifax County where he resided as a farmer prior to enlisting in Halifax County at age 17, May 16, 1861. Present or accounted for until discharged on or about September 12, 1862, by reason of being "under age." Reenlisted in the company on August 21, 1863. Present or accounted for until hospitalized at Richmond, Virginia, August 17, 1864, with a gunshot wound of the right wrist; however, place and date wounded not reported. Returned to duty on October 10, 1864, and was reported absent on hospital detail in November-December, 1864.

SLEDGE, JOHN L., Private

Resided in Halifax County and was by occupation a machinist prior to enlisting in Halifax County at age 35, April 25, 1861. Present or accounted for until discharged on May 16, 1862, by reason of being over age.

SMALLWOOD, PYLADIES, Private

Was by occupation a farmer prior to enlisting in Halifax County at age 30, April 25, 1861. Present or accounted for until he was "killed at home by a citizen" September 27, 1862.

SMITH, J. H., Private

Resided in Halifax County and enlisted at Norfolk, Virginia, at age 20, August 12, 1861. Present or accounted for until wounded at Gaines' Mill, Virginia, June 27, 1862. Reported absent wounded or absent sick until he died in Halifax County on March 8, 1863, of wounds and/or disease.

SNOW, HENRY A., Private

Resided in Halifax County and was by occupation a farmer prior to enlisting in Halifax County at age 22, April 25, 1861. Present or accounted for until captured at Winchester, Virginia, September 19, 1864. Confined at Point Lookout, Maryland, until released on June 3, 1865, after taking the Oath of Allegiance.

SNOW, SHUGAN, Private

Resided in Halifax County and was by occupation a farmer prior to enlisting in Halifax County at age 18, April 25, 1861. Present or accounted for until appointed Captain to rank from February 16, 1862,

and transferred to Company I of this regiment.

STAMPER, ROBERT J., Private

Resided in Halifax County and was by occupation a salesman prior to enlisting in Halifax County at age 21, May 16, 1861. Present or accounted for until mortally wounded at Gaines' Mill, Virginia, June 27, 1862. Roll of Honor indicates he was killed at Gaines' Mill; however, medical records indicate he died in hospital at Richmond, Virginia, July 23, 1862. No further records.

STOWE, J. A., Private

Resided in Catawba County and enlisted in Wake County on October 6, 1864, for the war. Present or accounted for until captured at Sayler's Creek, Virginia, April 6, 1865. Confined at Point Lookout, Maryland, until released on June 20, 1865, after taking the Oath of Allegiance.

SUITER, ARTHUR T., Sergeant

Resided in Halifax County and was by occupation a merchant prior to enlisting in Halifax County at age 24, April 25, 1861. Mustered in as Private and promoted to Sergeant in March-October, 1862. Present or accounted for until he died in hospital at Lynchburg, Virginia, March 13, 1863, of "pneumonia."

SUITER, JOSEPH LEONIDAS, Corporal

Resided in Halifax or Northampton counties and enlisted at Richmond, Virginia, at age 18, May 30, 1862, for the war. Mustered in as Private and promoted to Corporal on April 1, 1863. Present or accounted for until he deserted on August 23, 1863. Not listed again on the rolls of this company; however, records of the Federal Provost Marshal indicate he was wounded in the right leg and captured at Petersburg, Virginia, March 25, 1865. Hospitalized at Washington, D.C., until released on or about June 14, 1865, after taking the Oath of Allegiance.

TAYLOR, WILLIAM R., Private

Resided in Halifax County and was by occupation a salesman prior to enlisting in Halifax County at age 26, April 25, 1861. Present or accounted for until he died on or about September 5, 1861, of disease. Place of death not reported.

UNDERHILL, WILLIAM H., Sergeant

Resided in Halifax County and was by occupation a mechanic prior to enlisting in Halifax County at age 37, April 25, 1861. Mustered in as Sergeant. Present or accounted for until discharged on May 16, 1862, by reason of being over age.

WARREN, GEORGE L., Private

Resided in Halifax County and was by occupation a farmer prior to enlisting in Halifax County at age 22, April 25, 1861. Present or accounted for until hospitalized at Charlottesville, Virginia, July 25, 1864, with a contusion; however, place and date injured not reported. Furloughed for forty days on August 27, 1864.

WARREN, HENRY, Private

Resided in Halifax County and enlisted at Taylorsville, Virginia, February 22, 1864, for the war. Present or accounted for until wounded in the left leg at Spotsylvania Court House, Virginia, May 19, 1864. Reported absent wounded through April 7, 1865.

WARREN, ROBERT, Private

Enlisted in Halifax County on January 24, 1864, for the war. Present or accounted for until hospitalized at Richmond, Virginia, April 21, 1864, with a gunshot wound of the left side; however, place and date wounded not reported. Hospital records indicate he returned to duty on or about June 12, 1864; however, company records indicate he was absent without leave through December, 1864. No further records.

WARREN, THOMAS A., Private

Resided in Halifax County and was by occupation a farmer prior to enlisting in Halifax County at age 21, April 25, 1861. Present or accounted for until wounded in the thigh and captured at Hanover Court House, Virginia, May 27, 1862. Confined at Fort Monroe, Virginia, until exchanged at Aiken's Landing, James River, Virginia, August 5, 1862. Returned to duty at an unspecified date prior to March 2, 1863, and present or accounted for until he died in hospital at Richmond, Virginia, July 12, 1864. Cause of death not reported.

WELLER, JOSEPH M., Private

Resided in Halifax County and was by occupation a salesman prior to enlisting in Halifax County at age 19, May 16, 1861. Present or accounted for until discharged on or about July 20, 1862, by reason of disability.

WHITEHEAD, FREDERICK B., Color Sergeant

Resided in Halifax County and was by occupation a farmer prior to enlisting in Halifax County at age 22, April 25, 1861. Mustered in as Private and promoted to Color Sergeant on September 1, 1862. Present or accounted for until wounded in the neck and shoulder at Chancellorsville, Virginia, May 2, 1863. Reported absent wounded until retired to the Invalid Corps on April 25, 1864.

WHITEHEAD, GODWIN C., Corporal

Resided in Halifax County and was by occupation a farmer prior to enlisting in Halifax County at age 34, April 25, 1861. Mustered in as Corporal. Present or accounted for until discharged on July 15, 1862, by reason of being over age.

WILLCOX, LOGAN O., Sergeant

Resided in Halifax County and was by occupation a farmer prior to enlisting in Halifax County at age 21, April 25, 1861. Mustered in as Private and promoted to Sergeant in March-July, 1862. Present or accounted for until he died on or about July 16, 1862, of disease. Place of death not reported.

WILLIS, JOHN R., Private

Resided in Maryland and enlisted at Bunker Hill, Virginia, at age 21, September 25, 1862, for the war. Present or accounted for until reported absent without leave in August, 1863. Reported absent without leave through February, 1864. No further records.

WOOD, JOSEPH J., Private

Resided in Halifax County and was by occupation a farmer prior to enlisting in Halifax County at age 19, April 25, 1861. Present or accounted for until hospitalized at Charlottesville, Virginia, October 16, 1862, with a contusion of the chest; however, place and date injured not reported. Returned to duty on

November 24, 1862. Present or accounted for until he was reported transferred to Company D, 24th Regiment N.C.Troops (14th Regiment N.C.Volunteers), on or about January 7, 1865; however, records of the 24th Regiment do not indicate that he served therein. No further records.

WOOD, WILLIAM ROBERT, Private

Resided in Halifax County and was by occupation a printer prior to enlisting at Camp Carolina, Virginia, at age 20, July 9, 1861. Present or accounted for until wounded in the pelvis and captured at Hanover Court House, Virginia, May 27, 1862. Hospitalized at Gaines' Mill, Virginia, where he died May 31, 1862, of wounds.

1st COMPANY H

This company, known as "The Nash Boys," was raised in Nash County and enlisted at Nashville on or about April 22 or May 1, 1861. It tendered its service to the state and was ordered to Garysburg, where it was assigned to this regiment. The company was mustered in as Captain William T. Williams's Company and was designated Company G and Company I before it was designated Company H. It was referred to as 1st Company H after a second company was assigned to the regiment as Company H in May, 1862. The second company was transferred out of the regiment on July 22, 1862, but this company continued to be referred to as 1st Company H. After it was mustered into the regiment the company functioned as a part of the regiment, and its history for the war period is recorded as a part of the regimental history.

The information contained in the following roster of the company was compiled principally from company muster rolls for May 1, 1861-February 28, 1862, and November, 1862-December, 1864. No company muster rolls were found for March-October, 1862, or for the period after December, 1864. In addition to the company muster rolls, Roll of Honor records, receipt rolls, hospital records, prisoner of war records, and other primary records, supplemented by state pension applications, United Daughters of the Confederacy records, and postwar rosters and histories, all provided useful information.

OFFICERS
CAPTAINS

WILLIAMS, WILLIAM T.

Resided in Nash County and was by occupation a physician prior to enlisting in Nash County at age 21. Appointed Captain to rank from May 1, 1861. Present or accounted for until appointed Lieutenant Colonel to rank from September 26, 1861, and transferred to the 32nd Regiment N.C.Troops.

VICK, SAMUEL S.

Resided in Nash County and was by occupation a student prior to enlisting in Nash County at age 18. Appointed 1st Lieutenant on or about April 22, 1861, and was promoted to Captain to rank from

September 30, 1861. Died on or about October 26, 1861, of disease. Place of death not reported.

BLOUNT, WILLIAM H.
Resided in Nash County and was by occupation a cadet prior to enlisting in Nash County at age 18. Appointed 3rd Lieutenant on or about May 1, 1861, and was promoted to 2nd Lieutenant on May 18, 1861. Promoted to 1st Lieutenant to rank from September 30, 1861, and was promoted to Captain to rank from October 26, 1861. Present or accounted for until he was defeated for reelection when the regiment was reorganized on May 1, 1862. Later served as 2nd Lieutenant in Company D, 47th Regiment N.C.Troops.

BUNN, WILLIAM H.
Resided in Nash County and enlisted at Camp Morton at age 27, November 10, 1861. Mustered in as Private and was appointed Captain to rank from May 1, 1862. Present or accounted for until reported absent without leave in December, 1863. Court-martialed on or about March 26, 1864, and was dismissed from the service.

DRAKE, JOHN A.
Resided in Nash County and was by occupation a physician prior to enlisting at Camp Carolina, Virginia, at age 23, July 2, 1861. Mustered in as Private and was promoted to 1st Sergeant on September 28, 1861. Appointed 1st Lieutenant to rank from May 1, 1862. Present or accounted for until wounded in the knee at Morton's Ford, Virginia, October 11, 1863. Returned to duty prior to November 1, 1863. Promoted to Captain on April 26, 1864. Present or accounted for until wounded in the abdomen at or near Lynchburg, Virginia, in May-October, 1864. Reported absent wounded or absent sick through December, 1864, but rejoined the company prior to March 25, 1865, when he was captured at Petersburg, Virginia. Confined at Old Capitol Prison, Washington, D.C., until transferred to Fort Delaware, Delaware, March 30, 1865. Released at Fort Delaware on June 17, 1865, after taking the Oath of Allegiance.

LIEUTENANTS

ARRINGTON, HARDY H., 2nd Lieutenant
Resided in Nash County and was by occupation a farmer prior to enlisting in Nash County at age 24, April 23, 1861. Mustered in as Private and was appointed 2nd Lieutenant to rank from October 26, 1861. Present or accounted for until he was defeated for reelection when the regiment was reorganized on May 1, 1862.

AVENT, JAMES H., 2nd Lieutenant
Resided in Nash County and enlisted at age 23. Appointed 2nd Lieutenant on May 1, 1861. Resigned May 15, 1861. Reason he resigned not reported.

BARRETT, JOHN W., 1st Lieutenant
Resided in Nash County and was by occupation a student prior to enlisting in Nash County at age 25. Appointed 3rd Lieutenant on or about May 1, 1861, and was promoted to 2nd Lieutenant to rank from September 30, 1861. Promoted to 1st Lieutenant on October 26, 1861. Present or accounted for until

transferred to 2nd Company H of this regiment in March-June, 1862.

FOX, JACOB, 2nd Lieutenant
Resided in Nash County and enlisted at age 50. Elected 2nd Lieutenant on May 1, 1861. Died June 8, 1861, of disease. Place of death not reported.

GRIFFIN, SAMUEL H., 2nd Lieutenant
Resided in Nash County and was by occupation a clerk prior to enlisting in Nash County at age 25, May 1, 1861. Mustered in as Sergeant and was appointed 2nd Lieutenant to rank from May 1, 1862. Present or accounted for until captured at Sayler's Creek, Virginia, April 6, 1865. Confined at Old Capitol Prison, Washington, D. C., until transferred to Johnson's Island, Ohio, April 17, 1865. Released at Johnson's Island on June 18, 1865, after taking the Oath of Allegiance.

HARPER, JOHN CALHOUN, 1st Lieutenant
Born in Franklin County and resided in Franklin or Nash counties where he was by occupation a student prior to enlisting in Northampton County at age 21, May 15, 1861. Mustered in as Private and appointed 2nd Lieutenant to rank from May 1, 1862. Promoted to 1st Lieutenant on March 26, 1863. Present or accounted for until wounded in the left leg at Chancellorsville, Virginia, May 3, 1863. Returned to duty prior to September 1, 1863, and present or accounted for until paroled at Appomattox Court House, Virginia, April 9, 1865.

ROWLAND, WILLIS F., 2nd Lieutenant
Resided in Nash County and was by occupation a merchant prior to enlisting in Nash County at age 33, May 9, 1861. Mustered in as Private and promoted to 1st Sergeant on June 16, 1861. Appointed 2nd Lieutenant on September 28, 1861. Present or accounted for until he was defeated for reelection when the regiment was reorganized on May 1, 1862.

NONCOMMISSIONED OFFICERS AND PRIVATES

ARNOLD, JOSEPH, Private
Resided in Nash County and was by occupation a farmer prior to enlisting in Halifax County at age 21, May 6, 1861. Present or accounted for until killed in battle in May-October, 1864; however, battle in which killed not reported.

ARRINGTON, R. A., Private
Resided in Nash County and enlisted at Camp Arrington, Virginia, at age 22, April 20, 1862. Present or accounted for until discharged on December 9, 1862, after providing a substitute.

BAINES, A. L., Private
Resided in Nash County and enlisted at Camp Arrington, Virginia, at age 27, February 24, 1862. Present or accounted for until wounded in the left thigh and captured at or near Sayler's Creek, Virginia, April 6, 1865. Hospitalized at various Federal hospitals until transferred to Fort McHenry, Maryland, May 9, 1865. Released at Fort McHenry on June 9, 1865, after taking the Oath of Allegiance.

BARBEE, CLEM S., Private
Resided in Nash County and enlisted at Camp

Arrington, Virginia, at age 19, April 20, 1862. Present or accounted for until wounded in the arm at Chancellorsville, Virginia, May 1-3, 1863. Returned to duty prior to September 1, 1863, and present or accounted for until captured near Petersburg, Virginia, March 25, 1865. Confined at Point Lookout, Maryland, until released on June 23, 1865, after taking the Oath of Allegiance.

BARBEE, JAMES J., 1st Sergeant
Resided in Nash County and was by occupation a farmer prior to enlisting in Nash County at age 21, May 1, 1861. Mustered in as Private and promoted to 1st Sergeant on May 1, 1862. Present or accounted for until captured at Spotsylvania Court House, Virginia, May 12, 1864. Confined at Point Lookout, Maryland, until transferred to Elmira, New York, August 10, 1864. Died at Elmira on November 18, 1864, of "pneumonia."

BARBEE, WILLIAM C., Private
Resided in Nash County and enlisted at Camp Martin at age 18, November 18, 1861. Present or accounted for until killed in battle in May-October, 1864; however, battle in which killed not reported.

BARNES, ALEXANDER L. B., Corporal
Resided in Nash County and was by occupation a farmer prior to enlisting in Nash County at age 22, May 1, 1861. Mustered in as Private and promoted to Corporal in March-December, 1862. Present or accounted for through April, 1863. Nominated for the Badge of Distinction for gallantry at Chancellorsville, Virginia, May 1-3, 1863. Present or accounted for until captured at Cedar Creek, Virginia, October 19, 1864. Company records indicate he was also wounded at Cedar Creek; however, records of the Federal Provost Marshal do not substantiate that report. Confined at Point Lookout, Maryland, until released on June 23, 1865, after taking the Oath of Allegiance.

BARNES, B., Private
Place and date of enlistment not reported. Paroled at Appomattox Court House, Virginia, April 9, 1865.

BARNES, CULLEN E., Private
Resided in Nash County and was by occupation a mechanic prior to enlisting at Camp Carolina, Virginia, at age 25, June 15, 1861. Discharged on or about August 27, 1861, by reason of "ill health."

BARNES, GRANBERY B. R., Private
Resided in Nash County and was by occupation a farmer prior to enlisting in Nash County at age 23, May 1, 1861. Present or accounted for until wounded in the wrist at Chancellorsville, Virginia, May 2-3, 1863. Returned to duty in September-October, 1863. Present or accounted for until killed in battle in May-October, 1864; however, battle in which killed not reported.

BARNES, JOHN RICHARD, Private
Resided in Nash County and was by occupation a mechanic prior to enlisting at Camp Carolina, Virginia, at age 22, June 12, 1861. Present or accounted for until discharged on August 27, 1861, by reason of "ill health."

BARNES, ROBERT, Private
Resided in Nash County and was by occupation a farmer prior to enlisting in Nash County at age 19, May 1, 1861. Present or accounted for until wounded in the left thigh and captured at Cedar Creek, Virginia, October 19, 1864. Hospitalized at Baltimore, Maryland, until paroled and transferred to Venus Point, Savannah River, Georgia, where he was received November 15, 1864, for exchange. Paroled at Appomattox Court House, Virginia, April 9, 1865.

BARNES, WILLIAM, Private
Born in Nash County where he resided as a farmer prior to enlisting in Nash County at age 16, May 1, 1861. Present or accounted for until discharged on or about August 1, 1862, by reason of being under age.

BARNES, WILLIAM W., Private
Enlisted in Alexander County on March 7, 1864, for the war. Present or accounted for until killed in battle in May-October, 1864; however, battle in which killed not reported.

BASS, BENJAMIN F., Private
Resided in Nash County and was by occupation a farmer prior to enlisting in Northampton County at age 23, May 10, 1861. Present or accounted for until transferred to 2nd Company H of this regiment on May 1, 1862.

BASS, MARK C., Private
Resided in Nash County and was by occupation a farmer prior to enlisting at Camp Carolina, Virginia, at age 17, June 12, 1861. Present or accounted for until transferred to 2nd Company H of this regiment on May 1, 1862.

BATCHELOR, B. B., Private
Born in Nash County where he resided as a farmer or cooper prior to enlisting in Northampton County at age 30, May 10, 1861. Present or accounted for until transferred to 2nd Company H of this regiment on or about May 1, 1862.

BATCHELOR, RICHARD, Private
Resided in Nash County and was by occupation a farmer prior to enlisting in Nash County at age 19, May 1, 1861. Present or accounted for until discharged on or about August 27, 1861, by reason of "ill health."

BATTLE, DOSSEY, Sergeant
Previously served in 2nd Company D of this regiment. Transferred to this company on January 4, 1863, with the rank of Private. Promoted to Sergeant prior to March 1, 1863. Present or accounted for until promoted to Sergeant Major in March, 1863, and transferred to the Field and Staff of this regiment.

BATTLE, TIP, Corporal
Resided in Nash County and was by occupation a farmer prior to enlisting in Nash County at age 20, August 22, 1861. Mustered in as Private and promoted to Corporal on October 1, 1862. Present or accounted for until discharged on December 9, 1862, after providing a substitute.

BEAL, E. B. H., Private
Resided in Nash County and enlisted at age 25, May

1, 1861. North Carolina pension records indicate he was wounded in Virginia in 1863. No further records. [May have served later in Company H, 10th Regiment N.C. Troops (1st Regiment N.C. Artillery).]

BEAL, JAMES H., Corporal
Resided in Nash County and was by occupation a farmer prior to enlisting in Nash County at age 19, May 1, 1861. Mustered in as Private and promoted to Corporal in March-April, 1862. Present or accounted for until transferred to 2nd Company H of this regiment on or about May 1, 1862.

BEDGOOD, J., Private
Resided in Nash County and enlisted at age 17, February 24, 1862. Discharged on May 1, 1862, by reason of being under age.

BENTON, HENRY, Private
Born in Nash County where he resided as a farmer prior to enlisting in Nash County at age 17, May 1, 1861. Present or accounted for until discharged on or about August 1, 1862, by reason of being under age.

BLOUNT, BENJAMIN J., Sergeant
Resided in Nash County and was by occupation a student prior to enlisting in Nash County at age 23, May 1, 1861. Mustered in as Sergeant. Present or accounted for until he was reported transferred to the 47th Regiment N.C.Troops; however, records of the 47th Regiment do not indicate that he served therein. Later served as 2nd Lieutenant in Company H, 55th Regiment N. C.Troops.

BOTTOMS, RICHARD, Private
Resided in Nash County and was by occupation a farmer prior to enlisting in Nash County at age 22, May 1, 1861. Present or accounted for until he deserted on or about April 26, 1863. Court-martialed on or about December 26, 1863. No further records.

BRASWELL, HANS, Private
Resided in Nash County and was by occupation a farmer prior to enlisting in Nash County at age 48, May 1, 1861. Present or accounted for until discharged on February 15, 1862, by reason of disability.

BRASWELL, JOHN A., Private
Resided in Nash County and was by occupation a student prior to enlisting at Camp Carolina, Virginia, at age 21, June 24, 1861. Present or accounted for until he died on February 18, 1862, of disease. Place of death not reported.

BRASWELL, JOHN THOMAS, Private
Resided in Nash County where he enlisted at age 24, February 24, 1862. Discharged at an unspecified date after providing a substitute.

BREWER, JAMES, Jr., Private
Resided in Nash County and was by occupation a farmer prior to enlisting in Nash County at age 21, May 1, 1861. Present or accounted for until he died on or about January 19, 1862. Place and cause of death not reported.

BREWER, JORDAN, Corporal
Resided in Nash County and was by occupation a farmer prior to enlisting in Nash County at age 34,

April 22, 1861. Mustered in as Private and promoted to Corporal at an unspecified date. Present or accounted for until discharged on August 1, 1862, by reason of being over age.

BROWN, JOHN, Private
Resided in Ireland and enlisted at Gordonsville, Virginia, at age 25, December 9, 1862, for the war as a substitute. Deserted on or about December 27, 1862.

BRYAN, DEMPSEY T., Private
Born in Edgecombe County and resided in Nash County where he was by occupation a student prior to enlisting in Nash County at age 16, May 1, 1861. Present or accounted for until discharged on or about August 1, 1862, by reason of being under age. Later served in Company A, 63rd Regiment N.C. Troops (5th Regiment N.C.Cavalry).

BRYSON, J. M., Private
Resided in Jackson County. Place and date of enlistment not reported. Deserted to the enemy prior to April 12, 1865, when he was confined at Knoxville, Tennessee. Transferred to Chattanooga, Tennessee, April 14, 1865. Transferred to Louisville, Kentucky, where he took the Oath of Allegiance on April 18, 1865.

BUNN, ELIAS, Private
Resided in Nash County and enlisted at age 27, February 5, 1862. Appointed Adjutant on or about May 1, 1862, and transferred to the Field and Staff of this regiment.

CELLERS, JORDAN, Private
Enlisted at Fisher's Hill, Virginia, September 19, 1864, for the war. Company muster rolls dated April 30-December, 1864, indicate that he was a prisoner of war; however, place and date captured not reported. Records of the Federal Provost Marshal do not substantiate the report of his capture. No further records.

COGGIN, DANIEL C., Private
Resided in Nash County and was by occupation a clerk prior to enlisting in Nash County at age 21, May 1, 1861. Mustered in as Private and was promoted to 1st Sergeant on June 15, 1861. Reduced to ranks on August 6, 1861. Discharged September 25, 1861. Reason discharged not reported.

COLLINS, JONES, Sergeant
Resided in Nash County and was by occupation a clerk prior to enlisting in Nash County at age 25, May 1, 1861. Mustered in as Sergeant. Present or accounted for until transferred to 2nd Company H of this regiment on May 1, 1862.

COLLINS, PEYTON C., Sergeant
Resided in Nash County and was by occupation a farmer prior to enlisting in Nash County at age 23, May 1, 1861. Mustered in as Private and promoted to Sergeant in March-December, 1862. Present or accounted for until wounded in the arm at or near Bethesda Church, Virginia, on or about May 30, 1864. Reported absent wounded or absent on detail through December, 1864.

COOPER, SAMUEL T., Private
Resided in Nash County and was by occupation a student prior to enlisting at Camp Carolina, Virginia, at age 18, July 5, 1861. Present or accounted

for until transferred to 2nd Company H of this regiment on or about May 1, 1862.

COPPEDGE, C. H., Private
Resided in Nash County and enlisted at age 28, May 1, 1861. No further records. [May have served later in Company D, 47th Regiment N. C. Troops.]

CROWELL, WILLIAM D., Private
Resided in Nash County and enlisted at age 50, May 1, 1861. Discharged May 10, 1861, by reason of disability.

CULPEPPER, WILLIAM J., Corporal
Resided in Nash County where he enlisted at age 34, May 1, 1861. Mustered in as Private and promoted to Corporal on December 9, 1862. Present or accounted for until transferred to Company I, 30th Regiment N.C. Troops, October 1, 1863.

CULPEPPER, WILLIAM R., Private
Was by occupation a farmer prior to enlisting in Nash County at age 25, May 1, 1861. Present or accounted for through February, 1862. No further records.

CYRUS, F., Private
Enlisted in Montgomery County on October 28, 1864, for the war. Present or accounted for through December, 1864.

CYRUS, GEORGE, Private
Resided in Nash County and enlisted at Camp Arrington, Virginia, at age 18, February 24, 1862. Present or accounted for until wounded in the thigh at Chancellorsville, Virginia, May 3, 1863. Returned to duty in November-December, 1863, and present or accounted for until paroled at Appomattox Court House, Virginia, April 9, 1865.

CYRUS, WILLIAM H., Private
Born in Nash County where he resided as a farmer or mechanic prior to enlisting at Camp Arrington, Virginia, at age 22, February 24, 1862. Present or accounted for until wounded in the hip at or near Stevensburg, Virginia, on or about October 11, 1863. Reported absent wounded through December, 1864.

DANIEL, DAVID, Private
Resided in Nash County and was by occupation a farmer prior to enlisting in Northampton County at age 44, May 15, 1861. Present or accounted for until discharged on August 27, 1861, by reason of disability.

DAVIS, D. W., Private
Resided in Nash County and enlisted at Camp Arrington, Virginia, at age 24, April 13, 1862. Present or accounted for until killed in battle in May-October, 1864; however, battle in which killed not reported.

DAVIS, H. A., Private
Enlisted at New Market, Virginia, October 8, 1864, for the war. Present or accounted for until captured at Cedar Creek, Virginia, October 19, 1864. Confined at Point Lookout, Maryland, until paroled and transferred to Boulware's and Cox's Wharf, James River, Virginia, where he was received February 20-21, 1865, for exchange. Rejoined the company at an unspecified date subsequent to March 6, 1865.

Died in a Federal hospital at City Point, Virginia, April 24, 1865, of a gunshot wound which resulted in the amputation of his thigh. Place and date wounded and captured not reported.

DAVIS, JOHN W., Private
Resided in Nash County and was by occupation an artist prior to enlisting in Nash County at age 29, May 1, 1861. Present or accounted for until discharged on or about July 18, 1862, by reason of disability.

DAVIS, WILLIAM, Private
Enlisted at Orange Court House, Virginia, February 13, 1864, for the war. Present or accounted for through December, 1864.

DELBRIDGE, WILLIAM R., Private
Resided in Nash County and was by occupation a student prior to enlisting in Northampton County at age 22, May 17, 1861. Present or accounted for until captured at Gettysburg, Pennsylvania, July 1, 1863. Confined at Fort Delaware, Delaware, until transferred to Point Lookout, Maryland, October 15-18, 1863. Released at Point Lookout on or about February 24, 1864, after taking the Oath of Allegiance and joining the U.S. Army. Assigned to Company F, 1st Regiment U.S. Volunteer Infantry.

DENTON, WILLIE, Private
Resided in Edgecombe County and enlisted at Camp Carolina, Virginia, at age 19, June 12, 1861. Present or accounted for until transferred to 2nd Company H of this regiment on or about June 10, 1862.

DICK, T. C., Private
Resided in Nash County and enlisted on April 22, 1861. Discharged December 20, 1861, after furnishing a substitute.

DIXON, WESTON W., Private
Born in Nash County where he resided as a painter prior to enlisting in Nash County at age 40, May 1, 1861. Present or accounted for until discharged on or about August 1, 1862, by reason of being over age.

DRAKE, JOHN R., Private
Resided in Nash County and was by occupation a student prior to enlisting in Nash County at age 14, May 1, 1861. Present or accounted for until transferred to 2nd Company H of this regiment on or about May 1, 1862.

DRAKE, WILLIAM F., Private
Resided in Nash County and enlisted at Camp Arrington, Virginia, at age 45, April 20, 1862. Present or accounted for until paroled at Appomattox Court House, Virginia, April 9, 1865.

EDWARDS, BENNETT, Private
Resided in Franklin County where he enlisted at age 25, March 4, 1863, for the war. Present or accounted for until hospitalized at Richmond, Virginia, May 19, 1864, with a shell wound of the left foot; however, place and date wounded not reported. Reported absent wounded through October, 1864, and was reported absent without leave in November-December, 1864. North Carolina pension records indicate that he survived the war.

EDWARDS, HIRAM, Private
Resided in Nash County and enlisted at Camp Ar-

rington, Virginia, at age 21, April 20, 1862. Present or accounted for until captured at or near Sayler's Creek, Virginia, April 6, 1865. Confined at Point Lookout, Maryland, until released on June 11, 1865, after taking the Oath of Allegiance.

EDWARDS, R., Private

Resided in Nash County and enlisted at age 17, February 20, 1862. Discharged at an unspecified date by reason of disability.

EDWARDS, WILLIAM T. JEFF, Private

Resided in Nash County and was by occupation a farmer prior to enlisting in Nash County at age 18, May 1, 1861. Present or accounted for until he died on November 19, 1862. Place and cause of death not reported.

EVANS, BRYANT, Private

Resided in Nash County and enlisted at Gordonsville, Virginia, at age 25, March 10, 1863, for the war. Present or accounted for until wounded in the wrist at Chancellorsville, Virginia, May 3, 1863. Returned to duty in September-October, 1863, and present or accounted for through April, 1864. Company muster rolls dated April 30-December, 1864, indicate that he was a prisoner of war; however, records of the Federal Provost Marshal do not substantiate that report. No further records.

EVANS, DAVID, Private

Resided in Nash County and was by occupation a farmer prior to enlisting in Nash County at age 23, May 1, 1861. Present or accounted for until transferred to 2nd Company H of this regiment on or about May 1, 1862.

EVANS, IRA T., Private

Resided in Nash County and was by occupation a farmer prior to enlisting in Northampton County at age 23, May 15, 1861. Present or accounted for until he deserted on or about May 13, 1863. Returned to duty September 21, 1863, and was court-martialed on or about January 19, 1864. Rejoined the company prior to May 12, 1864, when he was captured at Spotsylvania Court House, Virginia. Confined at Point Lookout, Maryland, until paroled and transferred to Boulware's Wharf, James River, Virginia, where he was received March 16, 1865, for exchange.

EVANS, J. V., Private

Resided in Nash County. Place and date of enlistment not reported. Captured near Spotsylvania Court House, Virginia, May 12, 1864, and confined at Point Lookout, Maryland, until transferred to Elmira, New York, August 10, 1864. Released at Elmira on July 7, 1865, after taking the Oath of Allegiance.

FOX, ISHAM, Sergeant

Resided in Nash County where he enlisted at age 19, May 1, 1861. Mustered in as Private and promoted to Corporal on August 1, 1863. Promoted to Sergeant on November 1, 1863. Present or accounted for until killed in May-October, 1864; however, battle in which killed not reported.

GARDNER, BENJAMIN, Private

Resided in Nash County and was by occupation a farmer prior to enlisting in Nash County at age 27,

May 1, 1861. Present or accounted for through April, 1864. Company muster roll dated April 30-October 31, 1864, states that he was wounded and in the hands of the enemy; however, records of the Federal Provost Marshal do not substantiate that report. Company muster roll dated November-December, 1864, states that he died of wounds. Place and date of death not reported.

GARDNER, GEORGE A., Private

Born in Nash County where he resided as a farmer prior to enlisting at Camp Carolina, Virginia, at age 16, June 19, 1861. Present or accounted for until discharged on or about September 22, 1862, by reason of being under age. Later served in 2nd Company H, 32nd Regiment N.C. Troops.

GORDON, ISAAC W., Private

Resided in Nash County and enlisted at Gordonsville, Virginia, at age 17, March 15, 1862, as a substitute. Present or accounted for until captured at "Spotsylvania, Virginia, June 10, 1864." Confined at Point Lookout, Maryland, until released on or about June 24, 1864, after joining the U.S. service. Assigned to Company I, 1st Regiment U.S. Volunteer Infantry.

GOSSETT, ABRAHAM, Private

Place and date of enlistment not reported. Captured at Petersburg, Virginia, March 25, 1865, and confined at Point Lookout, Maryland, where he died on April 19, 1865. Cause of death not reported.

GRIFFIN, HENRY G., Private

Resided in Nash County and enlisted at Camp Arrington, Virginia, at age 28, February 24, 1862. Present or accounted for until paroled at Appomattox Court House, Virginia, April 9, 1865.

GRIFFIN, WILLIAM J., Private

Resided in Nash County and enlisted at Camp Arrington, Virginia, at age 30, February 24, 1862, for the war. Present or accounted for until wounded in the shoulder at Chancellorsville, Virginia, May 3, 1863. Returned to duty prior to September 1, 1863, and present or accounted for through December, 1864. Hospitalized at Danville, Virginia, subsequent to December 31, 1864, with a gunshot wound of the left knee; however, date and place wounded not reported. Discharged from hospital at Danville on May 5, 1865. No further records.

GURNEY, FORD, Private

Born in Ireland and resided in Nash County where he was by occupation a mechanic or saddler prior to enlisting in Nash County on May 1, 1861. Present or accounted for until discharged on or about August 3, 1862, by reason of being over age. Discharge certificate gives his age as 36.

HARPER, GEORGE H., Private

Resided in Nash County and was by occupation a clerk prior to enlisting in Nash County at age 19, May 1, 1861. Present or accounted for until transferred to 2nd Company H of this regiment on May 1, 1862.

HARPER, HENRY C., Private

Resided in Nash County and was by occupation a student prior to enlisting at Camp Carolina, Virginia, at age 17, July 2, 1861. Present or accounted for until transferred to 2nd Company H of this regiment on May 1, 1862.

HARPER, HIGDON, Private
Resided in Nash County and was by occupation a farmer prior to enlisting in Nash County at age 22, May 1, 1861. Present or accounted for until transferred to 2nd Company H of this regiment on May 1, 1862.

HARPER, SAMUEL T., Private
Born in Nash County where he resided as a farmer or mechanic prior to enlisting in Nash County at age 31, May 1, 1861. Present or accounted for until transferred to 2nd Company H of this regiment on May 1, 1862.

HEDGEPETH, GEORGE W., Private
Resided in Nash County and enlisted at Camp Carolina, Virginia, at age 28, July 1, 1861. Present or accounted for until captured at or near Sayler's Creek, Virginia, April 6, 1865. Confined at Point Lookout, Maryland, until released on June 28, 1865, after taking the Oath of Allegiance.

HEDGPETH, F. T., Private
Resided in Nash County and enlisted at Camp Arrington, Virginia, at age 24, February 24, 1862. Present or accounted for through April, 1864. Company muster roll dated April 30-December, 1864, states that he was a prisoner of war; however, records of the Federal Provost Marshal do not substantiate that report. No further records.

HUNTER, CORDA N., Private
Resided in Nash County and was by occupation a farmer prior to enlisting in Nash County at age 31, May 1, 1861. Present or accounted for until transferred to 2nd Company H of this regiment on May 1, 1862.

JONES, D. W., Private
Place and date of enlistment not reported. Captured at Spotsylvania Court House, Virginia, May 20, 1864. Confined at Point Lookout, Maryland, until transferred to Elmira, New York, July 3, 1864. Died at Elmira on December 2, 1864, of "pneumonia."

JOYNER, B. H., Private
Born in Nash County where he resided as a farmer prior to enlisting at Gordonsville, Virginia, at age 28, March 6, 1862. Present or accounted for until paroled at Appomattox Court House, Virginia, April 9, 1865.

JOYNER, BERRY F., Private
Resided in Nash County and was by occupation a farmer prior to enlisting in Nash County at age 24, May 1, 1861. Present or accounted for until killed at Gettysburg, Pennsylvania, July 1-3, 1863.

JOYNER, H. T., Private
Enlisted in Alexander County on March 29, 1864, for the war. Present or accounted for until killed in battle prior to November 1, 1864. Battle in which killed not reported.

JOYNER, ORREN H., Private
Resided in Nash County and was by occupation a farmer prior to enlisting in Nash County at age 25, May 1, 1861. Present or accounted for until he deserted on or about April 21, 1863. Court-martialed on or about December 26, 1863, but rejoined the company at an unspecified date. Captured at Fisher's Hill, Virginia, September 22, 1864, and confined at Point Lookout, Maryland, until released on May 13, 1865, after taking the Oath of Allegiance.

JOYNER, ROBERT W., Sergeant
Resided in Nash County and was by occupation a student prior to enlisting in Nash County at age 21, May 1, 1861. Mustered in as Private and was promoted to Corporal on June 4, 1861. Promoted to Sergeant on August 18, 1862. Present or accounted for until wounded in the back and captured at Gettysburg, Pennsylvania, July 1-2, 1863. Hospitalized at Gettysburg until transferred to Davids Island, New York Harbor, July 17-24, 1863. Paroled at Davids Island and transferred to City Point, Virginia, where he was received September 8, 1863, for exchange. Reported absent wounded through December, 1864. Captured in hospital at Richmond, Virginia, April 3, 1865, and was paroled on April 24, 1865.

JOYNER, WILLIAM P., Private
Resided in Nash County and enlisted at Camp Arrington, Virginia, at age 30, April 27, 1862. Present or accounted for through April, 1864. Company muster rolls dated April 30-December, 1864, indicate he was captured in an unspecified battle and died of disease. North Carolina pension records indicate that he died in Virginia on May 12, 1864. No further records.

LANCASTER, L. D., Private
Resided in Nash County and enlisted at age 32, February 4, 1862. Present or accounted for until he died in hospital at Gordonsville, Virginia, June 12, 1862, of "enteritis."

LAND, WILLIE G., Private
Resided in Nash County and was by occupation a farmer prior to enlisting in Nash County at age 19, May 1, 1861. Present or accounted for until wounded at Winchester, Virginia, September 19, 1864. Reported absent wounded or absent on detail through January 3, 1865.

MACLIN, R. L., Private
Resided in Nash County and enlisted at Camp Arrington, Virginia, at age 19, February 24, 1862. Present or accounted for until wounded in the left leg and captured at Winchester, Virginia, September 19, 1864. Hospitalized at Winchester until transferred to Baltimore, Maryland, November 20, 1864. Confined at Fort McHenry, Maryland, December 9, 1864, and was transferred to Point Lookout, Maryland, January 2, 1865. Released at Point Lookout on June 3, 1865, after taking the Oath of Allegiance.

MADEGAN, DANIEL, Private
Born in Ireland where he resided as a ditcher prior to enlisting at Richmond, Virginia, May 25, 1861. Present or accounted for until discharged on or about July 18, 1862, by reason of being over age and "not naturalized." Age given on discharge certificate as 38.

MADEGAN, DAVID, Private
Born in Ireland where he resided as a ditcher prior to enlisting at Richmond, Virginia, at age 25, May 25, 1861. Present or accounted for until discharged on or about July 18, 1862, by reason of his "owing

allegiance to the Queen of England."

MADEGAN, JAMES, Private
Born in Ireland where he resided as a ditcher prior to enlisting at Richmond, Virginia, May 25, 1861. Present or accounted for until discharged on or about July 18, 1862, by reason of being under age and because he was not a naturalized citizen. Age given on discharge certificate as 17.

MOSELEY, J. F., Private
Resided in Nash County and enlisted at Gordonsville, Virginia, at age 35, May 12, 1862, for the war. Present or accounted for until mortally wounded on July 5, 1864. Battle in which wounded and place and date of death not reported.

MURRAY, PRESLEY C., Private
Resided in Nash County and was by occupation a student prior to enlisting in Nash County at age 20, May 1, 1861. Present or accounted for until he died on or about October 5, 1861, of disease. Place of death not reported.

MURRAY, WILLIAM H., Sergeant
Resided in Nash County and was by occupation a farmer prior to enlisting in Nash County at age 26, May 1, 1861. Mustered in as Corporal and promoted to Sergeant on August 1, 1862. Present or accounted for until killed in battle in May-October, 1864; however, battle in which killed not reported.

PAYDON, JAMES, Private
Resided in Nash County and was by occupation a farmer prior to enlisting in Halifax County at age 33, May 7, 1861. Present or accounted for until discharged on May 1, 1863, by reason of disability.

PITMAN, JOHN A., Private
Resided in Nash County and was by occupation a farmer prior to enlisting in Nash County at age 20, May 1, 1861. Present or accounted for until wounded in the hand and leg at Chancellorsville, Virginia, May 2-3, 1863. Returned to duty in September-October, 1863, and present or accounted for until paroled at Appomattox Court House, Virginia, April 9, 1865.

PITMAN, N. W., Private
Enlisted in Alexander County on March 29, 1864, for the war. Present or accounted for until paroled at Appomattox Court House, Virginia, April 9, 1865.

POLIN, JAMES, Private
Resided in Nash County and was by occupation a farmer prior to enlisting in Nash County at age 22, May 1, 1861. Present or accounted for until captured at Cedar Creek, Virginia, October 19, 1864. Confined at Point Lookout, Maryland, until released on May 14, 1865, after taking the Oath of Allegiance.

POLIN, JOHN, Private
Enlisted at Hanover Junction, Virginia, May 26, 1864, for the war. Company muster roll dated April 30-October 31, 1864, states he was at home on furlough. Company muster roll dated November-December, 1864, states that he died of disease. Place and date of death not reported.

PRICE, ASA, Private
Resided in Nash County and was by occupation a

farmer prior to enlisting in Nash County at age 30, April 22, 1861. Present or accounted for until transferred to 2nd Company H of this regiment on May 1, 1862.

PRICE, ELBERT, Private
Resided in Nash County and was by occupation a farmer prior to enlisting in Nash County at age 20, April 22, 1861. Present or accounted for until he died on September 19, 1861, of disease. Place of death not reported.

PRICE, JACKSON C., Private
Resided in Nash County and was by occupation a farmer prior to enlisting in Nash County at age 23, April 22, 1861. Present or accounted for until transferred to 2nd Company H of this regiment on May 1, 1862.

PRICE, T. CARTER, Private
Resided in Nash County and was by occupation a farmer prior to enlisting in Nash County at age 26, April 22, 1861. Present or accounted for until transferred to 2nd Company H of this regiment on May 1, 1862.

PRICE, WILLIAM R., Sergeant
Resided in Nash County and was by occupation a farmer prior to enlisting in Nash County at age 22, April 22, 1861. Mustered in as Private and promoted to Sergeant on September 1, 1861. Present or accounted for until he died at Gordonsville, Virginia, on or about August 19, 1862. Cause of death not reported.

PRIDGEN, HARDY H., Private
Born in Nash County where he resided as a farmer prior to enlisting in Nash County on May 1, 1861. Present or accounted for until discharged on or about August 1, 1862, by reason of being over age. Discharge certificate gives his age as 36. Reenlisted in the company on March 10, 1863. Wounded in the hip at Chancellorsville, Virginia, May 3, 1863, and died at Richmond, Virginia, May 14, 1863, of wounds.

PRIDGEN, WILLIAM R., Private
Born in Nash County where he resided as a farmer prior to enlisting in Nash County at age 34, May 1, 1861. Present or accounted for until discharged at Gordonsville, Virginia, on or about August 1, 1862, by reason of being over age. Later served in 2nd Company H, 32nd Regiment N. C. Troops.

PRIVETT, ZACHARIAH F., Private
Resided in Nash County and was by occupation a farmer prior to enlisting in Nash County at age 25, May 1, 1861. Present or accounted for until killed in battle in May-October, 1864; however, battle in which killed not reported.

RACKLEY, L. D., Private
Resided in Nash County and enlisted at Camp Arrington, Virginia, at age 24, April 20, 1862. Present or accounted for until he deserted on or about May 16, 1863. Returned to duty on or about October 1, 1863, and was court-martialed on or about December 26, 1863. Reported absent undergoing sentence of court-martial through April, 1864. Returned to duty prior to September 19, 1864, when he was captured at Winchester, Virginia. Confined at Point

Lookout, Maryland, until paroled and transferred to Boulware's Wharf, James River, Virginia, where he was received March 18, 1865, for exchange.

ROWLAND, A. F., Private
Resided in Nash County and enlisted at Camp Arrington, Virginia, at age 17, February 24, 1862. Present or accounted for until wounded at Gettysburg, Pennsylvania, July 1, 1863. Returned to duty prior to September 1, 1863, and present or accounted for until captured at Winchester, Virginia, September 19, 1864. Confined at Point Lookout, Maryland, until paroled and transferred to Boulware's Wharf, James River, Virginia, where he was received March 18, 1865, for exchange.

ROWLAND, D. T., Private
Resided in Nash County and enlisted in Wake County. Date of enlistment not reported; however, he was first reported with this company on a muster roll dated April 30-October 31, 1864. Present or accounted for until captured near Petersburg, Virginia, March 25, 1865. Confined at Point Lookout, Maryland, until released on June 17, 1865, after taking the Oath of Allegiance.

ROWLING, J. T., Private
Place and date of enlistment not reported. Captured at Winchester, Virginia, September 19, 1864, and confined at Point Lookout, Maryland, until exchanged on March 15, 1865.

SEXTON, GEORGE W., Private
Resided in Nash County and was by occupation a farmer prior to enlisting at Camp Carolina, Virginia, at age 19, June 20, 1861. Present or accounted for until he deserted on or about July 21, 1862.

SOREY, DORSEY W., Corporal
Resided in Nash County and was by occupation a farmer prior to enlisting in Nash County at age 20, April 22, 1861. Mustered in as Private and promoted to Corporal in March-December, 1862. Present or accounted for until wounded in the lungs and captured at Gettysburg, Pennsylvania, July 1-3, 1863. Died in hospital at Gettysburg on July 11, 1863, of wounds.

STYLES, K., Private
Resided in Franklin County and enlisted at age 37, February 24, 1862. Discharged on August 1, 1862, by reason of being over age.

SUTHERS, J. J., Private
Place and date of enlistment not reported. Captured at Fisher's Hill, Virginia, September 22, 1864, and confined at Point Lookout, Maryland, until paroled and transferred to Boulware's Wharf, James River, Virginia, where he was received March 19, 1865, for exchange.

SUTTON, J. WEST, Private
Resided in Nash County and was by occupation a farmer prior to enlisting in Northampton County at age 21, May 16, 1861. Present or accounted for until he deserted on May 15, 1863. Confined at Castle Thunder Prison, Richmond, Virginia, on or about December 28, 1863, and was court-martialed on or about February 12, 1864. Reported in confinement until he was released on or about December 1, 1864. No further records.

TAYLOR, DANIEL A., Private
Resided in Nash County. Place and date of enlistment not reported. Captured at or near Sayler's Creek, Virginia, April 6, 1865. Confined at Point Lookout, Maryland, until released on June 21, 1865, after taking the Oath of Allegiance.

TAYLOR, JOHN R., Private
Resided in Nash County and was by occupation a farmer prior to enlisting in Nash County at age 21, May 1, 1861. Mustered in as Private and promoted to Corporal in January-February, 1863. Reduced to ranks on August 1, 1863. Present or accounted for until hospitalized at Richmond, Virginia, May 19, 1864, with a gunshot wound of the right hip; however, place and date wounded not reported. Reported absent wounded or absent sick through December, 1864.

THOMAS, JOSIAH, Private
Born in Edgecombe County and resided in Nash County where he was by occupation a farmer prior to enlisting at Camp Arrington, Virginia, at age 30, February 24, 1862. Present or accounted for through December, 1864.

TISDALE, GEORGE W., Private
Resided in Nash County and was by occupation a farmer prior to enlisting in Nash County at age 18, May 1, 1861. Present or accounted for until wounded in the left leg and captured at Monocacy, Maryland, July 9-10, 1864. Hospitalized at Baltimore, Maryland, until transferred to Point Lookout, Maryland, October 25, 1864. Paroled at Point Lookout and transferred to Venus Point, Savannah River, Georgia, where he was received November 15, 1864, for exchange.

TISDALE, NICHOLAS, Private
Resided in Nash County and was by occupation a farmer prior to enlisting in Northampton County at age 21, May 15, 1861. Present or accounted for until paroled at Appomattox Court House, Virginia, April 9, 1865.

TUCKER, HENRY C., Sergeant
Resided in Nash County and was by occupation a farmer prior to enlisting in Nash County at age 24, May 1, 1861. Mustered in as Private and promoted to Corporal in November-December, 1863. Promoted to Sergeant on May 13, 1864. Present or accounted for through December, 1864.

TUCKER, JOHN H., Private
Resided in Nash County and was by occupation a farmer prior to enlisting at Camp Carolina, Virginia, at age 19, July 10, 1861. Present or accounted for until paroled at Appomattox Court House, Virginia, April 9, 1865.

TUCKER, L. D., Private
Resided in Nash County and enlisted at Camp Arrington, Virginia, at age 15, February 24, 1862. Present or accounted for until captured at Spotsylvania Court House, Virginia, May 12, 1864. Confined at Point Lookout, Maryland, until transferred to Elmira, New York, August 10, 1864. Released at Elmira on June 23, 1865, after taking the Oath of Allegiance.

TURNER, H., Private
Resided in Nash County and enlisted at age 24, February 28, 1862. Present or accounted for until he died in hospital at Lynchburg, Virginia, July 17, 1862, of "meningitis."

VICK, JOSEPH J., Private
Resided in Nash County and was by occupation a farmer prior to enlisting in Nash County at age 22, May 1, 1861. Present or accounted for until he died on or about January 27, 1862, of disease. Place of death not reported.

VICK, T. CICERO, Sergeant
Was by occupation a farmer prior to enlisting in Nash County at age 21, April 22, 1861. Mustered in as Corporal and promoted to Sergeant in March-December, 1862. Present or accounted for until discharged on December 25, 1862, after providing a substitute.

WALKER, JOHN, Private
Resided in Ireland and enlisted at Gordonsville, Virginia, at age 28, December 9, 1862, for the war as a substitute. Deserted December 27, 1862.

WATERFIELD, BENJAMIN, Musician
Enlisted at Camp Carolina, Virginia, July 30, 1861. Mustered in as Musician. Present or accounted for through December, 1861. No further records.

WELLS, STEPHEN, Private
Resided in Nash County and was by occupation a farmer prior to enlisting in Nash County at age 28, May 1, 1861. Present or accounted for until he deserted on May 15, 1863. Court-martialed on or about December 26, 1863. Died at Orange Court House, Virginia, January 6, 1864. Cause of death not reported.

WESTRAY, RICHARD T., Private
Resided in Nash County and was by occupation a farmer prior to enlisting in Northampton County at age 20, May 15, 1861. Present or accounted for until transferred to 2nd Company H of this regiment on or about May 1, 1862.

WESTRAY, WILLIS, Private
Resided in Nash County and was by occupation a farmer prior to enlisting at Camp Carolina, Virginia, at age 48, June 12, 1861. Present or accounted for until discharged on August 1, 1862, by reason of being over age.

WHETLEY, ANDREW M. F., Private
Resided in Nash County and enlisted at Camp Arrington, Virginia, at age 35, February 24, 1862. Present or accounted for until he died at Gordonsville, Virginia, December 14, 1862, of "febris typhoides."

WHITAKER, HENRY, Private
Resided in Nash County and was by occupation a student prior to enlisting at Camp Carolina, Virginia, at age 22, June 10, 1861. Present or accounted for until discharged on November 22, 1861, by reason of disability.

WILLIAMS, ARCHIBALD HUNTER ARRINGTON, Private
Resided in Nash County and enlisted at Camp Martin at age 18, November 19, 1861. Present or accounted for until appointed 2nd Lieutenant on November 9, 1862, and transferred to Company F, 55th Regiment N.C. Troops.

WILLIAMS, CASWELL, Corporal
Born in Edgecombe County and resided in Nash County where he was by occupation a clerk prior to enlisting at Camp Arrington, Virginia, at age 20, April 6, 1862. Mustered in as Private. Present or accounted for until wounded at Gettysburg, Pennsylvania, July 1, 1863. Returned to duty in November-December, 1863, and was promoted to Corporal in May-October, 1864. Present or accounted for until captured at "High Bridge, Virginia, April 14, 1865." Hospitalized at various Federal hospitals with a "sprained left knee" until confined at Newport News, Virginia, April 23, 1865. Released at Newport News on June 30, 1865, after taking the Oath of Allegiance.

WILLIAMS, ELIJAH, Private
Resided in Edgecombe County and enlisted at Gordonsville, Virginia, at age 24, May 12, 1862, for the war. Present or accounted for until captured at Winchester, Virginia, September 19, 1864. Confined at Point Lookout, Maryland, until paroled and transferred to Boulware's Wharf, James River, Virginia, where he was received March 18, 1865, for exchange.

WILLIAMS, MICAJAH T., Corporal
Born in Nash County and was by occupation a farmer prior to enlisting in Wilson County at age 21, May 1, 1862, for the war. Mustered in as Corporal. Present or accounted for until wounded in the left arm at Cedar Creek, Virginia, October 19, 1864. Reported absent wounded until retired from service on or about February 21, 1865, by reason of disability.

WILLIAMS, NOAH, Private
Resided in Edgecombe County and enlisted at Gordonsville, Virginia, at age 22, May 10, 1862, for the war. Present or accounted for until he was reported missing and presumed captured at Chancellorsville, Virginia, May 3, 1863; however, records of the Federal Provost Marshal do not substantiate the report of his capture. Returned to duty prior to July 1, 1863. Present or accounted for until killed in battle in May-October, 1864; however, battle in which killed not reported.

WILLIAMS, THOMAS M., Private
Born in Franklin County and resided in Nash County where he was by occupation a student prior to enlisting in Halifax County at age 17, May 9, 1861. Present or accounted for until discharged on or about August 1, 1862, by reason of being under age.

WILLIAMSON, ISAAC, Private
Resided in Wilson County and enlisted at Winchester, Virginia, September 10, 1864, for the war. Present or accounted for until he deserted from hospital at Lynchburg, Virginia, November-December, 1864. Paroled at Goldsboro on May 9, 1865.

WILLS, STEPHEN, Private
Enlisted in Nash County on May 1, 1863, for the war. Dropped from the rolls of the company on May 13, 1863, for desertion.

WILSON, ANDREW, Private
Resided in Nash or Edgecombe counties and was by occupation a farmer prior to enlisting in Halifax County at age 24, May 1, 1861. Present or accounted for until transferred to 2nd Company H of this regiment on May 1, 1862.

WOODARD, LARK C., Private
Resided in Nash County and was by occupation a farmer prior to enlisting in Nash County at age 26, May 1, 1861. Present or accounted for until transferred to 2nd Company H of this regiment on May 1, 1862.

WORICK, MANLEY, Private
Resided in Albany County, New York, and enlisted on July 1, 1864, for the war Deserted to the enemy on or about July 31, 1864. Confined at Old Capitol Prison, Washington, D.C., and was transferred to Elmira, New York, August 28, 1864. No further records.

WRYAN, JAMES, Private
Resided in Ireland and enlisted at Gordonsville, Virginia, at age 26, December 26, 1862, for the war as a substitute. Deserted December 27, 1862.

2nd COMPANY H

This company was from Nash County and began organizing at Nashville in March, 1862. It tendered its service to the state and was mustered in as Captain John J. Drake's Company. It was assigned to this regiment in May, 1862, as Company H. Since it was the second company in the regiment to be designated Company H, the company was referred to as 2nd Company H. On July 22, 1862, the company was transferred to the 32nd Regiment N.C. Troops and became 2nd Company H of that regiment.

The information contained in the following roster of the company was compiled principally from company muster rolls for May 1, 1861-February 28, 1862, and May-June, 1862. No company muster rolls were found for March-April, 1862, or for the period after June, 1862. In addition to the company muster rolls, Roll of Honor records, receipt rolls, hospital records, prisoner of war records, and other primary records, supplemented by state pension applications, United Daughters of the Confederacy records, and postwar rosters and histories, all provided useful information.

OFFICERS
CAPTAIN

DRAKE, JOHN J.
Resided in Nash County where he enlisted at age 41. Appointed Captain on or about March 1, 1862. Present or accounted for until wounded in the left side at Malvern Hill, Virginia, July 1-2, 1862. Transferred to 2nd Company H, 32nd Regiment N.C. Troops, July 22, 1862.

LIEUTENANTS

ARRINGTON, GEORGE W., 2nd Lieutenant
Resided in Nash County where he enlisted at age 30. Appointed 2nd Lieutenant on or about March 1, 1862. Present or accounted for until transferred to 2nd Company H, 32nd Regiment N.C. Troops, July 22, 1862.

BARRETT, JOHN W., 1st Lieutenant
Previously served as 1st Lieutenant in 1st Company H of this regiment. Transferred to this company in March-June, 1862. Present or accounted for until transferred to 2nd Company H, 32nd Regiment N.C. Troops, July 22, 1862.

JENKINS, JOSEPH P., 2nd Lieutenant
Resided in Nash County where he enlisted at age 28. Appointed 2nd Lieutenant on or about March 1, 1862. Present or accounted for until wounded in the leg at or near Malvern Hill, Virginia, on or about July 1, 1862. Transferred to 2nd Company H, 32nd Regiment N.C. Troops, July 22, 1862, while absent wounded.

NONCOMMISSIONED OFFICERS AND PRIVATES

ARRINGTON, JOHN D., Private
Enlisted in Nash County on May 1, 1862, for the war. Present or accounted for until transferred to 2nd Company H, 32nd Regiment N.C. Troops, July 22, 1862.

ARRINGTON, RICHARD W., Sergeant
Born in Nash County where he resided as a farmer prior to enlisting in Nash County at age 28, March 1, 1862, for the war. Mustered in as Sergeant. Present or accounted for until transferred to 2nd Company H, 32nd Regiment N.C. Troops, July 22, 1862.

ARRINGTON, ROBERT W., Private
Enlisted in Nash County on May 1, 1862, for the war. No further records.

BARNES, JAMES H., Private
Born in Nash County where he resided prior to enlisting in Nash County at age 28, March 1, 1862, for the war. Present or accounted for until transferred to 2nd Company H, 32nd Regiment N.C. Troops, July 22, 1862.

BARRETT, ELIJAH E., Private
Resided in Nash County where he enlisted at age 28, May 1, 1862, for the war. Present or accounted for until transferred to 2nd Company H, 32nd Regiment N.C. Troops, July 22, 1862.

BARRETT, JAMES E., Private
Resided in Nash County where he enlisted at age 32, March 1, 1862, for the war. Present or accounted for until transferred to 2nd Company H, 32nd Regiment N.C. Troops, July 22, 1862.

BASS, BENJAMIN F., Corporal
Previously served as Private in 1st Company H of this regiment. Transferred to this company on May 1, 1862. Promotion record not reported. Present or accounted for until transferred to 2nd Company H, 32nd Regiment N.C. Troops, July 22, 1862.

BASS, GEORGE W., Private
Resided in Nash County where he enlisted at age 38, March 1, 1862, for the war. Present or accounted for until transferred to 2nd Company H, 32nd Regiment N.C. Troops, July 22, 1862.

BASS, MARK C., Private
Previously served in 1st Company H of this regiment. Transferred to this company on May 1, 1862. Present or accounted for until killed at or near Malvern Hill, Virginia, on or about July 1, 1862.

BATCHELOR, B. B., Private
Previously served in 1st Company H of this regiment. Transferred to this company on or about May 1, 1862. Present or accounted for until transferred to 2nd Company H, 32nd Regiment N.C. Troops, July 22, 1862.

BATCHELOR, THOMAS E., Private
Resided in Nash County where he enlisted at age 27, March 1, 1862, for the war. Present or accounted for until transferred to 2nd Company H, 32nd Regiment N.C. Troops, July 22, 1862.

BATTLE, LAWRENCE, Private
Born in Nash County where he resided as a farmer prior to enlisting in Nash County on May 1, 1862, for the war. Present or accounted for until transferred to 2nd Company H, 32nd Regiment N.C. Troops, July 22, 1862.

BEAL, JAMES H., Corporal
Previously served as Corporal in 1st Company H of this regiment. Transferred to this company on or about May 1, 1862. Present or accounted for until transferred to 2nd Company H, 32nd Regiment N.C Troops, July 22, 1862.

BEAL, JESSE, Private
Born in Nash County where he resided as a student prior to enlisting in Nash County at age 18, March 1, 1862, for the war. Present or accounted for until transferred to 2nd Company H, 32nd Regiment N.C. Troops, July 22, 1862.

BRADLEY, WILLIS, Private
Resided in Nash County where he enlisted at age 35, May 1, 1862, for the war. Present or accounted for until transferred to 2nd Company H, 32nd Regiment N.C. Troops, July 22, 1862.

BRASWELL, LEONIDAS C., Private
Resided in Nash County where he enlisted at age 22, March 1, 1862, for the war. Present or accounted for until transferred to 2nd Company H, 32nd Regiment N.C. Troops, July 22, 1862.

BRASWELL, OSCAR, Private
Resided in Nash County where he enlisted at age 33, March 1, 1862, for the war. Present or accounted for until transferred to 2nd Company H, 32nd Regiment N.C. Troops, July 22, 1862.

BRASWELL, SAMUEL, Private
Resided in Nash County where he enlisted at age 19, March 1, 1862, for the war. Present or accounted for until transferred to 2nd Company H, 32nd Regiment N.C. Troops, July 22, 1862.

BROWN, WILLIAM, Private
Resided in Nash County where he enlisted at age 28, March 1, 1862, for the war. Present or accounted for until transferred to 2nd Company H, 32nd Regiment N.C. Troops, July 22, 1862.

COGGIN, JOHN J., Private
Resided in Nash County where he enlisted at age 27, March 1, 1862, for the war. Present or accounted for until transferred to 2nd Company H, 32nd Regiment N.C. Troops, July 22, 1862.

COGGIN, WILLIE, Private
Resided in Nash County where he enlisted at age 19, March 1, 1862, for the war. Present or accounted for until transferred to 2nd Company H, 32nd Regiment N.C. Troops, July 22, 1862.

COGGIN, WILLIS, Private
Resided in Nash County where he enlisted at age 36, March 1, 1862, for the war. Present or accounted for until transferred to 2nd Company H, 32nd Regiment N.C. Troops, July 22, 1862.

COLLINS, JONES, Sergeant
Previously served as Sergeant in 1st Company H of this regiment. Transferred to this company on or about May 1, 1862. Present or accounted for until wounded at Gaines' Mill, Virginia, June 27, 1862, or at Malvern Hill, Virginia, July 1, 1862. Died in hospital at Richmond, Virginia, July 12, 1862, of wounds.

COOPER, SAMUEL T., Private
Previously served in 1st Company H of this regiment. Transferred to this company on or about May 1, 1862. Present or accounted for until transferred to 2nd Company H, 32nd Regiment N.C. Troops, July 22, 1862.

CULPEPPER, JETHRO D., Private
Resided in Nash County where he enlisted on March 1, 1862, for the war. Present or accounted for until transferred to 2nd Company H, 32nd Regiment N.C. Troops, July 22, 1862.

DENSON, DAVID M., Private
Resided in Nash County where he enlisted at age 34, March 1, 1862, for the war. Died in hospital at Richmond, Virginia, June 15, 1862. Cause of death not reported.

DENTON, WILLIE, Private
Previously served in 1st Company H of this regiment. Transferred to this company on or about June 10, 1862. Present or accounted for until transferred to 2nd Company H, 32nd Regiment N.C. Troops, July 22, 1862.

DOLES, WILLIAM F., 1st Sergeant
Resided in Nash County where he enlisted at age 37, March 1, 1862, for the war. Mustered in as 1st Sergeant. Present or accounted for until transferred to 2nd Company H, 32nd Regiment N.C. Troops, July 22, 1862.

DRAKE, BENJAMIN F., Sergeant
Resided in Nash County where he enlisted at age 20, March 1, 1862, for the war. Mustered in as Sergeant. Present or accounted for until transferred to 2nd Company H, 32nd Regiment N.C. Troops, July 22, 1862.

DRAKE, JOHN R., Private
Previously served in 1st Company H of this regiment. Transferred to this company on or about May 1,

1862. Present or accounted for until transferred to 2nd Company H, 32nd Regiment N.C. Troops, July 22, 1862.

EARL, JAMES M., Private
Resided in Nash County where he enlisted at age 28, May 1, 1862. Present or accounted for until transferred to 2nd Company H, 32nd Regiment N.C. Troops, July 22, 1862.

EDWARDS, JAMES WELDON, Private
Resided in Nash County where he enlisted at age 28, March 1, 1862, for the war. Present or accounted for until transferred to 2nd Company H, 32nd Regiment N.C. Troops, July 22, 1862.

ETHRIDGE, DAVID E., Private
Resided in Nash County where he enlisted at age 30, March 1, 1862, for the war. Present or accounted for until transferred to 2nd Company H, 32nd Regiment N.C. Troops, July 22, 1862.

ETHRIDGE, WILLIAM E., Corporal
Resided in Nash County where he enlisted at age 25, March 1, 1862, for the war. Mustered in as Corporal. Present or accounted for until transferred to 2nd Company H, 32nd Regiment N.C. Troops, July 22, 1862.

EVANS, DAVID, Private
Previously served in 1st Company H of this regiment. Transferred to this company on or about May 1, 1862. Present or accounted for until transferred to 2nd Company H, 32nd Regiment N.C. Troops, July 22, 1862.

GRIFFIN, A. J., Private
Resided in Nash County where he enlisted at age 32, March 1, 1862, for the war. Present or accounted for until transferred to 2nd Company H, 32nd Regiment N.C. Troops, July 22, 1862.

GRIFFIN, HILLMAN, Private
Resided in Nash County where he enlisted at age 34, March 1, 1862, for the war. Present or accounted for until transferred to 2nd Company H, 32nd Regiment N.C. Troops, July 22, 1862.

GRIFFIN, JOSEPH J., Private
Born in Nash County where he resided prior to enlisting in Nash County at age 34, March 1, 1862, for the war. Present or accounted for until he died in hospital at Charlottesville, Virginia, July 19, 1862, of "pneumonia."

GRIFFIN, PERRY, Private
Enlisted in Nash County on March 1, 1862, for the war. Present or accounted for until he died in hospital at Richmond, Virginia, July 17, 1862. Cause of death not reported.

GRIFFIN, WILLIE T., Private
Resided in Nash County where he enlisted at age 19, March 1, 1862, for the war. Present or accounted for until transferred to 2nd Company H, 32nd Regiment N.C. Troops, July 22, 1862.

HALL, JOHN W., Private
Resided in Nash County where he enlisted at age 28, March 1, 1862, for the war. Present or accounted for until he died in hospital at Richmond, Virginia, July 7, 1862, of disease.

HARPER, GEORGE H., Private
Previously served in 1st Company H of this regiment. Transferred to this company on May 1, 1862. Present or accounted for until transferred to 2nd Company H, 32nd Regiment N.C. Troops, July 22, 1862.

HARPER, HENRY C., Private
Previously served in 1st Company H of this regiment. Transferred to this company on May 1, 1862. Present or accounted for until transferred to 2nd Company H, 32nd Regiment N.C. Troops, July 22, 1862.

HARPER, HIGDON, Private
Previously served in 1st Company H of this regiment. Transferred to this company on May 1, 1862. Present or accounted for until transferred to 2nd Company H, 32nd Regiment N.C. Troops, July 22, 1862.

HARPER, SAMUEL T., Private
Previously served in 1st Company H of this regiment. Transferred to this company on May 1, 1862. Present or accounted for until transferred to 2nd Company H, 32nd Regiment N.C. Troops, July 22, 1862.

HEDGPETH, HENRY W., Private
Born in Nash County where he resided as a farmer prior to enlisting in Nash County at age 26, March 1, 1862, for the war. Present or accounted for until transferred to 2nd Company H, 32nd Regiment N.C. Troops, July 22, 1862.

HEDGPETH, LEWIS W., Private
Resided in Nash County where he enlisted at age 28, May 1, 1862, for the war. Present or accounted for until wounded in the thigh and captured at Hanover Court House, Virginia, May 27, 1862. Hospitalized at Portsmouth Grove, Rhode Island, July 7, 1862. Transferred to 2nd Company H, 32nd Regiment N.C. Troops, July 22, 1862, while a prisoner of war.

HUNTER, CORDA N., Private
Previously served in 1st Company H of this regiment. Transferred to this company on May 1, 1862. Present or accounted for until transferred to 2nd Company H, 32nd Regiment N.C. Troops, July 22, 1862.

JOHNSON, ELIAS, Private
Resided in Wake County and enlisted in Nash County at age 23, May 1, 1862, for the war. Present or accounted for until transferred to 2nd Company H, 32nd Regiment N.C. Troops, July 22, 1862.

JOHNSON, WILLIAM, Private
Enlisted in Nash County on March 1, 1862, for the war. Present or accounted for until he died in hospital at Richmond, Virginia, June 27, 1862. Cause of death not reported.

LAND, JOHN, Private
Resided in Nash County where he enlisted at age 19, March 1, 1862, for the war. Present or accounted for until transferred to 2nd Company H, 32nd Regiment N.C. Troops, July 22, 1862.

MEADOWS, GIDEON, Private
Resided in Nash County where he enlisted at age 19, March 1, 1862, for the war. Present or accounted for until he died in hospital at Richmond, Virginia, June 29, 1862, of "typhoid fever."

MEADOWS, WILLIAM, Private
Resided in Nash County where he enlisted at age 18, March 1, 1862, for the war. Present or accounted for

until he died in hospital at Richmond, Virginia, July 1, 1862, of "typhoid fever."

MOORE, RICHARD H., Private
Resided in Nash County where he enlisted at age 34, May 1, 1862, for the war. Present or accounted for until transferred to 2nd Company H, 32nd Regiment N.C. Troops, July 22, 1862.

PITTMAN, JOHN C., Private
Enlisted in Nash County on May 1, 1862, for the war. Present or accounted for until transferred to 2nd Company H, 32nd Regiment N.C. Troops, July 22, 1862.

POWELL, GEORGE W., Private
Resided in Nash County where he enlisted at age 20, March 1, 1862, for the war. Present or accounted for until transferred to 2nd Company H, 32nd Regiment N.C. Troops, July 22, 1862.

POWELL, JESSE A., Private
Resided in Nash County where he enlisted at age 21, March 1, 1862, for the war. Present or accounted for until transferred to 2nd Company H, 32nd Regiment N.C. Troops, July 22, 1862.

POWELL, JOHN, Private
Resided in Nash County where he enlisted at age 42, May 1, 1862, for the war. Present or accounted for until killed at Gaines' Mill, Virginia, June 27, 1862.

POWELL, JOHN W., Sergeant
Resided in Nash County where he enlisted at age 25, March 1, 1862, for the war. Mustered in as Sergeant. Present or accounted for until transferred to 2nd Company H, 32nd Regiment N.C. Troops, July 22, 1862.

PRICE, ASA, Private
Previously served in 1st Company H of this regiment. Transferred to this company on May 1, 1862. Present or accounted for until wounded at Malvern Hill, Virginia, July 1, 1862. Died in hospital at Richmond, Virginia, in July, 1862, of wounds.

PRICE, HENRY, Private
Resided in Nash County where he enlisted at age 16, March 1, 1862, for the war. Present or accounted for until he died in hospital at Richmond, Virginia, June 13, 1862, of disease.

PRICE, JACKSON C., Private
Previously served in 1st Company H of this regiment. Transferred to this company on May 1, 1862. Present or accounted for until transferred to 2nd Company H, 32nd Regiment N.C. Troops, July 22, 1862.

PRICE, T. CARTER, Private
Previously served in 1st Company H of this regiment. Transferred to this company on May 1, 1862. Present or accounted for until transferred to 2nd Company H, 32nd Regiment N.C. Troops, July 22, 1862.

PRICE, WILLIAM, Private
Born in Nash County where he resided prior to enlisting in Nash County at age 28, March 1, 1862, for the war. Present or accounted for until transferred to 2nd Company H, 32nd Regiment N.C. Troops, July 22, 1862.

RICHARDSON, PERRY, Private
Resided in Nash County where he enlisted at age 34, March 1, 1862, for the war. Present or acounted for until transferred to 2nd Company H, 32nd Regiment N.C. Troops, July 22, 1862.

RICKS, NERO, Corporal
Resided in Nash County where he enlisted at age 21, March 1, 1862, for the war. Mustered in as Corporal. Present or accounted for until he died in hospital at Richmond, Virginia, June 15, 1862, of "typhoid fever."

ROSE, ROBBIN, Private
Resided in Nash County where he enlisted at age 21, March 1, 1862, for the war. Present or accounted for until transferred to 2nd Company H, 32nd Regiment N.C. Troops, July 22, 1862.

SEXTON, JOHN THOMAS, Private
Resided in Nash County where he enlisted at age 38, March 1, 1862, for the war. Present or accounted for until transferred to 2nd Company H, 32nd Regiment N.C. Troops, July 22, 1862.

SEXTON, WILLIAM H., Private
Resided in Nash County where he enlisted at age 40, March 1, 1862, for the war. Present or accounted for until transferred to 2nd Company H, 32nd Regiment N.C. Troops, July 22, 1862.

SNEED, W. J., Private
Resided in Nash County where he enlisted at age 33, March 1, 1862, for the war. Present or accounted for until he died in hospital at Richmond, Virginia, July 4, 1862, of "typhoid fever."

TAYLOR, JOHN A., Private
Enlisted in Nash County on May 1, 1862, for the war. Present or accounted for until transferred to 2nd Company H, 32nd Regiment N.C. Troops, July 22, 1862.

TAYLOR, JOSEPH, Private
Resided in Nash County where he enlisted at age 28, March 1, 1862, for the war. Present or accounted for until transferred to 2nd Company H, 32nd Regiment N.C. Troops, July 22, 1862.

TAYLOR, THOMAS B., Private
Enlisted in Nash County on March 1, 1862, for the war. Present or accounted for until transferred to 2nd Company H, 32nd Regiment N. C. Troops, July 22, 1862.

TISDALE, JAMES T., Private
Enlisted in Nash County on March 1, 1862, for the war. Present or accounted for until transferred to 2nd Company H, 32nd Regiment N.C. Troops, July 22, 1862.

TODD, HENRY A., Private
Resided in Nash County where he enlisted at age 29, May 1, 1862, for the war. Present or accounted for until captured at Hanover Court House, Virginia, May 27, 1862. Confined at Fort Columbus, New York Harbor, June 4, 1862. Transferred to 2nd Company H, 32nd Regiment N.C. Troops, July 22, 1862, while a prisoner of war.

VICK, JAMES, Private
Resided in Nash County where he enlisted at age 22, March 1, 1862, for the war. Present or accounted for until transferred to 2nd Company H, 32nd Regiment N.C. Troops, July 22, 1862.

WARD, THOMAS M., Private
Resided in Nash County where he enlisted at age 36, March 1, 1862, for the war. Present or accounted for until transferred to 2nd Company H, 32nd Regiment N.C. Troops, July 22, 1862.

WESTRAY, RICHARD T., Private
Previously served in 1st Company H of this regiment. Transferred to this company on or about May 1, 1862. Present or accounted for until transferred to 2nd Company H, 32nd Regiment N.C. Troops, July 22, 1862.

WESTWRAY, JOHN, Private
Resided in Nash County where he enlisted at age 28, May 1, 1862, for the war. Present or accounted for until wounded in the thigh at Gaines' Mill, Virginia, June 27, 1862. Died in hospital at Richmond, Virginia, July 5, 1862, of wounds.

WHEELESS, JAMES, Private
Resided in Nash County where he enlisted at age 19, March 1, 1862, for the war. Present or accounted for until killed at Gaines' Mill, Virginia, June 27, 1862.

WHITFIELD, GEORGE V., Private
Resided in Nash County where he enlisted at age 31, May 1, 1862, for the war. Present or accounted for until transferred to 2nd Company H, 32nd Regiment N.C. Troops, July 22, 1862.

WILDER, TROY L., Private
Resided in Nash County where he enlisted at age 36, March 1, 1862, for the war. Present or accounted for until transferred to 2nd Company H, 32nd Regiment N.C. Troops, July 22, 1862.

WILLIAMS, JAMES, Private
Enlisted in Nash County on April 1, 1862, for the war. Present or accounted for until discharged on June 1, 1862. Reason discharged not reported.

WILSON, ANDREW, Private
Previously served in 1st Company H of this regiment. Transferred to this company on May 1, 1862. Present or accounted for until captured at Hanover Court House, Virginia, May 27, 1862. Transferred to 2nd Company H, 32nd Regiment N.C. Troops, July 22, 1862, while a prisoner of war.

WOODARD, LARK C., Private
Previously served in 1st Company H of this regiment. Transferred to this company on May 1, 1862. Present or accounted for until killed at Malvern Hill, Virginia, July 1, 1862.

COMPANY I

This company was from Halifax County and enlisted at Halifax on February 25, 1862. The company tendered its service to the state and was mustered in as Captain Shugan Snow's Company. It was assigned to the regiment in February, 1862, and was designated Company I. After it was mustered into the regiment the company functioned as a part of the regiment, and its history for the war period is recorded as a part of the regimental history.

The information contained in the following roster of the company was compiled principally from company muster rolls for June 30-October 31, 1862; February 1-August 31, 1863; and November, 1863-December, 1864. No company muster rolls were found for the period prior to June 30, 1862; for November, 1862-January, 1863; September-October, 1863; or for the period after December, 1864. In addition to the company muster rolls, Roll of Honor records, receipt rolls, hospital records, prisoner of war records, and other primary records, supplemented by state pension applications, United Daughters of the Confederacy records, and postwar rosters and histories, all provided useful information.

OFFICERS
CAPTAINS

SNOW, SHUGAN
Previously served as Private in Company G of this regiment. Transferred to this company upon appointment as Captain to rank from February 16, 1862. Present or accounted for until he resigned on November 2, 1862. Reason he resigned not reported. Resignation accepted November 21, 1862.

KITCHIN, WILLIAM HODGE
Previously served as Private in Company G of this regiment. Appointed 2nd Lieutenant in this company on January 15, 1863. Promoted to Captain on March 15, 1863. Present or accounted for until captured at Spotsylvania Court House, Virginia, May 10-12, 1864. Confined at Fort Delaware, Delaware, until transferred to Hilton Head, South Carolina, August 20, 1864. Received at Fort Pulaski, Georgia, October 20, 1864, and was transferred back to Hilton Head on November 19, 1864. Transferred back to Fort Delaware where he arrived March 12, 1865. Released at Fort Delaware on June 16, 1865, after taking the Oath of Allegiance.

LIEUTENANTS

ALSTON, EDWARD, 2nd Lieutenant
Previously served as Private in 2nd Company C of this regiment. Transferred to this company upon appointment as 2nd Lieutenant to rank from February 16, 1862. Present or accounted for until wounded at Gaines' Mill, Virginia, June 27, 1862. Reported absent wounded until he resigned on March 14, 1863, by reason of wounds received at Gaines' Mill. Resignation accepted March 25, 1863.

LONG, NICHOLAS M., 1st Lieutenant
Resided in Halifax County. Appointed 1st Lieutenant to rank from March 26, 1862. Present or accounted for until he resigned on May 5, 1862. Reason he resigned not reported.

SHEARIN, MARTIN LUTHER, 3rd Lieutenant
Resided in Halifax County where he enlisted at age 26, February 25, 1862. Mustered in as Sergeant. Present or accounted for until captured at South Mountain, Maryland, September 14, 1862. Paroled and exchanged at an unspecified date. Returned to duty prior to March 2, 1863, and was elected 3rd Lieutenant on May 26, 1863. Present or accounted for until wounded in the right leg at or near Sayler's

Creek, Virginia, April 6, 1865. Right leg amputated. Hospitalized at Washington, D.C., until released on or about June 10, 1865, after taking the Oath of Allegiance.

SNOW, THADDEUS C., 1st Lieutenant
Resided in Halifax County and enlisted in Wake County. Appointed 2nd Lieutenant to rank from February 16, 1862, and was promoted to 1st Lieutenant on May 5, 1862. Present or accounted for until wounded at Chancellorsville, Virginia, May 2, 1863. Reported absent wounded until he was reported absent without leave in June, 1863. Reported absent without leave until he was dropped from the rolls of the company on or about June 6, 1864.

NONCOMMISSIONED OFFICERS AND PRIVATES

AMBROSE, BENJAMIN F., Private
Resided in Washington County prior to enlisting in Wake County on September 10, 186[4], for the war. Present or accounted for until captured near Petersburg, Virginia, March 25, 1865. Confined at Point Lookout, Maryland, until released on June 22, 1865, after taking the Oath of Allegiance.

AMBROSE, J. A., Private
Resided in Washington County and enlisted in Wake County on September 10, 186[4], for the war. Present or accounted for until captured near Petersburg, Virginia, February 6, 1865. Confined at Point Lookout, Maryland, until released on June 22, 1865, after taking the Oath of Allegiance.

ARRINGTON, G. G., Corporal
Resided in Halifax County where he enlisted at age 18, February 25, 1862, for the war. Mustered in as Private and promoted to Corporal on July 1, 1863. Present or accounted for until captured near Petersburg, Virginia, March 25, 1865. Confined at Point Lookout, Maryland, until released on June 3, 1865, after taking the Oath of Allegiance.

ARRINGTON, JOHN W., Private
Resided in Halifax County where he enlisted at age 18, February 25, 1862, for the war. Present or accounted for through April, 1863. Nominated for the Badge of Distinction for gallantry at Chancellorsville, Virginia, May 1-3, 1863. Present or accounted for until wounded at Spotsylvania Court House, Virginia, May 10, 1864. Died May 20, 1864, of wounds. Place of death not reported.

BASS, JOHN, Private
Resided in Wayne County and enlisted in Wake County on September 10, 186[4], for the war. Present or accounted for until captured near Petersburg, Virginia, March 25, 1865. Confined at Point Lookout, Maryland, until released on June 24, 1865, after taking the Oath of Allegiance.

BOSWELL, JOSEPH, Private
Resided in Halifax County and enlisted at age 19, February 25, 1862, for the war. Died March 13, 1862. Place and cause of death not reported.

BURT, WILLIAM E., Private
Resided in Halifax County where he enlisted at age 21, February 25, 1862, for the war. Present or

accounted for until captured at Spotsylvania Court House, Virginia, May 12, 1864. Confined at Point Lookout, Maryland, until transferred to Elmira, New York, August 10, 1864. Died at Elmira on November 21, 1864, of "pneumonia."

CAPPS, WHITMAN, Private
Born in Warren County and resided in Halifax County where he was by occupation a farmer prior to enlisting in Halifax County at age 39, February 25, 1862, for the war. Present or accounted for until discharged on or about April 24, 1864, by reason of "general disability."

CARLISLE, C. C., Private
Resided in Halifax County and enlisted at Richmond, Virginia, at age 46, July 12, 1862, for the war as a substitute for "M.P. Perry." Present or accounted for until he died "at home" on July 9, 1864, of disease.

CARLISLE, ISHAM, Private
Resided in Halifax County where he enlisted at age 19, February 25, 1862, for the war. Present or accounted for until wounded in battle near Richmond, Virginia, on or about July 1, 1862. Died on or about July 10, 1862, of wounds. Place of death not reported.

CARLISLE, STERLING BROWN, Private
Resided in Halifax County where he enlisted at age 18, February 25, 1862, for the war. Present or accounted for until wounded in the left hand at Winchester, Virginia, on or about July 20, 1864. Returned to duty prior to November 1, 1864, and present or accounted for until captured at Petersburg, Virginia, April 3, 1865. Confined at Hart's Island, New York Harbor, until released on June 17, 1865, after taking the Oath of Allegiance.

CARTER, BOSTON W., Private
Resided in Halifax County where he enlisted at age 18, February 25, 1862, for the war. Died on or about March 20, 1862, of "measles." Place of death not reported.

CARTER, JESSE, Private
Resided in Halifax County where he enlisted at age 18, February 25, 1862, for the war. Present or accounted for until wounded in the left shoulder at Malvern Hill, Virginia, July 1, 1862. Reported absent wounded until discharged on or about March 23, 1863, by reason of wounds received at Malvern Hill.

CARTER, THEE, Private
Resided in Halifax County where he enlisted at age 30, February 25, 1862, for the war. Present or accounted for through December, 1864.

COLLINS, S. A., Private
Born in Halifax County where he resided as a planter prior to enlisting in Halifax County at age 19, February 25, 1862, for the war. Present or accounted for until captured at Hanover Court House, Virginia, May 27, 1862. Confined at Fort Monroe, Virginia, until exchanged at Aiken's Landing, James River, Virginia, August 5, 1862. Present or accounted for until wounded at Chancellorsville, Virginia, May 2, 1863. Died May 3, 1863, of wounds.

CRAWLEY, WILLIAM D., Private

Resided in Halifax County where he enlisted at age 27, February 25, 1862, for the war. Present or accounted for until captured at South Mountain, Maryland, September 14, 1862. Confined at Fort Delaware, Delaware, until transferred to Aiken's Landing, James River, Virginia, October 2, 1862, for exchange. Declared exchanged at Aiken's Landing on November 10, 1862. Present or accounted for until hospitalized at Richmond, Virginia, on or about August 9, 1864, with a wound; however, place and date wounded not reported. Furloughed for sixty days on or about August 10, 1864. Reported absent without leave on company muster rolls dated April 30-December, 1864.

DANIEL, W. W., Private

Resided in Halifax County where he enlisted at age 20, February 25, 1862, for the war. Present or accounted for until captured at Spotsylvania Court House, Virginia, May 12, 1864. Confined at Point Lookout, Maryland, until transferred to Elmira, New York, August 10, 1864. Died at Elmira on September 5, 1864, of "chronic diarrhoea."

DEBUAM, J. R., Private

Enlisted in Wake County on September 10, 186[4], for the war. Company muster roll dated April 30-October 31, 1864, states that he was wounded and a prisoner of war; however, records of the Federal Provost Marshal do not substantiate that report. Company muster roll dated November-December, 1864, states that he was absent sick. No further records.

DICKENS, HENRY B., Corporal

Resided in Halifax County where he enlisted at age 27, February 25, 1862, for the war. Mustered in as Private and promoted to Corporal in November, 1862-February, 1863. Present or accounted for until captured at Spotsylvania Court House, Virginia, May 12, 1864. Confined at Point Lookout, Maryland, until transferred to Elmira, New York, August 10, 1864. Paroled at Elmira and transferred to Venus Point, Savannah River, Georgia, where he was received November 15, 1864, for exchange.

DICKENS, J. D., Private

Resided in Halifax County and enlisted in Wake County on September 10, 186[4], for the war. Present or accounted for until captured at Petersburg, Virginia, April 2, 1865. Confined at Hart's Island, New York Harbor, until released on June 17, 1865, after taking the Oath of Allegiance.

DICKENS, J. J., Private

Resided in Halifax County where he enlisted at age 24, February 25, 1862, for the war. Present or accounted for until captured at South Mountain, Maryland, September 14, 1862. Confined at Fort Delaware, Delaware, until transferred to Aiken's Landing, James River, Virginia, October 2, 1862, for exchange. Declared exchanged at Aiken's Landing on November 10, 1862. Present or accounted for until hospitalized at Danville, Virginia, April 3, 1865, suffering from "shock by concussion." Place and date injured not reported. No further records.

DICKENS, WARREN, Private

Resided in Halifax County where he enlisted at age 49, February 25, 1862, for the war. Present or

accounted for until captured at Richmond, Virginia, April 3, 1865. Paroled at Richmond on April 21, 1865. Roll of Honor indicates that he was wounded at Malvern Hill, Virginia.

DRURY, WILLIAM H., Sergeant

Resided in Halifax County where he enlisted at age 27, February 25, 1862, for the war. Mustered in as Private. Present or accounted for until wounded at Malvern Hill, Virginia, July 1, 1862. Returned to duty prior to November 1, 1862, and was promoted to Corporal in March-April, 1863. Present or accounted for until wounded at Gettysburg, Pennsylvania, July 2, 1863. Returned to duty prior to September 1, 1863, and was promoted to Sergeant in September-December, 1863. Present or accounted for through February 25, 1865.

EDWARDS, A. E., Private

Place and date of enlistment not reported. Captured at Asheville on April 6, 1865. Confined at Knoxville, Tennessee, at an unspecified date and was transferred to Chattanooga, Tennessee, May 3, 1865. No further records.

FALKNER, S. C., Private

Resided in Halifax County where he enlisted at age 48, February 25, 1862, for the war as a substitute. Present or accounted for until wounded at Spotsylvania Court House, Virginia, on or about May 12, 1864. Died of wounds on or about May 15, 1864. Place of death not reported.

FELTS, WILLIAM RANSOM, Private

Born in Warren County and resided in Halifax County where he was by occupation a farmer prior to enlisting in Halifax County at age 28, February 25, 1862, for the war. Present or accounted for until discharged on or about January 7, 1863, by reason of "phthisis pulmonalis." Died in hospital at Richmond, Virginia, January 13, 1863, of "consumption."

FLETCHER, FLEMMING C., Private

Place and date of enlistment not reported. Paroled at Appomattox Court House, Virginia, April 9, 1865.

FLETCHER, JAMES, Private

Resided in Halifax County where he enlisted at age 20, February 25, 1862, for the war. Died on or about March 10, 1862, of "measles." Place of death not reported.

FLETCHER, JOHN, Private

Resided in Halifax County where he enlisted at age 27, February 25, 1862, for the war. Present or accounted for until discharged on or about December 4, 1863, by reason of "rheumatism."

FLETCHER, L. C., Private

Resided in Halifax County where he enlisted at age 18, February 25, 1862, for the war. Present or accounted for until paroled at Appomattox Court House, Virginia, April 9, 1865.

FLETCHER, WILLIAM E., Private

Resided in Halifax County where he enlisted at age 30, February 25, 1862, for the war. Present or accounted for until hospitalized at Richmond, Virginia, May 19, 1864, with a gunshot wound of the groin; however, place and date wounded not reported. Returned to duty on or about July 2, 1864, and present or accounted for until captured at Cedar Creek, Virginia, October 19, 1864. Confined at Point Lookout, Maryland, until released on June 3, 1865, after taking the Oath of Allegiance.

GLASGOW, JOHN, Private
Resided in Halifax County where he enlisted at age 31, February 25, 1862, for the war. Present or accounted for through March 1, 1863. No further records.

GLASGOW, S. A. J., Private
Resided in Halifax County where he enlisted at age 25, February 25, 1862, for the war. Present or accounted for until wounded in the right leg and captured at Gettysburg, Pennsylvania, July 1-4, 1863. Hospitalized at Gettysburg until transferred to Davids Island, New York Harbor, July 17-24, 1863. Exchanged at City Point, Virginia, on or about September 16, 1863. Rejoined the company prior to January 1, 1864, and present or accounted for until paroled at Appomattox Court House, Virginia, April 9, 1865.

GREEN, WILLIAM D., Private
Resided in Halifax County where he enlisted at age 42, February 25, 1862, for the war. Present or accounted for through December, 1864.

HALE, SAMUEL, Private
Resided in Halifax County where he enlisted at age 32, February 25, 1862, for the war. Present or accounted for until paroled at Gordonsville, Virginia, May 22, 1865.

HALE, WILLIS, Private
Resided in Halifax County where he enlisted at age 28, February 25, 1862, for the war. Present or accounted for until wounded and captured at South Mountain, Maryland, September 14, 1862. Confined at Fort McHenry, Maryland, and at Fort Monroe, Virginia, until transferred to Aiken's Landing, James River, Virginia, where he was received October 19, 1862, for exchange. Declared exchanged at Aiken's Landing on November 10, 1862. Present or accounted for until he died in hospital at Staunton, Virginia, October 27, 1863, of "febris typhoides."

HAMLET, BENJAMIN, Private
Resided in Halifax County where he enlisted at age 20, February 25, 1862, for the war. Present or accounted for until wounded at Malvern Hill, Virginia, July 1, 1862. Returned to duty prior to March 2, 1863, and present or accounted for until wounded in the finger at Chancellorsville, Virginia, May 2, 1863. Hospitalized at Richmond, Virginia, where he died on or about June 2, 1863, of wounds and/or "diphtheria."

HARDEE, J. J., Private
Resided in Halifax County where he enlisted at age 30, February 25, 1862, for the war. Mustered in as Corporal but was reduced to ranks at his own request on July 1, 1863. Present or accounted for through December, 1864.

HARLOW, AUGUSTUS, Private
Resided in Halifax County where he enlisted at age 22, February 25, 1862, for the war. Present or accounted for until wounded in the hand at Chancellorsville, Virginia, May 2, 1863. Returned to duty

prior to July 1, 1863, when he was wounded at Gettysburg, Pennsylvania. Returned to duty prior to November 27-28, 1863, when he was wounded in the hand at Payne's Farm, Virginia. Returned to duty in May-October, 1864, but was retired to the Invalid Corps on December 23, 1864, by reason of "t[otal] d[isability]."

HARPER, GEORGE W., Sergeant
Resided in Halifax County where he enlisted at age 21, February 25, 1862, for the war. Mustered in as Sergeant. Present or accounted for until wounded at Malvern Hill, Virginia, July 1, 1862. Died July 12, 1862, of wounds. Place of death not reported.

HARPER, W. G., Private
Resided in Halifax County where he enlisted on February 25, 1862, for the war. Present or accounted for until captured at Harrisonburg, Virginia, on or about October 1, 1864. Confined at Point Lookout, Maryland, until released on June 27, 1865, after taking the Oath of Allegiance.

HARPER, W. H., Private
Resided in Halifax County and enlisted at age 25, February 25, 1862, for the war. Present or accounted for until mortally wounded at Gaines' Mill, Virginia, June 27, 1862, or at Malvern Hill, Virginia, July 1, 1862. Place and date of death not reported.

HARPER, WILLIAM, Private
Enlisted in Halifax County on February 25, 1862, for the war. Present or accounted for until detailed as a courier and transferred to the staff of Major General Robert E. Rodes on May 25, 1863.

HARRISS, W. A., Private
Resided in Halifax County where he enlisted at age 24, February 25, 1862, for the war. Present or accounted for until killed at Malvern Hill, Virginia, July 1, 1862.

HASKINS, JAMES, Private
Resided in Halifax County where he enlisted at age 48, February 25, 1862, for the war. Present or accounted for through March 8, 1865; however, he was reported absent sick or absent on hospital duty during much of that period.

HAWKINS, WILLIAM, Private
Resided in Halifax County where he enlisted at age 40, February 25, 1862, for the war. Present or accounted for until captured at Hanover Court House, Virginia, May 27, 1862. Exchanged at Aiken's Landing, James River, Virginia, August 5, 1862. Present or accounted for through December, 1864; however, he was reported absent sick or absent on hospital duty during much of that period.

HERBERT, GEORGE, Private
Resided in Halifax County and enlisted at age 25, February 25, 1862, for the war. Discharged May 20, 1862, by reason of disability.

HOWARD, JAMES, Private
Enlisted in Wake County on September 10, 186[4], for the war. Present or accounted for through December, 1864.

HULL, JOHN, Private
Resided in Halifax County where he enlisted at age 29, February 25, 1862, for the war. Present or

accounted for through February 6, 1865.

JOHNSTON, JOHN P., 1st Sergeant
Resided in Warren County and enlisted in Halifax County at age 22, February 25, 1862, for the war. Mustered in as Sergeant and was promoted to 1st Sergeant in May-June, 1863. Present or accounted for until wounded at Malvern Hill, Virginia, May 1, 1862. Returned to duty prior to November 1, 1862, and present or accounted for until captured near Petersburg, Virginia, March 25, 1865. Confined at Point Lookout, Maryland, until released on June 3, 1865, after taking the Oath of Allegiance.

JORDAN, JAMES, Private
Resided in Halifax County where he enlisted at age 18, February 25, 1862, for the war. Present or accounted for until reported absent wounded in May-October, 1864; however, battle in which wounded not reported. Reported absent sick in November-December, 1864. No further records.

JORDAN, JOSEPH, Private
Resided in Halifax County where he enlisted at age 26, February 25, 1862, for the war. Present or accounted for until killed at Malvern Hill, Virginia, July 1, 1862.

KING, M. E., Private
Born in Halifax County where he resided as a farmer prior to enlisting in Halifax County at age 25, February 25, 1862, for the war. Present or accounted for until wounded in the hand at Chancellorsville, Virginia, May 2, 1863. Returned to duty prior to July 1, 1863, and present or accounted for until wounded in the left eye at Morton's Ford, Virginia, on or about October 11, 1863. Reported absent wounded until discharged on or about April 5, 1864, by reason of "the loss of one eye and insufficient vision of the other."

LANGISTON, G., Private
Resided in Halifax County where he enlisted at age 26, February 25, 1862, for the war. Died on or about March 5, 1862, of "measles." Place of death not reported.

LEE, E., Private
Enlisted in Halifax County on February 25, 1862, for the war. Present or accounted for until he died on August 27, 1862. Place and cause of death not reported.

LEE, ISRAEL, Private
Resided in Halifax County and enlisted at age 31, February 25, 1862, for the war. Present or accounted for until he died in hospital at Danville, Virginia, July 29, 1862, of "erysipelas"; "chronic diarrhoea"; and/or "typhoid fever."

LEE, JAMES H., Private
Resided in Halifax County and enlisted near Kelly's Ford, Virginia, at age 38, November 1, 1863, for the war. Present or accounted for until wounded in the left leg at Spotsylvania Court House, Virginia, on or about May 12, 1864. Hospitalized at Richmond, Virginia, where he died May 23, 1864, of wounds and "tetanus."

LEE, JOHN, Private
Resided in Halifax County where he enlisted at age 18, February 25, 1862, for the war. Present or

accounted for until wounded in the right side or right hip and captured at Spotsylvania Court House, Virginia, on or about May 12, 1864. Hospitalized at Washington, D.C., until transferred to Elmira, New York, October 24, 1864. Paroled at Elmira on February 25, 1865, and transferred to James River, Virginia, for exchange. Furloughed for sixty days from hospital at Richmond, Virginia, March 8, 1865.

LOVE, ROBERT, Private
Resided in Halifax County where he enlisted at age 19, February 25, 1862, for the war. Present or accounted for through December, 1864; however, he was reported absent on hospital duty during much of that period. Reported in hospital at Danville, Virginia, January 27, 1865, with a wound of the arm; however, place and date wounded not reported. No further records.

MABRY, JOHN B., Corporal
Resided in Halifax County and was by occupation a farmer prior to enlisting in Halifax County at age 28, February 25, 1862, for the war. Mustered in as Private. Present or accounted for until wounded at Malvern Hill, Virginia, July 1, 1862. Returned to duty prior to November 1, 1862, and was promoted to Corporal in March-April, 1863. Present or accounted for until wounded in the thigh at Chancellorsville, Virginia, May 2, 1863. Returned to duty in September-December, 1863, and present or accounted for until captured at Spotsylvania Court House, Virginia, May 12, 1864. Confined at Point Lookout, Maryland, until transferred to Elmira, New York, August 10, 1864. Died at Elmira on September 21, 1864, of "chronic diarrhoea."

McGUIRE, EDGAR H., Private
Resided in Halifax County where he enlisted at age 17, February 25, 1862, for the war. Present or accounted for through March, 1864. Company muster roll dated April 30-October 31, 1864, states that he was a prisoner of war; however, records of the Federal Provost Marshal do not substantiate that report. A company record dated June 30, 1864, states that he had died. No further records.

MADDEN, J. R., Private
Resided in Halifax County where he enlisted at age 20, February 25, 1862, for the war. Present or accounted for until he died in hospital at Richmond, Virginia, August 4, 1862, of "pneumonia."

MATHEWS, JAMES, Private
Resided in Halifax County where he enlisted at age 54, February 25, 1862, for the war. Present or accounted for until reported absent without leave in October, 1863. Reported absent without leave until he was discharged July 6, 1864, for reasons of "equity, justice, and necessity."

MATHEWS, T. H., Private
Resided in Halifax County where he enlisted at age 30, February 25, 1862, for the war. Present or accounted for until wounded in the right knee and captured at or near Cedar Creek, Virginia, October 19, 1864. Right leg amputated. Died in hospital at Baltimore, Maryland, November 14, 1864, of wounds.

MOHORN, JOSEPH S., Private
Resided in Halifax County and was by occupation a

farmer prior to enlisting in Halifax County at age 24, February 25, 1862, for the war. Present or accounted for until wounded in the hand at Malvern Hill, Virginia, July 1, 1862. Returned to duty prior to November 1, 1862, and present or accounted for until wounded in the thigh at Chancellorsville, Virginia, May 2, 1863. Returned to duty prior to July 1, 1863. Present or accounted for until reported absent wounded on company muster roll dated April 30-October 31, 1864; however, battle in which wounded not reported. Reported absent sick through December, 1864. No further records.

MOISE, W., Private
Place and date of enlistment not reported. Paroled at Greensboro on May 2, 1865. No further records.

NANNY, DOUGLAS D., Private
Born in Halifax County and resided in Northampton County where he was by occupation a farmer prior to enlisting in Halifax County at age 38, February 25, 1862, for the war. Present or accounted for until mortally wounded at Malvern Hill, Virginia, July 1, 1862. Died the same day.

NEWSOM, L. BROWNLOW, Sergeant
Resided in Halifax County where he enlisted at age 25, February 25, 1862, for the war. Mustered in as 1st Sergeant but was reduced to the rank of Sergeant on May 26, 1862. Present or accounted for until wounded in the head at Chancellorsville, Virginia, May 2, 1863. Returned to duty in September-December, 1863, and present or accounted for until killed at Spotsylvania Court House, Virginia, May 12, 1864.

PARKER, DAVID, Corporal
Resided in Halifax County and enlisted at age 19, February 25, 1862, for the war. Mustered in as Corporal. Present or accounted for until killed at Malvern Hill, Virginia, July 1, 1862.

PARKER, F. R., 1st Sergeant
Previously served in Company G of this regiment. Transferred to this company on March 30, 1862, with the rank of Private. Promoted to Sergeant prior to June 1, 1862, when he was promoted to 1st Sergeant. Present or accounted for until he died at Guinea Station, Virginia, May 10, 1863, of wounds. Place and date wounded not reported.

PULLEN, W. P., Private
Resided in Halifax County where he enlisted at age 25, February 25, 1862, for the war. Present or accounted for until wounded in the back or abdomen and captured at Hanover Court House, Virginia, May 27, 1862. Hospitalized at Gaines' Mill, Virginia, until transferred to Fort Monroe, Virginia, June 18, 1862. Paroled at Fort Monroe and transferred to Aiken's Landing, James River, Virginia, where he was received September 1, 1862, for exchange. Declared exchanged at Aiken's Landing on November 10, 1862. Reported absent wounded until he was detailed for light duty in January-February, 1864. Reported absent on detail through December, 1864.

RIGGS, JESSE, Private
Resided in Forsyth County and enlisted in Wake County on September 10, 1864, for the war. Present

or accounted for until captured near Petersburg, Virginia, March 25, 1865. Confined at Point Lookout, Maryland, until released on June 17, 1865, after taking the Oath of Allegiance.

ROOKER, JAMES P., Private
Resided in Northampton County and enlisted in Halifax County at age 20, February 25, 1862, for the war. Present or accounted for until wounded in the face at Chancellorsville, Virginia, May 2, 1863. Reported absent wounded until retired to the Invalid Corps on October 24, 1864.

SHEARIN, EDWARD A., Private
Resided in Warren County and enlisted in Halifax County at age 38, February 25, 1862, for the war. Present or accounted for until wounded at Fredericksburg, Virginia, December 13, 1862. Returned to duty prior to March 2, 1863, and present or accounted for until captured at Spotsylvania Court House, Virginia, May 20, 1864. Confined at Point Lookout, Maryland, until transferred to Elmira, New York, July 3, 1864. Paroled at Elmira and transferred to Venus Point, Savannah River, Georgia, where he was received November 15, 1864, for exchange.

SHEARIN, EDWIN H., Private
Resided in Halifax County where he enlisted at age 30, February 25, 1862, for the war. Present or accounted for until hospitalized at Richmond, Virginia, December 15, 1862, with a gunshot wound of the shoulder and hip; however, place and date wounded not reported. Returned to duty on February 16, 1863. Present or accounted for until hospitalized at Richmond on May 17, 1864, with a gunshot wound; however, place and date wounded not reported. Furloughed for sixty days on June 7, 1864. Reported absent without leave on October 31, 1864. Returned to duty prior to April 6, 1865, when he was captured at or near Sayler's Creek, Virginia. Confined at Point Lookout, Maryland, until released on June 20, 1865, after taking the Oath of Allegiance.

SHEARIN, GEORGE, Private
Resided in Halifax County where he enlisted at age 29, February 25, 1862, for the war. Present or accounted for until wounded at Malvern Hill, Virginia, July 1, 1862. Reported absent wounded until January 1, 1863, when he was reported absent without leave. No further records.

SHEARIN, PETER D., Sergeant
Previously served in 2nd Company C of this regiment. Transferred to this company in March, 1862, with the rank of Corporal. Hospitalized at Richmond, Virginia, July 7, 1862, with a wound; however, place and date wounded not reported. Returned to duty prior to November 1, 1862, and was promoted to Sergeant in March-April, 1863. Present or accounted for through December, 1864.

SMITH, THOMAS, Private
Resided in Halifax County and enlisted at age 43, February 25, 1862, for the war. Present or accounted for until he died in hospital at Lynchburg, Virginia, June 4, 1862, of "typhoid fever."

SMITH, THOMAS R., Private
Resided in Halifax County where he enlisted at age

48, February 25, 1862, for the war. Present or accounted for until wounded at Gaines' Mill, Virginia, June 27, 1862. Died the same day.

STALLINGS, GRAY, Private

Resided in Nash County and enlisted in Halifax County at age 26, February 25, 1862, for the war. Present or accounted for through December, 1864. North Carolina pension records indicate that he was wounded at Chancellorsville, Virginia.

TUCKER, JAMES H., Private

Resided in Halifax County where he enlisted at age 42, February 25, 1862, for the war. Present or accounted for until captured at South Mountain, Maryland, September 14, 1862. Confined at Fort Delaware, Delaware, until paroled and transferred to Aiken's Landing, James River, Virginia, October 2, 1862, for exchange. Declared exchanged at Aiken's Landing on November 10, 1862. Returned to duty prior to March 2, 1863. Present or accounted for through January 21, 1865; however, he was reported absent sick or absent on light duty during most of that period.

UPTON, JAMES B., Private

Born in Halifax County where he resided as a farmer prior to enlisting in Halifax County at age 42, February 25, 1862, for the war. Present or accounted for until reported absent without leave on May 15, 1863. Reported absent without leave until discharged on April 13, 1864, by reason of having been "mashed across the hips in the machinery of a steam engine."

WALKER, S. J., Private

Resided in Halifax County where he enlisted at age 26, February 25, 1862, for the war. Present or accounted for until wounded at Gaines' Mill, Virginia, June 27, 1862. Returned to duty prior to November 1, 1862, and present or accounted for until reported missing at Chancellorsville, Virginia, May 3, 1863. Returned to duty prior to July 1, 1863, and present or accounted for until wounded in both thighs and captured at Spotsylvania Court House, Virginia, on or about May 12, 1864. Left thigh amputated. Died on or about May 21, 1864, of wounds. Place of death not reported.

WALTERS, R., Private

Place and date of enlistment not reported. Captured at or near Sayler's Creek, Virginia, April 6, 1865. Confined at Point Lookout, Maryland, on or about April 15, 1865. No further records.

WATERS, H. B., Private

Resided in Washington County and enlisted in Wake County on September 10, 1864, for the war. Present or accounted for through December, 1864. Captured by the enemy at an unspecified date and confined at Point Lookout, Maryland. Released at Point Lookout on June 22, 1865, after taking the Oath of Allegiance.

WHEELERS, WILLIAM H., Private

Resided in Halifax County where he enlisted at age 31, February 25, 1862, for the war. Present or accounted for through December, 1864; however, he was reported absent sick or absent on hospital duty during most of that period.

WILLIAMS, JOSEPH B., Private

Resided in Halifax County where he enlisted at age 18, February 25, 1862, for the war. Present or accounted for until he died on or about April 6, 1862, of "measles." Place of death not reported.

WILLIAMS, SAMUEL F., Private

Resided in Halifax County where he enlisted at age 45, February 25, 1862, for the war. Present or accounted for until discharged on April 15, 1863, by reason of disability.

WILSON, A. J., Private

Resided in Halifax County where he enlisted at age 19, April 21, 1862, for the war. Present or accounted for until wounded in the left leg and captured at or near Monocacy Junction, Maryland, on or about July 9, 1864. Hospitalized at Frederick, Maryland, until transferred to hospital at Baltimore, Maryland, September 20, 1864. Transferred to Point Lookout, Maryland, October 27, 1864. Paroled and transferred to Venus Point, Savannah River, Georgia, where he was received November 15, 1864, for exchange. Reported absent wounded until furloughed for sixty days on March 3, 1865.

WILSON, ROBERT, Private

Resided in Halifax County where he enlisted at age 28, April 21, 1862, for the war. Present or accounted for until wounded in the arm at or near Malvern Hill, Virginia, on or about July 1, 1862. Hospitalized at Richmond, Virginia, where he died August 5, 1862, of wounds.

WOOD, BENJAMIN, Private

Born in Halifax County where he resided as a planter prior to enlisting in Halifax County at age 18, February 25, 1862, for the war. Present or accounted for until wounded at Malvern Hill, Virginia, July 1, 1862. Returned to duty prior to March 2, 1863, and present or accounted for until wounded in the right shoulder at Chancellorsville, Virginia, May 2, 1863. Reported absent wounded until discharged on April 5, 1864, by reason of disability from wounds.

WOOD, ELLIN, Private

Resided in Halifax County where he enlisted at age 35, February 25, 1862, for the war. Present or accounted for until captured at Hanover Court House, Virginia, May 27, 1862. Confined at Fort Columbus, New York Harbor, until paroled and transferred to Aiken's Landing, James River, Virginia, where he was exchanged on August 5, 1862. Died on or about August 17, 1862, of disease. Place of death not reported.

WOOD, WILLIAM, Private

Resided in Halifax County where he enlisted at age 26, February 25, 1862, for the war. Present or accounted for until killed at South Mountain, Maryland, September 14, 1862.

COMPANY K

This company was from Warren and Franklin counties and enlisted in February and March, 1862. The company tendered its service to the state and was mustered in as Captain Robert W. Alston's Company. It was assigned to the regiment in March, 1862, and designated Company K. After it was mustered into the regiment the company functioned as a part of the regiment, and its history for the war period is recorded as a part of the regimental history.

The information contained in the following roster of the company was compiled principally from company muster rolls for June 30-October 31, 1862; January-August, 1863; and November, 1863-December, 1864. No company muster rolls were found for the period prior to June 30, 1862; for November-December, 1862; September-October, 1863; or for the period after December, 1864. In addition to the company muster rolls, Roll of Honor records, receipt rolls, hospital records, prisoner of war records, and other primary records, supplemented by state pension applications, United Daughters of the Confederacy records, and postwar rosters and histories, all provided useful information.

OFFICERS
CAPTAINS

ALSTON, ROBERT W.
Resided in Warren County where he enlisted at age 25. Appointed Captain to rank from March 13, 1862. Present or accounted for until wounded at Boonsboro, Maryland, September 14, 1862. Appointed Major and transferred to the Field and Staff of this regiment on or about May 24, 1863.

WILLIAMS, ROBERT L.
Previously served as Private in 2nd Company C of this regiment. Transferred to this company upon appointment as 2nd Lieutenant to rank from March 25, 1862. Promoted to 1st Lieutenant on March 13, 1863, and was promoted to Captain on May 24, 1863. Present or accounted for until wounded at Spotsylvania Court House, Virginia, in May, 1864. Died June 9, 1864, of wounds. Place of death not reported.

ALSTON, PHILEMON G.
Previously served in 2nd Company C of this regiment. Transferred to this company on May 1, 1862, with the rank of Private. Promoted to 1st Sergeant on June 1, 1862. Hospitalized at Richmond, Virginia, July 4, 1862, with a gunshot wound; however, place and date wounded not reported. Returned to duty prior to September 14, 1862, when he was wounded at South Mountain, Maryland. Returned to duty prior to March 1, 1863, and was appointed 3rd Lieutenant on March 16, 1863. Promoted to 2nd Lieutenant on May 24, 1863. Present or accounted for until wounded at Spotsylvania Court House, Virginia, May 10-12, 1864. Promoted to 1st Lieutenant on May 25, 1864, and promoted to Captain on June 9, 1864. Reported absent wounded through February 27, 1865. Paroled at Richmond prior to August 9, 1865.

LIEUTENANTS

ALSTON, SAMUEL T., 1st Lieutenant
Previously served as Private in 2nd Company C of this regiment. Transferred to this company upon appointment as 3rd Lieutenant to rank from March 25, 1862. Present or accounted for until hospitalized at Richmond, Virginia, July 4, 1862, with a gunshot wound; however, place and date wounded not reported. Returned to duty in November, 1862-April, 1863, and was promoted to 2nd Lieutenant on March 12, 1863. Promoted to 1st Lieutenant on May 24, 1863. Present or accounted for until wounded at Spotsylvania Court House, Virginia, in May, 1864. Died on or about May 25, 1864, of wounds. Place of death not reported.

DAVIS, WILLIAM K., 1st Lieutenant
Resided in Franklin County where he enlisted at age 23. Appointed 1st Lieutenant to rank from March 13, 1862. Present or accounted for until he resigned on December 9, 1862, by reason of "ill health." Resignation accepted on or about January 13, 1863.

PICKFORD, THOMAS J., 2nd Lieutenant
Previously served as Private in 2nd Company C of this regiment. Transferred to this company on February 1, 1863, with the rank of Private. Promoted to Sergeant in March-June, 1863, and was appointed 2nd Lieutenant on September 11, 1864. Present or accounted for until captured at Cedar Creek, Virginia, October 19, 1864. Confined at Fort Delaware, Delaware, until released on June 7, 1865, after taking the Oath of Allegiance.

NONCOMMISSIONED OFFICERS AND PRIVATES

ALSTON, B., Private
Place and date of enlistment not reported. Paroled at Appomattox Court House, Virginia, April 9, 1865.

ALSTON, JOHN D., Sergeant
Resided in Warren County and enlisted at Gordonsville, Virginia, at age 20, May 13, 1862, for the war. Mustered in as Private and promoted to Corporal on June 1, 1862. Present or accounted for until hospitalized at Richmond, Virginia, July 4, 1862, with a gunshot wound; however, place and date wounded not reported. Discharged on October 11, 1862, "for rehabilitation." Reenlisted in the company on September 15, 1863, and was promoted to Sergeant in November-December, 1864. Present or accounted for until paroled at Appomattox Court House, Virginia, April 9, 1865.

ANDREWS, JAMES T., Private
Resided in Nash County and enlisted in Wake County at age 20, March 24, 1862, for the war. Present or accounted for until wounded in the left leg at Cedar Creek, Virginia, October 19, 1864. Left leg amputated. Company records indicate that he was also captured at Cedar Creek; however, records of the Federal Provost Marshal do not substantiate that report. North Carolina pension records indicate that he survived the war. No further records.

ARMSTRONG, H. S., Corporal
Born in Scotland and resided in Warren County where he enlisted at age 42, February 12, 1862, for the war. Mustered in as Corporal. Present or accounted for until he deserted to the enemy or was

captured at Hanover Court House, Virginia, May 27, 1862. Confined at Fort Delaware, Delaware, until released on or about August 10, 1862, after taking the Oath of Allegiance.

ASKEW, GEORGE W., Private

Resided in Franklin County and enlisted at Gordonsville, Virginia, at age 17, May 13, 1862, for the war. Present or accounted for until wounded and captured at South Mountain, Maryland, or at Sharpsburg, Maryland, September 14-17, 1862. Paroled on or about September 30, 1862, and was reported absent wounded through October, 1862. Discharged April 15, 1863. Died in hospital at Richmond, Virginia, April 26, 1863, of "pneumonia."

AYCOCK, SAMUEL, Private

Resided in Warren County and enlisted in Nash County at age 29, March 24, 1862, for the war. Present or accounted for until hospitalized at Richmond, Virginia, December 15, 1862, with a gunshot wound of the hip; however, place and date wounded not reported. Returned to duty on or about February 25, 1863, and present or accounted for until killed at Petersburg, Virginia, April 1, 1865.

AYCOCK, WILLIAM, Private

Resided in Warren County and was by occupation a merchant prior to enlisting in Warren County at age 39, February 12, 1862, for the war. Present or accounted for until captured at Cedar Creek, Virginia, October 19, 1864. Confined at Point Lookout, Maryland, until paroled and transferred to Boulware's Wharf, James River, Virginia, where he was received March 30, 1865, for exchange.

BARTHOLIMEW, SAMUEL, Private

Resided in Franklin County prior to enlisting in Lenoir County at age 28, February 26, 1862, for the war. Present or accounted for until captured at Hanover Court House, Virginia, May 27, 1862. Confined at Fort Columbus, New York Harbor, until transferred to Fort Delaware, Delaware, at an unspecified date. Died at Fort Delaware on August 10, 1862. Cause of death not reported.

BARTHOLOMEW, J. W., Private

Resided in Franklin County and enlisted at "Davis Crossroads" at age 23, February 25, 1862, for the war. Present or accounted for until captured at Spotsylvania Court House, Virginia, May 12, 1864. Confined at Point Lookout, Maryland, until transferred to Elmira, New York, August 10, 1864. Died at Elmira on September 3, 1864, of "typhoid fever."

BARTHOLOMEW, L. E., Private

Previously served in Company G, 15th Regiment N.C. Troops (5th Regiment N.C. Volunteers). Transferred to this company on June 25, 1862, in exchange for Private Isaac W. Gordon. Present or accounted for until wounded in the shoulder and captured at Spotsylvania Court House, Virginia, on or about May 12, 1864. Confined at various Federal hospitals until confined at Old Capitol Prison, Washington, D.C., June 8, 1864. Transferred to Fort Monroe, Virginia, July 5, 1864. No further records.

BASS, DAVID, Private

Resided in Nash County where he enlisted at age 27, March 1, 1862, for the war. Present or accounted for

until wounded and reported captured at Hanover Court House, Virginia, May 27, 1862; however, records of the Federal Provost Marshal do not substantiate the report of his capture. Sent to hospital at Winchester, Virginia, September 22, 1862, and rejoined the company prior to March 1, 1863. Present or accounted for until paroled at Lynchburg, Virginia, April 15, 1865.

BELL, W. H., Private

Resided in Franklin County and enlisted at age 42, February 25, 1862, for the war. Discharged March 25, 1862, by reason of disability.

BENNETT, JAMES, Private

Resided in Warren County and enlisted at age 24, February 12, 1862, for the war. Present or accounted for until he died in hospital at Lynchburg, Virginia, July 27, 1862, of "typhoid fever."

BENNETT, JOHN, Private

Resided in Warren County and enlisted at age 30, February 12, 1862, for the war. Died at Camp Arrington, Virginia, April 23, 1862, of "typhoid pneumonia."

BEST, HENRY, Corporal

Born in Franklin County where he resided as a farmer prior to enlisting in Lenoir County at age 41, February 26, 1862, for the war. Mustered in as Corporal. Present or accounted for until discharged on or about June 18, 1862, by reason of disability.

BOBBITT, J. R., Private

Resided in Franklin County and enlisted in Lenoir County at age 45, March 24, 1862, for the war. Present or accounted for until hospitalized at Richmond, Virginia, April 18, 1863, with "bronchitis (pneumonia)." Died May 1, 1863.

BRAKE, GEORGE W., Private

Resided in Nash County and enlisted in Northampton County at age 21, March 24, 1862, for the war. Present or accounted for until wounded "by the explosion of a shell . . . which left no visible mark" at Gettysburg, Pennsylvania, July 1-3, 1863. Returned to duty in September-December, 1863, and present or accounted for until he died in hospital at Richmond, Virginia, August 25, 1864, of "typhoid fever."

BREWER, E. G., Private

Resided in Chatham County and enlisted at Fredericksburg, Virginia, at age 50, April 5, 1863, for the war as a substitute. Present or accounted for until "sent to hospital" in June, 1863. Never rejoined the company. Company muster rolls dated March-December, 1864, state that he was "supposed to be dead." No further records.

BROADWELL, RUFFIN, Private

Resided in Wake County where he enlisted at age 39, February 4, 1863, for the war. Present or accounted for until captured near Spotsylvania Court House, Virginia, May 12, 1864. Confined at Point Lookout, Maryland, until transferred to Elmira, New York, August 10, 1864. Died at Elmira on November 10, 1864, of "pneumonia."

BURT, JOHN A., 1st Sergeant

Born in Warren County where he resided as a farmer prior to enlisting in Warren County at age 22, February 13, 1862, for the war. Mustered in as Sergeant and promoted to 1st Sergeant on March 2, 1863. Present or accounted for until wounded in the right forearm at Spotsylvania Court House, Virginia, May 12, 1864. Reported absent wounded until he was retired from service on or about March 3, 1865, by reason of disability from wounds.

CABLE, J., Private
Enlisted in Wake County on August 1, 1863, for the war. Present or accounted for until he deserted on August 10, 1864.

CAMP, C. A., Sergeant
Resided in Franklin County and enlisted at "Davis Crossroads" at age 18, March 24, 1862, for the war. Mustered in as Private. Present or accounted for until wounded at Chancellorsville, Virginia, May 1-3, 1863. Returned to duty prior to July 1, 1863, and was promoted to Sergeant in November-December, 1864. Present or accounted for until paroled at Appomattox Court House, Virginia, April 9, 1865.

CAMPBELL, J. D., Private
Resided in Chatham County where he enlisted at age 18, March 19, 1863, for the war. Present or accounted for until wounded at Gettysburg, Pennsylvania, July 1-3, 1863. Returned to duty prior to September 1, 1863, and present or accounted for until captured at Spotsylvania Court House, Virginia, May 12, 1864. Confined at Point Lookout, Maryland, until transferred to Elmira, New York, August 10, 1864. Hospitalized at Elmira on August 18, 1865, with "chronic diarrhoea" and died August 28, 1865.

CAMPBELL, J. P., Private
Enlisted in Wake County on June 18, 1864, for the war. Present or accounted for until wounded in the head at Cedar Creek, Virginia, October 19, 1864. Returned to duty November 11, 1864, and present or accounted for until paroled at Appomattox Court House, Virginia, April 9, 1865.

CARR, JOSEPH J., Sergeant
Resided in Franklin County where he enlisted at age 32, March 24, 1862, for the war. Mustered in as Sergeant. Present or accounted for until he died in hospital at Richmond, Virginia, April 15, 1863, of "typhoid fever."

CARR, ROBERT B., Private
Born in Franklin County where he resided as a farmer prior to enlisting at age 19, February 28, 1862, for the war. Present or accounted for until discharged on June 18, 1862, by reason of disability.

CARTER, J. W., Private
Resided in Warren County and enlisted at age 21, February 12, 1862, for the war. Present or accounted for until discharged in April, 1862, by reason of disability.

CHANDLER, S. H., Private
Resided in Person County and enlisted on August 12, 1864, for the war. Present or accounted for until captured at Petersburg, Virginia, April 3, 1865. Confined at Hart's Island, New York Harbor, until released June 19-20, 1865, after taking the Oath of Allegiance.

COLEY, J. C., Private
Resided in Nash County and enlisted at age 23, February 24, 1862, for the war. No further records.

COLEY, JOHN, Private
Resided in Nash County where he enlisted at age 28, March 24, 1862, for the war. Present or accounted for through December, 1864.

COOK, B. F., Private
Resided in Union County where he enlisted at age 30, March 23, 1863, for the war. Present or accounted for until reported captured at Spotsylvania Court House, Virginia, May 12, 1864; however, records of the Federal Provost Marshal do not substantiate that report. No further records.

CORDON, R. J., Private
Enlisted in Wake County on September 5, 1864, for the war. Present or accounted for until reported captured on October 14, 1864; however, records of the Federal Provost Marshal do not substantiate that report. Company muster roll dated November-December, 1864, states that he was present. Paroled at Greensboro on May 16, 1865.

DAVIS, GEORGE R., Private
Resided in Franklin County and was by occupation a shoemaker prior to enlisting in Franklin County at age 29, March 24, 1862, for the war. Present or accounted for until he died in hospital at Richmond, Virginia, January 23, 1864, of "variola."

DAVIS, J., Private
Place and date of enlistment not reported. Captured at Winchester, Virginia, September 19, 1864, and confined at Point Lookout, Maryland, until released on December 2, 1864, after taking the Oath of Allegiance.

DEARING, J. N., Private
Resided in Nash County where he enlisted at age 35, March 24, 1862, for the war. Present or accounted for until he died "at home" on December 5, 1862, of disease.

DENTON, HENRY, Private
Resided in Franklin County and enlisted at Camp Arrington, Virginia, at age 20, April 29, 1862, for the war. Present or accounted for until wounded in the thigh and captured at Hanover Court House, Virginia, May 27, 1862. Hospitalized at various Federal hospitals until confined at Fort Delaware, Delaware, on or about July 15, 1862. Exchanged at Aiken's Landing, James River, Virginia, August 5, 1862. Returned to duty in January-February, 1864, and present or accounted for through December, 1864.

DENTON, JACKSON, Private
Enlisted at Camp Holmes on July 15, 1862, for the war; however, he was not carried on the muster rolls of this company until his name appears on a roll dated April 30-October 31, 1864. Present or accounted for until December, 1864. No further records.

DENTON, JOHN B., Private
Born in Franklin County where he resided as a farmer prior to enlisting at Camp Holmes at age 19, July 15, 1862, for the war. Not listed on the rolls of this company until his name appears on a roll dated April 30-October 31, 1864. Present or accounted for until wounded in the right elbow and captured at Monocacy Junction, Maryland, July 9, 1864. Right

arm amputated. Hospitalized at various Federal hospitals until paroled and transferred for exchange. Exchanged on or about September 22, 1864. Reported absent wounded until discharged on or about March 9, 1865.

DUKE, J. L., Private
Resided in Warren County and enlisted at age 48, February 12, 1862, for the war. Discharged March 25, 1862, by reason of disability.

EMERSON, J. H., Private
Resided in Chatham County where he enlisted at age 38, March 19, 1863, for the war. Present or accounted for until captured at Wilderness, Virginia, May 6, 1864. Confined at Old Capitol Prison, Washington, D.C., until transferred to Fort Delaware, Delaware, June 15, 1864. Exchanged on September 18, 1864. Rejoined the company subsequent to December 31, 1864, but prior to April 6, 1865, when he was wounded in the left thigh and captured at Sayler's Creek, Virginia. Hospitalized at various Federal hospitals until hospitalized at Washington on April 19, 1865. Released on or about June 6, 1865, after taking the Oath of Allegiance.

EMERSON, JOHN M., Private
Resided in Chatham County and was by occupation a farmer prior to enlisting in Chatham County at age 36, March 19, 1863, for the war. Present or accounted for until he was "arrested" by the enemy at or near Winchester, Virginia, on or about July 20, 1864. Confined at Wheeling, West Virginia, until transferred to Camp Chase, Ohio, July 27, 1864. Died at Camp Chase on Decmeber 2, 1864, of "smallpox."

FREEMAN, ROBERT, Private
Resided in Franklin County and enlisted at Camp Holmes on July 14, 1864, for the war. Present or accounted for until wounded at or near Fisher's Hill, Virginia, September 22, 1864. Returned to duty in November-December, 1864, and present or accounted for until captured near Petersburg, Virginia, March 25, 1865. Confined at Point Lookout, Maryland, until released June 26-27, 1865, after taking the Oath of Allegiance.

FRUSHEE, L. S., Private
Enlisted at Camp Holmes on September 17, 1864, for the war. Present or accounted for until he died in hospital at Charlottesville, Virginia, November 26, 1864, of "typhoid fever."

GAY, SUMNER, Private
Resided in Franklin County and enlisted at Camp Arrington, Virginia, at age 20, April 15, 1862, for the war. Present or accounted for until wounded in the finger at Chancellorsville, Virginia, May 2, 1863. Returned to duty prior to July 1, 1863, and present or accounted for until captured at Spotsylvania Court House, Virginia, May 12, 1864. Confined at Point Lookout, Maryland, until paroled and transferred to Varina, Virginia, where he was received September 22, 1864, for exchange. No further records.

GORDON, ISAAC W., Private
Resided in Nash County and enlisted at age 16, March 20, 1862, for the war. Present or accounted

for until transferred to Company G, 15th Regiment N.C.Troops (5th Regiment N.C.Volunteers), June 25, 1862, in exchange for Private L. E. Bartholomew.

GRAPES, GEORGE T., Private
Place and date of enlistment not reported. Paroled at Greensboro on May 18, 1865.

GRAY, A. M., Private
Enlisted at Camp Holmes on September 8, 1864, for the war. Present or accounted for until paroled at Farmville, Virginia, April 11-21, 1865.

GUPTON, J. J., Private
Resided in Franklin County and enlisted in Lenoir County at age 23, March 24, 1862, for the war. Present or accounted for until he died in Franklin County on July 23, 1863, of disease.

GUPTON, JOSEPH, Private
Resided in Franklin County and enlisted at Camp Holmes on July 15, 1864, for the war. Present or accounted for until captured at or near Sayler's Creek, Virginia, April 6, 1865. Confined at Point Lookout, Maryland, until released on June 28, 1865, after taking the Oath of Allegiance.

GUPTON, NORFLEET, Private
Resided in Franklin County and enlisted in Lenoir County at age 26, March 24, 1862, for the war. Present or accounted for until he died "at home" on December 25, 1862, of disease.

GUPTON, PEYTON W., Sergeant
Born in Franklin County where he resided as a carpenter prior to enlisting in Lenoir County at age 30, March 24, 1862, for the war. Mustered in as Corporal and promoted to Sergeant on November 1, 1863. Present or accounted for until wounded in the fingers of the right hand at Spotsylvania Court House, Virginia, May 12, 1864. Several fingers amputated. Returned to duty in November-December, 1864, but was retired from service on or about December 28, 1864, by reason of disability.

GUPTON, ROBERT H., Private
Resided in Franklin County and enlisted in Lenoir County at age 43, March 24, 1862, for the war. Present or accounted for until captured near Petersburg, Virginia, March 25, 1865. Confined at Point Lookout, Maryland, until released on June 17, 1865, after taking the Oath of Allegiance.

GUPTON, STEPHEN, Private
Resided in Franklin County and enlisted at Camp Arrington, Virginia, at age 19, April 29, 1862, for the war. Present or accounted for until wounded at Gaines' Mill, Virginia, June 27, 1862. Returned to duty prior to March 1, 1863. Present or accounted for until reported captured at Spotsylvania Court House, Virginia, May 12, 1864; however, records of the Federal Provost Marshal do not substantiate that report. No further records.

HARRIS, A. B., Private
Resided in Warren County where he enlisted at age 25, March 24, 1862, for the war. Present or accounted for until he died in hospital at Gordonsville, Virginia, on or about May 21, 1862, of "typhoid fever."

HARRIS, B. O., Sergeant
Resided in Franklin County and enlisted at age 21,

March 24, 1862, for the war. Mustered in as Sergeant. Present or accounted for until discharged on or about June 3, 1862, after providing a substitute.

HOLLINGSWORTH, S. C., Private
Enlisted at Camp Holmes on July 20, 1864, for the war. Present or accounted for until discharged on September 15, 1864. Reason discharged not reported.

HOLLINGSWORTH, T. C., Private
Enlisted at Camp Holmes on July 30, 1864, for the war. Present or accounted for until killed at Cedar Creek, Virginia, October 19, 1864.

HORTON, GEORGE R., Private
Place and date of enlistment not reported. Captured at Cedar Creek, Virginia, October 19, 1864, and confined at Point Lookout, Maryland, where he died on May 5, 1865, of "chronic diarrhoea."

HORTON, JAMES H., Private
Enlisted at Camp Holmes on August 7, 1864, for the war. Present or accounted for until wounded at Cedar Creek, Virginia, October 19, 1864. Reported absent wounded through December, 1864.

HUFF, J., Private
Place and date of enlistment not reported. Captured in hospital at Richmond, Virginia, April 3, 1865, and died April 21, 1865, of "typhoid fever."

HUMPHRIES, T. J., Private
Enlisted at Camp Holmes on August 12, 1864, for the war. Present or accounted for until captured at Fisher's Hill, Virginia, September 22, 1864. Confined at Point Lookout, Maryland, where he died on December 21, 1864, of "typhoid fever."

INSCO, ARMISTEAD, Private
Resided in Franklin County prior to enlisting at "Davis Crossroads" at age 27, March 24, 1862, for the war. Present or accounted for until killed at Gaines' Mill, Virginia, June 27, 1862.

INSCO, HENRY, Private
Resided in Halifax County and enlisted in Warren County at age 29, March 24, 1862, for the war. Present or accounted for until captured at Winchester, Virginia, September 19, 1864. Confined at Point Lookout, Maryland, where he died on or about November 6, 1864, of "diarrhoea chronic."

INSCOE, B. B., Private
Enlisted at Camp Holmes on September 15, 1864, for the war. Present or accounted for until captured at Cedar Creek, Virginia, October 19, 1864. Confined at Point Lookout, Maryland, where he died on November 29, 1864, of "diarrh[oea] chr[onic]."

INSCOE, J., Private
Enlisted at Camp Holmes on September 18, 1864, for the war. Present or accounted for until captured at Cedar Creek, Virginia, October 19, 1864. Confined at Point Lookout, Maryland. Records of the Federal Provost Marshal indicate both that he died on November 7, 1864, of "chronic diarrhoea" and that he was paroled and transferred for exchange on March 17, 1865. No further records.

JOHNSON, HAYWOOD, Private
Resided in Franklin County and enlisted at "Camp A[rrington]" at age 21, April 29, 1862, for the war.

Present or accounted for until mortally wounded at South Mountain, Maryland, September 14, 1862. Place and date of death not reported.

JOHNSON, JOHN R., Private
Born in Franklin County where he resided prior to enlisting in Franklin County at age 28, March 24, 1862, for the war. Present or accounted for until killed at or near Chancellorsville, Virginia, on or about May 5, 1863. Nominated for the Badge of Distinction for gallantry at Chancellorsville. Company records indicate that he was a sharpshooter.

JONES, J. R., Private
Resided in Person County and enlisted at Camp Holmes on September 8, 1864, for the war. Present or accounted for until wounded in the left thigh and captured at Petersburg, Virginia, March 25, 1865. Hospitalized at Washington, D.C., until released on or about June 19, 1865, after taking the Oath of Allegiance. Hospital records give his age as 35.

JONES, M. S., Private
Enlisted at Camp Holmes on August 12, 1864, for the war. Present or accounted for until paroled at Appomattox Court House, Virginia, April 9, 1865.

JONES, THOMAS J., Private
Resided in Franklin County and enlisted at "Davis Crossroads" at age 19, March 24, 1862, for the war. Present or accounted for until wounded in the hip at Chancellorsville, Virginia, May 3, 1863. Returned to duty prior to July 1-3, 1863, when he was wounded at Gettysburg, Pennsylvania. Reported absent sick or absent wounded until he returned to duty in January-February, 1864. Present or accounted for until captured at Spotsylvania Court House, Virginia, May 12, 1864. Confined at Point Lookout, Maryland, until transferred to Elmira, New York, August 10, 1864. Paroled at Elmira and transferred to Venus Point, Savannah River, Georgia, where he was received November 15, 1864, for exchange. Died at Savannah on January 1, 1865, of "chronic diarrhoea."

JOYNER, A. P., Corporal
Resided in Franklin County and enlisted at Gordonsville, Virginia, at age 28, May 15, 1862, for the war. Mustered in as Private and promoted to Corporal on November 1, 1863. Present or accounted for until wounded in the left foot at Spotsylvania Court House, Virginia, May 12, 1864. Reported absent wounded through December, 1864.

JOYNER, JOHN, Private
Resided in Franklin County where he enlisted at age 31, March 24, 1862, for the war. Present or accounted for until captured at Petersburg, Virginia, April 2, 1865. Confined at Point Lookout, Maryland, until released on June 28, 1865, after taking the Oath of Allegiance.

JOYNER, WILLIS B., Private
Resided in Franklin County. Place and date of enlistment not reported. Wounded in the head and captured at Petersburg, Virginia, March 25, 1865. Hospitalized at Washington, D.C. Hospital records give his age as 40. Transferred to Old Capitol Prison, Washington, April 17, 1865, and was transferred to Elmira, New York, May 1, 1865. Prison records filed

at Elmira indicate he was conscripted on February 1, 1865. Released at Elmira on June 30, 1865, after taking the Oath of Allegiance.

LANCASTER, W. E., Private
Resided in Franklin County and enlisted in Lenoir County at age 35, March 24, 1862, for the war. Present or accounted for until hospitalized at Richmond, Virginia, July 23, 1862, with "typhoid fever." Died at Richmond on or about August 5, 1862.

LANIER, R. H., Private
Born in Franklin County and resided in Nash County where he was by occupation a farmer prior to enlisting at Hanover Court House, Virginia, at age 50, May 23, 1862, for the war as a substitute. Present or accounted for until discharged on October 22, 1862, by reason of "general infirmity & weakness."

LAUGHTER, R. W., Private
Resided in Halifax County where he enlisted at age 45, March 24, 1862, for the war. Present or accounted for until he died in hospital at Richmond, Virginia, May 15, 1863, of "typhoid pneumonia."

LEONARD, ELLEN, Private
Resided in Warren County prior to enlisting at Gordonsville, Virginia, at age 45, May 14, 1862, for the war as a substitute. Present or accounted for until mortally wounded near Mine Run, Virginia, November 28, 1863. Place and date of death not reported.

LEONARD, J., Private
Enlisted at Camp Holmes on August 7, 1864, for the war. Present or accounted for until captured at Winchester, Virginia, September 19, 1864. Confined at Point Lookout, Maryland, where he died on January 20, 1865, of "chronic diarrhoea."

LEONARD, WILLIAM H., Private
Resided in Franklin County and enlisted at Gordonsville, Virginia, at age 22, May 14, 1862, for the war. Present or accounted for until he was reported captured at Spotsylvania Court House, Virginia, May 12, 1864; however, records of the Federal Provost Marshal do not substantiate that report. No further records.

LEVERETT, GEORGE T., Corporal
Place and date of enlistment not reported. Captured in hospital at Petersburg, Virginia, April 3, 1865, and died April 7, 1865. Cause of death not reported.

LONG, EDWARD J., Corporal
Resided in Franklin County and enlisted at "Davis Crossroads" at age 38, March 24, 1862, for the war. Mustered in as Corporal. Present or accounted for until captured at Warrenton, Virginia, October 20, 1863. Confined at Old Capitol Prison, Washington, D.C., and was transferred to Point Lookout, Maryland, October 27, 1863. Released at Point Lookout on February 21, 1864, after taking the Oath of Allegiance and joining the U. S. Army. Assigned to Company F, 1st Regiment U.S. Volunteer Infantry.

McCRODEN, ROBERT, Private
Born in Maryland and resided in Warren County where he enlisted at age 18, March 24, 1862, for the war. Present or accounted for until captured at Hanover Court House, Virginia, May 27, 1862. Confined at Fort Columbus, New York Harbor, until paroled and transferred to Aiken's Landing, James

River, Virginia, where he was exchanged on August 5, 1862. Returned to duty prior to September 14, 1862, when he was captured at South Mountain, Maryland. Confined at Fort Delaware, Delaware, until transferred to Aiken's Landing on October 2, 1862, for exchange. Declared exchanged at Aiken's Landing on November 10, 1862. Rejoined the company prior to March 1, 1863, and present or accounted for until wounded in the right arm at Spotsylvania Court House, Virginia, May 10, 1864. Right arm amputated. Reported absent wounded until retired to the Invalid Corps on December 21, 1864.

MARSHALL, J. E., Private
Resided in Warren County and enlisted at age 29, February 12, 1862, for the war. Died at Camp Arrington, Virginia, on or about April 28, 1862, of disease.

MOSES, LUTHER H., Private
Born in Franklin County where he resided prior to enlisting at "Davis Crossroads" at age 19, March 24, 1862, for the war. Present or accounted for until wounded in the leg at Spotsylvania Court House, Virginia, May 10, 1864. Leg amputated. Reported absent wounded through December, 1864.

MURPHY, D. F., Private
Resided in Franklin County where he enlisted at age 25, March 24, 1862, for the war. Present or accounted for until captured at Spotsylvania Court House, Virginia, May 12, 1864. Confined at Point Lookout, Maryland, until transferred to Elmira, New York, August 10, 1864. Released at Elmira on June 27, 1865, after taking the Oath of Allegiance.

MURPHY, J. P., Private
Resided in Franklin County prior to enlisting at "Davis Crossroads" at age 18, March 24, 1862, for the war. Present or accounted for until he died in hospital at Danville, Virginia, November 26, 1862, of "variola."

MURRAY, W. O. C., Corporal
Resided in Franklin County and enlisted at Gordonsville, Virginia, at age 20, May 15, 1862, for the war. Mustered in as Private and promoted to Corporal on March 1, 1863. Present or accounted for until wounded at Spotsylvania Court House, Virginia, May 12, 1864. Died "at home" on June 1, 1864.

NEAL, E. L., Corporal
Resided in Warren County and enlisted in Northampton County at age 22, March 24, 1862, for the war. Mustered in as Private. Present or accounted for until hospitalized at Richmond, Virginia, May 17, 1864, with a gunshot wound of the right thigh; however, place and date wounded not reported. Returned to duty and was promoted to Corporal in November-December, 1864. Present or accounted for until paroled at Appomattox Court House, Virginia, April 9, 1865.

NEAL, J. H., Private
Resided in Warren County where he enlisted at age 30, March 24, 1862, for the war. Present or accounted for through November, 1862. Died prior to November 28, 1863. Place, exact date, and cause of death not reported.

NEAL, W. W., Private
Resided in Warren County and enlisted at age 33, February 26, 1862, for the war. Present or accounted for until discharged on March 25, 1862, by reason of disability.

NEWTON, JOHN, Private
Resided in Washington County prior to enlisting in Wake County on September 1, 1864, for the war. Present or accounted for until captured at Petersburg, Virginia, April 2, 1865. Confined at Point Lookout, Maryland, until released on June 29, 1865, after taking the Oath of Allegiance.

OVERTON, J. W., Private
Resided in Franklin County where he enlisted at age 24, May 24, 1862, for the war. Present or accounted for until he died in hospital at Lynchburg, Virginia, January 3, 1863, of "pneumonia."

PERRY, JOSEPH, Private
Resided in Franklin County where he enlisted at age 23, March 24, 1862, for the war. Present or accounted for until captured at Wilderness, Virginia, May 5-7, 1864. Paroled and exchanged at an unspecified date. Present or accounted for until wounded at Cedar Creek, Virginia, October 19, 1864. Reported absent wounded through December, 1864.

PERRY, WILLIAM, Private
Enlisted in Wake County on August 12, 1864, for the war. Present or accounted for until he "lost three fingers" of the left hand at Cedar Creek, Virginia, October 19, 1864. Reported absent wounded or absent on detail through February 21, 1865.

PIKE, EDWARD, Private
Resided in Warren County and enlisted at age 26, February 10, 1862, for the war. Present or accounted for until he died at Norfolk, Virginia, on or about April 28, 1862, of disease.

PITMAN, J. T., Private
Resided in Warren County where he enlisted at age 17, March 24, 1862, for the war as a substitute. Present or accounted for until hospitalized at Richmond, Virginia, December 16, 1862, with a gunshot wound of the right foot; however, place and date wounded not reported. Returned to duty prior to May 1, 1863, and present or accounted for until he died "at home" on February 18, 1864, of disease.

RADFORD, THEODORE, Private
Resided in Nash County where he enlisted at age 22, March 24, 1862, for the war. Present or accounted for until paroled at Appomattox Court House, Virginia, April 9, 1865.

REID, JOHN A. BYNUM, Private
Resided in Warren County where he enlisted at age 33, March 24, 1862, for the war. Present or accounted for until discharged on December 21, 1863, by reason of disability.

RIGGAN, J. F., Private
Resided in Warren County and enlisted at age 44, February 22, 1862, for the war. Discharged March 25, 1862, by reason of disability.

ROBERTSON, T. B., Private
Resided in Warren County where he enlisted at age 45, March 24, 1862, for the war. Present or account-ed for through December, 1864.

ROBERTSON, W. J., Private
Resided in Warren County where he enlisted at age 34, March 24, 1862, for the war. Present or accounted for until he died "at home" in July, 1864, of disease.

ROBERTSON, WILLIAM J., Private
Resided in Warren County where he enlisted at age 18, March 24, 1862, for the war. Present or accounted for until wounded in the toe at Chancellorsville, Virginia, May 2, 1863. Returned to duty prior to September 1, 1863, and present or accounted for until wounded in the left foot and ankle at Petersburg, Virginia, April 2, 1865. Hospitalized at Richmond, Virginia, where he was captured on April 3, 1865. Took the Oath of Allegiance at Richmond on June 27, 1865.

ROGERS, J. C., Private
Resided in Person County and enlisted in Wake County on August 12, 1864, for the war. Present or accounted for until captured near Petersburg, Virginia, March 25, 1865. Confined at Point Lookout, Maryland, until released on June 14, 1865, after taking the Oath of Allegiance.

SHEARIN, J., Private
Enlisted in Wake County on July 1, 1864, for the war. Present or accounted for until captured at Winchester, Virginia, or at Fisher's Hill, Virginia, September 19-22, 1864. Confined at Point Lookout, Maryland, until paroled and transferred to Boulware's Wharf, James River, Virginia, where he was received March 18, 1865, for exchange.

SMITH, SOL W., Sergeant
Born in Warren County where he resided as a farmer prior to enlisting in Warren County at age 31, March 24, 1862, for the war. Mustered in as Sergeant. Present or accounted for through January 17, 1865.

SNIPES, GEORGE, Private
Enlisted in Wake County on August 12, 1864, for the war. Present or accounted for through December, 1864.

STALLINGS, LANGDON C., Private
Resided in Franklin County prior to enlisting at "Davis Crossroads" at age 21, March 24, 1862, for the war. Present or accounted for until he died "at home" on or about July 15, 1862, of disease.

STAMPER, M. D., Private
Enlisted in Wake County on June 12, 1864, for the war. Present or accounted for through December, 1864.

SWANSON, W. C., Private
Resided in Franklin County where he enlisted at age 42, March 24, 1863, for the war. Present or accounted for until wounded in the scalp on or about April 28, 1863; however, battle in which wounded not reported. Returned to duty at an unspecified date and present or accounted for through December, 1864; however, he was reported absent on light duty during most of that period. Retired to the Invalid Corps on or about January 27, 1865.

TABLER, JESSE, Private
Conscripted on June 28, 1864. Deserted on or about August 11, 1864, and was "making his way to Winchester to give himself up to the Union forces when he laid down on the roadside within ½ mile of the town" and was captured by some Federal cavalrymen after he "accidentally fell asleep." Confined at Old Capitol Prison, Washington, D.C., until transferred to Elmira, New York, October 24, 1864. Died at Elmira on May 3, 1865, of "chro[nic] diarrhoea."

TALLEY, R. B., Private
Resided in Person County and enlisted at Camp Holmes on August 12, 1864, for the war. Present or accounted for until he was reported captured on October 19, 1864; however, records of the Federal Provost Marshal do not substantiate that report. Company muster roll dated November-December, 1864, indicates that he was present. Present or accounted for until captured near Petersburg, Virginia, March 25, 1865. Confined at Point Lookout, Maryland, until released on June 14, 1865, after taking the Oath of Allegiance.

THOMAS, B. F., Sergeant
Resided in Franklin County and enlisted at "Davis Crossroads" at age 23, March 24, 1862, for the war. Mustered in as 1st Sergeant but was reduced to the rank of Sergeant on June 1, 1862. Present or accounted for until he died in hospital at Richmond, Virginia, July 16, 1862, of "feb[ris] typh[oides]."

THOMAS, JAMES O'KELLY, Private
Resided in Franklin County where he enlisted at age 28, May 15, 1862, for the war. Present or accounted for until wounded in the thigh and captured at Hanover Court House, Virginia, May 27, 1862. Died May 28, 1862.

THOMAS, JOSEPH, Private
Born in Franklin County where he resided as a farmer prior to enlisting in Wake County at age 26, May 15, 1862, for the war. Present or accounted for until discharged on or about August 27, 1862, by reason of "an aberration of the mind following an attack of fever." Died at Richmond, Virginia, September 8, 1862, of disease.

THOMAS, SAMUEL, Private
Resided in Franklin County and enlisted at "Davis Crossroads" at age 20, March 24, 1862, for the war. Present or accounted for until hospitalized at Richmond, Virginia, July 6, 1862, with "diarrhoea." Died at Richmond on July 8, 1862.

THOMPSON, DRURY, Private
Resided in Warren County where he enlisted at age 48, March 24, 1862, for the war. Present or accounted for until he died at Richmond, Virginia, May 17, 1862, of disease.

THOMPSON, J. B., Private
Resided in Warren County where he enlisted at age 21, March 24, 1862, for the war. Present or accounted for until he died at Lynchburg, Virginia, on or about July 7, 1862, of "febris cont com."

TUCKER, G. W., Private
Resided in Warren County where he enlisted at age 34, March 24, 1862, for the war. Present or accounted for until hospitalized at Danville, Virginia, May 18, 1864, with a gunshot wound of the arm; however, place and date wounded not reported. Returned to duty prior to November 1, 1864, and present or accounted for until captured at Petersburg, Virginia, April 2, 1865. Confined at Point Lookout, Maryland, until released on June 21, 1865, after taking the Oath of Allegiance.

TUCKER, GEORGE M., Private
Resided in Franklin County and enlisted in Lenoir County at age 20, March 24, 1862, for the war. Present or accounted for until hospitalized at Richmond, Virginia, July 19, 1862, with "typhoid fever." Died at Richmond on July 24, 1862.

TUCKER, THOMAS, Private
Resided in Franklin County and enlisted in Lenoir County at age 19, March 24, 1862, for the war. Present or accounted for through December, 1864.

WARREN, A., Private
Enlisted in Wake County on August 29, 1864, for the war. Present or accounted for until "sent to hospital" on October 31, 1864. No further records.

WEBB, R. J., Private
Enlisted in Wake County on June 25, 1864, for the war. Present or accounted for until wounded in the left forearm at Cedar Creek, Virginia, October 19, 1864. Reported absent wounded until furloughed for sixty days on November 30, 1864.

WHITFIELD, ALEXANDER, Private
Enlisted in Wake County on August 27, 1864, for the war. Present or accounted for until paroled at Greensboro on May 11, 1865.

WHITLOW, JAMES S., Private
Resided in Caswell County and enlisted in Wake County on July 5, 1864, for the war. Present or accounted for until captured at Petersburg, Virginia, April 3, 1865. Confined at Hart's Island, New York Harbor, until released on June 17, 1865, after taking the Oath of Allegiance.

WILLIAMSON, CYRUS, Private
Resided in Union County where he enlisted at age 20, March 23, 1863, for the war. Present or accounted for until he was reported wounded and captured at Spotsylvania Court House, Virginia, May 12, 1864; however, records of the Federal Provost Marshal do not substantiate the report of his capture. No further records.

WOOD, WILLIAM F., Private
Resided in Franklin County and enlisted at "Davis Crossroads" at age 44, March 24, 1862, for the war. Present or accounted for until discharged on September 3, 1862, by reason of "permanent deafness & impaired health from organic disease of the heart with slight effusion in the lower extremities."

COMPANY L

This company was from Tyrrell County and enlisted at Columbia on May 16, 1861. It tendered its service to the state and was ordered to Garysburg, where it was assigned to this regiment. The company was mustered in as Captain Edmund C. Brabble's Company and was designated Company L. In October, 1861, the company was transferred out of the regiment and became Company A, afterwards Company F, 1st Battalion N.C. Infantry. The battalion was later raised to a regiment and designated the 32nd Regiment N.C. Troops. This company became Company A of that regiment. [The history of this company subsequent to October, 1861, together with the service records of its members, will appear in the roster for Company A, 32nd Regiment N.C. Troops, which will be published in a future volume.]

The information contained in the following roster of the company was compiled principally from a company muster roll for May 16 through August 31, 1861. No additional company muster rolls were found. In addition to the company muster roll, Roll of Honor records, receipt rolls, hospital records, prisoner of war records, and other primary records, supplemented by state pension applications, United Daughters of the Confederacy records, and postwar rosters and histories, all provided useful information.

OFFICERS
CAPTAIN

BRABBLE, EDMUND C.
Resided in Tyrrell County where he enlisted at age 29. Appointed Captain on May 16, 1861. Present or accounted for until transferred to Company A, 32nd Regiment N.C.Troops, in October, 1861.

LIEUTENANTS

DUGUID, JOHN C., 3rd Lieutenant
Resided in Tyrrell County and enlisted at age 40. Appointed 3rd Lieutenant on May 16, 1861. Present or accounted for until transferred to Company A, 32nd Regiment N.C.Troops, in October, 1861.

HASSELL, LEONARD L., 1st Lieutenant
Enlisted in Tyrrell County. Appointed 1st Lieutenant on May 16, 1861. Present or accounted for until transferred to Company A, 32nd Regiment N.C. Troops, in October, 1861.

LEWIS, HENRY G., 2nd Lieutenant
Resided in Tyrrell or Edgecombe counties and enlisted in Tyrrell County at age 22. Appointed 2nd Lieutenant on May 16, 1861. Present or accounted for until transferred to Company A, 32nd Regiment N.C.Troops, in October, 1861.

NONCOMMISSIONED OFFICERS AND PRIVATES

ALEXANDER, JOSHUA W., Private
Resided in Tyrrell County where he enlisted on May 16, 1861. Present or accounted for until transferred to Company A, 32nd Regiment N.C.Troops, in October, 1861.

ALEXANDER, NELSON, Private
Resided in Tyrrell County where he enlisted at age 22, May 16, 1861. Present or accounted for until transferred to Company A, 32nd Regiment N.C. Troops, in October, 1861.

ALEXANDER, WILLIAM E., Private
Resided in Tyrrell County where he enlisted at age 25, May 16, 1861. Present or accounted for until transferred to Company A, 32nd Regiment N.C. Troops, in October, 1861.

ALEXANDER, WILLIAM W., Private
Resided in Tyrrell or Northampton counties and enlisted in Tyrrell County at age 26, May 16, 1861. Present or accounted for until transferred to Company A, 32nd Regiment N.C.Troops, in October, 1861.

AMBROSE, JOSEPH H., Private
Resided in Tyrrell County where he enlisted at age 18, May 16, 1861. Present or accounted for until transferred to Company A, 32nd Regiment N.C. Troops, in October, 1861.

ARMSTRONG, CHARLES H., Private
Resided in Tyrrell County where he enlisted at age 22, May 16, 1861. Present or accounted for until transferred to Company A, 32nd Regiment N.C. Troops, in October, 1861.

ARMSTRONG, HENRY, Private
Resided in Tyrrell County where he enlisted at age 27, May 16, 1861. Present or accounted for until transferred to Company A, 32nd Regiment N.C. Troops, in October, 1861.

ARMSTRONG, HOLLOWAY A., Private
Resided in Tyrrell County where he enlisted at age 26, May 16, 1861. Present or accounted for until transferred to Company A, 32nd Regiment N.C. Troops, in October, 1861.

ARMSTRONG, WILLIAM B., Private
Resided in Tyrrell County where he enlisted at age 29, May 16, 1861. Present or accounted for until transferred to Company A, 32nd Regiment N.C. Troops, in October, 1861.

BARNES, JOSHUA L., Private
Resided in Tyrrell County where he enlisted at age 23, May 16, 1861. Present or accounted for until transferred to Company A, 32nd Regiment N.C. Troops, in October, 1861.

BASNIGHT, LEMUEL, Private
Resided in Tyrrell County where he enlisted on May 16, 1861. Present or accounted for until transferred to Company A, 32nd Regiment N.C.Troops, in October, 1861.

BASNIGHT, THOMAS, Private
Resided in Tyrrell County where he enlisted at age 30, May 16, 1861. Present or accounted for until transferred to Company A, 32nd Regiment N.C. Troops, in October, 1861.

BATEMAN, GEORGE W., Corporal
Resided in Tyrrell County where he enlisted at age 22, May 16, 1861. Mustered in as Corporal. Present or accounted for until transferred to Company A, 32nd Regiment N. C. Troops, in October, 1861.

BESS, LEMUEL B., Private
Resided in Tyrrell County where he enlisted at age 33, May 16, 1861. Present or accounted for until transferred to Company A, 32nd Regiment N.C. Troops, in October, 1861.

BOYLE, FRANCIS A., 1st Sergeant
Resided in Tyrrell or Washington counties and enlisted in Tyrrell County at age 25, May 16, 1861. Mustered in as 1st Sergeant. Present or accounted for until transferred to Company A, 32nd Regiment N.C. Troops, in October, 1861.

BRICKHOUSE, SAMUEL, Private
Resided in Tyrrell County where he enlisted at age 20, May 16, 1861. Present or accounted for until transferred to Company A, 32nd Regiment N.C. Troops, in October, 1861.

BRICKHOUSE, WILLIAM P., Corporal
Born in Tyrrell County where he resided as a farmer prior to enlisting in Tyrrell County at age 37, May 16, 1861. Mustered in as Corporal. Present or accounted for until transferred to Company A, 32nd Regiment N.C.Troops, in October, 1861.

CAHOON, BENJAMIN F., Private
Resided in Tyrrell County where he enlisted at age 21, May 16, 1861. Present or accounted for until transferred to Company A, 32nd Regiment N.C. Troops, in October, 1861.

CAHOON, CHARLES, Private
Resided in Tyrrell County where he enlisted at age 20, May 16, 1861. Present or accounted for until transferred to Company A, 32nd Regiment N.C. Troops, in October, 1861.

CAHOON, FRANKLIN, Private
Resided in Tyrrell County where he enlisted at age 27, May 16, 1861. Present or accounted for until transferred to Company A, 32nd Regiment N.C. Troops, in October, 1861.

CAHOON, HENRY, Private
Resided in Tyrrell County where he enlisted on May 16, 1861. Present or accounted for until transferred to Company A, 32nd Regiment N.C.Troops, in October, 1861.

CAHOON, JOHN S., Private
Resided in Tyrrell County where he enlisted at age 19, May 16, 1861. Present or accounted for until transferred to Company A, 32nd Regiment N.C. Troops, in October, 1861.

CAHOON, JOHN T., Private
Resided in Tyrrell County where he enlisted at age 18, May 16, 1861. Present or accounted for until transferred to Company A, 32nd Regiment N. C. Troops, in October, 1861.

COLSTON, WILLIAM G., Private
Resided in Maryland and enlisted in Tyrrell County at age 21, May 16, 1861. Present or accounted for until transferred to Company A, 32nd Regiment N.C. Troops, in October, 1861.

COMBS, THOMAS T., Private
Resided in Tyrrell County where he enlisted at age 30, May 16, 1861. Present or accounted for until transferred to Company A, 32nd Regiment N.C. Troops, in October, 1861.

COOPER, ELIJAH N., Private
Resided in Tyrrell County where he enlisted at age 21, May 16, 1861. Present or accounted for until transferred to Company A, 32nd Regiment N.C. Troops, in October, 1861.

COWAND, DAVID G., Sergeant
Resided in Tyrrell or Washington counties and enlisted in Tyrrell County at age 29, May 16, 1861. Mustered in as Sergeant. Present or accounted for until transferred to Company A, 32nd Regiment N.C. Troops, in October, 1861.

CRADDOCK, JAMES H., Private
Resided in Tyrrell County where he enlisted at age 22, May 16, 1861. Present or accounted for until he died in hospital at Norfolk, Virginia, October 3, 1861. Cause of death not reported.

CRAIN, GRIFFIN R., Private
Resided in Tyrrell County where he enlisted on May 16, 1861. Present or accounted for until transferred to Company A, 32nd Regiment N.C.Troops, in October, 1861.

CRAIN, JESSE, Private
Resided in Tyrrell County where he enlisted at age 21, May 16, 1861. Present or accounted for until transferred to Company A, 32nd Regiment N.C. Troops, in October, 1861.

DAVENPORT, BENJAMIN W., Private
Resided in Tyrrell County where he enlisted at age 21, May 16, 1861. Present or accounted for until transferred to Company A, 32nd Regiment N.C. Troops, in October, 1861.

DAVENPORT, WILSON S., Private
Born in Tyrrell County where he resided as a farmer prior to enlisting in Tyrrell County at age 24, May 16, 1861. Present or accounted for until transferred to Company A, 32nd Regiment N.C. Troops, in October, 1861.

DILLON, WILLIAM J., Private
Resided in Tyrrell County where he enlisted at age 30, May 16, 1861. Present or accounted for until transferred to Company A, 32nd Regiment N.C. Troops, in October, 1861.

DOZIER, JOHN A., Private
Resided in Tyrrell County where he enlisted on May 16, 1861. Present or accounted for until transferred to Company A, 32nd Regiment N.C. Troops, in October, 1861.

GRAY, WILLIAM M., Private
Resided in Tyrrell County where he enlisted at age 25, May 16, 1861. Present or accounted for until transferred to Company A, 32nd Regiment N.C. Troops, in October, 1861.

HARRIS, WILSON W., Private
Resided in Tyrrell County where he enlisted at age 25, May 16, 1861. Present or accounted for until transferred to Company A, 32nd Regiment N.C. Troops, in October, 1861.

HASSELL, ENOCH N., Private
Resided in Tyrrell County where he enlisted on May 16, 1861. Present or accounted for until transferred to Company A, 32nd Regiment N.C.Troops, in October, 1861.

HASSELL, JOHN P., Private
Enlisted in Tyrrell County on May 16, 1861. Died in hospital at Camp Carolina, Virginia, July 20, 1861. Cause of death not reported.

HOLLIDAY, SEBERN R., Private
Resided in Tyrrell County where he enlisted at age 25, May 16, 1861. Present or accounted for until transferred to Company A, 32nd Regiment N.C. Troops, in October, 1861.

HOOKER, DANIEL S., Private
Born in Tyrrell County where he resided as a farmer prior to enlisting in Tyrrell County at age 20, May 16, 1861. Present or accounted for until transferred to Company A, 32nd Regiment N.C.Troops, in October, 1861.

HORTON, JAMES H., Private
Resided in Virginia and enlisted in Tyrrell County at age 22, May 16, 1861. Present or accounted for until transferred to Company A, 32nd Regiment N.C. Troops, in October, 1861.

JONES, THOMAS L., Private
Resided in Tyrrell County where he enlisted at age 22, May 16, 1861. Present or accounted for until transferred to Company A, 32nd Regiment N.C. Troops, in October, 1861.

KEMP, ZEBULON W., Private
Resided in Tyrrell County where he enlisted at age 25, May 16, 1861. Present or accounted for until transferred to Company A, 32nd Regiment N.C. Troops, in October, 1861.

KENNEDY, WILLIAM, Private
Resided in Tyrrell County where he enlisted at age 22, May 16, 1861. Present or accounted for until transferred to Company A, 32nd Regiment N.C. Troops, in October, 1861.

KNIGHT, THOMAS W., Sergeant
Resided in Tyrrell County where he enlisted at age 42, May 16, 1861. Mustered in as Sergeant. Present or accounted for until transferred to Company A, 32nd Regiment N. C. Troops, in October, 1861.

LEWIS, HENRY B., Private
Resided in Tyrrell County where he enlisted on May 16, 1861. Present or accounted for until transferred to Company A, 32nd Regiment N.C. Troops, in October, 1861.

LIVERMAN, ENOS, Private
Resided in Tyrrell County where he enlisted at age 24, May 16, 1861. Present or accounted for until transferred to Company A, 32nd Regiment N.C. Troops, in October, 1861.

LIVERMAN, JORDAN S., Private
Resided in Tyrrell County where he enlisted at age 25, May 16, 1861. Present or accounted for until transferred to Company A, 32nd Regiment N.C. Troops, in October, 1861.

MEEKINS, FREDERIC, Private
Resided in Tyrrell County where he enlisted at age 39, May 16, 1861. Present or accounted for until transferred to Company A, 32nd Regiment N.C. Troops, in October, 1861.

MERRITT, ASA, Private
Resided in Tyrrell County where he enlisted at age 22, May 16, 1861. Present or accounted for until **transferred** to **Company A, 32nd Regiment N.C.** Troops, in October, 1861.

MERRITT, GEORGE, Private
Resided in Tyrrell County where he enlisted at age 30, May 16, 1861. Present or accounted for until transferred to Company A, 32nd Regiment N.C. Troops, in October, 1861.

NICHOLLS, JOHN H., Private
Resided in Tyrrell County where he enlisted at age 28, May 16, 1861. Present or accounted for until transferred to Company A, 32nd Regiment N. C. Troops, in October, 1861.

OWENS, HENRY C., Private
Resided in Tyrrell County where he enlisted at age 20, May 16, 1861. Present or accounted for until he died in hospital at Norfolk, Virginia, September 6, 1861. Cause of death not reported.

OWENS, JAMES BARTLETT, Private
Resided in Tyrrell County where he enlisted at age 31, May 16, 1861. Present or accounted for until transferred to Company A, 32nd Regiment N.C. Troops, in October, 1861.

PATRICK, FREDERICK F., Private
Resided in Tyrrell County where he enlisted at age 38, May 16, 1861. Present or accounted for until transferred to Company A, 32nd Regiment N.C. Troops, in October, 1861.

POOLE, THOMAS G., Private
Resided in Tyrrell County where he enlisted at age 37, May 16, 1861. Present or accounted for until transferred to Company A, 32nd Regiment N.C. Troops, in October, 1861.

QUICK, JAMES E., Private
Resided in Virginia and enlisted in Tyrrell County at age 28, May 16, 1861. Present or accounted for until transferred to Company A, 32nd Regiment N.C. Troops, in October, 1861.

ROUGHTON, DANIEL, Private
Resided in Tyrrell County where he enlisted on May 16, 1861. Present or accounted for until he deserted on September 16, 1861.

ROUGHTON, HEZEKIAH G., Corporal
Resided in Tyrrell County where he enlisted at age 27, May 16, 1861. Mustered in as Corporal. Present or accounted for until transferred to Company A, 32nd Regiment N. C. Troops, in October, 1861.

ROUGHTON, ZACHARIAH, Sergeant
Resided in Tyrrell County where he enlisted at age 40, May 16, 1861. Mustered in as Sergeant. Present or accounted for until transferred to Company A, 32nd Regiment N.C.Troops, in October, 1861.

SANDLIN, DANIEL S., Private
Resided in Tyrrell County where he enlisted at age 25, May 16, 1861. Present or accounted for until transferred to Company A, 32nd Regiment N.C. Troops, in October, 1861.

SAWYER, CHARLES H. H., Private
Resided in Tyrrell County where he enlisted at age 24, May 16, 1861. Present or accounted for until transferred to Company A, 32nd Regiment N.C. Troops, in October, 1861.

SAWYER, SAMUEL L., Private
Resided in Tyrrell County where he enlisted at age 27, May 16, 1861. Present or accounted for until

transferred to Company A, 32nd Regiment N.C. Troops, in October, 1861.

SAWYER, SIMEON T., Private
Resided in Washington County and enlisted in Tyrrell County at age 26, May 16, 1861. Present or accounted for until transferred to Company A, 32nd Regiment N.C.Troops, in October, 1861.

SAWYER, TILLMAN T., Private
Resided in Washington County and enlisted in Tyrrell County at age 24, May 16, 1861. Present or accounted for until transferred to Company A, 32nd Regiment N. C. Troops, in October, 1861.

SAWYER, WILLIAM H. H., Private
Enlisted in Tyrrell County on May 16, 1861. Present or accounted for until transferred to Company A, 32nd Regiment N. C. Troops, in October, 1861.

SMITH, CHARLES, Private
Resided in Tyrrell County where he enlisted at age 21, May 16, 1861. Present or accounted for until transferred to Company A, 32nd Regiment N. C. Troops, in October, 1861.

SMITH, SAMUEL, Private
Resided in Tyrrell County where he enlisted at age 23, May 16, 1861. Present or accounted for until transferred to Company A, 32nd Regiment N.C. Troops, in October, 1861.

SPENCER, BENJAMIN S., Private
Resided in Tyrrell County where he enlisted at age 26, May 16, 1861. Present or accounted for until transferred to Company A, 32nd Regiment N.C. Troops, in October, 1861.

TARKINTON, BENJAMIN F., Private
Resided in Tyrrell County where he enlisted on May 16, 1861. Present or accounted for until transferred to Company A, 32nd Regiment N.C.Troops, in October, 1861.

TARKINTON, HENRY Z., Private
Resided in Tyrrell County where he enlisted at age 20, May 16, 1861. Present or accounted for until transferred to Company A, 32nd Regiment N.C. Troops, in October, 1861.

THOMAS, JOHN H., Corporal
Resided in Tyrrell County where he enlisted at age 24, May 16, 1861. Mustered in as Corporal. Present or accounted for until transferred to Company A, 32nd Regiment N.C.Troops, in October, 1861.

TWIDDY, BENJAMIN A., Private
Born in Tyrrell County where he resided as a farmer prior to enlisting in Tyrrell County at age 20, May 16, 1861. Present or accounted for until transferred to Company A, 32nd Regiment N.C.Troops, in October, 1861.

TWIDDY, URIAH, Private
Resided in Tyrrell County where he enlisted at age 21, May 16, 1861. Present or accounted for until transferred to Company A, 32nd Regiment N.C. Troops, in October, 1861.

WALKER, DANIEL, Private
Enlisted in Tyrrell County on May 16, 1861. Present or accounted for until transferred to Company A, 32nd Regiment N.C.Troops, in October, 1861.

WARD, FRANKLIN J., Private
Resided in Tyrrell County where he enlisted on May 16, 1861. Present or accounted for until transferred to Company A, 32nd Regiment N.C.Troops, in October, 1861.

WHITE, JOSEPH T., Private
Resided in Tyrrell County where he enlisted on May 16, 1861. Present or accounted for until transferred to Company A, 32nd Regiment N.C.Troops, in October, 1861.

COMPANY M

This company, known as the "Camden Grays," was raised in Camden County and enlisted on May 30, 1861. It tendered its service to the state and was ordered to Garysburg, where it was assigned to this regiment. The company was mustered in as Captain Joseph G. Hughes's Company and was designated Company M. In October, 1861, the company was transferred out of the regiment and became Company B, afterward Company A, 1st Battalion N.C. Infantry. The battalion was later raised to a regiment and designated the 32nd Regiment N.C. Troops, and this company became 2nd Company B of that regiment. [The history of this company subsequent to October, 1861, together with the service records of its members, will appear in the roster for 2nd Company B, 32nd Regiment N.C. Troops, which will be published in a future volume.]

The information contained in the following roster of the company was compiled principally from a company muster roll for May 30 through August 31, 1861. No additional company muster rolls were found. In addition to the company muster roll, Roll of Honor records, receipt rolls, hospital records, prisoner of war records, and other primary records, supplemented by state pension applications, United Daughters of the Confederacy records, and postwar rosters and histories, all provided useful information.

OFFICERS
CAPTAIN

HUGHES, JOSEPH G.
Resided in Camden County where he enlisted at age 28. Appointed Captain on May 30, 1861. Present or accounted for until transferred to 2nd Company B, 32nd Regiment N.C.Troops, in October, 1861.

LIEUTENANTS

CHERRY, ADDISON P., 2nd Lieutenant
Resided in Camden County where he enlisted at age 26. Appointed 2nd Lieutenant on or about May 30, 1861. Present or accounted for until transferred to 2nd Company B, 32nd Regiment N.C.Troops, in October, 1861.

OVERTON, WILLIAM R., 1st Lieutenant
Resided in Camden County where he enlisted at age 31. Appointed 1st Lieutenant on or about May 30, 1861. Present or accounted for until transferred to 2nd Company B, 32nd Regiment N.C.Troops, in October, 1861.

PARKER, RICHARD H., 3rd Lieutenant
Resided in Camden County where he enlisted at age 25. Appointed 3rd Lieutenant on May 30, 1861. Present or accounted for until transferred to 2nd Company B, 32nd Regiment N.C.Troops, in October, 1861.

NONCOMMISSIONED OFFICERS AND PRIVATES

BANKS, WILLIAM H., Private
Resided in Camden County where he enlisted at age 30, May 30, 1861. Present or accounted for until transferred to 2nd Company B, 32nd Regiment N.C. Troops, in October, 1861.

BRIGHT, ELISHA, Private
Resided in Camden County where he enlisted at age 20, May 30, 1861. Present or accounted for until transferred to 2nd Company B, 32nd Regiment N.C. Troops, in October, 1861.

BRIGHT, HENRY, Private
Resided in Camden County where he enlisted at age 22, May 30, 1861. Present or accounted for until transferred to 2nd Company B, 32nd Regiment N.C. Troops, in October, 1861.

BRIGHT, HENRY C., Private
Resided in Camden County where he enlisted at age 23, May 30, 1861. Present or accounted for until transferred to 2nd Company B, 32nd Regiment N.C. Troops, in October, 1861.

BRIGHT, MARCUS, Private
Resided in Camden County where he enlisted at age 34, May 30, 1861. Present or accounted for until transferred to 2nd Company B, 32nd Regiment N.C. Troops, in October, 1861.

BRIGHT, WASHINGTON, Private
Resided in Camden County where he enlisted at age 24, May 30, 1861. Present or accounted for until transferred to 2nd Company B, 32nd Regiment N.C. Troops, in October, 1861.

BROWN, JAMES W., Private
Resided in Camden County where he enlisted at age 34, May 30, 1861. Present or accounted for until transferred to 2nd Company B, 32nd Regiment N.C. Troops, in October, 1861.

BULLOCH, ROBERT, Sergeant
Born in Scotland and resided in Camden County where he was by occupation a mechanic prior to enlisting in Camden County at age 35, May 30, 1861. Mustered in as Sergeant. Present or accounted for until transferred to 2nd Company B, 32nd Regiment N.C.Troops, in October, 1861.

BURNHAM, BENJAMIN, Corporal
Born in Camden County where he resided as a merchant prior to enlisting in Camden County at age 34, May 30, 1861. Mustered in as Corporal. Present or accounted for until transferred to 2nd Company B, 32nd Regiment N.C.Troops, in October, 1861.

CHERRY, OLIVER, Private
Resided in Camden County where he enlisted at age 20, May 30, 1861. Present or accounted for until transferred to 2nd Company B, 32nd Regiment N.C. Troops, in October, 1861.

CREEKMORE, JOSIAH, Private
Born in Virginia and resided in Camden County where he was by occupation a farmer prior to enlisting in Camden County at age 35, May 30, 1861. Present or accounted for until transferred to 2nd Company B, 32nd Regiment N.C. Troops, in October, 1861.

CREEKMORE, MARTIN, Private
Resided in Camden County where he enlisted at age 28, May 30, 1861. Present or accounted for until transferred to 2nd Company B, 32nd Regiment N.C. Troops, in October, 1861.

DEAL, ALBERT, Private
Resided in Camden County where he enlisted at age 25, May 30, 1861. Present or accounted for until transferred to 2nd Company B, 32nd Regiment N.C. Troops, in October, 1861.

DUKE, WILEY, Private
Resided in Camden County where he enlisted at age 22, May 30, 1861. Present or accounted for until transferred to 2nd Company B, 32nd Regiment N.C. Troops, in October, 1861.

DUNN, SAMUEL J., Private
Resided in Camden County where he enlisted at age 35, May 30, 1861. Present or accounted for until transferred to 2nd Company B, 32nd Regiment N.C. Troops, in October, 1861.

EDNEY, ALEXANDER, Private
Resided in Camden County where he enlisted at age 19, May 30, 1861. Present or accounted for until transferred to 2nd Company B, 32nd Regiment N.C. Troops, in October, 1861.

ETHERIDGE, JAMES W., Private
Resided in Camden County where he enlisted at age 22, May 30, 1861. Present or accounted for until transferred to 2nd Company B, 32nd Regiment N.C. Troops, in October, 1861.

FEREBEE, JAMES W., Private
Resided in Camden County where he enlisted at age 23, May 30, 1861. Present or accounted for until transferred to 2nd Company B, 32nd Regiment N.C. Troops, in October, 1861.

GREGORY, JOSEPH MORGAN, Private
Resided in Camden County where he enlisted at age 24, May 30, 1861. Present or accounted for until transferred to Company B, 32nd Regiment N.C. Troops, in October, 1861.

GREGORY, WILLIAM J., Private
Born in Camden County where he resided as a merchant prior to enlisting in Camden County at age 50, May 30, 1861. Present or accounted for until transferred to 2nd Company B, 32nd Regiment N.C. Troops, in October, 1861.

HENLEY, JAMES A., Corporal
Resided in Camden County where he enlisted at age 22, May 30, 1861. Mustered in as Corporal. Present or accounted for until transferred to 2nd Company B, 32nd Regiment N.C. Troops, in October, 1861.

HODGES, JAMES E., Sergeant
Resided in Camden County or at Norfolk, Virginia, prior to enlisting in Camden County at age 27, May 30, 1861. Mustered in as Sergeant. Present or

accounted for until transferred to 2nd Company B, 32nd Regiment N.C.Troops, in October, 1861.

HUGHES, JOB C., Private
Born in Camden County where he resided as a farmer prior to enlisting in Camden County at age 17, May 30, 1861. Present or accounted for until transferred to 2nd Company B, 32nd Regiment N.C. Troops, in October, 1861.

JACOBS, JOHN, Musician
Resided in Camden County where he enlisted at age 35, May 30, 1861. Mustered in as Musician (Drummer). Present or accounted for until transferred to 2nd Company B, 32nd Regiment N.C.Troops, in October, 1861.

JONES, WILLIAM B., Corporal
Resided in Camden County where he enlisted at age 40, May 30, 1861. Mustered in as Corporal. Present or accounted for until transferred to 2nd Company B, 32nd Regiment N.C.Troops, in October, 1861.

LINTON, JESSE, Private
Born in Camden County where he resided as a wheelwright prior to enlisting in Camden County at age 50, May 30, 1861. Present or accounted for until transferred to 2nd Company B, 32nd Regiment N.C. Troops, in October, 1861.

McCOY, DAVID, Private
Resided in Camden County where he enlisted at age 21, May 30, 1861. Present or accounted for until transferred to 2nd Company B, 32nd Regiment N.C. Troops, in October, 1861.

McCOY, JAMES S., Private
Resided in Camden County where he enlisted at age 34, May 30, 1861. Present or accounted for until transferred to 2nd Company B, 32nd Regiment N.C. Troops, in October, 1861.

McCOY, MALACHI, Private
Born in Camden County and resided in Camden County or at Portsmouth, Virginia, prior to enlisting in Camden County at age 17, May 30, 1861. Present or accounted for until transferred to 2nd Company B, 32nd Regiment N.C.Troops, in October, 1861.

McCOY, TIMOTHY, Private
Resided in Camden County where he enlisted at age 17, May 30, 1861. Present or accounted for until transferred to 2nd Company B, 32nd Regiment N.C. Troops, in October, 1861.

McDANIEL, ISAAC, Private
Resided in Camden County where he enlisted at age 26, May 30, 1861. Present or accounted for until transferred to 2nd Company B, 32nd Regiment N.C. Troops, in October, 1861.

McPHERSON, WILLIAM, Private
Resided in Camden County where he enlisted at age 22, May 30, 1861. Present or accounted for until transferred to 2nd Company B, 32nd Regiment N.C. Troops, in October, 1861.

MEGGS, JOSEPH, Private
Resided in Camden County where he enlisted at age 24, May 30, 1861. Present or accounted for until transferred to 2nd Company B, 32nd Regiment N.C. Troops, in October, 1861.

MEGGS, WILLIAM, Private
Resided in Camden County where he enlisted at age 22, May 30, 1861. Present or accounted for until transferred to 2nd Company B, 32nd Regiment N.C. Troops, in October, 1861.

MILLER, WILLIAM P., 1st Sergeant
Born in Norfolk County, Virginia, and resided in Camden County where he was by occupation a merchant prior to enlisting in Camden County at age 27, May 30, 1861. Mustered in as 1st Sergeant. Present or accounted for until transferred to 2nd Company B, 32nd Regiment N.C. Troops, in October, 1861.

MORGAN, JOHN S., Sergeant
Resided in Camden County where he enlisted at age 28, May 30, 1861. Mustered in as Sergeant. Present or accounted for until transferred to 2nd Company B, 32nd Regiment N.C.Troops, in October, 1861.

NASH, ENOCH, Private
Resided in Camden County where he enlisted at age 20, May 30, 1861. Present or accounted for until transferred to 2nd Company B, 32nd Regiment N.C. Troops, in October, 1861.

NIXON, GEORGE W., Private
Resided in Camden County where he enlisted at age 30, May 30, 1861. Present or accounted for until transferred to 2nd Company B, 32nd Regiment N.C. Troops, in October, 1861.

OLD, WALTER R., Private
Born in Camden County where he resided as a student prior to enlisting in Camden County at age 16, May 30, 1861. Present or accounted for until transferred to 2nd Company B, 32nd Regiment N.C. Troops, in October, 1861.

OVERTON, JAMES B., Private
Born in Camden County where he enlisted at age 44, May 30, 1861. Present or accounted for until transferred to 2nd Company B, 32nd Regiment N. C. Troops, in October, 1861.

PERKINS, RICHARD C., Private
Resided in Camden County where he enlisted at age 40, May 30, 1861. Present or accounted for until transferred to 2nd Company B, 32nd Regiment N.C. Troops, in October, 1861.

POWERS, JOHN, Private
Resided in Camden County where he enlisted at age 22, May 30, 1861. Present or accounted for until transferred to 2nd Company B, 32nd Regiment N.C. Troops, in October, 1861.

POWERS, WILLIAM, Private
Born in Camden County where he resided as a farmer prior to enlisting in Camden County at age 40, May 30, 1861. Present or accounted for until transferred to 2nd Company B, 32nd Regiment N.C. Troops, in October, 1861.

POWERS, WILSON, Private
Resided in Camden County where he enlisted at age 19, May 30, 1861. Present or accounted for until transferred to 2nd Company B, 32nd Regiment N.C. Troops, in October, 1861.

PRITCHARD, BENJAMIN C., Private
Resided in Camden County where he enlisted at age

20, May 30, 1861. Present or accounted for until transferred to 2nd Company B, 32nd Regiment N.C. Troops, in October, 1861.

PRITCHARD, DAVID T., Private
Resided in Camden County where he enlisted at age 20, May 30, 1861. Present or accounted for until transferred to 2nd Company B, 32nd Regiment N.C. Troops, in October, 1861.

RADFORD, JAMES E., Private
Resided in Camden County where he enlisted at age 20, May 30, 1861. Present or accounted for until transferred to 2nd Company B, 32nd Regiment N.C. Troops, in October, 1861.

RICHARDSON, E. GILBERT, Corporal
Resided in Camden County where he enlisted at age 25, May 30, 1861. Mustered in as Corporal. Present or accounted for until discharged in August, 1861. Reason discharged not reported.

RIGGS, ALPHEUS B., Private
Resided in Camden County where he enlisted at age 22, May 30, 1861. Present or accounted for until transferred to 2nd Company B, 32nd Regiment N.C. Troops, in October, 1861.

RIGGS, RICHARD, Private
Resided in Camden County where he enlisted at age 22, May 30, 1861. Present or accounted for until transferred to 2nd Company B, 32nd Regiment N.C. Troops, in October, 1861.

RIGGS, WILLIAM, Private
Resided in Camden County where he enlisted at age 25, May 30, 1861. Present or accounted for until transferred to 2nd Company B, 32nd Regiment N.C. Troops, in October, 1861.

RUDDER, JOSEPH C., Musician
Resided in Camden County where he enlisted at age 27, May 30, 1861. Mustered in as Musician (Fifer). Present or accounted for until transferred to 2nd Company B, 32nd Regiment N.C. Troops, in October, 1861.

SAVILLS, WILLIAM F., Private
Resided in Camden County where he enlisted at age 34, May 30, 1861. Present or accounted for until transferred to 2nd Company B, 32nd Regiment N.C. Troops, in October, 1861.

SAWYER, ARCHIBALD, Private
Born in Camden County where he resided as a farmer prior to enlisting in Camden County at age 35, May 30, 1861. Present or accounted for until transferred to 2nd Company B, 32nd Regiment N.C. Troops, in October, 1861.

SAWYER, ELIJAH, Private
Born in Camden County where he resided as a farmer prior to enlisting in Camden County at age 38, May 30, 1861. Present or accounted for until transferred to 2nd Company B, 32nd Regiment N.C. Troops, in October, 1861.

SAWYER, GEORGE, Private
Born in Camden County where he resided as a farmer prior to enlisting in Camden County at age 36, May 30, 1861. Present or accounted for until transferred to 2nd Company B, 32nd Regiment N.C. Troops, in October, 1861.

SAWYER, JAMES H., Private
Resided in Camden County where he enlisted at age 20, May 30, 1861. Present or accounted for until transferred to 2nd Company B, 32nd Regiment N.C. Troops, in October, 1861.

SAWYER, JOHN F., Private
Resided in Camden County where he enlisted at age 20, May 30, 1861. Present or accounted for until transferred to 2nd Company B, 32nd Regiment N.C. Troops, in October, 1861.

SAWYER, SAMUEL, Private
Born in Camden County where he resided as a farmer prior to enlisting in Camden County on May 30, 1861. Present or accounted for until transferred to 2nd Company B, 32nd Regiment N.C. Troops, in October, 1861.

SPENCE, JOSEPH, Private
Resided in Camden County where he enlisted at age 22, May 30, 1861. Present or accounted for until transferred to 2nd Company B, 32nd Regiment N.C. Troops, in October, 1861.

SPENCE, MILES, Private
Born in Camden County where he resided as a farmer prior to enlisting in Camden County at age 36, May 30, 1861. Present or accounted for until transferred to 2nd Company B, 32nd Regiment N.C. Troops, in October, 1861.

SPRUIL, BURTON, Private
Resided in Camden County where he enlisted at age 28, May 30, 1861. Present or accounted for until transferred to 2nd Company B, 32nd Regiment N.C. Troops, in October, 1861.

STEPHENS, JOSEPH, Private
Resided in Camden County where he enlisted at age 22, May 30, 1861. Present or accounted for until transferred to 2nd Company B, 32nd Regiment N.C. Troops, in October, 1861.

TAYLOR, WILLIAM, Private
Resided in Camden County where he enlisted at age 35, May 30, 1861. Present or accounted for until transferred to 2nd Company B, 32nd Regiment N.C. Troops, in October, 1861.

TINDALE, WILLIAM, Private
Resided in Camden County where he enlisted at age 50, May 30, 1861. Present or accounted for until transferred to 2nd Company B, 32nd Regiment N.C. Troops, in October, 1861.

TISDALE, BARNEY, Private
Resided in Camden County where he enlisted at age 28, May 30, 1861. Deserted August 14, 1861. Transferred to 2nd Company B, 32nd Regiment N.C. Troops, in October, 1861, while listed as a deserter.

TURNER, WILLIAM, Private
Resided in Camden County where he enlisted at age 31, May 30, 1861. Present or accounted for until transferred to 2nd Company B, 32nd Regiment N.C. Troops, in October, 1861.

TUTTLE, JOHN F., Private
Born in Camden County where he resided as a farmer prior to enlisting in Camden County at age 19, May 30, 1861. Present or accounted for until transferred to 2nd Company B, 32nd Regiment N.C.

Troops, in October, 1861.

WHITE, WILLIAM H., Private
Resided in Camden County where he enlisted at age 20, May 30, 1861. Present or accounted for until transferred to 2nd Company B, 32nd Regiment N.C. Troops, in October, 1861.

WHITEHURST, JOHN, Private
Born in Camden County where he resided as a farmer prior to enlisting in Camden County at age 35, May 30, 1861. Present or accounted for until transferred to 2nd Company B, 32nd Regiment N.C. Troops, in October, 1861.

WHITEHURST, WILLIAM R., Private
Resided in Camden County where he enlisted at age 20, May 30, 1861. Present or accounted for until transferred to 2nd Company B, 32nd Regiment N.C. Troops, in October, 1861.

WILLIAMS, ZEBEDEE, Private
Resided in Camden County where he enlisted at age 20, May 30, 1861. Present or accounted for until transferred to 2nd Company B, 32nd Regiment N.C. Troops, in October, 1861.

COMPANY N

This company was from Northampton County and enlisted at Pleasant Hill on July 29, 1861. It tendered its service to the state and was assigned to this regiment. The company was mustered in as Captain John M. Moody's Company and was designated Company N. In October, 1861, the company was transferred out of the regiment and became Company C, afterwards Company B, 1st Battalion N.C. Infantry. The battalion was later raised to a regiment and designated the 32nd Regiment N.C. Troops, and this company became Company C of that regiment. [The history of this company subsequent to October, 1861, together with the service records of its members, will appear in the roster for Company C, 32nd Regiment N.C. Troops, which will be published in a future volume.]

The information contained in the following roster of the company was compiled principally from a company muster roll for July 29 through August 31, 1861. No additional company muster rolls were found. In addition to the company muster roll, Roll of Honor records, receipt rolls, hospital records, prisoner of war records, and other primary records, supplemented by state pension applications, United Daughters of the Confederacy records, and postwar rosters and histories, all provided useful information.

OFFICERS
CAPTAIN

MOODY, JOHN M., Jr.
Resided in Northampton County where he enlisted at age 21. Appointed Captain on or about July 29, 1861. Present or accounted for until transferred to Company C, 32nd Regiment N.C. Troops, in October, 1861.

LIEUTENANTS

BELL, WILLIAM T., 3rd Lieutenant
Resided in Northampton County where he enlisted at age 21. Appointed 3rd Lieutenant on or about July 29, 1861. Present or accounted for until transferred to Company C, 32nd Regiment N.C. Troops, in October, 1861.

COKER, JOSEPH W., 1st Lieutenant
Resided in Northampton County where he enlisted at age 26. Appointed 1st Lieutenant on or about July 29, 1861. Present or accounted for until transferred to Company C, 32nd Regiment N.C. Troops, in October, 1861.

FURGURSON, BAKER L., 2nd Lieutenant
Resided in Northampton County where he enlisted at age 30. Appointed 2nd Lieutenant on or about July 29, 1861. Present or accounted for until transferred to Company C, 32nd Regiment N.C. Troops, in October, 1861.

NONCOMMISSIONED OFFICERS
AND PRIVATES

ALLEN, WILLIAM T., Private
Born in Northampton County where he resided as a farmer prior to enlisting in Northampton County at age 50, July 29, 1861. Present or accounted for until transferred to Company C, 32nd Regiment N.C. Troops, in October, 1861.

BASS, JAMES H., Private
Resided in Northampton County where he enlisted at age 36, July 29, 1861. Present or accounted for until transferred to Company C, 32nd Regiment N.C. Troops, in October, 1861.

BASS, MATTHEW T., Private
Born in Northampton County where he resided as a farmer prior to enlisting at "Lockhart's Grove" at age 33, August 8, 1861. Present or accounted for until transferred to Company C, 32nd Regiment N.C. Troops, in October, 1861.

BIRDSONG, HENRY H., Private
Resided in Northampton County and enlisted at "Lockhart's Grove" at age 27, August 8, 1861. Present or accounted for until transferred to Company C, 32nd Regiment N.C. Troops, in October, 1861.

BIRDSONG, SAMUEL N., Private
Resided in Northampton County where he enlisted at age 24, July 29, 1861. Present or accounted for until transferred to Company C, 32nd Regiment N.C. Troops, in October, 1861.

BIRDSONG, WILLIAM J., Private
Resided in Northampton County and enlisted at "Lockhart's Grove" at age 26, August 8, 1861. Present or accounted for until transferred to Company C, 32nd Regiment N.C. Troops, in October, 1861.

BRANTLEY, WILLIAM B., Private
Born in Northampton County where he resided as a farmer prior to enlisting in Northampton County at age 47, July 29, 1861. Present or accounted for until transferred to Company C, 32nd Regiment N.C. Troops, in October, 1861.

BURNETT, JOSEPH W., Private
Resided in Northampton County where he enlisted at age 22, July 29, 1861. Present or accounted for until transferred to Company C, 32nd Regiment N.C. Troops, in October, 1861.

CORNWELL, WILLIAM ANDREW J., Private
Enlisted in Northampton County on July 29, 1861. Killed "by a railroad accident" on August 23, 1861. Place of death not reported.

COX, HENRY, Private
Resided in Northampton County and was by occupation a farmer prior to enlisting in Northampton County at age 34, July 29, 1861. Present or accounted for until transferred to Company C, 32nd Regiment N.C.Troops, in October, 1861.

CREW, JOHN H., Private
Resided in Northampton County where he enlisted at age 18, July 29, 1861. Present or accounted for until transferred to Company C, 32nd Regiment N.C. Troops, in October, 1861.

DARDEN, JOHN M., Private
Resided in Northampton County and was by occupation a farmer prior to enlisting in Northampton County at age 18, July 29, 1861. Present or accounted for until transferred to Company C, 32nd Regiment N.C.Troops, in October, 1861.

DAVIS, JOHN F., 1st Sergeant
Resided in Northampton County where he enlisted on July 29, 1861. Mustered in as 1st Sergeant. Present or accounted for until transferred to Company C, 32nd Regiment N.C.Troops, in October, 1861.

DAVIS, JOSEPH, Private
Resided in Northampton County where he enlisted at age 38, August 15, 1861. Present or accounted for until transferred to Company C, 32nd Regiment N.C. Troops, in October, 1861.

DREWIT, JOHN W., Private
Resided in Northampton County where he enlisted at age 24, July 29, 1861. Present or accounted for until transferred to Company C, 32nd Regiment N.C. Troops, in October, 1861.

EDWARDS, JAMES E., Private
Resided in Northampton County and enlisted at "Lockhart's Grove" at age 30, August 8, 1861. Present or accounted for until transferred to Company C, 32nd Regiment N.C.Troops, in October, 1861.

EDWARDS, ROBERT J., Private
Resided in Northampton County where he enlisted at age 25, July 29, 1861. Present or accounted for until transferred to Company C, 32nd Regiment N.C. Troops, in October, 1861.

EPPES, JOHN, Private
Born in Northampton County where he resided as a farmer prior to enlisting in Northampton County at age 47, July 29, 1861. Present or accounted for until transferred to Company C, 32nd Regiment N.C. Troops, in October, 1861.

GARNER, ALBERT W., Private
Resided in Northampton County where he enlisted at age 34, July 29, 1861. Present or accounted for until transferred to Company C, 32nd Regiment N.C. Troops, in October, 1861.

GARNER, JOHN T., Private
Resided in Northampton County where he enlisted at age 21, July 29, 1861. Present or accounted for until transferred to Company C, 32nd Regiment N.C. Troops, in October, 1861.

GARNER, JOHN W., Private
Enlisted in Northampton County on July 29, 1861. Present or accounted for until transferred to Company C, 32nd Regiment N.C.Troops, in October, 1861.

GRIFFIN, BENJAMIN H., Private
Resided in Northampton County where he enlisted at age 23, July 29, 1861. Present or accounted for until transferred to Company C, 32nd Regiment N.C. Troops, in October, 1861.

GRIZZARD, WILLIAM H., Private
Resided in Northampton County where he enlisted at age 18, July 29, 1861. Present or accounted for until transferred to Company C, 32nd Regiment N.C. Troops, in October, 1861.

HARRIS, HUGH J., Private
Born in Northampton County where he resided as a mechanic prior to enlisting in Northampton County at age 40, July 29, 1861. Present or accounted for until transferred to Company C, 32nd Regiment N.C. Troops, in October, 1861.

HARRIS, M. D. L., Private
Resided in Northampton County where he enlisted at age 21, July 29, 1861. Present or accounted for until transferred to Company C, 32nd Regiment N.C. Troops, in October, 1861.

HARRIS, THOMAS J. L., Private
Resided in Northampton County where he enlisted at age 19, July 29, 1861. Present or accounted for until transferred to Company C, 32nd Regiment N.C. Troops, in October, 1861.

HARRIS, WILLIAM, Private
Resided in Northampton County where he enlisted at age 27, July 29, 1861. Present or accounted for until transferred to Company C, 32nd Regiment N.C. Troops, in October, 1861.

HARRISON, DAVID P., Private
Born in Virginia and resided in Northampton County where he was by occupation a farmer prior to enlisting in Northampton County at age 47, July 29, 1861. Present or accounted for until transferred to Company C, 32nd Regiment N.C.Troops, in October, 1861.

HART, WILLIAM RANDOLPH, Private
Resided in Northampton County where he enlisted at age 23, July 29, 1861. Present or accounted for until transferred to Company C, 32nd Regiment N.C. Troops, in October, 1861.

INGRAM, JAMES H., Private
Resided in Northampton County where he enlisted at age 21, July 29, 1861. Present or accounted for until transferred to Company C, 32nd Regiment N.C. Troops, in October, 1861.

JONES, JAMES, Private
Resided in Northampton County and enlisted at

"Lockhart's Grove" at age 18, August 8, 1861. Present or accounted for until transferred to Company C, 32nd Regiment N.C.Troops, in October, 1861.

JORDAN, JAMES, Jr., Private
Resided in Northampton County where he enlisted at age 24, July 29, 1861. Present or accounted for until transferred to Company C, 32nd Regiment N.C. Troops, in October, 1861.

KEE, CORNELIUS R., Private
Resided in Northampton County where he enlisted at age 22, July 29, 1861. Present or accounted for until transferred to Company C, 32nd Regiment N.C. Troops, in October, 1861.

MASSA, JOHN W., Private
Resided in Northampton County where he enlisted at age 19, July 29, 1861. Present or accounted for until transferred to Company C, 32nd Regiment N.C. Troops, in October, 1861.

MASSIE, JAMES W., Private
Resided in Northampton County where he enlisted at age 18, July 29, 1861. Present or accounted for until transferred to Company C, 32nd Regiment N.C. Troops, in October, 1861.

MATHEWS, JOHN H., Private
Resided in Northampton County where he enlisted at age 23, July 29, 1861. Present or accounted for until transferred to Company C, 32nd Regiment N.C. Troops, in October, 1861.

MORGAN, DANIEL M., Private
Born in Northampton County where he resided as a farmer prior to enlisting in Northampton County at age 38, July 29, 1861. Present or accounted for until transferred to Company C, 32nd Regiment N.C. Troops, in October, 1861.

MORGAN, HENRY P., Private
Resided in Northampton County where he enlisted at age 18, July 29, 1861. Present or accounted for until transferred to Company C, 32nd Regiment N.C. Troops, in October, 1861.

MORGAN, MATHEW W., Private
Resided in Northampton County where he enlisted at age 25, July 29, 1861. Present or accounted for until transferred to Company C, 32nd Regiment N.C. Troops, in October, 1861.

MULDER, JOHN J., Private
Resided in Northampton County and enlisted at Camp Carolina, Virginia, at age 34, August 15, 1861. Present or accounted for until transferred to Company C, 32nd Regiment N. C. Troops, in October, 1861.

NEWSOM, JOHN T., Private
Resided in Northampton County where he enlisted at age 19, July 29, 1861. Present or accounted for until transferred to Company C, 32nd Regiment N.C. Troops, in October, 1861.

PEARSON, JAMES G., Private
Resided in Northampton County where he enlisted at age 25, July 29, 1861. Present or accounted for until transferred to Company C, 32nd Regiment N.C. Troops, in October, 1861.

PORCH, WILLIAM D., Private
Resided in Northampton County and enlisted at "Lockhart's Grove" at age 24, August 8, 1861. Present or accounted for until transferred to Company C, 32nd Regiment N. C. Troops, in October, 1861.

ROOK, JAMES L., Private
Resided in Northampton County and enlisted at "Lockhart's Grove" at age 17, August 8, 1861. Present or accounted for until transferred to Company C, 32nd Regiment N.C.Troops, in October, 1861.

ROWELL, JOHN, Private
Born in Northampton County where he resided as a farmer prior to enlisting in Northampton County at age 50, July 29, 1861. Present or accounted for until transferred to Company C, 32nd Regiment N.C. Troops, in October, 1861.

SHEHORN, JOHN, Private
Resided in Northampton County where he enlisted at age 60, July 29, 1861. Present or accounted for until transferred to Company C, 32nd Regiment N. C. Troops, in October, 1861.

SHEHORN, JOHN W., Private
Born in Northampton County where he resided as a farmer prior to enlisting in Northampton County at age 28, July 29, 1861. Present or accounted for until transferred to Company C, 32nd Regiment N.C. Troops, in October, 1861.

SMITH, HENRY J., Private
Born in Northampton County where he resided as a farmer prior to enlisting in Northampton County at age 38, July 29, 1861. Present or accounted for until transferred to Company C, 32nd Regiment N.C. Troops, in October, 1861.

STARK, WILLIAM B., Private
Resided in Northampton County where he enlisted at age 17, July 29, 1861. Present or accounted for until transferred to Company C, 32nd Regiment N.C. Troops, in October, 1861.

SYKES, BENJAMIN S., Private
Resided in Northampton County where he enlisted at age 20, July 29, 1861. Present or accounted for until transferred to Company C, 32nd Regiment N.C. Troops, in October, 1861.

THOMPSON, ALBERT, Private
Born in Northampton County and was by occupation a farmer prior to enlisting in Northampton County on July 29, 1861. Present or accounted for until transferred to Company C, 32nd Regiment N.C. Troops, in October, 1861.

THOMPSON, PETER, Private
Born in Northampton County and was by occupation a farmer prior to enlisting at "Lockhart's Grove" on August 8, 1861. Present or accounted for until transferred to Company C, 32nd Regiment N.C. Troops, in October, 1861.

VASSER, JAMES H., Private
Resided in Northampton County and enlisted at "Lockhart's Grove" at age 19, August 8, 1861. Present or accounted for until transferred to Company C, 32nd Regiment N.C.Troops, in October, 1861.

VASSER, JOSEPH, Private

Resided in Northampton County where he enlisted at age 21, July 29, 1861. Present or accounted for until transferred to Company C, 32nd Regiment N.C. Troops, in October, 1861.

VICK, EDMOND M., Private

Resided in Northampton County where he enlisted at age 30, July 29, 1861. Present or accounted for until transferred to Company C, 32nd Regiment N.C. Troops, in October, 1861.

VINCENT, JAMES H., Private

Born in Northampton County where he resided as a mechanic prior to enlisting at "Lockhart's Grove" at age 40, August 8, 1861. Present or accounted for until transferred to Company C, 32nd Regiment N.C. Troops, in October, 1861.

WARRICK, JOHN J., Private

Resided in Northampton County and enlisted at "Lockhart's Grove" at age 25, August 8, 1861. Present or accounted for until transferred to Company C, 32nd Regiment N.C. Troops, in October, 1861.

WOODRUFF, RICHARD H., Private

Resided in Northampton County where he enlisted at age 20, July 29, 1861. Present or accounted for until transferred to Company C, 32nd Regiment N.C. Troops, in October, 1861.

WRIGHT, JOHN R., Private

Enlisted in Northampton County on July 29, 1861. Died in North Carolina on September 19, 1861. Cause of death not reported.

WRIGHT, SAMUEL J., Private

Resided in Northampton County and enlisted at "Lockhart's Grove" at age 30, August 8, 1861. Present or accounted for until transferred to Company C, 32nd Regiment N.C. Troops, in October, 1861.

COMPANY O

This company was from Northampton County and enlisted in Northampton County on August 1-5, 1861. It tendered its service to the state and was assigned to this regiment. The company was mustered in as Captain Emory A. Martin's Company and was designated Company O. In October, 1861, the company was transferred out of the regiment and became Company D, afterwards Company C, 1st Battalion N.C. Infantry. The battalion was later raised to a regiment and designated the 32nd Regiment N.C. Troops, and this company became Company D of that regiment. [The history of this company subsequent to October, 1861, together with the service records of its members, will appear in the roster for Company D, 32nd Regiment N.C. Troops, which will be published in a future volume.]

The information contained in the following roster of the company was compiled principally from a company muster roll for August, 1861. No additional company muster rolls were found. In addition to the company muster roll, Roll of Honor records, receipt rolls, hospital records, prisoner of war records, and other primary

records, supplemented by state pension applications, United Daughters of the Confederacy records, and postwar rosters and histories, all provided useful information.

OFFICERS
CAPTAIN

MARTIN, EMORY A.

Resided in Northampton County and enlisted at age 29. Appointed Captain on or about August 1, 1861. Present or accounted for until transferred to Company D, 32nd Regiment N.C. Troops, in October, 1861.

LIEUTENANTS

GARRIS, JOSEPH A., 1st Lieutenant

Resided in Northampton County where he enlisted at age 22. Appointed 1st Lieutenant on or about August 1, 1861. Present or accounted for until transferred to Company D, 32nd Regiment N. C. Troops, in October, 1861.

GILLIAM, JORDAN, 3rd Lieutenant

Resided in Northampton County where he enlisted at age 27. Appointed 3rd Lieutenant on or about August 1, 1861. Present or accounted for until transferred to Company D, 32nd Regiment N.C. Troops, in October, 1861.

HOLIDAY, JESSE GRAY, 2nd Lieutenant

Resided in Northampton County where he enlisted at age 30. Appointed 2nd Lieutenant on or about August 1, 1861. Present or accounted for until transferred to Company D, 32nd Regiment N.C. Troops, in October, 1861.

NONCOMMISSIONED OFFICERS AND PRIVATES

ALLEN, JERRY, Private

Resided in Northampton County where he enlisted at age 18, August 1, 1861. Present or accounted for until transferred to Company D, 32nd Regiment N.C. Troops, in October, 1861.

ASKEW, JAMES W., Private

Resided in Northampton County where he enlisted at age 46, August 5, 1861. Present or accounted for until transferred to Company D, 32nd Regiment N.C. Troops, in October, 1861.

ASKEW, JOSEPH, Private

Resided in Northampton County where he enlisted at age 34, August 5, 1861. Present or accounted for until transferred to Company D, 32nd Regiment N.C. Troops, in October, 1861.

ATKERSON, JAMES H., Private

Resided in Northampton County where he enlisted at age 24, August 8, 1861. Present or accounted for until transferred to Company D, 32nd Regiment N.C. Troops, in October, 1861.

BARBER, BENJAMIN F., Sergeant

Resided in Northampton or Hertford counties and enlisted in Northampton County at age 22, August

12, 1861. Mustered in as Sergeant. Present or accounted for until transferred to Company D, 32nd Regiment N.C.Troops, in October, 1861.

BARNES, DAVID T., Private
Resided in Northampton County where he enlisted at age 21, August 2, 1861. Present or accounted for until transferred to Company D, 32nd Regiment N.C. Troops, in October, 1861.

BARNES, FRANCIS A., Corporal
Resided in Northampton County where he enlisted at age 25, August 1, 1861. Mustered in as Corporal. Present or accounted for until transferred to Company D, 32nd Regiment N.C.Troops, in October, 1861.

BARNES, WILLIAM H., Private
Resided in Northampton County where he enlisted at age 19, August 2, 1861. Present or accounted for until transferred to Company D, 32nd Regiment N.C. Troops, in October, 1861.

BELCH, JOSEPH T., Corporal
Resided in Northampton County or at Boykin's Depot, Virginia, and enlisted in Northampton County at age 25, August 5, 1861. Mustered in as Corporal. Present or accounted for until transferred to Company D, 32nd Regiment N.C.Troops, in October, 1861.

BELCH, ROBERT D., Corporal
Resided in Northampton County where he enlisted at age 30, August 2, 1861. Mustered in as Corporal. Present or accounted for until transferred to Company D, 32nd Regiment N. C. Troops, in October, 1861.

BRIDGERS, LEMUEL H., Private
Resided in Northampton County or at Boykin's Depot, Virginia, prior to enlisting in Northampton County at age 21, August 5, 1861. Present or accounted for until transferred to Company D, 32nd Regiment N. C. Troops, in October, 1861.

BRIDGES, DANIEL E., Private
Resided in Northampton County or at Boykin's Depot, Virginia, prior to enlisting in Northampton County at age 17, August 2, 1861. Present or accounted for until transferred to Company D, 32nd Regiment N.C.Troops, in October, 1861.

BRITTON, JOHN W., Private
Resided in Northampton County where he enlisted at age 35, August 8, 1861. Present or accounted for until transferred to Company D, 32nd Regiment N.C. Troops, in October, 1861.

BROWN, JOSHUA B., Private
Resided in Northampton County or at Boykin's Depot, Virginia, prior to enlisting in Northampton County at age 23, August 6, 1861. Present or accounted for until transferred to Company D, 32nd Regiment N.C.Troops, in October, 1861.

BRYANT, AUGUSTUS M., Private
Resided in Northampton County where he enlisted at age 19, August 5, 1861. Present or accounted for until transferred to Company D, 32nd Regiment N.C. Troops, in October, 1861.

BRYANT, BENJAMIN W., Private
Resided in Northampton County or at Boykin's

Depot, Virginia, prior to enlisting in Northampton County at age 28, August 1, 1861. Present or accounted for until transferred to Company D, 32nd Regiment N.C.Troops, in October, 1861.

DAUGHTRY, WILLIAM H., Private
Resided in Northampton County where he enlisted at age 18, August 7, 1861. Present or accounted for until transferred to Company D, 32nd Regiment N.C. Troops, in October, 1861.

DAVIS, WILLIAM A., Private
Resided in Northampton County where he enlisted at age 20, August 10, 1861. Present or accounted for until transferred to Company D, 32nd Regiment N.C. Troops, in October, 1861.

EDWARDS, ALEXANDER, Private
Resided in Northampton County where he enlisted at age 17, August 5, 1861. Discharged on August 24, 1861, by reason of "inability, through sickness, to perform military duty."

EDWARDS, JOHN T., Private
Resided in Northampton County where he enlisted at age 18, August 2, 1861. Present or accounted for until transferred to Company D, 32nd Regiment N.C. Troops, in October, 1861.

FENNEL, JAMES H., Private
Resided in Northampton County where he enlisted at age 37, August 8, 1861. Present or accounted for until transferred to Company D, 32nd Regiment N.C. Troops, in October, 1861.

FLYTHE, JOHN J., Private
Resided in Northampton County where he enlisted at age 18, August 1, 1861. Present or accounted for until transferred to Company D, 32nd Regiment N.C. Troops, in October, 1861.

FUTRELL, ENOS, Private
Resided in Northampton County where he enlisted at age 21, August 5, 1861. Present or accounted for until transferred to Company D, 32nd Regiment N.C. Troops, in October, 1861.

FUTRELL, HEZEKIAH, Private
Resided in Northampton County where he enlisted at age 20, August 2, 1861. Present or accounted for until transferred to Company D, 32nd Regiment N.C. Troops, in October, 1861.

FUTRELL, NOAH, Private
Born in Northampton County where he resided prior to enlisting in Northampton County at age 29, August 1, 1861. Present or accounted for until transferred to Company D, 32nd Regiment N.C.Troops, in October, 1861.

FUTRELL, WILLIAM H., Private
Born in Northampton County where he resided as a farmer prior to enlisting in Northampton County at age 19, August 5, 1861. Present or accounted for until transferred to Company D, 32nd Regiment N.C. Troops, in October, 1861.

GRANT, ADBEAL, Private
Resided in Northampton County where he enlisted at age 16, August 6, 1861. Present or accounted for until transferred to Company D, 32nd Regiment N.C. Troops, in October, 1861.

GRIMES, WILLIAM L., Private
Resided in Northampton County where he enlisted at age 26, August 10, 1861. Present or accounted for until transferred to Company D, 32nd Regiment N.C. Troops, in October, 1861.

HEDGPETH, DAVID C., Private
Resided in Northampton County where he enlisted at age 18, August 5, 1861. Present or accounted for until transferred to Company D, 32nd Regiment N.C. Troops, in October, 1861.

HOBBS, JAMES E., Private
Born in Northampton County where he resided as a laborer prior to enlisting in Northampton County at age 25, August 8, 1861. Present or accounted for until transferred to Company D, 32nd Regiment N.C. Troops, in October, 1861.

HOBBS, MILLS T., Private
Resided in Northampton County where he enlisted at age 26, August 9, 1861. Died in hospital at Norfolk, Virginia, September 24, 1861, of disease.

HYATT, WILLIAM, Private
Resided in Northampton County where he enlisted at age 21, August 12, 1861. Present or accounted for until transferred to Company D, 32nd Regiment N.C. Troops, in October, 1861.

JENKINS, JEFFERSON, Private
Resided in Northampton County where he enlisted at age 30, August 2, 1861. Present or accounted for until transferred to Company D, 32nd Regiment N.C. Troops, in October, 1861.

JOHNSON, ELIAS J., Private
Resided in Northampton County where he enlisted at age 20, August 8, 1861. Present or accounted for until transferred to Company D, 32nd Regiment N.C. Troops, in October, 1861.

JOHNSON, JAMES H., Private
Resided in Northampton County where he enlisted at age 23, August 1, 1861. Present or accounted for until transferred to Company D, 32nd Regiment N.C. Troops, in October, 1861.

JOHNSON, MARCUS R., Private
Resided in Northampton County where he enlisted at age 20, August 1, 1861. Present or accounted for until transferred to Company D, 32nd Regiment N.C. Troops, in October, 1861.

JOYNER, ALFRED T., Private
Enlisted in Northampton County on August 10, 1861. Present or accounted for until transferred to Company D, 32nd Regiment N.C. Troops, in October, 1861.

KNIGHT, GEORGE W., Private
Resided in Northampton County where he enlisted at age 30, August 3, 1861. Present or accounted for until transferred to Company D, 32nd Regiment N.C. Troops, in October, 1861.

LANE, ANDREW J., Private
Resided in Northampton County where he enlisted at age 28, August 7, 1861. Present or accounted for until transferred to Company D, 32nd Regiment N.C. Troops, in October, 1861.

LASSITER, CALEB, Private
Resided in Northampton County where he enlisted at

age 33, August 6, 1861. Present or accounted for until transferred to Company D, 32nd Regiment N.C. Troops, in October, 1861.

MARTIN, HENRY T., Private
Resided in Northampton County where he enlisted at age 28, August 1, 1861. Present or accounted for until transferred to Company D, 32nd Regiment N.C. Troops, in October, 1861.

MARTIN, JAMES E., Private
Resided in Northampton County where he enlisted at age 16, August 2, 1861. Present or accounted for until transferred to Company D, 32nd Regiment N.C. Troops, in October, 1861.

MARTIN, JOHN E., Private
Resided in Northampton County where he enlisted at age 22, August 1, 1861. Present or accounted for until transferred to Company D, 32nd Regiment N.C. Troops, in October, 1861.

MARTIN, JOSEPH V., Sergeant
Resided in Northampton County or at Boykin's Depot, Virginia, prior to enlisting in Northampton County at age 18, August 1, 1861. Mustered in as Sergeant. Present or accounted for until transferred to Company D, 32nd Regiment N.C. Troops, in October, 1861.

MARTIN, MATHEW, Private
Resided in Northampton County where he enlisted at age 23, August 11, 1861. Present or accounted for until transferred to Company D, 32nd Regiment N.C. Troops, in October, 1861.

MORGAN, MATHIAS, Private
Resided in Northampton County where he enlisted at age 40, August 2, 1861. Present or accounted for until transferred to Company D, 32nd Regiment N.C. Troops, in October, 1861.

NELSON, RIDDICK, Private
Resided in Northampton County where he enlisted at age 42, August 2, 1861. Present or accounted for until transferred to Company D, 32nd Regiment N.C. Troops, in October, 1861.

NEWELL, JOSEPH, Private
Born in Northampton County where he resided as a farmer prior to enlisting in Northampton County at age 18, August 11, 1861. Present or accounted for until transferred to Company D, 32nd Regiment N.C. Troops, in October, 1861.

ODOM, BENJAMIN, Private
Born in Northampton County where he resided prior to enlisting in Northampton County at age 31, August 9, 1861. Present or accounted for until transferred to Company D, 32nd Regiment N.C. Troops, in October, 1861.

PILAND, SAMUEL J., Private
Resided in Northampton County where he enlisted at age 40, August 1, 1861. Present or accounted for until transferred to Company D, 32nd Regiment N.C. Troops, in October, 1861.

POPE, JAMES E., Private
Enlisted in Northampton County on August 2, 1861. Reported absent sick through August 31, 1861. No further records.

RICKS, THOMAS C., Private
Enlisted in Northampton County on August 8, 1861. Present or accounted for through August 31, 1861. No further records.

ROSE, MATHIAS, Private
Resided in Northampton County where he enlisted at age 18, August 7, 1861. Present or accounted for until transferred to Company D, 32nd Regiment N.C. Troops, in October, 1861.

STEPHENSON, BENJAMIN T., Private
Resided in Northampton County where he enlisted at age 18, August 5, 1861. Present or accounted for until transferred to Company D, 32nd Regiment N.C. Troops, in October, 1861.

STEPHENSON, JESSE B., Sergeant
Born in Northampton County where he resided prior to enlisting in Northampton County at age 22, August 2, 1861. Mustered in as Sergeant. Present or accounted for until transferred to Company D, 32nd Regiment N.C. Troops, in October, 1861.

STEPHENSON, WILLIAM K., 1st Sergeant
Resided in Northampton County where he enlisted at age 21, August 5, 1861. Mustered in as 1st Sergeant. Present or accounted for until transferred to Company D, 32nd Regiment N.C. Troops, in October, 1861.

TALLOR, HARRISON, Private
Born in Northampton County where he resided as a shoemaker prior to enlisting in Northampton County at age 47, August 8, 1861. Present or accounted for until transferred to Company D, 32nd Regiment N.C. Troops, in October, 1861.

VAUGHAN, ELIAS H., Private
Resided in Northampton County where he enlisted at age 40, August 5, 1861. Present or accounted for until transferred to Company D, 32nd Regiment N.C. Troops, in October, 1861.

VAUGHAN, JOHN T., Private
Resided in Northampton County where he enlisted at age 20, August 8, 1861. Present or accounted for until transferred to Company D, 32nd Regiment N.C. Troops, in October, 1861.

VAUGHAN, WILLIAM J., Private
Resided in Northampton County where he enlisted at age 20, August 1, 1861. Present or accounted for until transferred to Company D, 32nd Regiment N.C. Troops, in October, 1861.

VICK, ELISHA, Private
Resided in Northampton County where he enlisted at age 18, August 5, 1861. Present or accounted for until transferred to Company D, 32nd Regiment N.C. Troops, in October, 1861.

VICK, WILLIAM H., Private
Resided in Northampton County where he enlisted at age 21, August 1, 1861. Present or accounted for until transferred to Company D, 32nd Regiment N.C. Troops, in October, 1861.

VINSON, EXUM, Corporal
Resided in Northampton County where he enlisted at age 23, August 5, 1861. Mustered in as Corporal. Present or accounted for until transferred to Company D, 32nd Regiment N.C. Troops, in October, 1861.

WARREN, JOSHUA, Private
Resided in Northampton County where he enlisted at age 23, August 8, 1861. Present or accounted for until transferred to Company D, 32nd Regiment N.C. Troops, in October, 1861.

WARREN, PERRY, Private
Resided in Northampton County where he enlisted at age 16, August 8, 1861. Present or accounted for until transferred to Company D, 32nd Regiment N.C. Troops, in October, 1861.

WOODARD, GEORGE A., Private
Resided in Northampton County where he enlisted at age 34, August 8, 1861. Present or accounted for until transferred to Company D, 32nd Regiment N.C. Troops, in October, 1861.

MISCELLANEOUS

The following list of names was compiled from primary records which indicate that these men served in the 12th Regiment N.C. Troops (2nd Regiment N.C. Volunteers) but do not indicate the company to which they belonged.

BRIDGES, B. F., Private
Place and date of enlistment not reported. Deserted to the enemy on or about April 12, 1865.

CASWELL, WILLIAM, _____
Place and date of enlistment not reported. Reported in confinement as a prisoner of war at Newport News, Virginia, April 23, 1865. No further records.

POSTON, SAMUEL, Private
Enlisted in Cleveland County on October 16, 1864, for the war. Company in which he enlisted not reported. Transferred to Company E of this regiment on October 28, 1864.

13th BATTALION N. C. INFANTRY

This battalion was organized by Special Orders No. 56, Department of North Carolina, Major General D.H. Hill commanding, May 19, 1863, when four independent companies of bridge guards were organized into a battalion. Major Clement G. Wright was assigned to command the battalion, and it was referred to as Wright's Battalion. The battalion was reported as the 4th Battalion N.C. Infantry and as the North Carolina Partisan Battalion before it was officially designated the 13th Battalion N.C. Infantry.

When the order organizing the battalion was issued, the companies were on detached service along various railroads in eastern North Carolina. The companies rendezvoused at Goldsboro where the battalion was organized. On May 27, 1863, there were 300 men reported in the ranks. From Goldsboro the battalion was ordered to Franklin, Virginia, where it was stationed on outpost duty.

On October 2, 1863, by Special Orders No. 234, Adjutant and Inspector General's Office, Richmond, Virginia, the battalion was consolidated with the 8th Battalion N.C. Partisan Rangers to form the 66th Regiment N.C. Troops. When this order was carried out, the 13th Battalion N.C. Infantry ceased to exist as a separate unit. The history of the companies after that date are recorded in the history of the 66th Regiment N.C. Infantry.

FIELD AND STAFF

MAJOR

WRIGHT, CLEMENT G.
Previously served as Private in Company A, 63rd Regiment N.C. Troops (5th Regiment N.C. Cavalry) and as Aide-de-Camp (Captain) on the staff of General Robertson. Appointed Major of this battalion on or about August 3, 1863. Present or accounted for until transferred to the Field and Staff, 66th Regiment N.C. Troops, October 2, 1863.

ASSISTANT COMMISSARY OF SUBSISTENCE

JORDAN, WILLIAM C.
Previously served as Private in Company I, 41st Regiment N.C. Troops (3rd Regiment N.C. Cavalry). Transferred to this company in May, 1863, upon appointment as Acting Assistant Commissary of Subsistence (2nd Lieutenant) on April 27, 1863. Present or accounted for until transferred to the Field and Staff, 66th Regiment N.C. Troops, October 2, 1863.

SERGEANT MAJOR

WRIGHT, WILIE B.
Previously served as Private in Company D of this battalion. Promoted to Sergeant Major and transferred to the Field and Staff on June 1, 1863. Present or accounted for until transferred to the Field and Staff, 66th Regiment N C. Troops, October 2, 1863.

QUARTERMASTER SERGEANT

UPPERMAN, JOHN H.
Previously served as Private in Company B of this regiment. Promoted to Quartermaster Sergeant on June 16, 1863, and transferred to the Field and Staff. Present or accounted for until transferred to the Field and Staff, 66th Regiment N.C. Troops, October 2, 1863.

COMPANY A

This company was organized in Orange County and enlisted on November 20, 1861, as Captain Joseph W. Latta's Company (Railroad Guards), N.C. Volunteers. The company was assigned to the battalion on May 19, 1863, and was designated Company A. By Special Orders No. 234, Adjutant and Inspector General's Office, Richmond, October 2, 1863, the company was assigned to the 66th Regiment N.C. Troops and became Company A of that regiment.

The information contained in the following roster of the company was compiled principally from a company muster roll for May through June, 1863. No additional company muster rolls were found. In addition to the company muster roll, Roll of Honor records, receipt rolls, hospital records, prisoner of war records, and other primary records, supplemented by state pension applications, United Daughters of the Confederacy records, and postwar rosters and histories, all provided useful information.

OFFICERS

CAPTAIN

LATTA, JOSEPH W.
Enlisted in Orange County. Appointed Captain on or about November 20, 1861. Present or accounted for until transferred to Company A, 66th Regiment N.C. Troops, October 2, 1863.

LIEUTENANTS

FAUCETT, ALBERT G., 1st Lieutenant
Resided in Franklin County and enlisted in Orange County. Appointed 1st Lieutenant on or about November 20, 1861. Present or accounted for until transferred to Company A, 66th Regiment N.C. Troops, October 2, 1863.

LATTA, JAMES G., 2nd Lieutenant
Enlisted in Orange County on November 20, 1861, for the war. Rank at time he was mustered in not reported; however, he was promoted from 1st Sergeant to 2nd Lieutenant on August 24, 1863. Present or accounted for until transferred to Company A, 66th Regiment N.C. Troops, October 2, 1863.

LATTA, SIMPSON, 2nd Lieutenant
Enlisted in Person County. Appointed 2nd Lieutenant on or about January 30, 1862. Present or accounted for until transferred to Company A, 66th Regiment N.C. Troops, October 2, 1863.

LYNCH, JOHN E., 2nd Lieutenant
Enlisted in Orange County. Appointed 2nd Lieutenant on or about November 20, 1861. Present or

accounted for until transferred to Company A, 66th Regiment N.C.Troops, October 2, 1863.

McCOWN, WILLIAM, 2nd Lieutenant
Place and date of enlistment not reported. Name appears on a company record dated December 3, 1861. No further records.

NONCOMMISSIONED OFFICERS AND PRIVATES

BALDWIN, NELSON, Private
Enlisted in Orange County on April 15, 1863, for the war. Present or accounted for until transferred to Company A, 66th Regiment N.C.Troops, October 2, 1863.

BARBEE, JAMES, Private
Enlisted in Orange County on November 20, 1861, for the war. Present or accounted for until transferred to Company A, 66th Regiment N.C.Troops, October 2, 1863.

BARROW, WILLIAM J., Private
Resided in Johnston County where he enlisted on December 17, 1862, for the war. Present or accounted for until transferred to Company A, 66th Regiment N.C.Troops, October 2, 1863.

BASS, JOHN, Private
Enlisted in Lenoir County on September 11, 1863, for the war. Present or accounted for until transferred to Company A, 66th Regiment N.C.Troops, October 2, 1863.

BLACKWOOD, WILLIAM J., Private
Previously served in an unspecified engineering unit. Transferred to this company on August 17, 1863. Present or accounted for until transferred to Company A, 66th Regiment N.C.Troops, October 2, 1863.

BOOTH, NASH, Private
Enlisted in Orange County on December 20, 1861, for the war. Present or accounted for until transferred to Company A, 66th Regiment N. C. Troops, October 2, 1863.

BORLAND, ANDREW J., Private
Enlisted in Alamance County on December 17, 1862, for the war. Present or accounted for until transferred to Company A, 66th Regiment N.C.Troops, October 2, 1863.

BOWIN, WILLIAM, Private
Enlisted in Orange County on November 20, 1861, for the war. Present or accounted for until transferred to Company A, 66th Regiment N.C. Troops, October 2, 1863.

BROCKWELL, GEORGE W., Private
Enlisted in Orange County on November 26, 1862, for the war. Present or accounted for until transferred to Company A, 66th Regiment N.C.Troops, October 2, 1863.

BROCKWELL, JAMES, Private
Resided in Orange County where he enlisted on November 20, 1861, for the war. Present or accounted for until transferred to Company A, 66th Regiment N.C.Troops, October 2, 1863.

BROWNING, GASTIN, Private
Enlisted in Orange County on December 15, 1862, for the war. Present or accounted for until transferred to Company A, 66th Regiment N.C.Troops, October 2, 1863.

BROWNING, JAMES H., Private
Resided in Orange County where he enlisted on November 20, 1861, for the war. Present or accounted for until transferred to Company A, 66th Regiment N.C.Troops, October 2, 1863.

BROWNING, JEFFERSON, Private
Place and date of enlistment not reported. Name appears on a receipt roll for pay dated December 28, 1861-January 1, 1862. Died in hospital at Raleigh on March 14, 1863, of "strangulated hernia."

BROWNING, JOHN W., Private
Enlisted in Orange County on December 15, 1862, for the war. Present or accounted for until transferred to Company A, 66th Regiment N.C.Troops, October 2, 1863.

BROWNING, MOSES, Private
Enlisted in Orange County on November 20, 1861, for the war. Present or accounted for until transferred to Company A, 66th Regiment N.C.Troops, October 2, 1863.

BROWNING, SIDNEY, Private
Enlisted in Orange County on November 20, 1861, for the war. Present or accounted for until transferred to Company A, 66th Regiment N.C.Troops, October 2, 1863.

BROWNING, WILLIAM, Private
Enlisted in Alamance County on December 15, 1862, for the war. Present or accounted for until transferred to Company A, 66th Regiment N.C.Troops, October 2, 1863.

CARDIN, HENRY H., Private
Enlisted in Orange County on November 20, 1861, for the war. Present or accounted for until transferred to Company A, 66th Regiment N.C.Troops, October 2, 1863.

CARDIN, WILLIAM H., Private
Enlisted in Orange County on December 17, 1862, for the war. Present or accounted for until transferred to Company A, 66th Regiment N.C.Troops, October 2, 1863.

CARRELL, BENJAMIN, Private
Enlisted in Orange County on February 24, 1862, for the war. Present or accounted for until he died at Weldon on July 15, 1863, of "febris cont."

CARRINGTON, JAMES T., Private
Enlisted in Orange County on February 20, 1862, for the war. Present or accounted for until transferred to Company A, 66th Regiment N. C. Troops, October 2, 1863.

CARRINGTON, JOHN D., Private
Resided in Orange County where he enlisted. Enlistment date reported as April 20, 1861; however, he was not listed on the rolls of this company until May-June, 1863. Present or accounted for until transferred to Company A, 66th Regiment N.C. Troops, October 2, 1863.

CARRINGTON, RICHARD B., Private
Resided in Orange County where he enlisted on November 20, 1861, for the war. Present or accounted for until transferred to Company A, 66th Regiment N.C. Troops, October 2, 1863.

CARRINGTON, WILLIE P., Private
Enlisted in Orange County on November 20, 1861, for the war. Present or accounted for until transferred to Company A, 66th Regiment N.C. Troops, October 2, 1863.

CATES, JAMES, Private
Enlisted in Orange County on December 5, 1861, for the war. Present or accounted for until transferred to Company A, 66th Regiment N.C. Troops, October 2, 1863.

CATES, JEHU M., Private
Enlisted in Orange County on November 20, 1861, for the war. Present or accounted for until transferred to Company A, 66th Regiment N.C. Troops, October 2, 1863.

CATES, ROBERT H., Private
Enlisted in Orange County on November 20, 1861, for the war. Present or accounted for until transferred to Company A, 66th Regiment N.C. Troops, October 2, 1863.

CATES, THOMAS, Private
Resided in Orange County where he enlisted on December 17, 1862, for the war. Present or accounted for until transferred to Company A, 66th Regiment N.C. Troops, October 2, 1863.

CATES, WILIE, Private
Enlisted in Orange County on November 20, 1861, for the war. Present or accounted for until transferred to Company A, 66th Regiment N.C. Troops, October 2, 1863.

CATES, WILLIAM, Private
Enlisted in Orange County on November 20, 1861, for the war. Present or accounted for until transferred to Company A, 66th Regiment N.C. Troops, October 2, 1863.

CATES, WILLIAM J., Private
Enlisted in Orange County on December 17, 1862, for the war. Present or accounted for until transferred to Company A, 66th Regiment N.C. Troops, October 2, 1863.

CHISENHALL, LOUICO, Private
Enlisted in Orange County on November 20, 1861, for the war. Present or accounted for until transferred to Company A, 66th Regiment N.C. Troops, October 2, 1863.

CHISENHALL, SIDNEY, Private
Enlisted in Orange County on December 20, 1862, for the war. Present or accounted for until transferred to Company A, 66th Regiment N.C. Troops, October 2, 1863.

CHRISTIAN, JAMES NEWTON, Private
Resided in Orange County where he enlisted on February 24, 1862, for the war. Present or accounted for until transferred to Company A, 66th Regiment N.C. Troops, October 2, 1863.

COLE, WILLIAM DAVID, Private
Enlisted in Orange County on February 24, 1862, for the war. Present or accounted for until transferred to Company A, 66th Regiment N. C. Troops, October 2, 1863.

COUCH, DAVID W., Private
Enlisted in Orange County on November 20, 1861, for the war. Present or accounted for until transferred to Company A, 66th Regiment N.C. Troops, October 2, 1863.

COUCH, GEORGE H., Private
Enlisted in Orange County on November 20, 1861, for the war. Present or accounted for until transferred to Company A, 66th Regiment N.C. Troops, October 2, 1863.

COUCH, JOHN, Sergeant
Enlisted in Orange County on November 20, 1861, for the war. Promotion record not reported. Present or accounted for until transferred to Company A, 66th Regiment N.C. Troops, October 2, 1863.

COUCH, NATHAN, Private
Resided in Orange County where he enlisted on November 20, 1861, for the war. Present or accounted for until transferred to Company A, 66th Regiment N.C. Troops, October 2, 1863.

COUCH, THOMAS J., Private
Enlisted in Orange County on February 15, 1862, for the war. Present or accounted for until transferred to Company A, 66th Regiment N.C. Troops, October 2, 1863.

COUCH, WILLIAM, Private
Enlisted in Orange County on December 18, 1862, for the war. Present or accounted for until transferred to Company A, 66th Regiment N.C. Troops, October 2, 1863.

COUCH, WILLIAM G., Corporal
Enlisted in Orange County on November 20, 1861, for the war. Promotion record not reported. Present or accounted for until transferred to Company A, 66th Regiment N.C. Troops, October 2, 1863.

CRABTREE, ROBERT H., Private
Resided in Orange County where he enlisted on July 1, 1863, for the war. Present or accounted for until transferred to Company A, 66th Regiment N.C. Troops, October 2, 1863.

CRABTREE, WILLIAM R., Private
Resided in Orange County where he enlisted on November 20, 1861, for the war. Present or accounted for until transferred to Company A, 66th Regiment N.C. Troops, October 2, 1863.

CRISMOND, CRAVEN, Private
Enlisted in Alamance County on December 19, 1862, for the war. Present or accounted for until transferred to Company A, 66th Regiment N.C. Troops, October 2, 1863.

DIXON, JAMES T., Private
Enlisted in Orange County on November 20, 1861, for the war. Present or accounted for until transferred to Company A, 66th Regiment N.C. Troops, October 2, 1863.

DUNNAGAN, CHARLES L., Private
Enlisted in Orange County on February 2, 1862, for the war. Present or accounted for until transferred to Company A, 66th Regiment N.C. Troops, October 2, 1863.

FAUCETT, DAVID, Private

Enlisted in Orange County on January 15, 1863, for the war. Present or accounted for until transferred to Company A, 66th Regiment N.C.Troops, October 2, 1863.

FAUCETT, THOMAS, Private

Enlisted in Orange County on April 1, 186-, for the war. Present or accounted for until transferred to Company A, 66th Regiment N.C.Troops, October 2, 1863.

GARRARD, JOSEPH W., Private

Enlisted in Orange County on November 26, 1862, for the war. Present or accounted for until transferred to Company A, 66th Regiment N.C.Troops, October 2, 1863.

GARRETT, SKIDMORE J., Private

Resided in Orange County where he enlisted on February 24, 1862, for the war. Present or accounted for until transferred to Company A, 66th Regiment N.C.Troops, October 2, 1863.

GATES, WILIE P., Private

Enlisted in Orange County on February 24, 1862, for the war. Present or accounted for until transferred to Company A, 66th Regiment N.C.Troops, October 2, 1863.

GLENN, BRYANT, Private

Enlisted in Orange County on December 7, 1861, for the war. Present or accounted for until transferred to Company A, 66th Regiment N.C.Troops, October 2, 1863.

GLENN, HILLMAN, Private

Enlisted in Orange County on December 7, 1861, for the war. Present or accounted for until transferred to Company A, 66th Regiment N.C.Troops, October 2, 1863.

GLENN, WILLIAM T., Private

Enlisted in Orange County on December 7, 1861, for the war. Present or accounted for until transferred to Company A, 66th Regiment N. C.Troops, October 2, 1863.

GRISHAM, GEORGE F., Private

Enlisted in Orange County on November 20, 1861, for the war. Present or accounted for until transferred to Company A, 66th Regiment N.C.Troops, October 2, 1863.

GUESS, WILLIAM C., Private

Resided in Orange County where he enlisted on November 20, 1861, for the war. Present or accounted for until transferred to Company A, 66th Regiment N.C.Troops, October 2, 1863.

HALL, ANDREW, Private

Enlisted in Orange County on November 20, 1861, for the war. Present or accounted for until transferred to Company A, 66th Regiment N.C.Troops, October 2, 1863.

HALL, GASTIN W., Private

Enlisted in Orange County on February 15, 1862, for the war. Present or accounted for until transferred to Company A, 66th Regiment N.C.Troops, October 2, 1863.

HALL, JOHN, Sergeant

Enlisted in Orange County on November 20, 1861,

for the war. Promotion record not reported. Present or accounted for until transferred to Company A, 66th Regiment N.C. Troops, October 2, 1863.

HAMPTON, GASTIN, Private

Resided in Orange County where he enlisted on December 17, 1862, for the war. Present or accounted for until transferred to Company A, 66th Regiment N.C.Troops, October 2, 1863.

HERNDON, CHARLES M., Private

Resided in Orange County where he enlisted on February 6, 1862, for the war. Present or accounted for until transferred to Company A, 66th Regiment N.C.Troops, October 2, 1863.

HICKS, JAMES E., Private

Enlisted in Orange County on April 29, 1862, for the war. Present or accounted for until transferred to Company A, 66th Regiment N.C.Troops, October 2, 1863.

HOLLOWAY, JOHN A., Private

Enlisted in Orange County on February 24, 1862, for the war. Present or accounted for until transferred to Company A, 66th Regiment N.C.Troops, October 2, 1863.

HORNER, JAMES D., Corporal

Enlisted in Orange County on November 20, 1861, for the war. Promotion record not reported. Present or accounted for until transferred to Company A, 66th Regiment N.C.Troops, October 2, 1863.

HORNER, LITTLE D., Private

Enlisted in Orange County on December 7, 1861, for the war. Present or accounted for until transferred to Company A, 66th Regiment N.C.Troops, October 2, 1863.

HORNER, MOSES W., Private

Enlisted in Orange County on December 7, 1861, for the war. Present or accounted for until transferred to Company A, 66th Regiment N.C.Troops, October 2, 1863.

HOWELL, DUPREE H., Private

Enlisted in Johnston County on December 17, 1861, for the war. Present or accounted for until transferred to Company A, 66th Regiment N.C.Troops, October 2, 1863.

JAMES, JESSE W., Private

Enlisted in Orange County on December 15, 1861, for the war. Present or accounted for until transferred to Company A, 66th Regiment N.C.Troops, October 2, 1863.

JAMES, JOHN T., Private

Resided in Orange County where he enlisted on December 7, 1861, for the war. Present or accounted for until transferred to Company A, 66th Regiment N.C.Troops, October 2, 1863.

JAMES, THOMAS N., Private

Enlisted in Orange County on December 15, 1862, for the war. Present or accounted for until transferred to Company A, 66th Regiment N.C.Troops, October 2, 1863.

JEFFREYS, BENTON, Private

Enlisted in Orange County on November 20, 1861, for the war. Present or accounted for until transferred to Company A, 66th Regiment N.C.Troops,

October 2, 1863.

JOHNSON, DURELL, Private
Enlisted in Orange County on December 15, 1862, for the war. Present or accounted for until transferred to Company A, 66th Regiment N.C.Troops, October 2, 1863.

KING, WILLIAM C., Private
Enlisted in Alamance County on December 17, 1862, for the war. Present or accounted for until transferred to Company A, 66th Regiment N.C.Troops, October 2, 1863.

KIRKLAND, JOHN, Private
Enlisted in Orange County on December 17, 1862, for the war. Present or accounted for until transferred to Company A, 66th Regiment N.C.Troops, October 2, 1863.

LATTA, PHILLIP W., Private
Enlisted in Orange County on August 11, 1863, for the war. Present or accounted for until transferred to Company A, 66th Regiment N.C.Troops, October 2, 1863.

LATTA, WILLIAM, Private
Enlisted in Orange County on November 20, 1861, for the war. Present or accounted for until transferred to Company A, 66th Regiment N.C.Troops, October 2, 1863.

LYON, CADMUS H., Private
Resided in Orange County where he enlisted on November 20, 1861, for the war. Present or accounted for until transferred to Company A, 66th Regiment N.C.Troops, October 2, 1863.

McFARLIN, SIMEON, Private
Enlisted in Orange County on December 15, 1862, for the war. Present or accounted for until transferred to Company A, 66th Regiment N.C.Troops, October 2, 1863.

MANGUM, FIELDING, Private
Enlisted in Guilford County on February 4, 1862, for the war. Present or accounted for until transferred to Company A, 66th Regiment N.C.Troops, October 2, 1863.

MAYES, WILLIAM S., Private
Enlisted in Orange County on November 20, 1861, for the war. Present or accounted for until transferred to Company A, 66th Regiment N.C.Troops, October 2, 1863.

MAYHAN, WILLIAM F., Private
Enlisted in Alamance County on December 17, 1862, for the war. Present or accounted for until transferred to Company A, 66th Regiment N.C.Troops, October 2, 1863.

MITCHEL, ABEL R., Private
Enlisted in Alamance County on December 17, 1862 for the war. Present or accounted for until transferred to Company A, 66th Regiment N.C.Troops, October 2, 1863.

MONK, HENDERSON, Private
Resided in Orange County where he enlisted on September 15, 1863, for the war. Present or accounted for until transferred to Company A, 66th Regiment N.C.Troops, October 2, 1863.

MONK, JAMES, Private
Enlisted in Orange County on February 24, 1862, for the war. Present or accounted for until transferred to Company A, 66th Regiment N.C.Troops, October 2, 1863.

PEARCE, GEORGE B., Sergeant
Enlisted in Person County. Enlistment date reported as April 5, 1861; however, he was not listed on the rolls of this company until May-June, 1863. Rank first reported as Sergeant. Present or accounted for until transferred to Company A, 66th Regiment N.C. Troops, October 2, 1863.

PHIPPS, GREEN, Private
Resided in Orange County where he enlisted on November 20, 1861, for the war. Present or accounted for until transferred to Company A, 66th Regiment N.C.Troops, October 2, 1863.

PHIPPS, SIMEON, Private
Enlisted in Orange County on January 18, 1862, for the war. Present or accounted for until transferred to Company A, 66th Regiment N.C.Troops, October 2, 1863.

PHIPPS, STEPHEN P., Private
Enlisted in Orange County on November 20, 1861, for the war. Present or accounted for until transferred to Company A, 66th Regiment N.C.Troops, October 2, 1863.

POOL, JOHN, Private
Enlisted in Orange County on December 7, 1861, for the war. Present or accounted for until transferred to Company A, 66th Regiment N.C.Troops, October 2, 1863.

POOL, RANSOM, Private
Enlisted in Orange County on November 20, 1861, for the war. Present or accounted for until transferred to Company A, 66th Regiment N.C.Troops, October 2, 1863.

POOL, RUFUS, Private
Resided in Orange County where he enlisted on November 20, 1861, for the war. Present or accounted for until transferred to Company A, 66th Regiment N.C.Troops, October 2, 1863.

PROCTOR, HERBERT, Private
Enlisted in Orange County on November 20, 1861, for the war. Present or accounted for until transferred to Company A, 66th Regiment N.C.Troops, October 2, 1863.

PROCTOR, JOHN A., Private
Enlisted in Orange County on November 20, 1861, for the war. Present or accounted for until transferred to Company A, 66th Regiment N.C.Troops, October 2, 1863.

RHEW, JOHN W., Corporal
Enlisted in Orange County on November 20, 1861, for the war. Promotion record not reported. Present or accounted for until transferred to Company A, 66th Regiment N.C.Troops, October 2, 1863.

RHEW, SILAS M., Private
Enlisted in Orange County on November 20, 1861, for the war. Present or accounted for until transferred to Company A, 66th Regiment N.C.Troops, October 2, 1863.

RHEW, WILLIAM M., Private
Resided in Orange County where he enlisted on January 1, 1862, for the war. Present or accounted for until transferred to Company A, 66th Regiment N.C.Troops, October 2, 1863.

RHODES, ANDREW J., Private
Enlisted in Orange County on April 25, 1862, for the war. Present or accounted for until transferred to Company A, 66th Regiment N.C.Troops, October 2, 1863.

RHODES, GEORGE A., Private
Resided in Orange County where he enlisted on April 25, 1862, for the war. Present or accounted for until transferred to Company A, 66th Regiment N.C. Troops, October 2, 1863.

RILEY, THOMAS J., Private
Resided in Orange County where he enlisted on March 29, 1862, for the war. Present or accounted for until transferred to Company A, 66th Regiment N.C.Troops, October 2, 1863.

RILEY, WILLIAM L., Private
Resided in Orange County where he enlisted on January 11, 1863, for the war. Present or accounted for until transferred to Company A, 66th Regiment N.C.Troops, October 2, 1863.

SCARLETT, JAMES C., Private
Resided in Orange County where he enlisted on July 1, 1863, for the war. Present or accounted for until transferred to Company A, 66th Regiment N.C. Troops, October 2, 1863.

SCARLETT, WILLIAM R., Sergeant
Enlisted in Orange County on November 20, 1861, for the war. Promotion record not reported. Present or accounted for until transferred to Company A, 66th Regiment N.C.Troops, October 2, 1863.

SIMPSON, CHARLES, Private
Enlisted in Orange County on February 6, 1862, for the war. Present or accounted for until transferred to Company A, 66th Regiment N.C.Troops, October 2, 1863.

SIMPSON, WILLIAM, Private
Born in Edgecombe County and was by occupation a farmer prior to enlisting in Orange County at age 63, February 6, 1862, for the war. Present or accounted for until transferred to Company A, 66th Regiment N.C.Troops, October 2, 1863.

SIMPSON, WILLIAM, Jr., Private
Enlisted in Orange County on February 6, 1862, for the war. Present or accounted for until transferred to Company A, 66th Regiment N.C.Troops, October 2, 1863.

SMITH, JOHN W., Private
Enlisted in Orange County on November 20, 1861, for the war. Present or accounted for until transferred to Company A, 66th Regiment N.C.Troops, October 2, 1863.

STANLEY, JOHN W., Private
Enlisted in Orange County on January 27, 1862, for the war. Present or accounted for until transferred to Company A, 66th Regiment N.C.Troops, October 2, 1863.

STRAYHORN, SAMUEL M., Private
Enlisted in Orange County on December 17, 1862, for the war. Present or accounted for until transferred to Company A, 66th Regiment N.C.Troops, October 2, 1863.

TATE, ALBERT A., Private
Enlisted in Orange County on December 16, 1862, for the war. Present or accounted for until transferred to Company A, 66th Regiment N.C.Troops, October 2, 1863.

TEASLEY, WILLIE W., Private
Enlisted in Orange County on February 6, 1862, for the war. Present or accounted for until transferred to Company A, 66th Regiment N.C.Troops, October 2, 1863.

THOMPSON, FRANCIS M., Private
Enlisted in Orange County on May 1, 1862, for the war. Present or accounted for until transferred to Company A, 66th Regiment N.C.Troops, October 2, 1863.

UMSTEAD, HENRY L., Private
Enlisted in Orange County on November 20, 1861, for the war. Present or accounted for until transferred to Company A, 66th Regiment N.C.Troops, October 2, 1863.

VICKERS, MOSES, Private
Resided in Orange County where he enlisted on November 20, 1861, for the war. Present or accounted for until transferred to Company A, 66th Regiment N.C.Troops, October 2, 1863.

WALKER, HENRY H., Private
Enlisted in Orange County on May 12, 1862, for the war. Present or accounted for until transferred to Company A, 66th Regiment N.C.Troops, October 2, 1863.

WALKER, JOHN A., Private
Enlisted in Orange County on May 12, 1862, for the war. Present or accounted for until transferred to Company A, 66th Regiment N.C.Troops, October 2, 1863.

WARREN, CHESLEY P., Private
Enlisted in Orange County on November 26, 1862, for the war. Present or accounted for until transferred to Company A, 66th Regiment N.C.Troops, October 2, 1863.

WATSON, JAMES W., Private
Enlisted in Orange County on November 20, 186[1], for the war. Present or accounted for until transferred to Company A, 66th Regiment N.C.Troops, October 2, 1863.

WHITAKER, ANDREW J., Private
Enlisted in Orange County on November 20, 186[1], for the war. Present or accounted for until transferred to Company A, 66th Regiment N.C.Troops, October 2, 1863.

WHITAKER, ISAAC D., Corporal
Enlisted in Orange County on November 20, 1861, for the war. Promotion record not reported. Present or accounted for until transferred to Company A, 66th Regiment N.C.Troops, October 2, 1863.

WHITAKER, JOSEPH A., Private
Enlisted in Orange County on November 20, 186[1],

for the war. Present or accounted for until transferred to Company A, 66th Regiment N.C. Troops, October 2, 1863.

WOFFORD, WILLIAM W., Private
Resided in Cabarrus County and enlisted in Orange County on February 20, 1862, for the war. Present or accounted for until transferred to Company A, 66th Regiment N.C. Troops, October 2, 1863.

WOODS, JAMES M., Private
Enlisted in Orange County on March 29, 1862, for the war. Present or accounted for until transferred to Company A, 66th Regiment N.C. Troops, October 2, 1863.

WOODS, JAMES M., Jr., Private
Enlisted in Orange County on November 20, 1861, for the war. Present or accounted for until transferred to Company A, 66th Regiment N.C. Troops, October 2, 1863.

WOODS, JOHN, Private
Enlisted in Orange County on December 10, 1862, for the war. Present or accounted for until transferred to Company A, 66th Regiment N.C. Troops, October 2, 1863.

WOODS, JOHN M., Private
Enlisted in Orange County on February 6, 1862, for the war. Present or accounted for until transferred to Company A, 66th Regiment N.C. Troops, October 2, 1863.

WOODS, WILLIAM M., Private
Resided in Orange County where he enlisted on February 6, 1862, for the war. Present or accounted for until transferred to Company A, 66th Regiment N.C. Troops, October 2, 1863.

COMPANY B

This company was organized in Nash and Franklin counties and enlisted as Captain Possum Nichols's Company, Raleigh and Gaston Railroad Guard. The date the company was organized is not reported; however, it was assigned to the battalion on May 19, 1863, and was designated Company B. By Special Orders No. 234, Adjutant and Inspector General's Office, Richmond, October 2, 1863, the company was assigned to the 66th Regiment N.C. Troops and became Company B of that regiment.

The information contained in the following roster of the company was compiled principally from company muster rolls for August 31-December 31, 1862, and May-June, 1863. No company muster rolls were found for the period prior to August 31, 1862; for January-April, 1863; or for the period after June, 1863. In addition to the company muster rolls, Roll of Honor records, receipt rolls, hospital records, prisoner of war records, and other primary records, supplemented by state pension applications, United Daughters of the Confederacy records, and postwar rosters and histories, all provided useful information.

OFFICERS

CAPTAIN

NICHOLS, POSSUM
Resided in Burke County and enlisted in Franklin County. Appointed Captain on or about December 4, 1862. Present or accounted for until captured at Rocky Mount on July 20, 1863. Transferred to Company B, 66th Regiment N.C. Troops, October 2, 1863, while a prisoner of war.

LIEUTENANTS

BUNTING, JAMES V., 3rd Lieutenant
Resided in Nash County where he enlisted. Appointed 3rd Lieutenant on or about December 13, 1861. Present or accounted for until transferred to Company B, 66th Regiment N.C. Troops, October 2, 1863.

MITCHELL, W. S., 1st Lieutenant
Resided in Franklin County where he enlisted. Enlistment date and promotion record not reported. Promoted from 1st Sergeant to 1st Lieutenant on October 10, 1862. Present or accounted for until transferred to Company B, 66th Regiment N.C. Troops, October 2, 1863.

MOORE, WILLIAM A., 1st Lieutenant
Enlisted in Franklin County. Mustered in as 1st Lieutenant; however, his date of rank is not reported. Defeated for reelection on October 10, 1862.

SILLS, DAVID N., 2nd Lieutenant
Enlisted in Nash County. Appointed 2nd Lieutenant on or about December 13, 1861. Present or accounted for until transferred to Company B, 66th Regiment N.C. Troops, October 2, 1863.

NONCOMMISSIONED OFFICERS AND PRIVATES

ACREE, GEORGE R., Private
Enlisted in Franklin County on December 13, 1861, for the war. Mustered in as Corporal but was reduced to ranks in January-June, 1863. Present or accounted for until transferred to Company B, 66th Regiment N.C. Troops, October 2, 1863.

ALFORD, JOHN, Private
Resided in Franklin County where he enlisted on December 13, 1861, for the war. Present or accounted for until transferred to Company B, 66th Regiment N. C. Troops, October 2, 1863.

AVENT, JAMES T., Sergeant
Enlisted in Nash County on December 13, 1861, for the war. Mustered in as Sergeant. Present or accounted for through December, 1862. No further records.

BACHELOR, MERRIT, Private
Enlisted in Nash County on December 13, 1861, for the war. Present or accounted for until transferred to Company B, 66th Regiment N.C. Troops, October 2, 1863.

BACHELOR, RUFUS, Private
Resided in Franklin County where he enlisted on December 13, 1861, for the war. Present or accounted for until transferred to Company B, 66th Regiment N.C. Troops, October 2, 1863.

BAKER, JOSEPH C., Corporal
Resided in Franklin County and enlisted on January 1, 1863, for the war. Mustered in as Private and

promoted to Corporal on September 1, 1863. Present or accounted for until transferred to Company B, 66th Regiment N.C.Troops, October 2, 1863.

BAKER, SIMON, Private
Enlisted in Franklin County on May 8, 1863, for the war. Present or accounted for until transferred to Company B, 66th Regiment N.C. Troops, October 2, 1863.

BARTHOLOMEW, BENJAMIN B., Private
Enlisted in Franklin County on December 13, 1861, for the war. Present or accounted for until transferred to Company B, 66th Regiment N. C.Troops, October 2, 1863.

BARTHOLOMEW, GEORGE W., Private
Enlisted in Franklin County on August 30, 1863, for the war. Present or accounted for until transferred to Company B, 66th Regiment N.C.Troops, October 2, 1863.

BARTHOLOMEW, NICHOLAS, Private
Resided in Franklin County where he enlisted on December 13, 1861, for the war. Present or accounted for until transferred to Company B, 66th Regiment N.C.Troops, October 2, 1863.

BENNETT, J. WILLIAM, Private
Enlisted in Nash County on January 31, 1862, for the war. Present or accounted for until transferred to Company B, 66th Regiment N.C.Troops, October 2, 1863.

BOWDEN, J. W., Private
Enlisted in Franklin County on December 13, 1861, for the war. Present or accounted for until transferred to Company B, 66th Regiment N.C.Troops, October 2, 1863.

BOWDEN, JOHN A., Private
Resided in Franklin County where he enlisted on December 13, 1861, for the war. Present or accounted for until transferred to Company B, 66th Regiment N.C.Troops, October 2, 1863.

BOWDEN, MOSES B., Private
Enlisted in Franklin County on December 13, 1861, for the war. Present or accounted for until transferred to Company B, 66th Regiment N.C.Troops, October 2, 1863.

BOWDEN, ROBERT T. D., Private
Resided in Franklin County where he enlisted on December 13, 1861, for the war. Mustered in as Corporal but was reduced to ranks in January-June, 1863. Present or accounted for until transferred to Company B, 66th Regiment N.C.Troops, October 2, 1863.

BOWDEN, WILLIAM B., Private
Previously served in 1st Company C, 12th Regiment N.C.Troops (2nd Regiment N.C.Volunteers). Enlisted in this company on December 13, 1861, for the war. Present or accounted for until transferred to Company B, 66th Regiment N.C.Troops, October 2, 1863.

BRASWELL, JOSEPH R., Private
Resided in Nash County where he enlisted on January 31, 1862, for the war. Present or accounted for until transferred to Company B, 66th Regiment N.C.Troops, October 2, 1863.

BUNN, DAVID, Private
Resided in Franklin County where he enlisted on December 13, 1861, for the war. Present or accounted for until transferred to Company B, 66th Regiment N. C.Troops, October 2, 1863.

BUNTING, C. H. C., Corporal
Enlisted in Nash County on December 13, 1861, for the war. Mustered in as Private and promoted to Corporal in January-June, 1863. Present or accounted for until transferred to Company B, 66th Regiment N.C.Troops, October 2, 1863.

BUNTING, T. B., Private
Enlisted in Nash County on December 13, 1861, for the war. Present or accounted for until captured at or near Tarboro on or about July 21, 1863. Exchanged at Fort Monroe, Virginia, August 4, 1863. Present or accounted for until transferred to Company B, 66th Regiment N.C.Troops, October 2, 1863.

CHAMPION, JAMES M., Private
Enlisted in Franklin County on December 13, 1861, for the war. Present or accounted for until transferred to Company B, 66th Regiment N.C.Troops, October 2, 1863.

COLLINS, A. J., Private
Resided in Nash County and enlisted in Franklin County on January 14, 1862, for the war. Present or accounted for until transferred to Company B, 66th Regiment N.C.Troops, October 2, 1863.

COLLINS, G. W., Private
Resided in Nash County and enlisted in Franklin County on August 14, 1862, for the war. Present or accounted for until transferred to Company B, 66th Regiment N.C.Troops, October 2, 1863.

COLLINS, JOSEPH, Private
Enlisted in Franklin County on December 13, 1861, for the war. Mustered in as Corporal but was reduced to ranks in January-June, 1863. Present or accounted for until discharged on September 21, 1863. Reason discharged not reported.

COLVERT, JOHN H., Private
Resided in Rutherford County and enlisted in Franklin County on December 13, 1861, for the war. Present or accounted for until transferred to Company B, 66th Regiment N.C.Troops, October 2, 1863.

COOK, G. W., Private
Resided in Nash County and enlisted in Franklin County on December 13, 1861, for the war. Present or accounted for until transferred to Company B, 66th Regiment N.C.Troops, October 2, 1863.

COOK, JOSEPH B., Private
Resided in Franklin County where he enlisted on December 13, 1861, for the war. Present or accounted for until transferred to Company B, 66th Regiment N.C.Troops, October 2, 1863.

COOK, STEPHEN, Private
Enlisted in Franklin County on December 13, 1861, for the war. Present or accounted for until transferred to Company B, 66th Regiment N.C.Troops, October 2, 1863.

COPPEDGE, G. W., Private
Resided in Nash County where he enlisted on July 30, 1862, for the war. Present or accounted for until transferred to Company B, 66th Regiment N.C. Troops, October 2, 1863.

COPPEDGE, HIRAM J., Private
Previously served in Company K, 44th Regiment N.C. Troops. Transferred to this company on August 1, 1861, in exchange for Private J.C. Wood. Present or accounted for until transferred to Company B, 66th Regiment N.C. Troops, October 2, 1863.

COPPEDGE, JORDAN, Private
Resided in Nash County where he enlisted on December 13, 1861, for the war. Present or accounted for until transferred to Company B, 66th Regiment N.C. Troops, October 2, 1863.

COPPEDGE, JOSEPH, Private
Resided in Franklin County and enlisted in Nash County on December 13, 1861, for the war. Present or accounted for until transferred to Company B, 66th Regiment N.C. Troops, October 2, 1863.

CROWDER, JOHN R., Private
Enlisted in Franklin County on December 13, 1861, for the war. Present or accounted for until he died on May 9, 1863. Place and cause of death not reported.

CROWDER, T. J., Private
Enlisted in Franklin County. Date of enlistment not reported. Died October 2, 1862. Place and cause of death not reported.

CULPEPPER, J. M., Private
Resided in Franklin County where he enlisted on March 25, 1863, for the war. Present or accounted for until captured at or near Tarboro on or about July 21, 1863. Exchanged at Fort Monroe, Virginia, August 4, 1863. Present or accounted for until transferred to Company B, 66th Regiment N.C. Troops, October 2, 1863.

DAVIS, W. T., Private
Enlisted in Franklin County on December 13, 1861, for the war. Present or accounted for until transferred to Company B, 66th Regiment N.C. Troops, October 2, 1863.

DORSEY, EPHRAIM, Private
Resided in Franklin County where he enlisted on December 13, 1861, for the war. Present or accounted for until transferred to Company B, 66th Regiment N.C. Troops, October 2, 1863.

EDWARDS, J. O., Private
Enlisted in Nash County on January 31, 1862, for the war. Present or accounted for until transferred to Company B, 66th Regiment N.C. Troops, October 2, 1863.

EDWARDS, W. H., Private
Resided in Greene County and enlisted in Franklin County on December 13, 1861, for the war. Present or accounted for until transferred to Company B, 66th Regiment N.C. Troops, October 2, 1863.

FULLER, JAMES H., Private
Resided in Franklin County and enlisted in Nash County on December 13, 1861, for the war. Present

or accounted for until transferred to Company B, 66th Regiment N.C. Troops, October 2, 1863.

GAY, SIDNEY, Private
Enlisted in Franklin County on December 13, 1861, for the war. Present or accounted for until transferred to Company I, 55th Regiment N.C. Troops on or about November 17, 1862.

GAY, THOMAS, Private
Resided in Franklin County where he enlisted on December 13, 1861, for the war. Present or accounted for until transferred to Company B, 66th Regiment N.C. Troops, October 2, 1863.

GOOCH, JOSEPH S., Private
Enlisted in Nash County on May 8, 1863, for the war. Present or accounted for until transferred to Company B, 66th Regiment N.C. Troops, October 2, 1863.

GRIFFIN, B. F., Private
Enlisted in Nash County on December 13, 1861, for the war. Present or accounted for until transferred to Company B, 66th Regiment N.C. Troops, October 2, 1863.

GRIFFIN, DOLPHIN, Private
Enlisted in Wake County on May 8, 1863, for the war. Present or accounted for until he deserted on August 15, 1863. Transferred to Company B, 66th Regiment N.C. Troops, October 2, 1863, while listed as a deserter.

GRIFFIN, J. J., Corporal
Enlisted in Nash County on January 31, 1862, for the war. Mustered in as Private and promoted to Corporal in January-June, 1863. Present or accounted for until captured at Rocky Mount on July 20, 1863. Transferred to Company B, 66th Regiment N.C. Troops, October 2, 1863, while a prisoner of war.

GRIFFIN, PENEWELL, Private
Enlisted in Nash County on December 13, 1861, for the war. Present or accounted for until transferred to Company B, 66th Regiment N. C. Troops, October 2, 1863.

GRIFFIN, RICHARD B., Private
Enlisted in Nash County on January 31, 1862, for the war. Present or accounted for until he deserted on August 15, 1863.

HARPER, JOSEPH, Private
Resided in Franklin or Nash counties where he enlisted on March 15, 1863, for the war. Present or accounted for until transferred to Company B, 66th Regiment N.C. Troops, October 2, 1863.

HEDGEPETH, WILLIAM T., Private
Enlisted in Nash County on December 13, 1861, for the war. Present or accounted for through December, 1862. No further records.

HINES, A. D., Private
Enlisted in Nash County on December 13, 1861, for the war. Present or accounted for until transferred to Company B, 66th Regiment N.C. Troops, October 2, 1863.

HOUSE, EDMUND, Private
Enlisted in Nash County on January 31, 1862, for the war. Present or accounted for until reported absent

without leave on October 1, 1863. Transferred to Company B, 66th Regiment N.C.Troops, October 2, 1863, while absent without leave.

JONES, FENNER, Private
Enlisted in Franklin County on May 8, 1863, for the war. Present or accounted for until transferred to Company B, 66th Regiment N.C.Troops, October 2, 1863.

JOYNER, RICHARD, Private
Enlisted in Franklin County on July 30, 1862, for the war. Present or accounted for until transferred to Company B, 66th Regiment N.C.Troops, October 2, 1863.

JOYNER, SAMUEL, Private
Enlisted in Franklin County on January 22, 1862, for the war. Present or accounted for until transferred to Company B, 66th Regiment N.C. Troops, October 2, 1863.

LANCASTER, W. B., Private
Born in Franklin County and was by occupation a farmer prior to enlisting in Franklin County on December 13, 1861, for the war. Present or accounted for until transferred to Company B, 66th Regiment N.C.Troops, October 2, 1863.

LEONARD, J. J., Jr., Private
Born in Franklin County where he enlisted on March 25, 1863, for the war. Present or accounted for until transferred to Company B, 66th Regiment N.C. Troops, October 2, 1863.

LEONARD, J. J., Sr., Private
Enlisted in Franklin County on December 13, 1861, for the war. Present or accounted for until transferred to Company B, 66th Regiment N.C.Troops, October 2. 1863.

LEONARD, JOHN F., Private
Enlisted in Franklin County on December 13, 1861, for the war. Present or accounted for until transferred to Company B, 66th Regiment N.C.Troops October 2, 1863.

MATTHEWS, GEORGE E., Private
Resided in Nash County where he enlisted on March 25, 1863, for the war. Present or accounted for until transferred to Company B, 66th Regiment N.C. Troops, October 2, 1863.

MATTHEWS, JAMES, Private
Enlisted in Nash County on May 8, 1863, for the war. Present or accounted for until transferred to Company B, 66th Regiment N.C.Troops, October 2, 1863.

MAY, B. F., Private
Born in Nash County where he enlisted on December 13, 1861, for the war. Present or accounted for until he died at Wilson or at Goldsboro on September 14, 1863, of "typhoid fever."

MAY, JOHN S., Private
Enlisted in Nash County on January 31, 1862, for the war. Mustered in as Private and promoted to Corporal at an unspecified date. Reduced to ranks on August 31, 1863. Present or accounted for until transferred to Company B, 66th Regiment N.C. Troops, October 2, 1863.

MAY, S. K., Private
Enlisted in Nash County on December 13, 1861, for the war. Present or accounted for until transferred to Company B, 66th Regiment N.C.Troops, October 2, 1863.

MAY, THEOPHILUS CELKERT, Sergeant
Enlisted in Nash County on January 31, 1862, for the war. Promotion record not reported. Present or accounted for until transferred to Company B, 66th Regiment N.C.Troops, October 2, 1863.

MOORE, WILLIAM A., Private
Enlisted in Franklin County on December 13, 1861, for the war. Present or accounted for until transferred to Company B, 66th Regiment N.C.Troops, October 2, 1863.

MULLINS, J. CRAYTON, Private
Enlisted in Franklin County on January 22, 1862, for the war. Present or accounted for until transferred to Company B, 66th Regiment N.C.Troops, October 2, 1863.

MURPHEY, ALPHEUS, Corporal
Born in Franklin County where he enlisted on January 5, 1862, for the war. Mustered in as Private and promoted to Corporal in January-June, 1863. Present or accounted for until he died in hospital at Goldsboro on or about September 4, 1863, of "febris typhoides."

MURPHEY, JAMES M., Private
Resided in Franklin County and was by occupation a farmer prior to enlisting in Franklin County on December 13, 1861, for the war. Present or accounted for until transferred to Company B, 66th Regiment N. C. Troops, October 2, 1863.

NELMS, JAMES N., Private
Enlisted in Franklin County on March 25, 1863, for the war. Present or accounted for until transferred to Company B, 66th Regiment N.C.Troops, October 2, 1863.

ODUM, JOHN H., Private
Enlisted in Franklin County on December 31, 1861, for the war. Present or accounted for until transferred to Company B, 66th Regiment N.C.Troops, October 2, 1863.

PERRY, JOSEPH, Private
Enlisted in Franklin County on December 13, 1861, for the war. Present or accounted for until transferred to Company B, 66th Regiment N.C.Troops, October 2, 1863.

PITTS, G. H., 1st Sergeant
Resided in Nash County where he enlisted on January 31, 1862, for the war. Mustered in as Private and promoted to 1st Sergeant on October 10, 1862. Present or accounted for until transferred to Company B, 66th Regiment N.C.Troops, October 2, 1863.

PITTS, JOHN HENRY, Sergeant
Enlisted in Nash County on December 13, 1861, for the war. Mustered in as Private and promoted to Sergeant in January-June, 1863. Present or accounted for until transferred to Company B, 66th Regiment N.C.Troops, October 2, 1863.

PRIVETT, JOSEPH BRYANT, Private
Resided in Nash County where he enlisted on January 31, 1862, for the war. Present or accounted for until transferred to Company B, 66th Regiment N.C.Troops, October 2, 1863.

SILLS, JAMES G., Private
Enlisted in Nash County on August 27, 1863, for the war. Present or accounted for until transferred to Company B, 66th Regiment N.C.Troops, October 2, 1863.

STALLINGS, OLIVER C., Private
Previously served in Company L, 15th Regiment N.C. Troops. Enlisted in this company on March 25, 1863, for the war. Present or accounted for until transferred to Company B, 66th Regiment N.C. Troops, October 2, 1863.

STILES, JOHN, Private
Enlisted in Nash County on December 13, 1861, for the war. Present or accounted for until transferred to Company B, 66th Regiment N.C.Troops, October 2, 1863.

STRICKLAND, MATHEW C., Private
Enlisted in Nash County on December 13, 1861, for the war. Present or accounted for until transferred to Company B, 66th Regiment N.C.Troops, October 2, 1863.

TAYLOR, DANIEL, Private
Enlisted in Nash County on December 13, 1861, for the war. No further records.

THOMAS, G. W., Jr., Private
Enlisted in Franklin County on December 13, 1861, for the war. Present or accounted for until transferred to Company B, 66th Regiment N.C.Troops, October 2, 1863.

THOMAS, G. W., Sr., Private
Enlisted in Franklin County on March 25, 1863, for the war. Present or accounted for until transferred to Company B, 66th Regiment N.C.Troops, October 2, 1863.

TODD, H. H., Corporal
Enlisted in Franklin County on March 1, 1862, for the war. Mustered in as Private and promoted to Corporal in January-June, 1863. Present or accounted for until transferred to Company B, 66th Regiment N.C.Troops, October 2, 1863.

TODD, JAMES H., Private
Enlisted in Franklin County on December 13, 1861, for the war. Present or accounted for until transferred to Company B, 66th Regiment N.C.Troops, October 2, 1863.

TUCKER, JAMES P., Sergeant
Enlisted in Franklin County on December 31, 1862, for the war. Mustered in as Sergeant. Present or accounted for until transferred to Company B, 66th Regiment N.C.Troops, October 2, 1863.

UPCHURCH, BENJAMIN W., Private
Resided in Nash County where he enlisted on August 14, 1862, for the war. Present or accounted for until transferred to Company B, 66th Regiment N.C. Troops, October 2, 1863.

UPPERMAN, JOHN H., Private
Enlisted in Franklin County on December 13, 1861,

for the war. Mustered in as Private. Present or accounted for until appointed Quartermaster Sergeant on June 16, 1863, and transferred to the Field and Staff of this battalion.

WEATHERS, W. P., Private
Enlisted in Granville County on May 8, 1863, for the war. Present or accounted for until transferred to Company B, 66th Regiment N.C.Troops, October 2, 1863.

WESTER, B. E., Private
Enlisted in Franklin County on December 13, 1861, for the war. Present or accounted for until transferred to Company B, 66th Regiment N.C.Troops, October 2, 1863.

WESTER, EXUM, Private
Enlisted in Franklin County on July 31, 1862, for the war. Present or accounted for until transferred to Company B, 66th Regiment N.C.Troops, October 2, 1863.

WESTER, JOE J., Corporal
Enlisted in Franklin County on December 13, 1861, for the war. Mustered in as Private and promoted to Corporal on September 5, 1863. Present or accounted for until transferred to Company B, 66th Regiment N.C.Troops, October 2, 1863.

WESTER, T. C., Private
Resided in Franklin County where he enlisted on December 13, 1861, for the war. Present or accounted for until transferred to Company B, 66th Regiment N.C.Troops, October 2, 1863.

WIGGINS, E. C., Private
Enlisted in Franklin County on January 31, 1862, for the war. Present or accounted for until transferred to Company B, 66th Regiment N.C.Troops, October 2, 1863.

WIGGS, JAMES J., Sergeant
Resided in Franklin County where he enlisted on December 31, 1861, for the war. Promotion record not reported. Present or accounted for until transferred to Company B, 66th Regiment N.C.Troops, October 2, 1863.

WILLIAMS, JAMES W., Private
Enlisted in Nash County on May 8, 1863, for the war. Present or accounted for until transferred to Company B, 66th Regiment N.C.Troops, October 2, 1863.

WOOD, BENNETT, Private
Resided in Nash County and enlisted in Franklin County on December 13, 1861, for the war. Present or accounted for until transferred to Company B, 66th Regiment N.C.Troops, October 2, 1863.

WOOD, HENRY, Private
Enlisted in Franklin County on March 25, 1863, for the war. Present or accounted for until transferred to Company B, 66th Regiment N.C.Troops, October 2. 1863.

WOOD, J. C., Private
Born in Franklin County where he resided prior to enlisting in Franklin County on December 13, 1861, for the war. Present or accounted for until transferred to Company K, 44th Regiment N.C.Troops, August 1, 1863, in exchange for Private Hiram J.

Coppedge.

WOOD, JOSEPH H., Private
Enlisted in Franklin County on December 13, 1861, for the war. Present or accounted for until transferred to Company B, 66th Regiment N.C.Troops, October 2, 1863.

WOOD, W. H., Private
Enlisted in Nash County on March 25, 1863, for the war. Present or accounted for until captured at Tarboro or at Rocky Mount on or about July 20, 1863. Paroled at Fort Monroe, Virginia, August 4, 1863. Present or accounted for until transferred to Company B, 66th Regiment N.C.Troops, October 2, 1863.

YARBOROUGH, HENRY, Private
Enlisted in Nash County on December 13, 1861, for the war. Present or accounted for through December, 1862.

YELVINGTON, S. J., Private
Enlisted in Franklin County on December 13, 1861, for the war. Present or accounted for until transferred to Company B, 66th Regiment N.C.Troops, October 2, 1863.

COMPANY C

This company was organized in Wayne and Lenoir counties and enlisted on January 28, 1862, as Captain Guilford W. Cox's Independent Company of Bridge Guards, N.C. Troops. It was created for local defense duty and to guard bridges on the Atlantic and North Carolina Railroad. The company saw action at the battle of New Bern on March 14, 1862, and, following the battle, it was stationed at Goldsboro. Detachments were sent out from that place to guard strategic points along the Atlantic and North Carolina Railroad.

The company was assigned to the battalion on May 19, 1863, and was designated Company C. By Special Orders No. 234, Adjutant and Inspector General's Office, Richmond, October 2, 1863, the company was assigned to the 66th Regiment N.C. Troops and became Company E of that regiment.

The information contained in the following roster of the company was compiled principally from company muster rolls for January 28, 1862, through June, 1863. No company muster rolls were found for the period after June, 1863. In addition to the company muster -rolls, Roll of Honor records, receipt rolls, hospital records, prisoner of war records, and other primary records, supplemented by state pension applications, United Daughters of the Confederacy records, and postwar rosters and histories, all provided useful information.

OFFICERS

CAPTAIN

COX, GUILFORD W.
Previously served as 2nd Lieutenant in Company H, 27th Regiment N.C.Troops. Appointed Captain of this company on or about January 28, 1862. Present or accounted for until transferred to Company E, 66th Regiment N.C.Troops, October 2, 1863.

LIEUTENANTS

BELL, DURAND H. L., Brevet 2nd Lieutenant
Enlisted in Carteret County. Appointed Brevet 2nd Lieutenant on February 11, 1862. Present or accounted for until he was captured by the enemy or deserted at New Bern on March 14, 1862.

GRIMMER, WILLIAM L., 2nd Lieutenant
Previously served as Private in Company K, 10th Regiment N.C. State Troops (1st Regiment N.C. Artillery). Transferred to this company upon appointment as 2nd Lieutenant on January 28, 1862. Present or accounted for until transferred to Company E, 66th Regiment N.C.Troops, October 2, 1863.

QUINERLY, STEPHEN S., Brevet 2nd Lieutenant
Enlisted in Pitt County on January 28, 1862, for the war. Mustered in as 1st Sergeant and was appointed Brevet 2nd Lieutenant on August 23, 1862. Present or accounted for until transferred to Company E, 66th Regiment N.C.Troops, October 2, 1863.

WITHERINGTON, IVAN K., 1st Lieutenant
Enlisted in Pitt County. Appointed 1st Lieutenant on or about January 28, 1862. Present or accounted for until transferred to Company E, 66th Regiment N.C. Troops, October 2, 1863.

NONCOMMISSIONED OFFICERS AND PRIVATES

ABBOTT, JOHN, Private
Enlisted in Lenoir County on January 28, 1862, for the war. Present or accounted for until transferred to Company E, 66th Regiment N.C.Troops, October 2, 1863.

ALDRIDGE, JOSIAH W., Private
Resided in Lenoir County where he enlisted on January 28, 1862, for the war. Mustered in as Corporal but was reduced to ranks in January-February, 1863. Present or accounted for until transferred to Company E, 66th Regiment N.C.Troops, October 2, 1863.

BELL, HIRAM R., Private
Enlisted in Carteret County on February 11, 1862, for the war. Present or accounted for until he was captured by the enemy or deserted at New Bern on March 14, 1862. Dropped from the rolls of the company on July 31, 1862.

BELL, JOSIAH L., Private
Enlisted in Carteret County on February 11, 1862, for the war. Present or accounted for until discharged at an unspecified date after providing Private Hatch B. Hill as a substitute.

BELL, M. R., Private
Enlisted in Carteret County on February 11, 1862, for the war. Present or accounted for until he deserted or was captured on March 28, 1862. Dropped from the rolls of the company prior to September 1, 1862.

BELL, WILLIAM S., Private
Enlisted in Carteret County on February 11, 1862, for the war. Mustered in as Sergeant. Present or accounted for until he was captured by the enemy or

deserted at New Bern on March 14, 1862. Reduced to ranks and was dropped from the rolls of the company prior to September 1, 1862.

BOON, PINKNEY, Private
Enlisted in Lenoir County on March 11, 1863, for the war as a substitute for Private Archibald Cox. Present or accounted for until transferred to Company E, 66th Regiment N.C.Troops, October 2, 1863.

BOYETTE, JAMES W., Private
Enlisted in Lenoir County on January 28, 1862, for the war. Present or accounted for until he was "sent to Chapel Hill under a writ of habeus corpus" in July-August, 1863. No further records.

BRADLEY, JAMES T., Private
Enlisted in Edgecombe County on August 26, 1862, for the war. Present or accounted for until transferred to Company E, 66th Regiment N.C.Troops, October 2, 1863.

BROCK, JOHN J., Private
Enlisted in Lenoir County on January 28, 1862, for the war. Present or accounted for until transferred to Company A, 8th Battalion N.C. Partisan Rangers, June 7, 1862.

BROWN, FRANKLIN, Private
Enlisted in Lenoir County on January 28, 1862, for the war. Present or accounted for until transferred to Company E, 66th Regiment N.C.Troops, October 2, 1863.

BROWN, JESSE, Private
Enlisted in Lenoir County on January 28, 1862, for the war. Present or accounted for until transferred to Company E, 66th Regiment N.C.Troops, October 2, 1863.

BRYAN, ROBERT H., Private
Enlisted in Lenoir County on January 28, 1862, for the war. Present or accounted for until transferred to Company E, 66th Regiment N.C.Troops, October 2, 1863.

BURNEY, LEWIS B., Private
Enlisted in Pitt County on January 28, 1862, for the war. Present or accounted for until transferred to Company E, 66th Regiment N.C.Troops, October 2, 1863.

CARTER, JAMES B., Private
Born in Duplin County and was by occupation a farmer prior to enlisting in Lenoir County on January 28, 1862, for the war. Present or accounted for until discharged on July 23, 1862, by reason of "rupture." Age given on discharge papers as 28.

CARTER, JAMES C., Private
Previously served as Musician in Captain John B. Griswold's Company (Provost Guard), N.C.Local Defense Troops. Transferred to this company on September 26, 1863. Transferred to Company E, 66th Regiment N.C.Troops, October 2, 1863.

CASE, THOMAS, Private
Enlisted in Lenoir County on January 28, 1862, for the war. Present or accounted for until transferred to Company A, 8th Battalion N.C. Partisan Rangers, June 7, 1862.

COX, ABRAM, Private
Enlisted in Pitt County on January 28, 1862, for the war. Present or accounted for until discharged on or about August 5, 1862, after providing Private T. McGilbert Ross as a substitute.

COX, ARCHIBALD, Private
Enlisted in Pitt County on January 15, 1863, for the war. Present or accounted for until discharged on or about March 11, 1863, after providing Private Pinkney Boon as a substitute.

COX, FREDERICK, Private
Enlisted in Lenoir County on January 28, 1862, for the war. Present or accounted for until he was "sent to Chapel Hill under a writ of Habeus Corpus" in July-August, 1863. Later served in Company E, 66th Regiment N.C.Troops.

COX, JAMES, Private
Enlisted in Pitt County on January 28, 1862, for the war. Present or accounted for until discharged on or about July 31, 1862, after providing Private Oliver Smith as a substitute.

COX, JOHN M., Private
Enlisted in Pitt County on January 28, 1862, for the war. Mustered in as Corporal but was reduced to ranks on July 31, 1862. Present or accounted for until transferred to Company E, 66th Regiment N.C. Troops, October 2, 1863.

COX, JOSEPH, Private
Enlisted in Pitt County on January 28, 1862, for the war. Present or accounted for until transferred to Company E, 66th Regiment N.C.Troops, October 2, 1863.

COX, WILLIAM C., Private
Enlisted in Lenoir County on January 28, 1862, for the war. Present or accounted for through June, 1863; however, he was reported in confinement at Salisbury for "disloyalty" during most of that period. Transferred to Company E, 66th Regiment N.C. Troops, October 2, 1863.

DAVENPORT, PHINEAS, Private
Resided in Lenoir County where he enlisted on January 28, 1862, for the war. Mustered in as Private and promoted to Sergeant on July 31, 1862. Reduced to ranks in March-April, 1863. Present or accounted for until transferred to Company E, 66th Regiment N.C.Troops, October 2, 1863.

DAVIS, CHANCY M., Corporal
Enlisted in Carteret County on February 24, 1862, for the war. Mustered in as Private and promoted to Corporal in May-June, 1863. Present or accounted for until transferred to Company E, 66th Regiment N.C.Troops, October 2, 1863.

DAWSON, JOHN WOOTEN, Private
Enlisted in Lenoir County on January 28, 1862, for the war. Present or accounted for until transferred to Company E, 66th Regiment N.C.Troops, October 2, 1863.

DAWSON, WILEY, Private
Enlisted in Lenoir County on January 28, 1862, for the war. Present or accounted for until transferred to Company E, 66th Regiment N.C.Troops, October 2, 1863.

DENNIS, WILLIAM N., Sergeant
Resided at "Cartwright" and enlisted in Carteret County on February 11, 1862, for the war. Mustered in as Private and promoted to Sergeant on July 31, 1862. Present or accounted for until transferred to Company E, 66th Regiment N.C. Troops, October 2, 1863.

DUDLEY, WILLIAM G., Corporal
Resided in Pitt County where he enlisted on January 28, 1862, for the war. Promotion record not reported. Present or accounted for until transferred to Company E, 66th Regiment N.C. Troops, October 2, 1863.

DUPREE, FURNIFOLD, Private
Enlisted in Lenoir County on January 28, 1862, for the war. Present or accounted for until transferred to Company E, 66th Regiment N.C. Troops, October 2, 1863.

DUPREE, JESSE F., Private
Resided in Lenoir County where he enlisted on January 28, 1862, for the war. Present or accounted for until transferred to Company E, 66th Regiment N.C. Troops, October 2, 1863.

EDWARDS, LEWIS, Private
Resided in Pitt County where he enlisted on January 28, 1862, for the war. Present or accounted for until transferred to Company E, 66th Regiment N.C. Troops, October 2, 1863.

FOUNTAIN, NORFLEET, Private
Enlisted in Edgecombe County on October 28, 1862, for the war. Present or accounted for until transferred to Company E, 66th Regiment N.C. Troops, October 2, 1863.

GARNER, DEXTON G., Private
Enlisted in Carteret County on February 11, 1862, for the war. Present or accounted for until he was captured by the enemy or deserted at New Bern on March 14, 1862. Dropped from the rolls of the company prior to September 1, 1862.

GARNER, JOHN C., Private
Enlisted in Carteret County on February 24, 1862 for the war. Present or accounted for until transferred to Company E, 66th Regiment N.C. Troops, October 2, 1863.

GARNER, ZEMERIAH, Private
Enlisted in Carteret County on February 11, 1862, for the war. Present or accounted for until he was captured by the enemy or deserted at New Bern on March 14, 1862. Dropped from the rolls of the company on July 31, 1862.

GLANCY, RUFUS, Private
Enlisted in Carteret County on February 11, 1862, for the war. Present or accounted for until transferred to Company E, 66th Regiment N.C. Troops, October 2, 1863.

GLANCY, WILLIAM, Private
Enlisted in Carteret County on February 11, 1862, for the war. Present or accounted for until transferred to Company E, 66th Regiment N.C. Troops, October 2, 1863.

GOULD, JAMES D., Private
Enlisted in Carteret County on February 11, 1862,

for the war. Died in hospital in North Carolina on July 18, 1863, of "febris cont."

GOULD, MICHAEL, Private
Enlisted in Carteret County on February 11, 1862, for the war. Present or accounted for until he was captured by the enemy or deserted at New Bern on March 14, 1862. Dropped from the rolls of the company on July 31, 1862.

GRAY, THOMAS, Private
Enlisted in Lenoir County on January 28, 1862, for the war. Present or accounted for until transferred to Company E, 66th Regiment N.C. Troops, October 2, 1863.

GWALTNEY, FRANKLIN M., Corporal
Enlisted in Pitt County on January 28, 1862, for the war. Mustered in as Private and promoted to Corporal on July 31, 1862. Present or accounted for until transferred to Company E, 66th Regiment N.C. Troops, October 2, 1863.

HARDEE, ABRAM, Private
Enlisted in Pitt County on January 28, 1862, for the war. Present or accounted for until transferred to Company E, 66th Regiment N.C. Troops, October 2, 1863.

HARDEE, JOHN A., Private
Enlisted in Pitt County on January 28, 1862, for the war. Present or accounted for until transferred to Company E, 66th Regiment N.C. Troops, October 2, 1863.

HEATH, IRA, Private
Resided in Lenoir County where he enlisted on January 28, 1862, for the war. Present or accounted for until transferred to Company E, 66th Regiment N.C. Troops, October 2, 1863.

HIBBS, W. H., Private
Enlisted in Carteret County on February 11, 1862, for the war. Present or accounted for until he was captured by the enemy or deserted at New Bern on March 14, 1862. Dropped from the rolls of the company on July 31, 1862.

HIGGINS, RICHARD A., Private
Enlisted in Lenoir County on January 28, 1862, for the war. Present or accounted for until he was "sent to Chapel Hill under a writ of Habeus Corpus" in July-August, 1863. Later served in Company E, 66th Regiment N.C. Troops.

HILL, HATCH B., Private
Enlisted in Carteret County on or about February 11, 1862, for the war as a substitute for Private Josiah L. Bell. Present or accounted for until he was captured by the enemy or deserted at New Bern on March 14, 1862. Dropped from the rolls of the company on July 31, 1862.

HILL, ROBERT P., Private
Enlisted in Lenoir County on January 28, 1862, for the war. Present or accounted for until transferred to Company E, 66th Regiment N.C. Troops, October 2, 1863.

HILL, ROBERT R., Sergeant
Enlisted in Lenoir County on January 28, 1862, for the war. Mustered in as Private and promoted to Sergeant on July 31, 1862. Present or accounted for

until transferred to Company E, 66th Regiment N.C. Troops, October 2, 1863.

HILL, THOMAS, Private

Enlisted in Carteret County on February 11, 1862, for the war. Mustered in as Corporal. Present or accounted for until he was captured by the enemy or deserted at New Bern on March 14, 1862. Reduced to ranks and was dropped from the rolls of the company on July 31, 1862.

HINES, MARION, Private

Enlisted in Lenoir County on March 22, 1863, for the war as a substitute for Private Alexander Tilghman. Present or accounted for until transferred to Company E, 66th Regiment N.C. Troops, October 2, 1863.

HOWARD, WILLIAM, Private

Enlisted in Lenoir County on February 11, 1862, for the war. Present or accounted for until transferred to Company E, 66th Regiment N.C. Troops, October 2, 1863.

IRVIN, JOHN, Private

Enlisted in Lenoir County on January 28, 1862, for the war. Present or accounted for until transferred to Company E, 66th Regiment N.C. Troops, October 2, 1863.

JARRELL, JAMES M., Private

Enlisted in Pitt County on January 28, 1862, for the war. Present or accounted for until transferred to Company E, 66th Regiment N.C. Troops, October 2, 1863.

JENKINS, JOSEPH, Private

Enlisted in Lenoir County on January 28, 1862, for the war. Present or accounted for until transferred to Company E, 66th Regiment N.C. Troops, October 2, 1863.

JOHNSON, W. T., Private

Born in Lenoir County and was by occupation a mechanic prior to enlisting in Lenoir County on January 28, 1862, for the war. Present or accounted for until discharged on August 21, 1862, by reason of "chronic rheumatism." Age given on discharge papers as 25.

JONES, ALEXANDER, Private

Enlisted in Lenoir County on January 28, 1862, for the war. Present or accounted for until transferred to Company E, 66th Regiment N.C. Troops, October 2, 1863.

JONES, WILLIAM L., Private

Enlisted in Lenoir County on January 28, 1862, for the war. Present or accounted for until transferred to Company E, 66th Regiment N.C. Troops, October 2, 1863.

JUMP, FRANK, Private

Enlisted in Lenoir County on January 28, 1862, for the war. Present or accounted for until transferred to Company E, 66th Regiment N.C. Troops, October 2, 1863.

KILPATRICK, WARREN L., Private

Enlisted in Lenoir County on January 28, 1862, for the war. Present or accounted for until transferred to Company A, 8th Battalion N.C. Partisan Rangers, June 7, 1862.

KIRKMAN, LAFAYETTE, Private

Enlisted in Craven County on October 28, 1862, for the war. Present or accounted for until transferred to Company E, 66th Regiment N.C. Troops, October 2, 1863.

LEE, RICHARD, Private

Enlisted in Lenoir County on January 28, 1862, for the war. Present or accounted for until transferred to Company E, 66th Regiment N.C. Troops, October 2, 1863.

McCABE, THOMAS J., Private

Enlisted in Carteret County on February 11, 1862, for the war. Present or accounted for until he was captured by the enemy or deserted at New Bern on March 14, 1862. Dropped from the rolls of the company on July 31, 1862.

McKEEL, EDMUND, Private

Enlisted in Pitt County on July 28, 1862, for the war as a substitute for Private W. A. Speir. Present or accounted for until he deserted on or about December 20, 1862.

McPHERSON, N. J., Private

Enlisted in Lenoir County on January 28, 1862, for the war. Present or accounted for until he was "sent to Chapel Hill under a writ of Habeus Corpus" in July-August, 1863. Later served in Company E, 66th Regiment N.C. Troops.

MANN, JOSEPH B., Private

Enlisted in Carteret County on February 11, 1862, for the war. Present or accounted for until he was captured by the enemy or deserted at New Bern on March 14, 1862. Dropped from the rolls of the company on July 31, 1862.

MAY, J. D., Private

Enlisted in Craven County on February 24, 1862, for the war. Present or accounted for until he was captured by the enemy or deserted at New Bern on March 14, 1862. Dropped from the rolls of the company on July 31, 1862.

MAY, JAMES S., 1st Sergeant

Enlisted in Pitt County on July 10, 1862, for the war. Mustered in as Private and promoted to 1st Sergeant on August 23, 1862. Present or accounted for until transferred to Company E, 66th Regiment N.C. Troops, October 2, 1863.

MOORE, ALLEN, Private

Born in Lenoir County and was by occupation a mechanic prior to enlisting in Lenoir County at age 25, January 28, 1862, for the war. Present or accounted for until transferred to Company E, 66th Regiment N.C. Troops, October 2, 1863.

MOORE, EASON G., Private

Enlisted in Pitt County on January 28, 1862, for the war. Present or accounted for until transferred to Company E, 66th Regiment N.C. Troops, October 2, 1863.

MOORE, JAMES, Private

Enlisted in Jones County on January 28, 1862, for the war. Mustered in as Sergeant but was reduced to ranks prior to June 7, 1862, when he was transferred to Company A, 8th Battalion N.C. Partisan Rangers.

MORTON, CHRISTOPHER, Private
Enlisted in Carteret County on February 24, 1862, for the war. Present or accounted for until he was captured by the enemy or deserted at New Bern on March 14, 1862. Dropped from the rolls of the company on July 31, 1862.

MORTON, LEONARD, Private
Enlisted in Carteret County on February 11, 1862, for the war. Present or accounted for until he was captured by the enemy or deserted at New Bern on March 14, 1862. Dropped from the rolls of the company on July 31, 1862.

NELSON, MATTHEW, Private
Enlisted in Lenoir County on February 11, 1862, for the war. Present or accounted for until transferred to Company E, 66th Regiment N.C. Troops, October 2, 1863.

NOBLES, KINNEY, Private
Enlisted in Lenoir County on January 28, 1862, for the war. Reported absent in arrest at Salisbury for "disloyalty" through June, 1863. Transferred to Company E, 66th Regiment N.C. Troops, October 2, 1863.

OGLESBY, ELIJAH, Private
Enlisted in Carteret County on February 11, 1862, for the war. Present or accounted for until he was captured by the enemy or deserted at New Bern on March 14, 1862. Dropped from the rolls of the company on July 31, 1862.

OGLESBY, RUFUS, Private
Enlisted in Carteret County on February 11, 1862, for the war. Present or accounted for until he was captured by the enemy or deserted at New Bern on March 14, 1862. Dropped from the rolls of the company on July 31, 1862.

PATE, GATLIN, Private
Resided in Lenoir County where he enlisted on January 28, 1862, for the war. Present or accounted for until transferred to Company E, 66th Regiment N.C. Troops, October 2, 1863.

PATE, LENOIR, Private
Resided in Lenoir County where he enlisted on January 28, 1862, for the war. Present or accounted for until transferred to Company E, 66th Regiment N.C. Troops, October 2, 1863.

POWELL, ALFRED, Private
Enlisted in Lenoir County on January 28, 1862, for the war. Present or accounted for until transferred to Company E, 66th Regiment N.C. Troops, October 2, 1863.

QUINERLY, JAMES E., Private
Enlisted in Pitt County on December 19, 1862, for the war. Present or accounted for until he died on July 2, 1863. Place and cause of death not reported.

QUINERLY, JOHN P., Private
Enlisted in Pitt County on January 28, 1862, for the war. Present or accounted for until he died on March 30, 1862. Place and cause of death not reported.

QUINERLY, LEWIS B., Private
Enlisted in Pitt County on January 28, 1862, for the war. Present or accounted for until he died on July 22, 1862. Place and cause of death not reported.

QUINN, ROBERT S., Private
Enlisted in Carteret County on February 11, 1862, for the war. Present or accounted for until transferred to Company E, 66th Regiment N.C. Troops, October 2, 1863.

RANFORD, WILLIAM, Private
Enlisted in Lenoir County on September 27, 1863, for the war. Transferred to Company E, 66th Regiment N.C. Troops, October 2, 1863.

RIDGON, GEORGE W., Private
Enlisted in Craven County on February 24, 1862, for the war. Present or accounted for until he was captured by the enemy or deserted at New Bern on March 14, 1862. Dropped from the rolls of the company on July 31, 1862.

ROBERTS, JAMES, Private
Enlisted in Carteret County on February 11, 1862, for the war. Present or accounted for until he was captured by the enemy or deserted at New Bern on March 14, 1862. Dropped from the rolls of the company on July 31, 1862.

ROSS, T. McGILBERT, Private
Enlisted in Pitt County on August 5, 1862, for the war as a substitute for Private Abram Cox. Present or accounted for until transferred to Company E, 66th Regiment N.C. Troops, October 2, 1863.

ROUSE, ALEXANDER E., Private
Enlisted in Lenoir County on January 28, 1862, for the war. Mustered in as Sergeant but was reduced to ranks on July 31, 1862. Present or accounted for until transferred to Company E, 66th Regiment N.C. Troops, October 2, 1863.

SEVASTON, JOHN, Private
Enlisted in Carteret County on February 11, 1862, for the war. Present or accounted for until he was captured by the enemy or deserted at New Bern on March 14, 1862. Dropped from the rolls of the company on July 31, 1862.

SIMMONS, JOHN W., Private
Enlisted in Jones County on January 28, 1862, for the war. Present or accounted for until transferred to Company A, 8th Battalion N.C. Partisan Rangers, June 7, 1862.

SIMMONS, SIMEON, Private
Resided in Jones County where he enlisted on January 28, 1862, for the war. Present or accounted for until transferred to Company A, 8th Battalion N.C. Partisan Rangers, June 7, 1862.

SIMPKINS, JOHN, Private
Enlisted in Lenoir County on January 28, 1862, for the war. Present or accounted for until he was "detailed on engineer duty" on August 19, 1863. Later served in Company F, 66th Regiment N.C. Troops.

SMITH, HENRY, Private
Enlisted in Pitt County on January 28, 1862, for the war. Present or accounted for until transferred to Company E, 66th Regiment N.C. Troops, October 2, 1863.

SMITH, JOHN, Private
Enlisted in Pitt County on January 28, 1862, for the war. Present or accounted for until transferred to

Company E, 66th Regiment N.C. Troops, October 2, 1863.

SMITH, JOSEPH B., Private
Enlisted in Pitt County on January 28, 1862, for the war. Present or accounted for until transferred to Company E, 66th Regiment N.C. Troops, October 2, 1863.

SMITH, OLIVER, Private
Enlisted in Wayne County on July 31, 1862, for the war as a substitute for Private James Cox. Present or accounted for until transferred to Company D, 8th Battalion N.C. Partisan Rangers, May 12, 1863.

SPEIR, W. A., Private
Enlisted in Pitt County on January 28, 1862, for the war. Present or accounted for until discharged on or about July 28, 1862, after providing Private Edmund McKeel as a substitute.

STOKES, BENJAMIN F., Private
Enlisted in Pitt County on January 28, 1862, for the war. Present or accounted for until transferred to Company E, 66th Regiment N.C. Troops, October 2, 1863.

STOKES, CALVIN, Sergeant
Enlisted in Pitt County on January 28, 1862, for the war. Mustered in as Sergeant. Present or accounted for until discharged on or about August 9, 1862, after providing Private Edmund Stokes as a substitute.

STOKES, EDMUND, Private
Enlisted in Pitt County on August 9, 1862, for the war as a substitute for Sergeant Calvin Stokes. Present or accounted for until transferred to Company E, 66th Regiment N.C. Troops, October 2, 1863.

STOKES, GEORGE B., Private
Enlisted in Pitt County on January 28, 1862, for the war. Present or accounted for until he died on April 17, 1863. Place and cause of death not reported.

STOKES, GUILFORD, Private
Enlisted in Pitt County on December 26, 1862, for the war. Present or accounted for until transferred to Company E, 66th Regiment N.C. Troops, October 2, 1863.

STRICKLAND, CYRUS, Private
Enlisted in Lenoir County on January 28, 1862, for the war. Present or accounted for until transferred to Company E, 66th Regiment N.C. Troops, October 2, 1863.

SUGG, JAMES N., Private
Enlisted in Lenoir County on January 28, 1862, for the war. Present or accounted for until transferred to Company E, 66th Regiment N.C. Troops, October 2, 1863.

SUTTON, JOHN, Private
Enlisted in Lenoir County on January 28, 1862, for the war. Present or accounted for until transferred to Company E, 66th Regiment N.C. Troops, October 2, 1863.

SUTTON, RICHARD, Private
Enlisted in Lenoir County on January 28, 1862, for the war. Present or accounted for until transferred to Company E, 66th Regiment N.C. Troops, October 2, 1863.

TAYLOR, JOHN E., Sergeant
Resided in Lenoir County and was by occupation a farmer prior to enlisting in Lenoir County on January 28, 1862, for the war. Mustered in as Private and promoted to Corporal in January-February, 1863. Promoted to Sergeant in May-June, 1863. Present or accounted for until transferred to Company E, 66th Regiment N.C. Troops, October 2, 1863.

TAYLOR, THOMAS W., Private
Enlisted in Carteret County on February 11, 1862, for the war. Present or accounted for until he was captured by the enemy or deserted at New Bern on March 14, 1862. Dropped from the rolls of the company on July 31, 1862.

THIGPEN, JAMES, Private
Enlisted in Lenoir County on January 28, 1862, for the war. Present or accounted for until transferred to Company A, 8th Battalion N.C. Partisan Rangers, June 7, 1862.

TILGHMAN, ALEXANDER, Private
Enlisted in Jones County on January 28, 1862, for the war. Present or accounted for until discharged on or about March 22, 1863, after providing Private Marion Hines as a substitute.

TURNER, JOHN, Private
Enlisted in Lenoir County on January 28, 1862, for the war. Present or accounted for until transferred to Company A, 8th Battalion N.C. Partisan Rangers, June 7, 1862.

WADSWORTH, JOHN B., Private
Enlisted in Pitt County on February 17, 1862, for the war. Present or accounted for until he was captured by the enemy or deserted at New Bern on March 14, 1862. Dropped from the rolls of the company on July 31, 1862.

WARTERS, AUGUSTUS, Private
Enlisted in Lenoir County on January 28, 1862, for the war. Present or accounted for until transferred to Company E, 66th Regiment N.C. Troops, October 2, 1863.

WARTERS, JESSE, Private
Enlisted in Lenoir County on January 28, 1862, for the war. Mustered in as Private and promoted to Corporal on July 31, 1862. Reduced to ranks in May-June, 1863. Present or accounted for until he was "released by civil authority" on August 7, 1863.

WARTERS, WILLIAM D., Private
Enlisted in Lenoir County on January 28, 1862, for the war. Present or accounted for until he was "released by civil authority" on August 7, 1863.

WATSON, SPENCER O., Private
Enlisted in Lenoir County on January 28, 1862, for the war. Present or accounted for until transferred to Company E, 66th Regiment N.C. Troops, October 2, 1863.

WHITE, LEWIS C., Private
Enlisted in Lenoir County on January 28, 1862, for the war. Present or accounted for until reported absent without leave on May 24, 1862. Returned to duty in September-October, 1862, and present or accounted for until transferred to Company E, 66th Regiment N.C. Troops, October 2, 1863.

WILLIAMS, JOHN L., Private
Enlisted in Lenoir County on January 28, 1862, for the war. Present or accounted for until transferred to Company E, 66th Regiment N.C. Troops, October 2, 1863.

WILSON, ROBERT, Private
Enlisted in Pitt County on January 28, 1862, for the war. Present or accounted for until transferred to Company E, 66th Regiment N.C.Troops, October 2, 1863.

WITHERINGTON, JAMES G., Sergeant
Resided in Pitt County where he enlisted on January 28, 1862, for the war. Mustered in as Private and promoted to Sergeant on July 31, 1862. Present or accounted for until transferred to Company E, 66th Regiment N.C.Troops, October 2, 1863.

WITHERINGTON, LEMUEL K., Corporal
Enlisted in Pitt County on January 28, 1862, for the war. Mustered in as Private and promoted to Corporal in May-June, 1863. Present or accounted for until transferred to Company E, 66th Regiment N.C.Troops, October 2, 1863.

WOOD, ISAIAH, Private
Born in Jones County and was by occupation a jailer prior to enlisting in Lenoir County on January 28, 1862, for the war. Present or accounted for until discharged on August 18, 1862. Reason discharged not reported. Age given on discharge papers as 41.

WORLIE, DAVID, Private
Resided in Halifax County and was by occupation a farmer prior to enlisting in Lenoir County on January 28, 1862, for the war. Present or accounted for until transferred to Company E, 66th Regiment N.C. Troops, October 2, 1863.

COMPANY D

This company was from New Hanover County. It was mustered into Confederate States service at Wilmington on January 25, 1862, and was designated Captain John L. Cantwell's Company, N.C. Volunteers, Wilmington Railroad Guard. On January 27 the company was detailed to guard the bridge over the Roanoke River at Weldon and also the bridges on the Wilmington & Manchester and Wilmington & Weldon railroads from the South Carolina line to the Roanoke River. The company was stationed at Wilmington and detachments were sent out to protect strategic points along the two railroads. On April 15, 1862, thirty-eight members of the company were transferred to the 51st Regiment N.C. Troops. The headquarters of the company remained at Wilmington until May-June, 1862, when it was moved to Goldsboro. Detachments from the company continued to guard points along the railroads throughout 1862 and early 1863. During that period the company remained independent even though it was referred to as Company A, Wilmington & Weldon Railroad Guards, N.C. Infantry.

The company was assigned to the 13th Battalion N.C. Infantry on May 19, 1863, and was designated Company D. By Special Orders No. 234, Adjutant and Inspector General's Office, Richmond, October 2, 1863, the company was assigned to the 66th Regiment

N.C. Troops and became Company K of that regiment.

The information contained in the following roster of the company was compiled principally from company muster rolls for January 25, 1862, through June, 1863. No company muster rolls were found for the period after June, 1863. In addition to the company muster rolls, Roll of Honor records, receipt rolls, hospital records, prisoner of war records, and other primary records, supplemented by state pension applications, United Daughters of the Confederacy records, and postwar rosters and histories, all provided useful information.

OFFICERS

CAPTAINS

CANTWELL, JOHN LUCAS
Born at Charleston, South Carolina, and was by occupation a cotton broker prior to enlisting in New Hanover County at age 33. Appointed Captain on or about December 10, 1861. Present or accounted for until transferred to the 51st Regiment N.C.Troops upon appointment as Colonel to rank from April 30, 1862.

BRADBERRY, JOHN J.
Previously served as 2nd Lieutenant in Company D, 4th Regiment N.C. State Troops. Appointed 1st Lieutenant in this company on or about January 25, 1862. Promoted to Captain in May-June, 1862. Present or accounted for through April, 1863. No further records.

FREEMAN, WILLIAM H.
Place of enlistment not reported. Mustered in as 1st Lieutenant; however, date of rank not reported. First listed on the rolls of this company in May-June, 1862. Promoted to Captain in May-June, 1863. Present or accounted for until transferred to Company K, 66th Regiment N.C.Troops, October 2, 1863.

LIEUTENANTS

GILBERT, EUGENE F., 1st Lieutenant
Place of enlistment not reported. Mustered in as 2nd Lieutenant; however, date of rank not reported. First listed on the rolls of this company in May-June, 1862. Promoted to 1st Lieutenant in May-June, 1863. Present or accounted for until transferred to Company K, 66th Regiment N.C.Troops, October 2, 1863.

PRIVETT, WILLIAM R., 3rd Lieutenant
Enlisted in Wayne County on June 25, 1862, for the war. Mustered in as Private and appointed 3rd Lieutenant in May-June, 1863. Present or accounted for until transferred to Company K, 66th Regiment N.C.Troops, October 2, 1863.

SMITH, WILLIAM, 3rd Lieutenant
Born in New Hanover County and was by occupation an agent prior to enlisting in New Hanover County at age 27. Appointed 3rd Lieutenant on or about January 20, 1862. No further records.

SOUTHERLAND, EDWARD, 2nd Lieutenant
Previously served as Private in 1st Company C, 12th Regiment N.C.Troops (2nd Regiment N.C.Volunteers). Appointed 2nd Lieutenant in this company on

or about December 12, 1861. Present or accounted for until promoted to 1st Lieutenant on April 15, 1862, and transferred to Company A, 51st Regiment N.C.Troops.

SYKES, JOHN T., 2nd Lieutenant
Enlisted in New Hanover County on May 1, 1862, for the war. Mustered in as 1st Sergeant and was appointed 3rd Lieutenant in September-October, 1862. Promoted to 2nd Lieutenant in May-June, 1863. Present or accounted for until transferred to Company K, 66th Regiment N.C.Troops, October 2, 1863.

NONCOMMISSIONED OFFICERS AND PRIVATES

ADAMS, JOHN A., Private
Born in Johnston County and was by occupation a farmer prior to enlisting in Wayne County at age 17, December 28, 1861, for the war. Present or accounted for until he died in hospital at Wilmington on February 25, 1862, of "catarrhus."

ANDERSON, HENRY, Private
Born in Wayne County and was by occupation a farmer prior to enlisting in Wayne County at age 17, January 11, 1862, for the war. Present or accounted for until transferred to Company K, 66th Regiment N.C.Troops, October 2, 1863.

ATKINSON, THOMAS, Private
Born in Johnston County and was by occupation a farmer prior to enlisting in New Hanover County at age 34, January 25, 1862, for the war. Present or accounted for until transferred to Company A, 51st Regiment N.C.Troops, April 15, 1862.

BAGLEY, ALVIN, Private
Enlisted in Wayne County on July 5, 1862, for the war. Present or accounted for until transferred to Company K, 66th Regiment N.C.Troops, October 2, 1863.

BAILEY, ALFRED, Musician
Enlisted in Wayne County on June 21, 1862, for the war. Mustered in as Private and promoted to Musician (Drummer) in May-June, 1863. Present or accounted for until transferred to Company K, 66th Regiment N.C.Troops, October 2, 1863.

BAILEY, JOHN H., Private
Born in Edgecombe County and resided in Wilson County where he was by occupation a farmer prior to enlisting in Wilson County at age 19, January 1, 1862, for the war. Present or accounted for until transferred to Company K, 66th Regiment N.C. Troops, October 2, 1863.

BAILEY, WILLIAM W., Private
Born in Edgecombe County and was by occupation a farmer or musician prior to enlisting in Wilson County at age 20, January 1, 1862, for the war. Present or accounted for until transferred to Company K, 66th Regiment N.C.Troops, October 2, 1863.

BALKCUM, HARMON, Private
Born in Sampson County and was by occupation a farmer prior to enlisting in Duplin County at age 40, January 4, 1862, for the war. Present or accounted

for until he died on April 8, 1863. Place and cause of death not reported.

BARNES, CLINTON, Private
Born in Nash County and was by occupation a farmer prior to enlisting in New Hanover County at age 17, January 16, 1862, for the war. Present or accounted for until transferred to Company K, 66th Regiment N.C.Troops, October 2, 1863.

BARNES, EDWIN, Sergeant
Born in Wilson County* and was by occupation a farmer prior to enlisting in Wilson County at age 18, January 9, 1862, for the war. Mustered in as Private and promoted to Sergeant in June, 1863. Present or accounted for until transferred to Company K, 66th Regiment N.C.Troops, October 2, 1863.

BARRINGTON, JOSEPH J., Private
Enlisted in Wayne County on January 25, 1862, for the war. Present or accounted for until he deserted on August 16, 1863.

BEEZLEY, EZEKIEL, Private
Enlisted in Wayne County on September 7, 1862, for the war as a substitute. Present or accounted for until transferred to Company K, 66th Regiment N.C. Troops, October 2, 1863.

BLAND, WILLIAM W., Private
Resided in Duplin County and enlisted in Wayne County on July 12, 1862, for the war. Present or accounted for until transferred to Company K, 66th Regiment N.C.Troops, October 2, 1863.

BLANTON, ENOCH, Private
Born in Duplin County or in Horry District, South Carolina, and was by occupation a farmer prior to enlisting in Duplin County at age 29, December 29, 1861, for the war. Present or accounted for until transferred to Company G, 51st Regiment N.C. Troops, April 15, 1862.

BLANTON, JOSEPH J., Private
Born in New Hanover County and was by occupation a farmer prior to enlisting in Duplin County at age 39, December 29, 1861, for the war. Present or accounted for until transferred to Company G, 51st Regiment N.C.Troops, April 15, 1862.

BOSTICK, DANIEL J., Private
Born in Duplin County where he resided as a farmer prior to enlisting in Duplin County at age 21, December 20, 1861, for the war. Present or accounted for until transferred to Company C, 51st Regiment N.C.Troops, April 15, 1862.

BOSTICK, DAVID R., Private
Previously served in 1st Company C, 12th Regiment N.C.Troops (2nd Regiment N.C.Volunteers). Enlisted in this company on December 20, 1861, for the war. Present or accounted for until transferred to Company C, 51st Regiment N.C.Troops, April 15, 1862.

BOSWELL, JAMES T., Private
Born in Wilson County* and was by occupation a farmer prior to enlisting in Wilson County at age 18, January 20, 1862, for the war. Present or accounted for until transferred to Company K, 66th Regiment N.C.Troops, October 2, 1863.

BOSWELL, JOHN A., Private
Born in Wilson County* and was by occupation a farmer prior to enlisting in Wilson County at age 21, January 9, 1862, for the war. Present or accounted for until transferred to Company K, 66th Regiment N.C.Troops, October 2, 1863.

BRADLEY, BENJAMIN, Private
Born in Duplin County and was by occupation a farmer prior to enlisting in New Hanover County at age 40, January 20, 1862, for the war. Present or accounted for until transferred to Company K, 66th Regiment N.C.Troops, October 2, 1863.

BRADY, LEVI H., Private
Previously served in Company F, 10th Regiment N.C. State Troops (1st Regiment N.C. Artillery). Transferred to this company on August 28, 1863, in exchange for Private Mathew T. Johnson. Present or accounted for until transferred to Company K, 66th Regiment N.C. Troops, October 2, 1863.

BRINSON, JOHN, Private
Previously served in 1st Company C, 12th Regiment N.C.Troops (2nd Regiment N.C.Volunteers). Enlisted in this company on December 10, 1861, for the war. Present or accounted for until transferred to Company A, 51st Regiment N.C.Troops, April 15, 1862.

BROCK, DAVID, Private
Born in Wayne County and was by occupation a farmer prior to enlisting in Wayne County at age 24, January 1, 1862, for the war. Present or accounted for until transferred to Company K, 66th Regiment N.C.Troops, October 2, 1863.

BROGDEN, BENJAMIN H., Private
Enlisted in Wayne County on June 27, 1862, for the war. Present or accounted for until he died April 19, 1863. Place and cause of death not reported.

BROWN, RICHARD, Private
Born in Lenoir County and was by occupation a painter prior to enlisting in Wayne County at age 21, December 23, 1861, for the war. Present or accounted for through June, 1863. No further records.

BRYANT, ROBERT C., Private
Enlisted in Wayne County on February 11, 1863, for the war as a substitute. Present or accounted for until transferred to Company K, 66th Regiment N.C. Troops, October 2, 1863.

BYRD, BENJAMIN R., Private
Born in Lenoir County and was by occupation a farmer prior to enlisting in Wayne County at age 34, January 1, 1862, for the war. Present or accounted for until transferred to Company K, 66th Regiment N.C.Troops, October 2, 1863.

BYRD, JAMES F., Private
Born in Duplin County and was by occupation a farmer prior to enlisting in Duplin County at age 21, December 29, 1861, for the war. Present or accounted for until transferred to Company A, 51st Regiment N.C.Troops, April 15, 1862.

BYRD, WILLIAM BENJAMIN, Private
Born in Duplin County and was by occupation a farmer prior to enlisting in Duplin County at age 24, December 29, 1861, for the war. Present or accounted for until transferred to Company A, 51st Regiment N. C.Troops, April 15, 1862.

CANFEL, JOHN, Private
Born in Tipperary, Ireland, and was by occupation a laborer prior to enlisting in Duplin County at age 31, December 29, 1861, for the war. Present or accounted for until transferred to Company A, 51st Regiment N.C.Troops, April 15, 1862.

CAPPS, JOHN, Private
Enlisted in Wayne County on March 9, 1863, for the war. Present or accounted for until transferred to Company K, 66th Regiment N.C.Troops, October 2, 1863.

CAPPS, WILLIAM, Private
Enlisted in Wayne County on March 9, 1863, for the war. Present or accounted for until transferred to Company K, 66th Regiment N.C.Troops, October 2, 1863.

CARMACK, SAMUEL, Private
Born in Craven County and was by occupation a carriage maker prior to enlisting in Wayne County at age 19, January 11, 1862, for the war. Present or accounted for until transferred to Company A, 51st Regiment N.C.Troops, April 15, 1862.

CARROLL, JOHN C., Private
Born in Duplin County where he resided as a farmer prior to enlisting in Duplin County at age 18, December 29, 1861, for the war. Present or accounted for until transferred to Company B, 51st Regiment N.C.Troops, April 15, 1862.

CHESNUTT, JOHN K., Private
Born in Sampson County and was by occupation a farmer prior to enlisting in Duplin County at age 18, January 17, 1862, for the war. Present or accounted for until transferred to Company C, 51st Regiment N.C.Troops, April 15, 1862.

COKER, WINDSOR C., Private
Born in Lenoir County and was by occupation a farmer or painter prior to enlisting in Lenoir County at age 35, December 29, 1861, for the war. Present or accounted for through February, 1863. No further records.

CORNISH, BRITTON, Private
Born in Wilson County* and was by occupation a farmer prior to enlisting in Wilson County at age 19, January 2, 1862, for the war. Present or accounted for until he died at Wilson on or about February 28, 1862. Cause of death not reported.

CORNISH, WILEY, Private
Born in Wilson County* and was by occupation a farmer prior to enlisting in Wilson County at age 23, January 2, 1862, for the war. Present or accounted for until transferred to Company K, 66th Regiment N.C.Troops, October 2, 1863.

COX, JAMES WOODARD, Private
Enlisted in Wayne County on June 22, 1862, for the war. Present or accounted for until transferred to Company K, 66th Regiment N.C. Troops, October 2, 1863.

COX, W. B., Private
Place and date of enlistment not reported. Name appears on a company muster roll dated May-June, 1862, which states that he was present. [May have

served later in Company B, 8th Battalion N.C. Partisan Rangers.]

CRAFT, THOMAS C., Private
Born in Bertie County and was by occupation a farmer prior to enlisting in Wilson County at age 45, January 1, 1862, for the war. Present or accounted for until transferred to Company K, 66th Regiment N.C.Troops, October 2, 1863.

CRAWFORD, JOHN H., Private
Enlisted in Wayne County on June 27, 1862, for the war. Present or accounted for until he deserted at Sessom's Mill on June 18, 1863.

CRAWFORD, LEONARD H., Private
Enlisted in Wayne County on June 27, 1862, for the war. Present or accounted for until transferred to Company K, 66th Regiment N.C.Troops, October 2, 1863.

CREECH, HAYWOOD, Private
Enlisted in Wayne County on July 5, 1862, for the war. Present or accounted for until transferred to Company K, 66th Regiment N.C.Troops, October 2, 1863.

CREECH, JOSIAH, Private
Enlisted in Wayne County on July 5, 1862, for the war. Present or accounted for until transferred to Company K, 66th Regiment N.C.Troops, October 2, 1863.

CREECH, LARKIN, Private
Enlisted in Wayne County on February 28, 1863, for the war. Present or accounted for until transferred to Company K, 66th Regiment N.C.Troops, October 2, 1863.

CREECH, THOMAS, Private
Resided in Johnston County and enlisted in Wayne County on July 5, 1862, for the war. Present or accounted for until transferred to Company K, 66th Regiment N.C.Troops, October 2, 1863.

CROOM, WILLIAM H., Private
Born in Lenoir County and was by occupation a carriage maker prior to enlisting in Lenoir County at age 48, January 6, 1862, for the war. Present or accounted for until transferred to Company K, 66th Regiment N. C.Troops, October 2, 1863.

DANIEL, MATTHEW Mc., Private
Born in Wayne County and was by occupation a mechanic prior to enlisting in Wayne County at age 34, December 28, 1861, for the war. Present or accounted for until discharged on September 1, 1862, by reason of "an ulcer of the right leg with enlargement of the bone."

DEAN, FELIX G., Private
Enlisted in Wayne County on July 13, 1862, for the war. Present or accounted for until discharged on September 1, 1862. Reason discharged not reported.

DEANS, GEORGE C., Private
Enlisted in Wayne County on July 13, 1862, for the war. Died July 28, 1862. Place and cause of death not reported.

DICKSON, EVERETT, Private
Born in Wayne County and was by occupation a farmer prior to enlisting in Wayne County at age 17, January 11, 1862, for the war. Present or accounted

for until transferred to Company K, 66th Regiment N.C.Troops, October 2, 1863.

EDWARDS, E. A., Private
Enlisted in Wayne County on July 16, 1862, for the war. Present or accounted for through December, 1862. No further records.

EDWARDS, GABRIEL, Corporal
Born in Wayne County and was by occupation a farmer prior to enlisting in Wayne County at age 44, January 11, 1862, for the war. Mustered in as Private and promoted to Corporal prior to March 1, 1862. Present or accounted for through February, 1863. No further records.

EDWARDS, JAMES W., Private
Enlisted in Wayne County on July 16, 1862, for the war. Present or accounted for until transferred to Company K, 66th Regiment N.C.Troops, October 2, 1863.

ELLIS, THOMAS W., Corporal
Born in Wilson County* and was by occupation a teacher prior to enlisting in Wilson County at age 22, January 9, 1862, for the war. Mustered in as Private and promoted to Corporal in May-June, 1862. Present or accounted for until transferred to Company K, 66th Regiment N.C.Troops, October 2, 1863.

ELLISON, CHARLES W., Private
Born at "New Salem" and was by occupation a trader prior to enlisting in Lenoir County at age 17, August 17, 1863, for the war. Deserted to the enemy on September 11, 1863, and took the Oath of Allegiance at New Bern on September 29, 1863.

ENNIS, JAMES, Private
Born in Duplin County and was by occupation a farmer prior to enlisting in New Hanover County at age 22, January 21, 1862, for the war. Present or accounted for until transferred to Company A, 51st Regiment N.C.Troops, April 15, 1862.

EPPS, PETER, Private
Born in Greene County and was by occupation a coach maker prior to enlisting in New Hanover County at age 32, January 12, 1862, for the war. Present or accounted for until discharged on April 12, 1862. Reason discharged not reported.

EVANS, ELISHA, Private
Enlisted in Wayne County on July 1, 1862, for the war. Mustered in as Musician (Drummer) but was reduced to ranks in March-April, 1863. Present or accounted for until transferred to Company K, 66th Regiment N.C.Troops, October 2, 1863.

EVANS, JOHN D., Private
Born in Duplin County where he resided as a farmer prior to enlisting in Duplin County at age 22, January 17, 1862, for the war. Present or accounted for until transferred to Company K, 66th Regiment N.C.Troops, October 2, 1863.

FARMER, JAMES, Private
Born in Wilson County* and was by occupation a farmer prior to enlisting in Wilson County at age 18, January 2, 1862, for the war. Present or accounted for until he died at Wilson on January 14, 1862. Cause of death not reported.

FARMER, MOSES B., Private
Born in Wayne County and was by occupation a
farmer prior to enlisting in Wayne County at age 26,
December 24, 1861, for the war. Present or accounted for until transferred to Company K, 66th Regiment N.C.Troops, October 2, 1863.

FARMER, PHILIP R., Private
Resided in Wilson County and enlisted in Wayne
County on June 1, 1862, for the war. Present or
accounted for until transferred to Company K, 66th
Regiment N.C.Troops, October 2, 1863.

FIELDS, WILLIAM B., Private
Born in Wayne County where he resided as a farmer
prior to enlisting in Wayne County at age 16,
December 24, 1861, for the war. Present or accounted for until transferred to Company C, 51st Regiment N.C.Troops, April 15, 1862.

FLOREY, JAMES, Private
Born in Wilson County* and was by occupation a
farmer prior to enlisting in Wilson County at age 17,
January 2, 1862, for the war. Present or accounted
for until transferred to Company K, 66th Regiment
N.C. Troops, October 2, 1863.

FULGUM, ROBERT L., Private
Born in Wayne County and was by occupation a
farmer prior to enlisting in New Hanover County at
age 17, January 12, 1862, for the war. Present or
accounted for until transferred to Company A, 51st
Regiment N.C.Troops, April 15, 1862.

GARRIS, ICHABOD P., Corporal
Enlisted in Wayne County on June 27, 1862, for the
war. Mustered in as Private and promoted to
Corporal on June 1, 1863. Present or accounted for
until transferred to Company K, 66th Regiment
N.C. Troops, October 2, 1863.

GAY, HENRY, Private
Born in Edgecombe County and was by occupation a
farmer prior to enlisting in Wayne County at age 49,
December 29, 1861, for the war. Present or accounted for until he died on November 22, 1862. Place
and cause of death not reported.

GILBERT, FRED G., Private
Enlisted in Wayne County on March 15, 1863, for
the war. Present or accounted for until he died at
Goldsboro on June 6, 1863. Cause of death not
reported.

GLISSON, BRYANT, Private
Born in Duplin County and was by occupation a
farmer prior to enlisting in Wayne County at age 29,
January 20, 1862, for the war. Present or accounted
for until transferred to Company K, 66th Regiment
N.C.Troops, October 2, 1863.

GUY, JOHN J., Private
Previously served in 1st Company C, 12th Regiment
N.C.Troops (2nd Regiment N.C.Volunteers). Enlisted in this company on December 20, 1861, for the
war. Present or accounted for until transferred to
Company A, 51st Regiment N.C.Troops, April 15,
1862.

HALL, EDWARD J., Corporal
Previously served as Private in 1st Company C, 12th
Regiment N.C.Troops (2nd Regiment N.C.Volun-
teers). Enlisted in this company on January 10, 1862,

for the war. Promotion record not reported. Present
or accounted for until transferred to Company C,
51st Regiment N.C.Troops, April 15, 1862.

HALL, JEREMIAH P., 1st Sergeant
Previously served as Private in 1st Company C, 12th
Regiment N.C.Troops (2nd Regiment N.C.Volun-
teers). Enlisted in this company on December 20,
1861, for the war. Mustered in as 1st Sergeant.
Present or accounted for until transferred to Company A, 51st Regiment N.C.Troops, April 15, 1862.

HAMILTON, BARDON B., Private
Enlisted in Wayne County on June 1, 1862, for the
war. Present or accounted for until transferred to
Company K, 66th Regiment N.C.Troops, October 2,
1863.

HARRELL, JOHN W. W., Sergeant
Born in Wayne County and was by occupation a
farmer prior to enlisting in Wayne County at age 25,
January 1, 1862, for the war. Mustered in as Sergeant. Present or accounted for until transferred to
Company A, 51st Regiment N.C.Troops, April 15,
1862.

HAWES, REUBEN J. T., Sergeant
Previously served as Private in 1st Company C, 12th
Regiment N.C.Troops (2nd Regiment N.C.Volun-
teers). Enlisted in this company on December 18,
1861, for the war. Mustered in as Sergeant. Present
or accounted for until transferred to Company A,
51st Regiment N.C.Troops, April 15, 1862.

HAZELL, H. S., Private
Enlisted in Wayne County on June 26, 1862, for the
war. Present or accounted for through August, 1862.
No further records.

HIGGINS, I., Private
Place and date of enlistment not reported. Name
appears on an undated muster roll of this company.
No further records.

HILL, GEORGE, Private
Enlisted in Wayne County on June 26, 1862, for the
war. Present or accounted for until transferred to
Company K, 66th Regiment N.C.Troops, October 2,
1863.

HILL, WILLIAM F., Private
Enlisted in Wayne County on June 26, 1862, for the
war. Present or accounted for until transferred to
Company K, 66th Regiment N.C.Troops, October 2,
1863.

HINNANT, CLAUD S., Private
Resided in Johnston County and enlisted in Wayne
County on July 5, 1862, for the war. Present or
accounted for until transferred to Company K, 66th
Regiment N.C.Troops, October 2, 1862.

HINSON, ELIJAH, Private
Born in Wayne County and was by occupation a
farmer prior to enlisting in Wayne County at age 18,
January 2, 1862, for the war. Present or accounted
for until transferred to Company A, 51st Regiment
N.C.Troops, April 15, 1862.

HOWELL, JETHRO H., Private
Resided in Johnston County and was by occupation a
farmer prior to enlisting in Wayne County on July 5,
1862, for the war. Present or accounted for until

transferred to Company K, 66th Regiment N.C. Troops, October 2, 1863.

HUGGINS, CHARLES W., Private
Born in Duplin County and was by occupation a farmer prior to enlisting in Wayne County at age 45, January 1, 1862, for the war. Present or accounted for until transferred to Company K, 66th Regiment N.C.Troops, October 2, 1863.

HUGHES, JOSEPH, Private
Born in Wayne County and was by occupation a farmer prior to enlisting in New Hanover County at age 26, January 20, 1862, for the war. Present or accounted for until discharged on August 10, 1863. Reason discharged not reported.

HUNT, CALVIN, Private
Born in Wilson County* and was by occupation a farmer prior to enlisting in Wilson County at age 18, January 2, 1862, for the war. Present or accounted for until transferred to Company A, 51st Regiment N.C.Troops, April 15, 1862.

HUSSEY, JOHN E., Sergeant
Previously served as Corporal in 1st Company C, 12th Regiment N.C. Troops (2nd Regiment N.C. Volunteers). Enlisted in this company on December 20, 1861, for the war. Promotion record not reported. Present or accounted for until transferred to Company C, 51st Regiment N.C. Troops, April 15, 1862.

INGRAM, SHUBE S., Private
Enlisted in Wayne County on June 26, 1862, for the war. Present or accounted for until transferred to Company K, 66th Regiment N.C.Troops, October 2, 1863.

IRVING, JOHN, Private
Place and date of enlistment not reported. Name appears on an undated muster roll of this company. No further records.

JACKSON, MAJOR, Private
Born in Lenoir County and was by occupation a farmer prior to enlisting in Lenoir County at age 18, January 7, 1862, for the war. Present or accounted for until hospitalized at Wilmington on or about February 12, 1862, with "febris intermittens tert." Hospital records indicate he was "taken home by his mother" and died March 16, 1862. Place and cause of death not reported.

JACKSON, ORREN L., 1st Sergeant
Born in Edgecombe County and was by occupation a laborer prior to enlisting in New Hanover County at age 26, January 23, 1862, for the war. Mustered in as Private and promoted to Sergeant in May-June, 1862. Promoted to 1st Sergeant in September-October, 1862. Present or accounted for until transferred to Company K, 66th Regiment N.C.Troops, October 2, 1863.

JACKSON, WILLIAM M., Private
Born in Edgecombe County and was by occupation a carpenter prior to enlisting in Wilson County at age 45, January 9, 1862, for the war. Mustered in as Private and promoted to Corporal prior to March 1, 1862. Promoted to Sergeant in July-August, 1862, but was reduced to ranks on June 1, 1863. Present or accounted for until transferred to Company K, 66th

Regiment N.C.Troops, October 2, 1863.

JINNETT, JOHN G., Private
Enlisted in Wayne County on June 26, 1862, for the war. Present or accounted for until transferred to Company K, 66th Regiment N.C.Troops, October 2, 1863.

JOHNSON, HARDY, Private
Born in Sampson County and was by occupation a laborer prior to enlisting in Wayne County at age 49, January 11, 1862, for the war. Present or accounted for until discharged on February 2, 1863, by reason of disability.

JOHNSON, JOHN W., Private
Born in Wilson County* and was by occupation a farmer prior to enlisting in New Hanover County at age 24, January 9, 1862, for the war. Present or accounted for until transferred to Company K, 66th Regiment N.C.Troops, October 2, 1863.

JOHNSON, MATHEW T., Private
Enlisted in Wayne County on June 25, 1862, for the war. Present or accounted for until he was "exchanged" for Private Levi H. Brady of Company F, 10th Regiment N.C. State Troops (1st Regiment N.C. Artillery) on August 28, 1863. Records of the latter unit do not indicate that he served therein. No further records.

JONES, CRAVEN S., Private
Born in Lenoir County and was by occupation a carpenter prior to enlisting in Lenoir County at age 50, January 11, 1862, for the war. Present or accounted for through February, 1863. No further records.

JONES, STEPHEN H., Private
Born in Lenoir County and was by occupation a farmer prior to enlisting in Wayne County at age 24, January 1, 186-. No further records. [May have served later in Company C, 8th Battalion N.C. Partisan Rangers.]

JONES, WILLIAM D., Private
Born in Jones County and was by occupation a farmer prior to enlisting in Wayne County at age 36, January 11, 1862, for the war. Present or accounted for until transferred to Company K, 66th Regiment N.C.Troops, October 2, 1863.

KEATON, WILLIAM SOL, Private
Enlisted in Wayne County on June 25, 1862, for the war. Present or accounted for through October, 1862. No further records.

KING, JAMES A., Private
Enlisted in Wayne County on July 10, 1862, for the war. Present or accounted for until transferred to Company K, 66th Regiment N.C.Troops, October 2, 1863.

KNOWLES, DAVID J., Private
Enlisted in Wayne County on July 10, 1862, for the war. Present or accounted for until transferred to Company K, 66th Regiment N.C.Troops, October 2, 1863.

KNOWLES, STEPHEN, Private
Born in Duplin County and was by occupation a farmer prior to enlisting in Duplin County at age 25, December 29, 1861, for the war. Present or account-

ed for until transferred to Company G, 51st Regiment N.C.Troops, April 15, 1862.

LAMM, JONAS, Private
Resided in Wilson County where he enlisted on June 25, 1862, for the war. Present or accounted for until transferred to Company K, 66th Regiment N.C. Troops, October 2, 1863.

LAMM, THOMAS J., Private
Enlisted in Wilson County on June 21, 1862, for the war. Present or accounted for until transferred to Company K, 66th Regiment N.C. Troops, October 2, 1863.

LANE, DAVID B., Private
Born in Wayne County and was by occupation a farmer prior to enlisting in Wayne County at age 19, December 28, 1861, for the war. Present or accounted for until transferred to Company K, 66th Regiment N.C.Troops, October 2, 1863.

LANE, ISAAC M., Private
Enlisted in Wayne County on June 26, 1862, for the war. Present or accounted for through June, 1863. [May have served later in Company K, 66th Regiment N.C. Troops.]

LANE, JOHN, Private
Born in Wayne County where he resided as a farmer prior to enlisting in Wayne County at age 43, December 24, 1861, for the war. Present or accounted for until transferred to Company K, 66th Regiment N.C.Troops, October 2, 1863.

LANE, JOHN W., Private
Enlisted in Wayne County on June 28, 1862, for the war. Present or accounted for until transferred to Company K, 66th Regiment N.C. Troops, October 2, 1863.

LANGSTON, LITTLETON, Private
Born in Wayne County and was by occupation a farmer prior to enlisting in Wayne County at age 19, January 5, 1862, for the war. Present or accounted for until transferred to Company K, 66th Regiment N.C.Troops, October 2, 1863.

LEWIS, DAVID, Private
Enlisted in Wayne County on July 10, 1862, for the war. Present or accounted for until transferred to Company K, 66th Regiment N.C.Troops, October 2, 1863.

LEWIS, HILLSMAN, Private
Born in Wilson County* where he resided as a farmer prior to enlisting in Wilson County at age 19, January 9, 1862, for the war. Present or accounted for until transferred to Company A, 51st Regiment N.C.Troops, April 15, 1862.

LONG, WILLIAM HENRY, Private
Born in Granville County and was by occupation a farmer prior to enlisting in Wilson County at age 20, January 1, 1862, for the war. No further records.

MASSEY, BURWELL G., Private
Enlisted in Wayne County on July 5, 1862, for the war. Present or accounted for until transferred to Company K, 66th Regiment N.C.Troops, October 2, 1863.

MASSEY, DANIEL F., Private
Enlisted in Wayne County on July 5, 1862, for the war. Present or accounted for until transferred to Company K, 66th Regiment N.C.Troops, October 2, 1863.

MASSEY, JOHN J., Sergeant
Enlisted in Wayne County on July 5, 1862, for the war. Mustered in as Corporal and promoted to Sergeant in September-October, 1862. Present or accounted for until transferred to Company K, 66th Regiment N.C.Troops, October 2, 1863.

MASSEY, WEST, Jr., Private
Enlisted in Wayne County on July 5, 1862, for the war. Present or accounted for until transferred to Company K, 66th Regiment N.C.Troops, October 2, 1863.

MASSEY, WILLIAM, Private
Enlisted in Wayne County on July 5, 1862, for the war. Present or accounted for until transferred to Company K, 66th Regiment N.C.Troops, October 2, 1863.

MASSEY, WILLIAM C., Private
Enlisted in Wayne County on July 5, 1862, for the war. Present or accounted for until transferred to Company K, 66th Regiment N.C.Troops, October 2, 1863.

MATHEWS, NOEL, Private
Born in Wilson County* and was by occupation a cooper prior to enlisting in New Hanover County at age 28, January 15, 1862, for the war. Present or accounted for until transferred to Company K, 66th Regiment N.C.Troops, October 2, 1863.

MATHIS, NOEL, Private
Enlisted in Wayne County on July 5, 1862, for the war. Present or accounted for until transferred to Company K, 66th Regiment N.C.Troops, October 2, 1863.

MATHIS, RICHARD, Private
Born in Duplin County and was by occupation a grocer prior to enlisting in Duplin County at age 22, December 29, 1861, for the war. Present or accounted for until transferred to Company A, 51st Regiment N.C.Troops, April 15, 1862.

MATHIS, WELLS, Private
Enlisted in Duplin County on June 20, 1862, for the war. Present or accounted for until transferred to Company K, 66th Regiment N.C.Troops, October 2, 1863.

MERRITT, LOUIS S., Private
Enlisted in Wayne County on July 10, 1862, for the war. Present or accounted for until transferred to Company K, 66th Regiment N.C.Troops, October 2, 1863.

MERRITT, ROBERT HOOKS, Private
Born in Duplin or Sampson counties and was by occupation a farmer prior to enlisting in Duplin County at age 46, January 4, 1862, for the war. Present or accounted for until transferred to Company C, 51st Regiment N.C.Troops, April 15, 1862.

MILLARD, BENNETT, Jr., Private
Born in Wayne County and was by occupation a farmer prior to enlisting in New Hanover County at age 23, January 21, 1862, for the war. Present or accounted for until transferred to Company K, 66th Regiment N.C.Troops, October 2, 1863.

MILLIARD, JAMES J., Private
Born in Duplin County and was by occupation a farmer prior to enlisting in New Hanover County at age 37, January 21, 1862, for the war. Present or accounted for until transferred to Company K, 66th Regiment N.C. Troops, October 2, 1863.

NEWELL, DEMPSEY E., Private
Born in Wayne County and was by occupation a farmer prior to enlisting in New Hanover County at age 27, January 21, 1862, for the war. Present or accounted for until transferred to Company K, 66th Regiment N.C. Troops, October 2, 1863.

NEWELL, FRANKLIN, Private
Born in Lenoir County and was by occupation a painter prior to enlisting in Lenoir County at age 20, January 2, 1862, for the war. Present or accounted for through February, 1863. No further records.

NEWTON, WILLIAM B., Private
Born in New Hanover County and was by occupation a farmer prior to enlisting in New Hanover County at age 46, January 17, 1862, for the war. Present or accounted for until transferred to Company G, 51st Regiment N.C. Troops, April 15, 1862.

ODUM, NATHAN L., Private
Born in Wayne County and was by occupation a farmer prior to enlisting in New Hanover County at age 24, January 25, 1862, for the war. Present or accounted for until transferred to Company K, 66th Regiment N.C. Troops, October 2, 1863.

OLIVER, ASA W., Private
Resided in Johnston County and enlisted in Wayne County on July 5, 1862, for the war. Present or accounted for until transferred to Company K, 66th Regiment N.C. Troops, October 2, 1863.

OLIVER, HENRY UPTON, Private
Enlisted in Wayne County on July 5, 1862, for the war. Present or accounted for until transferred to Company K, 66th Regiment N.C. Troops, October 2, 1863.

OLIVER, THOMAS T., Private
Enlisted in Wayne County on July 5, 1862, for the war. Present or accounted for until transferred to Company K, 66th Regiment N.C. Troops, October 2, 1863.

OLIVER, WILLIAM B., Private
Enlisted in Wayne County on July 5, 1862, for the war. Present or accounted for until he deserted at Sessom's Mills on June 18, 1863. Later served in Company K, 66th Regiment N.C. Troops.

OVERMAN, EZEKIEL, Private
Resided in Wayne County where he enlisted at age 18, June 22, 1862, for the war. Present or accounted for until transferred to Company A, 27th Regiment N.C. Troops on or about May 22, 1863, in exchange for Private Wilie B. Wright.

PARKER, GEORGE FENNEL, Private
Enlisted in Wayne County on June 22, 1862, for the war. Present or accounted for until transferred to Company K, 66th Regiment N.C. Troops, October 2, 1863.

PARKER, WILEY, Jr., Private
Born in Duplin County and was by occupation a farmer prior to enlisting in New Hanover County at age 19, January 20, 1862, for the war. Present or accounted for until transferred to Company K, 66th Regiment N.C. Troops, October 2, 1863.

PARKER, WILEY, Sr., Private
Born in Duplin County and was by occupation a farmer prior to enlisting in Wayne County at age 48, January 11, 1862, for the war. Present or accounted for until transferred to Company K, 66th Regiment N.C. Troops, October 2, 1863.

PATE, E. TEMP, Private
Enlisted in Wayne County on June 25, 1862, for the war. Present or accounted for through February, 1863. No further records.

PATE, VAN H., Private
Born in Lenoir County and was by occupation a carriage maker prior to enlisting in Wayne County on June 26, 1862, for the war. Present or accounted for until he deserted to the enemy on September 15, 1863. Took the Oath of Allegiance on September 29, 1863.

PETERSON, WILLIAM S., Private
Previously served in Company C, 63rd Regiment N.C. Troops (5th Regiment N.C. Cavalry). Transferred to this company on September 26, 1862, in exchange for Private James R. Strickland. Present or accounted for through February, 1863. No further records.

PIPPINS, JORDAN, Private
Born in Franklin County and was by occupation a farmer prior to enlisting in New Hanover County at age 60, January 22, 1862, for the war. Present or accounted for through February, 1863. No further records.

PRICE, JAMES, Private
Born in Johnston County and was by occupation a carpenter prior to enlisting in Wayne County at age 31, January 1, 1862, for the war. Present or accounted for until transferred to Company K, 66th Regiment N.C. Troops, October 2, 1863.

RACKLEY, JOSEPH R., Private
Born in Sampson County and was by occupation a farmer prior to enlisting in Duplin County at age 19, December 29, 1861, for the war. Present or accounted for until transferred to Company A, 51st Regiment N.C. Troops, April 15, 1862.

RACKLEY, JOSHUA A., Private
Born in Sampson County and resided in Duplin County where he enlisted on December 29, 1861, for the war. Present or accounted for until transferred to Company A, 51st Regiment N.C. Troops, April 15, 1862.

ROBERTS, JOHN R., Private
Born in Wayne County and was by occupation a farmer prior to enlisting in Wayne County at age 26, December 29, 1861, for the war. Present or accounted for until transferred to Company A, 51st Regiment N.C. Troops, April 15, 1862.

ROBERTS, NATHAN W., Private
Born in Wayne County and was by occupation a student prior to enlisting in Wayne County at age 15, December 27, 1861, for the war. Present or accounted for until transferred to Company K, 66th

Regiment N.C.Troops, October 2, 1863.

ROGERS, WILEY WESLEY, Private
Born in Wilson County* and was by occupation a farmer prior to enlisting in Wilson County at age 30, January 9, 1862, for the war. Present or accounted for until transferred to Company K, 66th Regiment N.C.Troops, October 2, 1863.

ROWE, JOHN G., Corporal
Born in Wilson County* where he resided as a farmer prior to enlisting in Wilson County at age 25, January 2, 1862, for the war. Mustered in as Private and promoted to Corporal in September-October, 1862. Present or accounted for until transferred to Company K, 66th Regiment N.C.Troops, October 2, 1863.

RUFFIN, A. GRAY, Private
Enlisted in Wayne County on June 1, 1862, for the war. Present or accounted for until transferred to Company K, 66th Regiment N.C.Troops, October 2, 1863.

SASSER, WILLIAM, Private
Born in Johnston County and was by occupation a farmer prior to enlisting in Wayne County at age 36, December 25, 1861, for the war. Present or accounted for until transferred to Company K, 66th Regiment N.C.Troops, October 2, 1863.

SELLERS, DANIEL A., Private
Enlisted in Wayne County on February 28, 1863, for the war. Present or accounted for until he died in hospital at Wilson on September 19, 1863, of "diarrhoea chronica."

SEWELL, THOMAS, Private
Born in Duplin County and resided in Lenoir County where he was by occupation a farmer prior to enlisting in Lenoir County at age 17, January 1, 1862, for the war. Present or accounted for until transferred to Company A, 51st Regiment N.C.Troops, April 15, 1862.

SIMMS, A. J., Private
Enlisted in Wayne County on June 1, 1862, for the war. Present or accounted for through June, 1862. [May have served later in 2nd Company H, 40th Regiment N.C.Troops (3rd Regiment N.C. Artillery).]

SMITH, JOHN, Private
Enlisted in Wayne County on June 25, 1862, for the war. Present or accounted for until transferred to Company K, 66th Regiment N.C.Troops, October 2, 1863.

SOUTHERLAND, WILLIAM J., Sergeant
Previously served as Private in 1st Company C, 12th Regiment N.C.Troops (2nd Regiment N.C.Volunteers). Enlisted in this company on December 14, 1861, for the war. Mustered in as Sergeant. Present or accounted for until transferred to Company A, 51st Regiment N.C.Troops, April 15, 1862.

SPENCER, WILLIAM J., Private
Enlisted in Wayne County on July 12, 1862, for the war. Present or accounted for until he deserted at Sessom's Mills on June 18, 1863. Later served in Company K, 66th Regiment N.C.Troops.

STALLINGS, JOHN J., Private
Enlisted in Wayne County on July 5, 1862, for the war. Present or accounted for until transferred to Company K, 66th Regiment N. C. Troops, October 2, 1863.

STALLINGS, WILLIAM H., Private
Enlisted in Wayne County on July 5, 1862, for the war. Present or accounted for until transferred to Company K, 66th Regiment N.C.Troops, October 2, 1863.

STANLEY, DANIEL K., Private
Born in Lenoir County and was by occupation a farmer prior to enlisting in Wayne County at age 17, January 3, 1862, for the war. Present or accounted for until transferred to Company K, 66th Regiment N.C.Troops, October 2, 1863.

STANSELL, BENJAMIN F., Sergeant
Born in Wayne County and was by occupation a clerk prior to enlisting in Wayne County at age 17, January 1, 1862, for the war. Mustered in as Private and promoted to Sergeant in May-June, 1862. Present or accounted for until transferred to Company K, 66th Regiment N.C.Troops, October 2, 1863.

STANSELL, CHRISTOPHER C., Sergeant
Born in Wayne County and was by occupation a farmer prior to enlisting in Wayne County at age 19, December 20, 1861, for the war. Mustered in as Private and promoted to Sergeant in May-June, 1862. Present or accounted for until transferred to Company K, 66th Regiment N.C.Troops, October 2, 1863.

STANSELL, JAMES H., Private
Born in Wayne County where he resided as a laborer prior to enlisting in Wayne County at age 35, December 27, 1861, for the war. Present or accounted for until transferred to Company K, 66th Regiment N.C.Troops, October 2, 1863.

STANSELL, WILLIAM B., Ordnance Sergeant
Enlisted in Wayne County on June 25, 1862, for the war. Mustered in as Private and promoted to Ordnance Sergeant on June 1, 1863. Present or accounted for until transferred to Company K, 66th Regiment N.C.Troops, October 2, 1863.

STRICKLAND, JAMES R., Private
Enlisted in Wayne County on June 24, 1862, for the war. Present or accounted for until transferred to Company C, 63rd Regiment N.C.Troops (5th Regiment N.C. Cavalry), September 26, 1862, in exchange for Private William S. Peterson.

SUMMERLIN, JOHN, Private
Enlisted at Franklin, Virginia, August 2, 1863, for the war. Transferred to Company K, 66th Regiment N.C.Troops, October 2, 1863.

TAYLOR, LEVI, Private
Enlisted in Wayne County on September 16, 1863, for the war. Transferred to Company K, 66th Regiment N.C.Troops, October 2, 1863.

TAYLOR, WILLIAM T., Private
Enlisted in Wayne County on June 1, 1862, for the war. Present or accounted for through October, 1862. No further records.

TOMLINSON, RICHARD H., Private
Enlisted in Wayne County on June 1, 1862, for the

war. Present or accounted for until transferred to Company K, 66th Regiment N.C. Troops, October 2, 1863.

TOMLINSON, WILLIAM H., Private
Born in Wilson County* and was by occupation a farmer prior to enlisting in Wilson County at age 23, January 9, 1862, for the war. Present or accounted for until transferred to Company K, 66th Regiment N.C. Troops, October 2, 1863.

TURNER, JOHN W., Private
Previously served in 1st Company C, 12th Regiment N.C. Troops (2nd Regiment N.C. Volunteers). Enlisted in this company on January 20, 1862, for the war. Present or accounted for until transferred to Company A, 51st Regiment N.C. Troops, April 15, 1862.

VICK, SAMUEL, Private
Born in Wayne County where he resided as a farmer prior to enlisting in New Hanover County at age 21, December 25, 1861, for the war. Present or accounted for until transferred to Company A, 51st Regiment N.C. Troops, April 15, 1862.

WALLACE, JOHN P., Private
Previously served in 1st Company C, 12th Regiment N.C. Troops (2nd Regiment N.C. Volunteers). Enlisted in this company on January 21, 1862, for the war. Present or accounted for until transferred to Company A, 51st Regiment N.C. Troops, April 15, 1862.

WALLER, WILLIS, Private
Born in Duplin County and was by occupation a cooper prior to enlisting in Duplin County at age 50, January 4, 1862, for the war. Present or accounted for until transferred to Company K, 66th Regiment N.C. Troops, October 2, 1863.

WARTERS, BENJAMIN F., Private
Born in Lenoir County and was by occupation a carpenter prior to enlisting in Wayne County at age 43, January 1, 1862, for the war. Mustered in as Corporal but was reduced to ranks on June 1, 1863. Present or accounted for until transferred to Company K, 66th Regiment N.C. Troops, October 2, 1863.

WATSON, BENJAMIN, Private
Born in Lenoir County and was by occupation a mechanic prior to enlisting in Wayne County at age 23. Date of enlistment not reported. No further records.

WEBB, BENNETT, Private
Born in Johnston County and was by occupation a carpenter prior to enlisting in Wayne County at age 65, December 27, 1861, for the war. Present or accounted for through February, 1863. No further records.

WELLONS, ERASTUS, Private
Resided in Johnston County and enlisted in Wayne County on February 28, 1863, for the war. Present or accounted for until transferred to Company K, 66th Regiment N.C. Troops, October 2, 1863.

WEST, DAVID J., Private
Born in Duplin County and was by occupation a farmer prior to enlisting in Duplin County at age 21, December 27, 1861, for the war. Present or accounted for until transferred to Company A, 51st Regi-

ment N.C. Troops, April 15, 1862.

WHITLEY, BENJAMIN F., Corporal
Born in Wilson County* and was by occupation a farmer prior to enlisting in Wilson County at age 18, January 9, 1862, for the war. Mustered in as Private and promoted to Corporal in May-June, 1862. Present or accounted for until transferred to Company K, 66th Regiment N.C. Troops, October 2, 1863.

WHITLEY, JAMES T., Private
Born in Wilson County* and was by occupation a farmer prior to enlisting in Wilson County at age 20, January 9, 1862, for the war. Present or accounted for until transferred to Company K, 66th Regiment N.C. Troops, October 2, 1863.

WIGGS, NATHAN, Private
Enlisted in Wayne County on July 5, 1862, for the war. Present or accounted for until transferred to Company K, 66th Regiment N.C. Troops, October 2, 1863.

WILLIAMS, GEORGE W., Private
Enlisted in Wayne County on June 1, 1862, for the war. Present or accounted for until discharged on February 11, 1863, by reason of disability.

WILLIAMSON, ELEAZER W., Private
Born in Wilson County* and was by occupation a farmer prior to enlisting in Wilson County at age 23, January 2, 1862, for the war. Present or accounted for until transferred to Company K, 66th Regiment N.C. Troops, October 2, 1863.

WINBORN, DAVID, Private
Born in Johnston County and resided in Wayne County where he was by occupation a farmer prior to enlisting in New Hanover County at age 22, January 25, 1862, for the war. Present or accounted for until transferred to Company K, 66th Regiment N.C. Troops, October 2, 1863.

WOODARD, D. D., Private
Enlisted in Wayne County on February 28, 1863, for the war. Present or accounted for until he died at Raleigh on August 9, 1863. Cause of death not reported.

WOODARD, JOSEPH, Private
Enlisted in Wayne County on March 1, 1863, for the war. Present or accounted for until transferred to Company K, 66th Regiment N.C. Troops, October 2, 1863.

WOODARD, MONROE, Private
Resided in Johnston County and enlisted in Wayne County on July 5, 1862, for the war. Present or accounted for until he died at home in Johnston County on June 2, 1863. Cause of death not reported.

WOODARD, RICHARD G., Private
Enlisted in Wayne County on February 28, 1863, for the war. Present or accounted for until transferred to Company K, 66th Regiment N.C. Troops, October 2, 1863.

WOODARD, RUFUS D., Private
Enlisted in Wayne County on July 5, 1862, for the war. Present or accounted for until he died at

Goldsboro on May 29, 1863, of "pneumonia."

WRIGHT, WILIE B., Private

Previously served in Company A, 27th Regiment N.C. Troops. Transferred to this company on or about May 22, 1863, in exchanged for Private Ezekiel Overman. Promoted to Sergeant Major on June 1, 1863, and transferred to the Field and Staff of this regiment.

YOUNG, FURNEY G., Private

Born in Franklin County and resided in Johnston County where he was by occupation a teacher prior to enlisting in New Hanover County at age 21, January 22, 1862, for the war. Present or accounted for until appointed 2nd Lieutenant and transferred to Company C, 24th Regiment N.C. Troops (14th Regiment N.C. Volunteers), on or about May 8, 1862.

13th REGIMENT N. C. TROOPS
(3rd Regiment N. C. Volunteers)

This regiment was organized at Garysburg on May 27, 1861, as the 3rd Regiment N.C. Volunteers. On May 29 the regiment was ordered to Suffolk, Virginia, where it arrived on May 30. It was mustered into Confederate States service for twelve months' service on June 1, 1861.

The regiment went into camp at Suffolk and came under the command of General John C. Pemberton, commanding the department. Company A was detached for outpost duty on Barrett's Neck on June 2 and returned to the regiment on June 10. On June 13 Companies B and C marched to Fort Des Londe to man the battery and construct additional fortifications. The other companies remained at Suffolk until ordered to Benn's Church, six miles south of Smithfield, early in July.

While Companies B and C remained at Fort Des Londe the remainder of the regiment moved from Suffolk on July 4 and 5. Regimental headquarters were established at Camp Ruffin, Benn's Church, and companies from the regiment were sent on detached duty to various points along the James River. Company A moved on July 4 to Pagan Creek Battery. It remained until July 9, when it was moved to Ragged Island. On July 18 the company moved to Benn's Church. Companies D, F, and I, marched to Benn's Church on July 4 and remained there throughout July. Company E moved to Old Town Point on July 4 and from there to Smith's Creek on July 8. It returned to Old Town Point on July 17 and rejoined the regiment at Benn's Church on July 31. Companies G, H, and K, moved to Smith's Neck on July 5. Company K moved to Ragged Island on July 8 and remained there until July 17 when it moved to Benn's Church. Company G remained at Smith's Neck until July 17 when it moved to Benn's Church. Company H remained at Smith's Neck until July 19 when it moved to join the regiment at Benn's Church. On July 19 Company C moved from Fort Des Londe to Benn's Church.

The month of August, 1861, began with all but two of the companies at Benn's Church. Company B was at Fort Des Londe and did not rejoin the regiment until August 6; Company G had left Benn's Church on July 31 for Todd's Point and did not return until August 14. On August 9 Company C returned to Fort Des Londe where it remained through August. Company K left Benn's Church on August 15 for Pagan Creek Battery, where it remained until it returned to Benn's Church on September 3. For the remainder of 1861 the regiment camped at Benn's Church with companies rotating periods of service at Ragged Island and Pagan Creek Battery.

The regiment went into winter quarters at Benn's Church in November. By Special Orders No. 222, Adjutant and Inspector General's Office, Richmond, November 14, 1861, the regiment was redesignated the 13th Regiment N.C. Troops (3rd Regiment N.C. Volunteers). At about this time the regiment was brigaded with the 14th Regiment N.C. Troops (4th Regiment N.C. Volunteers) and the 3rd Regiment Virginia Infantry, under the command of General Raleigh E.

Colston. The companies of the regiment continued to rotate service on Ragged Island for the remainder of the winter of 1861-1862. Early in March, 1862, the Confederate authorities began moving troops to the Yorktown-Warwick line below Williamsburg to meet a Federal advance under General George B. McClellan. On April 4, 1862, General Colston moved his brigade across the James River to reinforce General John Magruder's troops on the Yorktown-Warwick line. The clerk for Company D reported the regiments movements as follows:

> The Co. with the Regt marched from Camp Ruffin on the 5 of Apl 1862 to Rock Warf on James River across the River [sic] to King's Landing in the Steamer W.W. Townes. Thence to Yorktown. Remaining at Yorktown a few days it marched to Winn's Mill thence to Mulberry Island. Remaining at Mulberry Island a few days it marched back to Yorktown. Remaining at Yorktown 3 weeks, it fell back to Williamsburg at which place on the 5 of May it had an engagement with the enemy.

During the month of April, 1862, the troops under General Joseph E. Johnston at Manassas were moved down to the Yorktown-Warwick line, and General Johnston was placed in command of all troops on the line. General Colston's brigade was assigned to General James Longstreet's division in the center of the line. On April 26 the regiment reorganized for the war and held an election of officers; on April 30 its strength was reported as 575 men.

On the night of May 3-4, 1862, General Johnston's troops began a general withdrawal from the Yorktown-Warwick line. The Confederates withdrew toward Williamsburg, and Colston's brigade served as rear guard of Longstreet's division. The brigade arrived at Williamsburg late on May 4 and went into camp on the western edge of the town. Early on the morning of May 5 the Federal advance began pressing the rear-guard elements in the fortifications east of the town. Longstreet held Colston's brigade in reserve and deployed the remainder of his division to meet the enemy advance. Colston's brigade was ordered forward around 3:30 P.M. to reinforce General A. P. Hill's brigade on the right of Fort Magruder, which was in the center of the Confederate line of fortifications. The 13th Regiment N.C.Troops (3rd Regiment N.C.Volunteers) was moved into one of the redoubts on the right where it received its baptism of fire. Three companies of the regiment charged, engaged the enemy with bayonets, and succeeded in driving them back. The companies then retired to the redoubt where the regiment continued to hold the enemy in check on its front. During the evening General Longstreet began withdrawing his troops to join the army, which was retiring toward Richmond. The entire force moved up the Peninsula unopposed and joined the Army of Northern Virginia just east of Richmond. At Williamsburg on May 5 this regiment lost seventy-five men killed, wounded, and missing.

Under pressure from President Davis to assume the offensive, General Johnston ordered an attack on the Federal position at Seven Pines. With Longstreet's division on the right of the Williamsburg road and D.H. Hill's division on the left of the road, the Confederates succeeded in driving the Federals from their defenses at Seven Pines on May 31. During the action Colston's brigade moved on the right of Longstreet's advance. However, around 5:00 **P.M.** the brigade was withdrawn with two other brigades from Longstreet's right and sent to support Hill on the left of the road. The next day, June 1, the Federals counterattacked, and only after hard fighting did the Confederates hold on to what they had gained. Two regiments of Colston's brigade were sent forward to reinforce General George Pickett's brigade, which succeeded in holding the line under heavy pressure. The battle ended with little gain for the Confederate forces. Upon finding that the Federals had been heavily reinforced, the Confederates withdrew to their former positions.

General Johnston was wounded during the battle of May 31, and General Gustavus W. Smith, commanding on June 1, fell sick. General Robert E. Lee was then put in command of the Army of Northern Virginia. At that time the army underwent many changes, and troops from the same state were brigaded together. This regiment was transferred to General Samuel Garland's brigade, General D. H. Hill's division. In addition to this regiment, the brigade consisted of the 5th Regiment N.C.State Troops, 12th Regiment N.C. Troops (2nd Regiment N.C.Volunteers), 20th Regiment N.C.Troops (10th Regiment N.C.Volunteers), and the 23rd Regiment N.C.Troops (13th Regiment N.C.Volunteers).

On June 25 Garland's brigade moved up the Williamsburg road to support the Confederates under General Benjamin Huger during the action at King's School House. The brigade occupied rifle pits in rear of the action and was exposed to artillery fire during the entire afternoon. However, the brigade was not ordered into action, and it retired to its old camp after dark.

At about 2:00 **A.M.** on the morning of June 26 the brigade moved along with the rest of D. H. Hill's division to the Chickahominy bridge on the Mechanicsville Turnpike. General Robert E. Lee was concentrating his troops to attack the Federal right at Mechanicsville. At 4:00 **P.M.** Brigadier General Roswell S. Ripley's brigade, D. H. Hill's division, crossed the bridge to aid General A. P. Hill's troops engaged at Mechanicsville. The remainder of the division followed but did not take an active part in the day's action. That night General D. H. Hill received orders to cooperate with Major General T. J. Jackson on the Cold Harbor road. General Jackson's troops were on the Confederate left. At daylight General Hill found his route blocked and sent Garland's and G. B. Anderson's brigades to the left to turn the enemy's position. The Federals abandoned their defenses when the two brigades began to move on their flank and rear, and Hill's whole division moved on toward Cold Harbor.

In the meantime, General Jackson had been forced to change his route and was proceeding on a road that would bring his troops behind and to the right of D.H. Hill's division. Hill advanced his troops to Cold Harbor and then deployed them along the edge of

Powhite Swamp. To his right, Jackson's troops came into position, and on their right the troops of A. P. Hill's and James Longstreet's divisions were engaging the enemy at Gaines' Mill. Jackson's and D.H. Hill's troops were ordered forward to the support of Longstreet and A. P. Hill. Garland's brigade was on the extreme left of the Confederate line. As Anderson's brigade on Garland's right met the enemy on the edge of the swamp, Garland's brigade moved to attack. After a short but bloody contest, the woods were cleared of the enemy. A general attack was ordered, and the Federals withdrew under pressure from the front and the threat of the attacks on their right. Night brought an end to the contest, and the Federals made good their escape.

From Gaines' Mill the Confederate left wing, under the command of General Jackson, moved to cross the Chickahominy at Grapevine Bridge. The bridge had been destroyed by the enemy in his retreat, and the position was defended to delay any attempted crossing. There the troops went into bivouac while the bridge was being rebuilt, June 28-29. On June 30 the troops advanced across Grapevine Bridge and marched to White Oak Bridge. There a strong Federal force prevented the Confederates from rebuilding the bridge and thus kept Jackson's men at bay while the battle of Frayser's Farm was raging. Following the battle the bridge was rebuilt. Jackson's men then joined forces with the right wing of the army and moved to meet the enemy at Malvern Hill, where General D. H. Hill's division was placed on the Confederate center. Late on the afternoon of July 1, 1862, a general assault was launched on the enemy positions at Malvern Hill. Hill's division advanced across an open field with the enemy batteries some 700-800 yards distant. Garland's brigade advanced until forced to halt and take cover about halfway to the objective. As support was not forthcoming, the brigade retired. During the night the Federals retired to Harrison's Landing. The battle of Malvern Hill was the last battle of the Seven Days' battles around Richmond, June 25-July 1, 1862. During this campaign the regiment lost 29 killed, 80 wounded, and 4 missing.

The brigade remained in bivouac near Malvern Hill until marched back to its original camp near Richmond on July 9-10. D.H. Hill's division was left in front of Richmond to watch McClellan's troops at Harrison's Landing while Jackson and then Longstreet moved to confront General John Pope in middle Virginia. In mid-August, General Garland's brigade was moved to Hanover Junction with two other brigades of the division. On August 26 the brigades at Hanover Junction moved to join the remainder of the division at Orange Court House, and on August 28 the entire division moved to join the Army of Northern Virginia. The division reached the army at Chantilly, September 2, 1862, after the second battle of Manassas, and crossed into Maryland on September 4-5.

Upon reaching Frederick, Maryland, the army halted, and General Lee determined to send Jackson to capture Harpers Ferry while Longstreet moved to Hagerstown. On September 10, D. H. Hill's division moved out of Frederick as the rear guard of Longstreet's column. Mounting pressure from the advancing Federals, plus the necessity of protecting Jackson at Harpers Ferry, resulted in the deployment of Hill's division along the South Mountain gaps below Boonsboro on September 13. Hill stationed Garland's brigade at Fox's Gap, where the brigade came under heavy fire. Lieutenant Colonel Thomas Ruffin, Jr., commanded the regiment during the battle and reported the regiment's activities as follows (*O.R.*, S.I., Vol. XIX, pt. 1, pp. 1045-1046):

Early in the morning of the 14th we were ordered by General Garland to go, in company with the Twentieth North Carolina, commanded by Colonel Iverson, out by a road leading along the top of the mountain, and then to occupy a position on the left of the old Sharpsburg road, which we did at about sunrise, and remained there about two hours. We were then ordered to move farther to the right to the support of the Fifth North Carolina Regiment, which we proceeded to do, and, being met by General Garland, were directed to take position in an open field upon the brow of a high hill. The enemy, we found, were posted upon a high hill densely wooded, and immediately facing the hill occupied by ourselves. There was also a regiment under cover of a rail fence upon our left. Not being able to see the enemy in our front, our whole fire was directed upon those upon the left, and, as our men were cool and fired with precision and effect, they soon drove that portion of the enemy entirely off the field. All this, while those in our front were firing constantly into us, and it was then that General Garland fell. Not deeming it prudent to advance down the hill in the face of an enemy so strongly posted, and whose force, though we could not see them, we judged, by their fire, to be very strong, the regiment was withdrawn about 50 yards from the brow of the hill. There I received an order from Colonel McRae, in person, he having succeeded to the command, to move by the left flank until our left was brought in contact with the right of General Anderson's brigade, which we did, and took our new position upon the road on the right of General Anderson, and supposed that our own brigade was extended in one continuous line on our right. The enemy advancing in our front, we became soon entirely engaged, and were evidently getting the advantage of him, but to our great surprise a heavy fire was opened upon us from the right, which we supposed to be occupied by our own brigade. Our adjutant was immediately dispatched to see what was the matter, and, returning, reported that the enemy had obtained the road on our right, and were coming down upon us from that direction. An order for a charge to the front was immediately given, and, the men obeying it with alacrity, we had the satisfaction to see the enemy give way. We pursued as far as it was thought to be prudent, and, falling back, changed front, so as to meet those on the right; charged them also and drove them back. While thus engaged, the enemy appeared upon our left, which position had been occupied by General Anderson's brigade, but which had been removed without our knowledge. Finding this to be so, our regiment aboutfaced, and charged, and, as it turned out to be but a party of the enemy's skirmishers, there was no difficulty in repulsing them. It was then determined to get into position somewhere from which we could communicate with our commanding officer, and with this view the regiment was removed to the Sharpsburg road, where we found General Anderson's brigade. Not being able to find Colonel McRae, and, indeed, hearing that he and his command had been cut

off, we reported to General Anderson, and asked to be taken under his command, to which he assented, and we remained with him the rest of the day. By him we were formed in line of battle in the old Sharpsburg road, our regiment being on the right of his brigade, and were moved up the side of the mountain. It is difficult to conceive a more arduous march than this was; but it was performed in good time, and, when we reached the top of the mountain, we found a road, along which we moved to the left until we came to a dense corn-field, on the right of the road. In this field we found the enemy in strong force, with a battery in position, which we were ordered to charge, and attempted to do, in conjunction with the Second North Carolina Regiment, but were repulsed with great loss. It then being dark, we were ordered to retire.

During the engagement on September 14 General Garland was mortally wounded, and Colonel McRae of the 5th Regiment N.C. State Troops assumed command of the brigade. Although the brigade was severely cut up, the arrival of reinforcements enabled the Confederates to hold the gap. The next morning the entire force withdrew under orders to concentrate at Sharpsburg. Upon arriving at Antietam Creek on September 15, the brigade went into position on the heights east of the creek. Later D. H. Hill's troops were moved into position on the Confederate line in front of Sharpsburg, between the troops of Jackson on the left and Longstreet on the right.

On the morning of September 17 the Confederate left was vigorously assaulted, and Garland's brigade, still under Colonel McRae, and two other brigades of Hill's division (Colquitt's and Ripley's) were ordered to support Jackson's right. Colonel McRae reported (*O.R.*, S.I., Vol. XIX, pt. 1, p. 1043):

The brigade was moved from its position, on the Hagerstown road, to the support of Colquitt's, which was then about engaging the enemy on our left front. This was about 10 o'clock. We moved by the left flank, until we reached a point near the woods, when line of battle was formed and the advance begun. Some confusion ensued, from conflicting orders. When the brigade crossed the fence, it was halted and formed and again advanced. Coming in sight of the enemy, the firing was commenced steadily and with good will, and from an excellent position, but, unaccountably to me, an order was given to cease fire—that General Ripley's brigade was in front. This produced great confusion, and in the midst of it a force of the enemy appearing on the right, it commenced to break, and a general panic ensued. It was in vain that the field and most of the company officers exerted themselves to rally it. The troops left the field in confusion, the field officers, company officers, and myself bringing up the rear. Subsequently several portions of the brigade, under Colonel Iverson, Captain Garrett, and others, were rallied and brought into action, rendering useful service.

Although the brigade broke and retired from the field, the line held and the men of Garland's brigade rallied and returned to the fight.

The main Federal attack then shifted to the Confederate center, which held until the battle shifted to the Confederate right. Although severely crippled, the Confederate line held during the battle of September

17. The following day the Army of Northern Virginia rested on the field; it retired across the Potomac River during the night of September 18 and went into camp. Regimental losses were not reported for Garland's brigade, but the brigade reported 40 killed, 210 wounded, and 187 missing during the Maryland campaign. The regiment reportedly lost one half of the men engaged, but only four of the company clerks reported losses on the individual company muster rolls. These four companies (A, C, D, and H) lost 7 killed, 25 wounded, and 3 missing. In addition, seven of the wounded were later reported as captured.

On October 17, 1862, as a result of ill feelings between the regimental commander and the temporary brigade commander, the regiment was transferred to General William D. Pender's brigade, General A. P. Hill's division, General Jackson's corps. In addition to this regiment, Pender's brigade consisted of the 16th Regiment N.C.Troops (6th Regiment N.C.Volunteers); 22nd Regiment N.C.Troops (12th Regiment N.C. Volunteers); 34th Regiment N.C. Troops; and 38th Regiment N.C.Troops.

The Army of Northern Virginia, in the meantime, remained in the Shenandoah Valley until the Army of the Potomac began crossing the Potomac River east of the Blue Ridge on October 26, 1862. By use of his cavalry, Lee sought to discover the enemy's intentions, and on October 28 he ordered Longstreet's corps to move east of the mountains and Jackson's corps to move closer to Winchester. When it became apparent that the Federals were concentrating opposite Fredericksburg, Lee ordered Longstreet's corps to that point on November 19. Jackson's corps crossed the Blue Ridge and encamped in the vicinity of Orange Court House until November 26, when Jackson was ordered to move to Fredericksburg. At Fredericksburg, Longstreet's corps was posted on the heights just west of the town. When Jackson's corps came up, D. H. Hill's division was sent to Port Royal below Fredericksburg to prevent any crossing of the Rappahannock River at or near that point. The balance of Jackson's corps was positioned between Longstreet and D.H. Hill so as to support either force. A. P. Hill's division encamped at Yerby's.

At about 2:00 A.M. on December 11 the Federals began constructing bridges across the river at Fredericksburg, and on the night of December 12-13 they began crossing. Anticipating the enemy's intention, General Lee had ordered Jackson to move his men to confront the enemy at Fredericksburg on December 12. A. P. Hill's division moved at dawn on that day and occupied a defensive line from Hamilton's Crossing to Deep Run Creek. Pender's brigade was on the left of Hill's line next to Deep Run Creek and connected with Longstreet's right on the creek.

The Federals launched an attack on Hill's line on December 13. Pender's brigade came under heavy artillery fire concentrated against two batteries in its front. The main attack was made to Pender's right, but one Federal brigade advanced up Deep Run Creek on Pender's left. This enemy force was driven back by an attack of the 16th Regiment N.C.Troops (6th Regiment N.C.Volunteers) of Pender's brigade and two regiments from Law's brigade, Hood's division, Longstreet's corps. The enemy retired from in front of Hill's position; and, during the night, Hill's division was

relieved. The Federal attack on Longstreet's front had also been repulsed. The enemy remained on the south bank of the river until the night of December 15-16, when all troops recrossed to the north bank. The regiment was in the line on December 13 and lost 7 killed and 30 wounded, principally from artillery fire.

Following the battle the regiment went into winter quarters at Camp Gregg, eight miles below Fredericksburg on the Rappahannock River. The regiment remained at Camp Gregg until April 23, 1863, when it marched to Gordonsville to perform provost duty. On April 29 General Lee began concentrating his army at Fredericksburg to confront a Federal force which had crossed over the river. Lee, concluding that the Federal crossing was a feint, began moving his army to oppose the main Federal force which had moved up the left bank of the Rappahannock to cross over behind the Confederates at Fredericksburg. Jackson's corps moved down the Orange and Fredericksburg Plank Road, on May 1, in the direction of Chancellorsville. On Jackson's right, Major General Richard H. Anderson's division engaged the enemy as the columns moved westward. About three miles from Chancellorsville, Jackson's column found the enemy retiring. Pushing forward, the Confederates found the Federal army in a defensive position around Chancellorsville.

After reports of the Federal position came in, Lee decided to send Jackson's corps around the Federal position to attack the exposed right flank. Jackson's column moved out early on the morning of May 2, and, after hard marching, succeeded in reaching a point about four miles west of Chancellorsville on the exposed right flank of Hooker's army. The regiment had received word of the impending battle on the evening of May 1 and was ordered to rejoin the brigade. Leaving Gordonsville late in the evening, the regiment marched all night and joined Jackson's corps as it moved into position to strike the Federal right on the following afternoon.

As the troops came up, Jackson deployed them in three lines for the attack. Pender's brigade was placed in the third line with its right on the road. This regiment was on the left of the brigade line. Heth's brigade was positioned on Pender's left in the third line. The attack began about 5:15 P.M. and the Federal troops, caught by surprise, were driven toward Chancellorsville. During the advance the first two lines merged as one and drove the enemy until strong resistance and darkness forced a halt. The third line was exposed to artillery fire as it advanced, and after the attack stalled the third line moved to the front and became the first line.

At about 6:00 A.M. on May 3, the Confederates renewed the attack. General Pender reported the brigade's action as follows (*O.R.*, S.I., Vol.XXV, pt.1, pp. 935-936):

My line had not advanced more than 150 yards before the firing became very heavy, but my men continued to advance, and soon it became apparent that the enemy were posted behind a breastwork of logs and brush. This we carried without once hesitating. Beyond the breastworks the resistance again became very obstinate, as if we had come in contact with a fresh line (but let me here say that the thickness of the undergrowth very much obstructed the view of operations the whole of this day), and this, in its turn, was driven back after a short contest; but farther on the resistance became so great from their infantry force, and the tremendous fire from artillery on my right regiments, that they were forced to fall back, but rallied at the breastworks about 150 yards in our rear. My left regiment (Thirteenth North Carolina) not being subjected to the artillery fire, did not fall back, but continued to advance for a long distance with the brigade on my left, and in this advance Lieutenant [John R.] Ireland, Company E, Thirteenth North Carolina, rushed gallantly forward, and captured Brigadier-General [William] Hays and staff, who were endeavoring to escape. Corpl. Monroe [Robertson], Company A, Thirteenth North Carolina, also about this time chased a colorbearer so closely that he tore off the colors, and threw down the staff, which was secured.

After the other four regiments fell back to the breastworks and were reformed, I advanced again, the men going forward with alacrity; but, after penetrating the woods about the same distance as before, had to fall back again. This, to some extent, was unavoidable, as our line on the right of the road had been driven back about this time, and the men thus found that the enemy were at least 100 yards in rear of them, on the opposite side of the road. The Thirteenth North Carolina, on the left, after advancing a long ways to the front, was finally compelled to fall back for want of support and ammunition, which it did in good order. When my line was forced back the second time, supports came up and took the advance. My men were about out of ammunition, broken down, and badly cut up, having lost about 700 officers and men in the short time we had been engaged. What field officers were left collected the men after they had fallen behind the front line, and were engaged at different times during the fight. Knowing the ground pretty well by this time, I remained in the fight with whatever troops came up, until about the close of the action, when I very readily got my men into shape again near the spot from where I commenced the advance.

As soon as reinforcements reached Pender's position after the failure of the second attack a general advance of the entire Confederate line took place. Aided by artillery, the Confederates converged on Chancellorsville, forcing the Federals to retire. Once Chancellorsville was occupied, the brigade was ordered to entrench.

While his army was converging on Chancellorsville, Lee received word that the Federal force at Fredericksburg under General John Sedgwick had broken through and was moving on his rear. He was forced to discontinue the attack after Chancellorsville was occupied and moved a portion of his army to confront the new threat. After defeating Sedgwick at Salem Church, Lee concentrated to attack the force at Chancellorsville. On May 6, after reconnoitering the enemy position, it was discovered that the Federals had recrossed the Rappahannock. Lee then moved his army back to Fredericksburg, and the regiment returned to Camp Gregg. During the Chancellorsville campaign the regiment lost 31 killed and 178 wounded of the 375 men present for duty on April 30.

Following the Chancellorsville campaign and the death of Jackson, the Army of Northern Virginia was organized into three corps under Generals James Longstreet, Richard S Ewell, and A.P. Hill. General

Pender was promoted to command a division in Hill's corps. Colonel Alfred Moore Scales of this regiment was promoted to brigadier general to command Pender's old brigade, which was assigned to Pender's division, Hill's corps.

General Lee put his army in motion on June 4 toward the Shenandoah Valley to begin the campaign that would end at Gettysburg. General Ewell's corps moved first and was followed by General Longstreet's corps. General Hill's corps remained at Fredericksburg to watch the Federal forces opposite the town. Ewell's corps moved into the valley and encountered the Federals at Winchester on June 13. Longstreet's corps occupied Culpeper Court House. On June 13 the Federal forces at Fredericksburg began moving north, and Hill's corps moved up the Rappahannock River to follow the army. Ewell's corps marched into Pennsylvania on June 22, and on June 24 Lee ordered Longstreet and Hill to follow. By June 27 Hill's corps was encamped near Chambersburg, Pennsylvania. On June 29 Hill was ordered to move to Cashtown, and Longstreet was directed to follow on the next day. Ewell's corps had proceeded eastward to Carlisle and was ordered to rejoin the army at Cashtown or Gettysburg as circumstances might require.

General Heth's division of A. P. Hill's corps reached Cashtown on June 29, and the next morning General James Johnston Pettigrew's brigade was sent to procure supplies at Gettysburg. Upon finding the town occupied by the enemy, Pettigrew retired to Cashtown. General Hill arrived at Cashtown with Pender's division during the evening of June 30 and decided to advance with Heth's and Pender's divisions the next morning. Heth's division was formed in line of battle, and Pender's division was formed in line behind Heth's men. Scales's brigade was second from the left with the left of the brigade on the turnpike. After marching about a quarter of a mile the line halted and the brigade on Scales's left was moved to the right of the division line. This left Scales's brigade on the extreme left of the division line. After about a thirty-minute wait the line moved forward.

The order to advance came and both lines moved forward to encounter the enemy. As Heth's division was engaged, General Ewell's corps came in from Carlisle to strike the enemy on his right flank. After driving the enemy from three lines, Heth's division was relieved by Pender's men, and the attack continued until the Federals retired through Gettysburg to Cemetery Hill just south of the town. General Scales reported the brigade's encounter with the enemy as follows (O. R., S. I., Vol. XXVII, pt. 2, pp. 669-670):

We pressed on until coming up with the line in our front, which was at a halt and lying down. I received orders to halt, and wait for the line to advance. This they soon did, and pressed forward in quick time. That I might keep in supporting distance, I again ordered an advance, and, after marching one-fourth of a mile or more, again came upon the front line, halted and lying down. The officers on this part of the line informed me that they were without ammunition, and would not advance farther. I immediately ordered my brigade to advance. We passed over them, up the ascent, crossed the ridge, and commenced the descent just opposite the theological seminary. Here the brigade encountered a most terrific fire of grape and shell on our flank, and grape and musketry in our front. Every discharge made sad havoc in our line, but still we pressed on at a double-quick until we reached the bottom, a distance of about 75 yards from the ridge we had just crossed, and about the same distance from the college, in our front. Here I received a painful wound from a piece of shell, and was disabled. Our line had been broken up, and now only a squad here and there marked the place where regiments had rested.

. . . .

In less than ten minutes after I was disabled and left the field, the enemy, as I learn, gave way, and the brigade, with the balance of the division, pursued them to the town of Gettysburg.

Every field officer of the brigade except one was disabled during the attack. General Scales reported that the brigade lost 9 officers killed, 45 wounded, and 1 missing. The ranks were thinned by the loss of 39 killed, 336 wounded, and 115 missing. Some of the missing and slightly wounded returned during the night, and Colonel William L. J. Lowrance of the 34th Regiment N.C.Troops, who assumed command of the brigade, reported that the brigade numbered about 500 men when he took command.

After nightfall the brigade was ordered to the extreme right of the army. The next morning it was ordered farther to the right on line with the artillery to defend the flank. About 1:00 **P.M.**, July 2, the brigade was relieved by General R. H. Anderson's division and ordered to rejoin Pender's division in the center of the line. General Pender had been mortally wounded on July 1, and General James H. Lane commanded the division until General Issac R. Trimble was assigned to command it. On the morning of July 3 Lane's and Scales's brigades were ordered to the right to take part in the attack to be launched against the Federal center. General Trimble arrived in time to take command of the two brigades as they formed in line behind the artillery. The attack was to be made with Pickett's division of Longstreet's corps on the right, supported by Wilcox's brigade on the right rear, and Heth's division (commanded by General Pettigrew) of Hill's corps on the left, supported by the two brigades of Pender's division under General Trimble.

A heavy cannonade began about 1:00 **P.M.** and continued for about two hours. The attack column then moved in front of the artillery and formed for the attack. Colonel Lowrance, still commanding Scales's brigade, reported (*O.R.*, S. I., Vol. XXVII, pt. 2, pp. 671-672):

Then we were ordered forward over a wide, hot, and already crimson plain.

We advanced upon the enemy's line, which was in full view, at a distance of 1 mile. Now their whole line of artillery was playing upon us, which was on an eminence in our front, strongly fortified and supported by infantry. While we were thus advancing, many fell, but I saw but few in that most hazardous hour who even tried to shirk duty. All went forward with a cool and steady step, but ere we had advanced over two-thirds of the way, troops from the front came tearing through our ranks, which caused many of our men to break, but with the remaining few we went forward until the right of the brigade touched the enemy's line of breastworks, as we marched in rather an oblique line. Now the pieces in our front were all silenced. Here many were shot down, being then exposed to a heavy fire of grape and musketry upon our right flank. Now all apparently had forsaken us. The two brigades (now reduced to mere squads, not numbering in all 800 guns) were the only line to be seen upon that vast field, and no support in view. The natural inquiry was, What shall we do? and none to answer. The men answered for themselves, and, without orders, the brigade retreated, leaving many on the field unable to get off, and some, I fear, unwilling to undertake the hazardous retreat. The brigade was then rallied on the same line where it was first formed.

Following the failure of the assault, Lee held his army ready to repulse an expected attack. On the night of July 4 the army took up line of march for Hagerstown and arrived there on July 7. A defensive line was established to hold the enemy while preparations were made to cross the Potomac. On July 13 the army began moving to cross the river, and Hill's corps was designated rear guard. As the army crossed, the rear guard retired under pressure from the enemy. During this move the entire brigade barely escaped capture. Colonel Lowrance reported (*O.R.*, S. I., Vol. XXVII, pt. 2, p. 672):

We retreated to Hagerstown, where we arrived on the 7th and remained until the 11th, and were then drawn out in line of battle, and remained so until the night of the 13th, during which time the enemy were drawn up in our front, but remained inactive, excepting some skirmishing, which resulted in loss on our part of 2 killed, several wounded, and several captured.

Then commenced our retreat to Falling Waters, and we arrived there at 10 o'clock on the morning of the 14th; and, while resting for a few hours ere we crossed, whether it was in order to cross over the wagon trains, artillery, &c., I cannot say, but just as we were moving out to cross the river, were attacked by a squad of cavalry, which caused some detention. Then, all being quiet, I moved off, as directed, toward the river, but ere I had gone more than 300 yards, I was ordered by General Heth to take the brigade back to the support of those who were acting as rear guard; and, having done so, I took a position on the right of the center, which point appeared to be threatened, but was immediately ordered by General Heth to form the brigade on the extreme left; and having formed the brigade, as directed, by moving there in quick time (being informed that that point was threatened), I found the men were quite exhausted from pressure of heat, want of sleep, want of food, and fatigue of marching; and at this very moment I found the troops on our right giving way, whereupon I sent Lieutenant [J.D.] Young, acting aide-de-camp, to rally them, which he did after some time. Then I was ordered to join on their right, and, while making a move to this effect, ere we had come to the top of the hill on which they were, I rode forward, and saw the whole line in full retreat some 200 or 300 yards to my rear; the enemy were pursuing, and directly between me and the bridge.

The move, I understand since, was made by order, but I received no such orders, in consequence of which I was cut off. But I filed directly to the rear, and struck the river some three-quarters of a mile above the bridge, and then marched down the river; but the enemy had penetrated the woods, and struck the river between us and the bridge, and so cut off many of our men who were unwilling to try to pass, and captured many more who failed from mere exhaustion; so in this unfortunate circumstance we lost nearly 200 men.

The brigade was saved from capture by the defensive stand of Pettigrew's brigade, during which General Pettigrew fell mortally wounded. Pettigrew's men crossed the bridge around noon, just as the bridge was cut. Thus ended Lee's invasion of Pennsylvania. The regimental losses were officially reported as 29 killed and 97 wounded; however, regimental adjutant N. S. Smith reported after the war (Clark's *Regiments*, Vol. I, pp. 698-699) that the regiment went into action with 180 men on July 1 and lost 150 killed and wounded. A detail of 15 men which had been left at Greencastle rejoined the regiment on July 2. Thus, the regiment numbered 45 men on July 3. Smith reported a loss of 23 killed and wounded in the charge against the Federal center on that day. Approximately one half of the survivors (including Smith) were captured at Falling Waters on July 14, and, according to Smith's estimate, only 11 men remained in the regiment when it recrossed the Potomac. Colonel J. H. Hyman reported in the Roll of Honor return on October 28, 1863, that the regiment lost 149 men on July 1-3 and 20 men on July 14. Only one company clerk reported the strength of his company after the campaign. Of the sixteen men in the ranks of Company C when the campaign started, 5 were killed, 6 wounded, and 1 was missing, leaving 4 present for duty on July 15, 1863.

Lee moved his army east of the Blue Ridge Mountains when the Federal army crossed into Virginia. By August 4 the Army of Northern Virginia occupied the Rapidan River line and the Federal army occupied the Rappahannock River line. General Cadmus M. Wilcox was assigned to command the division after General Trimble was captured on July 3, and General Pender's division became General Wilcox's division. General Scales returned after his wound healed and assumed command of his brigade.

On October 10 Lee's army moved to strike the right flank of the Federal army. The move compelled the Federal commander, General George Meade, to retire toward Centreville. On the march Scales's brigade was detailed to guard the corps train at Buckland while Heth's and Wilcox's divisions moved toward Bristoe Station. As the rear guard of Meade's army was passing through Bristoe Station on October 14, General A. P. Hill's corps, with Heth's division in front, came on the field. Without waiting for the rest of his corps to come up or to reconnoiter the situation, General Hill ordered an attack. The attack failed with heavy loss to the attacking brigades.

No further attempts were made to drive the enemy, and during the night the Federal rear guard continued its retreat to Centreville. Lee decided not to follow the Federals and ordered his army to retire to the Rappahannock. After the battle at Rappahannock Bridge on November 7, Lee moved his army back to the Rapidan River line. General Meade began moving his army on November 26 to cross the Rapidan below Lee's position, and Lee ordered his army to intercept the Federals. Finding the Federal army advancing toward him, Lee retired to Mine Run and entrenched. Meade moved up to Mine Run and also entrenched. As soon as he received reports that the Federal flank was exposed, Lee determined to attack on the morning of December 2. Wilcox's and Anderson's divisions were concentrated for the assault; however, when the troops moved out they found that the Federal army had retired. A pursuit was undertaken, but Meade recrossed the Rapidan unmolested. Lee then ordered his troops back, and the army went into winter quarters. This regiment spent the winter of 1863-1864 in camp with the brigade near Orange Court House.

On the morning of May 4, 1864, while the Federal army under General U. S. Grant was moving across the lower Rapidan, Scales's brigade was near Orange Court House. When information was received that Grant was crossing, Lee ordered Ewell's corps to move on the left down the Orange Turnpike and Hill's corps to move in the center on the Plank Road. Longstreet's corps, at Gordonsville, was ordered to move up on Hill's right. On the morning of May 5, with Heth's division in the lead, Hill's column encountered Federal cavalry near Parker's Store and succeeded in forcing the enemy back. Hill's men then occupied the crossroads at Parker's Store. Immediately north on the Orange Turnpike, Ewell encountered the enemy in corps strength. Hill ordered Heth's division to deploy in line of battle across the Plank Road and directed Wilcox to lead his division off by the left to contact Ewell's right. Wilcox posted Scales's and McGowan's brigades on Chewning Plateau and moved his other two brigades (Lane's and Thomas's) farther to the left.

Elements of the Federal II Corps assaulted Heth's line around 4:00 P.M. The attack was so strong that Heth was forced to commit his reserve brigade. Wilcox's division was ordered to support Heth's line, and Scales's and McGowan's brigades were ordered forward. Thomas's and Lane's brigades were also pulled out of the line and ordered to reinforce Heth, leaving a gap between Ewell's and Hill's corps. Heth's division was holding off seven enemy brigades, and more were moving against him. McGowan's brigade was deployed astride the road; Scales's brigade was deployed south of the road. The two brigades moved forward to the attack and passed over Heth's first line. Scales's men, after forcing the Federal troops on Heth's right to retire, advanced to the attack. Both brigades drove the enemy back until forced to retire under heavy pressure. As the pressure mounted, Thomas's and Lane's brigades arrived to reinforce McGowan and Scales respectively. The situation was very precarious as additional Federal troops pressured the thin Confederate line. On the right, Scales's and Lane's men thwarted a Federal effort to turn the Confederate right. Darkness brought an end to the battle, and during the night the line was re-formed. McGowan's brigade was placed on the left of the road with its right on the road. Scales's brigade was posted on the right of the road with its left on the road. Thomas's brigade was moved from McGowan's left and placed on Scales's right. Lane's brigade regrouped behind Scales's brigade. Davis's brigade of Heth's division was on McGowan's left. Kirkland's and Walker's brigades of Heth's division were on the left of the road behind Davis and McGowan. Heth's fourth brigade, Cooke's, was further to the rear in general reserve.

At 5:00 A.M. the next morning, May 6, Federal columns struck Hill's line in front and on the left flank.

Thirteen Federal brigades fell hard on Hill's eight brigades. There was not time for resistance. Scales's brigade broke, and the regiment lost its colors. The whole line fell back in disorder. The second line could not hold, and a general rout followed. Only the timely arrival of Longstreet's corps, moving up to reinforce Hill, saved the day. The Federal assault was blunted and driven back. Wilcox's and Heth's men re-formed behind Longstreet's left, and Scales's brigade went into position near Chewning Plateau. The battle continued throughout the day on Longstreet's front, and night brought an end to the fighting.

Late in the evening of May 7 orders came to close on the right. Grant was heading toward Spotsylvania Court House, and Lee began moving his army. Throughout the night of May 7-8 the Confederates moved to the right. The race for the courthouse was won by the Confederates on the morning of May 8. When the rest of the army came up, a strong defensive line was constructed. Hill's corps, under the temporary command of General Jubal Early, was positioned on the right of the line with Ewell's corps in the center and Longstreet's corps on the left. Wilcox's division formed the left of Hill's (Early's) line and connected with the right of Ewell's line, which was shaped like an inverted V. Lane's brigade was on the left of Wilcox's divisional line, and McGowan's brigade was on the right. Thomas's and Scales's brigades were in the center.

Early on the morning of May 12 the Federals launched a sudden attack against the Confederate center held by Ewell's corps. The attackers overran the apex of the line and began driving the survivors back. Reinforcements were ordered to counterattack, and Lane's brigade attacked along the right side of the salient. Thomas's and Scales's brigades reinforced Lane's men and succeeded in driving the enemy back. This attack, combined with the counterattack on the left and center of the salient, forced the enemy to retire from the salient. The enemy entrenched on the opposite side of the Confederate trenches at the apex of the inverted V-shaped line, and hand-to-hand fighting raged throughout the day. After a second line was completed across the base of the inverted V line, the Confederates retired from the first line. The brigades of Wilcox's division then returned to their former positions.

After several unsuccessful attempts against the Confederate line, General Grant began to move his army eastward. On May 21 Scales's and Thomas's brigades were ordered forward to reconnoiter the enemy position. A sharp skirmish ensued, and the brigades halted, regrouped, and advanced. The Federal skirmishers retired, and the Confederates advanced to find that the Federals had abandoned their line. Lee began moving his army eastward to the North Anna River just north of Hanover Junction, where he established a defensive line to block the Federal route of advance. General Hill had returned to command his corps on May 21 and moved his troops into position on the left of the position at North Anna on May 22.

General Grant moved his army up to North Anna opposite Lee's position, and the V Corps, under General G. K. Warren, crossed the river at Jericho Mills on May 23. General Hill ordered Wilcox's division forward to oppose the Federal advance, and Wilcox

deployed his division with three brigades on line and Scales's brigade behind the left brigade. The division advanced to the attack. As they engaged the enemy the left brigade gave way and Scales's brigade moved up on the front line but did not advance. The entire line assumed the defensive and retired at nightfall after suffering the loss of 642 men killed, wounded, and captured.

The center of Lee's line was anchored on the river with the flanks drawn back so that the line formed an inverted V. Grant crossed a force and moved against the right of Lee's line as the V Corps moved against the left. Unable to force the Confederate center back, Grant found that he could not unite the wings of his army. During the night of May 26-27 Grant withdrew his army and moved eastward to cross the Pamunkey River.

Lee began moving his army as soon as it was learned that Grant was again on the move. Ewell's corps, now commanded by General Jubal Early, marched some twenty-four miles on May 27 and entrenched between Beaver Dam Creek and Pole Green Church. Longstreet's corps came up on Early's right, and Hill's corps extended along the left of Early's line. On May 30, under orders from General Lee, Early moved to attack the Federal left at Bethesda Church. The attack failed to turn the Federal left but revealed that the enemy was moving to the Confederate right.

The two armies began to concentrate at Cold Harbor, and on June 1 a spirited engagement occurred. On June 2 Hill was ordered to leave Heth's division on the left to support Early's corps and to move Wilcox's and Mahone's divisions to the Confederate right. Wilcox's division arrived on the right of the line at 3:00 P.M., and two brigades from the division joined in General Breckinridge's attack on and occupation of Turkey Hill. Wilcox's division was then placed on the right of Breckinridge's command and extended the line to within a half mile of the Chickahominy River. McGowan's brigade was on the right of the division and Scales's brigade was on the left of McGowan's men. As Scales's brigade moved into position, it had to drive a Federal force from its assigned position. At 4:30 A.M. on June 3 the Federals launched a general assault against the six-mile-long Confederate line. Only Wilcox's division escaped the fury of the assault, which was easily repulsed by the entrenched Confederates. The attacks continued until 11:00 A.M., but infantry and artillery fire from defensive positions did not cease until 1:00 P.M. The battle of Cold Harbor was over, and over 7,000 Federals were dead or wounded.

The two armies settled down as if to rest and remained in position. Heth's division was moved from the left of the line and joined the other two divisions of Hill's corps on the right. When Grant moved south of the Chickahominy Lee followed, and Hill's corps made contact near Riddell's Shop on June 13. A defensive line was established, but no general engagement followed. Grant then crossed the James River and moved on Petersburg. Hill's corps remained north of the James until ordered to move to Petersburg on June 17. When it arrived on June 18 it went into position on the extreme right of the Petersburg line and extended the line to the Petersburg and Weldon Railroad. Wilcox's division was just south of Petersburg, and Scales's brigade occupied the works south of Sycamore

Street. McGowan's brigade of Wilcox's division was on the division's right near the railroad.

Four weeks after their arrival in the Petersburg trenches, this regiment was detached for picket duty along the west bank of the Appomattox River. The regiment returned to the brigade just prior to the unsuccessful effort to dislodge the Federals from the Petersburg and Weldon Railroad at Globe Tavern on August 21. Hill's entire corps took part in this action, but since Scales's brigade was not part of the assault force, reports do not record the brigade's activity. South of Globe Tavern another Federal force occupied the railroad at Reams' Station. Moving around the enemy position at Globe Tavern, Hill ordered Scales's brigade, six other brigades of his corps, and two divisions of cavalry to attack the Federal position at Reams' Station. The troops moved on the afternoon of August 24 and arrived before Reams' Station the next morning. About 2:00 P.M. Scales's and Lane's brigades were ordered to attack the right of the Federal position. Two attempts to carry the works failed. During these two attacks the regiment served as skirmishers and led the brigade. A combined attack by the entire Confederate force later in the afternoon was successful and forced the Federals to retire. That night Hill's entire command returned to its original position in the Petersburg trenches.

Wilcox's division did not see action in the field again until September 30, when it was engaged at Jones' Farm. Grant moved to extend his line to tie it in with the position at Globe Tavern. Each side advanced to the attack, and, although initially successful, the Confederates could not prevent the Federals from establishing their line. During the action, Scales's brigade escaped capture as Wilcox's division was hit on the left flank and forced to retire. This regiment, detailed as skirmishers, did not receive the order to retire until night and had to make its way back between two Federal forces on either flank. Except for picket skirmishing, the regiment did not see action for the remainder of the year.

Early in February, 1865, General Grant ordered a move on the left of his line to secure a position on the Boydton Plank Road at Hatcher's Run. Hill's troops were engaged on February 5 but met with little success. Wilcox's division was moved farther to the right as the Confederates extended the line to meet the Federal extension. Securing the position on Hatcher's Run, Grant planned his next move. It began on March 29 and terminated with the routing of a Confederate force at Five Forks on April 1. This victory opened the way for an advance on the Confederate line at Petersburg in flank and rear. On April 2 the Federals launched a general attack against the entire line. Scales's brigade was attacked and forced back to the second line of entrenchments. To the left of the brigade the Federals broke through and threatened to carry the main works. That night Lee decided to evacuate the Petersburg line, and his army pulled out of the trenches to take up the march to Amelia Court House. At this time General Scales was home on sick furlough. The brigade was commanded by Colonel Joseph H. Hyman of this regiment during the retreat to Appomattox Court House.

Lee's army concentrated at Amelia Court House on April 4-5 and continued the retreat on April 6. At Sayler's Creek, on April 6, the Confederates failed to hold the advancing Federals and sustained heavy losses. The remnants of two corps were defeated and captured. Lee's army moved through Farmville on April 7, and on that day Scales's brigade successfully drove off a body of Federal cavalry which had formed to attack the right of the retreating column. The retreat continued, and on the morning of April 9 Wilcox's division was moving to support General Gordon's attack on the Federals just west of Appomattox Court House when word came to cease fire. Lee surrendered his army at Appomattox Court House on that day. When the army was paroled on April 12, 216 men of the regiment were present to receive their paroles.

FIELD AND STAFF

COLONELS

PENDER, WILLIAM DORSEY

Born in Edgecombe County on February 6, 1834. Graduated from the U. S. Military Academy in 1854 and served in the U. S. Army until he resigned his 1st Lieutenant's commission on March 21, 1861. Elected Colonel of this regiment on May 16, 1861. Present or accounted for until appointed Colonel of the 6th Regiment N.C. State Troops to rank from August 17, 1861.

SCALES, ALFRED MOORE

Previously served as Captain of Company H of this regiment. Elected Colonel of this regiment on October 11, 1861, and was commissioned on October 12, 1861. Present or accounted for until wounded in the thigh at Chancellorsville, Virginia, May 1-3, 1863. Appointed Brigadier General on June 13, 1863, and transferred.

HYMAN, JOSEPH H.

Previously served as Captain of Company G of this regiment. Appointed Major on October 15, 1862, and transferred to the Field and Staff. Promoted to Lieutenant Colonel on March 2, 1863, and promoted to Colonel on June 13, 1863. Present or accounted for until wounded in the "right arch" at Gettysburg, Pennsylvania, July 1, 1863. Rejoined the company in September-October, 1863, and present or accounted for until paroled at Appomattox Court House, Virginia, April 9, 1865.

LIEUTENANT COLONELS

GUY, W. S.

Resided in Granville County and enlisted at age 29. Elected Lieutenant Colonel to rank from May 27, 1861. Present or accounted for until he was defeated for reelection when the regiment was reorganized on April 26, 1862.

RUFFIN, THOMAS, Jr.

Previously served as Captain of Company E of this regiment. Promoted to Lieutenant Colonel on May 1, 1862, and transferred to the Field and Staff. Present or accounted for until he resigned on February 21, 1863, upon appointment as a judge of the military court of the Trans-Mississippi Department, Lieutenant General Edmund Kirby Smith commanding. Resignation accepted March 2, 1863.

ROGERS, HENRY A.

Previously served as Captain of Company D of this regiment. Appointed Major on December 16, 1862, and transferred to the Field and Staff. Present or accounted for until wounded at Chancellorsville, Virginia, May 3, 1863. Promoted to Lieutenant Colonel on June 13, 1863, and rejoined the company in July-August, 1863. Wounded in the head at Barnett's Ford, Virginia, September 22, 1863. Reported absent wounded until retired to the Invalid Corps on October 19, 1864.

WITHERS, ELIJAH BENTON

Previously served as Captain of Company A of this regiment. Promoted to Major on June 13, 1863, and transferred to the Field and Staff. Present or accounted for until wounded at Gettysburg, Pennsylvania, July 1, 1863. Rejoined the company in November-December, 1863, and was promoted to Lieutenant Colonel on October 19, 1864. Present or accounted for until paroled at Appomattox Court House, Virginia, April 9, 1865.

MAJORS

HAMILTON, DANIEL HAYWARD, Jr.

Resided in Orange County and enlisted at age 26. Elected Major on May 26, 1861, and was commissioned on May 27, 1861. Present or accounted for until he was defeated for reelection when the regiment was reorganized on April 26, 1862. Later served as Adjutant of the 1st Regiment (McCreary's) South Carolina Infantry.

HAMBRICK, JOHN T.

Previously served as Captain of Company D of this regiment. Appointed Major on May 26, 1862, to rank from April 26, 1862, and assigned to the Field and Staff. Present or accounted for until he resigned on October 11, 1862, by reason of "a spinal affection [sic] of several years standing accompanied with Bright's disease of the kidneys." Resignation accepted October 15, 1862.

MARTIN, THOMAS A.

Previously served as Captain of Company E of this regiment. Appointed Major on January 19, 1865, and transferred to the Field and Staff. Paroled at Appomattox Court House, Virginia, April 9, 1865.

ADJUTANTS

FLEMING, JASPER

Previously served as 3rd Lieutenant in Company C of this regiment. Appointed Adjutant on June 3, 1861, and was promoted to Adjutant (1st Lieutenant) on December 31, 1861, to rank from November 20, 1861. Present or accounted for until he resigned on November 8, 1862, by reason of "typhoid fever." Resignation accepted December 20, 1862.

WALKER, HENRY A.

Previously served as Sergeant Major of this regiment. Appointed Adjutant (1st Lieutenant) on March 16, 1863, to rank from December 20, 1862. Wounded at Chancellorsville, Virginia, May 3, 1863, and report-

ed absent wounded until he resigned on August 13, 1863, by reason of wounds. Resignation accepted September 1, 1863. Later served as a 2nd Lieutenant in the Engineer Corps.

ANDERSON, GEORGE W.

Previously served as 1st Lieutenant in Company K of this regiment. Appointed Adjutant (1st Lieutenant) on November 10, 1863, to rank from October 23, 1863, and transferred to the Field and Staff. Present or accounted for until reported absent sick on May 14, 1864. Reported absent sick until dropped from the rolls of the company on August 27, 1864.

GRIER, CALVIN E.

Previously served as Sergeant Major of this regiment. Appointed Adjutant (1st Lieutenant) on October 17, 1864. Paroled at Appomattox Court House, Virginia, April 9, 1865.

ASSISTANT QUARTERMASTERS

PENDER, DAVID

Resided in Edgecombe County and enlisted at age 27. Appointed Assistant Quartermaster (Lieutenant) on or about May 16, 1861, and was promoted to Assistant Quartermaster (Captain) on or about June 1, 1861. Resigned on or about September 7, 1861.

HILL, CHARLES D.

Previously served as Quartermaster Sergeant of this regiment. Appointed Assistant Quartermaster (Captain) on September 20, 1861. Present or accounted for until appointed paymaster of Major General Cadmus M. Wilcox's division on September 15, 1864, and transferred.

ASSISTANT COMMISSARIES OF SUBSISTENCE

CAIN, THOMAS R.

Resided in Orange County and enlisted at age 27. Appointed Assistant Commissary of Subsistence (Captain) on or about May 16, 1861. Resigned on or about October 19, 1861.

SCALES, ERASMUS D.

Previously served as Commissary Sergeant of this regiment. Appointed Assistant Commissary of Subsistence (Captain) on November 14, 1861. Present or accounted for until promoted to Assistant Brigade Commissary on June 13, 1863, and transferred.

CHAPLAINS

ANDREWS, JOHN N.

Appointed Chaplain of this regiment on or about May 27, 1861. "Not commissioned" as of August 31, 1861, and resigned at an unspecified date.

SIMPSON, JAMES S.

Appointed Chaplain on January 28, 1862, to rank from December 10, 1861, but declined the appointment.

HILL, H. G.

Appointed Chaplain on June 24, 1862, to rank from June 18, 1862. Resigned October 16, 1863, by reason of "delicacy of constitution" and "present feeble state of health." Resignation accepted October 22, 1862.

WILLIAMS, GEORGE T.

Previously served as Chaplain of the 1st Regiment South Carolina Infantry. Transferred to this regiment on April 28, 1863, with the rank of Chaplain. Present or accounted for until he resigned on December 1, 1863.

VANN, WILLIAM A.

Appointed Chaplain on March 16, 1864, to rank from February 17, 1864. Died in hospital at Lynchburg, Virginia, April 29, 1864, of "febris typhoides."

SURGEONS

MONTGOMERY, DANIEL A.

Previously served as 1st Lieutenant in Company E of this regiment. Appointed Surgeon to rank from May 21, 1861. Present or accounted for until he resigned on November 21, 1861.

McADEN, JOHN HENRY

Previously served as Private in Company A of this regiment. Appointed Assistant Surgeon on June 1, 1861, to rank from May 27, 1861, and transferred to the Field and Staff. Promoted to Surgeon on or about November 16, 1861. Present or accounted for until captured at Gettysburg, Pennsylvania, July 3-5, 1863. Confined at Fort McHenry, Maryland, until transferred to Fort Delaware, Delaware, where he arrived July 20, 1863. Exchanged at an unspecified date and rejoined the company in November-December, 1863. Present or accounted for through October, 1864. Later served as Surgeon of Brigadier General Alfred M. Scales's brigade.

ASSISTANT SURGEONS

WALKER, FRANK A.

Resided in Virginia and enlisted at age 29. Appointed Assistant Surgeon on May 16, 1861. Present or accounted for until transferred to the C. S. Navy on February 16, 1863.

FOOTE, GEORGE A.

Appointed Assistant Surgeon on May 25, 1861. Resigned or was relieved from duty with this regiment on August 20, 1861.

CALDWELL, JOHN W.

Appointed Assistant Surgeon on July 19, 1861. Resigned November 30, 1861.

STEPHENS, WILLIAM G.

Previously served as 2nd Lieutenant in Company C of this regiment. Appointed Assistant Surgeon on February 14, 1863, and transferred to the Field and Staff. Present or accounted for until relieved by reason of ill health and ordered to report to the medical director at Charleston, South Carolina, February 25, 1865. Paroled at Greensboro on May 2, 1865.

ENSIGNS

ROAN, NATHANIEL K.

Previously served as Sergeant in Company A of this regiment. Promoted to Ensign (Color Sergeant) on July 1, 1861, and transferred to the Field and Staff. Present or accounted for until he was transferred back to Company A in January-February, 1862.

HOWARD, HENRY O.

Previously served as Sergeant in Company A of this regiment. Appointed Ensign (Color Sergeant) on December 1, 1863, and transferred to the Field and Staff. Promoted to Ensign (1st Lieutenant) on April 28, 1864. Captured at Wilderness, Virginia, May 6, 1864, and confined at Point Lookout, Maryland, until transferred to Elmira, New York, August 10, 1864. Released at Elmira on June 16, 1865, after taking the Oath of Allegiance.

SERGEANTS MAJOR

WALKER, HENRY A.

Previously served as Private in Company C of this regiment. Appointed Sergeant Major on June 10, 1861, and transferred to the Field and Staff. Present or accounted for until appointed Adjutant (1st Lieutenant) of this regiment on March 16, 1863, to rank from December 20, 1862.

WILLIAMSON, JOHN WILLIAM

Previously served as Private in Company A of this regiment. Appointed Sergeant Major on December 20, 1862, or April 4, 1863, and transferred to the Field and Staff. Present or accounted for until appointed 1st Lieutenant to rank from April 30, 1863, and transferred to Company D, 1st Regiment N.C. State Troops.

HOWARD, WILLIAM M.

Previously served as Private in Company A of this regiment. Appointed Sergeant Major on or about April 30, 1863, and transferred to the Field and Staff. Present or accounted for until appointed 1st Lieutenant in Company D, 1st Regiment N.C. State Troops to rank from October 5, 1863.

GRIER, CALVIN E.

Previously served as Private in Company C, 10th Regiment N.C. State Troops (1st Regiment N.C. Artillery). Appointed Sergeant Major of this regiment on November 6, 1863. Present or accounted for until reported absent wounded in January-February, 1864; however, place and date wounded not reported. Rejoined the company in May-June, 1864, and was wounded in the left lung at Reams' Station, Virginia, August 25, 1864. Reported absent wounded until appointed Adjutant (1st Lieutenant) of this regiment on October 17, 1864.

TROLLINGER, JACOB H.

Previously served as Corporal in Company K of this regiment. Detailed as Sergeant Major and transferred to the Field and Staff on February 16, 1864. Rejoined Company K on or about May 20, 1864.

QUARTERMASTER SERGEANTS

HILL, CHARLES D.

Previously served as Private in Company C of this regiment. Appointed Quartermaster Sergeant on June 3, 1861, and transferred to the Field and Staff. Present or accounted for until appointed Quartermaster (Captain) of this regiment on September 20, 1861.

LAWSON, ROBERT W.

Previously served as Private in Company A of this

regiment. Promoted to Quartermaster Sergeant on October 4, 1861, and transferred to the Field and Staff. Present or accounted for until discharged on December 1, 1861. Reason discharged not reported.

HILL, DANIEL C.

Previously served as Sergeant in Company C of this regiment. Promoted to Quartermaster Sergeant on December 1, 1861, and transferred to the Field and Staff. Present or accounted for until paroled at Appomattox Court House, Virginia, April 9, 1865.

COMMISSARY SERGEANTS

SCALES, ERASMUS D.

Previously served as Private in Company H of this regiment. Promoted to Commissary Sergeant on June 10, 1861, and transferred to the Field and Staff. Appointed Assistant Commissary of Subsistence (Captain) of this regiment on November 14, 1861.

GUERRANT, JOHN WYATT S.

Previously served as Corporal in Company K of this regiment. Detailed as Commissary Sergeant on August 1, 1863, and transferred to the Field and Staff. Present or accounted for through October, 1864. Paroled at Appomattox Court House, Virginia, April 9, 1865.

ORDNANCE SERGEANTS

MEBANE, WILLIAM N.

Previously served as Private in Company H of this regiment. Promoted to Ordnance Sergeant on June 15, 1862, and transferred to the Field and Staff. Present or accounted for until appointed "ordnance officer" (2nd Lieutenant) of Brigadier General John R. Cooke's brigade on or about September 2, 1864.

TROLLINGER, JACOB H.

Previously served as Corporal in Company K of this regiment. Detailed as Ordnance Sergeant on September 6, 1864, and transferred to the Field and Staff. Records of the Field and Staff do not indicate whether he rejoined Company K; however, he was captured at Dinwiddie Court House, Virginia, April 3, 1865. Confined at Point Lookout, Maryland, until released on June 21, 1865, after taking the Oath of Allegiance.

PATTERSON, ARMISTEAD H.

Previously served in Captain Pencik's Company, Virginia Light Artillery. Appointed Ordnance Sergeant of this regiment in January-February, 1865. Present or accounted for until paroled at Appomattox Court House, Virginia, April 9, 1865.

BAND

ALEXANDER, JASPER, Musician

Previously served as Musician in Company B of this regiment. Detailed for duty with the regimental band at an unspecified date subsequent to January 26, 1864. Rejoined his company at an unspecified date.

ALEXANDER, OSWALD, Musician

Previously served as Private in Company B of this regiment. Promoted to Musician and detailed for duty with the regimental band in March-June, 1862. Rejoined his company at an unspecified date.

ALEXANDER, ULYSSES C., Musician

Previously served as Private in Company B of this regiment. Detailed for duty with the regimental band in February, 1863. Rejoined his company at an unspecified date.

ALEXANDER, WILLIAM W., Musician

Previously served as Musician in Company B of this regiment. Detailed for duty with the regimental band at an unspecified date subsequent to January 22, 1864. Rejoined his company at an unspecified date.

ALEXANDER, WILSON WATSON, Musician

Previously served as Musician (Drummer) in Company B of this regiment. Detailed for duty with the regimental band in 1864. Rejoined his company at an unspecified date.

BROWN, JAMES WILLIAM, Musician

Previously served as Private in Company B of this regiment. Promoted to Musician and detailed for duty with the regimental band in September-October, 1863. Records do not indicate whether he rejoined his company; however, he was paroled at Appomattox Court House, Virginia, April 9, 1865.

FRAZER, JAMES N., Musician

Previously served as Musician in Company B of this regiment. Detailed for duty with the regimental band at an unspecified date subsequent to January 22, 1864. Rejoined his company at an unspecified date.

FRAZIER, ISAAC A., Musician

Previously served as Musician in Company B of this regiment. Detailed for duty in the regimental band at an unspecified date subsequent to January 13, 1863. Rejoined his company at an unspecified date.

FRAZIER, JOHN T., Musician

Previously served as Private in Company B of this regiment. Promoted to Musician and detailed for duty with the regimental band in September-October, 1862. Present or accounted for through June, 1862. Rejoined his company at an unspecified date.

FRAZIER, RICHARD J., Musician

Previously served as Private in Company B of this regiment. Promoted to Musician and detailed for duty with the regimental band in September-October, 1861. Present or accounted for through June, 1862. Rejoined his company at an unspecified date.

FRAZIER, WARREN F., Musician

Previously served as Private in Company B of this regiment. Promoted to Musician and detailed for duty with the regimental band in September-October, 1861. Present or accounted for through June, 1862. Rejoined his company at an unspecified date.

HAWKINS, JAMES F., Musician

Previously served as Musician in Company B of this regiment. Detailed for duty with the regimental band at an unspecified date subsequent to January 22, 1864. Rejoined his company at an unspecified date.

HAWKINS, JOSEPH P., Musician

Previously served as Private in Company B of this regiment. Promoted to Musician and detailed for duty with the regimental band in September-October, 1861. Present or accounted for through June, 1862. Rejoined his company at an unspecified date.

JOHNSTON, JAMES H., Musician

Previously served as Musician (Drummer) in Company A of this regiment. Detailed for duty with the regimental band in September-October, 1861. Promoted to Musician (Drum Major) on September 1, 1862. Reduced to ranks and transferred back to Company A in October, 1862.

KERR, JOHN T., Musician

Previously served as Private in Company B of this regiment. Promoted to Musician and detailed for duty with the regimental band in September-October, 1861. Present or accounted for through June, 1862. Rejoined his company at an unspecified date.

McCONNELL, JAMES H., Musician

Previously served as Private in Company B of this regiment. Promoted to Musician and detailed for duty with the regimental band in September-October, 1861. Present or accounted for through June, 1862. Rejoined his company at an unspecified date.

REID, JOHN WILLIAM, Musician

Previously served as Private in Company B of this regiment. Promoted to Musician and detailed for duty with the regimental band in September-October, 1861. Present or accounted for through June, 1862. Rejoined his company at an unspecified date.

STERLING, JOHN H., Musician

Previously served as Private in Company B of this regiment. Promoted to Musician and detailed for duty with the regimental band in September-October, 1861. Present or accounted for through June, 1862. Rejoined his company at an unspecified date.

TAYLOR, ARCHIBALD A., Musician

Previously served as Private in Company B of this regiment. Promoted to Musician and detailed for duty with the regimental band in September-October, 1861. Present or accounted for through June, 1862. Rejoined his company at an unspecified date.

THOMPSON, WILLIAM J., Musician

Previously served as Private in Company B of this regiment. Promoted to Musician and detailed for duty with the regimental band in September-October, 1861. Present or accounted for through June, 1862. Rejoined his company at an unspecified date.

TODD, JOHN A. N., Musician

Previously served as Private in Company B of this regiment. Promoted to Musician and detailed for duty with the regimental band in September-October, 1861. Present or accounted for until he died at Richmond, Virginia, June 6, 1862. Cause of death not reported.

WEARN, GEORGE H., Chief Musician

Previously served as Musician in Company B of this regiment. Detailed for duty with the regimental band in September-October, 1861. Promoted to Chief Musician (Drum Major) on November 1, 1863. Rejoined his company at an unspecified date. No further records.

COMPANY A

This company, known as the Yanceyville Grays, was from Caswell County and enlisted at Yanceyville on April 29, 1861. On May 4, 1861, it was ordered to Weldon and moved to Raleigh, where it remained until 7:00 A.M. on May 23 when it proceeded to Weldon. Upon its arrival at Weldon the regiment was ordered to proceed to Garysburg. There it was assigned to this regiment as Company A. After joining the regiment the company functioned as a part of the regiment, and its history for the war period is recorded as a part of the regimental history.

The information contained in the following roster of the company was compiled principally from company muster rolls for May 18, 1861, through October, 1864. No company muster rolls were found for the period after October, 1864. In addition to the company muster rolls, Roll of Honor records, receipt rolls, hospital records, prisoner of war records, and other primary records, supplemented by state pension applications, United Daughters of the Confederacy records, and postwar rosters and histories, all provided useful information.

OFFICERS

CAPTAINS

GRAVES, JOHN A.

Resided in Caswell County and was by occupation a lawyer prior to enlisting in Caswell County at age 38. Elected Captain to rank from April 29, 1861. Present or accounted for until promoted to Major on April 8, 1862, and transferred to the Field and Staff, 47th Regiment N.C. Troops.

WITHERS, ELIJAH BENTON

Resided in Caswell County and was by occupation a lawyer prior to enlisting in Caswell County at age 23, April 29, 1861. Mustered in as Private and was appointed Captain to rank from April 26, 1862. Present or accounted for until promoted to Major on June 13, 1863, and transferred to the Field and Staff of this regiment.

HENDERSON, LUDOLPHUS B.

Resided in Caswell County and was by occupation a dentist prior to enlisting in Caswell County at age 25, April 29, 1861. Mustered in as Private and promoted to Corporal on June 7, 1861. Elected 1st Lieutenant to rank from April 26, 1862, and promoted to Captain on June 13, 1863. Present or accounted for until wounded at Gettysburg, Pennsylvania, July 3, 1863. Returned to duty on September 10, 1863, and present or accounted for until hospitalized at Danville, Virginia, June 2, 1864, with a gunshot wound. Place and date wounded not reported. Returned to duty on September 1, 1864, and present or accounted for until captured at Hatcher's Run, Virginia, April 2, 1865. Confined at Old Capitol Prison, Washington, D.C., until transferred to Johnson's Island, Ohio, April 9, 1865. Released at Johnson's Island on June 18, 1865, after taking the Oath of Allegiance.

LIEUTENANTS

FOWLER, HENRY B., 2nd Lieutenant

Resided in Davie County and enlisted at Camp Ruffin, Virginia, at age 27, August 10, 1861. Mustered in as Private and was elected 2nd Lieutenant to rank from April 26, 1862. Present or accounted for until killed at Sharpsburg, Maryland, September 17, 1862.

GUNN, GEORGE W., 3rd Lieutenant
Resided in Caswell County and was by occupation a "physic" prior to enlisting in Caswell County at age 26. Elected 3rd Lieutenant on April 29, 1861. Reported "under arrest" on a company muster-in roll dated May 18-June 30, 1861. Resigned on July 5, 1861. Later enlisted in Company C, 41st Regiment N.C.Troops (3rd Regiment N.C.Cavalry).

LOCKETT, DAVID S., 2nd Lieutenant
Resided in Caswell County and was by occupation a laborer prior to enlisting in Caswell County at age 20. Mustered in as Private and elected 2nd Lieutenant on May 11, 1863. Present or accounted for until paroled at Appomattox Court House, Virginia, April 9, 1865.

McADEN, BARTLETT Y., 1st Lieutenant
Resided in Caswell County and was by occupation a farmer prior to enlisting at age 29. Elected 1st Lieutenant on April 29, 1861. Present or accounted for until he was defeated for reelection when the regiment was reorganized on April 26, 1862.

NORFLEET, MARMADUKE WILLIAMS,
2nd Lieutenant
Resided in Caswell County and was by occupation a "speculator" prior to enlisting in Caswell County at age 21. Elected 2nd Lieutenant on April 29, 1861. Present or accounted for until he was defeated for reelection when the regiment was reorganized on April 26, 1862. Later served as 2nd Lieutenant in Company C, 47th Regiment N.C.Troops.

POTEAT, FELIX L., 3rd Lieutenant
Resided in Caswell County and was by occupation a farmer prior to enlisting in Caswell County at age 22, April 29, 1861. Mustered in as Sergeant and was appointed 3rd Lieutenant to rank from July 13, 1861. Present or accounted for until he was defeated for reelection when the regiment was reorganized on April 26, 1862. [May have served later as 3rd Lieutenant of Company K, 47th Regiment N.C.Troops.]

ROBERTSON, WILEY P., 3rd Lieutenant
Born in Caswell County where he resided as a tobacconist prior to enlisting in Caswell County at age 18, April 29, 1861. Mustered in as Corporal and elected 3rd Lieutenant on April 26, 1862. Present or accounted for until killed at Gaines' Mill, Virginia, June 27, 1862.

WILLIAMSON, JAMES N., 1st Lieutenant
Resided in Caswell County and was by occupation a student prior to enlisting in Caswell County at age 18, May 13, 1861. Mustered in as Private and appointed 3rd Lieutenant on September 23, 1862. Present or accounted for until wounded at Chancellorsville, Virginia, May 1-3, 1863. Promoted to 2nd Lieutenant on June 7, 1863, to rank from May 21, 1863, and was promoted to 1st Lieutenant on June 13, 1863. Rejoined the company prior to July 1, 1863, when he was wounded in the thigh at Gettysburg, Pennsylvania. Rejoined the company in September-October, 1863, and present or accounted for until paroled at Appomattox Court House, Virginia, April 9, 1865.

WILLIAMSON, WALTER S., 2nd Lieutenant
Resided in Caswell County and was by occupation a farmer prior to enlisting in Caswell County at age 21, April 29, 1861. Mustered in as 1st Sergeant and appointed 2nd Lieutenant on September 23, 1862. Present or accounted for until he resigned on April 18, 1863, upon appointment as Adjutant (1st Lieutenant) of the 8th Regiment N.C.State Troops to rank from November 1, 1862.

NONCOMMISSIONED OFFICERS AND PRIVATES

BECK, J., Private
Place and date of enlistment not reported. Admitted to hospital at Greensboro in April, 1865. Paroled at Greensboro on May 8, 1865.

BOSWELL, GEORGE W., Private
Born in Caswell County where he resided as a farmer prior to enlisting in Caswell County at age 20, April 29, 1861. Present or accounted for until he died in hospital at Petersburg, Virginia, May 10, 1862, of "typhoid fever."

BOSWORTH, BEDFORD A., Private
Resided in Caswell County. Place and date of enlistment not reported. Captured in hospital at Richmond, Virginia, April 3, 1865. Confined at Newport News, Virginia, April 24, 1865. Released June 15, 1865, after taking the Oath of Allegiance.

BOWERS, _____, _____
Enlisted on August 1, 1862, as a substitute for Private Thomas S. Harrison. Deserted the same day.

BOWLIN, JEREMIAH, Private
Enlisted at Camp Vance on February 1, 1864, for the war. Present or accounted for until he deserted on April 12, 1864. Paroled at Morganton on May 27, 1865.

BRADY, JAMES W., Private
Enlisted in Wake County on November 22, 1863, for the war. Deserted near Petersburg, Virginia, June 22, 1864.

BRINCEFIELD, CALVIN, Private
Born in Caswell County where he resided as a carpenter prior to enlisting in Caswell County at age 34, April 29, 1861. Discharged on December 10, 1861, by reason of "chronic rheumatism" but reenlisted in this company on September 15, 1863. Present or accounted for through November 5, 1864.

BRINCEFIELD, MARTIN, Private
Resided in Caswell County and was by occupation a laborer prior to enlisting in Caswell County at age 20, April 29, 1861. Present or accounted for until he died in hospital at Charlottesville, Virginia, May 8, 1863, of "pneumonia."

BUSHNELL, HENRY W., Private
Resided in Caswell County and enlisted at Camp Ruffin, Virginia, at age 28, September 5, 1861. Present or accounted for through October, 1864; however, he was reported absent sick during most of that period.

BUSHNELL, JAMES M., Private
Resided in Caswell County. Place and date of enlistment not reported. Captured at Hatcher's Run, Vir-

ginia, April 2, 1865. Confined at Point Lookout, Maryland, until released on June 23, 1865, after taking the Oath of Allegiance.

BYERLY, JACOB, Private
Born in Davidson County where he resided prior to enlisting at Camp Holmes on February 24, 1864, for the war. Present or accounted for until captured at Hatcher's Run, Virginia, April 2, 1865. Confined at Point Lookout, Maryland, until released on June 23, 1865, after taking the Oath of Allegiance.

BYRD, THOMAS, Private
Resided in Caswell County and enlisted at Camp Holmes on January 28, 1864, for the war. Deserted on April 12, 1864. Company records do not indicate whether he rejoined the company; however, he was captured by the enemy at Petersburg, Virginia, April 2, 1865. Confined at Point Lookout, Maryland, until released on June 23, 1865, after taking the Oath of Allegiance.

CAPE, GEORGE, Private
Enlisted at Orange Court House, Virginia, April 1, 1864, for the war. Present or accounted for through December 23, 1864; however, he was reported absent sick during much of that period.

CAPPS, C. A., Private
Enlisted at Camp Vance on December 28, 1863, for the war. Deserted near Orange Court House, Virginia, on or about January 23, 1864, and deserted to the enemy on or about February 13, 1864.

CHANDLER, H. A., Private
Born in Caswell County and enlisted at Camp Holmes on April 10, 1864, for the war. Present or accounted for until he died in hospital at Richmond, Virginia, on or about June 4, 1864, of a gunshot wound. Place and date wounded not reported.

CLARK, PETER F., Private
Enlisted at Orange Court House, Virginia, March 17, 1864, for the war. Present or accounted for until paroled at Appomattox Court House, Virginia, April 9, 1865.

COOK, WILLIAM L., Private
Enlisted at Camp Holmes on April 10, 1864, for the war. Present or accounted for through November 23, 1864.

CORBETT, JAMES F., Private
Resided in Caswell County and was by occupation a student prior to enlisting in Caswell County at age 19, April 29, 1861. Present or accounted for until wounded in the hand at South Mountain, Maryland, September 14, 1862. Rejoined the company in March-April, 1863, and present or accounted for until transferred to Company C, 41st Regiment N.C. Troops (3rd Regiment N.C.Cavalry), January 23, 1865.

COVINGTON, GEORGE W., Private
Born in Caswell County where he resided as a student prior to enlisting in Caswell County at age 16, April 29, 1861. Present or accounted for until discharged on July 27, 1862, by reason of being under age.

DAVIS, JOHN G., Private
Resided in Caswell County and enlisted at Camp Ruffin, Virginia, at age 19, July 18, 1861. Present or

accounted for until he deserted on September 20, 1862. Returned from desertion on August 8, 1864. Captured at Hatcher's Run, Virginia, April 2, 1865. Confined at Point Lookout, Maryland, until released on June 9, 1865, after taking the Oath of Allegiance.

DEITZ, HENRY C., Private
Enlisted at Camp Vance on August 1, 1863, for the war. Present or accounted for through October, 1864. Paroled at Newton on April 19, 1865.

DENNIS, FRANKLIN JEFFERSON, Private
Resided in Caswell County and was by occupation a coach maker prior to enlisting in Caswell County at age 27, April 29, 1861. Present or accounted for until wounded at Gettysburg, Pennsylvania, July 1-3, 1863. Returned to duty prior to September 1, 1863, and present or accounted for until captured at the North Anna River, Virginia, May 23, 1864. Confined at Point Lookout, Maryland, until paroled and transferred to Boulware's Wharf, James River, Virginia, where he was received March 16, 1865, for exchange.

DICKINSON, GEORGE B., Private
Resided in Caswell County and enlisted at Camp Ruffin, Virginia, at age 18, July 27, 1861. Present or accounted for through October, 1863. May have served later as Sergeant Major of this regiment. No further records.

DUKE, JOHN W., Private
Resided in Caswell County and was by occupation a wagoner prior to enlisting in Caswell County at age 26, April 29, 1861. Present or accounted for until wounded at Gaines' Mill, Virginia, June 27, 1862. Rejoined the company in January-February, 1863, and present or accounted for until wounded at Spotsylvania Court House, Virginia, May 20, 1864. Reported absent wounded until retired to the Invalid Corps on December 31, 1864.

DUPREE, JOSEPH W., Private
Born in Caswell County where he resided as a carpenter or farmer prior to enlisting in Caswell County at age 34, April 29, 1861. Mustered in as Sergeant but was reduced to ranks when the regiment was reorganized on April 26, 1862. Present or accounted for until wounded at Gaines' Mill, Virginia, June 27, 1862, "while bearing the flag." Died at Richmond, Virginia, July 24, 1862, of wounds.

DUPREE, ROBERT H., Private
Resided in Caswell County and enlisted at Camp Ruffin, Virginia, at age 19, August 1, 1861. Present or accounted for until discharged on July 28, 1862, after providing Private John Thomas of Company H as a substitute.

ENOCH, JOHN C., Private
Resided in Caswell County and enlisted on April 15, 1864, for the war. Captured at Hatcher's Run, Virginia, April 2, 1865. Confined at Point Lookout, Maryland, until released on June 11, 1865, after taking the Oath of Allegiance.

ENOCH, WALKER L., Private
Resided in Caswell County and was by occupation a farmer prior to enlisting in Caswell County at age 21, April 29, 1861. Captured at Middletown, Maryland, on or about September 12, 1862. Confined at

Fort Delaware, Delaware, until transferred to Aiken's Landing, James River, Virginia, October 2, 1862, for exchange. Declared exchanged at Aiken's Landing on November 10, 1862. Rejoined the company prior to January 1, 1863, and present or accounted for until captured at Richmond, Virginia, April 3, 1865. Confined at Newport News, Virginia, until released on June 30, 1865, after taking the Oath of Allegiance.

EVANS, G. WILSON, Private
Born in Caswell County where he resided as a farmer prior to enlisting in Caswell County at age 24, April 29, 1861. Present or accounted for until he died in hospital at Richmond, Virginia, May 16, 1862, of disease.

EVANS, SAMUEL W., Private
Born in Caswell County where he resided as a farmer prior to enlisting in Caswell County at age 22, April 29, 1861. Present or accounted for until discharged near Burkeville, Virginia, October 27, 1862, by reason of "permanent deafness" and "double inguinal hernia."

EVANS, W. L., Private
Enlisted at Orange Court House, Virginia, March 27, 1864, for the war. Died "at home" on June 15, 1864. Cause of death not reported.

FERGUSON, JAMES T., Private
Resided in Caswell County and was by occupation a wagoner prior to enlisting in Caswell County at age 22, April 29, 1861. Present or accounted for until paroled at Appomattox Court House, Virginia, April 9, 1865.

FERRELL, WILLIAM F., Private
Resided in Caswell County or at Danville, Virginia, and was by occupation a farmer prior to enlisting in Caswell County at age 24, April 29, 1861. Mustered in as Private and promoted to Corporal on April 26, 1862. Reduced to ranks on December 15, 1862. Present or accounted for until captured at Gettysburg, Pennsylvania, July 1-4, 1863. Confined at Davids Island, New York Harbor, until transferred to City Point, Virginia, where he was received September 16, 1863, for exchange. Promoted to Corporal on March 25, 1864, but was reduced to ranks prior to June 12, 1864, when he was captured at Cold Harbor, Virginia. Confined at Point Lookout, Maryland, until transferred to Elmira, New York, July 27, 1864. Released at Elmira on June 16, 1865, after taking the Oath of Allegiance.

FITZGERALD, ELISHA B., Private
Resided in Caswell County and was by occupation a farmer prior to enlisting at Suffolk, Virginia, at age 18, June 10, 1861. Present or accounted for until he died "at home" or at Yorktown, Virginia, on or about June 12, 1862, of disease.

FITZGERALD, OBEDIAH N., Private
Resided in Caswell County and was by occupation a farmer prior to enlisting at Suffolk, Virginia, at age 27, June 10, 1861. Present or accounted for until killed at South Mountain, Maryland, September 14, 1862.

FITZGERALD, RICHARD THOMAS, Corporal
Resided in Caswell County and was by occupation a

farmer prior to enlisting at Suffolk, Virginia, at age 20, June 10, 1861. Mustered in as Private and promoted to Corporal on March 25, 1864. Present or accounted for until paroled at Appomattox Court House, Virginia, April 9, 1865.

GILLESPIE, JOSEPH M., Private
Resided in Caswell County and enlisted at Camp Ruffin, Virginia, at age 23, July 18, 1861. Present or accounted for until his left eye was "shot out" at Williamsburg, Virginia, May 5, 1862. Rejoined the company in January-February, 1863, and present or accounted for until paroled at Appomattox Court House, Virginia, April 9, 1865.

GOLD, A. J., Private
Enlisted at Camp Vance on February 16, 1864, for the war. Present or accounted for until he died in hospital at Salisbury on August 14, 1864, of "diarrhoea ch[ronic]."

GRAVES, FELIX R., Private
Born in Caswell County where he resided as a miller or farmer prior to enlisting in Caswell County at age 28, April 29, 1861. Present or accounted for until killed at Malvern Hill, Virginia, June 30-July 1, 1862.

GRAVES, GEORGE AUGUSTUS, Private
Resided in Caswell County and was by occupation a farmer prior to enlisting in Caswell County at age 23, April 29, 1861, for one year. Present or accounted for until appointed Captain on April 26, 1862, and transferred to Company G, 22nd Regiment N.C. Troops (12th Regiment N.C. Volunteers).

GRAVES, JOHN H. N. F., Sergeant
Born in Caswell County where he resided as a farmer prior to enlisting in Caswell County at age 20, April 29, 1861. Mustered in as Private and promoted to Sergeant on September 23, 1862. Present or accounted for until wounded at Fredericksburg, Virginia, December 13, 1862. Rejoined the company in January-February, 1863, and present or accounted for until killed at Chancellorsville, Virginia, May 3, 1863.

GRAVES, WILLIAM G., Private
Resided in Caswell County and was by occupation a farmer prior to enlisting in Caswell County at age 23, April 29, 1861. Present or accounted for until wounded by a "stray ball" at Yorktown, Virginia, April 27, 1862. Transferred on or about July 5, 1862, upon appointment as 1st Lieutenant in Company H, 56th Regiment N.C. Troops.

GUNN, FRANKLIN L., Corporal
Resided in Caswell County and was by occupation a student prior to enlisting in Caswell County at age 18, April 29, 1861. Mustered in as Corporal. Present or accounted for until transferred to Company H, 3rd Regiment Alabama Infantry in September-October, 1861.

GUYNN, RICHARD M., Private
Enlisted at Camp Holmes on April 10, 1864, for the war. Present or accounted for through November 5, 1864.

HALL, SYDNEY J., Private
Born in Caswell County and enlisted at Orange Court House, Virginia, May 19, 1864, for the war.

Captured in battle on the North Anna River, Virginia, May 23, 1864. Confined at Point Lookout, Maryland, until paroled and transferred to Aiken's Landing, James River, Virginia, September 18, 1864, for exchange. "Bro[ugh]t from the Flag of Truce Boat dead" on or about September 20, 1864. Place and cause of death not reported.

HARRALSON, ALLEN, Sergeant
Resided in Caswell County and was by occupation a clerk prior to enlisting in Caswell County at age 18, April 29, 1861. Mustered in as Private and appointed Sergeant on November 3, 1861. Reduced to ranks on April 26, 1862. Present or accounted for until wounded at Fredericksburg, Virginia, December 13, 1862. Rejoined the company in March-April, 1863, and was promoted to Sergeant on May 11, 1863. Present or accounted for until hospitalized at Danville, Virginia, May 23, 1864, with a gunshot wound of the shoulder; however, place and date wounded not reported. Returned to duty on June 21, 1864, and present or accounted for until captured at Hatcher's Run, Virginia, April 2, 1865. Confined at Point Lookout, Maryland, until released on June 27, 1865, after taking the Oath of Allegiance.

HARRALSON, BASELY, Private
Enlisted at Camp Holmes on April 10, 1864, for the war. Captured at Wilderness, Virginia, May 5-6, 1864. Confined at Point Lookout, Maryland, until transferred to Elmira, New York, August 10, 1864. Died at Elmira on January 19, 1865, of "variola."

HARRALSON, BRICE, Private
Born in Caswell County where he resided as a merchant prior to enlisting in Caswell County at age 30, April 29, 1861. Present or accounted for until transferred to the C. S. Navy for duty on the C.S.S. *Merrimac* on February 19, 1862.

HARRELSON, L. L., Private
Place and date of enlistment not reported. Reported in hospital at Danville, Virginia, April 5, 1865. Paroled at Raleigh on May 16, 1865.

HARRISON, THOMAS S., Private
Resided in Caswell County and was by occupation a farmer prior to enlisting in Caswell County at age 18, April 29, 1861. Mustered in as Private and promoted to Corporal on November 3, 1861. Reduced to ranks on April 26, 1862. Present or accounted for until discharged in May, 1862, or on August 1, 1862, after furnishing _____ Bowers as a substitute.

HATCHETT, WILLIAM H., Private
Born in Caswell County where he resided as a farmer prior to enlisting in Caswell County at age 21, April 29, 1861. Present or accounted for until wounded in the arm and captured at South Mountain, Maryland, September 14, 1862. Confined at Fort McHenry, Maryland, until paroled and transferred to Aiken's Landing, James River, Virginia, where he was received October 19, 1862, for exchange. Declared exchanged at Aiken's Landing on November 10, 1862. Reported absent wounded until discharged on January 30, 1864, by reason of a "gun shot wound of the arm causing paralysis of the limb."

HAWKINS, CHARLES O., Private
Resided in Caswell County and was by occupation a grocer prior to enlisting in Caswell County at age 23, April 29, 1861. Present or accounted for until killed at Fredericksburg, Virginia, December 13, 1862.

HENDERSON, JAMES A., Private
Born in Caswell County where he resided as a student or farmer prior to enlisting in Caswell County at age 19, April 29, 1861. Present or accounted for until discharged on August 23, 1862, by reason of "phthisis pulmonalis."

HENDERSON, NATHANIEL S., Private
Born in Caswell County where he resided as a physician prior to enlisting in Caswell County at age 23, April 29, 1861. Present or accounted for until discharged October 20, 1861, by reason of disability.

HENSLEY, HENRY, Private
Resided in Caswell County and was by occupation a farmer prior to enlisting in Caswell County at age 17, April 29, 1861. Present or accounted for until wounded in the left arm and left leg at Malvern Hill, Virginia, July 1, 1862. Discharged September 28, 1862, by reason of wounds received at Malvern Hill; however, he reenlisted in this company at Orange Court House, Virginia, September 5, 1863. Present or accounted for until paroled at Appomattox Court House, Virginia, April 9, 1865.

HODGES, YEWELL FRANKLIN, Private
Resided in Caswell County and enlisted at Camp Holmes on October 16, 1864, for the war. Records of the Federal Provost Marshal indicate both that he deserted on or about March 19, 1865, and that he was captured at Hatcher's Run, Virginia, April 2, 1865. Confined at Point Lookout, Maryland, until released on or about June 27, 1865, after taking the Oath of Allegiance.

HOOPER, JAMES HENRY, Private
Born in Caswell County where he resided as a farmer prior to enlisting in Caswell County at age 17, April 29, 1861. Discharged on or about July 29, 1862, by reason of being under age. Reenlisted in this company prior to April 9, 1865, when he was paroled at Appomattox Court House, Virginia.

HOWARD, HENRY O., Private
Resided in Caswell County and was by occupation a farmer prior to enlisting in Caswell County at age 20, April 29, 1861. Mustered in as Private. Present or accounted for until wounded at Barnett's Ford, Virginia, August 1, 1862. Returned to duty prior to November 1, 1862, and present or accounted for until wounded at Gettysburg, Pennsylvania, July 1-3, 1863. Returned to duty prior to September 1, 1863. Present or accounted for until promoted to Ensign (Color Sergeant) on December 1, 1863, and transferred to the Field and Staff of this regiment.

HOWARD, WILLIAM M., Private
Resided in Caswell County and was by occupation a farmer prior to enlisting in Caswell County at age 20, April 29, 1861. Mustered in as Private. Present or accounted for until appointed Sergeant Major on or about April 30, 1863, and transferred to the Field and Staff of this regiment.

HYMAN, GAVIN L., Private
Previously served in Company G, 41st Regiment N.C. Troops (3rd Regiment N.C. Cavalry). Transfer-

red to this company on January 24, 1865. No further records.

JEFFREYS, JOHN G., Private

Resided in Caswell County and was by occupation a farmer prior to enlisting in Caswell County at age 21, April 29, 1861. Present or accounted for until paroled at Appomattox Court House, Virginia, April 9, 1865.

JEFFRIES, LEA, Private

Place and date of enlistment not reported. First reported on records of this company on November 15, 1864. Paroled at Appomattox Court House, Virginia, April 9, 1865.

JOHNSON, JOHN J., Private

Resided in Indiana and enlisted at age 25. Roll of Honor indicates he enlisted on April 29, 1861; however, he was not listed in the records of this company until December, 1862, when he was reported as a deserter. Roll of Honor indicates he deserted at Boonsboro, Maryland. Records of the Federal Provost Marshal indicate he was captured at Sharpsburg, Maryland, on or about September 17, 1862, and refused to be exchanged. No further records.

JOHNSON, TOBIAS, Private

Born in Wilkes County where he resided prior to enlisting in Wake County at age 18, September 27, 1862, for the war. Present or accounted for until he died at Camp Gregg, Virginia, February 19, 1863, of disease.

JOHNSON, WILLIAM W., Private

Enlisted at Camp Holmes on December 8, 1863, for the war. Present or accounted for until he died in hospital at Gordonsville, Virginia, March 23-26, 1864. Cause of death not reported.

JOHNSTON, JAMES H., Private

Resided in Wilkes County and was by occupation a coach trimmer prior to enlisting in Caswell County at age 25, April 29, 1861. Mustered in as Musician (Drummer). Detailed for duty with the regimental band in September-October, 1861. Promoted to Musician (Drum Major) on September 1, 1862, while absent on detail with the band. Reduced to ranks and transferred back to this company in October, 1862. Present or accounted for until he died "in camp" or in hospital at Petersburg, Virginia, on or about February 8, 1863. Cause of death not reported.

JONES, EDWARD O., 1st Sergeant

Born in Caswell County where he resided as deputy postmaster prior to enlisting in Caswell County at age 23, April 29, 1861. Mustered in as Private and promoted to 1st Sergeant on December 15, 1862. Present or accounted for until killed at Chancellorsville, Virginia, May 3, 1863.

JONES, HENRY M., Private

Enlisted at Camp Holmes on August 26, 1864, for the war. Present or accounted for until paroled at Appomattox Court House, Virginia, April 9, 1865.

JONES, JOHN McCAIN, 1st Sergeant

Resided in Person County and enlisted in Caswell County at age 22, September 3, 1861. Mustered in as Private and promoted to Sergeant on December 15, 1862. Promoted to 1st Sergeant on May 1, 1863.

Present or accounted for until wounded at Gettysburg, Pennsylvania, July 1, 1863. Rejoined the company in November-December, 1863. Hospitalized at Danville, Virginia, May 28, 1864, with a gunshot wound of the hand; however, place and date wounded not reported. Returned to duty on June 21, 1864, and present or accounted for until paroled at Appomattox Court House, Virginia, April 9, 1865.

JONES, ROBERT W., Private

Resided in Person County and enlisted in Caswell County at age 23, September 3, 1861. Present or accounted for until wounded severely at Gaines' Mill, Virginia, June 27, 1862. Reported absent wounded until he rejoined the company in January-February, 1864. Retired to the Invalid Corps on April 15, 1864, by reason of wounds received at Gaines' Mill.

KENNON, WILLIAM G., Private

Born in Caswell County where he resided prior to enlisting at Camp Ruffin, Virginia, at age 18, July 18, 1861. Present or accounted for until wounded at Sharpsburg, Maryland, September 17, 1862. Rejoined the company in January-February, 1863, and present or accounted for until wounded in battle on May 29, 1864. Died prior to July 1, 1864, of wounds. Place of death not reported.

KERR, NATHANIEL R., Private

Resided in Caswell County and was by occupation a student prior to enlisting in Caswell County at age 18, April 29, 1861. Mustered in as Corporal but was reduced to ranks when the regiment was reorganized on April 26, 1862. Present or accounted for until killed at South Mountain, Maryland, September 14, 1862.

KIMBRO, JAMES W., Private

Resided in Caswell County and enlisted at Camp Ruffin, Virginia, at age 24, July 18, 1861. Mustered in as Private and promoted to Corporal on December 15, 1862. Present or accounted for until wounded in the left arm at Chancellorsville, Virginia, May 3, 1863. Reported absent wounded until March-April, 1864, when he was reduced to ranks. Retired to the Invalid Corps on April 29, 1864, by reason of wounds received at Chancellorsville.

KIMBRO, JOHN T., Corporal

Resided in Caswell County and was by occupation a farmer prior to enlisting in Caswell County at age 20, April 29, 1861. Mustered in as Private. Present or accounted for until wounded in the middle finger of the right hand and captured at Chancellorsville, Virginia, May 3, 1863. Confined at Old Capitol Prison, Washington, D.C., until paroled and transferred to City Point, Virginia, where he was received June 12, 1863, for exchange. Rejoined the company prior to September 1, 1863, and was promoted to Corporal on March 25, 1864. Present or accounted for until wounded in the left knee at Wilderness, Virginia, May 5, 1864. Reported absent wounded through October, 1864.

KIMBRO, RUFUS, Private

Born in Caswell County where he resided as a farmer prior to enlisting in Caswell County at age 24, April 29, 1861. Present or accounted for until he died in hospital at Richmond, Virginia, June 12, 1862, of "cont[inued] fever."

KIMBROUGH, ALEXANDER, Private

Resided in Caswell County and was by occupation a farmer prior to enlisting in Caswell County at age 17, April 29, 1861. Present or accounted for until wounded in the right hand at Chancellorsville, Virginia, May 1-3, 1863. Returned to duty May 29, 1863. Present or accounted for until admitted to hospital at Petersburg, Virginia, June 3, 1864, with a gunshot wound of the shoulder; however, place and date wounded not reported. Rejoined the company in September-October, 1864. Captured at Garrett Station, Virginia, April 3, 1865. Confined at Hart's Island, New York Harbor, until released on June 17, 1865, after taking the Oath of Allegiance.

LAWSON, ROBERT W., Private

Was by occupation a merchant prior to enlisting in Caswell County at age 23, May 13, 1861. Present or accounted for until appointed Quartermaster Sergeant on October 4, 1861, and transferred to the Field and Staff of this regiment.

LEA, CALVIN GRAVES, Private

Resided in Caswell County and was by occupation a "physic" prior to enlisting in Caswell County at age 26, April 29, 1861. Present or accounted for until wounded and captured at South Mountain, Maryland, September 14, 1862. Paroled and exchanged on or about October 3, 1862. Reported absent wounded until discharged on May 15, 1863, by reason of wounds received at South Mountain.

LEA, JAMES WELDON, Private

Resided in Caswell County and was by occupation a farmer prior to enlisting in Caswell County at age 25, April 29, 1861. Mustered in as Private and promoted to Sergeant on July 19, 1861. Reduced to ranks when the regiment was reorganized on April 26, 1862. Transferred to Company I, 5th Regiment N.C. State Troops, upon election as 2nd Lieutenant in that company to rank from April 1, 1863.

LEA, JOHN G., Private

Resided in Caswell County and was by occupation a "physic" prior to enlisting in Caswell County at age 22, April 29, 1861. Mustered in as Private and promoted to Sergeant on April 26, 1862. Wounded in the right arm and captured at South Mountain, Maryland, September 14, 1862. Hospitalized at Frederick, Maryland, and at Washington, D.C., until confined at Old Capitol Prison, Washington, September 30, 1862. Transferred to Fort McHenry, Maryland, prior to October 17, 1862, when he was paroled and transferred for exchange. Received at Aiken's Landing, James River, Virginia, October 19, 1862, for exchange. Declared exchanged at Aiken's Landing on November 10, 1862. Returned to duty in March-April, 1863, and was detailed in hospital at Danville, Virginia. Reduced to ranks in March-April, 1864. Reported absent on detail at Danville through October, 1864.

LEONARD, B. A., Private

Enlisted at Camp Holmes on February 28, 1864, for the war. Died in hospital at Gordonsville, Virginia, April 14, 1864, of "pneumonia."

LONG, DAVID C., Private

Resided in Caswell County and enlisted at Camp Ruffin, Virginia, at age 25, July 10, 1861. Present or accounted for until wounded at Gaines' Mill, Virginia, June 27, 1862. Rejoined the company in March-April, 1863, and present or accounted for until captured at Gettysburg, Pennsylvania, July 1-4, 1863. Confined at Davids Island, New York Harbor, until paroled and transferred to City Point, Virginia, where he was received September 8, 1863, for exchange. Rejoined the company in January-February, 1864, and present or accounted for until killed near Reams' Station, Virginia, August 25, 1864.

LYON, JOHN K., Private

Born in Caswell County where he resided prior to enlisting at Camp Ruffin, Virginia, at age 19, July 18, 1861. Present or accounted for until admitted to hospital at Richmond, Virginia, May 7, 1862, with diarrhoea. Died in hospital at Richmond on or about May 12, 1862, of "typhoid pneumonia."

LYON, WILLIAM W., Private

Born in Caswell County and resided in Rockingham County where he was by occupation a carpenter or mechanic prior to enlisting in Rockingham County at age 25, May 30, 1861. Present or accounted for until transferred to the C. S. Navy for duty on the C.S.S. *Merrimac* on February 14, 1862.

McADEN, JOHN HENRY, Private

Resided in Caswell County and enlisted at age 24, April 29, 1861. Transferred to the Field and Staff of this regiment upon appointment as Assistant Surgeon on June 1, 1861, to rank from May 27, 1861.

McCAIN, JAMES A., Private

Born in Caswell County where he resided as a student prior to enlisting in Caswell County at age 17, April 29, 1861. Present or accounted for until discharged on July 29, 1862, by reason of being under age. Enlisted in Company C, 41st Regiment N.C. Troops (3rd Regiment N.C. Cavalry), July 13, 1863. Transferred back to this company on January 23, 1865. Captured at Hatcher's Run, Virginia, April 1, 1865, and confined at Point Lookout, Maryland, until released on June 15, 1865, after taking the Oath of Allegiance.

McCRARY, CHRISTOPHER, Private

Resided in Wilkes County and enlisted in Wake County at age 22, September 27, 1862. Present or accounted for until wounded at Chancellorsville, Virginia, May 3, 1863. Reported in hospital at Richmond, Virginia, May 10, 1863. Died of wounds received at Chancellorsville; however, place and date of death not reported.

MASSEY, RAINEY C., Private

Enlisted at Camp Holmes on April 10, 1864, for the war. Present or accounted for until paroled at Appomattox Court House, Virginia, April 9, 1865.

MAYNARD, HENRY C., Private

Resided in Caswell County and was by occupation a farmer prior to enlisting in Caswell County at age 17, April 29, 1861. Present or accounted for until wounded in the hip and captured at South Mountain, Maryland, September 14, 1862. Hospitalized at Burkittsville, Maryland. Never rejoined the company and company records indicate that he was believed to be dead. No further records.

MERRITT, SOLOMON, Private

Resided in Caswell County and was by occupation a laborer prior to enlisting in Caswell County at age 34, April 29, 1861. Present or accounted for until discharged in August, 1862, under the provisions of the Conscript Act.

MITCHELL, WILLIAM D., Private

Born in Caswell County where he resided as a student prior to enlisting in Caswell County at age 17, April 29, 1861. Present or accounted for until discharged near Orange Court House, Virginia, April 27, 1864, by reason of "chronic rheumatism causing enlargement of the joints of the lower extremities."

MOFFITT, ABEL, Private

Enlisted at Camp Holmes on December 14, 1863, for the war. Present or accounted for until wounded at Wilderness, Virginia, May 5, 1864. Died in hospital "in Orange County" in May, 1864.

MOORE, ALEXANDER, Private

Previously served in Company B, 59th Regiment N.C.Troops (4th Regiment N.C.Cavalry). Transferred to this company on April 15, 1864. Deserted on June 22, 1864, but returned on September 3, 1864. Deserted to the enemy on or about December 17, 1864. Took the Oath of Amnesty at City Point, Virginia, December 20, 1864, and was furnished transportation to New Bern.

MOORE, JOSEPH B., Corporal

Resided in Caswell County and was by occupation a teacher prior to enlisting in Caswell County at age 20, April 29, 1861. Mustered in as Private. Present or accounted for until reported absent without leave in November-December, 1862. Rejoined the company in March-April, 1863. Promoted to Corporal on March 25, 1864. Present or accounted for until reported missing at Spotsylvania Court House, Virginia, May 20, 1864. Records of the U. D. C. indicate that he died of wounds received at Spotsylvania Court House.

MOORE, SPENCER A., Private

Resided in Caswell County where he enlisted at age 36, August 17, 1863, for the war. Present or accounted for until paroled at Appomattox Court House, Virginia, April 9, 1865.

MORRIS, JOHN Z., Private

Born in Charlotte County, Virginia, and resided in Caswell County or in Charlotte County, Virginia, where he was by occupation a clerk of coachman prior to enlisting in Caswell County at age 21, April 29, 1861. Present or accounted for until captured at Petersburg, Virginia, April 2, 1865. Confined at Point Lookout, Maryland, until released on June 15, 1865, after taking the Oath of Allegiance.

MORSE, ELAM, Private

Place and date of enlistment not reported. First reported in the records of this company on December 1, 1864. Paroled at Greensboro on May 8, 1865.

NEAL, FELIX M., Private

Resided in Caswell County and enlisted at Camp Ruffin, Virginia, at age 19, October 23, 1861. Mustered in as Private and was promoted to Corporal on April 26, 1862. Present or accounted for

until wounded in the left leg and captured at Sharpsburg, Maryland, September 17, 1862. Paroled and exchanged in November, 1862. Rejoined the company in March-April, 1863, and was detailed in hospital at Richmond, Virginia, May 3, 1863. Reduced to ranks in March-April, 1864. Reported absent on detail through March 16, 1865. Paroled at Appomattox Court House, Virginia, April 9, 1865.

NEAL, JAMES H., Private

Enlisted at Camp Holmes on April 10, 1864, for the war. Admitted to hospital at Richmond, Virginia, May 25, 1864, with "typhoid fever" and died May 29, 1864.

ORR, A. P., Private

Place and date of enlistment not reported. Paroled at or near Burkeville Junction, Virginia, April 14-17, 1865.

ORR, E., Private

Place and date of enlistment not reported. Paroled at or near Burkeville Junction, Virginia, April 14-17, 1865.

PAGE, JAMES W., Private

Born in Caswell County where he resided as a farmer prior to enlisting in Caswell County at age 24, April 29, 1861. Present or accounted for until killed at Gaines' Mill, Virginia, June 27, 1862.

PARK, JOHN S., Private

Resided in Caswell County and was by occupation a tailor prior to enlisting in Caswell County at age 29, May 13, 1861. Present or accounted for until he was detailed as a nurse for the wounded at Gettysburg, Pennsylvania, and was captured on July 4, 1863. Confined at Fort Delaware, Delaware, until transferred to Point Lookout, Maryland, October 15-18, 1863. Paroled at Point Lookout and transferred to Cox's Landing, James River, Virginia, where he was received February 14-15, 1865, for exchange. Rejoined the company prior to April 2, 1865, when he was captured at or near Sutherland's Station, Virginia. Confined at Point Lookout until released on June 9, 1865, after taking the Oath of Allegiance.

PATTILLO, WILLIAM H., Private

Resided in Caswell County and was by occupation a "sportsman" prior to enlisting in Caswell County at age 20, April 29, 1861. Present or accounted for until discharged on July 27, 1862, after providing Private Selita Ragle as a substitute.

PETTIGREW, THOMAS C., Private

Enlisted at Orange Court House, Virginia, March 19, 1864, for the war. Present or accounted for until wounded at Spotsylvania Court House, Virginia, May 20, 1864. Rejoined the company in July-August, 1864, and present or accounted for until paroled at Appomattox Court House, Virginia, April 9, 1865.

PINNIX, WILLIAM F., Private

Resided in Caswell County and was by occupation a "physic" prior to enlisting in Caswell County at age 20, April 29, 1861. Present or accounted for until "shot through the lungs" at Gaines' Mill, Virginia, June 27, 1862. Rejoined the company in March-April, 1863, and present or accounted for until wounded at Chancellorsville, Virginia, May 3, 1863. Died in hospital prior to July 1, 1863, of wounds;

however, place of death not reported.

PLEASANTS, JOHN A., Private
Enlisted at Bunker Hill, Virginia, July 15, 1863, for the war. Deserted near Bunker Hill on July 21, 1863.

POTEAT, JAMES M., Corporal
Born in Caswell County where he resided as a farmer prior to enlisting in Caswell County at age 23, April 29, 1861. Mustered in as Private and promoted to Corporal on April 26, 1862. Present or accounted for until wounded in the hip and captured at Sharpsburg, Maryland, September 17, 1862. Confined at Fort McHenry, Maryland. Paroled and exchanged at Aiken's Landing, James River, Virginia, in November, 1862. Reported absent wounded until discharged at camp near Orange Court House, Virginia, February 8, 1864, by reason of wounds received at Sharpsburg.

POTEAT, THOMAS, Private
Born in Caswell County and enlisted at Camp Holmes on April 10, 1864, for the war. Present or accounted for until he died in hospital at Richmond, Virginia, June 10, 1864, of "rubeola."

RAGLE, SELITA, Private
Resided in Virginia and enlisted at Richmond, Virginia, at age 37, August 8, 1862, for the war as a substitute for Private William H. Pattillo. Present or accounted for until August 25, 1864, when company records indicate he was captured by the enemy; however, records of the Federal Provost Marshal do not substantiate that report. No further records.

REAGAN, JOHN C., Private
Resided in Caswell County and was by occupation a farmer prior to enlisting in Caswell County at age 21, April 29, 1861. Present or accounted for until wounded at Fredericksburg, Virginia, December 13, 1862. Rejoined the company prior to March 1, 1863, and present or accounted for until captured at Gettysburg, Pennsylvania, July 3, 1863. Confined at Fort McHenry, Maryland, and at Fort Delaware, Delaware, until transferred to Point Lookout, Maryland, October 15-18, 1863. Paroled at Point Lookout on February 18, 1865, and transferred to Boulware's and Cox's Wharf, James River, Virginia, where he was received February 20-21, 1865, for exchange. Reported present with a detachment of paroled prisoners at Camp Lee, near Richmond, Virginia, February 28, 1865.

RICHMOND, HENRY, Private
Resided in Caswell County and was by occupation a clerk prior to enlisting in Wake County at age 20, May 18, 1861. Present or accounted for until he died at or near Richmond, Virginia, September 1, 1862, of "fever."

ROAN, NATHANIEL K., Sergeant
Resided in Caswell County and was by occupation a student prior to enlisting in Caswell County at age 17, April 29, 1861. Mustered in as Sergeant. Appointed Ensign (Color Sergeant) on July 1, 1861, and transferred to the Field and Staff. Rejoined the company in January-February, 1862, and was reported present through June 30, 1862. Discharged on or about August 3, 1862, after furnishing John Webster as a substitute.

ROBERTS, JOHN L., Private
Resided in Caswell County and was by occupation a farmer prior to enlisting in Caswell County at age 29, April 29, 1861. Present or accounted for until paroled at Appomattox Court House, Virginia, April 9, 1865.

ROBERTS, RUFUS L., Private
Enlisted at Camp Holmes on September 20, 1864, for the war. Paroled at Appomattox Court House, Virginia, April 9, 1865.

ROBERTS, WILLIAM H., Sergeant
Resided in Caswell County and was by occupation a farmer prior to enlisting in Caswell County at age 21, April 29, 1861. Mustered in as Private. Present or accounted for until detailed to care for the wounded and was captured at Gettysburg, Pennsylvania, July 1-5, 1863. Confined at Davids Island, New York Harbor, until paroled and transferred to City Point, Virginia, where he was received September 16, 1863, for exchange. Rejoined the company in January-February, 1864, and was promoted to Sergeant on March 25, 1864. Present or accounted for until paroled at Appomattox Court House, Virginia, April 9, 1865.

ROBERTSON, JOHN, Private
Resided in Caswell County and was by occupation a farmer prior to enlisting in Caswell County at age 21, April 29, 1861. Present or accounted for until wounded at Gettysburg, Pennsylvania, July 1-2, 1863. Died July 2, 1863, of wounds. Place of death not reported.

ROBERTSON, MONROE, Private
Resided in Caswell County and was by occupation a farmer prior to enlisting in Caswell County at age 19, April 29, 1861. Present or accounted for until wounded in battle at the North Anna River, Virginia, May 23, 1864. Rejoined the company in July-August, 1864, and present or accounted for until paroled at Appomattox Court House, Virginia, April 9, 1865. Roll of Honor indicates that "he was presented with a Whitworth Rifle for bravery."

SAWYERS, THOMAS L., Private
Born in Caswell County where he resided as a farmer prior to enlisting in Caswell County at age 19, April 29, 1861. Present or accounted for until killed at Fredericksburg, Virginia, December 13, 1862.

SCHNEIDER, MARTIN, Private
Place and date of enlistment not reported. Captured at Reams' Station, Virginia, August 25, 1864. Confined at Old Capitol Prison, Washington, D.C., until transferred to Elmira, New York, October 24, 1864. Released at Elmira on November 29, 1864, after taking the Oath of Allegiance.

SCOTT, PLEASANT S., Private
Enlisted in Caswell County on March 6, 1863, for the war. Present or accounted for until wounded in the right leg at Gettysburg, Pennsylvania, July 1, 1863. Reported absent wounded until retired to the Invalid Corps on January 10, 1865.

SHIELDS, THOMAS R., Private
Resided in Caswell County where he enlisted at age 20, April 29, 1861. Present or accounted for until wounded in the hand at Gaines' Mill, Virginia, on or

about June 27, 1862. Rejoined the company prior to November 1, 1862, and present or accounted for until wounded in the right arm at Chancellorsville, Virginia, May 3, 1863. Rejoined the company in January-February, 1864, but was retired on April 8, 1864, by reason of wounds received at Chancellorsville.

SINK, JOSEPH A., Private
Enlisted at Camp Holmes on February 28, 1864, for the war. Present or accounted for until wounded at Wilderness, Virginia, May 5, 1864. Rejoined the company in July-August, 1864. Died in hospital at Richmond, Virginia, December 11, 1864. Cause of death not reported.

SLEDGE, CRAWFORD, Private
Born in Caswell County where he resided as a farmer prior to enlisting in Caswell County at age 35, April 29, 1861. Present or accounted for until discharged July 29, 1862, by reason of being over age.

SMITH, A. J., Private
Place and date of enlistment not reported. Paroled at Greensboro on May 11, 1865.

SMITH, RICHARD S., Private
Resided in Caswell County where he enlisted on September 1, 1864, for the war. Present or accounted for until captured at Hatcher's Run, Virginia, April 2, 1865. Confined at Point Lookout, Maryland, until released on June 19, 1865, after taking the Oath of Allegiance.

STADLER, B. G., Private
Resided in Caswell County and enlisted in Person County at age 37, March 6, 1863, for the war. Present or accounted for until admitted to hospital at Charlottesville, Virginia, July 27, 1863, with a gunshot wound; however, place and date wounded not reported. Returned to duty August 5, 1863, and present or accounted for until he died in hospital at Richmond, Virginia, November 22, 1863, of "dysentery acute."

STONE, THOMAS, Private
Born in Caswell County where he resided prior to enlisting in Caswell County at age 32, March 6, 1863, for the war. Present or accounted for until hospitalized at Richmond, Virginia, December 20, 1863, with "rubeola." Died January 20, 1864.

SUMMERS, HEZEKIAH, Private
Enlisted at Camp Holmes on April 10, 1864, for the war. Captured in battle on the North Anna River, Virginia, May 23, 1864. Confined at Point Lookout, Maryland, where he died April 16, 1865, of "pneumonia."

TATE, ROBERT, Private
Born in Caswell County where he resided as a laborer prior to enlisting in Person County at age 29, March 6, 1863, for the war. Discharged April 16, 1863, by reason of "neuralgic affliction of the heart which often affects his mind."

THOMAS, JOHN, Private
Resided in Alabama and enlisted at age 37, July 28, 1862, for the war as a substitute for Private Robert H. Dupree. Arrested on October 30, 1862, as a deserter from the "2nd Alabama Battalion." No further records.

THOMPSON, HENRY C., Private
Resided in Caswell County and was by occupation a clerk prior to enlisting at Suffolk, Virginia, at age 25, June 6, 1861. Present or accounted for until wounded and captured at Williamsburg, Virginia, on or about May 5, 1862. Died in a Federal hospital at Williamsburg on May 9, 1862, of wounds.

THOMPSON, JOHN W., Private
Resided in Caswell County and was by occupation a student prior to enlisting in Caswell County at age 18, May 31, 1861. Present or accounted for until wounded at Chancellorsville, Virginia, May 1-3, 1863. Rejoined the company in September-October, 1863, and present or accounted for until wounded in the right arm on June 11, 1864. Rejoined the company on or about November 1, 1864. Paroled at Greensboro on May 8, 1865.

THOMPSON, JULIUS W., Private
Resided in Caswell County and was by occupation a clerk prior to enlisting in Caswell County at age 21, April 29, 1861. Mustered in as Private and promoted to Sergeant on April 26, 1862. Reduced to ranks in November-December, 1862. Present or accounted for until captured at or near Gettysburg, Pennsylvania, on or about July 3, 1863. Confined at Fort Delaware, Delaware, until transferred to Point Lookout, Maryland, October 15-18, 1863. Paroled at Point Lookout and transferred to Venus Point, Savannah River, Georgia, where he was received November 15, 1864, for exchange. Rejoined the company prior to April 2, 1865, when he was captured at Hatcher's Run, Virginia. Confined at Point Lookout until released on June 9, 1865, after taking the Oath of Allegiance.

TOTTEN, HENRY C., Private
Born in Caswell County where he resided as a farmer prior to enlisting at Camp Ruffin, Virginia, at age 19, July 18, 1861. Present or accounted for until killed at Williamsburg, Virginia, May 5, 1862.

TOTTEN, JOHN C., Jr., Private
Previously served in Company F of this regiment. Transferred to this company on December 15, 1862. Present or accounted for until wounded in the leg at Gettysburg, Pennsylvania, July 1-3, 1863. Died in hospital at Danville, Virginia, July 19, 1863, of "typhoid fever."

TOTTEN, LOGAN M., Private
Born in Caswell County where he resided as a student prior to enlisting at Camp Ruffin, Virginia, at age 18, July 18, 1861. Discharged January 8, 1861, by reason of "being a minor."

TOTTEN, THOMAS, Private
Born in Caswell County where he resided prior to enlisting at Camp Ruffin, Virginia, at age 22, July 18, 1861. Present or accounted for until killed at Chancellorsville, Virginia, May 3, 1863.

TROGDON, HENRY K., Private
Enlisted at Camp Holmes on November 20, 1863, for the war. Deserted in December, 1863.

TURNER, THOMAS J., Private
Born in Caswell County where he resided as a farmer prior to enlisting in Caswell County at age 24, April 29, 1861. Present or accounted for until he died in hospital at Richmond, Virginia, June 2, 1862, of "intermittent fever."

TUTTLE, GABE, Private

Resided in Stokes County and enlisted at Camp Holmes on March 26, 1864, for the war. Present or accounted for until captured at Hatcher's Run, Virginia, April 2, 1865. Confined at Point Lookout, Maryland, until released on June 20, 1865, after taking the Oath of Allegiance.

VADEN, WILLIAM H., Corporal

Born in Halifax County and resided in Caswell County where he was by occupation a tobacconist prior to enlisting in Caswell County at age 23, April 29, 1861. Mustered in and promoted to Corporal on April 26, 1862. Hospitalized at Richmond, Virginia, June 10, 1862, with a "wound"; however, place and date wounded not reported. Rejoined the company prior to September 14, 1862, when he was wounded in the groin and captured at South Mountain, Maryland. Confined at Fort McHenry, Maryland, until transferred to Aiken's Landing, James River, Virginia, where he was received October 19, 1862, for exchange. Declared exchanged at Aiken's Landing on November 10, 1862. Died on or about November 25, 1862, of wounds received at South Mountain. Place of death not reported.

WALKER, WILLIAM F., Private

Place and date of enlistment not reported. First reported on company records dated December 1, 1864. Captured at Hatcher's Run, Virginia, April 2, 1865. Confined at Point Lookout, Maryland, until released on June 3, 1865, after taking the Oath of Allegiance.

WALTERS, HENRY T., Corporal

Resided in Caswell County and was by occupation a farmer prior to enlisting in Caswell County at age 24, April 29, 1861. Mustered in as Private. Present or accounted for until wounded at Sharpsburg, Maryland, September 17, 1862. Rejoined the company in January-February, 1863, and promoted to Corporal on May 11, 1863. Present or accounted for until wounded at Gettysburg, Pennsylvania, July 2, 1863. Died July 3, 1863, of wounds.

WARE, SIDNEY G., Private

Resided in Rockingham County. Place and date of enlistment not reported. Captured at Hatcher's Run, Virginia, April 2, 1865. Confined at Point Lookout, Maryland, until released on June 22, 1865, after taking the Oath of Allegiance.

WARREN, ANGLIS M., Private

Resided in Caswell County and enlisted in Person County at age 18, March 6, 1863, for the war. Present or accounted for until wounded at Gettysburg, Pennsylvania, July 1, 1863. Reported absent wounded until reported absent without leave from September 1 through December 31, 1863. Rejoined the company in January-February, 1864, and was detailed in hospital at Richmond, Virginia, March 11, 1864. Reported absent on detail through October, 1864.

WEBSTER, JOHN, _____

Enlisted on August 3, 1862, as a substitute for Sergeant Nathaniel K. Roan. Deserted the same day.

WILLIAMS, JAMES W., Private

Enlisted at Camp Holmes on November 20, 1863, for the war. Present or accounted for until wounded at Wilderness, Virginia, May 5, 1864. Reported absent wounded until he died in hospital at Tarboro on December 30, 1864, of "febris typhoides."

WILLIAMSON, JAMES A., Private

Born in Caswell County where he resided as a teacher prior to enlisting in Caswell County at age 20, April 29, 1861. Present or accounted for until discharged on October 10, 1861, for disability.

WILLIAMSON, JOHN WILLIAM, Private

Resided in Caswell County and was by occupation a farmer prior to enlisting in Caswell County at age 25, April 29, 1861. Present or accounted for until appointed Sergeant Major on December 20, 1862, or April 4, 1863, and transferred to the Field and Staff of this regiment.

WOMACK, DAVID G., Private

Enlisted at Camp Holmes on April 10, 1864, for the war. Wounded in the hand at Wilderness, Virginia, May 5, 1864. Returned to duty July 2, 1864, and present or accounted for until paroled at Appomattox Court House, Virginia, April 9, 1865.

WOMACK, WILBUR F., Private

Resided in Caswell County and was by occupation a farmer prior to enlisting in Caswell County at age 21, April 29, 1861. Reported missing and "supposed killed" at Gaines' Mill, Virginia, June 27, 1862. No further records.

WOMACK, WILLIAM H., Private

Resided in Caswell County and was by occupation a farmer prior to enlisting in Caswell County at age 27, April 29, 1861. Present or accounted for until captured at Williamsport, Maryland, on or about September 15, 1862. Confined at Fort Delaware, Delaware, until transferred to Aiken's Landing, James River, Virginia, October 2, 1862, for exchange. Declared exchanged at Aiken's Landing on November 10, 1862. Present or accounted for until detailed in hospital at Danville, Virginia, March 4, 1863. Reported absent on detail through October, 1864.

WOOD, LEVIN H., Private

Born in Alamance County* and resided in Caswell County where he was by occupation a grocer prior to enlisting in Caswell County at age 27, April 29, 1861. Present or accounted for until transferred to the C. S. Navy for duty on the C. S. S. *Merrimac* on February 19, 1862.

COMPANY B

This company, known as the Ranaleburg Riflemen, was from Mecklenburg County and enlisted at Ranaleburg on April 3, 1861. The company left Ranaleburg on April 28 and arrived at Raleigh on April 30. Leaving Raleigh on May 23, the company arrived at Garysburg on the evening of the same day. There it was assigned to this regiment as Company B. After joining the regiment the company functioned as a part of the regiment, and its history for the war period is recorded as a part of the regimental history.

The information contained in the following roster of the company was compiled principally from company muster rolls for May 13, 1861, through October, 1864. No company muster rolls were found for the period after October, 1864. In addition to the company muster rolls, Roll of Honor records, receipt rolls, hospital records, prisoner of war records, and other primary records, supplemented by state pension applications, United Daughters of the Confederacy records, and postwar rosters and histories, all provided useful information.

OFFICERS

CAPTAINS

ERWIN, ALBERT A.

Resided in Mecklenburg County where he enlisted at age 33. Appointed Captain to rank from April 24, 1861. Present or accounted for until wounded in the right arm at Williamsburg, Virginia, May 5, 1862. Resigned February 18, 1863, by reason of wounds received at Williamsburg. Resignation accepted February 27, 1863.

ROBINSON, WILLIAM W.

Born in Mecklenburg County where he resided as a "m. student" or farmer prior to enlisting in Mecklenburg County at age 25, April 3, 1861. Mustered in as Private and promoted to Sergeant on April 26, 1862. Elected 3rd Lieutenant on July 26, 1862. Present or accounted for until wounded at Sharpsburg, Maryland, September 17, 1862. Promoted to 1st Lieutenant on December 23, 1862. Rejoined the company in January-February, 1863, and was promoted to Captain on February 27, 1863. Present or accounted for until wounded at Spotsylvania Court House, Virginia, May 21, 1864. Reported absent wounded through December 31, 1864.

LIEUTENANTS

ALEXANDER, SILAS W., 1st Lieutenant

Resided in Mecklenburg County and was by occupation a wagonmaker prior to enlisting in Mecklenburg County at age 32, July 17, 1861. Mustered in as Private and was elected 2nd Lieutenant on April 26, 1862, to rank from that date. Elected 1st Lieutenant on July 26, 1862. Present or accounted for until he resigned on September 23, 1862, by reason of "ill health." Resignation accepted November 9, 1862.

ERWIN, JOHN R., 1st Lieutenant

Resided in Mecklenburg County and was by occupation a merchant prior to enlisting in Mecklenburg County at age 23. Elected 1st Lieutenant on April 3, 1861. Present or accounted for until he was defeated for reelection when the regiment was reorganized on April 26, 1862. [May have served later as Captain of Company F, 63rd Regiment N.C. Troops (5th Regiment N.C. Cavalry).]

HART, WILLIAM S. M., 2nd Lieutenant

Resided in Mecklenburg County and was by occupation a farmer prior to enlisting in Mecklenburg County at age 25, April 3, 1861. Mustered in as Sergeant but was reduced to ranks in July-August, 1861. Elected 2nd Lieutenant on April 26, 1862. Present or accounted for until he died on June 22, 1862, of disease. Place of death not reported.

McLEAN, JOHN D., 1st Lieutenant

Resided in Mecklenburg County and was by occupation a physician prior to enlisting in Mecklenburg County at age 26, May 26, 1861. Mustered in as Private and was elected 2nd Lieutenant on October 14, 1862. Promoted to 1st Lieutenant on February 27, 1863. Present or accounted for until paroled at Appomattox Court House, Virginia, April 9, 1865.

PRESSLY, WILLIAM A., 3rd Lieutenant

Resided in Mecklenburg County and was by occupation a physician prior to enlisting in Mecklenburg County at age 48. Elected 3rd Lieutenant on May 25, 1861. Present or accounted for until he resigned or was defeated for reelection when the regiment was reorganized on April 26, 1862.

SMITH, EDWARD, 2nd Lieutenant

Born in Mecklenburg County where he resided as a. student or farmer prior to enlisting in Mecklenburg County at age 22, April 3, 1861. Mustered in as Private and promoted to Sergeant on July 26, 1862. Appointed 3rd Lieutenant on December 23, 1862, and was promoted to 2nd Lieutenant on February 27, 1863. Present or accounted for until captured at Gettysburg, Pennsylvania, July 1-3, 1863. Confined at Fort McHenry, Maryland, and at Fort Delaware, Delaware, until transferred to Johnson's Island, Ohio, July 18, 1863. Transferred to Point Lookout, Maryland, March 14, 1865, and was transferred to Cox's Wharf, James River, Virginia, where he was received on or about March 22, 1865, for exchange. Captured in Buchanan County, Virginia, March 25, 1865, and confined at Wheeling, West Virginia, until transferred to Camp Chase, Ohio, April 13, 1865. Released at Camp Chase on June 13, 1865, after taking the Oath of Allegiance.

THOMPSON, JOSEPH, 1st Lieutenant

Born in Mecklenburg County where he resided as a teacher prior to enlisting in Mecklenburg County at age 27, May 20, 1861. Mustered in as Private and was elected 1st Lieutenant on April 26, 1862. Present or accounted for until killed at Williamsburg, Virginia, May 5, 1862.

WALKER, HENRY J., 3rd Lieutenant

Resided in Mecklenburg County and was by occupation a teacher prior to enlisting in Mecklenburg County at age 24, May 20, 1861, for one year. Mustered in as Private and promoted to Sergeant on April 26, 1862. Appointed 3rd Lieutenant on May 14, 1863. Present or accounted for until wounded and captured near Hagerstown, Maryland, July 13, 1863, and left leg amputated. Admitted to hospital at Baltimore, Maryland, September 21, 1863, and transferred to Johnson's Island, Ohio, September 28, 1863. Transferred to Point Lookout, Maryland, April 22, 1864. Paroled at Point Lookout and transferred to Aiken's Landing, James River, Virginia, where he was received May 8, 1864, for exchange. Reported absent wounded through October, 1864.

WARREN, ROBERT S., 2nd Lieutenant

Resided in Mecklenburg County and enlisted at age 39. Elected 2nd Lieutenant on April 3, 1861. Present or accounted for until he resigned or was defeated for reelection when the regiment was reorganized on April 26, 1862.

NONCOMMISSIONED OFFICERS
AND PRIVATES

ADAIR, THOMAS, Private
Enlisted in Mecklenburg County on October 15, 1863, for the war. Present or accounted for until he deserted to the enemy on or about March 13, 1865. Took the Oath of Allegiance prior to March 18, 1865, and was furnished transportation to Knoxville, Tennessee.

ADAIR, WILLIAM, Private
Enlisted in Mecklenburg County on October 15, 1863, for the war. Present or accounted for through October, 1864.

ALEXANDER, HEZEKIAH C., Private
Resided in Mecklenburg County and was by occupation a farmer prior to enlisting in Mecklenburg County at age 21, July 17, 1861. Mustered in as Private and promoted to Corporal on April 26, 1862. Reduced to ranks October 14, 1862. Present or accounted for until killed at Gettysburg, Pennsylvania, July 1-3, 1863.

ALEXANDER, JASPER, Musician
Enlisted in Mecklenburg County on January 26, 1864, for the war. Mustered in as Musician. Detailed for duty with the regimental band. Rejoined the company at an unspecified date. Present or accounted for until hospitalized at Richmond, Virginia, June 19, 1864, with a gunshot wound; however, place and date wounded not reported. Rejoined the company prior to September 1, 1864. Admitted to hospital at Richmond on March 19, 1865, with chronic diarrhoea and was transferred to the Federal Provost Marshal on April 14, 1865.

ALEXANDER, OSWALD, Musician
Resided in Mecklenburg County and was by occupation a daguerreotypist prior to enlisting in Mecklenburg County at age 23, July 17, 1861. Mustered in as Private. Promoted to Musician and detailed for duty with the regimental band in March-June, 1862. Rejoined the company at an unspecified date. Present or accounted for until paroled at Appomattox Court House, Virginia, April 9, 1865.

ALEXANDER, OSWALD S. P., Sergeant
Resided in Mecklenburg County and was by occupation a wagonmaker prior to enlisting in Mecklenburg County at age 23, July 17, 1861. Mustered in as Private and promoted to Sergeant on April 26, 1862. Present or accounted for until wounded at Gaines' Mill, Virginia, June 27, 1862. Died July 9, 1862, of wounds. Place of death not reported.

ALEXANDER, ULYSSES C., Private
Resided in Mecklenburg County and was by occupation a blacksmith prior to enlisting in Mecklenburg County at age 27, July 17, 1861. Present or accounted for until detailed for duty with the regimental band in February, 1863. Rejoined the company at an unspecified date. Present or accounted for until captured at Richmond, Virginia, April 3, 1865. Confined at Libby Prison, Richmond, until transferred to Newport News, Virginia, April 23, 1865. Died at Newport News on June 27, 1865, of "diarrhoea chron[ic]."

ALEXANDER, WILLIAM W., Musician
Enlisted in Mecklenburg County on January 22, 1864, for the war. Mustered in as Musician. Detailed for duty with the regimental band. Rejoined the company at an unspecified date. Present or accounted for until paroled at Appomattox Court House, Virginia, April 9, 1865.

ALEXANDER, WILSON WATSON, Musician
Resided in Mecklenburg County and enlisted at Charlotte in 1864. Mustered in as Musician (Drummer). Detailed for duty with the regimental band. Rejoined the company at an unspecified date. Present or accounted for until paroled at Appomattox Court House, Virginia, April 9, 1865.

ATCHISON, JOHN G., Private
Resided in Mecklenburg County and was by occupation a farmer prior to enlisting in Mecklenburg County at age 23, May 20, 1861. Present or accounted for until he died in hospital at Richmond, Virginia, May 17, 1862. Cause of death not reported.

BAILES, GEORGE S., Private
Resided in South Carolina and was by occupation a farmer prior to enlisting in Mecklenburg County at age 22, April 3, 1861. Present or accounted for until he died in hospital at Lynchburg, Virginia, July 17, 1862, of "typhoid fever."

BAKER, JOHN C., Private
Born in Mecklenburg County where he resided as a farmer prior to enlisting in Mecklenburg County at age 21, June 12, 1861. Present or accounted for until transferred to the C. S. Navy for duty on the C.S.S. *Merrimac* on February 26, 1862.

BAKER, ROBERT G. C., Private
Born in Mecklenburg County where he resided as a farmer prior to enlisting in Mecklenburg County at age 20, July 17, 1861. Present or accounted for until killed at Williamsburg, Virginia, May 5, 1862.

BARNETT, RANDOLPH S., Private
Born in Wilkes County where he resided as a farmer prior to enlisting in Mecklenburg County at age 32, September 27, 1862, for the war. Present or accounted for until discharged on December 20, 1863, by reason of "indolent ulcer of both legs of seventeen years standing."

BARTLETT, JAMES H., Private
Resided in Mecklenburg County and was by occupation a farmer prior to enlisting in Mecklenburg County at age 16, May 17, 1862, for the war. Present or accounted for until wounded in the right shoulder at South Mountain, Maryland, September 14, 1862. Rejoined the company in January-February, 1863, and present or accounted for until captured near Petersburg, Virginia, March 25, 1865. Confined at Point Lookout, Maryland, until released on May 15, 1865, after taking the Oath of Allegiance.

BARTLETTE, WILLIAM F., Private
Resided in Mecklenburg County and was by occupation a farmer prior to enlisting in Mecklenburg County at age 18, July 17, 1861. Present or accounted for until reported missing in action at Gettysburg, Pennsylvania, July 3, 1863. Never

rejoined the company. Roll of Honor indicates he was wounded at Chancellorsville, Virginia. No further records.

BASON, JOSEPH H., Private

Was by occupation a farmer prior to enlisting in Mecklenburg County at age 21, April 3, 1861. Present or accounted for until promoted to Sergeant and transferred to Company F, 6th Regiment N.C. State Troops on May 20, 1861.

BEMAN, GEORGE C., Private

Enlisted in Mecklenburg County on March 1, 1864, for the war. Present or accounted for until paroled at Farmville, Virginia, April 11-21, 1865.

BERRYHILL, JAMES L., Private

Born in Mecklenburg County where he resided as a farmer prior to enlisting in Mecklenburg County at age 24, July 17, 1861. Present or accounted for until he died at Camp Ruffin, Virginia, or at Smithfield, Virginia, May 1, 1862. Cause of death not reported.

BERRYHILL, JOSEPH J., Private

Born in Mecklenburg County where he resided as a farmer prior to enlisting in Mecklenburg County at age 20, April 3, 1861. Present or accounted for until he died in hospital at Richmond, Virginia, June 6, 1862, of "typhoid fever."

BIGHAM, MADISON S., Private

Enlisted in Mecklenburg County on February 1, 1864, for the war. Present or accounted for until wounded in the right thigh at Wilderness, Virginia, May 5, 1864. Reported absent wounded through October, 1864.

BLACKWELDER, ALFRED, Private

Born in Mecklenburg or Cabarrus counties and resided in Mecklenburg County where he was by occupation a farmer prior to enlisting in Mecklenburg County at age 24, April 3, 1861. Present or accounted for until wounded "slightly" at South Mountain, Maryland, September 14, 1862. Died at home in Mecklenburg County on December 25, 1862. Cause of death not reported.

BLALOCK, JOHN W., Private

Place and date of enlistment not reported. Died in hospital at Richmond, Virginia, September 5, 1862, of "febris typhoides."

BOWDEN, SAMUEL D., Private

Resided in Mecklenburg County and was by occupation a farmer prior to enlisting in Mecklenburg County at age 21, April 3, 1861. Present or accounted for through June, 1862, and was reported absent sick from August 28, 1862, through June, 1863. Reported absent without leave from July, 1863, through October, 1864. Roll of Honor indicates that he "straggled" from his company while on the march on August 22, 1862. No further records.

BOYD, JAMES T., Private

Born in York District, South Carolina, and resided in Mecklenburg County where he was by occupation a farmer prior to enlisting in Mecklenburg County at age 25, May 20, 1861. Present or accounted for until wounded and captured at Williamsburg, Virginia, May 5, 1862. Confined at Old Capitol Prison, Washington, D.C., until transferred to Fort Monroe, Virginia, where he was received on August 1, 1862.

Received at Aiken's Landing, James River, Virginia, August 5, 1862, for exchange. Died at home in South Carolina on or about November 22, 1862, of "consumption."

BOYD, JESSE A., Private

Resided in Mecklenburg County and was by occupation a farmer prior to enlisting in Mecklenburg County at age 18, April 3, 1861. Present or accounted for until transferred to Company H, 18th Regiment South Carolina Infantry in July, 1862.

BOYD, JOHN, Private

Resided in Mecklenburg County and was by occupation a farmer prior to enlisting in Mecklenburg County at age 18, April 3, 1861. Present or accounted for until he died in hospital at Richmond, Virginia, July 8, 1862, of "typhoid fever."

BRIMER, ALFRED, Private

Resided in Gaston County and was by occupation a farmer prior to enlisting in Mecklenburg County at age 24, July 17, 1861. Present or accounted for until killed at Gettysburg, Pennsylvania, July 1, 1863.

BROWN, COLUMBUS W., Private

Born in Mecklenburg County where he resided as a farmer prior to enlisting in Mecklenburg County at age 23, July 17, 1861. Present or accounted for until wounded at Williamsburg, Virginia, May 5, 1862. Returned to duty prior to July 1, 1862, and present or accounted for until killed at South Mountain, Maryland, September 14, 1862.

BROWN, JAMES WILLIAM, Musician

Previously served as Private in Company H, 11th Regiment N.C. Troops (1st Regiment N.C. Volunteers). Transferred to this company on September 4, 1863, in exchange for Private James H. McConnell. Promoted to Musician and detailed for duty with the regimental band in September-October, 1863. Records do not indicate whether he rejoined the company; however, he was paroled at Appomattox Court House, Virginia, April 9, 1865.

BROWN, RUFUS E., Private

Enlisted in Mecklenburg County at age 17, October 27, 1863, for the war. Present or accounted for until admitted to hospital at Richmond, Virginia, May 24, 1864, with a gunshot wound; however, place and date wounded not reported. Reported absent wounded or absent sick until retired to the Invalid Corps on December 28, 1864.

BYRAM, THOMAS J., Private

Enlisted in Mecklenburg County on February 8, 1864, for the war. Present or accounted for until wounded at Wilderness, Virginia, May 5, 1864. Rejoined the company prior to April 3, 1865, when he was captured in Dinwiddie County, Virginia. Confined at Point Lookout, Maryland, until released on June 23, 1865, after taking the Oath of Allegiance.

BYRUM, JOHN M., Private

Resided in Mecklenburg County. Place and date of enlistment not reported. Captured at Dinwiddie Court House, Virginia, April 3, 1865. Confined at Point Lookout, Maryland, until released on June 23, 1865, after taking the Oath of Allegiance.

CAROTHERS, JOHN K., Private

Born in Mecklenburg County where he resided as a farmer or blacksmith prior to enlisting in Mecklenburg County at age 38, April 3, 1861. Present or accounted for until discharged on July 17, 1862, by reason of being over age.

CATE, R., Private

Place and date of enlistment not reported. Paroled at Greensboro on May 25, 1865.

CATHEY, HENRY, Private

Resided in Mecklenburg County and was by occupation a carpenter prior to enlisting in Mecklenburg County at age 30, May 20, 1861. Present or accounted for until wounded in the thigh at Gaines' Mill, Virginia, June 27, 1862. Rejoined the company in July-August, 1863, and present or accounted for until wounded on May 21, 1864. Rejoined the company in July-August, 1864, and present or accounted for until paroled at Appomattox Court House, Virginia, April 9, 1865.

CHOATE, A. DAVIDSON, Private

Resided in South Carolina and enlisted in Mecklenburg County at age 27, August 13, 1861. Present or accounted for until killed at Gaines' Mill, Virginia, June 27, 1862.

CHOATE, JOSINA MADISON, Private

Born in York District, South Carolina, and resided in Mecklenburg County where he was by occupation a farmer prior to enlisting in Mecklenburg County at age 38, April 3, 1861. Mustered in as 1st Sergeant but was reduced to ranks on April 26, 1862. Present or accounted for until discharged at Richmond, Virginia, July 16, 1862, by reason of being over age.

CHOATE, ROBERT W., Corporal

Resided in South Carolina and enlisted in Mecklenburg County at age 23, August 13, 1861, for one year. Mustered in as Private and promoted to Corporal on May 14, 1863. Present or accounted for until wounded and captured at Gettysburg, Pennsylvania, July 1-5, 1863. Hospitalized at Chester, Pennsylvania, until transferred to City Point, Virginia, where he was received August 20, 1863, for exchange. Rejoined the company in November-December, 1863, and present or accounted for until wounded and reported missing in action on May 21, 1864. Company records do not indicate that his absence was accounted for or that he rejoined the company. Reportedly transferred to Company E, 17th Regiment South Carolina Infantry on August 8, 1864; however, records of that unit do not indicate that he served therein. No further records.

CHOATE, WILLIAM F., Private

Resided in York District, South Carolina, and enlisted in Mecklenburg County at age 36, August 13, 1861. Present or accounted for until wounded in the chin at Chancellorsville, Virginia, May 1-3, 1863. Rejoined the company in November-December, 1863, and was transferred to Company E, 17th Regiment South Carolina Infantry, August 8, 1864.

CLANTON, WILLIAM D., Private

Resided in Mecklenburg County where he enlisted at age 27, May 20, 1861. Present or accounted for until retired to the Invalid Corps on December 28, 1864.

Nature of disability not reported.

CLARK, ROBERT F., Private

Born in Mecklenburg County where he resided as a farmer prior to enlisting in Mecklenburg County at age 43, July 17, 1861. Present or accounted for until he died at Camp Ruffin, Virginia, on or about October 10, 1861. Cause of death not reported.

CLARKE, ALEXANDER A., Private

Born in Mecklenburg County where he resided prior to enlisting in Mecklenburg County at age 18, March 12, 1863, for the war. Present or accounted for until he died at Gordonsville, Virginia, May 31, 1863, of disease.

CRANFORD, MICAJAH, Private

Enlisted in Mecklenburg County on November 21, 1863, for the war. Present or accounted for through December 9, 1864. Reported in a Federal hospital at Farmville, Virginia, from April 7 through June 15, 1865.

CROWELL, SAMUEL W., Private

Resided in Mecklenburg County where he enlisted at age 20, May 20, 1861. Present or accounted for until captured near Hanover Junction, Virginia, May 23, 1864. Confined at Point Lookout, Maryland, until transferred to Cox's Landing, James River, Virginia, where he was received February 14-15, 1865, for exchange. Paroled at Appomattox Court House, Virginia, April 9, 1865.

DARNELL, JAMES J., Private

Born in Mecklenburg County where he resided as a farmer prior to enlisting in Mecklenburg County at age 30, April 3, 1861. Present or accounted for until discharged at Richmond, Virginia, July 17, 1862, under the provisions of the Conscript Act.

DAVIS, F. T., Private

Place and date of enlistment not reported. Paroled at Farmville, Virginia, April 11-21, 1865.

DAVIS, JOSIAH C., Private

Born in Cocke County, Tennessee, and resided in Mecklenburg County where he was by occupation a farmer prior to enlisting in Mecklenburg County at age 23, May 20, 1861. Present or accounted for until transferred to the C. S. Navy for duty on the C.S.S. *Merrimac* on February 25, 1862.

EDWARDS, MATTHEW A., Corporal

Resided in Mecklenburg County and was by occupation a farmer prior to enlisting in Mecklenburg County at age 18, April 3, 1861. Mustered in as Private and promoted to Corporal on April 26, 1862. Present or accounted for until wounded at South Mountain, Maryland, September 14, 1862. Rejoined the company in January-February, 1863, and present or accounted for until wounded in the left shoulder at Chancellorsville, Virginia, May 1-3, 1863. Reported absent wounded until retired to the Invalid Corps on April 29, 1864.

ELLIS, WILLIAM H., Private

Enlisted in Mecklenburg County on April 1, 1864, for the war. Present or accounted for through October, 1864.

ERWIN, ARTHUR R., Private

Resided in Mecklenburg County and was by occupation a farmer prior to enlisting in Mecklenburg

County at age 29, June 12, 1861. Present or accounted for until paroled at Appomattox Court House, Virginia, April 9, 1865.

ERWIN, FRANCIS LEE, Sergeant
Resided in Mecklenburg County and was by occupation a farmer prior to enlisting in Mecklenburg County at age 26, April 3, 1861. Mustered in as Sergeant. Present or accounted for until transferred to the Signal Corps on or about April 25, 1862.

ERWIN, JAMES C., Private
Born in York District, South Carolina, and resided in Mecklenburg County where he was by occupation a farmer prior to enlisting in Mecklenburg County at age 18, April 3, 1861. Present or accounted for until he died at home in Mecklenburg County on or about October 24, 1862. Cause of death not reported.

ERWIN, JAMES M., Private
Born in York District, South Carolina, and resided in Mecklenburg County where he was by occupation a farmer prior to enlisting in Mecklenburg County at age 49, June 12, 1861. Present or accounted for until wounded at Williamsburg, Virginia, May 5, 1862. Discharged October 13, 1862, by reason of being over age.

FLENNIKEN, JOHN B., Private
Resided in Mecklenburg County and was by occupation a farmer prior to enlisting in Mecklenburg County at age 19, July 17, 1861. Present or accounted for until he died in hospital at Lynchburg, Virginia, on or about June 19, 1862, of "pneumonia."

FRAZER, JAMES N., Musician
Enlisted in Mecklenburg County on January 22, 1864, for the war. Mustered in as Musician. Detailed for duty with the regimental band. Rejoined the company at an unspecified date. Present or accounted for until paroled at Appomattox Court House, Virginia, April 9, 1865.

FRAZIER, ISAAC A., Musician
Previously served in Company G, 34th Regiment N.C.Troops. Transferred to this company on January 12, 1863, with the rank of Musician. Detailed for duty in the regimental band. Rejoined the company at an unspecified date. Present or accounted for until paroled at Appomattox Court House, Virginia, April 9, 1865.

FRAZIER, JOHN T., Musician
Resided in Mecklenburg County where he enlisted at age 23, August 7, 1861. Mustered in as Private. Promoted to Musician and detailed for duty with the regimental band in September-October, 1861. Rejoined the company at an unspecified date subsequent to June 30, 1862. Present or accounted for until paroled at Appomattox Court House, Virginia, April 9, 1865.

FRAZIER, RICHARD J., Musician
Resided in Mecklenburg County and enlisted at Camp Ruffin, Virginia, at age 19, August 7, 1861. Mustered in as Private. Promoted to Musician and detailed for duty with the regimental band in September-October, 1861. Rejoined the company at an unspecified date subsequent to June 30, 1862. Present or accounted for until paroled at Appomat-

tox Court House, Virginia, April 9, 1865.

FRAZIER, WARREN F., Musician
Resided in Mecklenburg County and enlisted at Camp Ruffin, Virginia, at age 22, August 7, 1861. Mustered in as Private. Promoted to Musician and detailed for duty with the regimental band in September-October, 1861. Rejoined the company at an unspecified date subsequent to June 30, 1862. Present or accounted for until paroled at Appomattox Court House, Virginia, April 9, 1865.

FREEMAN, WILLIAM A., Sergeant
Resided in Mecklenburg County and was by occupation a carpenter prior to enlisting in Mecklenburg County at age 22, July 17, 1861. Mustered in as Private and promoted to Corporal on April 26, 1862. Present or accounted for until wounded and captured at Williamsburg, Virginia, May 5-6, 1862. Confined at Old Capitol Prison, Washington, D.C., until transferred to Aiken's Landing, James River, Virginia, where he was received August 5, 1862, for exchange. Rejoined the company in January-February, 1863, and was promoted to Sergeant on May 14, 1863. Present or accounted for until paroled at Appomattox Court House, Virginia, April 9, 1865.

GALLANT, JONAS A., Sergeant
Born in Mecklenburg County and resided in Gaston County where he was by occupation a farmer prior to enlisting in Mecklenburg County at age 19, July 17, 1861. Mustered in as Private. Present or accounted for until wounded at Gaines' Mill, Virginia, June 27, 1862. Promoted to Corporal on October 14, 1862, and rejoined the company prior to November 1, 1862. Present or accounted for until wounded in the left lung at Chancellorsville, Virginia, May 3, 1863. Rejoined the company in September-October, 1863, and was promoted to Sergeant on April 25, 1864. Present or accounted for until paroled at Appomattox Court House, Virginia, April 9, 1865.

GALLANT, WILLIAM LAWRENCE, Private
Place and date of enlistment not reported. First reported on company records on November 5, 1864. Paroled at Appomattox Court House, Virginia, April 9, 1865.

GARNER, WILLIAM, Private
Enlisted in Mecklenburg County on December 30, 1863, for the war. Present or accounted for through October, 1864.

GLOVER, THOMAS M., Private
Born in York District, South Carolina, and resided in Mecklenburg County where he enlisted at age 17, August 13, 1861. Present or accounted for until he died in hospital at Richmond, Virginia, June 7, 1862, of "pneumonia."

GRANDFORD, M., Private
Place and date of enlistment not reported. Paroled at Farmville, Virginia, April 11-21, 1865.

GRIER, CALVIN E., Private
Resided in Mecklenburg County and was by occupation a student prior to enlisting in Mecklenburg County at age 16, June 23, 1861. Present or accounted for until discharged on July 17, 1862.

Reason discharged not reported. Later served in Company C, 10th Regiment N.C. State Troops (1st Regiment N.C. Artillery).

GRIER, SAMUEL M., Private
Born in Mecklenburg County where he resided as a student prior to enlisting in Mecklenburg County at age 19, June 23, 1861. Present or accounted for until killed at Gaines' Mill, Virginia, June 27, 1862.

GRIER, THOMAS M., Private
Resided in Mecklenburg County and was by occupation a student prior to enlisting in Mecklenburg County at age 16, July 17, 1861. Present or accounted for until discharged on July 17, 1862. Reason discharged not reported.

GROVES, JOHN RUSSELL, Private
Resided in Gaston or Cleveland counties and was by occupation a farmer prior to enlisting in Mecklenburg County at age 24, April 3, 1861. Present or accounted for until wounded in the left thigh and captured at Falling Waters, Maryland, July 14, 1863. Left thigh amputated. Confined at Point Lookout, Maryland, until exchanged on or about January 22, 1864. Reported absent wounded through October, 1864.

HALL, WILSON H., Private
Resided in Mecklenburg County and was by occupation a farmer prior to enlisting in Mecklenburg County at age 19, July 17, 1861. Present or accounted for until wounded at Chancellorsville, Virginia, May 1-3, 1863. Reported absent wounded until September-October, 1864, when he rejoined the company. Paroled at Charlotte on May 27, 1865.

HANNON, W. A., Private
Enlisted at Petersburg, Virginia, in October, 1864, for the war. Present or accounted for until paroled at Charlotte on May 13, 1865.

HAWKINS, FIELDS A., Private
Resided in Mecklenburg County and was by occupation a farmer prior to enlisting in Mecklenburg County at age 20, May 22, 1861. Present or accounted for until wounded at Williamsburg, Virginia, May 5, 1862. Rejoined the company prior to July 1, 1862, and present or accounted for until wounded in the right leg at Sharpsburg, Maryland, September 17, 1862. Right leg amputated. Reported absent wounded through October, 1864.

HAWKINS, JAMES F., Musician
Enlisted in Mecklenburg County on January 22, 1864, for the war. Mustered in as Musician. Detailed for duty with the regimental band. Rejoined the company at an unspecified date. Present or accounted for until paroled at Appomattox Court House, Virginia, April 9, 1865.

HAWKINS, JOSEPH P., Musician
Resided in Mecklenburg County and was by occupation a farmer prior to enlisting in Mecklenburg County at age 22, May 22, 1861. Mustered in as Private. Promoted to Musician and detailed for duty with the regimental band in September-October, 1861. Rejoined the company at an unspecified date subsequent to June 30, 1862. Present or accounted for until paroled at Appomattox Court House, Virginia, April 9, 1865.

HEITMAN, ORIN B., Private
Resided in Davidson County and enlisted in Mecklenburg County on March 1, 1864, for the war. Present or accounted for until reported absent wounded in September-October, 1864; however, place and date wounded not reported. Rejoined the company prior to April 2, 1865, when he was captured at or near Petersburg, Virginia. Confined at Point Lookout, Maryland, until released on June 13, 1865, after taking the Oath of Allegiance.

HILL, WILLIAM H., Private
Resided in Wilkes County and enlisted in Mecklenburg County at age 33, September 27, 1862, for the war. Present or accounted for until he died in hospital at Richmond, Virginia, December 26, 1862, of "typhoid fever."

HINSON, MARION, Private
Previously served in Company D, 63rd Regiment N.C. Troops (5th Regiment N.C. Cavalry). Transferred to this company on March 24, 1865. No further records.

HOTCHKISS, SETH A., Private
Born in York District, South Carolina, and resided in South Carolina where he was by occupation a farmer prior to enlisting in Mecklenburg County at age 18, April 3, 1861. Present or accounted for until transferred to the C. S. Navy for duty on the C.S.S. *Merrimac* on February 15, 1862.

JAMISON, EMORY A., Private
Born in Mecklenburg County where he resided as a farmer prior to enlisting in Mecklenburg County at age 19, August 13, 1861. Present or accounted for until discharged at Camp Ruffin, Virginia, November 2, 1861, by reason of disability.

JOHNSTON, HENRY F., Private
Born in South Carolina where he resided as a farmer prior to enlisting in Mecklenburg County at age 17, April 3, 1861. Present or accounted for until transferred to the C. S. Navy for duty on the C.S.S. *Merrimac* on February 15, 1862.

JORDAN, ALEXANDER, Private
Born in Moore County and was by occupation a farmer prior to enlisting in Mecklenburg County on November 20, 1863, for the war. Present or accounted for until discharged near Orange Court House, Virginia, April 24, 1864, by reason of "general debility & old age." Discharge records give his age as 43.

KERR, JOHN B., Private
Born in Mecklenburg County where he resided as a farmer prior to enlisting in Mecklenburg County at age 20, July 17, 1861. Present or accounted for until wounded at Williamsburg, Virginia, May 5, 1862. Discharged at Richmond, Virginia, September 28, 1862, by reason of "epileptic convulsions."

KERR, JOHN T., Musician
Resided in Mecklenburg County and enlisted at Camp Ruffin, Virginia, at age 22, August 7, 1861. Mustered in as Private. Promoted to Musician and detailed for duty with the regimental band in September-October, 1861. Rejoined the company at an unspecified date subsequent to June 30, 1862. Present or accounted for until paroled at Appomat-

tox Court House, Virginia, April 9, 1865.

KIMBRELL, JAMES L., Private

Born in York District, South Carolina, and resided in South Carolina where he was by occupation a farmer prior to enlisting in Mecklenburg County at age 20, April 3, 1861. Present or accounted for until wounded at South Mountain, Maryland, September 14, 1862. Rejoined the company in November-December, 1862, and present or accounted for until killed at Gettysburg, Pennsylvania, July 1, 1863.

KIRKPATRICK, JAMES F., Private

Resided in Mecklenburg County and was by occupation a farmer prior to enlisting in Mecklenburg County at age 28, July 17, 1861. Present or accounted for until wounded and captured at South Mountain, Maryland, September 14, 1862. Paroled September 23, 1862, and rejoined the company in November-December, 1862. Present or accounted for until wounded and captured at Gettysburg, Pennsylvania, July 1, 1863. Hospitalized at Chester, Pennsylvania, until transferred to City Point, Virginia, where he was exchanged on August 20, 1863. Rejoined the company in November-December, 1863, and present or accounted for until paroled at Appomattox Court House, Virginia, April 9, 1865.

KNOX, JAMES F., Private

Resided in Mecklenburg County and was by occupation a farmer prior to enlisting in Mecklenburg County at age 18, April 3, 1861. Mustered in as Corporal but was reduced to ranks on April 26, 1862. Present or accounted for until wounded in the leg and captured at Williamsburg, Virginia, May 5, 1862. Died in hospital near Fort Monroe, Virginia, May 16, 1862, of wounds.

KNOX, JOHN D., Private

Resided in Mecklenburg County and was by occupation a farmer prior to enlisting in Mecklenburg County at age 22, April 3, 1861. Present or accounted for until transferred to the Signal Corps on April 5, 1862.

KNOX, JOHN N., 1st Sergeant

Resided in Mecklenburg County and was by occupation a farmer prior to enlisting in Mecklenburg County at age 31, April 3, 1861. Mustered in as Private and promoted to 1st Sergeant on April 26, 1862. Present or accounted for until killed at Gettysburg, Pennsylvania, July 1, 1863.

KNOX, JOSEPH M., Private

Resided in Mecklenburg County and was by occupation a carpenter prior to enlisting in Mecklenburg County at age 24, April 3, 1861. Mustered in as Corporal but was reduced to ranks on April 26, 1862. Present or accounted for until wounded and captured at Williamsburg, Virginia, May 5, 1862. Never rejoined the company and company records indicate that he was believed to be dead. Roll of Honor states he was killed at Williamsburg. No further records.

KNOX, THOMAS N., Private

Resided in Mecklenburg County and was by occupation a farmer prior to enlisting in Mecklenburg County at age 31, April 3, 1861. Present or accounted for until transferred to the Signal Corps on April 15, 1862.

LEE, DAVID P., Private

Resided in Mecklenburg County where he enlisted at age 18, August 13, 1861. Present or accounted for until transferred to the Signal Corps on April 15, 1862.

LEWIS, LINDSAY GEORGE, Private

Records of Company D, 63rd Regiment N.C. Troops (5th Regiment N.C. Cavalry) indicate he served in that unit and transferred to this company on March 24, 1865; however, he was reported as a member of the 63rd Regiment when captured on the South Side Railroad, Virginia, April 2, 1865. No further records.

LIEBERMAN, CHARLES S., Private

Resided in Mecklenburg County and was by occupation a "dyester" prior to enlisting in Mecklenburg County at age 25, May 20, 1861. Present or accounted for until wounded at Malvern Hill, Virginia, on or about July 1, 1862. Returned to duty prior to September 17, 1862, when he was killed at Sharpsburg, Maryland.

McCONNELL, JAMES H., Musician

Resided in Mecklenburg County and enlisted at Camp Ruffin, Virginia, at age 29, August 7, 1861. Mustered in as Private. Promoted to Musician and detailed for duty with the regimental band in September-October, 1861. Rejoined the company at an unspecified date subsequent to June 30, 1862. "Left sick" at Boonsboro, Maryland, and was captured on or about September 12, 1862. Hospitalized at Frederick, Maryland, and at Baltimore, Maryland, until transferred to Aiken's Landing, James River, Virginia, where he was received October 12-13, 1862, for exchange. Reported absent without leave from December 6, 1862, until February 21, 1863. Present or accounted for until transferred to Company H, 11th Regiment N.C. Troops (1st Regiment N.C. Volunteers), September 4, 1863, in exchange for Private James William Brown.

McGINN, ISAAC H., Private

Resided in Mecklenburg County and was by occupation a wagonmaker prior to enlisting in Mecklenburg County at age 25, July 17, 1861. Present or accounted for until wounded in the foot and captured at Williamsburg, Virginia, May 5, 1862. Foot amputated. Hospitalized at Fort Monroe, Virginia, until exchanged in September, 1862. Reported absent wounded through October, 1864.

McGINN, LAWSON W., Private

Born in Mecklenburg County where he resided as a blacksmith prior to enlisting in Mecklenburg County at age 22, April 3, 1861. Present or accounted for until killed at Fredericksburg, Virginia, December 13, 1862.

McGINN, NEELY C., Private

Resided in Mecklenburg County where he enlisted at age 20, October 22, 1861. Present or accounted for until wounded at Gaines' Mill, Virginia, June 27, 1862. Rejoined the company prior to November 1, 1862, and present or accounted for until wounded and captured at Gettysburg, Pennsylvania, July 1-5, 1863. Hospitalized at Chester, Pennsylvania, until transferred to City Point, Virginia, where he was received on August 20, 1863, for exchange. Rejoined the company in November-December, 1863, and present or accounted for until paroled at Appomattox Court House, Virginia, April 9, 1865.

McGINN, WILLIAM A., Private
Resided in Mecklenburg County and was by occupation a farmer prior to enlisting in Mecklenburg County at age 30, June 23, 1861. Present or accounted for until wounded and captured at Gettysburg, Pennsylvania, July 1-5, 1863. Hospitalized at Chester, Pennsylvania, until paroled and transferred to City Point, Virginia, where he was received August 20, 1863, for exchange. Rejoined the company in January-February, 1864, and present or accounted for until paroled at Appomattox Court House, Virginia, April 9, 1865.

McGUIRE, JOHN W., Private
Born in Mecklenburg County where he resided as a farmer prior to enlisting in Mecklenburg County at age 44, May 26, 1861. Present or accounted for until discharged at Richmond, Virginia, on or about July 17, 1862, by reason of being over age.

McLEAN, JAMES LOGAN, Private
Resided in Gaston County and was by occupation a farmer prior to enlisting in Mecklenburg County at age 23, May 26, 1861. Present or accounted for until paroled at Appomattox Court House, Virginia, April 9, 1865.

McRUM, SAMUEL W., Private
Born in Mecklenburg County where he resided as a farmer prior to enlisting in Mecklenburg County at age 29, July 17, 1861. Present or accounted for until discharged at Camp Ruffin, Virginia, October 28, 1861, by reason of disability.

McRUM, STEPHEN J., Private
Resided in Mecklenburg County and was by occupation a farmer prior to enlisting in Mecklenburg County at age 23, April 3, 1861. Present or accounted for until killed at Gaines' Mill, Virginia, June 27, 1862.

MANESS, JAMES A., Private
Enlisted in Mecklenburg County on December 30, 1863, for the war. Present or accounted for until captured in battle on the North Anna River, Virginia, May 23, 1864, or at Hanover Junction, Virginia, May 24, 1864. Confined at Point Lookout, Maryland, until transferred to Boulware's Wharf, James River, Virginia, March 16, 1865, for exchange. No further records.

MANESS, JOHN, Private
Enlisted in Mecklenburg County on December 30, 1863, for the war. Present or accounted for through April, 1864. No further records.

MARKS, STEPHEN HARRISON, Private
Resided in Mecklenburg County and was by occupation a farmer prior to enlisting in Mecklenburg County at age 20, April 3, 1861. Present or accounted for until wounded at Sharpsburg, Maryland, September 17, 1862. Rejoined the company in November-December, 1862, and present or accounted for until wounded in the cheek and arm at Gettysburg, Pennsylvania, July 1, 1863. Rejoined the company in September-October, 1863, and present or accounted for until paroled at Appomat-

tox Court House, Virginia, April 9, 1865.

MARKS, THOMAS H., Private
Resided in Cleveland County and was by occupation a farmer prior to enlisting in Mecklenburg County at age 26, April 3, 1861. Present or accounted for until wounded and captured at South Mountain, Maryland, September 14, 1862. Paroled September 23, 1862, and rejoined the company in January-February, 1863. Reported absent sick from May-June, 1863, through December, 1863, and reported absent without leave from January-February, 1864, through October, 1864. No further records.

MARKS, WILLIAM S., Private
Resided in Mecklenburg County. Place and date of enlistment not reported. First reported on company records on November 5, 1864. Captured at Hatcher's Run, Virginia, April 2, 1865, and confined at Point Lookout, Maryland, until released June 29, 1865, after taking the Oath of Allegiance.

MORRISON, JAMES E., Private
Born in Mecklenburg County where he resided as a farmer prior to enlisting in Mecklenburg County at age 25, July 17, 1861. Present or accounted for until he died in hospital at Richmond, Virginia, May 16, 1862, of "typhoid fever."

MOSER, HENRY S., Private
Born in Catawba County* and resided in Mecklenburg County where he was by occupation a farmer prior to enlisting in Mecklenburg County at age 23, April 3, 1861. Present or accounted for until killed at Gettysburg, Pennsylvania, July 1, 1863.

MULWEE, JOHN W., Private
Resided in Mecklenburg County and was by occupation a farmer prior to enlisting in Mecklenburg County at age 21, May 20, 1861. Present or accounted for until wounded in the shoulder at Gettysburg, Pennsylvania, July 1, 1863. Rejoined the company in September-October, 1863, and present or accounted for until captured by Federal forces in hospital at Richmond, Virginia, April 3, 1865. Confined at Libby Prison, Richmond, until April 23, 1865, when he was transferred to Newport News, Virginia. Released at Newport News on June 16, 1865, after taking the Oath of Allegiance.

NEAGLE, JAMES H., Private
Resided in Mecklenburg County and was by occupation a student prior to enlisting in Mecklenburg County at age 17, July 17, 1861. Present or accounted for until wounded in the right leg and captured at Gettysburg, Pennsylvania, July 1-5, 1863. Hospitalized at Chester, Pennsylvania, until transferred to Point Lookout, Maryland, where he was received on October 4, 1863. Paroled at Point Lookout and transferred to City Point, Virginia, March 16, 1864, for exchange. Reported absent wounded until retired to the Invalid Corps on December 7, 1864.

NICHOLSON, RANDOLPH J., Private
Resided in Mecklenburg County and was by occupation a carpenter prior to enlisting in Mecklenburg County at age 26, April 3, 1861. Present or accounted for until reported missing in action at Gettysburg, Pennsylvania, July 3, 1863. Never

rejoined the company. No further records.

NIVENS, JOSEPH G., Private
Resided in Mecklenburg County and was by occupation a farmer prior to enlisting in Mecklenburg County at age 28, May 26, 1861. Present or accounted for until wounded at Malvern Hill, Virginia, on or about July 1, 1862. Returned to duty prior to November 1, 1862, and present or accounted for until transferred to 2nd Company B, 6th Regiment South Carolina Infantry, February 12, 1863.

OAKELY, CALOWAY, Private
Resided in Granville County and enlisted in Mecklenburg County on January 30, 1864, for the war. Present or accounted for until admitted to hospital at Petersburg, Virginia, July 25, 1864, with a gunshot wound; however, place and date wounded not reported. Reported absent wounded through October, 1864, but rejoined the company prior to April 2, 1865, when he was captured at Hatcher's Run, Virginia. Confined at Point Lookout, Maryland, until released on June 22, 1865, after taking the Oath of Allegiance.

ORR, THOMAS BENTON, Private
Resided in Mecklenburg County and was by occupation a farmer prior to enlisting in Mecklenburg County at age 23, April 3, 1861. Present or accounted for until killed at Gaines' Mill, Virginia, June 27, 1862.

PARKER, SAMUEL S., Private
Resided in Wilkes County and enlisted in Mecklenburg County at age 31, September 27, 1862, for the war. Present or accounted for until he died in hospital at Lynchburg, Virginia, January 27, 1863, of "febris remittens."

PARKS, DAVID K., Private
Resided in Mecklenburg County and was by occupation a farmer prior to enlisting in Mecklenburg County at age 22, April 3, 1861. Present or accounted for until captured at Dinwiddie Court House, Virginia, April 3, 1865. Confined at Point Lookout, Maryland, until released on June 16, 1865, after taking the Oath of Allegiance.

PARKS, GEORGE L., Private
Resided in Mecklenburg County where he enlisted at age 23, October 22, 1861. Present or accounted for until he died in hospital at Richmond, Virginia, July 15, 1862, of "cont[inued] fever."

PARNELL, AMOS T., Private
Enlisted in Mecklenburg County on November 20, 1863, for the war. Present or accounted for until wounded at Wilderness, Virginia, May 5, 1864. Reported absent wounded through October, 1864.

PERRY, L. H., Corporal
Place and date of enlistment and promotion record not reported. Captured at Fort Fisher on January 15, 1865. Confined at Elmira, New York, where he died July 6, 1865, of "diarrhoea."

POAG, WILLIAM J., Private
Enlisted in Mecklenburg County on May 15, 1864, for the war. Present or accounted for until paroled at Appomattox Court House, Virginia, April 9, 1865.

PORTER, SAMUEL A., Private
Resided in Mecklenburg County and was by occupation a farmer prior to enlisting in Mecklenburg County at age 20, July 17, 1861. Present or accounted for until transferred to the Signal Corps on April 15, 1862.

POTTS, WILLIAM M., Private
Was by occupation a student prior to enlisting in Mecklenburg County at age 17, April 3, 1861. Discharged May 29, 1861. Reason discharged not reported.

PRATHER, ELISHA L., Private
Resided in Mecklenburg County and was by occupation a farmer prior to enlisting in Mecklenburg County at age 24, April 3, 1861. Present or accounted for until wounded in the leg and captured at Williamsburg, Virginia, May 5, 1862. Died in a Federal hospital near Fort Monroe, Virginia, May 24, 1862, of wounds.

REECE, JOHN, Private
Enlisted in Mecklenburg County on February 1, 1864, for the war. Present or accounted for until he died in May-June, 1864. Place, exact date, and cause of death not reported.

REID, JOHN WILLIAM, Musician
Resided in Mecklenburg County and enlisted at Camp Ruffin, Virginia, at age 23, August 7, 1861. Mustered in as Private. Promoted to Musician and detailed for duty with the regimental band in September-October, 1861. Rejoined the company at an unspecified date subsequent to June 30, 1862. Present or accounted for until paroled at Appomattox Court House, Virginia, April 9, 1865.

SHEFFIELD, JAMES M., Private
Born in Henry County, Virginia, and resided in Mecklenburg County where he was by occupation a "tobacco mcf" prior to enlisting in Mecklenburg County at age 34, June 23, 1861. Present or accounted for until transferred to the C. S. Navy for duty on the C.S.S. Merrimac on February 15, 1862.

SLOAN, GEORGE W., Private
Resided in Mecklenburg County and was by occupation a farmer prior to enlisting in Mecklenburg County at age 23, July 17, 1861. Present or accounted for until wounded at Chancellorsville, Virginia, May 3, 1863. Rejoined the company in November-December, 1863, and present or accounted for until paroled at Appomattox Court House, Virginia, April 9, 1865.

SMITH, DAVID H., Private
Resided in Mecklenburg County and was by occupation a carpenter prior to enlisting in Mecklenburg County at age 26, April 3, 1861. Present or accounted for until wounded at Wilderness, Virginia, May 5, 1864. Reported absent wounded through October, 1864.

SMITH, JOHN W., Private
Resided in Mecklenburg County and was by occupation a farmer prior to enlisting in Mecklenburg County at age 18, July 17, 1861. Present or accounted for until discharged on September 27, 1862. Reason discharged not reported.

SPENCER, CLARK, Private

Enlisted in Mecklenburg County on December 30, 1863, for the war. Present or accounted for until captured at or near Hanover Junction, Virginia, May 24, 1864. Confined at Point Lookout, Maryland, until paroled and transferred to Venus Point, Savannah River, Georgia, where he was received November 15, 1864, for exchange. No further records.

STERLING, JOHN H., Musician

Resided in Mecklenburg County where he enlisted at age 35, September 15, 1861. Mustered in as Private. Promoted to Musician and detailed for duty with the regimental band in September-October, 1861. Rejoined the company at an unspecified date subsequent to June 30, 1862. Present or accounted for until paroled at Appomattox Court House, Virginia, April 9, 1865.

STOWE, RUFUS A., Private

Resided in Mecklenburg County where he enlisted at age 18, August 21, 1863, for the war. Present or accounted for until he died in hospital at Richmond, Virginia, November 5, 1863, of "febris typhoides."

STURGEON, CHARLES S., Private

Resided in Mecklenburg County and was by occupation a farmer prior to enlisting in Mecklenburg County at age 26, July 17, 1861. Present or accounted for until wounded in the right leg at Gaines' Mill, Virginia, June 27, 1862. Right leg amputated. Discharged at Richmond, Virginia, September 18, 1862.

SWANN, ROBERT L., Private

Born in York District, South Carolina, and resided in Mecklenburg County where he was by occupation a farmer prior to enlisting in Mecklenburg County at age 24, April 30, 1861. Mustered in as Corporal but was reduced to ranks on April 26, 1862. Present or accounted for until wounded and captured at Williamsburg, Virginia, May 5-6, 1862. Confined at Old Capitol Prison, Washington, D.C., until transferred to Aiken's Landing, James River, Virginia, where he was received August 5, 1862, for exchange. Rejoined the company in January-February, 1863, and present or accounted for until wounded at Chancellorsville, Virginia, May 3, 1863. Died May 4, 1863, of wounds.

TAYLOR, ARCHIBALD A., Musician

Resided in Mecklenburg County and enlisted at Camp Ruffin, Virginia, at age 36, August 7, 1861. Mustered in as Private. Promoted to Musician and detailed for duty with the regimental band in September-October, 1861. Rejoined the company at an unspecified date subsequent to June 30, 1862. Present or accounted for until paroled at Appomattox Court House, Virginia, April 9, 1865.

TAYLOR, WILLIAM J., Private

Resided in Mecklenburg County and was by occupation a farmer prior to enlisting in Mecklenburg County at age 18, July 17, 1861. Present or accounted for until wounded at Williamsburg, Virginia, on or about May 5, 1862. Rejoined the company prior to July 1, 1862, and present or accounted for until wounded at Gettysburg, Pennsylvania, July 1-2, 1863. Rejoined the company in November-December, 1863, and present or accounted for until

captured at Hatcher's Run, Virginia, April 2, 1865. Confined at Point Lookout, Maryland, until released on June 20, 1865, after taking the Oath of Allegiance.

THOMPSON, WILLIAM J., Musician

Resided in Mecklenburg County and enlisted at Camp Ruffin, Virginia, at age 29, August 7, 1861. Mustered in as Private. Promoted to Musician and detailed for duty with the regimental band in September-October, 1861. Rejoined the company at an unspecified date subsequent to June 30, 1862. Present or accounted for until paroled at Appomattox Court House, Virginia, April 9, 1865.

THORNBURG, FIELDS B., Private

Born in Mecklenburg County where he resided as a farmer prior to enlisting in Mecklenburg County at age 38, May 20, 1861. Present or accounted for until killed at Gaines' Mill, Virginia, June 27, 1862.

THORNBURG, GEORGE J., Private

Born in Gaston County* and resided in Wilkes County where he was by occupation a farmer prior to enlisting in Mecklenburg County at age 20, May 26, 1861. Present or accounted for until discharged at Camp Ruffin, Virginia, October 14, 1861, by reason of disability.

THORNBURG, HENRY M., Private

Born in Gaston County* and resided in Wilkes County where he was by occupation a farmer prior to enlisting in Mecklenburg County at age 25, May 26, 1861. Present or accounted for through January 27, 1865.

THORNBURG, S. LEWIS, Private

Born in Gaston* or Lincoln counties and resided in Mecklenburg County where he was by occupation a farmer prior to enlisting in Mecklenburg County at age 34, May 17, 1862, for the war. Present or accounted for until he died in hospital at Richmond, Virginia, on or about January 23, 1863, of "pneumonia."

TICER, ROBERT C. S., Private

Born in Mecklenburg County where he resided as a blacksmith prior to enlisting in Mecklenburg County at age 18, July 17, 1861. Present or accounted for until killed at South Mountain, Maryland, September 14, 1862.

TODD, JOHN A. N., Musician

Resided in Mecklenburg County and enlisted at Camp Ruffin, Virginia, at age 23, August 7, 1861. Mustered in as Private. Promoted to Musician and detailed for duty with the regimental band in September-October, 1861. Died at Richmond, Virginia, June 6, 1862, while absent on detail with the band. Cause of death not reported.

TODD, JOHN W., 1st Sergeant

Resided in Mecklenburg County and was by occupation a farmer prior to enlisting in Mecklenburg County at age 26, April 3, 1861. Mustered in as Sergeant and was reduced to ranks on April 26, 1862. Promoted to Sergeant on July 26, 1862. Present or accounted for until wounded at South Mountain, Maryland, on or about September 14, 1862. Rejoined the company in November-December, 1862, and was promoted to 1st Sergeant on July 1, 1863. Present or accounted for through October, 1864.

TORRENCE, WILLIAM B., Private
Born in Gaston County where he resided prior to enlisting in Mecklenburg County at age 16, February 3, 1863, for the war. Present or accounted for until he died in hospital at Richmond, Virginia, June 22, 1863, of "febris typh[oid]."

TREDENICK, NICHOLAS POLK, Private
Resided in Mecklenburg County and was by occupation a farmer prior to enlisting in Mecklenburg County at age 17, July 17, 1861. Present or accounted for until discharged on September 27, 1862. Reason discharged not reported. Later served in Company C, 9th Regiment N.C.State Troops (1st Regiment N.C.Cavalry).

WALKER, LEVI JASPER, Private
Resided in Mecklenburg County and was by occupation a farmer prior to enlisting in Mecklenburg County at age 19, May 20, 1861. Present or accounted for until wounded in the left leg and captured at Gettysburg, Pennsylvania, July 1-4, 1863. Left leg amputated. Hospitalized at Davids Island, New York Harbor, until paroled and transferred to City Point, Virginia, where he was received October 28, 1863, for exchange. Reported absent wounded until retired to the Invalid Corps on May 2, 1864.

WATTS, WILLIAM T., Private
Enlisted in Mecklenburg County on March 20, 1864, for the war. Present or accounted for until paroled at Appomattox Court House, Virginia, April 9, 1865.

WEARN, GEORGE H., Chief Musician
Resided in Mecklenburg County and enlisted at Camp Ruffin, Virginia, at age 27, August 7, 1861. Mustered in as Musician. Detailed for duty with the regimental band in September-October, 1861, and was promoted to Chief Musician (Drum Major) on November 1, 1863. Rejoined the company at an unspecified date. Present or accounted for until paroled at Appomattox Court House, Virginia, April 9, 1865.

WESNER, SAMUEL, Private
Enlisted in Mecklenburg County on March 1, 1864, for the war. Present or accounted for until killed at Spotsylvania Court House, Virginia, May 21, 1864.

WHYTE, WILLIAM, Sergeant
Resided in South Carolina and enlisted in Mecklenburg County at age 19, August 13, 1861. Mustered in as Private and promoted to Corporal on April 26, 1862. Promoted to Sergeant on December 23, 1862. Present or accounted for until wounded in the leg at Wilderness, Virginia, May 5, 1864. Reported absent wounded through October, 1864, but rejoined the company prior to January 1, 1865. Paroled at Farmville, Virginia, April 11-21, 1865.

WILEY, JOHN C., Private
Enlisted in Mecklenburg County on February 1, 1864, for the war. Present or accounted for until paroled at Appomattox Court House, Virginia, April 9, 1865.

WILSON, JAMES F., Private
Born in York District, South Carolina, and resided in Mecklenburg County where he was by occupation a farmer prior to enlisting in Mecklenburg County at age 18, April 3, 1861. Present or accounted for until killed at Williamsburg, Virginia, May 5, 1862.

WINGETT, NEELY J., Corporal
Resided in Mecklenburg County and was by occupation a farmer or cooper prior to enlisting in Mecklenburg County at age 24, April 3, 1861. Mustered in as Private and promoted to Corporal on December 23, 1862. Present or accounted for until wounded in the right hip at Chancellorsville, Virginia, May 2-3, 1863. Rejoined the company in November-December, 1863, and present or accounted for until captured at Dinwiddie Court House, Virginia, April 3, 1865. Confined at Point Lookout, Maryland, until released on June 22, 1865, after taking the Oath of Allegiance.

WINGETTE, JAMES R., Private
Born in Mecklenburg County where he resided as a farmer prior to enlisting in Mecklenburg County at age 21, April 3, 1861. Mustered in as Corporal but was reduced to ranks in March-May, 1862. Present or accounted for until killed at Williamsburg, Virginia, May 5, 1862.

WOLF, HENRY F., Private
Born in Mecklenburg County where he resided as a farmer prior to enlisting in Mecklenburg County at age 23, July 17, 1861. Present or accounted for until he suffered a bayonet wound and was captured at Williamsburg, Virginia, May 5-6, 1862. Hospitalized at Washington, D.C., until exchanged at Aiken's Landing, James River, Virginia, August 5, 1862. Rejoined the company in November-December, 1862, and present or accounted for until wounded and captured at Gettysburg, Pennsylvania, July 1-4, 1863. Hospitalized as Davids Island, New York Harbor, where he died July 19, 1863, of wounds.

WRYFIELD, JOHN R., Private
Born in Gaston County* where he resided as a farmer prior to enlisting in Mecklenburg County at age 20, April 3, 1861. Present or accounted for until wounded "slightly" at Chancellorsville, Virginia, May 3, 1863. Died in hospital at Guinea Station, Virginia, July 14, 1863. Cause of death not reported.

WRYFIELD, WILLIAM, Private
Previously served in Company D, 63rd Regiment N.C.Troops (5th Regiment N.C.Cavalry). Transferred to this company on March 24, 1865. No further records.

YOUNGBLOOD, SAMUEL C., Private
Born in York District, South Carolina, and resided in Mecklenburg County where he was by occupation a farmer prior to enlisting in Mecklenburg County at age 30, April 3, 1861. Mustered in as Sergeant but was reduced to ranks on April 26, 1862. Died at home in Mecklenburg County on or about November 12, 1862. Cause of death not reported.

COMPANY C

This company, known as the Milton Blues, was from Caswell County and enlisted at Milton on or about April 24, 1861. The company left Milton on April 26 under orders to proceed to Fort Macon, where it arrived the same day. It remained at Fort Macon until it moved to Raleigh on April 29. On May 23 the company moved to Garysburg, where it was assigned to the regiment as Company C. After joining the regiment the company functioned as a part of the regiment, and its history for the war period is recorded as a part of the regimental history.

The information contained in the following roster of the company was compiled principally from company muster rolls for May 15, 1861, through October, 1864. No company muster rolls were found for the period after October, 1864. In addition to the company muster rolls, Roll of Honor records, receipt rolls, hospital records, prisoner of war records, and other primary records, supplemented by state pension applications, United Daughters of the Confederacy records, and postwar rosters and histories, all provided useful information.

OFFICERS

CAPTAINS

MITCHELL, JAMES T.
Resided in Caswell County and was by occupation a mechanic prior to enlisting in Caswell County at age 33. Elected Captain on April 24, 1861. Present or accounted for until he was defeated for reelection when the regiment was reorganized on April 26, 1862. Later served as Captain of Company B, 59th Regiment N.C.Troops (4th Regiment N.C.Cavalry).

HUNT, LEONARD H.
Resided in Caswell County and was by occupation a druggist prior to enlisting in Caswell County at age 25. Elected 1st Lieutenant on April 24, 1861, and was elected Captain on April 26, 1862. Present or accounted for until wounded at Gaines' Mill, Virginia, on or about June 27, 1862. Returned to duty prior to November 1, 1862. Present or accounted for until he resigned on June 2, 1863, upon appointment as Major on the staff of Major General William D. Pender.

RAINEY, WILLIAM W.
Resided in Caswell County and was by occupation a farmer prior to enlisting in Caswell County at age 22, April 24, 1861. Mustered in as Corporal and promoted to Sergeant on September 24, 1861. Reduced to ranks on April 26, 1862, but was reappointed Sergeant on August 1, 1862. Appointed Color Sergeant in November-December, 1862, and was elected 2nd Lieutenant on February 14, 1863. Promoted to Captain on June 1, 1863. Present or accounted for until wounded and captured at Gettysburg, Pennsylvania, July 1-5, 1863. Died July 9, 1863, of wounds. Place of death not reported.

EVANS, THOMAS C.
Resided in Caswell County and was by occupation a lawyer prior to enlisting in Caswell County at age 21, April 24, 1861. Mustered in as Private and promoted to Corporal on August 19, 1861. Reduced to ranks on April 26, 1862, and was discharged on May 28, 1862, after being appointed Drillmaster. Elected Captain on August 9, 1863. Present or accounted for

until wounded in the mouth and neck at Spotsylvania Court House, Virginia, in May, 1864. Hospitalized at Richmond, Virginia, May 23, 1864. Returned to duty on September 13, 1864, and present or accounted for until paroled at Appomattox Court House, Virginia, April 9, 1865.

LIEUTENANTS

BRANDON, WILLIAM T., 1st Lieutenant
Resided in Virginia and was by occupation a farmer prior to enlisting in Caswell County at age 22, April 24, 1861. Mustered in as Private and promoted to Sergeant on January 1, 1863. Elected 2nd Lieutenant on March 5, 1863, and was promoted to 1st Lieutenant on June 1, 1863. Present or accounted for until wounded and captured at Gettysburg, Pennsylvania, July 1-5, 1863. Died on or about July 9, 1863, of wounds received at Gettysburg. Place of death not reported.

CHANDLER, WILLIAM B., 2nd Lieutenant
Resided in Caswell County and was by occupation a farmer prior to enlisting in Caswell County at age 21, April 24, 1861. Mustered in as Private. Present or accounted for until wounded and captured at Chancellorsville, Virginia, May 3, 1863. Confined at Washington, D.C., until transferred to City Point, Virginia, where he was received May 13, 1863, for exchange. Rejoined the company in July-August, 1863, and was elected 2nd Lieutenant on October 24, 1863. Present or accounted for until captured at or near Wilderness, Virginia, on or about May 6, 1864. Confined at Fort Delaware, Delaware, until transferred to Hilton Head, South Carolina, August 20, 1864. Transferred back to Fort Delaware where he arrived March 12, 1865. Released June 16, 1865, after taking the Oath of Allegiance.

DAVIS, CHAMPION T. N., 2nd Lieutenant
Resided in Caswell County and was by occupation a mechanic prior to enlisting in Caswell County at age 33, April 24, 1861. Mustered in as Private and was elected 2nd Lieutenant on April 26, 1862. Present or accounted for until he resigned on February 9, 1863, by reason of "exema." Resignation accepted February 24, 1863.

FLEMING, JASPER, 3rd Lieutenant
Resided in Caswell County where he enlisted at age 27. Elected 3rd Lieutenant on April 24, 1861. Appointed Adjutant on June 3, 1861, and transferred to the Field and Staff of this regiment.

HUNT, EUSTACE, 2nd Lieutenant
Resided in Caswell County and was by occupation a farmer prior to enlisting in Caswell County at age 23. Elected 2nd Lieutenant on April 24, 1861. Present or accounted for until he resigned on July 5, 1861.

RAINEY, JOHN P., Jr., 1st Lieutenant
Resided in Caswell County and was by occupation a farmer prior to enlisting in Caswell County at age 18, April 24, 1861. Mustered in as Private. Present or accounted for until wounded at Sharpsburg, Maryland, September 17, 1862. Returned to duty prior to November 1, 1862, and was promoted to Corporal on April 1, 1863. Present or accounted for

until wounded in the forearm and captured at Chancellorsville, Virginia, May 3, 1863. Hospitalized at Washington, D.C., until transferred to Old Capitol Prison, Washington, June 25, 1863. Paroled and transferred to City Point, Virginia, where he was received June 30, 1863, for exchange. Rejoined the company in July-August, 1863, and was appointed 1st Lieutenant on October 24, 1863. Present or accounted for until paroled at Appomattox Court House, Virginia, April 9, 1865.

STEPHENS, WILLIAM G., 2nd Lieutenant
Resided in Caswell County and was by occupation a physician prior to enlisting in Caswell County at age 21, April 24, 1861. Mustered in as Private and was elected 2nd Lieutenant on January 13, 1862. Present or accounted for until appointed Assistant Surgeon on February 14, 1863, and transferred to the Field and Staff of this regiment.

THORNTON, SAMUEL R., 1st Lieutenant
Resided in Caswell County and was by occupation a farmer prior to enlisting in Caswell County at age 27, April 24, 1861. Mustered in as 1st Sergeant and was elected 2nd Lieutenant on July 13, 1861. Elected 1st Lieutenant on April 26, 1862. Present or accounted for until wounded at Chancellorsville, Virginia, May 1-3, 1863. Died in May, 1863, of wounds. Place and exact date of death not reported.

NONCOMMISSIONED OFFICERS AND PRIVATES

ALEXANDER, NOAH, Private
Born in Gaston County* where he resided as a farmer prior to enlisting in Gaston County at age 38, March 5, 1863, for the war. Present or accounted for until discharged at Liberty, Virginia, August 31, 1863, by reason of "hypertrophy, with valvular disease of the heart."

ALLEN, JOHN, Private
Resided in Caswell County and was by occupation a trader prior to enlisting in Caswell County at age 25, April 24, 1861. Present or accounted for until wounded at Chancellorsville, Virginia, May 1-3, 1863. Rejoined the company prior to July 1-5, 1863, when he was wounded in the left foot and captured at Gettysburg, Pennsylvania. Left leg amputated. Hospitalized at Chester, Pennsylvania, until paroled and transferred to City Point, Virginia, where he was received September 23, 1863, for exchange. Reported absent wounded until retired to the Invalid Corps on August 30, 1864.

ALLEN, WILLIAM, Private
Resided in Caswell County and was by occupation a trader prior to enlisting in Caswell County at age 21, April 24, 1861. Present or accounted for until he was reported in the hands of the enemy on a company muster roll dated May-June, 1864. Records of the Federal Provost Marshal do not substantiate the report of his capture. Reported in hospital at Lynchburg, Virginia, on company muster roll dated July-August, 1864. Rejoined the company in September-October, 1864. Captured on the South Side Railroad, Virginia, April 2, 1865. Confined at Point Lookout, Maryland, until released on June 23, 1865,

after taking the Oath of Allegiance.

ATKINSON, ADOLPHUS, Private
Resided in Caswell County and was by occupation a silversmith prior to enlisting in Caswell County at age 17, April 24, 1861. Present or accounted for until wounded and captured at Gettysburg, Pennsylvania, or at Cashtown, Pennsylvania, July 1-5, 1863. Hospitalized at Chester, Pennsylvania, until paroled and transferred to City Point, Virginia, where he was received August 20, 1863, for exchange. Reported absent wounded through October, 1864.

ATKINSON, AUGUSTUS, Private
Resided in Caswell County where he enlisted at age 21, April 24, 1861. Present or accounted for until transferred to the Signal Corps on April 1, 1862.

BLACKBURN, J. T., Private
Enlisted at Camp Vance on January 30, 1864, for the war. Present or accounted for through February, 1864. No further records.

BRANDON, GEORGE W., Corporal
Resided in Virginia and enlisted in Caswell County at age 18, July 17, 1861. Mustered in as Private and promoted to Corporal on April 1, 1863. Present or accounted for until wounded and captured at Gettysburg, Pennsylvania, July 1, 1863. Hospitalized at Chester, Pennsylvania, where he died August 26, 1863, of wounds.

BRANDON, WILLIAM J., Corporal
Resided in Virginia and was by occupation a farmer prior to enlisting in Caswell County at age 18, August 24, 1861. Mustered in as Private. Present or accounted for until wounded in the right hand at Fredericksburg, Virginia, on or about December 13, 1862. Rejoined the company in March-April, 1863, and was promoted to Corporal in March-April, 1864. Present or accounted for until reported absent wounded in May-June, 1864; however, place and date wounded not reported. Rejoined the company in July-August, 1864, and present or accounted for until paroled at Appomattox Court House, Virginia, April 9, 1865.

BREWER, ROBERT E., Private
Resided in Caswell County where he enlisted at age 25, July 17, 1861. Present or accounted for until wounded in the left shoulder at Gaines' Mill, Virginia, June 27, 1862. Reported absent wounded until he rejoined the company in September-October, 1863. Present or accounted for through October, 1864. Paroled at Charlotte on May 24, 1865.

BROOKS, JOHN T., Private
Resided in Caswell County and was by occupation a student prior to enlisting in Caswell County at age 17, April 24, 1861. Present or accounted for through October, 1864; however, he was reported on detail as a courier during much of that period.

BUMGANER, WILLIAM C., Private
Resided in Wilkes County and enlisted in Wake County at age 27, September 27, 1862, for the war. Present or accounted for through October, 1864.

BURCH, ANGUS J., Corporal
Resided in Caswell County and was by occupation a mechanic prior to enlisting in Caswell County at age 21, April 24, 1861. Mustered in as Private and pro-

moted to Corporal in September-October, 1864. Present or accounted for until paroled at Appomattox Court House, Virginia, April 9, 1865.

BURKE, JOHN, Private
Resided in Caswell County where he enlisted at age 38, June 28, 1861. Present or accounted for until discharged on or about September 30, 1862, by reason of being over age.

BURTON, JOHN A., Sergeant
Resided in Caswell County where he enlisted at age 21, August 5, 1861. Mustered in as Private. Present or accounted for until wounded at Chancellorsville, Virginia, May 3, 1863. Rejoined the company in September-October, 1863, and was promoted to Corporal on October 29, 1863. Promoted to Sergeant on April 28, 1864. Present or accounted for until paroled at Appomattox Court House, Virginia, April 9, 1865.

BYRD, LEWIS, Private
Enlisted at Camp Vance on February 16, 1864, for the war. Present or accounted for until captured at Wilderness, Virginia, May 6, 1864. Confined at Point Lookout, Maryland, until released on May 23, 1864, after joining the U.S. Army. Unit to which assigned not reported.

CAMPBELL, WILLIAM C., Private
Born in Caswell County where he resided as a farmer or machinist prior to enlisting in Caswell County at age 21, April 24, 1861. Present or accounted for until killed at Fredericksburg, Virginia, December 13, 1862.

CARTER, JASPER N., Private
Resided in Caswell County where he enlisted at age 19, July 25, 1861. Present or accounted for until he died at home in Caswell County on or about November 21, 1862. Cause of death not reported.

CASE, NEEDHAM, Private
Resided in Craven County and enlisted at Camp Holmes on November 25, 1863, for the war. Present or accounted for until captured at Amelia Court House, Virginia, April 5, 1865. Confined at Point Lookout, Maryland, until released on June 26, 1865, after taking the Oath of Allegiance.

CAUDLE, LEWIS, Private
Resided in Yadkin County where he enlisted at age 25, March 3, 1863, for the war. Deserted on April 18, 1863, but rejoined the company in March-April, 1864. Reported "missing" on May 5, 1864. No further records.

CHANCE, YANCEY, Private
Born in Caswell County where he resided as a teamster or mechanic prior to enlisting in Caswell County at age 17, April 24, 1861. Present or accounted for until discharged on July 24, 1862, by reason of being under age. [May have served later in Company B, 59th Regiment N.C. Troops (4th Regiment N. C. Cavalry).]

COURTNEY, JAMES S., Private
Place and date of enlistment not reported. First listed on a company muster roll dated June 30-October 31, 1862, which states he deserted August 15, 1862.

COVINGTON, SAMUEL T., Private
Resided in Person County and was by occupation a farmer prior to enlisting in Caswell County at age 21, April 24, 1861. Present or accounted for until wounded at Fredericksburg, Virginia, on or about December 13, 1862. Rejoined the company prior to January 1, 1863, and present or accounted for until wounded and captured at Gettysburg, Pennsylvania, July 1-4, 1863. Hospitalized at Davids Island, New York Harbor, until paroled and transferred to City Point, Virginia, where he was received September 8, 1863, for exchange. Rejoined the company in January-February, 1864, and present or accounted for until paroled at Appomattox Court House, Virginia, April 9, 1865.

DAVIS, G. B., Private
Enlisted in Orange County on September 25, 1863, for the war. Present or accounted for until paroled at Appomattox Court House, Virginia, April 9, 1865.

DISMUKES, HENRY M., Private
Born in Caswell County where he resided as a farmer prior to enlisting in Caswell County at age 21, September 1, 1861. Present or accounted for until discharged at Richmond, Virginia, October 5, 1862, by reason of "chronic rheumatism."

DUKE, ARCHIBALD, Private
Born in Caswell County where he resided as a farmer prior to enlisting in Caswell County at age 21, April 24, 1861. Present or accounted for until he died in hospital at Guinea Station, Virginia, on or about February 28, 1863, of "smallpox."

DUNTON, AUGUSTUS T., Corporal
Resided in New York and was by occupation an "agent" prior to enlisting in Caswell County at age 31, April 24, 1861. Mustered in as Private and promoted to Corporal on December 1, 1861. Present or accounted for until he deserted in March, 1862.

EARP, LAWSON, Private
Resided in Caswell County and was by occupation a farmer prior to enlisting in Caswell County at age 51, April 24, 1861. Present or accounted for until discharged prior to July 1, 1861, by reason of "disability."

FARLEY, WILLIAM T., Sergeant
Resided in Caswell County and was by occupation a mechanic prior to enlisting in Caswell County at age 21, April 24, 1861. Mustered in as Private and promoted to Corporal on January 1, 1863. Promoted to Sergeant on April 1, 1863. Present or accounted for until wounded at Gettysburg, Pennsylvania, July 1-3, 1863. Captured at Falling Waters, West Virginia, July 14, 1863. Confined at Point Lookout, Maryland, until paroled and transferred to City Point, Virginia, where he was received March 6, 1864, for exchange. Rejoined the company in May-June, 1864, and present or accounted for until paroled at Appomattox Court House, Virginia, April 9, 1865.

FARMER, ENOCH H., Sergeant
Born in Halifax County, Virginia, and resided in Caswell County where he was by occupation a printer prior to enlisting in Caswell County at age 23, April 24, 1861. Mustered in as Private and promoted to 1st

Sergeant on April 26, 1862. Present or accounted for until wounded in the right arm at Gaines' Mill, Virginia, June 27, 1862. Right arm amputated. Reduced to the rank of Sergeant on November 1, 1862. Reported absent wounded or absent on furlough until discharged at Albany, Georgia, April 1, 1865. Paroled at Albany on May 19, 1865.

FERGUSON, ALLEN, Private
Enlisted at Camp Vance on August 25, 1863, for the war. Present or accounted for until captured at Wilderness, Virginia, May 6, 1864. Confined at Point Lookout, Maryland, until transferred to Elmira, New York, August 10, 1864. Died at Elmira on August 22, 1864, of "chronic diarrhoea." Records of the Federal Provost Marshal give his age as 43.

FORREST, JOHN B., Private
Resided in Stanly County where he enlisted at age 39, February 28, 1863, for the war. Present or accounted for until wounded in the left thigh at Chancellorsville, Virginia, May 3, 1863. Rejoined the company in September-October, 1863, and present or accounted for until captured at Spotsylvania Court House, Virginia, May 20-21, 1864. Confined at Point Lookout, Maryland, until paroled and transferred to Aiken's Landing, James River, Virginia, September 18, 1864, for exchange. Hospitalized at Richmond, Virginia, until furloughed for sixty days on October 5, 1864.

FREEMAN, JONATHAN, Private
Enlisted in Stokes County on September 25, 1863, for the war. Mustered in as 1st Sergeant but was reduced to ranks on June 4, 1864. Present or accounted for through October, 1864. Died at or near Richmond, Virginia, on or about November 14, 1864. Cause of death not reported.

FURGUSON, ROBERT F., Private
Resided in Caswell County and was by occupation a mechanic prior to enlisting in Caswell County at age 27, April 24, 1861. Present or accounted for until discharged on or about December 7, 1861. Reason discharged not reported.

GORDON, GEORGE W., Private
Born in Caswell County where he resided as a clerk prior to enlisting in Caswell County at age 17, April 24, 1861. Mustered in as Private and promoted to Corporal on April 26, 1862. Present or accounted for until wounded in the right arm at South Mountain, Maryland, September 14, 1862. Reduced to ranks on October 29, 1863. Reported absent wounded until he rejoined the company in November-December, 1863. Discharged on January 31, 1864, by reason of "paralysis" of the right arm.

GORDON, WILLIAM H., Private
Resided in Caswell County where he enlisted at age 20, June 26, 1861. Present or accounted for until discharged on or about October 1, 1862, under the provisions of the Conscript Act.

GORDON, WILLIAM W., Private
Resided in Caswell County and was by occupation a clerk prior to enlisting in Caswell County at age 19, April 24, 1861. Present or accounted for until he was "left sick" at Yorktown, Virginia, when the town was evacuated on May 3, 1862. Company records indicate that he was believed to have died in the hands

of the enemy. No further records.

HADDOCK, JOHN B., Private
Enlisted at Camp Holmes on April 10, 1864, for the war. Present or accounted for until captured at or near Wilderness, Virginia, May 5-8, 1864. Confined at Point Lookout, Maryland, until transferred to Elmira, New York, August 10, 1864. Died at Elmira on September 25, 1864, of "chronic diarrhoea."

HAMLETT, HENDERSON R., Private
Previously served in Company A, 24th Regiment N.C. Troops (14th Regiment N.C. Volunteers). Transferred to this company on February 16, 1865. No further records.

HAMLETT, HENRY C., Private
Resided in Person County and was by occupation a farmer prior to enlisting in Caswell County at age 27, April 24, 1861. Present or accounted for until wounded at Gaines' Mill, Virginia, or at Malvern Hill, Virginia, June 27-July 2, 1862. Rejoined the company in November-December, 1862, and present or accounted for until killed at Gettysburg, Pennsylvania, July 1, 1863.

HAMLETT, JAMES F., Private
Resided in Person County and enlisted in Caswell County at age 20, July 17, 1861. Present or accounted for until paroled at Appomattox Court House, Virginia, April 9, 1865.

HAMLETT, JAMES L., Sergeant
Born in Caswell County where he resided as a teacher prior to enlisting in Caswell County at age 24, April 24, 1861. Mustered in as Corporal and promoted to Sergeant on September 24, 1861. Present or accounted for until killed at Fredericksburg, Virginia, December 13, 1862.

HAMLETT, ROBERT T., Private
Born in Person County and resided in Caswell County where he was by occupation a farmer prior to enlisting in Caswell County at age 34, April 24, 1861. Present or accounted for until discharged at Richmond, Virginia, July 25, 1862, under the provisions of the Conscript Act. [May have served later in Company E, 35th Regiment N.C. Troops.]

HAMLETT, WILLIAM H., Private
Resided in Caswell County and was by occupation a farmer prior to enlisting in Caswell County at age 23, April 24, 1861. Present or accounted for until he died at "Smithfield" on or about September 5, 1861, of disease.

HARRIS, WILLIAM H., Private
Born in Caswell County where he resided as a merchant or farmer prior to enlisting in Caswell County at age 23, April 24, 1861. Present or accounted for until he died in hospital at Richmond, Virginia, May 18, 1862, of disease.

HART, ELISHA, Private
Enlisted at Camp Holmes on November 30, 1863, for the war. Present or accounted for through October, 1864; however, he was reported absent sick during most of that period.

HENDRICK, CHARLES M., Private
Resided in Caswell County and was by occupation a farmer prior to enlisting in Caswell County at age 23, April 24, 1861. Mustered in as Private and pro-

moted to Corporal on April 1, 1863. Present or accounted for until wounded at Chancellorsville, Virginia, May 3, 1863. Rejoined the company in January-February, 1864, and was reduced to ranks in March-April, 1864. Present or accounted for until retired to the Invalid Corps on October 20, 1864.

HENDRICK, JOHN G., Corporal
Resided in Caswell County and was by occupation a farmer prior to enlisting in Caswell County at age 24, April 24, 1861. Mustered in as Private. Present or accounted for until wounded at South Mountain, Maryland, September 14, 1862. Rejoined the company in January-February, 1863, and was promoted to Corporal on October 29, 1863. Present or accounted for until admitted to hospital at Farmville, Virginia, May 10, 1864, with a gunshot wound; however, place and date wounded not reported. Rejoined the company in July-August, 1864, and present or accounted for through October, 1864.

HILL, CHARLES D., Private
Resided in Caswell County where he enlisted at age 23, April 24, 1861. Present or accounted for until appointed Quartermaster Sergeant on June 3, 1861, and transferred to the Field and Staff of this regiment.

HILL, DANIEL C., Sergeant
Born in Caswell County where he resided as a clerk prior to enlisting in Caswell County at age 19, April 24, 1861. Mustered in as Corporal and was promoted to Sergeant on July 13, 1861. Present or accounted for until promoted to Quartermaster Sergeant on December 1, 1861, and transferred to the Field and Staff of this regiment.

HINES, EDWARD P., Private
Resided in Caswell County and was by occupation a clerk prior to enlisting in Caswell County at age 15, April 24, 1861. Present or accounted for until discharged on September 9, 1861, by reason of "disability."

HINES, SAMUEL H., Corporal
Born in Caswell County where he resided as a clerk prior to enlisting in Caswell County at age 25, April 24, 1861. Mustered in as Corporal. Present or accounted for until discharged at Camp Ruffin, Virginia, August 9, 1861, by reason of "disability." Later served as Captain of Company I, 45th Regiment N.C. Troops.

HOLBROOKS, WINFREY, Private
Resided in Wilkes County and enlisted in Wake County at age 33, September 27, 1862, for the war. Present or accounted for until wounded at Chancellorsville, Virginia, May 3, 1863. Reported absent wounded until he "deserted from hospital" in September-October, 1863. "Absent without leave" through October, 1864.

HOLCOMBE, JOEL J., Corporal
Resided in Caswell County and was by occupation a farmer prior to enlisting in Caswell County at age 26, April 24, 1861. Mustered in as Private. Present or accounted for until wounded at Chancellorsville, Virginia, May 3, 1863. Rejoined the company in September-October, 1863, and was promoted to Corporal on April 29, 1864. Present or accounted for

until killed in battle at the North Anna River, Virginia, May 24, 1864.

HOLLOWAY, JOHN, Private
Born in Wilkes County where he resided prior to enlisting in Wake County at age 23, September 27, 1862, for the war. Present or accounted for until he died in hospital at Richmond, Virginia, December 30, 1862, of "typhoid fever."

HORTON, THOMAS J., Private
Resided in Caswell County and was by occupation a farmer prior to enlisting in Caswell County at age 25, April 24, 1861. Present or accounted for until discharged on October 1, 1861, by reason of "disability."

HOWARD, WILLIAM A., Private
Born in Caswell County where he resided as a farmer or stonecutter prior to enlisting in Caswell County at age 24, April 24, 1861. Present or accounted for until discharged at Camp Ruffin, Virginia, December 10, 1861, by reason of "disease of a pulmonary character."

HUMPHREYS, ELLIOTT, Private
Resided in Rockingham County where he enlisted at age 37, February 28, 1863, for the war. Present or accounted for until wounded in the left hip at Chancellorsville, Virginia, May 3, 1863. Rejoined the company in September-October, 1863, and present or accounted for until captured at or near Wilderness, Virginia, on or about May 6, 1864. Confined at Point Lookout, Maryland, where he died on September 3, 1864, of "acute diarrhoea."

JAMES, WILLIAM H., Private
Resided in Virginia and was by occupation a trader prior to enlisting in Caswell County at age 21, April 24, 1861. Present or accounted for through September 1, 1862. Died prior to November 1, 1863. Place, exact date, and cause of death not reported.

JOHNSON, J. A., Private
Resided in Surry County where he enlisted at age 24, March 14, 1863, for the war. Deserted April 18, 1863.

JOHNSON, ROBERT, Private
Enlisted at Camp Vance on November 15, 1863, for the war. Died in hospital at Charlottesville, Virginia, January 6, 1864, of "pneumonia."

JOHNSON, SAMUEL M., Private
Born at Harpers Ferry, Virginia, and resided in Wilkes County where he was by occupation a teacher prior to enlisting in Wake County at age 27, September 27, 1862, for the war. Present or accounted for until reported absent without leave on February 26, 1864. Reported absent without leave through October, 1864.

JONES, WALTER J., Private
Born in Caswell County where he resided as a lawyer prior to enlisting in Caswell County at age 21, April 24, 1861. Present or accounted for until discharged at Camp Ruffin, Virginia, February 10, 1862, by reason of "an eruptive disease of long standing."

JONES, WILLIAM P., Private
Resided in Person County and was by occupation a farmer prior to enlisting in Caswell County at age

19, April 24, 1861. Present or accounted for until transferred to the Signal Corps on April 1, 1862.

KERSEY, LORENZO D., Private

Born in Caswell County where he resided as a mechanic prior to enlisting in Caswell County at age 20, April 24, 1861. Mustered in as Private. Present or accounted for until wounded and captured at Gettysburg, Pennsylvania, July 1-4, 1863. Hospitalized at Davids Island, New York Harbor, until paroled and transferred to City Point, Virginia, where he was received September 16, 1863, for exchange. Rejoined the company in March-April, 1864, and was wounded in the right arm in action near the North Anna River, Virginia, May 21, 1864. Promoted to Corporal on August 25, 1864, but was reported absent wounded through October, 1864. Reduced to ranks prior to March 25, 1865, when he was discharged by reason of wounds. Later paroled at Greensboro.

KISORT, WILLIE, Private

Born in Orange County and resided in Caswell County where he was by occupation a carpenter or mechanic prior to enlisting in Caswell County at age 34, April 24, 1861. Present or accounted for until discharged on July 24, 1862, under the provisions of the Conscript Act.

LALE, R. C., Private

Resided in Burke County where he enlisted at age 38, March 26, 1863, for the war. Present or accounted for until wounded at Chancellorsville, Virginia, May 3, 1863. Died at Richmond, Virginia, prior to September 11, 1863. Cause and exact date of death not reported.

LEFLER, ELI, Private

Resided in Stanly County where he enlisted at age 39, February 28, 1863, for the war. Present or accounted for until killed at Gettysburg, Pennsylvania, July 1, 1863.

LONG, HENRY M., 1st Sergeant

Resided in Person County and was by occupation a trader prior to enlisting in Caswell County at age 21, April 24, 1861. Mustered in as Private and promoted to Corporal on April 26, 1862. Present or accounted for until wounded at South Mountain, Maryland, September 14, 1862. Rejoined the company in January-February, 1863, and was promoted to Sergeant on April 1, 1863. Present or accounted for until wounded in the hand at Gettysburg, Pennsylvania, July 1, 1863. Rejoined the company in November-December, 1863, and was promoted to 1st Sergeant on April 29, 1864. Present or accounted for until captured in hospital at Richmond, Virginia, April 3, 1865. Confined at Libby Prison, Richmond, until transferred to Newport News, Virginia, April 23, 1865. Released at Newport News on June 16, 1865, after taking the Oath of Allegiance.

LONGWELL, DAVID, Private

Born in Baltimore, Maryland, and resided in Caswell County where he was by occupation a tailor prior to enlisting in Caswell County at age 32, April 24, 1861. Present or accounted for until discharged July 21, 1862, under the provisions of the Conscript Act.

MAAC, THOMAS, Private

Place and date of enlistment not reported. First listed on a company muster roll dated February 28-June 30, 1862, which states that he deserted on June 14, 1862.

MABE, WILLIAM T., Private

Enlisted at Camp Holmes on February 25, 1864, for the war. Present or accounted for until wounded in the left foot in August, 1864. Place and exact date wounded not reported. Rejoined the company in September-October, 1864, and present or accounted for through October, 1864.

McBERRY, CALEB, Private

Place and date of enlistment not reported. Deserted to the enemy or was captured at Kinston on March 15, 1865.

McCAIN, ALFRED P., Private

Resided in Caswell County and was by occupation a mechanic prior to enlisting in Caswell County at age 25, April 24, 1861. Mustered in as Private and promoted to Sergeant on August 1, 1862. Promoted to 1st Sergeant on January 1, 1863. Present or accounted for until wounded at Chancellorsville, Virginia, May 3, 1863. Rejoined the company in January-February, 1864, and was reduced to ranks in March-April, 1864. Reported absent on detail with the Provost Guard at Liberty, Virginia, from June 9, 1864, through October 31, 1864.

McCAIN, JOHN W., Sergeant

Resided in Virginia and enlisted in Caswell County at age 35, July 19, 1861. Mustered in as Private. Present or accounted for until wounded at Gaines' Mill, Virginia, June 27, 1862. Rejoined the company in May-June, 1863, and was promoted to Corporal on October 5, 1863. Promoted to Sergeant on April 28, 1864. Present or accounted for until paroled at Appomattox Court House, Virginia, April 9, 1865.

McCAIN, WILLIAM A., Private

Resided in Caswell County and was by occupation a mechanic prior to enlisting in Caswell County at age 26, April 24, 1861. Present or accounted for until wounded at Gaines' Mill, Virginia, June 27, 1862. Rejoined the company prior to November 1, 1862, and present or accounted for until paroled at Appomattox Court House, Virginia, April 9, 1865.

MARTIN, CLARENCE D., Sergeant

Resided in Caswell County and was by occupation a student prior to enlisting in Wayne County at age 16, April 26, 1861. Mustered in as Private and promoted to Corporal on December 1, 1861. Promoted to Sergeant on April 26, 1862. Present or accounted for until he died or was discharged in June, 1862. No further records.

MARTIN, JENKINS C., Private

Resided in New Hanover County and enlisted at age 17, April 26, 1861. Not listed in the records of this company; however, he is listed on the Roll of Honor. No further records.

MILLER, JOHN, Private

Enlisted at Camp Vance on February 21, 1864, for the war. Present or accounted for until he deserted in March, 1864.

MITCHELL, CHARLES G., Private

Resided in Rockingham County where he enlisted at age 37, February 28, 1863, for the war. Present or accounted for until wounded in the leg at Chancellorsville, Virginia, May 3, 1863. Reported absent wounded or absent sick until captured in hospital at Richmond, Virginia, April 3, 1865. Confined at Libby Prison, Richmond, until transferred to Newport News, Virginia, April 23, 1865. Released at Newport News on June 30, 1865, after taking the Oath of Allegiance.

MITCHELL, JOSIAH, Private
Resided in Rockingham County where he enlisted at age 37, February 28, 1863, for the war. Present or accounted for until wounded in the elbow at Chancellorsville, Virginia, May 3, 1863. Rejoined the company in January-February, 1864, and present or accounted for until paroled at Appomattox Court House, Virginia, April 9, 1865.

MOORE, LITTLETON R., Private
Resided in Caswell County and was by occupation a farmer prior to enlisting in Caswell County at age 22, April 24, 1861. Present or accounted for until discharged June 1, 1861, by reason of "disability."

NICHOLS, DAVID A., Private
Born in Caswell County where he resided as a mechanic or carpenter prior to enlisting in Caswell County at age 34, April 24, 1861. Present or accounted for until he died in hospital at Petersburg, Virginia, May 11, 1862, of "febris typhoides."

OWEN, HENRY C., Private
Born in Caswell County where he resided as a farmer prior to enlisting in Caswell County at age 50, July 27, 1861. Present or accounted for until discharged on July 26, 1862, by reason of "chronic rheumatism."

PALMER, JOHN C., Private
Born in Caswell County and resided in Wake County where he was by occupation a jeweler prior to enlisting in Northampton County at age 20, May 27, 1861. Present or accounted for until transferred to Company G, 53rd Regiment N.C.Troops, April 15, 1862.

PATTERSON, ARMISTEAD H., Private
Resided in Caswell County and was by occupation a student prior to enlisting in Caswell County at age 20, April 24, 1861. Mustered in as Private and promoted to Corporal on September 24, 1861. Reduced to ranks in November-December, 1861. Discharged on or about August 14, 1862, after providing a substitute. Later served in Captain Pincik's Company, Virginia Light Artillery.

PATTERSON, DAVID, Jr., Private
Born at Petersburg, Virginia, and resided in Caswell County where he was by occupation a clerk prior to enlisting in Caswell County at age 22, August 24, 1861. Present or accounted for until killed at Gaines' Mill, Virginia, June 27, 1862.

PHELPS, JAMES L., Private
Resided in Caswell County and was by occupation a farmer prior to enlisting in Caswell County at age 21, April 24, 1861. Present or accounted for until wounded at or near South Mountain, Maryland, on or about September 17, 1862. Rejoined the company in May-June, 1863, and present or accounted for until wounded in the hand at Wilderness, Virginia, May 6, 1864. Reported absent wounded through

October, 1864. Captured in hospital at Richmond, Virginia, April 3, 1865. Confined at Libby Prison, Richmond, until transferred to Newport News, Virginia, April 23, 1865. Released at Newport News on June 30, 1865, after taking the Oath of Allegiance.

PIPER, GEORGE, Private
Resided in Caswell County where he enlisted at age 17, June 28, 1861. Present or accounted for until discharged on or about September 30, 1862, under the provisions of the Conscript Act. [May have served later in Company I, 45th Regiment N.C.Troops).]

PIPER, ROBERT, Private
Born in Orange County and resided in Caswell County where he was by occupation a mason prior to enlisting in Caswell County at age 25, April 24, 1861. Present or accounted for until killed at Gaines' Mill, Virginia, June 27, 1862.

PITTARD, ADDISON L., Private
Resided in Caswell County where he enlisted at age 19, August 5, 1861. Present or accounted for until he died at home on May 25 or June 12, 1862, of disease.

PITTARD, JOSIAH R., Private
Resided in Caswell County where he enlisted at age 16, August 5, 1861. Present or accounted for until he died in hospital at Danville, Virginia, June 12, 1862, of "febris typhoides."

POWELL, HENRY E., Private
Resided in Caswell County and was by occupation a farmer prior to enlisting in Caswell County at age 21, April 24, 1861. Present or accounted for until wounded and captured at Gettysburg, Pennsylvania, July 1-5, 1863. Hospitalized at Davids Island, New York Harbor, until paroled and transferred to City Point, Virginia, where he was received September 16, 1863, for exchange. Rejoined the company in March-April, 1864, and present or accounted for through October, 1864.

POWELL, WATSON W., Private
Resided in Caswell County and was by occupation a farmer prior to enlisting in Caswell County at age 20, April 24, 1861. Present or accounted for until wounded at Malvern Hill, Virginia, on or about July 1, 1862. Reported absent wounded or absent sick through February, 1863, but rejoined the company prior to July 3-5, 1863, when he was captured at Gettysburg, Pennsylvania. Confined at Johnson's Island, Ohio, July 20, 1863. Transferred to Point Lookout, Maryland, April 22, 1864, and was transferred to Old Capitol Prison, Washington, D.C., August 4, 1864. Transferred to Fort Delaware, Delaware, August 11, 1864. Paroled at Fort Delaware on October 6, 1864, and transferred for exchange. Received at Cox's Landing, James River, Virginia, October 15, 1864, for exchange.

POWELL, WILLIAM M., Private
Resided in Caswell County and was by occupation a farmer prior to enlisting in Caswell County at age 19, April 24, 1861. Present or accounted for until wounded at Malvern Hill, Virginia, on or about July 1, 1862. Rejoined the company in March-April, 1863, and present or accounted for until wounded and captured at Gettysburg, Pennsylvania, July 1-3, 1863. Died on or about July 3, 1863, of wounds.

POWERS, ARCHIBALD, Private

Born in Wake County and resided in Caswell County where he was by occupation a trader prior to enlisting in Caswell County at age 18, April 24, 1861. Present or accounted for until killed at Fredericksburg, Virginia, December 13, 1862.

PRICE, ALEXANDER, Private

Enlisted in Wake County on November 26, 1863, for the war. Present or accounted for until paroled at Appomattox Court House, Virginia, April 9, 1865.

RAINEY, JOSIAH N., Private

Enlisted at "Springville" on May 25, 1864, for the war. Present or accounted for until paroled at Appomattox Court House, Virginia, April 9, 1865.

RASH, J. C., Private

Resided in Wilkes County and enlisted in Wake County at age 30, September 27, 1862, for the war. Present or accounted for until wounded in the left hip and left side and captured at Chancellorsville, Virginia, May 3, 1863. Hospitalized at Washington, D.C., until transferred to Baltimore, Maryland, August 22, 1863. Paroled at Baltimore on August 23, 1863, and transferred to City Point, Virginia, where he was received August 24, 1863, for exchange. Reported absent wounded until reported absent without leave from March-April, 1864, through October, 1864.

REDMAN, FRANKLIN, Private

Enlisted in Stokes County on September 25, 1863, for the war. Present or accounted for until paroled at Appomattox Court House, Virginia, April 9, 1865.

RICE, DAVID B., Private

Resided in Caswell County and was by occupation a tobacconist prior to enlisting in Caswell County at age 25, April 24, 1861. Present or accounted for until discharged on October 20, 1861, by reason of "disability."

RICHMOND, STEPHEN D., 1st Sergeant

Resided in Caswell County and was by occupation a farmer prior to enlisting in Caswell County at age 21, April 24, 1861. Mustered in as Sergeant and promoted to 1st Sergeant on July 13, 1861. Present or accounted for until appointed Adjutant and transferred to the Field and Staff, 49th Regiment N.C. Troops, on or about April 12, 1862.

ROBERTSON, JOHN E., Private

Resided in Caswell County and was by occupation a farmer prior to enlisting in Caswell County at age 21, April 24, 1861. Mustered in as Sergeant but was reduced to ranks on September 4, 1861. Present or accounted for until discharged on November 7, 1861, by reason of "disability."

SAUNDERS, J. J., Private

Place and date of enlistment not reported. Paroled at Appomattox Court House, Virginia, April 9, 1865.

SLOOP, CALEB, Private

Resided in Alexander County and enlisted in Wake County on November 3, 1863, for the war. Present or accounted for until he deserted to the enemy in Alexander County in September, 1864. Took the Oath of Allegiance at Knoxville, Tennessee, September 21, 1864, and at Louisville, Kentucky, October

16, 1864.

SMITH, JERRALD, Private

Resided in Caswell County and was by occupation a mechanic prior to enlisting in Caswell County at age 20, April 24, 1861. Present or accounted for until reported absent without leave on April 8, 1863. Reported absent without leave through October, 1864.

SMITH, JOHN B., Sergeant

Resided in Caswell County and was by occupation a student prior to enlisting in Caswell County at age 17, April 24, 1861. Mustered in as Private and promoted to Corporal on July 13, 1861. Promoted to Sergeant on December 1, 1861. Present or accounted for until transferred to the Signal Corps on April 1, 1862.

SMITH, JOHN E., Private

Enlisted in Caswell County on September 26, 1863, for the war. Present or accounted for through February, 1864. No further records.

SMITH, JOHN W., Private

Resided in Person County and was by occupation a farmer prior to enlisting in Caswell County at age 21, April 24, 1861. Present or accounted for until transferred to the Signal Corps on April 1, 1862.

SMITHEY, JETHRO, Private

Resided in Wilkes County and enlisted at Camp Vance on March 15, 1864, for the war. Present or accounted for until discharged on July 28, 1864, by reason of being "over age."

SPARKS, GEORGE W., Private

Resided in Wilkes County and enlisted in Wake County at age 34, September 27, 1862, for the war. Present or accounted for through October, 1864.

SPARKS, HUGH, Private

Resided in Wilkes County and enlisted in Wake County at age 30, September 27, 1862, for the war. Present or accounted for until reported absent without leave on May 3, 1863. Rejoined the company in November-December, 1863, and present or accounted for until captured at Wilderness, Virginia, May 6, 1864. Confined at Point Lookout, Maryland, until transferred to Elmira, New York, August 10, 1864. Died at Elmira on September 11, 1864, of "chronic diarrhoea."

SPICER, RANSOM C., Private

Resided in Wilkes County and enlisted in Wake County at age 21, September 27, 1862, for the war. Present or accounted for until wounded at Chancellorsville, Virginia, May 3, 1863. Reported absent wounded through October, 1864.

SPOONMAN, CHARLES, Private

Enlisted at Camp Vance on February 15, 1864, for the war. Present or accounted for through April, 1864. Reported absent without leave from May-June, 1864, through October, 1864.

STAMPS, EDWARD R., Private

Resided in Caswell County and was by occupation a student prior to enlisting in Caswell County at age 17, April 24, 1861. Present or accounted for until transferred to Captain Pencik's Company, Virginia Light Artillery, May 14, 1862.

STANFIELD, WILLIAM A., Corporal
Resided in Caswell County and was by occupation a farmer prior to enlisting in Caswell County at age 30, April 24, 1861. Mustered in as Private and promoted to Corporal on April 26, 1862. Present or accounted for until he deserted to the enemy or was captured at South Mountain, Maryland, September 14, 1862. Confined at Old Capitol Prison, Washington, D.C., until paroled and transferred to City Point, Virginia, where he was received June 12, 1863, for exchange. Never rejoined the company. No further records.

STEPHENS, ARCHIBALD G., Private
Resided in Caswell County and was by occupation a farmer prior to enlisting in Caswell County at age 19, April 24, 1861. Present or accounted for until wounded at Gaines' Mill, Virginia, June 27, 1862. Died in hospital at Richmond, Virginia, July 21, 1862, of wounds.

STEPHENS, ARMSTEAD, Private
Born in Halifax County, Virginia, and resided in Caswell County where he was by occupation a carpenter prior to enlisting in Caswell County at age 45, June 28, 1861. Present or accounted for until discharged at Camp Ruffin, Virginia, January 15, 1862, after he "fell in a pit and dislocated his shoulder."

STIGALL, FARMVILLE R., Private
Enlisted in Caswell County on August 25, 1864, for the war. Present or accounted for until paroled at Appomattox Court House, Virginia, April 9, 1865.

STONE, WILLIAM, Private
Resided in Rockingham County where he enlisted at age 36, March 5, 1863, for the war. Present or accounted for until reported absent wounded in May-June, 1864; however, place and date wounded not reported. Rejoined the company in July-August, 1864, and present or accounted for until paroled at Appomattox Court House, Virginia, April 9, 1865.

STREETER, SERENO M., Private
Resided in Georgia and was by occupation an "agent" prior to enlisting in Caswell County at age 21, April 24, 1861. Present or accounted for until he deserted to the enemy in March, 1862.

STRICKLIN, NATHAN C., Private
Enlisted in Guilford County on September 26, 1863, for the war. Present or accounted for until paroled at Appomattox Court House, Virginia, April 9, 1865.

TALLY, HENRY C., Private
Resided in Caswell County where he enlisted at age 18, June 28, 1861. Present or accounted for until he died at Danville, Virginia, June 6, 1862, of "febris typhoides."

TALLY, JOHN W., Private
Resided in Caswell County and was by occupation a farmer prior to enlisting in Caswell County at age 21, April 24, 1861. Present or accounted for until captured in March-June, 1862; however, place and date captured not reported. Reported in confinement at Fort Wool, Virginia, August 2, 1862. Transferred to Aiken's Landing, James River, Virginia, where he was received August 5, 1862, for exchange. Died at Richmond, Virginia, November 23, 1862, of

"typhoid fever."

TERRY, ABNER R., Sergeant
Born in Caswell County where he resided as an architect or mechanic prior to enlisting in Caswell County at age 31, April 24, 1861. Mustered in as Sergeant. Present or accounted for until discharged at Camp Ruffin, Virginia, September 8, 1861, by reason of "disability."

TERRY, JOSEPH D., Sergeant
Resided in Caswell County and was by occupation a mechanic prior to enlisting in Caswell County at age 18, April 24, 1861. Mustered in as Private and promoted to Corporal on September 24, 1861. Promoted to Sergeant on April 26, 1862. Present or accounted for until killed at Gaines' Mill, Virginia, June 27, 1862.

THOMAS, JAMES, Private
Born in Caswell County where he resided as a mechanic or farmer prior to enlisting in Caswell County at age 21, April 24, 1861. Present or accounted for until he died at Richmond, Virginia, May 6, 1862, of disease.

THOMPSON, WILLIAM H., Corporal
Resided in Caswell County and was by occupation a mechanic prior to enlisting in Caswell County at age 23, April 24, 1861. Mustered in as Private and promoted to Corporal on April 26, 1862. Present or accounted for until killed at South Mountain, Maryland, September 14, 1862.

WALKER, HENRY A., Private
Resided in Caswell County where he enlisted at age 20, April 24, 1861. Mustered in as Private. Present or accounted for until appointed Sergeant Major on June 10, 1861, and transferred to the Field and Staff of this regiment.

WALLACE, JAMES J., Private
Born in Halifax County, Virginia, and resided in Caswell County where he was by occupation a mechanic prior to enlisting in Caswell County at age 32, April 24, 1861. Present or accounted for until killed at Chancellorsville, Virginia, May 3, 1863.

WATKINS, JOHN L., Private
Resided in Caswell County and was by occupation a physician prior to enlisting in Caswell County at age 21, April 24, 1861. Present or accounted for until discharged on June 14, 1862, after providing a substitute.

WELCH, J. W., Private
Enlisted at Camp Vance on March 15, 1864, for the war. Present or accounted for until he died at Lynchburg, Virginia, June 26, 1864, of "diarrhoea ch[ronic]."

WHITE, T. P., Private
Born in Anson County and resided in Stanly County where he was by occupation a farmer prior to enlisting in Stanly County at age 28, February 28, 1863, for the war. Present or accounted for until killed at Chancellorsville, Virginia, May 3, 1863.

WILKERSON, MUNROE JAMES, Private
Resided in Person County and enlisted at age 28, May 10, 1861. "Promoted to office" and left the regiment on May 27, 1861. No further records.

WILLIAMS, JOHN D., Private

Enlisted at age 20, April 24, 1861. No further records.

WOOD, WILLIAM, Private

Enlisted at Camp Holmes on November 25, 1863, for the war. Present or accounted for until captured at Wilderness, Virginia, May 5, 1864. No further records.

WORSHAM, JOHN D., Private

Resided in Caswell County where he enlisted at age 21, June 28, 1861. Present or accounted for until paroled at Farmville, Virginia, April 11-21, 1865.

YARBROUGH, JOHN B., Private

Resided in Caswell County and was by occupation a mechanic prior to enlisting in Caswell County at age 20, April 24, 1861. Mustered in as Private and promoted to Sergeant on August 1, 1862. Present or accounted for until wounded in the right leg and captured at Gettysburg, Pennsylvania, July 1-4, 1863. Hospitalized at Davids Island, New York Harbor, until paroled and transferred to City Point, Virginia, where he was received September 16, 1863, for exchange. Reduced to ranks in March-April, 1864, and was reported absent wounded until retired to the Invalid Corps on November 25, 1864.

YATES, LEWIS, Private

Enlisted at Camp Vance on February 18, 1864, for the war. "Deserted from camp" in March, 1864, and was reported absent without leave through October, 1864.

COMPANY D

This company, known as the Leasburg Grays, was from Caswell County and enlisted at Leasburg on May 1, 1861. It departed for Raleigh the same day and arrived there on May 2. Leaving Raleigh on May 23, the company arrived at Garysburg the same day. There it was assigned to the regiment as Company D. After joining the regiment the company functioned as a part of the regiment, and its history for the war period is recorded as a part of the regimental history.

The information contained in the following roster of the company was compiled principally from company muster rolls for May 15, 1861, through October, 1864. No company muster rolls were found for the period after October, 1864. In addition to the company muster rolls, Roll of Honor records, receipt rolls, hospital records, prisoner of war records, and other primary records, supplemented by state pension applications, United Daughters of the Confederacy records, and postwar rosters and histories, all provided useful information.

OFFICERS

CAPTAINS

HAMBRICK, JOHN T.

Resided in Caswell County and was by occupation a merchant prior to enlisting in Caswell County at age 38. Elected Captain on May 1, 1861, but was defeated for reelection when the regiment was reorganized on April 26, 1862. Appointed Major on May 26, 1862, to rank from April 26, 1862, and assigned to the Field and Staff of this regiment.

ROGERS, HENRY A.

Resided in Caswell County and was by occupation a teacher prior to enlisting in Caswell County at age 26. Elected 2nd Lieutenant on April 17, 1861, to rank from May 1, 1861. Elected Captain on April 26, 1862, to rank from that date. Present or accounted for until wounded at Sharpsburg, Maryland, September 17, 1862. Promoted to Major on December 16, 1862, and transferred to the Field and Staff of this regiment.

STEPHENS, THOMAS J.

Resided in Caswell County and was by occupation a teacher prior to enlisting in Caswell County at age 22, May 1, 1861. Mustered in as 1st Sergeant and appointed 2nd Lieutenant on April 26, 1862. Promoted to 1st Lieutenant on July 1, 1862, and promoted to Captain on December 16, 1862. Present or accounted for until he resigned on December 14, 1863, by reason of "severe stomatitis."

WOODS, WILLIAM G.

Resided in Caswell County and was by occupation a student prior to enlisting in Caswell County at age 20, May 1, 1861. Mustered in as Private and appointed 3rd Lieutenant on April 26, 1862. Promoted to 2nd Lieutenant on July 1, 1862, and promoted to 1st Lieutenant on December 16, 1862. Present or accounted for until wounded and captured at Gettysburg, Pennsylvania, July 5, 1863. Hospitalized at Baltimore, Maryland, and at Chester, Pennsylvania, until transferred to Point Lookout, Maryland, where he arrived October 4, 1863. Transferred to Johnson's Island, Ohio, October 20, 1863. Promoted to Captain on December 15, 1863, while a prisoner of war. Transferred from Johnson's Island to Point Lookout on March 21, 1865, and was transferred to Fort Delaware, Delaware, on or about April 28, 1865. Released at Fort Delaware on June 12, 1865, after taking the Oath of Allegiance.

LIEUTENANTS

ALLEN, JOHN W., 2nd Lieutenant

Resided in Caswell County and was by occupation a farmer prior to enlisting in Caswell County at age 27, May 1, 1861. Mustered in as Private and was promoted to 1st Sergeant on April 26, 1862. Reported absent wounded on company muster roll dated July 1-October 31, 1862; however, place and date wounded not reported. Rejoined the company in November-December, 1862, and was elected 2nd Lieutenant on December 19, 1863. Present or accounted for until paroled at Appomattox Court House, Virginia, April 9, 1865.

CHAMBERS, THOMAS J., 2nd Lieutenant

Resided in Caswell County and was by occupation a clerk prior to enlisting in Caswell County at age 22, May 1, 1861. Mustered in as Sergeant and was elected 3rd Lieutenant on July 28, 1862. Promoted to 2nd Lieutenant on December 16, 1862. Present or accounted for until killed at Gettysburg, Pennsylvania, July 1, 1863.

HOLDEN, EMORY BROCK, 1st Lieutenant

Resided in Caswell County where he enlisted at age 30. Elected 1st Lieutenant on May 1, 1861. Present or accounted for until he was defeated for reelection when the regiment was reorganized on April 26, 1862. Later served as 1st Lieutenant in Company B, 59th Regiment N.C.Troops (4th Regiment N.C. Cavalry).

RICHMOND, DANIEL W. K., 3rd Lieutenant
Resided in Caswell County and was by occupation a clerk prior to enlisting in Caswell County at age 21. Elected 3rd Lieutenant on May 1, 1861, to rank from that date. Present or accounted for until he was defeated for reelection when the regiment was reorganized on April 26, 1862.

STEPHENS, WILLIAM Q., 1st Lieutenant
Born in Caswell County where he resided as a farmer or teacher prior to enlisting in Caswell County at age 24, May 1, 1861. Mustered in as Corporal and was promoted to Sergeant on June 7, 1861. Appointed 1st Lieutenant on April 26, 1862. Present or accounted for until he died in hospital at Richmond, Virginia, June 28, 1862, of "typhoid fever." "Always displayed great coolness and bravery."

WILLIAMS, ROBERT A., 1st Lieutenant
Resided in Person County and enlisted in Caswell County at age 22, July 30, 1861. Mustered in as Private. Present or accounted for until wounded in the arm and side at Gaines' Mill, Virginia, June 27, 1862. Returned to duty in November-December, 1862, and was appointed 2nd Lieutenant on August 1, 1863. Promoted to 1st Lieutenant on December 14, 1863. Present or accounted for until paroled at Appomattox Court House, Virginia, April 9, 1865.

NONCOMMISSIONED OFFICERS AND PRIVATES

ANDREWS, LINDSEY, Private
Resided in Henderson County and enlisted at Camp Vance on September 6, 1863, for the war. Present or accounted for until wounded at Wilderness, Virginia, May 5, 1864. Reported absent wounded through October, 1864, but rejoined the company prior to April 2, 1865, when he was captured on the South Side Railroad, Virginia. Confined at Hart's Island, New York Harbor, until released on June 17, 1865, after taking the Oath of Allegiance.

ATKINS, GASTON, Private
Resided in Caswell County and was by occupation a farmer prior to enlisting in Caswell County at age 19, May 1, 1861. Present or accounted for until he died in hospital at Richmond, Virginia, August 10, 1862. Cause of death not reported.

AUSTIN, GEORGE A., Private
Born in Caswell County where he resided as a farmer prior to enlisting in Caswell County at age 22, May 1, 1861. Present or accounted for until killed at Chancellorsville, Virginia, May 3, 1863.

BERRIER, ANDREW J., Private
Resided in Davidson County and enlisted at Camp Holmes on February 28, 1864, for the war. Deserted on April 19, 1864, but rejoined the company on September 23, 1864. Deserted to the enemy on or about November 6, 1864. Took the Oath of Allegiance at City Point, Virginia, November 9, 1864.

BLACKBURN, WILBURN, Private
Resided in Wilkes County and enlisted in Wake County at age 28, September 27, 1862, for the war. Present or accounted for until he deserted on May 10, 1863.

BOSHAMER, HENRY R., Private
Resided in Caswell County and was by occupation a confectioner prior to enlisting in Caswell County at age 18, May 1, 1861. Present or accounted for until killed at Chancellorsville, Virginia, May 3, 1863.

BRADFORD, WILLIAM H., Private
Resided in Orange County and was by occupation a farmer prior to enlisting in Caswell County at age 19, May 1, 1861. Present or accounted for until reported absent wounded on company muster roll dated March 1-June 30, 1862; however, place and date wounded not reported. Rejoined the company in July-October, 1862, and present or accounted for until captured at Fredericksburg, Virginia, May 3, 1863. Confined at Washington, D.C., until transferred to City Point, Virginia, where he was received May 13, 1863, for exchange. Rejoined the company prior to July 1-4, 1863, when he was wounded and captured at Gettysburg, Pennsylvania. Hospitalized at Davids Island, New York Harbor, until paroled and transferred to City Point, where he was received September 16, 1863, for exchange. Rejoined the company in January-February, 1864, and present or accounted for until he "died of wounds" on August 4, 1864. Place and date wounded and place of death not reported.

BRADSHAW, WILLIAM A., Private
Enlisted at Camp Vance on February 1, 1864, for the war. Present or accounted for until he died in a Federal hospital at Knoxville, Tennessee, April 27, 1865, of "typhoid fever."

BRADSHER, DOLPHUS G., Private
Born in Person County where he resided as a farmer prior to enlisting in Caswell County at age 29, May 1, 1861. Present or accounted for until discharged at Petersburg, Virginia, November 30, 1864, by reason of "physical disability."

BROACH, VINCENT, Private
Resided in Person County and enlisted in Caswell County at age 22, July 30, 1861. Present or accounted for until he died in hospital at Richmond, Virginia, July 3, 1862, of "cont[inue]d fever."

BURCH, CHARLES, Private
Resided in Caswell County and was by occupation a farmer prior to enlisting in Caswell County at age 21, May 1, 1861. Present or accounted for until wounded in the thigh at Chancellorsville, Virginia, May 3, 1863. Rejoined the company in July-August, 1863, and present or accounted for through January 7, 1865.

BURTON, GEORGE M., Private
Born in Person County and resided in Caswell County where he was by occupation a farmer prior to enlisting in Caswell County at age 17, July 30, 1861. Present or accounted for until discharged near Berryville, Virginia, November 10, 1862, by reason of being under age. [May have served later in Company B, 59th Regiment N.C. Troops (4th Regiment N.C. Cavalry).]

BURTON, JOHN H., Sergeant

Resided in Caswell County and was by occupation a farmer prior to enlisting in Caswell County at age 23, May 1, 1861. Mustered in as Sergeant but was reduced to ranks on June 6, 1861. Promoted to Sergeant on November 1, 1861. Present or accounted for until captured at Falling Waters, Maryland, July 14, 1863. Confined at Baltimore, Maryland, until transferred to Point Lookout, Maryland, where he arrived August 17, 1863. Paroled at Point Lookout and transferred to City Point, Virginia, where he was received March 6, 1864, for exchange. Rejoined the company in May-June, 1864, and present or accounted for until paroled at Appomattox Court House, Virginia, April 9, 1865. Roll of Honor indicates he was wounded in the hand in an unspecified battle.

BUTLER, JOSHUA H., Private

Resided in Caswell County and was by occupation a farmer prior to enlisting in Caswell County at age 27, May 1, 1861. Present or accounted for until he died at home in Caswell County on or about October 14, 1862. Cause of death not reported.

CAMPBELL, JOHN M., Private

Resided in Union County and enlisted at Camp Holmes on February 24, 1864, for the war. Present or accounted for until captured on the South Side Railroad, Virginia, April 2, 1865. Confined at Hart's Island, New York Harbor, April 7, 1865. Released at Hart's Island on June 19, 1865, after taking the Oath of Allegiance.

CASORT, HAYWOOD, Private

Born in Caswell County where he resided as a farmer prior to enlisting in Caswell County at age 16, August 15, 1861. Present or accounted for until discharged near Winchester, Virginia, November 15, 1862, by reason of being under age.

CATES, HIRAM, Private

Resided in Caswell County and was by occupation a farmer prior to enlisting in Caswell County at age 20, May 1, 1861. Present or accounted for until wounded at Chancellorsville, Virginia, May 3, 1863. Rejoined the company in March-April, 1864, but was retired to the Invalid Corps on May 2, 1864.

COLEMAN, ABNER G., Private

Resided in Person County and was by occupation a farmer prior to enlisting in Caswell County at age 21, May 1, 1861. Present or accounted for until discharged July 29, 1862, after providing a substitute.

COMPTON, SILAS, Private

Born in Orange County and resided in Caswell County where he was by occupation a farmer prior to enlisting in Caswell County at age 25, May 1, 1861. Present or accounted for until killed at Chancellorsville, Virginia, May 3, 1863.

COVENDER, E. H., Private

Born in Onslow County and was by occupation a farmer prior to enlisting at Camp Holmes on January 27, 1864, for the war. Present or accounted for until discharged near Orange Court House, Virginia, April 25, 1864, by reason of "physical disability." Age given on discharge certificate as 20.

CRAFT, ANDREW J., Sergeant

Born in Bedford County, Virginia, and resided in Caswell County where he was by occupation a painter prior to enlisting in Caswell County on May 1, 1861. Mustered in as Corporal and promoted to Sergeant on April 26, 1862. Present or accounted for until discharged on July 30, 1862, by reason of "being over thirty-five years of age."

CRAFT, VAN BUREN, Private

Resided in Caswell County and was by occupation a painter prior to enlisting in Caswell County at age 24, May 1, 1861. Present or accounted for until wounded in the left leg at Chancellorsville, Virginia, May 3, 1863. Rejoined the company in September-October, 1863, and present or accounted for until paroled at Appomattox Court House, Virginia, April 9, 1865.

CROWDER, SAMUEL, Private

Place and date of enlistment not reported. First listed on the records of this company on December 1, 1864. Deserted to the enemy on or about February 26, 1865. Took the Oath of Allegiance on or about March 1, 1865.

DONOHO, EDWIN L., Private

Resided in Caswell County where he enlisted at age 21, July 30, 1861. Present or accounted for until he died in hospital at Richmond, Virginia, May 24-25, 1862. Cause of death not reported.

DUNCAN, GEORGE, Private

Enlisted at Camp Holmes on February 14, 1864, for the war. Present or accounted for through October, 1864.

DUNNIVANT, ALEXANDER, Private

Born in Caswell County where he resided as a farmer prior to enlisting in Caswell County at age 23, May 1, 1861. Present or accounted for until he died at Richmond, Virginia, July 1, 1862, of disease.

EVANS, JOHN W., Private

Born in Caswell County where he resided as a farmer prior to enlisting in Caswell County at age 19, May 1, 1861. Present or accounted for until captured at Boonsboro, Maryland, September 15, 1862. Confined at Fort Delaware, Delaware, until transferred to Aiken's Landing, James River, Virginia, October 2, 1862, for exchange. Declared exchanged at Aiken's Landing on November 10, 1862. Rejoined the company in January-February, 1863, and present or accounted for until wounded at Chancellorsville, Virginia, May 1-3, 1863. Rejoined the company prior to July 1, 1863, when he was killed at Gettysburg, Pennsylvania.

FAUCETT, WILLIAM H., Private

Born in Alamance County* where he resided prior to enlisting in Alamance County at age 38, March 13, 1863, for the war. Present or accounted for until wounded and captured at Gettysburg, Pennsylvania, July 1, 1863. Died in hospital at Gettysburg, July 3-5, 1863, of wounds.

FEATHERSTON, THOMAS W., Sergeant

Resided in Caswell County and was by occupation a farmer prior to enlisting in Caswell County at age 24, May 1, 1861. Mustered in as Private and was promoted to Corporal on April 26, 1862. Present or accounted for until wounded in the arm and leg and captured at Sharpsburg, Maryland, September 17,

1862. Hospitalized at Frederick, Maryland. Reported in confinement at Fort McHenry, Maryland, October 20, 1862. Paroled and transferred to Aiken's Landing, James River, Virginia, where he was received October 22, 1862, for exchange. Declared exchanged at Aiken's Landing on November 10, 1862. Promoted to Sergeant in November, 1864-April, 1865. Present or accounted for until paroled at Appomattox Court House, Virginia, April 9, 1865.

FEATHERSTON, WILLIAM H., Private
Resided in Caswell or Person counties and was by occupation a farmer prior to enlisting in Caswell County at age 18, May 1, 1861. Present or accounted for until he died at home on June 14, 1862, of disease.

FOWLER, ZACHARY, Private
Enlisted at Camp Vance on October 6, 1863, for the war. Present or accounted for until hospitalized at Richmond, Virginia, June 15, 1864, with a gunshot wound. Place and date wounded not reported. Died "at home" on August 15, 1864, of disease.

FULLER, JOHN L., Private
Resided in Caswell County and was by occupation a physician prior to enlisting in Caswell County at age 25, May 1, 1861. Present or accounted for until he died at Smithfield, Virginia, May 10, 1862, of disease.

GLENN, JOHN D., Private
Enlisted at Camp Holmes on February 24, 1864, for the war. Present or accounted for until paroled at Appomattox Court House, Virginia, April 9, 1865.

GORDON, ALEXANDER H., Corporal
Resided in Person County and enlisted in Caswell County at age 19, July 1, 1861. Mustered in as Private and promoted to Corporal on April 26, 1862. Present or accounted for until wounded at Gaines' Mill, Virginia, on or about June 27, 1862. Rejoined the company prior to July 1, 1862, and present or accounted for until killed at Gettysburg, Pennsylvania, July 1, 1863.

GORDON, JAMES, Private
Resided in Caswell County and was by occupation a farmer prior to enlisting in Caswell County at age 32, May 1, 1861. Present or accounted for until he died in hospital at Lynchburg, Virginia, July 8, 1862, of "dyptheria."

GRAHAM, WILLIAM R., Private
Resided in Caswell County and was by occupation a carpenter prior to enlisting in Caswell County at age 24, May 1, 1861. Present or accounted for through October, 1864; however, he was reported on detail as a pioneer or engineer during most of that period.

GRINSTEAD, LARKIN L., Private
Resided in Person County and was by occupation a farmer prior to enlisting in Caswell County at age 28, July 30, 1861. Present or accounted for until paroled at Appomattox Court House, Virginia, April 9, 1865.

HAFNER, JAMES B., Private
Enlisted at Camp Vance on November 26, 1863, for the war. Present or accounted for until he deserted to the enemy on February 9, 1864.

HAGWOOD, WILLIAM, Private
Resided in Caswell County and was by occupation a farmer prior to enlisting in Caswell County at age 25, May 1, 1861. No further records.

HAIR, JOHN, Private
Born in Harnett County* and enlisted at Camp Vance on November 30, 1863, for the war. Present or accounted for until he died in hospital at Charlottesville, Virginia, January 1, 1864, of "hydrothorax."

HAMILTON, JOHN T., Private
Resided in Caswell County and was by occupation a farmer prior to enlisting in Caswell County at age 22, May 1, 1861. Present or accounted for until wounded at Malvern Hill, Virginia, on or about July 1, 1862. Rejoined the company prior to November 1, 1862. Present or accounted for until wounded at Cold Harbor, Virginia, June 1, 1864. Rejoined the company in September-October, 1864, and present or accounted for through October, 1864.

HARRISON, JOHN A., 1st Sergeant
Resided in Caswell County and was by occupation a trader prior to enlisting in Caswell County at age 28, May 1, 1861. Mustered in as Private and promoted to Corporal on October 1, 1861. Reduced to ranks on April 26, 1862, but was promoted to Sergeant on August 1, 1862. Promoted to 1st Sergeant on December 19, 1863. Present or accounted for until captured near Mine Run, Virginia, May 5-7, 1864. Confined at Point Lookout, Maryland, until transferred to Elmira, New York, August 3, 1864. Paroled at Elmira and transferred to Venus Point, Savannah River, Georgia, where he was received on November 15, 1864, for exchange. Company records do not indicate whether he rejoined the company; however, he was paroled at Lynchburg, Virginia, April 15, 1865.

HINKLE, EMANUEL, Private
Enlisted at Camp Holmes on February 28, 1864, for the war. Discharged March 27, 1864. Reason discharged not reported.

HINKLE, MATHIAS H., Private
Enlisted at Camp Holmes on February 28, 1864, for the war. Deserted April 19, 1864, but returned on October 7, 1864. Paroled at Greensboro on May 8, 1865.

HOLDEN, LUCIAN J., Private
Born in Caswell County where he resided as a clerk prior to enlisting in Caswell County at age 18, August 15, 1861. Discharged at Camp Ruffin, Virginia, October 29, 1861, by reason of disability.

HOLT, CALVIN, Private
Enlisted at Camp Vance on December 28, 1863, for the war. Deserted to the enemy on or about February 9, 1864.

HOOD, ABEL T., Private
Born in Orange County where he resided as a farmer prior to enlisting in Caswell County at age 24, May 1, 1861. Present or accounted for until discharged at Camp Ruffin, Virginia, September 23, 1861, by reason of disability.

HOOPER, SIDNEY Y., Private
Previously served in Company C, 41st Regiment N.C. Troops (3rd Regiment N.C. Cavalry). Transferred to

this company on November 24, 1864. No further records.

HOWARD, JOHN H., Private
Resided in Caswell County and was by occupation a sawyer prior to enlisting in Caswell County at age 19, July 30, 1861. Present or accounted for until wounded in the arm at Wilderness, Virginia, May 5, 1864. Reported absent wounded or absent on detail through October, 1864. Captured in hospital at Richmond, Virginia, April 3, 1865. Confined at Libby Prison, Richmond, until transferred to Newport News, Virginia, April 23, 1865. Released at Newport News on June 30, 1865, after taking the Oath of Allegiance.

HUDGINS, LEVI, Private
Resided in Person County where he enlisted at age 38, March 10, 1863, for the war. Present or accounted for until wounded in the shoulder at Chancellorsville, Virginia, May 3, 1863. Rejoined the company in July-August, 1863, and present or accounted for until wounded accidentally in the left foot on or about April 14, 1864. Reported absent wounded or absent on light duty through October, 1864. Paroled at Appomattox Court House, Virginia, April 9, 1865.

HUGHES, JERRY, Private
Born in Orange County and enlisted at Richmond, Virginia, August 3, 1862, for the war as a substitute for Private Jasper J. James. Present or accounted for until captured at Gettysburg, Pennsylvania, July 1-4, 1863. Confined at Davids Island, New York Harbor, until paroled and transferred to City Point, Virginia, where he was received September 16, 1863, for exchange. Rejoined the company in January-February, 1864, and present or accounted for until he died July 23, 1864, of disease. Place of death not reported.

JAMES, JASPER J., Private
Resided in Caswell County and was by occupation a merchant prior to enlisting in Caswell County at age 19, May 1, 1861. Mustered in as Corporal but was reduced to ranks on April 26, 1862. Present or accounted for until discharged on August 3, 1862, after providing Private Jerry Hughes as a substitute.

JOHNSON, JAMES, Private
Resided in Caswell County or at Danville, Virginia, and was by occupation a farmer prior to enlisting in Caswell County at age 20, May 1, 1861. Present or accounted for until wounded at Chancellorsville, Virginia, May 3, 1863. Rejoined the company in July-August, 1863, and present or accounted for until captured in battle at the North Anna River, Virginia, May 23-24, 1864. Confined at Point Lookout, Maryland, until transferred to Elmira, New York, July 8, 1864. Released at Elmira on June 30, 1865, after taking the Oath of Allegiance.

JOHNSTON, WILLIAM, Private
Born in Caswell County where he resided as a farmer prior to enlisting in Caswell County at age 19, May 1, 1861. Present or accounted for until wounded in the right heel at Chancellorsville, Virginia, May 1-3, 1863. Rejoined the company prior to July 1-5, 1863, when he was wounded and captured at Gettysburg, Pennsylvania. Hospitalized at Chester, Pennsylvania, until transferred to City Point, Virginia, where he

was received September 23, 1863, for exchange. Rejoined the company in March-April, 1864, and present or accounted for until killed near Nance's Shop, Virginia, June 12, 1864.

JOHNSTON, WILLIAM, Private
Enlisted near Richmond, Virginia, June 7, 1862, for the war. Deserted at an unspecified date.

JONES, JOHN W., Private
Born in Person County where he resided as a teacher prior to enlisting in Caswell County at age 24, July 30, 1861. Present or accounted for until wounded in the left leg at Chancellorsville, Virginia, May 3, 1863. Reported absent wounded until discharged near Orange Court House, Virginia, March 28, 1864, by reason of wounds received at Chancellorsville.

JONES, ROBERT J., Private
Resided in Person County and enlisted in Caswell County at age 28, July 30, 1861. Present or accounted for until captured at Williamsport, Maryland, September 15, 1862. Confined at Fort Delaware, Delaware, until transferred to Aiken's Landing, James River, Virginia, October 2, 1862, for exchange. Declared exchanged at Aiken's Landing on November 10, 1862. Rejoined the company in January-February, 1863, and present or accounted for until wounded at Chancellorsville, Virginia, May 1-3, 1863. Rejoined the company prior to July 1, 1863, and present or accounted for until paroled at Appomattox Court House, Virginia, April 9, 1865.

JONES, ROBERT M., Corporal
Resided in Caswell or Wake counties and was by occupation a farmer prior to enlisting in Caswell County at age 24, May 1, 1861. Mustered in as Private. Present or accounted for until wounded at Chancellorsville, Virginia, May 3, 1863. Rejoined the company in July-August, 1863, and was promoted to Corporal on December 26, 1863. Present or accounted for until captured at Butler's Mills, Virginia, May 23-24, 1864. Confined at Point Lookout, Maryland, until transferred to Elmira, New York, July 8, 1864. Released at Elmira on June 19, 1865, after taking the Oath of Allegiance.

JONES, THOMAS L., Private
Enlisted at Camp Vance on December 28, 1863, for the war. Dropped from the rolls in January-February, 1864. Reason he was dropped not reported.

LEA, DAVID, Private
Born in Person County where he resided as a farmer prior to enlisting in Caswell County at age 22, May 1, 1861. Present or accounted for until wounded and captured at Sharpsburg, Maryland, on or about September 17, 1862. Died at Shepherdstown, Virginia, October 15, 1862, of wounds.

LEA, GREEN D., Corporal
Born in Person County and resided in Caswell County where he was by occupation a saddler prior to enlisting in Caswell County at age 18, May 1, 1861. Mustered in as Private. Present or accounted for until wounded at Gettysburg, Pennsylvania, July 1, 1863. Rejoined the company in September-October, 1863, and was promoted to Corporal on December 26, 1863. Present or accounted for until wounded in

a skirmish at Barnett's Ford, Virginia. Date of skirmish not reported. Died at Orange Court House, Virginia, February 10, 1864, of wounds.

LOVE, JAMES, Private
Born in Caswell County where he resided as a farmer prior to enlisting in Caswell County at age 21, May 1, 1861. Present or accounted for until discharged at Camp Ruffin, Virginia, September 23, 1861, by reason of disability.

McFARLAND, WALKER, Private
Born in Caswell County where he resided as a farmer prior to enlisting in Caswell County at age 19, May 1, 1861. Present or accounted for until captured at Williamsburg, Virginia, on or about May 5, 1862. Confined at Fort Monroe, Virginia. Exchanged prior to October 2, 1862. Rejoined the company in November-December, 1862, and present or accounted for until wounded and captured at Gettysburg, Pennsylvania, July 1-3, 1863. Died in hospital at Gettysburg on or about July 10, 1863.

MARTIN, JAMES, Private
Resided in Caswell County and was by occupation a farmer prior to enlisting in Caswell County at age 18, May 1, 1861. Present or accounted for until he died at Camp Ruffin, Virginia, December 7, 1861, of "pneumonia."

MATLOCK, WILLIAM, Private
Resided in Caswell County and enlisted at age 38, March 14, 1863, for the war. Discharged April 23, 1863, by reason of disability.

MITCHELL, C. J., Private
Place and date of enlistment not reported. Captured in hospital at Richmond, Virginia, April 3, 1865, and was transferred to the Federal Provost Marshal on April 21, 1865.

MORROW, JESSE, Private
Resided in Orange County and enlisted at age 19, May 1, 1861. Discharged on or about August 1, 1861, by reason of disability.

MURPHY, W. E., Private
Place and date of enlistment not reported. Paroled at Lynchburg, Virginia, April 15, 1865.

NELSON, JAMES, Private
Place and date of enlistment not reported. Paroled at Appomattox Court House, Virginia, April 9, 1865.

NELSON, JOHN T., Private
Resided in Person County and was by occupation a farmer prior to enlisting in Caswell County at age 22, May 1, 1861. Present or accounted for until wounded in the right thigh at Chancellorsville, Virginia, May 3, 1863. Rejoined the company in September-October, 1863, and present or accounted for until wounded at Wells' Farm, Virginia, June 22, 1864. Rejoined the company on or about November 1, 1864. No further records.

NORMAN, ANTHONY, Private
Resided in Caswell County where he enlisted at age 19, August 15, 1861. Present or accounted for until wounded at Gaines' Mill, Virginia, on or about June 27, 1862. Rejoined the company prior to November 1, 1862, and present or accounted for until wounded at Chancellorsville, Virginia, May 1-3, 1863. Re-

joined the company prior to July 1, 1863, when he was killed at Gettysburg, Pennsylvania.

OAKLEY, HENDERSON, Private
Resided in Person County and was by occupation a farmer prior to enlisting in Caswell County at age 18, May 1, 1861. Present or accounted for until he died at Smithfield, Virginia, May 7, 1862, of disease.

OAKLEY, WILLIAM R., Private
Born in Person County where he resided as a farmer prior to enlisting in Caswell County at age 24, May 1, 1861. Present or accounted for until killed at Gettysburg, Pennsylvania, July 1, 1863.

O'BRIEN, ELIJAH MASTEN, Sergeant
Resided in Person County and enlisted in Caswell County at age 19, July 1, 1861. Mustered in as Private and promoted to Corporal on April 26, 1862. Present or accounted for until wounded at Sharpsburg, Maryland, September 17, 1862. Rejoined the company in September-October, 1863, and was promoted to Sergeant on December 26, 1863. Present or accounted for until paroled at Appomattox Court House, Virginia, April 9, 1865.

O'BRIEN, JAMES W., Private
Resided in Person County and was by occupation a farmer prior to enlisting in Caswell County at age 24, May 1, 1861. Present or accounted for until wounded at Malvern Hill, Virginia, on or about July 1, 1862. Died at Richmond, Virginia, July 9-10, 1862, of wounds.

O'BRIEN, JOHN R., Private
Resided in Person County and was by occupation a clerk prior to enlisting in Caswell County at age 20, May 1, 1861. Present or accounted for until wounded at Gettysburg, Pennsylvania, July 1, 1863. Rejoined the company in November-December, 1863, and present or accounted for until paroled at Appomattox Court House, Virginia, April 9, 1865.

PARROTT, ADOLPHUS B., Private
Resided in Person County and was by occupation a farmer prior to enlisting in Caswell County at age 20, May 1, 1861. Present or accounted for until wounded in battle at or near the North Anna River, Virginia, May 22, 1864. Died the same day.

PAYLOR, JOHN D., Private
Born in Person County where he resided as a student prior to enlisting in Caswell County at age 19, May 1, 1861. Present or accounted for until discharged at Camp Ruffin, Virginia, September 23, 1861, by reason of disability.

PIGG, ANDREW J., Private
Resided in Union County and enlisted at Camp Holmes on February 24, 1864, for the war. Present or accounted for until captured at Dinwiddie Court House, Virginia, April 4, 1865. Confined at Point Lookout, Maryland, until released on June 16, 1865, after taking the Oath of Allegiance.

PITTARD, ELIJAH, Private
Resided in Caswell County and was by occupation a trader prior to enlisting in Caswell County at age 31, May 1, 1861. Present or accounted for until he deserted on September 25, 1862, or was discharged on that date by the Conscript Act.

PITTARD, SIDNEY T., Private
Born in Caswell County where he resided as a farmer prior to enlisting in Caswell County at age 23, July 30, 1861. Present or accounted for until captured at Warrenton, Virginia, in September, 1862. Rejoined the company in November-December, 1862, and present or accounted for until wounded in the right elbow at Chancellorsville, Virginia, May 3, 1863. Rejoined the company in January-February, 1864, but was discharged near Orange Court House, Virginia, March 7, 1864, by reason of "anchylosis" of the right elbow and "partial paralysis of the limb."

PLEASANT, ALVIS L., Private
Resided in Caswell County and was by occupation a farmer prior to enlisting in Caswell County at age 21, May 1, 1861. Present or accounted for until wounded at Chancellorsville, Virginia, May 3, 1863. Rejoined the company in January-February, 1864, and present or accounted for until admitted to hospital at Danville, Virginia, on or about June 3, 1864, with a gunshot wound of the head. Place and date wounded not reported. Returned to duty on June 24, 1864, and present or accounted for until captured at Farmville, Virginia, April 6, 1865. Confined at Newport News, Virginia, April 14, 1865. Released at Newport News on June 25, 1865, after taking the Oath of Allegiance.

PRUITT, SQUIRE, Private
Resided in Wilkes County and enlisted in Wake County at age 28, September 27, 1862, for the war. Present or accounted for until he died in hospital at Richmond, Virginia, September 22, 1864, of "pneumonia."

RAINS, JAMES, Private
Resided in Polk County and enlisted at Camp Vance on October 16, 1863, for the war. Present or accounted for until captured at Dinwiddie Court House, Virginia, April 4, 1865. Confined at Point Lookout, Maryland, until released on June 19, 1865, after taking the Oath of Allegiance.

RICE, STEPHEN C., Private
Previously served in Company C, 41st Regiment N.C. Troops (3rd Regiment N.C. Cavalry). Transferred to this company on November 24, 1864. Paroled at Appomattox Court House, Virginia, April 9, 1865.

RICHMOND, JAMES B., Private
Born in Caswell County where he resided as a farmer prior to enlisting in Caswell County at age 18, May 1, 1861. Present or accounted for until discharged on July 31, 1862, under the provisions of the Conscript Act. [May have served later in Company B, 59th Regiment N.C. Troops (4th Regiment N.C. Cavalry).]

ROBERTS, REASON, Private
Born in Buncombe County and was by occupation a mechanic prior to enlisting at Camp Vance on September 10, 1863, for the war. Present or accounted for through January 28, 1865.

ROGERS, JAMES, Private
Resided in Cleveland County and enlisted at Orange Court House, Virginia, February 22, 1864, for the war. Present or accounted for until captured at Petersburg, Virginia, April 3, 1865. Confined at Davids Island, New York Harbor, where he died April 28, 1865, of "pneumonia" or "chronic diarrhoea." Age given on Federal hospital records as 17.

ROGERS, JOSEPH, Private
Enlisted at Camp Vance on October 14, 1863, for the war. Present or accounted for until captured in battle at the North Anna River, Virginia, May 23, 1864. Confined at Point Lookout, Maryland, until transferred to Aiken's Landing, James River, Virginia, where he was received March 16, 1865, for exchange. North Carolina pension records indicate he was wounded in the left knee at Wilderness, Virginia, on or about May 7, 1864.

SCOTT, GEORGE W., Private
Resided in Person County and enlisted in Caswell County at age 32, July 30, 1861. Present or accounted for until discharged on June 7, 1862, after providing a substitute.

SCOTT, WILLIAM D., Private
Resided in Person County and enlisted in Caswell County at age 19, July 30, 1861. Present or accounted for until wounded at Gaines' Mill, Virginia, on or about June 27, 1862. Rejoined the company in November-December, 1862, and present or accounted for until wounded in the right foot and captured at Gettysburg, Pennsylvania, July 1-5, 1863. Right foot amputated. Hospitalized at Chester, Pennsylvania, until paroled and transferred to City Point, Virginia, where he was received September 23, 1863, for exchange. Reported absent wounded until retired to the Invalid Corps on May 16, 1864.

SERGEANT, ROBERT W., Private
Resided in Person County and was by occupation a merchant prior to enlisting in Caswell County at age 26, May 1, 1861. Mustered in as Corporal but was reduced to ranks on September 30, 1861. Present or accounted for through October, 1864.

SHIELDS, WILLIAM, Private
Born in Halifax County, Virginia, and resided in Caswell County where he was by occupation a farmer prior to enlisting in Caswell County at age 28, May 1, 1861. Present or accounted for until discharged near Richmond, Virginia, July 31, 1862, under the provisions of the Conscript Act. Reenlisted in this company at Richmond on June 17, 1864, and present or accounted for until paroled at Farmville, Virginia, May 2, 1865.

SOLOMON, JOHN, Private
Resided in Caswell County and was by occupation a farmer prior to enlisting in Caswell County at age 24, May 1, 1861. Present or accounted for until he died in hospital at Richmond, Virginia, May 19, 1862, of "typhoid fever."

SOLOMON, THOMAS, Private
Resided in Caswell County and was by occupation a farmer prior to enlisting in Caswell County at age 21, May 1, 1861. Present or accounted for until wounded in the forehead at Chancellorsville, Virginia, May 3, 1863. Rejoined the company in September-October, 1863, and present or accounted for through October, 1864.

STACK, MILTON, Private
Born in Guilford County and was by occupation a

farmer prior to enlisting at Camp Holmes on March 24, 1864, for the war. Discharged near Orange Court House, Virginia, April 27, 1864, by reason of "contraction of the tendons about the knee joint caused from disease of the bones and . . . membranes." Age given on discharge certificate as 39.

STEPHENS, ANDREW W., Private
Born in Caswell County where he resided as a farmer prior to enlisting in Caswell County at age 30, May 1, 1861. Present or accounted for until killed at Gettysburg, Pennsylvania, July 1, 1863.

STEPHENS, BEDFORD M., Corporal
Born in Caswell County where he resided as a teacher prior to enlisting in Caswell County at age 19, May 1, 1861. Mustered in as Corporal. Present or accounted for until wounded at Gettysburg, Pennsylvania, July 1, 1863. Rejoined the company in January-February, 1864, and present or accounted for until killed near Spotsylvania Court House, Virginia, May 22, 1864.

STEPHENS, JOHN C., Private
Resided in Caswell County where he enlisted at age 17, July 1, 1861. Present or accounted for until discharged on October 1, 1862, by reason of being under age.

STEPHENS, THOMAS, Private
Place and date of enlistment not reported. Paroled at Appomattox Court House, Virginia, April 9, 1865.

TERRELL, JONATHAN R., Sergeant
Resided in Caswell County where he enlisted at age 25, July 1, 1861. Mustered in as Private and was promoted to Sergeant on August 1, 1862. Present or accounted for until wounded at Sharpsburg, Maryland, September 17, 1862. Rejoined the company in November-December, 1862, and present or accounted for until wounded in the hand at Chancellorsville, Virginia, May 3, 1863. Rejoined the company in September-October, 1863, and present or accounted for until transferred to the C. S. Navy on April 3, 1864.

TERRELL, SIDNEY M., Private
Resided in Caswell County and was by occupation a farmer prior to enlisting in Caswell County at age 21, May 1, 1861. Present or accounted for until discharged on September 24, 1864. Reason discharged not reported.

TILMAN, DANIEL, Private
Resided in Person County where he enlisted at age 36, March 10, 1863, for the war. Present or accounted for until wounded at Chancellorsville, Virginia, May 1-3, 1863. Died in hospital at Richmond, Virginia, June 3, 1863, of wounds or "erysipelas."

TURNER, WILLIAM, Private
Resided in Caswell County and was by occupation a farmer prior to enlisting in Caswell County at age 24, May 1, 1861. Present or accounted for until he died at home on October 15 or November 1, 1862. Cause of death not reported.

WADE, JOHN, Private
Born in Person County where he resided prior to enlisting in Person County at age 38, March 10, 1863, for the war. Present or accounted for until

wounded at Chancellorsville, Virginia, May 3, 1863. Died in hospital at Staunton, Virginia, August 6, 1863, of "febris typhoides."

WADE, JOHN C., Private
Born in Caswell County where he resided as a trader prior to enlisting in Caswell County at age 32, May 1, 1861. Present or accounted for until discharged at Camp Ruffin, Virginia, December 14, 1861, by reason of "general debility."

WAGSTAFF, CLEM M. G., Corporal
Resided in Person County and enlisted in Caswell County at age 21, July 30, 1861. Mustered in as Private. Present or accounted for until wounded and captured at Gettysburg, Pennsylvania, July 1-5, 1863. Confined at Baltimore, Maryland, until transferred to Point Lookout, Maryland, where he arrived August 17, 1863. Paroled at Point Lookout on March 3, 1864, and transferred to City Point, Virginia, where he was received March 6, 1864, for exchange. Rejoined the company prior to May 1, 1864, and was promoted to Corporal in November, 1864-April, 1865. Present or accounted for until captured at Burkeville, Virginia, April 3, 1865. Confined at Point Lookout until released on June 21, 1865, after taking the Oath of Allegiance.

WARREN, BARTLETT Y., Private
Resided in Caswell County and was by occupation a farmer prior to enlisting in Caswell County at age 27, May 1, 1861. Present or accounted for until wounded in the left arm at Malvern Hill, Virginia, on or about July 1, 1862. Returned to duty on July 22, 1862, and present or accounted for until killed at Gettysburg, Pennsylvania, July 1, 1863.

WARREN, JAMES M., Private
Previously served in Company C, 41st Regiment N.C. Troops (3rd Regiment N.C. Cavalry). Transferred to this company on November 24, 1864. Wounded at or near Petersburg, Virginia, on or about March 30, 1865. Hospitalized at Petersburg where he was captured on April 3, 1865. Confined at Fort Monroe, Virginia, until released on July 2, 1865.

WATKINS, DAVID W., Private
Resided in Wilkes County and enlisted in Wake County at age 26, September 27, 1862, for the war. Present or accounted for until wounded in the chest at Chancellorsville, Virginia, May 3, 1863. Reported absent wounded until he deserted from hospital at Petersburg, Virginia, on or about August 1, 1863.

WATKINS, JOHN W., Private
Resided in Wilkes County and enlisted in Wake County at age 30, September 27, 1862, for the war. Present or accounted for until wounded at Chancellorsville, Virginia, May 3, 1863. Reported absent wounded until he deserted from hospital at Petersburg, Virginia, on or about August 1, 1863.

WEDDON, HENRY A., Private
Born in Wake County and resided in Caswell County where he was by occupation a farmer prior to enlisting in Caswell County at age 24, May 1, 1861. Present or accounted for until killed at Ellerson's Mill, Virginia, June 26, 1862.

WHITLOW, JOHN N., Private
Resided in Caswell County where he enlisted at age

27, August 15, 1861. Present or accounted for until wounded in the left arm at Spotsylvania Court House, Virginia, May 22, 1864. Rejoined the company in September-October, 1864, and present or accounted for through October, 1864.

WHITLOW, WILLIAM, Private
Born in Caswell County where he resided as a painter or farmer prior to enlisting in Caswell County at age 31, May 1, 1861. Present or accounted for until discharged on July 31, 1862, under the provisions of the Conscript Act. [May have served later in Company B, 59th Regiment N.C. Troops (4th Regiment N.C. Cavalry).]

WILLIAMS, HENRY S., Corporal
Resided in Caswell or Person counties and was by occupation a farmer prior to enlisting in Caswell County at age 25, May 1, 1861. Mustered in as Private. Present or accounted for until wounded at Chancellorsville, Virginia, May 3, 1863. Rejoined the company in November-December, 1863, and was promoted to Corporal in November, 1864-April, 1865. Captured at Dinwiddie Court House, Virginia, April 3, 1865. Confined at Point Lookout, Maryland, until released on June 21, 1865, after taking the Oath of Allegiance.

WOODS, JAMES M., Private
Resided in Caswell County where he enlisted at age 19, July 1, 1861. Present or accounted for until wounded and captured at Williamsburg, Virginia, May 5, 1862. Hospitalized at Fort Monroe, Virginia, until exchanged on or about August 31, 1862. Rejoined the company prior to November 1, 1862, and present or accounted for until killed at Chancellorsville, Virginia, May 3, 1863.

WOODS, JOHN, Private
Resided in Caswell County and was by occupation a mason prior to enlisting in Caswell County at age 28, May 1, 1861. Present or accounted for until wounded at Wells' Farm, Virginia, June 22, 1864. Rejoined the company in September-October, 1864, but was retired to the Invalid Corps on November 10, 1864.

WOODS, JOHN S. S., Private
Born in Caswell County where he resided as a student prior to enlisting in Caswell County at age 18, May 1, 1861. Present or accounted for until he died in hospital at Richmond, Virginia, May 18, 1862, of "typhoid fever."

WOODY, TENSLEY, Private
Resided in Person County and enlisted at age 36, March 10, 1863, for the war. Discharged April 23, 1863, by reason of disability.

WRIGHT, SIDNEY R., Private
Born in Caswell County where he resided as a painter or carpenter prior to enlisting in Caswell County at age 25, May 1, 1861. Mustered in as Sergeant but was reduced to ranks on October 31, 1861. Present or accounted for until transferred to the C. S. Navy for duty on the C.S.S. *Merrimac* on February 15, 1862.

YARBROUGH, DAVID, Private
Resided in Person County where he enlisted at age 37, March 10, 1863, for the war. Present or accounted for until wounded in the right thigh at Chancel-

lorsville, Virginia, May 3, 1863. Rejoined the company in July-August, 1863, and present or accounted for until captured at Richmond, Virginia, April 3, 1865. Confined at Libby Prison, Richmond, until transferred to Newport News, Virginia, April 23, 1865. Released at Newport News on June 30, 1865, after taking the Oath of Allegiance.

YARBROUGH, JORDAN W., Private
Previously served in Company A, 50th Regiment N.C. Troops. Enlisted in this company in Person County on March 10, 1863, for the war. Present or accounted for until wounded at Chancellorsville, Virginia, May 3, 1863. Rejoined the company in July-August, 1863, and present or accounted for until wounded in the left arm on August 22, 1864. Battle in which wounded not reported. Reported absent wounded until discharged near Petersburg, Virginia, March 15, 1865, by reason of a "gun shot wound [of the] left arm injuring the nerve . . . and producing partial paralysis of limb."

COMPANY E

This company, known as the Alamance Regulators, was from Alamance County and enlisted at Graham on May 8, 1861. It was ordered to Weldon on May 8 and arrived there the same day. It was ordered to Garysburg on May 10. There it was assigned to the regiment as Company E. After joining the regiment the company functioned as a part of the regiment, and its history for the war period is recorded as a part of the regimental history.

The information contained in the following roster of the company was compiled principally from company muster rolls for May 15, 1861, through October, 1864. No company muster rolls were found for the period after October, 1864. In addition to the company muster rolls, Roll of Honor records, receipt rolls, hospital records, prisoner of war records, and other primary records, supplemented by state pension applications, United Daughters of the Confederacy records, and postwar rosters and histories, all provided useful information.

OFFICERS
CAPTAINS

RUFFIN, THOMAS, Jr.
Resided in Alamance County where he enlisted at age 36. Elected Captain on or about May 8, 1861, to rank from April 26, 1861. Present or accounted for until he resigned on or about October 30, 1861. Resignation accepted on or about December 9, 1861. Temporarily assigned as Captain of Company H, 6th Regiment N.C. State Troops, from January 14, 1862, until April 26, 1862, when he was reelected Captain of this company. Promoted to Lieutenant Colonel and transferred to the Field and Staff of this regiment on May 1, 1862.

MURRAY, JOHN A.
Born in Alamance County* where he resided prior to enlisting at age 31. Elected 3rd Lieutenant on or about May 8, 1861, and was elected 1st Lieutenant on June 21, 1861. Elected Captain on December 9, 1861. Present or accounted for until he was defeated

for reelection when the regiment was reorganized on April 26, 1862.

COOK, ELBRIDGE

Resided in Alamance County and was by occupation a clerk prior to enlisting in Alamance County at age 22, May 8, 1861. Appointed Corporal on May 9, 1861, and was promoted to 1st Sergeant prior to July 1, 1861. Elected Captain on June 23, 1862. Present or accounted for until killed at Malvern Hill, Virginia, July 1, 1862.

MARTIN, THOMAS A.

Resided in Franklin County and was by occupation a student prior to enlisting in Alamance County at age 20, May 8, 1861. Appointed Corporal on May 9, 1861, and was promoted to Sergeant on July 12, 1861. Appointed 3rd Lieutenant to rank from April 26, 1862, and was promoted to 1st Lieutenant on June 23, 1862. Promoted to Captain on November 17, 1862. Present or accounted for until wounded in the left hip at Gettysburg, Pennsylvania, July 1, 1863. Reported absent wounded through October, 1863, and reported absent on detail from November-December, 1863, through June, 1864. Rejoined the company in July-August, 1864, and present or accounted for through October, 1864. Promoted to Major on January 19, 1865, and transferred to the Field and Staff of this regiment.

BASON, JAMES D.

Resided in Alamance County and was by occupation a clerk prior to enlisting in Alamance County at age 25, May 8, 1861. Mustered in as Sergeant and was elected 2nd Lieutenant to rank from November 5, 1861. Appointed 1st Lieutenant to rank from April 26, 1862. Present or accounted for until wounded at Chancellorsville, Virginia, May 3, 1863. Returned to duty on June 9, 1863, and was wounded at Gettysburg, Pennsylvania, July 3, 1863. Rejoined the company prior to September 1, 1863, and present or accounted for until promoted to Captain on or about January 19, 1865. Paroled at Appomattox Court House, Virginia, April 9, 1865.

LIEUTENANTS

ANDREWS, WILLIAM MURPHY, 2nd Lieutenant

Resided in Alamance County and was by occupation a laborer prior to enlisting in Alamance County at age 25, May 8, 1861. Mustered in as Private and appointed 3rd Lieutenant on June 23, 1862. Promoted to 2nd Lieutenant on November 17, 1862. Present or accounted for until paroled at Appomattox Court House, Virginia, April 9, 1865.

FAUCETT, WILLIAM H., 1st Lieutenant

Resided in Alamance County where he enlisted at age 31. Elected 2nd Lieutenant to rank from May 3, 1861, and was promoted to 1st Lieutenant to rank from December 9, 1861. Present or accounted for until he was defeated for reelection when the regiment was reorganized on April 26, 1862.

HURDLE, HENRY C., 3rd Lieutenant

Resided in Alamance County and was by occupation a trader prior to enlisting in Alamance County at age 36, May 8, 1861. Mustered in as Corporal and was elected 3rd Lieutenant to rank from December 9, 1861. Present or accounted for until he was defeated for reelection when the regiment was reorganized on April 26, 1862.

IRELAND, JOHN RICH, 3rd Lieutenant

Resided in Alamance County and was by occupation a student prior to enlisting in Alamance County at age 20, May 8, 1861. Mustered in as Private and promoted to Sergeant on September 25, 1862. Appointed 3rd Lieutenant on November 17, 1862. Present or accounted for until wounded in the right leg at Gettysburg, Pennsylvania, July 3, 1863. Reported absent wounded through October, 1863, and reported absent on detail from November 26, 1863, through October, 1864. Rejoined the company prior to March 28, 1865, when he was hospitalized at Richmond, Virginia, with a gunshot wound of the back and left shoulder; however, place and date wounded not reported. Returned to duty April 2, 1865.

MONTGOMERY, DANIEL A., 1st Lieutenant

Resided in Alamance County and enlisted at age 38. Elected 1st Lieutenant on or about May 8, 1861. Appointed Surgeon to rank from May 21, 1861, and transferred to the Field and Staff of this regiment.

MONTGOMERY, WILLIAM V., 3rd Lieutenant

Resided in Alamance County where he enlisted at age 20, May 8, 1861. Mustered in as Private and was elected 3rd Lieutenant on June 22, 1861. Present or accounted for until he resigned on October 19, 1861. Reason he resigned not reported.

NONCOMMISSIONED OFFICERS AND PRIVATES

ADAMS, JOHN J., Private

Resided in Alamance County and was by occupation a laborer prior to enlisting in Alamance County at age 21, May 8, 1861. Present or accounted for until wounded in the right thigh and captured at Gettysburg, Pennsylvania, July 1-4, 1863. Hospitalized at Davids Island, New York Harbor, July 17-24, 1863. Paroled at Davids Island and transferred to City Point, Virginia, where he was received September 8, 1863, for exchange. Rejoined the company in January-February, 1864, and present or accounted for until he deserted to the enemy on or about March 8, 1865. Took the Oath of Allegiance on or about March 10, 1865.

ADAMS, JOHN R., Sergeant

Resided in Alamance County and was by occupation a laborer prior to enlisting in Alamance County at age 21, May 8, 1861. Mustered in as Private. Present or accounted for until wounded in the right side and captured at South Mountain, Maryland, September 14, 1862. Confined at Fort McHenry, Maryland, until transferred to Aiken's Landing, James River, Virginia, where he was received October 19, 1862, for exchange. Declared exchanged at Aiken's Landing on November 10, 1862. Rejoined the company in March-April, 1863, and was promoted to Corporal in September-October, 1863. Promoted to Sergeant on April 30, 1864. Present or accounted for until captured at Petersburg, Virginia, April 2, 1865. Confined at Point Lookout, Maryland, until released on June 23, 1865, after taking the Oath of Allegiance.

ALLEN, BARTLETT, Private
Enlisted at Camp Holmes on February 24, 1864, for the war. Present or accounted for until reported absent without leave from June 22, 1864, through October, 1864. Deserted to the enemy on or about March 8, 1865. Took the Oath of Allegiance on or about March 10, 1865. North Carolina pension records indicate he was wounded at Wilderness, Virginia, May 5, 1864.

ANDREWS, ALEXANDER A., Private
Resided in Alamance County and was by occupation a laborer prior to enlisting in Alamance County at age 24, May 8, 1861. Present or accounted for until he deserted to the enemy on or about March 8, 1865. Took the Oath of Allegiance on or about March 10, 1865.

ANDREWS, CADWALLADER J., Private
Resided in Alamance County and was by occupation a laborer prior to enlisting in Alamance County at age 18, May 8, 1861. Present or accounted for until wounded at Gettysburg, Pennsylvania, July 1-3, 1863. Rejoined the company prior to September 1, 1863, and present or accounted for until killed at Cold Harbor, Virginia, June 3, 1864.

ANDREWS, HENRY R., Private
Born in Alamance County* where he resided as a farmer prior to enlisting at Richmond, Virginia, at age 30, August 1, 1862. Present or accounted for until discharged at Camp Gregg, Virginia, April 16, 1863, by reason of "tubercular disease of the lungs."

ANTHONY, JACOB, Private
Resided in Alamance County and was by occupation a laborer prior to enlisting in Alamance County at age 21, May 8, 1861. Mustered in as Musician but was reduced to ranks in March-April, 1864. Present or accounted for until killed at Wilderness, Virginia, May 5, 1864.

ATKINS, ALFRED A., Private
Born in Alamance County* where he resided as a laborer or farmer prior to enlisting in Alamance County at age 20, May 8, 1861. Present or accounted for until wounded in the ankle at Gaines' Mill, Virginia, June 27, 1862. Died in hospital at Richmond, Virginia, July 15, 1862, of wounds.

BARNETT, DANIEL L., Private
Born in Alamance County* where he resided as a laborer prior to enlisting in Alamance County at age 24, May 8, 1861. Present or accounted for until killed at Chancellorsville, Virginia, May 3, 1863.

BASON, W. H., Private
Place and date of enlistment not reported. Paroled at Appomattox Court House, Virginia, April 9, 1865.

BERRY, JOHN, Jr., Hospital Steward
Resided in Orange County and was by occupation a doctor prior to enlisting in Alamance County at age 22, May 8, 1861. Mustered in as Sergeant and was appointed Hospital Steward in August, 1861. Appointed Assistant Surgeon in April, 1863, and transferred to an unspecified unit or hospital. Later served as Assistant Surgeon of the 26th Regiment N.C. Troops.

BILLINGS, JOHN A., Private
Resided in Wilkes County and was by occupation a farmer prior to enlisting at Bunker Hill, Virginia, at age 18, September 27, 1862, for the war. Present or accounted for until discharged on February 7, 1863, by reason of "phthisis pulmonalis."

BIRD, GEORGE M., Private
Resided in Alamance County and was by occupation a laborer prior to enlisting in Alamance County at age 19, May 8, 1861. Present or accounted for until "drummed out July 15, 1861." [May have served later in Company K, 6th Regiment N.C. State Troops.]

BOGGS, WILLIAM B., Private
Resided in Alamance County and was by occupation a laborer prior to enlisting in Alamance County at age 18, May 8, 1861. Present or accounted for until wounded and captured at Gettysburg, Pennsylvania, July 1, 1863. Died July 8 or July 25, 1863, of wounds. Place of death not reported.

BOWER, CHARLES, Private
Resided in Louisiana and enlisted near Richmond, Virginia, at age 35, July 29, 1862, for the war as a substitute for Private James M. Dickey. Deserted prior to November 1, 1862.

BOYD, JAMES E., Private
Resided in Alamance County and enlisted at Camp Ruffin, Virginia, at age 17, September 10, 1861. Present or accounted for until hospitalized at Richmond, Virginia, July 4, 1862, with a gunshot wound; however, place and date wounded not reported. Discharged September 25, 1862, under the provisions of the Conscript Act.

BRADSHAW, JAMES M., Private
Resided in Alamance County and was by occupation a student prior to enlisting in Alamance County at age 22, May 8, 1861. Present or accounted for until discharged on September 18, 1861. Reason discharged not reported.

BRADSHAW, JAMES P., Sergeant
Resided in Alamance County and was by occupation a carpenter prior to enlisting in Alamance County at age 25, May 8, 1861. Mustered in as Private and promoted to Corporal on May 1, 1862. Admitted to hospital at Richmond, Virginia, June 28, 1862, with a gunshot wound; however, place and date wounded not reported. Promoted to Sergeant on September 25, 1862, and rejoined the company prior to November 1, 1862. Present or accounted for until wounded and captured at Gettysburg, Pennsylvania, July 1, 1863. Hospitalized at Davids Island, New York Harbor, where he died August 9, 1863, of "pyaemia."

BRADSHAW, JOSEPH, Private
Enlisted at Camp Gregg, Virginia, May 10, 1863, for the war. Reported absent sick from May-June, 1863, through April, 1864, and reported absent without leave from May-June, 1864, through October, 1864.

CAUSEY, JAMES A., Private
Resided in Alamance County and enlisted at Camp Gregg, Virginia, at age 37, March 13, 1863, for the war. Present or accounted for until discharged June 5, 1863, by reason of disability.

CHATHAM, JAMES, Private
Resided in Alamance County and enlisted near Richmond, Virginia, at age 15, July 23, 1862, for the war as a substitute for Private John Marion Tapscott. Deserted prior to November 1, 1862. Reported in hospital at Richmond on April 13, 1863, and was sent to Castle Thunder Prison, Richmond, April 21, 1863. Reported present on a company muster roll dated January-February, 1864, but deserted again on March 2, 1864.

CLENDENIN, ROBERT J., Private
Born in Alamance County* where he resided as a laborer prior to enlisting in Alamance County at age 18, May 8, 1861. Present or accounted for until killed at South Mountain, Maryland, September 14, 1862.

CLENDENIN, WILLIAM, Private
Born in Alamance County* where he resided as a laborer or farmer prior to enlisting in Alamance County at age 22, May 8, 1861. Present or accounted for until killed at Chancellorsville, Virginia, May 3, 1863.

COBLE, ALFRED M., Private
Resided in Randolph County and enlisted at Bunker Hill, Virginia, at age 20, September 27, 1862, for the war. Present or accounted for until paroled at Appomattox Court House, Virginia, April 9, 1865.

COBLE, DANIEL O., Private
Resided in Randolph County and enlisted at Bunker Hill, Virginia, at age 22, September 27, 1862, for the war. Present or accounted for until paroled at Appomattox Court House, Virginia, April 9, 1865.

COOK, MUNROE, 1st Sergeant
Born in Alamance County* where he resided as a laborer or student prior to enlisting in Alamance County at age 18, May 8, 1861. Mustered in as Private and promoted to Corporal on December 15, 1862. Present or accounted for until wounded in the left arm at Chancellorsville, Virginia, May 3, 1863. Rejoined the company in July-August, 1863, and was promoted to Sergeant on August 15, 1863. Promoted to 1st Sergeant on March 8, 1864. Present or accounted for until transferred to another unit on January 7, 1865, upon appointment as 2nd Lieutenant. Unit to which transferred not reported.

CRUTCHFIELD, ALGERNON S., Private
Resided in Alamance County and was by occupation a laborer prior to enlisting in Alamance County at age 18, May 8, 1861. Present or accounted for until he deserted on or about July 31, 1862.

CRUTCHFIELD, FELIX GRUNDY, Private
Resided in Alamance County and was by occupation a clerk prior to enlisting in Alamance County at age 18, May 8, 1861. Present or accounted for until appointed Sergeant Major and transferred to the Field and Staff, 8th Regiment N.C. State Troops, November 24, 1864.

CRUTCHFIELD, JAMES A., Private
Resided in Alamance County and enlisted at Camp Ruffin, Virginia, at age 24, July 27, 1861. Present or accounted for until wounded at Malvern Hill, Virginia, on or about July 1, 1862. Died on or about July 10, 1862, of wounds. Place of death not reported.

DANIEL, BARNEY, Private
Resided in Alamance County and was by occupation a laborer prior to enlisting in Alamance County at age 19, May 8, 1861. Present or accounted for until captured at Sharpsburg, Maryland, on or about September 18, 1862. Paroled September 21, 1862. Reported absent without leave from November 20, 1862, until he was dropped from the rolls of the company in September-October, 1863.

DANIEL, PLEASANT, Private
Resided in Alamance County and was by occupation a laborer prior to enlisting in Alamance County at age 20, May 8, 1861. Present or accounted for until he died in hospital at Richmond, Virginia, June 4, 1862, of "febris typhoides."

DICKEY, JAMES A., Sergeant
Resided in Alamance County and was by occupation a wagonmaker prior to enlisting in Alamance County at age 19, May 8, 1861. Mustered in as Private and promoted to Corporal on November 17, 1862. Promoted to Sergeant on May 3, 1863. Present or accounted for until wounded in the right arm and captured at Gettysburg, Pennsylvania, July 1-4, 1863. Right arm amputated. Hospitalized at Davids Island, New York Harbor, until paroled and transferred to City Point, Virginia, where he was received October 28, 1863, for exchange. Reported absent wounded until retired to the Invalid Corps on May 13, 1864.

DICKEY, JAMES M., Private
Resided in Alamance County and was by occupation a wagonmaker prior to enlisting in Alamance County at age 20, May 8, 1861. Present or accounted for until discharged on August 29, 1862, after providing Private Charles Bower as a substitute.

DICKEY, SAMUEL J., Private
Resided in Alamance County and was by occupation a harness maker prior to enlisting in Alamance County at age 21, May 8, 1861. Present or accounted for until he died on May 10, 1862, "while on the march near Chickahominy River." Cause of death not reported.

DICKEY, THOMAS, Private
Born in Orange County and resided in Alamance County where he was by occupation a blacksmith prior to enlisting in Alamance County at age 36, May 8, 1861. Present or accounted for until discharged at Suffolk, Virginia, July 3, 1861, by reason of disability.

DUPONT, LUCIAN, Private
Resided in Virginia and enlisted near Richmond, Virginia, at age 38, July 28, 1862, for the war as a substitute for Private John S. Faucett. Deserted prior to November 1, 1862.

EVANS, JAMES R., Private
Enlisted at Camp Holmes on January 26, 1864, for the war. Present or accounted for until he died in hospital at Richmond, Virginia, May 30, 1864, of "pneumonia."

FAUCETT, JOHN C., Sergeant
Born in Alamance County* where he resided as a merchant or clerk prior to enlisting in Alamance County at age 21, May 8, 1861. Appointed Sergeant on May 9, 1861. Present or accounted for until reported transferred to the 47th Regiment N.C. Troops on July 26, 1862; however, records of the 47th Regiment do not indicate that he served therein. No further records.

FAUCETT, JOHN S., Private
Resided in Alamance County and was by occupation a student prior to enlisting in Alamance County at age 19, May 8, 1861. Present or accounted for until discharged on August 29, 1862, after providing Private Lucian Dupont as a substitute.

FAUCETT, THOMAS U., Private
Enlisted at Camp Gregg, Virginia, April 18, 1863, for the war. Present or accounted for until wounded in the leg at Chancellorsville, Virginia, May 3, 1863. Reported absent wounded through June, 1864. Reported on detail as a provost guard at Danville, Virginia, from July-August, 1864, until January 27, 1865. Company records dated January 27, 1865, give his age as 38. Retired to the Invalid Corps at an unspecified date. Paroled at Greensboro on May 16, 1865.

FAUCETT, WILLIAM, _____
Enlisted in May-June, 1863, for the war. Died of wounds received at Gettysburg, Pennsylvania, July 1-3, 1863. Place and date of death not reported.

FAUCETTE, GEORGE W., Private
Resided in Alamance County and was by occupation a laborer prior to enlisting in Alamance County at age 18, May 8, 1861. Present or accounted for until discharged on or about August 2, 1862, under the provisions of the Conscript Act.

FAUCETTE, ROBERT G., 1st Sergeant
Resided in Alamance County and was by occupation a laborer prior to enlisting in Alamance County at age 25, May 8, 1861. Mustered in as Private and promoted to Corporal on June 24, 1862. Promoted to Sergeant on November 17, 1862. Present or accounted for until wounded at Fredericksburg, Virginia, on or about December 13, 1862. Rejoined the company prior to January 1, 1863, and present or accounted for until wounded at Chancellorsville, Virginia, May 3, 1863. Rejoined the company in January-February, 1864, and promoted to 1st Sergeant in November, 1864-April, 1865. Paroled at Appomattox Court House, Virginia, April 9, 1865.

FAUCETTE, WILLIAM F., Color Sergeant
Resided in Alamance County and was by occupation a saddler prior to enlisting in Alamance County at age 28, May 8, 1861. Mustered in as Private and promoted to Corporal on May 3, 1863. Promoted to Color Sergeant on June 29, 1863. Present or accounted for until wounded in the left arm and captured at Gettysburg, Pennsylvania, July 1-5, 1863. Left arm amputated. Hospitalized at Chester, Pennsylvania,

until transferred to Point Lookout, Maryland, October 2, 1863. Paroled at Point Lookout and transferred to City Point, Virginia, where he was received March 20, 1864, for exchange. Retired in September-October, 1864. Paroled at Greensboro on May 16, 1865.

FONVILLE, THOMAS G., Private
Born in Alamance County* where he resided as a saddler prior to enlisting in Alamance County at age 22, May 8, 1861. Present or accounted for until captured at Sharpsburg, Maryland, on or about September 18, 1862. Paroled at Sharpsburg on September 21, 1862. Rejoined the company in November-December, 1862, and present or accounted for until killed at Gettysburg, Pennsylvania, July 1, 1863.

FOOSHEE, R. B., Private
Resided in Alamance County and enlisted at Camp Gregg, Virginia, at age 18, April 18, 1863, for the war. Present or accounted for until wounded at Gettysburg, Pennsylvania, July 1-3, 1863, and left in the hands of the enemy. Confined at Fort Delaware, Delaware, where he died September 7, 1863, of "bronchitis acute."

FOSTER, JAMES J., Private
Resided in Alamance County and was by occupation a laborer prior to enlisting in Alamance County at age 26, May 8, 1861. Present or accounted for until hospitalized at Richmond, Virginia, April 15, 1864, with a gunshot wound of the head; however, place and date wounded not reported. Rejoined the company prior to May 1, 1864, and present or accounted for until captured at Petersburg, Virginia, April 2, 1865. Confined at Point Lookout, Maryland, until released on June 26, 1865, after taking the Oath of Allegiance.

FOSTER, STEPHEN M., Private
Resided in Alamance County and was by occupation a saddler prior to enlisting in Alamance County at age 24, May 8, 1861. Present or accounted for until wounded in the cranium at Chancellorsville, Virginia, May 3, 1863. Rejoined the company in July-August, 1863. Detailed for light duty on September 22, 1863, and reported absent on detail through October, 1864. Paroled at Greensboro on May 11, 1865.

FREDRICK, BEDFORD B., Private
Resided in Alamance County and was by occupation a laborer prior to enlisting in Alamance County at age 20, May 8, 1861. Present or accounted for until he died in hospital at Lynchburg, Virginia, September 30, 1863, of "morbu varai."

GARRISON, GEORGE W., Private
Enlisted in Alamance County on March 5, 1864, for the war. Wounded at Spotsylvania Court House, Virginia, May 21, 1864. Rejoined the company in September-October, 1864, and present or accounted for until captured at Petersburg, Virginia, April 2, 1865. Confined at Point Lookout, Maryland, April 4, 1865. Records of the Federal Provost Marshal indicate he was a prisoner who had taken an assumed name. No further records.

GARRISON, JAMES H., Corporal
Resided in Alamance County and was by occupation a blacksmith prior to enlisting in Alamance County

at age 21, May 8, 1861. Mustered in as Private and promoted to Corporal on July 1, 1863. Present or accounted for until he deserted to the enemy on or about March 8, 1865. Took the Oath of Allegiance on or about March 10, 1865.

GARRISON, LEVI, Private
Resided in Alamance County and was by occupation a laborer or farmer prior to enlisting in Alamance County at age 22, May 8, 1861. Present or accounted for until wounded at Chancellorsville, Virginia, May 3, 1863. Rejoined the company in September-October, 1863, and present or accounted for until wounded in the thorax or left shoulder at Wilderness, Virginia, on or about May 6, 1864. Rejoined the company in September-October, 1864. Captured at Petersburg, Virginia, April 2, 1865, and confined at Point Lookout, Maryland, until released on June 27, 1865, after taking the Oath of Allegiance.

GENTRY, DANIEL, Private
Resided in Wilkes County and enlisted at Bunker Hill, Virginia, at age 24, September 27, 1862, for the war. Present or accounted for until he died in hospital at Gordonsville, Virginia, December 29, 1863, of "pneumonia."

GERRINGER, FELTY, Private
Born in Alamance County* where he resided prior to enlisting at Camp Gregg, Virginia, at age 39, March 13, 1863, for the war. Present or accounted for until killed at Gettysburg, Pennsylvania, July 1, 1863.

GERRINGER, JOHN, Private
Resided in Alamance County and enlisted at Camp Gregg, Virginia, at age 37, March 13, 1863, for the war. Present or accounted for until wounded "severely" at Chancellorsville, Virginia, May 3, 1863. Reported absent wounded until discharged on or about February 9, 1864. Reason discharged not reported.

GILLIAM, JAMES S., Sergeant
Resided in Alamance County and was by occupation a laborer prior to enlisting in Alamance County at age 22, May 8, 1861. Mustered in as Private. Present or accounted for until wounded and captured at South Mountain, Maryland, September 14, 1862. Paroled October 3, 1862, and rejoined the company in January-February, 1863. Promoted to Corporal on May 3, 1863, and was wounded at Chancellorsville, Virginia, the same date. Rejoined the company in November-December, 1863, and was promoted to Sergeant on March 8, 1864. Wounded at Wilderness, Virginia, May 5, 1864, and was reported absent wounded through October, 1864. Took the Oath of Allegiance at Richmond, Virginia, June 20, 1865.

HALEY, JAMES A., Private
Resided in Alamance County and was by occupation a laborer prior to enlisting in Alamance County at age 23, May 8, 1861. Present or accounted for until wounded at Chancellorsville, Virginia, May 3, 1863. Died in hospital at Richmond, Virginia, June 12, 1863, of "typhoid fever."

HALL, HENRY, Private
Resided in Alamance County and was by occupation a laborer prior to enlisting in Alamance County at age 22, May 8, 1861. Present or accounted for until captured and paroled at Warrenton, Virginia, Sep-

tember 29, 1862. Hospitalized at Richmond, Virginia, October 3, 1862, with a contused wound. Place and date wounded not reported. Rejoined the company in January-February, 1863, and present or accounted for until wounded at Chancellorsville, Virginia, May 3, 1863. Rejoined the company in July-August, 1863, and present or accounted for until wounded at Wilderness, Virginia, May 5, 1864. Rejoined the company in July-August, 1864, and present or accounted for until paroled at Appomattox Court House, Virginia, April 9, 1865.

HARRIS, HENRY C., Private
Resided in Alamance County and enlisted at Camp Gregg, Virginia, at age 22, May 13, 1863, for the war. Deserted April 18, 1863.

HERRING, HENDERSON, Private
Resided in Alamance County and enlisted at Camp Gregg, Virginia, at age 37, May 13, 1863, for the war. Present or accounted for until wounded at Chancellorsville, Virginia, May 3, 1863. Rejoined the company in January-February, 1864, and present or accounted for until hospitalized at Charlottesville, Virginia, May 10, 1864, with a gunshot wound of the right hand. Place and date wounded not reported. Rejoined the company prior to June 5-6, 1864, when he deserted to the enemy at Cold Harbor, Virginia. Confined at Point Lookout, Maryland, until transferred to Elmira, New York, July 25, 1864. Released at Elmira on September 19, 1864, after taking the Oath of Allegiance.

HICKS, DANIEL, Private
Enlisted at Camp Vance on February 15, 1864, for the war. Present or accounted for until captured at Wilderness, Virginia, May 6, 1864. Confined at Point Lookout, Maryland, until released on May 17, 1864, after joining the U.S. Navy.

HICKS, JAMES M., Corporal
Born in Alamance County* where he resided as a laborer prior to enlisting in Alamance County at age 27, May 8, 1861. Mustered in as Private and promoted to Corporal on May 3, 1863. Present or accounted for until killed at Gettysburg, Pennsylvania, July 1, 1863.

HOLT, DANIEL C., Private
Enlisted at Camp Holmes on March 6, 1864, for the war. Present or accounted for until captured at Wilderness, Virginia, May 5-6, 1864. Confined at Point Lookout, Maryland, until transferred to Elmira, New York, August 10, 1864. Died at Elmira on February 14, 1865, of "variola."

HOLT, GEORGE W., Private
Previously served in Company E, 1st Regiment N.C. State Troops. Enlisted in this company at Camp Gregg, Virginia, April 18, 1863, for the war. Present or accounted for until wounded at Gettysburg, Pennsylvania, July 1-3, 1863. Rejoined the company prior to September 1, 1863, and present or accounted for until he was reported absent on wounded furlough on June 7, 1864. Place and date wounded not reported. Rejoined the company in July-August, 1864, and present or accounted for until paroled at Appomattox Court House, Virginia, April 9, 1865.

HOLT, HENRY S., Private
Resided in Alamance County and was by occupation

a laborer prior to enlisting in Alamance County at age 19, May 8, 1861. Present or accounted for until paroled at Appomattox Court House, Virginia, April 9, 1865.

HOLT, JOSEPH R., Sergeant
Resided in Alamance County and was by occupation a student prior to enlisting in Alamance County at age 18, May 8, 1861. Mustered in as Corporal and was promoted to Sergeant on December 9, 1861. Present or accounted for until discharged on August 29, 1862, after providing Private John Kelly as a substitute.

HORN, ABEL, Private
Resided in Alamance County and was by occupation a laborer prior to enlisting in Alamance County at age 28, May 8, 1861. Present or accounted for until paroled at Appomattox Court House, Virginia, April 9, 1865.

HORN, JEHU, Private
Resided in Alamance County and was by occupation a wheelwright prior to enlisting in Alamance County at age 30, May 8, 1861. Present or accounted for until discharged on August 2, 1862, under the provisions of the Conscript Act.

HUFFMAN, ADAM, Private
Resided in Alamance County and was by occupation a laborer prior to enlisting in Alamance County at age 23, May 8, 1861. Present or accounted for until wounded in the instep at Chancellorsville, Virginia, May 3, 1863. Rejoined the company in July-August, 1863, and present or accounted for until killed at Spotsylvania Court House, Virginia, May 21, 1864.

HUFFMAN, JOHN S., Private
Enlisted at Camp Holmes on March 27, 1864, for the war. Present or accounted for until paroled at Appomattox Court House, Virginia, April 9, 1865.

HUGHES, JEREMIAH, Private
Resided in Alamance County and was by occupation a laborer prior to enlisting in Alamance County at age 41, May 8, 1861. Present or accounted for until discharged on August 2, 1862, by reason of being over age.

HURDLE, BENJAMIN F., Private
Resided in Alamance County and was by occupation a laborer prior to enlisting in Alamance County at age 21, May 8, 1861. Present or accounted for through October, 1864; however, he was reported absent on detail as a Hospital Steward during much of that period.

HURDLE, WILLIAM J., Private
Resided in Alamance County and was by occupation a laborer prior to enlisting in Alamance County at age 19, May 8, 1861. Present or accounted for until he died in hospital at Danville, Virginia, May 31, 1862, of "febris typhoides."

KECK, GEORGE A., Private
Resided in Alamance County and was by occupation a laborer prior to enlisting in Alamance County at age 24, May 8, 1861. Present or accounted for until wounded in the left arm at Gettysburg, Pennsylvania, July 1, 1863. Rejoined the company in November-December, 1863. Present or accounted for until reported captured by the enemy on May 23, 1864;

however, records of the Federal Provost Marshal do not substantiate that report. No further records.

KELLY, JOHN, Private
Resided in Virginia and enlisted near Richmond, Virginia, at age 35, July 29, 1862, for the war as a substitute for Sergeant Joseph R. Holt. Deserted prior to November 1, 1862.

KING, WILLIAM E., Private
Resided in Alamance County and was by occupation a blacksmith prior to enlisting in Alamance County at age 19, May 8, 1861. Present or accounted for until wounded at Seven Pines, Virginia, September 17, 1862. Rejoined the company in March-April, 1863, and was wounded at Chancellorsville, Virginia, May 1-3, 1863. Died in hospital at Richmond, Virginia, June 13, 1863, of "erysipelas."

KINNEY, MEBANE, Private
Born in Alamance County* where he resided as a farmer prior to enlisting at Camp Ruffin, Virginia, at age 35, July 27, 1861. Present or accounted for until killed at Malvern Hill, Virginia, on or about June 30, 1862.

LACKEY, JAMES M., Private
Resided in Alamance County and was by occupation a laborer prior to enlisting in Alamance County at age 21, May 8, 1861. Present or accounted for until captured at Culpeper, Virginia, in July-October, 1862. Paroled prior to November 1, 1862, and rejoined the company in November-December, 1862. Present or accounted for until wounded at Gettysburg, Pennsylvania, July 1-3, 1863. Rejoined the company prior to September 1, 1863, and present or accounted for until killed at Spotsylvania Court House, Virginia, May 21, 1864.

LIGGINS, WILL, _____
Negro. North Carolina pension records indicate that he "went as servant" to James E. Boyd, Clay Hazell, and Jim Vincent in 1863. No further records.

LONG, JOHN A., Private
Born in Alamance County* where he resided as a farmer or laborer prior to enlisting in Alamance County at age 18, May 8, 1861. Present or accounted for until killed at South Mountain, Maryland, September 14, 1862.

LONG, JOSEPH G., 1st Sergeant
Born in Alamance County* where he resided as a farmer or student prior to enlisting in Alamance County at age 19, May 8, 1861. Mustered in as Private and promoted to Corporal on December 9, 1861. Promoted to 1st Sergeant on June 24, 1862. Present or accounted for until wounded at Sharpsburg, Maryland, September 17, 1862. Rejoined the company in January-February, 1863, and present or accounted for until killed at Chancellorsville, Virginia, May 3, 1863.

McCLURE, WILLIAM D., Private
Enlisted at Camp Orange, Virginia, December 16, 1863, for the war. Present or accounted for through April 3, 1865. Paroled at Greensboro on May 22, 1865.

McCLUSKEY, RICHARD, Private
Resided in Kentucky and enlisted at Camp Gregg, Virginia, at age 30, March 13, 1863, for the war.

Present or accounted for until wounded at Chancellorsville, Virginia, May 3, 1863. Rejoined the company in November-December, 1863, and present or accounted for until he deserted on May 4, 1864.

MARTINDALE, BRYANT B., Private
Resided in Alamance County and was by occupation a laborer prior to enlisting in Alamance County at age 18, May 8, 1861. Present or accounted for until reported absent without leave on October 10, 1862. Rejoined the company in January-February, 1863, and was wounded at Chancellorsville, Virginia, May 3, 1863. Reported absent wounded until detailed for light duty at Charlotte on November 18, 1863. Reported absent on detail through October, 1864.

MARTINDALE, DANIEL W., Private
Resided in Alamance County and was by occupation a laborer prior to enlisting in Alamance County at age 19, May 8, 1861. Present or accounted for until wounded in the thigh at Chancellorsville, Virginia, May 3, 1863. Rejoined the company in November-December, 1863. Company muster rolls dated July-October, 1864, indicate he was at home on wounded furlough.

MATHIS, JAMES M., Private
Resided in Alamance County and was by occupation a laborer prior to enlisting in Alamance County at age 28, May 8, 1861. Present or accounted for until wounded and captured at Gettysburg, Pennsylvania, July 1-4, 1863. Hospitalized at Davids Island, New York Harbor, where he died on August 6, 1863, of "typhoid fever."

MAY, CALEB E., Private
Resided in Alamance County and was by occupation a laborer prior to enlisting in Alamance County at age 26, May 8, 1861. Present or accounted for until wounded and captured at Gettysburg, Pennsylvania, July 1-4, 1863. Hospitalized at Davids Island, New York Harbor, until transferred to City Point, Virginia, where he was received August 28, 1863, for exchange. Rejoined the company in January-February, 1864, and present or accounted for until paroled at Appomattox Court House, Virginia, April 9, 1865.

MAY, HENDERSON, Private
Resided in Alamance County and was by occupation a laborer prior to enlisting in Alamance County at age 31, May 8, 1861. Present or accounted for until discharged on August 2, 1862, under the provisions of the Conscript Act. [May have served later in Company I, 63rd Regiment N.C. Troops (5th Regiment N.C. Cavalry).]

MAYNARD, RICHARD L., Corporal
Resided in Alamance County and was by occupation a laborer prior to enlisting in Alamance County at age 21, May 8, 1861. Mustered in as Private and promoted to Corporal on June 24, 1862. Present or accounted for until appointed 2nd Lieutenant and transferred to Company I, 57th Regiment N.C. Troops, July 26, 1862.

MITCHELL, RICHARD A., Private
Born in Caswell County and resided in Alamance County where he was by occupation a laborer prior to enlisting in Alamance County at age 25, May 8, 1861. Present or accounted for until transferred to

the C. S. Navy for duty on the C.S.S. *Merrimac* on February 19, 1862.

MOIZE, JAMES M., Private
Born in Alamance County* where he resided as a laborer or farmer prior to enlisting in Alamance County at age 19, May 8, 1861. Present or accounted for until he died at home in Alamance County on or about September 23, 1862, of "typhoid fever."

MURRAY, JOHN A., Private
Resided in Alamance County and was by occupation a laborer prior to enlisting in Alamance County at age 24, May 8, 1861. Present or accounted for through October, 1864; however, he was on detail as a teamster during most of that period. Captured at or near Appomattox, Virginia, April 3, 1865. Confined at Hart's Island, New York Harbor, until released on June 19, 1865, after taking the Oath of Allegiance.

MURRAY, JOHN A., Corporal
Born in Alamance County* where he resided as a laborer prior to enlisting in Alamance County at age 19, May 8, 1861. Mustered in as Private and promoted to Corporal on December 15, 1862. Present or accounted for until killed at Chancellorsville, Virginia, May 3, 1863.

MURRAY, WILLIAM W., Private
Born in Alamance County* where he resided prior to enlisting at Camp Ruffin, Virginia, at age 19, July 27, 1861. Present or accounted for until wounded at Gaines' Mill, Virginia, June 27, 1862. Rejoined the company in March-April, 1863, and present or accounted for until killed at Gettysburg, Pennsylvania, July 1, 1863.

NEASE, GEORGE M., Private
Born in Alamance County* where he resided as a laborer prior to enlisting in Alamance County at age 22, May 8, 1861. Present or accounted for until he died at home in Alamance County on or about August 14, 1862, of "typhoid fever."

NEASE, ISAAC M., Private
Born in Alamance County* where he resided as a coach maker prior to enlisting in Alamance County at age 23, May 8, 1861. Present or accounted for until reported missing on the retreat from Yorktown, Virginia, May 10, 1862. No further records.

PATTERSON, ARMISTEAD J., Corporal
Resided in Alamance County and was by occupation a laborer prior to enlisting in Alamance County at age 19, May 8, 1861. Mustered in as Private and promoted to Corporal on April 30, 1861. Present or accounted for until captured at Petersburg, Virginia, April 2, 1865. Confined at Point Lookout, Maryland, until released on June 16, 1865, after taking the Oath of Allegiance.

PATTERSON, JAMES M., 1st Sergeant
Resided in Alamance County and was by occupation a clerk prior to enlisting in Alamance County at age 24, May 8, 1861. Mustered in as Private and promoted to Corporal on July 12, 1861. Promoted to Sergeant on June 24, 1862. Present or accounted for until wounded at Seven Pines, Virginia, September 17, 1862. Rejoined the company in January-February, 1863. Promoted to 1st Sergeant on May 3, 1863, and was wounded in the left arm at Chancel-

lorsville, Virginia, the same day. Rejoined the company in July-August, 1863, and present or accounted for until· appointed 3rd Lieutenant in Company I, 8th Regiment N.C. State Troops, on February 13, 1864.

PATTON, MATTHEW, Private
Resided in Alamance County and enlisted at Camp Gregg, Virginia, at age 37, April 18, 1863, for the war. Present or accounted for until captured at Gettysburg, Pennsylvania, July 1-4, 1863. Confined at Fort Delaware, Delaware, where he died August 11, 1863, of "disease of heart."

PHILLIPS, BENJAMIN R., Private
Resided in Alamance County and was by occupation a laborer prior to enlisting in Alamance County at age 22, May 8, 1861. Present or accounted for until killed at Gaines' Mill, Virginia, June 27, 1862.

PHILLIPS, THOMAS M., Private
Resided in Alamance County and was by occupation a laborer prior to enlisting in Alamance County at age 18, May 8, 1861. Present or accounted for until he died in hospital at Richmond, Virginia, June 2, 1862, of "cont[inued] fever."

PICKETT, DAVID H., Private
Resided in Alamance County and enlisted at Camp Gregg, Virginia, at age 37, March 13, 1863, for the war. Present or accounted for until April 26, 1863, when he was reported absent sick. Reported absent sick or absent without leave through October, 1864.

PRATHER, JOHN A., Private
Resided in Alamance County and enlisted on October 22, 1863, for the war. Present or accounted for until captured at or near Petersburg, Virginia, April 2, 1865. Confined at Point Lookout, Maryland, until released on June 16, 1865, after taking the Oath of Allegiance.

PYLE, ANDREW J., Private
Resided in Alamance County and was by occupation a laborer prior to enlisting in Alamance County at age 20, May 8, 1861. Present or accounted for until captured at or near Petersburg, Virginia, April 2, 1865. Confined at Point Lookout, Maryland, until released on June 16, 1865, after taking the Oath of Allegiance.

RICH, DANIEL R., Private
Resided in Alamance County and enlisted at Camp Ruffin, Virginia, at age 18, September 15, 1861. Present or accounted for until killed at Gaines' Mill, Virginia, June 27, 1862.

RICH, HENRY M., Corporal
Resided in Alamance County and was by occupation a farmer prior to enlisting in Alamance County at age 28, May 8, 1861. Mustered in as Musician. Present or accounted for until wounded in the right thigh at Chancellorsville, Virginia, May 3, 1863. Rejoined the company in July-August, 1863, and was promoted to Corporal on March 8, 1864. Present or accounted for until paroled at Appomattox Court House, Virginia, April 9, 1865. North Carolina pension records indicate that his right shoulder was dislocated and he was wounded in the right leg at Fort Harrison, Virginia, September 29-30, 1864.

RICH, JAMES A., Private
Resided in Alamance County and was by occupation a laborer prior to enlisting in Alamance County at age 22, May 8, 1861. Present or accounted for until he died at home in Alamance County on June 11, 1862, of "typhoid fever."

RIKE, ANDREW J., Private
Resided in Alamance County and enlisted at Camp Gregg, Virginia, at age 30, April 18, 1863, for the war. Present or accounted for until wounded at Gettysburg, Pennsylvania, July 1-3, 1863. Rejoined the company prior to September 1, 1863, and present or accounted for until captured at Hatcher's Run, Virginia, April 2, 1865. Confined at Point Lookout, Maryland, until released on June 17, 1865, after taking the Oath of Allegiance.

RIKE, BENJAMIN L., Corporal
Resided in Alamance County and was by occupation a laborer prior to enlisting in Alamance County at age 26, May 8, 1861. Mustered in as Private. Present or accounted for until wounded at Malvern Hill, Virginia, July 1, 1862. Rejoined the company in January-February, 1863, and was wounded at Chancellorsville, Virginia, May 3, 1863. Promoted to Corporal on August 15, 1863, and rejoined the company in September-October, 1863. Present or accounted for until captured at Wilderness, Virginia, May 6, 1864. Confined at Point Lookout, Maryland, until transferred to Elmira, New York, August 10, 1864. Released at Elmira on or about July 11, 1865, after taking the Oath of Allegiance.

RIKE, EMANUEL, Private
Resided in Alamance County and was by occupation a laborer prior to enlisting in Alamance County at age 24, May 8, 1861. Present or accounted for until wounded in the thigh at Chancellorsville, Virginia, May 3, 1863. Rejoined the company in July-August, 1863, and was detailed as a blacksmith on August 10, 1863. Reported absent on detail until paroled at Appomattox Court House, Virginia, April 9, 1865.

RIPPEY, JAMES A., Private
Resided in Alamance County and was by occupation a laborer prior to enlisting in Alamance County at age 19, May 8, 1861. Present or accounted for until captured at Gettysburg, Pennsylvania, July 1-4, 1863. Confined at Fort Delaware, Delaware, until transferred to Point Lookout, Maryland, October 15-18, 1863. Paroled at Point Lookout and transferred to City Point, Virginia, where he was received March 20, 1864, for exchange. Rejoined the company in May-June, 1864, and present or accounted for until he deserted to the enemy on or about March 8, 1865. Took the Oath of Allegiance on or about March 10, 1865.

RONEY, DANIEL M., Sergeant
Born in Alamance County* where he resided as a carpenter or mechanic prior to enlisting in Alamance County at age 20, May 8, 1861. Mustered in as Private and promoted to Corporal on June 22, 1861. Promoted to Sergeant on May 1, 1862. Died at Richmond, Virginia, June 15, 1862, of "typhoid fever."

RUMBLEY, JOHN S., Private
Born in Alamance County* where he resided as a grocer prior to enlisting in Alamance County at age

24, May 8, 1861. Present or accounted for until wounded at Chancellorsville, Virginia, May 3, 1863. Died on or about May 8, 1863, of wounds. Place of death not reported.

SHARP, DANIEL E., Private
Resided in Alamance County and enlisted at Camp Gregg, Virginia, at age 36, April 18, 1863, for the war. Wounded at Chancellorsville, Virginia, May 3, 1863, and died in hospital at Richmond, Virginia, June 1, 1863, of wounds.

SHAPPE, ROBERT P., Private
Resided in Alamance County and was by occupation a laborer prior to enlisting in Alamance County at age 21, May 8, 1861. Present or accounted for until paroled at Appomattox Court House, Virginia, April 9, 1865. North Carolina pension records indicate he was wounded in the chest at Petersburg, Virginia, in 1865.

SHEPHERD, MARTIN, Private
Enlisted at Camp Holmes on February 28, 1864, for the war. A hospital record dated 1864 gives his age as 34. Present or accounted for until hospitalized at Richmond, Virginia, May 19, 1864, with a gunshot wound; however, place and date wounded not reported. Returned to duty May 23, 1864. Present or accounted for until paroled at Appomattox Court House, Virginia, April 9, 1865.

SHOFFNER, JOHN, Private
Resided in Alamance County and enlisted at Camp Gregg, Virginia, at age 37, April 18, 1863, for the war. Wounded at Chancellorsville, Virginia, May 3, 1863, and died in hospital at Richmond, Virginia, May 14, 1863, of wounds.

SHOFFNER, MICHAEL MORGAN, Private
Resided in Alamance County and enlisted at Camp Gregg, Virginia, at age 24, April 18, 1863, for the war. Wounded in the head at Chancellorsville, Virginia, May 3, 1863. Rejoined the company in November-December, 1863, and present or accounted for until retired to the Invalid Corps on April 29, 1864.

SIMPSON, GEORGE W., Private
Resided in Alamance County. Place and date of enlistment not reported. Captured at Hatcher's Run, Virginia, April 2, 1865, and confined at Point Lookout, Maryland, until released on June 19, 1865, after taking the Oath of Allegiance.

SIMPSON, HARDY, Private
Born in Alamance County* where he resided as a laborer prior to enlisting in Alamance County at age 21, May 8, 1861. Present or accounted for until he died at home in Alamance County on February 23, 1863, of "consumption."

SPARKES, JOHN, Private
Resided in Wilkes County and enlisted at Bunker Hill, Virginia, at age 25, September 27, 1862, for the war. Present or accounted for until he deserted on May 10, 1863.

SPARKS, WILLIAM, Private
Resided in Wilkes County and enlisted at Bunker Hill, Virginia, at age 19, September 27, 1862, for the war. Present or accounted for until he deserted on May 10, 1863.

SPOON, JOHN A., Private
Born in Alamance County* where he resided as a farmer prior to enlisting at Camp Ruffin, Virginia, at age 22, July 27, 1861. Present or accounted for until discharged on October 25, 1861, by reason of disability.

STALEY, DANIEL S., Private
Born in Alamance County* where he resided prior to enlisting at Camp Ruffin, Virginia, at age 24, July 27, 1861. Present or accounted for until killed at Chancellorsville, Virginia, May 3, 1863.

STOCKARD, ROBERT J., Private
Born in Alamance County* where he resided as a farmer prior to enlisting at Camp Ruffin, Virginia, at age 23, September 14, 1861. Present or accounted for until he died at home in Alamance County on August 6, 1862, of "typhoid fever."

STOCKARD, SAMUEL C., Corporal
Born in Alamance County* where he resided as a farmer or laborer prior to enlisting in Alamance County at age 23, May 8, 1861. Mustered in as Private and promoted to Corporal on December 9, 1861. Present or accounted for until killed at Chancellorsville, Virginia, May 3, 1863.

SUTTON, CHESLEY W., Private
Resided in Alamance County and was by occupation a laborer prior to enlisting in Alamance County at age 27, May 8, 1861. Present or accounted for until killed at Sharpsburg, Maryland, September 17, 1862.

SUTTON, JOHN M., Private
Born in Alamance County* where he resided as a shoemaker prior to enlisting in Alamance County at age 26, May 8, 1861. Present or accounted for until he died in hospital at Richmond, Virginia, June 18, 1862, of "feb[ris] typh[oides]."

TAPSCOTT, JOHN MARION, Private
Resided in Alamance County and was by occupation a laborer prior to enlisting in Alamance County at age 20, May 8, 1861. Present or accounted for until wounded at Ellerson's Mill, Virginia, June 26, 1862. Discharged August 29, 1862, after providing Private James Chatham as a substitute.

TATE, JAMES T., Private
Resided in Alamance County where he enlisted on February 5, 1864, for the war. Present or accounted for until captured at Petersburg, Virginia, April 3, 1865. Confined at Point Lookout, Maryland, until released on June 21, 1865, after taking the Oath of Allegiance.

THOMPSON, WILLIAM, Private
Resided in Alamance County and enlisted at Camp Gregg, Virginia, at age 18, April 18, 1863, for the war. Present or accounted for until wounded in the foot and captured at Gettysburg, Pennsylvania, July 1-5, 1863. Hospitalized at Gettysburg and at Chester, Pennsylvania. Died in hospital at Chester on July 30, 1863, of "nervous exhaustion, the result of gun shot wound."

THOMPSON, WILLIAM M., Private
Resided in Alamance County and was by occupation a laborer prior to enlisting in Alamance County at age 19, May 8, 1861. Present or accounted for until wounded in both thighs at Chancellorsville, Virginia,

May 3, 1863. Rejoined the company in November-December, 1863, and present or accounted for until transferred to Company F, 19th Regiment N.C. Troops (2nd Regiment N.C. Cavalry), March 23, 1865. Detailed as a courier during most of his period of service with this company.

TOOMEY, MICHAEL C., Private
Born in Cork County, Ireland, and resided in Alamance County where he was by occupation a peddler or laborer prior to enlisting in Alamance County at age 22, May 8, 1861. Present or accounted for until discharged near Richmond, Virginia, August 6, 1862, by reason of being an "unnaturalized foreigner."

WADE, ELZA J., Private
Resided in Alamance County and was by occupation a grocer prior to enlisting in Alamance County at age 33, May 8, 1861. Appointed 1st Sergeant on May 9, 1861, but was reduced to ranks on June 1, 1861. Present or accounted for until discharged on or about August 2, 1862, under the provisions of the Conscript Act.

WARD, WILLIAM H., Private
Born in Alamance County* where he resided as a laborer prior to enlisting in Alamance County at age 20, May 1, 1861. Present or accounted for until transferred to the C. S. Navy for duty on the C.S.S. *Merrimac* on February 19, 1862.

WAY, WILLIAM H., Private
Resided in Alamance County and enlisted at Camp Gregg, Virginia, at age 37, March 13, 1863, for the war. Present or accounted for until wounded in the head at Chancellorsville, Virginia, May 3, 1863. Reported absent wounded through October, 1864. Paroled at Appomattox Court House, Virginia, April 9, 1865.

WEEDON, DANIEL W., Private
Resided in Alamance County and was by occupation a laborer prior to enlisting in Alamance County at age 23, May 8, 1861. Present or accounted for until wounded at Chancellorsville, Virginia, May 3, 1863. Rejoined the company in July-August, 1863, and present or accounted for until captured at or near Petersburg, Virginia, April 2, 1865. Confined at Point Lookout, Maryland, until released on June 21, 1865, after taking the Oath of Allegiance.

WHITAKER, F. P., Private
Resided in Buncombe County. Place and date of enlistment not reported. Deserted to the enemy at Waynesville on February 24, 1865. Took the Oath of Allegiance at Knoxville, Tennessee, March 21, 1865.

WHITSELL, MILTON, Private
Born in Alamance County* where he resided prior to enlisting at Camp Gregg, Virginia, at age 18, March 27, 1863, for the war. Died in hospital at Guinea Station, Virginia, April 11, 1863, of "typhoid fever."

WHITSELL, SIMPSON R., Private
Born in Alamance County* where he resided as a laborer prior to enlisting in Alamance County at age 22, May 8, 1861. Present or accounted for until killed at Chancellorsville, Virginia, May 3, 1863.

WILLIAMS, LUTHER J., Private
Resided in Alamance County and was by occupation

a laborer prior to enlisting in Alamance County at age 23, May 8, 1861. Present or accounted for until he died in hospital at Richmond, Virginia, June 13, 1862, of "typhoid fever."

WILLIAMS, WILLIAM, Private
Resided in Alamance County and enlisted at Camp Gregg, Virginia, at age 25, March 13, 1863, for the war. Reported absent sick, absent without leave, or absent in arrest from April 18, 1863, through February, 1864. Rejoined the company in March-April, 1864, and present or accounted for until paroled at Appomattox Court House, Virginia, April 9, 1865.

COMPANY F

This company, known as the Davie Greys, was from Davie County and enlisted at Mocksville on April 26, 1861. The company left Mocksville on May 1, 1861, and arrived at Weldon on May 4. On May 8 it moved from Weldon to Garysburg. There it was assigned to the regiment as Company F. After joining the regiment the company functioned as a part of the regiment, and its history for the war period is recorded as a part of the regimental history.

The information contained in the following roster of the company was compiled principally from company muster rolls for May 15, 1861, through October, 1864. No company muster rolls were found for the period after October, 1864. In addition to the company muster rolls, Roll of Honor records, receipt rolls, hospital records, prisoner of war records, and other primary records, supplemented by state pension applications, United Daughters of the Confederacy records, and postwar rosters and histories, all provided useful information.

OFFICERS
CAPTAINS

CLEMENTS, JESSE A.
Resided in Davie County and was by occupation a farmer prior to enlisting in Davie County at age 51. Appointed Captain to rank from May 5, 1861. Present or accounted for until he was defeated for reelection when the regiment was reorganized on April 26, 1862.

FOSTER, GEORGE
Resided in Davie County and was by occupation a farmer prior to enlisting in Davie County at age 26, April 26, 1861. Mustered in as Corporal and was elected Captain to rank from April 26, 1862. Present or accounted for until he resigned on May 11, 1863, by reason of "rheumatism." Resignation accepted on or about June 5, 1863.

WILLIAMS, FRANKLIN
Resided in Davie County and was by occupation a teacher prior to enlisting in Davie County at age 23, April 26, 1861. Mustered in as Private and was elected 1st Lieutenant to rank from April 26, 1862. Present or accounted for until wounded at Fredericksburg, Virginia, on or about December 13, 1862. Rejoined the company prior to January 1, 1863, and was promoted to Captain on June 5, 1863. Present or

accounted for until wounded in the left leg and captured at Gettysburg, Pennsylvania on or about July 1, 1863. Hospitalized at various Federal hospitals until transferred to Johnson's Island, Ohio, where he arrived December 9, 1863. Confined at various Federal prisons until transferred from Point Lookout, Maryland, to Cox's Wharf, James River, Virginia, where he was received October 15, 1864, for exchange. Reported absent wounded through October, 1864.

ROESSLER, JULIUS

Resided in Davie County and was by occupation a merchant prior to enlisting in Davie County at age 33. Elected 1st Lieutenant to rank from May 5, 1861, but was defeated for reelection when the regiment was reorganized on April 26, 1862. Rejoined the company on or about August 1, 1863, when he was elected 1st Lieutenant. Present or accounted for until admitted to hospital at Danville, Virginia, May 9, 1864, with a gunshot wound of the head; however, place and date wounded not reported. Rejoined the company prior to July 1, 1864, and present or accounted for until paroled at Appomattox Court House, Virginia, April 9, 1865. Records of the Federal Provost Marshal indicate he was promoted to Captain in November, 1864-April, 1865.

LIEUTENANTS

CLEMENT, WILEY A., 2nd Lieutenant

Resided in Davie County and was by occupation a student prior to enlisting in Davie County at age 21. Elected 2nd Lieutenant to rank from May 5, 1861. Present or accounted for until he resigned on March 21, 1862, by reason of having raised his own company. Later served as Captain of Company F, 42nd Regiment N.C. Troops.

DRIVER, JOHN E., 2nd Lieutenant

Resided in Davie County and was by occupation a tobacconist prior to enlisting in Davie County at age 23, April 26, 1861. Promoted to 1st Sergeant from an unspecified rank on June 1, 1861. Elected 2nd Lieutenant on April 26, 1862. Present or accounted for until wounded in the left arm at Williamsburg, Virginia, May 5, 1862. Resigned August 4, 1862, by reason of wounds resulting in "paralysis of the fingers." Resignation accepted on or about August 22, 1862.

SAIN, CHESHIRE, 3rd Lieutenant

Resided in Davie County and was by occupation a blacksmith prior to enlisting in Davie County at age 40. Elected 3rd Lieutenant to rank from May 5, 1861. Present or accounted for until he was defeated for reelection when the regiment was reorganized on April 26, 1862. [May have served later as Captain of Company A, 4th Regiment N.C. Senior Reserves.]

SAIN, NIMROD B., 2nd Lieutenant

Resided in Davie County and was by occupation a carpenter prior to enlisting in Davie County at age 32, April 26, 1861. Promoted to Sergeant from an unspecified rank on June 1, 1861. Elected 2nd Lieutenant to rank from April 26, 1862. Present or accounted for until wounded at Gettysburg, Pennsylvania, July 1, 1863. Rejoined the company in

September-October, 1863, and present or accounted for until he resigned on February 28, 1864, by reason of "chronic rheumatism." Resignation accepted on March 11, 1864.

THOMPSON, WILLIAM GRAHAM, 2nd Lieutenant

Resided in Davie County and was by occupation a farmer prior to enlisting in Davie County at age 19, April 26, 1861. Mustered in as Private and promoted to 1st Sergeant on April 28, 1862. Elected 3rd Lieutenant on April 12, 1863. Present or accounted for until wounded in the thigh at Chancellorsville, Virginia, May 3, 1863. Rejoined the company in March-April, 1864, and was promoted to 2nd Lieutenant. Present or accounted for until paroled at Appomattox Court House, Virginia, April 9, 1865.

NONCOMMISSIONED OFFICERS AND PRIVATES

ALLEN, JAMES P., Private

Enlisted at Camp Holmes on September 29, 1864, for the war. Present or accounted for through October, 1864.

ALLEN, MATHEW A., Private

Enlisted at Camp Holmes on September 29, 1864, for the war. Present or accounted for through October, 1864.

ANDERSON, CHARLES S., Private

Born in Davie County* where he resided as a farmer prior to enlisting in Davie County at age 36, April 26, 1861. Present or accounted for until he died in hospital at Richmond, Virginia, June 2, 1862, of "typhoid fever."

BAITY, THOMAS B., Private

Resided in Davie County where he enlisted at age 26, August 6, 1861. Present or accounted for until he died in hospital on July 3, 1862, of wounds received in battle near Richmond, Virginia. Date wounded and place of death not reported.

BECK, WILLIAM, Private

Resided in Davidson County and enlisted at Camp Holmes on February 24, 1864, for the war. Present or accounted for until captured at Sutherland's Station, Virginia, on or about April 3, 1865. Confined at Point Lookout, Maryland, until hospitalized at Washington, D.C., July 24, 1865. Died July 25, 1865, of "ch[ronic] diarrhoea & scurvy." Federal hospital records give his age as 30.

BELL, N. R., Private

Enlisted at Camp Vance on January 25, 1864, for the war. Present or accounted for until he died in hospital at Gordonsville, Virginia, April 15, 1864. Cause of death not reported.

BESSENT, DANIEL D., Private

Born in Davie County where he resided as a tobacconist prior to enlisting in Davie County at age 17, April 26, 1861. Present or accounted for until killed at Chancellorsville, Virginia, May 3, 1863.

BLACKWOOD, JOHN B., Private

Resided in Davie County and was by occupation a farmer prior to enlisting in Davie County at age 18, May 21, 1861. Present or accounted for until wounded in the left hand at Gaines' Mill, Virginia, June

27, 1862. Rejoined the company in November-December, 1862. Present or accounted for through April 28, 1864; however, he was reported absent sick or absent on detail during most of that period. Retired to the Invalid Corps on April 29, 1864, by reason of wounds received at Gaines' Mill.

BOLES, JAMES D., Private
Resided in Davie County and was by occupation a farmer prior to enlisting in Davie County at age 28, April 26, 1861. Present or accounted for until hospitalized at Richmond, Virginia, August 29, 1862, with a wound of the hand; however, place and date wounded not reported. Reported absent wounded, absent sick, or absent on detail until captured at Hanover Junction, Virginia, May 23, 1864. Confined at Point Lookout, Maryland, until transferred to Cox's Landing, James River, Virginia, where he was received February 14-15, 1865, for exchange. Paroled at Salisbury in 1865.

BOOE, GEORGE W., Sergeant
Resided in Davie County and was by occupation a student prior to enlisting in Davie County at age 19, April 26, 1861. Mustered in as Corporal and was promoted to Sergeant on April 28, 1862. Present or accounted for until transferred to Company H, 63rd Regiment N.C. Troops (5th Regiment N.C. Cavalry), on or about October 31, 1862.

BOOE, GEORGE W., Private
Resided in Davie County and was by occupation a farmer prior to enlisting in Davie County at age 19, April 26, 1861. Present or accounted for until wounded in the left arm and captured at South Mountain, Maryland, September 14, 1862. Exchanged at Aiken's Landing, James River, Virginia, on or about October 12, 1862. Rejoined the company in November-December, 1862, and present or accounted for until wounded in the hip at Chancellorsville, Virginia, May 3, 1863. Rejoined the company in November-December, 1863, and present or accounted for until wounded at or near Spotsylvania Court House, Virginia, May 21, 1864. Rejoined the company in July-August, 1864, and present or accounted for until captured at Hatcher's Run, Virginia, April 2, 1865. Confined at Point Lookout, Maryland, until released on June 23, 1865, after taking the Oath of Allegiance.

BOYD, JAMES S., Private
Born in Randolph County and resided in Davie County where he was by occupation a blacksmith or farmer prior to enlisting in Davie County at age 23, April 26, 1861. Present or accounted for until killed at Gaines' Mill, Virginia, June 27, 1862.

BRANK, WASHINGTON J., Private
Enlisted at Camp Holmes on November 21, 1863, for the war. Present or accounted for through February 2, 1865.

BRINIGER, JOHN, Private
Resided in Davie County where he enlisted at age 19, August 6, 1861. Present or accounted for until hospitalized at Richmond, Virginia, June 10, 1862, with a wound; however, place and date wounded not reported. Rejoined the company prior to November 1, 1862, and present or accounted for until he died on November 4, 1868. Place and cause of death not

reported.

BURTON, DANIEL P., Private
Resided in Davie County where he enlisted at age 24, July 4, 1861. Present or accounted for until paroled at Appomattox Court House, Virginia, April 9, 1865. Paroled again at Salisbury on May 25, 1865.

BURTON, NOEL E., Private
Enlisted at Petersburg, Virginia, June 23, 1864, for the war. Present or accounted for until paroled at Appomattox Court House, Virginia, April 9, 1865.

BUTLER, THOMAS S., Private
Resided in Davie County and was by occupation a teacher prior to enlisting in Davie County at age 21, April 26, 1861. Present or accounted for until wounded at Chancellorsville, Virginia, May 3, 1863. Rejoined the company prior to July 14, 1863, when he was captured at Falling Waters, Maryland. Confined at Baltimore, Maryland, and at Point Lookout, Maryland, until paroled and transferred to City Point, Virginia, where he was received March 6, 1864, for exchange. Rejoined the company in May-June, 1864, and present or accounted for until captured on the South Side Railroad, Virginia, April 3, 1865. Confined at Point Lookout until released on June 23, 1865, after taking the Oath of Allegiance.

CAMPBELL, GEORGE W., Private
Born in Davie County* where he resided as a farmer prior to enlisting in Davie County at age 42, August 6, 1861. Present or accounted for until discharged at Camp Gregg, Virginia, May 9, 1863, by reason of "being over forty years of age."

CARTNER, JAMES F., Private
Born in Davie County where he resided as a farmer prior to enlisting in Davie County at age 19, August 6, 1861. Present or accounted for until he died in hospital at Richmond, Virginia, June 28, 1862, of "typhoid fever."

CHANDLER, SOLOMON, Private
Enlisted at Camp Holmes on November 21, 1863, for the war. Died December 2, 1863. Place and cause of death not reported.

CHAPLIN, ALEXANDER, Private
Born in Davie County* where he resided as a farmer prior to enlisting in Davie County at age 33, April 26, 1861. Present or accounted for until discharged near Richmond, Virginia, July 26, 1862, under the provisions of the Conscript Act.

CHURCH, WILLIAM, Private
Resided in Wilkes County and enlisted at Camp Vance on March 14, 1864, for the war. Deserted on May 24, 1864, but was reported sick in hospital on company muster roll dated July-August, 1864. Died in hospital at Richmond, Virginia, September 5, 1864, of "colitis acuta."

CLICK, DANIEL W., Private
Born in Davie County where he resided as a tobacconist or constable prior to enlisting in Davie County at age 21, April 26, 1861. Present or accounted for until he died in hospital at Richmond, Virginia, July 10, 1862, of "typhoid fever."

CLONINGER, ALONZO, Private
Previously served in Company B, 42nd Regiment

N.C. Troops. Transferred to this company on February 18, 1863. Killed at Chancellorsville, Virginia, May 3, 1863.

DANNER, ELI, Private
Born in Davie County where he resided as a farmer prior to enlisting in Davie County at age 22, August 6, 1861. Present or accounted for until wounded at Chancellorsville, Virginia, May 3, 1863. Rejoined the company in July-August, 1863, and present or accounted for until wounded in the right thigh at Petersburg, Virginia, June 22, 1864. Reported absent wounded until retired on February 8, 1865, by reason of wounds received at Petersburg. Paroled at Salisbury in 1865.

DAVIS, ALFRED, Private
Place and date of enlistment not reported. Name appears on a list of prisoners paroled at Salisbury in 1865.

DAVIS, FRANKLIN, Private
Born in Randolph County and resided in Davie County where he was by occupation a farmer prior to enlisting in Davie County at age 23, August 6, 1861. Present or accounted for until he died in hospital at Richmond, Virginia, June 30, 1862, of "febris typhoides" and/or "int[ermittent] fev[er]."

DAYWALT, ALFRED J., Private
Born in Davie County where he resided as a farmer prior to enlisting in Davie County at age 20, August 6, 1861. Present or accounted for until wounded in the breast at Gettysburg, Pennsylvania, July 1, 1863. Rejoined the company in November-December, 1863, and present or accounted for until paroled at Appomattox Court House, Virginia, April 9, 1865.

DEDMAN, THOMAS H., Private
Resided in Davie County where he enlisted at age 17, August 6, 1861. Present or accounted for until discharged on November 10, 1862, under the provisions of the Conscript Act.

DINGLER, JAMES, Private
Resided in Davie County and was by occupation a shoemaker prior to enlisting in Davie County at age 31, April 26, 1861. Present or accounted for until discharged on July 26, 1862, under the provisions of the Conscript Act.

DIVIRE, DANIEL, Corporal
Resided in Davie County and was by occupation a farmer prior to enlisting in Davie County at age 27, April 26, 1861. Mustered in as Private and promoted to Corporal on July 1, 1864. Present or accounted for until paroled at Appomattox Court House, Virginia, April 9, 1865.

DOBBINS, ALFRED M. C., Private
Resided in Davie County and was by occupation a doctor prior to enlisting in Davie County at age 32, April 26, 1861. Present or accounted for until reported absent wounded in May-June, 1862; however, battle in which wounded not reported. Elected 3rd Lieutenant on October 7, 1862, and rejoined the company prior to November 1, 1862. "Cashiered by sentence of court martial" on or about March 20, 1863, and was reduced to ranks. Deserted to the enemy near Fredericksburg, Virginia, May 2-4, 1863. Took the Oath of Allegiance on May 4, 1863.

ECCLES, JOHN C., Private
Enlisted at Camp Holmes on February 20, 1864, for the war. Present or accounted for until wounded and captured at Wilderness, Virginia, May 6, 1864. Confined at Point Lookout, Maryland, until transferred to Elmira, New York, July 25, 1864. Died at Elmira on March 13, 1865, of "inflammation of lungs." Records of the Federal Provost Marshal give his age as 43.

ELLIS, THOMAS N., Private
Resided in Davie County where he enlisted at age 19, August 6, 1861. Present or accounted for until wounded at Chancellorsville, Virginia, May 3, 1863. Rejoined the company in July-August, 1863, and present or accounted for until captured at Reams' Station, Virginia, August 25, 1864. Confined at Point Lookout, Maryland, until paroled and transferred to Cox's Landing, James River, Virginia, where he was received February 14-15, 1865, for exchange. Paroled at Mocksville on June 9, 1865.

ELLISON, DONALSON, Private
Resided in Davie County and was by occupation a farmer prior to enlisting in Davie County at age 18, June 18, 1861. Present or accounted for until he died in hospital at Richmond, Virginia, August 12, 1862, of disease.

FLETCHER, MATHEW, Private
Resided in Davie or Wilkes counties and was by occupation a farmer prior to enlisting in Davie County at age 22, April 26, 1861. Present or accounted for until captured at Gill's Mill, Virginia, April 6, 1865. Confined at Point Lookout, Maryland, until released on June 26, 1865, after taking the Oath of Allegiance.

FOSTER, HENRY, Private
Resided in Davie County where he enlisted at age 30, July 16, 1862. Present or accounted for until paroled at Appomattox Court House, Virginia, April 9, 1865.

FOSTER, HENRY C., Sergeant
Resided in Davie County and was by occupation a farmer prior to enlisting in Davie County at age 18, April 26, 1861. Mustered in as Private. Present or accounted for until wounded at Gaines' Mill, Virginia, June 27, 1862. Rejoined the company prior to March 1, 1863, and was promoted to Sergeant on April 17, 1863. Present or accounted for until wounded at Chancellorsville, Virginia, May 3, 1863. Rejoined the company in July-August, 1863, and was reduced to ranks prior to September 1, 1863, when he was reappointed Sergeant. Present or accounted for until paroled at Appomattox Court House, Virginia, April 9, 1865.

FOSTER, JACOB, Private
Resided in Davie County and was by occupation a farmer prior to enlisting in Davie County at age 23, April 26, 1861. Present or accounted for until wounded in battle near Richmond, Virginia, in May-June, 1862. Battle in which wounded not reported. Rejoined the company prior to November 1, 1862, and present or accounted for until wounded and captured at or near Fredericksburg, Virginia, May 3, 1863. Sent to Washington, D.C. Transferred to City Point, Virginia, where he was received May 13,

1863, for exchange. Rejoined the company prior to July 1, 1863, and present or accounted for until captured at Hatcher's Run, Virginia, April 2, 1865. Confined at Point Lookout, Maryland, until released on June 26, 1865, after taking the Oath of Allegiance.

FOSTER, SAMUEL, Private
Resided in Davie County and was by occupation a farmer prior to enlisting in Davie County at age 18, April 26, 1861. Present or accounted for until wounded in the thigh at Gaines' Mill, Virginia, June 27, 1862. Reported absent wounded until September-October, 1864, when he rejoined the company. Retired to the Invalid Corps on November 2, 1864.

FURCHES, SAMUEL W., Private
Resided in Davie County where he enlisted at age 25, August 6, 1861. Present or accounted for until captured at Frederick, Maryland, September 12, 1862. Confined at Fort Delaware, Delaware, until transferred to Aiken's Landing, James River, Virginia, October 2, 1862, for exchange. Declared exchanged at Aiken's Landing on November 10, 1862. Rejoined the company prior to March 1, 1863, and was wounded in the right hand and right wrist at Chancellorsville, Virginia, May 3, 1863. Rejoined the company in March-April, 1864, but was retired to the Invalid Corps on April 20, 1864. Paroled at Mocksville on June 9, 1865.

FURCHES, THOMAS W., Private
Born in Davie County where he resided prior to enlisting in Davie County at age 22, August 6, 1861. Present or accounted for until wounded and captured at Williamsburg, Virginia, May 5, 1862. Hospitalized at Washington, D.C., until transferred to Old Capitol Prison, Washington, June 11, 1862. Exchanged at Aiken's Landing, James River, Virginia, August 5, 1862. Rejoined the company prior to March 1, 1863. Killed at Chancellorsville, Virginia, May 3, 1863.

GATTON, FRANKLIN, Private
Born in Davie County where he resided as a farmer prior to enlisting in Davie County at age 21, April 26, 1861. Present or accounted for until wounded at Chancellorsville, Virginia, May 3, 1863. Rejoined the company in November-December, 1863. Died in hospital at Gordonsville, Virginia, January 14, 1864, of "pneumonia."

GATTON, HARRISON, Private
Resided in Davie County and was by occupation a farmer prior to enlisting in Davie County at age 21, April 26, 1861. Present or accounted for until wounded at Chancellorsville, Virginia, May 3, 1863. Rejoined the company in September-October, 1863, and present or accounted for until paroled at Appomattox Court House, Virginia, April 9, 1865. Paroled again at Mocksville on June 9, 1865.

GRAVES, JOHN W., Private
Born in Davie County where he resided as a farmer prior to enlisting in Davie County at age 19, August 6, 1861. Present or accounted for until wounded in the left hand at Fredericksburg, Virginia, December 13, 1862. Left hand amputated. Reported absent wounded or absent on detail as a guard until discharged at Petersburg, Virginia, December 8, 1864,

by reason of wounds received at Fredericksburg.

GRAY, G. F., Private
Place and date of enlistment not reported. First listed in the records of this company on December 1, 1864. Paroled at Appomattox Court House, Virginia, April 9, 1865.

HARRIS, JOHN W., Private
Born in Wilkes County and resided in Davie County where he was by occupation a farmer prior to enlisting in Davie County at age 22, April 26, 1861. Present or accounted for until wounded in the left thigh and captured at Gettysburg, Pennsylvania, July 1-4, 1863. Hospitalized at Davids Island, New York Harbor, until paroled and transferred to City Point, Virginia, where he was received September 8, 1863, for exchange. Reported absent wounded or absent sick until he rejoined the company in September-October, 1864.

HARRISON, RICHARD, Private
Born in Davie or Surry counties and resided in Davie County where he was by occupation a farmer prior to enlisting in Davie County at age 17, April 26, 1861. Present or accounted for until discharged at Camp Ruffin, Virginia, March 2, 1862, by reason of "epilepsy."

HENDREN, ARTHUR N., 1st Sergeant
Resided in Davie County and was by occupation a farmer prior to enlisting in Davie County at age 23, April 26, 1861. Mustered in as Musician. Present or accounted for until captured at or near Sharpsburg, Maryland, on or about September 17, 1862. Paroled September 20, 1862. Rejoined the company in November-December, 1862. Promoted to 1st Sergeant on May 1, 1864. Present or accounted for until paroled at Appomattox Court House, Virginia, April 9, 1865.

HENDRIX, JEHU, Private
Resided in Davie County where he enlisted at age 36, July 16, 1862, for the war. Present or accounted for until captured at Amelia Court House, Virginia, April 5, 1865. Confined at Point Lookout, Maryland, until released on June 27, 1865, after taking the Oath of Allegiance.

HENLEY, WILLIAM, Private
Enlisted at Camp Holmes on February 13, 1864, for the war. Present or accounted for through October, 1864. Paroled at Greensboro on May 16, 1865.

HEPLER, BENJAMIN F., Private
Resided in Davidson County and enlisted in Guilford County at age 17, March 13, 1863, for the war. Present or accounted for until wounded in the hip at Chancellorsville, Virginia, May 3, 1863. Reported absent wounded or absent sick until he rejoined the company in March-April, 1864. Killed at or near Cold Harbor, Virginia, June 1, 1864.

HINKLE, GEORGE W., Private
Resided in Davie County where he enlisted at age 18, August 6, 1861. Present or accounted for until wounded and captured at Gettysburg, Pennsylvania, July 1-4, 1863. Hospitalized at Davids Island, New York Harbor, until paroled and transferred to City Point, Virginia, where he was received September 8, 1863, for exchange. Rejoined the company in May-

June, 1864, and present or accounted for until captured at the Appomattox River, Virginia, April 3, 1865. Confined at Hart's Island, New York Harbor, until released on June 19, 1865, after taking the Oath of Allegiance.

HOBBS, JULIUS, Sergeant
Born in Davie County where he resided as a student or farmer prior to enlisting in Davie County at age 22, April 26, 1861. Mustered in as Private and promoted to Sergeant on April 28, 1862. Present or accounted for until he died in hospital at Charlottesville, Virginia, December 9, 1862, of "pneumonia."

HODGES, JOSEPH, Private
Born in Davie County* where he resided prior to enlisting in Davie County at age 26, August 6, 1861. Present or accounted for until wounded at Fredericksburg, Virginia, on or about December 13, 1862. Rejoined the company prior to January 1, 1863, and present or accounted for until killed at Chancellorsville, Virginia, May 3, 1863.

HOLT, ROBERT A., Private
Resided in Davie County and was by occupation a farmer prior to enlisting in Davie County at age 22, April 26, 1861. Present or accounted for until wounded in the left foot and captured at Gettysburg, Pennsylvania, July 1-4, 1863. Hospitalized at Davids Island, New York Harbor, until paroled and transferred to City Point, Virginia, where he was received October 28, 1863, for exchange. Reported absent wounded or absent sick until retired to the Invalid Corps on August 13, 1864.

HOUSE, JOHN W., Private
Resided in Davie County and was by occupation a farmer prior to enlisting in Davie County at age 20, April 26, 1861. Present or accounted for until transferred to Company B, 42nd Regiment N.C. Troops, April 22, 1863.

HOWARD, HARRISON H., Corporal
Resided in Davie County and was by occupation a painter prior to enlisting in Davie County at age 20, April 26, 1861. Mustered in as Private. Present or accounted for until wounded in the right arm at Chancellorsville, Virginia, May 3, 1863. Rejoined the company in July-August, 1863, and was promoted to Corporal on September 1, 1863. Present or accounted for until captured at Wilderness, Virginia, May 6, 1864. Confined at Point Lookout, Maryland, until transferred to Elmira, New York, August 10, 1864. Died at Elmira on February 13, 1865, of "variola."

HUDSON, JAMES, Private
Enlisted at Camp Vance on November 21, 1863, for the war. Present or accounted for through August, 1864. Reported absent sick without leave on company muster roll dated September-October, 1864. No further records.

HUNTER, JOHN W., Private
Resided in Davie County where he enlisted at age 26, August 6, 1861. Present or accounted for until wounded in the arm, leg, and side at Chancellorsville, Virginia, May 3, 1863. Reported absent wounded or absent on detail as a guard until he rejoined the company in March-April, 1864. Retired to the Invalid Corps on April 30, 1864. Paroled at Salisbury in 1865.

IJAMS, JAMES D., Sergeant
Resided in Davie County and was by occupation a farmer prior to enlisting in Davie County at age 20, April 26, 1861. Mustered in as Corporal. Present or accounted for until captured at Williamsburg, Virginia, on or about May 6, 1862. Exchanged and rejoined the company prior to November 1, 1862. Present or accounted for until wounded at Chancellorsville, Virginia, May 3, 1863. Rejoined the company in July-August, 1863, and was promoted to Sergeant on September 1, 1863. Present or accounted for until paroled at Appomattox Court House, Virginia, April 9, 1865.

IJAMS, MATTHEW N., Corporal
Resided in Davie County where he enlisted at age 19, August 6, 1861. Mustered in as Private. Present or accounted for until wounded and captured at Williamsburg, Virginia, on or about May 6, 1862. Hospitalized at Washington, D.C., until transferred to Old Capitol Prison, Washington, June 27, 1862. Transferred to Aiken's Landing, James River, Virginia, where he was received August 5, 1862, for exchange. Rejoined the company prior to November 1, 1862, and was promoted to Corporal on December 6, 1862. Present or accounted for until captured at Falling Waters, Maryland, July 14, 1863. Confined at Point Lookout, Maryland, until paroled and transferred to City Point, Virginia, where he was received March 20, 1864, for exchange. Rejoined the company in May-June, 1864, and present or accounted for through October, 1864. Paroled at Salisbury in 1865.

JONES, ANDERSON W., Private
Enlisted at Camp Holmes on October 12, 1863, for the war. Present or accounted for until discharged on January 22, 1864. Reason discharged not reported.

JONES, DAVID H., Private
Enlisted at Camp Holmes on December 12, 1863, for the war. Discharged January 22, 1864. Reason discharged not reported.

JONES, KINSEY, Private
Enlisted at Camp Holmes on February 15, 1864, for the war. Present or accounted for until he deserted in March-April, 1864.

JONES, MADISON, Private
Enlisted at Camp Holmes on December 12, 1863, for the war. Discharged in January-February, 1864. Reason discharged not reported.

JONES, SAMUEL G., Private
Place and date of enlistment not reported. First listed in the records of this company on November 5, 1864. Paroled at Appomattox Court House, Virginia, April 9, 1865.

JONES, WILEY G., Private
Enlisted at Camp Holmes on October 5, 1863, for the war. Present or accounted for until paroled at Appomattox Court House, Virginia, April 9, 1865.

KAHNWEILER, K., Private
Place and date of enlistment not reported. Paroled at or near Burkeville Junction, Virginia, April 14-17, 1865.

KENT, DAVID, Private
Place and date of enlistment not reported. Reported present on the muster rolls of this company during March-June, 1864. No further records.

KURFEES, CALEB W., Private
Born in Davie County where he resided as a farmer prior to enlisting in Davie County at age 19, August 6, 1861. Present or accounted for until he died in hospital at Richmond, Virginia, June 3, 1862, of "continued fever."

KURFEES, FRANKLIN J., Private
Resided in Davie County and was by occupation a farmer prior to enlisting in Davie County at age 21, April 26, 1861. Present or accounted for until wounded at South Mountain, Maryland, September 14, 1862. Died September 17-18, 1862, of wounds. Place of death not reported.

KURFEES, ZEDOCK C., Private
Resided in Davie County where he enlisted at age 18, August 6, 1861. Present or accounted for until wounded at Chancellorsville, Virginia, May 3, 1863. Rejoined the company in July-August, 1863, and present or accounted for until paroled at Appomattox Court House, Virginia, April 9, 1865.

LASSITER, ETHADRA W., Private
Resided in Davie County where he enlisted at age 35, March 26, 1863, for the war. Deserted April 29, 1863. Reported absent in arrest on company muster roll dated March-April, 1864, and reported absent in confinement on company muster rolls dated May-October, 1864. Paroled at Mocksville on June 9, 1865.

LEACH, DAVID, Private
Resided in Davie County where he enlisted at age 25, August 6, 1861. Present or accounted for until wounded at Chancellorsville, Virginia, May 3, 1863. Rejoined the company in September-October, 1863, and present or accounted for until wounded in action on October 6, 1864. Reported absent wounded through October, 1864.

LEACH, JOHN, Sergeant
Born in Davie County* where he resided as a farmer prior to enlisting in Davie County at age 30, August 6, 1861. Mustered in as Private and promoted to Corporal on December 6, 1862. Promoted to Sergeant on January 2, 1863. Present or accounted for until wounded in the right thigh at Chancellorsville, Virginia, May 3, 1863. Died in hospital at Richmond, Virginia, August 22, 1863, of wounds.

LEACH, JOHN W., Private
Resided in Davie County where he enlisted at age 22, August 6, 1861. Present or accounted for until killed at Sharpsburg, Maryland, September 17, 1862.

LEONARD, EMANUEL, Private
Resided in Davie County and was by occupation a farmer prior to enlisting in Davie County at age 28, April 26, 1861. Present or accounted for until killed at Gettysburg, Pennsylvania, July 1, 1863.

LITTLE, ROBERT A., Private
Resided in Davie County and was by occupation a farmer prior to enlisting in Davie County at age 21, April 26, 1861. Present or accounted for until wounded near Richmond, Virginia, in March-June,

1862. Rejoined the company prior to November 1, 1862, and present or accounted for until wounded at Chancellorsville, Virginia, May 3, 1863. Rejoined the company in January-February, 1864, and present or accounted for until wounded in the right thigh and right shoulder at Wilderness, Virginia, May 5, 1864. Died in hospital at Charlottesville, Virginia, May 13, 1864, of "sec[ondary] hemorrhage."

McCARTER, THOMAS, Private
Resided in Davie County and was by occupation a farmer prior to enlisting in Davie County at age 19, April 26, 1861. Present or accounted for until he died in hospital at Richmond, Virginia, on or about June 5, 1862, of "typhoid fever."

McCLENAN, MATHEW A., Corporal
Resided in Davie County where he enlisted at age 22, August 6, 1861. Mustered in as Private and promoted to Corporal on April 28, 1862. Present or accounted for until wounded in the thigh and hand at or near Malvern Hill, Virginia, on or about June 30, 1862. Hospitalized at Richmond, Virginia, where he died July 27, 1862, of wounds.

McDONALD, JAMES, Private
Resided in Davie County where he enlisted at age 19, August 6, 1861. Present or accounted for until killed at Gettysburg, Pennsylvania, July 1, 1863. Roll of Honor indicates he was wounded "three different times . . . without leaving the field" at Chancellorsville, Virginia, May 1-3, 1863, and was "brave in all the battles."

McGUIRE, WILLIAM F., Sergeant
Resided in Davie County and was by occupation a farmer prior to enlisting in Davie County at age 18, April 26, 1861. Mustered in as Private and promoted to Corporal on January 2, 1863. Present or accounted for until wounded at Chancellorsville, Virginia, May 1-3, 1863. Rejoined the company prior to July 1, 1863, and was wounded at Gettysburg, Pennsylvania, July 1-3, 1863. Rejoined the company prior to September 1, 1863, when he was promoted to Sergeant. Present or accounted for until captured at Reams' Station, Virginia, August 24-25, 1864. Confined at Point Lookout, Maryland, until paroled and transferred to Boulware's and Cox's Wharf, James River, Virginia, where he was received February 20-21, 1865, for exchange.

MADRA, WILLIAM H., Private
Resided in Davie County and was by occupation a farmer prior to enlisting in Davie County at age 21, April 26, 1861. Present or accounted for until killed at Gaines' Mill, Virginia, June 27, 1862.

MARLIN, JOHN L., Private
Resided in Davie County and was by occupation a farmer prior to enlisting in Davie County at age 18, April 26, 1861. Present or accounted for until he died in hospital at Richmond, Virginia, on or about July 20, 1862, of disease.

MARTIN, DAVID W., Private
Born in Davie County where he resided as a farmer prior to enlisting in Davie County at age 21, April 26, 1861. Present or accounted for until killed at Gaines' Mill, Virginia, June 27, 1862.

MASON, A. J., Private
Enlisted at Camp Vance on January 25, 1864, for the war. Present or accounted for through February, 1864, but deserted prior to May 1, 1864.

MASON, GRIEF G., Corporal
Resided in Davie County and was by occupation a tobacconist prior to enlisting in Davie County at age 21, April 26, 1861. Mustered in as Private and promoted to Corporal on June 1, 1861. Present or accounted for until killed at Wilderness, Virginia, May 5, 1864, "while gallantly carrying the Regimental Colors."

MAY, URBAN C., Private
Resided in Davie County where he enlisted at age 19, August 4, 1862, for the war. Present or accounted for until wounded and captured at Gettysburg, Pennsylvania, July 1-5, 1863. Hospitalized at Davids Island, New York Harbor, until transferred to Fort Wood, Bedloe's Island, New York Harbor, on or about October 24, 1863. Transferred to Point Lookout, Maryland, December 17, 1863. Released at Point Lookout on January 23, 1864, after taking the Oath of Allegiance and joining the U. S. service. Unit to which assigned not reported.

MILLER, JAMES W., Private
Resided in Davie County where he enlisted at age 17, August 6, 1861. Present or accounted for until wounded at South Mountain, Maryland, on or about September 14, 1862. Discharged in November-December, 1862. Reason discharged not reported. Later served in Company F, 42nd Regiment N.C. Troops.

MOCK, HENRY A., Private
Resided in Davie County where he enlisted at age 30, March 26, 1863, for the war. Deserted April 29, 1863. Reported as a deserter until he was reported in confinement in January-February, 1864. Reported in confinement through April, 1864, but rejoined the company prior to May 6, 1864, when he allowed himself to be "captured purposely" at Wilderness, Virginia. Confined at Point Lookout, Maryland, until transferred to Elmira, New York, July 25, 1864. Died at Elmira on March 8, 1865, of "chro[nic] diarr[hoea]."

MONDAY, WILLIAM, Private
Resided in Davie County and was by occupation a farmer prior to enlisting in Davie County at age 21, April 26, 1861. Present or accounted for until wounded in the right side and back and captured at South Mountain, Maryland, September 14, 1862. Confined at various Federal hospitals until confined at Fort McHenry, Maryland, on or about November 17, 1862. Paroled and transferred to City Point, Virginia, where he was received November 21, 1862, for exchange. Rejoined the company prior to May 1, 1863. Wounded at Chancellorsville, Virginia, May 1-3, 1863, and "went into the fight when he could scarcely bear his gun from the effects of his wounds." Rejoined the company prior to July 1, 1863. Present or accounted for through October, 1864; however, he was reported absent sick or absent on detail during most of that period. Captured in hospital at Richmond, Virginia, April 3, 1865, and was paroled on April 20, 1865.

NAIL, ABRAHAM M., Sergeant
Born in Davie County* where he resided as a carpenter prior to enlisting in Davie County at age 34, April 26, 1861. Appointed Sergeant on June 1, 1861. Present or accounted for until discharged at Richmond, Virginia, July 26, 1862, under the provisions of the Conscript Act.

NAIL, JASPER H. Y., Musician
Resided in Davie County and was by occupation a farmer prior to enlisting in Davie County at age 19, April 26, 1861. Mustered in as Private and was appointed Musician on September 1, 1861. Present or accounted for until paroled at Richmond, Virginia, on or about April 17, 1865. North Carolina pension records indicate he was wounded in the left thigh at Malvern Hill, Virginia, in "June, 1863."

NAIL, JOHN A., Sergeant
Resided in Davie or Rowan counties and was by occupation a farmer prior to enlisting in Davie County at age 21, April 26, 1861. Mustered in as Private and was promoted to Corporal on April 28, 1862. Present or accounted for until captured at Sharpsburg, Maryland, September 17, 1862. Confined at Fort Delaware, Delaware, until transferred to Aiken's Landing, James River, Virginia, October 2, 1862, for exchange. Declared exchanged at Aiken's Landing on November 10, 1862. Rejoined the company in November-December, 1862, and was promoted to Sergeant prior to January 1, 1863. Present or accounted for until wounded at Chancellorsville, Virginia, May 1-3, 1863. Rejoined the company prior to July 1-3, 1863, when he was wounded in the right shoulder and captured at Gettysburg, Pennsylvania. Hospitalized at Chester, Pennsylvania. Promoted to 1st Sergeant on September 1, 1863, while a prisoner of war. Paroled at Chester and transferred to City Point, Virginia, where he was received September 23, 1863, for exchange. Rejoined the company in March-April, 1864, and was reduced to the rank of Sergeant in May-June, 1864. Present or accounted for until paroled at Appomattox Court House, Virginia, April 9, 1865. Paroled again at Salisbury on July 8, 1865.

NAIL, PHILIP A., Private
Born in Rowan County and resided in Davie County where he was by occupation a farmer prior to enlisting in Davie County at age 20, August 6, 1861. Present or accounted for until he died in hospital at Richmond, Virginia, June 28, 1862 of "cont[inued] fever."

PENRY, BOONE T., 1st Sergeant
Born in Davie County where he resided prior to enlisting in Davie County at age 24, August 6, 1861. Mustered in as Private. Present or accounted for until hospitalized at Richmond, Virginia, June 13, 1862, with a gunshot wound of the foot; however, place and date wounded not reported. Returned to duty on or about September 2, 1862, and was promoted to Sergeant on December 6, 1862. Promoted to 1st Sergeant on April 17, 1863. Present or accounted for until killed at Chancellorsville, Virginia May 3, 1863.

PENRY, WILLIAM H., Private
Resided in Davie County and was by occupation a

farmer prior to enlisting in Davie County at age 25, April 26, 1861. Present or accounted for until captured at or near Frederick City, Maryland, September 10-12, 1862. Confined at Fort Delaware, Delaware, until transferred to Aiken's Landing, James River, Virginia, October 2, 1862, for exchange. Declared exchanged at Aiken's Landing on November 10, 1862. Rejoined the company prior to January 1, 1863, and present or accounted for until killed at Gettysburg, Pennsylvania, July 1, 1863.

POOL, BENJAMIN F., Private
Born in Randolph County and resided in Davie County where he was by occupation a farmer prior to enlisting in Davie County at age 21, August 6, 1861. Present or accounted for until he died in hospital at Richmond, Virginia, August 5, 1862, of disease.

POOL, RANDOLPH, Private
Resided in Davie County where he enlisted at age 23, August 6, 1861. Present or accounted for until wounded in the left knee at Chancellorsville, Virginia, May 3, 1863. Rejoined the company prior to July 14, 1863, when he was captured at Falling Waters, Maryland. Confined at Old Capitol Prison, Washington, D.C., until transferred to Point Lookout, Maryland, August 8, 1863. Transferred to Elmira, New York, August 16, 1864. Paroled at Elmira on March 10, 1865, and transferred to Boulware's Wharf, James River, Virginia, March 15, 1865, for exchange. Paroled at Mocksville on June 9, 1865.

RABEN, SAMUEL W., Private
Resided in Davie County where he enlisted at age 26, August 6, 1861. Present or accounted for until killed at Gaines' Mill, Virginia, June 27, 1862.

RHIDENHOUR, JOHN W., Private
Resided in Davidson County and enlisted in Davie County at age 34, July 16, 1862, for the war. Present or accounted for until wounded and captured at Gettysburg, Pennsylvania, July 1, 1863. Hospitalized at Chester, Pennsylvania, where he died August 12, 1863, of "traumatic erysipelas."

RIDENHOUR, ANDERSON J., Private
Resided in Davidson County and enlisted in Davie County at age 30, January 3, 1863, for the war. Present or accounted for until wounded and captured at Gettysburg, Pennsylvania, July 1, 1863. Hospitalized at Chester, Pennsylvania, where he died September 10, 1863, of "chronic diarrhoea."

RIDENHOUR, LOSSON, Private
Resided in Davie County and was by occupation a farmer prior to enlisting in Davie County at age 26, April 26, 1861. Present or accounted for until he died in hospital at Richmond, Virginia, July 2, 1862, of "typhoid fever."

SAIN, ANDREW, Private
Resided in Davie County where he enlisted at age 21, August 6, 1861. Mustered in as Private and promoted to Corporal on September 1, 1863. Reduced to ranks in May-June, 1864. Present or accounted for until paroled at Appomattox Court House, Virginia, April 9, 1865.

SAIN, JACOB, Private
Born in Davie County where he resided as a farmer

prior to enlisting in Davie County at age 20, April 26, 1861. Present or accounted for until he died in hospital at Richmond, Virginia, on or about August 4, 1862, of disease.

SAIN, JOSEPH, Private
Born in Davie County where he resided as a miller prior to enlisting in Davie County at age 23, April 26, 1861. Present or accounted for until he died in hospital or "on the road between Winchester and Staunton" on or about October 24, 1862, of disease.

SAIN, WILLIAM, Private
Born in Davie County* where he resided prior to enlisting in Davie County at age 27, August 6, 1861. Present or accounted for until he died in hospital at Petersburg, Virginia, May 13, 1862, of disease.

SEAGRAVES, FRANK, Private
Resided in Yadkin County and enlisted at Camp Vance on March 16, 1864, for the war. Present or accounted for until reported missing from May 6, 1864, through October, 1864. Took the Oath of Allegiance at Salisbury on June 15, 1865.

SHAW, AUGUSTUS, Private
Resided in Davie County where he enlisted at age 34, March 26, 1863, for the war. Deserted April 12, 1863.

SHAW, WILLIAM, Private
Resided in Davie County where he enlisted at age 36, March 26, 1863, for the war. Deserted April 12, 1863, but was reported in confinement from September-October, 1863, through February, 1864. "Shot by order of court martial" on April 26, 1864.

SHEEK, ALBERT A., Private
Resided in Davie County and was by occupation a clerk prior to enlisting in Davie County at age 17, June 18, 1861. Present or accounted for until wounded near Richmond, Virginia, in March-June, 1862. Rejoined the company prior to November 1, 1862, but was discharged prior to January 1, 1863. Reason discharged not reported.

SHEETS, JOHN, Private
Resided in Davie County where he enlisted at age 21, August 6, 1861. Present or accounted for until wounded and captured at Gettysburg, Pennsylvania, July 1-5, 1863. Confined at Fort Delaware, Delaware, until transferred to Point Lookout, Maryland, October 15-18, 1863. Released at Point Lookout on February 24, 1864, after taking the Oath of Allegiance and joining the U.S. Army. Unit to which assigned not reported.

SHIVES, A. C., Private
Enlisted on or about August 1, 1864, for the war. Paroled at Appomattox Court House, Virginia, April 9, 1865.

SIMMONS, HENRY, Private
Resided in Davie County where he enlisted at age 23, August 6, 1861. Present or accounted for until he died at home in Davie County in September, 1862, of disease.

SMITH, WILLIAM A., Private
Resided in Davie County and was by occupation a farmer prior to enlisting in Davie County at age 24, April 26, 1861. Mustered in as Private and appointed

Musician on June 1, 1861. Reduced to ranks in September-October, 1861. Present or accounted for until killed at Gaines' Mill, Virginia, June 27, 1862.

SPAUGH, GUTLIP, Private
Enlisted at Camp Holmes on February 28, 1864, for the war. Present or accounted for until wounded in the right arm at Malvern Hill, Virginia, June 13, 1864. Reported absent wounded until retired to the Invalid Corps on November 30, 1864.

STONESTREET, JOHN H., Private
Resided in Davie County where he enlisted at age 25, August 6, 1861. Present or accounted for until wounded at Spotsylvania Court House, Virginia, May 21, 1864. Rejoined the company in July-August, 1864, and present or accounted for until paroled at Appomattox Court House, Virginia, April 9, 1865.

SWARINGEN, SAMUEL T., Private
Previously served in Company H, 63rd Regiment N.C. Troops (5th Regiment N.C. Cavalry). Transferred to this company on July 25, 1864. Deserted to the enemy or was captured at Point of Rocks, Virginia, August 13, 1864. Confined at Fort Monroe, Virginia, until transferred to Point Lookout, Maryland, August 16, 1864. Paroled at Point Lookout and transferred to Boulware's Wharf, James River, Virginia, where he was received March 19, 1865, for exchange.

TAYLOR, LORENZO D., Private
Previously served in Company H, 3rd Regiment Georgia Infantry. "Drummed out" of that unit on June 18, 1861, and enlisted in this company the same day. Present or accounted for until transferred back to Company H, 3rd Regiment Georgia Infantry, December 29, 1862.

THOMAS, JOHN B., Private
Resided in Davie County and was by occupation a farmer prior to enlisting in Davie County at age 22, April 26, 1861. Present or accounted for until he died at Ben's Church, near Smithfield, Virginia, on or about July 26, 1861, of disease.

TOTTEN, JOHN C., Jr., Private
Resided in Davie or Caswell counties and was by occupation a farmer prior to enlisting in Davie County at age 26, August 6, 1861. Present or accounted for until captured at South Mountain, Maryland, September 14, 1862. Confined at Fort Delaware, Delaware, until transferred to Aiken's Landing, James River, Virginia, October 2, 1862, for exchange. Declared exchanged at Aiken's Landing on November 10, 1862. Transferred to Company A of this regiment on December 15, 1862.

TURNER, PINKNEY, Private
Resided in Davie County where he enlisted at age 27, August 6, 1861. Present or accounted for until captured at Falling Waters, Maryland, July 14, 1863. Confined at Point Lookout, Maryland, until paroled and transferred to City Point, Virginia, where he was received March 6, 1864, for exchange. Reported absent without leave until he rejoined the company in July-August, 1864. Present or accounted for until captured at Appomattox, Virginia, April 6, 1865. Confined at Point Lookout, Maryland, until released on June 21, 1865, after taking the Oath of Allegiance.

TUTTAROW, GEORGE W., Private
Resided in Davie County and was by occupation a blacksmith prior to enlisting in Davie County at age 20, April 26, 1861. Present or accounted for until wounded near Richmond, Virginia, in March-June, 1862. Battle in which wounded not reported. Rejoined the company in November-December, 1862, and present or accounted for until wounded at Chancellorsville, Virginia, May 3, 1863. Rejoined the company in January-February, 1864, and present or accounted for until paroled at Appomattox Court House, Virginia, April 9, 1865.

TUTTEROW, JOHN V., Private
Resided in Davie County where he enlisted at age 21, August 6, 1861. Present or accounted for until wounded in the left ankle at Gettysburg, Pennsylvania, July 1, 1863. Rejoined the company in March-April, 1864, and present or accounted for until wounded in the right lung at Spotsylvania Court House, Virginia, May 10, 1864. Rejoined the company in July-August, 1864, and present or accounted for until captured near Petersburg, Virginia, March 25, 1865. Confined at Point Lookout, Maryland, until released on June 21, 1865, after taking the Oath of Allegiance.

VERBER, PETER, Private
Enlisted at Camp Holmes on January 11, 1864, for the war. Present or accounted for until wounded at Wilderness, Virginia, May 5, 1864. Died in September-October, 1864, of wounds. Place of death not reported.

VINAGUM, DANIEL V., Private
Resided in Davie County and was by occupation a tailor prior to enlisting in Davie County at age 21, April 26, 1861. Present or accounted for until wounded at South Mountain, Maryland, September 14, 1862. Reported on detail as a teamster from October 25, 1862, through October, 1863. Rejoined the company in November-December, 1863, and present or accounted for until wounded at or near Petersburg, Virginia, June 22, 1864. Rejoined the company in September-October, 1864, and present or accounted for until paroled at Appomattox Court House, Virginia, April 9, 1865.

VINAGUM, THOMAS V., Private
Resided in Davie County and was by occupation a tobacconist prior to enlisting in Davie County at age 22, April 26, 1861. Present or accounted for until wounded at Gettysburg, Pennsylvania, July 1, 1863. Died in hospital at Staunton, Virginia, August 28, 1863, of wounds. Roll of Honor indicates that he "distinguished himself as a scout in several hard fought battles."

VON EATON, JOHN I., Sergeant
Born in Davie County where he resided as a farmer prior to enlisting in Davie County at age 22, April 26, 1861. Mustered in as Sergeant. Present or accounted for until "killed by the accidental discharge of his own gun" near Orange Court House, Virginia, November 29, 1862.

VON EATON, SAMUEL P., Private
Resided in Davie County and was by occupation a student prior to enlisting in Davie County at age 26,

June 18, 1861. Present or accounted for until he died in hospital at Richmond, Virginia, July 1, 1862, of "continued fever."

WALLACE, DANIEL C., Private
Resided in Davie County and was by occupation a tobacconist prior to enlisting in Davie County at age 30, April 26, 1861. Present or accounted for until wounded near Richmond, Virginia, in March-June, 1862. Rejoined the company prior to November 1, 1862, and present or accounted for until wounded at Gettysburg, Pennsylvania, July 3, 1863. Died in Pennsylvania, July 7-8, 1863, of wounds.

WALSH, THOMAS F., Private
Enlisted at Camp Vance on March 14, 1864, for the war. Present or accounted for through October, 1864.

WEST, JILES, Private
Resided in Davie County where he enlisted at age 30, July 16, 1862, for the war. Present or accounted for until furloughed for sixty days from hospital at Richmond, Virginia, December 14, 1864. Paroled at Mocksville on June 9, 1865.

WHITAKER, ALFRED, Private
Born in Davie County where he resided as a farmer prior to enlisting in Davie County at age 18, April 26, 1861. Present or accounted for until killed in a skirmish on the Potomac River on September 5, 1862.

WHITAKER, NOAH, Private
Resided in Davie County and was by occupation a carpenter prior to enlisting in Davie County at age 34, April 26, 1861. Present or accounted for until discharged on July 26, 1862, under the provisions of the Conscript Act.

WHITE, MICHAEL, Private
Born in "Wadford" County, Ireland, and resided in Davie County where he was by occupation a farmer or laborer prior to enlisting in Davie County at age 30, April 26, 1861. Present or accounted for until discharged on August 12, 1862, by reason of being an "unnaturalized foreigner."

WILLIAMS, DANIEL M., Corporal
Resided in Davie County and was by occupation a clerk prior to enlisting in Davie County at age 20, April 26, 1861. Mustered in as Private. Present or accounted for until wounded and captured at Gettysburg, Pennsylvania, July 1-4, 1863. Hospitalized at Davids Island, New York Harbor, until paroled and transferred to City Point, Virginia, where he was received September 16, 1863, for exchange. Rejoined the company in March-April, 1864, and was promoted to Corporal on May 1, 1864. Present or accounted for until captured at Wilderness, Virginia, May 6, 1864. Confined at Point Lookout, Maryland, until transferred to Elmira, New York, August 10, 1864. Paroled at Elmira and transferred to James River, Virginia, February 20, 1865, for exchange. Hospitalized at Richmond, Virginia, until furloughed for thirty days on March 13, 1865. Paroled at Salisbury on May 23, 1865, and took the Oath of Allegiance on July 7, 1865.

WINTER, JAMES, Private
Enlisted at Camp Vance on January 25, 1864, for the war. Deserted in March-April, 1864.

WOODLIEF, JONATHAN E., Private
Born in Granville County and was by occupation a farmer prior to enlisting at Camp Holmes on February 19, 1864, for the war. Present or accounted for until discharged on April 10, 1864, by reason of "spasmodic contraction of the muscles of respiration, resembling epilepsy." Discharge papers give his age as 36.

COMPANY G

This company, known as the Edgecombe Rifles, was from Edgecombe County and enlisted at Tarboro on May 8, 1861. It left for Garysburg the same day. There it was assigned to the regiment as Company G. After joining the regiment the company functioned as a part of the regiment, and its history for the war period is recorded as a part of the regimental history.

The information contained in the following roster of the company was compiled principally from company muster rolls for May 16, 1861, through October, 1864. No company muster rolls were found for the period after October, 1864. In addition to the company muster rolls, Roll of Honor records, receipt rolls, hospital records, prisoner of war records, and other primary records, supplemented by state pension applications, United Daughters of the Confederacy records, and postwar rosters and histories, all provided useful information.

OFFICERS
CAPTAINS

HYMAN, JOSEPH H.
Resided in Edgecombe County and enlisted at age 26. Elected Captain to rank from May 1, 1861. Present or accounted for until promoted to Major on October 15, 1862, and transferred to the Field and Staff of this regiment.

FUQUA, JOHN A.
Resided in Edgecombe County and enlisted at age 22. Elected 1st Lieutenant to rank from May 1, 1861, and promoted to Captain on October 15, 1862. Present or accounted for until wounded in the left arm at Chancellorsville, Virginia, May 3, 1863. Reported absent wounded through February, 1864, and reported absent on detail from March-April, 1864, through June, 1864. Retired to the Invalid Corps on August 8, 1864. Later served on the staff of Brigadier General Bradley T. Johnson as Assistant Commandant of the prison at Salisbury.

BROWN, GREY L.
Resided in Edgecombe County and was by occupation a farmer prior to enlisting in Edgecombe County at age 26, May 8, 1861. Mustered in as Sergeant and promoted to 1st Sergeant on October 15, 1861. Present or accounted for until wounded at Williamsburg,

Virginia, on or about May 5, 1862. Rejoined the company prior to July 1, 1862. Appointed 2nd Lieutenant on March 8, 1863. Present or accounted for until wounded in the left thigh and captured at Chancellorsville, Virginia, May 3, 1863. Hospitalized at Washington, D.C., until transferred to Old Capitol Prison, Washington, June 25, 1863. Paroled on or about June 30, 1863. Rejoined the company in September-October, 1863, and was promoted to 1st Lieutenant on November 14, 1863. Promoted to Captain on August 8, 1864. Present or accounted for until paroled at Appomattox Court House, Virginia, April 9, 1865.

LIEUTENANTS

ATKINSON, RUFUS, 2nd Lieutenant
Resided in Edgecombe County and was by occupation a teacher prior to enlisting in Edgecombe County at age 21, May 8, 1861. Mustered in as Corporal and promoted to Sergeant on October 15, 1861. Elected 3rd Lieutenant to rank from April 26, 1862, and was promoted to 2nd Lieutenant on October 15, 1862. Present or accounted for until wounded at Gettysburg, Pennsylvania, July 1, 1863. Captured on or about July 30, 1863. Died in a Federal hospital at Winchester, Virginia, August 2-3, 1863, of wounds received at Gettysburg.

CIVALLIER, CHARLES N., 1st Lieutenant
Resided in Edgecombe County and enlisted at age 24. Elected 2nd Lieutenant to rank from May 1, 1861, and was promoted to 1st Lieutenant on October 15, 1862. Present or accounted for until wounded in the left elbow at Boonsboro, Maryland, September 14, 1862. Reported absent wounded or absent without leave until he resigned on November 14, 1863, by reason of wounds received at Boonsboro.

JENKINS, BENNETT P., 2nd Lieutenant
Resided in Edgecombe County and was by occupation a farmer prior to enlisting in Edgecombe County at age 20, May 8, 1861. Mustered in as 1st Sergeant and was elected 2nd Lieutenant to rank from October 15, 1861. Present or accounted for until he was defeated for reelection when the regiment was reorganized on April 26, 1862.

McNAIR, WILLIAM T., 2nd Lieutenant
Resided in Edgecombe County and enlisted at age 27. Elected 2nd Lieutenant on April 25, 1861, to rank from May 1, 1861. Present or accounted for until he resigned on or about October 10, 1861. Reason he resigned not reported.

STANCILL, GEORGE W., 1st Lieutenant
Resided in Edgecombe County and was by occupation a farmer prior to enlisting in Edgecombe County at age 20, May 8, 1861. Mustered in as Corporal. Present or accounted for until wounded at Williamsburg, Virginia, on or about May 5, 1862. Promoted to Sergeant on May 25, 1862, and rejoined the company prior to July 1, 1862. Promoted to 1st Sergeant on May 8, 1863. Present or accounted for until wounded at Gettysburg, Pennsylvania, July 1-3, 1863. Rejoined the company prior to September 1, 1863, and was appointed 2nd Lieutenant on November 20, 1863. Promoted to 1st Lieutenant on August 8,

1864. Present or accounted for until paroled at Appomattox Court House, Virginia, April 9, 1865.

NONCOMMISSIONED OFFICERS AND PRIVATES

ANDERSON, VAN BUREN, Private
Resided in Edgecombe County and was by occupation a farmer prior to enlisting in Edgecombe County at age 20, May 8, 1861. Present or accounted for until captured at Williamsburg, Virginia, May 5, 1862. Confined at Fort Monroe, Virginia. Paroled prior to July 1, 1862, and rejoined the company prior to November 1, 1862. Present or accounted for until reported absent sick on June 1, 1863. Reported absent sick through April, 1864. No further records.

ANDREWS, EDMOND, Sergeant
Resided in Edgecombe County and was by occupation a farmer prior to enlisting in Edgecombe County at age 18, May 8, 1861. Mustered in as Private. Present or accounted for until wounded at Williamsburg, Virginia, on or about May 5, 1862. Promoted to Corporal on September 17, 1862, and rejoined the company in November-December, 1862. Promoted to Sergeant on May 6, 1864. Present or accounted for until paroled at Appomattox Court House, Virginia, April 9, 1865.

ANDREWS, KENNETH, Private
Resided in Edgecombe County and was by occupation a farmer prior to enlisting in Edgecombe County at age 25, May 8, 1861. Present or accounted for until admitted to hospital at Richmond, Virginia, May 9, 1862, with a gunshot wound; however, place and date wounded not reported. Returned to duty on June 1, 1862, and present or accounted for until he died in hospital at Richmond on or about January 10, 1863, of "variola confluent" and "erysipelas."

ANDREWS, WILSON J., Corporal
Born in Edgecombe County where he resided as a painter prior to enlisting in Edgecombe County at age 28, May 8, 1861. Mustered in as Private and promoted to Corporal on October 15, 1861. Present or accounted for until wounded and captured at Williamsburg, Virginia, May 5, 1862. Confined at Old Capitol Prison, Washington, D.C., until transferred to Aiken's Landing, James River, Virginia, where he was received August 5, 1862, for exchange. Reported absent wounded through October, 1862, but rejoined the company prior to December 13, 1862, when he was killed at Fredericksburg, Virginia.

ATKINS, LAWRENCE, Private
Resided in Edgecombe County and was by occupation a carpenter prior to enlisting in Edgecombe County at age 26, May 8, 1861. Present or accounted for until wounded and captured at Williamsburg, Virginia, May 5, 1862. Hospitalized at Washington, D.C., until transferred to Old Capitol Prison, Washington, June 27, 1862. Transferred to Aiken's Landing, James River, Virginia, where he was exchanged on August 5, 1862. Captured at Boonsboro, Maryland, September 14, 1862. Exchanged at an unspecified date and rejoined the company prior to January 1, 1863. Present or accounted for until wounded at

Chancellorsville, Virginia, May 1-3, 1863. Rejoined the company prior to July 1, 1863, when he was wounded at Gettysburg, Pennsylvania. Rejoined the company in September-October, 1863, and present or accounted for until paroled at Appomattox Court House, Virginia, April 9, 1865.

ATKINS, WILLIAM H., Private

Resided in Edgecombe County and was by occupation a painter prior to enlisting in Edgecombe County at age 24, May 8, 1861. Present or accounted for until wounded and captured at Williamsburg, Virginia, May 5, 1862. Confined at Fort Delaware, Delaware, until transferred to Aiken's Landing, James River, Virginia, where he was received August 5, 1862, for exchange. Rejoined the company in November-December, 1863, and present or accounted for until wounded at Chancellorsville, Virginia, May 3, 1863. Rejoined the company in September-October, 1863, and present or accounted for until paroled at Appomattox Court House, Virginia, April 9, 1865.

ATKINSON, MARK B., Private

Resided in Edgecombe County where he enlisted at age 18, August 11, 1861. Present or accounted for until captured at Boonsboro, Maryland, September 15, 1862. Confined at Fort Delaware, Delaware, until transferred to Aiken's Landing, James River, Virginia, October 2, 1862, for exchange. Declared exchanged at Aiken's Landing on November 10, 1862. Rejoined the company prior to January 1, 1863, and present or accounted for until captured at Gettysburg, Pennsylvania, July 3-4, 1863. Confined at Fort Delaware until transferred to Point Lookout, Maryland, October 15-18, 1863. Paroled at Point Lookout on February 18, 1865, and transferred to Boulware's and Cox's Wharf, James River, where he was received February 20-21, 1865, for exchange.

BARNHILL, JESSE C., Private

Resided in Edgecombe County and was by occupation a farmer prior to enlisting in Edgecombe County at age 21, May 8, 1861. Present or accounted for until discharged at Richmond, Virginia, September 6, 1862, by reason of "repeated and severe attacks of rheumatism." Died in Edgecombe County on November 18, 1862. Cause of death not reported.

BARNHILL, MARTIN VAN BUREN, Corporal

Resided in Edgecombe County and was by occupation a farmer prior to enlisting in Edgecombe County at age 19, May 8, 1861. Mustered in as Private. Present or accounted for until wounded and captured at Gettysburg, Pennsylvania, July 1-4, 1863. Hospitalized at Davids Island, New York Harbor, until paroled and transferred to City Point, Virginia, where he was received August 28, 1863, for exchange. Rejoined the company in November-December, 1863, and was promoted to Corporal on May 6, 1864. Present or accounted for until hospitalized at Richmond, Virginia, June 8, 1864, with a gunshot wound; however, place and date wounded not reported. Rejoined the company in September-October, 1864, and present or accounted for until paroled at Burkeville Junction, Virginia, April 14-17, 1865.

BELL, BENJAMIN, Private

Born in Edgecombe County where he resided as a farmer prior to enlisting in Edgecombe County at age 17, May 8, 1861. Present or accounted for until he died in hospital at Richmond, Virginia, June 21, 1862, of "typhoid fever."

BELL, NOAH, Private

Born in Edgecombe County where he resided as a farmer prior to enlisting in Edgecombe County at age 15, May 8, 1861. Present or accounted for until discharged on August 4, 1862, by reason of being under age. [May have served later in Company D, 40th Regiment N.C. Troops (3rd Regiment N.C. Artillery).]

BELL, THEODORE, Private

Resided in Edgecombe or Halifax counties and was by occupation a carpenter prior to enlisting in Edgecombe County at age 24, May 8, 1861. Present or accounted for until wounded in the arm and shoulder and captured at Boonsboro, Maryland, September 14, 1862. Confined at Fort McHenry, Maryland, until paroled and transferred to Aiken's Landing, James River, Virginia, on or about October 14, 1862. Declared exchanged at Aiken's Landing on November 10, 1862. Reported absent wounded through June, 1863. Admitted to hospital at Farmville, Virginia, July 6, 1863, with a wound of the right side and returned to duty on July 16, 1863. Present or accounted for until captured at Appomattox, Virginia, April 3, 1865. Confined at Point Lookout, Maryland, until released on June 23, 1865, after taking the Oath of Allegiance.

BLACKWOOD, NATHANIEL, Corporal

Resided in Edgecombe County and was by occupation a teamster prior to enlisting in Edgecombe County at age 24, May 8, 1861. Mustered in as Private and promoted to Corporal on December 20, 1862. Present or accounted for until wounded in the right leg at Chancellorsville, Virginia, May 1-3, 1863. Died in hospital at Richmond, Virginia, June 10, 1863, of "pneumonia."

BLOUNT, L. WILLIAM, Private

Resided in Edgecombe County and was by occupation a farmer prior to enlisting in Edgecombe County at age 17, May 8, 1861. Present or accounted for until captured at or near Chancellorsville, Virginia, on or about May 1-3, 1863. Paroled May 4, 1863. Rejoined the company prior to July 1, 1863, when he was wounded and captured at Gettysburg, Pennsylvania. Died in hospital at Davids Island, New York Harbor, August 13, 1863, of "pyamia."

BOSEMAN, JAMES H., Private

Born in Edgecombe County where he resided as a farmer prior to enlisting in Edgecombe County at age 16, May 8, 1861. Present or accounted for until discharged on August 4, 1862, by reason of being under age.

BOZEMAN, ISAAC, Private

Resided in Edgecombe County and was by occupation a wheelwright prior to enlisting in Edgecombe County at age 24, May 8, 1861. Present or accounted for until "drummed out of service Nov[ember] 7, 1861 for dishonorable conduct."

BRANTLY, BENJAMIN F., Private
Enlisted in Wake County on August 12, 1864, for the war. Present or accounted for until paroled at Farmville, Virginia, April 11-21, 1865.

BRASSNELL, C. S., Private
Place and date of enlistment not reported. Paroled at Appomattox Court House, Virginia, April 9, 1865.

BRASWELL, JAMES F., Private
Resided in Edgecombe County where he enlisted at age 44, August 11, 1861. Present or accounted for until he died in hospital at Huguenot Springs, Virginia, September 28, 1862, of "debilitas."

BROWN, G. J., Private
Place and date of enlistment not reported. Paroled at Appomattox Court House, Virginia, April 9, 1865.

BURGESS, GEORGE, Private
Resided in Edgecombe County where he enlisted at age 18, October 25, 1862, for the war. Present or accounted for until wounded in the thigh at or near Petersburg, Virginia, June 22, 1864. Reported absent wounded through October, 1864. Paroled at Greensboro in 1865.

BURGESS, LAWRENCE, Private
Resided in Edgecombe County and was by occupation a farmer prior to enlisting in Edgecombe County at age 18, May 8, 1861. Present or accounted for until wounded in the right thigh at Chancellorsville, Virginia, May 3, 1863. Died at home in Edgecombe County on August 6, 1863, of wounds.

CHAMBERLAIN, LEWIS L., Private
Resided in Yadkin County and enlisted in Wake County at age 27, September 27, 1862, for the war. Present or accounted for until reported absent without leave from March 20, 1863, through August, 1864. Reported "in arrest" in September-October, 1864.

CHAPEL, SILAS C., Private
Born in Wilkes County where he resided as a farmer prior to enlisting in Wake County at age 30, September 27, 1862, for the war. Present or accounted for until wounded in the left forearm and captured at Chancellorsville, Virginia, May 3, 1863. Hospitalized at Washington, D.C., until paroled and transferred to City Point, Virginia, where he was received June 30, 1863, for exchange. Reported absent wounded until discharged on April 25, 1864, by reason of wounds received at Chancellorsville.

CLARK, HENRY T., Private
Resided in Edgecombe County and was by occupation a farmer prior to enlisting in Edgecombe County at age 27, May 8, 1861. Present or accounted for until he died in hospital near Richmond, Virginia, on August 12, 1862. Cause of death not reported.

COBB, G. W., Private
Enlisted in Wake County on May 7, 1864, for the war. Present or accounted for through June, 1864. No further records.

COGINS, THOMAS, Private
Born in Edgecombe County where he resided as a farmer prior to enlisting in Edgecombe County at age 21, May 8, 1861. Present or accounted for until transferred to the C. S. Navy on February 20, 1862.

DENTON, W. J., Private
Place and date of enlistment not reported. Paroled at Appomattox Court House, Virginia, April 9, 1865.

DRIVER, RICHARDSON, Private
Resided in Franklin County and enlisted in Wake County on November 25, 1863, for the war. Present or accounted for until captured in hospital at Richmond, Virginia, April 3, 1865. Confined at Libby Prison, Richmond, until transferred to Newport News, Virginia, April 23, 1865. Released at Newport News on June 30, 1865, after taking the Oath of Allegiance.

DUPREE, WILLIAM T., Sergeant
Resided in Edgecombe County and was by occupation a farmer prior to enlisting in Edgecombe County at age 28, May 8, 1861. Mustered in as Corporal and was promoted to Sergeant on October 15, 1861. Present or accounted for until wounded at Williamsburg, Virginia, May 5, 1862. Rejoined the company in November-December, 1862, and present or accounted for until wounded in the left shoulder at Chancellorsville, Virginia, May 3, 1863. Reported absent wounded until captured by the enemy at Tarboro on June 21, 1863. Confined at Fort Monroe, Virginia, where he was paroled on August 4, 1863. Rejoined the company in September-October, 1863, and present or accounted for until wounded at Spotsylvania Court House, Virginia, May 18, 1864. Reported absent wounded through October, 1864. Captured in hospital at Richmond, Virginia, April 3, 1865, and confined at Libby Prison, Richmond, until transferred to Newport News, Virginia, April 23, 1865. Released at Newport News on June 30, 1865, after taking the Oath of Allegiance.

DURHAM, CALVIN, Private
Enlisted in Wake County on January 28, 1864, for the war. Present or accounted for until reported absent without leave from June 25, 1864, through October, 1864. No further records.

EHEARN, JERRY, Private
Resided in Edgecombe County and was by occupation a plumber prior to enlisting in Edgecombe County at age 19, May 8, 1861. Present or accounted for until hospitalized at Richmond, Virginia, June 4, 1862, with a gunshot wound of the foot; however, place and date wounded not reported. Reported absent wounded until discharged on February 10, 1863.

ELIXON, JOHN B., Private
Born in Edgecombe County where he resided as a teamster prior to enlisting in Edgecombe County at age 18, May 8, 1861. Present or accounted for until wounded at Boonsboro, Maryland, September 14, 1862. Rejoined the company in November-December, 1862, and present or accounted for until wounded and captured at Gettysburg, Pennsylvania, July 1-5, 1863. Hospitalized at Davids Island, New York Harbor, until paroled and transferred to City Point, Virginia, where he was received August 28, 1863, for exchange. Rejoined the company in November-December, 1863, and present or accounted for until captured at Sutherland's Station, Virginia, April 3, 1865. Confined at Point Lookout,

Maryland, until released on June 11, 1865, after taking the Oath of Allegiance.

FRANKLIN, ISAAC, Private
Enlisted at Camp Vance on August 26, 1863, for the war. Present or accounted for until wounded at or near Petersburg, Virginia, June 18, 1864. Died "at home" prior to November 19, 1864. Cause and exact date of death not reported.

GARDNER, BENJAMIN, Private
Resided in Edgecombe County and was by occupation a carpenter prior to enlisting in Edgecombe County at age 22, May 8, 1861. Present or accounted for until discharged on or about September 29, 1861, by reason of disability.

GARRETT, A., Private
Place and date of enlistment not reported. Name appears on a list of prisoners paroled at Appomattox Court House, Virginia, April 9, 1865.

GARRETT, WILLIAM E., Corporal
Resided in Edgecombe County where he enlisted at age 19, August 1, 1861. Mustered in as Private and promoted to Corporal on September 1, 1863. Present or accounted for until paroled at Appomattox Court House, Virginia, April 9, 1865. Roll of Honor indicates he was wounded at Fredericksburg, Virginia, and was wounded in the thigh at Chancellorsville, Virginia.

GAY, SILAS H., Corporal
Born in Edgecombe County where he resided as a farmer prior to enlisting in Edgecombe County at age 16, August 11, 1861. Mustered in as Private. Discharged on or about November 15, 1862, by reason of being under age. Reenlisted in this company at Camp Gregg, Virginia, June 1, 1863. Promoted to Corporal in November, 1864-April, 1865. Present or accounted for until paroled at Appomattox Court House, Virginia, April 9, 1865.

GREGORY, SANDFORD B., Private
Enlisted in Wake County on March 26, 1864, for the war. Present or accounted for through October, 1864.

GRIFFIN, BENJAMIN, Private
Resided in Edgecombe County and was by occupation a farmer prior to enlisting in Edgecombe County at age 21, May 8, 1861. Present or accounted for until he died in hospital at Lynchburg, Virginia, December 24, 1862, of "pneumonia."

GRIMES, WILLIAM B., Private
Born in Edgecombe County where he resided as a farmer prior to enlisting in Edgecombe County at age 21, May 8, 1861. Present or accounted for until killed at Gaines' Mill, Virginia, June 27, 1862.

HAMME, F., Private
Place and date of enlistment not reported. Captured at Spotsylvania Court House, Virginia, May 20, 1864, and confined at Point Lookout, Maryland, until transferred to Elmira, New York, July 3, 1864. Released at Elmira on June 30, 1865.

HARRELL, J. H., Private
Enlisted at Camp Holmes on January 28, 1864, for the war. Present or accounted for through February, 1864. No further records.

HARRIS, IRVIN T., Private
Resided in Edgecombe County and was by occupation a farmer prior to enlisting in Edgecombe County at age 22, May 8, 1861. Present or accounted for until captured at Sutherland's Station, Virginia, April 2, 1865. Confined at Hart's Island, New York Harbor, until released on June 17, 1865, after taking the Oath of Allegiance.

HARRIS, SHERWOOD, Private
Resided in Edgecombe County and was by occupation a teamster prior to enlisting in Edgecombe County at age 18, May 8, 1861. Present or accounted for through April, 1864.

HEDGEPETH, JOSEPH S., Private
Resided in Edgecombe County and was by occupation a farmer prior to enlisting in Edgecombe County at age 18, May 8, 1861. Present or accounted for until transferred to the C. S. Navy on February 20, 1862.

HICKS, REDDEN, Private
Born in Edgecombe County where he resided as a farmer prior to enlisting in Edgecombe County at age 21, May 8, 1861. Present or accounted for until hospitalized at Richmond, Virginia, June 2, 1862, with a gunshot wound; however, place and date wounded not reported. Discharged September 13, 1862, by reason of "typhoid fever, general debility, [and] extreme emaciation."

HINSHAW, MOSES E., Private
Enlisted at Camp Holmes on January 29, 1864, for the war. Present or accounted for until reported captured on May 6, 1864; however, records of the Federal Provost Marshal do not substantiate that report. Company muster rolls indicate he was a prisoner of war through October, 1864. No further records.

HOLDEN, JOHN U., Private
Enlisted in Wake County on December 16, 1863, for the war. Present or accounted for until captured in battle at the North Anna River, Virginia, May 24, 1864. Confined at Point Lookout, Maryland, until released on June 7, 1864, after joining the U.S. Army. Assigned to Company A, 1st Regiment U.S. Volunteer Infantry.

HOWARD, CALVIN W., Corporal
Born in Edgecombe County where he resided as a farmer prior to enlisting in Edgecombe County at age 20, May 8, 1861. Mustered in as Private and promoted to Corporal on October 15, 1861. Present or accounted for until he died in hospital at Richmond, Virginia, July 12, 1862, of "typh[oi]d fever."

HOWARD, JAMES T., 1st Sergeant
Resided in Edgecombe County and was by occupation a farmer prior to enlisting in Edgecombe County at age 18, May 8, 1861. Mustered in as Private and promoted to Corporal on May 25, 1862. Present or accounted for until wounded at Gettysburg, Pennsylvania, July 1-3, 1863. Rejoined the company prior to September 1, 1863, when he was promoted to Sergeant. Promoted to 1st Sergeant on November 20, 1863. Present or accounted for until wounded at or near Petersburg, Virginia, June 22, 1864. Reported absent wounded through October, 1864.

HUSSEY, WILLIAM M., Private

Born in Edgecombe County where he resided as a shoemaker prior to enlisting in Edgecombe County at age 29, May 8, 1861. Present or accounted for until killed at Williamsburg, Virginia, May 5, 1862.

HYDE, JOHN, Private

Resided in Edgecombe County and was by occupation a farmer prior to enlisting in Edgecombe County at age 44, May 8, 1861. Present or accounted for until discharged on or about September 29, 1861, by reason of disability.

JONES, ELISHA R., Private

Resided in Edgecombe County and was by occupation a farmer prior to enlisting in Edgecombe County at age 22, May 8, 1861. Present or accounted for until wounded at Gettysburg, Pennsylvania, July 3, 1863. Died of wounds the same day.

KEEL, JOSEPH H., Sergeant

Resided in Edgecombe County and was by occupation a farmer prior to enlisting in Edgecombe County at age 27, May 8, 1861. Mustered in as Corporal and promoted to Sergeant on April 26, 1862. Present or accounted for until wounded in the left hand and/or left elbow at Gettysburg, Pennsylvania, July 1, 1863. Little finger amputated. Reported absent wounded until he returned to duty in November-December, 1863. Present or accounted for until paroled at Appomattox Court House, Virginia, April 9, 1865.

LANGLEY, FRANKLIN SHADY, Private

Born in Edgecombe County where he resided as a farmer prior to enlisting in Edgecombe County at age 17, May 8, 1861. Present or accounted for until discharged on August 4, 1862, under the provisions of the Conscript Act.

LANGLEY, WILLIS P., Private

Born in Edgecombe County where he resided as a farmer prior to enlisting in Edgecombe County at age 19, May 8, 1861. Present or accounted for until wounded in the thigh and captured at Williamsburg, Virginia, May 5, 1862. Hospitalized at Fort Monroe, Virginia, where he died August 29, 1862, of wounds and/or remittent fever.

LAWRENCE, JESSE, Private

Born in Edgecombe County where he resided as a farmer prior to enlisting in Edgecombe County at age 28, May 8, 1861. Present or accounted for until killed at Williamsburg, Virginia, May 5, 1862.

LEWIS, JAMES T., Corporal

Resided in Edgecombe County where he enlisted at age 21, August 10, 1861. Mustered in as Private. Present or accounted for until captured at Williamsburg, Virginia, May 5, 1862. Confined at Fort Monroe, Virginia. Exchanged at an unspecified date and rejoined the company in November-December, 1862. Promoted to Corporal on November 20, 1863, and present or accounted for until wounded in the arm at Spotsylvania Court House, Virginia, May 18, 1864. Rejoined the company in September-October, 1864, and present or accounted for through October, 1864.

LILLY, HENRY D., Private

Resided in Edgecombe County and was by occupation a farmer prior to enlisting in Edgecombe County

at age 24, May 8, 1861. Present or accounted for until wounded "through both jaws" at Gettysburg, Pennsylvania, July 1, 1863. Rejoined the company in September-October, 1863, and present or accounted for until wounded at Petersburg, Virginia, June 22, 1864. Rejoined the company in September-October, 1864, and present or accounted for until paroled at Appomattox Court House, Virginia, April 9, 1865.

LOGAN, WINSTON, Private

Enlisted in Wake County on March 22, 1864, for the war. Present or accounted for until wounded at or near Petersburg, Virginia, June 22, 1864. Reported absent wounded until he returned to duty on August 24, 1864. Reported absent without leave on October 18, 1864. No further records.

MARSHALL, JESSE E., Private

Born in Edgecombe County where he resided as a farmer prior to enlisting in Edgecombe County at age 17, May 8, 1861. Present or accounted for until wounded and captured at Williamsburg, Virginia, May 5, 1862. Hospitalized at Washington, D.C., where he died June 12, 1862, of wounds.

MATHEWS, CALVIN, Private

Resided in Edgecombe County and was by occupation a miller prior to enlisting in Northampton County at age 40, May 17, 1861. Present or accounted for until he died at Richmond, Virginia, August 15, 1862. Cause of death not reported.

MAYO, JAMES R., Sergeant

Resided in Edgecombe County and was by occupation a farmer prior to enlisting in Edgecombe County at age 21, May 8, 1861. Mustered in as Private and promoted to Corporal on December 13, 1862. Present or accounted for until wounded and captured at Gettysburg, Pennsylvania, July 1, 1863. Hospitalized at Chester, Pennsylvania, until transferred to City Point, Virginia, where he was received August 20, 1863, for exchange. Rejoined the company in November-December, 1863, and was promoted to Sergeant on November 20, 1863. Present or accounted for through April, 1864. No further records.

MEDFORD, JAMES R., Private

Resided in Edgecombe County and was by occupation a miller prior to enlisting in Edgecombe County at age 21, May 8, 1861. Present or accounted for until captured at Boonsboro, Maryland, or at South Mountain, Maryland, September 14, 1862. Confined at Fort Delaware, Delaware, until transferred to Aiken's Landing, James River, Virginia, October 2, 1862, for exchange. Declared exchanged at Aiken's Landing on November 10, 1862. Reported absent without leave from November-December, 1862, through February, 1863, but rejoined the company in March-April, 1863. Present or accounted for until wounded at Gettysburg, Pennsylvania, July 1, 1863. Rejoined the company in November-December, 1863, and present or accounted for until wounded in the left leg at or near Cold Harbor, Virginia, May 31, 1864. Reported absent wounded or absent sick through October, 1864, but rejoined the company prior to April 2, 1865, when he was captured on the South Side Railroad. Confined at Hart's Island, New York Harbor, until released on June 17, 1865, after taking the Oath of Allegiance.

MEHEGAN, ROBERT N., Private
Enlisted in the "fall" of 1864 for the war. Paroled at Appomattox Court House, Virginia, April 9, 1865.

MICHAEL, HENRY, Private
Born in Davidson County* and was by occupation a farmer prior to enlisting in Wake County at age 43, February 28, 1864, for the war. Present or accounted for until discharged on April 2, 1864, by reason of "tubercular disease of the lungs."

MICRARY, WILLIAM, Private
Enlisted in Wake County on February 28, 1864, for the war. Present or accounted for through February 25, 1865.

MILLS, CHURCHWELL, Private
Resided in Edgecombe County and was by occupation a farmer prior to enlisting in Edgecombe County at age 21, May 8, 1861. Present or accounted for until he died in Edgecombe County on July 3 or July 23, 1863. Cause of death not reported.

MOORE, MOSES, Private
Resided in Edgecombe County and was by occupation a farmer prior to enlisting in Edgecombe County at age 30, May 8, 1861. Present or accounted for until wounded in the hand at Gaines' Mill, Virginia, June 27, 1862. Captured at Warrenton, Virginia, September 29, 1862, and paroled. Rejoined the company in November-December, 1862, and present or accounted for until wounded in the hand at Chancellorsville, Virginia, May 1-3, 1863. Rejoined the company in July-August, 1863, and present or accounted for until wounded in the right hand at Wilderness, Virginia, May 6, 1864. Rejoined the company in September-October, 1864. Captured at Petersburg, Virginia, April 3, 1865, and confined at Hart's Island, New York Harbor, until released on June 17, 1865, after taking the Oath of Allegiance.

MORGAN, LAFAYETTE, Private
Resided in Edgecombe County and was by occupation a farmer prior to enlisting in Edgecombe County at age 17, May 8, 1861. Present or accounted for until killed at Williamsburg, Virginia, May 5, 1862.

MORRIS, ELIJAH, Private
Enlisted in Wake County on November 20, 1863, for the war. Present or accounted for until paroled at Appomattox Court House, Virginia, April 9, 1865.

MOSELEY, WILLIAM J., Private
Born in Edgecombe County where he resided as a wheelwright prior to enlisting in Edgecombe County at age 21, May 8, 1861. Present or accounted for until killed at Chancellorsville, Virginia, May 3, 1863.

MOXLEY, T., Private
Resided in Rockingham County. Place and date of enlistment not reported. Captured at Petersburg, Virginia, April 2, 1865, and confined at Point Lookout, Maryland, until released on June 29, 1865, after taking the Oath of Allegiance.

NICHOLS, MARTIN S., Private
Resided in Yadkin County and enlisted in Wake County at age 27, September 27, 1862, for the war. Present or accounted for until reported absent without leave from April 15, 1863, through October, 1863. Rejoined the company in November-Decem-

ber, 1863, and present or accounted for until wounded in the left arm and left side at Wilderness, Virginia, May 6, 1864. Reported absent wounded through October, 1864.

OBERRY, GREEN, Private
Enlisted in Wake County on October 17, 1864, for the war. Present or accounted for until furloughed for sixty days from hospital at Richmond, Virginia, December 19, 1864.

PARKER, ARTHUR THOMAS, Private
Resided in Edgecombe County and was by occupation a farmer prior to enlisting in Edgecombe County at age 20, May 8, 1861. Present or accounted for until captured at Sutherland's Station, Virginia, April 3, 1865. Confined at Point Lookout, Maryland, until released June 16-17, 1865, after taking the Oath of Allegiance.

PARKER, BENJAMIN F., Private
Born in Edgecombe County where he resided as a carpenter prior to enlisting in Edgecombe County at age 27, May 8, 1861. Present or accounted for until wounded at Williamsburg, Virginia, on or about May 5, 1862. Returned to duty prior to June 27, 1862, when he was wounded at Gaines' Mill, Virginia. Died June 28, 1862, of wounds.

PARKER, HENRY, Private
Resided in Edgecombe County and was by occupation a farmer prior to enlisting in Edgecombe County at age 27, May 8, 1861. Present or accounted for until wounded and captured at Gettysburg, Pennsylvania, July 1-4, 1863. Hospitalized at Davids Island, New York Harbor, until paroled and transferred to City Point, Virginia, where he was received September 27, 1863, for exchange. Rejoined the company in January-February, 1864, and present or accounted for until paroled at Appomattox Court House, Virginia, April 9, 1865.

PEEL, WILLIAM, Jr., Sergeant
Born in Edgecombe County where he resided as a farmer prior to enlisting in Edgecombe County at age 26, May 8, 1861. Mustered in as Sergeant. Present or accounted for until wounded in the thigh and captured at Williamsburg, Virginia, May 5, 1862. Hospitalized at Fort Monroe, Virginia, where he died May 25, 1862, of wounds.

PENDER, C. McLARRY, Private
Resided in Edgecombe County and was by occupation a laborer prior to enlisting in Edgecombe County at age 16, May 8, 1861. Present or accounted for until discharged on August 1, 1862, by reason of being under age.

PHELPS, HENDERSON, Private
Enlisted in Wake County on November 24, 1863, for the war. Present or accounted for until he died in hospital at Richmond, Virginia, June 15, 1864, of a gunshot wound. Place and date wounded not reported.

PIPPEN, SILAS M., Private
Resided in Edgecombe County and was by occupation a farmer prior to enlisting in Edgecombe County at age 25, May 8, 1861. Present or accounted for until wounded and captured at Williamsburg, Virginia, May 5, 1862. Hospitalized at Washington, D.C., un-

til transferred to Old Capitol Prison, Washington, June 27, 1862. Transferred to Aiken's Landing, James River, Virginia, where he was received August 5, 1862, for exchange. Rejoined the company in November-December, 1862, and present or accounted for until captured at Falling Waters, Maryland, July 14, 1863. Confined at Old Capitol Prison until transferred to Point Lookout, Maryland, August 8, 1863. Released at Point Lookout on January 26, 1864, after taking the Oath of Allegiance and joining the U.S. service. Reportedly assigned to the 1st Regiment U.S. Volunteer Infantry; however, records of that unit do not indicate that he served therein.

PIPPIN, GEORGE H., Private
Previously served in Company H, 63rd Regiment N.C. Troops (5th Regiment N.C. Cavalry). Transferred to this company on July 25, 1864. No further records.

PIPPIN, GEORGE H., Private
Resided in Martin County where he enlisted on May 6, 1863, for the war. Present or accounted for until captured at Amelia Court House, Virginia, April 3, 1865. Confined at Point Lookout, Maryland, until released on June 17, 1865, after taking the Oath of Allegiance.

PRICE, WILLIAM, Private
Born in Edgecombe County where he resided as a carpenter or cabinetmaker prior to enlisting in Edgecombe County at age 24, May 8, 1861. Present or accounted for until transferred to the C.S. Navy on February 20, 1862.

PROCTOR, WILLIAM H., Private
Born in Edgecombe County where he resided as a blacksmith or farmer prior to enlisting in Edgecombe County at age 21, May 8, 1861. Present or accounted for until wounded at Williamsburg, Virginia, May 5, 1862. Rejoined the company in November-December, 1862, and present or accounted for until wounded in the left arm, left hand, and both knees and captured at Gettysburg, Pennsylvania, July 1-4, 1863. Hospitalized at Davids Island, New York Harbor, until paroled and transferred to City Point, Virginia, where he was received October 28, 1863, for exchange. Reported absent wounded until he was retired from service on February 8, 1865, by reason of being "unable to walk without the aid of a crutch" as a result of wounds received at Gettysburg.

REASONS, REDDEN W., Private
Born in Edgecombe County where he resided as a farmer or laborer prior to enlisting in Edgecombe County at age 18, May 8, 1861. Present or accounted for until discharged on August 1, 1862, under the provisions of the Conscript Act.

REID, HENRY, Private
Enlisted in Wake County on December 18, 1863, for the war. Present or accounted for until he deserted on April 20, 1864.

RICE, WILLIAM, Private
Enlisted in Wake County on December 28, 1863, for the war. Deserted January 16, 1864.

RITTER, JOHN, Private
Resided in Edgecombe County and was by occupation a laborer prior to enlisting in Edgecombe Coun-

ty at age 23, May 8, 1861. Present or accounted for until captured at Falling Waters, Maryland, July 14, 1863. Confined at Baltimore, Maryland, until transferred to Point Lookout, Maryland, August 17, 1863. Released at Point Lookout on January 26, 1864, after taking the Oath of Allegiance and joining the U.S. service. Reportedly assigned to Company G, 1st Regiment U.S. Volunteer Infantry; however, records of that unit do not indicate that he served therein.

ROGERS, JOHN T., Private
Resided in Edgecombe County where he enlisted at age 17, August 13, 1861. Present or accounted for until wounded at Chancellorsville, Virginia, May 1-3, 1863. Rejoined the company prior to July 1-3, 1863, when he was wounded in the leg at Gettysburg, Pennsylvania. Rejoined the company prior to September 1, 1863, and present or accounted for until wounded at Wilderness, Virginia, May 6, 1864. Rejoined the company in September-October, 1864, and present or accounted for until paroled at Appomattox Court House, Virginia, April 9, 1865.

SATTERTHWAITE, MAJOR J., Private
Resided in Edgecombe County and was by occupation a farmer prior to enlisting in Edgecombe County at age 31, May 8, 1861. Present or accounted for until wounded in the shoulder at Chancellorsville, Virginia, May 3, 1863. Rejoined the company in September-October, 1863, and present or accounted for until captured at Reams' Station, Virginia, August 25, 1864. Confined at Point Lookout, Maryland, until paroled and transferred to Boulware's Wharf, James River, Virginia, where he was received March 16, 1865, for exchange.

SAVAGE, JOHN, Private
Resided in Edgecombe County and was by occupation a farmer prior to enlisting in Edgecombe County at age 21, May 8, 1861. Present or accounted for until reported captured at Williamsburg, Virginia, May 5, 1862; however, records of the Federal Provost Marshal do not substantiate that report. Present or accounted for until captured at Gettysburg, Pennsylvania, July 2-6, 1863. Confined at Fort Delaware, Delaware, until transferred to Point Lookout, Maryland, October 15-18, 1863. Reported in confinement at Fort Delaware through December, 1864. No further records.

SAWYER, JOHN R., Private
Resided in Edgecombe County and was by occupation a farmer prior to enlisting in Northampton County at age 21, May 17, 1861. Present or accounted for until he "wounded himself intentionally" on December 13, 1862. Hospitalized at Richmond, Virginia, until furloughed on January 8, 1863. Never rejoined the company and was listed as a deserter.

SHERROD, ROBERT WILSON, Private
Resided in Edgecombe County and was by occupation a farmer prior to enlisting in Edgecombe County at age 28, May 8, 1861. Present or accounted for until wounded in the left shoulder at Gaines' Mill, Virginia, June 27, 1862. Rejoined the company in July-October, 1862, and present or accounted for through October, 1864.

STALLINGS, RICHARD J., Sergeant
Resided in Edgecombe County and was by occupa-

tion a clerk prior to enlisting in Edgecombe County at age 25, May 8, 1861. Mustered in as Sergeant but was reduced to ranks on October 10, 1861. Reappointed Sergeant on March 8, 1863. Present or accounted for until killed at Gettysburg, Pennsylvania, July 3, 1863.

STARLING, JOHN, Private
Resided in Wayne County and enlisted in Wake County on November 16, 1863, for the war. Present or accounted for until captured at Wilderness, Virginia, May 6, 1864. Confined at Point Lookout, Maryland, until transferred to Elmira, New York, August 10, 1864. Released at Elmira on May 29, 1865, after taking the Oath of Allegiance.

STATON, REDDEN, Corporal
Resided in Edgecombe County and was by occupation a farmer prior to enlisting in Edgecombe County at age 20, May 8, 1861. Mustered in as Private and promoted to Corporal on May 25, 1862. Present or accounted for until killed at Sharpsburg, Maryland, September 17, 1862.

STILLY, FRANCIS, Private
Enlisted at Orange Court House, Virginia, April 21, 1864, for the war. Present or accounted for through April 1, 1865.

STONE, ANTHONY J., Private
Born in Somersetshire, England, and was by occupation a brickmaker prior to enlisting in Edgecombe County at age 28, May 8, 1861. Present or accounted for until discharged on August 4, 1862, under the provisions of the Conscript Act.

SUMMERLIN, JOHN, Private
Born in Edgecombe County where he resided as a farmer prior to enlisting in Edgecombe County at age 24, May 8, 1861. Present or accounted for through April, 1864. No further records.

TANNER, WILLIAM JAMES, Private
Resided in Edgecombe County and was by occupation a farmer prior to enlisting in Edgecombe County at age 19, May 8, 1861. Present or accounted for until he died on October 5, 1862. Place and cause of death not reported.

TUCKER, ROBERT B., Private
Born in Yadkin County* where he resided as a farmer prior to enlisting in Wake County at age 24, September 27, 1862, for the war. Present or accounted for until discharged at Danville, Virginia, July 23, 1863, by reason of "ascites."

WALSTON, RUFUS, Private
Born in Edgecombe County where he resided as a farmer prior to enlisting in Edgecombe County at age 17, May 8, 1861. Present or accounted for until wounded and captured at Williamsburg, Virginia, May 5, 1862. Hospitalized at Washington, D.C., where he died June 10, 1862, of wounds.

WALTERS, HARDY, Private
Resided in Edgecombe County where he enlisted at age 22, August 10, 1861. Present or accounted for through October, 1862. Reported absent without leave from November-December, 1862, through October, 1864.

WARREN, JAMES A., Private
Born in Edgecombe County where he resided as a

farmer prior to enlisting in Edgecombe County at age 21, May 8, 1861. Present or accounted for until he died in hospital at Richmond, Virginia, July 5, 1862, of "bronchitis."

WEAKS, WILLIAM A. J., Private
Enlisted in Wake County on August 12, 1864, for the war. Present or accounted for through October, 1864.

WHITEHEART, WILLIS, Private
Enlisted in Wake County on September 29, 1863, for the war. Present or accounted for until captured at or near Wilderness, Virginia, on or about May 6, 1864. Confined at Point Lookout, Maryland, until transferred to Elmira, New York, July 24, 1864. Died at Elmira on September 13, 1864, of "chronic diarrhoea."

WHITEHURST, JOHN H., Corporal
Resided in Pitt or Edgecombe counties and was by occupation a farmer prior to enlisting in Edgecombe County at age 24, May 8, 1861. Mustered in as Private. Present or accounted for until captured at Sharpsburg, Maryland, September 17, 1862. Paroled on or about September 20, 1862. Rejoined the company in November-December, 1862, and present or accounted for until wounded in the thigh and captured at Gettysburg, Pennsylvania, July 1-5, 1863. Hospitalized at Davids Island, New York Harbor, until paroled and transferred to City Point, Virginia, where he was received August 28, 1863, for exchange. Rejoined the company in September-October, 1863, and was promoted to Corporal on September 1, 1863. Present or accounted for until captured at Beverly's Bridge, Virginia, April 2, 1865. Confined at Point Lookout, Maryland, until released on June 22, 1865, after taking the Oath of Allegiance.

WILKERSON, HUGH E., Corporal
Resided in Wilson County and enlisted in Edgecombe County at age 17, August 11, 1861. Mustered in as Private and promoted to Corporal on April 26, 1862. Present or accounted for until wounded in the abdomen at Fredericksburg, Virginia, December 13, 1862. Died in hospital at Richmond, Virginia, December 19, 1862, of wounds or "pneumonia."

WILLIAMS, JAMES R., Private
Resided in Edgecombe County and was by occupation a farmer prior to enlisting in Edgecombe County at age 31, May 8, 1861. Present or accounted for until admitted to hospital at Richmond, Virginia, October 23, 1862, with a wound of the left side; however, place and date wounded not reported. Rejoined the company in March-April, 1863, and was wounded in both knees at Chancellorsville, Virginia, May 3, 1863. Reported absent wounded until he rejoined the company in March-April, 1864. Present or accounted for until paroled at Appomattox Court House, Virginia, April 9, 1865.

WILLIAMS, JOHN, Private
Resided in Edgecombe County and was by occupation a miner prior to enlisting in Edgecombe County at age 41, May 8, 1861. Present or accounted for until discharged on August 1, 1862, by reason of being over age.

WILLIAMS, JOHN B., Private
Resided in Edgecombe County and was by occupa-

tion a farmer prior to enlisting in Edgecombe County at age 22, May 8, 1861. Present or accounted for until wounded and captured at Boonsboro, Maryland, or at South Mountain, Maryland, on or about September 14, 1862. Confined at Fort McHenry, Maryland, until paroled and transferred to Aiken's Landing, James River, Virginia, where he was received October 17, 1862, for exchange. Declared exchanged at Aiken's Landing on November 10, 1862. Rejoined the company in January-February, 1863, and present or accounted for until he died at Orange Court House, Virginia, March 12, 1864. Cause of death not reported.

WOOTEN, JAMES, Private

Born in Edgecombe County where he resided as a farmer prior to enlisting in Edgecombe County at age 36, August 4, 1861. Present or accounted for until he died in hospital at Richmond, Virginia, May 17, 1862, of "rubeola."

COMPANY H

This company, known as the Rockingham Guards, was from Rockingham County and enlisted at Wentworth on May 3, 1861. The company received orders to march to Garysburg the same day and began the march on May 10. It arrived at Garysburg on May 14. There it was assigned to the regiment as Company H. After joining the regiment the company functioned as a part of the regiment, and its history for the war period is recorded as a part of the regimental history.

The information contained in the following roster of the company was compiled principally from company muster rolls for May 18, 1861, through October, 1864. No company muster rolls were found for the period after October, 1864. In addition to the company muster rolls, Roll of Honor records, receipt rolls, hospital records, prisoner of war records, and other primary records, supplemented by state pension applications, United Daughters of the Confederacy records, and postwar rosters and histories, all provided useful information.

OFFICERS

CAPTAINS

SCALES, ALFRED MOORE

Born in Rockingham County on November 26, 1827. Was by occupation a lawyer and served as a member of the North Carolina General Assembly and the U.S. House of Representatives prior to enlisting as a Private in this company on or about April 30, 1861. Elected Captain the same date. Date of rank reported as May 3, 1861. Present or accounted for until elected Colonel to rank from October 12, 1861, and transferred to the Field and Staff of this regiment.

McGEHEE, HENRY J.

Resided in Rockingham County and was by occupation a merchant prior to enlisting at age 33. Elected 1st Lieutenant on April 30, 1861, to rank from May 3, 1861. Elected Captain to rank from October 15, 1861. Present or accounted for until he was defeated for reelection when the regiment was reorganized on April 26, 1862.

JOHNS, ANTHONY BENNING, Jr.

Resided in Rockingham County and was by occupation a physician prior to enlisting in Rockingham County at age 25, May 3, 1861. Mustered in as Sergeant and was elected 1st Lieutenant to rank from November 5, 1861. Elected Captain to rank from April 26, 1862. Present or accounted for until wounded at Malvern Hill, Virginia, on or about July 1, 1862. Returned to duty prior to November 1, 1862, and present or accounted for until he resigned on January 6, 1863. Later served as Assistant Surgeon of the 45th Regiment N.C. Troops.

LAWSON, THOMAS T.

Resided in Rockingham County and enlisted at Camp Ruffin, Virginia, at age 21, September 11, 1861. Mustered in as Private and was elected 1st Lieutenant to rank from April 26, 1862. Reported captured in March-June, 1862; however, records of the Federal Provost Marshal do not substantiate that report. Rejoined the company prior to November 1, 1862, and present or accounted for until promoted to Captain to rank from January 6, 1863. Present or accounted for until he died near Orange Court House, Virginia, February 24, 1864, of disease.

MOIR, ROBERT L.

Resided in Rockingham County and was by occupation a clerk prior to enlisting in Rockingham County at age 21, May 3, 1861. Mustered in as Private and promoted to Sergeant on September 24, 1861. Promoted to 1st Sergeant on April 26, 1862, and was elected 3rd Lieutenant on November 17, 1862. Promoted to 2nd Lieutenant on January 6, 1863. Present or accounted for until wounded at Chancellorsville, Virginia, May 1-3, 1863. Rejoined the company prior to July 3, 1863, when he was wounded at Gettysburg, Pennsylvania. Rejoined the company prior to September 1, 1863, and was promoted to Captain on May 6, 1864. Present or accounted for until paroled at Appomattox Court House, Virginia, April 9, 1865.

LIEUTENANTS

CARDWELL, JOEL R., 2nd Lieutenant

Resided in Rockingham County and was by occupation a student prior to enlisting in Rockingham County at age 18, May 3, 1861. Mustered in as Corporal and was promoted to Sergeant on June 30, 1861. Promoted to 1st Sergeant on November 5, 1861, and elected 2nd Lieutenant to rank from January 9, 1862. Present or accounted for until he was defeated for reelection when the regiment was reorganized on April 26, 1862.

JOYCE, JOHN C., 3rd Lieutenant

Resided in Rockingham County and was by occupation a tobacconist prior to enlisting in Rockingham County at age 28, May 3, 1861. Mustered in as Private and promoted to Sergeant on November 6, 1861. Elected 3rd Lieutenant to rank from April 26, 1862. Present or accounted for until killed at South Mountain, Maryland, September 14, 1862.

SCALES, JOHN L., 2nd Lieutenant

Resided in Rockingham County and was by occupation a farmer prior to enlisting in Rockingham County at age 33. Elected 2nd Lieutenant on April

30, 1861, to rank from May 3, 1861. Present or accounted for until he resigned on December 4, 1861. Reason he resigned not reported.

SETTLE, DAVID, 2nd Lieutenant
Resided in Rockingham County and was by occupation a lawyer prior to enlisting at age 21. Elected 2nd Lieutenant to rank from May 3, 1861. Present or accounted for until he was defeated for reelection when the regiment was reorganized on April 26, 1862.

SMITH, JAMES MACKLIN, 1st Lieutenant
Resided in Rockingham County and was by occupation a medical student prior to enlisting in Rockingham County at age 23, May 3, 1861. Mustered in as Private and was elected 2nd Lieutenant to rank from April 26, 1862. Promoted to 1st Lieutenant on January 6, 1863. Present or accounted for until wounded in the ankle at Gettysburg, Pennsylvania, July 1, 1863. Reported absent wounded until he was retired to the Invalid Corps on April 30, 1864.

SMITH, NATHANIEL S., 1st Lieutenant
Resided in Rockingham County and was by occupation a student prior to enlisting in Northampton County at age 22, May 18, 1861. Mustered in as Private and was appointed 3rd Lieutenant on January 6, 1863. Present or accounted for until captured at Falling Waters, Maryland, July 14, 1863. Confined at Old Capitol Prison, Washington, D.C., until transferred to Johnson's Island, Ohio, August 8, 1863. Promoted to 1st Lieutenant on May 6, 1864, while a prisoner of war. Released at Johnson's Island on June 11, 1865, after taking the Oath of Allegiance.

NONCOMMISSIONED OFFICERS AND PRIVATES

ALLEN, JAMES A., 1st Sergeant
Resided in Rockingham County and was by occupation a merchant prior to enlisting in Rockingham County at age 24, May 3, 1861. Mustered in as 1st Sergeant. Present or accounted for until discharged on October 31, 1861, by reason of disability.

ALLEN, JESSIE, Private
Enlisted at Camp Vance on November 19, 1863, for the war. Present or accounted for until he deserted on January 15, 1864.

ANDERSON, NATHANIEL, Private
Resided in Rockingham County and was by occupation a farmer prior to enlisting in Rockingham County at age 18, May 3, 1861. Present or accounted for until he died in hospital at Richmond, Virginia, May 16 or June 16, 1862, of "typhoid."

BARNES, WILLIAM, Private
Born in Rockingham County where he resided as a laborer prior to enlisting in Rockingham County at age 22, May 3, 1861. Present or accounted for until he died in hospital at Richmond, Virginia, September 11 or October 10, 1862, of disease.

BARNES, WILLIAM H. H., Private
Resided in Rockingham County and was by occupation a student prior to enlisting in Rockingham County at age 22, May 3, 1861. Present or accounted for until discharged July 29, 1862, after providing a substitute.

BAUGHN, ROBERT K., Private
Resided in Rockingham County and was by occupation a farmer prior to enlisting in Rockingham County at age 25, May 3, 1861. Present or accounted for until paroled at Appomattox Court House, Virginia, April 9, 1865.

BAUGHN, WILLIAM G., Private
Resided in Rockingham County and was by occupation a farmer prior to enlisting in Rockingham County at age 27, May 3, 1861. Present or accounted for until he died in hospital at Richmond, Virginia, June 8, 1862, of "cont[inued] fever."

BELTON, JOHN H., Private
Resided in Rockingham County where he enlisted at age 40, May 3, 1863, for the war. Present or accounted for until paroled at Appomattox Court House, Virginia, April 9, 1865.

BENNETT, J. W., Private
Resided in Rockingham County. Place and date of enlistment not reported. Captured at Appomattox, Virginia, April 3, 1865. Confined at Hart's Island, New York Harbor, until released June 19-20, 1865, after taking the Oath of Allegiance.

BENTON, WILLIAM W., Private
Born in Stokes County and resided in Rockingham County where he was by occupation a wagoner or laborer prior to enlisting in Rockingham County at age 32, May 3, 1861. Present or accounted for until discharged on August 1, 1862, under the provisions of the Conscript Act.

BETHEL, GEORGE J., Private
Resided in Rockingham County and was by occupation a student prior to enlisting at Suffolk, Virginia, at age 18, May 3, 1861. Present or accounted for until appointed drillmaster and assigned to duty at Raleigh. Later served as a 2nd Lieutenant in Company B, 55th Regiment N.C. Troops.

BETHEL, WILLIAM P., Corporal
Born in Person County and resided in Rockingham County where he was by occupation a student prior to enlisting in Rockingham County at age 16, May 3, 1861. Mustered in as Private and promoted to Corporal on April 26, 1862. Present or accounted for until discharged on August 1, 1862, by reason of being under age.

BOOKER, GEORGE W., Private
Born in Prince Edward County, Virginia, and resided in Rockingham County where he was by occupation a house painter prior to enlisting in Rockingham County at age 36, May 3, 1861. Present or accounted for until wounded at Malvern Hill, Virginia, on or about July 1, 1862. Discharged on August 1, 1862, by reason of being over age.

BOSLER, JOHN, Private
Place and date of enlistment not reported. Paroled at Appomattox Court House, Virginia, April 9, 1865.

BROWN, JACOB, Private
Born in Rowan County and resided in Rockingham County where he was by occupation a laborer prior to enlisting in Rockingham County at age 21, May 3, 1861. Present or accounted for until transferred to the C.S. Navy for duty on the C.S.S. *Merrimac* on

February 19, 1862.

BURTON, WILLIAM J., Private
Born in Halifax County, Virginia, and resided in Rockingham County where he was by occupation a clerk prior to enlisting in Rockingham County at age 16, May 3, 1861. Present or accounted for until discharged on August 1, 1862, by reason of being under age.

CALHOUN, OBEDIAH C., Private
Born in Prince Edward County, Virginia, and resided in Rockingham County where he was by occupation a stonemason prior to enlisting in Rockingham County at age 39, May 3, 1861. Mustered in as Private and promoted to Sergeant on or about April 30, 1861. Reduced to ranks on June 26, 1861. Present or accounted for until discharged on August 1, 1862, by reason of being over age.

CALLAHAN, ROBERT, Private
Enlisted at Camp Vance on May 10, 1864, for the war. Present or accounted for until he deserted on August 20, 1864.

CARDWELL, JOSEPH N., Private
Born in Rockingham County where he resided as a tobacconist prior to enlisting in Rockingham County at age 20, May 3, 1861. Present or accounted for until he died in hospital at Richmond, Virginia, May 8 or June 8, 1862, of "pneumonia."

CARTER, PLEASANT HENRY, Private
Born in Stokes County and resided in Rockingham County where he was by occupation a farmer prior to enlisting in Rockingham County at age 18, May 3, 1861. Present or accounted for until wounded in the right hand at Chancellorsville, Virginia, May 3, 1863. Discharged on February 6, 1864, by reason of "gun shot wound of hand destroying the fingers."

CARTER, SAMUEL W., Corporal
Resided in Rockingham County and was by occupation a farmer prior to enlisting in Rockingham County at age 19, May 3, 1861. Mustered in as Private. Present or accounted for until wounded in the right thigh at Chancellorsville, Virginia, May 1-3, 1863. Rejoined the company in July-August, 1863, and was promoted to Corporal on October 25, 1863. Present or accounted for until reported absent wounded in May-June, 1864; however, place and date wounded not reported. Rejoined the company in July-August, 1864, and present or accounted for until paroled at Appomattox Court House, Virginia, April 9, 1865.

CARTER, W. H., Sergeant
Enlisted in Rockingham County on May 3, 1862, for the war. Mustered in with an unspecified rank and was promoted to Sergeant on August 28, 1862. Killed at South Mountain, Maryland, September 14, 1862.

CARTER, WILLIAM BROWN, Private
Enlisted at Orange Court House, Virginia, April 10, 1864, for the war. Present or accounted for until paroled at Appomattox Court House, Virginia, April 9, 1865.

CARTER, WILLIAM F., Private
Resided in Rockingham County and was by occupation a farmer prior to enlisting in Rockingham County at age 21, May 3, 1861. Present or accounted

for until killed at South Mountain, Maryland, September 14, 1862.

CARTER, WILLIAM T. B., Sergeant
Born in Stokes County where he resided as a farmer prior to enlisting in Rockingham County at age 20, May 3, 1861. Mustered in as Private. Present or accounted for until wounded at Gaines' Mill, Virginia, June 27, 1862. Rejoined the company in July-October, 1862, and was promoted to Sergeant on October 1, 1862. Present or accounted for until killed at Fort Harrison, Virginia, September 29, 1864.

CASHWELL, NATHANIEL, Private
Enlisted at Camp Vance on July 15, 1863, for the war. Present or accounted for until captured at Wilderness, Virginia, May 6, 1864. Confined at Point Lookout, Maryland, until transferred to Elmira, New York, July 23, 1864. Died at Elmira on March 6, 1865, of "pneumonia."

CHAPMAN, JAMES, Private
Resided in Rockingham County where he enlisted at age 18, February 28, 1863, for the war. Present or accounted for until reported absent without leave on December 1, 1863. Reported absent without leave through October, 1864.

CLARKE, MABORN, Private
Enlisted in Wake County on March 26, 1864, for the war. Present or accounted for through October, 1864.

CLER, ANTHONY, Private
Resided in Rockingham County and was by occupation a laborer prior to enlisting in Rockingham County at age 16, May 3, 1861. Present or accounted for until discharged on August 3, 1862, by reason of being under age.

CLUBB, W. J., Private
Enlisted at Camp Vance on December 28, 1863, for the war. Deserted on January 15, 1864.

COMBS, ALBERT W., Sergeant
Resided in Rockingham County and was by occupation a farmer prior to enlisting in Rockingham County at age 20, May 3, 1861. Mustered in as Private and promoted to Corporal on May 3, 1863. Present or accounted for until admitted to hospital at Richmond, Virginia, May 24, 1864, with a gunshot wound; however, place and date wounded not reported. Rejoined the company in July-August, 1864, and was promoted to Sergeant on October 1, 1864. Present or accounted for until captured near Petersburg, Virginia, March 25, 1865. Confined at Point Lookout, Maryland, until released on June 24, 1865, after taking the Oath of Allegiance.

COOPER, ISAAC, Private
Enlisted at Camp Holmes on December 16, 1863, for the war. Present or accounted for until killed at Wilderness, Virginia, May 5, 1864.

CORRUM, R. J., Private
Place and date of enlistment not reported. First reported in the records of this company on November 15, 1864. Deserted to the enemy on or about February 22, 1865. Took the Oath of Allegiance on or about February 24, 1865.

CORRUM, W. D., Private
Place and date of enlistment not reported. Deserted

to the enemy on or about February 22, 1865. No further records.

COVINGTON, ROBERT, Private

Resided in Rockingham County and was by occupation a farmer prior to enlisting in Rockingham County at age 20, May 3, 1861. Present or accounted for until captured at Winchester, Virginia, on or about December 5, 1862. Confined at various Federal prisons until transferred from Camp Chase, Ohio, to City Point, Virginia, where he was received on April 1, 1863, for exchange. Rejoined the company prior to July 1-5, 1863, when he was wounded in the left thigh and captured at Gettysburg, Pennsylvania. Hospitalized at Chester, Pennsylvania, until paroled and transferred to City Point where he was received September 23, 1863, for exchange. Rejoined the company in March-April, 1864. Reported absent wounded on company muster roll dated May-June, 1864; however, place and date wounded not reported. Rejoined the company in July-August, 1864, and present or accounted for until paroled at Appomattox Court House, Virginia, April 9, 1865.

COX, JOHN H., Private

Resided in Rockingham County and was by occupation a laborer prior to enlisting in Rockingham County at age 27, May 3, 1861. Present or accounted for through October, 1864.

COX, SMITH, Private

Resided in Wilkes County and enlisted in Wake County at age 25, September 27, 1862, for the war. Present or accounted for until wounded at Spotsylvania Court House, Virginia, May 20, 1864. Died in hospital at Gordonsville, Virginia, May 27, 1864, of wounds.

CRESON, JAMES, Private

Enlisted at Camp Holmes on February 1, 1864, for the war. Deserted March 8, 1864.

CROUCH, JOHN Y., Private

Resided in Iredell County and enlisted at Camp Vance on March 7, 1864, for the war. Present or accounted for until captured at Wilderness, Virginia, May 5-6, 1864. Confined at Point Lookout, Maryland, until transferred to Elmira, New York, July 25, 1864. Released at Elmira on May 29, 1865, after taking the Oath of Allegiance.

CUMMINGS, GEORGE W., Private

Born in Surry County where he resided prior to enlisting in Wake County at age 23, September 27, 1862, for the war. Present or accounted for until wounded at Chancellorsville, Virginia, May 3, 1863. Died of wounds the same day.

DALTON, CHARLES R., Corporal

Born in Rockingham County where he resided as ·a tobacconist prior to enlisting in Rockingham County at age 18, May 3, 1861. Mustered in as Private. Present of accounted for until wounded at Malvern Hill, Virginia, on or about July 1, 1862. Returned to duty prior to November 1, 1862, and was promoted to Corporal on January 10, 1863. Present of accounted for until killed at Chancellorsville, Virginia, May 3, 1863.

DALTON NICHOLAS H., Private

Resided in Rockingham County and was by occupa-

tion a tobacconist prior to enlisting in Rockingham County at age 23, May 3, 1861. Mustered in as Private and was promoted to Corporal on November 6, 1861. Reduced to ranks on or about April 26, 1862. Present or accounted for until mortally wounded at South Mountain, Maryland, September 14, 1862. Place and date of death not reported.

DALTON, SAMUEL P., Private

Born in Patrick County, Virginia, and resided in Rockingham County where he was by occupation a mechanic or carpenter prior to enlisting in Rockingham County at age 34, May 3, 1861. Mustered in as Private and promoted to Corporal on May 22, 1861. Reduced to ranks in March-June, 1862. Present or accounted for until discharged on August 4, 1862, under the provisions of the Conscript Act.

DANIEL, THOMAS, Private

Enlisted at Camp Holmes on June 4, 1864, for the war. Present or accounted for through October, 1864.

DELANEY, THOMAS, Private

Place and date of enlistment not reported. First reported on the records of this company on November 26, 1864. Paroled at Appomattox Court House, Virginia, April 9, 1865.

DILLION, WILLIAM T., Private

Enlisted in Stokes County on February 12, 1864, for the war. Present or accounted for until paroled at Appomattox Court House, Virginia, April 9, 1865.

DIX, WILLIAM P., Private

Resided in Rockingham County and was by occupation a farmer prior to enlisting at age 37, February 28, 1863, for the war. Present or accounted for through November 22, 1864.

EASLEY, JAMES M., Musician

Resided in Rockingham County where he enlisted at age 23, May 3, 1861. Mustered in as Musician. Present or accounted for until reported absent wounded in May-June, 1864; however, place and date wounded not reported. Rejoined the company in September-October, 1864, but was retired to the Invalid Corps on November 23, 1864.

EDWARDS, WILLIAMSON M., Private

Resided in Rockingham County and was by occupation a clerk prior to enlisting in Rockingham County at age 32, May 3, 1861. Present or accounted .for until discharged on July 29, 1862, after providing a substitute.

ELLINGTON, ALFRED B., Private

Resided in Rockingham County and was by occupation a student prior to enlisting in Rockingham County at age 18, May 3, 1861. Present or accounted for until transferred to Company I of this regiment on November 1, 1861.

ELLINGTON, CHARLES, Private

Place and date of enlistment not reported. First reported on the records of this company on November 15, 1864. Captured at Dinwiddie Court House, Virginia, April 2, 1865. Confined at Point Lookout, Maryland, where he died June 25, 1865, of "erysipelas."

ELLINGTON, DAVID S., Private

Resided in Rockingham County and was by occupation a law student prior to enlisting in Rockingham County at age 22, May 3, 1861. Present or accounted for until transferred to Company I of this regiment on November 1, 1861.

FEATHERSTON, THOMAS S., Private
Resided in Rockingham County and was by occupation a farmer prior to enlisting in Rockingham County at age 20, May 3, 1861. Present or accounted for until wounded in the knee at Fredericksburg, Virginia, December 13, 1862. Rejoined the company in January-February, 1863, and present or accounted for until killed in a skirmish near Mechanicsville, Virginia, June 1, 1864.

FODDRILL, WILLIAM, Private
Enlisted at Camp Holmes on April 7, 1864, for the war. Present or accounted for through October, 1864.

FOY, PLEASANT J. M., Private
Resided in Rockingham County and was by occupation a student prior to enlisting in Rockingham County at age 17, May 3, 1861. Present or accounted for until wounded at Gaines' Mill, Virginia, June 27, 1862. Discharged on August 11, 1862, after providing William Ball as a substitute.

FRAZIER, DANIEL S., Private
Resided in Rockingham County and was by occupation a physician prior to enlisting in Rockingham County at age 21, May 3, 1861. Present or accounted for until killed at Gaines' Mill, Virginia, June 27, 1862.

FRENCH, DAVID P., Private
Resided in Rockingham County. Place and date of enlistment not reported. First reported on the records of this company on November 15, 1864. Captured at Dinwiddie Court House, Virginia, April 2, 1865. Confined at Point Lookout, Maryland, until released on June 26, 1865, after taking the Oath of Allegiance.

FUQUA, JOHN H., Private
Resided in Caswell County. Place and date of enlistment not reported. Captured at Hatcher's Run, Virginia, April 2, 1865. Confined at Point Lookout, Maryland, until released on June 26, 1865, after taking the Oath of Allegiance.

GARDNER, J. B., Private
Enlisted at Camp Holmes on December 31, 1863, for the war. Deserted on January 15, 1864, but returned prior to May 6, 1864, when he was captured at Wilderness, Virginia. Confined at Point Lookout, Maryland, until released on or about May 17, 1864, after joining the U.S. Navy.

GATEWOOD, JEREMIAH, Private
Born in Stokes County and was by occupation a farmer prior to enlisting in Stokes County on February 12, 1864, for the war. Present or accounted for until wounded in the right hand at Spotsylvania Court House, Virginia, in May, 1864. Reported absent wounded or absent sick until discharged on February 22, 1865, by reason of wounds received at Spotsylvania Court House. Discharge papers give his age as 17.

GROGAN, DANIEL, Private
Born in Rockingham County where he resided as a laborer or stonemason prior to enlisting in Rocking-

ham County at age 37, May 15, 1861. Present or accounted for until discharged on July 3, 1861, by reason of disability.

GUERRANT, JOHN C., Private
Resided in Rockingham County and was by occupation a silversmith prior to enlisting in Rockingham County at age 20, May 3, 1861. Present or accounted for until transferred to Company K of this regiment on July 1, 1861.

HAMBY, HENRY M., Private
Resided in Surry County and enlisted in Wake County at age 22, September 27, 1862, for the war. Present or accounted for until wounded in the shoulder at Chancellorsville, Virginia, May 3, 1863. Rejoined the company in September-October, 1863, and present or accounted for until captured at Spotsylvania Court House, Virginia, May 18, 1864. Confined at Point Lookout, Maryland, until paroled and transferred to Boulware's and Cox's Wharf, James River, Virginia, February 20-21, 1865, for exchange.

HAMINGTON, J. L., Private
Place and date of enlistment not reported. Captured at Spotsylvania Court House, Virginia, May 20, 1864. Confined at Point Lookout, Maryland, until transferred to Elmira, New York, July 3, 1864. Died at Elmira on February 7, 1865, of "variola."

HAMLIN, THOMAS, Private
Born in Rockingham County where he resided as a student prior to enlisting at Suffolk, Virginia, at age 15, June 21, 1861. Present or accounted for until discharged on November 10, 1862, by reason of being under age.

HATHCOCK, J. Z. A., Private
Resided in Stanly County where he enlisted at age 19, February 28, 1863, for the war. Present or accounted for until captured at Fredericksburg, Virginia, May 3, 1863. Confined at Washington, D.C., until transferred to City Point, Virginia, where he was received May 13, 1863, for exchange. Rejoined the company prior to July 1-4, 1863, when he was wounded at Gettysburg, Pennsylvania. Rejoined the company in September-October, 1863, and present or accounted for until captured at Wilderness, Virginia, May 6, 1864. Confined at Point Lookout, Maryland, until transferred to Elmira, New York, August 10, 1864. Released at Elmira on June 27, 1865, after taking the Oath of Allegiance.

HAYGOOD, J. C., Private
Enlisted at Camp Holmes on September 27, 1863, for the war. Deserted on January 15, 1864, but rejoined the company prior to May 6, 1864, when he was captured at Wilderness, Virginia. Confined at Point Lookout, Maryland, until released on May 17, 1864, after joining the U.S. Navy.

HEATH, JOHN, Private
Place and date of enlistment not reported. Deserted to the enemy on or about October 11, 1864. Took the Oath of Allegiance on or about October 12, 1864.

HEGGIE, ARCHIBALD, Corporal
Resided in Rockingham County and was by occupation a student prior to enlisting in Rockingham County at age 18, May 3, 1861. Mustered in as

Private. Present or accounted for until wounded in the right hand at Chancellorsville, Virginia, May 1-3, 1863. Rejoined the company in September-October, 1863, and was promoted to Corporal on July 1, 1864. Present or accounted for until paroled at Appomattox Court House, Virginia, April 9, 1865.

HEGGIE, SAMUEL S., Corporal
Born in Rockingham County where he resided as a tobacconist prior to enlisting in Rockingham County at age 22, May 3, 1861. Mustered in as Private and was promoted to Corporal on October 1, 1864. Present or accounted for until paroled at Appomattox Court House, Virginia, April 9, 1865.

HEGGIE, WILLIAM Z., Corporal
Born in Rockingham County where he resided as a physician prior to enlisting in Rockingham County at age 25, May 3, 1861. Mustered in as Private and promoted to Corporal in November, 1864-April, 1865. Present or accounted for until paroled at Appomattox Court House, Virginia, April 9, 1865.

HERBIN, JAMES M., Private
Resided in Rockingham County and was by occupation a farmer prior to enlisting at Suffolk, Virginia, at age 23, May 30, 1861. Present or accounted for until wounded at Gaines' Mill, Virginia, June 27, 1862. Died July 17, 1862, of wounds. Place of death not reported.

HOWARD, F. H., Private
Place and date of enlistment not reported. Captured at Spotsylvania Court House, Virginia, May 20, 1864. Confined at Point Lookout, Maryland, until transferred to Elmira, New York, July 3, 1864. Paroled at Elmira on October 11, 1864, and transferred to Venus Point, Savannah River, Georgia, where he was received November 15, 1864, for exchange. No further records.

HUDSON, JOHN, Private
Born in Rockingham County where he resided prior to enlisting in Rockingham County at age 36, February 28, 1863, for the war. Present or accounted for until he died in hospital at Gordonsville, Virginia, June 7, 1863, of "febris typhoides."

HUNEYCUTT, R. G. H., Private
Born in Stanly County where he resided as a farmer prior to enlisting in Stanly County at age 22, February 28, 1863, for the war. Present or accounted for until wounded in the left arm at Chancellorsville, Virginia, May 3, 1863. Reported absent wounded until discharged on April 10, 1864, by reason of "partial paralysis" of the left arm.

JAMES, W. A., Private
Place and date of enlistment not reported. Deserted to the enemy on or about February 22, 1865.

JARRELL, R. T., Private
Place and date of enlistment not reported. First reported on the records of this company on November 15, 1864. Deserted to the enemy on or about February 22, 1865, and took the Oath of Allegiance on or about February 24, 1865.

JEFFERSON, JAMES T., Private
Born in Pittsylvania County, Virginia, and was by occupation a student prior to enlisting in Rockingham County at age 21, May 3, 1861. Present or

accounted for until reported absent without leave on September 13, 1862. Rejoined the company in January-February, 1863. Transferred to Company E, 57th Regiment Virginia Infantry, March 15, 1863.

JOYCE, JOSEPH H., Private
Resided in Rockingham County and was by occupation a farmer prior to enlisting in Rockingham County at age 22, May 3, 1861. Present or accounted for until wounded at Gaines' Mill, Virginia, June 27, 1862. Died July 10, 1862, of wounds. Place of death not reported.

JOYCE, JOSEPH S., Private
Resided in Rockingham County and was by occupation a farmer prior to enlisting in Rockingham County at age 23, May 3, 1861. Present or accounted for until he died in hospital at Richmond, Virginia, June 25, 1862, of "typhoid fever."

JOYCE, OWEN, Corporal
Resided in Rockingham County and was by occupation a farmer prior to enlisting in Rockingham County at age 24, May 3, 1861. Mustered in as Private. Present or accounted for until wounded at Gettysburg, Pennsylvania, July 1, 1863. Rejoined the company prior to September 1, 1863, and was promoted to Corporal on July 1, 1864. Present or accounted for until paroled at Appomattox Court House, Virginia, April 9, 1865. North Carolina pension records indicate he was wounded at Sharpsburg, Maryland, September 17, 1862.

KEELE, MARTIN L., Corporal
Resided in Rockingham County and was by occupation a tobacco roller prior to enlisting in Rockingham County at age 18, May 3, 1861. Mustered in as Corporal. Present or accounted for until he died in hospital at Richmond, Virginia, on or about May 28, 1862, of disease.

LEWIS, JOHN T., Private
Born in Rockingham County where he resided as a farmer prior to enlisting in Rockingham County at age 18, May 3, 1861. Present or accounted for until discharged on August 1, 1862, under the provisions of the Conscript Act.

LEWIS, MARCUS L., Private
Resided in Rockingham County and was by occupation a farmer prior to enlisting in Rockingham County at age 22, May 3, 1861. Present or accounted for until reported absent without leave on July 10, 1863. Reported absent without leave through October, 1864.

LEWIS, POWHATAN G., Private
Born in Rockingham County where he resided as a farmer prior to enlisting in Rockingham County at age 25, May 3, 1861. Present or accounted for until discharged on January 27, 1865, by reason of disability.

LEWIS, WILLIAM, Private
Previously served in Company D, 63rd Regiment N.C. Troops (5th Regiment N.C. Cavalry). Transferred to this company on October 29, 1863, in exchange for Private John A. Watson. Present or accounted for until wounded at or near Spotsylvania Court House, Virginia, May 1-11, 1864. Died in hospital at Gordonsville, Virginia, May 11, 1864, of wounds.

LYONS, ABSALOM, Private

Born in Surry County where he resided as a farmer prior to enlisting in Wake County at age 23, September 27, 1862, for the war. Present or accounted for until he died in hospital at Charlottesville, Virginia, February 5, 1863, of "pneumonia."

McCOY, WILLIAM P., Private

Resided in Rockingham County where he enlisted at age 23, May 3, 1861. Present or accounted for until he died in hospital at Lynchburg, Virginia, June 1, 1862, of "febris."

MARSHALL, WILLIAM, Private

Enlisted at Camp Holmes on February 13, 1864, for the war. Present or accounted for until captured at Wilderness, Virginia, May 6, 1864. Confined at Point Lookout, Maryland, until transferred to Elmira, New York, August 10, 1864. Died at Elmira on August 22, 1864, of "chronic diarrhoea."

MARTIN, JACKSON M., 1st Sergeant

Born in Rockingham County where he resided as a student prior to enlisting in Rockingham County at age 19, May 3, 1861. Mustered in as Private and promoted to 1st Sergeant on January 10, 1862. Reduced to ranks on April 26, 1862, but was reappointed 1st Sergeant on November 17, 1862. Present or accounted for until wounded in the right hand at Chancellorsville, Virginia, May 1-3, 1863. Rejoined the company in July-August, 1863, and present or accounted for until captured at Wilderness, Virginia, May 6, 1864. Confined at Point Lookout, Maryland, until transferred to Elmira, New York, August 10, 1864. Paroled at Elmira and transferred to Venus Point, Savannah River, Georgia, where he was received November 15, 1864, for exchange. Rejoined the company prior to April 9, 1865, when he was paroled at Appomattox Court House, Virginia.

MARTIN, MILTON V., Sergeant

Resided in Rockingham County and was by occupation a medical student prior to enlisting in Rockingham County at age 23, May 3, 1861. Mustered in as Private and promoted to Corporal on May 3, 1863. Promoted to Sergeant on November 25, 1863. Present or accounted for until captured at Wilderness, Virginia, May 6, 1864. Confined at Point Lookout, Maryland, until transferred to Elmira, New York, August 10, 1864. Paroled at Elmira and transferred to Boulware's Wharf, James River, Virginia, where he was received March 15, 1865, for exchange.

MEBANE, WILLIAM N., Private

Resided in Rockingham County and enlisted at Camp Ruffin, Virginia, at age 21, October 4, 1861. Present or accounted for until appointed Ordnance Sergeant on June 15, 1862, and transferred to the Field and Staff of this regiment.

MELTON, HENRY H., Private

Resided in Stanly County where he enlisted at age 18, February 28, 1863, for the war. Present or accounted for until wounded and captured at Gettysburg, Pennsylvania, July 1-5, 1863. Hospitalized at Chester, Pennsylvania, until transferred to City Point, Virginia, where he was received August 20, 1863, for exchange. Rejoined the company in May-June, 1864, and present or accounted for until wounded in the head at or near Petersburg, Virgin-

ia, on or about April 3, 1865. Died in hospital at Petersburg on April 16, 1865 of wounds.

MILES, LAWSON H., Private

Resided in Rockingham County where he enlisted at age 36, March 3, 1863, for the war. Present or accounted for until captured at Falling Waters, Maryland, July 14, 1863. Paroled at Baltimore, Maryland, and transferred to City Point, Virginia, where he was received August 24, 1863, for exchange. Deserted from hospital at Farmville, Virginia, August 31-September 1, 1863.

MINER, JAMES A., Private

Resided in Rockingham County and was by occupation a student prior to enlisting at Suffolk, Virginia, at age 19, May 30, 1861. Present or accounted for until he "shot himself" at Gaines' Mill, Virginia, on or about June 27, 1862, and deserted.

MINER, JASPER D., Private

Born in Rockingham County and was by occupation a student prior to enlisting in Rockingham County at age 16, May 3, 1861. Mustered in as Sergeant but was reduced to ranks on September 1, 1861. Present or accounted for until discharged on August 1, 1862, by reason of being under age.

MITCHELL, JOHN B., Private

Resided in Rockingham County. Place and date of enlistment not reported. First reported on the records of this company when he was hospitalized at Richmond, Virginia, March 13, 1865. Captured in hospital at Richmond on April 3, 1865, and confined at Libby Prison, Richmond, until transferred to Newport News, Virginia, April 23, 1865. Released at Newport News on June 30, 1865, after taking the Oath of Allegiance.

MITCHELL, WILLIAM A., Private

Resided in Rockingham County. Place and date of enlistment not reported. Captured at or near Petersburg, Virginia, April 2, 1865, and confined at Point Lookout, Maryland, until released on June 29, 1865, after taking the Oath of Allegiance.

MOIR, HENRY C., Private

Resided in Rockingham County and was by occupation a student prior to enlisting in Rockingham County at age 18, May 3, 1861. Present or accounted for until hospitalized at Danville, Virginia, May 8, 1863, with gunshot wound; however, place and date wounded not reported. Returned to duty June 19, 1863, and was wounded and captured at Gettysburg, Pennsylvania, July 1-4, 1863. Confined at Fort Delaware, Delaware, until transferred to Point Lookout, Maryland, October 15-18, 1863. Confined at Point Lookout until paroled and transferred to Boulware's and Cox's Wharf, James River, Virginia, where he was received February 20-21, 1865, for exchange. Paroled at Greensboro on May 16, 1865.

MONTGOMERY, ALVIS D., Private

Resided in Rockingham County and enlisted at Suffolk, Virginia, at age 23, July 5, 1861. Present or accounted for until appointed Aide-de-Camp to Brigadier General Alfred M. Scales on June 15, 1863, and transferred.

MOORE, RICHARD, Private

Resided in Rockingham County where he enlisted at

age 28, May 3, 1861. Present or accounted for until he died in hospital at Richmond, Virginia, June 18, 1862, of "typhoid fever."

MOORE, SAMUEL P., Private
Born in Caswell County and resided in Rockingham County where he was by occupation a student prior to enlisting in Rockingham County at age 17, May 3, 1861. Present or accounted for until he died in hospital at Richmond, Virginia, on or about June 25, 1862, of disease.

MORPHIS, G. B., Private
Place and date of enlistment not reported. Paroled at Appomattox Court House, Virginia, April 9, 1865.

MORPHIS, STEPHEN F., Private
Enlisted at Camp Holmes on October 17, 1864, for the war. Present or accounted for until paroled at Appomattox Court House, Virginia, April 9, 1865.

MOXLY, WILLIAM H., Corporal
Resided in Rockingham County and was by occupation a student prior to enlisting in Rockingham County at age 24, May 3, 1861. Mustered in as Private and promoted to Corporal on April 26, 1862. Present or accounted for until wounded in the thigh at Chancellorsville, Virginia, May 3, 1863. Hospitalized at Richmond, Virginia, where he died on or about May 28, 1863, of wounds.

OAKLEY, ROBERT R., Private
Born in Rockingham County where he resided as a laborer prior to enlisting in Rockingham County at age 18, May 3, 1861. Present or accounted for until he died in hospital at Charlottesville, Virginia, April 27, 1863, of "pneumonia."

ODLE, JAMES A., Private
Born in Rockingham County where he resided as a laborer prior to enlisting in Rockingham County at age 26, May 3, 1861. Present or accounted for until discharged at Suffolk, Virginia, July 4, 1861, by reason of disability.

OLIVER, W. W., Private
Place and date of enlistment not reported. First reported on company records on November 17, 1864. Captured in hospital at Richmond, Virginia, April 3, 1865, and paroled on April 18, 1865.

PASCHALL, HENRY C., Private
Born in Warren County where he resided as a painter prior to enlisting in Wake County at age 19, September 27, 1862, for the war. Present or accounted for until discharged on August 21, 1863, by reason of "phthisis pulmonalis accompanied with chronic diarrhoea."

PATRICK, DAVID S., Private
Resided in Rockingham County where he enlisted at age 24, May 3, 1861. Present or accounted for until discharged on July 10, 1862, after providing August Shearen as a substitute.

PRICE, PLEASANT H., Private
Resided in Rockingham County. Place and date of enlistment not reported. Captured at or near Petersburg, Virginia, April 2, 1865, and confined at Point Lookout, Maryland, until released on June 17, 1865, after taking the Oath of Allegiance.

PROFFIT, LUTHER C., Private
Born in Wilkes County where he resided prior to enlisting in Wake County at age 20, September 27, 1862, for the war. Present or accounted for until he died at Camp Gregg, Virginia, March 25, 1863, of "brain fever."

RAMSAY, JOHN, Private
Enlisted at Camp Holmes on January 29, 1864, for the war. Present or accounted for until reported absent without leave on October 12, 1864.

RATLIFF, JAMES C., Sergeant
Resided in Rockingham County and was by occupation a farmer prior to enlisting in Rockingham County at age 23, May 3, 1861. Mustered in as Private and promoted to Sergeant on April 26, 1862. Present or accounted for until wounded at or near Mechanicsville, Virginia, on or about June 26, 1862. Rejoined the company prior to July 1, 1862, and present or accounted for until wounded and captured at Gettysburg, Pennsylvania, July 1-5, 1863. Hospitalized at Chester, Pennsylvania, until transferred to City Point, Virginia, where he was received August 20, 1863, for exchange. Rejoined the company in November-December, 1863, and present or accounted for until paroled at Appomattox Court House, Virginia, April 9, 1865.

REED, THOMAS S., Private
Resided in Rockingham County and was by occupation a laborer prior to enlisting in Rockingham County at age 20, May 3, 1861. Present or accounted for until wounded in the left arm at Chancellorsville, Virginia, May 3, 1863. Hospitalized at Richmond, Virginia, where he died May 11, 1863, of wounds.

REYNOLDS, EVANS, Private
Enlisted at Camp Holmes on December 15, 1863, for the war. Present or accounted for until he died in hospital at Staunton, Virginia, May 11, 1864, of a gunshot wound. Place and date wounded not reported.

REYNOLDS, WILLIAM P., Musician
Born in Rockingham County where he resided as a student prior to enlisting in Rockingham County at age 15, May 3, 1861. Mustered in as Musician. Present or accounted for until discharged on August 1, 1862, by reason of being under age.

ROBERTSON, JOHN F. M., Corporal
Born in Stokes County and resided in Rockingham County where he was by occupation a farmer or student prior to enlisting in Rockingham County at age 18, May 3, 1861. Mustered in as Private and promoted to Corporal on April 26, 1862. Present or accounted for until wounded in the hip at Gaines' Mill, Virginia, or at Malvern Hill, Virginia, June 27-July 1, 1862. Rejoined the company in May-June, 1863, and was wounded in the leg and captured at Gettysburg, Pennsylvania, July 1-4, 1863. Leg amputated. Hospitalized at Davids Island, New York Harbor, until paroled and transferred to City Point, Virginia, where he was received September 8, 1863, for exchange. Reported absent wounded until discharged on March 22, 1864, by reason of wounds received at Gettysburg.

ROBERTSON, PETER D., Private
Born in Montgomery County and resided in Rocking-

ham County where he was by occupation a farmer prior to enlisting in Guilford County at age 29, March 20, 1863, for the war. Present or accounted for until wounded in the left arm and captured at Gettysburg, Pennsylvania, July 3-4, 1863. Confined at Fort Delaware, Delaware, until paroled and transferred to City Point, Virginia, where he was received August 1, 1863, for exchange. Discharged on December 16, 1863, by reason of wounds received at Gettysburg.

ROGERS, JAMES T., Private
Born in Pittsylvania County, Virginia, and resided in Rockingham County where he was by occupation a student prior to enlisting in Rockingham County at age 15, May 3, 1861. Present or accounted for until discharged on August 1, 1862, by reason of being under age.

RUSSELL, GEORGE W., Private
Enlisted at Camp Holmes on March 26, 1864, for the war. Company muster rolls indicate he was absent sick from May-June, 1864, through October, 1864; however, medical records indicate he was hospitalized at Farmville, Virginia, May 6-7, 1864, and deserted May 9-10, 1864. No further records.

SCALES, EDWARD F., Private
Born in Rockingham County where he resided as a tobacconist prior to enlisting in Rockingham County at age 19, May 3, 1861. Present or accounted for until wounded and captured at South Mountain, Maryland, or at Sharpsburg, Maryland, in September, 1862. Died in the hands of the enemy of wounds. Place and date of death not reported.

SCALES, ERASMUS D., Private
Resided in Rockingham County and enlisted at Suffolk, Virginia, at age 21, May 30, 1861. Present or accounted for until appointed Commissary Sergeant on June 10, 1861, and transferred to the Field and Staff of this regiment.

SCALES, HENRY W., Private
Born in Rockingham County where he resided as a farmer prior to enlisting at Suffolk, Virginia, at age 26, May 30, 1861. Present or accounted for until wounded at or near Malvern Hill, Virginia, on or about July 1, 1862. Died July 3, 1862, of wounds. Place of death not reported.

SCALES, NICHOLAS D., Private
Born in Rockingham County where he resided as a student prior to enlisting in Rockingham County at age 20, May 3, 1861. Present or accounted for until discharged on November 29, 1861, by reason of disability.

SHARP, CALVIN, Private
Resided in Rockingham County. Place and date of enlistment not reported. First reported in the records of this company on November 26, 1864. Captured on the South Side Railroad, Virginia, April 2, 1865. Confined at Hart's Island, New York Harbor, until released on June 18, 1865, after taking the Oath of Allegiance.

SHELTON, WILLIAM R., Private
Enlisted at Camp Holmes on December 28, 1863, for the war. Present or accounted for until he deserted on March 8, 1864.

SHUMAKER, BURRIS, Private
Enlisted at Camp Vance on November 20, 1863, for the war. Present or accounted for until he deserted on January 15, 1864.

SIMS, JAMES T., Private
Resided in Rockingham County and was by occupation a laborer prior to enlisting in Rockingham County at age 23, May 3, 1861. Present or accounted for until killed at Gaines' Mill, Virginia, June 27, 1862.

SIMS, JOHN B., Private
Resided in Rockingham County and was by occupation a laborer prior to enlisting in Rockingham County at age 18, May 3, 1861. Present or accounted for until he died at Smithfield, Virginia, April 18, 1862, of disease.

SMITH, GEORGE W., Corporal
Born in Mecklenburg County, Virginia, and enlisted at Camp Ruffin, Virginia, September 1, 1861. Mustered in as Private and promoted to Corporal on April 26, 1862. Present or accounted for until wounded at Gaines' Mill, Virginia, June 27, 1862. Rejoined the company in January-February, 1863, and present or accounted for until killed at Chancellorsville, Virginia, May 3, 1863.

SMITH, JOSHUA R., Sergeant
Born in Rockingham County where he resided as a student prior to enlisting in Rockingham County at age 17, May 3, 1861. Mustered in as Corporal and promoted to Sergeant on November 6, 1861. Present or accounted for until discharged on November 25, 1863, by reason of disability.

SPARKS, MATHEW T., Private
Resided in Rockingham County where he enlisted at age 39, February 28, 1863, for the war. Present or accounted for until paroled at Appomattox Court House, Virginia, April 9, 1865.

STEPHENS, JAMES R., Private
Resided in Rockingham County and was by occupation a mechanic prior to enlisting in Rockingham County at age 24, May 3, 1861. Present or accounted for until captured at Falling Waters, Maryland, July 14, 1863. Confined at Baltimore, Maryland, until transferred to Point Lookout, Maryland, on or about August 17, 1863. Confined at Point Lookout until exchanged on or about February 28, 1865. Paroled at Appomattox Court House, Virginia, April 9, 1865.

STEPHENS, WILLIAM HENRY, Private
Resided in Rockingham County and enlisted at Camp Ruffin, Virginia, at age 18, July 7, 1861. Mustered in as Private and promoted to Corporal on August 10, 1862. Reduced to ranks on January 10, 1863. Present or accounted for until paroled at Appomattox Court House, Virginia, April 9, 1865.

STONE, WILLIAM, Private
Born in Rockingham County where he resided prior to enlisting at Camp Ruffin, Virginia, at age 21, October 13, 1861. Present or accounted for until wounded in the head at Gaines' Mill, Virginia, June 27, 1862. Hospitalized at Danville, Virginia, where he died on or about July 21, 1862, of wounds.

TERRY, JOHN D., Private
Resided in Rockingham County and was by occupation a laborer prior to enlisting in Rockingham County at age 23, May 3, 1861. Present or accounted for until captured at Sharpsburg, Maryland, September 17, 1862. Confined at Fort Delaware, Delaware, until transferred to Aiken's Landing, James River, Virginia, October 2, 1862, for exchange. Declared exchanged at Aiken's Landing on November 10, 1862. Rejoined the company prior to January 1, 1863, and present or accounted for until wounded in the right thigh at Chancellorsville, Virginia, May 1-3, 1863. Rejoined the company in July-August, 1863, and present or accounted for until paroled at Appomattox Court House, Virginia, April 9, 1865.

THOMAS, JAMES F., Private
Enlisted at Camp Holmes on October 16, 1864, for the war. Paroled at Appomattox Court House, Virginia, April 9, 1865.

THOMAS, JOHN, Private
Resided in Gadsden County, Florida. Place and date of enlistment nor reported. Captured near Petersburg, Virginia, March 25, 1865. Confined at Point Lookout, Maryland, until released on May 14, 1865, after taking the Oath of Allegiance. [May have been the same John Thomas who served in Company A of this regiment.]

THOMAS, ROBERT B., Private
Resided in Rockingham County and was by occupation a laborer prior to enlisting in Rockingham County at age 20, May 3, 1861. Present or accounted for until he died on or about August 11, 1862, of "fever." Place of death not reported.

THOMAS, WILLIAM Y., Private
Enlisted in Rockingham County on September 25, 1863, for the war. Present or accounted for until paroled at Appomattox Court House, Virginia, April 9, 1865.

THOMASON, HUGHEY, Private
Resided in Davidson County and enlisted at Camp Holmes on January 27, 1864, for the war. Present or accounted for until reported absent without leave from March 8, 1864, until September 24, 1864. Deserted to the enemy on or about November 6, 1864. Took the Oath of Allegiance at City Point, Virginia, November 9, 1864.

VAUGHN, JAMES T., Private
Born in Rockingham County where he resided as a laborer prior to enlisting in Rockingham County at age 19, May 3, 1861. Present or accounted for until wounded at Gaines' Mill, Virginia, June 27, 1862. Rejoined the company prior to November 1, 1862, and present or accounted for until killed at Gettysburg, Pennsylvania, July 1, 1863.

VERNON, GREEN, Private
Resided in Rockingham County and was by occupation a laborer prior to enlisting in Rockingham County at age 23, May 3, 1861. Present or accounted for until he died in hospital at Danville, Virginia, on or about June 14, 1862, of "febris typhoides."

WALKER, J. THOMPSON, Private
Born in Rockingham County where he resided as a farmer prior to enlisting in Rockingham County at

age 25, May 3, 1861. Present or accounted for until discharged on March 9, 1864, by reason of a "fractured thigh." Paroled at Greensboro on May 8, 1865.

WALL, GEORGE W., Private
Enlisted at Camp Holmes on March 25, 1864, for the war. Company muster rolls indicate he was absent sick from May-June, 1864, through October, 1864; however, medical records indicate that he deserted from hospital at Farmville, Virginia, May 9, 1864. No further records.

WALL, JOSEPH M., Private
Resided in Rockingham County and was by occupation a farmer prior to enlisting in Rockingham County at age 27, May 3, 1861. Present or accounted for until wounded at South Mountain, Maryland, September 14, 1862. Rejoined the company in January-February, 1863, and present or accounted for until wounded in the right shoulder or right arm and captured at Chancellorsville, Virginia, May 3, 1863. Hospitalized at Washington, D.C., until paroled at Old Capitol Prison, Washington, June 25, 1863. Received at City Point, Virginia, June 30, 1863, for exchange. Rejoined the company in September-October, 1863, and present or accounted for until killed at Spotsylvania Court House, Virginia, May 21,1864.

WALLS, PETER, Private
Resided in Surry County and enlisted in Wake County at age 25, September 27, 1862, for the war. Present or accounted for until reported absent without leave in March-April, 1864. Reported absent without leave through October, 1864. North Carolina pension records indicate he was wounded at Fredericksburg, Virginia, and that he survived the war.

WALSER, ALBERT, Private
Resided in Davidson County and enlisted at Camp Holmes on January 29, 1864, for the war. Present or accounted for until March 8, 1864, when he was reported absent without leave. Rejoined the company on September 11, 1864. Captured at Petersburg, Virginia, April 3, 1865, and confined at Hart's Island, New York Harbor, until released June 19-20, 1865, after taking the Oath of Allegiance.

WALSH, THOMAS, Private
Resided in Wilkes County and enlisted in Wake County at age 23, September 27, 1862, for the war. Present or accounted for until wounded at Chancellorsville, Virginia, May 1-3, 1863. Rejoined the company in July-August, 1863, and present or accounted for until he died in hospital at Charlottesville, Virginia, October 14, 1863. Cause of death not reported.

WALTERS, JOHN M., Private
Resided in Guilford County and enlisted at Camp Holmes on March 26, 1864, for the war. Present or accounted for until captured at Wilderness, Virginia, May 6, 1864. Confined at Point Lookout, Maryland, until transferred to Elmira, New York, July 25, 1864. Released at Elmira on May 29, 1865, after taking the Oath of Allegiance.

WALTHALL, LAWSON B., Sergeant
Born in Lowndes County, Mississippi, and resided in Rockingham County where he was by occupation a student prior to enlisting in Rockingham County at age 17, May 3, 1861. Mustered in as Private and

promoted to Corporal on June 30, 1861. Promoted to Sergeant on April 26, 1862. Present or accounted for until discharged on August 1, 1862, under the provisions of the Conscript Act.

WATSON, DAVID, Private
Born in Rockingham County where he resided as a carpenter or mechanic prior to enlisting in Rockingham County at age 26, May 3, 1861. Present or accounted for until wounded in the left shoulder and right thigh and captured at South Mountain, Maryland, September 14, 1862, or at Sharpsburg, Maryland, September 17, 1862. Hospitalized at Frederick, Maryland, until transferred to Fort McHenry, Maryland, December 13, 1862. Paroled at Fort McHenry on December 14, 1862, and transferred for exchange. Reported absent wounded until discharged from service on March 19, 1864, by reason of wounds received in September, 1862.

WATSON, JOHN A., Private
Resided in Rockingham County and was by occupation a farmer prior to enlisting in Rockingham County at age 20, May 3, 1861. Present or accounted for until wounded at Gaines' Mill, Virginia, June 27, 1862. Rejoined the company in November-December, 1862, and was reported "in guardhouse" through February, 1863. Wounded in the hand at Chancellorsville, Virginia, May 1-3, 1863. Rejoined the company in July-August, 1863, and present or accounted for until transferred to Company D, 63rd Regiment N.C. Troops (5th Regiment N.C. Cavalry), October 29, 1863, in exchange for Private William Lewis.

WEBSTER, JOHN R., Private
Born in Rockingham County where he resided as a student prior to enlisting in Rockingham County at age 15, May 3, 1861. Present or accounted for until discharged on August 1, 1862, by reason of being under age.

WEST, WILLIAM, Private
Resided in Surry County and enlisted in Wake County at age 33, September 27, 1862, for the war. Present or accounted for until wounded at Chancellorsville, Virginia, May 1-3, 1863. Died in hospital at Richmond, Virginia, May 21, 1863, of wounds or "fever."

WESTMORELAND, ALEXANDER, Private
Enlisted at Camp Holmes on February 1, 1864, for the war. Deserted March 8, 1864. "Killed . . . for desertion" on September 9, 1864.

WILLIAMS, A. L., Private
Enlisted at Camp Vance on March 4, 1864, for the war. Present or accounted for through October, 1864.

WINSTON, THOMAS F., Private
Resided in Rockingham County and was by occupation a farmer prior to enlisting in Rockingham County at age 18, May 3, 1861. Present or accounted for until wounded in the "right great toe" at Chancellorsville, Virginia, May 1-3, 1863. Returned to duty on June 19, 1863, and was captured at Gettysburg, Pennsylvania, July 3-4, 1863. Confined at Fort Delaware, Delaware, until transferred to Point Lookout, Maryland, October 15-18, 1863. Confined at Point Lookout until paroled on February 18, 1865,

and transferred to Boulware's and Cox's Wharf, James River, Virginia, where he was received February 20-21, 1865, for exchange. Paroled at Appomattox Court House, Virginia, April 9, 1865.

WITHERS, ROBERT E., Private
Born in Stokes County and resided in Rockingham County where he was by occupation a student prior to enlisting in Rockingham County at age 17, May 3, 1861. Present or accounted for until discharged on August 1, 1862, under the provisions of the Conscript Act.

COMPANY I

This company, known as the Rockingham Rangers, was from Rockingham County and enlisted at Wentworth on May 3, 1861. The company received orders to march to Garysburg the same day and began the march on May 13. It arrived at Garysburg on May 17. There is was assigned to the regiment as Company I. After joining the regiment the company functioned as a part of the regiment, and its history for the war period is recorded as a part of the regimental history.

The information contained in the following roster of the company was compiled principally from company muster rolls for May 18, 1861, through October, 1864. No company muster rolls were found for the period after October, 1864. In addition to the company muster rolls, Roll of Honor records, receipt rolls, hospital records, prisoner or war records, and other primary records, supplemented by state pension applications, United Daughters of the Confederacy records, and postwar rosters and histories, all provided useful information.

OFFICERS

CAPTAINS

SETTLE, THOMAS
Resided in Rockingham County and was by occupation a lawyer prior to enlisting at age 30. Appointed Captain on May 3, 1861. Present or accounted for until April 26, 1862, when he was reelected at the reorganization of the regiment. Declined the position and "went home."

GLENN, CHALMERS
Resided in Rockingham County and was by occupation a lawyer prior to enlisting in Rockingham County at age 30. Elected 1st Lieutenant on April 30, 1861, to rank from May 3, 1861, and was elected Captain to rank from April 26, 1862. Present or accounted for until killed at South Mountain, Maryland, September 14, 1862. "A very gallant officer."

WARD, ROBERT H.
Resided in Rockingham County and was by occupation a lawyer prior to enlisting in Rockingham County at age 27. Elected 3rd Lieutenant on April 30, 1861, to rank from May 3, 1861, and was elected 1st Lieutenant on April 26, 1862. Promoted to Captain on September 14, 1862. Present or accounted for until wounded in the left arm at Chancellorsville, Virginia, May 3, 1863. Rejoined the company in January-February, 1864, and present or accounted

for until wounded in the right leg at Wilderness, Virginia, May 5, 1864. Reported absent wounded through October, 1864.

WILLIAMS, ROWLAND S.

Resided in Rockingham County and was by occupation a farmer prior to enlisting in Rockingham County at age 21, May 3, 1861. Mustered in as Private. Present or accounted for until wounded in the finger at Malvern Hill, Virginia, on or about July 2, 1862. Rejoined the company prior to November 1, 1862, and was promoted to Sergeant on October 22, 1862. Promoted to 1st Sergeant on December 6, 1862, and was elected 3rd Lieutenant on December 28, 1862. Promoted to 1st Lieutenant on March 30, 1864, and was promoted to Captain in November, 1864-April, 1865. Present or accounted for until paroled at Appomattox Court House, Virginia, April 9, 1865.

LIEUTENANTS

BURROUGHS, WILLIAM C., 2nd Lieutenant

Resided in Rockingham County and was by occupation a farmer prior to enlisting in Rockingham County at age 32, May 3, 1861. Mustered in as 1st Sergeant and was elected 2nd Lieutenant to rank from April 26, 1862. Present or accounted for until captured at or near Gaines' Mill, Virginia, on or about June 27, 1862. Confined at Fort Monroe, Virginia, and at Fort Delaware, Delaware, until exchanged at Aiken's Landing, James River, Virginia, August 5, 1862. Resigned December 8, 1862. Resignation accepted December 23, 1862.

HANCOCK, EZEKIEL W., 2nd Lieutenant

Resided in Rockingham County and was by occupation a farmer prior to enlisting in Rockingham County at age 44. Elected 2nd Lieutenant on April 30, 1861, to rank from May 3, 1861. Present or accounted for until he was defeated for reelection when the regiment was reorganized on April 26, 1862. Later served as Colonel of the 7th Regiment N.C. Senior Reserves.

NEAL, ABNER F., 1st Lieutenant

Resided in Rockingham County and was by occupation a laborer prior to enlisting in Rockingham County at age 22, May 3, 1861. Mustered in as Private and was promoted to Sergeant in March-April, 1862. Promoted to 1st Sergeant on August 12, 1862. Captured at or near Sharpsburg, Maryland, on or about September 17, 1862. Paroled September 19, 1862. Rejoined the company in November-December, 1862, and was elected 2nd Lieutenant on or about December 6, 1862. Promoted to 1st Lieutenant on July 10, 1863. Present or accounted for until he resigned on March 21, 1864. Resignation accepted March 30, 1864.

WINCHESTER, WILLIAM H., 1st Lieutenant

Resided in Rockingham County and was by occupation a clerk prior to enlisting in Rockingham County at age 21, May 3, 1861. Mustered in as Corporal and was elected 2nd Lieutenant on April 26, 1862. Promoted to 1st Lieutenant on September 17, 1862. Present or accounted for until wounded at Chancellorsville, Virginia, May 1-3, 1863. Rejoined the company prior to July 1-3, 1863, when his "right foot was shot off at the ankle" and he was captured at Gettysburg, Pennsylvania. Hospitalized at Baltimore, Maryland, until transferred to Chester, Pennsylvania, July 18, 1863. Died in hospital at Chester on August 1, 1863, of "pyaemia."

NONCOMMISSIONED OFFICERS AND PRIVATES

ADAMS, JOHN, Private

Resided in Virginia and enlisted at age 36, August 7, 1862, for the war. "Whipped out of the company" at an unspecified date.

ALDRID, M. J., Private

Enlisted in Randolph County on December 3, 1863, for the war. Present or accounted for until captured at Wilderness, Virginia, May 5-6, 1864. Confined at Point Lookout, Maryland, where he died July 1, 1864, of "dysentery acute."

APPLE, EDWIN R., Corporal

Resided in Rockingham County and was by occupation a farmer prior to enlisting in Rockingham County at age 32, May 3, 1861. Mustered in as Private. Present or accounted for until wounded in the hip at Gaines' Mill, Virginia, June 27, 1862. Rejoined the company in November-December, 1862, and present or accounted for until wounded in the right thigh at Chancellorsville, Virginia, May 3, 1863. Rejoined the company in January-February, 1864, and was promoted to Corporal on January 1, 1864. Present or accounted for until paroled at Appomattox Court House, Virginia, April 9, 1865.

APPLE, MADISON, Private

Resided in Rockingham County and was by occupation a laborer prior to enlisting in Rockingham County at age 30, May 3, 1861. Present or accounted for until killed at Malvern Hill, Virginia, July 1, 1862.

BAILEY, JOHN, Private

Born in Rockingham County where he resided as a laborer prior to enlisting in Rockingham County at age 25, May 3, 1861. Present or accounted for until he died at home on or about January 15, 1863, of disease.

BAILEY, MILTON, Private

Resided in Rockingham County and was by occupation a laborer prior to enlisting in Rockingham County at age 19, May 3, 1861. Present or accounted for until accidentally wounded in the hip and abdomen. Place and date wounded not reported. Died in hospital at Richmond, Virginia, June 20, 1862, of wounds.

BAILEY, ROBERT, Private

Resided in Rockingham County and was by occupation a laborer prior to enlisting in Rockingham County at age 22, May 3, 1861. Present or accounted for until he died in hospital at Richmond, Virginia, June 19, 1862, of "diarrhoea" or "typhoid pneumonia."

BAILEY, WILLIAM, Private

Resided in Rockingham County and was by occupation a laborer prior to enlisting in Rockingham County at age 21, May 3, 1861. Present or accounted for until wounded at Gaines' Mill, Virginia, June 27, 1862. Died July 4, 1862, or January 15, 1863, of disease. Place of death not reported.

BAKER, CHARLES, Private
Resided in Rockingham County and was by occupation a laborer prior to enlisting in Rockingham County at age 23, May 3, 1861. Present or accounted for until transferred to Company L, 21st Regiment N.C. Troops (11th Regiment N.C. Volunteers) on March 4, 1863, in exchange for Private John E. Winchester.

BANES, JAMES, Private
Place and date of enlistment not reported. Paroled at Greensboro on May 16, 1865.

BARHAM, WILLIAM N., Private
Born in Rockingham County where he resided as a farmer or laborer prior to enlisting in Rockingham County at age 23, May 3, 1861. Present or accounted for until wounded at Gaines' Mill, Virginia, June 27, 1862. Reported absent wounded until discharged at Danville, Virginia, July 12, 1863, by reason of "tuberculosis and ascites and paralysis of [the] right fore arm." Discharge papers indicate he was wounded at Fredericksburg, Virginia, December 13, 1862.

BENNETT, JAMES H., 1st Sergeant
Resided in Rockingham County and was by occupation a farmer prior to enlisting in Rockingham County at age 27, May 3, 1861. Mustered in as Corporal and promoted to 1st Sergeant on April 26, 1862. Present or accounted for until discharged on July 29, 1862, after providing a substitute.

BENTON, JAMES M., Sergeant
Resided in Rockingham County and was by occupation a ditcher prior to enlisting in Rockingham County at age 27, May 3, 1861. Mustered in as Private. Present or accounted for until wounded at Gettysburg, Pennsylvania, July 1-3, 1863. Rejoined the company prior to September 1, 1863, when he was promoted to Sergeant. Present or accounted for until captured on the South Side Railroad, Virginia, April 2, 1865. Confined at Hart's Island, New York Harbor, until released on June 18, 1865.

BIRD, W. W., Private
Enlisted at Camp Holmes on February 26, 1864, for the war. Present or accounted for until wounded at or near Petersburg, Virginia, June 22, 1864. Died July 22, 1864, of wounds. Place of death not reported.

BLACK, CHARLES, Private
Resided in Rockingham County and was by occupation a laborer prior to enlisting in Rockingham County at age 38, May 3, 1861. Present or accounted for until he died in hospital at Danville, Virginia, July 5, 1862, of "febris typhoides."

BRIM, RICHARD, Private
Born in Rockingham County where he resided as a farmer prior to enlisting in Rockingham County at age 17, May 3, 1861. Present or accounted for until wounded in the hip at Gaines' Mill, Virginia, June 27, 1862. Discharged August 1, 1862, under the provisions of the Conscript Act.

CANTRELL, GEORGE W., Private
Resided in Rockingham County and was by occupation a laborer prior to enlisting in Rockingham County at age 16, May 3, 1861. Present or accounted for until "whipped out of the company" on October 10, 1861, "for committing larceny." Later served honorably in Company E, 45th Regiment N.C. Troops.

CANTRELL, NATHANIEL H., Private
Born in Rockingham County where he resided as a farmer prior to enlisting in Rockingham County at age 37, May 3, 1861. Present or accounted for until discharged on August 1, 1862, by reason of being over age. [May have served later in Company D, 63rd Regiment N.C. Troops (5th Regiment N.C. Cavalry).]

CARTER, DANIEL L., Sergeant
Resided in Rockingham County and was by occupation a laborer prior to enlisting in Rockingham County at age 22, May 3, 1861. Mustered in as Private and promoted to Sergeant on April 26, 1862. Present or accounted for until discharged on August 9, 1862, after providing a substitute.

CARTER, HENRY, Private
Resided in Rockingham County and was by occupation a laborer prior to enlisting in Rockingham County at age 20, May 3, 1861. Present or accounted for until captured at or near Sharpsburg, Maryland, on or about October 1, 1862. Confined at Fort McHenry, Maryland, and at Fort Monroe, Virginia, until transferred to Aiken's Landing, James River, Virginia, where he was received October 25, 1862, for exchange. Declared exchanged at Aiken's Landing on November 10, 1862. Rejoined the company prior to January 1, 1863, and present or accounted for until wounded at Gettysburg, Pennsylvania, July 1-3, 1863. Rejoined the company prior to November 1, 1863, and present or accounted for until paroled at Appomattox Court House, Virginia, April 9, 1865.

CARTER, THOMAS B., Private
Resided in Rockingham County and was by occupation a laborer prior to enlisting in Rockingham County at age 22, May 3, 1861. Present or accounted for until discharged on August 3, 1861, by reason of "bad health."

CAYTON, PHILIP, Private
Resided in Rockingham County and was by occupation a laborer prior to enlisting in Rockingham County at age 21, May 3, 1861. Present of accounted for until reported absent without leave on August 1, 1863. Reported absent without leave through October, 1864.

CHANCE, DAVID, Private
Resided in Rockingham County and was by occupation a laborer prior to enlisting in Rockingham County at age 30, May 3, 1861. Present or accounted for until accidentally wounded in the leg on February 12, 1863. Rejoined the company in July-August, 1863, and present or accounted for through December, 1864.

COBB, ANDREW J., Private
Resided in Rockingham County and was by occupation a farmer prior to enlisting in Rockingham

County at age 23, May 3, 1861. Present or accounted for until hospitalized at Charlottesville, Virginia, October 16, 1862, with a gunshot wound; however, place and date wounded not reported. Returned to duty on November 10, 1862, and present or accounted for until wounded at Spotsylvania Court House, Virginia, May 21, 1864. Died in hospital at Lynchburg, Virginia, June 27, 1864, of wounds.

COBLER, ELIJAH, Private
Enlisted at Orange Court House, Virginia, November 23, 1863, for the war. Present or accounted for through October, 1864; however, he was reported absent sick during most of that period.

COBLER, HARVEY, Private
Enlisted in Rockingham County on September 1, 1861. Present or accounted for until he died in hospital at Richmond, Virginia, June 11, 1862, of "diarrhoea."

COBLER, ROBERT, Private
Enlisted in Rockingham County on September 1, 1861. Present or accounted for until transferred to the C.S. Navy on April 16, 1864.

COLEMAN, BARTLETT Y., Private
Resided in Rockingham County and was by occupation a laborer prior to enlisting in Rockingham County at age 21, May 3, 1861. Present or accounted for until killed at Gaines' Mill, Virginia, June 27, 1862.

COLEMAN, MILTON, Private
Born in Rockingham County where he resided as a farmer prior to enlisting in Rockingham County at age 17, May 3, 1861. Present or accounted for until discharged on August 1, 1862, under the provisions of the Conscript Act. Roll of Honor indicates he was wounded in battle near Richmond, Virginia, at an unspecified date. Clark's Regiments indicates he was killed at Gaines' Mill, Virginia. No further records.

COTTRELL, JOHN, Private
Resided in Guilford County and was by occupation a painter prior to enlisting in Guilford County at age 23, May 3, 1861. Present or accounted for until captured at Burgess' Mill, Virginia, April 2, 1865. Confined at Point Lookout, Maryland, until released on June 24, 1865, after taking the Oath of Allegiance.

COX, C. C., Private
Enlisted at Camp Holmes on November 6, 1863, for the war. Present or accounted for until he deserted near Orange Court House, Virginia, February 12, 1864. Reported in confinement on company muster roll dated March-April, 1864. Present or accounted for until he deserted again near Petersburg, Virginia, August 20, 1864. Paroled at Greensboro on May 20, 1865.

COX, HARDIN, Private
Resided in Rockingham County and was by occupation a shoemaker prior to enlisting at Camp Gregg, Virginia, at age 27, March 24, 1863, for the war. Wounded in the hand at Chancellorsville, Virginia, May 3, 1863. Reported absent sick or absent without leave through October, 1864. Paroled at Appomattox Court House, Virginia, April 9, 1865. Paroled again at Greensboro in 1865.

CUMMINGS, B. YANCEY, Private
Enlisted in Rockingham County on March 29, 1864, for the war. Present or accounted for until wounded in battle on the Weldon Railroad, near Petersburg, Virginia, August 21, 1864. Died August 22, 1864, of wounds. Place of death not reported.

CURRIE, WALKER, Private
Resided in Rockingham County and was by occupation a laborer prior to enlisting in Rockingham County at age 23, May 3, 1861. Present or accounted for until he died at Suffolk, Virginia, May 10, 1862, of disease.

DABBS, WILLIAM, Private
Born in Caswell County where he resided prior to enlisting in Rockingham County at age 36, February 28, 1863, for the war. Present or accounted for until he died in hospital at Richmond, Virginia, June 27, 1863, of "typhoid pneumonia."

DAVIS, CHARLES A., Private
Resided in Rockingham County and was by occupation a laborer prior to enlisting in Rockingham County at age 21, May 3, 1861. Present or accounted for until captured at South Mountain, Maryland, September 14, 1862. Confined at Fort Delaware, Delaware, until transferred to Aiken's Landing, James River, Virginia, October 2, 1862, for exchange. Declared exchanged at Aiken's Landing on November 10, 1862. Rejoined the company prior to December 13, 1862, when he was wounded in the left hand at Fredericksburg, Virginia. Reported absent wounded or absent sick through October, 1864. Paroled at Charlotte on May 13, 1865.

DEAL, MILUS, Private
Resided in Alexander County and enlisted in Wake County at age 37, September 27, 1862, for the war. Present or accounted for until captured on the South Side Railroad, Virginia, April 2, 1865. Confined at Hart's Island, New York Harbor, until released on June 18, 1865, after taking the Oath of Allegiance.

EDWARDS, JOHN W., Private
Born in Rockingham County where he resided as a carpenter prior to enlisting in Rockingham County at age 30, May 3, 1861. Present or accounted for until discharged on August 1, 1862, under the provisions of the Conscript Act.

ELLINGTON, ALFRED B., Sergeant
Previously served in Company H of this regiment. Transferred to this company on November 1, 1861, with the rank of Private. Promoted to Sergeant on April 26, 1862. Discharged on July 9, 1862, after providing Private Lewis Gudenburg as a substitute.

ELLINGTON, DAVID S., Private
Previously served in Company H of this regiment. Transferred to this company on November 1, 1861. Present or accounted for until appointed 3rd Lieutenant and transferred to Company G, 45th Regiment N.C. Troops, April 14, 1862.

ELLINGTON, JOHN M., Private
Born in Rockingham County where he resided as a farmer prior to enlisting in Rockingham County at age 35, May 3, 1861. Mustered in as Sergeant but was reduced to ranks in March-June, 1862. Present or accounted for until discharged on August 1, 1862, under the provisions of the Conscript Act.

FRIDDLE, JOHN A., Private

Resided in Rockingham County and was by occupation a laborer prior to enlisting in Rockingham County at age 19, May 3, 1861. Present or accounted for until he died at Camp Ruffin, Virginia, September 21, 1861, of disease.

FRY, LEMUEL R., Private

Resided in Rockingham County and was by occupation a laborer prior to enlisting in Rockingham County at age 22, May 3, 1861. Present or accounted for until wounded at Gettysburg, Pennsylvania, July 1, 1863. Rejoined the company in September-October, 1863, and present or accounted for until he deserted to the enemy on or about February 18, 1865. Took the Oath of Allegiance on or about February 21, 1865.

FUQUA, QUINTON, Private

Resided in Rockingham County and was by occupation a mason prior to enlisting in Rockingham County at age 20, May 3, 1861. Present or accounted for until wounded in the abdomen at Chancellorsville, Virginia, May 3, 1863. Reported absent wounded until retired to the Invalid Corps on October 4, 1864.

GENTRY, RICHARD J., Private

Previously served in Company G, 22nd Regiment N.C. Troops (12th Regiment N.C. Volunteers). Transferred to this company on or about October 24, 1864. Captured at Petersburg, Virginia, April 3, 1865, and confined at Hart's Island, New York Harbor, until released June 19-20, 1865, after taking the Oath of Allegiance.

GILBERT, JAMES, Private

Resided in Wake County and was by occupation a printer. Place and date of enlistment not reported. Captured in Loudoun County, Virginia, June 3, 1864. Confined at Wheeling, West Virginia, until transferred to Camp Chase, Ohio, on or about October 6, 1864. Released at Camp Chase on May 13, 1865, after taking the Oath of Allegiance. Records of the Federal Provost Marshal give his age as 23.

GRADY, WILLIAM O., Private

Born in Rockingham County where he resided as a shoemaker prior to enlisting in Rockingham County at age 32, May 3, 1861. Present or accounted for until discharged on August 1, 1862, under the provisions of the Conscript Act. [May have served later in Company F, 45th Regiment N.C. Troops.]

GREAR, CHARLES, Private

Resided in Rockingham County and was by occupation a laborer prior to enlisting in Rockingham County at age 34, May 3, 1861. Present or accounted for until discharged on August 3, 1862, under the provisions of the Conscript Act. Reenlisted at Orange Court House, Virginia, November 23, 1863. Present or accounted for until wounded at Wilderness, Virginia, May 5, 1864. Reported absent wounded until August 3, 1864, when he was reported absent without leave. Reported absent without leave through October, 1864.

GREAR, JAMES, Private

Enlisted at Orange Court House, Virginia, November 23, 1863, for the war. Present or accounted for until

he deserted near Orange Court House on February 12, 1864.

GUDENBURG, LEWIS, Private

Resided in Louisiana and enlisted at Richmond, Virginia, at age 36, July 11, 1862, for the war as a substitute for Private Alfred B. Ellington. Present or accounted for until wounded and captured at Gettysburg, Pennsylvania, July 1-4, 1863. Hospitalized at Davids Island, New York Harbor, July 17-24, 1863. No further records.

HAINES, JAMES M., Private

Enlisted in Rockingham County on January 26, 1864, for the war. Present or accounted for until paroled at Appomattox Court House, Virginia, April 9, 1865.

HARFIELD, JAMES S., Private

Resided in Rockingham County and was by occupation a laborer prior to enlisting in Rockingham County at age 19, May 3, 1861. Present or accounted for until accidentally wounded in the left arm on or about June 13, 1862. Hospitalized at Richmond, Virginia, the same date. Died in hospital at Richmond on July 6, 1862, of "typhoid fever" and wounds.

HARRIS, RICHARD E. S., Private

Resided in Rockingham County and was by occupation a laborer prior to enlisting in Rockingham County at age 20, May 3, 1861. Present or accounted for until he was "whipped out of the company" on or about October 10, 1861, "for committing larceny."

HASKELL, THOMAS B., Private

Born in England and resided in Anson County where he was by occupation a farmer prior to enlisting in Stanly County at age 46, February 28, 1863, for the war. Present or accounted for until wounded at Gettysburg, Pennsylvania, July 1-3, 1863. Rejoined the company prior to September 1, 1863, and present or accounted for until discharged on April 14, 1864, by reason of "asthma."

HENDERSON, JOHN M., Private

Enlisted at Orange Court House, Virginia, March 29, 1864, for the war. Present or accounted for until paroled at Appomattox Court House, Virginia, April 9, 1865.

HICKS, JAMES, Private

Born in Caldwell County and was by occupation a farmer prior to enlisting at Camp Vance on February 14, 1864, for the war. Present or accounted for until discharged on April 25, 1864, by reason of "malformation of the knee joint." Age given on discharge papers as 18.

HOPKINS, PINKNEY J., Private

Resided in Rockingham County and was by occupation a farmer prior to enlisting in Rockingham County on August 21, 1861. Present or accounted for until wounded in the thigh at Chancellorsville, Virginia, May 3, 1863. Rejoined the company in January-February, 1864, and present or accounted for until paroled at Appomattox Court House, Virginia, April 9, 1865. Hospital record dated 1863 gives his age as 20.

HOSFORD, CRAVEN, Private

Resided in Rockingham County where he enlisted at age 30, February 28, 1863, for the war. Present or accounted for through October, 1864. Paroled at Greensboro on May 15, 1865.

HUDSON, JOEL J., Private
Resided in Rockingham County and was by occupation a laborer prior to enlisting in Rockingham County at age 21, May 3, 1861. Mustered in as Private and promoted to Corporal on April 26, 1862. Promoted to Sergeant on August 1, 1862, but was reduced to ranks on October 22, 1862. Present or accounted for until killed at Gettysburg, Pennsylvania, July 1, 1863.

INGRAM, CHARLES, Private
Resided in Caswell County or in Halifax County, Virginia, and was by occupation a farmer prior to enlisting in Caswell County at age 20, May 3, 1861. Present or accounted for until captured at or near Petersburg, Virginia, April 2, 1865. Confined at Point Lookout, Maryland, until released on June 14, 1865, after taking the Oath of Allegiance.

JONES, DANIEL, Private
Resided in Rockingham County and was by occupation a laborer prior to enlisting in Rockingham County at age 23, May 3, 1861. Present or accounted for until reported absent without leave from August 10, 1863, through October, 1864. Paroled at Appomattox Court House, Virginia, April 9, 1865.

JONES, GILES W., Private
Resided in Rockingham County and was by occupation a cooper prior to enlisting in Rockingham County at age 20, May 3, 1861. Mustered in as Private and promoted to Color Sergeant on June 27, 1862. Present or accounted for until wounded at South Mountain, Maryland, September 14, 1862. Rejoined the company in January-February, 1863, and was reduced to ranks on June 27, 1863. Present or accounted for until wounded in the left leg and captured at Gettysburg, Pennsylvania, July 1-4, 1863. Died in hospital at Davids Island, New York Harbor, August 22, 1863, following the amputation of his left leg.

JONES, WILLIAM A. T., Private
Born in Person County and resided in Rockingham County where he was by occupation a carpenter prior to enlisting in Rockingham County at age 39, May 3, 1861. Present or accounted for until discharged on August 5, 1862, by reason of being over age.

LAMBERT, E. F., Private
Enlisted in Wake County on September 27, 1862, for the war. Present or accounted for through October, 1864; however, he was reported absent sick during most of that period.

LAMBERT, JOHN, Private
Resided in Alexander County and enlisted at age 36, September 28, 1862, for the war. No further records.

LANE, DAVID, Corporal
Resided in Wilkes County and enlisted at Camp Vance on February 14, 1864, for the war. Mustered in as Private and promoted to Corporal in November, 1864-April, 1865. Present or accounted for until captured on the South Side Railroad, Virginia, April 2, 1865. Confined at Hart's Island, New York Har-

bor, until released June 19-20, 1865, after taking the Oath of Allegiance.

LESTER, OLIVER L., Private
Born in Pittsylvania County, Virginia, and resided in Rockingham County where he was by occupation a miller prior to enlisting in Rockingham County at age 36, May 3, 1861. Present or accounted for until discharged on August 1, 1862, by reason of being over age.

LIMBERGER, CHARLES, Private
Enlisted at Richmond, Virginia, July 29, 1862, for the war. Deserted August 19, 1862.

LIMBERGER, JOHN, Private
Resided in Louisiana and enlisted at age 36, July 28, 1862, for the war. Deserted July 29, 1862.

LISK, P. J., Private
Born in Anson County where he resided prior to enlisting in Stanly County at age 21, February 28, 1863, for the war. Present or accounted for until wounded at Chancellorsville, Virginia, May 3, 1863. Rejoined the company in January-February, 1864, and present or accounted for until hospitalized at Charlottesville, Virginia, February 9, 1865, with a gunshot wound of the right foot. Place and date wounded not reported. Paroled at Appomattox Court House, Virginia, April 9, 1865.

LOUDER, GEORGE, Private
Resided in Alexander County and enlisted in Wake County at age 24, September 27, 1862, for the war. Present or accounted for until he died in hospital at Richmond, Virginia, on or about December 25, 1862, of "pneumonia." Clark's *Regiments* states that he "had gotten so badly frozen" at Fredericksburg, Virginia, December 13, 1862, that "he died that night."

LOVELACE, PINKNEY, Private
Resided in Rockingham County where he enlisted at age 22, February 28, 1863, for the war. Present or accounted for until wounded at Chancellorsville, Virginia, May 3, 1863. Died in hospital at Richmond, Virginia, June 13, 1863, of "ty[phoid] fever."

McCALLUM, J. Y., Private
Place and date of enlistment not reported. Paroled at Appomattox Court House, Virginia, April 9, 1865.

McCOLLUM, DAVID, Private
Resided in Rockingham County and was by occupation a farmer prior to enlisting in Rockingham County at age 23, May 3, 1861. Present or accounted for until captured at Gettysburg, Pennsylvania, July 1, 1863, or at Falling Waters, Maryland, July 14, 1863. Confined at Point Lookout, Maryland, until paroled and transferred to City Point, Virginia, where he was received March 6, 1864, for exchange. Rejoined the company prior to June 22, 1864, when he was wounded at or near Petersburg, Virginia. Rejoined the company in September-October, 1864, and was captured at Sutherland's Station, Virginia, April 2, 1865. Confined at Hart's Island, New York Harbor, until released on June 18, 1865, after taking the Oath of Allegiance.

McCOY, JOSIAH K., Private
Born in Chatham County and resided in Rocking-

ham County where he was by occupation a bricklayer prior to enlisting in Rockingham County at age 33, May 3, 1861. Mustered in as Sergeant but was reduced to ranks in March-June, 1862. Present or accounted for until discharged on August 1, 1862, under the provisions of the Conscript Act.

MALCOM, E. D., Private
Enlisted in Rockingham County on May 3, 1862, for the war. Discharged August 3, 1862, under the provisions of the Conscript Act.

MANLEY, WILLIAM M., Private
Resided in Rockingham County and was by occupation a laborer prior to enlisting in Rockingham County at age 16, May 3, 1861. Present or accounted for until discharged on October 1, 1862, by reason of being under age.

MANLY, JAMES M., Private
Resided in Rockingham County and was by occupation a farmer prior to enlisting in Rockingham County at age 21, May 3, 1861. Present or accounted for until wounded in the knee at Chancellorsville, Virginia, May 3, 1863. Rejoined the company in September-October, 1863, and present or accounted for until wounded at Spotsylvania Court House, Virginia, May 21, 1864. Reported absent wounded until retired to the Invalid Corps on January 11, 1865.

MANLY, JOHN, Private
Resided in Rockingham County and was by occupation a farmer prior to enlisting in Rockingham County at age 18, May 3, 1861. Present or accounted for until captured at South Mountain, Maryland, on or about September 15, 1862. Confined at Fort Delaware, Delaware, until transferred to Aiken's Landing, James River, Virginia, October 2, 1862, for exchange. Declared exchanged at Aiken's Landing on November 10, 1862. Rejoined the company prior to January 1, 1863, and present or accounted for until he deserted near Culpeper Court House, Virginia, June 19, 1863. Confined at Fort Delaware until transferred to Point Lookout, Maryland, October 15-18, 1863. Records of the Federal Provost Marshal indicate he remained in confinement until February 18, 1865; however, it is unclear whether he was paroled and transferred for exchange on that date or if he remained in confinement through April, 1865. Paroled at Greensboro on May 5, 1865.

MANLY, WILLIAM J., Private
Resided in Rockingham County and was by occupation a farmer prior to enlisting in Rockingham County at age 24, May 3, 1861. Mustered in as Sergeant but was reduced to ranks on or about March 7, 1862. Present or accounted for until wounded at Gaines' Mill, Virginia, June 27, 1862. Rejoined the company prior to November 1, 1862, and present or accounted for until wounded in the face and/or foot at Chancellorsville, Virginia, May 3, 1863. Rejoined the company in November-December, 1863, and present or accounted for until wounded at or near Reams' Station, Virginia, August 26, 1864. Rejoined the company in September-October, 1864, and present or accounted for until he deserted to the enemy on or about February 18, 1865. Took the Oath of Allegiance on or about February 21, 1865.

MARCRUM, FREEMAN, Private
Born in Rockingham County where he resided as a farmer prior to enlisting in Rockingham County at age 32, May 3, 1861. Present or accounted for until discharged on August 1, 1862, under the provisions of the Conscript Act.

MEADOR, WILLIAM W., Private
Resided in Rockingham County and was by occupation a laborer prior to enlisting in Rockingham County at age 22, May 3, 1861. Present or accounted for until wounded at Gaines' Mill, Virginia, June 27, 1862. Rejoined the company prior to September 14, 1862, when he was captured at South Mountain, Maryland. Confined at Fort Delaware, Delaware, until transferred to Aiken's Landing, James River, Virginia, October 2, 1862, for exchange. Declared exchanged at Aiken's Landing on November 10, 1862. Rejoined the company in January-February, 1863, and present or accounted for until captured on the South Side Railroad, near Petersburg, Virginia, April 2, 1865. Confined at Hart's Island, New York Harbor, until released on June 18, 1865, after taking the Oath of Allegiance.

MERIDITH, J. M., Private
Resided in Guilford County and enlisted at Camp Holmes on October 13, 1864, for the war. Deserted on October 27, 1864, and deserted to the enemy on or about January 29, 1865. Took the Oath of Amnesty at City Point, Virginia, February 1, 1865.

MILLER, JAMES, Private
Resided in Rockingham County and was by occupation a laborer prior to enlisting in Rockingham County at age 21, May 3, 1861. Present or accounted for until he died at Shepardstown, Virginia. Date and cause of death not reported.

NEWMAN, HIRAM, Private
Born in Rockingham County where he resided as a ditcher prior to enlisting in Rockingham County at age 29, May 3, 1861. Present or accounted for until discharged on August 1, 1862, under the provisions of the Conscript Act.

NUNN, WILLIAM J., Private
Resided in Rockingham County and was by occupation a laborer prior to enlisting in Rockingham County at age 23, May 3, 1861. Present or accounted for through December, 1863. Reported absent without leave from January-February, 1864, through October, 1864.

PADGETT, JOEL J., Private
Born in Rutherford County and resided in Alexander County where he was by occupation a farmer prior to enlisting in Wake County at age 18, September 27, 1862, for the war. Present or accounted for until discharged on November 12, 1863, by reason of "hypertrophy of the heart with ascites."

PEAY, JOHN Y., Private
Resided in Rockingham County and was by occupation a laborer prior to enlisting in Rockingham County at age 21, May 3, 1861. Present or accounted for through December, 1863. Reported absent without leave from January-February, 1864, through October, 1864.

PELOGINO, JOSEPH, Private

Resided in Virginia and enlisted at Richmond, Virginia, at age 36, August 1, 1862. Deserted on or about August 19, 1862.

PERDUE, HAZZARD, Private

Born in Lenoir County and resided in Rockingham County where he was by occupation a harness maker prior to enlisting in Rockingham County at age 27, May 3, 1861. Present or accounted for until killed at Fredericksburg, Virginia, December 13, 1862.

PICKERELL, JAMES, Private

Born in Pittsylvania County, Virginia, and resided in Rockingham County where he enlisted at age 28, February 28, 1863, for the war. Present or accounted for until killed at Chancellorsville, Virginia, May 3, 1863.

PIRTLE, ANDREW J., Musician

Born in Rockingham County where he resided as a laborer or carpenter prior to enlisting in Rockingham County at age 33, May 3, 1861. Mustered in as Musician. Present or accounted for until discharged on August 1, 1862, under the provisions of the Conscript Act. Later served in Company H, 45th Regiment N.C. Troops.

POWERS, W. D., Private

Resided in Wake County where he enlisted on February 14, 1864, for the war. Present or accounted for until wounded in the left thumb and right shoulder at or near Petersburg, Virginia, August 19-25, 1864. Reported absent wounded until he returned to duty on November 8, 1864. Paroled at Raleigh on May 12, 1865.

PRATT, JOSEPHUS, Sergeant

Resided in Rockingham County and was by occupation a laborer prior to enlisting in Rockingham County at age 18, May 3, 1861. Mustered in as Private and promoted to Sergeant on February 25, 1863. Present or accounted for until wounded in the left thigh and captured at Gettysburg, Pennsylvania, July 1-5, 1863. Hospitalized at Chester, Pennsylvania, until transferred to City Point, Virginia, where he was received September 23, 1863, for exchange. Rejoined the company in January-February, 1864, and present or accounted for until captured on the South Side Railroad, near Petersburg, Virginia, April 2, 1865. Confined at Hart's Island, New York Harbor, until released on June 18, 1865, after taking the Oath of Allegiance.

PRATT, WILLIAM J., Private

Born in Rockingham County where he resided as a farmer prior to enlisting in Rockingham County at age 40, May 3, 1861. Present or accounted for until discharged on August 1, 1862, by reason of being over age. Paroled at Greensboro on May 18, 1865.

PULLIAM, JAMES N., Private

Enlisted in Rockingham County on September 1, 1861. Present or accounted for until he died in Rockingham County on November 1, 1862. Cause of death not reported.

PURCELL, JAMES T., Sergeant

Resided in Rockingham County and was by occupation a laborer prior to enlisting in Rockingham County at age 24, May 3, 1861. Mustered in as

Private and promoted to Sergeant on April 26, 1862. Present or accounted for until wounded in the right shoulder at Chancellorsville, Virginia, May 3, 1863. Reported absent wounded or absent on detail until retired to the Invalid Corps on July 12, 1864.

PURCELL, WILLIAM W., Private

Resided in Rockingham County and was by occupation a laborer prior to enlisting in Rockingham County at age 25, May 3, 1861. Present or accounted for until wounded in the arm at Gaines' Mill, Virginia, June 27, 1862. Died in hospital at Richmond, Virginia, July 28, 1862, of wounds.

RHODES, INGRAM, Corporal

Resided in Rockingham County and was by occupation a carpenter prior to enlisting in Rockingham County at age 21, May 3, 1861. Mustered in as Private. Present or accounted for until wounded at Gaines' Mill, Virginia, June 27, 1862. Rejoined the company prior to November 1, 1862, and was promoted to Corporal on December 6, 1862. Present or accounted for until wounded in the right leg at Chancellorsville, Virginia, May 3, 1863. Rejoined the company in July-August, 1863, and present or accounted for until paroled at Appomattox Court House, Virginia, April 9, 1865.

RHODES, NOEL, Private

Resided in Rockingham County and was by occupation a carpenter prior to enlisting in Rockingham County at age 30, May 3, 1861. Present or accounted for until killed at Gaines' Mill, Virginia, June 27, 1862.

ROGERS, JAMES, Private

Resided in Rockingham County and was by occupation a laborer prior to enlisting in Rockingham County at age 25, May 3, 1861. Present or accounted for until captured at "Smithfield" in March-June, 1862. Received at Aiken's Landing, James River, Virginia, August 5, 1862, for exchange. Rejoined the company prior to November 1, 1862, and present or accounted for until wounded and captured at Gettysburg, Pennsylvania, July 1-4, 1863. Hospitalized at Davids Island, New York Harbor, until paroled and transferred to City Point, Virginia, where he was received September 8, 1863, for exchange. Rejoined the company in January-February, 1864, and present or accounted for until paroled at Appomattox Court House, Virginia, April 9, 1865.

SCRUGGS, JAMES, Sergeant

Born in Rockingham County where he resided as a laborer prior to enlisting in Rockingham County at age 19, May 3, 1861. Mustered in as Private and promoted to Sergeant on December 30, 1862. Present or accounted for until he died at Guinea Station, Virginia, on or about January 31, 1863, of disease.

SCRUGGS, THOMAS B., Private

Resided in Rockingham County and was by occupation a farmer prior to enlisting in Rockingham County at age 41, May 3, 1861. Mustered in as Corporal but was reduced to ranks in March-June, 1862. Present or accounted for until wounded in the knee at Gaines' Mill, Virginia, June 27, 1862. Died in hospital at Richmond, Virginia, July 16, 1862, of wounds.

SETLIFF, ALEXANDER, Private
Resided in Rockingham County and was by occupation a laborer prior to enlisting in Rockingham County at age 32, May 3, 1861. Present or accounted for until hospitalized at Richmond, Virginia, July 3, 1862, with a gunshot wound; however, place and date wounded not reported. Died July 8, 1862.

SHARP, HENRY J., Sergeant
Resided in Rockingham County and was by occupation a laborer prior to enlisting in Rockingham County at age 19, May 3, 1861. Mustered in as Private and promoted to Corporal on August 12, 1862. Captured at Williamsport, Maryland, September 16, 1862. Confined at Fort Delaware, Delaware, until transferred to Aiken's Landing, James River, Virginia, October 2, 1862, for exchange. Declared exchanged at Aiken's Landing on November 10, 1862. Rejoined the company in January-February, 1863, and promoted to Sergeant on September 1, 1864. Present or accounted for until captured at or near Petersburg, Virginia, April 2, 1865. Confined at Point Lookout, Maryland, until released on June 20, 1865, after taking the Oath of Allegiance.

SHEA, THOMAS, Private
Resided in Maryland and was by occupation a tobacconist prior to enlisting in Guilford County at age 30, May 3, 1861. Mustered in as Corporal but was reduced to ranks on June 6, 1861. Present or accounted for until discharged on or about March 2, 1862, "by reason of being a Marylander."

SHRIEVES, JAMES S., Corporal
Born in Rockingham County where he resided as a laborer prior to enlisting in Rockingham County at age 23, May 3, 1861. Mustered in as Private and promoted to Corporal on April 26, 1862. Present or accounted for until he died in hospital at Staunton, Virginia, October 31, 1862, of "febris typhoides."

SIMPSON, POWHATTAN D., 1st Sergeant
Resided in Rockingham County and was by occupation a farmer prior to enlisting in Rockingham County at age 22, May 3, 1861. Mustered in as Corporal. Present or accounted for until wounded at or near Frayser's Farm, Virginia, on or about June 30, 1862. Rejoined the company prior to November 1, 1862, and was promoted to Sergeant on December 6, 1862. Promoted to 1st Sergeant on December 30, 1862. Present or accounted for until wounded in the toe at Chancellorsville, Virginia, May 3, 1863. Rejoined the company in September-October, 1863, and present or accounted for until paroled at Appomattox Court House, Virginia, April 9, 1865.

SIMPSON, STARLING, Private
Resided in Rockingham County and was by occupation a laborer prior to enlisting in Rockingham County at age 20, May 3, 1861. Discharged on August 1, 1862, after providing a substitute.

SMOTHERS, GARLAND D., Sergeant
Resided in Rockingham County and was by occupation a laborer prior to enlisting in Rockingham County at age 26, May 3, 1861. Mustered in as Private and promoted to Corporal in April, 1862. Promoted to Sergeant prior to September 14, 1862, when he was killed at South Mountain, Maryland.

SMOTHERS, THOMAS MADISON, Private
Enlisted in Rockingham County on August 21, 1861. Present or accounted for until captured at Gettysburg, Pennsylvania, July 1-3, 1863. Confined at Fort Delaware, Delaware, until released on or about September 22, 1863, after joining the U.S. Army. Assigned to Company E, 3rd Regiment Maryland Cavalry.

SOWELL, ERASMUS, Private
Resided in Rockingham County and was by occupation a laborer prior to enlisting in Rockingham County at age 23, May 3, 1861. Present or accounted for until he died at Farmville, Virginia, September 1, 1862, of "phthisis."

STANLY, ALFRED, Private
Resided in Virginia and enlisted in Rockingham County at age 25, February 28, 1863, for the war. Present or accounted for until paroled at Appomattox Court House, Virginia, April 9, 1865. North Carolina pension records indicate that he "lost his right eye" at Gettysburg, Pennsylvania.

STEWART, ROBERT M., Private
Resided in Rockingham County and was by occupation a laborer prior to enlisting in Rockingham County at age 19, May 3, 1861. Present or accounted for until killed at Wilderness, Virginia, May 5, 1864.

STIER, BEDFORD B., Private
Resided in Rockingham County and was by occupation a laborer prior to enlisting in Rockingham County at age 36, May 3, 1861. Present or accounted for until wounded at Gaines' Mill, Virginia, June 27, 1862. Died at Richmond, Virginia, July 2, 1862, of wounds.

STIER, FREDERICK, Musician
Resided in Rockingham County and was by occupation a blacksmith prior to enlisting in Rockingham County at age 60, May 3, 1861. Mustered in as Musician (Drummer). Present or accounted for until discharged on October 9, 1861, by reason of disability.

STIER, WILLIAM, Private
Enlisted in Rockingham County on February 16, 1864, for the war. Present or accounted for until captured at Wilderness, Virginia, May 6, 1864. Confined at Point Lookout, Maryland, where he died June 22, 1864. Cause of death not reported.

STONE, ALFRED T., Private
Resided in Rockingham County and was by occupation a laborer prior to enlisting in Rockingham County at age 19, May 3, 1861. Present or accounted for until he died in hospital at Danville, Virginia, July 20, 1862, of "phthisis pulmonalis."

STONE, WILLIAM, Private
Enlisted at Spotsylvania Court House, Virginia, May 8, 1864, for the war. Present or accounted for until captured at Petersburg, Virginia, August 3, 1864. Confined at Point Lookout, Maryland, until transferred to Elmira, New York, August 8, 1864. Died at

Elmira on September 10, 1864, of "chronic diarrhoea."

SUITS, GEORGE W., Private
Resided in Rockingham County and was by occupation a laborer prior to enlisting in Rockingham County at age 20, May 3, 1861. Present or accounted for until paroled at Appomattox Court House, Virginia, April 9, 1865.

SUTLIFF, ABRAHAM, Private
Born in Rockingham County where he resided as a farmer prior to enlisting in Rockingham County at age 37, May 3, 1861. Present or accounted for until discharged on November 13, 1861, by reason of disability.

SUTLIFF, JOSEPH, Private
Resided in Rockingham County and was by occupation a laborer prior to enlisting in Rockingham County at age 30, May 3, 1861. Present or accounted for until captured at Appomattox, Virginia, April 3, 1865. Confined at Hart's Island, New York Harbor, until released June 19-20, 1865, after taking the Oath of Allegiance.

TATE, WILLIAM, Private
Resided in Caswell County and enlisted at age 37, September 28, 1862, for the war. No further records.

TAYLOR, SAMUEL, Private
Born in Rockingham County where he resided as a farmer prior to enlisting in Rockingham County at age 15, May 3, 1861. Present or accounted for until discharged on August 1, 1862, by reason of being under age.

THOMAS, J. N., Private
Enlisted at Camp Holmes on February 26, 1864, for the war. Present or accounted for through October, 1864.

THOMAS, JOHN A., Corporal
Resided in Rockingham County and was by occupation a laborer prior to enlisting in Rockingham County at age 24, May 3, 1861. Mustered in as Private and promoted to Musician on October 9, 1861. Promoted to Corporal on August 12, 1862. Present or accounted for until wounded in the left hand at Fredericksburg, Virginia, December 13, 1862. Rejoined the company in September-October, 1863, and present or accounted for until paroled at Greensboro on May 13, 1865.

THOMAS, JOSEPH, Private
Resided in Bertie County. Place and date of enlistment not reported. Captured at Hatcher's Run, Virginia, April 1, 1865. Confined at Point Lookout, Maryland, until released on June 21, 1865, after taking the Oath of Allegiance.

THOMAS, PETER, Private
Resided in Rockingham County and was by occupation a laborer prior to enlisting in Rockingham County at age 21, May 3, 1861. Present or accounted for through October, 1864; however, he was reported absent sick during most of that period.

TOLLOCK, P., Private
A company muster roll dated March-April, 1863, states he enlisted in Rockingham County on February 28, 1862, and was discharged on April 7, 1863. Reason discharged not reported. No further records.

TROXLER, CALVIN, Private
Resided in Rockingham County and was by occupation a laborer prior to enlisting in Rockingham County at age 22, May 3, 1861. Present or accounted for until he died in hospital at Suffolk, Virginia, June 30, 1861, of disease.

TROXLER, GEORGE, Private
Resided in Rockingham County and was by occupation a carpenter prior to enlisting in Rockingham County at age 21, May 3, 1861. Present or accounted for until wounded in the right side and left hip at Chancellorsville, Virginia, May 3, 1863. Reported absent wounded through October, 1864. Paroled at Greensboro on May 13, 1865.

VERNON, RICHARD, Private
Enlisted at Orange Court House, Virginia, November 23, 1863, for the war. Present or accounted for until he deserted on February 12, 1864. Reported present in confinement on company muster roll dated March-April, 1864. Deserted again on May 21, 1864.

WALL, BOOKER, Private
Resided in Rockingham County and was by occupation a laborer prior to enlisting in Rockingham County at age 22, May 3, 1861. Present or accounted for until wounded at Fredericksburg, Virginia, December 13, 1862. Rejoined the company in November-December, 1863, and present or accounted for until paroled at Appomattox Court House, Virginia, April 9, 1865.

WARREN, MICAJAH, Private
Resided in Rockingham County and was by occupation a ditcher prior to enlisting in Rockingham County at age 26, May 3, 1861. Present or accounted for until he died in hospital at Lynchburg, Virginia, July 4, 1863, of "febris remittens." Clark's *Regiments* indicates that he "fell" at Gaines' Mill, Virginia, on or about June 27, 1862. No further records.

WATLINGTON, E. R., Private
Enlisted at Camp Holmes on October 17, 1864, for the war. Paroled at Appomattox Court House, Virginia, April 9, 1865.

WEBSTER, THOMAS H., Private
Resided in Alexander County and enlisted in Wake County at age 36, September 27, 1862, for the war. Present or accounted for until wounded at Spotsylvania Court House, Virginia, May 21, 1864. Reported absent wounded until August 3, 1864, when he was reported absent without leave. Reported absent without leave through October, 1864.

WILLIAMS, H. H., Private
Enlisted at Camp Holmes on February 26, 1864, for the war. Present or accounted for until captured at Appomattox, Virginia, April 8, 1865. Confined at Point Lookout, Maryland, where he died May 10, 1865, of "scurvy."

WILSON, WILLIAM S., Private
Resided in Rockingham County and was by occupation a ditcher prior to enlisting in Rockingham County at age 28, May 3, 1861. Present or accounted for until he deserted on July 20, 1863. Reported in confinement without pay for six months at hard labor on company muster roll dated May-June, 1864. Captured in hospital at Richmond, Virginia, April 3, 1865, and paroled April 27, 1865.

WINCHESTER, GREENVILLE, 1st Sergeant
Enlisted at Camp Holmes on October 19, 1864, for the war. Mustered in as Private. Promoted to 1st Sergeant prior to April 9, 1865, when he was paroled at Appomattox Court House, Virginia.

WINCHESTER, JOHN E., Private
Previously served in Company L, 21st Regiment N.C. Troops (11th Regiment N.C. Volunteers). Transferred to this company on March 4, 1863, in exchange for Private Charles Baker. Present or accounted for until wounded in the left hand at Wilderness, Virginia, May 5, 1864. Rejoined the company on September 15, 1864, and present or accounted for until captured at Sutherland's Station, Virginia, April 2, 1865. Confined at Hart's Island, New York Harbor, until released June 17-18, 1865, after taking the Oath of Allegiance.

WRAY, JAMES D., Private
Enlisted in Rockingham County on August 21, 1861. Present or accounted for until reported missing at Gettysburg, Pennsylvania, July 1, 1863. No further records.

YORK, JOSEPH, Private
Resided in Rockingham County and was by occupation a laborer prior to enlisting in Rockingham County at age 21, May 3, 1861. Present or accounted for until he died at Camp Ruffin, Virginia, September 16, 1861, of disease.

COMPANY K

This company, known as the Dixie Boys, was from Rockingham County and enlisted at Lawsonville on May 22, 1861. It tendered its service the same day and was ordered to proceed to Weldon. It departed for that town on May 30 and arrived the next day. At Weldon it was informed that it had been assigned to the regiment as Company K and that the regiment had moved to Suffolk, Virginia. The company proceeded to Suffolk and joined the regiment on the night of May 31. After joining the regiment the company functioned as a part of the regiment, and its history for the war period is recorded as a part of the regimental history.

The information contained in the following roster of the company was compiled principally from company muster rolls for June 3, 1861-June, 1863, and September, 1863-October, 1864. No company muster rolls were found for July-August, 1863, or for the period after October, 1864. In addition to the company muster rolls, Roll of Honor records, receipt rolls, hospital records, prisoner of war records, and other primary records, supplemented by state pension applications, United Daughters of the Confederacy records, and postwar rosters and histories, all provided useful information.

OFFICERS
CAPTAINS

BAILEY, GILES P.
Resided in Rockingham County and was by occupation a physician prior to enlisting in Rockingham County at age 36. Elected Captain May 22, 1861. Present or accounted for until "shot and stabbed in a hand-to-hand fight" and captured at Williamsburg, Virginia, May 5, 1862, "while gallantly leading his co[mpany] in the charge." Hospitalized at Williamsburg and at Fort Monroe, Virginia, until transferred to Fort Delaware, Delaware, on or about July 15, 1862. Exchanged at Aiken's Landing, James River, Virginia, August 5, 1862. Reported absent wounded until he resigned on October 15, 1862, by reason of wounds received at Williamsburg.

WATT, ROBERT L.
Resided in Rockingham County and was by occupation a cadet prior to enlisting in Rockingham County at age 18. Elected 1st Lieutenant on May 4, 1861, and was commissioned on May 22, 1861. Present or accounted for until wounded at Williamsburg, Virginia, on or about May 5, 1862. Rejoined the company in November-December, 1862, and was appointed Captain to rank from November 8, 1862. Present or accounted for until he died at Camp Gregg, Virginia, January 15, 1863, of "pneumonia."

GUERRANT, HUGH LINDSAY
Resided in Rockingham County and was by occupation a merchant prior to enlisting in Rockingham County at age 26. Elected 2nd Lieutenant to rank from May 22, 1861, and was promoted to 1st Lieutenant on November 8, 1862. Promoted to Captain on January 15, 1863. Present or accounted for until wounded at Chancellorsville, Virginia, May 3, 1863. Rejoined the company prior to July 1, 1863, and present or accounted for until "shot in the hand" at Wilderness, Virginia, in May, 1864. Rejoined the company prior to July 1, 1864, and present or accounted for until paroled at Appomattox Court House, Virginia, April 9, 1865.

LIEUTENANTS

ANDERSON, GEORGE W., 1st Lieutenant
Resided in Rockingham County and was by occupation a plasterer prior to enlisting in Rockingham County at age 20, May 22, 1861. Mustered in as Corporal and promoted to 1st Sergeant on July 17, 1861. Present or accounted for until wounded at Gaines' Mill, Virginia, on or about June 27, 1862. Rejoined the company prior to November 1, 1862, and was elected 3rd Lieutenant on November 8, 1862. Promoted to 2nd Lieutenant on January 15, 1863, and promoted to 1st Lieutenant on July 1, 1863. Present or accounted for until appointed Adjutant (1st Lieutenant) on November 10, 1863, to rank from October 23, 1863, and transferred to the Field and Staff of this regiment.

McCOLLUM, ROBERT F., 2nd Lieutenant
Resided in Rockingham County and was by occupation a trader prior to enlisting in Rockingham County at age 28, May 22, 1861. Mustered in as Private and promoted to Sergeant on April 26, 1862. Present or accounted for until captured at Williamsburg, Virginia, May 6, 1862. Exchanged at Aiken's Landing, James River, Virginia, August 5, 1862. Rejoined the company prior to November 1, 1862, and was promoted to 1st Sergeant on May 3, 1863. Appointed 2nd Lieutenant on August 1, 1863. Present or accounted for until he resigned on February 15, 1865,

by reason of "a severe contusion of the left foot injuring the dorsal bones." Resignation accepted March 16, 1865.

NUNNALLY, JOHN H., 3rd Lieutenant
Resided in Rockingham County and was by occupation a farmer prior to enlisting at age 30. Elected 3rd Lieutenant on May 4, 1861, and was commissioned on May 22, 1861. Present or accounted for until he resigned on July 9, 1861. Reason he resigned not reported.

NUNNALLY, WILLIAM M., 1st Lieutenant
Resided in Rockingham County and was by occupation a merchant prior to enlisting in Rockingham County at age 26, May 22, 1861. Mustered in as 1st Sergeant and was elected 3rd Lieutenant on July 13, 1861. Promoted to 2nd Lieutenant on November 8, 1862, and was promoted to 1st Lieutenant on January 15, 1863. Present or accounted for until killed at Gettysburg, Pennsylvania, July 1, 1863.

RAWLEY, TAYLOR L., 1st Lieutenant
Previously served as Sergeant in Company G, 14th Regiment N.C. Troops (4th Regiment N.C. Volunteers). Elected 1st Lieutenant in this company on or about November 25, 1863. Present or accounted for until paroled at Appomattox Court House, Virginia, April 9, 1865.

TOTTEN, WILLIAM R., 3rd Lieutenant
Resided in Rockingham County and was by occupation a trader prior to enlisting in Rockingham County at age 23, May 22, 1861. Mustered in as Private. Wounded and captured at Williamsburg, Virginia, on or about May 6, 1862. Hospitalized at Washington, D.C. Exchanged at Aiken's Landing, James River, Virginia, August 5, 1862. Promoted to Corporal on September 30, 1862, and rejoined the company prior to November 1, 1862. Promoted to 1st Sergeant on November 8, 1862, and was appointed 3rd Lieutenant on March 8, 1863. Present or accounted for until wounded in the leg at Gettysburg, Pennsylvania, July 1, 1863. Leg amputated. Died July 10, 1863. Place of death not reported.

NONCOMMISSIONED OFFICERS AND PRIVATES

ALLEN, WILLIAM P., Private
Born in Rockingham County where he resided as a farmer prior to enlisting in Rockingham County at age 19, May 22, 1861. Present or accounted for until he died in hospital at Richmond, Virginia, June 4, 1862, of "feb[ris] typh[oid]."

AMOS, JESSE E., Private
Resided in Rockingham County and was by occupation a blacksmith prior to enlisting in Rockingham County at age 35, May 22, 1861. Mustered in as Sergeant but was reduced to ranks on or about April 26, 1862. Present or accounted for until wounded at South Mountain, Maryland, September 14, 1862. Rejoined the company in November-December, 1862, and was detailed as a blacksmith at Richmond, Virginia, December 9, 1862. Reported absent on detail through June, 1864. Rejoined the company on or about July 13, 1864, and present or accounted for until he died near Petersburg, Virginia, February 1, 1865, of disease.

BATEMAN, JOHN, Private
Resided in Rockingham County and was by occupation a farmer prior to enlisting in Rockingham County at age 21, May 22, 1861. Present or accounted for until captured at Williamsburg, Virginia, on or about May 5, 1862. Confined at Fort Monroe, Virginia. Exchanged prior to November 1, 1862, and rejoined the company prior to January 1, 1863. Present or accounted for until captured at Gettysburg, Pennsylvania, July 1-4, 1863. Confined at Fort Delaware, Delaware, where he died September 27, 1863, of "remittent fever."

BENTON, JOSEPH, Private
Enlisted in Wake County on October 19, 1864, for the war. Present or accounted for through October, 1864.

BIGGS, WILLIAM R., Private
Enlisted in Wake County on November 24, 1863, for the war. Deserted December 20, 1863, but rejoined the company prior to May 1, 1864. Present or accounted for until captured in hospital at Richmond, Virginia, April 3, 1865. Confined at Libby Prison, Richmond, until transferred to Newport News, Virginia, April 23, 1865. Released at Newport News on June 30, 1865, after taking the Oath of Allegiance.

BILLINGS, J., Private
Place and date of enlistment not reported. Paroled at Appomattox Court House, Virginia, April 9, 1865.

BOWMAN, GEORGE R., Private
Resided in Rockingham County where he enlisted at age 26, August 5, 1861. Mustered in as Private and was promoted to Corporal prior to April 26, 1862, when he was reduced to ranks. Promoted to Corporal on November 8, 1862. Deserted at Fredericksburg, Virginia, December 13, 1862, and was reduced to ranks on that date. No further records.

BOWMAN, THOMAS P., Private
Resided in Rockingham County and was by occupation a farmer prior to enlisting in Rockingham County at age 24, May 22, 1861. Present or accounted for until wounded at South Mountain, Maryland, September 14, 1862. "Took the woods" on or about December 20, 1862, and was reported as a deserter from March 1, 1863, until he was "sent back to his command" on February 20, 1864. Wounded at Wilderness, Virginia, May 5, 1864, and was reported absent wounded through October, 1864.

BOYLES, DAVID A., Sergeant
Born in Rockingham County where he resided as a farmer prior to enlisting in Rockingham County at age 17, May 22, 1861. Mustered in as Private and was elected Corporal on April 26, 1862. Promoted to Sergeant on September 18, 1862. Present or accounted for until he died in hospital at Staunton, Virginia, December 5, 1862, of "diphtheria."

BOYLES, JOHN W., Private
Resided in Rockingham County and was by occupation a farmer prior to enlisting in Rockingham County at age 18, May 22, 1861. Present or accounted for until captured at Williamsburg, Virginia, on or about May 5, 1862. Confined at Fort Monroe, Virginia, until exchanged prior to November 1, 1862. Rejoined the company prior to January 1,

1863, and present or accounted for until captured at Gettysburg, Pennsylvania, July 1-4, 1863. Confined at Fort Delaware, Delaware, until transferred to Point Lookout, Maryland, October 18-20, 1863. Died in hospital at Point Lookout on January 3, 1864, of "scorbutis & chronic diarrh[oea]."

BRAN, COLEMAN, Private
Resided in Rockingham County and was by occupation a farmer prior to enlisting in Rockingham County at age 25, May 22, 1861. Present or accounted for until discharged on August 9, 1862, after providing Private John Roberson as a substitute. Records of the Federal Provost Marshal indicate he was captured at Dinwiddie, Virginia, April 3, 1865. Confined at Point Lookout, Maryland, until released on June 23, 1865, after taking the Oath of Allegiance.

BRANN, JOHN V., Private
Resided in Rockingham County where he enlisted at age 24, August 5, 1861. Present or accounted for until he died on May 20, 1863, of disease. Place of death not reported.

BRAY, HENRY J., Private
Resided in Rockingham County and was by occupation a mechanic prior to enlisting in Rockingham County at age 19, May 22, 1861. Present or accounted for until wounded in the left thigh at Chancellorsville, Virginia, May 3, 1863. Reported absent wounded through December 13, 1864.

BRINSFIELD, GRANDERSON H., Private
Resided in Rockingham County and was by occupation a farmer prior to enlisting in Rockingham County at age 20, May 22, 1861. Present or accounted for until paroled at Appomattox Court House, Virginia, April 9, 1865.

BROWN, JAMES W., Private
Born in Rockingham County where he resided prior to enlisting in Rockingham County at age 18, August 4, 1862, for the war. Present or accounted for until he died at Mount Jackson, Virginia, October 24, 1862, or at Gordonsville, Virginia, April 2, 1863, of "small pox."

BROWN, THOMPSON, Private
Enlisted in Wake County on October 19, 1864, for the war. Present or accounted for until captured at Appomattox, Virginia, April 4, 1865. Confined at Hart's Island, New York Harbor, until released on June 19, 1865, after taking the Oath of Allegiance.

BROWN, WILLIAM, Private
Enlisted in Wake County on December 16, 1863, for the war. Present or accounted for until captured at Wilderness, Virginia, May 5, 1864, or at Beaver Dam Station, Virginia, May 9, 1864. Confined at Point Lookout, Maryland, until transferred to Elmira, New York, July 28, 1864. Died at Elmira on February 28, 1865, of "variola."

BURCHFIELD, CHARLES, Private
Enlisted at Camp Holmes on February 13, 1864, for the war. Present or accounted for until he died on April 4, 1864, of disease. Place of death not reported.

BURTON, THOMAS J., Private
Resided in Rockingham County where he enlisted at age 18, August 5, 1861. Present or accounted for

until wounded and captured at Williamsburg, Virginia, on or about May 5, 1862. Confined at Fort Monroe, Virginia, until exchanged on September 1, 1862. Returned to duty on or about February 10, 1863, and was detailed in hospital at Richmond, Virginia. Rejoined the company on or about November 1, 1864. Captured at Appomattox, Virginia, April 4, 1865, and confined at Hart's Island, New York Harbor, until released June 19-20, 1865, after taking the Oath of Allegiance.

CALL, JAMES H., Private
Resided in Wilkes County and enlisted in Wake County at age 18, September 27, 1862, for the war. Present or accounted for until captured at Wilderness, Virginia, May 6, 1864. Confined at Point Lookout, Maryland, until transferred to Elmira, New York, August 10, 1864. Died at Elmira on December 10, 1864, of "pneumonia."

CAPE, HENRY, Private
Resided in Rockingham County and was by occupation a trader prior to enlisting in Rockingham County at age 20, May 22, 1861. Present or accounted for until wounded at Chancellorsville, Virginia, May 3, 1863. Rejoined the company in May-June, 1864, and present or accounted for until captured in hospital at Richmond, Virginia, April 3, 1865. Paroled at Richmond on May 3, 1865, and took the Oath of Allegiance on May 25, 1865.

CAPE, JOHN T., Private
Born in Orange County and resided in Rockingham County where he was by occupation a trader prior to enlisting in Rockingham County at age 21, May 22, 1861. Present or accounted for until he died in hospital at Richmond, Virginia, October 28, 1862, of "febris typhoides."

CARTER, BENJAMIN T., Private
Resided in Rockingham County and was by occupation a hireling prior to enlisting in Rockingham County at age 33, May 22, 1861. Present or accounted for until wounded and captured at or near Gettysburg, Pennsylvania, July 1-6, 1863. Hospitalized at Chester, Pennsylvania, where he died August 29, 1863, of "pyaemia."

CHAMBERS, JAMES F., Private
Resided in Rockingham County and was by occupation a hireling prior to enlisting in Rockingham County at age 16, May 22, 1861. Present or accounted for until discharged on October 1, 1862, by reason of being under age.

CHAMBERS, JOHN, Private
Resided in Rockingham County where he enlisted at age 27, August 4, 1862, for the war. Present or accounted for until captured near Hanover Junction, Virginia, May 23, 1864. Confined at Point Lookout, Maryland, until paroled and transferred to Aiken's Landing, James River, Virginia, March 14, 1865, for exchange. Exchanged at Boulware's Wharf, James River, March 16, 1865.

CHAMBERS, PEYTON, Private
Born in Rockingham County where he resided as a farmer or trader prior to enlisting in Rockingham County at age 25, May 22, 1861. Present or accounted for until killed at Sharpsburg, Maryland, on or about September 17, 1862.

CHANCE, ANDREW JACKSON, 1st Sergeant
Born in Rockingham County where he resided prior to enlisting in Rockingham County at age 30, August 5, 1861. Mustered in as Private and promoted to Sergeant on April 26, 1862. Present or accounted for until captured at South Mountain, Maryland, on or about September 15, 1862, or at Sharpsburg, Maryland, September 17, 1862. Confined at Fort Delaware, Delaware, until transferred to Aiken's Landing, James River, Virginia, October 2, 1862, for exchange. Declared exchanged at Aiken's Landing on November 10, 1862. Rejoined the company prior to January 1, 1863, and was promoted to 1st Sergeant on March 8, 1863. Present or accounted for until killed at Chancellorsville, Virginia, May 3, 1863.

CHANCE, TILMON F., Private
Resided in Rockingham or Rowan counties and enlisted in Rockingham County at age 21, August 5, 1861. Present or accounted for until captured at or near Williamsport, Maryland, on or about September 15, 1862. Confined at Fort Delaware, Delaware, until transferred to Aiken's Landing, James River, Virginia, October 2, 1862, for exchange. Declared exchanged at Aiken's Landing on November 10, 1862. Rejoined the company prior to March 1, 1863, and present or accounted for until wounded at or near Chancellorsville, Virginia, May 3, 1863. Reported absent wounded through October, 1864. Paroled at Salisbury on May 16, 1865, and took the Oath of Allegiance at Salisbury on June 10, 1865.

CHANCE, WILLIAM A., Private
Born in Rockingham County where he resided as a farmer prior to enlisting in Rockingham County at age 24, August 4, 1862, for the war. Present or accounted for until he died in hospital at Staunton, Virginia, October 17, 1862, of "dyphtheria." A North Carolina widow's pension indicates that "his last letter said he had been struck by a ball on the head and I never heard from him again." Place and date wounded not reported.

COBB, ARCHIBALD, Private
Born in Caswell County and resided in Rockingham County where he was by occupation a farmer prior to enlisting in Rockingham County at age 28, October 11, 1861. Present or accounted for until discharged at Danville, Virginia, November 28, 1863, by reason of "complete paralysis of right arm."

COGHILL, GEORGE, Private
Enlisted in Wake County on November 24, 1863, for the war. Present or accounted for until captured near Hanover Junction, Virginia, May 23, 1864. Confined at Point Lookout, Maryland, where he died June 21, 1864. Cause of death not reported.

COLLINS, LEWIS C., Private
Resided in Rockingham County and was by occupation a farmer prior to enlisting in Rockingham County at age 23, May 22, 1861. Mustered in as Private and promoted to Corporal on April 26, 1862. Reduced to ranks on September 30, 1862. Present or accounted for until wounded at Gettysburg, Pennsylvania, July 1-3, 1863. Returned to duty prior to November 1, 1863, and present or accounted for through October, 1864. Paroled at Greensboro on May 4, 1865.

COLLINS, ROBERT, Private
Resided in Rockingham County where he enlisted at age 30, August 5, 1861. Present or accounted for until wounded in the hand at Spotsylvania Court House, Virginia, May 22, 1864. Reported absent wounded or absent sick through November 13, 1864.

COOPER, JAMES, Private
Resided in Wilkes County and enlisted at Camp Vance on March 14, 1864, for the war. Present or accounted for until he deserted on May 6, 1864. "Returned under guard" on October 30, 1864. Captured by the enemy at Dinwiddie Court House, Virginia, April 3, 1865. Confined at Point Lookout, Maryland, until released on June 26, 1865, after taking the Oath of Allegiance.

DAWSON, JOHN W., Private
Born in Rockingham County where he resided as a farmer prior to enlisting in Rockingham County at age 28, May 22, 1861. Present or accounted for until wounded in the knee at Gaines' Mill, Virginia, June 27, 1862. Died in hospital at Richmond, Virginia, August 3 or August 15, 1862, of wounds.

DUNAWAY, SAMUEL H., Private
Born in Rockingham County where he enlisted on November 5, 1863, for the war. Present or accounted for until killed at Wilderness, Virginia, May 5, 1864.

ELMORE, JAMES W., Private
Resided in Rockingham County where he enlisted at age 24, August 5, 1861. Present or accounted for until captured at Reams' Station, Virginia, August 25, 1864. Confined at Point Lookout, Maryland, until paroled and transferred to Aiken's Landing, James River, Virginia, March 14, 1865, for exchange. Received for exchange at Boulware's Wharf, James River, March 16, 1865.

GORRELL, RALPH W., Private
Resided in Rockingham County and was by occupation a hireling prior to enlisting in Rockingham County at age 35, May 22, 1861. Present or accounted for until hospitalized at Danville, Virginia, February 15-16, 1863, with a gunshot "injury of hands." Place and date wounded not reported. Returned to duty on June 16, 1863, but was discharged August 22, 1863. Reason discharged not reported.

GREGORY, NATHANIEL H., Private
Resided in Rockingham County and was by occupation a hireling prior to enlisting in Rockingham County at age 38, May 22, 1861. Present or accounted for until wounded in the left leg at Sharpsburg, Maryland, September 17, 1862. Left leg amputated. Reported absent wounded until retired to the Invalid Corps on May 10, 1864.

GUERRANT, JOHN C., Private
Previously served in Company H of this regiment. Transferred to this company on July 1, 1861, and present or accounted for until detailed in the "gun factory" at Danville, Virginia, on or about February 5, 1862. Reported absent on detail through October, 1864.

GUERRANT, JOHN WYATT S., Corporal
Resided in Rockingham County where he enlisted at age 19, July 3, 1861. Mustered in as Private and promoted to Corporal on December 13, 1862. De-

tailed as Commissary Sergeant on August 1, 1863, and transferred to the Field and Staff of this regiment. Reported absent on detail through October, 1864. Paroled at Appomattox Court House, Virginia, April 9, 1865.

HARRISON, HENRY M., Corporal
Resided in Rockingham County and was by occupation a farmer prior to enlisting in Rockingham County at age 23, May 22, 1861. Mustered in as Corporal but was reduced to ranks of April 26, 1862. Present or accounted for until wounded at Chancellorsville, Virginia, May 1-3, 1863. Rejoined the company in September-October, 1863, and present or accounted for until wounded in the left leg at or near Petersburg, Virginia, June 22, 1864. Reported absent wounded through October, 1864. Paroled at Appomattox Court House, Virginia, April 9, 1865. Rank given on parole as Corporal.

HARVILLE, JAMES C., Private
Born in Caswell County and resided in Rockingham County where he was by occupation a shoemaker or hireling prior to enlisting in Rockingham County at age 25, May 22, 1861. Present or accounted for until wounded in both legs at Chancellorsville, Virginia, May 3, 1863. Died in hospital at Richmond, Virginia, June 28, 1863, of wounds.

HARVILLE, THOMAS C., Corporal
Resided in Rockingham County and was by occupation a trader prior to enlisting in Rockingham County at age 23, May 22, 1861. Mustered in as Private and promoted to Corporal on March 8, 1863. Present or accounted for until paroled at Appomattox Court House, Virginia, April 9, 1865. Paroled again at Greensboro on May 9, 1865.

HINES, MADISON D., Private
Born in Guilford County and resided in Rockingham County where he was by occupation a farmer prior to enlisting in Rockingham County at age 22, May 22, 1861. Present or accounted for until killed at Williamsburg, Virginia, May 5, 1862.

HINTON, J. E., Private
Place and date of enlistment not reported. Captured on the South Side Railroad, Virginia, April 2, 1865. Confined at Hart's Island, New York Harbor, until released on June 16, 1865.

HORNBUCKLE, ROBERT F., Private
Resided in Rockingham County and enlisted in Wake County on October 19, 1864, for the war. Captured at Petersburg, Virginia, April 4, 1865, and confined at Hart's Island, New York Harbor, until released June 19-20, 1865, after taking the Oath of Allegiance.

HORNBUCKLE, THOMAS W., Sergeant
Resided in Rockingham County and was by occupation a shoemaker prior to enlisting in Rockingham County at age 19, May 22, 1861. Mustered in as Private and promoted to Corporal on April 26, 1862. Promoted to Sergeant prior to September 16-17, 1862, when he was killed at Sharpsburg, Maryland.

HUMBLE, PETER C., Private
Enlisted at Camp Holmes on February 6, 1864, for the war. Present or accounted for through October, 1864. Paroled at Greensboro on May 12, 1865.

HUTCHINSON, CLEVELAND, Private
Enlisted at Camp Vance on March 18, 1864, for the war. Company muster rolls indicate he was captured by the enemy on May 6, 1864; however, records of the Federal Provost Marshal do not substantiate that report. No further records.

JACKSON, JOHN, Private
Born in Guilford County and resided in Rockingham County where he was by occupation a farmer prior to enlisting in Rockingham County at age 20, May 22, 1861. Present or accounted for until he died in hospital at Richmond, Virginia, on or about May 9, 1862, of "feb[ris] typh[oid]."

JONES, DAVID C., Private
Previously served in Company D, 48th Regiment Virginia Infantry. Transferred to this company on or about May 18, 1864. Present or accounted for until paroled at Appomattox Court House, Virginia, April 9, 1865.

JONES, JAMES A., 1st Sergeant
Resided in Rockingham County and was by occupation a farmer prior to enlisting in Rockingham County at age 26, May 22, 1861. Mustered in as Private and promoted to Corporal on April 26, 1862. Present or accounted for until captured at Sharpsburg, Maryland, September 17, 1862. Confined at Fort Delaware, Delaware, until transferred to Aiken's Landing, James River, Virginia, October 2, 1862, for exchange. Declared exchanged at Aiken's Landing on November 10, 1862. Rejoined the company prior to January 1, 1863, and was promoted to Sergeant on March 8, 1863. Promoted to 1st Sergeant in September-October, 1863. Present or accounted for until paroled at Appomattox Court House, Virginia, April 9, 1865.

JOURDAN, JOHN H., Private
Born in Rockingham County where he resided as a farmer prior to enlisting in Rockingham County at age 22, May 22, 1861. Present or accounted for until he died on May 3, 1863. Place and cause of death not reported.

JUSTICE, JOHN W., Sergeant
Resided in Rockingham County and was by occupation a farmer prior to enlisting in Rockingham County at age 24, May 22, 1861. Mustered in as Sergeant but was reduced to ranks on April 26, 1862. Present or accounted for until wounded at Williamsburg, Virginia, on or about May 5, 1862. Promoted to Corporal on September 30, 1862, and rejoined the company prior to November 1, 1862. Promoted to Sergeant on March 8, 1863. Present or accounted for until wounded at Chancellorsville, Virginia, May 1-3, 1863. Rejoined the company prior to November 1, 1863, and present or accounted for until wounded at or near Cold Harbor, Virginia, May 31, 1864. Rejoined the company in September-October, 1864, and present or accounted for until paroled at Appomattox Court House, Virginia, April 9, 1865.

KNOTT, JOHN H., Private
Resided in Rockingham County where he enlisted at age 35, August 5, 1861. Present or accounted for until captured at Williamsburg, Virginia, on or about May 5, 1862. Confined at Fort Monroe, Virgin-

ia, but was paroled prior to July 1, 1862. Reported absent on parole until reported absent without leave on December 1, 1862. Rejoined the company in September-October, 1863, but was again reported absent without leave in January-February, 1864. Rejoined the company in March-April, 1864, and present or accounted for until paroled at Appomattox Court House, Virginia, April 9, 1865.

LOFTIS, THOMAS, Private

Resided in Rockingham County where he enlisted at age 18, August 5, 1861. Present or accounted for until he was "shot and bayoneted" at Williamsburg, Virginia, on or about May 5, 1862. Rejoined the company prior to July 1, 1862, and present or accounted for until wounded in the left breast at Sharpsburg, Maryland, on or about September 16, 1862. Rejoined the company in November-December, 1862, and present or accounted for until wounded at Wilderness, Virginia, May 5, 1864. Reported absent wounded until retired to the Invalid Corps on November 23, 1864. Paroled at Greensboro on May 4, 1865. North Carolina pension records indicate he was wounded at Sweet Mountain, Virginia; at Malvern Hill, Virginia; and at Gettysburg, Pennsylvania.

LOVE, HENRY D., Private

Resided in Rockingham County and was by occupation a blacksmith prior to enlisting in Rockingham County at age 28, May 22, 1861. Present or accounted for until wounded at Spotsylvania Court House, Virginia, May 12, 1864. Reported absent wounded until retired to the Invalid Corps on December 7, 1864. Paroled at Greensboro on May 5, 1865.

LOVE, JULIUS S., Private

Resided in Rockingham County and was by occupation a blacksmith prior to enlisting in Rockingham County at age 19, May 22, 1861. Present or accounted for until wounded in the hand at South Mountain, Maryland, September 14, 1862. Rejoined the company in March-April, 1863, and present or accounted for until wounded in the left elbow and captured at Gettysburg, Pennsylvania, July 1-3, 1863. Hospitalized at Chester, Pennsylvania, until transferred to Point Lookout, Maryland, where he arrived October 4, 1863. Paroled at Point Lookout and transferred to City Point, Virginia, March 16, 1864, for exchange. Reported absent wounded until retired to the Invalid Corps on October 27, 1864. Paroled at Greensboro on May 5, 1865.

LOVE, ROBERT, Private

Born in Orange County and resided in Rockingham County where he was by occupation a blacksmith prior to enlisting in Rockingham County at age 39, May 22, 1861. Present or accounted for until discharged on July 1, 1864, by reason of disability.

LOVELES, ELIAS, Private

Born in Rockingham County where he resided as a hireling prior to enlisting in Rockingham County at age 30, May 22, 1861. Present or accounted for until killed at Chancellorsville, Virginia, May 3, 1863. Roll of Honor indicates that he "acted bravely in many battles."

McCALLUM, C. S., Private

Place and date of enlistment not reported. Paroled at Greensboro on May 17, 1865.

McCOY, JOHN W., Private

Resided in Macon County and enlisted in Wake County at age 27, September 27, 1862, for the war. Present or accounted for until he died on January 20, 1863, of disease. Place of death not reported.

MANSFIELD, JONATHAN, Private

Born in Rockingham County where he resided prior to enlisting in Rockingham County at age 28, August 5, 1861. Present or accounted for until hospitalized at Richmond, Virginia, September 28, 1862, with a shell wound of the right shoulder. Place and date wounded not reported. Returned to duty on October 24, 1862, but "shot his finger off to keep out of the fight" at an unspecified date. Reported absent without leave or absent wounded from December 1, 1862, through December, 1863. Reported in confinement at hard labor at Richmond from January-February, 1864, through October, 1864. "Shot [and killed] in attempting to desert" on November 10, 1864.

MANSFIELD, SAMUEL, Private

Resided in Rockingham County and was by occupation a hireling prior to enlisting in Rockingham County at age 19, May 22, 1861. Present or accounted for until he died at Hanover Junction, Virginia, on or about June 15, 1863, of "pneumonia."

MANSFIELD, SIDNEY, Private

Resided in Rockingham County where he enlisted at age 17, August 5, 1861. Present or accounted for until discharged on October 6, 1862, under the provisions of the Conscript Act. [May have served later in Company H, 45th Regiment N.C. Troops.]

MANSFIELD, WILLIAM JAMES, Private

Born in Rockingham County where he resided as a miller prior to enlisting in Rockingham County at age 18, August 4, 1862, for the war. Present or accounted for until discharged on January 8, 1863, by reason of "mental incapacity."

MARTIN, JOHN M., Private

Resided in Rockingham County where he enlisted at age 22, August 5, 1861. Present or accounted for until wounded and captured at Williamsburg, Virginia, on or about May 5, 1864. Confined at Washington, D.C., until paroled and transferred to Aiken's Landing, James River, Virginia, where he was exchanged on August 5, 1862. Rejoined the company prior to November 1, 1862, and present or accounted for until he died on or about January 20, 1863, of disease. Place of death not reported.

MAXWELL, ROBERT A., Sergeant

Resided in Rockingham County and was by occupation a wheelwright or mechanic prior to enlisting in Rockingham County at age 21, May 22, 1861. Mustered in as Private. Present or accounted for until wounded and captured at Williamsburg, Virginia, on or about May 6, 1862. Confined at Old Capitol Prison, Washington, D.C., until transferred to Aiken's Landing, James River, Virginia, where he was received August 5, 1862, for exchange. Promoted to Corporal on September 30, 1862, and rejoined the company prior to November 1, 1862. Present or accounted for until wounded at Fredericksburg, Virginia, December 13, 1862. Rejoined the company prior to May 1, 1863. Promoted to Sergeant on May 3,

1863, and was wounded in the arm at Chancellorsville, Virginia, the same day. "Left the hosp[ita]l before his wound was well and followed the army to Penn[sylvania]." Rejoined the company prior to July 1, 1863, and present or accounted for until captured at Dinwiddie Court House, Virginia, April 3, 1865. Confined at Point Lookout, Maryland, until released on June 15, 1865, after taking the Oath of Allegiance.

MURRY, JONATHAN, Private
Resided in Rockingham County and was by occupation a farmer prior to enlisting in Rockingham County at age 28, May 4, 1861. Present or accounted for until discharged on June 17, 1861, by reason of disability.

NUNN, CALTON, Private
Resided in Rockingham County where he enlisted at age 22, August 5, 1861. Present or accounted for until wounded and captured at Gettysburg, Pennsylvania, July 1-3, 1863. Died in hospital at Chester, Pennsylvania, July 24, 1863, of "exhaustion, consequent on gunshot wound."

NUNN, THOMAS, Private
Born in Rockingham County where he resided prior to enlisting in Rockingham County at age 23, October 8, 1862, for the war. Present or accounted for until killed at Chancellorsville, Virginia, May 3, 1863.

OAKLY, WILLIAM A., Private
Born in Rockingham County where he resided as a hireling prior to enlisting in Rockingham County at age 17, May 22, 1861. Present or accounted for until he died in hospital at Richmond, Virginia, May 21, 1862, of "diarrhoea."

OSBORNE, CHRISTIAN, Private
Resided in Maryland and enlisted at Richmond, Virginia, at age 20, June 14, 1862, for the war as a substitute for Private A. Banks Powell. Deserted the same day.

PAMPLIN, JAMES, Private
Resided in Rockingham County and was by occupation a hireling prior to enlisting in Rockingham County at age 21, May 22, 1861. Present or accounted for until wounded and captured at Sharpsburg, Maryland, September 17, 1862. Confined at Fort Delaware, Delaware, until transferred to Aiken's Landing, James River, Virginia, October 2, 1862, for exchange. Declared exchanged at Aiken's Landing on November 10, 1862. Rejoined the company in January-February, 1863, and present or accounted for until wounded in the hip at Chancellorsville, Virginia, May 3, 1863. Reported absent wounded through October, 1864. Captured in hospital at Richmond, Virginia, April 3, 1865, and confined at Libby Prison, Richmond, until transferred to Newport News, Virginia, April 23, 1865. Released at Newport News on June 16, 1865, after taking the Oath of Allegiance.

PARISH, S. H., Private
Born in Wake County and enlisted at Camp Holmes on February 6, 1864, for the war. Present or accounted for until killed at Wilderness, Virginia, May 5, 1864.

PASCHAL, DAVID S., Private
Resided in Rockingham County and was by occupation a farmer prior to enlisting in Rockingham County at age 30, May 22, 1861. Mustered in as Corporal but was reduced to ranks on April 26, 1862. Present or accounted for through October, 1862. Roll of Honor indicates that he "abandoned his company while in line of battle at Fredericksburg," Virginia, December 13, 1862; however, he was hospitalized at Richmond, Virginia, December 14, 1862, with a shell wound of the back. Reported absent without leave until he rejoined the company in November-December, 1863. Present or accounted for until wounded in the shoulder at or near Wilderness, Virginia, on or about May 5, 1864. Returned to duty on July 18, 1864, and present or accounted for through October, 1864. Paroled at Greensboro on May 15, 1865.

PETTIGREW, FRANKLIN, Private
Born in Orange County and resided in Rockingham County where he was by occupation a farmer or hireling prior to enlisting in Rockingham County at age 23, May 22, 1861. Present or accounted for until wounded at Chancellorsville, Virginia, May 1-3, 1863. Rejoined the company in September-October, 1863, and present or accounted for until wounded in the right leg at or near Petersburg, Virginia, May 31, 1864. Right leg amputated. Reported absent wounded until retired to the Invalid Corps on November 8, 1864.

PICKRELL, JAMES W., Private
Resided in Rockingham County where he enlisted at age 32, August 5, 1861. Present or accounted for until discharged on November 8, 1861, by reason of disability.

POWELL, A. BANKS, Private
Resided in Rockingham County and was by occupation a farmer prior to enlisting in Rockingham County at age 24, May 22, 1861. Present or accounted for until wounded at Williamsburg, Virginia, on or about May 5, 1862. Returned to duty on May 15, 1862, and was discharged on June 14, 1862, after providing Private Christian Osborne as a substitute.

PRITCHET, T. H., Private
Place and date of enlistment not reported. Paroled at Appomattox Court House, Virginia, April 9, 1865.

PRITCHETT, BARTLETT Y., Private
Born in Rockingham County where he resided as a farmer prior to enlisting in Rockingham County at age 41, May 22, 1861. Present or accounted for until discharged on March 6, 1863, by reason of being over age.

RAMSEY, JOHN, Private
Enlisted in Wake County on November 24, 1863, for the war. "Deserted" on December 20, 1863, but returned "under guard" on August 28, 1864. Acquitted by a military court on October 3, 1864. No further records.

RAMSEY, RICHARD, Private
Resided in Rockingham County and was by occupation a farmer prior to enlisting in Rockingham County at age 20, May 22, 1861. Present or account-

ed for until killed at Gettysburg, Pennsylvania, July 1, 1863.

RENAN, T. P., Private
Place and date of enlistment not reported. Paroled at Greensboro on May 13, 1865.

RENN, JOHN, Private
Enlisted in Wake County on October 19, 1864, for the war. Paroled at Appomattox Court House, Virginia, April 9, 1865.

ROBERSON, JOHN, Private
Resided in Virginia and enlisted at age 18, August 11, 1862, for the war as a substitute for Private Coleman Bran. Deserted on October 29, 1862, but was arrested. No further records.

SANDERS, DAVID L., Private
Resided in Rockingham County where he enlisted at age 23, October 11, 1861. Present or accounted for until captured at Williamsburg, Virginia, on or about May 5, 1862. Confined at Fort Monroe, Virginia, until paroled and transferred for exchange at an unspecified date. Rejoined the company in November-December, 1862, and present or accounted for until killed at Chancellorsville, Virginia, May 3, 1863.

SANDERS, HENSON C., Private
Resided in Rockingham County and was by occupation a farmer prior to enlisting in Rockingham County at age 25, May 22, 1861. Present or accounted for until he died June 1, 1862, of disease. Place of death not reported.

SANDERS, RICHARD, Private
Born in Caswell County and resided in Rockingham County where he was by occupation a farmer or hireling prior to enlisting in Rockingham County at age 22, May 22, 1861. Present or accounted for until killed "in front of his company" at Malvern Hill, Virginia, on or about July 1, 1862.

SANDERS, ROBERSON C., Private
Resided in Rockingham County where he enlisted at age 20, August 5, 1861. Present or accounted for until captured at Gettysburg, Pennsylvania, July 1-5, 1863. Confined at Fort Delaware, Delaware, until paroled and transferred to City Point, Virginia, July 30, 1863, for exchange. Rejoined the company in January-February, 1864, and present or accounted for until wounded in the left shoulder at Spotsylvania Court House, Virginia, May 12, 1864. Returned to duty on September 9, 1864, and present or accounted for through October, 1864.

SARTIN, ELLIS, Private
Resided in Caswell County and enlisted in Wake County on March 27, 1864, for the war. Present or accounted for until wounded at Wilderness, Virginia, May 5, 1864. Rejoined the company in September-October, 1864. Captured at Appomattox, Virginia, April 4, 1865. Confined at Hart's Island, New York Harbor, until released on or about July 12, 1865, after taking the Oath of Allegiance. Age given on Oath as 21.

SARTIN, THOMAS J. E., Private
Resided in Rockingham County and was by occupation a farmer prior to enlisting in Rockingham County at age 23, May 22, 1861. Present or account-

ed for until wounded in the right leg at Chancellorsville, Virginia, May 1-3, 1863. Rejoined the company in September-October, 1863, and present or accounted for until wounded at Spotsylvania Court House, Virginia, May 12, 1864. Rejoined the company in September-October, 1864, and present or accounted for until paroled at Appomattox Court House, Virginia, April 9, 1865.

SILLS, JOSEPH P., Private
Enlisted at Camp Vance on October 14, 1863, for the war. Present or accounted for until wounded in the shoulder at Wilderness, Virginia, May 5, 1864. Reported absent wounded until he returned to duty on or about November 1, 1864. No further records.

SLADE, JESSE F., Private
Born in Rockingham County where he resided as a farmer prior to enlisting in Rockingham County at age 37, May 22, 1861. Mustered in as Sergeant but was reduced to ranks on April 26, 1862. Present or accounted for until killed at Gettysburg, Pennsylvania, July 1, 1863.

STANFIELD, ROBERT W., Corporal
Born in Virginia and resided in Rockingham County where he enlisted at age 20, August 5, 1861. Mustered in as Private. Present or accounted for until wounded and captured at Williamsburg, Virginia, May 5-6, 1862. Confined at Fort Monroe, Virginia, and at Fort Delaware, Delaware, until transferred to Aiken's Landing, James River, Virginia, August 5, 1862, for exchange. Rejoined the company prior to November 1, 1862, and was promoted to Corporal on May 3, 1863. Present or accounted for until captured at Gettysburg, Pennsylvania, July 1-3, 1863. Confined at Fort Delaware until released on or about September 22, 1863, after joining the U.S. Army. Assigned to Company E, 3rd Regiment Maryland Cavalry.

STEPHENS, PETER, Private
Resided in Rockingham County and was by occupation a hireling prior to enlisting in Rockingham County at age 37, May 22, 1861. Present or accounted for until he deserted on December 12, 1862.

STOKES, JAMES, Private
Enlisted at Camp Vance on October 7, 1863, for the war. Present or accounted for until reported absent without leave on May 4, 1864.

STRADER, STEPHEN N., Private
Resided in Rockingham County where he enlisted at age 25, August 5, 1861. Present or accounted for until captured at Hatcher's Run, Virginia, April 2, 1865. Confined at Point Lookout, Maryland, until released on June 19, 1865, after taking the Oath of Allegiance. Oath of Allegiance indicates he was "blind in left eye."

SUMMERS, PINKNEY, Private
Resided in Rockingham County and was by occupation a farmer prior to enlisting in Rockingham County at age 20, May 22, 1861. Present or accounted for until wounded at Gettysburg, Pennsylvania, July 1, 1863. Rejoined the company in November-December, 1863, and present or accounted for until paroled at Appomattox Court House, Virginia, April 9, 1865.

SUMMERS, WILLIAM N., Private

Born in Caldwell County* and resided in Rockingham County where he was by occupation a farmer prior to enlisting in Rockingham County at age 22, May 22, 1861. Present or accounted for until captured at Williamsburg, Virginia, on or about May 5, 1862. Paroled prior to July 1, 1862, and rejoined the company in November-December, 1862. Present or accounted for until wounded in the right leg at Gettysburg, Pennsylvania, July 1, 1863. Reported absent wounded until discharged on January 28, 1865, by reason of wounds received at Gettysburg.

TATE, ANDREW JACKSON, Private

Resided in Alamance County and enlisted near Orange Court House, Virginia, February 28, 1864, for the war. Present or accounted for until wounded in the chest at Wilderness, Virginia, May 5, 1864. Rejoined the company in July-August, 1864, and present or accounted for until captured at "Chesterfield," Virginia, April 6, 1865. Confined at Point Lookout, Maryland, until released on June 21, 1865, after taking the Oath of Allegiance.

TATE, JAMES M., Private

Born in Caswell County and resided in Rockingham County where he was by occupation a farmer or hireling prior to enlisting in Rockingham County at age 21, May 22, 1861. Present or accounted for until discharged on September 25, 1861, by reason of disability.

TATE, WILLIAM G., Private

Resided in Rockingham County and was by occupation a hireling prior to enlisting in Rockingham County at age 18, May 22, 1861. Present or accounted for until wounded at Chancellorsville, Virginia, May 1-3, 1863. Rejoined the company in September-October, 1863, and present or accounted for until paroled at Appomattox Court House, Virginia, April 9, 1865.

TAYLOR, GEORGE, Private

Resided in Rockingham County where he enlisted at age 32, August 5, 1861. Present or accounted for until wounded in the left arm at Williamsburg, Virginia, on or about May 5, 1862. Rejoined the company prior to November 1, 1862, and present or accounted for until captured at Gettysburg, Pennsylvania, July 1-3, 1863, or at Falling Waters, Maryland, July 14, 1863. Confined at Point Lookout, Maryland, until paroled and transferred to City Point, Virginia, March 3, 1864, for exchange. Rejoined the company prior to July 1, 1864, and present or accounted for until captured at Hatcher's Run, Virginia, April 2, 1865. Confined at Point Lookout until released on June 5, 1865, after taking the Oath of Allegiance.

THACKER, OSCAR J., Private

Born in Rockingham County where he resided prior to enlisting in Rockingham County at age 18, August 4, 1862, for the war. Present or accounted for until captured at South Mountain, Maryland, September 14, 1862. Confined at Fort Delaware, Delaware, until transferred to Aiken's Landing, James River, Virginia, October 2, 1862, for exchange. Declared exchanged at Aiken's Landing on November 10, 1862. Rejoined the company in January-February, 1863,

and present or accounted for until killed at Chancellorsville, Virginia, May 3, 1863.

TROLLINGER, JACOB H., Corporal

Resided in Rockingham or Alamance counties and was by occupation a clerk prior to enlisting in Rockingham County at age 20, May 22, 1861. Mustered in as Private and promoted to Corporal on March 8, 1863. Present or accounted for until wounded in the thigh at Chancellorsville, Virginia, May 1-3, 1863. Rejoined the company prior to July 1, 1863, and present or accounted for until reported absent without leave from August 25, 1863, through October, 1863. Rejoined the company in November-December, 1863, and present or accounted for until detailed as Sergeant Major on February 16, 1864, and transferred to the Field and Staff of this regiment. Rejoined the company on or about May 20, 1864. Detailed as Ordnance Sergeant on September 6, 1864, and transferred to the Field and Staff of this regiment. Records of the Field and Staff do not indicate whether he rejoined Company K; however, he was captured at Dinwiddie Court House, Virginia, April 3, 1865. Confined at Point Lookout, Maryland, until released on June 21, 1865, after taking the Oath of Allegiance.

TULLOCH, JAMES, Private

Resided in Rockingham County where he enlisted at age 27, April 26, 1863, for the war. Present or accounted for until wounded at Gettysburg, Pennsylvania, July 1, 1863. Reported absent wounded until July-August, 1864, when he was reported present but under arrest. Rejoined the company in September-October, 1864, and present or accounted for until captured on the South Side Railroad, Virginia, April 2, 1865. Confined at Hart's Island, New York Harbor, until released June 19-20, 1865, after taking the Oath of Allegiance.

TULLOCH, JOHN R., Private

Resided in Rockingham County and was by occupation a hireling prior to enlisting in Rockingham County at age 22, May 22, 1861. Present or accounted for until wounded in the left ankle at Fredericksburg, Virginia, December 13, 1862. Reported absent wounded until retired to the Invalid Corps on December 7, 1864.

TULLUCH, DAVID, Private

Resided in Rockingham County where he enlisted at age 18, August 5, 1861. Present or accounted for until wounded in the left hand at Malvern Hill, Virginia, on or about July 1, 1862. Rejoined the company prior to November 1, 1862, but was detailed for hospital duty on December 6, 1862. Reported absent on detail until retired to the Invalid Corps on December 7, 1864. Paroled at Greensboro on May 19, 1865.

UPTON, ISOM, Private

Born in Randolph County and resided in Rockingham County where he was by occupation a shoemaker prior to enlisting in Rockingham County at age 28, August 4, 1862, for the war. Present or accounted for until killed at Gettysburg, Pennsylvania, July 1, 1863.

UPTON, THOMAS, Private

Born in Chatham County and resided in Rockingham County where he enlisted at age 30, August 4, 1862, for the war. Present or accounted for until he died in hospital at Charlottesville, Virginia, December 18, 1862, of "pneumonia."

WALKER, ALEXANDER W., Private
Resided in Rockingham County and was by occupation a farmer prior to enlisting in Rockingham County at age 20, May 22, 1861. Present or accounted for until captured at Gettysburg, Pennsylvania, July 1-4, 1863. Confined at Fort Delaware, Delaware, until transferred to Point Lookout, Maryland, where he arrived October 15, 1863. Died in hospital at Point Lookout on November 27, 1863, of "diarrhoea chronic."

WALKER, JAMES W., Private
Born in Rockingham County where he resided prior to enlisting in Rockingham County at age 32, December 15, 1862, for the war. Present or accounted for until killed at Gettysburg, Pennsylvania, July 1, 1863.

WALKER, WILLIAM A., Private
Born in Rockingham County where he resided as a farmer prior to enlisting in Rockingham County at age 37, August 5, 1861. Present or accounted for until wounded in the thigh and captured at Williamsburg, Virginia, May 5, 1862. Confined at Fort Monroe, Virginia, until paroled on an unspecified date and transferred for exchange. Reported absent wounded or absent on furlough until discharged on January 4, 1865, by reason of wounds received at Williamsburg.

WALKER, WILLIAM M., Private
Resided in Rockingham County and was by occupation a trader prior to enlisting in Rockingham County at age 26, May 22, 1861. Present or accounted for until paroled at Appomattox Court House, Virginia, April 9, 1865. Roll of Honor indicates that he was "awarded a medal for gallant and meritorius conduct on the battle field."

WARD, JAMES L., Private
Born in Caswell County and resided in Rockingham County where he was by occupation a farmer prior to enlisting in Rockingham County at age 26, May 22, 1861. Present or accounted for until wounded in the left wrist and captured at Williamsburg, Virginia, May 5, 1862. Hospitalized at Washington, D.C. Exchanged at Aiken's Landing, James River, Virginia, November 10, 1862. Rejoined the company in March-April, 1863, and was discharged on June 1, 1863, by reason of wounds received at Williamsburg.

WARD, MADISON M., Private
Born in Rockingham County where he resided as a farmer prior to enlisting in Rockingham County at age 20, May 22, 1861. Present or accounted for until killed at Williamsburg, Virginia, May 5, 1862.

WARE, GEORGE W., Private
Resided in Rockingham County and was by occupation a hireling prior to enlisting in Rockingham County at age 31, May 22, 1861. Present or accounted for until captured at Middletown, Maryland, September 14, 1862, or at Sharpsburg, Maryland, on or about September 16, 1862. Confined at Fort Delaware, Delaware, until transferred to Aiken's Land-

ing, James River, Virginia, October 2, 1862, for exchange. Declared exchanged at Aiken's Landing on November 10, 1862. Rejoined the company in January-February, 1863, and present or accounted for until wounded in the knee and captured at Gettysburg, Pennsylvania, July 1-3, 1863. Leg amputated. Died in hospital at Gettysburg on July 12, 1863.

WARREN, GREEN, Private
Resided in Rockingham County and was by occupation a farmer prior to enlisting in Rockingham County at age 23, May 22, 1861. Present or accounted for through October, 1864.

WARREN, JAMES, Private
Resided in Rockingham County and was by occupation a mechanic prior to enlisting in Rockingham County at age 21, May 22, 1861. Present or accounted for until paroled at Appomattox Court House, Virginia, April 9, 1865. Roll of Honor indicates that he was "the only man of this company who came out of the battle at Gettysburg unhurt."

WATKINS, AUGUSTUS J., Private
Resided in Rockingham County and was by occupation a farmer prior to enlisting in Rockingham County at age 19, May 22, 1861. Present or accounted for until killed at Williamsburg, Virginia, May 5, 1862.

WINDSOR, GEORGE T., Corporal
Resided in Rockingham County where he enlisted at age 22, August 5, 1861. Mustered in as Private. Present or accounted for until wounded in the chest at Chancellorsville, Virginia, May 3, 1863. Promoted to Corporal on August 1, 1863, and rejoined the company prior to November 1, 1863. Present or accounted for until wounded at Wilderness, Virginia, May 5, 1864. Rejoined the company in September-October, 1864, and present or accounted for until captured at or near Petersburg, Virginia, April 4, 1865. Confined at Hart's Island, New York Harbor, until released on June 19, 1865, after taking the Oath of Allegiance.

WRIGHT, PHILANDER R., Sergeant
Resided in Rockingham County and was by occupation a carpenter prior to enlisting in Rockingham County at age 24, May 22, 1861. Mustered in as Private and promoted to Corporal on June 5, 1861. Promoted to Sergeant on April 26, 1862. Present or accounted for until wounded and captured at Williamsburg, Virginia, May 5, 1862. Died in hospital at Williamsburg on or about May 15, 1862, of wounds.

WRIGHT, WILLIAM D., Private
Resided in Rockingham County and was by occupation a farmer prior to enlisting in Rockingham County at age 20, May 22, 1861. Present or accounted for until wounded at Seven Pines, Virginia, on or about June 1, 1862. Rejoined the company prior to November 1, 1862, and present or accounted for until wounded at Gettysburg, Pennsylvania, July 1-3, 1863. Rejoined the company prior to March 1, 1864, and present or accounted for through October, 1864. Paroled at Greensboro on May 18, 1865.

MISCELLANEOUS

The following list of names was compiled from primary records which indicate that these men served in the 13th Regiment N.C. Troops but do not specify the company to which they belonged.

HODGES, W. T., Private

Place and date of enlistment not reported. Deserted to the enemy on or about March 22, 1865. Took the Oath of Allegiance on or about March 25, 1865.

HOOPER, S. Y., Private

Place and date of enlistment not reported. First listed in the records of this company on December 25, 1864. Deserted to the enemy on or about March 31, 1865. Took the Oath of Allegiance on or about April 6, 1865.

JARRELL, W. A., Private

Place and date of enlistment not reported. Deserted to the enemy on or about February 23, 1865, and took the Oath of Allegiance on or about February 24, 1865.

JEFFRIES, JAMES H., Private

Place and date of enlistment not reported. Deserted to the enemy on or about February 22, 1865, and took the Oath of Allegiance on or about February 24, 1865.

SUN, J. A., Private

Place and date of enlistment not reported. Records of the Federal Provost Marshal dated April 12, 1865, indicate that he was a deserter.

TISDALE, MATHEW, Sergeant

Place and date of enlistment not reported. Records of the Federal Provost Marshal dated April 10, 1865, indicate that he was a deserter who had taken the "Oath."

14th REGIMENT N. C. TROOPS

(4th Regiment N. C. Volunteers)

This regiment was organized at Garysburg on June 6, 1861, as the 4th Regiment N.C. Volunteers and was mustered in to Confederate States service for a period of twelve months. Five days later, on June 11, the newly organized unit was ordered to Suffolk, Virginia, where it arrived on the same day and set up camp at Camp Bragg, just outside of the town. While the regiment was undergoing its initial training it was attached to the forces under General John C. Pemberton, commanding at Smithfield, Virginia.

On July 9 the regiment moved to Camp Ellis, two miles from Suffolk. There it remained until August 10, when it moved to Camp Bee at Bidgood's Church, near Smithfield. While the regiment was stationed at Camp Bee some of the companies were detached for short periods of time. Company D was detailed on guard duty at Stone House Wharf for one week and rejoined the regiment on August 28. Company F relieved Company D at Stone House Wharf on August 28 and remained for about a week. At about this time a Virginia company, the Prince George Cavalry, which became Company F, 5th Regiment Virginia Cavalry, was attached to this regiment and served at Camp Lookout. The company remained attached to the regiment through November, 1861. On October 2 Companies D and K were ordered to Fort Ellen on Burwell Bay. The eight remaining companies of the regiment remained at Camp Bee until November 15 when they moved to Fort Bee, a quarter of a mile from Camp Bee, and went into winter quarters. Companies D and K went into winter quarters at Fort Ellen.

By Special Orders No. 222, Adjutant and Inspector General's Office, Richmond, November 14, 1861, the regiment was redesignated the 14th Regiment N.C. Troops (4th Regiment N.C. Volunteers). At about this time the regiment was brigaded with the 13th Regiment N.C. Troops (3rd Regiment N.C. Volunteers) and the 3rd Regiment Virginia Infantry. General Raleigh E. Colston was assigned to command the brigade, which became known as Colston's brigade.

Early in March, 1862, Confederate authorities began moving troops to the Yorktown-Warwick line below Williamsburg to meet a Federal force advancing under General George B. McClellan. On March 11, 1862, the regiment moved from Fort Bee to Camp Redick, where it remained until March 21 when it returned to Fort Bee. It moved to Camp Pryor, near Yorktown, on March 27, and returned to Fort Bee on April 3. The next day, General Colston began moving his brigade across the James River to reinforce General John B. Magruder's force on the Yorktown-Warwick line. The regiment moved to Green's Farm, Mulberry Point, on April 5, and skirmished with the enemy on April 6 and 7. It remained there until April 12, when it was ordered to move toward Yorktown. The next day, April 13, it camped near that place.

During the month of April, 1862, the troops under General Joseph E. Johnston at Manassas moved down to the Yorktown-Warwick line, and General Johnston was placed in command. General Colston's brigade was assigned to General James Longstreet's division in the center of the line. On April 25 and 26 the regiment reorganized for the war and held an election of officers.

Fearing the mounting pressure against his defensive line, General Johnston began a general withdrawal from the Yorktown-Warwick line on the night of May 3-4, 1862. The Confederates withdrew toward Williamsburg, and Colston's brigade served as rear guard of Longstreet's division. The brigade arrived at Williamsburg late on May 4 and went into camp on the western edge of the town. Early the next morning the Federal advance began pressing the rearguard elements in the fortifications east of the town. Longstreet held Colston's brigade in reserve and deployed the balance of his division to meet the enemy advance. Colston's brigade was ordered forward around 3:30 **P.M.** to reinforce General A.P. Hill's brigade on the right of Fort Magruder, which was in the center of the Confederate line of fortifications. The regiment, after moving into one of the redoubts, received its baptism of fire and held the enemy back on its front. Although the Federals maintained pressure on the Confederate line throughout the day, they failed to break through. That evening General Longstreet began withdrawing his troops to join the army as it retired toward Richmond. The entire force moved up the Peninsula unopposed and joined the Army of Northern Virginia just east of Richmond. At Williamsburg on May 5 the regiment lost 8 killed and 9 wounded.

General McClellan's army advanced up the Peninsula and confronted the Confederates in their defensive positions just east of Richmond. Under pressure from President Jefferson Davis to assume the offensive, General Johnston ordered an attack on the Federal position at Seven Pines. With Longstreet's division on the right of the Williamsburg road and D. H. Hill's division on the left of the road, the Confederates succeeded in driving the Federals from their defenses at Seven Pines on May 31. During the action Colston's brigade moved on the right of Longstreet's advance. However, around 5:00 **P.M.** the brigade was withdrawn with two other brigades from Longstreet's right and sent to support Hill on the left of the road. The next day, June 1, the Federals counterattacked, and only after hard fighting did the Confederates hold on to what they had gained. Two regiments of Colston's brigade were sent forward to reinforce General George Pickett's brigade, and the combined force succeeded in holding the line under heavy pressure. The battle ended with little gain for the Confederate forces, which were ordered to withdraw to their former positions after it was learned that the Federals had been heavily reinforced.

During the battle of May 31 General Johnston had been wounded, and General Gustavus W. Smith, commanding on June 1, fell sick. General Robert E. Lee was then put in command of the Army of Northern Virginia. After the battle the army underwent many changes as troops from the same state were brigaded together. This regiment was assigned to Brigadier General George B. Anderson's brigade, Major General D.H. Hill's division, on June 9, 1862. In addition to this regiment, the brigade consisted of the 2nd Regiment N.C. State Troops, 4th Regiment N.C. State Troops, and 30th Regiment N.C. Troops. Although the brigade would later undergo a change in commanders, the regiment served in the same brigade for the remainder of the war.

On the morning of June 26, 1862, the brigade moved from its camp near the Williamsburg road, about five miles from Richmond, to the Chickahominy Bridge on the Mechanicsville Turnpike. General Lee was concentrating his troops to attack the Federal right at Mechanicsville. At 4:00 P.M. Brigadier General Roswell S. Ripley's brigade, D. H. Hill's division, crossed the bridge to aid General A. P. Hill's troops engaged at Mechanicsville. The remainder of the division followed but did not take an active part in the day's action. That night General D. H. Hill received orders to cooperate with Major General T. J. Jackson on the Cold Harbor road on the Confederate left. At daylight General Hill found his route blocked and sent Samuel Garland's and Anderson's brigades to the left to turn the enemy's position. The Federals abandoned their defenses when the two brigades began to move on their flank and rear, and Hill's whole division moved on toward Cold Harbor.

In the meantime, General Jackson had been forced to change his route and was proceeding on a road that would bring his troops in behind and to the right of Hill's division. Hill advanced his troops to Cold Harbor and then deployed them along the edge of Powhite Swamp. To his right Jackson's troops came into position, and on their right the troops of A. P. Hill's and James Longstreet's divisions were engaging the enemy at Gaines' Mill. Jackson's and D. H. Hill's troops were ordered forward to the support of Longstreet and A. P. Hill. Anderson's brigade was second from the end on the left of the line and met the enemy on the edge of the swamp. After a short but bloody contest the woods were cleared of the enemy. Between the edge of the wooded swamp and the Federal position was an open field some 400 yards wide. A general attack was ordered, and the Federals withdrew under pressure from the front and the threat of the attacks on their right. Night brought an end to the contest, and the Federals made good their escape.

From Gaines' Mill the Confederates, now commanded by General Jackson, moved to cross the Chickahominy at Grapevine Bridge. The bridge had been destroyed by the enemy in his retreat, and the position was defended to delay any attempted crossing. There the troops went into bivouac while the bridge was being rebuilt, June 28-29. On June 30 the troops advanced across Grapevine Bridge and marched to White Oak Bridge, which they also found destroyed. There a strong Federal force prevented the Confederates from rebuilding the bridge and thus kept Jackson's men at bay while the battle of Frayser's Farm was raging. Following the battle White Oak Bridge was rebuilt. Jackson's men then joined forces with the right wing of the army and moved to meet the enemy at Malvern Hill. As the Confederates moved up, General D. H. Hill's division was placed on the Confederate center. Late on the afternoon of July 1, 1862, a general assault was launched by Hill's division. The troops advanced across an open field and reached within 200 yards of the enemy's batteries before halting and falling back. During the night the Federals retired to Harrison's Landing. The battle of Malvern Hill was the last of the Seven Days' battles around Richmond, June 25-July 1, 1862. During this campaign the regiment lost 17 killed and 85 wounded.

The brigade bivouacked near Malvern Hill until marched back to its original camp near Richmond on July 9-10. It marched to Malvern Hill on August 6 and returned the night of August 7. D. H. Hill's division had been left in front of Richmond to watch McClellan's troops at Harrison's Landing while Jackson and then Longstreet moved to confront General John Pope in middle Virginia. In mid-August, General Anderson's brigade marched to Hanover Junction. On August 26 the brigade moved to join the division at Orange Court House, and on August 28 the entire division marched to join the Army of Northern Virginia. The division reached the army at Chantilly, September 2, 1862, after the battle of Second Manassas, and crossed into Maryland on September 4-5.

Upon reaching Frederick, Maryland, the army halted, and General Lee determined to send Jackson to capture Harpers Ferry while Longstreet moved to Hagerstown. On September 10 D. H. Hill's division moved out of Frederick as the rear guard of Longstreet's column. Mounting pressure from the advancing Federals, plus the necessity of protecting Jackson at Harpers Ferry, resulted in the deployment of Hill's division along the South Mountain gaps below Boonsboro on September 13. This regiment, as part of Anderson's brigade, saw heavy action at Fox's Gap on September 14. Captain A.J. Griffith, commanding the regiment on September 14, reported its movements as follows (O.R., S.I., Vol. XIX, pt. 1, pp. 1049-1050):

> Early in the morning of the 14th the regiment took up line of march down the turnpike in the direction of Crampton's Pass. It was in front of the brigade, and rested on the left of the road at the pass for a short time, and then received orders to march back and pass to the right of the turnpike to re-enforce General [Samuel] Garland. Coming upon a squad of the enemy, it formed line, but, by some mistake in orders, marched back to the turnpike without firing on the enemy, at which place it received orders to face about and march back to the field, where it was joined by General [Roswell S.] Ripley and thrown on his right. The whole line then moved forward on the enemy, who had taken position on the mountain. Before coming upon the enemy the second time, it being nearly night, it received orders to fall back to an old road, with only 1 man wounded, and await orders to re-enforce General Ripley, if necessary. No orders arriving, the regiment was not called into action.

The next day General Hill withdrew his troops under general orders to concentrate at Sharpsburg. When the brigade arrived at Antietam Creek on September 15 it went into position on the heights east of the creek. Later D. H. Hill's troops were moved into position between the troops of Jackson and Longstreet on the Confederate line in front of Sharpsburg.

On the morning of September 17 the Confederate left was vigorously assaulted, and the three brigades of Hill's division on the left of his line were ordered to support Jackson's right. Anderson's regiments were ordered to extend to the left to fill the area vacated by the troops that had been ordered to support Jackson's right. When the Federal attack fell on the Confederate center, Anderson's and Rodes's brigades were in the sunken road later called the Bloody Lane. Several determined assaults were repulsed, but the Federals succeeded in enfilading the right of Rodes's brigade. An order for the right regiment to form perpendicular to the road to protect the flank was misconstrued as an order for a general withdrawal. As Rodes's brigade retired, General Anderson's men held their ground until forced to retire. As the enemy moved in on their front and flank, General Anderson was mortally wounded, and the brigade was routed from its position. During the retreat the regimental colors were captured. The remnants took up position about 200 yards in rear of the road, where the survivors on both sides began to dig in as the battle shifted to the Confederate right. Captain Griffith reported the regiment's action as follows (*O.R.*, S. I., Vol. XIX, pt. 1, p. 1050):

> About 8 o'clock received orders to move by the left flank, passing through a corn-field into an old road; filed to the left, and took position in front of the enemy, which was well protected by banks. The enemy advanced immediately, and a heavy fire opened on both sides. At this position it drove the enemy back three times, disorganizing their lines, with heavy loss. About 11 o'clock received orders from the right that a new line of the enemy was advancing in the rear. The regiment fell back to a road, and took position behind a stone fence, losing many men while changing position. Having but few men, it rallied with other regiments and drove the enemy back, and remained in line in front of the enemy until late at night; then marched a short distance to the rear to rally. . . .
>
> The casualties were 213 killed, wounded, and missing, including Col. R. T. Bennett, blown up by a shell (severely shocked), and Lieut. Col. William A. Johnston, wounded in the arm.

After the men rallied, General Hill attempted to lead an assault on the Federal position with about 200 men, but it failed. This ended any serious fighting on that part of the line. The next day the troops rested on the field. They retired across the Potomac during the night of September 18 and went into camp.

The Army of Northern Virginia remained in the Shenandoah Valley until the Army of the Potomac crossed the Potomac River east of the Blue Ridge. By use of his cavalry, Lee sought to discover the enemy's intentions. On October 28, 1862, Longstreet's corps moved east of the mountains to Culpeper Court House while Jackson's corps moved closer to Winchester. D.H. Hill's division was posted at the forks of the Shenandoah River to guard the mountain passes. General Anderson died of his wound on October 16, 1862, and on November 7 Colonel Stephen D. Ramseur, 49th Regiment N.C. Troops, was promoted to brigadier general and assigned to command Anderson's brigade. General Ramseur was absent wounded at the time and did not assume active command until March, 1863. In the interim, Colonel Bryan Grimes of the 4th Regiment N.C. State Troops commanded the brigade.

When the enemy's intention was discerned, Lee moved Longstreet to Fredericksburg and ordered Jackson to prepare to move. Hill's division was pulled back and moved to Strasburg. From there the division took up the line of march to Gordonsville on November 21 and from Gordonsville it moved to Fredericksburg. On December 3 Hill's division was sent to Port Royal below Fredericksburg to prevent any crossing of the Rappahannock River at or near that point. It remained there until ordered to Fredericksburg on December 12. Arriving in the morning on December 13, the division was placed in the third defensive line. During the battle of

that day the division was subjected to heavy artillery fire but saw little action. After the battle it was advanced to the second line, where it remained throughout the next day. On December 15 it went into the first line, where it remained for two days. While on the field the regiment was never actually engaged but suffered the loss of 4 men wounded from the artillery fire.

A few days after the battle the regiment went into winter quarters near the Gordon House, seven miles from Fredericksburg. On January 4, 1863, it was assigned to picket duty at Taylor's Farm, eight miles below Fredericksburg. It returned to camp on January 10. From January 31 to February 3 it served a second tour at Taylor's Farm. Twelve days later, February 15, the regiment moved from near Gordon House to permanent quarters near Hamilton's Crossing, and later that month it served two tours of duty (February 18-20 and February 24-28) one mile below Fredericksburg. On March 29 the regiment was ordered to Bowling Green, Caroline County, Virginia, to guard the bridges over the Mattaponi River. It remained at Bowling Green until April 20, when it returned to its old camp near Hamilton's Crossing.

Early in 1863 there were some changes in the division's high command. In January General D. H. Hill was ordered to report to the adjutant general in Richmond for reassignment. His division was assigned to General Edward Johnson, who was absent wounded. The senior brigadier, Robert E. Rodes, assumed command until General Johnson returned to active duty. In March, 1863, General Ramseur reported and assumed command of the brigade.

On April 29, 1863, the division received orders to march to Hamilton's Crossing. There it was placed in position on the right of the forces in the Fredericksburg entrenchments and extended the line to Massaponax Creek. Ramseur's brigade was placed on the south side of the creek to guard the ford near its mouth. On April 29 and 30 the brigade was subjected to occasional shelling, but no general action occurred. Lee, concluding that the enemy activity at Massaponax Creek was a feint, ordered the brigade to move up to Hamilton's Crossing during the evening of April 30.

General Hooker's Federal army had moved up the left bank of the Rappahannock to cross over behind the Confederates at Fredericksburg, and General Lee began to move a portion of his army to oppose Hooker. Jackson's corps moved down the Orange and Fredericksburg Plank Road in the direction of Chancellorsville on May 1. After advancing about seven miles, Ramseur's brigade was detached and ordered to report to Major General Richard H. Anderson, whose division was engaged on the right of Jackson's column. Upon joining with Anderson's division, Ramseur's brigade took part in the advance against the enemy and drove them back about two miles. Night brought an end to the attack. At about sunrise, May 2, Ramseur's brigade was relieved from duty with Anderson's division and ordered to rejoin Johnson's division. The brigade rejoined the division in time to participate in Jackson's flank march. After hard marching, Jackson's corps succeeded in reaching a point about four miles west of Chancellorsville on the exposed right flank of Hooker's army.

As the troops came up, Jackson deployed them in three lines for the attack. Four brigades of the division were placed in the first line, and Ramseur's brigade was placed on the right of the second line to secure the right flank of the first line. The attack began at about 5:15 **P.M.** During the advance the brigade in front of Ramseur's failed to maintain the pace, and thus the right of the line failed to bring its full weight against the enemy positions. Soon after the attack began the second line began to catch up to the first line and the two became one as they drove in Hooker's right flank. The advance continued until darkness and strong resistance forced a halt. The lines were re-formed, and Ramseur's brigade was placed on the right side of the Plank Road in the third line. The activities of the brigade on May 3, 1863, were reported by General Ramseur as follows (*O.R.*, S. I., Vol. XXV, pt. 1, pp. 995-996):

Saturday night our division occupied the last line of battle within the intrenchments from which the routed corps of Sigel had fled in terror. My brigade was placed perpendicular to the Plank road, the left resting on the road, General Doles on my right and Colonel [E. A.] O'Neal, commanding Rodes' brigade, on my left. I placed Colonel [F.M.] Parker, Thirtieth North Carolina, on the right of my brigade; Colonel [R.T.] Bennett, Fourteenth North Carolina, on right center; Colonel [W. R.] Cox, Second North Carolina, left center; and Colonel [Bryan] Grimes, Fourth North Carolina, on left.

Sunday, May 3, the division being, as stated, in the third line of battle, advanced about 9 o'clock to the support of the second line. After proceeding about one-fourth of a mile, I was applied to by Major [W. J.] Pegram for a support to his battery, when I detached Colonel Parker, Thirtieth North Carolina, for this purpose, with orders to advance obliquely to his front and left, and rejoin me after his support should be no longer needed, or to fight his regiment as circumstances might require. I continued to advance to the first line of breastworks, from which the enemy had been driven, and behind which I found a small portion of Paxton's brigade and Jones' brigade, of Trimble's division. . . . At the command "Forward," my brigade, with a shout, cleared the breastworks, and charged the enemy. The Fourth North Carolina (Colonel Grimes) and seven companies of the Second North Carolina (Colonel Cox) drove the enemy before them until they had taken the last line of his works, which they held under a severe, direct, and enfilading fire, repulsing several assaults on this portion of our front. The Fourteenth North Carolina (Colonel Bennett) and three companies of the Second were compelled to halt some 150 or 200 yards in rear of the troops just mentioned, for the reason that the troops on my right had failed to come up, and the enemy was in heavy force on my right flank. Had Colonel Bennett advanced, the enemy could easily have turned my right. As it was, my line was subjected to a horrible enfilade fire, by which I lost severely. I saw the danger threatening my right, and sent several times to Jones' brigade to come to my assistance; and I also went back twice myself and exhorted and ordered it (officers and men) to fill up the gap (some 500 or 600 yards) on my right, but all in vain. I then reported to General Rodes that unless support was sent to drive the enemy from my right, I would have to fall back.

In the meantime Colonel Parker, of the Thirtieth [North Carolina], approaching my position from the battery on the right, suddenly fell upon the flank and handsomely repulsed a heavy column of the enemy who were moving to get in my rear by my right flank, some 300 or 400 of them surrendering to him as prisoners of war. The enemy still held his strong position in the ravine on my right, so that the Fourteenth [North Carolina] and the three companies of the Second [North Carolina] could not advance. The enemy discovered this situation of affairs, and pushed a brigade to the right and rear of Colonel Grimes, and seven companies of Colonel Cox's (Second [North Carolina]), with the intention of capturing their commands. This advance was made under a terrible direct fire of musketry and artillery. The move necessitated a retrograde movement on the part of Colonels Grimes and Cox, which was executed in order, but with the loss of some prisoners, who did not hear the command to retire. Colonel Bennett held his position until ordered to fall back, and, in common with all the others, to replenish his empty cartridge-boxes. The enemy did not halt at this position, but retired to his battery, from which he was quickly driven, Colonel Parker, of the Thirtieth [North Carolina], sweeping over it with the troops on my right.

After refilling cartridge boxes, the brigade was ordered to the left to meet an expected enemy attack. The entire Confederate line was converging on Chancellorsville, forcing the Federals to retire. Once Chancellorsville was occupied, the division was ordered to entrench along the Plank Road. It occupied this position until Hooker's army recrossed the Rappahannock and Lee moved his army back to Fredericksburg. On May 6 the brigade encamped near Hamilton's Crossing. During the Chancellorsville campaign the regiment lost 23 killed and 120 wounded.

Following the Chancellorsville campaign and the death of Jackson, the Army of Northern Virginia was divided into three corps under Generals James Longstreet, Richard S. Ewell, and A. P. Hill. Ramseur's brigade was assigned to Major General Robert E. Rodes's division, Lieutenant General Ewell's 2nd Corps. The brigade composition remained the same. The division left camp on June 3 and reached a point just beyond Culpeper Court House on June 7. Ewell's corps, with Rodes's division leading, was on the march to Pennsylvania. From Culpeper Court House the division moved to Brandy Station on June 9 to assist the cavalry but arrived after the battle was over. It then resumed its march toward the Shenandoah Valley. Rodes's division received orders on June 12 to proceed to Cedarville by way of Chester Gap in advance of the other two divisions of the corps. At Cedarville, Rodes was ordered to move on Berryville and Martinsburg and into Maryland while the other two divisions of the corps moved on Winchester. Berryville was occupied on June 13, after its defenders made good their escape. On June 14 Rodes's division deployed before the defenses in front of Martinsburg. Fearing the defenders might escape, Rodes ordered a charge. Ramseur's brigade, being in the lead, drove the enemy at almost a run for two miles beyond the town. However, the enemy infantry escaped by taking the Shepherdstown road while the Confederates concentrated on the Federal cavalry and artillery on the Williamsport road. On June 15 Rodes heard of the victory at Winchester and moved his men to Williamsport. Ramseur's brigade was one of the three that Rodes ordered across the Potomac River. The division remained at Williamsport until the remainder of the corps moved up. On June 19 Rodes's division was put in motion and marched to Hagerstown, where it remained two days. The division resumed its march on June 22, crossed into Pennsylvania, and bivouacked at Greencastle. The next day the division moved toward Chambersburg and passed through that town on June 24. There Major General Edward Johnson's division joined Rodes's, and together they moved to Carlisle, arriving there on June 27.

On the night of June 30 Rodes's division was at Heidlersburg, where General Ewell received orders to proceed to Cashtown or Gettysburg, as circumstances might dictate. Rodes's division moved on the morning of July 1 for Cashtown. While en route, word came that A. P. Hill's corps was moving on Gettysburg, and General Ewell directed Rodes to proceed to that town. When Rodes's division arrived on the field, A. P. Hill's men were already engaged. Rodes moved his division into position on Hill's left, placing four brigades on the line and Ramseur's brigade in reserve. The timely arrival of Major General Jubal Early's division, on the left of Rodes's, combined with the assaults launched from Hill's and Rodes's lines, drove the enemy through the town of Gettysburg. General Ramseur reported the activities of his brigade on that day as follows (O.R., S. I., Vol. XXVII, pt. 2, p. 587):

> July 1, in rear of the division train, as a guard on the march from Heidlersburg to Gettysburg. My brigade arrived on the field after the division had formed line of battle. I was then held in reserve to support General Doles, on the left; Colonel [E. A.] O'Neal, left center; or General [Alfred] Iverson, on the right center, according to circumstances.
>
> After resting about fifteen minutes, I received orders to send two regiments to the support of Colonel O'Neal, and with the remaining two to support Iverson. I immediately detached the Second and Fourth North Carolina troops to support O'Neal, and with the Fourteenth and Thirtieth hastened to the support of Iverson. I found three regiments of Iverson's command almost annihilated, and the Third Alabama Regiment coming out of the fight from Iverson's right. I requested Colonel [C. A.] Battle, Third Alabama, to join me, which he cheerfully did. With these regiments (Third Alabama, Fourteenth and Thirtieth North Carolina), I turned the enemy's strong position in a body of woods, surrounded by a stone fence, by attacking en masse on his right flank, driving him back, and getting in his rear. At the time of my advance on the enemy's right, I sent to the commanding officer of the Twelfth North Carolina, of Iverson's brigade, to push the enemy in front. This was done. The enemy seeing his right flank turned, made but feeble resistance to the front attack, but ran off the field in confusion, leaving his killed and wounded and between 800 and 900 prisoners

in our hands. The enemy was pushed through Gettysburg to the heights beyond, when I received an order to halt, and form line of battle in a street in Gettysburg running east and west.

Major J. H. Lambeth, commanding the 14th Regiment N.C. Troops (4th Regiment N.C. Volunteers) reported the movements of the regiment at Gettysburg as follows (O.R., S.I., Vol. XXVII, pt. 2, pp. 590-591):

> On July 1, about 2 p.m., the command was moved to the front, and engaged the enemy, driving in their sharpshooters and skirmishers, and advanced on the strong positions behind stone walls and other well-selected obstructions, completely routing them, killing, wounding, and capturing an immense number of the enemy, driving them through the town of Gettysburg to their fortified heights on the eastern side of the town. The men being so much fatigued by the forced march of 14 miles on the morning before entering the field, the pursuit was discontinued.
>
> The command remained in town in line of battle during the night and until late in the evening of the succeeding day, when the command was moved to the extreme right of the division, where it connected with General A.P. Hill's left, and remained in line, occupying an old road entering the town on the southeast side. Remained there until the morning of the 4th, all of which time we were exposed to the fire from the enemy's batteries. Our sharpshooters in front were constantly engaged.
>
> On the morning of the 4th, our position was changed to a more formidable one at the theological seminary, which position we occupied until the morning of the 5th, when the line of march was again resumed in the direction of Hagerstown.

Ramseur's brigade did not take part in any major fighting on July 2 and 3. General Ramseur's report on Gettysburg quoted above continued as follows (O.R., S.I., Vol. XXVII, pt. 2, pp. 587-588):

> July 2, remained in line of battle all day, with very heavy skirmishing in front. At dark, I received an order from Major-General Rodes to move by the right flank until Brigadier-General Doles' troops cleared the town, and then to advance in line of battle on the enemy's position on the Cemetery Hill. Was told that the remaining brigades of the division would be governed by my movements. Obeyed this order until within 200 yards of the enemy's position, where batteries were discovered in position to pour upon our lines direct, cross, and enfilade fires. Two lines of infantry behind stone walls and breastworks were supporting these batteries. The strength and position of the enemy's batteries and their supports induced me to halt and confer with General Doles, and, with him, to make representation of the character of the enemy's position, and ask further instructions.
>
> In answer, received an order to retire quietly to a deep road some 300 yards in rear, and be in readiness to attack at daylight; withdrew accordingly.
>
> July 3, remained in line all day, with severe and damaging skirmishing in front, exposed to the artillery of the enemy and our own short-range guns, by the careless use or imperfect ammunition

of which I lost 7 men killed and wounded. Withdrew at night, and formed line of battle near Gettysburg, where we remained on July 4. Commenced retreat with the army on the night of the 4th instant.

On the night of July 4-5, the division began to move toward Hagerstown by way of Fairfield. On the morning of July 6 it became the rear guard of the army and was engaged in several brief skirmishes on that day. Upon reaching Hagerstown on July 7, a line of battle was established, but no general engagement occurred. On the night of July 14 the division recrossed the Potomac and marched to near Darkesville. During the Gettysburg campaign the regiment lost 5 killed, 37 wounded, and 2 missing or captured.

When the Federal army began crossing the Potomac River east of the Blue Ridge, General Lee moved his army east of the mountains to interpose it between the enemy and Richmond. By August 1, 1863, the Army of Northern Virginia was encamped near Orange Court House, and the Army of the Potomac was at Warrenton. By August 4 Lee had withdrawn his army to the Rapidan River line. In October Lee attempted to turn the flank of the Federal army. The movement maneuvered the Federal commander into falling back, and on October 14 the Federal rear guard was intercepted at Bristoe Station. Failure to coordinate the attack resulted in heavy casualties to troops of A.P. Hill's corps and in the escape of the Federals. The regiment took part in the movement with the brigade and division, but Ewell's corps was not engaged at Bristoe Station. However, the regiment was engaged in a skirmish at Warrenton Springs on October 12 and in a skirmish two miles from Warrenton Court House on October 14. The casualties during these two engagements were not reported, but the casualty report for the period October 10-21 shows that the regiment lost 1 killed and 4 wounded.

With the escape of the Federal army to Centreville, Lee withdrew his army to the upper Rappahannock River. Rodes's division was positioned opposite Kelly's Ford. The Federal army followed the Confederates and launched an attack at Kelly's Ford on November 7. On that day the 2nd Regiment N.C. State Troops of Ramseur's brigade was on picket duty at Kelly's Ford and received the brunt of the assault. The 30th Regiment N.C. Troops of the brigade was ordered forward to support the regiment while the 4th Regiment N.C. State Troops and 14th Regiment N.C. Troops (4th Regiment N.C. Volunteers) were held in reserve. The two regiments at the ford lost heavily in killed, wounded, and captured before retiring on the reserves and leaving the ford in Federal hands. Further up the river the Confederates also lost their bridgehead at Rappahannock Bridge.

Lee withdrew his army south across the upper Rapidan River toward Orange Court House, where the army went into camp. Ramseur's brigade encamped near Morton's Ford, and companies from the regiment went on picket duty at various fords on the river. On November 26 the Federal army crossed the lower Rapidan and turned west to face Lee's army. Lee thought the Federal army was moving south to a position between the Confederate army and Richmond and put his army in motion to strike the Federal army on its flank. The activities of Ramseur's brigade in the move

and the resulting Mine Run campaign were described in Ramseur's report as follows (*O.R.*, S. I., Vol. XXIX, pt. 1, pp. 886-887):

My brigade moved with the division about 3 o'clock on the morning of November 27. Formed line of battle along ridge road leading by Zoar Church; remained here several hours, right resting near the chuch, left near right of Major-General Johnson's intrenchments, and then took up line of march toward Locust Grove. Met the enemy in heavy force near and this side of Locust Grove. Division was again formed in line of battle and advanced a short distance, developing the enemy in strong force; then halted, and my brigade, on the right, was thrown forward so as to connect with the left of Major-General Early's division, Brigadier-General Gordon's brigade. Remained thus in line of battle, with sharp skirmishing in front, until dark. My brigade was then moved from the right to the left of the division, partially covering a wide gap between Major-General Rodes and Major-General Johnson.

About 12 o'clock at night the division fell back from its advanced position near Locust Grove, and took up line of battle again on Mine Run. My brigade was left to cover this movement. This line was strongly and rapidly fortified, and here we awaited the onset of the enemy, November 28, 29, and 30, and December 1. This he declined to make, and during the night of the 1st retreated to the north bank of the Rapidan.

At daylight Wednesday morning, December 2, advanced with my brigade and followed the retreating enemy as far as the river, picking up some 50 or 60 stragglers. Returned to camp at Morton's Ford December 3.

Thus ended the Mine Run campaign during which the regiment lost 1 killed and 1 wounded. Both armies went into winter quarters. Ramseur's brigade built winter quarters near Orange Court House, and on December 20 the regiment was detached to cut lumber for use in planking the roads. Companies C, D, and F were ordered to Bell's Mill, and the remainder of the regiment was ordered to Bond's Saw Mill. The companies remained on detached service until February 1, 1864, when the regiment was ordered to rejoin the brigade. For the balance of the winter the regiment did picket duty at Morton's Ford.

On the morning of May 4, 1864, while the Federal army under General U. S. Grant was moving across the lower Rapidan, Ramseur's brigade was at Raccoon Ford. When the division moved to oppose the Federal advance, Ramseur's brigade was left to guard the fords from Rapidan Station to Mitchell's Ford. It remained in position during the first day of the battle of the Wilderness, May 5. Rejoining the corps on the evening of May 6, the brigade was placed on the extreme left of the line to protect the flank. On the morning of May 7 it was moved to the rear as a reserve. When Burnside's IX Corps appeared to be moving into the gap between Ewell's and A. P. Hill's corps, Ramseur's brigade was sent in to check the enemy and did so. At the same time it closed the gap between the two corps.

Late in the evening of May 7 orders came to close up on the right. Throughout the night of May 7-8 the troops moved to the right. On May 8 the division arrived on the field at Spotsylvania Court House and formed on the right of Brigadier General Benjamin G. Humphrey's brigade, Major General Kershaw's division, Longstreet's corps. By a vigorous charge Ramseur's brigade drove the enemy from Humphrey's right for half a mile. It was then recalled and placed on the right of Kershaw's division, to the left of the famous Mule Shoe. Here the brigade was subjected to heavy skirmishing with the enemy on May 9, 10, 11.

When the Federal assault broke through the angle of the Mule Shoe on the morning of May 12, Ramseur's brigade was ordered to check the enemy's advance and to drive him back. To do this he formed his brigade in a line parallel to the lines captured by the enemy. When the command to charge was given, the entire brigade moved forward and drove the enemy out of the captured works. This was accomplished by 7:30 A.M. on May 12, and the brigade held the lines until 3:00 A.M. on May 13, when it was withdrawn to a new line in its rear. There it remained until moved out on May 19. On May 15, 1864, the remnants of the 1st and 3rd Regiments N.C. State Troops were assigned to the brigade. These two regiments had been in Brigadier General George H. Steuart's brigade, Major General Edward Johnson's division, Ewell's corps. Steuart's brigade had been in position in the Mule Shoe on the morning of May 12 and had been overrun and captured. Only a few escaped. The 1st and 3rd Regiments N.C. State Troops mustered about thirty men each when they joined Ramseur's brigade. General Ramseur was promoted to major general and assigned to command a division on May 27, and Colonel William R. Cox of the 2nd Regiment N.C. State Troops was promoted to brigadier general and assigned to command the brigade. Thus Ramseur's brigade became known as Cox's brigade.

After several unsuccessful attempts against the Confederate line, General Grant began to move his army eastward. Because of the increased Federal activity to the east, Ewell's corps was ordered to reconnoiter and attempt to discover the enemy's intentions. With Ramseur's brigade leading, Ewell's corps moved out of the entrenchments and engaged the rear elements of the Federal army on May 19. An attack was made but was repulsed, and, with reinforcements coming up, the Federals began to press Ewell's men. The Confederates held and took advantage of night to break off the fighting and retire. This engagement disclosed the enemy's movement, and Lee moved his army accordingly. On May 22 Ewell's corps arrived at Hanover Junction with Longstreet's corps. Hill's corps arrived on the morning of May 23. From Hanover Junction the Army of Northern Virginia marched to the North Anna River, where it blocked the Federal army once again. At North Anna, May 24-25, Ewell's corps, now commanded by General Jubal Early, was on the Confederate right and was not engaged. Grant withdrew during the night of May 26-27 and crossed the Pamunkey River, again sidestepping to the Confederate right. Early's corps marched some 24 miles on May 27 and entrenched between Beaver Dam Creek and Pole Green Church. Longstreet's corps came up on Early's right, and Hill's corps extended along the left of Early's line. On May 30, under orders from General Lee, Early moved to attack the Federal left at Bethesda Church. The attack failed to turn the Federal left but revealed that the enemy was moving to the Confederate right.

The two armies began to concentrate at Cold Harbor, and on June 1 a spirited engagement occurred. Again Lee moved to his right, and the new alignment left Early's corps on the Confederate left. Early was ordered to move out on June 2 to strike the Federal right. The attack was led by Rodes's division and met with partial success until Federal reinforcements arrived to drive it back. During the battle of Cold Harbor, June 3, 1864, Early's corps was under attack by General A. E. Burnside's IX Corps and a part of General G. K. Warren's V Corps. The men of Warren's corps struck the line held by Rodes's division and were repulsed. Following the battle, the armies remained in position, observing and skirmishing until June 12, when Grant began moving his army to cross the James River. General Early's corps was withdrawn from the line on June 11 and was ordered to Lynchburg on June 12 to defend that city against an anticipated attack by troops under General David Hunter. Early was directed to remain in the Shenandoah Valley after striking Hunter's force.

General Early's troops began arriving at Lynchburg on June 17. By the next day Early's entire command was there. Hunter retired, and, after an unsuccessful attempt to overtake the retreating Federals, Early proceeded into the Shenandoah Valley. Still in Cox's brigade, Rodes's division, this regiment took part in Early's Valley campaign of 1864. On July 6, 1864, Early crossed into Maryland and advanced on Washington, D.C. At the battle of Monocacy River, July 9, 1864, Rodes's division operated on the Baltimore road while the main fighting occurred on the Washington road to the division's right. Rodes's division was in the vanguard when the defenses of Washington came in sight on July 11. Upon finding the defenses heavily manned on the morning of July 12, Early called off a planned assault, and during the night of July 12 he began to withdraw. Moving back into the Shenandoah Valley by way of Snicker's Gap, Early's men were engaged in skirmishes at Snicker's Gap on July 18, at Stephenson's Depot on July 20, and at Kernstown on July 24, before he moved to Martinsburg to give his men a rest.

In August, 1864, the Federals began concentrating a large force under General Phil Sheridan at Harpers Ferry. On August 10 Early began a series of maneuvers to create the impression of a larger force than he had. His men were northeast of Winchester when Sheridan began to move. On September 19 contact was made, and Early concentrated his forces to receive the attack. The Confederates were making a determined defense east of Winchester when the left came under heavy attack and the whole line began to retire. During the initial stages of the battle General Rodes was killed as he deployed his division between Gordon's and Ramseur's divisions. These three divisions held the main line against repeated assaults, and only when the left appeared to be turned did they begin to retire to a defensive line close to the town. Again the Federals assaulted the front and left of the line. Word of a Federal column turning the right caused Early to issue orders for a general withdrawal; however, upon finding the troops moving on the right were his own men adjusting the alignment, Early tried to counter the order. It was too late. The troops continued to the rear through Winchester and rallied south of the town. From there they retreated to Fisher's Hill near Strasburg.

At Fisher's Hill, Major General Stephen D. Ramseur was placed in command of Rodes's division. Sheridan struck Early's left and center at Fisher's Hill on September 22 and forced a general retreat. Early regrouped at Waynesboro on September 28. There he received reinforcements and again began to move down the valley. On October 7 his troops occupied New Market. Moving to Fisher's Hill on October 12-13, Early found the enemy on the north bank of Cedar Creek. On October 19, 1864, Early launched a surprise attack against the Federal camp. The attack was initially successful, and the Confederates succeeded in driving the Federals from two defensive lines; however, Early delayed the attack on the third line and assumed the defensive. Sheridan, rallying his troops, launched a devastating counterattack and routed Early's army. In this battle the three divisions of the 2nd Corps were commanded by General John B. Gordon. While attempting to rally the men, General Ramseur was mortally wounded and captured. Brigadier General Bryan Grimes, as senior brigadier, was assigned to command the division. Thus, when the 2nd Corps regrouped at New Market, this regiment was in Cox's brigade, Grimes's division. With the exception of minor skirmishing and the repulse of a Federal cavalry force on November 22, the army remained inactive.

On December 9 two divisions of the 2nd Corps moved under orders to return to Richmond. A few days later the Rodes-Ramseur division, under Grimes, was ordered to return to the main army in the Richmond-Petersburg line. On December 14 it marched to Staunton and took the train to Petersburg. The brigade arrived on December 16 and went into winter quarters at Swift Creek, about three miles north of Petersburg. There it remained until ordered to the right of the line about February 20, 1865. Grimes's division had been placed on alert to be ready to move at a moment's notice. On February 17 three brigades moved to Sutherland's Depot on the right of the line. Cox's brigade covered the division front at Swift Creek until relieved and then joined the division at Sutherland's. In mid-March, the division was ordered into the trenches in front of Petersburg. There it remained until the night of March 24, when the 2nd Corps, still under General Gordon, was massed for an attack on Fort Stedman. Although initially successful, the attack the following day was quickly repulsed by the concentrated firepower and manpower of the Federal army.

The remnants of the regiment returned to the trenches with the rest of the brigade and division. During the general assault on the morning of April 2, 1865, the Federals reached the divisional line near Fort Mahone. Grimes's division attacked and reoccupied its trenches only to have other portions of the line fall to the Federal assault. Retreat was necessary, and it began the night of April 2-3. Gordon's corps acted as rear guard as the army moved to Amelia Court House. It camped five miles east of the town on April 4, while the army awaited the collection of supplies. The next day the retreat resumed and continued through the night of April 5-6. As the rear guard, Gordon's corps was subjected to attacks by Federal cavalry and infantry. At a crossing of Sayler's Creek, on April 6, Gordon's men made a stand and repulsed the assault on their front. To the south of Gordon's position the Con-

federates under Generals Ewell and Anderson were severely defeated and captured. The Federals then moved on Gordon's right. The pressure forced the line to break in confusion, but Gordon rallied the survivors west of the creek and rejoined the army. At Farmville, on April 7, the men of Gordon's corps went to the relief of General Mahone's division. The Federals were held, and the army continued the retreat.

On the night of April 7-8 Gordon's corps moved to the advance of the army. His lead elements reached Appomattox Court House in the late afternoon of April 8 and halted. Later that evening they found the Federal cavalry in their front. It was decided that an attack should be made the next morning to cut through the enemy. Gordon's men moved into position west of the town during the night. At 5:00 A.M. the advance began, and the Federal cavalry was driven from the crossroads. The Confederates then took up a defensive position and came under attack by Federal infantry and cavalry. Gordon held his line until word came of the truce. A cease-fire was arranged, and Gordon began to withdraw. Cox's brigade did not receive the cease-fire order, and as it moved back the men turned and fired on an advancing Federal cavalry force. After hearing the volley, General Gordon sent word of the truce. The last shot had been fired. The Army of Northern Virginia was surrendered on that day, and on April 12, 1865, 115 men of the 14th Regiment N.C. Troops (4th Regiment N.C. Volunteers) were paroled.

FIELD AND STAFF

COLONELS

DANIEL, JUNIUS
Born in Halifax County on June 27, 1828. Was by occupation a U.S. Army officer and planter prior to enlisting in Northampton County at age 32. Appointed Colonel to rank from June 3, 1861. Present or accounted for until elected Colonel of the 45th Regiment N.C. Troops on or about April 14, 1862.

ROBERTS, PHILETUS W.
Previously served as Captain of Company F of this regiment. Elected Colonel on or about April 27, 1862, and transferred to the Field and Staff. Present or accounted for until he died July 5, 1862. Place and cause of death not reported.

BENNETT, RISDEN TYLER
Previously served as Assistant Commissary of Subsistence of this regiment. Elected Lieutenant Colonel to rank from April 27, 1862, and was promoted to Colonel on July 5, 1862. Present or accounted for until wounded in the groin at Gettysburg, Pennsylvania, July 2-3, 1863. Rejoined the company at an unspecified date. Wounded in the right shoulder at or near Cold Harbor, Virginia, June 2, 1864. Rejoined the company at an unspecified date. Captured at Winchester, Virginia, September 19, 1864. Confined at Fort Delaware, Delaware, until paroled and transferred to City Point, Virginia, February 27, 1865, for exchange. Clark's *Regiments* indicates he was wounded in the mouth at Spotsylvania Court House, Virginia, in May, 1864.

LIEUTENANT COLONELS

LOVEJOY, GEORGE S.
Resided in Wake County and was by occupation a

"U.S. cadet" prior to enlisting in Northampton County at age 21. Elected Lieutenant Colonel to rank from June 3, 1861. Present or accounted for through March, 1862. Company records indicate he was defeated for reelection when the regiment was reorganized on April 26, 1862; however, records of the North Carolina Adjutant General indicate he died July 20, 1862. No further records.

JOHNSTON, WILLIAM A.

Previously served as Captain of Company A of this regiment. Appointed Lieutenant Colonel to rank from July 5, 1862, and transferred to the Field and Staff. Present or accounted for until wounded in the right arm at Chancellorsville, Virginia, May 3, 1863. Rejoined the company at an unspecified date. Wounded in a skirmish at Petersburg, Virginia, in 1864-1865, and "disabled." Paroled at Appomattox Court House, Virginia, April 9, 1865.

MAJORS

FAISON, PAUL F.

Resided in Northampton County and was by occupation a "U.S. cadet" prior to enlisting in Northampton County at age 21. Appointed Major to rank from May 28, 1861. Present or accounted for until he was defeated for reelection when the regiment was reorganized on April 26, 1862. Later served as Colonel of the 56th Regiment N.C. Troops.

DIXON, EDWARD

Previously served as Captain of Company D of this regiment. Elected Major on April 27, 1862, and transferred to the Field and Staff. Present or accounted for until he died at Richmond, Virginia, July 8, 1862, of disease.

LAMBETH, JOSEPH HARRISON

Previously served as Captain of Company B of this regiment. Promoted to Major on July 5, 1862, and transferred to the Field and Staff. Present or accounted for until wounded in the right thigh and captured at Winchester, Virginia, September 19, 1864. Hospitalized at Winchester and at Baltimore, Maryland, until confined at Point Lookout, Maryland, at an unspecified date. Transferred to Venus Point, Savannah River, Georgia, where he was received November 15, 1864, for exchange. Paroled at Greensboro on May 2, 1865.

ADJUTANTS

GALES, SEATON E.

Previously served as 2nd Lieutenant in Company K of this regiment. Appointed Adjutant (2nd Lieutenant) on June 3, 1861, and transferred to the Field and Staff. Present or accounted for until he defeated for reelection or declined reelection when the regiment was reorganized, April 25-26, 1862. Later served as Assistant Adjutant General on the staff of Brigadier General Stephen D. Ramseur.

JOHNSTON, ROBERT BRUCE

Previously served as 1st Lieutenant in Company C, 16th Regiment N.C. Troops (6th Regiment N.C. Volunteers). Appointed Adjutant (1st Lieutenant) of this regiment on June 15, 1862. Resigned on or about August 2, 1862. Reason he resigned not reported.

MARSHALL, JAMES C.

Previously served as 1st Lieutenant in Company A, 23rd Regiment N.C. Troops (13th Regiment N.C. Volunteers). Appointed Adjutant (1st Lieutenant) on or about August 25, 1862, and transferred to this company. Present or accounted for until captured at Fisher's Hill, Virginia, September 22, 1864. Confined at Fort Delaware, Delaware, until released on June 8, 1865, after taking the Oath of Allegiance.

ASSISTANT QUARTERMASTERS

LOCKHART, BENJAMIN FRANKLIN

Resided in Northampton County and was by occupation a farmer prior to enlisting in Northampton County at age 34. Appointed Assistant Quartermaster on or about June 3, 1861. Discharged on August 20, 1861, after his appointment was not confirmed by the Confederate government.

BROWN, WILLIAM C.

Previously served as Private in Company F of this regiment. Appointed Assistant Quartermaster (Captain) on September 28, 1861, and transferred to the Field and Staff. Present or accounted for until he died at Richmond, Virginia, July 6, 1862, of disease.

SMITH, BENJAMIN F.

Previously served in Company E, 5th Regiment Texas Infantry. Appointed Assistant Quartermaster (Captain) to rank from July 14, 1862, and transferred to this regiment. Present or accounted for until assigned to duty at Fort Fisher on October 11, 1864.

ASSISTANT COMMISSARIES
OF SUBSISTENCE

DANIEL, ERASMUS A.

Previously served as Private in 2nd Company C, 12th Regiment N.C. Troops (2nd Regiment N.C. Volunteers). Transferred to this regiment on or about June 3, 1861, upon appointment as Assistant Commissary of Subsistence; however, his appointment to that position was not confirmed by the Confederate government.

BENNETT, RISDEN TYLER

Previously served as Sergeant in Company C of this regiment. Appointed Assistant Commissary of Subsistence (Captain) of September 28, 1861, and transferred to the Field and Staff. Present or accounted for until elected Lieutenant Colonel of this regiment on April 27, 1862.

LILLY, ROBERT J.

Previously served as Sergeant in Company C of this regiment. Appointed Assistant Commissary of Subsistence (Captain) on or about April 27, 1862, and transferred to the Field and Staff. Captured at or near Frederick, Maryland, September 17, 1862, and confined at Fort McHenry, Maryland, until paroled on November 6, 1862. Transferred to Aiken's Landing, James River, Virginia, where he was declared exchanged on November 10, 1862. Present or accounted for until he was "reassigned" on September 17, 1863.

SURGEONS

HUTCHINGS, JOHN WILLIAM

Resided in Hertford County and was by occupation a doctor prior to enlisting at age 40. Appointed Surgeon to rank from June 1, 1861. Present or accounted for until he resigned on June 25, 1862. Later served as Surgeon of the 59th Regiment N.C. Troops.

GREEN, BENJAMIN T.

Appointed Surgeon to rank from June 24, 1861. Resigned at an unspecified date. Reason he resigned not reported.

TRACY, JAMES WRIGHT

Previously served as Assistant Surgeon of the 37th Regiment N.C. Troops. Transferred to this regiment on or about July 1, 1862, and was appointed Surgeon on or about July 25, 1862. Present or accounted for until transferred for reassignment on or about April 23, 1864.

RAMSEUR, DAVID P.

Resided in Lincoln County and enlisted at age 25. Appointed Surgeon on April 23, 1864. Captured near Washington, D.C., July 13, 1864, and confined at Old Capitol Prison, Washington, until transferred to Fort Delaware, Delaware, July 22, 1864. Transferred to City Point, Virginia, for exchange. Received at Aiken's Landing, James River, Virginia, August 12, 1864, for exchange. Captured at Richmond, Virginia, on or about April 3, 1865, and was paroled on April 19, 1865.

ASSISTANT SURGEONS

NEILSON, MORGAN L.

Previously served as Private in Company F of this regiment. Appointed Assistant Surgeon on or about June 1, 1861, and transferred to the Field and Staff. Discharged August 20, 1861. Reason discharged not reported.

WINGFIELD, THURMER H.

Resided in Virginia and was by occupation a doctor prior to enlisting in Wake County at age 32. Appointed Assistant Surgeon on June 3, 1861. Present or accounted for until appointed Surgeon in November, 1861, and transferred to the 5th Regiment N.C. State Troops.

LOGAN, JOHN E.

Resided in Guilford County. Appointed Assistant Surgeon to rank from October 21, 1861. Paroled at Appomattox Court House, Virginia, April 9, 1865.

GOODE, REGINALD H.

Served as Assistant Surgeon of the 49th Regiment N.C. Troops. Records of the Federal Provost Marshal indicate that he was serving as Assistant Surgeon of this regiment when he was captured in May, 1864. No further records.

CHAPLAINS

COBB, NEEDHAM BRYAN

Resided in Wake County and was by occupation a preacher prior to enlisting at age 25. Appointed Chaplain to rank from June 12, 1861. Present or accounted for until he resigned in August-September, 1861. Reason he resigned not reported.

POWER, WILLIAM CARR

Born in South Carolina and resided in South Carolina or in Anson County prior to enlisting at age 33. Appointed Chaplain on September 23, 1861. Present or accounted for until paroled at Appomattox Court House, Virginia, April 9, 1865.

ENSIGN

ROGERS, JOSEPH T.

Served as Private in Company E of this regiment. Appointed Ensign on June 22, 1864, to rank from June 17, 1864. Records do not indicate whether he was transferred to the Field and Staff; however, he was present or accounted for with the regiment through December 29, 1864.

SERGEANTS MAJOR

BADGER, RICHARD C.

Previously served as Sergeant in Company K of this regiment. Appointed Sergeant Major on June 3, 1861, and transferred to the Field and Staff. Present or accounted for until appointed Assistant Commissary of Subsistence (Captain) to rank from June 2, 1862, and transferred to the 45th Regiment N.C. Troops.

TURNER, PRESTON H.

Previously served as Sergeant in Company H of this regiment. Appointed Sergeant Major on April 27, 1862, and transferred to the Field and Staff. Present or accounted for until transferred to Company K, 28th Regiment N.C. Troops, upon appointment as 2nd Lieutenant on or about October 15, 1863.

JENKINS, NEWSOM EDWARD

Previously served as 1st Sergeant of Company A of this regiment. Appointed Sergeant Major on or about January 15, 1864, and transferred to the Field and Staff. Present or accounted for until paroled at Appomattox Court House, Virginia, April 9, 1865.

QUARTERMASTER SERGEANTS

FORTUNE, WILLIAM P.

Previously served as Private in Company F of this regiment. Promoted to Quartermaster Sergeant on June 3, 1861, and transferred to the Field and Staff. Present of accounted for until appointed Captain to rank from September 1, 1863, and transferred to Company C, 69th Regiment N.C. Troops (7th Regiment N.C. Cavalry).

SMITH, THOMAS

Previously served as Private in Company C of this regiment. Appointed Quartermaster Sergeant on or about August 1, 1863, and transferred to the Field and Staff. Present or accounted for until paroled at Appomattox Court House, Virginia, April 9, 1865.

COMMISSARY SERGEANTS

SKINNER, WILLIAM L.

Served as Private in Company K of this regiment. Detailed as Commissary Sergeant on June 25, 1861, and transferred to the Field and Staff. Present or accounted for until appointed Ordnance Sergeant and transferred to the Field and Staff, 56th Regiment N.C. Troops, September 15, 1862.

DUNLAP, GEORGE B.

Served as Private in Company C of this regiment.

Detailed as Commissary Sergeant on or about August 1, 1863, and transferred to the Field and Staff. Records do not indicate whether he rejoined his company; however, he was present or accounted for until reported captured at Snicker's Gap, Virginia, on or about July 8, 1864. Records of the Federal Provost Marshal do not substantiate the report of his capture. No further records.

HOSPITAL STEWARDS

COVINGTON, ELIJAH A.
Served as Private in Company C of this regiment. Detailed as Hospital Steward on April 8, 1862, and transferred to the Field and Staff. Records do not indicate whether he rejoined his company; however, he was present or accounted for until captured at Winchester, Virginia, September 19, 1864. Confined at Point Lookout, Maryland, until paroled and transferred to Boulware's Wharf, James River, Virginia, where he was received March 19, 1865, for exchange. "A good hospital steward."

HUSSEY, T. C.
Place and date of enlistment not reported. Paroled at Appomattox Court House, Virginia, on or about April 10, 1865.

BAND

The following members of this regiment are believed to have served at one time or another in the regimental band.

CARTER, ALBERT D., Chief Musician (Company E)

FREIBE, HENRY, Musician (Company K)

HAHN, HENRY, Musician (Company K)

KREIGER, CHARLES, Musician (Company K)

LEWIS, JAMES J., Musician (Company E)

ROBERTS, EDWARD M., Musician (Company K)

RUTH, RUFUS H., Musician (Company K)

SPITTMAN, J. W., Musician
Place and date of enlistment not reported. Captured in hospital at Petersburg, Virginia, April 3, 1865. Reported in various Federal hospitals through May 17, 1865. No further records.

SUGGS, PETER, Musician (Company K)

VAUGHAN, WILLIAM H., Chief Musician (Company E)

ZIEGLER, WILLIAM, Musician (Company K)

COMPANY A

This company, known as the Roanoke Minute Men, was from Warren and Halifax counties and enlisted at Littleton on March 30, 1861. On May 1, 1861, it left Littleton for Raleigh, where it arrived the same day. The next day, May 2, the company moved from Raleigh to Garysburg. There it was assigned to this regiment as Company A. After joining the regiment the company functioned as a part of the regiment, and its history for the war period is recorded as a part of the regimental history.

The information contained in the following roster of the company was compiled principally from company muster rolls for July, 1861, through August 31, 1864. No company muster rolls were found for the period prior to July, 1861, or for the period after August 31, 1864. In addition to the company muster rolls, Roll of Honor records, receipt rolls, hospital records, prisoner of war records, and other primary records, supplemented by state pension applications, United Daughters of the Confederacy records, and postwar rosters and histories, all provided useful information.

OFFICERS

CAPTAINS

JOHNSTON, WILLIAM A.
Resided in Halifax County and enlisted in Warren County at age 26. Elected Captain on March 30, 1861. Present or accounted for until promoted to Lieutenant Colonel to rank from July 5, 1862, and transferred to the Field and Staff of this regiment.

CHERRY, JAMES J.
Resided in Halifax County and was by occupation a farmer prior to enlisting in Warren County at age 22, March 30, 1861. Mustered in as Private and was elected 2nd Lieutenant to rank from April 27, 1862. Promoted to 1st Lieutenant on July 1, 1862, and was promoted to Captain on July 8, 1862. Present or accounted for until wounded at or near Chancellorsville, Virginia, on or about April 29, 1863. Died May 2, 1863, of wounds. Place of death not reported.

JENKINS, WILSON T.
Resided in Halifax or Warren counties and was by occupation a farmer prior to enlisting in Warren County at age 21, March 30, 1861. Mustered in as Private and promoted to Sergeant on November 1, 1861. Elected 3rd Lieutenant to rank from April 27, 1862, and promoted to 1st Lieutenant on July 6, 1862. Promoted to Captain on March 1, 1864. Present or accounted for until paroled at Appomattox Court House, Virginia, April 9, 1865.

LIEUTENANTS

BOBBITT, BURGE B., 2nd Lieutenant
Resided in Halifax County and enlisted in Warren County at age 20. Elected 2nd Lieutenant to rank from February 23, 1861. Present or accounted for until defeated for reelection when the regiment was reorganized on April 26, 1862.

KEARNEY, WILLIAM T., 1st Lieutenant
Resided in Halifax County and was by occupation a farmer prior to enlisting in Northampton County at age 33, June 5, 1861. Mustered in as Private and elected 1st Lieutenant to rank from April 27, 1862. Present or accounted for until killed at Malvern Hill, Virginia, July 1, 1862.

MYRICK, ROBERT A., 3rd Lieutenant
Resided in Halifax County and enlisted in Warren County at age 30. Elected 3rd Lieutenant on March 30, 1861, to rank from January 25, 1861. Present or accounted for until defeated for reelection when the regiment was reorganized on April 25, 1862.

PEARSON, WILLIAM A., 1st Lieutenant

Resided in Halifax County and enlisted at age 26. Elected 1st Lieutenant on March 30, 1861, to rank from January 25, 1861. Present or accounted for until defeated for reelection when the regiment was reorganized on April 25, 1862.

PUGH, WILLIAM J., 1st Lieutenant

Resided in Northampton or Gaston counties and was by occupation a merchant prior to enlisting in Warren County at age 17, March 30, 1861. Mustered in as Private and elected 2nd Lieutenant to rank from October 1, 1862. Present or accounted for until wounded at Chancellorsville, Virginia, May 3, 1863. Rejoined the company in July-August, 1863, and was promoted to 1st Lieutenant on March 1, 1864. Present or accounted for until captured in hospital at Petersburg, Virginia, April 3, 1865. Transferred to Newport News, Virginia, April 22, 1865, and was transferred to Old Capitol Prison, Washington, D.C., April 28, 1865. Transferred to Johnson's Island, Ohio, May 11, 1865, and was released on June 19, 1865, after taking the Oath of Allegiance.

WILLIAMS, JOHN J., 3rd Lieutenant

Resided in Halifax or Warren counties and was by occupation a farmer prior to enlisting in Warren County at age 19, March 30, 1861. Mustered in as Private and promoted to Sergeant on April 25, 1862. Elected 3rd Lieutenant on October 1, 1862. Present or accounted for until wounded at Chancellorsville, Virginia, May 3, 1863. Rejoined the company in September-October, 1863, and was detailed as a Provost Guard in November-December, 1863. Reported absent on detail through February 25, 1865.

NONCOMMISSIONED OFFICERS AND PRIVATES

ADAMS, STEPHEN O., Private

Resided in Halifax County and enlisted at Camp Bragg, Virginia, at age 26, July 4, 1861. Present or accounted for until captured at Petersburg, Virginia, April 3, 1865. Confined at Hart's Island, New York Harbor, until released June 17-18, 1865, after taking the Oath of Allegiance.

ALES, JAMES H., Private

Was by occupation a tobacconist prior to enlisting in Warren County at age 27, March 30, 1861. Present or accounted for until he deserted or was captured at Gettysburg, Pennsylvania, July 3, 1863. Confined at Fort Delaware, Delaware, until released on July 7, 1863, after taking the Oath of Allegiance.

ALLEN, MARCUS A., Private

Born in Halifax County and was by occupation a farmer prior to enlisting in Northampton County at age 17, May 23, 1861. Present or accounted for until discharged on February 3, 1862, by reason of "chills and fever."

ALLSBROOK, HARTWELL, Private

Enlisted at Camp Holmes at age 33, September 1, 1863, for the war. Present or accounted for through April 1, 1864. No further records.

AYCOCK, JAMES H., Private

Enlisted at Camp Bragg, Virginia, at age 22, July 4, 1861. Present or accounted for through August, 1864.

AYCOCK, RICHARD T., Private

Born in Warren County and enlisted at Camp Bragg, Virginia, at age 31, July 4, 1861. Present or accounted for until he died at Richmond, Virginia, June 9 or June 27, 1862, of disease.

BARKLEY, THOMAS J., Private

Enlisted at Camp Holmes at age 18, July 28, 1863, for the war. Present or accounted for until he died "at home" on March 7, 1864, of disease.

BOBBITT, GIDEON C., Private

Born in Warren County and was by occupation a farmer prior to enlisting in Warren County at age 36, March 30, 1861. Present or accounted for until discharged July 16, 1862, by reason of being over age.

BOBBITT, STEPHEN E., Private

Resided in Warren County and was by occupation a farmer prior to enlisting in Halifax County at age 31, May 8, 1861. Present or accounted for until captured at Petersburg, Virginia, April 3, 1865. Confined at Hart's Island, New York Harbor, until released on June 17, 1865, after taking the Oath of Allegiance.

BOLTON, JOHN, Private

Place and date of enlistment not reported. Captured in hospital at Petersburg, Virginia, April 3, 1865. Reported in hospital at Petersburg on May 25, 1865. No further records. [It is unclear whether this soldier served in Company A, H, or K of this regiment.]

BOON, THOMAS, Private

Was by occupation a farmer prior to enlisting in Northampton County at age 44, May 23, 1861. Present or accounted for until discharged on or about September 16, 1862, by reason of being over age.

BOSWELL, PETER, Private

Was by occupation a farmer prior to enlisting in Northampton County at age 30, June 1, 1861. Present or accounted for until captured on or about September 30, 1862, when he was paroled at Shepherdstown, Virginia. Present or accounted for until he died at Weldon on May 20 or June 21, 1863, of wounds. Place and date wounded not reported.

BROWN, WILLIAM, Private

Born in Halifax County and was by occupation a farmer prior to enlisting at Camp Ellis, Virginia, at age 38, August 8, 1861. Present or accounted for until he died in hospital at Fort Bee, Virginia, December 26, 1861, of "pneumonia."

BROWN, WILLIAM E., Private

Was by occupation a farmer prior to enlisting in Northampton County at age 24, May 13, 1861. Present or accounted for until wounded at or near Malvern Hill, Virginia, on or about July 2, 1862. Rejoined the company in March-April, 1863, and was detailed in hospital at Richmond, Virginia, May 11, 1863. Reported absent on detail through March 30, 1864. No further records.

BURGE, WASHINGTON B., Private

Born in Warren County and was by occupation a clerk or merchant prior to enlisting in Northampton County at age 23, May 23, 1861. Present or accounted for until he deserted or was captured at Gettysburg, Pennsylvania, July 1-5, 1863. Confined at Fort Delaware, until transferred to Point Lookout, Maryland, October 15-18, 1863. Released at Point Lookout on January 22, 1864, after taking the Oath of Allegiance and joining the U.S. service. Unit to which assigned not reported.

BURGE, WILLIAM, Private
Was by occupation a preacher prior to enlisting in Warren County at age 61, March 30, 1861. Present or accounted for until discharged on or about September 12, 1861. Reason discharged not reported.

BURROWS, JAMES A., Sergeant
Enlisted at Camp Bragg, Virginia, at age 22, July 6, 1861. Mustered in as Private and promoted to Sergeant on October 1, 1862. Present or accounted for until wounded at or near Chancellorsville, Virginia, May 1-3, 1863. Died May 5, 1863, of wounds. Place of death not reported.

CAMP, GEORGE W., Private
Was by occupation a merchant prior to enlisting in Warren County at age 27, March 30, 1861. Mustered in as Private and promoted to Corporal on June 1, 1861. Reduced to ranks on January 13, 1862. Present or accounted for until killed at Sharpsburg, Maryland, September 17, 1862.

CARLENA, AUGUSTUS, Private
Born in Italy and was by occupation a "warrior" prior to enlisting in Northampton County at age 26, May 20, 1861. Present or accounted for until captured at Harrison's Landing, Virginia, July 1, 1862. Confined at Fort Columbus, New York Harbor, and at Fort Delaware, Delaware, until exchanged at Aiken's Landing, James River, Virginia, August 5, 1862. Discharged on or about November 5, 1862, under the provisions of the Conscript Act.

CARROLL, WILLIAM S., Private
Born in Franklin County and resided in Halifax County where he was by occupation a merchant or carpenter prior to enlisting in Northampton County at age 22, June 1, 1861. Present or accounted for until discharged on October 5, 1862, by reason of "disease of kidneys." Died at home in December, 1862, of disease.

CLEMENTS, WILLIAM E., Private
Was by occupation a farmer prior to enlisting in Northampton County at age 19, May 22, 1861. Present or accounted for until wounded in the left forearm at Payne's Farm, Virginia, November 27-28, 1863. Reported absent wounded through August, 1864. Reported on detail as Forage Sergeant from January 16, 1865, through February 21,1865.

DAY, JOHN W., Private
Was by occupation a farmer prior to enlisting in Northampton County at age 18, June 1, 1861. Present or accounted for until paroled at Lynchburg, Virginia, April 13, 1865.

DEATON, DAVID, Private
Enlisted in Wake County at age 37, July 16, 1862, for the war. Present or accounted for until sent to hospital at Winchester, Virginia, October 20, 1862. Reported absent sick until November-December, 1863, when he was reported dead. Survivor's records

indicate he died at Jordan's Springs, Virginia. Date and cause of death not reported.

EATON, CHARLES, Private
Born in Warren County and was by occupation a farmer prior to enlisting in Warren County at age 40, March 30, 1861. Present or accounted for until discharged on June 9, 1862, by reason of "a generally broken down condition." Died at Richmond on or about June 29, 1862, of disease.

EDMONDS, WILLIAM H., Private
Enlisted at Camp Bragg, Virginia, at age 29, July 6, 1861. Present or accounted for until he died in hospital at Richmond, Virginia, March 14, 1863, of "pneumonia."

EDWARDS, JAMES H., Private
Enlisted in Wake County at age 35, July 16, 1862, for the war as a substitute. Present or accounted for until killed at Sharpsburg, Maryland, September 17, 1862.

FELTZ, THOMAS, Private
Born in Warren County and was by occupation a farmer prior to enlisting in Warren County at age 21, March 30, 1861. Present or accounted for until he died in hospital at Richmond, Virginia, June 30, 1862, of "feb[ris] typh[oid]."

FLOORE, E., Private
Resided in Wilson County. Place and date of enlistment not reported. Paroled at Goldsboro in 1865.

FLOYD, JAMES H., Private
Was by occupation a farmer prior to enlisting in Warren County at age 21, March 30, 1861. Present or accounted for until he died in hospital at Danville, Virginia, August 4, 1862, of "chronic diarrhoea."

FORREST, JAMES, Private
Place and date of enlistment not reported. Captured at Five Forks, Virginia, April 1, 1865, and confined at Point Lookout, Maryland, until released June 26, 1865.

GOODSON, CORNELIUS W., Private
Enlisted in Wake County at age 30, July 16, 1862, for the war. Records of the Federal Provost Marshal indicate he was wounded in the breast in an unspecified battle and was paroled on September 27, 1862; however, company muster rolls indicate he was killed at Sharpsburg, Maryland, September 17, 1862. No further records.

HARDISTER, EZEKIEL, Private
Enlisted in Wake County at age 38, July 16, 1862, for the war. Present or accounted for until wounded in the left shoulder at Spotsylvania Court House, Virginia, May 8, 1864. Reported absent wounded through August, 1864. Captured in hospital at Richmond, Virginia, April 3, 1865, but escaped on April 24, 1865. Paroled on or about May 18, 1865.

HARDY, CURTIS, Sergeant
Born in Warren County and was by occupation a merchant prior to enlisting at Camp Bragg at age 22, July 6, 1861. Mustered in as Private and promoted to Sergeant on November 28, 1861. Present or accounted for until wounded at Sharpsburg, Maryland, September 17, 1862. Died at "S. H. Groves

farm," near Sharpsburg, October 5 or October 16, 1862.

HARDY, DANIEL C., Corporal
Was by occupation a farmer prior to enlisting in Warren County at age 33, March 30, 1861. Mustered in as Corporal but was reduced to ranks in March-December, 1862. Present or accounted for until wounded at Gettysburg, Pennsylvania, July 1-3, 1863. Rejoined the company in September-October, 1863, and was promoted to Corporal on April 12, 1864. Present or accounted for until captured at Winchester, Virginia, September 19, 1864. Confined at Point Lookout, Maryland, until transferred to Boulware's Wharf, James River, Virginia, where he was received March 18, 1865, for exchange.

HARDY, JOSEPH R., Corporal
Was by occupation a farmer prior to enlisting in Warren County at age 21, March 30, 1861. Mustered in as Private and promoted to Corporal on December 1, 1862. Present or accounted for until wounded in Virginia on May 30, 1864. Reported absent wounded through August, 1864. Paroled at Appomattox Court House, Virginia, April 9, 1865.

HARPER, JOHN W., Sergeant
Was by occupation a farmer prior to enlisting in Warren County at age 24, March 30, 1861. Mustered in as Sergeant. Present or accounted for until wounded in the left ankle and captured at Winchester, Virginia, September 19, 1864. Hospitalized at various Federal hospitals until transferred to Point Lookout, Maryland, where he arrived January 8, 1865. Released on June 3, 1865, after taking the Oath of Allegiance.

HARRIS, THOMAS WALKER, Private
Born in Halifax County where he resided as a farmer prior to enlisting in Warren County at age 32, March 30, 1861. Present or accounted for until reported in confinement from November 18, 1861, through February, 1862. Discharged July 16, 1862, under the provisions of the Conscript Act. Reenlisted in this company on June 23, 1863. Present or accounted for until reported absent without leave from May 20, 1864, until September 14, 1864. Captured at Petersburg, Virginia, April 3, 1865, and confined at Hart's Island, New York Harbor, until released June 16-17, 1865, after taking the Oath of Allegiance.

HARRISS, ANDREW J., Private
Was by occupation a farmer prior to enlisting in Warren County at age 22, March 30, 1861. Present or accounted for through August, 1864; however, he was reported on detail as a teamster during most of that period.

HARRISS, CHARLES E., Private
Was by occupation a mechanic prior to enlisting in Warren County at age 18, March 30, 1861. Mustered in as Private and promoted to Corporal on June 1, 1861. Reduced to ranks in March-December, 1862. Present or accounted for until captured at Williamsport, Maryland, July 14, 1863. Confined at various Federal prisons until confined at Point Lookout, Maryland, on or about October 18, 1863. Died at Point Lookout on February 6, 1864, of disease.

HARRISS, MAJOR D., Private
Was by occupation a farmer prior to enlisting in Warren County at age 26, March 30, 1861. Mustered in as Corporal but was reduced to ranks on June 1, 1861. Present or accounted for until paroled at Appomattox Court House, Virginia, April 9, 1865.

HARRISS, ROBERT H., Private
Was by occupation a farmer prior to enlisting in Warren County at age 18, March 30, 1861. Present or accounted for until he died in hospital at Richmond, Virginia, June 13, 1862, of "febris typhoides."

HERBERT, GEORGE W., Private
Enlisted in Halifax County at age 26, June 23, 1863, for the war. Present or accounted for until he died in hospital at Gordonsville, Virginia, April 9, 1864, of a gunshot wound. Place and date wounded not reported.

HICKS, DANIEL T., Private
Was by occupation a farmer prior to enlisting in Warren County at age 20, March 30, 1861. Present or accounted for until paroled at Appomattox Court House, Virginia, April 9, 1865.

HOLT, BENJAMIN J., Private
Was by occupation a coach maker prior to enlisting in Warren County at age 25, March 30, 1861. Present or accounted for until he died in camp near Fredericksburg, Virginia, February 27, 1863, of disease.

HOUSE, ISAAC F., Private
Born in Halifax County and was by occupation a farmer prior to enlisting in Warren County at age 17, March 30, 1861. Present or accounted for until killed at Malvern Hill, Virginia, July 1, 1862.

HOUSE, THOMAS E., Private
Was by occupation a merchant prior to enlisting in Warren County at age 20, March 30, 1861. Mustered in as Sergeant but was reduced to ranks in March-December, 1862. Present or accounted for until wounded in the knee at Gettysburg, Pennsylvania, July 2-3, 1863. Reported absent wounded or absent sick through August, 1864.

HURLEY, CORNELIUS, Private
Enlisted in Wake County at age 23, July 16, 1862, for the war. Present or accounted for until he deserted on or about October 15, 1862. Paroled at Troy on May 22, 1865.

INGRAM, BENJAMIN G., Private
Was by occupation a farmer prior to enlisting in Northampton County at age 28, May 21, 1861. Present or accounted for until paroled at Appomattox Court House, Virginia, April 9, 1865.

JARRALD, ADDISON, Private
Was by occupation a farmer prior to enlisting in Northampton County at age 32, May 22, 1861. Present or accounted for until he died at Richmond, Virginia, on or about June 4, 1862, of disease.

JENKINS, BRADFORD S., Private
Enlisted near Fredericksburg, Virginia, at age 18, January 5, 1863, for the war. Present or accounted for through August, 1864.

JENKINS, GEORGE F., Private
Was by occupation a mechanic prior to enlisting

Warren County at age 24, March 30, 1861. Present or accounted for until he died at Richmond, Virginia, on or about June 16, 1862, of disease.

JENKINS, JOHN F., Private

Was by occupation a farmer prior to enlisting in Warren County at age 26, March 30, 1861. Mustered in as Private and promoted to Corporal in January-May, 1862. Hospitalized at Richmond, Virginia, July 6, 1862, with "thumb shot off"; however, place and date wounded not reported. Reduced to ranks on December 1, 1862. Rejoined the company prior to January 1, 1863, and present or accounted for until he died in hospital at Lynchburg, Virginia, July 27, 1863, of "phthisis pul[monalis]."

JENKINS, NEWSOM EDWARD, 1st Sergeant

Was by occupation a schoolteacher prior to enlisting in Warren County at age 24, March 30, 1861. Mustered in as 1st Sergeant. Present or accounted for until wounded at Chancellorsville, Virginia, May 1-3, 1863. Returned to duty prior to July 1, 1863, and present or accounted for until appointed Sergeant Major on or about January 15, 1864, and transferred to the Field and Staff of this regiment.

JENKINS, ROBERT T., Private

Was by occupation a farmer prior to enlisting in Warren County at age 21, March 30, 1861. Present or accounted for through August, 1864. Reported on duty with Captain Samuel D. Haslett's Provost Guard Company in September-October, 1864. Paroled at Farmville, Virginia, April 11-21, 1865.

JENKINS, WILLIAM C., Private

Was by occupation a farmer prior to enlisting in Warren County at age 27, March 30, 1861. Present or accounted for until discharged on or about September 8, 1861, by reason of disability.

JENKINS, WILLIAM F., Private

Enlisted at "Chickahominy," Virginia, May 15, 1862, for the war. Present or accounted for until reported absent on wounded furlough since October 1, 1862. Place and date wounded not reported. Returned to duty on March 9, 1863, and present or accounted for through October, 1863. Died prior to January 1, 1864. Place, exact date, and cause of death not reported.

JOHNSTON, ANTHONY M., Private

Born in Warren County and was by occupation a farmer prior to enlisting in Warren County at age 18, March 30, 1861. Present or accounted for until discharged on or about April 20, 1862, by reason of "chronic intermittent fever."

JOHNSTON, FRANCIS M., Private

Previously served in Company E, Mallett's Battalion (Camp Guard). Enlisted in this company at Camp Holmes on June 16, 1864, for the war. Present or accounted for until paroled at Appomattox Court House, Virginia, April 9, 1865. North Carolina pension records indicate he was wounded at Winchester, Virginia, September 19, 1864.

JOHNSTON, JAMES T., Private

Was by occupation a farmer prior to enlisting in Northampton County at age 28, June 1, 1861. Present or accounted for until killed at Chancellorsville, Virginia, May 3, 1863.

JOHNSTON, THOMAS M., Private

Was by occupation a farmer prior to enlisting in Warren County at age 18, March 30, 1861. Mustered in as Private and promoted to Corporal on April 5, 1862. Present or accounted for until hospitalized at Richmond, Virginia, July 5, 1862, with a gunshot wound; however, place and date wounded not reported. Reduced to ranks on December 1, 1862, and was reported absent sick until he rejoined the company in July-August, 1863. Reported absent sick from September-October, 1863, until February 7, 1864, when he was discharged. Reason discharged not reported.

JOHNSTON, WHITMEL A., Sergeant

Was by occupation a farmer prior to enlisting in Warren County at age 18, March 30, 1861. Mustered in as Private and promoted to Sergeant on April 25, 1862. Present or accounted for until killed at Sharpsburg, Maryland, September 17, 1862.

JOHNSTON, WILLIS R., Sergeant

Born in Warren County and was by occupation a schoolteacher prior to enlisting in Warren County at age 20, March 30, 1861. Mustered in as Sergeant. Present or accounted for until he died at Camp Bee, Virginia, November 1, 1861, of "congestive chill."

KEARNEY, AUGUSTUS A., Private

Was by occupation a farmer prior to enlisting in Northampton County at age 29, June 5, 1861. Present or accounted for until wounded at Sharpsburg, Maryland, September 17, 1862. Returned to duty prior to January 1, 1863, and present or accounted for until killed at Gettysburg, Pennsylvania, July 1, 1863.

KING, NATHANIEL E., Private

Resided in Halifax County and enlisted near Orange Court House, Virginia, February 18, 1864, for the war. Present or accounted for until captured at Amelia Court House, Virginia, April 6, 1865. Confined at Point Lookout, Maryland, until released on July 6, 1865, after taking the Oath of Allegiance.

KING, RICHARD M., Sergeant

Was by occupation a farmer prior to enlisting in Warren County at age 22, March 30, 1861. Mustered in as Corporal but was reduced to ranks on June 1, 1861. Present or accounted for until captured at Frederick, Maryland, September 12, 1862. Promoted to Sergeant on September 20, 1862, while a prisoner of war. Confined at Fort Delaware, Delaware, until transferred to Aiken's Landing, James River, Virginia, October 2, 1862, for exchange. Declared exchanged at Aiken's Landing in November 10, 1862. Rejoined the company in January-February, 1863, and present or accounted for until wounded in the right arm at Spotsylvania Court House, Virginia, May 12, 1864. Reported absent wounded through August, 1864. Paroled at Appomattox Court House, Virginia, April 9, 1865.

KING, THOMAS E., Private

Was by occupation a farmer prior to enlisting in Warren County at age 18, March 30, 1861. Present or accounted for until wounded in the left leg and captured at or near Sharpsburg, Maryland, on or about September 17, 1862. Confined at Fort McHenry, Maryland, until paroled and transferred to Aiken's

Landing, James River, Virginia, where he was received October 19, 1862, for exchange. Declared exchanged at Aiken's Landing on November 10, 1862. Rejoined the company in January-February, 1863, and present or accounted for until wounded in the chest and captured at Winchester, Virginia, September 19, 1864. Hospitalized at Baltimore, Maryland, December 21, 1864. Paroled at Baltimore and transferred for exchange on or about February 16, 1865. Furloughed from hospital at Richmond, Virginia, March 15, 1865.

LANCASTER, JAMES J., Private
Was by occupation a mechanic prior to enlisting in Warren County at age 33, March 30, 1861. Mustered in as Private and promoted to Corporal on June 1, 1861. Present or accounted for until wounded in the thorax and captured at Sharpsburg, Maryland, September 17, 1862. Exchanged on or about October 6, 1862, and was reduced to ranks prior to January 1, 1863. Rejoined the company in January-February, 1863, and present or accounted for until killed at Spotsylvania Court House, Virginia, May 12, 1864.

LATHAM, DAVID L., Private
Born in Granville County and was by occupation a mechanic or blacksmith prior to enlisting in Northampton County at age 26, June 1, 1861. Present or accounted for until he died in hospital at Lynchburg, Virginia, January 17, 1863, of "typ[hoi]d pneumonia."

LEWIS, DAVID, Private
Enlisted in Wake County on July 16, 1862, for the war. Present or accounted for until he died in November-December, 1863. Place and cause of death not reported.

LEWIS, ROBERT J., Private
Was by occupation a merchant prior to enlisting in Warren County at age 23, March 30, 1861. Present or accounted for until wounded at Malvern Hill, Virginia, on or about July 2, 1862. Rejoined the company in January-February, 1863, and present or accounted for through January 21, 1865; however, he was reported absent sick or absent on detail during most of that period. Captured in hospital at Richmond, Virginia, April 3, 1865, and was paroled on April 20, 1865.

LYNCH, RICHARD, Private
Was by occupation a farmer prior to enlisting in Northampton County at age 20, June 1, 1861. Present or accounted for until wounded at Spotsylvania Court House, Virginia, May 19, 1864. Reported absent wounded through August, 1864. Paroled at Appomattox Court House, Virginia, April 9, 1865.

McCARSON, ARTHUR M., Private
Resided in Henderson County. Place and date of enlistment not reported. Took the Oath of Allegiance at Louisville, Kentucky, March 10, 1865.

McCASKILL, MARTIN, Private
Enlisted in Wake County at age 32, July 16, 1862, for the war. Present or accounted for through October, 1863. Died prior to January 1, 1864. Place, cause, and exact date of death not reported.

McCASKILL, NATHANIEL, Private
Enlisted in Wake County at age 34, July 16, 1862,

for the war. Present or accounted for through October, 1863. Died prior to January 1, 1864. Place, cause, and exact date of death not reported.

MARLOW, WILLIAM H., Private
Was by occupation a farmer prior to enlisting in Northampton County at age 17, June 1, 1861. Present or accounted for until he lost the use of his right eye as a result of a wound received at Malvern Hill, Virginia, on or about July 1, 1862. Rejoined the company in March-April, 1863. Present or accounted for through September 9, 1864; however, he was reported absent sick or absent on detail during much of that period.

MATHEWS, JOHN R., Private
Was by occupation a farmer prior to enlisting in Warren County at age 24, March 30, 1861. Present or accounted for until hospitalized at Richmond, Virginia, June 7, 1862, with "laryngitis." Died in hospital at Richmond on June 14, 1862, of disease.

MOORE, WILLIAM A., Private
Was by occupation a farmer prior to enlisting in Warren County at age 18, March 30, 1861. Present or accounted for until he died at Richmond, Virginia, on or about July 1, 1862, of disease.

MORRISS, JAMES N., Private
Was by occupation a farmer prior to enlisting in Northampton County at age 26, May 13, 1861. Present or accounted for until discharged on March 18, 1863. Reason discharged not reported.

MORRISS, JOHN A:, Private
Resided in Wilson County and enlisted in Wake County at age 28, July 16, 1862, for the war. Present or accounted for until captured on or about September 19, 1862, when he was hospitalized at Frederick, Maryland. Rejoined the company prior to January 1, 1863, and present or accounted for until captured at Petersburg, Virginia, April 2, 1865. Confined at Hart's Island, New York Harbor, until released on June 18, 1865, after taking the Oath of Allegiance.

MORRISS, NORMAN G., Private
Was by occupation a farmer prior to enlisting in Warren County at age 20, March 30, 1861. Present or accounted for until paroled at Appomattox Court House, Virginia, April 9, 1865.

MORRISS, THOMAS, Private
Born in Halifax County and was by occupation a farmer prior to enlisting in Warren County at age 36, March 30, 1861. Present or accounted for until discharged on July 16, 1862, under the provisions of the Conscript Act.

MORRISS, WILLIAM H., Private
Enlisted in Wake County at age 36, July 16, 1862, for the war. Present or accounted for until captured at or near Sharpsburg, Maryland, on or about September 17, 1862. Confined at Fort McHenry, Maryland, until paroled and transferred to Aiken's Landing, James River, Virginia, where he was received October 19, 1862, for exchange. Declared exchanged at Aiken's Landing on November 10, 1862. Rejoined the company in January-February, 1863, and present or accounted for until reported absent without leave on June 11, 1863. Reported absent without leave through August, 1864.

MORRISS, WILLIAM P., Private
Was by occupation a farmer prior to enlisting in Warren County at age 21, March 30, 1861. Present or accounted for until he died in hospital at Richmond, Virginia, May 22, 1862, of "pneumonia."

MUNN, DANIEL A., Private
Enlisted in Wake County at age 32, July 16, 1862, for the war. Present or accounted for until he died in hospital at Lynchburg, Virginia, January 17, 1863, of "pneumonia."

MYRICK, ALEXANDER W., Private
Born in Warren County and was by occupation a farmer prior to enlisting in Warren County at age 22, March 30, 1861. Present or accounted for until he died in hospital at Richmond, Virginia, June 5, 1862, of disease.

MYRICK, FLETCHER H., Private
Born in Warren County and was by occupation a farmer prior to enlisting in Warren County at age 24, March 30, 1861. Mustered in as Corporal but was reduced to ranks on June 1, 1861. Present or accounted for until he died in hospital at Richmond, Virginia, June 10, 1862, of disease.

MYRICK, JESSE R., Private
Was by occupation a merchant prior to enlisting in Warren County at age 20, March 30, 1861. Present or accounted for until captured at Frederick, Maryland, September 12, 1862. Confined at Fort Delaware, Delaware, until transferred to Aiken's Landing, James River, Virginia, October 2, 1862, for exchange. Declared exchanged at Aiken's Landing on November 10, 1862. Rejoined the company in January-February, 1863, and present or accounted for until wounded at Fredericksburg, Virginia, May 1, 1863. Hospitalized at Richmond, Virginia, where he died on or about May 14, 1863, of wounds.

NEVILL, ANDERSON, Cook
Was by occupation a farmer prior to enlisting in Warren County at age 41, March 30, 1861. Mustered in as Private. Discharged on June 16, 1862, under the provisions of the Conscript Act. Reenlisted in this company on February 17, 1863, with the rank of Cook. Present or accounted for through August, 1864; however, he was reported absent sick during much of that period.

NEWSOM, JAMES W., Sergeant
Was by occupation a farmer prior to enlisting in Warren County at age 20, March 30, 1861. Mustered in as Private and promoted to Sergeant on May 13, 1863. Present or accounted for until he died in Virginia on October 19, 1864. Place and cause of death not reported.

NEWSOM, JESSE FAULCON, Corporal
Resided in Halifax County and enlisted at Camp Ellis, Virginia, at age 18, August 8, 1861. Mustered in as Private and promoted to Corporal on September 17, 1862. Present or accounted for until hospitalized at Charlottesville, Virginia, October 24, 1864, with a gunshot wound of the right side; however, place and date wounded not reported. Rejoined the company prior to April 6, 1865, when he was captured at Amelia Court House, Virginia. Confined at Point Lookout, Maryland, until released on June 29, 1865, after taking the Oath of Allegiance.

NEWSOM, LEMUEL C., Sergeant
Was by occupation a farmer prior to enlisting in Warren County at age 20, March 30, 1861. Mustered in as Private and promoted to Corporal on December 1, 1862. Promoted to Sergeant on April 12, 1864. Present or accounted for until he died May 22, 1864, of wounds. Place and date wounded and place of death not reported.

PARSONS, A. L., Private
Enlisted in Wake County at age 36, July 16, 1862, for the war. Present or accounted for until sent to hospital at Winchester, Virginia, September 20, 1862. Died prior to January 1, 1864. Place, cause, and exact date of death not reported.

PARSONS, JAMES L., Private
Enlisted in Wake County at age 30, July 16, 1862, for the war. Present or accounted for until sent to hospital at Winchester, Virginia, September 20, 1862. Died at Jordan's Springs, Virginia, prior to January 1, 1864. Cause and exact date of death not reported.

PENDERGRASS, RICHARD J., Private
Enlisted in Wake County at age 18, July 21, 1863, for the war. Present or accounted for until wounded in the right hand at Spotsylvania Court House, Virginia, May 10, 1864. Reported absent wounded until retired to the Invalid Corps on December 1, 1864.

PETERSON, CORNELIUS W., Private
Born in Halifax County and was by occupation a clerk or telegraph operator prior to enlisting in Halifax County at age 18, May 10, 1861. Mustered in as Private and promoted to Corporal on April 25, 1862. Present or accounted for until wounded in the left arm at Malvern Hill, Virginia, July 1, 1862. Left arm amputated. Reduced to ranks on December 1, 1862. Reported absent on detail from January-February, 1863, through August, 1864.

PITTARD, WILLIAM G., Private
Was by occupation a farmer prior to enlisting in Warren County at age 29, March 30, 1861. Present or accounted for until he died in hospital at Lynchburg, Virginia, March 1, 1863, of "erysipelas."

PRYOR, THOMAS A., Private
Was by occupation a farmer prior to enlisting in Warren County at age 16, March 30, 1861. Present or accounted for until discharged on July 16, 1862, under the provisions of the Conscript Act.

RIGGAN, DANIEL R., Private
Resided in Warren County and enlisted at Camp Bragg, Virginia, at age 27, July 6, 1861. Present or accounted for until discharged on or about October 16, 1861, by reason of disability.

ROBERTS, BENJAMIN, Private
Enlisted in Wake County on July 16, 1862, for the war. Present or accounted for until sent to hospital at Leesburg, Virginia, September 5, 1862. Reported absent sick through February, 1863. No further records.

ROBERTS, JAMES L., Private
Enlisted in Wake County at age 30, July 15, 1862, for the war. Present or accounted for through April 1, 1864; however, he was reported absent sick or

absent on detail during much of that period. "Transferred on detail" on April 1, 1864. No further records.

ROBERTS, WILLIAM A., Private
Enlisted in Wake County on July 16, 1862, for the war. Present or accounted for through August, 1864; however, he was reported absent sick or absent without leave during most of that period.

RODGERS, JOHN E., Private
Resided in Wilkes County where he enlisted on November 5, 1863, for the war. Present or accounted for until captured at or near the North Anna River, Virginia, May 23, 1864. Confined at Old Capitol Prison, Washington, D.C., until transferred to Fort Delaware, Delaware, June 15, 1864. Released June 7-8, 1865, after taking the Oath of Allegiance.

RODGERS, LETCHER, Private
Enlisted in Wilkes County on November 5, 1863, for the war. No further records.

ROOKER, DAVID T., Private
Was by occupation a farmer prior to enlisting in Northampton County at age 17, May 15, 1861. Present or accounted for until wounded and captured at or near Sharpsburg, Maryland, on or about September 17, 1862. Died in hospital at Frederick, Maryland, September 24, 1862, of wounds.

ROOKER, GEORGE W., Corporal
Was by occupation a mechanic prior to enlisting in Warren County at age 21, March 30, 1861. Mustered in as Private. Present or accounted for until wounded in the thorax and captured at Sharpsburg, Maryland, September 17, 1862. Hospitalized at Frederick, Maryland, until transferred to Fort Delaware, Delaware, at an unspecified date. Paroled at Fort Delaware and transferred to City Point, Virginia, where he was received December 18, 1862, for exchange. Rejoined the company in January-February, 1863, and present or accounted for until wounded in the right arm or right shoulder at Chancellorsville, Virginia, May 3, 1863. Rejoined the company in July-August, 1863, and present or accounted for until wounded in the right arm at or near Spotsylvania Court House, Virginia, on or about May 12, 1864. Reported absent wounded through August, 1864. Promoted to Corporal prior to April 9, 1865, when he was paroled at Appomattox Court House, Virginia.

ROOKER, WILLIAM T., Corporal
Was by occupation a farmer prior to enlisting in Northampton County at age 18, May 13, 1861. Mustered in as Private. Present or accounted for until wounded at Sharpsburg, Maryland, September 17, 1862. Promoted to Corporal on December 1, 1862, and returned to duty prior to January 1, 1863. Present or accounted for until wounded in the left foot at Chancellorsville, Virginia, May 1-3, 1863. Discharged March 9-10, 1864. Reason discharged not reported.

SCARLETT, FELIX, Private
Enlisted in Wake County at age 20, July 16, 1862, for the war. Present or accounted for until captured at or near Sharpsburg, Maryland, on or about September 17, 1862. Died November 12, 1862, of disease. Place of death not reported.

SHEARIN, ELBERT J., Private
Born in Warren County and was by occupation a farmer prior to enlisting in Warren County at age 24, March 30, 1861. Present or accounted for until he died at Camp Ellis, Virginia, July 9, 1861, of "measles" and "dysentery."

SHEARIN, HENRY W., Private
Resided in Halifax County where he enlisted at age 28, June 23, 1863, for the war. Present or accounted for until captured at Petersburg, Virginia, April 2, 1865. Confined at Hart's Island, New York Harbor, until released on June 17, 1865, after taking the Oath of Allegiance.

SHEARIN, JOSEPH J., Private
Born in Warren County and was by occupation a farmer prior to enlisting in Northampton County at age 17, May 23, 1861. Present or accounted for until killed at Malvern Hill, Virginia, July 1, 1862.

SHEARIN, ROBERT A., Corporal
Born in Warren County and was by occupation a farmer prior to enlisting in Warren County at age 28, March 30, 1861. Mustered in as Private and promoted to Corporal on January 13, 1862. Present or accounted for until killed at Sharpsburg, Maryland, September 17, 1862.

SHEARIN, SEBASTIAN C., Private
Was by occupation a farmer prior to enlisting in Warren County at age 22, March 30, 1861. Present or accounted for until wounded in the left arm and left foot at Harpers Ferry, West Virginia, July 4, 1864. Reported absent wounded until retired to the Invalid Corps on November 29, 1864.

SHEARIN, ZACHARIAH E., Private
Born in Warren County and was by occupation a teacher prior to enlisting in Warren County at age 21, March 30, 1861. Present or accounted for until discharged on November 22, 1861, by reason of disability.

SHEARIN, ZACHARIAH T., 1st Sergeant
Was by occupation a farmer prior to enlisting in Warren County at age 19, March 30, 1861. Mustered in as Private and promoted to Sergeant on April 25, 1862. Promoted to 1st Sergeant on April 12, 1864. Present or accounted for until wounded in the left arm and captured at Spotsylvania Court House, Virginia, May 8, 1864. Confined at Point Lookout, Maryland, until transferred to Elmira, New York, August 10, 1864. Paroled at Elmira on March 10, 1865, and transferred to Boulware's Wharf, James River, Virginia, where he was received March 15, 1865, for exchange.

TUCKER, JOSEPH, Private
Was by occupation a mechanic prior to enlisting in Warren County at age 20, March 30, 1861. Present or accounted for until wounded in the right arm and captured at Gettysburg, Pennsylvania, July 1-3, 1863. Hospitalized at Gettysburg until transferred to Fort McHenry, Maryland, August 22-23, 1863. Transferred to Point Lookout, Maryland, September 15, 1863. Confined at Point Lookout until paroled and transferred to Cox's Landing, James River, Virginia, where he was received February 14-15, 1865. Reported present with a detachment of paroled and ex-

changed prisoners at Camp Lee, near Richmond, Virginia, February 17, 1865.

TUCKER, MERIDITH, Private

Was by occupation a farmer prior to enlisting in Northampton County at age 21, May 13, 1861. Present or accounted for through April, 1863. Reported absent sick from May-June, 1863, through August, 1864.

TURNER, JOHN J., Private

Enlisted in Wake County at age 25, July 16, 1862, for the war. Present or accounted for until he died in hospital at Danville, Virginia, October 22, 1862, of "chr[onic] diarrhoea."

VICK, JOHN W., Private

Born in Greensville County, Virginia, and was by occupation a merchant prior to enlisting in Halifax County at age 29, May 6, 1861. Present or accounted for until he died "at home" in Northampton or Halifax counties on or about November 19, 1862, of disease.

WALKER, JOSEPH R., Private

Born in Halifax County and was by occupation a farmer prior to enlisting in Warren County at age 16, March 30, 1861. Present or accounted for until he died in hospital at Richmond, Virginia, July 3, 1862, of "diarrhoea ch[ronic]."

WEBB, WILLIAM E., Private

Enlisted in Halifax County at age 40, June 23, 1863, for the war. Present or accounted for until paroled at Appomattox Court House, Virginia, April 9, 1865.

WILLIAMS, WILLIAM G., Private

Was by occupation a farmer prior to enlisting in Northampton County at age 22, May 13, 1861. Present or accounted for until he died in hospital at Richmond, Virginia, June 1, 1862, of "feb[ris] typh-[oid]."

WILSON, NATHANIEL, Private

Enlisted at Camp Ellis, Virginia, at age 23, August 8, 1861. Present or accounted for until "sent home wounded" on October 20, 1862. Place and date wounded not reported. Rejoined the company in March-April, 1863, and present or accounted for until wounded in the right thigh at or near Reams' Station, Virginia on or about August 26, 1864. Reported absent wounded until furloughed for sixty days on March 15, 1865.

WRIGHT, DRUREY S., Private

Resided in Warren County and enlisted at Camp Bragg, Virginia, at age 22, July 6, 1861. Present or accounted for until captured at Petersburg, Virginia, April 2, 1865. Confined at Hart's Island, New York Harbor, until released on June 18, 1865, after taking the Oath of Allegiance.

YARBROUGH, BENJAMIN, Private

Enlisted in Wake County at age 34, July 16, 1862, for the war. Present or accounted for until he died in hospital at Richmond, Virginia, November 10, 1862, of "typhoid fever" and/or "chronic diarrhoea."

YARBROUGH, SAMUEL, Private

Enlisted in Wake County at age 32, July 16, 1862, for the war. Present or accounted for until he died in North Carolina on April 28, 1863, of disease.

YARBROUGH, WILLIAM P., Private

Resided in Montgomery County and enlisted in Wake County at age 35, July 16, 1862, for the war. Present or accounted for until "sent home wounded" on November 10, 1862. Place and date wounded not reported. Rejoined the company in January-February, 1863, and present or accounted for until captured at Petersburg, Virginia, April 3, 1865. Confined at Hart's Island, New York Harbor, until released on June 17, 1865, after taking the Oath of Allegiance.

YEOURNS, STARKEY, Private

Enlisted in Wake County at age 30, July 16, 1862, for the war. Present or accounted for until sent to hospital at Leesburg, Virginia, September 5, 1862. Died prior to January 1, 1864. Place, cause, and exact date of death not reported.

COMPANY B

This company, known as the Thomasville Rifles, was from Davidson County and enlisted at Thomasville and at Lexington on April 23, 1861. It was ordered to Raleigh, where it arrived on the same day. The company remained at Raleigh until May 23, 1861, when it was moved to Garysburg. There it was assigned to this regiment as Company B. After joining the regiment the company functioned as a part of the regiment, and its history for the war period is recorded as a part of the regimental history.

The information contained in the following roster of the company was compiled principally from company muster rolls for April 23, 1861, through August 31, 1864. No company muster rolls were found for the period after August 31, 1864. In addition to the company muster rolls, Roll of Honor records, receipt rolls, hospital records, prisoner of war records, and other primary records, supplemented by state pension applications, United Daughters of the Confederacy records, and postwar rosters and histories, all provided useful information.

OFFICERS
CAPTAINS

MILLER, WILLIS L.

Resided in Davidson County and was by occupation a minister prior to enlisting in Davidson County at age 30. Appointed Captain on April 23, 1861. Present or accounted for until he resigned or was defeated for reelection when the regiment was reorganized on April 25, 1862.

LAMBETH, JOSEPH HARRISON

Resided in Davidson County and was by occupation a clerk prior to enlisting in Davidson County at age 21, April 23, 1861. Mustered in as Private and was appointed 3rd Lieutenant to rank from May 26, 1861. Promoted to Captain on April 25, 1862. Present or accounted for until promoted to Major on July 5, 1862, and transferred to the Field and Staff of this regiment.

LIEUTENANTS

AYER, HENRY W., 2nd Lieutenant
Resided in Davidson County and was by occupation a clerk prior to enlisting in Davidson County at age 26, April 23, 1861. Mustered in as 1st Sergeant and appointed 2nd Lieutenant to rank from May 26, 1861. Present or accounted for until he resigned or was defeated for reelection when the regiment was reorganized April 25-26, 1862.

CROSS, MOSES H., 2nd Lieutenant
Resided in Davidson County and was by occupation a farmer prior to enlisting in Davidson County at age 18, April 23, 1861. Mustered in as Private and promoted to 1st Sergeant on October 5, 1862. Appointed 3rd Lieutenant on November 4, 1863, and promoted to 2nd Lieutenant on May 18, 1864. Present or accounted for until paroled at Appomattox Court House, Virginia, April 9, 1865.

HEPLER, SAMUEL J., 1st Lieutenant
Resided in Davidson County and was by occupation a farmer prior to enlisting in Davidson County at age 19, April 23, 1861. Mustered in as Sergeant and was promoted to 1st Sergeant on May 26, 1861. Reduced to ranks on September 26, 1861, but was appointed 2nd Lieutenant to rank from April 27, 1862. Present or accounted for until wounded in the left arm at Sharpsburg, Maryland, September 17, 1862. Left arm amputated. Promoted to 1st Lieutenant on October 4, 1862, but resigned on May 15, 1863, by reason of wounds received at Sharpsburg. Resignation accepted June 1, 1863.

JONES, CYRUS P., 2nd Lieutenant
Resided in Davidson County and was by occupation a shoemaker prior to enlisting in Davidson County at age 19, April 23, 1861. Mustered in as Corporal and promoted to 1st Sergeant on April 27, 1862. Appointed 3rd Lieutenant on October 4, 1862. Present or accounted for until wounded at Chancellorsville, Virginia, May 1-3, 1863. Returned to duty prior to July 1, 1863, and was promoted to 2nd Lieutenant on November 4, 1863. Present or accounted for until killed at Spotsylvania Court House, Virginia, May 19, 1864.

LAMBETH, DAVID THOMAS, 3rd Lieutenant
Resided in Davidson County and was by occupation a farmer. Appointed 3rd Lieutenant on or about April 23, 1861. Resigned on May 2, 1861, and/or was discharged on or about May 22, 1861. Reason he resigned and/or was discharged not reported.

LEACH, ALEXANDER A., 1st Lieutenant
Resided in Moore or Davidson counties and was by occupation a carpenter prior to enlisting in Davidson County at age 27, April 23, 1861. Mustered in as Corporal but was reduced to ranks on July 31, 1861. Elected 3rd Lieutenant on April 25, 1862, and was promoted to 2nd Lieutenant on October 4, 1862. Promoted to 1st Lieutenant on November 4, 1863. Present or accounted for through April 2, 1865.

SHELBY, ROMULUS W., 1st Lieutenant
Resided in Davidson County and was by occupation a shoemaker. Appointed 1st Lieutenant on or about April 23, 1861, but resigned and/or was discharged May 2-7, 1861. Reason he resigned and/or was discharged not reported.

THOMAS, PLEASANT C., 1st Lieutenant
Resided in Davidson County and was by occupation a merchant prior to enlisting at age 23. Elected 2nd Lieutenant on April 23, 1861, and was promoted to 1st Lieutenant to rank from May 26, 1861. Present or accounted for until he resigned or was defeated for reelection when the regiment was reorganized April 25-26, 1862.

WILBURN, LAMMA, 1st Lieutenant
Born in Randolph County where he resided as a student prior to enlisting in Davidson County at age 24, April 23, 1861. Mustered in as Private and promoted to Corporal on December 19, 1861. Promoted to Sergeant on January 11, 1862, and was elected 1st Lieutenant on April 25, 1862. Present or accounted for until he died in hospital at Richmond, Virginia, June 26, 1862, of "fever."

NONCOMMISSIONED OFFICERS AND PRIVATES

ALLRED, CLEMMONS M., Private
Resided in Davidson County and was by occupation a carpenter prior to enlisting in Davidson County at age 23, April 23, 1861. Mustered in as Corporal and promoted to Sergeant on April 27, 1862. Reduced to ranks on March 1, 1863. Present or accounted for until wounded at Chancellorsville, Virginia, May 1-3, 1863. Reported absent wounded through October, 1863. Detailed as a Provost Guard in November-December, 1863, and reported absent on detail through August, 1864. Paroled at Appomattox Court House, Virginia, April 9, 1865.

ALLRED, WILLIAM, Private
Resided in Davidson County and was by occupation a carpenter prior to enlisting in Davidson County at age 19, April 23, 1861. Present or accounted for until wounded at Sharpsburg, Maryland, September 17, 1862. Rejoined the company in January-February, 1863, and present or accounted for until reported absent without leave from July 20, 1863, until November 6, 1863. Present or accounted for from November 7, 1863, through August, 1864.

ANDERSON, JESSE A., Private
Resided in Davidson County and was by occupation a carpenter prior to enlisting in Davidson County at age 23, April 23, 1861. Present or accounted for until wounded in the left arm at Sharpsburg, Maryland, September 17, 1862. Rejoined the company in March-April, 1863. Hospitalized at Richmond, Virginia, May 22, 1863, with a gunshot wound of the right arm; however, place and date wounded not reported; returned to duty May 23, 1863, and was captured at Gettysburg, Pennsylvania, July 1, 1863. Died in Pennsylvania on or about July 10, 1863. Cause of death not reported.

ANDREWS, THOMAS D., Private
Resided in Guilford County and enlisted in Wake County on July 16, 1863, for the war. Present or accounted for until wounded in the left ankle and captured at or near Fisher's Hill, Virginia, on or

about September 22, 1864. Hospitalized at Baltimore, Maryland, until transferred to Point Lookout, Maryland, where he arrived October 18, 1864. Paroled at Point Lookout and transferred to Venus Point, Savannah River, Georgia, where he was received November 15, 1864, for exchange. Rejoined the company prior to April 3, 1865, when he was captured at Petersburg, Virginia. Confined at Hart's Island, New York Harbor, until released on June 17, 1865, after taking the Oath of Allegiance.

ATKINS, WILLIAM M., Private
Resided in Moore County and enlisted in Wake County on July 16, 1862, for the war. Present or accounted for through August, 1864; however, he was reported absent sick or absent on light duty during most of that period. Paroled at Troy on May 22, 1865.

BABCOCK, EDWARD WARREN, Private
Resided in Davidson County and was by occupation a boot maker prior to enlisting in Wake County at age 24, April 27, 1861. Mustered in as Private and promoted to Sergeant in March-April, 1863. Present or accounted for until wounded in the left thigh at Chancellorsville, Virginia, May 1-3, 1863. Rejoined the company in November-December, 1863, and was promoted to 1st Sergeant in January-April, 1864. Reduced to ranks on August 1, 1864. Present or accounted for through August, 1864.

BAKER, DAVID, Private
Enlisted in Davidson County on April 27, 1861. Died at Lexington in November, 1862. Cause of death not reported.

BAKER, GEORGE, Private
Enlisted at Bond's Mill, Virginia, December 14, 1863, for the war. Present or accounted for until killed at Spotsylvania Court House, Virginia, May 12, 1864.

BAKER, PHILLIP, Private
Resided in Davidson County and was by occupation a farmer prior to enlisting in Davidson County at age 25, April 27, 1861. Present or accounted for until wounded and captured at Sharpsburg, Maryland, September 17, 1862. Confined at Fort McHenry, Maryland, until paroled and transferred to Aiken's Landing, James River, Virginia, where he was received October 19, 1862, for exchange. Declared exchanged at Aiken's Landing on November 10, 1862. Rejoined the company in September-October, 1863, but was detailed for light duty at Gordonsville, Virginia, on or about December 17, 1863. Retired to the Invalid Corps on April 27, 1864. Paroled at Greensboro on April 28, 1865.

BAKER, RUFUS, Private
Resided in Davidson County and was by occupation a farmer prior to enlisting in Davidson County at age 20, April 27, 1861. Present or accounted for through February 17, 1865; however, he was reported absent sick, absent on furlough, or absent on light duty during most of that period. Paroled at Lynchburg, Virginia, in April, 1865.

BAKER, WILLIAM, Private
Resided in Davidson County and enlisted at Camp Bee, Virginia, September 10, 1861. Present or ac-

counted for until wounded in the left arm and hip at Spotsylvania Court House, Virginia, May 12, 1864. Reported absent wounded through August, 1864. Took the Oath of Allegiance at or near Washington, D.C., on or about April 10, 1865.

BARTON, JOHN R., Private
Resided in Guilford County and was by occupation a miller prior to enlisting at age 22. Place and date of enlistment not reported. Captured at New Creek, West Virginia, November 20, 1864, and confined at Wheeling, West Virginia, until transferred to Camp Chase, Ohio, December 13, 1864. Released at Camp Chase on or about April 22, 1865, after joining the U.S. Army. Assigned to Company E, 5th Regiment U.S. Volunteer Infantry.

BECK, JACOB H. R., Private
Resided in Davidson County where he enlisted on July 29, 1861. Present or accounted for until he deserted on or about July 1, 1862. Reported "present in arrest" on February 23, 1863, and was reported in confinement through June, 1863. Rejoined the company prior to September 1, 1863, and present or accounted for until killed at Spotsylvania Court House, Virginia, May 15, 1864.

BEMISTER, THOMAS, Private
Resided in Rowan County and was by occupation a painter prior to enlisting in Wake County at age 25, May 1, 1861. Present or accounted for until transferred to Company D of this regiment on or about November 30, 1862.

BERRIER, HENRY J., Sergeant
Resided in Davidson County where he enlisted on August 15, 1861. Mustered in as Private and promoted to Sergeant on September 26, 1861. Reduced to ranks on April 27, 1862, but was promoted to Sergeant in January-April, 1864. Present or accounted for until captured at Farmville, Virginia, April 6, 1865. Confined at Point Lookout, Maryland, until released on June 24, 1865, after taking the Oath of Allegiance.

BLACK, AMOS, Private
Resided in Davidson County and enlisted in Wake County on July 16, 1862, for the war. Present or accounted for until he died in "the valley of Virginia" on November 22, 1862, of disease.

BLAIR, ARRIS, Private
Enlisted in Davidson County on April 23, 1861. Present or accounted for until he deserted prior to September 1, 1861.

BRAXTON, HIRAM, Private
Resided in Chatham County and enlisted in Wake County on June 22, 1863, for the war. Present or accounted for through August, 1864.

BRAXTON, JOHN, Private
Resided in Chatham County and enlisted in Wake County on June 22, 1863, for the war. Present or accounted for until killed at Spotsylvania Court House, Virginia, May 12, 1864.

BRITT, FRANK J., Private
Resided in Maine and was by occupation a shoemaker prior to enlisting in Davidson County at age 20, April 23, 1861. Mustered in as Sergeant but was reduced to ranks on July 27, 1861. Present or ac-

counted for until killed at Malvern Hill, Virginia, July 1, 1862.

BRYANT, THOMAS, Private
Born in Davidson County where he resided as a farmer prior to enlisting in Davidson County at age 29, April 27, 1861. Present or accounted for until wounded and captured at Sharpsburg, Maryland, September 17, 1862. Died in hospital at Frederick, Maryland, October 19, 1862, of wounds.

BUIE, JOHN A., Private
Resided in Moore County and enlisted in Wake County at age 41, October 19, 1863, for the war. Present or accounted for through August, 1864.

COLLETT, WILLIAM J., Private
Resided in Davidson County and was by occupation a farmer prior to enlisting in Davidson County at age 20, April 27, 1861. Present or accounted for until mortally wounded at Winchester, Virginia, September 19, 1864. Place and exact date of death not reported.

DALTON, W. A., Sergeant
Place and date of enlistment not reported. Deserted to the enemy prior to March 3, 1865, when he was confined at Knoxville, Tennessee. Released March 4, 1865, after taking the Oath of Allegiance.

DAVIS, HENRY J., Sergeant
Resided in Davidson County and was by occupation a farmer prior to enlisting in Davidson County at age 20, May 10, 1861. Mustered in as Private and promoted to Corporal on November 2, 1862. Promoted to Sergeant on August 1, 1864. Present or accounted for until captured at Winchester, Virginia, September 19, 1864, or at Strasburg, Virginia, September 22-23, 1864. Confined at Point Lookout, Maryland, until paroled on February 18, 1865, and transferred to Boulware's and Cox's Wharf, James River, Virginia, for exchange. Reported present with a detachment of paroled and exchanged prisoners at Camp Lee, near Richmond, Virginia, February 28, 1865.

DORSETT, WILLIAM H., Private
Resided in Davidson County and was by occupation a carpenter prior to enlisting in Davidson County at age 17, April 23, 1861. Mustered in as Private and promoted to Sergeant on April 27, 1862. Reduced to ranks on November 20, 1862. Present or accounted for until wounded in the head at Gettysburg, Pennsylvania, July 1-3, 1863. Rejoined the company prior to September 1, 1863, and present or accounted for until he deserted on February 15, 1864.

ELLINGTON, GEORGE B., Corporal
Resided in Davidson County and was by occupation a carpenter prior to enlisting in Davidson County at age 24, April 23, 1861. Mustered in as Private. Present or accounted for until wounded at Sharpsburg, Maryland, September 17, 1862. Rejoined the company in January-February, 1863, and was promoted to Corporal on March 1, 1863. Present or accounted for until he was listed as a deserter on August 7, 1864. Paroled at Gordonsville, Virginia, June 17, 1865.

ELLINGTON, JAMES F., Private
Resided in Davidson County and was by occupation a coach maker prior to enlisting in Wake County at age 24, May 9, 1861. Present or accounted for until

discharged on or about August 30, 1861, by reason of disability.

EPPS, BEVERLY R., Corporal
Resided in Davidson County and was by occupation a farmer prior to enlisting in Davidson County at age 19, April 23, 1861. Mustered in as Private and promoted to Corporal on August 1, 1864. Present or accounted for until wounded in the calf of the right leg and captured at Winchester, Virginia, September 19, 1864. Hospitalized at Winchester and at Baltimore, Maryland, until transferred to Point Lookout, Maryland, where he arrived October 18, 1864. Paroled at Point Lookout and transferred to Venus Point, Savannah River, Georgia, where he was received November 15, 1864, for exchange. Rejoined the company prior to April 2, 1865, when he was captured at Petersburg, Virginia. Confined at Hart's Island, New York Harbor, until released on June 17, 1865, after taking the Oath of Allegiance.

EPPS, JAMES W., Corporal
Born in Halifax County and resided in Davidson County where he was by occupation a carpenter prior to enlisting in Davidson County at age 22, April 23, 1861. Mustered in as Private and promoted to Corporal on April 28, 1862. Present or accounted for until he died in hospital at Richmond, Virginia, June 29, 1862, of "feb[ris] typh[oid]."

EPPS, THOMAS G., Private
Born in Person County and resided in Davidson County where he was by occupation a farmer prior to enlisting in Davidson County at age 20, April 23, 1861. Present or accounted for until he died in hospital at Richmond, Virginia, or at Farmville, Virginia, on or about July 1, 1862, of "feb[ris] typh[oid]."

FALKNER, BENJAMIN, Private
Resided in Davidson County and enlisted in Wake County on July 16, 1862, for the war. Present or accounted for until captured at Wilderness, Virginia, May 6, 1864. Confined at Point Lookout, Maryland, until transferred to Elmira, New York, August 10, 1864. Died at Elmira on December 6, 1864, of "chronic diarrhoea."

FITCHETT, EDWARD G., Private
Resided in Guilford County and was by occupation a shoemaker prior to enlisting in Guilford County at age 27, May 30, 1861. Mustered in as Private and promoted to Sergeant on July 29, 1861. Reduced to ranks on April 27, 1862, and deserted on May 28, 1862. Rejoined the company on February 11, 1863, and present or accounted for until he deserted again on June 28, 1864.

FOLKNER, JAMES, Private
Resided in Davidson County and was by occupation a farmer or carpenter prior to enlisting in Davidson County at age 22, April 23, 1861. Present or accounted for until he died in hospital at Richmond, Virginia, June 19, 1862, of "febris typhoides."

FOUST, JOSEPH S., Private
Resided in Guilford County and was by occupation a farmer prior to enlisting in Guilford County at age 33, May 30, 1861. Present or accounted for until transferred out of this company and assigned to hospital duty at Liberty, Virginia, November 15, 1862.

GREENWOOD, ABEL T., Private

Resided in Wake County and enlisted on February 11, 1864, for the war. Present or accounted for until he deserted to the enemy at or near Spotsylvania Court House, Virginia, on or about June 17, 1864. Confined at Fort Monroe, Virginia, until transferred to Elmira, New York, July 23, 1864. Released at Elmira on May 17, 1865, after taking the Oath of Allegiance.

GUYER, HARPER F., Private

Resided in Davidson County and was by occupation a farmer prior to enlisting in Davidson County at age 19, April 23, 1861. Present or accounted for until wounded at Malvern Hill, Virginia, on or about July 1, 1862. Died at or near Gaines' Mill, Virginia, July 15, 1862, of wounds or "fever."

HALL, CHARLES, Private

Resided in Guilford County and was by occupation a miner prior to enlisting in Guilford County at age 22, April 23, 1861. Present or accounted for through September 15, 1862. Company muster rolls indicate he died in Maryland on October 1, 1862, of disease; however, records of the Federal Provost Marshal indicate he was captured at Sharpsburg, Maryland, on or about September 17, 1862, and was paroled on October 5, 1862. Roll of Honor indicates he died in Maryland of wounds received at Sharpsburg. No further records.

HAMMILL, JAMES B., Corporal

Resided in Guilford County and was by occupation a miner prior to enlisting in Guilford County at age 21, May 30, 1861. Mustered in as Private and promoted to Corporal on April 27, 1862. Present or accounted for until killed at Sharpsburg, Maryland, September 17, 1862.

HANCOCK, JOSEPH, Private

Born in Randolph County where he resided prior to enlisting in Davidson County on August 5, 1861. Present or accounted for until killed at Malvern Hill, Virginia, July 1, 1862.

HEDRICK, JOHN F., Corporal

Resided in Davidson County and was by occupation a student prior to enlisting in Davidson County at age 18, April 23, 1861. Mustered in as Private and promoted to Corporal on July 29, 1861. Present or accounted for until he died at Fort Bee, Virginia, December 12-13, 1861, of disease.

HEPLER, THOMAS, Private

Resided in Davidson County and was by occupation a carpenter prior to enlisting in Davidson County at age 24, April 23, 1861. Present or accounted for until captured at Winchester, Virginia, September 19, 1864. Confined at Point Lookout, Maryland, until paroled and transferred to Boulware's Wharf, James River, Virginia, where he was received March 18, 1865, for exchange.

HEPLER, WILLIAM J., Private

Born in Davidson County where he resided prior to enlisting in Davidson County on July 29, 1861. Present or accounted for until killed at Sharpsburg, Maryland, September 17, 1862.

HURLEY, CHARLES G., Private

Born in Montgomery County and resided in Moore County prior to enlisting in Wake County on July 16, 1862, for the war. Present or accounted for until he died in hospital at Richmond, Virginia, October 25, 1862, of "chron[ic] dysentery."

HUTSON, ROBERT C., Private

Resided in Davidson County and was by occupation a shoemaker prior to enlisting in Davidson County at age 24, April 23, 1861. Present or accounted for until captured in hospital at Richmond, Virginia, April 3, 1865. Paroled at Richmond on April 18, 1865.

JACKSON, WILLIS, Private

Resided in Guilford County and was by occupation a farmer prior to enlisting in Guilford County at age 52, May 30, 1861. Present or accounted for until discharged on August 30, 1861, by reason of disability.

JOHNSON, ANDREW, Private

Enlisted in Wake County on December 2, 1863, for the war. Died in hospital at Orange Court House, Virginia, January 12, 1864. Cause of death not reported.

JONES, ALBY, Private

Resided in Guilford County and enlisted at New Market on August 27, 1861. Present or accounted for through August, 1864; however, he was reported absent sick, absent on furlough, or absent without leave during much of that period. Paroled at Greensboro on May 9, 1865.

JONES, JAMES W., Private

Resided in Davidson County and was by occupation a machine operator prior to enlisting in Davidson County at age 24, April 23, 1861. Mustered in as Sergeant but was reduced to ranks on June 27, 1861. Present or accounted for until discharged on or about September 9, 1861. Reason discharged not reported.

JORDAN, JOHN M., Private

Resided in Davidson County and enlisted in Wake County on July 16, 1862, for the war. Present or accounted for through August, 1864.

KNOY, WILLIAM, Private

Born in Davidson County where he resided prior to enlisting in Wake County on July 16, 1862, for the war. Present or accounted for until killed at Sharpsburg, Maryland, September 17, 1862.

LAMBETH, DUDLEY M., Private

Born in Davidson County where he resided as a farmer prior to enlisting in Davidson County at age 21, May 10, 1861. Present or accounted for until killed at Malvern Hill, Virginia, July 1, 1862.

LAMBETH, JONES H., _____

Enlisted in Davidson County at age 19, on or about March 17, 1862. "Rejected by [the] medical surgeons."

LANNING, MARION, Private

Born in Davidson County where he resided prior to enlisting in Davidson County on August 15, 1861. Present or accounted for until he died in hospital at Richmond, Virginia, June 26, 1862, of "measles."

LEACH, ROBERT D., Private

Resided in Moore County and enlisted in Wake County on July 16, 1862, for the war. Present or accounted for until hospitalized at Farmville, Virginia, January 16, 1863, with a gunshot wound of the hand; however, place and date wounded not reported. Rejoined the company in March-April, 1863, and present or accounted for until wounded at Hanover Junction, Virginia, on or about May 24, 1864. Reported absent in hospital through August, 1864.

LEDFORD, PRESTON LAFAYETTE, Corporal
Resided in Davidson County and enlisted in Wake County on July 16, 1862, for the war. Mustered in as Private and promoted to Corporal on August 1, 1864. Present or accounted for until captured at Jarratt's Station, Virginia, April 3, 1865. Confined at Hart's Island, New York Harbor, until released on June 17, 1865, after taking the Oath of Allegiance.

LENARD, JACOB R., Private
Resided in Davidson County and was by occupation a farmer prior to enlisting in Davidson County at age 23, April 23, 1861. Mustered in as Corporal but resigned and was reduced to ranks on June 29, 1861. Present or accounted for until captured at Winchester, Virginia, September 19, 1864. Confined at Point Lookout, Maryland, until paroled and transferred to Boulware's Wharf, James River, Virginia, where he was received March 18, 1865, for exchange.

LEONARD, WINT, Private
Resided in Davidson County and was by occupation a farmer prior to enlisting in Davidson County at age 20, April 23, 1861. Present or accounted for until wounded at Sharpsburg, Maryland, September 17, 1862. Died in Maryland on November 15, 1862, of wounds.

LINES, CHARLES L., Private
Resided in Davidson County where he enlisted at age 28, March 17, 1862. Mustered in as Private and promoted to Sergeant on April 27, 1862. Present or accounted for until wounded at Sharpsburg, Maryland, September 17, 1862. Rejoined the company in January-February, 1863, and present or accounted for until wounded in the left leg at Gettysburg, Pennsylvania, July 2-3, 1863. Rejoined the company in September-October, 1863, and present or accounted for until wounded in the right foot and captured at Winchester, Virginia, September 19, 1864. Hospitalized at various Federal hospitals until confined at Point Lookout, Maryland, October 26, 1864. Paroled at Point Lookout and transferred to Venus Point, Savannah River, Georgia, where he was received November 15, 1864, for exchange. Paroled at Appomattox Court House, Virginia, April 9, 1865. Rank given on parole as Private.

LINK, S., Private
Resided in Davidson County and enlisted at age 26, July 16, 1862, for the war. Present or accounted for until he died in Maryland or at Winchester, Virginia, September 8, 1862. Cause of death not reported.

LITTLE, GREEN B., Corporal
Born in Guilford County where he resided as a miner prior to enlisting in Guilford County at age 22, May 30, 1861. Mustered in as Private and promoted to Corporal on July 31, 1861. Present or accounted for until discharged on November 23, 1861, by reason of "the effects of severe and protracted typhoid fever."

LONG, JOHN L., Private
Born in Davidson County where he resided prior to enlisting in Wake County on July 16, 1862, for the war. Present or accounted for until he died in hospital at Staunton, Virginia, November 10, 1862, of "acute diarrhoea."

LOOKABILL, BARNEY, Private
Born in Davidson County where he resided as a miner prior to enlisting in Davidson County at age 21, April 23, 1861. Present or accounted for until wounded in the right hand at Malvern Hill, Virginia, July 1, 1862. Reported absent wounded until discharged on November 24, 1862, by reason of wounds received at Malvern Hill. Paroled at Greensboro on May 10, 1865.

LYONS, E. N., Private
Place and date of enlistment not reported. Died in hospital at Farmville, Virginia, April 26, 1865. Cause of death not reported.

McCUTCHAN, ROBERT M., Private
Resided in Davidson County and was by occupation a shoe cutter prior to enlisting in Davidson County at age 19, April 23, 1861. Mustered in as Sergeant and promoted to 1st Sergeant on September 26, 1861. Reduced to ranks on April 27, 1862. Court-martialed on or about April 9, 1863; however, reason he was court-martialed not reported. Present or accounted for until wounded at Spotsylvania Court House, Virginia, May 8, 1864. Died June 1, 1864. Place of death not reported.

McEWING, EDWARD A., Private
Born at Paisley, Scotland, and resided in Davidson County where he was by occupation a shoemaker prior to enlisting in Davidson County at age 22, April 23, 1861. Present or accounted for until discharged on July 22, 1862, by reason of "being a foreigner."

McGUIRE, HAMILTON J., Private
Resided in Davidson County and was by occupation a student prior to enlisting in Davidson County at age 18, April 23, 1861. Present or accounted for until discharged on or about August 30, 1861, by reason of disability.

McKNIGHT, JAMES G., Private
Resided in Forsyth County and enlisted in Wake County at age 18, July 16, 1862, for the war. Present or accounted for until captured at Petersburg, Virginia, April 3, 1865. Confined at Hart's Island, New York Harbor, until released on June 17, 1865, after taking the Oath of Allegiance.

McRARY, WILLIAM F., Private
Resided in Wilkes County and was by occupation a farmer prior to enlisting in Davidson County at age 22, May 10, 1861. Present or accounted for until wounded in the shoulder at Gettysburg, Pennsylvania, July 1-3, 1863. Rejoined the company prior to September 1, 1863. Present or accounted for until reported absent wounded on company muster roll dated December 31, 1863-August 31, 1864; however, place and date wounded not reported. No further records.

MARSHALL, JOSEPH, Private
Enlisted in Wake County on July 23, 1863, for the war. Present or accounted for until he deserted on

August 20, 1863. Rejoined the company prior to July 28, 1864, when he deserted a second time.

MAY, JOSHUA B., Private
Born in Davidson County where he resided as a farmer prior to enlisting in Davidson County at age 18, April 27, 1861. Mustered in as Private and promoted to Corporal on December 19, 1861. Reduced to ranks on April 27, 1862. Present or accounted for until he died in hospital at Richmond, Virginia, June 17, 1862, of "fever" and/or "dysenteria."

MEADOWS, JOHN D., Private
Resided in Guilford County and was by occupation a farmer prior to enlisting in Guilford County at age 16, June 5, 1861. Present or accounted for until discharged at Camp Bee, Virginia, on or about September 8, 1861, by reason of disability.

MOORE, GEORGE H., Private
Resided in Davidson County and was by occupation a carpenter prior to enlisting in Davidson County at age 19, April 23, 1861. Present or accounted for until killed at Spotsylvania Court House, Virginia, May 12, 1864.

MOORE, ROBERT A., Sergeant
Resided in Randolph County and enlisted at Fort Bee, Virginia, December 1, 1861. Mustered in as Private and promoted to Corporal of April 28, 1862. Promoted to Sergeant on April 26, 1864. Present or accounted for until "killed on picket" on May 26, 1864. Place of death not reported.

MOORE, WALTER J., Corporal
Resided in Davidson County and was by occupation an artist prior to enlisting in Davidson County at age 17, May 21, 1861. Mustered in as Private and promoted to Corporal on October 6, 1862. Present or accounted for until captured at Gettysburg, Pennsylvania, July 3, 1863, or at Hagerstown, Maryland, July 5, 1863. Confined at Fort Delaware, Delaware, until transferred to Point Lookout, Maryland, October 15-18, 1863. Died at Point Lookout on June 13, 1864. Cause of death not reported.

MORGAN, JABEZ F., Private
Resided in Davidson County and was by occupation a carpenter prior to enlisting in Davidson County at age 22, April 27, 1861. Present or accounted for until wounded at Sharpsburg, Maryland, September 17, 1862. Died in Maryland on November 15, 1862, of wounds.

MORRIS, GREEN RICHARDSON, Private
Previously served in Company E, 28th Regiment N.C. Troops. Transferred to this company on April 14, 1864. Present or accounted for through August, 1864. Paroled at Troy on May 22, 1865.

MORRIS, JOHN W., Private
Resided in Davidson County and enlisted in Wake County at age 23, July 16, 1862, for the war. Deserted at Hanover Junction, Virginia, August 26, 1862.

MURPHY, JOSEPH, Private
Resided in Davidson County and enlisted in Wake County at age 26, July 16, 1862, for the war. Deserted prior to September 12, 1862, when he was reported under arrest. Died March 10, 1863, of "pneumonia." Place of death not reported.

MYERS, AMBROSE, Private
Resided in Davidson County and enlisted in Wake County at age 39, November 4, 1863, for the war. Present or accounted for until wounded in the left thigh and captured at Winchester, Virginia, September 19, 1864. Hospitalized at Winchester and at Baltimore, Maryland, until transferred to Point Lookout, Maryland, where he arrived October 26, 1864. Paroled at Point Lookout and transferred to Venus Point, Savannah River, Georgia, where he was received November 15, 1864, for exchange.

MYERS, CLARKSON W., Corporal
Born in Davidson County where he resided as a farmer prior to enlisting in Davidson County at age 20, April 27, 1861. Mustered in as Private and promoted to Corporal on April 28, 1862. Present or accounted for until wounded and captured at Sharpsburg, Maryland, September 17, 1862. Hospitalized at Frederick, Maryland, where he died October 17-18, 1862, of wounds.

MYERS, FELIX, Private
Resided in Davidson County and enlisted in Wake County on July 16, 1862, for the war. Present or accounted for until killed at Chancellorsville, Virginia, May 3, 1863.

MYERS, JEFFERSON C., Private
Born in Davidson County where he resided as a farmer prior to enlisting in Davidson County at age 20, April 23, 1861. Present or accounted for until discharged at Fort Bee, Virginia, December 12, 1861, by reason of "severe and protracted typhoid fever."

MYERS, JESSE A., Private
Resided in Davidson County and enlisted in Wake County at age 37, November 6, 1863, for the war. Present or accounted for through August, 1864; however, he was reported absent on light duty during most of that period.

MYERS, LEMUEL J., Sergeant
Enlisted in Wake County on July 16, 1862, for the war. Mustered in as Private. Present or accounted for until wounded at Sharpsburg, Maryland, September 17, 1862. Rejoined the company in January-February, 1863, and present or accounted for until wounded in the hip at Gettysburg, Pennsylvania, July 2-3, 1863. Rejoined the company in September-October, 1863. Promoted to Corporal on April 26, 1864, and promoted to Sergeant on August 1, 1864. Present or accounted for until captured at Winchester, Virginia, September 19, 1864. Confined at Point Lookout, Maryland, until paroled and transferred to Boulware's Wharf, James River, Virginia, where he was received March 18, 1865, for exchange.

NOWELL, JONATHAN, Private
Resided in Davidson County and was by occupation a shoe cutter prior to enlisting in Davidson County at age 38, April 23, 1861. Present or accounted for until he deserted on April 27, 1862.

ODELL, WILLIAM H., Private
Born in Guilford County where he resided as a farmer prior to enlisting in Guilford County at age 37, May 5, 1861. Present or accounted for until wounded at Sharpsburg, Maryland, September 17, 1862. Died in Maryland on November 30, 1862, of wounds.

PARISH, JOHN C., Private
Enlisted at Bond's Mills, Virginia, January 12, 1864, for the war. Present or accounted for through August, 1864.

PARR, MARTIN V., Private
Resided in Guilford County and was by occupation a farmer prior to enlisting in Wake County at age 25, April 30, 1861. Present or accounted for until captured at Petersburg, Virginia, April 2, 1865. Confined at Hart's Island, New York Harbor, until released on June 18, 1865, after taking the Oath of Allegiance.

PICKETT, ALEXANDER, Private
Resided in Davidson County and was by occupation a farmer prior to enlisting in Davidson County at age 22, May 13, 1861. Present or accounted for until he died in hospital at Richmond, Virginia, June 17, 1862, of "febris typhoides & cont[inued]."

RAKER, DAVID, Private
Born in Davidson County where he resided as a farmer prior to enlisting in Davidson County at age 20, April 27, 1861. Present or accounted for until he died at Lexington, North Carolina, November 14-15, 1862. Cause of death not reported.

ROBINS, MADISON, Private
Born in Guilford County where he resided as a miner prior to enlisting in Guilford County at age 25, May 30, 1861. Present or accounted for until he died at Richmond, Virginia, May 24, 1862, of "fever."

ROBINS, PLEASANT, Private
Born in Guilford County where he resided as a miner prior to enlisting in Guilford County at age 26, April 23, 1861. Present or accounted for until he died at Fort Bee, Virginia, January 18, 1862, of "brain fever."

RUSSELL, ZACHARIAH, Private
Enlisted in Wake County at age 21, July 16, 1862, for the war. Present or accounted for until wounded in the chin and right hand at Sharpsburg, Maryland September 17, 1862. Rejoined the company in May-June, 1863, and present or accounted for through August, 1864.

SECHRIST, AMBROSE, Private
Enlisted in Wake County on December 2, 1863, for the war. Died at Orange Court House, Virginia, December 28, 1863. Cause of death not reported.

SECHRIST, ANDREW, Private
Resided in Davidson County and enlisted in Wake County at age 24, July 16, 1862, for the war. Present or accounted for until captured at Boonsboro, Maryland, on or about September 17, 1862. Confined at Fort Delaware, Delaware, until transferred to Aiken's Landing, James River, Virginia, October 2, 1862, for exchange. Declared exchanged at Aiken's Landing on November 10, 1862. Rejoined the company in January-February, 1863, and present or accounted for until captured at Winchester, Virginia, September 19, 1864. Confined at Point Lookout, Maryland, until exchanged on March 15, 1865.

SECHRIST, CONRAD, Private
Born in Davidson County where he resided as a laborer prior to enlisting in Davidson County at age 16, March 20, 1862. Present or accounted for until

"drummed out of service" by sentence of court-martial on or about November 13, 1863. No further records.

SHAW, ALBERT W., Private
Was by occupation a stage driver prior to enlisting in Guilford County at age 18, April 23, 1861. Present or accounted for until he deserted on February 22, 1863. Reported "in arrest" on company muster roll dated March-April, 1863, but deserted again on May 4, 1863.

SHELLY, WILLIAM W., Sergeant
Resided in Davidson County and was by occupation a shoe cutter prior to enlisting in Davidson County at age 18, April 23, 1861. Mustered in as Private and promoted to Corporal prior to July 29, 1861, when he was promoted to Sergeant. Present or accounted for until discharged on January 1, 1862, after providing a substitute.

SHOUP, JULIUS L., 1st Sergeant
Resided in Davidson County and was by occupation a student prior to enlisting in Davidson County at age 18, April 27, 1861. Mustered in as Private and promoted to Corporal on January 11, 1862. Promoted to Sergeant on November 2, 1862, and promoted to 1st Sergeant on August 1, 1864. Present or accounted for until paroled at Appomattox Court House, Virginia, April 9, 1865.

SIDES, CALVIN T., Private
Resided in Forsyth County and enlisted in Wake County at age 18, July 16, 1863, for the war. Present or accounted for until transferred to Company E, 28th Regiment N.C. Troops, April 14, 1864.

SINK, ANDREW, Private
Resided in Davidson County where he enlisted at age 21, August 29, 1861. Present or accounted for until wounded in the neck and captured at Gettysburg, Pennsylvania, July 1-5, 1863. Confined at Davids Island, New York Harbor, until paroled and transferred to City Point, Virginia, where he was received August 28, 1863, for exchange. Rejoined the company in January-April, 1864, and present or accounted for until wounded in the right arm at Spotsylvania Court House, Virginia, in May, 1864. Reported absent wounded until retired to the Invalid Corps on December 12, 1864.

SMITH, ALFRED H., Private
Resided in Davidson County and was by occupation a farmer prior to enlisting in Davidson County at age 18, April 23, 1861. Mustered in as Private and promoted to Corporal on October 6, 1862. Reduced to ranks on November 19, 1862. Present or accounted for until captured at or near Mechanicsville, Virginia, on or about May 30, 1864. Confined at Point Lookout, Maryland, until transferred to Elmira, New York, July 5, 1864. Released at Elmira on June 19, 1865, after taking the Oath of Allegiance.

SMITH, GEORGE E., Private
Resided in Guilford County and enlisted at Fort Bee, Virginia, at age 23, January 1, 1862. Present or accounted for until wounded in the right leg at Sharpsburg, Maryland, September 17, 1862. Reported absent wounded or absent on detail through January 14, 1865.

SMITH, JOHN C., Private

Resided in Guilford County and was by occupation a farmer prior to enlisting in Guilford County at age 24, April 27, 1861. Present or accounted for until hospitalized at Richmond, Virginia, May 20, 1863, with a gunshot wound of the head; however, place and date wounded not reported. Rejoined the company in July-August, 1863. Present or accounted for until hospitalized at Richmond on July 17, 1864, with an unspecified wound; however, place and date wounded not reported. Rejoined the company prior to September 1, 1864, and present or accounted for until paroled at Farmville, Virginia, April 11-21, 1865.

SNIDER, ROMULUS S., Private

Resided in Forsyth County and was by occupation a carpenter prior to enlisting in Davidson County at age 24, April 23, 1861. Mustered in as Private and promoted to Sergeant on April 27, 1862. Present or accounted for until wounded in the right arm at Williamsburg, Virginia, May 5, 1862. Rejoined the company prior to January 1, 1863. Reduced to ranks on August 5, 1863. Present or accounted for until wounded in the neck and left shoulder and captured at Winchester, Virginia, September 19, 1864. Hospitalized at Winchester and at Baltimore, Maryland, until confined at Point Lookout, Maryland, October 18, 1864. Paroled at Point Lookout and transferred to Venus Point, Savannah River, Georgia, where he was received November 15, 1864, for exchange. Rejoined the company prior to April 3, 1865, when he was captured at Petersburg, Virginia. Confined at Hart's Island, New York Harbor, until released on June 21, 1865, after taking the Oath of Allegiance.

SOWERS, WILLIAM A., Private

Resided in Davidson County and was by occupation a farmer prior to enlisting in Davidson County at age 20, May 13, 1861. Present or accounted for through January 31, 1865. Paroled at Greensboro on May 1, 1865.

SPAUGH, SOLOMON, Private

Born in Davidson County where he resided prior to enlisting in Wake County at age 23, July 16, 1862, for the war. Present or accounted for until he died at or near Culpeper Court House, Virginia, September 16, 1862. Cause of death not reported.

STONE, JOHN, Private

Enlisted in Wake County on July 16, 1862, for the war. Present or accounted for until he died "in the Valley of Virginia" on October 13, 1862. Cause of death not reported.

STRAYHORN, HILLERY, Private

Enlisted in Davidson County on August 26, 1861. Present or accounted for until he deserted on February 22, 1863. Assumed the name of Thomas M. Strayhorn and enlisted in Company A, 10th Battalion N.C. Heavy Artillery, March 30, 1863. Arrested as a deserter and was returned to this company in January-February, 1864. Reported in arrest in April, 1864, but deserted again on June 28, 1864.

SUMNER, ASA, Private

Enlisted in Davidson County on August 26, 1861. Present or accounted for until he died at Richmond, Virginia, August 28, 1862, of "fever."

TAYLOR, CALEB, Private

Born in Northampton County and resided in Wake County where he was by occupation a laborer prior to enlisting at Fort Bee, Virginia, at age 33, March 1, 1862. Present or accounted for through October 13, 1862. Discharge records indicate he was discharged at Huguenot Springs, Virginia, October 14, 1862, by reason of "varix & hernia"; however, company records indicate he was absent in hospital until he was reported dead on a company muster roll dated December 31, 1863-August 31, 1864. No further records.

THOMAS, HENRY C., Private

Born in Davidson County where he resided as a clerk prior to enlisting in Davidson County at age 16, April 23, 1861. Mustered in as Private and promoted to Sergeant on November 17, 1861. Reduced to ranks on April 29, 1862. Present or accounted for until discharged on July 22, 1862, by reason of being under age.

TYSINGER, ALEXANDER, Private

Resided in Randolph County and was by occupation a farmer prior to enlisting in Davidson County at age 16, May 13, 1861. Present or accounted for until wounded in the right arm at Malvern Hill, Virginia, July 1, 1862. Rejoined the company in January-February, 1863, and present or accounted for until discharged on January 25, 1864. Reason discharged not reported.

TYSINGER, FARLEY, Private

Born in Davidson County and resided in Randolph County prior to enlisting in Davidson County at age 21, August 26, 1861. Present or accounted for until killed at Sharpsburg, Maryland, September 17, 1862.

VANSTORY, LINDSAY M., Private

Resided in Guilford County and was by occupation a farmer prior to enlisting in Wake County at age 17, May 9, 1861. Present or accounted for until he died in hospital at Richmond, Virginia, June 20, 1862, of "febris cont[inued]."

VAUGHN, AZARIAH A., Private

Born in Rockingham County and resided in Davidson County where he was by occupation a carpenter or mechanic prior to enlisting in Davidson County at age 23, April 23, 1861. Present or accounted for until discharged on December 18, 1861, by reason of "debility resulting from severe and protracted typhoid fever." Later served in Company D, 45th Regiment N.C. Troops.

VEACH, WILLIAM D., Private

Resided in Davidson County and enlisted in Wake County at age 22, July 16, 1862, for the war. Present or accounted for until paroled at Appomattox Court House, Virginia, April 9, 1865.

WAGGONER, EMANUEL, Private

Resided in Davidson County and was by occupation a farmer prior to enlisting in Davidson County at age 18, May 13, 1861. Present or accounted for until discharged in March-April, 1863, by reason of disability.

WAGGONER, JACOB, Private

Resided in Davidson County and was by occupation a farmer prior to enlisting in Wake County on July

16, 1862, for the war. Present or accounted for until hospitalized at Richmond, Virginia, May 28, 1864, with a gunshot wound; however, place and date wounded not reported. Furloughed from hospital for sixty days on June 7, 1864. Rejoined the company prior to September 19, 1864, when he was captured at Winchester, Virginia. Confined at Point Lookout, Maryland, until released May 12-14, 1865, after taking the Oath of Allegiance.

WAGGONER, JOHN W., Private
Born in Davidson County where he resided prior to enlisting in Wake County at age 25, July 16, 1862, for the war. Present or accounted for until killed at Sharpsburg, Maryland, September 17, 1862.

WARREN, ED, Private
Place and date of enlistment not reported. Retired to the Invalid Corps on November 29, 1864. Paroled at Greensboro, May 4-5, 1865.

WATFORD, GREEN D., Private
Born in Randolph County and resided in Davidson County where he was by occupation a carpenter prior to enlisting in Davidson County at age 22, April 23, 1861. Present or accounted for until wounded at Sharpsburg, Maryland, September 17, 1862. Died in Maryland on October 31, 1862, of wounds.

WEST, AUGUSTUS F., Private
Resided in Davidson or Wake counties and was by occupation a printer prior to enlisting in Davidson County at age 23, April 23, 1861. Present or accounted for until he deserted on December 6, 1862. Returned from desertion on March 3, 1863, and was reported "in arrest" until he was released at an unspecified date. Rejoined the company prior to September 1, 1863. Transferred to Company K of this regiment on September 8, 1863.

WILBURN, JOHN C., Private
Was by occupation a farmer prior to enlisting in Davidson County at age 18, April 27, 1861. Present or accounted for through August, 1864. Paroled at Greensboro on May 5, 1865.

WILLIAMS, ALFRED W., Private
Resided in Moore County and enlisted in Wake County at age 30, July 16, 1862, for the war. Present or accounted for until his left foot was "cut off" near Orange Court House, Virginia, January 25, 1864. Reported absent wounded until retired to the Invalid Corps on December 12, 1864.

WILLIAMS, GEORGE W., Private
Resided in Davidson County where he enlisted at age 21, August 13, 1861. Present or accounted for until wounded at Sharpsburg, Maryland, September 17, 1862. Rejoined the company in January-February, 1863, but was reported absent without leave from July-August, 1863, through October, 1863. Rejoined the company in November-December, 1863, and present or accounted for until he deserted on June 28, 1864.

WINBURN, R. W., Private
Enlisted in Guilford County on April 27, 1861. Present or accounted for until he deserted or was transferred to another company prior to September 1, 1861.

WRENN, HENRY R., Private
Resided in Guilford County and was by occupation a printer prior to enlisting in Guilford County at age 18, April 27, 1861. Mustered in as Private and appointed Musician on August 23, 1861. Reduced to ranks on December 11, 1861. Promoted to Sergeant on August 5, 1863. Present or accounted for until reported absent wounded in November-December, 1863; however, place and date wounded not reported. Deserted March 10, 1864, and was reduced to ranks on April 26, 1864.

COMPANY C

This company, known as the Anson Guard, was from Anson County and enlisted at Wadesboro on April 22, 1861. On April 30 it left Wadesboro for Raleigh, where it arrived on May 2. Two days later the company moved to Garysburg. There it was assigned to this regiment as Company C. After joining the regiment the company functioned as a part of the regiment, and its history for the war period is recorded as a part of the regimental history.

The information contained in the following roster of the company was compiled principally from company muster rolls for May, 1861, through August 31, 1864. No company muster rolls were found for the period after August 31, 1864. In addition to the company muster rolls, Roll of Honor records, receipt rolls, hospital records, prisoner of war records, and other primary records, supplemented by state pension applications, United Daughters of the Confederacy records, and postwar rosters and histories, all provided useful information.

OFFICERS
CAPTAINS

HALL, ROBERT T.
Born in Anson County and was by occupation clerk of the superior court prior to enlisting at age 37. Appointed Captain on or about April 30, 1861. Resigned June 15, 1861. Reason he resigned not reported.

SMITH, CHARLES E.
Resided in Anson County and was by occupation a businessman prior to enlisting in Anson County at age 24. Elected 1st Lieutenant on or about April 22, 1861, and was appointed Captain to rank from June 15, 1861. Present or accounted for until he declined to be reelected when the regiment was reorganized on April 25, 1862.

FREEMAN, ELI
Born in Ohio and resided in Anson County where he was by occupation a metal craftsman prior to enlisting in Anson County at age 26, April 22, 1861. Mustered in as Sergeant and promoted to 1st Sergeant on October 18, 1861. Elected 2nd Lieutenant on November 25, 1861. Elected 1st Lieutenant on April 25, 1862, and was promoted to Captain the same day. Present or accounted for until wounded

and captured at Sharpsburg, Maryland, on or about September 16, 1862. Confined at Fort Delaware, Delaware, until transferred to Aiken's Landing, James River, Virginia, October 2, 1862, for exchange. Declared exchanged at Aiken's Landing on November 10, 1862. Rejoined the company prior to January 1, 1863, and present or accounted for until killed at or near Bethesda Church, Virginia, May 30, 1864.

LIEUTENANTS

BOGGAN, WALTER J., 2nd Lieutenant
Born in Anson County where he resided as a merchant or "soldier" prior to enlisting at age 20. Elected 2nd Lieutenant to rank from April 20, 1861. Present or accounted for until he resigned on December 1, 1861. Later served as Captain of Company H, 43rd Regiment N.C. Troops.

HAMMOND, WILLIAM M., 1st Lieutenant
Resided in Anson County and was by occupation a lawyer prior to enlisting in Anson County at age 23, April 22, 1861. Mustered in as Private and appointed 1st Lieutenant to rank from June 15, 1861. Present or accounted for until he declined reelection or was defeated for reelection when the regiment was reorganized April 25-26, 1862. Later served as Adjutant (1st Lieutenant) of the 45th Regiment N.C. Troops.

LANE, ALEX, 3rd Lieutenant
Place and date of enlistment not reported. Paroled at Greensboro on May 11, 1865.

LILES, WILLIAM A., 1st Lieutenant
Resided in Anson County and was by occupation a farmer prior to enlisting in Anson County at age 27. Appointed 3rd Lieutenant on or about April 22, 1861, and was elected 2nd Lieutenant to rank from April 20, 1861. Promoted to 1st Lieutenant to rank from April 26, 1862. Present or accounted for until hospitalized at Richmond, Virginia, June 1, 1864, with a gunshot wound; however, place and date wounded not reported. Furloughed for sixty days on June 6, 1864. Rejoined the company prior to September 1, 1864. Hospitalized at Danville, Virginia, on or about April 9, 1865, with a gunshot wound of the scalp; however, place and date wounded not reported. No further records.

McGREGOR, JOHN W., 3rd Lieutenant
Resided in Anson County and was by occupation a "minor" prior to enlisting in Anson County at age 19, April 22, 1861. Mustered in as Private and promoted to Corporal on September 10, 1862. Promoted to Sergeant on September 17, 1862, and was captured at Sharpsburg, Maryland, the same day. Confined at Fort Delaware, Delaware, until transferred to Aiken's Landing, James River, Virginia, October 2, 1862, for exchange. Declared exchanged at Aiken's Landing on November 10, 1862. Rejoined the company prior to January 1, 1863, and present or accounted for until wounded at Chancellorsville, Virginia, May 3, 1863. Rejoined the company in November-December, 1863, and was promoted to 1st Sergeant on January 1, 1864. Present or accounted for until wounded in the leg at Spotsylvania Court House, Virginia, May 19, 1864. Reported absent wounded through August, 1864. Promoted to 3rd

Lieutenant prior to April 9, 1865, when he was wounded at Appomattox Court House, Virginia. A "recklessly brave" officer.

MEACHUM, WILLIAM GASTON, 3rd Lieutenant
Resided in Anson County and enlisted at Camp Ellis, Virginia, at age 28, August 6, 1861. Mustered in as Private and was elected 3rd Lieutenant to rank from April 27, 1862. Present or accounted for until wounded at Malvern Hill, Virginia, July 1, 1862. Returned to duty at an unspecified date. Present or accounted for until reported wounded and captured at Sharpsburg, Maryland, September 17, 1862; however, records of the Federal Provost Marshal do not substantiate that report. Wounded and captured at Shepherdstown, Virginia, November 25, 1862. Reported in confinement at Fort McHenry, Maryland, April 10, 1863. Transferred to Fort Delaware, Delaware, on or about April 19, 1863. Paroled at Fort Delaware and transferred to City Point, Virginia, where he was received May 4, 1863, for exchange. Reported absent wounded until he rejoined the company in September-October, 1863. Present or accounted for through April 29, 1864; however, he was reported absent sick or absent on light duty during much of that period. Retired to the Invalid Corps on April 30, 1864.

THREADGILL, WILLIAM A., 2nd Lieutenant
Resided in Anson County and was by occupation a farmer prior to enlisting in Anson County at age 29, April 22, 1861. Mustered in as Private and was elected 3rd Lieutenant on April 25, 1862. Appointed 2nd Lieutenant to rank from April 27, 1862. Present or accounted for until wounded in the right hip and captured at Sharpsburg, Maryland, on or about September 17, 1862. Confined at Fort McHenry, Maryland, and at Fort Monroe, Virginia, until transferred to City Point, Virginia, where he was received December 10, 1862, for exchange. Reported absent wounded until he resigned on or about August 25, 1863, by reason of wounds received at Sharpsburg.

NONCOMMISSIONED OFFICERS AND PRIVATES

ALFORD, JOSEPH H., Private
Resided in Anson County and was by occupation a mechanic prior to enlisting in Anson County at age 26, April 22, 1861. Present or accounted for until wounded at Spotsylvania Court House, Virginia, May 8, 1864. Reported absent wounded through August, 1864.

BALDWIN, DUDLEY M., Private
Resided in Richmond County and enlisted in Wake County at age 23, July 16, 1862, for the war. Present or accounted for until captured at Sharpsburg, Maryland, September 17, 1862. Confined at Fort Delaware, Delaware, until transferred to Aiken's Landing, James River, Virginia, October 2, 1862, for exchange. Declared exchanged at Aiken's Landing on November 10, 1862. Sent to hospital on or about December 7, 1862. Company muster roll dated March-April, 1863, states that he was thought to be dead. No further records.

BALDWIN, HIRAM, Private

Resided in Montgomery County and enlisted in Wake County at age 21, July 16, 1862, for the war. Present or accounted for until captured at Sharpsburg, Maryland, September 17, 1862. Confined at Fort Delaware, Delaware, until transferred to Aiken's Landing, James River, Virginia, October 2, 1862, for exchange. Declared exchanged at Aiken's Landing on November 10, 1862. Rejoined the company prior to January 1, 1863, and present or accounted for until paroled at Appomattox Court House, Virginia, April 9, 1865.

BALLARD, JOHN, Private

Was by occupation a farmer prior to enlisting in Anson County at age 38, April 22, 1861. Present or accounted for until discharged on August 17, 1861. Reason discharged not reported. Later served in Company I, 43rd Regiment N.C. Troops.

BALLARD, MATTHEW T., Private

Resided in Anson County and enlisted at Fredericksburg, Virginia, at age 36, March 1, 1863, for the war. Present or accounted for until paroled at Farmville, Virginia, April 11-21, 1865.

BENNETT, DAVID NEVIL, Private

Resided in Anson County and enlisted at Camp Ellis, Virginia, at age 18, July 22, 1861. Mustered in as Private and promoted to Sergeant on October 18, 1861. Promoted to Ordnance Sergeant on August 25, 1862, but was reduced to ranks on May 1, 1864. Present or accounted for until wounded at Charles Town, West Virginia, on or about August 2, 1864. Reported absent wounded until retired to the Invalid Corps on February 15, 1865.

BENNETT, NEVIL J., Private

Resided in Anson County where he enlisted at age 35, March 1, 1863, for the war. Present or accounted for through August, 1864; however, he was reported absent sick or absent on detail during most of that period.

BENNETT, RISDEN TYLER, Sergeant

Resided in Anson County and was by occupation a lawyer prior to enlisting in Anson County at age 21, April 22, 1861. Mustered in as Corporal and promoted to Sergeant on June 1, 1861. Present or accounted for until appointed Assistant Commissary of Subsistence (Captain) on September 28, 1861, and transferred to the Field and Staff of this regiment.

BILLINGSLEY, EDMUND F., Private

Born in Anson County where he resided as a farmer prior to enlisting in Anson County at age 24, April 22, 1861. Present or accounted for until captured at Sharpsburg, Maryland, September 17, 1862. Confined at Fort Delaware, Delaware, until transferred to Aiken's Landing, James River, Virginia, October 2, 1862, for exchange. Declared exchanged at Aiken's Landing on November 10, 1862. Rejoined the company prior to January 1, 1863, and present or accounted for until wounded at Chancellorsville, Virginia, May 1-3, 1863. Rejoined the company prior to July 1, 1863, and present or accounted for until killed at Spotsylvania Court House, Virginia, May 12, 1864.

BILLINGSLEY, JAMES J., Private

Resided in Anson County and was by occupation a "minor" prior to enlisting in Anson County at age 20, April 22, 1861. Present or accounted for until wounded in the arm at Sharpsburg, Maryland, September 17, 1862. Rejoined the company in January-February, 1863, and present or accounted for until paroled at Appomattox Court House, Virginia, April 9, 1865.

BLUM, HENRY, Private

Born in New Orleans, Louisiana, and resided in Louisiana prior to enlisting in Wake County at age 24, July 16, 1862, for the war as a substitute. Present or accounted for until wounded in the arm and shoulder and captured at Sharpsburg, Maryland, on or about September 17, 1862. Arm amputated. Hospitalized at Frederick, Maryland, and at Baltimore, Maryland, until transferred to Fort Monroe, Virginia, October 27, 1862. Paroled and transferred to Aiken's Landing, James River, Virginia, where he was received November 2, 1862, for exchange. Died in hospital at Richmond, Virginia, November 8, 1862, of wounds received at Sharpsburg.

BOGGAN, WILLIAM H., Private

Resided in Anson County and was by occupation a "minor" prior to enlisting in Anson County at age 18, April 22, 1861. Present or accounted for until discharged on May 2, 1862, by reason of disability.

BOWMAN, CORNELIUS C., Private

Resided in Anson County and enlisted at Strasburg, Virginia, July 23, 1864, for the war. Present or accounted for until captured at Petersburg, Virginia, April 3, 1865. Confined at Hart's Island, New York Harbor, until released June 17-18, 1865, after taking the Oath of Allegiance.

BOWMAN, JOHN, Private

Resided in Anson County and was by occupation a farmer prior to enlisting in Anson County at age 24, April 22, 1861. Present or accounted for until paroled at Appomattox Court House, Virginia, April 9, 1865.

BOYD, B. S., Private

Enlisted at Orange Court House, Virginia, April 13, 1864, for the war. Present or accounted for through October, 1864; however, he was reported on detail as a nurse or guard during most of that period.

BRIGMAN, JAMES, Private

Resided in Robeson County and was by occupation a farmer prior to enlisting in Anson County at age 28, April 22, 1861. Present or accounted for until reported in confinement from November-December, 1861, through February, 1862. Rejoined the company prior to January 1, 1863, and present or accounted for until wounded at Chancellorsville, Virginia, May 3, 1863. Rejoined the company in September-October, 1863, and present or accounted for until wounded at Spotsylvania Court House, Virginia, May 12, 1864. Died May 17, 1864, of wounds. Place of death not reported.

BRITTAIN, JESSE J., Private

Resided in Montgomery County and enlisted in Wake County at age 25, July 16, 1862, for the war. Present or accounted for until he died in hospital at Richmond, Virginia, December 16, 1862, of "pneumonia."

BROWER, JOHN A., Private
Resided in Anson County and was by occupation a mechanic prior to enlisting in Anson County at age 24, April 22, 1861. Present or accounted for until killed at Gaines' Mill, Virginia, June 27, 1862.

BROWER, WILLIAM H., Private
Enlisted in December, 1864, at age 16. Paroled at Appomattox Court House, Virginia, April 9, 1865.

BRUNER, JOSEPH J., Private
Resided in Anson County and enlisted in Wake County at age 19, June 19, 1863, for the war. Present or accounted for through March 17, 1865; however, he was reported on detail as a hospital guard or as a member of President Jefferson Davis's guard during most of that period. Paroled at Albemarle on May 19, 1865.

BUCHANAN, FREDERICK A., Private
Born in Anson County where he resided as a farmer prior to enlisting in Anson County at age 22, April 22, 1861. Mustered in as Sergeant but was reduced to ranks on April 25, 1862. Present or accounted for until wounded in the right arm at Sharpsburg, Maryland, September 17, 1862. Rejoined the company in January-February, 1863, and present or accounted for until wounded at Chancellorsville, Virginia, May 3, 1863. Died May 4, 1863, of wounds.

CAMERON, EVANDER McNAIR, Private
Resided in Moore County and was by occupation a farmer prior to enlisting in Anson County at age 22, April 22, 1861. Present or accounted for until captured at or near Kelly's Ford, Virginia, November 8, 1863. Confined at Old Capitol Prison, Washington, D.C. Hospitalized at Washington on December 22, 1863, with "smallpox" and died January 16, 1864.

CARPENTER, HEZEKIAH B., Private
Resided in Anson County and was by occupation a farmer prior to enlisting in Anson County at age 23, April 22, 1861. Present or accounted for until paroled at Appomattox Court House, Virginia, April 9, 1865.

CATES, _____, Private
Resided in Montgomery County and enlisted in Wake County at age 18, July 16, 1862, for the war. Present or accounted for until reported absent sick on September 4, 1862. Company muster roll dated March-April, 1863, states that he was thought to be dead. Roll of Honor indicates that he was "lost in 1st Maryland Campaign." No further records.

CLARK, ZACHARIAH D., Private
Born in Anson County where he resided as a farmer or clerk prior to enlisting in Anson County at age 33, April 22, 1861. Present or accounted for until discharged on July 21, 1862, under the provisions of the Conscript Act. Later served in Company I, 6th Regiment N.C. Senior Reserves.

COIER, JOHN C., Private
Resided in Montgomery County and enlisted in Wake County at age 29, July 16, 1862, for the war. Present or accounted for until captured at Sharpsburg, Maryland, September 17, 1862. Confined at Fort Delaware, Delaware, until transferred to Aiken's Landing, James River, Virginia, October 2, 1862, for exchange. Declared exchanged at Aiken's Landing

on November 10, 1862. Rejoined the company in January-February, 1863, and present or accounted for until wounded at Chancellorsville, Virginia, May 1-3, 1863. Rejoined the company prior to July 1, 1863, and was wounded in the arm at Gettysburg, Pennsylvania, July 2-3, 1863. Rejoined the company in September-October, 1863, and present or accounted for through August, 1864.

COVINGTON, ELIJAH A., Private
Resided in Anson County and was by occupation a doctor prior to enlisting in Anson County at age 23, April 22, 1861. Present or accounted for until detailed as a Hospital Steward on April 8, 1862, and transferred to the Field and Staff of this regiment. Records do not indicate whether he rejoined the company; however, he was present or accounted for until captured at Winchester, Virginia, September 19, 1864. Confined at Point Lookout, Maryland, until paroled and transferred to Boulware's Wharf, James River, Virginia, where he was received March 19, 1865, for exchange.

COVINGTON, JAMES, Private
Resided in Richmond County and enlisted in Wake County at age 25, July 16, 1862, for the war. Present or accounted for until reported absent sick on September 5, 1862. Company muster roll dated March-April, 1863, states that he was thought to be dead. Roll of Honor indicates that he was "lost" during the Sharpsburg campaign of 1862.

COX, CHARLES H., Sergeant
Resided in Anson County and enlisted at Camp Ellis, Virginia, at age 18, August 6, 1861. Mustered in as Private. Present or accounted for until captured at Sharpsburg, Maryland, September 17, 1862. Confined at Fort Delaware, Delaware, until transferred to Aiken's Landing, James River, Virginia, October 2, 1862, for exchange. Declared exchanged at Aiken's Landing on November 10, 1862. Rejoined the company prior to January 1, 1863, and present or accounted for until wounded in battle near Warrenton, Virginia, October 14, 1863. Rejoined the company in November-December, 1863, and was promoted to Sergeant on January 15, 1864. Present or accounted for until wounded at or near Charles Town, West Virginia, August 2, 1864. Died August 3, 1864, of wounds.

CRUMP, THOMAS B., Private
Resided in Anson County and was by occupation a farmer prior to enlisting in Anson County at age 21, April 22, 1861. Mustered in as Private and promoted to Corporal on September 10, 1862. Present or accounted for until he "lost an arm" at Sharpsburg, Maryland, September 17, 1862. Reduced to ranks on November 30, 1862. Reported absent wounded until retired to the Invalid Corps on February 13, 1865. Took the Oath of Allegiance at Salisbury on May 30, 1865.

DARLEY, FRANK, Private
Resided in Anson County and was by occupation an editor prior to enlisting in Anson County at age 35, April 22, 1861. Present or accounted for until discharged on July 2, 1862, under the provisions of the Conscript Act. Reenlisted in this company on December 17, 1862. Present or accounted for until ap-

pointed Drillmaster (2nd Lieutenant) on October 17, 1863, to rank from September 25, 1863, and assigned to enrolling duty in North Carolina.

DAVIS, THOMAS, Private
Resided in Buncombe County. Place and date of enlistment not reported. Deserted to the enemy at Asheville on March 4, 1865. Took the Oath of Allegiance at Louisville, Kentucky, March 5, 1865.

DUMAS, JOHN C., Corporal
Resided in Anson County and was by occupation a farmer prior to enlisting in Anson County at age 21, April 22, 1861. Mustered in as Private and promoted to Corporal in September, 1864-April, 1865. Present or accounted for until paroled at Appomattox Court House, Virginia, April 9, 1865. Roll of Honor indicates he was wounded at Cold Harbor, Virginia.

DUMAS, JOSEPH PICKET, Private
Born in Richmond County and resided in Anson County where he was by occupation a student prior to enlisting in Anson County at age 15, April 22, 1861. Present or accounted for until discharged on July 21, 1862, by reason of being under age. Paroled at Salisbury on June 16, 1865. [May have served later in Company B, 31st Regiment N.C. Troops.]

DUNLAP, GEORGE B., Private
Resided in Anson County and was by occupation a "minor" prior to enlisting in Anson County at age 20, April 22, 1861. Present or accounted for until detailed as Commissary Sergeant on or about August 1, 1863, and transferred to the Field and Staff of this regiment. Records do not indicate whether he rejoined the company; however, he was present or accounted for until captured at Snicker's Gap, Virginia, July 8, 1864. Released in 1865 after the Confederate surrender.

DUNLAP, JOHN JENNINGS, Private
Resided in Anson County and was by occupation a farmer prior to enlisting in Anson County at age 21, April 22, 1861. Present or accounted for through August, 1864; however, he was reported on duty as a teamster or forage master during most of that period. Paroled at Appomattox Court House, Virginia, April 9, 1865.

EDWARDS, SIMON J., Private
Resided in Anson County and was by occupation a "minor" prior to enlisting in Anson County at age 19, April 22, 1861. Mustered in as Private and promoted to Corporal on September 10, 1862. Present or accounted for until wounded and captured at Sharpsburg, Maryland, September 17, 1862. Hospitalized at Washington, D.C., until transferred to Old Capitol Prison, Washington, September 30, 1862. Date exchanged not reported; however, he rejoined the company in May-June, 1863. Reduced to ranks on September 7, 1863. Present or accounted for through August, 1864; however, he was reported on detached duty as a postmaster during most of that period.

EWING, DANIEL J., Private
Resided in Montgomery County and enlisted in Wake County at age 22, July 16, 1862, for the war. Present or accounted for until wounded at Chancellorsville, Virginia, May 3, 1863. Rejoined the

company in January-March, 1864, but was retired to the Invalid Corps on April 12, 1864. Paroled at Lynchburg, Virginia, April 15, 1865.

FENTON, EDMUND F., Private
Born in Philadelphia, Pennsylvania, and resided in Anson County where he was by occupation a "minor" prior to enlisting in Anson County at age 19, April 22, 1861. Present or accounted for until wounded at Malvern Hill, Virginia, July 1, 1862. Returned to duty prior to March 1, 1863, and present or accounted for until he "lost" his left arm at Chancellorsville, Virginia, May 3, 1863. Reported absent wounded until retired to the Invalid Corps on April 26, 1864.

FLAKE, ELIJAH W., Private
Born in Anson County where he resided as a farmer prior to enlisting at Camp Bee, Virginia, at age 20, September 5, 1861. Present or accounted for until transferred to the C.S. Navy for duty on the C.S.S. *Merrimac* on February 15, 1862.

GADDY, EDMUND D., Private
Resided in Anson County and was by occupation a farmer prior to enlisting in Anson County at age 23, April 22, 1861. Present or accounted for until wounded in the leg and captured at Sharpsburg, Maryland, September 17, 1862. Paroled on September 27, 1862. Reported absent wounded until detailed for light duty in North Carolina, June 9-10, 1863. Reported absent on detail through August, 1864. Paroled at Charlotte on April 30, 1865.

GADDY, STEPHEN H., Private
Resided in Anson County and enlisted at Morton's Ford, Virginia, at age 16, October 1, 1863, for the war. Present or accounted for until hospitalized at Richmond, Virginia, May 17, 1864, with a gunshot wound of the left thigh; however, place and date wounded not reported. Rejoined the company prior to September 1, 1864, and was captured at Petersburg, Virginia, April 3, 1865. Confined at Hart's Island, New York Harbor, until released on June 17, 1865, after taking the Oath of Allegiance.

GIBSON, GEORGE D., Private
Born in New York City and resided in Anson County where he was by occupation a coach maker or mechanic prior to enlisting in Anson County at age 33, April 22, 1861. Present or accounted for until discharged on July 21, 1862, under the provisions of the Conscript Act.

HAILEY, HINSON BROOKS, Private
Resided in Anson County and was by occupation a farmer prior to enlisting in Anson County at age 22, April 22, 1861. Present or accounted for until he died in hospital at Richmond, Virginia, June 23, 1862, of disease.

HAMILTON, IRA J., Private
Resided in Montgomery County and enlisted in Wake County at age 21, July 16, 1862, for the war. Present or accounted for until captured at Sharpsburg, Maryland, September 17, 1862. Confined at Fort Delaware, Delaware, until transferred to Aiken's Landing, James River, Virginia, October 2, 1862, for exchange. Declared exchanged at Aiken's Landing on November 10, 1862. Rejoined the company in March-April, 1863, and present or accounted for through January 21, 1865; however, he was reported

absent sick or absent on duty as a nurse during most of that period.

HAMILTON, S. I., Private
Place and date of enlistment not reported. Captured in hospital at Richmond, Virginia, April 3, 1865, and paroled on April 20, 1865.

HAMMOND, HAMPTON B., Jr., Private
Resided in Anson County and was by occupation a clerk prior to enlisting in Anson County at age 22, April 22, 1861. Mustered in as Private and promoted to Corporal on September 7, 1863. Reduced to ranks in January-August, 1864. Present or accounted for through August, 1864; however, he was reported on duty as a Provost Guard during much of that period. Reported on duty with Captain Samuel D. Haslett's Company, Provost Guard, in September-October, 1864. Paroled at Appomattox Court House, Virginia, April 9, 1865.

HENRY, JULIUS A., Corporal
Resided in Anson County and was by occupation an artist prior to enlisting in Anson County at age 24, April 22, 1861. Mustered in as Private. Present or accounted for until wounded at Chancellorsville, Virginia, May 1-3, 1863. Rejoined the company prior to July 1, 1863, and was promoted to Corporal on December 19, 1863. Present or accounted for until wounded at Spotsylvania Court House, Virginia, May 12, 1864. Reported absent wounded or absent on hospital duty through January 21, 1865. Captured in hospital at Richmond, Virginia, April 3, 1865, and was paroled at Richmond on April 17, 1865.

HILL, JOSHUA C., Corporal
Born in Montgomery County and resided in Anson County where he was by occupation a farmer prior to enlisting in Anson County at age 23, April 22, 1861. Mustered in as Private and promoted to Corporal on April 25, 1862. Present or accounted for until he died at Richmond, Virginia, June 3, 1862, of disease.

HOOKER, JAMES D., Private
Born in Anson County where he resided as a farmer prior to enlisting at Camp Bee, Virginia, at age 28, October 10, 1861. Present or accounted for until wounded in the right thigh and captured at Sharpsburg, Maryland, on or about September 17, 1862. Hospitalized at Frederick, Maryland, until transferred to Fort McHenry, Maryland, prior to October 14, 1862. Paroled and transferred to Aiken's Landing, James River, Virginia, October 17, 1862, for exchange. Declared exchanged at Aiken's Landing on November 10, 1862. Reported absent wounded until discharged on November 15, 1863, by reason of disability.

HORTON, REUBEN BLOOMFIELD, Private
Resided in Anson County and was by occupation a "minor" prior to enlisting in Anson County at age 20, April 22, 1861. Present or accounted for until captured at or near Martinsburg, West Virginia, on or about July 23, 1863. Confined at Fort McHenry, Maryland, until transferred to Point Lookout, Maryland, November 1, 1863. Paroled at Point Lookout on March 9, 1864, and transferred to City Point, Virginia, where he was received March 15,

1864, for exchange. Reported absent sick through August, 1864.

HUTCHINSON, BENJAMIN C., Private
Born in Anson County where he resided as a trader or farmer prior to enlisting in Anson County at age 32, April 22, 1861. Mustered in as Private and promoted to Sergeant on October 18, 1861. Present or accounted for until discharged on July 21, 1862, under the provisions of the Conscript Act. Reenlisted in this company with the rank of Private on January 15, 1863. Present or accounted for until captured at Farmville, Virginia, April 6, 1865. Confined at Point Lookout, Maryland, until released on June 27, 1865, after taking the Oath of Allegiance.

HUTCHINSON, WILLIAM G., Musician
Born in Darlington District, South Carolina, and resided in Anson County where he was by occupation a shoemaker or mechanic prior to enlisting in Anson County at age 34, April 22, 1861. Mustered in as Musician (Fifer). Present or accounted for until discharged on July 21, 1862, under the provisions of the Conscript Act.

JOHNSON, CAREY, Private
Resided in Robeson or Montgomery counties and enlisted in Wake County at age 36, June 19, 1863, for the war. Present or accounted for until wounded in the left knee at or near the North Anna River, Virginia, May 25, 1864. Reported absent wounded until he returned to duty on December 8, 1864.

JONES, ISAAC A., Sergeant
Resided in Anson County and was by occupation a "minor" prior to enlisting in Anson County at age 18, April 22, 1861. Mustered in as Sergeant. Present or accounted for until transferred to Company H, 5th Regiment N.C. State Troops on June 8, 1861, upon appointment as 2nd Lieutenant to rank from May 16, 1861.

KENDALL, BENJAMIN D., Private
Resided in Anson County and enlisted at Richmond, Virginia, at age 25, August 1, 1862, for the war. Present or accounted for through August, 1864; however, he was reported absent on detail as a teamster during most of that period. Hospitalized at Danville, Virginia, on or about April 5, 1865, with a gunshot wound of the right elbow; however, place and date wounded not reported. Furloughed for sixty days on April 8, 1865.

KENDALL, HENRY E., Private
Born in Anson County where he resided prior to enlisting at Camp Bee, Virginia, at age 20, August 31, 1861. Present or accounted for until killed at Sharpsburg, Maryland, September 17, 1862.

KIRBY, WILLIAM H., Private
Resided in Anson County and was by occupation a farmer prior to enlisting in Anson County at age 28, April 22, 1861. Present or accounted for until captured at Hanover Junction, Virginia, May 22, 1864. Confined at Point Lookout, Maryland, until transferred to Elmira, New York, July 8, 1864. Died at Elmira on August 7, 1864, of "chronic diarrhoea."

KNOTTS, WILSON, Private
Born in Anson County where he resided as a farmer prior to enlisting in Anson County at age 24, April

22, 1861. Present or accounted for until he died in hospital at Richmond, Virginia, June 28, 1862, of "chronic diarrhoea."

LAMONDS, NEILL, Private
Resided in Montgomery County and enlisted in Wake County at age 28, July 16, 1862, for the war. Present or accounted for until captured at Sharpsburg, Maryland, September 17, 1862. Confined at Fort Delaware, Delaware, until transferred to Aiken's Landing, James River, Virginia, October 2, 1862, for exchange. Declared exchanged at Aiken's Landing on November 10, 1862. Rejoined the company prior to January 1, 1863, and present or accounted for until wounded at Chancellorsville, Virginia, May 1-3, 1863. Rejoined the company prior to July 1, 1863, and present or accounted for until paroled at Appomattox Court House, Virginia, April 9, 1865.

LEAK, WILLIAM P., Private
Enlisted in Anson County on July 1, 1864, for the war. Present or accounted for until paroled at Appomattox Court House, Virginia, April 9, 1865.

LEON, J. R., _____
Enlisted on or about August 30, 1861. No further records.

LILES, CHARLES M., Private
Place and date of enlistment not reported. Paroled at Appomattox Court House, Virginia, April 9, 1865.

LILLY, ATLAS DARGAN, Private
Resided in Rowan or Stanly counties and enlisted at Orange Court House, Virginia, March 13, 1864, for the war. Present or accounted for until captured at Wilderness, Virginia, May 5, 1864, or at Spotsylvania Court House, Virginia, May 8, 1864. Confined at Point Lookout, Maryland, until transferred to Elmira, New York, where he arrived July 26, 1864. Released at Elmira on May 29, 1865, after taking the Oath of Allegiance.

LILLY, PETER B., Private
Resided in Anson County and was by occupation a farmer prior to enlisting in Anson County at age 21, April 22, 1861. Present or accounted for until discharged on or about October 4, 1861, by reason of disability.

LILLY, ROBERT J., Sergeant
Resided in Anson County and was by occupation a medical student prior to enlisting in Anson County at age 21, April 22, 1861. Mustered in as Private and promoted to Sergeant on September 1, 1861. Present or accounted for until appointed Assistant Commissary of Subsistence (Captain) on or about April 27, 1862, and transferred to the Field and Staff of this regiment.

LITTLE, GEORGE BADGER, Sergeant
Born in Anson County where he resided as a "minor" prior to enlisting in Anson County at age 19, April 22, 1861. Mustered in as Private and promoted to Corporal on April 25, 1862. Promoted to Sergeant on July 21, 1862. Present or accounted for until killed at Sharpsburg, Maryland, September 17, 1862, "while bravely bearing the flag of the regiment."

LITTLE, GEORGE T., Corporal
Resided in Anson County and was by occupation a

"minor" prior to enlisting in Anson County at age 17, April 22, 1861. Mustered in as Private and promoted to Corporal on April 25, 1862. Present or accounted for until discharged on August 25, 1862, by reason of disability.

LITTLE, WILLIAM CALVIN, Private
Resided in Anson County and enlisted at Richmond, Virginia, at age 23, August 1, 1862, for the war. Present or accounted for until captured at Sharpsburg, Maryland, September 17, 1862. Confined at Fort Delaware, Delaware, until transferred to Aiken's Landing, James River, Virginia, October 2, 1862, for exchange. Declared exchanged at Aiken's Landing on November 10, 1862. Rejoined the company prior to January 1, 1863, and present or accounted for until killed near Bethesda Church, Virginia, on or about June 2, 1864.

McAULEY, GEORGE WASHINGTON, Private
Resided in Montgomery County and enlisted in Wake County at age 18, July 16, 1862, for the war. Present or accounted for until wounded in the right arm at Sharpsburg, Maryland, September 17, 1862. Rejoined the company in March-April, 1863, and present or accounted for until wounded at Fisher's Hill, Virginia, September 19, 1864. Final disposition not reported; however, he survived the war.

McCALLUM, A. S., Private
Born in Montgomery County where he resided prior to enlisting in Wake County at age 20, July 16, 1862, for the war. Present or accounted for until captured at Sharpsburg, Maryland, September 17, 1862. Confined at Fort Delaware, Delaware, where he died on or about October 4, 1862, of "measles."

McCASKILL, JAMES A., Private
Resided in Montgomery County and enlisted in Wake County at age 18, July 16, 1862, for the war. Present or accounted for until wounded at Chancellorsville, Virginia, May 3, 1863. Reported absent wounded until he deserted from hospital on July 1, 1863. Reported as a deserter through August, 1864. Paroled at Appomattox Court House, Virginia, April 9, 1865.

McGREGOR, MALCOLM, Private
Enlisted at Kelly's Ford, Virginia, November 1, 1863, for the war. Present or accounted for through August, 1864.

McKASKALL, EDWARD A., Private
Place and date of enlistment not reported. Paroled at Appomattox Court House, Virginia, April 9, 1865.

McKAY, DANIEL C., Lance Corporal
Born in Montgomery County and resided in Anson County where he was by occupation a farmer prior to enlisting in Anson County at age 24, April 22, 1861. Mustered in as Private and promoted to Lance Corporal on April 25, 1862. Present or accounted for until killed at Malvern Hill, Virginia, July 1, 1862.

McKAY, MARTIN, Private
Born in Montgomery County and resided in Anson County where he was by occupation a farmer prior to enlisting at age 23, April 22, 1861. Present or accounted for until captured at Sharpsburg, Maryland, on or about September 17, 1862. Paroled September 20, 1862. Rejoined the company prior to

January 1, 1863, and present or accounted for until wounded in the right thigh at Chancellorsville, Virginia, May 3, 1863. Reported absent wounded until he died in hospital at Richmond, Virginia, August 30, 1863, of wounds.

McLENDON, JOEL FRANKLIN, Private
Born in Anson County where he resided as a farmer prior to enlisting in Anson County at age 24, April 22, 1861. Present or accounted for until killed at Malvern Hill, Virginia, July 1, 1862.

McLENDON, JOHN J., Private
Resided in Anson County and was by occupation a "minor" prior to enlisting in Anson County at age 19, April 22, 1861. Present or accounted for until paroled at Appomattox Court House, Virginia, April 9, 1865. According to one report, "the last musket fired by Lee's army [at Appomattox] was discharged by this brave [man]." [W.A. Smith, *The Anson Guards.*]

McNAIR, DUNCAN E., 1st Sergeant
Born in Robeson County where he resided as a civil engineer prior to enlisting in Anson County at age 27, April 22, 1861. Mustered in as 1st Sergeant. Present or accounted for until transferred to Company H, 3rd Regiment N.C. State Troops, on or about October 18, 1861, upon appointment as 1st Lieutenant.

McPHERSON, WILLIAM D., Private
Resided in Cumberland County where he enlisted at age 22, July 5, 1862, for the war. Present or accounted for until captured at Sharpsburg, Maryland, on or about September 17, 1862. Paroled at Keedysville, Maryland, September 20, 1862. Rejoined the company prior to January 1, 1863, and present or accounted for until wounded at Spotsylvania Court House, Virginia, May 12, 1864. Died May 18, 1864, of wounds. Place of death not reported.

MASK, JOHN D., Private
Resided in Montgomery County and enlisted in Wake County at age 29, July 16, 1862, for the war. Present or accounted for until captured at Sharpsburg, Maryland, September 17, 1862. Confined at Fort Delaware, Delaware, until transferred to Aiken's Landing, James River, Virginia, October 2, 1862, for exchange. Declared exchanged at Aiken's Landing on November 10, 1862. Rejoined the company in January-February, 1863, and present or accounted for until wounded at Gettysburg, Pennsylvania, July 1-3, 1863. Rejoined the company prior to September 1, 1863, and present or accounted for until captured at Cedar Creek, Virginia, October 19, 1864. Confined at Point Lookout, Maryland, until released on June 15, 1865, after taking the Oath of Allegiance.

MEDLEY, BENJAMIN FRANK, Private
Resided in Anson County and was by occupation a farmer prior to enlisting in Anson County at age 27, April 22, 1861. Present or accounted for until paroled at Appomattox Court House, Virginia, April 9, 1865.

MITCHELL, RAYFORD, Private
Resided in Anson or Robeson counties and was by occupation a farmer prior to enlisting in Anson County at age 22, April 22, 1861. Present or accounted for

until he deserted to the enemy or was captured at or near Kelly's Ford, Virginia, November 7-8, 1863. Confined at Old Capitol Prison, Washington, D.C., until transferred to Point Lookout, Maryland, February 3, 1864. Released at Point Lookout on February 27, 1864, after taking the Oath of Allegiance and joining the U.S. Army. Assigned to Company F, 1st Regiment U.S. Volunteer Infantry.

MORRISON, ALEXANDER S., Private
Resided in Anson County and was by occupation a farmer prior to enlisting in Anson County at age 25, April 22, 1861. Mustered in as Private and promoted to 1st Sergeant on November 25, 1861. Present or accounted for until captured at Sharpsburg, Maryland, September 17, 1862. Confined at Fort Delaware, Delaware, until transferred to Aiken's Landing, James River, Virginia, October 2, 1862, for exchange. Declared exchanged at Aiken's Landing on November 10, 1862. Rejoined the company in January-February, 1863, and present or accounted for until wounded at Chancellorsville, Virginia, May 1-3, 1863. Rejoined the company prior to July 1, 1863, and was reduced to ranks on November 19, 1863. Present or accounted for until paroled at Appomattox Court House, Virginia, April 9, 1865.

MORRISON, THOMAS W., Private
Enlisted in the autumn of 1864 at age 16. Present or accounted for until paroled at Appomattox Court House, Virginia, April 9, 1865.

MORTON, ALEXANDER B., Corporal
Resided in Anson County and was by occupation a mechanic prior to enlisting in Anson County at age 26, April 22, 1861. Mustered in as Private and promoted to Corporal on September 10, 1862. Present or accounted for until hospitalized at Richmond, Virginia, May 18, 1864, with a gunshot wound of the left hip; however, place and date wounded not reported. Rejoined the company prior to August 21, 1864, when he was wounded in the chest on the Weldon Railroad, near Petersburg, Virginia. Reported absent wounded until furloughed on September 29, 1864. Paroled at Appomattox Court House, Virginia, April 9, 1865.

MORTON, GEORGE A., Private
Resided in Anson County and was by occupation a farmer prior to enlisting in Anson County at age 24, April 22, 1861. Present or accounted for until wounded in the left shoulder and captured at Sharpsburg, Maryland, on or about September 17, 1862. Paroled September 25, 1862. Rejoined the company prior to January 1, 1863, and present or accounted for until paroled at Appomattox Court House, Virginia, April 9, 1865.

MORTON, GEORGE D., Private
Born in Montgomery County and resided in Anson County where he was by occupation a mechanic or shoemaker prior to enlisting in Anson County at age 33, April 22, 1861. Present or accounted for until wounded at Malvern Hill, Virginia, July 1, 1862. Discharged on July 21, 1862, under the provisions of the Conscript Act.

MORTON, PETER F., Sergeant
Resided in Anson County and enlisted at Camp Bee, Virginia, at age 19, October 10, 1861. Mustered in

as Private. Present or accounted for until he was detailed as an attendant for the wounded at Sharpsburg, Maryland, September 17, 1862. Captured at Shepherdstown, Virginia, November 25, 1862. Hospitalized at Baltimore, Maryland, April 4, 1863, with a gunshot wound; however, place and date wounded not reported. Paroled at Fort McHenry, Maryland, April 19, 1863, and transferred to City Point, Virginia, for exchange. Rejoined the company prior to May 1, 1863, and was wounded at Chancellorsville, Virginia, May 1-3, 1863. Rejoined the company prior to July 1, 1863, and present or accounted for until paroled at Appomattox Court House, Virginia, April 9, 1865.

MORTON, WILLIAM H., Private
Resided in Anson County and was by occupation a mechanic prior to enlisting in Anson County at age 24, April 22, 1861. Present or accounted for until he "lost an arm" at Malvern Hill, Virginia, July 1, 1862. Reported absent wounded until discharged in February, 1863, by reason of disability.

MURCHISON, A. B., Private
Enlisted in Wake County on July 16, 1862, for the war. Present or accounted for until he died in Virginia on October 15, 1862, of disease.

NAPIER, HENRY J., Corporal
Resided in Anson County and was by occupation a mechanic prior to enlisting in Anson County at age 25, April 22, 1861. Mustered in as Private. Present or accounted for until captured at Sharpsburg, Maryland, September 17, 1862. Paroled at Keedysville, Maryland, September 20, 1862. Promoted to Corporal on December 1, 1862, and rejoined the company prior to January 1, 1863. Present or accounted for until wounded in both hands at Chancellorsville, Virginia, May 3, 1863. Rejoined the company in September-October, 1863, but was discharged December 19, 1863. Reason discharged not reported.

PINKSTON, ROBERT R., Private
Resided in Anson County and was by occupation a mechanic prior to enlisting in Anson County at age 22, April 22, 1861. Present or accounted for until detailed as an attendant to the wounded at Sharpsburg, Maryland, September 17, 1862. Captured at Shepherdstown, Virginia, November 25, 1862. Reported in confinement at Fort McHenry, Maryland, January 25, 1863. Exchanged and rejoined the company prior to March 1, 1863. Present or accounted for through March 31, 1865; however, he served as a guard at the Confederate White House at Richmond, Virginia, during most of that period.

RAGSDALE, DANIEL, Private
Resided in Montgomery County and enlisted in Wake County at age 20, July 16, 1862, for the war. Present or accounted for until captured at or near Sharpsburg, Maryland, on or about September 17, 1862. Paroled September 27, 1862. Rejoined the company in March-April, 1863, and present or accounted for until he died in hospital at Richmond, Virginia, June 20, 1863, of "febris typhoides."

REDFEARN, JOHN W., Private
Resided in Anson County and was by occupation a

farmer prior to enlisting in Anson County at age 23, April 22, 1861. Present or accounted for until he died in hospital at Richmond, Virginia, June 28, 1862, of disease.

ROBINSON, HENRY W., Private
Born in Marlboro District, South Carolina, and resided in Anson County where he was by occupation a dentist prior to enlisting at Camp Ellis, Virginia, at age 24, July 22, 1861. Present or accounted for until discharged on October 20, 1863, by reason of disability.

ROGERS, GEORGE L., Private
Born in Wythe County, Virginia, and resided in Anson County where he was by occupation a mechanic prior to enlisting in Anson County at age 23, April 22, 1861. Present or accounted for until he died in hospital at Richmond, Virginia, July 13, 1862, of "feb[ris] typhoid."

ROGERS, THOMAS C., Private
Resided in Anson County and was by occupation a physician prior to enlisting in Anson County at age 23, April 22, 1861. Mustered in as Private and promoted to Sergeant on April 25, 1862. Present or accounted for until captured and paroled at Warrenton, Virginia, September 29, 1862. Reduced to ranks October 5, 1862. Present or accounted for until appointed Hospital Steward and transferred to the Field and Staff, 44th Regiment N.C. Troops, November 2, 1863.

RYE, WILLIAM W., Private
Born in Richmond County and resided in Anson County where he was by occupation a "minor" prior to enlisting in Anson County at age 20, April 22, 1861. Present or accounted for until discharged on November 12, 1861, by reason of "chronic diarrhoea and intermittent fever."

SANDERS, JOHN HENRY DURANT, Private
Resided in Anson County and enlisted in Wake County at age 18, July 24, 1863, for the war. Present or accounted for until hospitalized at Charlottesville, Virginia, October 23, 1864, with a gunshot wound of the right thigh; however, place and date wounded not reported. Rejoined the company prior to April 2, 1865, when he was captured at or near Petersburg, Virginia. Confined at Point Lookout, Maryland, until released on June 8, 1865, after taking the Oath of Allegiance.

SAUNDERS, HENRY B., Private
Resided in Anson County and was by occupation a farmer prior to enlisting in Anson County at age 22, April 22, 1861. Present or accounted for until wounded in the left hand and captured at or near Sharpsburg, Maryland, on or about September 17, 1862. Paroled September 25, 1862. Rejoined the company prior to January 1, 1863. Nominated for the Badge of Distinction for gallantry at Chancellorsville, Virginia, May 1-3, 1863. Present or accounted for until captured at Cedar Creek, Virginia, October 19, 1864. Confined at Point Lookout, Maryland, until paroled and transferred to Cox's Landing, James River, Virginia, where he was received February 14-15, 1865, for exchange.

SAUNDERS, WILLIAM H., Private
Resided in Anson County and was by occupation a

farmer prior to enlisting in Anson County at age 21, April 22, 1861. Present or accounted for until wounded at Chancellorsville, Virginia, May 1-3, 1863. Rejoined the company prior to July 1, 1863, and present or accounted for until wounded in the left leg at Spotsylvania Court House, Virginia, May 14, 1864. Reported absent wounded through August, 1864. Paroled at Appomattox Court House, Virginia, April 9, 1865. Roll of Honor indicates he was wounded at Cold Harbor, Virginia.

SIBLEY, HENRY CLAY, Private
Born in Anson County where he resided as a student prior to enlisting in Anson County at age 20, April 22, 1861. Present or accounted for until discharged on December 2, 1861, by reason of "inguinal hernia."

SIBLEY, JEREMIAH B., Private
Born in Anson County where he resided as a farmer prior to enlisting in Anson County at age 25, April 22, 1861. Present or accounted for until wounded in the arm and shoulder at Malvern Hill, Virginia, July 1, 1862. Reported absent wounded until he died in hospital at Richmond, Virginia, December 7, 1862, of wounds.

SIMONS, THOMAS D., Private
Born in Montgomery County and resided in Anson County where he was by occupation a "minor" prior to enlisting in Anson County at age 20, April 22, 1861. Present or accounted for until wounded at Malvern Hill, Virginia, July 1, 1862. Died on July 14, 1862, of wounds. Place of death not reported.

SMART, JAMES A., Sergeant
Resided in Anson County and was by occupation a mechanic prior to enlisting in Anson County at age 24, April 22, 1861. Mustered in as Corporal and promoted to Sergeant on September 10, 1862. Present or accounted for until wounded in the chest at Spotsylvania Court House, Virginia, May 12-14, 1864. Reported absent wounded through August, 1864. Paroled at Appomattox Court House, Virginia, April 9, 1865.

SMITH, EDMUND J., Private
Resided in Anson County and was by occupation a "minor" prior to enlisting in Anson County at age 20, April 22, 1861. Mustered in as Private and promoted to Lance Corporal on December 1, 1862. Present or accounted for until wounded at Chancellorsville, Virginia, May 1-3, 1863. Rejoined the company prior to July 1, 1863, and present or accounted for until wounded at Spotsylvania Court House, Virginia, May 12, 1864. Reported absent wounded through August, 1864, and was reduced to ranks prior to September 1, 1864. Retired to the Invalid Corps on October 14, 1864.

SMITH, JAMES L., Private
Resided in Anson County and enlisted at Camp Ellis, Virginia, at age 20, August 6, 1861. Present or accounted for until captured at Sharpsburg, Maryland, September 17, 1862. Confined at Fort Delaware, Delaware, until transferred to Aiken's Landing, James River, Virginia, October 2, 1862, for exchange. Declared exchanged at Aiken's Landing on November 10, 1862. Rejoined the company in January-February, 1863, and present or accounted for

for until wounded at Chancellorsville, Virginia, May 1-3, 1863. Rejoined the company prior to July 1, 1863, and present or accounted for until paroled at Appomattox Court House, Virginia, April 9, 1865.

SMITH, JAMES M., Private
Born in Anson County where he resided prior to enlisting at Camp Ellis, Virginia, at age 21, August 6, 1861. Present or accounted for until wounded at Williamsburg, Virginia, May 5, 1862. Died "at home" on May 27, 1862, of "fever."

SMITH, JAMES TILLMAN, Private
Resided in Anson County and enlisted at Camp Ellis, Virginia, at age 19, July 22, 1861. Present or accounted for until wounded at Sharpsburg, Maryland, September 17, 1862. Rejoined the company in January-February, 1863, and present or accounted for until wounded at Chancellorsville, Virginia, May 3, 1863. Reported absent wounded until discharged on October 20, 1863.

SMITH, STERLING L., Private
Born in Stanly County* and resided in Anson County where he was by occupation a farmer prior to enlisting in Anson County at age 21, April 22, 1861. Present or accounted for until wounded at Chancellorsville, Virginia, May 3, 1863. Died May 5, 1863, of wounds.

SMITH, THOMAS, Private
Resided in Anson County and enlisted at Camp Ellis, Virginia, at age 21, August 6, 1861. Present or accounted for until appointed Quartermaster Sergeant on or about August 1, 1863, and transferred to the Field and Staff of this regiment.

SMITH, WILLIAM ALEXANDER, Private
Born in Anson County where he resided as a student prior to enlisting at Camp Ellis, Virginia, at age 18, July 22, 1861. Present or accounted for until wounded in the left leg at Malvern Hill, Virginia, July 1, 1862. Reported absent wounded until discharged on November 11, 1862, by reason of wounds received at Malvern Hill.

STALLINGS, CASWELL, Private
Resided in Anson or Robeson counties and was by occupation a farmer prior to enlisting in Anson County at age 24, April 22, 1861. Present or accounted for until paroled at Appomattox Court House, Virginia, April 9, 1865.

STANBACK, GEORGE L., Sergeant
Born in Richmond County where he resided as a "minor" prior to enlisting in Anson County at age 20, April 22, 1861. Mustered in as Private and promoted to Sergeant on October 5, 1862. Present or accounted for until wounded at Chancellorsville, Virginia, May 1-3, 1863. Rejoined the company prior to July 1, 1863, and present or accounted for until killed at Bethesda Church, Virginia, in May, 1864.

STANBACK, WILLIAM L., Private
Resided in Richmond County and enlisted in Anson County at age 18, September 17, 1863, for the war. Present or accounted for until hospitalized at Richmond, Virginia, May 18, 1864, with a gunshot wound of the left thigh; however, place and date wounded not reported. Rejoined the company prior

to September 1, 1864, and was killed at Winchester, Virginia, September 19, 1864.

SUMNER, R. A., Private
Resided in Buncombe County. Place and date of enlistment not reported. Deserted to the enemy at Asheville on December 5, 1864. Took the Oath of Allegiance at Knoxville, Tennessee, March 21, 1865.

TAYLOR, BURKET, Private
Resided in Edgecombe County and enlisted in Wake County at age 25, July 16, 1862, for the war. Present or accounted for until captured at Sharpsburg, Maryland, September 17, 1862. Confined at Fort Delaware, Delaware, until transferred to Aiken's Landing, James River, Virginia, October 2, 1862, for exchange. Declared exchanged at Aiken's Landing on November 10, 1862. Rejoined the company prior to January 1, 1863, and present or accounted for until killed at Spotsylvania Court House, Virginia, May 12, 1864.

TEAL, ALEXANDER C., Private
Resided in Anson County and enlisted in Wake County at age 18, July 20, 1863, for the war. Present or accounted for until hospitalized at Richmond, Virginia, August 21, 1864, with a wound; however, place and date wounded not reported. Paroled at Appomattox Court House, Virginia, April 9, 1865.

THREADGILL, BENJAMIN K., Private
Resided in Anson County and was by occupation a farmer prior to enlisting in Anson County at age 21, April 22, 1861. Present or accounted for until captured at Sharpsburg, Maryland, September 17, 1862. Paroled at Keedysville, Maryland, September 20, 1862. Rejoined the company and was wounded in the right shoulder at Fredericksburg, Virginia, on or about December 13, 1862. Rejoined the company prior to January 1, 1863, and present or accounted for until wounded at Chancellorsville, Virginia, May 1-3, 1863. Rejoined the company prior to July 1, 1863, and present or accounted for until captured at Petersburg, Virginia, April 3, 1865. Confined at Hart's Island, New York Harbor, until released on June 17, 1865, after taking the Oath of Allegiance.

THREADGILL, JOHN, _____
Resided in Anson County and enlisted at age 16, September 19, 1864, for the war. Present or accounted for until captured at Petersburg, Virginia, April 3, 1865. Confined at Hart's Island New York Harbor, until released on June 17, 1865, after taking the Oath of Allegiance.

THREADGILL, MILES, Private
Previously served in Company H, 43rd Regiment N.C. Troops. Transferred to this company on October 1, 1863. Present or accounted for until wounded at Spotsylvania Court House, Virginia, May 12, 1864. Reported absent wounded until he returned to duty on October 31, 1864.

THREADGILL, WILLIAM C., Corporal
Resided in Anson County and was by occupation a "minor" prior to enlisting in Anson County at age 17, April 22, 1861. Mustered in as Private. Present or accounted for until wounded at Malvern Hill, Virginia, July 1, 1862. Hospitalized at Farmville, Virginia, June 11, 1863, with a gunshot wound of the left leg; however, place and date wounded not reported. Rejoined the company in November-December, 1863, and present or accounted for until hospitalized at Richmond, Virginia, May 18, 1864, with a gunshot wound of the left side. Place and date wounded not reported. Rejoined the company prior to September 1, 1864. Captured at Petersburg, Virginia, April 3, 1865. Confined at Point Lookout, Maryland, until released on June 20, 1865, after taking the Oath of Allegiance. Rank given on Oath as Corporal.

TILLMAN, DAVID C., Private
Resided in Anson County and was by occupation a farmer prior to enlisting in Anson County at age 24, April 22, 1861. Present or accounted for until captured at Sharpsburg, Maryland, September 17, 1862. Confined at Fort Delaware, Delaware, until transferred to Aiken's Landing, James River, Virginia, October 2, 1862, for exchange. Declared exchanged at Aiken's Landing on November 10, 1862. Rejoined the company prior to January 1, 1863, and present or accounted for until wounded in the shoulder at Gettysburg, Pennsylvania, July 3, 1863. Captured at Gettysburg or at Waterloo, Pennsylvania, July 3-5, 1863. Confined at Fort McHenry, Maryland, and at Fort Delaware until transferred to Point Lookout, Maryland, October 15-18, 1863. Paroled at Point Lookout and transferred to City Point, Virginia, where he was received April 30, 1864, for exchange. Rejoined the company prior to September 1, 1864. No further records.

TILLMAN, JAMES D., Private
Resided in Anson County and was by occupation a "minor" prior to enlisting in Anson County at age 18, April 22, 1861. Present or accounted for until captured at Amelia Court House, Virginia, April 6, 1865. Confined at Point Lookout, Maryland, until released on June 30, 1865, after taking the Oath of Allegiance.

TURNER, JOHN W., Sergeant
Resided in Anson County and was by occupation a mechanic prior to enlisting in Anson County at age 25, April 22, 1861. Mustered in as Corporal but was reduced to ranks on October 1, 1861. Promoted to Sergeant on August 1, 1864. Present or accounted for until paroled at Appomattox Court House, Virginia, April 9, 1865.

TYSON, MARTIN V., Private
Born in Anson County where he resided as a farmer prior to enlisting in Anson County at age 21, April 22, 1861. Present or accounted for until captured at Sharpsburg, Maryland, September 17, 1862. Paroled on September 21, 1862, and rejoined the company prior to January 1, 1863. Present or accounted for until killed at Spotsylvania Court House, Virginia, May 12, 1864.

WADDELL, ADOLPHUS A., Private
Resided in Anson County and was by occupation a clerk prior to enlisting in Anson County at age 22, April 22, 1861. Mustered in as Private and promoted to Corporal on June 1, 1861. Reduced to ranks on April 25, 1862. Present or accounted for through August, 1864.

WADDILL, JOHN B., Corporal
Resided in Anson County and was by occupation a "minor" prior to enlisting in Anson County at age 20, April 22, 1861. Mustered in as Private. Present or accounted for until wounded and captured at Sharpsburg, Maryland, September 17, 1862. Paroled at Keedysville, Maryland, September 20, 1862. Rejoined the company in January-February, 1863, and was promoted to Corporal on September 7, 1863. Present or accounted for until hospitalized at Charlottesville, Virginia, July 25, 1864, with a gunshot wound of the leg; however, place and date wounded not reported. Rejoined the company prior to September 1, 1864. Paroled at Appomattox Court House, Virginia, April 9, 1865.

WATKINS, CULPEPPER R., Private
Born in Stanly County and resided in Anson County where he was by occupation a student prior to enlisting in Anson County at age 18, April 22, 1861. Present or accounted for until discharged on December 3, 1862, by reason of disability.

WATKINS, JAMES M., Private
Enlisted at Fredericksburg, Virginia, at age 17, March 15, 1863, for the war. Present or accounted for until captured at Mechanicsville, Virginia, May 30, 1864. Confined at Point Lookout, Maryland, until transferred to Elmira, New York, July 8, 1864. Died at Elmira on August 26, 1864, of "rubeola."

WATKINS, ROBERT D., Private
Born in Anson County where he resided as a student prior to enlisting in Anson County at age 14, April 22, 1861. Present or accounted for until discharged July 21, 1862, under the provisions of the Conscript Act. Later served in Captain Abner A. Moseley's Company (Sampson Artillery).

WATKINS, THOMAS J., Private
Resided in Anson County and was by occupation a "minor" prior to enlisting in Anson County at age 20, April 22, 1861. Present or accounted for until wounded in the finger at Chancellorsville, Virginia, May 1-4, 1863. Returned to duty prior to July 1-3, 1863, when he was wounded in the ankle at Gettysburg, Pennsylvania. Returned to duty prior to September 1, 1863, and present or accounted for until wounded in the mouth at Spotsylvania Court House, Virginia, May 12, 1864. Returned to duty prior to September 19, 1864, when he was wounded in the shoulder and captured at Winchester, Virginia. Hospitalized at Winchester and at Baltimore, Maryland, until confined at Point Lookout, Maryland, October 28-29, 1864. Paroled at Point Lookout on October 30, 1864, and transferred to Venus Point, Savannah River, Georgia, where he was received November 15, 1864, for exchange.

WATKINS, WILLIAM H., Private
Resided in Anson or Stanly counties and was by occupation a farmer prior to enlisting in Anson County at age 21, April 22, 1861. Mustered in as Private and promoted to Corporal on October 1, 1861. Promoted to Sergeant on April 25, 1862, but was reduced to ranks on May 1, 1864. Present or accounted for through August, 1864. Paroled at Appomattox Court House, Virginia, April 9, 1865.

WHEELER, JOSEPH H., Private
Born in Vermont and "seemed to detest the Yankees more than a native-born Southerner." Resided in Anson County and was by occupation a mechanic prior to enlisting in Anson County at age 27, April 22, 1861. Mustered in as Corporal but was reduced to ranks on April 25, 1862. Present or accounted for until wounded in the left leg and captured at Winchester, Virginia, September 19, 1864. Hospitalized at Winchester and at Baltimore, Maryland, until transferred to Fort McHenry, Maryland, February 16, 1865, for exchange. Exchanged prior to March 4, 1865, when he was hospitalized at Richmond, Virginia. Furloughed for sixty days from hospital at Richmond on March 8, 1865.

WILLIAMS, SETH A., Private
Resided in Montgomery County and enlisted in Wake County at age 25, July 16, 1862, for the war. Present or accounted for until paroled at Appomattox Court House, Virginia, April 9, 1865.

COMPANY D

This company, known as the Cleveland Blues, was from Cleveland County and enlisted at White Plains on April 26, 1861. On May 9 it left White Plains for Raleigh, where it arrived on May 17. The company left Raleigh for Garysburg on May 21 and arrived there the same day. It was then assigned to this regiment as Company D. After joining the regiment the company functioned as a part of the regiment, and its history for the war period is recorded as a part of the regimental history.

The information contained in the following roster of the company was compiled principally from company muster rolls for April 26, 1861, through August 31, 1864. No company muster rolls were found for the period after August 31, 1864. In addition to the company muster rolls, Roll of Honor records, receipt rolls, hospital records, prisoner of war records, and other primary records, supplemented by state pension applications, United Daughters of the Confederacy records, and postwar rosters and histories, all provided useful information.

OFFICERS
CAPTAINS

DIXON, EDWARD
Born in Cleveland County* where he resided as a farmer prior to enlisting in Surry County at age 30. Elected Captain to rank from April 26, 1861. Present or accounted for until elected Major on April 27, 1862, and transferred to the Field and Staff of this regiment.

WEIR, WILLIAM M.
Resided in Cleveland County and was by occupation a mechanic prior to enlisting in Surry County at age 22. Elected 3rd Lieutenant to rank from April 26, 1861, and was elected Captain, April 25-27, 1862.

Present or accounted for through August, 1864. Clark's *Regiments* indicates that he "perished in 1864." No further records.

LIEUTENANTS

GAMBLE, JOHN F., 1st Lieutenant
Resided in Cleveland County and was by occupation a farmer prior to enlisting in Surry County at age 22, April 26, 1861. Mustered in as Private and elected 2nd Lieutenant to rank from April 27, 1862. Present or accounted for until hospitalized at Richmond, Virginia, July 2, 1862, with a gunshot wound; however, place and date wounded not reported. Rejoined the company prior to September 16-17, 1862, when he was captured at Sharpsburg, Maryland. Confined at Fort Delaware, Delaware, until transferred to Aiken's Landing, James River, Virginia, October 2, 1862, for exchange. Declared exchanged at Aiken's Landing on November 10, 1862. Rejoined the company prior to January 1, 1863, and was promoted to 1st Lieutenant on March 1, 1864. Present or accounted for until captured at Spotsylvania Court House, Virginia, May 12 or May 19, 1864. Confined at Old Capitol Prison, Washington, D.C., until transferred to Fort Delaware on June 15, 1864. Transferred to Hilton Head, South Carolina, August 20, 1864. Transferred back to Fort Delaware where he arrived March 12, 1865. Released at Fort Delaware on June 18, 1865, after taking the Oath of Allegiance.

HARMAN, DAVID, 2nd Lieutenant
Resided in Cleveland County and was by occupation a student prior to enlisting in Surry County at age 23, April 26, 1861. Mustered in as Corporal and promoted to 1st Sergeant on July 18, 1861. Present or accounted for until captured at Malvern Hill, Virginia, July 2, 1862. Exchanged prior to September 17, 1862, when he was captured at Sharpsburg, Maryland. Confined at Fort Delaware, Delaware, until transferred to Aiken's Landing, James River, Virginia, October 2, 1862, for exchange. Appointed 2nd Lieutenant to rank from October 2, 1862. Declared exchanged at Aiken's Landing on November 10, 1862. Present or accounted for until wounded and captured at Winchester, Virginia, September 19, 1864. Died September 20, 1864, of wounds.

PATTERSON, ROBERT S., 1st Lieutenant
Resided in Cleveland County and was by occupation a student prior to enlisting in Surry County at age 21. Elected 1st Lieutenant to rank from April 26, 1861. Present or accounted for until he died on April 25, 1862. Place and cause of death not reported.

ROARK, RUFUS R., 1st Lieutenant
Resided in Cleveland County and was by occupation a student prior to enlisting in Surry County at age 21. Elected 2nd Lieutenant to rank from April 26, 1861, and elected 1st Lieutenant on April 26, 1862. Present or accounted for until he died June 10, 1862, of disease. Place of death not reported.

WEIR, ALEXANDER F., 1st Lieutenant
Resided in Cleveland County and was by occupation a student prior to enlisting in Surry County at age 22, April 26, 1861. Mustered in as Private and was promoted to Corporal on July 18, 1861. Elected 2nd

Lieutenant to rank from April 27, 1862, and was promoted to 1st Lieutenant on October 2, 1862. Present or accounted for until "dropped from the rolls" on or about February 5, 1863, by reason of "chr[onic] bronchitis."

NONCOMMISSIONED OFFICERS AND PRIVATES

ADDERTON, W. S., Private
Resided in Davidson County and enlisted in Wake County at age 24, July 16, 1862, for the war. Present or accounted for until captured at Spotsylvania Court House, Virginia, May 17, 1864. Died at Point Lookout, Maryland, October 30, 1864. Cause of death not reported.

ALLEN, J. T., Private
Born in Cleveland County where he resided as a farmer prior to enlisting in Cleveland County at age 20, July 24, 1861. Present or accounted for until reported in hospital at Frederick, Maryland, September 19, 1862; however, place and date captured not reported. Paroled prior to October 8, 1862, when he was hospitalized at Richmond, Virginia. Died in hospital at Richmond on or about January 20, 1863, of "typhoid fever."

ALLEN, M. S., Private
Resided in Person County and enlisted at Camp Holmes at age 45, September 18, 1863, for the war. Present or accounted for until he died January 21, 1864, of disease. Place of death not reported.

ANTHONY, JOHN, Private
Resided in Cleveland County and enlisted at Camp Holmes on October 28, 1863, for the war. Present or accounted for until captured at Petersburg, Virginia, April 3, 1865. Confined at Hart's Island, New York Harbor, until released on June 17, 1865, after taking the Oath of Allegiance.

BEAM, A. H., Private
Resided in Montgomery County and enlisted in Wake County at age 33, July 16, 1862, for the war. Present or accounted for until he died in hospital at Staunton, Virginia, November 26, 1862, of "diarrhoea chronica." Roll of Honor indicates he was missing since the battle of Sharpsburg, Maryland.

BEAM, ABRAM, Private
Resided in Cleveland County where he enlisted at age 21, July 29, 1861. Present or accounted for until he died on January 1, 1863, of disease. Place of death not reported.

BELL, TILMON, Corporal
Born in Cleveland County* where he resided as a farmer prior to enlisting in Surry County at age 25, April 26, 1861. Mustered in as Corporal. Present or accounted for until he died at or near Richmond, Virginia, May 9 or May 29, 1862, of disease.

BEMISTER, THOMAS, Private
Previously served in Company B of this regiment. Transferred to this company on or about November 30, 1862. Present or accounted for until captured in hospital at Richmond, Virginia, April 3, 1865. Paroled May 3, 1865.

BENNETT, JOSEPH, Sergeant
Resided in Cleveland County and was by occupation a mechanic or carpenter prior to enlisting in Surry County at age 24, April 26, 1861. Mustered in as Private and promoted to Corporal on December 1, 1862. Promoted to Sergeant on November 1, 1863. Present or accounted for until captured in hospital at Richmond, Virginia, April 3, 1865. Confined at Point Lookout, Maryland, until released on or about June 26, 1865, after taking the Oath of Allegiance.

BENNETT, WILLIAM, Private
Resided in Cleveland County and was by occupation an engineer prior to enlisting in Surry County at age 21, April 26, 1861. Present or accounted for through August, 1864. North Carolina pension records indicate he was wounded on September 15, 1864. No further records.

BLAKE, D., Private
Born in Montgomery County and resided in Davidson County prior to enlisting in Wake County at age 19, July 16, 1862, for the war. Present or accounted for until he died in hospital at Lynchburg, Virginia, on or about July 5, 1863, of "morbi varii."

BLALOCK, LAWSON C., Private
Resided in Cleveland County and was by occupation a farmer prior to enlisting in Surry County at age 23, April 26, 1861. Mustered in as Musician but was reduced to ranks in September-October, 1861. Present or accounted for until he died July 16, 1862, of disease. Place of death not reported.

BLANCHARD, WILLIAM, Private
Born in Lincoln County and resided in Cleveland County where he was by occupation a farmer prior to enlisting in Surry County at age 25, April 26, 1861. Present or accounted for until killed at Malvern Hill, Virginia, July 1, 1862.

BOLICK, NOAH, Private
Resided in Cleveland County and enlisted in Surry County at age 25, July 27, 1861. Present or accounted for until he died in hospital at Richmond, Virginia, July 4, 1862, of "pneumonia."

BONDS, NEWTON, Private
Previously served in Company B, 20th Regiment N.C. Troops (10th Regiment N.C. Volunteers). Transferred to this company on August 7, 1863, in exchange for Private Haywood Strickland. Deserted September 14, 1863, but returned to duty prior to March 14, 1864. Present or accounted for until captured at Cedar Creek, Virginia, October 19, 1864. Confined at Point Lookout, Maryland, until paroled and transferred to Boulware's Wharf, James River, Virginia, where he was received March 30, 1865, for exchange.

BOOKOUT, DAVID H., Private
Resided in Cleveland County and was by occupation a farmer prior to enlisting in Surry County at age 22, April 26, 1861. Present or accounted for through July 7, 1862. Company muster rolls indicate he died July 8, 1862, of disease; however, records of the U.D.C. indicate that he survived the war. Not listed in company records after 1862. No further records.

BORDERS, JAMES A., Sergeant
Born in York District, South Carolina, and resided in Cleveland County where he was by occupation a student prior to enlisting in Surry County at age 20, April 26, 1861. Mustered in as Sergeant. Present or accounted for until he died at or near Manassas, Virginia, on or about December 14, 1861. Cause of death not reported.

BORDERS, MICHAEL, Private
Resided in Cleveland County where he enlisted at age 27, July 27, 1861. Mustered in as Private and promoted to Sergeant on or about November 17, 1861. Present or accounted for until discharged on May 10, 1862, after providing a substitute.

BORDERS, WILLIAM, Corporal
Resided in Cleveland County and was by occupation a farmer prior to enlisting in Surry County at age 19, April 26, 1861. Mustered in as Corporal. Present or accounted for until discharged on June 2, 1862, after providing a substitute.

CAMENELA, F. B., Private
Place and date of enlistment not reported. Paroled at Greensboro on May 9, 1865.

CATHEY, FRANKLIN, Private
Resided in Cleveland County and was by occupation a miner prior to enlisting in Surry County at age 24, April 26, 1861. Present or accounted for until discharged on or about May 29, 1862, by reason of "ascites."

CEHERR, J. C., Private
Resided at Mack's Meadows, Virginia. Place and date of enlistment not reported. Captured at or near Bethesda Church, Virginia, May 30, 1864. Confined at Point Lookout, Maryland, until transferred to Elmira, New York, July 9, 1864. Released at Elmira on May 29, 1865, after taking the Oath of Allegiance.

CHANEY, JAMES H., Private
Resided in Cleveland County and was by occupation a miner prior to enlisting in Surry County at age 23, April 26, 1861. Mustered in as Private and promoted to Sergeant on December 1, 1862. Present or accounted for until he "deserted from line of battle" on September 14, 1863. Reduced to ranks in January-April, 1864. Rejoined the company prior to April 7, 1864, but deserted in July, 1864. Took the Oath of Allegiance at Charleston, West Virginia, December 14, 1864. [May have served also in Ward's Battalion, C. S. Prisoners.]

COBB, R. C., Private
Enlisted at Orange Court House, Virginia, January 1, 1864, for the war. Present or accounted for until hospitalized at Charlotte on June 4, 1864, with a gunshot wound; however, place and date wounded not reported. Returned to duty on June 25, 1864, and present or accounted for through August, 1864.

COLLINS, PETER H., Private
Resided in Cleveland County and was by occupation a farmer prior to enlisting in Surry County at age 22, April 26, 1861. Present or accounted for until wounded in the thigh at Gettysburg, Pennsylvania, July 1-3, 1863. Died July 8, 1863, of wounds. Place of death not reported.

CONNER, JACOB, Private
Born in Cleveland County* where he resided as a

farmer prior to enlisting in Surry County at age 23, April 26, 1861. Present or accounted for until he died at Camp Bee, Virginia, September 24-25, 1861. Cause of death not reported.

CORNELISON, R. W., Private
Resided in Montgomery County and enlisted in Wake County at age 30, July 16, 1862, for the war. Present or accounted for until wounded in the right hip and captured at Sharpsburg, Maryland, on or about September 17, 1862. Paroled at Fort McHenry, Maryland, on October 14, 1862, and transferred to Aiken's Landing, James River, Virginia, where he was received October 19, 1862, for exchange. Declared exchanged at Aiken's Landing on November 10, 1862. Reported absent wounded until he rejoined the company in September-October, 1863. Reported absent on detached service from December 16, 1863, through August 31, 1864.

COSTNER, JOHN C., Private
Resided in Cleveland County and was by occupation a farmer prior to enlisting in Surry County at age 23, April 26, 1861. Present or accounted for through August, 1864

CROW, JOHN D., Private
Resided in Cleveland County and was by occupation a farmer prior to enlisting in Surry County at age 26, April 26, 1861. Present or accounted for until captured at Sharpsburg, Maryland, September 17, 1862. Confined at Fort Delaware, Delaware, until transferred to Aiken's Landing, James River, Virginia, October 2, 1862, for exchange. Declared exchanged at Aiken's Landing on November 10, 1862. Returned to duty prior to January 1, 1863, and present or accounted for until wounded at Chancellorsville, Virginia, May 3, 1863. Reported absent wounded through August, 1864.

DAMERON, W. M., Private
Enlisted at Camp Holmes at age 42, September 25, 1863, for the war. Present or accounted for through August, 1864.

DAVIS, F., Private
Enlisted at Camp Holmes at age 44, September 25, 1863, for the war. Present or accounted for until February 15, 1864, when he was reported absent without leave. Reported absent without leave through August, 1864.

DEVINE, G. M., Private
Resided in Cleveland County where he enlisted at age 21, July 24, 1861. Present or accounted for until he died in hospital at Richmond, Virginia, September 10, 1862, of "febris typhoides."

DILLINGHAM, JOHN, Private
Born in York District, South Carolina, and resided in Cleveland County where he was by occupation a farmer prior to enlisting in Surry County at age 30, April 26, 1861. Present or accounted for until he died in hospital at Danville, Virginia, July 5, 1862, of "febris typhoides."

DIXON, A. I., Private
Born in Cleveland County* where he resided as a farmer prior to enlisting in Cleveland County at age 22, July 24, 1861. Present or accounted for until he died in hospital at Richmond, Virginia, September 5, 1862, of "febris typhoides."

DIXON, BENJAMIN, Private
Born in Cleveland County where he resided as a student or farmer prior to enlisting in Surry County at age 16, April 26, 1861. Present or accounted for until hospitalized at Richmond, Virginia, July 12, 1862, with a gunshot wound of the arm; however, place and date wounded not reported. Discharged at Richmond the same day by reason of being under age.

DIXON, JOHN F., Private
Resided in Cleveland County and was by occupation a millwright prior to enlisting at Camp Bragg, Virginia, at age 33, June 26, 1861. Present or accounted for through March, 1864; however, he was reported absent sick during much of that period. Retired to the Invalid Corps on or about April 22, 1864. Paroled at Appomattox Court House, Virginia, April 9, 1865.

DIXON, W. O., Private
Resided in Cleveland County where he enlisted at age 20, July 24, 1861. Present or accounted for until captured at Sharpsburg, Maryland, September 17, 1862. Confined at Fort Delaware, Delaware, until transferred to Aiken's Landing, James River, Virginia, October 2, 1862, for exchange. Declared exchanged at Aiken's Landing on November 10, 1862. Reported absent sick until he rejoined the company in November-December, 1863. Present or accounted for until wounded in the thigh and groin and captured at Spotsylvania Court House, Virginia, May 9-16, 1864. Hospitalized at Washington, D.C., where he died May 21, 1864.

DIXON, WILLIAM J., 1st Sergeant
Resided in Cleveland County and was by occupation a farmer prior to enlisting in Surry County at age 27, April 26, 1861. Mustered in as Sergeant and promoted to 1st Sergeant on October 3, 1862. Present or accounted for until wounded in the breast at Spotsylvania Court House, Virginia, May 19, 1864. Reported absent wounded through August, 1864.

DOBY, A., Private
Resided in Davidson County and enlisted in Wake County at age 25, July 16, 1862, for the war. Present or accounted for until wounded in the thigh and captured at Winchester, Virginia, September 19, 1864. Thigh amputated. Died in hospital at Winchester on October 8, 1864, of wounds.

DOBY, J. P., Private
Resided in Davidson or Rowan counties and enlisted in Wake County at age 28, July 16, 1862, for the war. Present or accounted for until captured at Spotsylvania Court House, Virginia, May 19-20, 1864. Confined at Point Lookout, Maryland, until transferred to Elmira, New York, July 3, 1864. Released at Elmira on June 30, 1865, after taking the Oath of Allegiance.

DOVER, FREDERICK, Private
Born in York District, South Carolina, and resided in Cleveland County where he was by occupation a farmer prior to enlisting in Surry County at age 22, April 26, 1861. Present or accounted for until he

died in hospital at Richmond, Virginia, in May, 1862, of disease.

DOVER, JAMES, Private

Resided in Cleveland County and was by occupation a farmer prior to enlisting at Camp Bragg, Virginia, at age 20, June 26, 1861. Present or accounted for until wounded in the shoulder at Gettysburg, Pennsylvania, July 1-3, 1863. Reported absent wounded until discharged on or about February 20, 1864.

ELLIS, CHARLES H., Private

Resided in Cleveland County and was by occupation a farmer prior to enlisting in Surry County at age 18, April 26, 1861. Present or accounted for until wounded in the head at Sharpsburg, Maryland, September 17, 1862. Rejoined the company in January-February, 1863, and present or accounted for until he "deserted from line of battle" on September 14, 1863. Returned from desertion on December 19, 1863, and present or accounted for until captured at Petersburg, Virginia, April 3, 1865. Confined at Hart's Island, New York Harbor, until released on June 17, 1865, after taking the Oath of Allegiance.

ELLIS, R. M., Private

Born in Cleveland County where he resided as a farmer or student prior to enlisting in Surry County at age 20, April 26, 1861. Mustered in as Private and promoted to Lance Corporal in November-December, 1861. Reduced to ranks prior to July 22, 1862, when he died at Richmond, Virginia, of disease.

ELMORE, MANASSA, Private

Resided in Cleveland County where he enlisted at age 25, July 24, 1861. Present or accounted for until he died in July, 1862, of disease. Place of death not reported.

ELWOOD, WILLIAM H., Sergeant

Resided in Cleveland County and was by occupation a miner prior to enlisting in Surry County at age 20, April 26, 1861. Mustered in as Private and promoted to Corporal on September 1, 1863. Promoted to Sergeant in November-December, 1863. Present or accounted for until paroled at Appomattox Court House, Virginia, April 9, 1865.

EPPS, E., Private

Resided in Davidson County and enlisted in Wake County at age 29, July 16, 1862, for the war. Present or accounted for until captured at Spotsylvania Court House, Virginia, May 19-20, 1864. Confined at Point Lookout, Maryland, until transferred to Elmira, New York, July 3, 1864. Died at Elmira on August 16, 1864, of "remittent fever."

EPPS, J. B., Private

Resided in Davidson County and enlisted in Wake County at age 20, July 16, 1862, for the war. Present or accounted for until he died in hospital at Liberty, Virginia, September 18, 1862, of "diarrhoea chronic."

ERWIN, C. C., Private

Resided in Anson County where he enlisted at age 44, August 21, 1863, for the war. Present or accounted for until reported absent sick on June 11,

1864. Reported absent sick through February 24, 1865. Paroled at Salisbury on May 11, 1865. North Carolina pension records indicate that he was "attacked with a stroke of blindness in both eyes" at Spotsylvania Court House, Virginia, on or about May 12, 1864, and "from [this] infirmity he lost his eyesight entirely."

FALLS, GEORGE C., Private

Born in Cleveland County where he resided as a farmer prior to enlisting in Surry County at age 19, April 26, 1861. Present or accounted for until wounded at Malvern Hill, Virginia, on or about July 1, 1862. Died in hospital at Richmond, Virginia, on or about July 20, 1862, of wounds and/or disease.

FALLS, JOSEPH O., Private

Resided in Cleveland County and was by occupation a farmer prior to enlisting in Surry County at age 23, April 26, 1861. Present or accounted for until wounded in the right arm and captured at Gettysburg, Pennsylvania, July 2-3, 1863. Right arm amputated. Hospitalized at Gettysburg and at Baltimore, Maryland. Transferred to City Point, Virginia, or or about November 12, 1863, for exchange. Reported absent wounded until retired to the Invalid Corps on December 29, 1864.

FERGUSON, SIMON, Private

Born in Ireland and resided in Cleveland County where he was by occupation a miner prior to enlisting in Surry County at age 26, April 26, 1861. Present or accounted for until wounded in the left leg at Sharpsburg, Maryland, September 17, 1862. Left leg amputated. Reported absent wounded until discharged on March 16, 1865, by reason of disability.

FOUST, L., Private

Resided in Davidson County and enlisted in Wake County at age 35, July 16, 1862, for the war. Present or accounted for until reported missing at Sharpsburg, Maryland, September 17, 1862. Rejoined the company in January-February, 1863. Present or accounted for until reported absent without leave from April 20, 1863, until December 6, 1863. Wounded in battle in Virginia on May 30, 1864, and died in hospital at Richmond, Virginia, June 11, 1864, of wounds.

FRANKLIN, J. J., Private

Resided in Person County and enlisted at Camp Holmes at age 43, September 18, 1863, for the war. Present or accounted for until wounded at Spotsylvania Court House, Virginia, May 19 1864. Reported absent wounded until retired to the Invalid Corps on November 29, 1864.

GADDY, JOSEPH THOMAS, Private

Previously served in Company I, 43rd Regiment N.C. Troops Enlisted in this company on August 21, 1863, for the war. Present or accounted for through January, 1864. Medical records dated February 18, 1864, state he was suffering from a gunshot wound of the left leg; however, place and date wounded not reported. Captured at Winchester, Virginia, September 19, 1864, and confined at Point Lookout, Maryland, until paroled and transferred to Venus Point, Savannah River, Georgia, where he was received November 15, 1864, for exchange. Paroled at Appomattox Court House, Virginia, April 9, 1865.

GAMBLE, ANDREW J., Sergeant
Resided in Cleveland County and was by occupation a farmer prior to enlisting in Surry County at age 23, April 26, 1861. Mustered in as Private and promoted to Sergeant on or about September 18, 1862. Present or accounted for until hospitalized at Richmond, Virginia, June 10, 1864, with a gunshot wound; however, place and date wounded not reported. Rejoined the company prior to September 1, 1864. Paroled at Appomattox Court House, Virginia, April 9, 1865

GARDNER, A. K., Private
Born in Cleveland County* where he resided as a farmer prior to enlisting in Surry County at age 21, April 26, 1861. Present or accounted for until wounded in the knee at Malvern Hill, Virginia, on or about July 1, 1862. Died in hospital at Richmond, Virginia, August 8, 1862, of wounds.

GILL, GEORGE R., Private
Born in Chester District, South Carolina, and was by occupation a farmer prior to enlisting in Surry County at age 34, April 26, 1861. Present or accounted for until discharged on July 26, 1862, under the provisions of the Conscript Act.

GIVINS, ROBERT, Private
Born in York District, South Carolina, and resided in Cleveland County where he was by occupation a farmer prior to enlisting in Surry County at age 26, April 26, 1861. Present or accounted for until he died July 25, 1862, of disease. Place of death not reported.

GLADDEN, W. L., Private
Enlisted at Camp Holmes on November 15, 1863, for the war. Present or accounted for until wounded near Bethesda Church, Virginia, May 30, 1864. Reported absent wounded through August, 1864.

GOFORTH, HENRY W., Private
Resided in Cleveland County and was by occupation a farmer prior to enlisting in Cleveland County at age 18, January 1, 1863, for the war. Present or accounted for until wounded in the chest and captured at Hagerstown, Maryland, July 13-14, 1863. Hospitalized at Frederick, Maryland, and at Baltimore, Maryland, until paroled on or about August 22, 1863. Received at City Point, Virginia, August 24, 1863, for exchange. Reported absent wounded through December, 1863, but returned to duty prior to September 1, 1864.

GOFORTH, JOHN F., Sergeant
Resided in Cleveland County and was by occupation a farmer prior to enlisting in Surry County at age 19, April 26, 1861. Mustered in as Private. Nominated for the Badge of Distinction for gallantry at Chancellorsville, Virginia, May 1-3, 1863. Promoted to Sergeant on May 10, 1863. Present or accounted for until furloughed for sixty days from hospital at Richmond, Virginia, January 8-9, 1865.

GORDON, REUBEN B., Private
Resided in Cleveland County and was by occupation a miner prior to enlisting in Surry County at age 21, April 26, 1861. Mustered in as Private and promoted to Sergeant on May 10, 1863. Present or accounted

for until he "deserted from line of battle" on September 14, 1863. Rejoined the company and was reduced to ranks in January-April, 1864. Deserted again on or about July 1, 1864. Reported on duty with Company A, Ward's Battalion C. S. Prisoners in July, 1864. Ordered to rejoin this company on July 30, 1864. No further records.

GRIFFIN, CORNELIUS, Private
Resided in Cleveland County where he enlisted at age 21, July 29, 1861. Present or accounted for until he "deserted from line of battle" on September 14, 1863. Reported absent without leave until he rejoined the company on December 13, 1863. Present or accounted for until he died May 12, 1864, of wounds. Place and date wounded and place of death not reported.

HAHN, A., Private
Resided in Stanly County and enlisted at Camp Holmes at age 40, September 10, 1863, for the war. Present or accounted for until he died in hospital at Richmond, Virginia, February 22, 1864, of "febr[is] typhoides."

HAMBRIGHT, C. V., Private
Born in Cleveland County* where he resided prior to enlisting in Cleveland County at age 24, July 29, 1861. Present or accounted for until killed at Gaines' Mill, Virginia, June 27, 1862.

HARMON, A. N., Private
Enlisted at Orange Court House, Virginia, March 28, 1864, for the war. Present or accounted for until wounded at Spotsylvania Court House, Virginia, May 12, 1864. Reported absent wounded until retired to the Invalid Corps on January 12, 1865.

HARMON, AUGUSTA, Corporal
Resided in Cleveland County and was by occupation a farmer prior to enlisting in Surry County at age 27, April 26, 1861. Mustered in as Private. Present or accounted for until captured at Frederick, Maryland, September 12, 1862. Confined at Fort Delaware, Delaware, until transferred to Aiken's Landing, James River, Virginia, October 2, 1862, for exchange. Declared exchanged at Aiken's Landing on November 10, 1862. Promoted to Corporal on December 1, 1862. Present or accounted for until he died in hospital at Richmond, Virginia, on or about May 30, 1863. Cause of death not reported.

HARMON, JOHN J., Private
Resided in Cleveland County and was by occupation a farmer prior to enlisting in Surry County at age 22, April 26, 1861. Present or accounted for until wounded at Chancellorsville, Virginia, May 3, 1863. Reported absent wounded until August 10, 1863, when he was reported absent without leave. Rejoined the company prior to November 1, 1863, and present or accounted for until paroled at Appomattox Court House, Virginia, April 9, 1865.

HARMON, JOHN L., Private
Born in Cleveland County* where he resided as a farmer prior to enlisting in Surry County at age 26, July 29, 1861. Present or accounted for until discharged on November 21, 1861, by reason of "cystitis and prostatic derangement."

HARMON, PRESTON, Private

Born in Cleveland County* where he resided as a farmer prior to enlisting in Surry County at age 21, April 26, 1861. Present or accounted for until paroled at Leesburg, Virginia, October 2, 1862; however, place and date captured not reported. Died at Winchester, Virginia, November 2, 1862, of disease.

HARMON, REUBEN L., Corporal

Resided in Cleveland County and was by occupation a farmer prior to enlisting in Surry County at age 21, April 26, 1861. Mustered in as Private and promoted to Corporal on November 1, 1863. Present or accounted for until captured at Bethesda Church, Virginia, May 30, 1864. Confined at Point Lookout, Maryland, until transferred to Elmira, New York, July 9, 1864. Paroled at Elmira on October 11, 1864, and transferred to Venus Point, Savannah River, Georgia, where he was received November 15, 1864, for exchange.

HEAVNER, JOHN R., Private

Resided in Cleveland County and was by occupation a carpenter prior to enlisting in Surry County at age 26, April 26, 1861. Present or accounted for until wounded at Chancellorsville, Virginia, May 1-3, 1863. Died in hospital at Richmond, Virginia, June 2, 1863, of wounds and/or disease.

HENDERSON, W., Private

Resided in Davidson County and enlisted in Wake County at age 28, July 16, 1862, for the war. Present or accounted for until captured at Spotsylvania Court House, Virginia, May 20, 1864. Confined at Point Lookout, Maryland, until transferred to Elmira, New York, July 3, 1864. Paroled at Elmira on October 11, 1864, and transferred to Venus Point, Savannah River, Georgia, where he was received November 15, 1864, for exchange. Paroled at Troy on May 23, 1865.

HORTON, JOSEPH, Private

Resided in Cleveland County where he enlisted at age 21, July 29, 1861. Present or accounted for until wounded at Malvern Hill, Virginia, July 1, 1862. Reported absent wounded until discharged on or about February 19, 1863.

HOWELL, DREWRY D., Private

Resided in Cleveland County and was by occupation a farmer prior to enlisting in Surry County at age 21, April 26, 1861. Present or accounted for until wounded in the left hand at or near Cold Harbor, Virginia, June 2, 1864. Reported absent wounded through August, 1864. Paroled at Appomattox Court House, Virginia, April 9, 1865.

HUGHS, JOHN B., Private

Born in Cleveland County where he resided as a farmer prior to enlisting in Surry County at age 17, April 26, 1861. Present or accounted for until killed at Malvern Hill, Virginia, July 1, 1862.

KENDRICK, D. D., Private

Resided in Cleveland County where he enlisted at age 23, July 26, 1861. Present or accounted for until he died in hospital at Richmond, Virginia, July 12, 1862, of "feb[ris] typh[oid]."

KENDRICK, JOSEPH C., Private

Resided in Cleveland County and was by occupation a farmer prior to enlisting in Surry County at age 21, April 26, 1861. Present or accounted for until he died at Richmond, Virginia, June 24, 1862, of disease.

KENDRICK, WILLIAM, Private

Born in Cleveland County* where he resided as a farmer prior to enlisting in Cleveland County at age 25, July 26, 1861. Present or accounted for until discharged on September 21, 1861, by reason of disability.

KINNEY, A. D., Private

Resided in Davidson or Rowan counties and enlisted in Wake County at age 19, July 16, 1862, for the war. Present or accounted for until hospitalized at Charlottesville, Virginia, October 16, 1862, with a gunshot wound; however, place and date wounded not reported. Returned to duty on November 10, 1862, and present or accounted for until wounded at Chancellorsville, Virginia, May 3, 1863. Reported absent wounded until August 10, 1863, when he was reported absent without leave. Rejoined the company prior to November 1, 1863, and present or accounted for until captured at Bethesda Church, Virginia, May 30, 1864. Confined at Elmira, New York, until released on June 30, 1865, after taking the Oath of Allegiance.

KINNEY, B. R., Corporal

Resided in Davidson County and enlisted at Fredericksburg, Virginia, at age 29, May 9, 1863, for the war. Mustered in as Private and promoted to Corporal on November 1, 1863. Present or accounted for until killed at Spotsylvania Court House, Virginia, May 12, 1864.

KIRKMAN, A. C., Private

Resided in Guilford County and enlisted at Camp Holmes on October 5, 1863, for the war. Present or accounted for until captured at Petersburg, Virginia, April 3, 1865. Confined at Hart's Island, New York Harbor, until released on June 17, 1865, after taking the Oath of Allegiance.

LACKEY, DIXON, Private

Resided in Cleveland County and was by occupation a farmer prior to enlisting in Surry County at age 21, April 26, 1861. Present or accounted for until discharged on September 21, 1861. Reason discharged not reported.

LAWSON, WILLIAM, Private

Resided in Cleveland County and was by occupation a coach trimmer prior to enlisting in Surry County at age 26, April 26, 1861. Present or accounted for until he deserted on May 5, 1862.

LOFTON, J. C., Private

Born in Davidson County where he resided prior to enlisting in Wake County at age 21, July 16, 1862, for the war. Present or accounted for until he died in hospital at Richmond, Virginia, November 17, 1862, of "gangrene of leg" or "erysipelas."

LONG, JACOB F., Corporal

Resided in Cleveland County and was by occupation a student prior to enlisting in Surry County at age 22, April 26, 1861. Mustered in as Sergeant but was reduced to ranks on December 1, 1862. Promoted to Corporal on November 1, 1863. Present or accounted for until captured at Cedar Creek, Virginia, October 19, 1864. Confined at Point Lookout, Maryland, until paroled and transferred to Cox's Landing, James River, Virginia, where he was received February 14-15, 1865, for exchange. Reported present with a detachment of paroled and exchanged prisoners at Camp Lee, near Richmond, Virginia, February 20, 1865.

LONG, W. A., Private
Resided in Cleveland County where he enlisted at age 21, July 24, 1861. Present or accounted for until wounded in the arm at Chancellorsville, Virginia, May 3, 1863. Arm amputated. Died in hospital at Richmond, Virginia, July 27-28, 1863, of wounds.

LOWE, JOHN, Private
Born in Gaston County* and resided in Cleveland County where he was by occupation a farmer prior to enlisting in Cleveland County at age 16, July 29, 1861. Present or accounted for until discharged on January 12, 1863, by reason of being under age.

MARTIN, M., Private
Resided in Wake County where he enlisted at age 40, July 16, 1862, for the war as a substitute. Present or accounted for through August, 1864.

MAYFIELD, JAMES, Private
Born in Rutherford County and resided in Cleveland County where he was by occupation a miner prior to enlisting in Surry County at age 18, April 26, 1861. Present or accounted for until he died in hospital at Lynchburg, Virginia, on or about July 16, 1862, of "ictus solis."

MICHAM, HUGH C., Private
Resided in Cleveland County and was by occupation a farmer prior to enlisting in Surry County at age 22, April 26, 1861. Present or accounted for until hospitalized at Richmond, Virginia, September 27, 1862, with a gunshot wound; however, place and date wounded not reported. Rejoined the company prior to January 1, 1863, and present or accounted for until he "deserted from line of battle" on September 14, 1863. Deserted to the enemy near Washington, North Carolina, on or about March 13, 1864. Released on or about March 20, 1864.

MILLS, J. Q., Private
Resided in Anson County and enlisted in Wake County on July 18, 1863, for the war. Present or accounted for until paroled at Appomattox Court House, Virginia, April 9, 1865.

MOORE, F., Private
Enlisted at Camp Holmes on October 28, 1863, for the war. Present or accounted for until paroled at Appomattox Court House, Virginia, April 9, 1865.

MORGAN, J. M., Private
Enlisted at Camp Holmes on October 3, 1863, for the war. Present or accounted for until transferred on November 1, 1863. Unit to which transferred not reported.

MOSS, A. G., Private
Resided in Cleveland County where he enlisted at age 25, July 26, 1861. Present or accounted for through August, 1864.

MOSS, H. S., Private
Resided in Cleveland or Gaston counties and enlisted at Orange Court House, Virginia, at age 18, August 21, 1863, for the war. Present or accounted for until hospitalized at Danville, Virginia, on or about May 19, 1864, with a gunshot wound of the hand; however, place and date wounded not reported. Rejoined the company prior to September 1, 1864. Captured at Petersburg, Virginia, April 3, 1865, and confined at Hart's Island, New York Harbor, until released on June 17, 1865, after taking the Oath of Allegiance.

MOTLEY, T., Private
Resided in Stanly County and enlisted at Camp Holmes at age 44, September 10, 1863, for the war. Present or accounted for until captured at Petersburg, Virginia, April 3, 1865. Confined at Hart's Island, New York Harbor, until released on June 17, 1865, after taking the Oath of Allegiance.

PARKER, HUMPHREY, Private
Born in Cleveland County* where he resided as a blacksmith prior to enlisting in Surry County at age 21, April 26, 1861. Present or accounted for until wounded and captured at or near Malvern Hill, Virginia, on or about July 1, 1862. Confined at Fort Columbus, New York Harbor, until exchanged at Aiken's Landing, James River, Virginia, August 5, 1862. Died on or about August 10, 1862, of disease. Place of death not reported.

PARKER, JOSEPH, Private
Born in York District, South Carolina, and resided in Cleveland County where he was by occupation a farmer prior to enlisting in Cleveland County at age 21, July 29, 1861. Present or accounted for until he died June 19, 1862, of disease. Place of death not reported.

PARKER, L., Private
Born in Sampson County where he resided prior to enlisting in Wake County at age 23, July 16, 1862, for the war. Present or accounted for until killed at Chancellorsville, Virginia, May 3, 1863.

PATTERSON, ALLISON, Private
Resided in Cleveland County where he enlisted at age 24, July 29, 1861. Present or accounted for until he died in hospital at Richmond, Virginia, March 12, 1863, of "compd cerebri."

PATTERSON, DIXON C., Private
Born in Cleveland County* where he resided as a farmer prior to enlisting in Northampton County at age 27, June 9, 1861. Present or accounted for until discharged on September 19, 1861, by reason of disability.

PATTERSON, MARTIN V., Private
Born in Cleveland County* where he resided as a farmer prior to enlisting in Surry County at age 24, April 26, 1861. Mustered in as Corporal but was reduced to ranks on December 1, 1862. Present or accounted for until he died in hospital at Lynchburg, Virginia, January 3, 1863, of "pneumonia."

PATTERSON, PRESTON G., Private
Resided in Cleveland County and was by occupation a farmer prior to enlisting in Surry County at age 24,

April 26, 1861. Present or accounted for until killed at Malvern Hill, Virginia, July 1, 1862.

PATTERSON, ROBERT B., Private
Born in Cleveland County* where he resided as a farmer prior to enlisting in Surry County at age 22, April 26, 1861. Present or accounted for until he died at Camp Ellis, Virginia, August 6, 1861. Cause of death not reported.

PATTERSON, T. V., Musician
Resided in Cleveland County and was by occupation a farmer prior to enlisting in Surry County at age 19, April 26, 1861. Mustered in as Musician. Present or accounted for until he died on July 22, 1862, of disease. Place of death not reported.

PATTERSON, THOMAS C., Private
Resided in Cleveland County and was by occupation a farmer prior to enlisting in Surry County at age 23, April 26, 1861. Present or accounted for until he deserted on September 5, 1862.

PATTERSON, WILLIAM P., Private
Resided in Cleveland County and was by occupation a farmer prior to enlisting in Surry County at age 22, April 26, 1861. Present or accounted for until hospitalized at Richmond, Virginia, April 23, 1863, with "typhoid pneumonia." Died in hospital at Richmond on May 5, 1863.

RANDALL, J. A., Private
Resided in Cleveland County where he enlisted at age 21, July 26, 1861. Present or accounted for until discharged on or about August 9, 1862. Reason discharged not reported.

RANDALL, J. P., Private
Resided in Cleveland County where he enlisted at age 23, July 26, 1861. Mustered in as Private and promoted to Corporal in March-November, 1862. Present or accounted for until wounded at or near Malvern Hill, Virginia, July 1, 1862. Reduced to ranks on December 1, 1862, and rejoined the company in January-February, 1863. Present or accounted for until wounded at Hagerstown, Maryland, in July, 1863. Died in hospital at Richmond, Virginia, August 7, 1863, of wounds and/or "meningitis."

RANDALL, JOHN C., Sergeant
Resided in Cleveland County where he enlisted at age 31, July 26, 1861. Mustered in as Private and promoted to Sergeant on December 26, 1861. Present or accounted for until wounded in the left arm and captured at Sharpsburg, Maryland, September 17, 1862. Left arm amputated. Confined at Fort McHenry, Maryland, until paroled and transferred to Aiken's Landing, James River, Virginia, where he was received October 19, 1862, for exchange. Declared exchanged at Aiken's Landing on November 10, 1862. Discharged on March 8, 1863, by reason of disability.

REAVES, C. A., Private
Resided in Davidson County and enlisted in Wake County at age 21, July 16, 1862, for the war. Present or accounted for until wounded at Sharpsburg, Maryland, September 17, 1862. Died of wounds the same day.

RHEA, WILLIAM S., Private
Born in York District, South Carolina, and resided in Cleveland County where he was by occupation a farmer prior to enlisting in Surry County at age 27, April 26, 1861. Present or accounted for until he died at Fredericksburg, Virginia, on or about December 25, 1862, of disease.

ROBERTS, H. K., Private
Enlisted at Camp Holmes on October 28, 1861. Present or accounted for until captured at Winchester, Virginia, September 19, 1864. Confined at Point Lookout, Maryland, until paroled and transferred to Cox's Landing, James River, Virginia, where he was received February 14-15, 1865, for exchange. Reported present with a detachment of paroled and exchanged prisoners at Camp Lee, near Richmond, Virginia, February 18, 1865.

SHEAHEN, JOHN, Private
Resided in Cleveland County and was by occupation a farmer prior to enlisting in Surry County at age 18, April 26, 1861. Present or accounted for until he "deserted from the line of battle" on September 14, 1863. Rejoined the company on December 14, 1863. Present or accounted for until reported captured on May 3, 1864; however, records of the Federal Provost Marshal do not substantiate that report. No further records.

SIMS, JOHN A., Private
Resided in Cleveland or Lincoln counties and enlisted in Cleveland County at age 20, July 29, 1861. Present or accounted for until wounded at Chancellorsville, Virginia, May 3, 1863. Reported absent wounded or absent sick through February 26, 1865. Captured in hospital at Richmond, Virginia, April 3, 1865. Confined at Libby Prison, Richmond, until transferred to Newport News, Virginia, April 23, 1865. Released at Newport News on June 30, 1865, after taking the Oath of Allegiance.

SKATES, GEORGE G., Private
Born in York District, South Carolina, and resided in Cleveland County where he was by occupation a farmer prior to enlisting in Surry County at age 19, April 26, 1861. Present or accounted for until he died in hospital at Petersburg, Virginia, on or about June 12, 1862, of "rubeola."

SLAUGHTER, S. J., Private
Resided in Person County and enlisted at Camp Holmes on September 18, 1863, for the war. Present or accounted for until he died in hospital at Richmond, Virginia, on or about July 1, 1864, of disease.

SMITH, ALFRED, Private
Resided in Davidson County and enlisted at Fredericksburg, Virginia, at age 35, May 9, 1863, for the war. Present or accounted for until captured at Spotsylvania Court House, Virginia, May 19-20, 1864. Confined at Point Lookout, Maryland, until transferred to Elmira, New York, on or about July 3, 1864. Paroled at Elmira on October 11, 1864, and transferred to Venus Point, Savannah River, Georgia, where he was received November 15, 1864, for exchange. Took the Oath of Allegiance at Salisbury on June 24, 1865.

SMITH, FREDERICK, Private
Resided in Davidson County and enlisted in Wake County at age 22, July 16, 1862, for the war. Present or accounted for until captured at Sharpsburg, Maryland, or at Boonsboro, Maryland, September 17-19, 1862. Confined at Fort Delaware, Delaware, until transferred to Aiken's Landing, James River, Virginia, October 2, 1862, for exchange. Declared exchanged at Aiken's Landing on November 10, 1862. Rejoined the company in May-June, 1863, and was wounded in the hand at Gettysburg, Pennsylvania, July 1-3, 1863. Rejoined the company in January-April, 1864, and was captured at Spotsylvania Court House, Virginia, May 20, 1864. Confined at Point Lookout, Maryland, until transferred to Elmira, New York, on or about July 3, 1864. Died at Elmira on or about March 1, 1865, of "chro[nic] diarrhoea."

SMITH, P. D., Private
Born in Davidson County where he resided as a farmer prior to enlisting in Wake County at age 29, July 16, 1862, for the war. Present or accounted for until captured at Sharpsburg, Maryland, September 17, 1862. Received at Aiken's Landing, James River, Virginia, October 6, 1862, for exchange. Declared exchanged at Aiken's Landing on November 10, 1862. Died on or about December 1, 1862, of disease. Place of death not reported.

SNIPES, N. B., Private
Resided in Caswell County and enlisted at Camp Holmes on September 25, 1863, for the war. Present or accounted for until he died at or near Richmond, Virginia, on or about July 28, 1864, of disease.

SOON, JAMES J., Private
Born in Orange County where he resided as a farmer prior to enlisting in Orange County on March 1, 1862. Present or accounted for until killed at Sharpsburg, Maryland, September 17, 1862. Death records give his age as 26.

SPAKE, PERRY G., Private
Resided in Cleveland County and was by occupation a blacksmith prior to enlisting in Surry County at age 22, April 26, 1861. Present or accounted for until wounded at Sharpsburg, Maryland, September 17, 1862. Died prior to March 1, 1863, of wounds. Place and exact date of death not reported.

SPARKS, THOMAS T., Private
Born in Cleveland County* where he resided as a farmer prior to enlisting in Cleveland County at age 21, July 25, 1861. Present or accounted for until wounded at Malvern Hill, Virginia, on or about July 1, 1862. Died at Richmond, Virginia, on or about July 16, 1862, of wounds.

STRICKLAND, HAYWOOD, Private
Not listed in the records of this company; however, records of Company B, 20th Regiment N.C. Troops (10th Regiment N.C. Volunteers) indicate that he served herein and was transferred to the 20th Regiment on August 7, 1863, in exchange for Private Newton Bonds. Records of the U.D.C. also indicate that he served in this unit. No further records.

STRICKLAND, JOHN, Private
Resided in Cleveland County and was by occupation

a "minor" prior to enlisting in Surry County at age 18, April 26, 1861. Present or accounted for until wounded in the arm at Gaines' Mill, Virginia, June 27, 1862. Died in hospital at Richmond, Virginia, on or about October 2, 1862, of "enteritis & amputated arm."

STRIDER, I., Private
Resided in Montgomery County and enlisted in Wake County at age 27, July 16, 1862, for the war. Present or accounted for until wounded in the thigh and captured at Sharpsburg, Maryland, September 17, 1862. Leg amputated. Paroled on September 27, 1862. Died at Frederick City, Maryland, prior to January 1, 1863. Exact date of death not reported.

STROUP, ALFORD A., Private
Born in Gaston County* and resided in Cleveland County where he was by occupation a farmer prior to enlisting in Surry County at age 22, April 26, 1861. Present or accounted for until transferred to the C.S. Navy for duty on the C.S.S. *Merrimac* on February 19, 1862.

SURRATT, W. M., Private
Enlisted at Camp Holmes on October 22, 1863, for the war. Present or accounted for through August, 1864.

SUTHERLAND, B., Private
Born in Madison County, Tennessee, and resided in Cleveland County where he was by occupation a farmer prior to enlisting at Richmond, Virginia, at age 42, May 10, 1862, for the war. Present or accounted for through January, 1865; however, he was reported absent on detached service during much of that period.

TAYLOR, CALEB, Private
Born in Davidson County where he resided as a farmer prior to enlisting at "Jackson," North Carolina, at age 24, February 11, 1862. Present or accounted for until he died October 16, 1862, of wounds. Place and date wounded and place of death not reported.

TAYLOR, E. W., Private
Born in Montgomery County and resided in Davidson County prior to enlisting in Wake County at age 21, July 16, 1862, for the war. Present or accounted for until wounded at Sharpsburg, Maryland, September 17, 1862. Rejoined the company in March-April, 1863, and present or accounted for until wounded at Chancellorsville, Virginia, May 1-3, 1863. Died at Chancellorsville of wounds. Date of death not reported.

THAMES, D., Private
Enlisted at Camp Holmes on October 1, 1863, for the war. Present or accounted for until he died in hospital at Charlottesville, Virginia, September 2, 1864, of "chronic diarrhoea."

TIPPETT, D. F., Private
Resided in Davidson County and enlisted in Wake County at age 20, July 16, 1862, for the war. Present or accounted for until wounded in the left leg at Chancellorsville, Virginia, May 1, 1863. Captured and paroled on or about May 24, 1863. Reported absent wounded through August, 1864. Retired to the Invalid Corps on December 9, 1864.

WADE, W. H., Private

Resided in Davidson County and enlisted in Wake County at age 30, July 16, 1862, for the war. Present or accounted for until he died on October 1, 1862, of disease. Place of death not reported.

WARE, ROBERT J., Corporal

Born in Cleveland County where he resided as a farmer prior to enlisting in Surry County at age 19, April 26, 1861. Mustered in as Private and promoted to Corporal on December 1, 1862. Present or accounted for until wounded at Chancellorsville, Virginia, May 1-3, 1863. Died May 20, 1863, of wounds. Place of death not reported.

WATTERSON, VARDRA M., Private

Born in Cleveland County* where he resided as a farmer prior to enlisting in Surry County at age 24, April 26, 1861. Present or accounted for until wounded in the left thigh at Malvern Hill, Virginia, July 1, 1862. Reported absent wounded until discharged on October 15, 1863, by reason of "atrophy & partial paralysis of [the left] leg."

WEAR, J. F., Private

Born in Cleveland County where he resided prior to enlisting in Cleveland County at age 20, July 29, 1861. Present or accounted for until he died on April 26, 1862, of disease. Place of death not reported.

WEBSTER, JOHN, Private

Resided in Yadkin County and enlisted at Camp Holmes at age 28, August 9, 1863, for the war. Present or accounted for until hospitalized at Richmond, Virginia, June 10, 1864, with a gunshot wound; however, place and date wounded not reported. Rejoined the company prior to September 1, 1864. Paroled at Appomattox Court House, Virginia, April 9, 1865.

WHITE, RUFUS, Private

Resided in Cleveland County where he enlisted at age 20, July 29, 1861. Present or accounted for until wounded in the scalp at Spotsylvania Court House, Virginia, May 12, 1864. Reported absent wounded through August, 1864. Paroled at Burkeville Junction, Virginia, April 14-17, 1865.

WHITLEY, E., Private

Enlisted at Camp Holmes on October 3, 1863, for the war. Present or accounted for through March 24, 1865.

WILSON, JOHN SCOTT, Private

Born in Mecklenburg County and resided in Cleveland County where he was by occupation a miner prior to enlisting in Surry County at age 21, April 26, 1861. Present or accounted for until wounded at Malvern Hill, Virginia, July 1, 1862. Died in hospital at Richmond, Virginia, on or about September 1, 1862, of wounds.

WILSON, SAMUEL A., Private

Enlisted at Camp Holmes on October 28, 1863, for the war. Present or accounted for through August, 1864.

WILSON, SILAS, Private

Resided in Montgomery County and enlisted at Camp Holmes at age 37, September 25, 1863, for the war. Present or accounted for through August, 1864.

WINTER, JOHN W., Private

Born in Gaston County* and resided in Cleveland County where he was by occupation a farmer prior to enlisting in Surry County at age 19, April 26, 1861. Present or accounted for until he died on October 8, 1862, of disease. Place of death not reported.

WRIGHT, JAMES, Private

Resided in Cleveland County and enlisted at Richmond, Virginia, at age 51, June 2, 1862, for the war. Present or accounted for through January 27, 1865; however, he was reported absent sick or absent without leave during much of that period.

WRIGHT, JOHN, Private

Resided in Cleveland County where he enlisted at age 26, July 29, 1861. Present or accounted for until wounded at Sharpsburg, Maryland, September 17, 1862. Died of wounds prior to May 1, 1863. Place and exact date of death not reported.

COMPANY E

This company, known as the Oak City Guards, was from Wake County and enlisted at Raleigh on May 1, 1861. It remained in Raleigh until moved to Garysburg on June 1, 1861. There it was assigned to this regiment as Company E. After joining the regiment the company functioned as a part of the regiment, and its history for the war period is recorded as a part of the regimental history.

The information contained in the following roster of the company was compiled principally form company muster rolls for May 1, 1861, through August 31, 1864. No company muster rolls were found for the period after August 31, 1864. In addition to the company muster rolls, Roll of Honor records, receipt rolls, hospital records, prisoner of war records, and other primary records, supplemented by state pension applications, United Daughters of the Confederacy records, and postwar rosters and histories, all provided useful information.

OFFICERS

CAPTAINS

FARIBAULT, GEORGE H.

Resided in Wake County and was by occupation a planter prior to enlisting in Wake County at age 31. Elected Captain to rank from May 1, 1861. Present or accounted for until appointed Lieutenant Colonel on April 9, 1862, and transferred to the Field and Staff of the 47th Regiment N.C. Troops.

POOLE, WILLIAM T.

Resided in Wake County and was by occupation a planter prior to enlisting in Wake County at age 23, May 1, 1861. Mustered in as Sergeant and was promoted to 1st Sergeant on June 1, 1861. Elected Captain to rank from April 25, 1862. Present or accounted for until killed at Charles Town, West Virginia, August 24, 1864.

HENSON, JEFFERSON M.

Resided in Wake or Rutherford counties and was by occupation a printer prior to enlisting in Wake County at age 28, May 1, 1861. Mustered in as Corporal and promoted to Sergeant on June 1, 1861. Appointed 2nd Lieutenant to rank from April 27, 1862, and was promoted to 1st Lieutenant on June 27, 1862. Promoted to Captain subsequent to September 1, 1864, but prior to April 9, 1865, when he was paroled at Appomattox Court House, Virginia.

LIEUTENANTS

De CARTERET, JOHN Q., 3rd Lieutenant

Was by occupation a bookbinder prior to enlisting in Wake County. Appointed 3rd Lieutenant on or about May 1, 1861. Resigned May 28, 1861. Reason he resigned not reported.

HARRISON, JOHN W., 2nd Lieutenant

Resided in Wake County and was by occupation a merchant prior to enlisting in Wake County at age 26. Elected 2nd Lieutenant to rank from May 1, 1861. Present or accounted for until he was defeated for reelection when the regiment was reorganized April 25-26, 1862.

LEMAY, THOMAS S., 3rd Lieutenant

Resided in Wake County and was by occupation a farmer prior to enlisting in Wake County at age 22, May 1, 1861. Mustered in as Private and was promoted to Commissary Sergeant on August 1, 1862. Appointed 3rd Lieutenant to rank from October 4, 1862. Present or accounted for until wounded at Chancellorsville, Virginia, May 3, 1863. Rejoined the company in September-October, 1863, and present or accounted for until killed near Bethesda Church, Virginia, May 30, 1864.

MITCHELL, JOSEPH L., 2nd Lieutenant

Resided in Wake County and was by occupation a teacher prior to enlisting in Wake County at age 25, May 1, 1861. Mustered in as Private and appointed 3rd Lieutenant to rank from April 27, 1862. Promoted to 2nd Lieutenant on June 27, 1862. Present or accounted for until wounded in the right leg near Bethesda Church, Virginia, May 30, 1864. Reported absent wounded or absent sick through January 29, 1865. Paroled at Raleigh on May 18, 1865.

ROYSTER, JAMES M., 3rd Lieutenant

Resided in Wake County and was by occupation a clerk prior to enlisting in Wake County at age 27, May 1, 1861. Mustered in as 1st Sergeant and appointed 3rd Lieutenant on June 1, 1861, to rank from May 1, 1861. Present or accounted for until defeated for reelection when the regiment was reorganized on April 25, 1862. Later served as Private in Company C, 47th Regiment N.C. Troops.

THOMPSON, WILLIAM MARCELLUS, 1st Lieutenant

Resided in Wake County and was by occupation a planter prior to enlisting in Wake County at age 31. Elected 1st Lieutenant to rank from May 1, 1861. Present or accounted for until killed at Gaines' Mill, Virginia, June 27, 1862.

NONCOMMISSIONED OFFICERS AND PRIVATES

ALLEN, DANIEL S., Private

Resided in Wake County and was by occupation a farmer prior to enlisting in Wake County at age 20, May 1, 1861. Mustered in as Corporal and promoted to Sergeant on November 13, 1861. Reduced to ranks on April 25, 1862. Present or accounted for until he died "at home" in Raleigh on August 5, 1862. Cause of death not reported.

BARLOW, WILLIAM, Private

Resided in Wake County and was by occupation a farmer prior to enlisting in Wake County at age 29, May 1, 1861. Mustered in as Private and promoted to Corporal on April 25, 1862. Present or accounted for until wounded in the arm at Chancellorsville, Virginia, May 3, 1863. Arm amputated. Reduced to ranks in November, 1863-March, 1864. Reported absent wounded until retired to the Invalid Corps on November 11, 1864.

BECK, JOHN M., Private

Resided in Wake County and was by occupation a farmer prior to enlisting in Wake County at age 20, May 1, 1861. Present or accounted for until captured at Sharpsburg, Maryland, September 17, 1862. Confined at Fort Delaware, Delaware, until transferred to Aiken's Landing, James River, Virginia, October 2, 1862, for exchange. Declared exchanged at Aiken's Landing on November 10, 1862. Rejoined the company prior to March 1, 1863, and was wounded at Chancellorsville, Virginia, May 3, 1863. Reported absent wounded through August, 1863. Rejoined the company in September-October, 1863, and present or accounted for until paroled at Appomattox Court House, Virginia, April 9, 1865.

BEDDINGFIELD, JOHN S., Private

Resided in Wake County where he enlisted at age 22, July 1, 1861. Present or accounted for until he died in hospital at Richmond, Virginia, August 2, 1862, of "typhoid fever."

BEDDINGFIELD, JOSEPH H., Private

Born in Wake County where he resided as a farmer prior to enlisting in Wake County at age 29, July 1, 1861. Present or accounted for until killed at Sharpsburg, Maryland, September 17, 1862.

BETHUNE, ANGUS, Private

Resided in Montgomery County and enlisted in Wake County at age 30, July 16, 1862, for the war. Present or accounted for until paroled at Leesburg, Virginia, October 2, 1862; however, place and date captured not reported. Present or accounted for until he died in camp near Fredericksburg, Virginia, January 19, 1863. Cause of death not reported.

BISHOP, WILLIAM G., Private

Resided in Wake County and was by occupation a farmer prior to enlisting in Wake County at age 20, May 1, 1861. Present or accounted for through December 31, 1864; however, he was reported absent sick during most of that period. Captured in hospital at Richmond, Virginia, April 3, 1865, and was paroled at Richmond on April 17, 1865.

BOYKIN, JAMES M., Private

Resided in Wake County and was by occupation a farmer prior to enlisting in Wake County at age 18, May 1, 1861. Present or accounted for until he deserted to the enemy at Clear Springs, Maryland, on or about July 13, 1863. Confined at Wheeling, West Virginia, until transferred to Camp Chase, Ohio, July 22, 1863. Released at Camp Chase on July 21, 1864, after joining the U.S. Navy.

BRUTON, D. ALEXANDER, Private

Resided in Montgomery County and enlisted in Wake County at age 29, July 16, 1862, for the war. Present or accounted for until he deserted at White Hall on October 10, 1862.

CARROLL, JOHN, Private

Resided in Johnston County and enlisted at Camp Holmes at age 38, July 16, 1863, for the war. Present or accounted for until captured at Petersburg, Virginia, April 3, 1865. Confined at Hart's Island, New York Harbor, where he died on May 20, 1865, of "chronic diarrhoea."

CARROLL, RANSOM, Private

Resided in Johnston County and enlisted at Camp Holmes at age 36, September 23, 1863, for the war. Present or accounted for until captured at Winchester, Virginia, September 19, 1864. Confined at Point Lookout, Maryland, where he died February 21, 1865, of "diarrhoea."

CARSON, JOSEPH F., Private

Born in Franklin County and resided in Wake County where he was by occupation a farmer prior to enlisting in Wake County at age 21, May 11, 1861. Present or accounted for until discharged on February 5, 1863. Reason discharged not reported.

CARTER, ALBERT D., Musician

Resided in Wake County and was by occupation a painter prior to enlisting in Wake County at age 20, May 1, 1861. Mustered in as Musician. Present or accounted for until paroled at Appomattox Court House, Virginia, April 9, 1865.

CARTER, CLAIBORNE, Private

Resided in Chatham County and enlisted in Wake County at age 21, July 16, 1862, for the war. Present or accounted for until captured at Sharpsburg, Maryland, September 17, 1862. Confined at Fort Delaware, Delaware, until transferred to Aiken's Landing, James River, Virginia, October 2, 1862, for exchange. Declared exchanged at Aiken's Landing on November 10, 1862. Rejoined the company in January-February, 1863, and present or accounted for until wounded at Spotsylvania Court House, Virginia, May 8, 1864. Reported absent wounded through October, 1864.

CARTER, PETERSON, Private

Resided in Chatham County and enlisted in Wake County at age 26, July 16, 1862, for the war. Present or accounted for until captured at Sharpsburg, Maryland, September 17, 1862. Confined at Fort Delaware, Delaware, until transferred to Aiken's Landing, James River, Virginia, October 2, 1862, for exchange. Declared exchanged at Aiken's Landing on November 10, 1862. Rejoined the company in January-February, 1863, and present or accounted

for until wounded in the left lung and captured at Winchester, Virginia, September 19, 1864. Died in hospital at Winchester on October 6, 1864, of "exhaustion."

CHANCEY, ABRAHAM, Private

Born in Montgomery County where he resided as a farmer prior to enlisting in Wake County at age 32, July 16, 1862, for the war. Present or accounted for until captured at Sharpsburg, Maryland, September 17, 1862. Paroled September 25, 1862. Returned to duty October 8-9, 1862. Discharged February 19, 1863. Reason discharged not reported.

CHISMAN, THOMAS P., Private

Resided in Wake County and was by occupation a druggist prior to enlisting in Wake County at age 22, June 28, 1861. Present or accounted for until he died at Raleigh on January 20, 1863. Cause of death not reported.

COGDILL, JOHN, Private

Place and date of enlistment not reported. Captured in Madison County, July 21, 1864. Confined at Camp Chase, Ohio, where he died September 27, 1864, of "chronic diarrhoea."

COOK, JOHN, Private

Resided in Montgomery County and enlisted in Wake County at age 28, July 16, 1862, for the war. Present or accounted for until captured at Sharpsburg, Maryland, September 17, 1862. Received for exchange at Aiken's Landing, James River, Virginia, October 6, 1862, and declared exchanged at Aiken's Landing on November 10, 1862. Rejoined the company prior to January 1, 1863, and present or accounted for through December, 1864. Paroled at Lynchburg, Virginia, April 13, 1865.

COOLEY, WILLIAM C., Private

Resided in Wake County and was by occupation a farmer prior to enlisting in Wake County at age 21, May 24, 1861. Present or accounted for until captured at Gettysburg, Pennsylvania, July 3-5, 1863. Confined at Fort McHenry, Maryland, and at Fort Delaware, Delaware, until paroled and transferred to City Point, Virginia, where he was received August 1, 1863, for exchange. Rejoined the company in November-December, 1863, and present or accounted for until captured near Bethesda Church, Virginia, May 30, 1864. Confined at Point Lookout, Maryland, until transferred to Elmira, New York, July 9, 1864. Died at Elmira on June 10, 1865, of "chro[nic] diarr[hoea]."

COPE, JOHN S., Private

Resided in Wake County and was by occupation a farmer prior to enlisting in Wake County at age 23, June 28, 1861. Present or accounted for until he died at Guinea Station, Virginia, on or about December 30, 1862. Cause of death not reported.

COZART, BENJAMIN HUBERT, Private

Resided in Orange County and enlisted in Wake County at age 23, July 16, 1862, for the war. Present or accounted for until discharged on April 13, 1863, after providing a substitute.

DAVIS, LEWIS B., Private

Resided in Wake County and was by occupation a farmer prior to enlisting in Wake County at age 25,

May 8, 1861. Present or accounted for until captured at Fisher's Hill, Virginia, September 22, 1864. Confined at Point Lookout, Maryland, until paroled and transferred to Boulware's Wharf, James River, Virginia, where he was received March 19, 1865, for exchange.

DODSON, JEREMIAH, Private
Resided in Stokes County and enlisted at Camp Holmes at age 30, September 11, 1863, for the war. Present or accounted for until wounded in the shoulder while constructing breastworks near Hanover Junction, Virginia, May 24, 1864. Died in hospital at Richmond, Virginia, June 11, 1864. of wounds and/or pneumonia.

DONHOE, WILLIAM, Private
Resided in Montgomery County and enlisted in Wake County at age 23, July 16, 1862, for the war. Present or accounted for until wounded at Sharpsburg, Maryland, September 17, 1862. Reported absent wounded until he died in Caswell County in January, 1863.

EDDINS, JOSEPH H., Private
Born in Wake County where he resided as a farmer prior to enlisting in Wake County at age 37, May 10, 1861. Present or accounted for until discharged July 29, 1862, by reason of being over age.

ELLIS, JASPER, Private
Resided in Montgomery County and enlisted in Wake County at age 25, July 16, 1862, for the war. Present or accounted for until January 1, 1863, when he was reported absent without leave. Reported absent without leave until he rejoined the company on or about January 15, 1864. Present or accounted for through August, 1864. Deserted to the enemy or was captured in North Carolina on or about April 25, 1865. North Carolina pension records indicate he was wounded in the right forearm at Winchester, Virginia, September 19, 1864.

ESTIS, JOHN, Private
Resided in Wake County and was by occupation a farmer prior to enlisting in Wake County at age 18, May 1, 1861. Present or accounted for until he died in camp near Fredericksburg, Virginia, February 5, 1863. Cause of death not reported.

EVANS, WILLIAM Y., Private
Was by occupation a farmer prior to enlisting in Wake County on May 1, 1861. Transferred to Company D, 3rd Regiment N.C. State Troops, on or about June 11, 1861.

FELTON, JOHN H., Sergeant
Resided in Wake County and enlisted at Suffolk, Virginia, at age 21, June 30, 1861. Mustered in as Private. Present or accounted for until wounded and captured at Sharpsburg, Maryland, September 17, 1862. Confined at Fort Delaware, Delaware, until transferred to Aiken's Landing, James River, Virginia, October 2, 1862, for exchange. Declared exchanged at Aiken's Landing on November 10, 1862. Rejoined the company prior to January 1, 1863, and present or accounted for until wounded and captured at Gettysburg, Pennsylvania, July 3, 1863, or at South Mountain, Pennsylvania, July 4-5, 1863. Confined at Fort Delaware. Promoted to

Sergeant in July-August, 1863, while a prisoner of war. Transferred from Fort Delaware to Point Lookout, Maryland, October 15-18, 1863. Paroled at Point Lookout and transferred to Boulware's and Cox's Wharf, James River, Virginia, where he was received February 20-21, 1865, for exchange. Reported present with a detachment of paroled and exchanged prisoners at Camp Lee, near Richmond, Virginia, February 23, 1865.

FERRELL, JESSE J., Private
Born in Wake County where he resided as a farmer prior to enlisting in Wake County at age 24, May 1, 1861. Present or accounted for until discharged on September 26, 1861, by reason of "general debility."

FERRELL, SIMEON D., Private
Born in Wake County where he resided as a schoolteacher prior to enlisting in Wake County at age 20, May 10, 1861. Present or accounted for until captured at Sharpsburg, Maryland, September 17, 1862. Confined at Fort Delaware, Delaware, where he died on or about December 10, 1862. Cause of death not reported.

FINCH, WILLIAM H., Private
Resided in Wake County and was by occupation a clerk prior to enlisting in Wake County at age 24, May 1, 1861. Mustered in as Sergeant but was reduced to ranks in November-December, 1861. Present or accounted for until discharged on July 1, 1862, by reason of being a justice of the peace.

FLOWERS, HARRIS, Private
Born in Wake County where he resided as a farmer prior to enlisting in Wake County at age 28, May 1, 1861. Present or accounted for until discharged on July 27, 1862, under the provisions of the Conscript Act.

FOWLER, JOHN R., Private
Resided in Wake County and was by occupation a hireling prior to enlisting in Wake County at age 23, May 1, 1861. Present or accounted for through August, 1864.

FOX, MOSES M., Private
Resided in Montgomery County and enlisted in Wake County at age 21, July 16, 1862, for the war. Present or accounted for until he deserted at "Charlestown" on October 26, 1862. Reported absent sick in January-February, 1863. Died in hospital at Richmond, Virginia, April 9, 1863, of "pneumonia."

GOODIN, GEORGE L., Private
Born in Wake County where he resided as a carpenter prior to enlisting in Wake County at age 36, May 1, 1861. Present or accounted for until discharged on July 28, 1862, by reason of being over age.

GRADY, BLAKE, Private
Resided in Wake County and was by occupation a farmer prior to enlisting in Wake County at age 21, June 10, 1861. Present or accounted for until captured at Sharpsburg, Maryland, September 17, 1862. Confined at Fort Delaware, Delaware, until transferred to Aiken's Landing, James River, Virginia, October 2, 1862, for exchange. Declared exchanged at Aiken's Landing on November 10, 1862. Rejoined the company prior to January 1,

1863, and present or accounted for until wounded in the leg and captured at Winchester, Virginia, September 19, 1864. Died in hospital at Winchester on October 3, 1864, of "tetanus."

GULLY, JOSEPH G. W., Private
Resided in Wake County and was by occupation a sawyer prior to enlisting in Wake County at age 24, May 1, 1861. Present or accounted for until discharged on or about September 14, 1861. Reason discharged not reported.

HAMILTON, WILLIAM HENRY, Sergeant
Resided in Wake County and was by occupation a gardener prior to enlisting in Wake County at age 28, May 1, 1861. Mustered in as Sergeant. Present or accounted for until wounded in the head and captured at Williamsburg, Virginia, May 5, 1862. "Lost both eyes" as a result of wounds received at Williamsburg. Hospitalized at Williamsburg until transferred to Fort Monroe, Virginia, May 9-11, 1862. Paroled and transferred to City Point, Virginia, June 10, 1862, for exchange. Reduced to ranks prior to January 1, 1863. Reported absent wounded through August, 1864.

HARRISON, HOWELL W., Private
Born in Johnston County where he resided as a cooper prior to enlisting in Wake County at age 21, May 1, 1861. Present or accounted for until transferred to the C.S. Navy for duty on the C.S.S. *Merrimac* on February 15, 1862.

HAYES, WELLINGTON, Private
Resided in Wake County and was by occupation a student prior to enlisting in Wake County at age 19, May 24, 1861. Present or accounted for until he died at Richmond, Virginia, on or about June 1, 1862. Cause of death not reported.

HICKS, JAMES H., Sergeant
Resided in Wake County and was by occupation a farmer prior to enlisting in Wake County at age 19, May 1, 1861. Mustered in as Private and promoted to Sergeant on April 25, 1862. Present or accounted for until captured at Sharpsburg, Maryland, September 17, 1862. Confined at Fort Delaware, Delaware, until transferred to Aiken's Landing, James River, Virginia, October 2, 1862, for exchange. Declared exchanged at Aiken's Landing on November 10, 1862. Rejoined the company prior to January 1, 1863, and present or accounted for until wounded at Chancellorsville, Virginia, May 3, 1863. Died May 4, 1863, of wounds.

HILL, FRANKLIN H., Private
Resided in Montgomery County and enlisted in Wake County at age 38, July 16, 1862, for the war. Present or accounted for until he died at Winchester, Virginia, October 11, 1862. Cause of death not reported.

HILL, JAMES R., Private
Resided in Rabun County, Georgia. Place and date of enlistment not reported. Deserted to the enemy on or about March 18, 1865. Took the Oath of Allegiance at Louisville, Kentucky, March 21, 1865.

HOLDER, JOHN, Private
Resided in Wake County and was by occupation a hireling prior to enlisting in Wake County at age 20,

May 1, 1861. Present or accounted for until wounded and captured at Gettysburg, Pennsylvania, July 3, 1863, or at South Mountain, Pennsylvania, July 4, 1863. Confined at Fort McHenry, Maryland, and at Fort Delaware, Delaware, until transferred to Point Lookout, Maryland, October 15-18, 1863. Released at Point Lookout on January 24, 1864, after taking the Oath of Allegiance and joining the U.S. service. Unit to which assigned not reported.

HOLMES, SIDNEY, Private
Resided in Wake County and was by occupation a hireling prior to enlisting in Wake County at age 18, May 1, 1861. Present or accounted for until killed at Williamsburg, Virginia, May 5, 1862.

HOWELL, NELSON, Private
Born in Wayne County where he resided as a farmer prior to enlisting at Camp Holmes at age 39, September 11, 1863, for the war. Present or accounted for until discharged on January 5, 1864, by reason of "chronic rheumatism." Records of the Federal Provost Marshal indicate he was captured at Goldsboro in March, 1865, and confined at Point Lookout, Maryland, until released on June 19, 1865.

HUBBARD, CULLEN, Private
Resided in Wake County and was by occupation a hireling prior to enlisting in Wake County at age 24, May 1, 1861. Present or accounted for through August, 1864; however, he was reported absent on detached duty as a pioneer during most of that period.

HUBBARD, HENRY, Private
Resided in Orange County. Place and date of enlistment not reported. Deserted to the enemy at Chambersburg, Pennsylvania, or at Hagerstown, Maryland, August 2, 1864. Confined at Fort Delaware, Delaware, until released on May 10, 1865, after taking the Oath of Allegiance.

HUBBARD, JOHN N., Private
Resided in Wake County and was by occupation a farmer prior to enlisting in Wake County at age 20, May 1, 1861. Present or accounted for until hospitalized at Richmond, Virginia, July 7, 1862, with a gunshot wound of the hand; however, place and date wounded not reported. Rejoined the company prior to January 1, 1863. Present or accounted for through August, 1864; however, he was reported on detail as a teamster during most of that period.

HUBBARD, WILLIAM H., Private
Enlisted in Wake County on March 10, 1864, for the war. Present or accounted for until killed near Spotsylvania Court House, Virginia, May 12, 1864.

IVY, CALVIN, Private
Resided in Montgomery County and enlisted at Camp Holmes at age 35, July 16, 1863, for the war. Present or accounted for through October 6, 1864.

JACKSON, CALVIN, Private
Resided in Wayne County and enlisted at Camp Holmes at age 30, September 11, 1863, for the war. Present or accounted for until he died in hospital at Richmond, Virginia, November 21, 1863, of "pneumonia."

JONES, GEORGE, Private

Resided in Wake County and was by occupation a farmer prior to enlisting in Wake County at age 19, May 1, 1861. Present or accounted for until killed at Gaines' Mill, Virginia, June 27, 1862.

KEENER, JAMES M., Private

Place and date of enlistment not reported. Captured in Madison County on July 22, 1864. Confined at Camp Chase, Ohio, where he died November 18, 1864, of "congestion of lungs."

KNIGHT, WILLIAM M., Private

Resided in Montgomery County and enlisted in Wake County at age 35, July 16, 1862, for the war. Present or accounted for until killed at Chancellorsville, Virginia, May 3, 1863.

LAFAYTER, SAMUEL, Private

Resided in Wake County and was by occupation a painter prior to enlisting in Wake County at age 21, May 1, 1861. Present or accounted for until wounded at Seven Pines, Virginia, June 1, 1862. Died in hospital at Richmond, Virginia, June 2, 1862.

LASSITER, GENADIOUS W., Private

Resided in Wake County and was by occupation a farmer prior to enlisting in Wake County at age 20, May 1, 1861. Present or accounted for until he died in hospital at Smithfield, Virginia, April 5, 1862. Cause of death not reported.

LASSITER, HENRY C., Private

Resided in Wake County and was by occupation a carpenter prior to enlisting in Wake County at age 25, May 1, 1861. Mustered in as Private and promoted to Corporal on November 13, 1861. Reduced to ranks in March-December, 1862. Present or accounted for until captured in hospital at Jordan Springs, Virginia, July 26, 1863. Paroled at Jordan Springs on August 2, 1863. Admitted to hospital at Richmond, Virginia, September 7, 1863, with a gunshot wound; however, place and date wounded not reported. Rejoined the company in November-December, 1863, and present or accounted for through August, 1864.

LASSITER, JAMES F., Sergeant

Resided in Wake County and was by occupation a carpenter prior to enlisting in Wake County at age 23, June 11, 1861. Mustered in as Private. Present or accounted for until wounded at Seven Pines, Virginia, May 31-June 1, 1862. Returned to duty prior to December 5, 1862, and was promoted to Sergeant on July 1, 1863. Present or accounted for until paroled at Appomattox Court House, Virginia, April 9, 1865.

LASSITER, WILLIAM T., Private

Resided in Wake County and was by occupation a hireling prior to enlisting in Wake County at age 19, May 13, 1861. Present or accounted for until reported absent without leave in September-December, 1863. Rejoined the company prior to April 1, 1864, and present or accounted for through August, 1864. Deserted to the enemy or was captured prior to April 12, 1865, when he was received at City Point, Virginia. No further records.

LESTER, JOHN, Private

Place and date of enlistment not reported. Captured at Cedar Creek, Virginia, October 19, 1864. Confined at Point Lookout, Maryland, until paroled and transferred to Boulware's Wharf, James River, Virginia, where he was received March 30, 1865, for exchange.

LEWIS, HENRY, Private

Was by occupation a harness maker prior to enlisting in Wake County at age 20, May 1, 1861. Present or accounted for through February, 1862. No further records.

LEWIS, JAMES J., Musician

Resided in Wake County and was by occupation a printer prior to enlisting in Wake County at age 24, May 1, 1861. Mustered in as Musician. Present or accounted for until reported absent without leave from August 20, 1862, through December, 1862. Reduced to ranks in March-December, 1862. Reported under arrest in January-February, 1863, but rejoined the company in March-April, 1863. Hospitalized at Richmond, Virginia, May 20, 1863, with a wound of the left shoulder; however, place and date wounded not reported. Returned to duty on May 23, 1863, and was promoted to Sergeant on November 1, 1863. Reduced to the rank of Musician on July 31, 1864. Present or accounted for until paroled at Appomattox Court House, Virginia, April 9, 1865.

LEWIS, RICHARD H., Private

Resided in Wake County where he enlisted at age 21, May 1, 1861. Present or accounted for until killed near Bethesda Church, Virginia, May 30, 1864.

LOVEJOY, CHARLES, Private

Enlisted on or about January 1, 1862, but was discharged on January 2, 1862, after "declining to take the Oath."

McGRADY, WILLIAM E., Private

Resided in Wake County and was by occupation a teacher prior to enlisting in Wake County at age 26, May 1, 1861. Present or accounted for until discharged on or about September 26, 1861. Reason discharged not reported.

MACON, ISAAC, Private

Resided in Montgomery or Rowan counties and enlisted in Wake County at age 24, July 16, 1862, for the war. Present or accounted for until captured at Sharpsburg, Maryland, September 17, 1862. Confined at Fort Delaware, Delaware, until transferred to Aiken's Landing, James River, Virginia, October 2, 1862, for exchange. Declared exchanged at Aiken's Landing on November 10, 1862. Rejoined the company in January-February, 1863, and was wounded at Chancellorsville, Virginia, May 3, 1863. Reported absent wounded through December, 1863. Rejoined the company prior to April 1, 1864, and present or accounted for until captured in battle at or near the North Anna River, Virginia, on or about May 23, 1864. Confined at Fort Monroe, Virginia, and at Point Lookout, Maryland, until transferred to Elmira, New York, July 25, 1864. Released at Elmira on June 12, 1865, after taking the Oath of Allegiance.

MARTIN, HUGH P., Private
Resided in Rockingham County and enlisted at Camp Holmes at age 21, September 18, 1863, for the war. Present or accounted for until he died in hospital at Richmond, Virginia, June 1, 1864, of "diarrh[oea] chron[ic]."

MARTIN, JOHN M., Private
Born in Wake County where he resided as a coach maker prior to enlisting in Wake County at age 24, May 1, 1861. Present or accounted for until captured at Sharpsburg, Maryland, September 17, 1862. Confined at Fort Delaware, Delaware, until transferred to Aiken's Landing, James River, Virginia, October 2, 1862, for exchange. Declared exchanged at Aiken's Landing on November 10, 1862. Rejoined the company prior to January 1, 1863, and present or accounted for until transferred to the C.S. Navy on or about April 5, 1864.

MARTIN, JOSEPH B., Sergeant
Resided in Wake County and was by occupation a student prior to enlisting in Wake County at age 20, May 1, 1861. Mustered in as Private and promoted to Corporal in July-August, 1863. Promoted to Sergeant on November 1, 1863. Present or accounted for until wounded in the left thigh and captured at Winchester, Virginia, September 19, 1864. Hospitalized at Winchester until transferred to hospital at Baltimore, Maryland, on or about October 19, 1864. Transferred to Point Lookout, Maryland, on or about October 29, 1864. Confined at Point Lookout until paroled and transferred to Venus Point, Savannah River, Georgia, where he was received November 15, 1864, for exchange.

MASON, WILLIAM, Private
Born in Montgomery County where he resided as a farmer prior to enlisting in Wake County at age 30, July 16, 1862, for the war. Present or accounted for until captured at Frederick, Maryland, September 12, 1862. Confined at Fort Delaware, Delaware, until transferred to Aiken's Landing, James River, Virginia, October 2, 1862, for exchange. Declared exchanged at Aiken's Landing on November 10, 1862. Reported absent sick until he died in hospital at Richmond, Virginia, May 1, 1863. Cause of death not reported.

MEARS, JOEL, Private
Resided in Montgomery County and enlisted in Wake County at age 30, July 16, 1862, for the war. Present or accounted for until captured at or near Sharpsburg, Maryland, on or about September 17, 1862. Confined at Fort Delaware, Delaware, until transferred to Aiken's Landing, James River, Virginia, October 2, 1862, for exchange. Died in hospital at Richmond, Virginia, October 24, 1862, of "diarrhoea chronica."

MESSER, ALEXANDER, Private
Resided in Johnston County and enlisted at Camp Holmes at age 38, July 16, 1863, for the war. Present or accounted for until hospitalized at Charlottesville, Virginia, October 24, 1864, with a gunshot wound of the face; however, place and date wounded not reported. Died prior to January 1, 1865. Place, cause, and exact date of death not reported.

MOONEYHAM, WILLIAM A., Private
Born in Wake County where he resided as a farmer prior to enlisting in Wake County at age 24, May 13, 1861. Present or accounted for until discharged on August 3, 1862, under the provisions of the Conscript Act.

MOORE, JOSEPH J., Private
Resided in Moore County and enlisted in Wake County at age 26, July 16, 1862, for the war. Present or accounted for until he deserted at Leesburg, Virginia, August 27, 1862.

NICHOLS, WILLIAM R., Private
Resided in Wake County and was by occupation a farmer prior to enlisting in Wake County at age 18, May 15, 1861. Present or accounted for until wounded in a skirmish at Warrenton, Virginia, on or about October 14, 1863. Reported absent wounded until retired to the Invalid Corps on April 26, 1864. Took the Oath of Allegiance at Salisbury on June 10, 1865.

NORWOOD, THOMAS L., Private
Resided in Wake County and was by occupation a farmer prior to enlisting in Wake County at age 23, May 21, 1861. Present or accounted for until wounded at Chancellorsville, Virginia, May 1-3, 1863. Rejoined the company prior to July 1, 1863, and present or accounted for until he deserted to the enemy or was captured on or about April 12, 1865.

NORWOOD, WILLIAM L., Private
Resided in Haywood County. Place and date of enlistment not reported. Deserted to the enemy on or about February 28, 1865. Took the Oath of Allegiance at Louisville, Kentucky, March 10, 1865.

OVERBY, WASHINGTON W., Private
Resided in Wake County and was by occupation a farmer prior to enlisting in Wake County at age 23, May 1, 1861. Present or accounted for until wounded near Bethesda Church, Virginia, May 30, 1864. Reported absent wounded until retired to the Invalid Corps on December 1, 1864.

OVERTON, SAMUEL, Private
Resided in Montgomery County and enlisted in Wake County at age 23, July 16, 1862, for the war. Present or accounted for until wounded and captured at Sharpsburg, Maryland, September 17, 1862. Paroled September 23, 1862. Died of wounds received at Sharpsburg; however, place and date of death not reported.

PAGE, JOHN W., Private
Resided in Wake County and was by occupation a doctor prior to enlisting in Wake County at age 28, May 1, 1861. Present or accounted for until discharged on June 27, 1863, when he was promoted and transferred to the C.S.A. Medical Department.

PARKER, WILLIAM C., Sergeant
Born in Guilford County and resided in Wake County where he was by occupation a tailor or city policeman prior to enlisting in Wake County at age 35, May 1, 1861. Mustered in as Corporal and was promoted to Sergeant on April 25, 1862. Present or accounted for until discharged on July 29, 1862, by reason of being over age.

PARKS, AUGUSTUS W., Private

Born in Rowan County and was by occupation a cabinetmaker prior to enlisting at Camp Holmes on August 1, 1863, for the war. Present or accounted for until reported absent wounded on September 10, 1863. Battle in which wounded not reported. Discharged on December 2, 1863, by reason of "ascites." Discharge papers give his age as 38.

PENNY, CALVIN D., Private

Resided in Wake County and was by occupation a farmer prior to enlisting in Wake County at age 20, May 1, 1861. Present or accounted for until killed at Malvern Hill, Virginia, July 1, 1862.

PENNY, JOHN A. J., Private

Resided in Wake County and was by occupation a doctor prior to enlisting in Wake County at age 19, May 1, 1861. Present or accounted for until paroled at Appomattox Court House, Virginia, April 9, 1865; however, he was reported on detail as a hospital attendant or apothecary during most or that period.

PENNY, JOHN H., Private

Resided in Wake County and was by occupation a clerk prior to enlisting in Wake County at age 21, June 11, 1861. Mustered in as Private and promoted to Sergeant on October 1, 1862. Present or accounted for until wounded in the right thigh at Chancellorsville, Virginia, May 3, 1863. Reduced to ranks in November-December, 1863. Reported absent wounded until retired to the Invalid Corps on February 13, 1865.

POLLARD, BARZILLIA B., Private

Enlisted in Wake County on January 29, 1864, for the war. Present or accounted for until wounded in the left leg and captured at Cedar Creek, Virginia, October 19, 1864. Hospitalized at Baltimore, Maryland, until confined at Point Lookout, Maryland, October 26, 1864. Paroled at Point Lookout and transferred to Venus Point, Savannah River, Georgia, where he was received November 15, 1864, for exchange.

POOLE, HINTON, Private

Resided in Wake County and was by occupation a farmer prior to enlisting in Wake County at age 27, May 16, 1861. Present or accounted for until reported absent without leave on October 19, 1862. Rejoined the company in January-February, 1863, and present or accounted for until wounded in the forehead and captured at Gettysburg, Pennsylvania, July 2-3, 1863, or at South Mountain, Maryland, July 5, 1863. Confined at Fort McHenry, Maryland, and at Fort Delaware, Delaware, until transferred to Point Lookout, Maryland, October 15-18, 1863. Confined at Point Lookout until he died on May 1, 1865, of "chronic diarrhoea."

POOLE, JOHN M., Private

Born in Orange County and resided in Wake County where he was by occupation a farmer or planter prior to enlisting in Wake County at age 54, May 1, 1861. Present or accounted for until discharged on July 29, 1862, by reason of being over age.

POOLE, RUFUS, Corporal

Resided in Wake County and was by occupation a

farmer prior to enlisting in Wake County at age 19, May 1, 1861. Mustered in as Private. Present or accounted for until wounded in the right arm at Chancellorsville, Virginia, May 3, 1863. Rejoined the company in November-December, 1863, and present or accounted for until captured at Petersburg, Virginia, April 2, 1865. Confined at Hart's Island, New York Harbor, until released on June 17, 1865, after taking the Oath of Allegiance. Rank given on Oath as Corporal. North Carolina pension records indicate he was wounded at Winchester, Virginia.

POOLE, WILLIAM URIAS, 1st Sergeant

Resided in Wake County and was by occupation a student prior to enlisting in Wake County at age 19, May 1, 1861. Mustered in as Private and promoted to 1st Sergeant on April 25, 1862. Present or accounted for until killed at Chancellorsville, Virginia, May 3, 1863. Nominated for the Badge of Distinction for gallantry at Chancellorsville.

POWERS, LEWIS H., Private

Resided in Wake County and was by occupation a farmer prior to enlisting in Wake County at age 22, June 28, 1861. Present or accounted for until killed at Williamsburg, Virginia, May 5, 1862.

RAY, CHARLES W., Private

Resided in Wake County and was by occupation a farmer prior to enlisting in Wake County at age 22, May 1, 1861. Mustered in as Private and promoted to Corporal on November 13, 1861. Reduced to ranks on April 23, 1862. Present or accounted for until killed at Payne's Farm, Virginia, November 27-28, 1863.

RAY, WILEY P., Private

Resided in Wake County and enlisted at Camp Holmes at age 38, October 16, 1863, for the war. Present or accounted for through August, 1864.

RIGSBY, THOMAS, Private

Resided in Wake County and enlisted at Bowling Green, Virginia, at age 45, April 13, 1863, for the war as a substitute. Present or accounted for until captured at Petersburg, Virginia, April 3, 1865. Confined at Hart's Island, New York Harbor, until released on June 17, 1865, after taking the Oath of Allegiance.

ROBERTSON, JAMES M., Private

Resided in Montgomery County and enlisted in Wake County at age 28, July 16, 1862, for the war. Present or accounted for until he deserted at White Hall on October 10, 1862. Rejoined the company in July-August, 1863, and present or accounted for until wounded at or near Spotsylvania Court House, Virginia, May 19, 1864. Reported absent wounded until retired to the Invalid Corps on December 13, 1864.

ROGERS, GEORGE S., Corporal

Resided in Wake County and was by occupation a student prior to enlisting in Wake County at age 18, May 1, 1861. Mustered in as Private and promoted to Corporal on October 1, 1862. Present or accounted for until killed at Chancellorsville, Virginia, May 3, 1863.

ROGERS, JOSEPH T., Ensign

Resided in Wake County and was by occupation a

farmer prior to enlisting in Wake County at age 25, May 1, 1861. Mustered in as Private and promoted to Corporal on May 30, 1861. Reduced to ranks on April 25, 1862. Present or accounted for until wounded in the right shoulder and captured at Malvern Hill, Virginia, on or about July 2, 1862. Confined at Fort Delaware, Delaware, until exchanged at Aiken's Landing, James River, Virginia, August 5, 1862. Present or accounted for until appointed Ensign on June 22, 1864, to rank from June 17, 1864. Company records do not indicate whether he was transferred to the Field and Staff; however, he was present or accounted for through December 29, 1864.

ROSS, LUICO R., Private
Resided in Wake County and was by occupation a farmer prior to enlisting in Wake County at age 23, May 1, 1861. Present or accounted for until wounded at Chancellorsville, Virginia, May 3, 1863. Rejoined the company in September-October, 1863, and present or accounted for until wounded in the left arm at Spotsylvania Court House, Virginia, May 8, 1864. Reported absent wounded until retired to the Invalid Corps on February 13, 1865.

ROSS, RICHARD S., Private
Resided in Wake County and was by occupation a farmer prior to enlisting in Wake County at age 46, May 26, 1861. Present or accounted for until discharged on or about September 4, 1861. Reason discharged not reported.

RUSSELL, MORTON, Private
Resided in Montgomery County and enlisted in Wake County at age 20, July 16, 1862, for the war. Present or accounted for until killed at Sharpsburg, Maryland, September 17, 1862.

RUSSELL, ZACHARIAH, Private
Resided in Montgomery County and enlisted in Wake County at age 19, July 16, 1862, for the war. Present or accounted for until killed at Sharpsburg, Maryland, September 17, 1862.

SAUNDERS, AARON, Private
Resided in Montgomery County and enlisted in Wake County at age 25, July 16, 1862, for the war. Present or accounted for until killed at Sharpsburg, Maryland, September 17, 1862

SHAW, WILLIAM H. H., Private
Resided in Wake County and was by occupation a farmer prior to enlisting in Wake County at age 18, May 1, 1861. Mustered in as Private and promoted to Sergeant on October 1, 1862. Present or accounted for until wounded in the leg at Chancellorsville, Virginia, May 3, 1863. Reduced to ranks in November-December, 1863. Reported absent wounded until retired to the Invalid Corps on December 1, 1864.

SMITH, ELIJAH D., Private
Resided in Wake County and was by occupation a farmer prior to enlisting in Wake County at age 24, May 21, 1861. Present or accounted for until killed at Malvern Hill, Virginia, July 1, 1862.

SMITH, RUFUS, Sergeant
Resided in Wake County and was by occupation a farmer prior to enlisting in Wake County at age 23,

May 1, 1861. Mustered in as Private. Present or accounted for until wounded at Chancellorsville, Virginia, May 3, 1863. Promoted to Corporal on May 12, 1863. Rejoined the company in November-December, 1863, and was promoted to Sergeant in September, 1864-April, 1865. Present or accounted for until wounded in the right thigh and captured at Appomattox Court House, Virginia, April 9, 1865. Hospitalized at various Federal hospitals until confined at Fort McHenry, Maryland, May 9, 1865. Released June 12, 1865, after taking the Oath of Allegiance.

SMITH, RUFUS WADSWORTH, Private
Resided in Wake County and was by occupation a butcher prior to enlisting in Wake County at age 23, May 22, 1861. Mustered in as Private and promoted to Corporal on April 25, 1862. Reduced to ranks in July-August, 1863, but was promoted to Corporal on December 1, 1863. Reduced to ranks on May 30, 1864. Present or accounted for until captured at Port Republic, Virginia, September 25-26, 1864. Confined at Point Lookout, Maryland, until paroled and transferred to Boulware's Wharf, James River, Virginia, where he was received March 19, 1865, for exchange.

SMITH, THOMAS J., 1st Sergeant
Resided in Wake County and was by occupation a nurseryman prior to enlisting in Wake County at age 21, May 1, 1861. Mustered in as Private and promoted to Corporal on April 25, 1862. Promoted to Sergeant on October 1, 1862, and promoted to 1st Sergeant on May 12, 1863. Present or accounted for until wounded in the left leg at Gettysburg, Pennsylvania, July 3, 1863. Rejoined the company in November-December, 1863, and present or accounted for until captured at Spotsylvania Court House, Virginia, May 20, 1864. Confined at Point Lookout, Maryland, until transferred to Venus Point, Savannah River, Georgia, where he was received November 15, 1864, for exchange. Rejoined the company prior to April 6, 1865, when he was captured at Amelia Court House, Virginia. Confined at Point Lookout until released on June 20, 1865, after taking the Oath of Allegiance.

STEPHENSON, ALVIN, Private
Enlisted at Camp Holmes on July 16, 1863, for the war. Present or accounted for until furloughed for thirty days on September 2, 1864.

STURDIVANT, WILLIAM A., Private
Resided in Wake County and was by occupation a farmer prior to enlisting in Wake County at age 24, May 1, 1861. Mustered in as Private and promoted to Corporal on October 1, 1862. Reduced to ranks in July-August, 1863. Present or accounted for until wounded at Wilderness, Virginia, May 6, 1864. Reported absent wounded or absent sick until he returned to duty on October 9, 1864. Paroled at Appomattox Court House, Virginia, April 9, 1865. Roll of Honor indicates that he received the Badge of Honor for meritorious conduct in battle.

TAYLOR, SIDNEY R., Private
Born in Wake County where he resided as a printer prior to enlisting in Wake County at age 20, May 1, 1861. Mustered in as Private and promoted to Lance

Corporal in November-December, 1861. Reduced to ranks on April 25, 1862. Present or accounted for until he died in hospital at Richmond, Virginia, December 25-26, 1862, of "pneumonia."

TERRELL, THOMAS G., Corporal

Resided in Wake County where he enlisted at age 20, July 1, 1861. Mustered in as Private and was promoted to Corporal in March-September, 1862. Present or accounted for until he died at Leesburg, Virginia, on or about September 25, 1862. Cause of death not reported.

THOMAS, WILLIAM O., Private

Resided in Wake County and was by occupation a farmer prior to enlisting in Wake County at age 21, June 10, 1861. Present or accounted for until he died at Staunton, Virginia, December 12-13, 1862, of "carditis."

THOMPSON, MICHAEL SHELL, Private

Resided in Wake County and was by occupation a farmer prior to enlisting in Wake County at age 19, May 1, 1861. Present or accounted for through September 29, 1864; however, he was reported absent sick or absent on detail during most of that period.

TURNER, E. N., Private

Place and date of enlistment not reported. Hospitalized at Farmville, Virginia, April 7, 1865, and died April 26, 1865. Cause of death not reported.

UTLEY, JOHN R., Private

Resided in Wake County and was by occupation a farmer prior to enlisting in Wake County at age 34, May 1, 1861. Present or accounted for until killed at Malvern Hill, Virginia, July 1, 1862.

VAUGHAN, WILLIAM H., Chief Musician

Born in Franklin County and resided in Wake County where he was by occupation a "moulder" prior to enlisting in Wake County at age 29, May 1, 1861. Mustered in as Musician and appointed Drum Major on June 3, 1861. Promoted to Chief Musician in November-December, 1861. Present or accounted for until discharged on August 18, 1862, by reason of disability.

WADFORD, WILLIAM, Private

Resided in Wake County and was by occupation a farmer prior to enlisting in Wake County at age 23, May 1, 1861. Present or accounted for until captured at South Mountain, Maryland, September 14, 1862. Confined at Fort Delaware, Delaware, until transferred to Aiken's Landing, James River, Virginia, October 2, 1862, for exchange. Declared exchanged at Aiken's Landing on November 10, 1862. Reported "in arrest" in January-February, 1863, but rejoined the company prior to May 1, 1863. Present or accounted for through August, 1864.

WARD, E. W., Private

Resided in Chatham County and enlisted at Camp Holmes at age 38, September 11, 1863, for the war. Present or accounted for until he died at Lynchburg, Virginia, November 20, 1863, of "diarrhoea chron[ic]."

WARD, WILLIAM T., Private

Resided in Chatham County and enlisted at Camp Holmes at age 20, October 1, 1863, for the war.

Present or accounted for until paroled at Appomattox Court House, Virginia, April 9, 1865.

WARREN, JOHN, Private

Born in Wake or Nash counties and resided in Wake County where he was by occupation a farmer prior to enlisting in Wake County at age 30, May 1, 1861. Present or accounted for until discharged on January 28, 1862, by reason of "debility resulting from typhoid fever, and chronic dyspepsia."

WATKINS, DAVID, Private

Resided in Wake County and was by occupation a farmer prior to enlisting in Wake County at age 28, May 7, 1861. Present or accounted for until wounded in the right arm and captured at Gettysburg, Pennsylvania, July 1-3, 1863. Right arm amputated. Hospitalized at Gettysburg and at Baltimore, Maryland, until paroled and transferred to City Point, Virginia, where he was received September 27, 1863, for exchange. Reported absent wounded through August, 1864.

WATKINS, WILEY W. W., Private

Resided in Wake County and was by occupation a millwright prior to enlisting in Wake County at age 27, May 10, 1861. Present or accounted for until wounded in the left arm and right knee at Chancellorsville, Virginia, May 3, 1863. Left arm amputated. Reported absent wounded through August, 1864.

WHITAKER, RUFUS H., Private

Resided in Wake County and was by occupation a farmer prior to enlisting in Wake County at age 23, June 29, 1861. Present or accounted for until captured at Sharpsburg, Maryland, September 17, 1862. Confined at Fort Delaware, Delaware, until transferred to Aiken's Landing, James River, Virginia, October 2, 1862, for exchange. Declared exchanged at Aiken's Landing on November 10, 1862. Rejoined the company prior to January 1, 1863, and present or accounted for until wounded in the back at Spotsylvania Court House, Virginia, May 12, 1864. Died in hospital at Richmond, Virginia, May 24, 1864, of wounds.

WILSON, JEFFERSON J., Private

Resided in Wake County and was by occupation a student prior to enlisting in Wake County at age 18, May 1, 1861. Present or accounted for until discharged on or about August 5, 1862, under the provisions of the Conscript Act.

WOODRO, JOSEPH, Private

Born in Orange County and resided in Wake County where he was by occupation a student prior to enlisting in Wake County at age 18, May 4, 1861. Present or accounted for until discharged on July 29, 1862, under the provisions of the Conscript Act.

WOODS, JAMES M., Private

Resided in Wake County and was by occupation a farmer prior to enlisting in Wake County at age 30, May 1, 1861. Mustered in as Corporal and promoted to Sergeant on November 13, 1861. Reduced to ranks on April 25, 1862. Present or accounted for until wounded at Chancellorsville, Virginia, May 3, 1863. Rejoined the company in September-October, 1863, and present or accounted for until killed at Wilderness, Virginia, May 6, 1864.

WOODS, LAMBERT, Sergeant

Resided in Wake County and was by occupation a farmer prior to enlisting in Wake County at age 28, May 1, 1861. Mustered in as Private and promoted to Sergeant on April 25, 1862. Present or accounted for until killed at Seven Pines, Virginia, May 31-June 1, 1862.

WOOLEY, ROBERT, Private

Resided in Montgomery County and enlisted in Wake County at age 34, July 16, 1862, for the war. Present or accounted for until wounded and captured at Sharpsburg, Maryland, September 17, 1862. Paroled at Keedysville, Maryland, September 20, 1862. Roll of Honor indicates he died in hospital at Winchester, Virginia. Date and cause of death not reported.

WORKMAN, ADDISON F., Private

Resided in Chatham County and enlisted in Wake County at age 18, November 25, 1863, for the war. Present or accounted for until wounded near Bethesda Church, Virginia, May 30, 1864. Reported absent wounded through August, 1864, but rejoined the company prior to September 22, 1864, when he was captured at Fisher's Hill, Virginia. Confined at Point Lookout, Maryland, until paroled and transferred to Cox's Landing, James River, Virginia, where he was received February 14-15, 1865, for exchange. Rejoined the company prior to April 3, 1865, when he was captured at Petersburg, Virginia. Confined at Point Lookout until released on June 17, 1865, after taking the Oath of Allegiance.

YARBOROUGH, BAILEY M., Private

Resided in Wake County and was by occupation a hotel keeper prior to enlisting in Wake County at age 21, May 1, 1861. Present or accounted for until he died in hospital at Richmond, Virginia, January 14, 1863, of "pneumonia typhoides."

YEARGIN, WYATT M., Private

Resided in Wake County and was by occupation a farmer prior to enlisting in Wake County at age 23, June 27, 1861. Present or accounted for until discharged on September 1, 1861. Reason discharged not reported.

YEARLY, LEMUEL A. M., Private

Born in Wake County where he resided as a merchant's clerk prior to enlisting in Wake County at age 22, May 1, 1861. Present or accounted for until discharged December 1, 1861, by reason of "the effects of severe and protracted typhoid fever."

YOUNG, WILLIAM T., Corporal

Resided in Wake County and was by occupation a farmer prior to enlisting in Wake County at age 25, May 1, 1861. Mustered in as Private. Present or accounted for until captured at Sharpsburg, Maryland, September 17, 1862. Confined at Fort Delaware, Delaware, until transferred to Aiken's Landing, James River, Virginia, October 2, 1862, for exchange. Declared exchanged at Aiken's Landing on November 10, 1862. Rejoined the company prior to March 1, 1863, and promoted to Corporal in July-August, 1863. Present or accounted for until wounded in the head and captured at Gettysburg, Pennsylvania, July 3, 1863. Confined at Fort Delaware and at Point Lookout, Maryland, until

paroled and transferred to City Point, Virginia, where he was received April 30, 1864, for exchange. Rejoined the company prior to September 22, 1864, when he was captured at Fisher's Hill, Virginia. Confined at Point Lookout until paroled and transferred to Boulware's Wharf, James River, Virginia, where he was received March 19, 1865, for exchange.

COMPANY F

This company, known as the Rough and Ready Guards, was from Buncombe County and enlisted at Asheville on May 3, 1861. It left Asheville for Statesville on the same day and arrived there on May 6. From Statesville the company moved to Raleigh, where it arrived on May 25. On June 1 it moved from Raleigh to Garysburg. There it was assigned to this regiment as Company F. After joining the regiment the company functioned as part of the regiment, and its history for the war period is recorded as a part of the regimental history.

The information contained in the following roster of the company was compiled principally from company muster rolls for May, 1861, through August 31, 1864. No company muster rolls were found for the period after August 31, 1864. In addition to the company muster rolls, Roll of Honor records, receipt rolls, hospital records, prisoner of war records, and other primary records, supplemented by state pension applications, United Daughters of the Confederacy records, and postwar rosters and histories, all provided useful information.

OFFICERS
CAPTAINS

VANCE, ZEBULON BAIRD

Born in Buncombe County where he resided as a lawyer prior to enlisting in Buncombe County at age 30. Elected Captain on May 3, 1861. Present or accounted for until elected Colonel of the 26th Regiment N.C. Troops on August 27, 1861.

ROBERTS, PHILETUS W.

Resided in Buncombe County and was by occupation a lawyer prior to enlisting at age 37. Elected 1st Lieutenant on May 3, 1861, and was elected Captain to rank from September 20, 1861. Present or accounted for until promoted to Colonel on or about April 27, 1862, and transferred to the Field and Staff of this regiment.

GUDGER, JAMES M.

Resided in Buncombe County and was by occupation a farmer prior to enlisting in Buncombe County at age 24. Elected 2nd Lieutenant to rank from May 4, 1861, and was promoted to Captain on or about April 27, 1862. Present or accounted for until wounded at or near Seven Pines, Virginia, "June 23, 1862." Rejoined the company in March-April, 1863, and present or accounted for until wounded at Spotsylvania Court House, Virginia, May 12, 1864. Reported absent wounded through February 25, 1865.

LIEUTENANTS

BROWN, SAMUEL S., 3rd Lieutenant
Resided in Buncombe County and was by occupation a farmer prior to enlisting in Buncombe County at age 24. Elected 3rd Lieutenant to rank from May 4, 1861. Present or accounted for until he died on or about February 28, 1862. Place and cause of death not reported.

GUDGER, WILLIAM McCREE, 2nd Lieutenant
Resided in Buncombe County and was by occupation a farmer prior to enlisting in Buncombe County at age 19, May 3, 1861. Mustered in as Private and promoted to Corporal on April 25, 1862. Promoted to Sergeant on December 10, 1863, and was elected 2nd Lieutenant on October 5, 1864. Present or accounted for until paroled at Appomattox Court House, Virginia, April 9, 1865.

HARNEY, FRANK M., 1st Lieutenant
Resided in Buncombe County and was by occupation a carpenter prior to enlisting in Buncombe County at age 23, May 3, 1861. Mustered in as 1st Sergeant and was appointed 2nd Lieutenant to rank from March 7, 1862. Elected 1st Lieutenant on or about April 27, 1862. Present or accounted for until wounded at Gettysburg, Pennsylvania, July 1, 1863, after capturing "with his own hands" the colors of the 68th Michigan Regiment or the 150th Pennsylvania Regiment. Died July 2, 1863, of wounds.

HERNDON, EDWARD W., 1st Lieutenant
Resided in Buncombe County where he enlisted at age 22, May 3, 1861. Mustered in as Private and appointed 1st Lieutenant to rank from September 20, 1861. Present or accounted for until defeated for reelection when the regiment was reorganized on April 25, 1862. Later served as Assistant Quartermaster (Major) on the staff of Brigadier General Robert B. Vance.

JOHNSTON, THOMAS DILLARD, 2nd Lieutenant
Resided in Buncombe County and was by occupation a lawyer prior to enlisting in Buncombe County at age 21, May 3, 1861. Mustered in as Sergeant and was appointed 2nd Lieutenant to rank from April 27, 1862. Present or accounted for until wounded at Malvern Hill, Virginia, July 1, 1862. Reported absent wounded until transferred to Thomas's Legion in December, 1862-April, 1863, upon appointment as Assistant Quartermaster (Captain).

MURRAY, GEORGE W., 1st Lieutenant
Resided in Buncombe County and was by occupation a farmer prior to enlisting in Buncombe County at age 27, May 3, 1861. Mustered in as Private and was elected 3rd Lieutenant to rank from April 27, 1862. Promoted to 2nd Lieutenant on April 27, 1863. Present or accounted for until wounded at Chancellorsville, Virginia, May 1-3, 1863. Rejoined the company prior to July 1, 1863, and was promoted to 1st Lieutenant on March 1, 1864. Present or accounted for until killed at Spotsylvania Court House, Virginia, May 12, 1864.

WILLIAMS, GAY M., 2nd Lieutenant
Resided in Buncombe County and was by occupation a farmer prior to enlisting in Buncombe County at age 24, May 17, 1861. Mustered in as Private and promoted to Sergeant in March-April, 1862. Appointed 3rd Lieutenant on April 27, 1862. Present or accounted for until wounded at Chancellorsville, Virginia, May 3, 1863. Rejoined the company in September-October, 1863, and was promoted to 2nd Lieutenant on March 1, 1864. Present or accounted for until wounded at Spotsylvania Court House, Virginia, May 19, 1864. Reported absent wounded through August, 1864, but rejoined the company prior to September 19, 1864, when he was captured at Winchester, Virginia. Confined at Fort Delaware, Delaware, until released on June 14, 1865, after taking the Oath of Allegiance.

NONCOMMISSIONED OFFICERS AND PRIVATES

ALEXANDER, JAMES M., Private
Resided in Buncombe County and was by occupation a merchant prior to enlisting in Buncombe County at age 24, May 3, 1861. Present or accounted for until transferred to Company K, 60th Regiment N.C. Troops, on or about September 25, 1862.

ALLEN, ROBERT M., Private
Born in Alamance County* and resided in Buncombe County where he was by occupation a mechanic or coach maker prior to enlisting in Buncombe County at age 29, May 3, 1861. Present or accounted for until discharged on August 15, 1861, by reason of disability.

BAIRD, ISRAEL VICTOR, Private
Born in Buncombe County where he resided as a farmer prior to enlisting in Buncombe County at age 20, May 3, 1861. Mustered in as Corporal but was reduced to ranks in March-April, 1862. Present or accounted for until appointed 2nd Lieutenant on or about April 27, 1862, and transferred to Company G, 64th Regiment N.C. Troops.

BIAS, WILLIAM M., Private
Born in Buncombe County and was by occupation a farmer prior to enlisting at Camp Ellis, Virginia, August 7, 1861. Present or accounted for until discharged January 18, 1863, by reason of being under age. Discharge papers give his age as 17.

BRITTAIN, J. H., Private
Resided in Buncombe County and enlisted at Camp Ellis, Virginia, at age 27, August 7, 1861. Present or accounted for until he died in hospital at Richmond, Virginia, on or about June 24, 1862, of "feb[ris] remitt[ent]."

BRITTAIN, JAMES, Private
Born in Buncombe County where he resided as a tanner prior to enlisting in Buncombe County at age 58, May 3, 1861. Present or accounted for until discharged on August 2, 1862, by reason of being over age.

BRITTAIN, JOSEPH McCORD, Private
Born in Buncombe County where he resided as a farmer prior to enlisting in Buncombe County at age 23, May 3, 1861. Present or accounted for until discharged on December 10, 1861, by reason of "a severe cut with an axe across and just above the toes

of the right foot." Date of injury given as October 10, 1861.

BROADSTREET, JOSEPH R., Private

Born in Cass County, Georgia, and resided in Buncombe County where he was by occupation a farmer prior to enlisting in Buncombe County at age 16, May 3, 1861. Present or accounted for until discharged on August 2, 1862, by reason of being under age.

BROOKS, THOMAS B., Private

Resided in Buncombe County and was by occupation a farmer prior to enlisting in Buncombe County at age 23, June 17, 1861. Present or accounted for until captured at or near Sharpsburg, Maryland, on or about September 15, 1862. Confined at Fort Delaware, Delaware, until transferred to Aiken's Landing, James River, Virginia, October 2, 1862, for exchange. Declared exchanged at Aiken's Landing on November 10, 1862. Rejoined the company in January-February, 1863, and present or accounted for until wounded in the left thigh at Gettysburg, Pennsylvania, July 1, 1863. Captured at Gettysburg, July 3-5, 1863, or at South Mountain, Maryland, July 5, 1863. Confined at Fort Delaware until paroled and transferred to City Point, Virginia, where he was received August 1, 1863, for exchange. Reported absent wounded until he deserted on January 20, 1864. Took the Oath of Allegiance at Nashville, Tennessee, April 5, 1865.

BROWN, WILLIAM C., Private

Resided in Buncombe County and was by occupation a lawyer prior to enlisting in Buncombe County at age 29, June 17, 1861. Present or accounted for until appointed Assistant Quartermaster (Captain) on September 28, 1861, and transferred to the Field and Staff of this regiment.

BYERS, CHARLES R. P., Private

Resided in Buncombe County and was by occupation an editor prior to enlisting in Buncombe County at age 29, May 3, 1861. Present or accounted for until captured at Hagerstown, Maryland, in September, 1862. Received at Aiken's Landing, James River, Virginia, October 6, 1862, for exchange. Declared exchanged at Aiken's Landing on November 10, 1862. Died at Asheville on November 27, 1862, of disease.

BYRD, JAMES T., Private

Resided in Montgomery County and enlisted in Wake County on July 24, 1863, for the war. Present or accounted for until paroled at Appomattox Court House, Virginia, April 9, 1865.

CAMPBELL, E., Private

Resided in Montgomery County and enlisted in Wake County at age 20, July 16, 1862, for the war. Present or accounted for until reported absent without leave on September 19, 1862. Rejoined the company in January-February, 1863, and present or accounted for until wounded at Spotsylvania Court House, Virginia, May 12, 1864. Reported absent wounded through August, 1864. Paroled at Appomattox Court House, Virginia, April 9, 1865.

CANDLER, CHARLES Z., Sergeant

Previously served in Company I, 25th Regiment N.C.

Troops. Transferred to this company on or about September 24, 1861, with the rank of Private. Promoted to Sergeant on April 27, 1862. Present or accounted for until he died in hospital at Richmond, Virginia, July 16, 1862, of disease.

CANDLER, THOMAS J., Private

Resided in Buncombe County and was by occupation a farmer prior to enlisting in Buncombe County at age 20, May 3, 1861. Present or accounted for until appointed 1st Lieutenant on July 15, 1862, and transferred to Company E, 60th Regiment N.C. Troops.

CAUBLE, HENRY W., Private

Resided in Buncombe County and was by occupation a farmer prior to enlisting in Buncombe County at age 30, May 3, 1861. Present or accounted for until wounded at Malvern Hill, Virginia, July 1, 1862. Rejoined the company prior to December 1, 1862, and present or accounted for through August, 1864. Paroled at Greensboro on or about April 29, 1865.

CAUBLE, PETER, Private

Born in Buncombe County where he resided as a farmer prior to enlisting in Buncombe County at age 28, May 3, 1861. Present or accounted for until he died in hospital at Richmond, Virginia, July 3, 1862, of "feb[ris] typh[oid]."

CHAMBERS, ELIHU, Private

Resided in Buncombe County and was by occupation a farmer prior to enlisting in Buncombe County at age 26, May 3, 1861. Present or accounted for until transferred to the 16th Regiment N.C. Troops (6th Regiment N.C. Volunteers), May 27, 1862; however, records of that unit do not indicate that he served therein.

CLARKE, WILLIAM H., Private

Resided in Buncombe or Haywood counties and was by occupation a farmer or carpenter prior to enlisting in Buncombe County at age 23, May 3, 1861. Present or accounted for until reported absent without leave from November 1, 1862, through December, 1862. Reported absent sick until reported absent without leave from July 1, 1863, through December, 1863. Rejoined the company prior to May 12, 1864, when he was wounded in the hand at Spotsylvania Court House, Virginia. Reported absent wounded through August, 1864. Deserted to the enemy at New Market, Virginia, October 9, 1864, and took the Oath of Allegiance at or near New Creek, West Virginia, in October, 1864.

COOPER, COLUMBUS, Private

Resided in Buncombe County and was by occupation a farmer prior to enlisting in Buncombe County at age 19, May 3, 1861. Present or accounted for until wounded in the left leg at Chancellorsville, Virginia, May 3, 1863. Reported absent wounded until March 18, 1864, when he was reported absent on detached service at Staunton, Virginia. Reported absent on detached service through August, 1864. Paroled at Appomattox Court House, Virginia, April 9, 1865.

CRAIG, WILLIAM PLEASANT, Private

Born in Buncombe County where he resided as a shoemaker prior to enlisting in Buncombe County at age 22, May 3, 1861. Present or accounted for until transferred to the C.S. Navy for duty on the C.S.S. *Merrimac* on February 18, 1862.

DALTON, W. M., Private
Enlisted in Buncombe County on May 3, 1861. Present or accounted for through December, 1862. No further records.

DARNOLD, WILLIAM E., Private
Born in Buncombe County where he resided as a farmer prior to enlisting in Buncombe County at age 20, May 3, 1861. Present or accounted for until he died in hospital at Richmond, Virginia, July 7, 1862, of "typhoid fever."

DAVIS, ANDREW W., Corporal
Resided in Buncombe County and was by occupation a farmer prior to enlisting in Buncombe County at age 21, May 3, 1861. Mustered in as Private and promoted to Corporal on March 27, 1864. Present or accounted for until wounded in the right leg and captured near Washington, D.C., July 13, 1864. Hospitalized at Washington and right leg amputated. Died in hospital at Washington on August 10, 1864, of "pyaemia."

DAVIS, HENRY K., Private
Resided in Buncombe County and was by occupation a farmer prior to enlisting in Buncombe County at age 20, May 3, 1861. Present or accounted for until he deserted to the enemy at the Rapidan River, Virginia, on or about September 2, 1862. Took the Oath of Allegiance at Knoxville, Tennessee, in December, 1864.

DEBOARD, J. R., Private
Resided in Buncombe County and enlisted at Camp Ellis, Virginia, at age 21, August 7, 1861. Present or accounted for until he died in hospital at Richmond, Virginia, June 10, 1862, of "cont[inued] fever."

DUNN, E. T., Private
Resided in Montgomery County and enlisted in Wake County at age 19, September 10, 1863, for the war. Present or accounted for until he died on or about May 15, 1864, of disease. Place of death not reported.

EARWOOD, LEWIS A., Private
Resided in Buncombe County and was by occupation a farmer prior to enlisting in Buncombe County at age 25, May 3, 1861. Present or accounted for until he deserted at or near Boonsboro, Maryland, September 14-15, 1862.

FLEMING, SIMON, Private
Resided in Edgecombe County and enlisted in Wake County at age 35, July 16, 1862, for the war. Present or accounted for until he died in hospital at Gordonsville, Virginia, December 25, 1862, of "anasarca."

FORTUNE, BENJAMIN F., Private
Resided in Buncombe County and was by occupation a farmer prior to enlisting in Buncombe County at age 22, May 3, 1861. Present or accounted for until discharged on February 24, 1863. Reason discharged not reported. [May have served later in Company C, 65th Regiment N.C. Troops (6th Regiment N.C. Cavalry) and/or in Company D, 7th Battalion N.C. Cavalry.]

FORTUNE, WILLIAM P., Private
Resided in Buncombe County and was by occupation a farmer prior to enlisting in Buncombe County at age 26, May 3, 1861. Present or accounted for until promoted to Quartermaster Sergeant on June 3, 1861, and transferred to the Field and Staff of this regiment.

FOUST, N., Private
Resided in Davidson County and enlisted in Wake County at age 30, July 16, 1862, for the war. Present or accounted for until wounded at Chancellorsville, Virginia, May 1-3, 1863. Rejoined the company prior to July 1, 1863, and present or accounted for until wounded at Spotsylvania Court House, Virginia, May 12, 1864. Reported absent wounded through August, 1864. Paroled at Greensboro on May 4, 1865.

FOX, JAMES F., Sergeant
Resided in Buncombe County and was by occupation a farmer prior to enlisting in Buncombe County at age 22, May 3, 1861. Mustered in as Private and promoted to Sergeant on May 2, 1863. Present or accounted for until wounded in the lung and thigh and captured at Gettysburg, Pennsylvania, July 1-3, 1863. Hospitalized at Davids Island, New York Harbor, where he died July 30, 1863, of "pyaemia."

FREEMAN, R., Private
Resided in Montgomery County and enlisted in Wake County at age 39, July 16, 1862, for the war. Present or accounted for until wounded in the left thigh at Chancellorsville, Virginia, May 1, 1863. Left leg amputated. Reported absent wounded until furloughed for sixty days from hospital at Richmond, Virginia, December 5, 1864.

GARRISON, WILLIAM C., Private
Resided in Buncombe County and was by occupation a farmer prior to enlisting in Buncombe County at age 26, May 3, 1861. Present or accounted for until appointed 2nd Lieutenant in Company D, 64th Regiment N.C. Troops, July 15, 1862.

GASH, LUCIUS W., Private
Resided in Buncombe County and was by occupation a farmer prior to enlisting in Buncombe County at age 17, May 17, 1861. Present or accounted for until discharged on September 16, 1861. Reason discharged not reported.

GASTON, JOSIAH PERRY, Private
Resided in Buncombe County and was by occupation a farmer prior to enlisting in Buncombe County at age 27, May 3, 1861. Present or accounted for until captured at Malvern Hill, Virginia, July 1, 1862. Confined at Fort Delaware, Delaware. Appointed 3rd Lieutenant in Company I, 64th Regiment N.C. Troops, July 15, 1862, while a prisoner of war. Paroled at Fort Delaware and transferred to Aiken's Landing, James River, Virginia, August 5, 1862, for exchange. Transferred to his new unit prior to February 1, 1863.

GOODLAKE, THOMAS W., Private
Born in England and resided in Buncombe County where he was by occupation a farmer prior to enlisting in Buncombe County at age 35, May 3, 1861. Present or accounted for until discharged on August 2, 1862, by reason of being over age.

GREEN, ALFRED J., Private
Resided in Buncombe County and was by occupation a farmer prior to enlisting in Buncombe County at age 18, May 3, 1861. Present or accounted for until wounded at Chancellorsville, Virginia, May 1-3, 1863. Rejoined the company prior to July 1, 1863, and present or accounted for until he deserted on March 5, 1864.

GREEN, AMOS J., Private
Born in Buncombe County where he resided as a farmer prior to enlisting in Buncombe County at age 41, May 3, 1861. Present or accounted for until he died at Suffolk, Virginia, September 2, 1861, of disease.

GREEN, JESSE M., Corporal
Resided in Buncombe County and was by occupation a farmer prior to enlisting in Buncombe County at age 21, May 3, 1861. Mustered in as Private. Present or accounted for until wounded in the arm at Boonsboro, Maryland, on or about September 15, 1862. Rejoined the company in March-April, 1863, and promoted to Corporal on October 1, 1863. Present or accounted for until he deserted to the enemy at New Market, Virginia, October 9, 1864.

GREEN, JOSEPH, Private
Resided in Montgomery County and enlisted in Wake County at age 30, July 16, 1862, for the war. Present or accounted for until he deserted on September 5, 1862.

GUDGER, CHARLES C., Private
Born in Buncombe County where he resided as a farmer prior to enlisting in Buncombe County at age 18, June 17, 1861. Present or accounted for until he died in hospital at Lynchburg, Virginia, July 9, 1862, of "typhoid fever."

GUDGER, DAVID M., Private
Resided in Buncombe County and was by occupation a civil engineer prior to enlisting in Buncombe County at age 20, May 3, 1861. Mustered in as Corporal but was reduced to ranks in March-December, 1862. Present or accounted for until wounded at Malvern Hill, Virginia, July 1, 1862. Reported absent wounded until discharged on April 25, 1863.

HAREN, ADEN GAINEY, Private
Born in Buncombe County where he resided as a farmer prior to enlisting in Buncombe County at age 33, May 3, 1861. Mustered in as Corporal but was reduced to ranks in March-August, 1862. Present or accounted for until discharged on August 4, 1862, under the provisions of the Conscript Act.

HARPER, JOHN R., Private
Resided in Buncombe County and was by occupation a farmer prior to enlisting in Buncombe County at age 22, June 17, 1861. Present or accounted for until wounded and captured at Sharpsburg, Maryland, September 17, 1862. Paroled on September 27, 1862. Died at Sharpsburg on October 17, 1862, of wounds.

HARRIS, ABEL FRANK, Corporal
Born in Buncombe County where he resided as a farmer prior to enlisting in Buncombe County at age 26, May 3, 1861. Mustered in as Corporal. Present or accounted for until discharged on July 11, 1861, by reason of disability.

HART, ALBERT C., Private
Was by occupation a farmer prior to enlisting in Buncombe County at age 17, May 3, 1861. Present or accounted for until discharged at Richmond, Virginia, August 16, 1862, by reason of "aberration of mind and deafness" incurred in battle "below Richmond." Date of battle not reported.

HASKINS, W. C., Private
Resided in Granville County and enlisted in Wake County at age 35, July 16, 1862, for the war. Present or accounted for through August, 1864.

HELMS, GIDEON B., Private
Resided in Buncombe County and was by occupation a farmer prior to enlisting in Buncombe County at age 20, May 3, 1861. Present or accounted for through August, 1864; however, he was reported absent sick or absent on detail during much of that period.

HOLOBY, _____, Private
Resided in Montgomery County and enlisted in Wake County at age 33, July 16, 1862, for the war. Present or accounted for until he deserted on September 6, 1862.

HOLTOM, T. L., Private
Resided in Montgomery County and enlisted in Wake County at age 22, July 16, 1862, for the war. Present or accounted for until wounded at Kelly's Ford, Virginia, November 6, 1863. Reported absent wounded until he was reported as a deserter from January 19, 1864, through August, 1864. Paroled at Troy on May 22, 1865.

HOLTOM, W. D., Private
Resided in Montgomery County and enlisted in Wake County at age 25, July 16, 1862, for the war. Present or accounted for until he deserted on July 1, 1863. Paroled at Troy on May 23, 1865.

JONES, A. T., Private
Enlisted at Bunker Hill, Virginia, August 1, 1864, for the war. Wounded in the neck and captured at Fisher's Hill, Virginia, September 22, 1864, or at Harrisonburg, Virginia, September 25, 1864. Hospitalized at various Federal hospitals until confined at Point Lookout, Maryland, October 18, 1864. Paroled at Point Lookout and transferred to Venus Point, Savannah River, Georgia, where he was received November 15, 1864, for exchange. Medical records dated 1864 give his age as 18.

JONES, ANON H., Corporal
Resided in Buncombe County where he enlisted at age 22, October 20, 1861. Mustered in as Private and promoted to Sergeant on April 28, 1862. Resigned as Sergeant on August 9, 1863, but was promoted to Corporal in January-March, 1864. Present or accounted for until wounded at Spotsylvania Court House, Virginia, May 19, 1864.

JONES, FIDILLA W., Private
Previously served in Company F, 16th Regiment N.C. Troops (6th Regiment N.C. Volunteers). Transferred to this company on May 27, 1862. Wounded at Malvern Hill, Virginia, on or about July 1, 1862, and died at Richmond, Virginia, July 10, 1862, of wounds.

JONES, WILLIAM J., Corporal
Resided in Buncombe County and was by occupation a farmer prior to enlisting in Buncombe County at age 22, May 3, 1861. Mustered in as Private and promoted to Corporal on April 25, 1862. Present or accounted for until hospitalized at Richmond, Virginia, September 18, 1864, with a wound; however, place and date wounded not reported. Rejoined the company prior to April 6, 1865, when he was captured at Amelia Court House, Virginia. Confined at Point Lookout, Maryland, until released on June 28, 1865, after taking the Oath of Allegiance.

KIRKENDALL, NEWTON, Private
Resided in Henderson County and was by occupation a farmer prior to enlisting at Orange Court House, Virginia, February 29, 1864, for the war. Present or accounted for until he deserted to the enemy at New Market, Virginia, October 9, 1864. Took the Oath of Allegiance at New Creek, West Virginia, in October, 1864. Records of the Federal Provost Marshal give his age as 18.

LEMONS, A. N., Private
Resided in Montgomery County and enlisted in Wake County at age 23, July 16, 1862, for the war. Present or accounted for until he deserted on July 1, 1863.

LEVERETT, THOMAS, Private
Resided in Buncombe County and was by occupation a farmer prior to enlisting in Buncombe County at age 35, May 3, 1861. Present or accounted for until he died at Richmond, Virginia, May 27, 1862, of disease.

LEWIS, W. F., Private
Resided in Montgomery County and enlisted in Wake County at age 19, July 24, 1863, for the war. Present or accounted for until wounded at Spotsylvania Court House, Virginia, May 12, 1864. Reported absent wounded until retired to the Invalid Corps on December 9, 1864. Paroled at Greensboro on May 5, 1865.

McFEE, ANDREW H., Private
Resided in Buncombe County and was by occupation a farmer prior to enlisting in Buncombe County at age 19, July 17, 1861. Present or accounted for until he deserted on or about March 11, 1864. Deserted to the enemy prior to September 26, 1864, when he took the Oath of Allegiance at Louisville, Kentucky.

McFEE, THOMAS M., Private
Resided in Buncombe County and was by occupation a farmer prior to enlisting in Buncombe County at age 18, May 3, 1861. Mustered in as Private and promoted to Corporal on August 1, 1863. Deserted March 3, 1864, and was reduced to ranks prior to April 1, 1864.

McGALLIARD, DAVID W., Corporal
Resided in Buncombe or McDowell counties and was by occupation a farmer prior to enlisting in Buncombe County at age 23, May 3, 1861. Mustered in as Private. Present or accounted for until wounded in the thigh at or near Warrenton Springs on or about October 11, 1863. Rejoined the company prior to April 1, 1864, and present or accounted for until wounded at Spotsylvania Court House, Virginia, May 19, 1864. Reported absent wounded through August, 1864. Rejoined the company and was promoted to Corporal prior to April 3, 1865, when he was captured at Petersburg, Virginia. Confined at Hart's Island, New York Harbor, until released on June 17, 1865, after taking the Oath of Allegiance.

MELTON, J. C., Private
Resided in Buncombe County and enlisted at Camp Ellis, Virginia, at age 21, August 7, 1861. Present or accounted for until captured at Sharpsburg, Maryland, September 17, 1862. Confined at Fort Delaware, Delaware, until transferred to Aiken's Landing, James River, Virginia, October 2, 1862, for exchange. Declared exchanged at Aiken's Landing on November 10, 1862. Rejoined the company prior to January 1, 1863, and present or accounted for through August, 1864.

MELTON, J. M., Private
Resided in Buncombe County and enlisted at Camp Ellis, Virginia, at age 18, August 7, 1861. Present or accounted for until killed at Sharpsburg, Maryland, September 17, 1862.

MERRILL, BENJAMIN W., 1st Sergeant
Born in Buncombe County where he resided as a farmer prior to enlisting in Buncombe County at age 24, May 3, 1861. Mustered in as Private and promoted to 1st Sergeant on April 27, 1862. Present or accounted for until wounded at Malvern Hill, Virginia, on or about July 1, 1862. Died in hospital at Richmond, Virginia, July 11, 1862, of wounds.

MERRIMON, AUGUSTUS P., Private
Was by occupation a lawyer prior to enlisting in Buncombe County on May 3, 1861. Appointed Captain and transferred to the Commissary Department in June, 1861.

MERRIMON, BRANCH A., Private
Resided in Buncombe County and was by occupation a merchant prior to enlisting in Buncombe County at age 24, May 3, 1861. Mustered in as Sergeant but was reduced to ranks in March-May, 1862. Present or accounted for until discharged on May 2, 1862, by reason of disability.

MERRIMON, EMORY H., Private
Born in Buncombe County where he resided as a farmer or law student prior to enlisting in Buncombe County at age 20, May 3, 1861. Present or accounted for until promoted to Quartermaster Sergeant and transferred to the Field and Staff, 64th Regiment N.C. Troops, November 5, 1862.

MILLER, JEPTHA I., Private
Resided in Buncombe County and was by occupation a farmer prior to enlisting in Buncombe County at age 20, May 3, 1861. Present or accounted for through August, 1864; however, he was reported absent sick or absent on detached service during most of that period.

MILLSAPS, PETER P., Private
Resided in Montgomery County and enlisted in Wake County at age 18, July 24, 1863, for the war. Present or accounted for until transferred to Company K, 34th Regiment N.C. Troops, on or about February 25, 1865.

MOOSE, J. J., Private
Enlisted in Wake County on June 16, 1863, for the war. Present or accounted for until hospitalized at Richmond, Virginia, December 17, 1863, with a gunshot wound; however, place and date wounded not reported. Discharged in December, 1863, by reason of wounds.

MURCHISON, D. P., Private
Resided in Montgomery County and enlisted in Wake County at age 27, July 16, 1862, for the war. Present or accounted for until he died at Fredericksburg, Virginia, December 29, 1862. Cause of death not reported.

MURPHY, WILLIAM M., Private
Resided in Buncombe County and was by occupation a farmer prior to enlisting in Buncombe County at age 20, June 17, 1861. Mustered in as Private and promoted to Corporal on April 25, 1862. Present or accounted for through August 31, 1863. Reduced to ranks on October 6, 1863. Deserted to the enemy prior to November 9, 1863, when he was confined at Knoxville, Tennessee. Released on November 17, 1863, after taking the Oath of Allegiance.

MURRELL, THOMAS W., Private
Resided in Buncombe County and was by occupation a mechanic prior to enlisting in Buncombe County at age 46, May 17, 1861. Present or accounted for until discharged on October 27, 1862, "on account of promotion."

NEILSON, MORGAN L., Private
Was by occupation a physician prior to enlisting at age 38, on or about June 1, 1861. Appointed Assistant Surgeon on or about June 1, 1861, and transferred to the Field and Staff of this regiment.

PATTON, GEORGE N., Private
Born in Buncombe County where he resided as a farmer prior to enlisting in Buncombe County at age 35, May 3, 1861. Present or accounted for until discharged on January 28, 1862, by reason of "chronic disease of the kidneys, and greatly impaired vision."

PATTON, JACOB E., Sergeant
Resided in Buncombe County and was by occupation a farmer prior to enlisting in Buncombe County at age 24, May 3, 1861. Mustered in as Private and promoted to Sergeant on April 25, 1862. Present or accounted for until wounded in the left foot and left leg at Spotsylvania Court House, Virginia, May 19, 1864. Reported absent wounded until furloughed for sixty days on September 7, 1864.

PATTON, WILLIAM M., Private
Resided in Buncombe County and was by occupation a farmer prior to enlisting in Buncombe County at age 22, May 3, 1861. Present or accounted for until wounded at Chancellorsville, Virginia, May 1-3, 1863. Died in hospital at Richmond, Virginia, May 21, 1863, of wounds.

PENLAND, GEORGE N., Private
Resided in Buncombe County and was by occupation a farmer prior to enlisting in Buncombe County at age 22, May 3, 1861. Present or accounted for until captured at Petersburg, Virginia, April 3, 1865. Confined at Hart's Island, New York Harbor, until

released on June 17, 1865, after taking the Oath of Allegiance.

PENLAND, JAMES C., Private
Resided in Buncombe County and was by occupation a farmer prior to enlisting in Buncombe County at age 20, June 17, 1861. Present or accounted for until wounded at Sharpsburg, Maryland, September 17, 1862. Died at Hagerstown, Maryland, of wounds; however, date of death not reported.

PENLAND, SAMUEL E., Private
Resided in Buncombe County and was by occupation a merchant prior to enlisting in Buncombe County at age 24, May 3, 1861. Mustered in as Private and promoted to Sergeant on July 10, 1862. Present or accounted for until reported absent without leave on October 1, 1862. Reduced to ranks on or about November 10, 1862. Rejoined the company in January-February, 1863, and present or accounted for until captured at Gettysburg, Pennsylvania, July 3-5, 1863, after being "left as [a] nurse for the wounded." Confined at Fort McHenry, Maryland, until transferred to Point Lookout, Maryland, January 23, 1864. Confined at Point Lookout until paroled and transferred to Venus Point, Savannah River, Georgia, where he was received November 15, 1864, for exchange.

PETILLO, JOHN R., Private
Resided in Buncombe County and was by occupation a farmer prior to enlisting in Buncombe County at age 20, June 17, 1861. Present or accounted for until paroled at Appomattox Court House, Virginia, April 9, 1865.

PHELTS, DANIEL M., Private
Resided in Buncombe County and was by occupation a mechanic prior to enlisting in Buncombe County at age 23, May 3, 1861. Present or accounted for until wounded in the head at Malvern Hill, Virginia, July 1, 1862. Rejoined the company in May-June, 1863, and present or accounted for until wounded at Gettysburg, Pennsylvania, July 1-3, 1863. Reported absent wounded through December, 1863, but rejoined the company prior to April 1, 1864. Wounded in the right hip at Spotsylvania Court House, Virginia, May 12, 1864. Reported absent wounded through August, 1864.

PLESS, JOHN H., Private
Resided in Buncombe or Haywood counties and was by occupation a carpenter prior to enlisting in Buncombe County at age 20, May 3, 1861. Present or accounted for until he deserted to the enemy on October 9, 1864.

POE, Z., Private
Resided in Montgomery County and enlisted in Wake County at age 34, July 16, 1862, for the war. Present or accounted for until reported absent without leave from September 14, 1862, through December, 1862. Rejoined the company in January-February, 1863, and present or accounted for until wounded at Chancellorsville, Virginia, May 1-3, 1863. Rejoined the company prior to June 4, 1863, and present or accounted for until captured at Kelly's Ford, Virginia, November 8, 1863. Confined at Old Capitol Prison, Washington, D.C., until

transferred to Point Lookout, Maryland, February 3, 1864. Died at Point Lookout on March 25, 1865, of "consumption."

PORTER, JOSEPH G., Private
Resided in Buncombe County and was by occupation a carpenter prior to enlisting in Buncombe County at age 23, May 3, 1861. Present or accounted for until he died in hospital at Richmond, Virginia, September 2, 1862, of "typhoid fever."

PORTER, WILLIAM HENRY HARRISON, Sergeant
Resided in Buncombe County and was by occupation a farmer prior to enlisting in Buncombe County at age 20, May 17, 1861. Mustered in as Private and promoted to Sergeant on January 18, 1863. Present or accounted for until killed at Chancellorsville, Virginia, May 3, 1863.

POWERS, WILLIAM R., Private
Born in Buncombe County where he resided as a farmer prior to enlisting in Buncombe County at age 21, May 3, 1861. Present or accounted for until transferred to the C.S. Navy for duty on the C.S.S. *Merrimac* on February 18, 1862.

PRICE, RICHARD NYE, Private
Resided in Buncombe County and was by occupation a minister prior to enlisting in Buncombe County at age 31, May 3, 1861. Present or accounted for until discharged on December 23, 1861. Reason discharged not reported. Later served as Chaplain of the 26th Regiment N.C. Troops.

RANDAL, JOSEPH W., Private
Born in Buncombe County where he resided as a farmer prior to enlisting in Buncombe County at age 30, May 3, 1861. Present or accounted for until discharged on August 19, 1861, by reason of "the peculiar condition of his family."

REAGAN, DANIEL H., Private
Resided in Buncombe County and was by occupation a farmer prior to enlisting in Buncombe County at age 19, May 3, 1861. Mustered in as Private and promoted to Corporal on January 18, 1863. Present or accounted for until he deserted on July 2, 1863. Reduced to ranks on August 9, 1863.

RECTOR, JAMES P., Private
Resided in Buncombe County and was by occupation a farmer prior to enlisting in Buncombe County at age 22, May 3, 1861. Present or accounted for until wounded at Malvern Hill, Virginia, July 1, 1862. Rejoined the company prior to January 1, 1863. Present or accounted for through August, 1864; however, he was reported on duty as a teamster during most of that period.

RECTOR, SAMUEL L., Private
Born in Buncombe County where he resided as a farmer prior to enlisting in Buncombe County at age 17, May 3, 1861. Present or accounted for until discharged on August 3, 1862, under the provisions of the Conscript Act.

RICE, ALFRED, Private
Resided in Buncombe County and was by occupation a farmer prior to enlisting in Buncombe County at age 24, May 3, 1861. Present or accounted for until captured at Malvern Hill, Virginia, on or about July 2, 1862. Confined at Fort Delaware, Delaware, until

exchanged at Aiken's Landing, James River, Virginia, August 5, 1862. Died in hospital at Staunton, Virginia, November 25, 1862, of "pneumonia."

SIMMONS, A., Private
Resided in Montgomery County and enlisted in Wake County at age 30, July 16, 1862, for the war. Present or accounted for until reported absent without leave from August 1, 1863, through October, 1863. Rejoined the company in November-December, 1863, and present or accounted for until captured at Winchester, Virginia, September 19, 1864. Confined at Point Lookout, Maryland, where he died January 13, 1865, of "acute dysentery."

SINGLETON, S. P., Private
Resided in Montgomery County and enlisted in Wake County at age 26, July 16, 1862, for the war. Present or accounted for through January 15, 1863. Died at Lynchburg, Virginia, prior to January 1, 1864, of disease. Exact date of death not reported.

SKINNER, JOHN, Private
Resided in Edgecombe County and enlisted in Wake County at age 25, July 16, 1862, for the war. Present or accounted for until captured at Petersburg, Virginia, April 3, 1865. Confined at Hart's Island, New York Harbor, until released on June 17, 1865, after taking the Oath of Allegiance.

SMITH, JAMES M., Private
Born in Buncombe County where he resided as a farmer prior to enlisting in Buncombe County at age 19, May 3, 1861. Present or accounted for until appointed 2nd Lieutenant and transferred to the 64th Regiment N.C. Troops on November 5, 1862; however, records of the 64th Regiment do not indicate that he served therein. Later served in Company A, 5th Battalion N.C. Cavalry.

SMITH, WILLIAM BEADON, Private
Resided in Buncombe County and was by occupation a civil engineer prior to enlisting in Buncombe County at age 26, May 3, 1861. Mustered in as Private and promoted to Corporal on July 1 or August 9, 1861. Reduced to ranks in March-July, 1862. Present or accounted for until wounded in the right shoulder at Malvern Hill, Virginia, July 1, 1862. Appointed Captain and transferred to the Commissary Department in July, 1862.

SOUTHER, RICHARD G., Private
Resided in Buncombe County and was by occupation a farmer prior to enlisting in Buncombe County at age 19, May 3, 1861. Present or accounted for until reported absent without leave from November 1, 1862, through February, 1863. Rejoined the company in March-April, 1863, and present or accounted for until he deserted on November 1, 1863. Deserted to the enemy prior to September 18, 1864, when he was confined at Knoxville, Tennessee. Took the Oath of Allegiance at Knoxville on September 20, 1864.

SPENCE, ANDREW P., Private
Resided in Buncombe County and was by occupation a farmer prior to enlisting in Buncombe County at age 25, May 3, 1861. Present or accounted for until he died in hospital at Danville, Virginia, August 7, 1862, of "chronic diarrhoea."

STEPP, J. P., Private
Resided in Buncombe County where he enlisted at

age 18, July 18, 1863, for the war. Present or accounted for until wounded in the left leg in battle at or near the North Anna River, Virginia, May 24, 1864. Reported absent wounded through August, 1864.

STEPP, JESSE, Private
Resided in Buncombe County and enlisted at Camp Ellis, Virginia, at age 23, July 25, 1861. Present or accounted for until wounded at or near Spotsylvania Court House, Virginia, on or about May 8, 1864. Died prior to September 1, 1864, of wounds. Place and exact date of death not reported.

STEPP, TISDALE, Private
Resided in Buncombe County and was by occupation a farmer prior to enlisting in Buncombe County at age 20, May 3, 1861. Present or accounted for until killed at Spotsylvania Court House, Virginia, May 12, 1864. Clark's *Regiments* indicates that he was "shot dead by an awkward soldier in our rear rank."

STEVENS, MERRITT FOSTER, Private
Resided in Buncombe County and was by occupation a farmer prior to enlisting in Buncombe County at age 26, May 3, 1861. Present or accounted for until transferred to Company F, 60th Regiment N.C. Troops, October 8, 1862.

STEVENS, THOMAS N., Private
Resided in Buncombe County and was by occupation a farmer prior to enlisting in Buncombe County at age 31, May 3, 1861. Mustered in as Sergeant but was reduced to ranks in March-October, 1862. Present or accounted for until transferred to Company F, 60th Regiment N.C. Troops, October 8, 1862.

STEWART, R., Private
Resided in Montgomery County and enlisted in Wake County at age 22, July 16, 1862, for the war. Present or accounted for until he died at Frederick City, Maryland, on or about October 6, 1862, of disease.

STRADLEY, EBENEZER C., Private
Born in Buncombe County where he resided as a blacksmith or farmer prior to enlisting in Buncombe County at age 20, May 3, 1861. Present or accounted for until he died at Suffolk, Virginia, July 31, 1861, of disease.

SUGGS, WILEY, Private
Resided in Montgomery County and enlisted in Wake County at age 30, July 16, 1862, for the war. Present or accounted for until he died in hospital at Mount Jackson, Virginia, November 22, 1862, of "anasarca."

SWAN, THOMAS W., Private
Resided in Buncombe County and was by occupation a farmer prior to enlisting in Buncombe County at age 21, May 3, 1861. Present or accounted for until wounded at Malvern Hill, Virginia, July 1, 1862. Reported absent without leave from November 1, 1862, through February, 1863. Rejoined the company in March-April, 1863, and present or accounted for through August, 1864; however, he was reported absent sick during much of that period.

TABOR, CALVIN, Private
Resided in Buncombe County and was by occupation a farmer prior to enlisting in Buncombe County at

age 19, May 3, 1861. Present or accounted for until transferred to Company G, 56th Regiment N.C. Troops, January 4, 1865.

TYSINGER, DANIEL, Private
Resided in Davidson County and enlisted in Wake County at age 26, November 26, 1863, for the war. Present or accounted for until captured at Port Republic, Virginia, September 28, 1864. Confined at Point Lookout, Maryland, until released October 14-19, 1864, after joining the U.S. Army. Assigned to Company D, 4th Regiment U.S. Volunteer Infantry.

WALKER, J. H., Sergeant
Resided in Buncombe County and was by occupation a farmer prior to enlisting in Buncombe County at age 23, May 3, 1861. Mustered in as Private and promoted to Sergeant on August 9, 1863. Present or accounted for until paroled at Appomattox Court House, Virginia, April 9, 1865.

WALTON, ALFRED F., Private
Resided in Buncombe County and was by occupation a farmer prior to enlisting in Buncombe County at age 19, May 3, 1861. Present or accounted for until reported absent without leave on August 12, 1863. Rejoined the company on or about January 1, 1864, and present or accounted for until wounded in the right arm at Bethesda Church, Virginia, May 30, 1864. Reported absent wounded through August, 1864, but rejoined the company prior to April 2, 1865, when he was captured at Petersburg, Virginia. Confined at Hart's Island, New York Harbor, until released on June 17, 1865, after taking the Oath of Allegiance.

WALTON, JAMES M., Private
Born in McDowell County and resided in Buncombe County where he was by occupation a farmer prior to enlisting in Iredell County at age 17, May 13, 1861. Present or accounted for until discharged on August 2, 1862, under the provisions of the Conscript Act. [May have served later in Company C, 69th Regiment N.C. Troops (7th Regiment N.C. Cavalry).]

WEAVER, J. C. FULTON, Private
Resided in Buncombe County and was by occupation a farmer prior to enlisting in Buncombe County at age 24, May 3, 1861. Present or accounted for until he died in hospital at Richmond, Virginia, June 20, 1862, of "typhoid fever."

WEAVER, WILEY W., Private
Resided in Buncombe County and was by occupation a farmer prior to enlisting in Buncombe County at age 17, May 3, 1861. Present or accounted for until killed at Malvern Hill, Virginia, July 1, 1862.

WEBB, WILLIAM H., Private
Resided in Buncombe County and was by occupation a farmer prior to enlisting in Buncombe County at age 22, May 3, 1861. Present or accounted for until reported absent without leave from June 20, 1864, through August, 1864. Rejoined the company prior to April 3, 1865, when he was captured at Petersburg, Virginia. Confined at Hart's Island, New York Harbor, until released on June 17, 1865, after taking the Oath of Allegiance.

WESTALL, NOBLE B., Sergeant

Resided in Buncombe County and was by occupation a farmer prior to enlisting in Buncombe County at age 23, May 3, 1861. Mustered in as Private and promoted to Sergeant on April 25, 1862. Present or accounted for until wounded at Spotsylvania Court House, Virginia, May 19, 1864. Reported absent wounded through August, 1864, but rejoined the company prior to April 3, 1865, when he was captured at Petersburg, Virginia. Confined at Hart's Island, New York Harbor, until released on June 17, 1865, after taking the Oath of Allegiance.

WHITE, GEORGE M., Private

Resided in Buncombe County and was by occupation a farmer prior to enlisting in Buncombe County at age 25, May 3, 1861. Present or accounted for until discharged on July 26, 1864, after being appointed a commissioned officer. No further records.

WHITE, JAMES J., Private

Resided in Buncombe County and was by occupation a farmer prior to enlisting in Buncombe County at age 23, May 3, 1861. Present or accounted for until wounded in the abdomen and left hand at Chancellorsville, Virginia, May 3, 1863. Rejoined the company prior to July 1, 1863, and was captured at Gettysburg, Pennsylvania, July 3, 1863, or at Williamsport, Maryland, July 14, 1863. Confined at various Federal prisons until transferred from Fort Delaware, Delaware, to Point Lookout, Maryland, October 15-18, 1863. Confined at Point Lookout until paroled and transferred to Boulware's and Cox's Wharf, James River, Virginia, where he was received February 20-21, 1865, for exchange. Reported present with a detachment of paroled and exchanged prisoners at Camp Lee, near Richmond, Virginia, February 28, 1865.

WHITMIRE, JEREMIAH M., 1st Sergeant

Resided in Buncombe County or in Greenville District, South Carolina, and was by occupation a mechanic prior to enlisting in Buncombe County at age 23, May 3, 1861. Mustered in as Private and promoted to Sergeant on September 1, 1861. Reduced to ranks on April 25, 1862, but was promoted to Sergeant on July 15, 1862. Promoted to 1st Sergeant on April 28, 1863. Nominated for the Badge of Distinction for gallantry at Chancellorsville, Virginia, May 1-3, 1863. Present or accounted for until wounded in the right breast at or near Spotsylvania Court House, Virginia, on or about May 8, 1864. Reported absent wounded through August, 1864, but rejoined the company prior to April 6, 1865, when he was captured at Burkeville, Virginia. Confined at Point Lookout, Maryland, until released on June 21, 1865, after taking the Oath of Allegiance.

WHITTAKER, JESSE C., Private

Resided in Buncombe County and was by occupation a farmer prior to enlisting in Buncombe County at age 30, June 17, 1861. Present or accounted for until wounded in the thigh and chest at Malvern Hill, Virginia, July 1, 1862. Died in hospital at Richmond, Virginia, on or about July 19, 1862, of wounds.

WILLIAMS, ROBERT, Private

Resided in Buncombe County and was by occupation a farmer prior to enlisting in Buncombe County at age 26, May 3, 1861. Present or accounted for until wounded at Chancellorsville, Virginia, May 3, 1863. Rejoined the company in November-December, 1863, and present or accounted for through January 18, 1865.

WILLOBY, B., Private

Resided in Montgomery County and enlisted in Wake County at age 22, July 16, 1862, for the war. Present or accounted for until reported absent without leave from September 3, 1862, until January 1, 1863. Died at Camp Gordon, Virginia, February 27, 1863, of disease.

WILLSON, THOMAS B., Private

Resided in Buncombe County and was by occupation a farmer prior to enlisting in Buncombe County at age 23, May 3, 1861. Present or accounted for until wounded in the left arm at Chancellorsville, Virginia. May 3, 1863. Left arm amputated. Reported absent wounded until retired to the Invalid Corps on April 28, 1864. Deserted to the enemy prior to March 10, 1865, when he was confined at Knoxville, Tennessee. Took the Oath of Allegiance at Chattanooga, Tennessee, and was released on March 13, 1865.

WISE, JOHN, Private

Resided in Buncombe County and was by occupation a farmer prior to enlisting in Buncombe County at age 22, May 3, 1861. Present or accounted for until wounded at Sharpsburg, Maryland, September 17, 1862. Reported absent wounded until he was listed as a deserter on July 1, 1863. North Carolina pension records indicate he was wounded in the head and right thigh at Richmond, Virginia, in July, 1862.

WISE, JOSIAH H., Private

Resided in Buncombe County and was by occupation a farmer prior to enlisting in Buncombe County at age 20, May 3, 1861. Present or accounted for until wounded at Malvern Hill, Virginia, on or about July 1, 1862. Died at Richmond, Virginia, July 6, 1862, of wounds.

YARBOROUGH, J. C., Private

Resided in Montgomery County and enlisted in Wake County at age 26, July 16, 1862, for the war. Present or accounted for through January 15, 1863. Died at Lynchburg, Virginia, prior to January 1, 1864, of disease. Exact date of death not reported.

YOUNG, WATSON G., Private

Born in Buncombe County where he resided as a farmer prior to enlisting in Buncombe County at age 20, May 3, 1861. Present or accounted for until killed at Malvern Hill, Virginia, July 1, 1862.

COMPANY G

This company, known as the Reid Guard, was from Rockingham County and enlisted at Rawlingsburg on May 10, 1861. The company moved to Oregon Hill at an unspecified date and departed for Raleigh on May 20, 1861. It arrived at Raleigh on May 22 and moved to Garysburg on May 29. There it was assigned to this regiment as Company G. After joining the regiment the company functioned as a part of the regiment, and its history for the war period is recorded as a part of the regimental history.

The information contained in the following roster of the company was compiled principally from company muster rolls for May 10, 1861-December 31, 1862, and March, 1863-August 31, 1864. No company muster rolls were found for January-February, 1863, or for the period after August 31, 1864. In addition to the company muster rolls, Roll of Honor records, receipt rolls, hospital records, prisoner of war records, and other primary records, supplemented by state pension applications, United Daughters of the Confederacy records, and postwar rosters and histories, all provided useful information.

OFFICERS
CAPTAINS

SLADE, THOMAS T.

Resided in Rockingham County and was by occupation a farmer prior to enlisting at age 38. Elected Captain to rank from May 10, 1861. Present or accounted for until he was "not reelected" when the regiment was reorganized on April 25, 1862. [May have served later in Company H, 22nd Regiment N.C. Troops.]

GRIFFITH, ANDREW J.

Resided in Rockingham County and was by occupation a merchant prior to enlisting in Rockingham County at age 24. Elected 1st Lieutenant to rank from May 11, 1862, and was elected Captain on April 25, 1862. Present or accounted for until reported captured at or near Cedar Creek, Virginia, October 19, 1864; however, records of the Federal Provost Marshal do not substantiate that report. Hospitalized at Richmond, Virginia, February 24, 1865, with a gunshot wound of the left leg; however, place and date wounded not reported. Reported absent wounded through March 21, 1865.

LIEUTENANTS

GILLIAM, JOHN J., 3rd Lieutenant

Resided in Rockingham County and was by occupation a farmer prior to enlisting in Rockingham County at age 21. Elected 3rd Lieutenant to rank from May 10, 1861. Present or accounted for until wounded in the leg at Yorktown, Virginia, in April, 1862. Leg amputated. Died in Rockingham County on April 26, 1862, of wounds.

GRIFFITH, JAMES A., 3rd Lieutenant

Resided in Rockingham County and was by occupation a student prior to enlisting in Rockingham County at age 20, May 10, 1861. Mustered in as Private and elected 3rd Lieutenant to rank from April 27, 1862. Present or accounted for until killed at Gettysburg, Pennsylvania, July 1, 1863.

JOHNSTON, JOHN S., 2nd Lieutenant

Resided in Rockingham County and was by occupation a clerk prior to enlisting in Rockingham County at age 19. Elected 2nd Lieutenant to rank from May 10, 1861. Present or accounted for until he was "not [re]elected" when the regiment was reorganized on April 25, 1862.

LEFTWICH, GEORGE W., 2nd Lieutenant

Resided in Rockingham County and was by occupation a farmer prior to enlisting in Rockingham County at age 20, May 10, 1861. Mustered in as Sergeant and elected 2nd Lieutenant to rank from April 27, 1862. Present or accounted for until captured at Petersburg, Virginia, April 2, 1865. Confined at Old Capitol Prison, Washington, D.C., until transferred to Johnson's Island, Ohio, April 9, 1865. Released at Johnson's Island on June 18, 1865, after taking the Oath of Allegiance.

PATTERSON, JOSEPH A., 1st Lieutenant

Resided in Rockingham County and was by occupation a clerk prior to enlisting in Rockingham County at age 23, May 10, 1861. Mustered in as Sergeant and was elected 1st Lieutenant to rank from April 27, 1862. Present or accounted for until captured at or near Sharpsburg, Maryland, on or about September 16, 1862. Confined at Fort Delaware, Delaware, until transferred to Aiken's Landing, James River, Virginia, October 2, 1862, for exchange. Declared exchanged at Aiken's Landing on November 10, 1862. Rejoined the company in January-April, 1863, and present or accounted for until wounded at or near Cold Harbor, Virginia, June 3, 1864. Died in hospital at Richmond, Virginia, June 28, 1864, of wounds.

NONCOMMISSIONED OFFICERS AND PRIVATES

ADAMS, JOHN W., Private

Resided in Rockingham County where he enlisted at age 18, July 5, 1861. Present or accounted for through December, 1864.

ADAMS, WILLIAM P., Private

Resided in Rockingham County and was by occupation a trader prior to enlisting in Rockingham County at age 20, May 10, 1861. Present or accounted for until killed at Sharpsburg, Maryland, September 17, 1862.

ALEXANDER, J. N., Private

Resided in Hertford County and enlisted in Wake County at age 36, July 16, 1862, for the war. Present or accounted for until reported absent without leave from December 1, 1862, through August, 1864.

ALEXANDER, W. B., Private

Resided in Hertford County and enlisted in Wake County at age 24, July 16, 1862, for the war. Present or accounted for through August, 1864.

ASTIN, JETTISON J., Private

Born in Rockingham County where he resided as a mason prior to enlisting in Rockingham County on May 10, 1861. Present or accounted for until discharged on October 18, 1861, by reason of "debility resulting from extreme old age." Age given on discharge papers as 56.

ATKINSON, DAVID J., Private

Born in Rockingham County where he resided as a mason prior to enlisting in Rockingham County at age 26, May 10, 1861. Present or accounted for until discharged on October 29, 1861, by reason of "phthisis pulmonalis."

BADGETT, JOHN D., Private
Resided in Caswell County and enlisted in Rockingham County at age 24, August 10, 1861. Present or accounted for until killed at Williamsburg, Virginia, May 5, 1862.

BAILEY, ALLEN, Private
Resided in Rockingham County and was by occupation a farmer prior to enlisting in Rockingham County at age 22, May 10, 1861. Present or accounted for through September, 1864; however, he was reported absent sick during much of that period.

BEGLES, E. B., Private
Place and date of enlistment not reported. Hospitalized at Danville, Virginia, April 5, 1865, with a gunshot wound of the left side; however, place and date wounded not reported. Furloughed for thirty days on April 9, 1865.

BRAGG, A. J., Private
Resided in Rockingham County and enlisted at Morton's Ford, Virginia, at age 17, April 10, 1864, for the war. Present or accounted for until paroled at Appomattox Court House, Virginia, April 9, 1865.

BRAGG, JOHN H., Corporal
Resided in Rockingham County and was by occupation a millwright prior to enlisting in Rockingham County at age 24, May 10, 1861. Mustered in as Private and promoted to Corporal on November 1, 1862. Present or accounted for until captured at Petersburg, Virginia, April 3, 1865. Confined at Hart's Island, New York Harbor, until released on June 17, 1865, after taking the Oath of Allegiance.

BRANSON, W. H., Sergeant
Place and date of enlistment not reported. Deserted to the enemy prior to March 3, 1865, when he was confined at Knoxville, Tennessee. Released on March 4, 1865, after taking the "Oath." Rank given on "Oath" as Sergeant.

BRANTLEY, J. M., Private
Resided in Montgomery County and enlisted in Wake County at age 25, July 16, 1862, for the war. Present or accounted for until reported missing in August, 1862. Reported missing through August, 1864. No further records.

BRITT, W., Private
Resided in Montgomery County and enlisted in Wake County at age 33, July 16, 1862, for the war. Present or accounted for until wounded at Sharpsburg, Maryland, on or about September 17, 1862. Died September 29, 1862, of wounds. Place of death not reported.

BRITTEN, M., Private
Enlisted in Wake County on July 16, 1862, for the war. Deserted August 6, 1862, "before arriving at Regiment."

BROWN, JOSEPH, Private
Resided in Virginia and enlisted at Richmond, Virginia, at age 35, June 4, 1862, for the war as a substitute for Private J. C. Mills. Deserted the same day.

CHANDLER, J. C., Private
Enlisted in Rockingham County on October 22, 1864, for the war. Present or accounted for until captured in hospital at Richmond, Virginia, April 3, 1865. Paroled at Richmond on April 20, 1865.

CHILTON, JOHN, Private
Resided in Rockingham County and enlisted in Wake County at age 38, July 28, 1863, for the war. Present or accounted for until he died in hospital at Richmond, Virginia, January 24, 1864, of "typhoid pneumonia."

CORUM, PINKNEY, Private
Resided in Rockingham County and was by occupation a farmer prior to enlisting in Rockingham County at age 38, May 10, 1861. Present or accounted for until discharged on or about August 11, 1862, under the provisions of the Conscript Act.

CRABTREE, A. C., Private
Resided in Orange County and enlisted in Wake County at age 23, August 14, 1863, for the war. Present or accounted for until paroled at Appomattox Court House, Virginia, April 9, 1865.

CRANFORD, J. M., Private
Resided in Montgomery County and enlisted in Wake County at age 22, July 16, 1862, for the war. Present or accounted for until captured at Frederick City, Maryland, September 11, 1862. Confined at Fort Delaware, Delaware, until paroled and transferred to City Point, Virginia, where he was received December 18, 1862, for exchange. Rejoined the company prior to March 1, 1863, and present or accounted for until wounded in the arm at Chancellorsville, Virginia, May 1-3, 1863. Died in Montgomery County on June 12, 1863, of wounds.

DEATON, MARTIN S., Private
Resided in Montgomery County and enlisted in Wake County at age 23, July 16, 1862, for the war. Present or accounted for until he "left the regiment" on the march to Maryland in August, 1862. North Carolina pension records indicate that he died at Leesburg, Virginia, in December, 1862-January, 1863, of disease.

DICKENS, JOSEPH W., Private
Resided in Rockingham County where he enlisted at age 32, July 5, 1861. Present or accounted for until wounded and captured at Sharpsburg, Maryland, September 17, 1862. Died of wounds. Place and date of death not reported.

DIX, JAMES H., Private
Resided in Rockingham County and was by occupation a farmer prior to enlisting in Rockingham County at age 19, May 10, 1861. Present or accounted for until killed at Bethesda Church, Virginia, May 30, 1864.

DIX, JAMES R., Private
Resided at Danville, Virginia, and enlisted in Rockingham County on July 15, 1861. Present or accounted for until captured at or near Bethesda Church, Virginia, May 30, 1864. Confined at Point Lookout, Maryland, until transferred to Elmira, New York, July 9, 1864. Released at Elmira on June 30, 1865, after taking the Oath of Allegiance.

DIX, TANDY, Private
Resided in Rockingham County and was by occupation a farmer prior to enlisting in Rockingham County at age 21, May 10, 1861. Present or

accounted for until he died in hospital at Richmond, Virginia, April 14, 1863, of "typhoid pneumonia."

DODSON, PETER S., Private
Resided in Rockingham County and was by occupation a farmer prior to enlisting in Rockingham County at age 20, May 10, 1861. Present or accounted for until captured at Fisher's Hill, Virginia, September 22, 1864. Confined at Point Lookout, Maryland, until released on June 11, 1865, after taking the Oath of Allegiance.

DRISCOLL, J. C., Private
Resided in Virginia and enlisted in Rockingham County at age 21, March 19, 1862, for the war as a substitute. Deserted near Richmond, Virginia, June 12, 1862.

DUETT, WILLIAM P., Private
Resided in Rockingham County and was by occupation a farmer prior to enlisting in Rockingham County at age 20, May 10, 1861. Present or accounted for until he died in Rockingham County on February 7, 1863, of disease.

ELLINGTON, JOHN R., Private
Resided in Rockingham County and was by occupation a farmer prior to enlisting in Rockingham County at age 23, May 10, 1861. Present or accounted for until he died in hospital at Richmond, Virginia, July 7, 1862, of disease.

FITZGERALD, JOHN W., Private
Resided in Rockingham County where he enlisted at age 23, August 10, 1861. Present or accounted for until discharged on July 31, 1862, after providing Private James Hubbard as a substitute.

FITZGERALD, RUFUS B., Private
Resided in Rockingham County and was by occupation a tobacconist prior to enlisting in Rockingham County at age 21, May 10, 1861. Mustered in as Private and promoted to Sergeant on November 18, 1861. Reduced to ranks on April 25, 1862. Present or accounted for until captured at Winchester, Virginia, September 19, 1864. Confined at Point Lookout, Maryland, until paroled and transferred to Boulware's and Cox's Wharf, James River, Virginia, where he was received February 20-21, 1865, for exchange. Reported present with a detachment of paroled and exchanged prisoners at Camp Lee, near Richmond, Virginia, February 28, 1865.

FLOODS, F. R., Private
Resided in Rockingham County and was by occupation a farmer prior to enlisting at age 17. Place and date of enlistment not reported. "Arrested" by U.S. forces at Martinsburg, West Virginia, July 21, 1864. Confined at Wheeling, West Virginia, until released on July 25, 1864, after taking the "Oath."

FORTNER, E. W., Private
Resided in Alexander County and enlisted in Wake County at age 27, July 28, 1863, for the war. Present or accounted for until he deserted near Orange Court House, Virginia, August 27, 1863.

FOSTER, THOMAS J., Private
Born in Orange County and resided in Rockingham County where he was by occupation a schoolteacher

prior to enlisting in Rockingham County at age 27, May 10, 1861. Present or accounted for until discharged on July 29, 1862, by reason of disability.

FRASIER, JAMES H., Private
Resided in Rockingham County and was by occupation a farmer prior to enlisting at Camp Bragg, Virginia, at age 21, June 23, 1861. Present or accounted for until wounded at Sharpsburg, Maryland, September 17, 1862. Rejoined the company in January-April, 1863, and was wounded in the left thigh at Chancellorsville, Virginia, May 3, 1863. Rejoined the company in July-August, 1863, and present or accounted for until wounded in the left arm at Fisher's Hill, Virginia, on or about September 22, 1864. Reported absent wounded until retired to the Invalid Corps on February 14, 1865.

FRENCH, DAVID P., Private
Born in Rockingham County where he resided as a farmer prior to enlisting in Rockingham County at age 38, May 10, 1861. Mustered in as Corporal but was reduced to ranks in March-December, 1862. Present or accounted for until discharged on August 6, 1862, by reason of being over age.

FRENCH, WILLIAM F., Private
Resided in Rockingham County and was by occupation a farmer prior to enlisting in Rockingham County at age 33, May 10, 1861. Mustered in as Private and promoted to Corporal on November 1, 1862. Reduced to ranks on November 1, 1863. Present or accounted for until captured at Spotsylvania Court House, Virginia, May 12, 1864. Confined at Point Lookout, Maryland, until released on June 4, 1864, after joining the U.S. Army. Assigned to Company G, 1st Regiment U.S. Volunteer Infantry.

GILLIAM, WILLIAM R., Private
Resided in Rockingham County and was by occupation a farmer prior to enlisting in Rockingham County at age 26, May 10, 1861. Mustered in as Sergeant but was reduced to ranks in March-December, 1862. Present or accounted for until he died in hospital at Lynchburg, Virginia, December 13, 1862, of "bronchitis chron[ic]."

GRIER, WILLIAM A. B., Private
Born in Franklin County, Virginia, and resided in Rockingham County where he was by occupation a farmer prior to enlisting in Rockingham County at age 26, May 10, 1861. Present or accounted for until discharged on August 6, 1862, under the provisions of the Conscript Act.

GRIFFITH, A. A., Private
Enlisted in Rockingham County on November 17, 1863, for the war. Present or accounted for through August, 1864.

GRIFFITH, WILLIAM W., Sergeant
Resided in Rockingham County where he enlisted at age 30, March 25, 1862, for the war. Mustered in as Private and promoted to Sergeant on December 1, 1863. Present or accounted for until wounded near Charles Town, West Virginia, August 24, 1864. Died August 25, 1864, of wounds.

HALL, C. N., Private
Resided in Montgomery County and enlisted in Wake County at age 30, July 16, 1862, for the war.

Present or accounted for until he left the regiment in Maryland on September 9, 1862, by reason of sickness. Captured prior to October 14-15, 1862, when he died at Fort Delaware, Delaware, of disease.

HARDY, ROBERT H., Private
Resided in Rockingham County and was by occupation a farmer prior to enlisting in Rockingham County at age 38, May 10, 1861. Present or accounted for until paroled on April 25, 1865.

HARPER, JOSEPH P., Private
Resided in Montgomery County and enlisted in Wake County at age 23, July 16, 1862, for the war. Present or accounted for through August, 1864; however, he was reported absent sick during most of that period. Paroled at Appomattox Court House, Virginia, April 9, 1865. North Carolina pension records indicate that he was wounded at Petersburg, Virginia, April 1, 1865.

HARRELL, MANGRUM, Private
Resided in Montgomery County and enlisted in Wake County at age 34, July 16, 1862, for the war. Present or accounted for through July, 1862. Captured prior to October 2, 1862, when he was paroled at Leesburg, Virginia. Died at Leesburg on or about October 6, 1862, of disease.

HARRIS, EDWIN RUFFIN, Private
Resided in Rockingham County where he enlisted at age 17, March 25, 1864, for the war. Present or accounted for until wounded at Bethesda Church, Virginia, May 30, 1864. Reported absent wounded through August, 1864. Paroled at Appomattox Court House, Virginia, April 9, 1865.

HARRIS, JAMES M., Private
Resided in Rockingham County where he enlisted at age 21, July 5, 1861. Present or accounted for until wounded in the leg at Spotsylvania Court House, Virginia, May 19, 1864. Reported absent wounded until retired to the Invalid Corps on March 3, 1865.

HARRIS, WILLIAM D., Sergeant
Resided in Rockingham County where he enlisted at age 26, August 10, 1861. Mustered in as Private and promoted to Sergeant on November 1, 1862. Present or accounted for until captured at Winchester, Virginia, September 19, 1864. Confined at Point Lookout, Maryland, until paroled and transferred to Cox's Landing, James River, Virginia, where he was received February 14-15, 1865, for exchange.

HOBBS, CORNELIUS, Private
Resided in Rockingham County and was by occupation a farmer prior to enlisting in Rockingham County at age 28, May 10, 1861. Present or accounted for until killed at Williamsburg, Virginia, May 5, 1862.

HOLDERBY, JAMES P., Private
Resided in Rockingham County and was by occupation a lawyer prior to enlisting in Rockingham County at age 25, May 10, 1861. Present or accounted for until he died at Reidsville, May 10-18, 1862, of "morbi varii."

HOLT, HENRY G., Private
Resided in Rockingham County and was by occupation a mechanic prior to enlisting in Rockingham County at age 27, May 10, 1861.

Present or accounted for until discharged in August, 1861, by reason of disability.

HUBBARD, JAMES, Private
Resided in Virginia and enlisted at Richmond, Virginia, at age 31, July 31, 1862, for the war as a substitute for Private John W. Fitzgerald. Deserted August 6, 1862.

HUMPHLET, D., Private
Resided in Hertford County and enlisted in Wake County at age 20, July 16, 1862, for the war. Present or accounted for until he "left the regiment" on the march to Maryland in August, 1862. Never rejoined the company. No further records.

HUMPHREYS, JONATHAN B., Private
Born in Caswell County and resided in Rockingham County where he was by occupation a tobacconist prior to enlisting in Rockingham County at age 36, May 10, 1861. Mustered in as Sergeant but was reduced to ranks in March-December, 1862. Present or accounted for until discharged on August 6, 1862, by reason of being over age.

HUTSON, JAMES W., Private
Resided in Rockingham County and was by occupation a farmer prior to enlisting in Rockingham County at age 22, May 10, 1861. Present or accounted for until he died in hospital at Richmond, Virginia, September 6, 1862, of "chronic diarrhoea."

JEFFREYS, JAMES HENRY, Private
Born in Rockingham County where he resided as a farmer prior to enlisting in Rockingham County at age 22, May 10, 1861. Present or accounted for until discharged November 20, 1861, by reason of "general debility with a decided tendency to phthisis pulmonalis."

JOHNSON, JOHN, Private
Resided in Virginia and enlisted at Richmond, Virginia, at age 32, May 30, 186[2], for the war as a substitute for Private William Bethel Motley. Deserted near Richmond, Virginia, June 4, 1862.

JOHNSTON, RICHARD, Private
Resided in Rockingham County where he enlisted at age 21, August 10, 1861. Present or accounted for until he died at Danville, Virginia, June 24, 1862, of "typhoid fever."

JONES, JASPER L., Private
Resided in Rockingham County and was by occupation a farmer prior to enlisting in Rockingham County at age 18, May 10, 1861. Present or accounted for until wounded on November 12, 1864. Battle in which wounded not reported. Died in hospital at Mount Jackson, Virginia, November 15, 1864.

JONES, JOHN O. B., Private
Resided in Rockingham County and was by occupation a farmer prior to enlisting in Rockingham County at age 30, May 10, 1861. Present or accounted for until wounded in the right arm and captured at Gettysburg, Pennsylvania, July 1-4, 1863. Hospitalized at Gettysburg until transferred to Davids Island, New York Harbor, July 17-24, 1863. Paroled at Davids Island and transferred to City Point, Virginia, where he was received September 8, 1863, for exchange. Reported absent wounded through Decem-

ber, 1863, but rejoined the company prior to April 1, 1864. Killed at Spotsylvania Court House, Virginia, May 12, 1864.

JONES, SAMUEL F., Corporal

Resided in Rockingham County and was by occupation a farmer prior to enlisting in Rockingham County at age 26, May 10, 1861. Mustered in as Private and promoted to Corporal on November 1, 1862. Present or accounted for until wounded at or near Spotsylvania Court House, Virginia, on or about May 6, 1864. Rejoined the company prior to September 1, 1864. Paroled at Appomattox Court House, Virginia, April 9, 1865. North Carolina pension records indicate he was wounded at Appomattox on April 9, 1865.

JONES, THOMAS J., Private

Resided in Caswell County and enlisted in Wake County at age 24, July 16, 1862, for the war. Present or accounted for through August, 1864; however, he was reported absent sick during most of that period.

JORDAN, A. J., Private

Resided in Hertford County and enlisted in Wake County at age 25, July 16, 1862, for the war. Present or accounted for until wounded at Sharpsburg, Maryland, September 17, 1862. Rejoined the company prior to January 1, 1863, and present or accounted for until wounded at Chancellorsville, Virginia, May 1-3, 1863. Died in hospital at Richmond, Virginia, on or about June 7, 1863, of wounds.

LEA, JOHN W., Corporal

Resided in Rockingham County and was by occupation a mechanic prior to enlisting in Rockingham County at age 22, May 10, 1861. Mustered in as Private and promoted to Corporal on April 25, 1862. Present or accounted for until wounded at or near Gaines' Mill, Virginia, on or about June 27, 1862. Rejoined the company prior to September 17, 1862, when he was wounded at Sharpsburg, Maryland. Reported absent wounded through December, 1862, but rejoined the company prior to May 1, 1863. Present or accounted for until wounded in the arm at Gettysburg, Pennsylvania, July 2-3, 1863. Rejoined the company prior to November 1, 1863, and present or accounted for until paroled at Appomattox Court House, Virginia, April 9, 1865.

LEA, ROBERT A., Private

Resided in Rockingham County and was by occupation a farmer prior to enlisting in Rockingham County at age 20, May 10, 1861. Present or accounted for until wounded at Chancellorsville, Virginia, May 1-3, 1863. Died in hospital at Richmond, Virginia, May 27-28, 1863, of wounds and/or disease.

LEA, THOMAS M., Private

Resided in Rockingham County and was by occupation a mechanic prior to enlisting in Rockingham County at age 24, May 10, 1861. Mustered in as Corporal but was reduced to ranks on November 1, 1862. Present or accounted for until wounded in the right shoulder at or near Hanover Junction, Virginia, on or about May 24, 1864. Reported absent wounded through August, 1864.

LEA, W. R., Private

Resided in Rockingham County where he enlisted at age 18, March 23, 1862, for the war. Present or accounted for until killed near Warrenton, Virginia, October 14, 1863.

LEFTWICH, JAMES B., Private

Resided in Rockingham County where he enlisted at age 17, March 25, 1864, for the war. Present or accounted for until wounded in the hip and captured at Winchester, Virginia, September 19, 1864. Hospitalized at Winchester until transferred to an unspecified hospital on November 8, 1864. Confined at Point Lookout, Maryland, March 31, 1865. Released at Point Lookout on June 28, 1865.

LEFTWICH, T. B., Private

Resided in Rockingham County where he enlisted at age 22, July 5, 1861. Present or accounted for until wounded at or near Gaines' Mill, Virginia, on or about June 27, 1862. Rejoined the company prior to January 1, 1863, and present or accounted for until wounded in the leg at Gettysburg, Pennsylvania, July 1-3, 1863. Rejoined the company prior to September 1, 1863, and present or accounted for until wounded in the left hip and captured at Winchester, Virginia, September 19, 1864. Hospitalized at various Federal hospitals until confined at Point Lookout, Maryland, January 8, 1865. Released at Point Lookout on June 28, 1865, after taking the Oath of Allegiance.

LONDON, JOHN C., Private

Resided in Rockingham County and was by occupation a farmer prior to enlisting in Rockingham County at age 29, May 10, 1861. Present or accounted for until paroled at Lynchburg, Virginia, in April, 1865.

LYON, J. R., Private

Resided in Rockingham County where he enlisted at age 20, August 10, 1861. Present or accounted for until paroled at Appomattox Court House, Virginia, April 9, 1865.

LYONS, ALBERT M., Private

Resided in Rockingham County and was by occupation a farmer prior to enlisting in Rockingham County at age 21, May 10, 1861. Mustered in as Corporal but was reduced to ranks on April 25, 1862. Present or accounted for until mortally wounded and captured at Sharpsburg, Maryland, September 17, 1862. Place and date of death not reported.

McKINNEY, GEORGE C., Private

Born in Rockingham County where he resided as a farmer prior to enlisting in Rockingham County at age 22, May 10, 1861. Present or accounted for until discharged on October 7, 1862, by reason of an "injury of [the] left knee from the kick of a mule" which he received on or about November 1, 1861.

MAYS, J. C., Private

Enlisted in Wake County on July 21, 1863, for the war. Present or accounted for until furloughed for sixty days on February 20, 1865.

MILLER, JAMES W., Private

Born in Rockingham County where he resided as a farmer prior to enlisting in Rockingham County at age 22, May 10, 1861. Present or accounted for until discharged on September 25, 1861, by reason of disability.

MILLER, ROBERT MARTIN, Private
Resided in Rockingham County and was by occupation a farmer prior to enlisting in Rockingham County at age 25, May 10, 1861. Present or accounted for until wounded in the head at Sharpsburg, Maryland, September 17, 1862. Rejoined the company in March-April, 1863, and present or accounted for until wounded in the right leg at Chancellorsville, Virginia, May 3, 1863. Right leg amputated. Reported absent wounded until retired to the Invalid Corps on December 8, 1864. Paroled at Greensboro on May 17, 1865.

MILLS, J. C., Private
Resided in Caswell County and enlisted in Rockingham County at age 20, August 10, 1861. Present or accounted for until discharged on June 4, 1862, after providing Private Joseph Brown as a substitute.

MITCHELL, PINKNEY, Private
Resided in Rockingham County and enlisted in Wake County at age 34, September 24, 1863, for the war. Present or accounted for until wounded in the left arm and captured at Winchester, Virginia, September 19, 1864. Hospitalized at Winchester and at Baltimore, Maryland, until transferred to Point Lookout, Maryland, November 22, 1864. Died in hospital at Point Lookout on June 11, 1865, of "scurvy."

MITCHUM, BENJAMIN C., Private
Resided in Rockingham County and was by occupation a farmer prior to enlisting in Rockingham County at age 20, May 10, 1861. Present or accounted for until he died in hospital at Richmond, Virginia, July 10, 1862, of "feb[ris] typhoides."

MORRIS, JOHN, Private
Resided in Montgomery County and enlisted in Wake County at age 28, July 16, 1862, for the war. Present or accounted for until captured at or near Boonsboro, Maryland, September 17, 1862. Confined at Fort Delaware, Delaware, until transferred to Aiken's Landing, James River, Virginia, October 2, 1862, for exchange. Declared exchanged at Aiken's Landing on November 10, 1862. Rejoined the company prior to January 1, 1863, and present or accounted for until captured at Petersburg, Virginia, April 3, 1865. Confined at Hart's Island, New York Harbor, until released on June 17, 1865, after taking the Oath of Allegiance.

MOTLEY, JOHN M., Private
Resided in Rockingham County and was by occupation a farmer prior to enlisting in Rockingham County at age 23, May 10, 1861. Present or accounted for until he died at Suffolk, Virginia, July 20, 1861, of disease.

MOTLEY, WILLIAM BETHEL, Private
Resided in Rockingham County where he enlisted at age 21, August 10, 1861. Present or accounted for until discharged on May 30, 1862, after providing Private John Johnson as a substitute.

MURPHY, JOHN, Private
Resided in Rockingham County and was by occupation a farmer prior to enlisting in Rocking-

ham County at age 32, May 10, 1861. Present or accounted for until he drowned in the James River on September 18, 1861.

PALMER, LUKE, Private
Born in Rockingham County where he resided as a student prior to enlisting in Rockingham County at age 16, May 10, 1861. Present or accounted for until discharged on August 11, 1862, by reason of being under age.

POOL, ATLAS, Private
Resided in Montgomery County and enlisted in Wake County at age 27, July 16, 1862, for the war. Present or accounted for until he died in hospital at Richmond, Virginia, September 2, 1862, of "double pneumonia."

POOL, W. R., Private
Resided in Montgomery County and enlisted in Wake County at age 32, July 16, 1862, for the war. Present or accounted for until wounded in the hand and captured in Maryland in September, 1862. Confined at Fort McHenry, Maryland, until paroled and transferred to Aiken's Landing, James River, Virginia, where he was received October 19, 1862, for exchange. Declared exchanged at Aiken's Landing on November 10, 1862. Rejoined the company prior to May 1, 1863, and present or accounted for until captured near Washington, D.C., July 12, 1864. Confined at Old Capitol Prison, Washington, until transferred to Elmira, New York, July 23, 1864. Paroled at Elmira on March 10, 1865, and transferred to Boulware's Wharf, James River, Virginia, where he was received March 15, 1865, for exchange.

PRITCHETT, B. Y., Private
Resided in Rockingham County where he enlisted at age 38, September 28, 1863, for the war. Present or accounted for until paroled at Lynchburg, Virginia, April 13-15, 1865.

RAWLEY, HUGH S., Private
Resided in Rockingham County where he enlisted at age 22, May 10, 1861. Mustered in as Corporal but was reduced to ranks on April 25, 1862. Present or accounted for until killed at Charles Town, West Virginia, August 24, 1864.

RAWLEY, J. W., 1st Sergeant
Resided in Rockingham County where he enlisted at age 28, August 10, 1861. Mustered in as Private and promoted to 1st Sergeant on April 25, 1862. Present or accounted for until captured at Frederick, Maryland, September 12, 1862. Confined at Fort Delaware, Delaware, until transferred to Aiken's Landing, James River, Virginia, October 2, 1862, for exchange. Declared exchanged at Aiken's Landing on November 10, 1862. Rejoined the company prior to January 1, 1863, and present or accounted for until wounded at Chancellorsville, Virginia, May 1-3, 1863. Rejoined the company prior to July 1, 1863, and present or accounted for until paroled at Appomattox Court House, Virginia, April 9, 1865.

RAWLEY, TAYLOR L., Sergeant
Resided in Rockingham County and was by occupation a student prior to enlisting in Rockingham County at age 19, May 10, 1861. Mustered in as Private and promoted to Sergeant on June 1, 1863.

Present or accounted for until appointed 1st Lieutenant and transferred to Company K, 13th Regiment N.C. Troops (3rd Regiment N.C. Volunteers) on or about November 25, 1863.

REYNOLDS, J. M., Private
Resided in Hertford County and enlisted in Wake County at age 23, July 16, 1862, for the war. Present or accounted for until he died in hospital at Richmond, Virginia, November 13, 1862, of "typhoid fever."

RICH, J. M., Private
Resided in Hertford County and enlisted in Wake County at age 25, July 16, 1862, for the war. Present or accounted for until captured at Frederick City, Maryland, September 11, 1862. Confined at Fort Delaware, Delaware, where he died December 15, 1862, of disease.

ROBERTSON, ELIJAH H., Corporal
Resided in Rockingham County where he enlisted at age 19, July 5, 1861. Mustered in as Private and promoted to Corporal on April 25, 1862. Present or accounted for until wounded and captured at Sharpsburg, Maryland, September 17, 1862. Died in hospital at Frederick, Maryland, November 2, 1862, of wounds.

ROSS, JOHN MONTGOMERY, Private
Enlisted in Stanly County on April 25, 1864, for the war. Present or accounted for until paroled at Albemarle on May 19, 1865.

SATTERFIELD, W. D., Private
Resided in Person County and enlisted in Wake County at age 25, July 16, 1862, for the war. Present or accounted for through March, 1865; however, he was reported absent sick or absent on light duty during most of that period. Captured in hospital at Richmond, Virginia, April 3, 1865, and was paroled on April 24, 1865.

SCARLETT, GEORGE W., Private
Resided in Rockingham County and was by occupation a farmer prior to enlisting in Rockingham County at age 33, May 10, 1861. Present or accounted for until he died in hospital at Mount Jackson, Virginia, December 10, 1862, of "erysipelas."

SCARLETT, JAMES I., Sergeant
Born in Rockingham County where he resided as a farmer prior to enlisting in Rockingham County at age 21, May 10, 1861. Mustered in as Private. Present or accounted for until wounded in the leg at Malvern Hill, Virginia, July 1, 1862. Promoted to Sergeant on November 1, 1862, and rejoined the company prior to January 1, 1863. Present or accounted for until wounded in the forehead at Chancellorsville, Virginia, May 3, 1863. Rejoined the company prior to July 1, 1863, and present or accounted for until wounded in the right elbow at Winchester, Virginia, September 19, 1864. Discharged March 21, 1865, by reason of wounds received at Winchester.

SIDDLE, JESSE, Private
Resided in Caswell County and enlisted in Rockingham County at age 36, August 10, 1861. Present or accounted for until hospitalized at Richmond,

Virginia, June 16, 1862, with "acute diarrhoea." Died in hospital at Richmond on June 29, 1862.

SMITH, CALEB, Private
Born in Rockingham County where he resided as a farmer prior to enlisting in Rockingham County at age 23, May 10, 1861. Present or accounted for until discharged on or about September 19, 1861, by reason of "inguinal hernia."

SMITH, G. M., Private
Place and date of enlistment not reported. Wounded in the thigh and captured at Winchester, Virginia, September 19, 1864. Died in hospital at Winchester on October 10, 1864, of "febris typhoid."

SMITH, GEORGE W., Private
Resided in Rockingham County and was by occupation a farmer prior to enlisting in Rockingham County at age 21, May 10, 1861. Present or accounted for until captured at Sharpsburg, Maryland, September 17, 1862. Confined at Fort Delaware, Delaware, until transferred to Aiken's Landing, James River, Virginia, October 2, 1862, for exchange. Declared exchanged at Aiken's Landing on November 10, 1862. Rejoined the company prior to January 1, 1863, and present or accounted for until wounded in the right thigh and captured at Winchester, Virginia, September 19, 1864. Hospitalized at Baltimore, Maryland, and was confined at Point Lookout, Maryland, October 26, 1864. Paroled at Point Lookout on October 30, 1864, and transferred to Venus Point, Savannah River, Georgia, where he was received November 15, 1864, for exchange.

SMITH, JAMES W., Private
Resided in Rockingham County and was by occupation a clerk prior to enlisting in Rockingham County at age 25, May 10, 1861. Present or accounted for until killed at Malvern Hill, Virginia, July 1, 1862.

SMITH, JOSEPH R., Sergeant
Resided in Rockingham County and was by occupation a farmer prior to enlisting in Rockingham County at age 25, May 10, 1861. Mustered in as Private and promoted to Sergeant on June 17, 1862. Present or accounted for until wounded at Malvern Hill, Virginia, July 1, 1862. Rejoined the company prior to January 1, 1863, and present or accounted for until killed at Chancellorsville, Virginia, May 3, 1863. Nominated for the Badge of Distinction for gallantry at Chancellorsville.

SNOW, L. A., Private
Resided in Rockingham County where he enlisted at age 21, March 25, 1862. Present or accounted for until he died in hospital at Richmond, Virginia, June 23, 1862, of "febris typhoides & parotitis."

SNOW, W. G., Private
Resided in Rockingham County where he enlisted at age 26, March 25, 1862, for the war. Present or accounted for until wounded in the left hand at Spotsylvania Court House, Virginia, May 12, 1864. Reported absent wounded through August, 1864. Paroled at Farmville, Virginia, April 11-21, 1865.

STANLY, WILLIAM R., Private
Resided in Rockingham County where he enlisted at

age 31, August 10, 1861. Present or accounted for until he died at Fort Bee, Virginia, or at Smithfield, Virginia, February 16-18, 1862, of disease.

STRADER, JOHN S., Private

Born in Caswell County and resided in Rockingham County where he was by occupation a farmer prior to enlisting in Rockingham County at age 25, May 10, 1861. Present or accounted for until discharged on August 6, 1862, under the provisions of the Conscript Act. Reenlisted in this company on July 28, 1863, and present or accounted for until captured at Cedar Creek, Virginia, October 19, 1864. Confined at Point Lookout, Maryland, until released on June 20, 1865, after taking the Oath of Allegiance.

STRADER, WILLIAM, Private

Resided in Rockingham County where he enlisted at age 20, August 10, 1861. Present or accounted for until wounded at Williamsport, Maryland, on or about July 7, 1863. Died of wounds. Place and date of death not reported.

STUBBLEFIELD, WILLIAM N., Private

Resided in Caswell County and enlisted in Rockingham County at age 20, August 10, 1861. Present or accounted for until he died in hospital at Richmond, Virginia, May 31, 1862, of "feb[ris] typh[oid]."

STUBBLEFIELD, WILLIAM W., Private

Resided in Rockingham County and was by occupation a farmer prior to enlisting in Rockingham County at age 30, May 10, 1861. Mustered in as Private and promoted to Sergeant on April 25, 1862. Reduced to ranks on November 1, 1862. Present or accounted for until wounded at Spotsylvania Court House, Virginia, May 12, 1864. Rejoined the company prior to July 1, 1864, and present or accounted for until wounded at Cedar Creek, Virginia, October 19, 1864. Company records do not indicate whether he returned to duty; however, he was hospitalized at Richmond, Virginia, March 12, 1865, with a gunshot wound of the face. Place and date wounded not reported. Captured at Richmond on April 3, 1865. Confined at Newport News, Virginia, April 24, 1865, and was released at Newport News on June 30, 1865, after taking the Oath of Allegiance.

SWANN, JAMES J., Private

Born in Caswell County and resided in Rockingham County where he was by occupation a mason prior to enlisting in Rockingham County at age 20, May 10, 1861. Present or accounted for until discharged on August 8, 1863, by reason of "phthisis pulmonalis" and/or "valvular disease of the heart."

SWANN, WILLIAM L., Private

Resided in Rockingham County and was by occupation a millwright prior to enlisting in Rockingham County at age 17, May 10, 1861. Present or accounted for until he died in hospital at Richmond, Virginia, February 23, 1863, of "typhoid fever."

TAYLOR, A. P., Private

Resided in Rockingham County where he enlisted at age 18, March 18, 1862. Present or accounted for until wounded in the right hip at Chancellorsville, Virginia, May 1-3, 1863. Rejoined the company in

September-October, 1863, and present or accounted for until wounded in the left hand at Spotsylvania Court House, Virginia, in May, 1864. Reported absent wounded through October 23, 1864. Paroled at Appomattox Court House, Virginia, April 9, 1865.

TAYLOR, BENJAMIN F., Private

Resided in Rockingham County and was by occupation a farmer prior to enlisting in Rockingham County at age 22, May 10, 1861. Present or accounted for until wounded in the left arm and captured at Sharpsburg, Maryland, September 17, 1862. Left arm amputated. Confined at Fort McHenry, Maryland, until paroled and transferred to Aiken's Landing, James River, Virginia, where he was received October 19, 1862, for exchange. Declared exchanged at Aiken's Landing on November 10, 1862. Reported absent wounded until retired to the Invalid Corps on November 25, 1864.

TAYLOR, DOCTOR W., Private

Resided in Rockingham County and was by occupation a farmer prior to enlisting in Rockingham County at age 23, May 10, 1861. Present or accounted for until captured at Williamsport, Maryland, September 15, 1862. Confined at Fort Delaware, Delaware, until transferred to Aiken's Landing, James River, Virginia, October 2, 1862, for exchange. Declared exchanged at Aiken's Landing on November 10, 1862. Rejoined the company prior to January 1, 1863, and present or accounted for until captured at or near Petersburg, Virginia, April 2, 1865. Confined at Hart's Island, New York Harbor, until released on June 17, 1865, after taking the Oath of Allegiance.

TAYLOR, GEORGE W., Private

Resided in Rockingham County and was by occupation a farmer prior to enlisting in Rockingham County at age 19, May 10, 1861. Present or accounted for until wounded in the face and neck at Williamsburg, Virginia, May 5, 1862. Reported absent wounded until discharged on August 23, 1862, by reason of wounds received at Williamsburg.

TAYLOR, WILLIAM W., Private

Born in Caswell County and resided in Rockingham County where he was by occupation a shoemaker prior to enlisting in Rockingham County at age 26, May 10, 1861. Present or accounted for until discharged on September 9, 1863, by reason of "phthisis pulmonalis [and] general debility."

TIGUE, JACOB, Private

Resided in Montgomery County and enlisted in Wake County at age 21, July 16, 1862, for the war. Present or accounted for until wounded and captured at or near Sharpsburg, Maryland, on or about September 17, 1862. Confined at Fort McHenry, Maryland. Transferred to Aiken's Landing, James River, Virginia, prior to November 10, 1862, when he was declared exchanged at Aiken's Landing. Reported absent without leave from December 1, 1862, until November 12, 1863, when he rejoined the company. Reported absent sick from November-December, 1863, until December 30, 1864, when he was reported as an "escaped prisoner." No further records.

WALKER, JAMES H., Corporal

Resided in Alamance County and was by occupation a farmer prior to enlisting in Rockingham County at age 19, May 10, 1861. Mustered in as Private and promoted to Corporal on December 1, 1863. Present or accounted for until captured at Petersburg, Virginia, April 3, 1865. Confined at Hart's Island, New York Harbor, until released on June 17, 1865, after taking the Oath of Allegiance.

WALKER, JOHN M., Jr., Sergeant

Born in Caswell County and resided in Rockingham County where he was by occupation a farmer prior to enlisting in Rockingham County at age 19, May 10, 1861. Mustered in as Private and promoted to Sergeant on April 25, 1862. Present or accounted for until he died in hospital at Richmond, Virginia, June 12, 1862, of "febris typhoides & cont[inued]."

WALKER, WILLIAM J., Sergeant

Resided in Alamance County and was by occupation a merchant prior to enlisting in Rockingham County at age 29, May 10, 1861. Mustered in as Private and promoted to Sergeant on April 25, 1862. Present or accounted for until wounded at Boonsboro, Maryland, September 15, 1862, or at Sharpsburg, Maryland, September 17, 1862. Reported absent wounded until paroled at Lynchburg, Virginia, in April, 1865.

WALLER, L. C., Private

Resided in Southampton County, Virginia, and enlisted in Montgomery County at age 45, August 27, 1863, for the war as a substitute. Present or accounted for until wounded in the left foot at Petersburg, Virginia, March 21, 1865. Captured at or near Petersburg on April 2, 1865, and hospitalized at various Federal hospitals until confined at Camp Hamilton, Virginia, May 6, 1865. Transferred to Newport News, Virginia, where he arrived May 8, 1865. Released at Newport News on June 15, 1865, after taking the Oath of Allegiance.

WELLS, GEORGE B., Private

Resided in Alamance County and was by occupation a farmer prior to enlisting in Rockingham County at age 16, May 10, 1861. Present or accounted for until wounded at Sharpsburg, Maryland, September 17, 1862. Rejoined the company prior to January 1, 1863, and present or accounted for until wounded in the chin at Gettysburg, Pennsylvania, July 2-3, 1863. Rejoined the company in November-December, 1863, and present or accounted for until killed at Spotsylvania Court House, Virginia, May 12, 1864.

WILBORN, WILLIAM C., Private

Resided in Alamance County and was by occupation a farmer prior to enlisting in Rockingham County at age 18, May 10, 1861. Present or accounted for through August, 1864; however, he was reported absent sick or absent on light duty during most of that period.

WILLIAMS, WILLIAM W., Private

Born in Rockingham County where he resided as a farmer prior to enlisting in Rockingham County at age 24, May 10, 1861. Present or accounted for until discharged on September 2, 1861, by reason of disability.

WILLOWBY, W. H., Private

Resided in Hertford County and enlisted in Wake County at age 24, July 16, 1862, for the war. Present or accounted for until wounded at Sharpsburg, Maryland, September 17, 1862. Reported absent wounded until he died at Harrisonburg, Virginia, in October, 1862, or on February 19, 1863.

WILSON, J. M., Private

Resided in Rockingham County where he enlisted at age 21, August 10, 1861. Mustered in as Private and promoted to Sergeant on April 25, 1862. Reduced to ranks on November 1, 1862. Present or accounted for until captured at Winchester, Virginia, September 19, 1864. Confined at Point Lookout, Maryland, until paroled and transferred to Boulware's Wharf, James River, Virginia, where he was received March 18, 1865, for exchange.

WILSON, WILLIAM L., Private

Resided in Rockingham County and was by occupation a farmer prior to enlisting in Rockingham County at age 23, May 10, 1861. Mustered in as Private and promoted to Corporal on April 25, 1862. Reduced to ranks on November 1, 1862. Present or accounted for until killed at Bethesda Church, Virginia, May 30, 1864.

WRIGHT, E. A., Private

Resided in Montgomery County where he enlisted at age 37, August 27, 1863, for the war. Present or accounted for until captured at Spotsylvania Court House, Virginia, May 19, 1864. Confined at Point Lookout, Maryland, until paroled and transferred to Aiken's Landing, James River, Virginia, September 18, 1864, for exchange. Hospitalized at Richmond, Virginia, September 22, 1864. No further records.

WRIGHT, J. M., Private

Resided in Montgomery County and enlisted in Wake County at age 33, July 16, 1862, for the war. Present or accounted for through August, 1864.

WRIGHT, W. B., Private

Resided in Caswell County and enlisted in Rockingham County at age 24, August 10, 1861. Present or accounted for until wounded at Winchester, Virginia, on or about September 19, 1864. Rejoined the company at an unspecified date and was paroled at Appomattox Court House, Virginia, April 9, 1865.

YATES, LAWSON, Private

Resided in Rockingham County and was by occupation a farmer prior to enlisting in Rockingham County at age 25, May 10, 1861. Present or accounted for until discharged on or about August 11, 1862, under the provisions of the Conscript Act.

YOUNG, ALEXANDER, Private

Resided in Rockingham County where he enlisted at age 26, March 17, 1862, for the war. Present or accounted for until wounded at Chancellorsville, Virginia, May 1-3, 1863. Rejoined the company in November-December, 1863, and present or accounted for until wounded in the left side and captured at Winchester, Virginia, September 19, 1864. Hospitalized at Winchester and at Baltimore, Maryland, until confined at Point Lookout, Maryland, November 23, 1864. Released at Point Lookout on May 14, 1865.

YOUNG, JOSIAH, Private
Resided in Rockingham County and was by occupation a farmer prior to enlisting in Rockingham County at age 23, May 10, 1861. Present or accounted for through April, 1864; however, he was reported absent sick during most of that period. Captured at Bethesda Church, Virginia, May 30, 1864. Confined at Point Lookout, Maryland, until paroled and transferred to Boulware's Wharf, James River, Virginia, where he was received March 19, 1865, for exchange.

YOUNG, PINKNEY, Private
Resided in Rockingham County and was by occupation a farmer prior to enlisting in Rockingham County at age 21, May 10, 1861. Present or accounted for through August, 1864; however, he was reported absent sick during much of that period. Paroled on May 11, 1865.

YOUNG, WILLIAM, Private
Born in Rockingham County where he resided as a farmer prior to enlisting in Rockingham County at age 24, May 10, 1861. Present or accounted for until discharged on November 28, 1861, by reason of "disease of the heart."

COMPANY H

This company, known as the Stanly Marksmen, was from Stanly County and enlisted at Albemarle on May 5, 1861. On May 23 the company left Albemarle for Raleigh, where it arrived the next day. It moved to Garysburg on June 1. There it was assigned to this regiment as Company H. After joining the regiment the company functioned as a part of the regiment, and its history for the war period is recorded as part of the regimental history.

The information contained in the following roster of the company was compiled principally from company muster rolls for June 30, 1861, through August 31, 1864. No company muster rolls were found for the period after August 31, 1864. In addition to the company muster rolls, Roll of Honor records, receipt rolls, hospital records, prisoner of war records, and other primary records, supplemented by state pension applications, United Daughters of the Confederacy records, and postwar rosters and histories, all provided useful information.

OFFICERS

CAPTAINS

ANDERSON, RICHARD
Resided in Stanly County and enlisted at age 28. Elected Captain to rank from May 13, 1861. Present or accounted for until he resigned or was defeated for reelection when the regiment was reorganized April 25-27, 1862.

DEBERRY, JAMES R.
Resided in Stanly County and was by occupation a clerk prior to enlisting in Stanly County at age 20, May 5, 1861. Mustered in as 1st Sergeant and was appointed 1st Lieutenant to rank from July 24, 1861. Elected Captain to rank from April 25-27, 1862. Present or accounted for until wounded at Sharpsburg, Maryland, September 17, 1862. Rejoined the company prior to January 1, 1863, and present or accounted for until killed in the "very forefront of battle" at Winchester, Virginia, September 19, 1864.

LIEUTENANTS

HEARNE, WILLIAM H., 1st Lieutenant
Resided in Stanly County and was by occupation a clerk prior to enlisting in Stanly County at age 20, May 5, 1861. Mustered in as Private and promoted to Sergeant on August 26, 1861. Elected 2nd Lieutenant to rank from April 27, 1862. Present or accounted for until wounded at Malvern Hill, Virginia, on or about July 1, 1862. Rejoined the company prior to January 1, 1863, and was promoted to 1st Lieutenant on March 1, 1864. Present or accounted for until wounded in the left foot and captured at Winchester, Virginia, September 19, 1864. Hospitalized at Winchester and at Baltimore, Maryland, until confined at Point Lookout, Maryland, November 23, 1864. Transferred to Old Capitol Prison, Washington, D.C., January 2, 1865, and was transferred to Fort Delaware, Delaware, February 3, 1865. Released at Fort Delaware on June 14, 1865, after taking the Oath of Allegiance.

KENDALL, JULIUS A., 2nd Lieutenant
Resided in Stanly County where he enlisted at age 31. Elected 2nd Lieutenant to rank from May 13, 1861. Present or accounted for until he resigned or was defeated for reelection when the regiment was reorganized, April 25-27, 1862. [May have served later as Private in Company I, 52nd Regiment N.C. Troops.]

LOCKE, JAMES M., 2nd Lieutenant
Born in Stanly County* where he resided as a farmer prior to enlisting in Stanly County at age 27, May 5, 1861. Mustered in as Corporal and was elected 2nd Lieutenant to rank from April 27, 1862. Present or accounted for until he died in hospital at Richmond, Virginia, June 11, 1862, of "typhoid fever."

McLESTER, JEREMIAH D., 3rd Lieutenant
Resided in Stanly County and was by occupation a farmer prior to enlisting in Stanly County at age 23, May 5, 1861. Mustered in as Private and promoted to Sergeant on April 27, 1862. Elected 3rd Lieutenant to rank from October 3, 1862. Present or accounted for until wounded in the head and captured at or near Gettysburg, Pennsylvania, July 2-4, 1863. Confined at Fort Delaware, Delaware, until transferred to Johnson's Island, Ohio, July 18, 1863. Confined at Johnson's Island until paroled on March 14, 1865, and transferred to Cox's Wharf, James River, Virginia, where he was received March 22, 1865, for exchange.

SHANKLE, DEWITT C., 1st Lieutenant
Born in Stanly County* where he resided as a merchant prior to enlisting in Stanly County at age 26, May 5, 1861. Mustered in as Sergeant and promoted to 1st Sergeant on July 26, 1861. Elected 1st Lieutenant to rank from April 27, 1862. Present or accounted for until captured at Sharpsburg, Maryland, on or about September 16, 1862. Confined at Fort Delaware, Delaware, until transferred to Aiken's Landing, James River, Virginia, October 2, 1862, for exchange. Declared exchanged at Aiken's Landing on November 10, 1862. Rejoined

the company prior to January 1, 1863, and present or accounted for until wounded at Chancellorsville, Virginia, May 3, 1863. Died May 4, 1863, of wounds.

SHOFFNER, MARTIN, 1st Lieutenant
Resided in Stanly County where he enlisted at age 41. Elected 1st Lieutenant on May 5, 1861. Resigned July 20-24, 1861. Reason he resigned not reported.

SIMPSON, JOHN B., 3rd Lieutenant
Resided in Stanly County and enlisted at age 38. Elected 3rd Lieutenant to rank from May 13, 1861. Present or accounted for until he resigned on April 23, 1862, "for good and sufficient reasons."

NONCOMMISSIONED OFFICERS AND PRIVATES

ALLEN, JOHN, Sergeant
Resided in Stanly County and was by occupation a farmer prior to enlisting in Stanly County at age 30, May 5, 1861. Mustered in as Sergeant. Present or accounted for until discharged on August 26, 1861. Reason discharged not reported.

ALMOND, CYRUS W., Private
Resided in Stanly County and was by occupation a farmer prior to enlisting in Stanly County at age 19, May 5, 1861. Present or accounted for until transferred to Company F, 5th Regiment N.C. State Troops, on or about November 15, 1862.

ALMOND, GREEN, Private
Born in Stanly County* where he resided as a farmer prior to enlisting in Stanly County at age 31, May 5, 1861. Present or accounted for until reported absent without leave from December 1, 1862, through February, 1863. Wounded in the right arm at Chancellorsville, Virginia, May 3, 1863, and right arm amputated. Discharged October 25, 1863, by reason of disability.

AUSTIN, JACOB, Private
Enlisted in Wake County on October 8, 1863, for the war. Present or accounted for until wounded at Spotsylvania Court House, Virginia, May 12, 1864. Reported absent wounded through August, 1864.

AVETT, J. H., Private
Resided in Stanly County where he enlisted at age 20, September 5, 1861. Present or accounted for until wounded in battle near Richmond, Virginia, in June-July, 1862. Rejoined the company prior to December 5, 1862, and present or accounted for until wounded at Spotsylvania Court House, Virginia, May 12, 1864. Died May 14, 1864, of wounds. Place of death not reported.

AVITTE, EDMUND F., Private
Born in Anson County and resided in Stanly County where he was by occupation a farmer prior to enlisting in Stanly County at age 23, May 5, 1861. Mustered in as Private and promoted to Corporal on August 26, 1861. Reduced to ranks on April 27, 1862, but was appointed Sergeant on December 8, 1862. Present or accounted for until wounded in the left leg at Fredericksburg, Virginia, December 13, 1862. Rejoined the company in September-October, 1863, and present or accounted for until wounded in the right knee at Mine Run, Virginia, November 26,

1863. Reported absent wounded through February, 1864, and was reduced to ranks "by his consent" on July 1, 1864. Discharged March 1, 1865, by reason of wounds received at Mine Run. Captured in hospital at Richmond, Virginia, April 3, 1865. No further records.

BARRINGER, D. GREENE, Private
Resided in Stanly County and was by occupation a farmer prior to enlisting in Stanly County at age 26, May 5, 1861. Present or accounted for until wounded in the left leg at Spotsylvania Court House, Virginia, May 12, 1864. Reported absent wounded through August, 1864. Took the Oath of Allegiance at Salisbury on July 6, 1865.

BATSON, B., _____
Place and date of enlistment not reported. Died in hospital at Asheville on September 20, 1864. Cause of death not reported.

BILES, HUTSON THOMAS, Private
Resided in Stanly County and enlisted in Wake County at age 43, September 10, 1863, for the war. Present or accounted for until hospitalized at Richmond, Virginia, April 14, 1864, with a gunshot wound of the left foot; however, place and date wounded not reported. Reported absent wounded through August, 1864. Paroled at Appomattox Court House, Virginia, April 9, 1865.

BILES, ISAAC E., Private
Resided in Stanly County and was by occupation a farmer prior to enlisting in Stanly County at age 24, May 5, 1861. Present or accounted for until he died at Camp Bee, Virginia, on or about September 9, 1861. Cause of death not reported.

BIRD, BENJAMIN F., Private
Born in Montgomery County and resided in Stanly County where he was by occupation a farmer prior to enlisting in Stanly County at age 22, May 5, 1861. Present or accounted for until he died "at home" on December 9, 1862, of "chronic diarrhoea."

BLAYLOCK, CALVIN, Private
Enlisted in Stanly County on February 10, 1864, for the war. Present or accounted for until captured near Washington, D.C., on or about July 13, 1864. Confined at Old Capitol Prison, Washington, and was transferred to Elmira, New York, August 27, 1864. Died at Elmira on March 29, 1865, of "variola." Federal medical records give his age as 19.

BROWN, C., Private
Enlisted in Wake County on July 16, 1862, for the war. Present or accounted for until he deserted at or near Richmond, Virginia, August 18, 1862.

BURLEYSON, LEE, Private
Born in Montgomery County and resided in Stanly County where he was by occupation a farmer prior to enlisting in Stanly County at age 36, May 5, 1861. Present or accounted for until discharged on August 5, 1862, by reason of being over age.

BURLEYSON, NATHAN, Private
Resided in Stanly County and was by occupation a farmer prior to enlisting in Stanly County at age 28, May 5, 1861. Present or accounted for until he died in hospital at Richmond, Virginia, June 16, 1863, of "ulcus."

BURNS, JOSHUA A., Private

Resided in Stanly or Anson counties and was by occupation a farmer prior to enlisting in Stanly County at age 23, May 5, 1861. Present or accounted for until wounded in the thigh and captured at Gettysburg, Pennsylvania, July 1-4, 1863. Confined at Davids Island, New York Harbor, until paroled and transferred to City Point, Virginia, where he was received August 28, 1863, for exchange. Returned to duty in November-December, 1863, and present or accounted for until captured at Petersburg, Virginia, April 3, 1865. Confined at Hart's Island, New York Harbor, until released on or about June 17, 1865, after taking the Oath of Allegiance.

CAGLE, DAVID D., Private

Resided in Stanly County and was by occupation a farmer prior to enlisting in Stanly County at age 20, May 5, 1861. Present or accounted for until he died at Camp Ellis, Virginia, August 24, 1861. Cause of death not reported.

CARTER, JULIUS F., Private

Resided in Stanly County and was by occupation a farmer prior to enlisting in Stanly County at age 22, May 5, 1861. Present or accounted for until wounded in battle near Richmond, Virginia, in June-July, 1862. Rejoined the company prior to September 17, 1862, when he was captured at Sharpsburg, Maryland. Confined at Fort Delaware, Delaware, until transferred to Aiken's Landing, James River, Virginia, October 2, 1862, for exchange. Declared exchanged at Aiken's Landing on November 10, 1862. Rejoined the company prior to January 1, 1863, and present or accounted for until paroled at Appomattox Court House, Virginia, April 9, 1865.

CARTER, ROBERT A., Private

Resided in Stanly County and was by occupation a farmer prior to enlisting in Stanly County at age 24, May 5, 1861. Present or accounted for until discharged September 18-19, 1861. Reason discharged not reported.

CAUDLE, J. W., Private

Enlisted in Wake County on October 8, 1863, for the war. Present or accounted for until captured in hospital at or near Petersburg, Virginia, on or about April 3, 1865. Died in hospital at Point of Rocks, Virginia, April 29, 1865, of "chronic diarrhoea."

CLARK, W. G., Private

Place and date of enlistment not reported. Paroled at Greensboro on May 16, 1865.

CLARK, YANCY, Private

Enlisted in Wake County on October 1, 1863, for the war. Reported absent without leave on October 20, 1863, but was reported "in arrest" on October 30, 1863. Court-martialed on or about January 8, 1864, and was reported in confinement at Salisbury through August, 1864.

CLARKE, WILLIAM P., Private

Born in Davidson County* and resided in Stanly County where he was by occupation a blacksmith or farmer prior to enlisting in Stanly County at age 43, May 5, 1861. Present or accounted for until discharged on August 5, 1862, under the provisions of the Conscript Act.

CLODFELTER, HENRY, Private

Enlisted in Wake County on February 1, 1864, for the war. Present or accounted for until captured at Spotsylvania Court House, Virginia, May 19-20, 1864. Confined at Point Lookout, Maryland, until transferred to Elmira, New York, July 23, 1864. Died at Elmira on October 24, 1864, of "pneumonia."

CLODFELTER, JACOB H., Private

Resided in Davidson County and enlisted in Wake County at age 27, July 16, 1862, for the war. Present or accounted for until wounded in the hip at Spotsylvania Court House, Virginia, May 8, 1864. Reported absent wounded through August, 1864.

COLEY, ISHAM, Private

Born in Stanly County* where he resided as a blacksmith prior to enlisting in Stanly County at age 27, September 5, 1861. Present or accounted for until he died in hospital at Richmond, Virginia, June 28, 1862, of disease.

COX, C. D., Private

Resided in Anson County and enlisted in Wake County at age 43, August 20, 1863, for the war. Present or accounted for until wounded at or near Cold Harbor, Virginia, May 31, 1864. Reported absent wounded through August, 1864.

DAVIS, WILLIAM E. H., Private

Resided in Granville County and enlisted in Wake County at age 18, June 11, 1863, for the war. Present or accounted for until captured at Winchester, Virginia, September 19, 1864. Confined at Point Lookout, Maryland, until paroled and transferred to Cox's Landing, James River, Virginia, where he was received February 14-15, 1865, for exchange. Reported present with a detachment of paroled and exchanged prisoners at Camp Lee, near Richmond, Virginia, February 18, 1865.

DEES, W. E., Private

Enlisted in Wake County on October 8, 1863, for the war. Present or accounted for until wounded in the right leg and captured at Cedar Creek, Virginia, October 19, 1864. Hospitalized at Baltimore, Maryland, until transferred to Point Lookout, Maryland, on or about October 26, 1864. Paroled at Point Lookout on October 30, 1864, and transferred to Venus Point, Savannah River, Georgia, where he was received November 15, 1864, for exchange. Paroled at Appomattox Court House, Virginia, April 9, 1865. Federal medical records give his age as 19.

DRY, JOHN, Private

Resided in Stanly County and was by occupation a farmer prior to enlisting in Stanly County at age 23, May 5, 1861. Present or accounted for through August, 1864. North Carolina pension records indicate he was wounded on September 19, 1864. No further records.

DUNN, JOHN D., Private

Resided in Nash County and was by occupation a farmer prior to enlisting in Wake County at age 36, June 11, 1863, for the war. Present or accounted for until hospitalized at Danville, Virginia, July 16, 1863, with a gunshot wound; however, place and date wounded not reported. Returned to duty prior to September 1, 1863, and present or accounted for until captured at Staunton, Virginia, September

27-28, 1864. Confined at Point Lookout, Maryland, until released on May 13, 1865, after taking the "Oath."

EDWARDS, JOSEPH, Private

Enlisted in Wake County on October 1, 1863, for the war. Reported absent without leave on October 20, 1863, and was reported "in arrest" on October 30, 1863. Court-martialed for desertion on or about January 8, 1864. Died on February 12, 1864, of "pneumonia." Place of death not reported.

EFIRD, SIDNEY L., Private

Born in Stanly County* where he resided as a farmer prior to enlisting in Stanly County at age 29, May 5, 1861. Present or accounted for until he died in hospital at Richmond, Virginia, July 19, 1862, of disease.

ELLIOTT, J. C., Private

Resided in Montgomery County and enlisted in Wake County at age 31, July 16, 1862, for the war. Present or accounted for until he died at camp near Port Royal, Virginia, December 10-11, 1862. Cause of death not reported.

ELLIOTT, R. H., Private

Resided in Montgomery or Rowan counties and enlisted in Wake County at age 29, July 16, 1862, for the war. Present or accounted for until captured at Berryville, Virginia, August 10, 1864. Confined at Old Capitol Prison, Washington, D.C., until transferred to Elmira, New York, August 28, 1864. Released at Elmira on or about June 21, 1865, after taking the Oath of Allegiance.

FORREST, THOMAS FRANK, Private

Resided in Stanly or Rowan counties and was by occupation a farmer prior to enlisting in Stanly County at age 20, May 5, 1861. Present or accounted for until wounded and captured at or near Sharpsburg, Maryland, on or about September 17, 1862. Received at Aiken's Landing, James River, Virginia, October 12, 1862, for exchange. Rejoined the company in January-February, 1863, and present or accounted for until wounded in the right hip at Chancellorsville, Virginia, May 3, 1863. Reported absent wounded until retired to the Invalid Corps on May 2, 1864.

FORREST, WILLIAM M., Private

Born in Stanly County* where he resided as a farmer prior to enlisting in Stanly County at age 22, May 5, 1861. Present or accounted for until discharged on October 16, 1861, by reason of "incipient phthisis."

FORT, W. H., Private

Place and date of enlistment not reported. Died at Elmira, New York, December 18, 1864. Cause of death not reported.

FOUTS, ABSALOM, Private

Resided in Davidson County and enlisted in Wake County at age 28, July 16, 1862, for the war. Present or accounted for through January 31, 1865; however, he was reported absent sick during much of that period.

FRY, CALVIN, Private

Resided in Stanly County and was by occupation a farmer prior to enlisting in Stanly County at age 33, May 5, 1861. Present or accounted for until

wounded in the right arm at Malvern Hill, Virginia, July 1, 1862. Reported absent wounded until discharged on or about August 5, 1862, under the provisions of the Conscript Act.

GUNTER, CHARLES, Private

Place and date of enlistment not reported. Captured at Orange Court House, Virginia, February 5, 1864, and confined at Old Capitol Prison, Washington, D.C., until released on March 15, 1864, after taking the "Oath."

HALL, JAMES, Private

Born in Stanly County* where he resided as a farmer prior to enlisting in Stanly County at age 23, May 5, 1861. Present or accounted for until captured at Sharpsburg, Maryland, September 17, 1862. Confined at Fort Delaware, Delaware, until transferred to Aiken's Landing, James River, Virginia, October 2, 1862, for exchange. Declared exchanged at Aiken's Landing on November 10, 1862. Rejoined the company prior to January 1, 1863, and present or accounted for until wounded in the right leg at Chancellorsville, Virginia, May 3, 1863. Right leg amputated. Reported absent wounded until retired to the Invalid Corps on August 10, 1864. Pension records indicate that he died of injuries received at Chancellorsville; however, place and date of death not reported.

HALL, WILLIAM S., Private

Resided in Montgomery County and enlisted in Wake County at age 28, July 16, 1862, for the war. Present or accounted for until wounded at Chancellorsville, Virginia, May 3, 1863. Rejoined the company in July-August, 1863, and present or accounted for until paroled at Appomattox Court House, Virginia, April 9, 1865.

HAMILTON, W. S., Private

Resided in Davidson County and enlisted in Wake County at age 19, July 16, 1862, for the war. Present or accounted for until he died on or about December 14, 1862. Place and cause of death not reported.

HARRIS, ALEXANDER, Private

Resided in Montgomery County and enlisted in Wake County at age 26, July 16, 1862, for the war. Present or accounted for until reported absent without leave from December 14, 1862, through April, 1863. Present or accounted for until wounded in the face at Gettysburg, Pennsylvania, July 2-3, 1863. Transferred to Company F, 44th Regiment N.C. Troops, August 30, 1863.

HATHCOCK, JESSE, Private

Resided in Stanly County and was by occupation a farmer prior to enlisting in Stanly County at age 27, May 5, 1861. Present or accounted for until captured at Sharpsburg, Maryland, September 17, 1862. Confined at Fort Delaware, Delaware, until transferred to Aiken's Landing, James River, Virginia, October 2, 1862, for exchange. Declared exchanged at Aiken's Landing on November 10, 1862. Rejoined the company in March-April, 1863, and present or accounted for until wounded in the thigh and captured at Charles Town, West Virginia, August 24, 1864. Paroled at Charleston, West Virginia, May 5, 1865.

HATHCOCK, TILMON, Private
Born in Stanly County* where he resided as a mechanic or farmer prior to enlisting in Stanly County at age 25, May 5, 1861. Mustered in as Private and promoted to Corporal on August 26, 1861. Reduced to ranks in March-June, 1862. Present or accounted for until he died in hospital at Richmond, Virginia, on or about June 1, 1862, of "feb[ris] remit[tent]."

HATLEY, GILFORD, Private
Born in Montgomery County and resided in Stanly County where he was by occupation a farmer prior to enlisting in Stanly County at age 51, May 5, 1861. Present or accounted for until discharged on August 5, 1862, by reason of being over age.

HATLEY, JAMES, Private
Enlisted in Stanly County on February 1, 1864, for the war. Present or accounted for through August, 1864. Name appears on a court-martial record dated January 28, 1865. No further records.

HATLEY, TILMON, Private
Resided in Stanly County and was by occupation a farmer prior to enlisting in Stanly County at age 20, May 5, 1861. Present or accounted for through August, 1864. Paroled at Albemarle on May 19, 1865.

HATLY, GREEN, Private
Born in Stanly County* where he resided as a farmer prior to enlisting in Stanly County at age 21, May 5, 1861. Present or accounted for until he died in hospital at Richmond, Virginia, May 23, 1862. Cause of death not reported.

HATLY, ISAAC, Private
Born in Montgomery County and resided in Stanly County where he was by occupation a farmer prior to enlisting in Stanly County at age 35, May 5, 1861. Present or accounted for until discharged on August 5, 1862, by reason of being over age.

HATLY, WILLIAM B., Sergeant
Resided in Stanly County and was by occupation a farmer prior to enlisting in Stanly County at age 28, May 5, 1861. Mustered in as Private and was promoted to Sergeant on April 27, 1862. Present or accounted for until he died in hospital at Richmond, Virginia, June 12, 1862, of "feb[ris] typhoid."

HERRIN, JOHN F., Private
Resided in Stanly County and enlisted in Wake County at age 42, September 10, 1863, for the war. Present or accounted for through January 20, 1865; however, he was reported absent on light duty during much of that period.

HILDRETH, EDMUND, Private
Resided in Anson County and enlisted in Wake County at age 40, July 24, 1863, for the war. Present or accounted for until he died in hospital at Richmond, Virginia, June 23, 1864, of "ch[ronic] dysentery."

HINSON, JOSHUA, Private
Resided in Stanly County and was by occupation a farmer prior to enlisting in Stanly County at age 22, May 5, 1861. Present or accounted for until killed at Sharpsburg, Maryland, September 17, 1862.

HOLT, HENRY H., Private
Born in Stanly County* where he resided as a farmer prior to enlisting in Stanly County at age 24, May 5, 1861. Present or accounted for until discharged at Camp Ellis, Virginia, August 23, 1861, by reason of "physical disability."

HOLT, WILLIAM, Private
Born in Stanly County* where he resided as a farmer prior to enlisting in Stanly County at age 21, May 5, 1861. Present or accounted for until he died in hospital at Richmond, Virginia, June 4, 1862, of "feb[ris] remit[tent]."

HOWELL, EDMUND H., Corporal
Resided in Stanly County and was by occupation a farmer prior to enlisting in Stanly County at age 24, May 5, 1861. Mustered in as Private. Present or accounted for until wounded in the foot at Seven Pines, Virginia, June 3, 1862. Promoted to Corporal on December 8, 1862, and rejoined the company prior to January 1, 1863. Present or accounted for until detailed for light duty on May 27, 1863. Reported on detail through August, 1864.

HOWELL, LEMUEL M., Private
Resided in Stanly County and was by occupation a farmer prior to enlisting in Stanly County at age 30, May 5, 1861. Present or accounted for until he died at Camp Ellis, Virginia, August 17, 1861. Cause of death not reported.

HURLEY, CALVIN, Private
Resided in Montgomery County and enlisted in Wake County at age 30, July 16, 1862, for the war. Present or accounted for until he died in hospital at Richmond, Virginia, September 6, 1862, of "typhoid dysentery."

INGRAM, PRESLEY NELMS, Private
Born in Anson County where he resided as a farmer prior to enlisting in Wake County at age 42, August 20. 1863, for the war. Present or accounted for until discharged on November 21, 1864, by reason of "disability."

JACKSON, HENRY, Private
Resided in Stanly County and was by occupation a farmer prior to enlisting in Stanly County at age 16, May 15, 1861. Present or accounted for until reported missing May 15-18, 1862. Company muster rolls indicate that he was thought to be dead. No further records.

JOLIE, D. I., Private
Place and date of enlistment not reported. Paroled at Salisbury on May 16, 1865.

KANOY, JOHN A., Private
Resided in Davidson County and enlisted in Wake County at age 33, July 16, 1862, for the war. Present or accounted for until captured at Sharpsburg, Maryland, September 17, 1862. Confined at Fort Delaware, Delaware, until transferred to Aiken's Landing, James River, Virginia, October 2, 1862, for exchange. Declared exchanged at Aiken's Landing on November 10, 1862. Rejoined the company in March-April, 1863, and present or accounted for until wounded in the thigh at Chancellorsville, Virginia, May 1-3, 1863. Died in hospital at Richmond, Virginia, June 7, 1863, of wounds.

KANOY, JOHN W., Private
Resided in Davidson County and enlisted in Wake County at age 32, July 16, 1862, for the war. Present or accounted for until wounded at Sharpsburg, Maryland, September 17, 1862. Died October 1, 1862, of wounds. Place of death not reported.

KEITH, JOHN, Private
Resided in Stanly County and was by occupation a farmer prior to enlisting in Stanly County at age 28, May 5, 1861. Present or accounted for through August, 1864; however, he was reported absent on duty as a pioneer during most of that period. Paroled at Appomattox Court House, Virginia, April 9, 1865.

KENDALL, HENRY A., Sergeant
Resided in Stanly County and was by occupation a farmer prior to enlisting in Stanly County at age 27, May 5, 1861. Mustered in as Corporal but was reduced to ranks on July 6, 1861. Present or accounted for until captured at Sharpsburg, Maryland, September 17, 1862. Confined at Fort Delaware, Delaware, until transferred to Aiken's Landing, James River, Virginia, October 2, 1862, for exchange. Declared exchanged at Aiken's Landing on November 10, 1862. Rejoined the company in January-February, 1863, and was promoted to Sergeant on May 10, 1863. Present or accounted for until captured at Petersburg, Virginia, April 3, 1865. Confined at Hart's Island, New York Harbor, until released on June 17, 1865, after taking the Oath of Allegiance. Clark's *Regiments* indicates he was wounded in the throat at Spotsylvania Court House, Virginia, May 19, 1864.

KIRK, JAMES F., Private
Resided in Stanly County and was by occupation a farmer prior to enlisting in Stanly County at age 20, May 5, 1861. Present or accounted for until captured at Williamsburg, Virginia, May 5, 1862. Reported in hospital at Williamsburg on or about May 9-11, 1862. No further records.

LANIER, WILLIAM W., Sergeant
Resided in Stanly County and was by occupation a farmer prior to enlisting in Stanly County at age 19, May 5, 1861. Mustered in as Corporal and was promoted to Sergeant on July 25, 1861. Reduced to ranks on April 27, 1862, but was promoted to Sergeant on December 8, 1862. Present or accounted for until killed at Chancellorsville, Virginia, May 3, 1863.

LAYTON, FRANKLIN M., Private
Resided in Stanly County and was by occupation a farmer prior to enlisting in Stanly County at age 27, May 5, 1861. Present or accounted for until captured at Sharpsburg, Maryland, September 17, 1862. Confined at Fort Delaware, Delaware, until transferred to Aiken's Landing, James River, Virginia, October 2, 1862, for exchange. Declared exchanged at Aiken's Landing on November 10, 1862. Rejoined the company in January-February, 1863, and present or accounted for until hospitalized at Richmond, Virginia, July 6, 1863, with a gunshot wound. Place and date wounded not reported. Furloughed for thirty days on August 29, 1863, and died "at home" in Stanly County on September 12, 1863, of disease.

LEFLER, DANIEL, Private
Resided in Montgomery County and enlisted in Wake County at age 26, July 16, 1862, for the war. Present or accounted for until wounded at Chancellorsville, Virginia, May 1-3, 1863. Rejoined the company prior to July 1, 1863, and present or accounted for until he was reported absent wounded on July 4, 1864. Place and date wounded not reported. Reported absent wounded through August, 1864.

LEFLER, FRANKLIN, Private
Resided in Stanly or Rowan counties and was by occupation a farmer prior to enlisting in Stanly County at age 21, May 5, 1861. Present or accounted for until wounded at Malvern Hill, Virginia, on or about July 1, 1862. Rejoined the company in January-February, 1863, and present or accounted for until wounded on December 16, 1863. Battle in which wounded not reported. Rejoined the company prior to September 1, 1864, and present or accounted for until hospitalized at Richmond, Virginia, February 25, 1865, with a gunshot wound of the right leg. Place and date wounded not reported. Captured in hospital at Richmond on April 3, 1865. Confined at Libby Prison, Richmond, until transferred to Newport News, Virginia, April 23, 1865. Released at Newport News on June 30, 1865, after taking the Oath of Allegiance.

LEFLER, J. M., Private
Resided in Montgomery County and enlisted in Wake County at age 28, July 16, 1862, for the war. Present or accounted for until captured at Sharpsburg, Maryland, September 17, 1862. Confined at Fort Delaware, Delaware, until transferred to Aiken's Landing, James River, Virginia, October 2, 1862, for exchange. Declared exchanged at Aiken's Landing on November 10, 1862. Rejoined the company in January-February, 1863. Present or accounted for until wounded at Chancellorsville, Virginia, May 1-3, 1863. Rejoined the company prior to June 8, 1863. Present or accounted for until reported captured near Richmond, Virginia, May 31, 1864; however, records of the Federal Provost Marshal do not substantiate that report. No further records.

LEONARD, ALFRED, Private
Enlisted in Wake County on October 1, 1863, for the war. Present or accounted for until discharged on November 13, 1863, by reason of disability.

LILLY, JOHN A., Private
Resided in Stanly County and was by occupation a farmer prior to enlisting in Stanly County at age 29, May 5, 1861. Present or accounted for until wounded at Chancellorsville, Virginia, May 3, 1863. Rejoined the company in July-August, 1863, and present or accounted for until captured at Winchester, Virginia, September 19, 1864. Confined at Point Lookout, Maryland, until transferred to Boulware's Wharf, James River, Virginia, where he was received March 18, 1865, for exchange. Furloughed for thirty days from hospital at Richmond, Virginia, March 28, 1865.

LIVINGSTON, J. R., Private
Born in Montgomery County and resided in Stanly County where he was by occupation a farmer prior

to enlisting in Stanly County at age 28, September 5, 1861. Present or accounted for until he died in hospital at Richmond, Virginia, June 11, 1862, of "typhoid fever."

LOWDER, EBEN, Corporal

Resided in Stanly County and was by occupation a farmer prior to enlisting in Stanly County at age 22, May 5, 1861. Mustered in as Private. Present or accounted for until wounded and captured at Williamsburg, Virginia, on or about May 6, 1862. Exchanged prior to September 17, 1862, when he was captured at Sharpsburg, Maryland. Confined at Fort Delaware, Delaware, until transferred to Aiken's Landing, James River, Virginia, October 2, 1862, for exchange. Declared exchanged at Aiken's Landing on November 10, 1862. Promoted to Corporal on December 8, 1862, and rejoined the company prior to January 1, 1863. Present or accounted for until wounded at Chancellorsville, Virginia, May 3, 1863. Rejoined the company in September-October, 1863, and present or accounted for until wounded in the left leg and captured at Appomattox Court House, Virginia, April 9, 1865. Hospitalized at various Federal hospitals until released on June 14, 1865.

LOWERY, JOHN, Private

Place and date of enlistment not reported. Wounded in the left leg at or near Appomattox Court House, Virginia, on or about April 9, 1865. Left leg amputated. Paroled at Farmville, Virginia, April 27, 1865.

MABERY, BENJAMIN M., Private

Company records indicate that he previously served in Mallett's Battalion (Camp Guard) and transferred to this company on April 15, 1863; however, records of Mallett's Battalion do not indicate that he served therein. Present or accounted for from March-April, 1863, until paroled at Appomattox Court House, Virginia, April 9, 1865.

MABRY, EBEN, Private

Resided in Stanly County and was by occupation a farmer prior to enlisting in Stanly County at age 21, May 5, 1861. Mustered in as Private and promoted to Corporal on April 27, 1862. Present or accounted for until wounded in battle near Richmond, Virginia, in June-July, 1862. Rejoined the company prior to January 1, 1863, and present or accounted for until paroled at Appomattox Court House, Virginia, April 9, 1865. Rank given on parole as Private. North Carolina pension records indicate he was wounded in the right shoulder at Winchester, Virginia, September 19, 1864.

MABRY, JOSEPH, Private

Resided in Stanly County where he enlisted at age 25, July 28, 1861. Mustered in as Private and promoted to Lance Corporal on November 17, 1861. Present or accounted for until wounded accidentally in the neck and chest near Richmond, Virginia, on or about July 10, 1862. Reduced to ranks prior to January 1, 1863. Rejoined the company in January-February, 1863, but was discharged on or about March 8, 1863, by reason of disability.

MABRY, THOMAS F., Private

Born in Stanly County where he resided as a farmer prior to enlisting in Stanly County at age 16, May 5,

1861. Present or accounted for until discharged on August 5, 1862, by reason of being under age. Reenlisted in this company on April 1, 1864. Died in hospital at Lynchburg, Virginia, April 30, 1864, of "acute dysentery."

McCLURE, JAMES H., Private

Resided in Stanly County and was by occupation a farmer prior to enlisting in Stanly County at age 25, May 5, 1861. Present or accounted for until wounded in the head and foot at Gettysburg, Pennsylvania, July 2-3, 1863. Died at Gettysburg on July 5, 1863, of wounds.

MANERS, JOHN W., Corporal

Resided in Stanly County and was by occupation a farmer prior to enlisting in Stanly County at age 23, May 5, 1861. Mustered in as Private and promoted to Corporal on April 27, 1862. Present or accounted for until wounded in the right shoulder and captured near Richmond, Virginia, June 23, 1862. Hospitalized at Davids Island, New York Harbor, until exchanged on October 11, 1862. Rejoined the company prior to January 1, 1863, and was reduced to ranks prior to March 26, 1863, when he was reappointed Corporal. Present or accounted for until wounded at Chancellorsville, Virginia, May 1-3, 1863. Died May 5, 1863, of wounds. Place of death not reported.

MANERS, WILLIAM A., Sergeant

Resided in Stanly County and was by occupation a farmer prior to enlisting in Stanly County at age 24, May 5, 1861. Mustered in as Private and promoted to Corporal on November 17, 1861. Promoted to Sergeant on April 27, 1862. Present or accounted for through August, 1864.

MANERS, WILLIAM M., Private

Born in Montgomery County and resided in Stanly County where he was by occupation a farmer prior to enlisting in Stanly County at age 47, September 5, 1861. Present or accounted for until discharged on August 5, 1862, by reason of being over age.

MARSHALL, GEORGE M., Private

Resided in Stanly County and was by occupation a farmer prior to enlisting in Stanly County at age 18, May 5, 1861. Present or accounted for until he died at Camp Ellis, Virginia, August 8 or August 19, 1861. Cause of death not reported.

MAULDEN, N. M., Private

Company records indicate that he served previously in Mallett's Battalion (Camp Guard) and transferred to this company on April 15, 1863; however, records of Mallett's Battalion do not indicate that he served therein. Present or accounted for from March-April, 1863, until wounded at Chancellorsville, Virginia, May 3, 1863. Rejoined the company in November-December, 1863, and present or accounted for until wounded in the abdomen and captured between Petersburg, Virginia, and Farmville, Virginia, March 29-April 9, 1865. Died on or about April 11, 1865, of wounds. Place of death not reported.

MELCHOR, C. G., Private

Previously served in Company F, 5th Regiment N.C. State Troops. Transferred to this company on October 2, 1862. Present or accounted for through December 9, 1864.

MELCHOR, LEONARD E., Private
Resided in Stanly County and was by occupation a farmer prior to enlisting in Stanly County at age 25, May 5, 1861. Present or accounted for until wounded at Chancellorsville, Virginia, May 3, 1863. Rejoined the company in September-October, 1863, and present or accounted for through August, 1864. Paroled at Albemarle on May 19, 1865, and took the Oath of Allegiance at Salisbury on June 21, 1865.

MELCHOR, WILLIAM H., Private
Resided in Stanly County and was by occupation a farmer prior to enlisting in Stanly County at age 20, May 5, 1861. Present or accounted for until wounded at Sharpsburg, Maryland, September 17, 1862. Rejoined the company in January-February, 1863, and present or accounted for through August, 1864. Paroled at Albemarle on May 19, 1865.

MELTON, ATLAS D., Private
Born in Stanly County where he resided as a farmer prior to enlisting in Stanly County at age 16, May 5, 1861. Present or accounted for until discharged on August 5, 1862, by reason of being under age. Later served in Company I, 52nd Regiment N.C. Troops.

MELTON, GREEN, Private
Resided in Stanly County where he enlisted at age 24, July 28, 1861. Present or accounted for until wounded in the hip and/or right foot at Gettysburg, Pennsylvania, July 3, 1863. Rejoined the company in November-December, 1863. Present or accounted for until hospitalized at Richmond, Virginia, May 15, 1864, with a gunshot wound of the right arm; however, place and date wounded not reported. Rejoined the company prior to September 1, 1864. Present or accounted for until paroled at Albemarle on May 19, 1865.

MELTON, JOSEPH, Private
Born in Montgomery County and resided in Stanly County where he was by occupation a shoemaker prior to enlisting in Stanly County at age 45, May 5, 1861. Present or accounted for until discharged on August 5, 1862, by reason of being over age.

MISENHIMER, GREENE A., Private
Resided in Stanly or Rowan counties and was by occupation a farmer prior to enlisting in Stanly County at age 19, May 5, 1861. Present or accounted for until reported missing and presumed captured on May 12, 1864; however, records of the Federal Provost Marshal do not substantiate the report of his capture. No further records.

MORRIS, COLUMBUS BRIGHT, Private
Resided in Stanly County and was by occupation a farmer prior to enlisting in Stanly County at age 21, May 5, 1861. Present or accounted for until captured at Sharpsburg, Maryland, September 17, 1862. Confined at Fort Delaware, Delaware, until transferred to Aiken's Landing, James River, Virginia, October 2, 1862, for exchange. Declared exchanged at Aiken's Landing on November 10, 1862. Reported absent sick or absent on detached duty until he rejoined the company in September-October, 1863. Present or accounted for until he deserted to the enemy at or near Bermuda Hundred, Virginia, on or about January 25, 1865. Took the Oath of Allegiance on or about January 30, 1865.

MORRIS, JAMES, Private
Resided in Montgomery County and enlisted in Wake County at age 18, July 24, 1863, for the war. Present or accounted for until captured at Petersburg, Virginia, April 3, 1865. Confined at Hart's Island, New York Harbor, where he died May 11, 1865, of "typhoid pneumonia."

MORRIS, NOAH, Private
Previously served in Company F, 44th Regiment N.C. Troops. Transferred to this company on August 30, 1863. Present or accounted for until paroled at Farmville, Virginia, April 11-21, 1865.

MORRIS, RICHARD, Private
Resided in Stanly County and enlisted in Wake County at age 18, September 10, 1863, for the war. Present or accounted for through August, 1864.

MORRIS, W. E., Private
Enlisted in Stanly County on August 8, 1864, for the war. Present or accounted for until paroled at Appomattox Court House, Virginia, April 9, 1865.

MORRIS, WHITSON, Private
Resided in Montgomery County and enlisted in Wake County at age 32, July 16, 1862, for the war. Present or accounted for until he deserted on June 14, 1864.

MORTON, HENRY A., Private
Born in Stanly County* where he resided as a farmer prior to enlisting in Stanly County at age 22, May 5, 1861. Present or accounted for until discharged on or about October 20, 1861, by reason of "the effects of severe and protracted typhoid fever."

MYERS, J. G., Private
Resided in Anson County and enlisted in Wake County at age 42, July 18, 1863, for the war. Present or accounted for until he died in hospital at Richmond, Virginia, October 12, 1863, of "febris typhoides."

NOBLES, DAVID D., Private
Resided in Stanly County and was by occupation a farmer prior to enlisting in Stanly County at age 26, May 5, 1861. Present or accounted for until wounded in the left thigh at Chancellorsville, Virginia, May 1-3, 1863. Rejoined the company in September-October, 1863, and present or accounted for until captured at Petersburg, Virginia, April 2, 1865. Confined at Point Lookout, Maryland, until released on June 29, 1865, after taking the Oath of Allegiance.

PALMER, DeMARCUS, Private
Resided in Stanly County and was by occupation a farmer prior to enlisting in Stanly County at age 23, May 5, 1861. Present or accounted for until killed at Malvern Hill, Virginia, July 1, 1862.

PALMER, HEZEKIAH W., Private
Resided in Stanly County and was by occupation a farmer prior to enlisting in Stanly County at age 25, May 5, 1861. Present or accounted for until discharged on August 23, 1861. Reason discharged not reported. Later served in Company A, 59th Regiment N.C. Troops (4th Regiment N.C. Cavalry).

PALMER, PIERSON G., Private
Born in Stanly County where he resided as a farmer prior to enlisting in Stanly County at age 19, May 5, 1861. Present or accounted for until killed at Gaines' Mill, Virginia, June 27, 1862.

PALMER, THOMAS A., Private
Born in Stanly County* where he resided as a farmer prior to enlisting in Stanly County at age 22, May 5, 1861. Present or accounted for until discharged on November 2, 1861, by reason of "great debility resulting from a severe and protracted attack of typhoid fever."

PARKER, DAVID G., Sergeant
Resided in Stanly County and was by occupation a farmer prior to enlisting in Stanly County at age 19, May 5, 1861. Mustered in as Private and promoted to Sergeant on April 27, 1862. Present or accounted for until he died at Richmond, Virginia, June 13, 1862. Cause of death not reported.

POOL, CALDWELL, Private
Resided in Montgomery County and enlisted in Wake County at age 32, July 16, 1862, for the war. Present or accounted for until he died October 20 or November 15, 1862, of disease. Place of death not reported.

POOL, H. S., Private
Resided in Montgomery County and enlisted in Wake County at age 34, July 16, 1862, for the war. Present or accounted for until he died at Charles Town, West Virginia, November 9, 1862. Cause of death not reported.

POPLIN, JESSE, Private
Born in Stanly County where he resided as a farmer prior to enlisting in Stanly County at age 20, May 5, 1861. Present or accounted for until wounded at Chancellorsville, Virginia, May 3, 1863. Died May 4, 1863, of wounds.

PRIVETT, E. B., Private
Resided in Anson County and enlisted in Wake County at age 18, July 24, 1863, for the war. Present or accounted for until captured at Petersburg, Virginia, April 2, 1865. Confined at Point Lookout, Maryland, until released on June 16, 1865, after taking the Oath of Allegiance.

PURSER, HUGH, Private
Resided in Union County and enlisted in Wake County on October 8, 1863, for the war. Present or accounted for until killed at Spotsylvania Court House, Virginia, May 8, 1864.

RANDLE, EDMUND D., Private
Resided in Stanly County and was by occupation a farmer prior to enlisting in Stanly County at age 19, May 5, 1861. Present or accounted for until discharged on or about September 26, 1861. Reason discharged not reported.

RATLIFF, W. T., Private
Resided in Anson County and enlisted in Wake County at age 43, July 24, 1863, for the war. Present or accounted for until he died in hospital at Richmond, Virginia, June 20, 1864, of "rubeola."

RITCHIE, IVY, Sergeant
Resided in Stanly County and was by occupation a farmer prior to enlisting in Stanly County at age 22,

May 5, 1861. Mustered in as Private. Present or accounted for until captured at Sharpsburg, Maryland, on or about September 17, 1862. Confined at Fort Delaware, Delaware, until transferred to Aiken's Landing, James River, Virginia, October 2, 1862, for exchange. Declared exchanged at Aiken's Landing on November 10, 1862. Rejoined the company prior to January 1, 1863, and present or accounted for until wounded at Chancellorsville, Virginia, May 3, 1863. Promoted to Corporal on May 12, 1863, and rejoined the company in July-August, 1863. Promoted to Sergeant on July 1, 1864. Present or accounted for through August, 1864. Clark's *Regiments* indicates he was killed near Appomattox, Virginia. Date of death not reported.

ROSS, THOMAS K., Private
Resided in Stanly or Wake counties and was by occupation a farmer prior to enlisting in Stanly County at age 17, May 5, 1861. Present or accounted for until he died at Camp Bee, Virginia, August 31, 1861. Cause of death not reported.

RUMAGE, WILLIAM R., Private
Resided in Stanly County and was by occupation a farmer prior to enlisting in Stanly County at age 18, May 5, 1861. Present or accounted for until wounded at Chancellorsville, Virginia, May 3, 1863. Died in hospital at Richmond, Virginia, July 19, 1863, of wounds.

RUSSELL, BENNETT, Sergeant
Resided in Stanly County and was by occupation a farmer prior to enlisting in Stanly County at age 28, May 5, 1861. Mustered in as Private and promoted to Corporal on April 27, 1862. Promoted to Sergeant on December 8, 1862. Present or accounted for until wounded in the head at Chancellorsville, Virginia, May 3, 1863. Rejoined the company prior to July 1, 1863, and present or accounted for until paroled at Appomattox Court House, Virginia, April 9, 1865.

SECHRIST, NOAH, Private
Resided in Davidson County and enlisted in Wake County at age 31, July 16, 1862, for the war. Present or accounted for until he died on or about October 20, 1862, of disease. Place of death not reported.

SELL, HENRY C., Private
Born in Stanly County* where he resided as a farmer prior to enlisting in Stanly County at age 24, May 5, 1861. Mustered in as Private and promoted to Corporal on April 27, 1862. Present or accounted for until he died at Gold Hill on July 7, 1862, of disease.

SHANKLE, CLAUDIUS A., 1st Sergeant
Resided in Stanly County and was by occupation a merchant prior to enlisting in Stanly County at age 24, May 5, 1861. Mustered in as Sergeant and promoted to 1st Sergeant on April 27, 1862. Present or accounted for until wounded on or about April 29, 1863; however, battle in which wounded not reported. Rejoined the company prior to May 1, 1863, and present or accounted for until hospitalized at Charlottesville, Virginia, October 23, 1864, with a gunshot wound of the right arm. Place and date wounded not reported. Reported absent wounded until furloughed for sixty days on January 21, 1865.

SHANKLE, GEORGE A., Private
Resided in Stanly County and was by occupation a

farmer prior to enlisting in Stanly County at age 23, May 5, 1861. Present or accounted for until wounded at Chancellorsville, Virginia, May 3, 1863. Died at Richmond, Virginia, May 12-14, 1863, of wounds.

SHANKLE, J. A., Private
Resided in Stanly County where he enlisted on March 4, 1864, for the war. Present or accounted for until captured at Petersburg, Virginia, April 3, 1865. Confined at Hart's Island, New York Harbor, until released on June 17, 1865, after taking the Oath of Allegiance.

SHANKLE, JAMES W., Private
Born in Stanly County where he resided as a farmer prior to enlisting in Stanly County at age 16, May 5, 1861. Present or accounted for until discharged on August 5, 1862, by reason of being under age. Later served in Company I, 52nd Regiment N.C. Troops.

SHANKLE, MARTIN, Private
Resided in Stanly County and was by occupation a farmer prior to enlisting in Stanly County at age 28, May 5, 1861. Present or accounted for until he died in hospital at Richmond, Virginia, August 15, 1862, of disease.

SIDES, CHRISTOPHER, Private
Resided in Stanly County and was by occupation a farmer prior to enlisting in Stanly County at age 23, May 5, 1861. Present or accounted for until captured at Sharpsburg, Maryland, September 17, 1862. Confined at Fort Delaware, Delaware, until transferred to Aiken's Landing, James River, Virginia, October 2, 1862, for exchange. Declared exchanged at Aiken's Landing on November 10, 1862. Rejoined the company prior to January 1, 1863, and present or accounted for until wounded in the thigh and right arm at Chancellorsville, Virginia, May 3, 1863. Died in hospital at Richmond, Virginia, July 4, 1863, of wounds.

SIDES, EDMUND, Private
Resided in Stanly County and was by occupation a farmer prior to enlisting in Stanly County at age 22, May 5, 1861. Present or accounted for until killed at Sharpsburg, Maryland, September 17, 1862.

SIDES, TILMON, Private
Resided in Stanly County where he enlisted at age 20, July 28, 1861. Present or accounted for until killed at Sharpsburg, Maryland, September 17, 1862.

SINGLETON, WILLIAM W., Private
Resided in Stanly County and was by occupation a farmer prior to enlisting in Stanly County at age 22, May 5, 1861. Present or accounted for until killed at Malvern Hill, Virginia, July 1, 1862.

SINK, GEORGE, Private
Resided in Davidson County and enlisted in Wake County at age 29, July 16, 1862, for the war. Present or accounted for until he died in hospital at Richmond, Virginia, December 28, 1862, of "variola."

SMITH, CORNELIUS, Private
Resided in Stanly County and was by occupation a farmer prior to enlisting in Stanly County at age 22, May 5, 1861. Present or accounted for until he died

at Camp Ellis, Virginia, August 8, 1861. Cause of death not reported.

SMITH, EDMUND P., Corporal
Resided in Stanly County and was by occupation a farmer prior to enlisting in Stanly County at age 28, May 5, 1861. Mustered in as Private and promoted to Corporal on April 27, 1862. Present or accounted for until wounded in battle near Richmond, Virginia, in June-July, 1862. Rejoined the company prior to September 17, 1862, when he was captured at Sharpsburg, Maryland. Confined at Fort Delaware, Delaware, until transferred to Aiken's Landing, James River, Virginia, October 2, 1862, for exchange. Declared exchanged at Aiken's Landing on November 10, 1862. Reduced to ranks "by his own request" on March 26, 1863. Rejoined the company in May-June, 1863. Promoted to Corporal in September, 1864-April, 1865. Present or accounted for until captured at Farmville, Virginia, April 6, 1865. Confined at Point Lookout, Maryland, where he died June 24, 1865, of "dia[rrhoea] chronic."

SMITH, JOHN F., Private
Born in Stanly County* where he resided as a farmer prior to enlisting in Stanly County at age 29, May 5, 1861. Present or accounted for until he died at Scottsville, Virginia, August 15, 1862, of disease.

SNUGGS, BENJAMIN F., Private
Resided in Stanly County and was by occupation a farmer prior to enlisting in Stanly County at age 20, May 5, 1861. Present or accounted for until wounded in the hip and hand at Spotsylvania Court House, Virginia, May 12, 1864. Rejoined the company prior to September 1, 1864. Captured at Petersburg, Virginia, April 2, 1865, and confined at Hart's Island, New York Harbor, until released on June 17, 1865.

SNUGGS, I. W., Private
Enlisted in Stanly County on or about March 4, 1864, for the war. Present or accounted for until wounded in the right leg and captured at Spotsylvania Court House, Virginia, May 12, 1864. Right leg amputated. Hospitalized at various Federal hospitals until confined at Old Capitol Prison, Washington, D.C., October 17, 1864. Transferred to Elmira, New York, October 24, 1864. Paroled at Elmira on February 9, 1865, and transferred to Boulware's and Cox's Wharf, James River, Virginia, where he was received February 20-21, 1865, for exchange. Hospitalized at Richmond, Virginia, the same day. Federal medical records give his age as 18.

SULLIVAN, W. B., Private
Resided in Anson County and enlisted in Wake County at age 43, July 24, 1863, for the war. Present or accounted for until captured at Waynesboro, Virginia, March 2, 1865. Confined at Fort Delaware, Delaware, until released on June 19, 1865, after taking the Oath of Allegiance.

SWEARINGEN, JAMES L. B., Private
Resided in Stanly County and was by occupation a farmer prior to enlisting in Stanly County at age 24, May 5, 1861. Present or accounted for until he died at Camp Ellis, Virginia, July 20, 1861. Cause of death not reported.

THOMPSON, JOHN, Private

Born in Stanly County where he resided as a farmer prior to enlisting in Stanly County at age 19, May 5, 1861. Present or accounted for until wounded and captured at Sharpsburg, Maryland, on or about September 17, 1862. Received at Aiken's Landing, James River, Virginia, October 12, 1862, for exchange. Rejoined the company prior to January 1, 1863, and present or accounted for until wounded in the thigh and head at Chancellorsville, Virginia, May 3, 1863. Reported absent wounded until retired to the Invalid Corps on August 3, 1864. Discharged February 20, 1865, by reason of wounds received at Chancellorsville. Paroled at Greensboro on May 3, 1865.

TOLBERT, B. H., Private

Resided in Montgomery County and enlisted in Wake County at age 29, July 16, 1862, for the war. Present or accounted for until captured at or near Sharpsburg, Maryland, on or about September 15, 1862. Confined at Fort Delaware, Delaware, until transferred to Aiken's Landing, James River, Virginia, October 2, 1862, for exchange. Declared exchanged at Aiken's Landing on November 10, 1862. Reported absent sick until he died in the smallpox hospital at Richmond, Virginia, May 25, 1863.

TURNER, PRESTON H., Sergeant

Resided in Stanly County and was by occupation a farmer prior to enlisting in Stanly County at age 20, May 5, 1861. Mustered in as Corporal and promoted to Sergeant on November 17, 1861. Present or accounted for until appointed Sergeant Major on April 27, 1862, and transferred to the Field and Staff of this regiment.

WALLER, LAWRENCE, Private

Born in Rowan County and resided in Stanly County where he was by occupation a farmer prior to enlisting in Stanly County at age 50, May 5, 1861. Present or accounted for until discharged on August 5, 1862, by reason of being over age.

WHITLEY, WILLEY, Private

Resided in Nash County and enlisted in Wake County at age 18, June 11, 1863, for the war. Present or accounted for until captured at Petersburg, Virginia, April 3, 1865. Confined at Hart's Island, New York Harbor, until released on June 17, 1865, after taking the Oath of Allegiance. North Carolina pension records indicate he was wounded in the left leg at Wilderness, Virginia.

WILLIAMS, ISAAC, Private

Resided in Stanly County and was by occupation a farmer prior to enlisting in Stanly County at age 19, May 5, 1861. Present or accounted for until captured at Sharpsburg, Maryland, September 17, 1862. Confined at Fort Delaware, Delaware, until transferred to Aiken's Landing, James River, Virginia, October 2, 1862, for exchange. Declared exchanged at Aiken's Landing on November 10, 1862. Rejoined the company in January-February, 1863, and present or accounted for until captured at or near Cold Harbor, Virginia, May 31, 1864. Records of the Federal Provost Marshal do not substantiate the report of his capture; however, Confederate medical records indicate he was a paroled prisoner who was

hospitalized at Richmond, Virginia, March 10, 1865. No further records.

COMPANY I

This company, known as the Lexington Wild Cats, was from Davidson County and enlisted at Lexington on May 14, 1861. On May 24 it left Lexington for Garysburg, where it arrived on May 25. There it was assigned to this regiment as Company I. After joining the regiment the company functioned as a part of the regiment, and its history for the war period is recorded as a part of the regimental history.

The information contained in the following roster of the company was compiled principally from company muster rolls for June 6, 1861, through August 31, 1864. No company muster rolls were found for the period after August 31, 1864. In addition to the company muster rolls, Roll of Honor records, receipt rolls, hospital records, prisoner of war records, and other primary records, supplemented by state pension applications, United Daughters of the Confederacy records, and postwar rosters and histories, all provided useful information.

OFFICERS
CAPTAINS

HARGRAVE, JESSE

Resided in Davidson County and was by occupation a lawyer prior to enlisting in Davidson County at age 23. Elected Captain to rank from May 14, 1861. Present or accounted for until he declined reelection or was defeated for reelection when the regiment was reorganized, April 25-26, 1862.

BEALL, THOMAS B.

Resided in Davidson County and was by occupation a farmer prior to enlisting in Davidson County at age 25. Elected 3rd Lieutenant to rank from May 14, 1861, and was elected Captain to rank from April 25-27, 1862. Present or accounted for until wounded in the right lung at Cedar Creek, Virginia, October 19, 1864. Reported absent wounded through February 17, 1865.

LIEUTENANTS

BRASINGTON, SAMUEL W., 1st Lieutenant

Resided in Davidson County and was by occupation a machinist prior to enlisting in Davidson County at age 25, May 14, 1861. Mustered in as Corporal and promoted to Sergeant on November 13, 1861. Elected 2nd Lieutenant to rank from April 27, 1862, and was promoted to 1st Lieutenant on or about June 17, 1862. Present or accounted for until wounded at Sharpsburg, Maryland, September 17, 1862. Rejoined the company in May-June, 1863, and present or accounted for until retired to the Invalid Corps on September 6, 1864.

HOLT, WILLIAM M., 1st Lieutenant

Resided in Davidson County and was by occupation a farmer prior to enlisting in Davidson County at age 23. Appointed 2nd Lieutenant to rank from May 14,

1861, and was elected 1st Lieutenant, April 25-27, 1862. Present or accounted for until he died on June 17, 1862. Place and cause of death not reported.

HUNT, CHARLES ANDREW, 2nd Lieutenant
Resided in Davidson County and was by occupation a student prior to enlisting in Davidson County at age 17, May 14, 1861. Mustered in as Sergeant and was elected 3rd Lieutenant to rank from April 27, 1862. Promoted to 2nd Lieutenant on October 1, 1862. Present or accounted for until wounded at Chancellorsville, Virginia, May 3, 1863. Rejoined the company prior to July 1, 1863, and present or accounted for until wounded in the right foot and captured at Winchester, Virginia, September 19, 1864. Hospitalized at Winchester and at Baltimore, Maryland, until transferred to Fort Delaware, Delaware, January 10, 1865. Paroled at Fort Delaware and transferred to City Point, Virginia, February 27, 1865, for exchange. Reported in hospital until furloughed for thirty days on March 7, 1865.

MILLER, OBEDIAH C., 3rd Lieutenant
Resided in Davidson County and was by occupation a farmer prior to enlisting in Davidson County at age 25, May 14, 1861. Mustered in as Private and promoted to 3rd Lieutenant to rank from October 20, 1862. Present or accounted for through October 30, 1864.

WEVERE, HORACE N., 1st Lieutenant
Resided in Davidson County and was by occupation an artist prior to enlisting in Davidson County at age 26. Elected 1st Lieutenant to rank from May 14, 1861. Present or accounted for until he resigned or was defeated for reelection when the regiment was reorganized on April 25, 1862.

NONCOMMISSIONED OFFICERS AND PRIVATES

BALL, HENRY, Private
Resided in Davidson County and was by occupation a coach maker prior to enlisting in Davidson County at age 20, May 14, 1861. Present or accounted for until he died at Camp Ellis, Virginia, July 28, 1861. Cause of death not reported.

BARNES, ALEXANDER, Private
Resided in Davidson County and was by occupation a farmer prior to enlisting in Davidson County at age 25, May 14, 1861. Present or accounted for until captured at South Mountain, Maryland, September 15, 1862. Confined at Fort Delaware, Delaware, until transferred to Aiken's Landing, James River, Virginia, October 2, 1862, for exchange. Declared exchanged at Aiken's Landing on November 10, 1862. Rejoined the company prior to January 1, 1863, and present or accounted for until wounded in the right cheek at Chancellorsville, Virginia, May 3, 1863. Rejoined the company in July-August, 1863, and present or accounted for until captured at Fisher's Hill, Virginia, September 22, 1864. Confined at Point Lookout, Maryland, until released on June 24, 1865, after taking the Oath of Allegiance.

BEASLY, I. F., Private
Place and date of enlistment not reported. Paroled at Charlotte on May 12, 1865.

BECK, D. M., Private
Place and date of enlistment not reported. Paroled at Greensboro on May 6, 1865.

BECK, DANIEL, Private
Born in Davidson County where he resided as a farmer prior to enlisting in Davidson County at age 21, May 14, 1861. Present or accounted for until discharged on January 28, 1862, by reason of "frequent attacks of intermittent fever and partial paralysis of the lower extremities."

BECK, GEORGE, Private
Resided in Davidson County and enlisted in Wake County at age 25, July 16, 1862, for the war. Present or accounted for until reported absent without leave from March 25, 1863, until November 26, 1863. Deserted on February 23, 1864.

BECK, HENRY B., Private
Resided in Davidson County and enlisted in Wake County at age 27, July 16, 1862, for the war. Present or accounted for until captured at Frederick, Maryland, September 12, 1862. Confined at Fort Delaware, Delaware, until transferred to Aiken's Landing, James River, Virginia, October 2, 1862, for exchange. Declared exchanged at Aiken's Landing on November 10, 1862. Rejoined the company in January-February, 1863, and present or accounted for through August, 1864.

BECK, JOHN LINDSAY, Private
Resided in Davidson County and was by occupation a miner prior to enlisting in Davidson County at age 29, May 14, 1861. Present or accounted for until wounded at Malvern Hill, Virginia, July 2, 1862. Reported on detail as a miner from October 30, 1862, through August, 1864.

BECK, TRAVIS D., Private
Resided in Davidson County and was by occupation a carpenter prior to enlisting in Davidson County at age 27, May 14, 1861. Mustered in as Private and promoted to Corporal on April 25, 1862. Present or accounted for until wounded at Malvern Hill, Virginia, July 1, 1862. Rejoined the company at an unspecified date and was detailed as a miner on October 30, 1862. Reduced to ranks on November 1, 1862. Reported absent on detail through August, 1864.

BECK, WILLIAM, Private
Born in Davidson County and was by occupation a farmer prior to enlisting in Wake County on July 16, 1862, for the war. Present or accounted for until discharged on October 2, 1862, by reason of "a deposit . . . in his right lung." Discharge papers give his age as 30.

BILLINGS, MERIDITH B., Corporal
Resided in Davidson County and was by occupation a miner prior to enlisting in Davidson County at age 19, May 14, 1861. Mustered in as Corporal. Present or accounted for until wounded in the arm at Malvern Hill, Virginia, on or about July 1, 1862. Arm amputated. Died in hospital at Richmond, Virginia, July 21, 1862.

BOWERS, DAVID, Private
Enlisted in Wake County on July 16, 1862, for the war. Present or accounted for until he died in Davidson County on November 8, 1862. Cause of death not reported.

BOWERS, LORENZO W., Private
Resided in Davidson County and was by occupation a farmer prior to enlisting in Davidson County at age 18, May 14, 1861. Present or accounted for until captured at Martinsburg, West Virginia, July 23, 1863. Confined at Martinsburg until transferred to Fort McHenry, Maryland, where he was confined on September 21, 1863. Transferred to Point Lookout, Maryland, November 1, 1863. Confined at Point Lookout until paroled and transferred to Boulware's Wharf, James River, Virginia, where he was received on or about March 16, 1865, for exchange.

BRIGGS, E., Private
Place and date of enlistment not reported. Paroled at Greensboro on May 6, 1865.

BRITTINGHAM, JOHN W., 1st Sergeant
Resided in Davidson County and was by occupation a mason prior to enlisting in Davidson County at age 36, May 14, 1861. Mustered in as 1st Sergeant. Present or accounted for until discharged on or about September 2, 1861, by reason of disability.

BROADWAY, WILLIAM HENRY, Private
Born in Davidson County where he resided as a farmer prior to enlisting in Davidson County at age 21, May 14, 1861. Present or accounted for until captured at Petersburg, Virginia, April 3, 1865. Confined at Hart's Island, New York Harbor, until released on June 17, 1865, after taking the Oath of Allegiance.

BRUCE, G. W., Private
Enlisted in Wake County on July 20, 1863, for the war. Present or accounted for until captured at Farmville, Virginia, April 6, 1865. Confined at Point Lookout, Maryland, where he died April 25, 1865, of "scurvy."

BRYANT, CORNELIUS, Private
Resided in Davidson County and was by occupation a carpenter prior to enlisting in Davidson County at age 22, May 14, 1861. Present or accounted for until paroled at Appomattox Court House, Virginia, April 9, 1865.

BURKHARDT, OBADIAH, Private
Resided in Davidson County and was by occupation a farmer prior to enlisting in Davidson County at age 21, May 14, 1861. Present or accounted for through August, 1864; however, he was reported absent on detail as a nurse or ambulance driver during much of that period. Paroled at Greensboro on May 3, 1865.

BYERLY, ANDREW, Private
Born in Davidson County where he resided as a farmer prior to enlisting in Davidson County at age 23, May 14, 1861. Present or accounted for until paroled on September 30, 1862; however, place and date captured not reported. Rejoined the company in January-February, 1863, and present or accounted for through December 14, 1864. Paroled at Greensboro on May 5, 1865.

CHAPELL, WILLIAM, Private
Resided in Davidson County and was by occupation a miner prior to enlisting in Davidson County at age 19, May 14, 1861. Present or accounted for until he died on or about March 10, 1862, "of a stab received in a fight." Place of death not reported.

CLODFELTER, ADAM E., Private
Enlisted in Wake County on July 16, 1862, for the war. Present or accounted for until reported absent without leave from April 19, 1863, until November 20, 1863. Present or accounted for until he deserted to the enemy on February 23, 1864.

CLODFELTER, DAVID C., Private
Resided in Davidson County and enlisted in Wake County at age 19, July 16, 1862, for the war. Present or accounted for until killed at or near Spotsylvania Court House, Virginia, May 10, 1864.

CONRAD, JAMES, Private
Enlisted on March 20, 1863, for the war. Present or accounted for through August, 1864. Paroled at Greensboro on May 5, 1865.

CONRAD, WILLIAM, Private
Resided in Davidson County and enlisted in Wake County at age 26, July 16, 1862, for the war. Present or accounted for until hospitalized at Richmond, Virginia, February 27, 1865, with a gunshot wound of the left arm; however, place and date wounded not reported. Captured in hospital at Richmond on April 3, 1865, and confined at Libby Prison, Richmond, until transferred to Newport News, Virginia, April 23, 1865. Released at Newport News on June 30, 1865, after taking the Oath of Allegiance.

CORNELISON, BURGESS B., Private
Resided in Davidson County and was by occupation a carpenter prior to enlisting in Davidson County at age 18, May 14, 1861. Present or accounted for until wounded in battle on the Weldon Railroad, near Petersburg, Virginia, August 21, 1864. Reported absent wounded until retired to the Invalid Corps on November 15, 1864.

COX, JOHN F., Private
Resided in Davidson County and was by occupation a farmer prior to enlisting in Davidson County at age 18, May 14, 1861. Present or accounted for until he died at Mount Jackson, Virginia, November 23, 1862, of "pneumonia."

CUTTING, LEANDER D., Corporal
Resided in Davidson County and was by occupation a carpenter prior to enlisting in Davidson County at age 17, May 14, 1861. Mustered in as Private and promoted to Corporal on January 1, 1863. Present or accounted for until wounded in the left knee and captured at Winchester, Virginia, September 19, 1864. Hospitalized at Winchester until transferred to hospital at Baltimore, Maryland, December 10, 1864. Transferred to Fort McHenry, Maryland, January 5, 1865, and was transferred to Point Lookout, Maryland, February 20, 1865, for exchange. Hospitalized at Richmond, Virginia, until furloughed for sixty days on March 10, 1865.

DARR, HENRY, Private
Enlisted in Wake County on October 16, 1863, for

the war. Present or accounted for until wounded in the "4th finger" of the left hand at Spotsylvania Court House, Virginia, May 21, 1864. Reported absent wounded through August, 1864.

DEMPSEY, E., Private
Enlisted in Wake County on July 20, 1863, for the war. Present or accounted for through August, 1864.

FORSHEE, JOSEPH, Private
Resided in Davidson County and was by occupation a miner prior to enlisting in Davidson County at age 29, May 14, 1861. Present or accounted for until captured at or near Gettysburg, Pennsylvania, July 3, 1863. Confined at Fort Delaware, Delaware, until transferred to Point Lookout, Maryland, September 26, 1863. Paroled at Point Lookout and transferred to City Point, Virginia, where he was received April 30, 1864, for exchange. Reported absent on furlough through August, 1864. Paroled at Appomattox Court House, Virginia, April 9, 1865.

FORSHEE, KEARNEY, Private
Resided in Davidson County and was by occupation a miner prior to enlisting in Davidson County at age 20, May 14, 1861. Present or accounted for until detailed as a miner on October 30, 1863. Reported absent on detail through August, 1864.

FORSHEE, WILLIAM, Private
Resided in Davidson County and was by occupation a miner prior to enlisting in Davidson County at age 22, May 14, 1861. Present or accounted for until reported absent without leave from September 14, 1863, until November 20, 1863. Present or accounted for until wounded in the left leg and captured at Spotsylvania Court House, Virginia, May 18, 1864. Left leg amputated. Hospitalized at Washington, D.C., where he died June 17, 1864, of "gangrene."

FRITTS, AMOS, Private
Resided in Davidson County and enlisted in Wake County at age 30, July 16, 1862, for the war. Present or accounted for through August, 1864; however, he was reported absent sick during much of that period. Paroled at Greensboro on May 5, 1865.

GALLIMORE, BENJAMIN F., Private
Resided in Davidson County and was by occupation a miner prior to enlisting in Davidson County at age 20, May 14, 1861. Present or accounted for through August, 1864.

GALLIMORE, BURGESS, Private
Enlisted in Wake County on July 16, 1862, for the war. Present or accounted for until reported absent without leave from April 19, 1863, until November 20, 1863. Present or accounted for until he deserted to the enemy on February 23, 1864.

GALLIMORE, DANIEL W., Private
Resided in Davidson County and was by occupation a miner prior to enlisting in Davidson County at age 22, May 14, 1861. Present or accounted for through August, 1864; however, he was reported on duty as a teamster during much of that period. Paroled at Greensboro on May 15, 1865.

GALLIMORE, EBENEZER, Private
Resided in Davidson County and was by occupation a farmer prior to enlisting in Davidson County at age

22, May 14, 1861. Present or accounted for until killed at Gettysburg, Pennsylvania, July 3, 1863.

GALLIMORE, JAMES, Private
Born in Davidson County* where he resided as a miner or farmer prior to enlisting in Davidson County at age 41, May 14, 1861. Present or accounted for until discharged on August 14, 1862, by reason of being over age.

GALLIMORE, WILSON J., Private
Resided in Davidson County and was by occupation a miner prior to enlisting in Davidson County at age 23, May 14, 1861. Mustered in as Private and promoted to Sergeant on April 25, 1862. Reduced to ranks on October 30, 1862, when he was detailed as a miner. Reported absent on detail through August, 1864.

GARDNER, W., Private
Place and date of enlistment not reported. Deserted to the enemy on or about April 6, 1865.

GATTIS, NATHAN, Private
Resided in Davidson County and was by occupation a farmer prior to enlisting in Davidson County at age 19, May 14, 1861. Present or accounted for until he deserted to the enemy on or about February 23, 1864.

GIBBINS, HAMILTON, Private
Resided in Davidson County and was by occupation a farmer prior to enlisting in Davidson County at age 19, May 14, 1861. Present or accounted for until he died at Goldsboro on or about October 20, 1862. Cause of death not reported.

GOSS, GEORGE W., Private
Resided in Davidson County and was by occupation a farmer prior to enlisting in Davidson County at age 18, May 28, 1861. Present or accounted for until wounded at Gaines' Mill, Virginia, June 27, 1862. Rejoined the company in January-February, 1863, and present or accounted for until killed at Spotsylvania Court House, Virginia, May 12, 1864.

GOSS, LEONARD C., Private
Enlisted on June 1, 1863, for the war. Present or accounted for until wounded at Spotsylvania Court House, Virginia, May 12, 1864. Reported absent wounded through August, 1864. Paroled at Appomattox Court House, Virginia, April 9, 1865.

HANNAH, JOHN, Private
Born in Davidson County where he resided as a coach driver prior to enlisting in Davidson County at age 22, May 14, 1861. Present or accounted for until discharged on August 15, 1861, by reason of disability.

HARGRAVE, ROBERT B., Sergeant
Resided in Davidson County and was by occupation a student prior to enlisting in Davidson County at age 19, May 14, 1861. Mustered in as Private and promoted to Sergeant on April 25, 1862. Present or accounted for until killed at Chancellorsville, Virginia, May 3, 1863.

HARRIS, JESSE FRANK, Private
Resided in Davidson County and was by occupation a farmer prior to enlisting in Davidson County at age 22, May 14, 1861. Present or accounted for until

detailed as a miner on October 30, 1862. Reported absent on detail through August, 1864.

HEADRICK, MICHAEL, Private
Resided in Davidson County and enlisted in Wake County at age 25, July 16, 1862, for the war. Present or accounted for through August, 1864.

HEARTLEY, WILLIAM W., Private
Resided in Davidson County and was by occupation a farmer prior to enlisting in Northampton County at age 18, June 4, 1861. Present or accounted for until he died at Fort Bee, Virginia, January 29, 1862. Cause of death not reported.

HEDRICK, GEORGE A., Private
Resided in Davidson County and was by occupation a farmer prior to enlisting in Davidson County at age 21, May 14, 1861. Present or accounted for until wounded at Spotsylvania Court House, Virginia, May 8, 1864. Reported absent wounded until retired to the Invalid Corps on October 31, 1864. Paroled at Greensboro on May 8, 1865.

HIATT, WESLEY, Private
Resided in Davidson County and was by occupation a blacksmith prior to enlisting in Davidson County at age 21, May 14, 1861. Present or accounted for through May 24, 1863; however, he was reported absent sick or on duty as a teamster during most of that period. Discharged from field service on May 25, 1863, and was reported absent on detached service through August, 1864.

HILB, LEOPOLD, Private
Resided in Germany and was by occupation a peddler prior to enlisting in Davidson County at age 19, May 14, 1861. Present or accounted for until discharged on September 25, 1862, by reason of being an "unnaturalized foreigner."

HIX, JOHN H., Private
Resided in Davidson County and was by occupation a student prior to enlisting in Davidson County at age 20, May 14, 1861. Present or accounted for until killed at Chancellorsville, Virginia, May 3, 1863.

HIX, THOMAS F., Corporal
Born in Stanly County* and resided in Davidson County where he was by occupation a medical student prior to enlisting in Davidson County at age 22, May 14, 1861. Mustered in as Corporal. Present or accounted for until discharged on September 7, 1861, by reason of disability.

HORN, CORNELIUS, Private
Resided in Davidson County and was by occupation a laborer prior to enlisting in Davidson County at age 40, May 14, 1861. Present or accounted for until discharged on August 7, 1862, under the provisions of the Conscript Act.

HUMPHREYS, ROBERT H., Sergeant
Resided in Davidson County and was by occupation a student prior to enlisting in Davidson County at age 17, May 14, 1861. Mustered in as Sergeant but was reduced to ranks on April 25, 1862. Present or accounted for until wounded in the scalp at Sharpsburg, Maryland, September 17, 1862. Rejoined the company in March-April, 1863, and was promoted to Sergeant on May 10, 1863. Present or

accounted for through August, 1864. Paroled at Thomasville on May 1, 1865.

HUNT, OBEDIAH, Private
Born in Davidson County where he resided as a blacksmith prior to enlisting in Davidson County at age 21, May 14, 1861. Present or accounted for until he died in hospital at Lynchburg, Virginia, June 28, 1862, of "diphtheria."

HUNT, WILLIAM H., Sergeant
Resided in Davidson County and was by occupation a student prior to enlisting in Northampton County at age 20, May 28, 1861. Mustered in as Private and promoted to Sergeant on September 12, 1861. Present or accounted for until wounded in the right leg and captured at or near Gettysburg, Pennsylvania, July 3-5, 1863. Confined at Fort Delaware, Delaware, until released on June 19, 1865, after taking the Oath of Allegiance.

INGRAM, JAMES W., Private
Resided in Davidson County and was by occupation a miner prior to enlisting in Davidson County at age 21, May 14, 1861. Present or accounted for until transferred to the C.S. Navy on or about April 5, 1864.

JENNINGS, ISAAC, Private
Place and date of enlistment not reported. Paroled at Greensboro on May 17, 1865.

JOHNSON, ELI W., Private
Resided in Davidson County and was by occupation a farmer prior to enlisting in Davidson County at age 21, May 14, 1861. Present or accounted for until wounded at Sharpsburg, Maryland, September 17, 1862. Died in hospital near Antietam, Maryland, September 20, 1862, of wounds. Roll of Honor states that he was "as gallant a man as ever fought."

KEPLEY, ANDREW, Private
Born in Davidson County and enlisted in Wake County on July 16, 1862, for the war. Present or accounted for until wounded and captured at Sharpsburg, Maryland, on or about September 17, 1862. Died in hospital at Shepherdstown, Virginia, October 7, 1862, of wounds.

KEPLY, MATHIAS, Private
Enlisted in Wake County on July 16, 1862, for the war. Present or accounted for until killed at Sharpsburg, Maryland, September 17, 1862.

KESLER, ROBERT, Private
Resided in Davidson County and enlisted in Wake County at age 35, July 16, 1862, for the war. Present or accounted for until paroled at Appomattox Court House, Virginia, April 9, 1865.

KESTLER, ALFRED, Private
Resided in Davidson County and was by occupation a farmer prior to enlisting in Davidson County at age 24, May 14, 1861. Present or accounted for until captured at Farmville, Virginia, April 6, 1865. Confined at Point Lookout, Maryland, until released on June 28, 1865, after taking the Oath of Allegiance.

KOONTS, EZEKIEL, Private
Resided in Davidson County and enlisted in Wake County on July 16, 1862, for the war. Present or accounted for until reported missing on September

17, 1862. Reported absent without leave until he was dropped from the rolls in November-December, 1863.

KOONTS, WILLIAM F., Private
Resided in Davidson County and was by occupation a carpenter prior to enlisting in Northampton County at age 28, June 4, 1861. Present or accounted for until reported missing on September 17, 1862. Reported absent sick or absent without leave until he was dropped from the rolls in November-December, 1863.

LANIER, WILLIAM R., Private
Resided in Davidson County and enlisted at Camp Daniel at age 18, September 12, 1861. Present or accounted for until reported absent without leave from May 25, 1863, until November 20, 1863. Present or accounted for until he deserted to the enemy at or near Bermuda Hundred, Virginia, on or about January 25, 1865. Took the Oath of Allegiance on or about January 27, 1865.

LEATHCO, JAMES P., Private
Resided in Davidson County and was by occupation a farmer prior to enlisting in Davidson County at age 23, May 14, 1861. Present or accounted for until hospitalized at Richmond, Virginia, September 30, 1862, with a gunshot wound; however, place and date wounded not reported. Rejoined the company prior to January 1, 1863, and present or accounted for until he deserted on June 1, 1863. Deserted to the enemy prior to December 5, 1863, when he took the Oath of Allegiance in West Virginia.

LEONARD, OBEDIAH, Private
Resided in Davidson County and enlisted in Wake County at age 24, July 16, 1862, for the war. Present or accounted for until reported missing on September 17, 1862. Reported missing or absent sick until dropped from the rolls in November-December, 1863.

LEONARD, VALENTINE, Private
Born in Davidson County where he resided as a farmer prior to enlisting in Davidson County at age 24, May 14, 1861. Present or accounted for until he died at Richmond, Virginia, on or about July 13, 1862. Cause of death not reported.

LEWIS, GEORGE T., Private
Resided in Davidson County and was by occupation a carpenter prior to enlisting in Davidson County at age 28, May 14, 1861. Present or accounted for until he died at Camp Ellis on July 31, 1861. Cause of death not reported.

LONG, EZRA, Private
Enlisted in Wake County on September 17, 1863, for the war. Present or accounted for until captured at Spotsylvania Court House, Virginia, in May, 1864. Confined at Point Lookout, Maryland, until transferred to Elmira, New York, July 25, 1864. Died at Elmira on August 31, 1864, of "chronic diarrhoea."

LOPP, JACOB, Private
Resided in Davidson County and enlisted in Wake County at age 20, July 16, 1862, for the war. Present or accounted for until wounded in the left arm and captured at or near Gettysburg, Pennsylvania, July 2-5, 1863. Confined at Fort Delaware, Delaware, until transferred to Point Lookout, Maryland,

October 15-18, 1863. Paroled at Point Lookout on February 18, 1865, and transferred to Boulware's and Cox's Wharf, James River, Virginia, for exchange. Reported present with a detachment of paroled and exchanged prisoners at Camp Lee, near Richmond, Virginia, February 28, 1865.

LOPP, MATHIAS, Private
Resided in Davidson County and enlisted in Wake County at age 25, July 16, 1862, for the war. Present or accounted for through December 20, 1864.

MILLER, JOHN Q., Private
Resided in Davidson County and enlisted in Wake County at age 28, July 16, 1862, for the war. Present or accounted for until killed at Spotsylvania Court House, Virginia, May 19, 1864.

MIZE, BURGESS H., Private
Resided in Davidson County and was by occupation a farmer prior to enlisting in Davidson County at age 22, May 14, 1861. Present or accounted for until wounded at Malvern Hill, Virginia, July 1, 1862. Rejoined the company in May-June, 1863. Present or accounted for until he was reported captured on May 19, 1864; however, records of the Federal Provost Marshal do not substantiate that report. No further records.

MIZE, JOHN, Private
Resided in Davidson County and was by occupation a farmer prior to enlisting in Davidson County at age 18, May 14, 1861. Present or accounted for until hospitalized at Richmond, Virginia, June 1, 1864, with a gunshot wound of the finger; however, place and date wounded not reported. Returned to duty on June 14, 1864, and present or accounted for until captured at Petersburg, Virginia, April 3, 1865. Confined at Hart's Island, New York Harbor, until released on June 17, 1865, after taking the Oath of Allegiance.

MORRIS, MURPHY, Private
Resided in Davidson County and was by occupation a farmer prior to enlisting in Davidson County at age 23, May 14, 1861. Present or accounted for until he died at Richmond, Virginia, August 30, 1862. Cause of death not reported.

MYERS, HENRY, Private
Resided in Davidson County and was by occupation a farmer prior to enlisting in Davidson County at age 25, May 14, 1861. Present or accounted for until captured at Petersburg, Virginia, April 3, 1865. Confined at Hart's Island, New York Harbor, until released on June 17, 1865, after taking the Oath of Allegiance.

MYERS, WILLIAM A., Private
Resided in Davidson County and was by occupation a farmer prior to enlisting in Davidson County at age 22, May 14, 1861. Present or accounted for until captured at Petersburg, Virginia, April 3, 1865. Confined at Hart's Island, New York Harbor, until released on June 17, 1865, after taking the Oath of Allegiance.

MYERS, WILLIAM H., Private
Resided in Davidson County and enlisted in Wake County at age 18, July 16, 1862, for the war. Present or accounted for until hospitalized at Richmond,

Virginia, December 24, 1864, with an injury of the foot. Place and date injured not reported. Returned to duty on December 27, 1864, and was captured prior to May 1, 1865. Confined at Hart's Island, New York Harbor, until released on June 17, 1865, after taking the Oath of Allegiance.

MYRICK, JESSE H., Private
Resided in Davidson County and was by occupation a farmer prior to enlisting in Davidson County at age 20, May 14, 1861. Present or accounted for until captured at Strasburg, Virginia, or at Woodstock, Virginia, September 23, 1864. Confined at Point Lookout, Maryland, until released on June 3, 1865, after taking the Oath of Allegiance.

MYRICK, JOHN S., Private
Resided in Davidson County and was by occupation a farmer prior to enlisting in Davidson County at age 18, May 14, 1861. Present or accounted for until killed at Sharpsburg, Maryland, September 17, 1862.

MYRICK, LAWSON, Private
Enlisted in Wake County on October 14, 1863, for the war. Present or accounted for until discharged in April, 1864. Reason discharged not reported.

OSBORNE, ZACHIAS, Private
Resided in Davidson County and was by occupation a farmer prior to enlisting in Davidson County at age 25, May 14, 1861. Present or accounted for until captured at Boonsboro, Maryland, September 15, 1862. Confined at Fort Delaware, Delaware, until transferred to Aiken's Landing, James River, Virginia, October 2, 1862, for exchange. Declared exchanged at Aiken's Landing on November 10, 1862. Died November 24, 1862. Place and cause of death not reported.

PAFSHEE, CARNEY, Private
Place and date of enlistment not reported. Paroled at Greensboro on May 4, 1865.

PENNINGER, MONROE, Private
Resided in Davidson County and was by occupation a farmer prior to enlisting in Davidson County at age 18, May 14, 1861. Present or accounted for until he died on August 20, 1862. Place and cause of death not reported.

PENRY, RICHARD A., Private
Resided in Davidson County and was by occupation a farmer prior to enlisting in Northampton County at age 15, May 28, 1861. Present or accounted for until killed at Williamsburg, Virginia, May 5, 1862.

PRUTT, H., Private
Place and date of enlistment not reported. Captured at Fisher's Hill, Virginia, September 22, 1864. Confined at Point Lookout, Maryland, until released on or about October 18, 1864, after joining the U.S. service. Unit to which assigned not reported.

REID, GEORGE W., Private
Resided in Davidson County and was by occupation a farmer prior to enlisting in Davidson County at age 22, May 14, 1861. Present or accounted for until wounded in the right leg at Spotsylvania Court House, Virginia, May 12, 1864. Reported absent wounded through August, 1864. Captured in hospital at Richmond, Virginia, April 3, 1865, and confined at Libby Prison, Richmond, until April 23,

1865, when he was transferred to Newport News, Virginia. Released at Newport News on June 30, 1865, after taking the Oath of Allegiance.

RICHARD, D. E. S., Private
Enlisted in Wake County on July 8, 1862, for the war. Present or accounted for until he died in hospital at Richmond, Virginia, October 17, 1862, of "pneumonia."

ROLAND, JOHN W., Private
Resided in Davidson County and was by occupation a farmer prior to enlisting in Davidson County at age 24, May 14, 1861. Present or accounted for until he deserted near Hamilton's Crossing, Virginia, April 6, 1863.

RUSH, ABNER E., Private
Resided in Davidson County or in Henderson County, Tennessee, and was by occupation a farmer prior to enlisting in Davidson County at age 24, May 14, 1861. Mustered in as Private and promoted to Corporal on April 25, 1862. Present or accounted for until wounded at Malvern Hill, Virginia, July 1, 1862. Reduced to ranks on October 1, 1862. Rejoined the company prior to January 1, 1863, and present or accounted for until wounded in the thorax at Chancellorsville, Virginia, May 3, 1863. Returned to duty on June 4, 1863, and was captured at Gettysburg, Pennsylvania, July 1-4, 1863. Confined at Fort Delaware, Delaware, until transferred to Point Lookout, Maryland, October 15-18, 1863. Transferred back to Fort Delaware at an unspecified date and was released at Fort Delaware on May 4, 1865, after taking the Oath of Allegiance.

SEACHRIST, AMOS, Private
Resided in Davidson County and was by occupation a farmer prior to enlisting in Davidson County at age 24, May 14, 1861. Present or accounted for until captured at Boonsboro, Maryland, September 17, 1862. Received at Aiken's Landing, James River, Virginia, October 6, 1862, for exchange. Declared exchanged at Aiken's Landing on November 10, 1862. Rejoined the company prior to January 1, 1863, and present or accounted for until he deserted in Maryland on July 11, 1864. Confined at Old Capitol Prison, Washington, D.C., until transferred to Elmira, New York, July 23, 1864. Released at Elmira on May 29, 1865, after taking the Oath of Allegiance.

SEACHRIST, DANIEL, Private
Resided in Davidson County and was by occupation a farmer prior to enlisting in Davidson County at age 20, May 14, 1861. Present or accounted for until paroled at Appomattox Court House, Virginia, April 9, 1865.

SEACHRIST, JAMES, Private
Resided in Davidson County and was by occupation a farmer prior to enlisting in Davidson County at age 19, May 14, 1861. Present or accounted for until wounded at Sharpsburg, Maryland, September 17, 1862. Rejoined the company prior to January 1, 1863, and present or accounted for until he deserted in Maryland on July 11, 1864. Confined at Old Capitol Prison, Washington, D.C., until transferred to Elmira, New York, July 23, 1864. Died at Elmira on May 10, 1865, of "chro[nic] diarrhoea."

SEMONE, JAMES, Private

Resided in Davidson County and was by occupation a farmer prior to enlisting in Davidson County at age 22, May 14, 1861. Present or accounted for until wounded and captured at Gettysburg, Pennsylvania, July 3-4, 1863. Confined at Fort Delaware, Delaware, until transferred to Point Lookout, Maryland, October 15-18, 1863. Paroled at Point Lookout on February 18, 1865, and transferred to Boulware's and Cox's Wharf, James River, Virginia, February 20-21, 1865, for exchange. Reported present with a detachment of paroled and exchanged prisoners at Camp Lee, near Richmond, Virginia, February 28, 1865.

SHAW, HENRY, Private

Resided in Davidson County and was by occupation a carpenter prior to enlisting in Davidson County at age 25, May 14, 1861. Present or accounted for until paroled at Appomattox Court House, Virginia, April 9, 1865.

SINK, GASHEM, Private

Resided in Davidson County and was by occupation a blacksmith prior to enlisting in Davidson County at age 19, May 14, 1861. Present or accounted for until he died in hospital at Richmond, Virginia, June 8, 1862, of "feb[ris] typhoides."

SMITH, CALHOUN M., Corporal

Resided in Davidson County and was by occupation a wheelwright prior to enlisting in Davidson County at age 20, May 14, 1861. Mustered in as Private and promoted to Corporal on April 25, 1862. Nominated for the Badge of Distinction for gallantry at Chancellorsville, Virginia, May 1-3, 1863. Present or accounted for until paroled at Appomattox Court House, Virginia, April 9, 1865.

SMITH, YARBROUGH H., Private

Born in Guilford County and resided in Davidson County where he was by occupation a tailor prior to enlisting in Davidson County at age 41, May 14, 1861. Present or accounted for until discharged on August 14, 1862, by reason of being over age.

STEVENS, MARTIN, Private

Place and date of enlistment not reported. Paroled at Greensboro on May 9, 1865.

STONER, JOHN, Corporal

Enlisted in Wake County on July 16, 1862, for the war. Mustered in as Private and promoted to Corporal on October 1, 1862. Present or accounted for until he died in hospital at White Sulpher Springs, Virginia, November 23, 1862, of "pneumonia."

STRANGE, BURGESS S., Private

Resided in Davidson County and was by occupation a farmer prior to enlisting in Davidson County at age 20, May 14, 1861. Mustered in as Private and promoted to Corporal on September 12, 1861. Promoted to Sergeant on April 25, 1862. Present or accounted for until wounded at Malvern Hill, Virginia, on or about July 1, 1862. Rejoined the company in January-February, 1863, and present or accounted for through August, 1864. Reduced to ranks prior to April 9, 1865, when he was paroled at Appomattox Court House, Virginia.

SULLIVAN, WESLEY E., Private

Resided in Davidson County and was by occupation a farmer prior to enlisting in Davidson County at age 22, May 14, 1861. Present or accounted for until he deserted to the enemy at or near Williamsport, Maryland, on or about July 10, 1863. Confined at Fort Delaware, Delaware, until released on September 22, 1863, after joining the U.S. Army. Assigned to Company G, 3rd Regiment Maryland Cavalry.

SULLIVAN, WILLIAM A., Private

Resided in Davidson County and was by occupation a student prior to enlisting in Davidson County at age 17, May 14, 1861. Present or accounted for until wounded at Sharpsburg, Maryland, September 17, 1862. Rejoined the company in January-February, 1863, and present or accounted for until paroled at Appomattox Court House, Virginia, April 9, 1865.

SWICEGOOD, GEORGE WASHINGTON, Corporal

Resided in Davidson County and was by occupation a farmer prior to enlisting in Davidson County at age 24, May 14, 1861. Mustered in as Private and promoted to Corporal on November 18, 1861. Reduced to ranks on April 25, 1862, but was promoted to Corporal in September, 1864. Present or accounted for until captured at Strasburg, Virginia, September 23-24, 1864. Confined at Point Lookout, Maryland, until released on May 13, 1865.

SWICEGOOD, JAMES A., Private

Resided in Davidson County and was by occupation a farmer prior to enlisting in Davidson County at age 26, May 14, 1861. Mustered in as Private and promoted to Corporal on June 18, 1863. Reduced to ranks in September, 1864-April, 1865. Present or accounted for until captured at Petersburg, Virginia, April 3, 1865. Confined at Hart's Island, New York Harbor, until released on June 17, 1865, after taking the Oath of Allegiance.

SWING, JOHN H., Private

Resided in Davidson County and was by occupation a carpenter prior to enlisting in Davidson County at age 24, May 14, 1861. Present or accounted for until wounded in both hips and captured at Sharpsburg, Maryland, on or about September 17, 1862. Confined at Fort McHenry, Maryland, until transferred to City Point, Virginia, where he was received November 21, 1862, for exchange. Rejoined the company in January-February, 1863, and present or accounted for until paroled at Appomattox Court House, Virginia, April 9, 1865.

THOMPSON, CHARLES M., Private

Born in Davidson County where he resided as a student prior to enlisting in Davidson County at age 17, May 14, 1861. Present or accounted for until wounded in the right arm at Spotsylvania Court House, Virginia, May 12, 1864. Right arm amputated. Reported absent wounded until discharged on March 18, 1865.

THOMPSON, WILLIAM L., Corporal

Resided in Davidson County and was by occupation a student prior to enlisting in Davidson County at age 19, May 14, 1861. Mustered in as Private and promoted to Corporal on November 1, 1862. Present or accounted for until furloughed for sixty days on

February 25, 1865; however, he was reported absent sick or absent on detail during much of that period.

TODD, MILO G., Private
Resided in Davidson County and was by occupation a carpenter prior to enlisting in Davidson County at age 27, May 14, 1861. Present or accounted for until he died at home in Rowan County on January 3, 1863. Cause of death not reported.

TREXLER, DAVID L., Private
Enlisted in Davidson County on January 27, 1863, for the war. Present or accounted for through October, 1864.

TYSINGER, PETER N., 1st Sergeant
Resided in Davidson County and was by occupation a farmer prior to enlisting in Davidson County at age 24, May 14, 1861. Mustered in as Sergeant and promoted to 1st Sergeant on September 12, 1861. Present or accounted for until wounded in the left leg at or near Bethesda Church, Virginia, May 30, 1864. Reported absent wounded through August, 1864. Paroled at Appomattox Court House, Virginia, April 9, 1865.

WEAVER, HENRY C., Private
Place and date of enlistment not reported. Captured at Spotsylvania Court House, Virginia, May 20, 1864. Confined at Point Lookout, Maryland, until transferred to Elmira, New York, July 5, 1864. Paroled at Elmira on February 9, 1865, and transferred to Boulware's and Cox's Wharf, James River, Virginia, where he was received on February 20, 1865, for exchange. Furloughed from hospital at Richmond, Virginia, February 25, 1865.

WEAVER, PRESTON D., Sergeant
Resided in Davidson County and was by occupation a harness maker prior to enlisting in Davidson County at age 18, May 14, 1861. Mustered in as Corporal but was reduced to ranks on April 25, 1862. Present or accounted for until wounded at Malvern Hill, Virginia, July 1, 1862. Promoted to Sergeant on November 1, 1862, and rejoined the company prior to January 1, 1863. Present or accounted for until wounded in battle on the Weldon Railroad, near Petersburg, Virginia, August 21, 1864. Paroled at Appomattox Court House, Virginia, April 9, 1865.

WILLIFORD, JESSE A., Private
Born in Cabarrus County and resided in Davidson County where he was by occupation a tailor prior to enlisting in Davidson County at age 34, May 14, 1861. Present or accounted for until discharged on August 15, 1861, by reason of disability.

WILSON, GILES, Private
Resided in Davidson County and enlisted in Wake County at age 35, July 16, 1862, for the war. Present or accounted for until captured at South Mountain, Maryland, September 15, 1862. Confined at Fort Delaware, Delaware, until transferred to Aiken's Landing, James River, Virginia, October 2, 1862, for exchange. Declared exchanged at Aiken's Landing on November 10, 1862. Rejoined the company prior to January 1, 1863, and present or accounted for until captured at Strasburg, Virginia, September 23, 1864. Confined at Point Lookout, Maryland, until

released on June 21, 1865, after taking the Oath of Allegiance.

WILSON, JOHN H., Private
Resided in Davidson County and was by occupation an artist prior to enlisting in Davidson County at age 25, May 14, 1861. Present or accounted for until wounded in the left arm at Malvern Hill, Virginia, July 1, 1862. Reported absent wounded until discharged on August 10, 1862, by reason of wounds received at Malvern Hill.

WOOD, RICHARD W., Private
Resided in Davidson County and was by occupation a farmer prior to enlisting in Davidson County at age 23, May 14, 1864. Present or accounted for until he died at home in Davidson County on September 16, 1862. Cause of death not reported.

WORKMAN, JAMES E., Private
Resided in Davidson County and was by occupation a farmer prior to enlisting in Davidson County at age 21, May 14, 1861. Present or accounted for until captured at or near Boonsboro, Maryland, on or about September 15, 1862. Confined at Fort Delaware, Delaware, until transferred to Aiken's Landing, James River, Virginia, October 2, 1862, for exchange. Declared exchanged at Aiken's Landing on November 10, 1862. Reported absent without leave until November 20, 1863. Present or accounted for until wounded at Spotsylvania Court House, Virginia, May 8, 1864. Reported absent wounded through August, 1864.

YOUNG, FRANKLIN, Private
Resided in Davidson County and was by occupation a farmer prior to enlisting in Davidson County at age 23, May 14, 1861. Present or accounted for until he died in hospital at Richmond, Virginia, July 6, 1862. Cause of death not reported.

YOUNG, GEORGE H., Private
Resided in Davidson County and was by occupation a farmer prior to enlisting in Davidson County at age 26, May 14, 1861. Present or accounted for until he died in hospital at Richmond, Virginia, July 6, 1862, of a gunshot wound of the side. Place and date wounded not reported.

YOUNG, JAMES J., Private
Resided in Davidson County and was by occupation a farmer prior to enlisting in Davidson County at age 23, May 14, 1861. Present or accounted for until wounded in the left side at Malvern Hill, Virginia, on or about July 1, 1862. Returned to duty July 9, 1862, and present or accounted for until captured at Spotsylvania Court House, Virginia, May 19-20, 1864. Confined at Point Lookout, Maryland, until released on May 28, 1864, after joining the U.S. Army. Assigned to Company I, 1st Regiment U.S. Volunteer Infantry.

YOUNG, LARY, Private
Enlisted in Wake County on July 14, 1863, for the war. Present or accounted for until paroled at Appomattox Court House, Virginia, April 9, 1865.

YOUNG, WILLIAM M., Private
Resided in Davidson County and was by occupation a farmer prior to enlisting in Davidson County at age 25, May 14, 1861. Present or accounted for until he

died at Richmond, Virginia, July 12, 1862. Cause of death not reported.

YOUNTZ, JOHN F., Private

Resided in Davidson County and was by occupation a farmer prior to enlisting in Davidson County at age 19, May 14, 1861. Present or accounted for through August, 1864. Paroled at Greensboro on May 16, 1865.

YOUNTZ, WILLIAM C., Private

Resided in Davidson County and was by occupation a farmer prior to enlisting in Davidson County at age 17, May 14, 1861. Present or accounted for until wounded on October 15, 1863; however, battle in which wounded not reported. Rejoined the company in January-March, 1864, and present or accounted for until paroled at Appomattox Court House, Virginia, April 9, 1865.

COMPANY K

This company, known as the Raleigh Rifles, was from Wake County and enlisted at Raleigh on May 21, 1861. On June 2 it left Raleigh for Garysburg, where it arrived the same day. There it was assigned to this regiment as Company K. After joining the regiment the company functioned as a part of the regiment, and its history for the war period is recorded as a part of the regimental history.

The information contained in the following roster of the company was compiled principally from company muster rolls for June 30, 1861, through August 31, 1864. No company muster rolls were found for the period after August 31, 1864. In addition to the company muster rolls, Roll of Honor records, receipt rolls, hospital records, prisoner of war records, and other primary records, supplemented by state pension applications, United Daughters of the Confederacy records, and postwar rosters and histories, all provided useful information.

OFFICERS
CAPTAINS

HARRISON, WILLIAM H.

Resided in Wake County and was serving as mayor of Raleigh when he enlisted in Wake County at age 33. Elected Captain to rank from May 21, 1861. Present or accounted for until he resigned or was not reelected when the regiment was reorganized, April 25-26, 1862.

JONES, JOSEPH

Resided in Wake County and was by occupation a druggist prior to enlisting in Wake County at age 23. Elected 2nd Lieutenant to rank from May 21, 1861, and was elected 1st Lieutenant on March 7, 1862. Elected Captain on or about April 27, 1862. Present or accounted for until wounded and captured at Sharpsburg, Maryland, on or about September 16, 1862. Confined at Fort Delaware, Delaware, until transferred to Aiken's Landing, James River, Virginia, October 2, 1862, for exchange. Declared

exchanged at Aiken's Landing on November 10, 1862. Rejoined the company prior to January 1, 1863, and present or accounted for until hospitalized at Richmond, Virginia, May 15, 1864, with a gunshot wound of the left arm and side. Place and date wounded not reported. Rejoined the company prior to September 1, 1864. No further records.

LIEUTENANTS

BEVERS, CHARLES WESLEY, 2nd Lieutenant

Resided in Wake County and was by occupation an engineer prior to enlisting in Wake County at age 23, May 21, 1861. Mustered in as Corporal and promoted to Sergeant on November 15, 1861. Elected 2nd Lieutenant to rank from April 27, 1862. Present or accounted for until captured at Sharpsburg, Maryland, on or about September 16, 1862. Confined at Fort Delaware, Delaware, until transferred to Aiken's Landing, James River, Virginia, October 2, 1862, for exchange. Declared exchanged at Aiken's Landing on November 10, 1862. Rejoined the company in January-February, 1863, and present or accounted for until wounded in the head at Spotsylvania Court House, Virginia, May 12, 1864. Rejoined the company prior to September 19-22, 1864, when he was captured at Winchester, Virginia, or at Fisher's Hill, Virginia. Confined at Fort Delaware until released on June 17, 1865, after taking the Oath of Allegiance.

BRYAN, JOHN S., 2nd Lieutenant

Resided in Wake County and was by occupation a farmer prior to enlisting at Camp Bragg, Virginia, at age 23, June 28, 1861. Mustered in as Private and promoted to Sergeant on November 15, 1861. Elected 2nd Lieutenant to rank from April 27, 1862. Present or accounted for until wounded at Chancellorsville, Virginia, May 3, 1863. Rejoined the company prior to July 1, 1863, and present or accounted for until captured at Bethesda Church, Virginia, May 30, 1864. Confined at Point Lookout, Maryland, until transferred to Fort Delaware, Delaware, June 23, 1864. Released at Fort Delaware on June 16, 1865, after taking the Oath of Allegiance.

BUSBEE, QUENTIN, 1st Lieutenant

Resided in Wake County and was by occupation a lawyer prior to enlisting in Wake County at age 35, May 21, 1861. Mustered in as Private and was appointed 1st Lieutenant to rank from November 25, 1861. Present or accounted for until he resigned on February 24, 1862, after being charged with absence without leave and "intoxication."

GALES, SEATON E., 2nd Lieutenant

Resided in Wake County and was by occupation a lawyer prior to enlisting in Wake County at age 33. Appointed 2nd Lieutenant to rank from May 21, 1861. Appointed Adjutant (2nd Lieutenant) on June 3, 1861, and transferred to the Field and Staff of this regiment.

HARDIE, PINCKNEY, 1st Lieutenant

Resided in Wake County and was by occupation an express agent prior to enlisting in Wake County at age 29, May 21, 1861. Mustered in as Corporal and promoted to Sergeant on June 5, 1861. Promoted to

1st Sergeant on December 22, 1861, and was elected 3rd Lieutenant to rank from March 7, 1862. Elected 1st Lieutenant on or about April 26, 1862. Present or accounted for until wounded at Gettysburg, Pennsylvania, July 1, 1863. Rejoined the company prior to September 1, 1863, and present or accounted for through September 30, 1864. Company records dated February 25, 1865, indicate he was a prisoner of war; however, records of the Federal Provost Marshal do not substantiate that report.

ROGERS, SION HART, 1st Lieutenant
Born in Wake County where he resided as a lawyer prior to enlisting in Wake County at age 35. Elected 1st Lieutenant to rank from May 21, 1861. Present or accounted for until he resigned on or about November 20, 1861. Later served as Colonel of the 47th Regiment N.C. Troops.

NONCOMMISSIONED OFFICERS AND PRIVATES

ADAMS, ARCHIBALD M., Private
Resided in Montgomery County and enlisted in Wake County at age 32, July 16, 1862, for the war. Present or accounted for until he deserted in May, 1863. Reported "in arrest" through August, 1863. Reported absent sick until January 14, 1864, when he was sent to Castle Thunder Prison, Richmond, Virginia. Rejoined the company prior to September 1, 1864. No further records.

ADAMS, CULBERT, Private
Resided in Wake County and was by occupation a farmer prior to enlisting in Wake County at age 19, May 21, 1861. Mustered in as Private and promoted to Sergeant on April 26, 1862. Reduced to ranks on July 1, 1862. Present or accounted for until wounded in the hand, face, and right leg at Gettysburg, Pennsylvania, July 1-3, 1863. Rejoined the company in September-October, 1863, and present or accounted for until captured at Winchester, Virginia, September 19, 1864. Confined at Point Lookout, Maryland, until transferred to Aiken's Landing, James River, Virginia, where he was received March 16, 1865, for exchange. Reported in hospital at Richmond, Virginia, March 19, 1865.

ALLEN, DANIEL B., Private
Born in Halifax County and resided in Wake County where he was by occupation a clerk prior to enlisting in Wake County at age 20, May 21, 1861. Present or accounted for until discharged on September 20, 1861, by reason of disability.

ALLEN, JOSIAH L., Corporal
Resided in Montgomery County and enlisted in Wake County at age 20, July 16, 1862, for the war. Mustered in as Private. Present or accounted for until captured at Sharpsburg, Maryland, September 17, 1862. Confined at Fort Delaware, Delaware, until transferred to Aiken's Landing, James River, Virginia, October 2, 1862, for exchange. Declared exchanged at Aiken's Landing on November 10, 1862. Reported "in arrest charged with desertion" on or about January 1, 1863, but rejoined the company prior to March 1, 1863. Present or accounted for through August, 1864. Promoted to Corporal prior to April 3, 1865, when he was captured at

Petersburg, Virginia. Confined at Hart's Island, New York Harbor, until released on June 17, 1865, after taking the Oath of Allegiance.

ARMSTRONG, WILLIAM H., Private
Born in Richmond, Virginia, and resided in Wake County where he was by occupation a gas fitter prior to enlisting in Wake County at age 27, May 21, 1861. Mustered in as Corporal but was reduced to ranks in March-October, 1862. Present or accounted for until discharged on October 7, 1862, by reason of "double hernia."

BADGER, RICHARD C., Sergeant
Resided in Wake County and was by occupation a lawyer prior to enlisting in Wake County at age 21, May 21, 1861. Mustered in as Sergeant. Present or accounted for until promoted to Sergeant Major on June 3, 1861, and transferred to the Field and Staff of this regiment.

BARHAM, JOHN Q. A., Private
Resided in Wake County and was by occupation a merchant prior to enlisting in Wake County at age 31, May 21, 1861. Mustered in as Private and promoted to Sergeant on December 22, 1861. Reduced to ranks on April 26, 1862. Present or accounted for through December 20, 1864; however, he was reported absent on detail as a hospital clerk during much of that period.

BAUER, JOHN N. C., Private
Resided in Wake County and was by occupation a wagonmaker prior to enlisting at Camp Bragg, Virginia, at age 38, June 23, 1861. Present or accounted for until discharged on September 2, 1862. Reason discharged not reported.

BEASLEY, CHARLES J., Private
Resided in Wake County where he enlisted at age 17, November 20, 1862, for the war. Present or accounted for until discharged on February 10, 1863. Reason discharged not reported.

BEASLEY, SAMUEL L., Sergeant
Born in Wake County where he resided as a wheelwright or coach maker prior to enlisting in Wake County at age 18, May 21, 1861. Mustered in as Private and promoted to Sergeant on December 28, 1862. Present or accounted for until captured at Sharpsburg, Maryland, September 17, 1862. Confined at Fort Delaware, Delaware, until transferred to Aiken's Landing, James River, Virginia, October 2, 1862, for exchange. Declared exchanged at Aiken's Landing on November 10, 1862. Rejoined the company prior to January 1, 1863, and present or accounted for until killed at Chancellorsville, Virginia, May 3, 1863.

BEASLEY, WILLIAM R., Private
Resided in Wake County and was by occupation a carpenter prior to enlisting in Wake County at age 24, May 21, 1861. Mustered in as Private and promoted to Corporal on April 26, 1862. Reduced to ranks on December 26, 1862. Present or accounted for until captured at Gettysburg, Pennsylvania, July 2-4, 1863. Confined at Fort Delaware, Delaware, until transferred to Point Lookout, Maryland, October 15-18, 1863. Died at Point Lookout on January 12, 1864, of disease.

BELL, HILLIARD, _____
Place and date of enlistment not reported. Detailed as a gunsmith in the Ordnance Department. No further records.

BELL, WILLIAM R., Corporal
Resided in Wake County and was by occupation a butcher prior to enlisting in Wake County at age 23, May 21, 1861. Mustered in as Private and promoted to Corporal on December 28, 1862. Present or accounted for until wounded at Chancellorsville, Virginia, May 1-3, 1863. Reported absent sick, absent on detail, or absent disabled through August, 1864.

BEVERS, FABIUS G., Private
Born in Wake County where he resided as an engineer prior to enlisting in Wake County at age 25, May 21, 1861. Present or accounted for until discharged on September 16, 1861, by reason of "sickness."

BIRD, ALFRED, Private
Resided in Pitt County and enlisted in Wake County at age 18, July 16, 1862, for the war. Present or accounted for until he died in hospital at Lynchburg, Virginia, June 28, 1863, of "febris congestiva."

BLUM, PETER, Private
Resided in Wake County and was by occupation a shoemaker prior to enlisting in Wake County at age 46, May 21, 1861. Present or accounted for until discharged on or about September 2, 1862. Reason discharged not reported.

BODEKER, FERDINAND W., 1st Sergeant
Resided in Wake County and was by occupation a druggist prior to enlisting in Wake County at age 25, May 21, 1861. Mustered in as Private and promoted to Sergeant on July 1, 1862. Present or accounted for until captured at Sharpsburg, Maryland, September 17, 1862. Confined at Fort Delaware, Delaware, until transferred to Aiken's Landing, James River, Virginia, October 2, 1862, for exchange. Declared exchanged at Aiken's Landing on November 10, 1862. Rejoined the company prior to January 1, 1863, and present or accounted for until wounded at Chancellorsville, Virginia, May 1-3, 1863. Rejoined the company prior to September 1, 1863, and was promoted to 1st Sergeant in January-April, 1864. Present or accounted for until hospitalized at Charlottesville, Virginia, October 23, 1864, with a gunshot wound of the right thigh. Place and date wounded not reported. Reported absent wounded until furloughed on April 6, 1865.

BOSCHA, GIOVANNI, Private
Enlisted in Long Bridge, Virginia, at age 36, May 14, 1862, for the war as a substitute. Deserted May 20, 1862, and was reported "in arrest" at Richmond, Virginia, on or about January 1, 1863.

BROWN, GEORGE, Private
Resided in Hertford County and enlisted in Wake County at age 22, July 16, 1862, for the war. Present or accounted for until he deserted on or about August 20, 1862.

BRYANT, JOHN QUINT, Private
Resided in Wake County and was by occupation a

painter prior to enlisting in Wake County at age 21, May 21, 1861. Present or accounted for until discharged on or about October 4, 1861. Reason discharged not reported.

CAUDLE, CHRISTOPHER COLUMBUS, Corporal
Resided in Wake County and was by occupation a cabinetmaker prior to enlisting in Wake County at age 18, May 21, 1861. Mustered in as Private. Present or accounted for until captured at Williamsport, Maryland, July 10, 1863. Confined at Wheeling, West Virginia, until transferred to Camp Chase, Ohio, July 22, 1863. Confined at Camp Chase until released on or about July 21, 1864, after joining the U.S. Navy. Records of the Federal Provost Marshal give his rank as Corporal.

CAUDLE, MARION, Private
Resided in Wake County and was by occupation a laborer prior to enlisting in Wake County at age 26, May 21, 1861. Present or accounted for until reported absent without leave on May 26, 1863. Reported absent without leave until he was reported absent in arrest on April 1, 1864. Reported on duty with Ward's Battalion (C. S. Prisoners) in July, 1864. Rejoined the company prior to September 1, 1864. Paroled at Raleigh on April 20, 1865, and took the Oath of Allegiance at Raleigh on May 22, 1865.

CHAMBLEE, WILLIAM H., Private
Resided in Wake County and was by occupation a farmer prior to enlisting at Camp Bragg, Virginia, at age 21, June 24, 1861. Mustered in as Private and promoted to Corporal on April 26, 1862. Reduced to ranks on July 1, 1862. Present or accounted for until wounded and captured at Chancellorsville, Virginia, May 1-3, 1863. Paroled on or about June 30, 1863. Rejoined the company prior to January 1, 1864, and present or accounted for until transferred to the C.S. Navy on or about April 5, 1864.

CHAMPION, WILLIAM, Private
Resided in Wake County and was by occupation a farmer prior to enlisting in Wake County at age 30, May 21, 1861. Mustered in as Private and promoted to Corporal on December 28, 1862. Reduced to ranks in May-June, 1863. Present or accounted for until reported absent without leave from June 3, 1863, until November-December, 1863, when he was reported absent in arrest. Reported absent in arrest through April 1, 1864, but rejoined the company prior to September 1, 1864. No further records.

CLARKE, CHARLES D., Private
Was by occupation a clerk prior to enlisting in Wake County at age 23, May 21, 1861. Present or accounted for until promoted to Quartermaster Sergeant and transferred to the Field and Staff, 24th Regiment N.C. Troops (14th Regiment N.C. Volunteers), July 18, 1861.

CONRAD, JACOB, Private
Place and date of enlistment not reported. Captured at Deep Bottom, Virginia, August 16-20, 1864. Confined at Point Lookout, Maryland, until released on October 15, 1864, after joining the U.S. Army. Unit to which assigned not reported.

COOK, KASIMER, Private
Born in Germany and resided in Wake County where

he was by occupation a barber or farmer prior to enlisting in Wake County at age 36, May 21, 1861. Mustered in as Private and appointed Acting Hospital Steward prior to July 1, 1861. Present or accounted for until discharged on August 16, 1861. Reason discharged not reported.

COOPER, JOHN L., Private
Resided in Wake County and was by occupation an engineer prior to enlisting in Wake County at age 34, May 21, 1861. Present or accounted for until discharged on or about September 2, 1862. Reason discharged not reported.

CORBETT, JEREMIAH, Private
Resided in Randolph County and enlisted in Wake County at age 36, July 16, 1863, for the war. Present or accounted for until he died in hospital at Lynchburg, Virginia, October 27, 1863, of "cardiorhuma-metastasisex rheum extremitatum."

COX, JEREMIAH, Private
Resided in Johnston County and enlisted in Wake County at age 43, September 24, 1863, for the war. Present or accounted for until he died in hospital at Richmond, Virginia, July 14, 1864, of wounds. Place and date wounded not reported.

DARR, IRENEUS, Private
Resided in Montgomery County and enlisted at age 21, July 16, 1862, for the war. Present or accounted for until he died at Lovettsville, Virginia, or at Scottsville, Virginia, September 10, 1862, of disease.

DAVIS, ALLEN F., Private
Resided in Wake County where he enlisted at age 36, October 8, 1863, for the war. Present or accounted for until he died in hospital at Richmond, Virginia, September 2, 1864, of "diarrhoea chronica."

DAVIS, L. A., Private
Resided in Moore County where he enlisted at age 26, July 16, 1862, for the war. Present or accounted for until reported absent without leave on August 18, 1862. Reported absent without leave through April, 1863. No further records.

DENNIS, GEORGE, Private
Resided in Montgomery County and enlisted in Wake County on July 16, 1862, for the war. Present or accounted for until captured at Gettysburg, Pennsylvania, July 3-5, 1863. Confined at Fort Delaware, Delaware, until transferred to Point Lookout, Maryland, October 15-18, 1863. Confined at Point Lookout until paroled and transferred to Boulware's and Cox's Wharf, James River, Virginia, where he was received February 20-21, 1865, for exchange. Reported present with a detachment of paroled and exchanged prisoners at Camp Lee, near Richmond, Virginia, February 28, 1865.

DINKINS, BRYANT, Private
Resided in Wake County and was by occupation a carpenter prior to enlisting in Wake County at age 40, May 21, 1861. Present or accounted for until discharged on September 2, 1862. Reason discharged not reported.

DRIVER, JOHN, Private
Resided in Wake County or at Bowling Green, Virginia, and was by occupation a laborer prior to

enlisting in Wake County at age 21, May 21, 1861. Present or accounted for until wounded and captured at Sharpsburg, Maryland, September 17, 1862. Hospitalized at Baltimore, Maryland, and was received at Aiken's Landing, James River, Virginia, November 5, 1862, for exchange. Declared exchanged at Aiken's Landing on November 10, 1862. Rejoined the company prior to March 1, 1863, and present or accounted for until captured at or near Bethesda Church, Virginia, May 30, 1864. Confined at Point Lookout, Maryland, until transferred to Elmira, New York, July 7, 1864. Released at Elmira on May 17, 1865, after taking the Oath of Allegiance.

EASON, SOLOMON, Private
Resided in Johnston County and enlisted in Wake County at age 18, July 11, 1863, for the war. Present or accounted for until hospitalized at Richmond, Virginia, June 4, 1864, with a gunshot wound of the back; however, place and date wounded not reported. Died in hospital at Richmond on June 6, 1864, of wounds.

ELLEN, ELI, Private
Resided in Wake County and was by occupation a shoemaker prior to enlisting in Wake County at age 47, May 21, 1861. Present or accounted for until discharged on September 2, 1862. Reason discharged not reported.

EVERETT, THOMAS, Private
Resided in Bertie County and enlisted in Wake County at age 28, June 26, 1863, for the war. Present or accounted for until discharged on September 5, 1863, by reason of "both physical & mental debility."

FINNELL, RICHARD N., Private
Resided in Wake County and was by occupation an engineer prior to enlisting in Wake County at age 32, May 21, 1861. Present or accounted for through April 1, 1864; however, he was reported absent on detail during much of that period.

FORT, DAVID, Private
Resided in Wake County where he enlisted at age 43, September 3, 1863, for the war. Present or accounted for until hospitalized at Richmond, Virginia, June 4, 1864, with a gunshot wound; however, place and date wounded not reported. Died in Wake County on July 10, 1864, of wounds.

FOWLER, THOMAS H., Private
Resided in Wake County and was by occupation a silverplater prior to enlisting in Wake County at age 42, May 21, 1861. Present or accounted for until discharged on October 10, 1862, by reason of being over age.

FREEDLE, WILLIAM L., Private
Resided in Davidson County and enlisted in Wake County at age 32, July 16, 1862, for the war. Present or accounted for until wounded in the back and captured at or near Sharpsburg, Maryland, on or about September 17, 1862. Paroled September 23, 1862. Present or accounted for through April 1, 1864. Wounded prior to August 31, 1864, and was reported absent wounded through August 31, 1864. Paroled at Appomattox Court House, Virginia, April 9, 1865.

FREIBE, HENRY, Musician

Born in Prussia and resided in Wake County where he was by occupation a butcher prior to enlisting in Wake County at age 24, May 21, 1861. Mustered in as Private and promoted to Musician in September-October, 1861. Present or accounted for until discharged on October 8, 1862, by reason of disability.

GOOCH, WILLIAM L., Private

Born in Wake County where he resided as a butcher prior to enlisting in Wake County at age 21, May 21, 1861. Present or accounted for until discharged on August 9, 1862, by reason of "syphilis consecutiva." Reenlisted in this company on July 31, 1863, and present or accounted for until hospitalized at Richmond, Virginia, May 22, 1864, with a gunshot wound. Place and date wounded not reported. Returned to duty on September 5, 1864, and was captured at Burkeville, Virginia, April 6, 1865. Confined at Point Lookout, Maryland, until released on June 27, 1865, after taking the Oath of Allegiance.

GRUBBS, ANDERSON, Private

Resided in Wake County and was by occupation an engineer prior to enlisting in Wake County at age 47, June 18, 1863, for the war as a substitute. Present or accounted for through February 17, 1865.

HAHN, HENRY, Musician

Resided in Wake County and was by occupation a shoemaker prior to enlisting in Wake County at age 22, May 21, 1861. Mustered in as Private and promoted to Musician in November-December, 1861. Present or accounted for until discharged on October 27, 1862. Reason discharged not reported.

HALL, ALVIS, Private

Resided in Montgomery County and enlisted at age 34, July 16, 1862, for the war. Captured prior to September 20, 1862, when he died of disease in a Federal hospital at Frederick, Maryland. Place and date captured not reported.

HALL, JOHN, Private

Resided in Montgomery County and enlisted at age 33, July 16, 1862, for the war. Present or accounted for until he died at Frederick, Maryland, September 15, 1862, of disease.

HALL, WILLIAM J., Private

Born in Wake County where he resided as a clerk prior to enlisting in Wake County at age 18, May 21, 1861. Present or accounted for until discharged on August 12, 1861, by reason of disability. Later served in Company C, 47th Regiment N.C. Troops.

HAMILTON, ELI, Private

Resided in Montgomery County and enlisted in Wake County at age 23, July 16, 1862, for the war. Present or accounted for until wounded at Chancellorsville, Virginia, May 1-3, 1863. Rejoined the company prior to July 2-5, 1863, when he was wounded in the thigh and captured at Gettysburg, Pennsylvania. Confined at Point Lookout, Maryland, until paroled and transferred to Aiken's Landing, James River, Virginia, where he was received May 8, 1864, for exchange. Reported absent with leave through August, 1864, but rejoined the company

prior to September 22-23, 1864, when he was captured at Fisher's Hill, Virginia. Confined at Point Lookout until released on June 27, 1865, after taking the Oath of Allegiance.

HAMILTON, ELI W., Private

Resided in Montgomery County and enlisted in Wake County at age 28, July 16, 1862, for the war. Present or accounted for until captured at Boonsboro, Maryland, September 14, 1862. Confined at Fort Delaware, Delaware, until transferred to Aiken's Landing, James River, Virginia, October 2, 1862, for exchange. Declared exchanged at Aiken's Landing on November 10, 1862. Reported absent without leave from November 12, 1862, through February, 1863, but rejoined the company in March-April, 1863. Wounded at Chancellorsville, Virginia, May 1-3, 1863, and died in hospital at Richmond, Virginia, June 1, 1863, of wounds.

HARDIE, GEORGE D., Private

Was by occupation a railroad agent prior to enlisting in Wake County at age 31, May 21, 1861. Mustered in as Private and promoted to Corporal on June 5, 1861. Promoted to 1st Sergeant on April 26, 1862, but was reduced to ranks on December 28, 1862. Present or accounted for through January 3, 1865; however, he was reported absent on detail as a nurse during much of that period.

HARLING, JAMES, Private

Place and date of enlistment not reported. Captured prior to January 10, 1864, when he was hospitalized at Point Lookout, Maryland, with a gunshot wound of the left thigh; however, place and date wounded not reported. Exchanged on April 27, 1864. Died in hospital at Richmond, Virginia, May 4, 1864, of "bronchitis."

HARRIS, ISHAM B., Private

Resided in Wake County where he enlisted at age 18, June 25, 1863, for the war. Present or accounted for until captured at Spotsylvania Court House, Virginia, May 20, 1864. Confined at Point Lookout, Maryland, until paroled and transferred to Aiken's Landing, James River, Virginia, September 18, 1864, for exchange. Reported in hospital at Richmond, Virginia, September 22, 1864. No further records.

HARRISON, MALCOLM, Private

Born in Wake County where he resided as a saddlemaker prior to enlisting in Wake County at age 22, May 21, 1861. Present or accounted for until discharged on January 27, 1862, by reason of "great debility resulting from frequent attacks of intermittent fever."

HENRY, THADEUS, Private

Born in Wake County where he resided as a laborer prior to enlisting in Wake County at age 18, May 21, 1861. Present or accounted for until discharged on December 14, 1861, by reason of "debility resulting from chronic intermittent fever." Reenlisted in the company on November 20, 1862, and present or accounted for until wounded in the arm and captured at Gettysburg, Pennsylvania, July 3, 1863. Confined at Fort Delaware, Delaware, until transferred to Point Lookout, Maryland, October

15-18, 1863. Died at Point Lookout on March 3, 1865, of "diarrhoea."

HIGH, GEORGE W., Private
Resided in Wake County and was by occupation a tinner prior to enlisting in Wake County at age 22, May 21, 1861. Present or accounted for through September 28, 1864.

HOGAN, ZACK, Private
Resided in Montgomery County and enlisted in Wake County at age 47, July 16, 1862, for the war as a substitute. Present or accounted for until he deserted on October 14, 1862. Reported absent without leave until hospitalized at Richmond, Virginia, March 16, 1863. Died in hospital at Richmond on April 4, 1863, of "pneumonia."

HOLLISTER, JAMES D., 1st Sergeant
Resided in Wake County where he enlisted on May 21, 1861. Mustered in as 1st Sergeant. Discharged June 4, 1861, by reason of "being a machinist."

HONEYCUTT, WILLIS, Private
Resided in Wake County where he enlisted at age 24, July 16, 1862, for the war. Present or accounted for until wounded at Chancellorsville, Virginia, May 1-3, 1863. Reported absent sick through April, 1864. Roll of Honor indicates he was "disabled by wounds."

HOOD, GEORGE A., Musician
Resided in Wake County and was by occupation a printer prior to enlisting in Wake County at age 18, May 21, 1861. Mustered in as Private and promoted to Musician in March-December, 1862. Present or accounted for until he died in the District of Columbia on July 20, 1864, of wounds. Place and date wounded and captured not reported.

HOOD, WILLIAM H., Jr., Private
Resided in Wake County and was by occupation a farmer prior to enlisting in Wake County at age 18, May 21, 1861. Mustered in as Private and promoted to Corporal on December 28, 1862. Promoted to Sergeant in May, 1863. Present or accounted for until wounded in the hand and face and captured at or near Gettysburg, Pennsylvania, July 3-5, 1863. Confined at Fort Delaware, Delaware, until transferred to Point Lookout, Maryland, October 15-18, 1863. Paroled at Point Lookout and transferred to Cox's Landing, James River, Virginia, where he was received February 14-15, 1865, for exchange. Reduced to ranks in February-April, 1865. Deserted to the enemy on or about April 25, 1865.

HORNE, JAMES W., Private
Resided in Wake County and was by occupation a clerk prior to enlisting in Wake County at age 24, May 21, 1861. Present or accounted for until transferred to Company D, 12th Battalion Virginia Light Artillery, June 4, 1862. Later served in Company A, 13th Battalion N.C. Light Artillery.

HORTON, MONROE M., Private
Born in Wake County where he resided as a gardener prior to enlisting in Wake County at age 18, May 21, 1861. Present or accounted for until discharged on December 13, 1861, by reason of

"debility resulting from chronic intermittent fever."

HOWARD, WILLIAM H., Private
Resided in Wake County and was by occupation a farmer prior to enlisting in Wake County at age 32, May 21, 1861. Present or accounted for until wounded at Malvern Hill, Virginia, July 1, 1862. Died at Newton on August 24, 1862, of wounds.

INGRAM, JOEL, Sergeant
Resided in Wake or Johnston counties and was by occupation a wheelwright prior to enlisting in Wake County at age 22, May 21, 1861. Mustered in as Private and promoted to Sergeant on July 1, 1862. Present or accounted for until wounded and captured at Chancellorsville, Virginia, May 1-3, 1863. Paroled June 30, 1863. Rejoined the company in November-December, 1863, and present or accounted for until captured at Fisher's Hill, Virginia, September 22, 1864. Confined at Point Lookout, Maryland, until paroled and transferred to Aiken's Landing, James River, Virginia, March 17, 1865, for exchange. Paroled at Goldsboro on May 8, 1865. "Came in for parole."

JENKINS, THOMAS G., Private
Resided in Wake County and was by occupation a clerk prior to enlisting in Wake County at age 21, May 21, 1861. Present or accounted for until transferred to Company C, 46th Regiment N.C. Troops, on or about May 15, 1862.

JOHNSON, ADDISON, Private
Resided in Wake County and was by occupation a carpenter prior to enlisting in Wake County at age 27, May 21, 1861. Present or accounted for until discharged on or about August 23, 1861. Reason discharged not reported. Later served in Company I, 6th Regiment N.C. State Troops.

JOHNSON, ELBRIDGE A., Private
Resided in Wake County and was by occupation a carpenter prior to enlisting in Wake County at age 37, May 21, 1861. Present or accounted for until discharged on September 2, 1862. Reason discharged not reported.

JOHNSON, JOHN W., Private
Resided in Wake County and was by occupation a lawyer prior to enlisting in Wake County at age 35, May 21, 1861. Present or accounted for until discharged on September 2, 1862. Reenlisted in the company prior to April 7, 1865, when he was hospitalized at Farmville, Virginia, with a gunshot wound. Place and date wounded not reported. Paroled at Farmville on or about May 14, 1865.

JOLLY, JOHNSON J., Private
Resided in Wake County and was by occupation a laborer prior to enlisting in Wake County at age 17, May 21, 1861. Present or accounted for until he died at Richmond, Virginia, on or about May 30, 1862, of disease.

JOLLY, THOMAS J., Corporal
Resided in Wake County and was by occupation a laborer prior to enlisting in Wake County at age 22, May 21, 1861. Mustered in as Private. Present or accounted for until paroled at Leesburg, Virginia, October 2, 1862; however, place and date captured

not reported. Rejoined the company prior to January 1, 1863, and present or accounted for until reported absent wounded on company muster roll dated December 31, 1863-August 31, 1864. Place and date wounded not reported. Paroled at Raleigh on May 8, 1865.

JONES, ADDISON, Private
Resided in Wake County and was by occupation a blacksmith prior to enlisting in Wake County at age 25, May 21, 1861. Present or accounted for until he deserted to the enemy in June-July, 1863. Took the Oath of Allegiance prior to August 1, 1863.

KEITH, JOHN H., Private
Resided in Wake County and was by occupation a farmer prior to enlisting in Wake County at age 24, May 21, 1861. Present or accounted for until wounded at Chancellorsville, Virginia, May 1-3, 1863. Rejoined the company in September-October, 1863, and present or accounted for through August, 1864. North Carolina pension records indicate he was wounded at Winchester, Virginia, September 19, 1864.

KEITH, LEONIDAS N., 1st Sergeant
Resided in Wake County and was by occupation a printer prior to enlisting in Wake County at age 28, May 21, 1861. Mustered in as Private and promoted to Sergeant on April 26, 1862. Promoted to 1st Sergeant on December 28, 1862. Present or accounted for until wounded at Chancellorsville, Virginia, May 2, 1863. Nominated for the Badge of Distinction for gallantry at Chancellorsville. Reported absent wounded until retired to the Invalid Corps on November 18, 1864. Paroled at Raleigh on May 11, 1865.

KENNEDY, DAVID R., Private
Resided in Montgomery County and enlisted in Wake County at age 42, September 24, 1863, for the war. Reported absent sick until reported absent without leave on April 1, 1864. Reported absent without leave through August, 1864.

KREIGER, CHARLES, Private
Born in Wake County where he resided as a bookbinder prior to enlisting in Wake County at age 40, May 21, 1861. Mustered in as Private and promoted to Musician on November 1, 1861. Reduced to ranks on December 22, 1861. Present or accounted for until discharged on August 21, 1862, by reason of being over age.

KUESTER, FERDINAND, Private
Resided in Wake County and was by occupation a locksmith prior to enlisting in Wake County at age 26, May 21, 1861. Present or accounted for until discharged on June 9, 1861. Reason discharged not reported.

LASSITER, JOHN, Private
Resided in Wake County and was by occupation a merchant prior to enlisting in Wake County at age 36, May 21, 1861. Present or accounted for until killed at Williamsburg, Virginia, May 5, 1862.

LEATHERMAN, WILLIAM, Private
Resided in Davidson County and enlisted in Wake County at age 28, June 17, 1863, for the war. Present

or accounted for through August, 1864. Paroled at Greensboro on May 4, 1865.

LEGGETT, JAMES W., Private
Resided in Martin County and enlisted in Wake County at age 32, July 15, 1863, for the war. Present or accounted for through April 9, 1865; however, he was reported absent sick during most of that period.

LITTLE, WILLIAM, Private
Born in Wake County where he resided as a laborer prior to enlisting in Wake County at age 20, May 21, 1861. Present or accounted for until transferred to the C.S. Navy for duty on the C.S.S. *Merrimac* on February 15, 1862.

LIVINGOOD, W. L., Private
Resided in Davidson County and enlisted in Wake County at age 30, July 16, 1862, for the war. Present or accounted for until captured at Sharpsburg, Maryland, September 17, 1862. Confined at Fort Delaware, Delaware, until transferred to Aiken's Landing, James River, Virginia, October 2, 1862, for exchange. Declared exchanged at Aiken's Landing on November 10, 1862. Deserted on or about November 12, 1862.

MARKHAM, JOHN L., Private
Resided in Wake County and was by occupation a laborer prior to enlisting in Wake County at age 20, May 21, 1861. Present or accounted for until wounded in the right hand and captured at or near Gettysburg, Pennsylvania, July 3-5, 1863. Confined at Fort Delaware, Delaware, until transferred to Point Lookout, Maryland, October 15-18, 1863. Paroled at Point Lookout on February 18, 1865, and transferred to Boulware's and Cox's Wharf, James River, Virginia, for exchange. Reported present with a detachment of paroled and exchanged prisoners at Camp Lee, near Richmond, Virginia, February 28, 1865.

MARTIN, JOHN, Private
Resided in Anson County and enlisted in Wake County at age 43, August 21, 1863, for the war. Court-martialed in November-December, 1863, for absence without leave. Rejoined the company prior to April 1, 1864, and was killed at Spotsylvania Court House, Virginia, May 1-2, 1864.

MARTIN, LEMUEL, Private
Resided in Anson County and enlisted in Wake County at age 35, August 21, 1863, for the war. Present or accounted for until hospitalized at Richmond, Virginia, May 22, 1864, with a gunshot wound; however, place and date wounded not reported. Reported absent sick until he was retired on March 17, 1865, by reason of "haemoptysis."

MARTINDALE, HENRY H., Private
Resided in Wake County and was by occupation a clerk prior to enlisting in Wake County at age 18, May 21, 1861. Present or accounted for through June, 1864; however, he was absent on detail during much of that period. Captured in Loudoun County, Virginia, July 16, 1864, and confined at Old Capitol Prison, Washington, D.C., until transferred to Elmira, New York, July 23, 1864. Paroled at Elmira on February 25, 1865, and transferred to James River, Virginia, for exchange. No further records.

MELTON, ISAAC, Private
Resided in Wake County where he enlisted at age 31, July 16, 1862, for the war. Present or accounted for until he deserted on or about December 1, 1862.

MILLER, GEORGE DEVEREUX, Private
Previously served in Company D, 31st Regiment N.C. Troops. Transferred to this company on November 7, 1863. Present or accounted for until captured in hospital at Richmond, Virginia, April 3, 1865. Transferred to the Federal Provost Marshal on May 9, 1865, and was paroled prior to May 16, 1865.

MILLER, J. F., Private
Resided in Wake County. Place and date of enlistment not reported. Captured at Petersburg, Virginia, April 3, 1865, and confined at Hart's Island, New York Harbor, until released on June 18, 1865, after taking the Oath of Allegiance.

MOORE, JOSEPH E., Private
Resided in Caswell County and enlisted in Wake County at age 42, September 24, 1863, for the war. Present or accounted for until wounded in the left shoulder and captured at Cedar Creek, Virginia, October 19, 1864. Hospitalized at Winchester, Virginia, where he died on December 4, 1864.

MOORE, WILLIAM H., 1st Sergeant
Born in Orange County and resided in Wake County where he was by occupation a printer prior to enlisting in Wake County at age 29, May 21, 1861. Mustered in as 1st Sergeant. Present or accounted for until discharged on December 21, 1861. Reason discharged not reported.

MORGAN, N. W., Private
Resided in Montgomery County and enlisted at age 30, July 16, 1862, for the war. Present or accounted for until he died at Lynchburg, Virginia, December 8, 1862, of "congestion [of] lungs."

MOSS, AUSTIN, Musician
Resided in Wake County and was by occupation a carpenter prior to enlisting in Wake County at age 25, May 21, 1861. Mustered in as Private and was promoted to Musician on March 17, 1864. Present or accounted for until he deserted to the enemy on or about March 21, 1865.

MOSS, WILLIAM THOMAS, Private
Born in Wake County where he resided as a carpenter prior to enlisting in Wake County at age 26, May 21, 1861. Present or accounted for until discharged on January 27, 1862, by reason of "great debility with a decided tendency to phthisis pulmonalis."

NELSON, AZERIAH, Private
Resided in Caswell County and enlisted in Wake County at age 42, September 24, 1863, for the war. Present or accounted for until he died in Caswell County on February 15, 1864, of disease.

NOWELL, JOSIAH H., Private
Resided in Wake County and enlisted at Camp Holmes at age 27, July 23, 1863, for the war. Present or accounted for until wounded in the left leg at Spotsylvania Court House, Virginia, May 12, 1864. Reported absent wounded until he returned to duty on November 1, 1864. No further records.

NOWELL, RANSOM G., Private
Resided in Wake County and was by occupation a machinist prior to enlisting in Wake County at age 19, May 21, 1861. Present or accounted for until killed at Gettysburg, Pennsylvania, July 1, 1863.

NOWELL, WILLIAM L., Private
Resided in Wake County and was by occupation an engineer prior to enlisting in Wake County at age 21, May 21, 1861. Present or accounted for through August 9, 1864.

NYE, THOMAS, Private
Resided in Robeson County and enlisted in Wake County at age 41, June 25, 1863, for the war. Present or accounted for until discharged on August 20, 1863. Reason discharged not reported.

OVERBY, JAMES, Private
Born in Wake County where he resided as a clerk prior to enlisting in Wake County at age 21, May 21, 1861. Present or accounted for until killed at Chancellorsville, Virginia, May 3, 1863.

PARRISH, JAMES, Private
Resided in Chatham County and enlisted in Wake County at age 28, July 16, 1862, for the war. Present or accounted for until captured at Sharpsburg, Maryland, September 17, 1862. Confined at Fort Delaware, Delaware, until transferred to Aiken's Landing, James River, Virginia, October 2, 1862, for exchange. Declared exchanged at Aiken's Landing on November 10, 1862. Rejoined the company in January-February, 1863, and present or accounted for until killed at Chancellorsville, Virginia, May 3, 1863.

PENNINGTON, HENRY, Private
Resided in Wake County and was by occupation a carpenter prior to enlisting in Wake County at age 36, May 21, 1861. Present or accounted for until discharged on June 12, 1862. Reason discharged not reported.

PERKINSON, JOHN B., Private
Resided in Wake County and was by occupation a coach maker prior to enlisting in Wake County at age 25, May 21, 1861. Present or accounted for until wounded at Malvern Hill, Virginia, on or about July 1, 1862. Died at Raleigh on July 18, 1862, of wounds.

POLLARD, SIDNEY, Private
Born in Wake County where he resided as a farmer prior to enlisting in Wake County at age 30, July 20, 1863, for the war. Present or accounted for until discharged on November 12, 1863, by reason of "hypertrophy of the heart."

POWELL, JOSEPH, Private
Born in Wake County where he resided as a laborer prior to enlisting in Wake County at age 22, May 21, 1861, for one year. Present or accounted for until killed at Chancellorsville, Virginia, May 3, 1863.

PUTNEY, WILLIAM H., Jr., Private
Resided in Wake County and was by occupation a clerk prior to enlisting in Wake County at age 22, May 21, 1861. Present or accounted for through February 7, 1865; however, he was reported absent sick during most of that period.

PUTTICK, JAMES A., Musician
Born in Wake County where he resided as a printer prior to enlisting in Wake County at age 18, May 21, 1861. Mustered in as Private and promoted to Musician in July-August, 1861. Present or accounted for until transferred to the C.S. Navy for duty on the C.S.S. *Merrimac* on February 15, 1862.

RAMSAY, WALTER JONES, Private
Resided in Wake County and enlisted at Rapidan, Virginia, at age 21, August 11, 1862, for the war. Present or accounted for until reported "absent" at Gettysburg, Pennsylvania, July 1-3, 1863. Never rejoined the company.

RENN, JAMES RANSOM, Private
Resided in Wake County and was by occupation a carpenter prior to enlisting in Wake County at age 39, May 21, 1861. Present or accounted for until discharged on or about September 2, 1862. Reason discharged not reported.

ROBERTS, EDWARD M., Private
Resided in Wake County and was by occupation a painter prior to enlisting in Wake County at age 29, May 21, 1861. Mustered in as Sergeant but was reduced to the rank of Musician on November 14, 1861. Reduced to ranks on June 1, 1864. Present or accounted for until wounded in the pelvis and captured at Winchester, Virginia, September 19, 1864. Hospitalized at Winchester where he died November 17, 1864.

ROBERTSON, CHARLES W., Sergeant
Resided in Wake County and was by occupation a farmer prior to enlisting in Wake County at age 18, May 21, 1861. Mustered in as Private and promoted to Sergeant in March-December, 1862. Present or accounted for until he died at Richmond, Virginia, on or about May 15, 1862, of disease.

ROBERTSON, ROBERT, Private
Resided in Granville County and enlisted in Wake County at age 20, June 22, 1863, for the war. Present or accounted for until captured at or near Bethesda Church, Virginia, May 30, 1864. Confined at Point Lookout, Maryland, until transferred to Elmira, New York, July 9, 1864. Paroled at Elmira on February 9, 1865, and transferred to Boulware's and Cox's Wharf, James River, Virginia, where he was received February 20-21, 1865, for exchange. Reported in hospital at Richmond, Virginia, February 25, 1865.

ROGERS, ALVIS, Private
Resided in Wake County and was by occupation a laborer prior to enlisting in Wake County at age 21, May 21, 1861. Present or accounted for until discharged on or about January 23, 1863. Reason discharged not reported.

ROGERS, JACOB M., Private
Born in Wake County where he resided as a clerk prior to enlisting in Wake County at age 18, May 21, 1861. Present or accounted for until he died in hospital at Richmond, Virginia, July 14-15, 1862, of disease.

ROYSTER, DAVID W., Private
Resided in Wake County and was by occupation a tailor prior to enlisting in Wake County at age 28,

May 21, 1861. Present or accounted for until wounded in the right arm at Chancellorsville, Virginia, May 2, 1863. Rejoined the company in September-October, 1863, and present or accounted for until paroled at Appomattox Court House, Virginia, April 9, 1865. North Carolina pension records indicate he was wounded in the left hip at Sharpsburg, Maryland.

RUSSELL, A. L., Private
Enlisted in Wake County on July 16, 1862, for the war. Present or accounted for until he died at Old Capitol Prison, Washington, D.C., October 12, 1862, of "pneumonia." Place and date captured not reported.

RUTH, RUFUS H., Private
Resided in Wake County and was by occupation a tailor prior to enlisting in Wake County at age 23, May 21, 1861. Mustered in as Private. Reported on duty as a Musician with the regimental band from September, 1861, through February, 1862. Reduced to ranks and rejoined the company at an unspecified date. Present or accounted for until hospitalized at Richmond, Virginia, May 20, 1863, with a wound of the left breast; however, place and date wounded not reported. Rejoined the company prior to July 1-5, 1863, when he was wounded in the arm and captured at Gettysburg, Pennsylvania. Arm amputated. Hospitalized at Davids Island, New York Harbor, until paroled and transferred to City Point, Virginia, where he was received August 28, 1863, for exchange. Reported absent wounded through August, 1864. Paroled at Raleigh on May 13, 1865.

SANDERS, J. Z., Private
Resided in Montgomery County and enlisted in Wake County at age 24, July 16, 1862, for the war. Present or accounted for until wounded at Chancellorsville, Virginia, May 1-3, 1863. Died in hospital at Richmond, Virginia, May 15, 1863, of wounds.

SANDERS, JACOB, Private
Resided in Montgomery County and enlisted in Wake County at age 30, July 16, 1862, for the war. Present or accounted for until wounded in the left breast and captured at Gettysburg, Pennsylvania, July 2-4, 1863. Confined at Fort Delaware, Delaware, until transferred to Point Lookout, Maryland, October 15-18, 1863. Paroled at Point Lookout and transferred to City Point, Virginia, where he was received March 20, 1864, for exchange. Rejoined the company prior to September 1, 1864, and was captured at or near Fisher's Hill, Virginia, September 22, 1864. Confined at Point Lookout until paroled and transferred to Aiken's Landing, James River, Virginia, where he was received March 19, 1865, for exchange.

SAULS, WILEY, Corporal
Resided in Wake County and was by occupation a coach trimmer prior to enlisting in Wake County at age 37, May 21, 1861. Mustered in as Private and promoted to Corporal on November 15, 1861. Present or accounted for until captured at Malvern Hill, Virginia, July 1, 1862. Confined at Fort Delaware, Delaware, until exchanged at Aiken's Landing, James River, Virginia, August 5, 1862.

Discharged September 2, 1862. Reason discharged not reported.

SCARBOROUGH, JOHN C., Private
Resided in Wake County and was by occupation a farmer prior to enlisting in Wake County at age 19, May 21, 1861. Present or accounted for until captured at Sharpsburg, Maryland, September 17, 1862. Received at Aiken's Landing, James River, Virginia, October 6, 1862, for exchange. Declared exchanged at Aiken's Landing on November 10, 1862. Present or accounted for until promoted to Corporal and transferred to Company I, 1st Regiment N.C. State Troops, December 31, 1862.

SKINNER, WILLIAM L., Private
Previously served in Company F, 12th Regiment N.C. Troops (2nd Regiment N.C. Volunteers). Transferred to this company on June 28, 1861. Present or accounted for until detailed as Commissary Sergeant on June 25, 1861, and transferred to the Field and Staff of this regiment.

SMITH, ISAAC D., Private
Resided in Wake County and was by occupation a constable prior to enlisting in Wake County at age 42, May 21, 1861. Present or accounted for until discharged on or about September 2, 1862. Reason discharged not reported.

SMITH, MARION, Sergeant
Resided in Wake County and was by occupation a machinist prior to enlisting in Wake County at age 21, May 21, 1861. Mustered in as Private and promoted to Sergeant in March-June, 1862. Present or accounted for until killed at Malvern Hill, Virginia, July 1, 1862.

SMITH, SAMUEL W., Private
Born in Wake County where he resided as a farmer prior to enlisting in Wake County at age 23, July 12, 1861. Present or accounted for until transferred to the C.S. Navy for duty on the C.S.S. *Merrimac* on February 15, 1862.

SMITH, SIMEON A., Private
Resided in Wake County and was by occupation a farmer prior to enlisting in Wake County at age 21, May 21, 1861. Mustered in as Private and promoted to Corporal on January 1, 1862. Reduced to ranks on January 1, 1863. Present or accounted for until paroled at Appomattox Court House, Virginia, April 9, 1865.

SOLOMON, JOHN W., Private
Resided in Wake County and was by occupation a stage driver prior to enlisting in Wake County at age 22, May 21, 1861. Mustered in as Private and promoted to Corporal on April 26, 1862. Reported absent without leave from November 15, 1862, through February, 1863, and was reduced to ranks on December 28, 1863. Rejoined the company in May-June, 1863, and was wounded in the side at Gettysburg, Pennsylvania, July 2-3, 1863. Rejoined the company in November-December, 1863, and present or accounted for through August, 1864.

STALLINGS, H. B., Private
Resided in Nash County and enlisted in Wake County at age 30, June 19, 1863, for the war. Present or accounted for until he died in hospital at

Charlottesville, Virginia, December 17, 1863, of "pneumonia."

STERNE, PETER J., Private
Resided in Wake County and was by occupation a trader or laborer prior to enlisting in Wake County at age 29, May 21, 1861. Present or accounted for until discharged on or about May 1, 1862, after providing a substitute.

STRONACH, GEORGE W., Ordnance Sergeant
Resided in Wake County and was by occupation a jeweler prior to enlisting in Wake County at age 19, May 21, 1861. Mustered in as Private and promoted to Ordnance Sergeant on May 1, 1864. Present or accounted for until paroled at Appomattox Court House, Virginia, April 9, 1865.

SUGGS, PETER, Musician
Resided in Wake County and was by occupation a laborer prior to enlisting in Wake County at age 18, May 21, 1861. Mustered in as Private and promoted to Musician on December 22, 1861. Present or accounted for until discharged on or about September 2, 1862. Reason discharged not reported.

SYKES, JOHN W., Private
Resided in Montgomery County and enlisted at age 27, July 16, 1862, for the war. Present or accounted for until killed at Sharpsburg, Maryland, September 17, 1862.

SYME, JOHN CAMERON, Private
Born at Petersburg, Virginia, and resided in Wake County where he was by occupation a student or "drill master" prior to enlisting at Camp Bragg, Virginia, at age 18, May 21, 1861. Present or accounted for until discharged on or about October 18, 1861. Reason discharged not reported. Later served in Company C, 47th Regiment N.C. Troops.

TAYLOR, WILLIAM H., Private
Resided in Stanly County and enlisted in Wake County at age 35, September 3, 1863, for the war. Present or accounted for until he deserted on October 22, 1863.

THOMPSON, JOHN D., Sergeant
Resided in Wake County and was by occupation a blacksmith prior to enlisting in Wake County at age 28, May 21, 1861. Mustered in as Private and promoted to Sergeant on June 1, 1862. Present or accounted for until wounded and captured at Cedar Creek, Virginia, October 19, 1864. Confined at Point Lookout, Maryland, until paroled and transferred to Cox's Landing, James River, Virginia, where he was received February 14-15, 1865, for exchange. Paroled at Raleigh on May 6, 1865.

TILLEY, SOLOMON D., Private
Born in Wake County where he resided as a clerk prior to enlisting in Wake County at age 21, May 21, 1861. Present or accounted for until discharged on September 21, 1861, by reason of disability.

TOWLES, JAMES, Private
Place and date of enlistment not reported. Paroled at Appomattox Court House, Virginia, April 9, 1865.

WAGSTAFF, EMANUEL M., Private
Born in Granville County and resided in Wake

County where he was by occupation a carpenter prior to enlisting in Wake County at age 26, May 21, 1861. Present or accounted for until wounded at Malvern Hill, Virginia, July 1, 1862. Died in hospital at Richmond, Virginia, July 12, 1862, of wounds and/or "feb[ris] typhoides."

WAITT, HORATIO A., Private
Born in Wake County where he resided as a farmer prior to enlisting in Wake County at age 20, May 21, 1861. Present or accounted for until killed at Sharpsburg, Maryland, September 17, 1862.

WARD, WILSON, Private
Born in Wake County where he resided as a farmer prior to enlisting at Camp Bragg, Virginia, at age 18, June 17, 1861. Present or accounted for until discharged on July 20, 1861, by reason of "extreme youth and inability to perform the duties of a soldier."

WATKINS, JAMES H., Private
Previously served in Company I, 1st Regiment N.C. State Troops. Transferred to this company on December 31, 1862. Present or accounted for until hospitalized at Wake Forest on April 10, 1865, with a gunshot wound of the right leg; however, place and date wounded not reported. No further records.

WEATHERS, REUBEN D., Sergeant
Resided in Wake County where he enlisted at age 19, July 2, 1861. Mustered in as Private. Present or accounted for until captured at Sharpsburg, Maryland, September 17, 1862. Confined at Fort Delaware, Delaware, until transferred to Aiken's Landing, James River, Virginia, October 2, 1862, for exchange. Declared exchanged at Aiken's Landing on November 10, 1862. Rejoined the company in January-February, 1863, when he was promoted to Corporal. Promoted to Sergeant in September, 1864-April, 1865. Present or accounted for until captured at Amelia Court House, Virginia, April 6, 1865. Confined at Point Lookout, Maryland, until released on June 21, 1865, after taking the Oath of Allegiance.

WEST, AUGUSTUS F., Private
Previously served in Company B of this regiment. Transferred to this company on September 8, 1863. Reported "in arrest" from November-December, 1863, through April 1, 1864. Rejoined the company prior to September 1, 1864, and was captured at Cedar Creek, Virginia, October 19, 1864. Confined at Point Lookout, Maryland, where he died on February 4, 1865, of "cerebritis."

WHITE, SAMUEL C., Private
Resided in Wake County and was by occupation a clerk prior to enlisting in Wake County at age 20, May 21, 1861. Mustered in as Private and promoted to Corporal on April 26, 1862. Reduced to ranks on December 28, 1862. Present or accounted for until wounded at Chancellorsville, Virginia, May 1-3, 1863. Rejoined the company in September-October, 1863, and present or accounted for until paroled at Appomattox Court House, Virginia, April 9, 1865.

WILKERSON, H. L., Private
Resided in Person County and enlisted in Wake County at age 26, July 16, 1862, for the war. Present

or accounted for until captured at Gettysburg, Pennsylvania, July 3, 1863. Died at Fort Delaware, Delaware, September 9, 1863, of disease.

WILSON, J. L., Private
Resided in Caswell County and enlisted in Wake County at age 26, July 16, 1862, for the war. Present or accounted for until wounded at Sharpsburg, Maryland, September 17, 1862. Never rejoined the company. Roll of Honor indicates he was killed at Sharpsburg; however, records of the Federal Provost Marshal indicate he was paroled at Greensboro on May 16, 1865. No further records.

WYNNE, WILLIAM W., Private
Born in Wake County where he resided as a farmer prior to enlisting in Wake County at age 21, May 21, 1861. Present or accounted for until discharged on September 19, 1861, by reason of disability.

WYNNE, WILLIAM W., Private
Resided in Wake County and was by occupation a carpenter prior to enlisting in Wake County at age 21, May 21, 1861. Mustered in as Corporal and promoted to Sergeant in January, 1862. Reduced to ranks on April 26, 1862. Present or accounted for through August, 1864; however, he was reported absent on detail during much of that period.

YATES, THOMAS S. P., Private
Resided in Wake County where he enlisted at age 29, September 26, 1863, for the war. Present or accounted for until he deserted on January 15, 1864.

ZIEGLER, WILLIAM, Musician
Resided in Wake County and was by occupation a butcher prior to enlisting in Wake County at age 24, May 21, 1861. Mustered in as Corporal and promoted to Sergeant on June 5, 1861. Reduced to the rank of Musician on December 21, 1861. Present or accounted for until he deserted on May 15, 1862.

MISCELLANEOUS

The following list of names was compiled from primary records which indicate that these men served in the 14th Regiment N.C. Troops but do not specify the company to which they belonged.

COX, H. S., Private
Place and date of enlistment not reported. Deserted to the enemy on or about April 12, 1865.

LEWIS, ALFRED, Private
Place and date of enlistment not reported. Deserted to the enemy on or about April 12, 1865.

LOWERY, ATLAS DARGAN, _____
Place and date of enlistment not reported. Wounded near Appomattox, Virginia. Date wounded not reported.

MARKS, JOS., Private
Place and date of enlistment not reported. Died at Point Lookout, Maryland, April 5, 1865. Cause of death not reported.

THREADGILL, JOHN, Private
Resided in Anson County. Place and date of enlistment not reported. Captured at Petersburg, Virginia, April 3, 1865, and confined at Hart's Island, New York

Harbor, until released on June 17, 1865, after taking
the Oath of Allegiance.

15th REGIMENT N. C. TROOPS

(5th Regiment N. C. Volunteers)

This regiment was organized at Garysburg and was mustered into Confederate States service for twelve months' service as the 5th Regiment N.C. Volunteers on June 11, 1861. When the regiment was mustered in it consisted of twelve companies, A through M — two over the required number. The regiment remained at Garysburg until ordered to Yorktown, Virginia, on June 29, 1861. Moving by way of Richmond, Virginia, the regiment arrived at Yorktown on July 1 and camped southwest of the old British works on the edge of town.

At Yorktown the regiment continued its training while some of the companies were sent to reconnoiter the lower Peninsula. The clerk of Company H reported the company's movements on the June 17-30, 1861, muster roll:

Co. H marched from Yorktown Va. to Warwick C[ourt] House, August 2nd 1861. From Warwick C H to Bethell [sic] Church, Aug. 5th '61. From Bethell C to Hampton, Augt 6th 1861. From Hampton to Bethell C. Augt 8th 1861. From Bethel C. to Warwick C. H., Agt. 12th /61. From Warwick C. House to Yorktown, Agt 13th '61. All in Virginia.

While at Yorktown the men of the regiment suffered severely from camp fever and other diseases. On August 9, 1861, there were less than 400 men present for duty out of the more than 1,000 men on the rolls. As a result of the high rate of sickness the regiment was moved north of the York River to Hobdy's Point, Gloucester County. Some of the companies were dispersed to King and Queen Court House and some to Gloucester Court House. The clerk for Company G reported on the July-August, 1861, muster roll:

This company has been prostrated by sickness. The arms and accoutrement and clothing have suffered thereby.

On September 7 the regiment was reported at a healthy location six miles from Gloucester Point with only 230 men present for duty out of 1,150. The regiment remained in Gloucester County until the first of October when it returned to Yorktown; there it was brigaded with the 1st Regiment N.C. Infantry (6 months) on October 3, 1861. These two regiments formed the 6th Brigade, which was commanded by the colonel of this regiment. Ten companies of the regiment were assigned to the position at Harrod's Mill, and two companies were stationed at Ship Point. Regimental headquarters were established at Camp Dudley, near Yorktown. On November 14, 1861, the regimental designation was changed from 5th Regiment N.C. Volunteers to 15th Regiment N.C. Troops (5th Regiment N.C. Volunteers) by Special Orders No. 222, Adjutant and Inspector General's Office, Richmond. The regiment went into winter quarters at Camp Dudley where it remained until March, 1862. The troops on the Peninsula were placed under the command of General John B. Magruder, and on January 31, 1862, the regiment was reported in the 1st Division, General G. J. Rains commanding.

In North Carolina a Federal force under General A. E. Burnside captured Roanoke Island on February 8, 1862. After this victory, General Burnside moved his troops toward New Bern. To support the numerically weaker Confederate forces in the New Bern area, troops were moved from Virginia. On March 6, 1862, some 5,000 troops were ordered from Yorktown to Suffolk to replace troops sent to North Carolina and to strengthen the positions in the Suffolk area. This regiment was ordered to Suffolk and moved to that place by way of City Point and Petersburg. The troops sent to Suffolk were placed under command of General Howell Cobb and became known as Cobb's brigade. In addition to this regiment, the brigade consisted of the 2nd Regiment Louisiana Infantry, 11th Regiment Georgia Infantry, 16th Regiment Georgia Infantry, and Cobb's Georgia Legion.

Burnside's troops succeeded in taking New Bern on March 14, and the Confederates, under General L. O'B. Branch, fell back to Goldsboro. Late in March, 1862, Cobb's brigade was ordered to reinforce General Branch at Goldsboro. The brigade remained at Goldsboro until ordered back to Yorktown, where it arrived April 15, 1862, and was assigned to the 2nd Division, General Lafayette McLaws commanding.

On the Peninsula the Confederates were preparing for the advance of General George B. McClellan's army from Fort Monroe. The Federals advanced to test the Confederate defenses and struck the line on April 16 at Lee's Mill or Dam No. 1, on Warwick Creek, where Cobb's brigade had gone into position. During the battle which ensued, a Federal force succeeded in crossing a pond on the regiment's flank, and a heavy fight developed before the Federals were forced back. Colonel Robert M. McKinney was killed while gallantly leading the regiment. Lieutenant Colonel Ross R. Ihrie reported the regiment's activities as follows (O.R., S.I., Vol. XI, pt. 1, pp. 421-422):

On the morning of the 16th cannonading along the line toward Wynn's Mill, and also some of the enemy's guns being brought to bear upon our batteries at Dam No. 1, and as the day progressed other indications of an attack by the enemy upon our line induced Colonel McKinney to call the regiment into line on the Military road running in front of where the regiment was lying.

About 10 a.m., calling in a working party of 100 men, and keeping the regiment in this state of readiness for two hours or more, he ordered the arms stacked, and had the whole regiment detailed for work upon a heavy intrenchment which he had been ordered to have erected in front of the encampment, and about 200 yards in the rear of the rifle pits skirting the water thrown back by Dam No. 2, making arrangements for carrying on the work the whole of the ensuing night. Our pickets were in front of the rifle pits, close along the water's edge. From the best information I have at the point the enemy charged the depth of the water was about 4 feet and its width from 150 to 200 yards, and covered with heavy timber and thick undergrowth.

About 3 P.M., the regiment being engaged upon the works alluded to, the pickets gave the alarm that the enemy were charging rapidly across the water and making to [sic] our rifle pits. The regiment was immediately thrown in line of battle, and, being ordered by Colonel McKinney, advanced at a double-quick and with a yell upon the enemy, who had taken partial shelter behind the earth thrown from our pits before the regiment could reach them, and opened a terrible fire upon us as we advanced. Their fire was returned with promptness and with deadly effect upon the enemy. Volley after volley in rapid succession immediately followed from both sides, amid which Colonel McKinney gallantly fell in the early part of the engagement, shot through the forehead. He fell near the center of the line, and his death was not known to either officers or men for some time after it occurred, and a deadly fire was kept up by both sides until about 5 .P.M.

Not knowing the strength of the enemy at the commencement of the engagement, Colonel McKinney dispatched an orderly to Brigadier-General Cobb for re-enforcements, and after having been engaged about two hours in close conflict, the enemy having given away on our right, the Seventh Georgia Regiment, under Colonel Wilson, came to our assistance, and at this moment the enemy gave way in precipitate retreat and did not again rally at any point on our line. The regiment had about 500 men engaged.

The Federals did not renew the attack and retired from the field.

During the month of April, 1862, the troops under General Joseph E. Johnston at Manassas moved down to the Yorktown-Warwick line and General Johnston was placed in command. General Magruder remained in command of his troops as the divisions of Johnston's army arrived on the line. On May 2, 1862, this regiment reorganized for the war. At this time Cobb's brigade was reported in Magruder's division of Magruder's corps.

Fearing the mounting pressure against his defensive line, General Johnston began to withdraw from the Yorktown-Warwick line on the night of May 3-4, 1862. Magruder's command retired through Williamsburg, and, although two brigades of his corps were ordered back to assist in the defense of the rearguard on May 5, Cobb's brigade continued on toward Richmond. The brigade moved through New Kent Court House, crossed the Chickahominy River, and encamped on the turnpike to Mechanicsville. After the battle at Williamsburg on May 5, the entire Confederate army retired up the Peninsula toward Richmond.

General McClellan's army advanced up the Peninsula and confronted the Confederates in their defensive positions just east of Richmond. Under pressure from President Jefferson Davis to assume the offensive, General Johnston concentrated his troops for an attack on the Federal position at Seven Pines. Magruder's division was moved to the Nine Mile Road on the left of the attacking column on the Williamsburg road but was not engaged during the battle of May 31-June 1, 1862.

During the battle of May 31 General Johnston had been wounded, and General Gustavus W. Smith, commanding on June 1, fell sick. General Robert E. Lee was then put in command of the Army of Northern Virginia. On June 24 Lee issued orders for an attack on McClellan's right. Leaving Magruder's command on the Williamsburg road and General Huger's command on the Charles City road, Lee shifted the bulk of the army north of Richmond, across the Chickahominy. General T.J. Jackson's command moved east from the Shenandoah Valley to cooperate with the troops north of the city, and on the afternoon of June 26 the Confederates attacked the Federals at Mechanicsville. After a bitter defense, the Federals retired to Gaines' Mill. There they again stubbornly resisted the full weight of Lee's combined forces until late in the evening of June 27, when they retired to cross the Chickahominy to join the main body of McClellan's army.

South of the Chickahominy Generals Magruder and Huger were under orders to hold their positions and observe the enemy — if McClellan began to retire, Magruder and Huger were to follow him. The defeat of his right wing forced McClellan to retire from in front of Magruder and Huger, and he did so without being detected on June 28. Early on the morning of June 29, Lee ordered two divisons (Longstreet's and A.P. Hill's) from north of the Chickahominy to recross the river and move down the Darbytown road and cooperate with Magruder and Huger. His third division (D.H. Hill's) remained with Jackson, who was under orders to move down the north side of the river and cross in an attempt to cut off the enemy's retreat or to hit him in flank.

After reconnoitering the Federal lines south of the river during the morning of June 29 it was found that McClellan was retiring. Magruder and Huger were ordered to move down the Williamsburg road and Charles City road respectively. Magruder, reaching the vicinity of Savage Station about noon, came upon the rear guard of the retreating enemy. When word reached him that the enemy was advancing, Magruder halted and sent for reinforcements. Two brigades from Huger's command were sent to Magruder, but these were withdrawn when it became apparent the enemy was not advancing. Late in the afternoon Magruder attacked with one of his three divisions and two regiments of another. After two hours of fighting the Federal rear guard retired under cover of darkness. During the battle, Cobb's brigade was on the left of the railroad and did not participate actively in the fighting, which occurred on the right of the railroad.

General Jackson's command crossed the Chickahominy and reached Savage Station early on June 30. Lee then ordered Longstreet and A.P. Hill to follow the enemy down the Darbytown road and directed Magruder to move over to the Darbytown road to support Longstreet. Jackson was ordered to move on Longstreet's left, and Huger was instructed to continue down the Charles City road on Longstreet's right. To the right of General Huger a small force under General T.H. Holmes was moving down the River Road. Longstreet and A.P. Hill encountered the enemy at Frayser's Farm. Huger's route of advance would bring him in on the enemy's right; Jackson's would bring him in on the enemy's rear. On the River Road General Holmes met with resistance, and Magruder was ordered to move his command to reinforce Holmes. Unfortunately, Magruder did not reach Holmes in time for an attack. The battle of Frayser's Farm began when Longstreet launched an assault after hearing firing on Huger's front. Huger was trying to drive back a Federal force in his front so that he could get into position to cooperate with Longstreet and A.P. Hill. The troops of these two divisions fought the battle alone as Jackson was prevented from crossing White Oak Swamp, and Huger never came up.

After the engagement Magruder was recalled to relieve the troops of Longstreet and Hill. His men, much fatigued by their long, hot march, arrived during the night. Early on the morning of July 1 General Jackson reached the battlefield of Frayser's Farm and was directed to continue the pursuit of the enemy with his command. He found the enemy strongly entrenched at Malvern Hill. Jackson formed his command in line, and two of Huger's brigades took position on his right. Magruder's command was ordered forward and formed on the right of these brigades. Late in the afternoon a general assault was ordered. General Cobb reported the activities of his brigade as follows (O.R., S.I., Vol. XI, pt. 2, pp. 748-749):

[We] reached the battle-field of the 1st. Here a portion of my command, the Georgia Legion, was placed in support of the artillery. The remaining regiments were posted to the right of Mrs. Carter's house, in a ravine. Another regiment of my command, the Sixteenth Georgia, was detached and sent forward to occupy a ravine on the right to prevent any attempt of the enemy to advance in that direction. My command was thus posted at three different points, rendering my own position, in endeavoring to look after each, an embarrassing one.

While at this point I received a message from General [Lewis A.] Armistead [of Huger's division], who occupied with his brigade the advance position in our front, that he needed support, and I immediately moved to his support with the remaining regiments of the brigade — the Twenty-fourth Georgia, Second Louisiana, and Fifteenth North Carolina. To reach that point we had to pass through the open field in our front under the fire of the enemy, which was done in double-quick and good order, and had to pass through dense woods and almost impassable ravines, which separated us from General Armistead's position, all of which was done in quick-time and with alacrity by the three regiments. On reaching this point I immediately posted my command on the crest of the hill in front of batteries of the enemy, which continued to pour a deadly fire upon that point, as well as the entire distance which we had traversed from the ravine near Mrs. Carter's house. Our duty was to prevent any advance of the enemy and to unite at the proper time in the effort to carry the batteries of the enemy. We had not occupied this position long when General Magruder was informed that the enemy was advancing in our front, and under his order I at once advanced these three regiments to the open field in front of the batteries of the enemy. The advance of the enemy was repulsed and the regiments united in the general assault on the batteries.

The conduct of both officers and men throughout was all that could be asked and even more than could be expected of men. The best evidence I can offer of the daring and courage of the men of my command is the fact that after the battle their dead were found mingled with those of other brigades nearest the batteries of the enemy.

It was at this point in the battle that Colonel Norwood, of the Second Louisiana, while gallantly leading his regiment, fell severely, but, I am happy to say, not mortally, wounded. Major Ashton, of the same regiment, had seized the colors of the regiment after three brave men had been shot down in the act of bearing them forward, and was bravely cheering on his men and rallying them to their standard, when, pierced by several balls, he fell and died instantly. In the same action the brave and gallant commander of the Fifteenth North Carolina, Colonel Dowd, was severely, but not mortally, wounded, and his regiment, for the present, deprived of his invaluable services.

The attack was repulsed, and during the night the Federals retired to Harrison's Landing. The battle of Malvern Hill was the last of the Seven Days' battles around Richmond, June 25-July 1, 1862. The regiment saw action only at Malvern Hill, but its loss in that one engagement was very heavy. Of 692 men reported as present for duty, the regiment lost 30 killed and 110 wounded.

The brigade marched back to the Williamsburg road near Richmond and went into camp. While there Companies L and M were transferred to the 32nd Regiment N.C. Troops in accordance with orders dated July 4, 1862. This reduced the regiment to ten companies, and the addition of some 250 recruits replaced the men lost in battle and by normal attrition. After the army returned to Richmond, General Magruder was transferred to the Trans-Mississippi area, and the brigades in his command were assigned to other divisions. Cobb's brigade was assigned to General McLaws's division, which was assigned to General Longstreet's command.

On July 13 Lee ordered General Jackson with his own and Ewell's division to Gordonsville to confront the Federal force under General John Pope. General A.P. Hill's division was sent to reinforce Jackson on July 27. McClellan's force reoccupied Malvern Hill on August 5, and Lee ordered Longstreet's, McLaws's, Ripley's, and Jones's divisions to move down to confront the enemy. After a brief skirmish the Federals were driven back, and during the night of August 6-7 they retired to their old position at Harrison's Landing. Lee then recalled his troops from Malvern Hill.

On August 9 Jackson defeated Pope at Cedar Mountain, and McClellan was ordered to reinforce Pope. Upon receiving information that McClellan was embarking, Lee ordered Longstreet to reinforce Jackson on August 13. Leaving McLaws's and D.H. Hill's divisions to observe McClellan, Lee transferred his headquarters to Gordonsville and concentrated to attack Pope before McClellan could reinforce him.

To protect Richmond from any movement from Fredericksburg, McLaws's division and two brigades from D.H. Hill's division were moved up to the South Anna River. Lee ordered Jackson to move around Pope's right flank and strike him in rear. This Jackson did and retired to a position north of Manassas. Lee then moved Longstreet to reinforce Jackson and ordered McLaws's and D.H. Hill's troops to move to Gordonsville. While Jackson held the Federals in check on August 28, Longstreet came up on his right flank on August 29, and the combined forces routed the Federals from the field. McLaws's division moved up from Gordonsville and joined the army on September 2.

Lee then moved his army across the Potomac River into Maryland and camped at Frederick on September 7. Not wishing to leave the Federal garrison at Harpers Ferry in his rear, Lee decided to send Jackson to capture that position while Longstreet moved to Hagerstown. On September 10 Lee issued the orders to carry out this move. Jackson was directed to move to Martinsburg and then down the south side of the Potomac to Harpers Ferry. General McLaws, with his own and R.H. Anderson's division, was ordered to seize Maryland Heights on the north side of the Potomac opposite Harpers Ferry. General John G. Walker was ordered to take possession of Loudoun Heights on the east side of the Shenandoah River where it unites with the Potomac. Thus Harpers Ferry would be surrounded and forced to surrender.

Unfortunately, a copy of Lee's order describing the movements of his army was found by the enemy, and McClellan pushed his troops forward. Longstreet's command was forced to return to the South Mountain gaps to protect the troops moving on Harpers Ferry. Behind McLaws's position on Maryland Heights the

Federals broke through at Crampton's Pass on September 14 and moved to strike the position on Maryland Heights in rear. Cobb's brigade was ordered to assist in the defense of Crampton's Pass and was routed from the field. General Cobb reported the action to General McLaws as follows (O.R., S.I., Vol. XIX, pt. 1, p. 870):

On the 14th my command was ordered by you to return to our former camp, at Brownsville. This order was received about 1 o'clock **P.M.,** and the brigade was immediately marched to that point, reaching there about 4 **P.M.** I had been in camp about an hour when I received a message from Colonel Munford, at Crampton's Gap, distant about 2 miles, recommending the removal of my command to that point, as the enemy were pressing the small force at the gap. I immediately ordered my two strongest regiments to march to their support. Before, however, the head of the column had filed into the road I received a message from Colonel Parham, who was in command of Mahone's brigade at the gap, to the effect that the enemy was pressing him hard with overwhelming numbers, and appealing for all the support I could bring him. I immediately ordered the remaining two regiments to march, and accompanied the command in person. As I was marching the last of the column, I received a message from you, through your assistant adjutant-general (Major McIntosh) that I must hold the gap if it cost the life of every man in my command. Thus impressed with the importance of the position, I went forward with the utmost dispatch. When I reached the top of the mountain, I found that the enemy had been repulsed and driven back in the center and had been pursued down the other side of the mountain by Mahone's brigade. I soon discovered, however, that the enemy, by their greatly superior numbers, were flanking us both upon the right and left. Two of my regiments were sent to the right and two to the left to meet these movements of the enemy. In this we were successful, until the center gave way, pressed by fresh troops of the enemy and increased numbers. Up to this time the troops had fought well, and maintained their ground against greatly superior forces. The Tenth Georgia Regiment, of General Semmes' brigade, had been ordered to the gap from their position at the foot of the mountain, and participated in the battle with great courage and energy. After the lines were broken, all my efforts to rally the troops were unsuccessful. I was enabled to check their advance by momentary rallies, and, the night coming on, I made a successful stand near the foot of the mountain, which position we held during the night, and until a new position was taken about day-dawn the next morning, in the rear of Brownsville, which position was held until the surrender of Harpers Ferry.

The mounting Federal pressure forced Lee to concentrate his army at Sharpsburg. When Harpers Ferry fell on September 14, Jackson left A.P. Hill's division to receive the surrender and moved the balance of his command to Sharpsburg. Longstreet's and D.H. Hill's divisions arrived at Sharpsburg on the morning of September 15, and Jackson arrived early the next day. General McLaws moved his men through Harpers Ferry and did not arrive until after the battle of Sharpsburg started on September 17.

Early on the morning of September 17 the Federals launched a devastating attack against Lee's left under Jackson. Fresh troops were sent in by both sides, and the battle seesawed back and forth. When McLaws's men arrived at Sharpsburg they were given a short rest and then ordered to support Jackson. Lieutenant Colonel William MacRae reported the movements of Cobb's brigade to General Cobb as follows (O.R., S.I., Vol. XIX, pt. 1, pp. 871-872):

General McLaws' division, after marching all the previous night, was ordered, about 8 **A.M.,** to take position on the left, your brigade, numbering 357 men, commanded by Lieutenant-Colonel Sanders, Twenty-fourth Georgia, in front. In about half an hour we arrived in front of the enemy and in range of his musketry, when the head of the brigade was ordered to file right when the rear had filed. General McLaws commanded us to march by the left flank. Colonel Sanders, being in front, did not hear the order, but marched on and joined the left of General Rodes' command. (I will here state that we were thus separated from the division, and did not join it until the next morning.) We halted and took position behind a fence, covered from the enemy's musketry by a hill in front, but not protecting us from the heavy shelling of his several batteries planted on the side of the mountain on our right. For an hour we remained here inactive, suffering considerably, when we were ordered forward; the men, eager to meet the foe upon a more equal footing, gallantly pressed forward with a cheer, the top of the hill gained amid a galling and destructive shower of balls. There we remained, unfaltering, until Colonel Sanders, finding himself unsupported, ordered us to fall back behind the fence. The command was executed in admirable order. We remained here until the force on our right gave way. To prevent flanking, we changed front to the rear on the Fourth Battalion, and took position behind a stone fence, our extreme left remaining unchanged. We had scarcely executed the movement when General D.H. Hill rode up and ordered us forward to check the advance of the enemy. Colonel Sanders, though very unwell, had gallantly remained on the field, cheering his men by words and example until this moment, when he was too much exhausted to remain any longer. Being next in rank, the command devolved upon me.

The brigade, numbering now about 250 men, moved eagerly and unfalteringly forward to within about 100 yards, then opened a destructive fire upon the enemy, largely outnumbering us. He made a short stand, and then fell back behind the hill. Three times did he try to advance, and was as often driven back by the galling fire of our gallant little band. We held them in check (momentarily expecting re-enforcements) until our ammunition was expended. Seeing no sign of support, I was constrained to give the command to fall back. We left the field with not more than 50 of the 250 men. We fell back about 300 yards and joined Colonel Cooke, of the Twenty-seventh North Carolina, remaining with his shattered regiment until he was relieved about 3 **P.M.**

McLaws's men were forced to retire after driving the Federals back to their original position. As the Confederates regrouped on the left, the Federals launched an attack on the center, and the fighting shifted to that part of the line. Although the Federals continued to pressure the center and then the right, the Confederate line held. The next day the two armies rested, and on the night of September 18 Lee began moving his army back across the Potomac. During the Maryland campaign the regiment lost heavily. At Crampton's Pass the regiment lost 11 killed, 48 wounded, 124 captured of 402 engaged. At Sharpsburg it lost 3 killed, 52 wounded, and 8 captured.

The Army of Northern Virginia remained in the Shenandoah Valley until the Army of the Potomac crossed the Potomac River east of the Blue Ridge. By use of his cavalry, Lee sought to discover the enemy's intentions. On October 28 Longstreet's corps moved east of the mountains to Culpeper Court House while Jackson's corps moved closer to Winchester. When the enemy's intention was discovered, Lee moved Longstreet to Fredericksburg and ordered Jackson to prepare to move. McLaws's and Ransom's divisions were ordered to Fredericksburg on November 17, and two days later the remainder of Longstreet's corps was ordered to Fredericksburg. Jackson was ordered to move to Fredericksburg on November 26. On that day the 15th Regiment N.C. Troops (5th Regiment N.C. Volunteers) was transferred to General John R. Cooke's brigade, General Robert Ransom's division, Longstreet's corps. In addition to this regiment, the brigade contained the 27th Regiment N.C. Troops, 46th Regiment N.C. Troops, and the 48th Regiment N.C. Troops.

General A.E. Burnside moved his army opposite Fredericksburg to force the passage of the Rappahannock River and to advance on Richmond, and General Lee positioned his army to oppose any advance. Longstreet's corps was stationed on the heights behind the town, and D.H. Hill's division was sent to Port Royal down the Rappahannock to prevent any crossing of the river at that point. The rest of Jackson's corps was disposed so as to support Hill or Longstreet as might be required. Ransom's division of Longstreet's corps was positioned to support the batteries on Marye's Heights and Willis' Hill, at the foot of which a brigade was stationed behind a stone wall.

On the morning of December 11 the Federals began building bridges across the river, and that evening they drove the Confederate pickets from the town. It was apparent to Lee that Burnside intended to force his way through at Fredericksburg, so he ordered Jackson and D.H. Hill to move and form on Longstreet's right. Cooke's brigade was positioned 200 yards in rear of the batteries on Marye's Heights and Willis' Hill. During the night of December 11-12 and the next day, the Federals crossed and formed for the attack.

The attack came early on the morning of December 13 as one Federal column advanced against Lee's right under Jackson. About 11:00 **A.M.** the Federals advanced from the town to attack the position behind the stone wall in an effort to capture the defenses on Marye's Heights and Willis' Hill. In all, six attacks were launched against the position and were repulsed. Cooke's brigade was moved up to the crest to support the troops at the base of the hill behind the stone wall. There the brigade came under heavy artillery fire directed at the Confederate artillery on the hill. General Cooke was wounded, and Colonel Edward D. Hall, 46th Regiment N.C. Troops, assumed command of the brigade. Colonel Hall reported the brigade's activities as follows (*O.R.*, S.I., Vol. XXI, pp. 629-630):

Early on the morning of the 11th instant, the brigade, under the command of General Cooke, was

ordered to the front, opposite Fredericksburg, where we remained in position until about 12 o'clock Saturday, the 13th, at which time the engagement was going on in our front. The brigade was formed in line of battle as follows: The Twenty-seventh on the right; Forty-eighth next; Forty-sixth next; Fifteenth on the left. We moved into action by regiments. After advancing about 200 yards under a heavy fire of shell and musketry, we arrived at the crest of Willis' Hill, which overlooks the battlefield, on which hill several batteries were placed. With the exception of the Twenty-seventh, the brigade was halted on the crest of the hill, and delivered its fire on the advancing column of the enemy, who was then engaged in making a furious assault on our front lines, which were covered by a long stone wall at the foot of the hill, which assault, on the arrival of the brigade, was repulsed, with great loss to the enemy. The enemy that time succeeded in getting up to within 40 yards of the wall. After the repulse of the enemy, the Forty-sixth was moved down the hill behind the fence, supporting [T.R.R.] Cobb's brigade, the Twenty-seventh and Forty-sixth remaining behind the fence, and the Forty-eighth and Fifteenth on the top of the hill all day. Six different times during the day did the enemy advance his heavily re-enforced columns, and each time was driven back with immense loss. The action ceased at night, when the brigade was withdrawn, and resumed the position they occupied previous to the action. I regret to have to state that our brave commander was severely wounded early in the action.

It gives me great pleasure to state that, without exception, the conduct of the different regiments composing the brigade was deserving of the most unqualified approbation.

No engagement having taken place the next day, the commanders of the different regiments were ordered to intrench themselves that night, and before day each had opened ditches sufficient to cover their whole commands; and the night after two additional works were completed sufficient for two more regiments.

On Sunday morning, the brigade was relieved by General [Micah] Jenkins, and ordered back to camp.

After being repulsed all along the line, the Federals fell back to the town and the river bank, where they remained until they recrossed the river on the night of December 15-16. The Confederates then reoccupied the town and advanced positions on the river bank. The battle of Fredericksburg was a defensive victory in which not all of Lee's army was engaged. However, those troops on the front line suffered heavy casualties. The 15th Regiment N.C. Troops (5th Regiment N.C. Volunteers) lost 20 killed and 101 wounded. Following the battle the army went into winter quarters.

The regiment underwent one final change in its organization on January 9, 1863, when Company D was transferred to the 49th Regiment N.C. Troops in a mutual exchange for Company B of that regiment. This exchange may have occurred while the regiment was on the move. Cooke's brigade had been ordered to South Carolina on January 3 and was at Petersburg on January 15. It left that city for Warsaw, North Carolina, on that day and arrived at Warsaw on January 20. From Warsaw it moved to Burgaw, North Carolina, and on February 20 it left that place for Coosawhatchie, South Carolina. Moving by way of Wilmington and Charleston, the brigade arrived at Coosawhatchie on February 22. There it was assigned to the Third Military District, Department of South Carolina, Georgia, and Florida, commanded by General P.G.T. Beauregard.

The Federals were applying pressure all along the coast and were preparing to launch an attack on Charleston. The brigade supported Clingman's brigade at James Island during the bombardment of Fort Sumter and the naval engagement at Charleston but did not see any combat. On April 23, 1863, the brigade left Coosawhatchie for Wilmington, where it arrived on April 26. Five days later, May 1, the brigade moved to Kinston to reinforce General D.H. Hill's command. On May 22 Cooke's and Ransom's brigades were sent to support the 56th Regiment N.C. Troops, which was being severely pressed by a brigade-size force. The regiment took an active part in driving the Federals back at Gum Swamp and lost 2 killed and 14 wounded. The enemy was forced back to his defenses, and the Confederates returned to Kinston. There the brigade remained until ordered to return to Richmond. Leaving Kinston on June 7, the brigade arrived at Richmond on June 8.

During the Gettysburg campaign Cooke's brigade remained in the defenses around Richmond and was assigned to the Department of Richmond, General Arnold Elzey commanding. One regiment, the 46th Regiment N.C. Troops, was sent to Hanover Junction; the rest of the brigade was stationed on the Meadow Bridge Road north of the city. Two regiments from the brigade were later sent to New Bridge. When a Federal force moved against the position at South Anna Bridge, General Cooke was sent to defend that position on July 4. This regiment moved up to South Anna Bridge, and the 46th Regiment N.C. Troops moved over from Hanover Junction. The enemy tried to force the Confederates back but were thwarted in their efforts. General Cooke reported the action as follows (*O.R.*, S.I., Vol. XXVII, pt. 2, pp. 857-858):

The enemy, commanded by Brigadier-Generals Foster, Getty, and Wardrop (consisting of three brigades of infantry, 1,500 cavalry, and three batteries of artillery, the cavalry under Spear), attacked me last night about dark, and continued it at intervals during the night along the line of the South Anna, covering a front of some 2½ miles.

The principal point of attack was at the railroad bridge, where they were met by companies of Colonels [E.D.] Hall's [46th Regiment N.C. Troops] and [William] MacRae's [15th Regiment N.C. Troops (5th Regiment N.C. Volunteers)] regiments, under Major [A.C.] McAlister, who repulsed them repeatedly in handsome style. Colonel [John A.] Baker's regiment occupied the right of our line, and behaved very well. They tore up a portion of the track toward Ashland, and from the light seen just before day would not be surprised had they burned that place. They have all disappeared this morning; but as the cavalry sent to follow them has as yet made no report, I am not certain in what direction. I presume, however, they are making their way back toward the White House, as the line to Gordonsville is not cut. During the day, I expect to gain fuller information, and will inform you further to-night.

Our loss, owing to our rifle-pits, is very small — 1 killed and 6 wounded. Theirs is not known, though during the firing groans were frequently heard, and this morning much blood and places where men have been dragged are reported to me as visible.

Cooke's brigade remained at South Anna until ordered to Fredericksburg when Lee moved the Army of Northern Virginia back into Virginia after the Gettysburg campaign. The brigade moved back to Hanover Junction after being relieved early in September, and it remained in the Hanover Junction-South Anna area until ordered to Gordonsville about September 27. There it was attached to A.P. Hill's corps, Army of Northern Virginia. On about October 3 the brigade was assigned to General Henry Heth's division of that corps.

When the brigade joined Heth's division the army was on the Rapidan River line and the Federal army occupied the Rappahannock River line. On October 10 Lee's army moved to strike the right flank of the Federal army. The move compelled the Federal commander, General George Meade, to order his army to retire toward Centreville. As the rear guard of Meade's army was passing through Bristoe Station, General A.P. Hill's corps, with Heth's division in front, came on the field. Without waiting for the rest of the army to come up or to reconnoiter the situation, General Hill ordered an attack. General W. W. Kirkland's brigade was placed on the left of the road, and General Cooke's brigade was put on the right. The brigades advanced to the attack down an open hill toward the Federal troops entrenched behind the railroad embankment. Cooke's brigade was caught in the open and forced to retire with heavy casualties. Kirkland's brigade continued to advance with both flanks exposed but was forced to retire under heavy fire. During the engagement General Cooke was wounded, and Colonel Edward D. Hall, 46th Regiment N.C. Troops, assumed command of the brigade. Colonel Hall reported the action as follows (*O.R.*, S.I., Vol. XXIX, pt. 1, pp. 434-436):

I have the honor to report that on the 14th instant, on arriving within 1 or 2 miles of Bristoe Station, the brigade formed a line of battle on the right of the road in the following order: First, Forty-sixth North Carolina; second, Fifteenth North Carolina; third, Twenty-seventh North Carolina; and the Forty-eighth North Carolina on the left. After forming we advanced through a very thick undergrowth. On clearing the woods and arriving in the first opening the brigade was halted a few moments to correct the alignment. The enemy was discovered massed upon our left beyond the railroad and to the left of the road leading to the station. Being then in command of the extreme right regiment, I immediately discovered that the enemy was in heavy force on my right and busily engaged in getting in position. In a few moments we were ordered to advance, and soon after the enemy's skirmishers commenced firing on my right flank. I discovered the line of battle behind the railroad, extending as far on my right as I could see; also a mass of troops lying perpendicular to the road and on the side next to us, from which body an advance was made on my right in considerable numbers. I then sent word to General Cooke that I was much annoyed by the fire and seriously threatened. I sent my right company to engage the skirmishers on my right, but they were soon driven in. I then changed the front of my regiment on the first company and checked their advance.

The brigade had again halted just before getting under fire, and I moved back just in time to join the line in its final advance. Soon after getting under fire I found that the left of the brigade had commenced firing as they advanced, which was taken up along the whole line.

Shortly afterward information was brought me that General Cooke was wounded and that I was in command. I ordered my regiment to cease firing and passed up to the center of the brigade, stopping the firing as I went. The brigade was then within 200 yards of the railroad. On getting on the top of the hill, I found the brigade suffering from a heavy flank fire of artillery from the right. The number of guns I cannot say; evidently more than one battery. Also the guns on the left and rear of the railroad had an enfilading fire on us. The musketry fire from the line of railroad was very heavy. I soon saw that a rapid advance must be made or a withdrawal. I chose the former. I passed the word to the right regiments to charge, which was done in what I conceive to be in good style. The fourth regiment was somewhat confused, but I sent the lieutenant-colonel commanding word to follow the line, which he did with about two-thirds of his regiment, the balance giving way.

The brigade charged up to within 40 yards of the railroad, and from the severity of the fire, and from their seeing the extreme left of the line falling back, they fell back—the two right regiments in good order, the third (Twenty-seventh North Carolina) in an honorable confusion, from the fact that between one-half and two-thirds of the regiment had been killed and wounded, they being in a far more exposed position than the other two regiments and having gone farther. The Forty-eighth, in advancing, encountered the whole line falling back. I halted the brigade in the first field we came to, about 400 yards from the enemy's line, from which position we fell back beyond the second field on seeing the enemy come out on our right and left. After a short time the brigade of General Davis joined us on the right, when we again advanced to within 400 yards of the enemy, and on seeing the right brigade halt I halted, where we remained during the night.

As there was a battery of artillery lost during the engagement, and from its proximity to the brigade the loss may be laid to it, I will state that I knew nothing of the guns being there until we had fallen back to the second field. The guns may have been in our rear, but they must certainly have been placed there after we advanced; and in retreating, our losses both by casualties and straggling, shortened our line so much that with the addition of one of General Kirkland's regiments (Forty-fourth North Carolina), which joined our left, the left of the brigade was some distance to the right of the guns. On learning the guns were there and in danger, I dispatched a portion of one regiment to the relief, but the guns had been taken off before the relief arrived.

I would respectfully state that I have been with the brigade during some of the heaviest engagements of the war, and have never seen the men more cool and determined, and that their falling back resulted from no fault of theirs, but from the great superiority in number and position of the enemy, and entire want of support, both in rear and prolongation of our lines.

During the unsuccessful attack the regiment lost 14 killed and 87 wounded.

No further attempts were made to attack the enemy, and during the night the Federal rear guard continued its retreat to Centreville. Lee decided not to follow and ordered his army to retire to the Rappahannock. After the battle at Rappahannock Bridge, November 7, Lee moved his army back to the Rapidan River line. General Meade began moving his army on November 26 to cross the Rapidan below Lee's position. Lee ordered his army to intercept the Federal army. Finding the Federals advancing toward him, Lee retired to Mine Run and entrenched. Meade moved up and entrenched. Receiving reports that the Federal flank was exposed, Lee determined to attack on the morning of December 2. When the troops moved out they found that the Federal army had retired. A pursuit was undertaken, but Meade recrossed the Rapidan unmolested. Lee then ordered his troops back, and the army went into winter quarters. This regiment spent the winter of 1863-1864 in camp with the brigade near Orange Court House.

On the morning of May 4, 1864, while the Federal army under General U.S. Grant was moving across the lower Rapidan, Cooke's brigade was near Orange Court House. When information was received that Grant was crossing, Lee ordered Ewell's corps to move on the left on the Orange Turnpike and Hill's corps to move in the center on the Plank Road. Longstreet's corps, at Gordonsville, was ordered to move up on Hill's right. On the morning of May 5, with Kirkland's brigade in the lead, Hill's column encountered Federal cavalry near Parker's Store. The Federals were forced back, and the Confederates occupied the crossroads at Parker's Store. Immediately north on the Orange Turnpike, Ewell encountered the enemy in corps strength. Hill ordered Heth's division to deploy in line of battle across the Plank Road. Cooke's brigade was in the center with this regiment on the right of the brigade line. General Davis's brigade was on Cooke's left, and General Walker's brigade was on Cooke's right. Kirkland's brigade was held in reserve on the road behind Cooke's. Elements of the Federal II Corps attacked Heth's line around 4:00 P.M. During the attack Kirkland's brigade was sent to the relief of Cooke's hard-pressed men. The line held under repeated assaults, and Kirkland's brigade charged over the line in an unsuccessful effort to dislodge the enemy. It then retired back to the Confederate line. Heth's division was holding off seven enemy brigades, and more were moving against it. Wilcox's division was ordered to the support of Heth, and the four brigades of that division arrived in time to stabilize the line.

During the night Cooke's brigade was withdrawn and placed in reserve to the left rear of the position behind the three other brigades of Heth's division on the left of the road. Wilcox's division formed on the right of the road. The next morning at 5:00 A.M., May 6, Federal columns struck Hill's line in front and on the left flank. The attack was so swift that units were overrun, and the line began to fall back. The men of Heth's division fell back to the entrenched position held by Cooke's brigade. Other units joined in support of Cooke's position and succeeded in throwing the enemy advance into confusion. As the Federal pressure increased, Cooke's brigade was forced to retire. Only the timely arrival of Longstreet's corps prevented the collapse of Lee's right. Longstreet's fresh troops blunted the Federal attack and drove it back. Hill's troops regrouped and were ordered to close the gap between Ewell's right and Longstreet's left. Heth's division went into position on the right of the gap on the immediate left of Longstreet's line. The battle continued throughout the day on Longstreet's front; only night brought an end to the fighting. During the battle of the Wilderness, May 5-6, the regiment lost 240 men killed and wounded.

Late in the evening of May 7 orders came to close on the right. General Grant was heading toward

Spotsylvania Court House, and Lee was moving to intercept him. Throughout the night of May 7-8 the Confederates moved to the right. The race for the courthouse was won by Lee's cavalry and infantry on the morning of May 8. When the rest of the army came up, a strong defensive line was constructed. Hill's corps was positioned on the right of the line, with Ewell's corps in the center and Longstreet's corps on the left. Heth's division formed the right of the line. On May 10 Heth's division was pulled out of the line and moved to the left, where it turned back a Federal reconnaissance force on the Shady Grove road. The division was moved back to the right of the line at Spotsylvania Court House on the morning of May 11. Early on May 12 the Federals launched a sudden attack on the Confederate center, which was known as the Mule Shoe. Reinforcements were thrown in to check the Federal advance, and after heavy fighting the Confederates held until a new line to the rear of the apex of the salient was completed. Cooke's brigade remained on the right and extended to cover the line as the troops on its left were sent to drive the Federals out of the Mule Shoe.

After several unsuccessful attempts against the Confederate line, General Grant began to move his army eastward. Lee moved his army to block Grant at North Anna River, where Lee set up a strong defensive position with Hill's corps on the left. Wilcox's division of Hill's corps engaged the enemy on May 23, but Heth's division was not directly engaged. Grant withdrew during the night of May 26-27 and crossed the Pamunkey River, again sidestepping to the Confederate right. Ewell's corps, now commanded by General Jubal Early, marched some twenty-four miles on May 27 and entrenched between Beaver Dam Creek and Pole Green Church. Longstreet's corps came up on Early's right, and Hill's corps extended along the left of Early's line. On May 30, under orders from General Lee, Early moved to attack the Federal left at Bethesda Church. The attack failed to turn the Federal left but revealed that the enemy was moving to the Confederate right. On the afternoon of June 1 Cooke's and Kirkland's brigades repulsed an attack launched to conceal the Federal shift.

The two armies began to concentrate at Cold Harbor, and on June 1 a spirited engagement occurred. On June 2 Hill was ordered to leave Heth's division on the left to support Early's corps and to move his other two divisions to the Confederate right. While Hill moved to anchor the right, Heth's division joined Early's two divisions in striking the Federal right flank. After driving them from their first line of entrenchments, darkness halted the action, and the Confederates retired to their former position. The next day Grant launched an unsuccessful general assault against the six-mile-long Confederate line. One point of concentration was against the Confederate left in an attempt to flank the position and get in the rear of the main line. At least three attacks were launched against Heth's division. Each was repulsed with loss. This regiment lost about 60 men killed and wounded. Late in the day Heth was ordered to move to the right and join Hill's corps at Turkey Hill. Early on the morning of June 4 Heth moved and rejoined the other divisions of the corps.

When Grant moved south of the Chickahominy, Lee followed, and Hill's corps made contact near Riddell's Shop on June 13. A defensive line was established, but no general engagement followed. Grant then crossed the James River and moved on Petersburg. Hill's corps remained north of the James until ordered to move to Petersburg on June 17. When it arrived on June 18 it went into position on the extreme right of the Petersburg line and extended the line beyond the Weldon Railroad. Heth's division began entrenching and remained in the line until ordered to the north side of the James River on July 28 to confront a Federal feint. On July 30 the Federal mine was exploded at Petersburg, and the attack which followed the explosion was turned back. The feint north of the James was withdrawn, and Heth's division returned to the Petersburg line on August 2. Following this move, Heth's men enjoyed three weeks of comparative quiet.

On August 18 the Federals took possession of the Weldon Railroad at Globe Tavern, and all efforts by troops under Hill failed to dislodge them. South of Globe Tavern another Federal force occupied the railroad at Reams' Station. Moving around the enemy position at Globe Tavern, Hill moved Cooke's brigade and six other brigades of his corps and two divisions of cavalry to attack the Federal position at Reams' Station. The troops moved on the afternoon of August 24 and arrived before Reams' Station the next morning. An assault by two brigades was repulsed, but a stronger attack on the Federal right in which Cooke's brigade took part succeeded in breaking through the Federal line. Some 2,000 men and 9 pieces of artillery were captured as the Federals were driven back in disorder. This regiment lost 23 men killed and 91 wounded. Following the battle, Hill withdrew his men and returned to Petersburg that night.

Heth's division did not see action in the field again until September 30 when it was engaged at Jones' Farm. Grant moved to extend his line to tie it in with the position at Globe Tavern. Each side advanced to the attack, and, although initially successful, the Confederates could not prevent the Federals from establishing their line. On October 27 a Federal force moved to gain possession of the high ground north of Hatcher's Run in the vicinity of Burgess' Mill. General Hill concentrated Heth's and Mahone's divisions of infantry and General Wade Hampton's cavalry force to oppose the advance. Mahone was sent to strike the Federal right; Hampton moved to attack the left; and Heth held the front. The attack on the Federal right failed, but the simultaneous attack on the left was pressed vigorously until dark. The next day the Federal force withdrew and returned to its former position, and Cooke's brigade moved with the balance of Heth's division to near Hatcher's Run and went into winter quarters. On December 8 Hill's corps was ordered to move to Belfield to oppose a Federal advance on the Weldon Railroad. The Confederates, marching through sleet and snow, were within a few miles of Belfield when it was learned that the Federals had retired. Hill then moved his men to cut off the route of retreat and intercepted the Federal cavalry at Jarratt's Station. After a brief skirmish they pushed on, only to find that the Federal infantry was three hours ahead of them. Hill then called off the pursuit. After bivouacking for the night, Hill started back to Hatcher's Run, which he reached on the afternoon of December 13. Except for picket duty, there was no action on the line for the remainder of the year.

Early in February, 1865, General Grant ordered a move on the left of his line to secure a position on the Boydton Plank Road at Hatcher's Run. Cooke's brigade led the assault on the Federal position on February 5. As the brigade advanced it found that it was not supported on the left. When the supporting brigade failed to move into position, the attack stalled, and Federal pressure on the right flank forced the brigade to withdraw. Retiring from the field, the brigade returned to its former camp. There it remained until the night of March 24 when the brigade was ordered to move to Petersburg. Arriving after midnight, the brigade bivouacked near the water works. As General John B. Gordon's troops launched an attack on Fort Stedman early on March 25, Cooke's brigade occupied the trenches vacated by the assault troops. After the failure of the attack the survivors reoccupied the trenches, and Cooke's brigade was pulled out and ordered to return to its camp. When the brigade returned to its old camp it had to recapture its picket line, which had been overrun while the brigade was at Petersburg.

On March 29 a large Federal force moved against the Confederate right. Lee sent his reserves under General George E. Pickett to the right of Hatcher's Run. Pickett's men, reinforced by cavalry, were initially successful in driving the Federal cavalry back to Dinwiddie Court House before retiring back to Five Forks. Reinforced with a corps of infantry, the Federals succeeded in routing Pickett's men at Five Forks on April 1. This victory opened the way for an advance on the Confederate line at Petersburg in flank and rear. On April 2 the Federals launched a general attack against the line. They broke through to the left of Cooke's brigade and swept down the trenches. The brigade fell back to the next line, and that night Lee decided to evacuate the Petersburg line. The Army of Northern Virginia pulled out of the trenches to take up the march to Amelia Court House.

Lee's army concentrated at Amelia Court House on April 4-5 and continued the retreat on April 6. At Sayler's Creek, on April 6, the Confederates failed to hold the advancing Federals and sustained heavy losses. The remnants of two corps were defeated and captured. Lee's army moved through Farmville on April 7; on the march Cooke's brigade assisted in protecting the wagon trains from Federal cavalry hit-and-run attacks. Lee surrendered his army at Appomattox Court House on April 9, 1865. When the army was paroled on April 12, only 138 men of the regiment were present to receive their paroles.

FIELD AND STAFF

COLONELS

LEE, STEPHEN

Elected Colonel of this regiment on or about June 17, 1861; however, he was elected Colonel of the 16th Regiment N.C. Troops (6th Regiment N.C. Volunteers) at the same time and chose to serve with the latter unit.

McKINNEY, ROBERT M.

Previously served as Captain of Company A, 6th Regiment N.C. State Troops. Elected Colonel of this regiment on June 24, 1861. Present or accounted for until killed at Lee's Mill, Virginia, April 16, 1862.

DOWD, HENRY A.

Previously served as Adjutant of this regiment. Elected

Colonel on April 20, 1862. Present or accounted for until wounded at Malvern Hill, Virginia, July 1, 1862. Reported absent wounded until he resigned on February 27, 1863, by reason of disability from wounds. Later served as Assistant Quartermaster (Captain) in the Quartermaster's Department.

MacRAE, WILLIAM

Previously served as Captain of Company B of this regiment. Promoted to Lieutenant Colonel on May 2, 1862, and transferred to the Field and Staff. Promoted to Colonel on February 27, 1863. Present or accounted for until promoted to the temporary rank of Brigadier General on June 22, 1864. Promoted to the permanent rank of Brigadier General on November 4, 1864.

YARBOROUGH, WILLIAM H.

Previously served as Captain of Company L. Appointed Major to rank from May 2, 1862, and transferred to the Field and Staff. Promoted to Lieutenant Colonel on February 27, 1863, and was promoted to Colonel on November 4, 1864. Present or accounted for until paroled at Appomattox Court House, Virginia, April 9, 1865. Roll of Honor indicates that he "received four slight wounds" during the war.

LIEUTENANT COLONELS

IHRIE, ROSS R.

Previously served as Captain of Company M of this regiment. Appointed Lieutenant Colonel to rank from June 11, 1861, and transferred to the Field and Staff. Present or accounted for until he was defeated for reelection when the regiment was reorganized on May 2, 1862.

HAMMOND, GRAY W.

Previously served as Captain of Company K of this regiment. Promoted to Major on February 27, 1863, and transferred to the Field and Staff. Promoted to Lieutenant Colonel on January 12, 1865, to rank from November 4, 1864. Present or accounted for until paroled at Appomattox Court House, Virginia, April 9, 1865.

MAJORS

GREEN, WILLIAM F.

Previously served as Captain of Company L of this regiment. Promoted to Major to rank from June 11, 1861, and transferred to the Field and Staff. Present or accounted for until he was defeated for reelection when the regiment was reorganized on May 2, 1862.

JEROME, ROBERT P.

Previously served as Captain of Company B of this regiment. Promoted to Major on November 4, 1864, and transferred to the Field and Staff. Present or accounted for until paroled at Greensboro on May 1, 1865.

ADJUTANTS

MANNING, JOHN, Jr.

Previously served as 1st Lieutenant in Company M of this regiment. Appointed Adjutant on or about July 1, 1861, and transferred to the Field and Staff. Present or accounted for until he resigned on or about October 7,

1861, to become a Confederate "Agent for Confiscation."

DOWD, HENRY A.
Previously served as 1st Lieutenant in Company I of this regiment. Promoted to Adjutant on October 7, 1861, and transferred to the Field and Staff. Present or accounted for until elected Colonel of this regiment on April 20, 1862.

GORDON, GEORGE L.
Previously served as Private in Company I of this regiment. Appointed Adjutant (1st Lieutenant) on June 10, 1862, and transferred to the Field and Staff. Killed at Malvern Hill, Virginia, July 1, 1862.

HOUSTON, ALEXANDER H.
Previously served as 1st Lieutenant in Company B of this regiment. Reported on detail as Acting Adjutant from January-February, 1863, through April, 1863. Appointed Adjutant (1st Lieutenant) on April 30, 1863, to rank from October 1, 1862, and permanently transferred to the Field and Staff. Present or accounted for until paroled at Appomattox Court House, Virginia, April 9, 1865.

ASSISTANT QUARTERMASTERS

CABANISS, HARVEY D.
Previously served as 1st Lieutenant in 1st Company D of this regiment. Appointed Assistant Quartermaster (Captain) on July 19, 1861, and transferred to the Field and Staff. Present or accounted for until he was dismissed by order of the Secretary of War on or about February 24, 1862, "for failure to give bond."

THOMAS, CHARLES H.
Previously served as Private in Company L of this regiment. Appointed Assistant Quartermaster (Captain) on March 13, 1862, to rank from March 1, 1862, and transferred to the Field and Staff. Present or accounted for until appointed Assistant to the Quartermaster of Brigadier General John R. Cooke's brigade on September 15, 1864.

ASSISTANT COMMISSARIES OF SUBSISTENCE

WALCH, T. C.
Resided in Virginia. Appointed Assistant Commissary of Subsistence on July 19, 1861. Present or accounted for until he resigned on October 14, 1861. Reason he resigned not reported.

MASSENBURG, ARCHIBALD CARGILL
Previously served as 1st Sergeant in Company L of this regiment. Appointed Assistant Commissary of Subsistence (Captain) on November 14, 1861, and transferred to the Field and Staff. Present or accounted for until his position was abolished and he was appointed 2nd Lieutenant in 2nd Company D of this regiment on September 13, 1863.

SURGEONS

GREEN, BENJAMIN T.
Previously served as 1st Lieutenant in Company E of this regiment. Appointed Surgeon on June 1, 1861, and transferred to the Field and Staff. Present or

accounted for until he resigned in September, 1861. Later served as Surgeon of the 55th Regiment N.C Troops.

LANGDON, SAMUEL W.
Resided in New Hanover County. Appointed Surgeon to rank from September 20, 1861. Present or accounted for until paroled at Appomattox Court House, Virginia, April 9, 1865.

ASSISTANT SURGEONS

MOTT, WALTER B.
Resided in Iredell County. Appointed Assistant Surgeon on June 1, 1861. Present or accounted for until he resigned in July, 1862. Reason he resigned not reported.

CLIFTON, JAMES BEVERLY
Born in Franklin County where he resided as a physician prior to enlisting at age 25. Appointed Assistant Surgeon in June, 1861. Present or accounted for until transferred for duty at a hospital at Williamsburg, Virginia, in November, 1861.

LEWIS, JOEL BATTLE
Served as Private in Company I of this regiment. Name appears on a pay voucher which indicates that he served as Assistant Surgeon of this regiment from August 29 until December 29, 1861.

BONNER, WILLIAM V.
Previously served as Private in Company I of this regiment. Appointed Assistant Surgeon on September 26, 1862, to rank from July 30, 1862, and transferred to the Field and Staff. Present or accounted for until he resigned on April 3, 1863. Resignation accepted July 23, 1863.

WILLIAMS, DONALD
Previously served as Private in Company I of this regiment. Appointed Assistant Surgeon on June 1, 1864, to rank from December 11, 1863, and transferred to the Field and Staff. Present or accounted for through October, 1864.

CHAPLAINS

McRAE, JOHN C.
Appointed Chaplain in August, 1861, and resigned in October, 1861.

HOWERTON, SAMUEL W.
Resided in Davidson County. Appointed Chaplain on April 10, 1863, to rank from February 24, 1863. Present or accounted for until he resigned on December 10, 1864.

ENSIGN

LOVE, JOHN B.
Previously served as Private in Company C of this regiment. Detailed as Ensign on various occasions prior to his appointment as Ensign and transfer to the Field and Staff on or about April 23, 1864. Present or accounted for until paroled at Appomattox Court House, Virginia, April 9, 1865. "Displayed great courage and coolness in every engagement."

SERGEANTS MAJOR

GRAYSON, R. O.

Resided in Virginia and enlisted at Richmond, Virginia, June 29, 1861. Mustered in as Sergeant Major. Present or accounted for through August, 1861. Appointed Lieutenant in an unspecified Virginia regiment prior to May 1, 1862.

LEWIS, EXUM

Previously served as Private in Company I of this regiment. Promoted to Sergeant Major on July 6, 1862, and transferred to the Field and Staff. Present or accounted for until reduced to ranks on January 1, 1863, "for prolonged absence" and transferred back to Company I.

PORTER, JOSEPH E.

Previously served as Corporal in Company I of this regiment. Promoted to Sergeant Major on January 1, 1863, and transferred to the Field and Staff. Present or accounted for through October, 1864.

QUARTERMASTER SERGEANTS

HALL, C. LANDON

Resided in Virginia and enlisted at Richmond, Virginia, June 29, 1861. Present or accounted for until transferred to an unspecified Virginia regiment in March, 1862.

COFFIELD, JOSEPH BRYANT

Previously served as Sergeant in Company I of this regiment. Promoted to Quartermaster Sergeant on December 1, 1862, and transferred to the Field and Staff. Present or accounted for until appointed 2nd Lieutenant to rank from February 9, 1864, and transferred to Company H, 1st Regiment N.C. State Troops.

BRITT, THOMAS A.

Previously served as Private in Company A of this regiment. Promoted to Quartermaster Sergeant in March-October, 1864, and transferred to the Field and Staff. Present or accounted for until paroled at Appomattox Court House, Virginia, April 9, 1865.

ORDNANCE SERGEANT

MOSS, PETER M.

Previously served as Corporal in Company E of this regiment. Promoted to Ordnance Sergeant on May 10, 1862, and transferred to the Field and Staff. Present or accounted for until paroled at Appomattox Court House, Virginia, April 9, 1865.

HOSPITAL STEWARD

SUGG, JOSEPH P.

Previously served as Private in Company I of this regiment. Appointed Hospital Steward on May 5, 1863, and transferred to the Field and Staff. Present or accounted for until paroled at Appomattox Court House, Virginia, April 9, 1865.

COMPANY A

This company was from Northampton County and enlisted at Garysburg on May 23, 1861. It was mustered in on June 10, 1861, and was assigned to this regiment as Company A. After joining the regiment the company functioned as a part of the regiment, and its history for the war period is recorded as a part of the regimental history.

The information contained in the following roster of the company was compiled principally from company muster rolls for June 10-August, 1861; November, 1862-April, 1864; and September-October, 1864. No company muster rolls were found for September, 1861-October, 1862; May-August, 1864; or for the period after October, 1864. In addition to the company muster rolls, Roll of Honor records, receipt rolls, hospital records, prisoner of war records, and other primary records, supplemented by state pension applications, United Daughters of the Confederacy records, and postwar rosters and histories, all provided useful information.

OFFICERS

CAPTAINS

STANCELL, SAMUEL T.

Resided in Northampton County and enlisted at age 33. Appointed Captain on or about June 10, 1861, to rank from February 18, 1861. Present or accounted for until wounded at Lee's Mill, Virginia, April 16, 1862. Defeated for reelection when the regiment was reorganized on May 2, 1862.

RANDOLPH, JAMES B.

Resided in Northampton County where he enlisted at age 24, May 23, 1861. Mustered in as Corporal and was elected 2nd Lieutenant on October 3, 1861. Elected Captain on May 2, 1862. Present or accounted for until killed at Malvern Hill, Virginia, July 1, 1862.

PEELE, JOHN H.

Resided in Northampton County where he enlisted at age 31, May 23, 1861. Mustered in as Private and was elected 1st Lieutenant on May 2, 1862. Promoted to Captain on July 1, 1862. Present or accounted for through October, 1864.

LIEUTENANTS

BOYKIN, LITTLEBERRY W., 2nd Lieutenant

Resided in Northampton County where he enlisted at age 35. Appointed 2nd Lieutenant on or about May 23, 1861. Present or accounted for until he resigned on August 26, 1861. Died September 15, 1861, of disease. Place of death not reported.

DeBERRY, EDWARD A., 1st Lieutenant

Resided in Northampton County where he enlisted at age 21. Appointed 1st Lieutenant on or about May 23, 1861. Present or accounted for until he resigned on or about August 19, 1861. "Died soon thereafter." Place, date, and cause of death not reported.

JACOBS, JAMES W., 1st Lieutenant

Resided in Northampton County where he enlisted at age 27, May 23, 1861. Mustered in as Private and was elected 1st Lieutenant on October 9, 1861. Present or accounted for until he was defeated for reelection when the regiment was reorganized on May 2, 1862.

PARKER, WILLIAM H., 1st Lieutenant
Resided in Northampton County where he enlisted at age 25, May 23, 1861. Mustered in as Sergeant and was elected 2nd Lieutenant to rank from May 2, 1862. Promoted to 1st Lieutenant to rank from July 1, 1862, and was wounded in the side at Malvern Hill, Virginia, the same day. Rejoined the company prior to January 1, 1863, and present or accounted for until he resigned on February 21, 1865. Reason he resigned not reported.

VICK, WILLIAM P., 2nd Lieutenant
Resided in Northampton County where he enlisted at age 24. Appointed 2nd Lieutenant on or about June 10, 1861, to rank from February 18, 1861. Present or accounted for until he was defeated for reelection when the regiment was reorganized on May 2, 1862.

WOOD, SPIER W., 2nd Lieutenant
Resided in Northampton or Halifax counties and enlisted in Northampton County at age 21, May 23, 1861. Mustered in as Private and was appointed 2nd Lieutenant to rank from May 2, 1862. Present or accounted for until wounded at Sharpsburg, Maryland, September 17, 1862. Returned to duty prior to January 1, 1863, and present or accounted for until he resigned on or about December 19, 1864. Reason he resigned not reported.

WOODRUFF, WILLIAM E., 2nd Lieutenant
Resided in Northampton County where he enlisted at age 22, May 23, 1861. Mustered in as Private and was promoted to Corporal on May 2, 1862. Elected 2nd Lieutenant on July 10, 1862. Present or accounted for until wounded at Sharpsburg, Maryland, September 17, 1862. Returned to duty in January-February, 1863, and present or accounted for until captured at Jackson on July 27, 1863. Paroled at Fort Monroe, Virginia, August 4, 1863. Rejoined the company prior to October 14, 1863, when he was wounded in the shoulder and left arm at Bristoe Station, Virginia. Returned to duty on or about October 21, 1863, and present or accounted for through October, 1864.

NONCOMMISSIONED OFFICERS AND PRIVATES

ALLEN, CHARLTON Y., Private
Resided in Northampton County where he enlisted at age 30, May 23, 1861. Present or accounted for until he died in North Carolina on March 4, 1862, of disease.

ALLEN, JOHN, Private
Resided in Northampton County and enlisted in Wake County at age 20, July 15, 1862, for the war. Present or accounted for until wounded at Sharpsburg, Maryland, September 17, 1862. Returned to duty prior to January 1, 1863, and present or accounted for through October, 1864.

ALLEN, JUNIUS A., Private
Born in Northampton County where he resided as a farmer prior to enlisting in Rowan County at age 25, May 23, 1861. Present or accounted for until discharged on July 6, 1862, after providing Private John R. Matthews as a substitute.

BARNES, ISAIAH, Private
Resided in Northampton County and enlisted in Wake County at age 23, July 15, 1862, for the war. Present or accounted for until wounded at or near Crampton's Pass, Maryland, September 14, 1862. Captured prior to September 20, 1862, and paroled; however, place and date captured not reported. Returned to duty prior to January 1, 1863, and present or accounted for until wounded at Bristoe Station, Virginia, October 14, 1863. Reported absent wounded or absent sick until he returned to duty on October 11, 1864. Present or accounted for until captured in Amelia County, Virginia, April 3, 1865. Confined at Point Lookout, Maryland, until released on June 24, 1865, after taking the Oath of Allegiance.

BARNES, JAMES B., Private
Resided in Northampton County where he enlisted at age 25, May 23, 1861. Present or accounted for until killed at Sharpsburg, Maryland, September 17, 1862.

BARNES, JOSEPH, Private
Resided in Northampton County and enlisted in Wake County at age 19, July 15, 1862, for the war. Present or accounted for until wounded and captured at Sharpsburg, Maryland, September 17, 1862. Died at or near Sharpsburg on September 29, 1862.

BARNES, JOSEPH S., Private
Resided in Northampton County where he enlisted at age 19, May 23, 1861. Present or accounted for until he died at Yorktown, Virginia, September 27, 1861, of disease.

BARNES, WILLIAM R., Private
Resided in Northampton County where he enlisted at age 23, May 23, 1861. Present or accounted for until reported absent without leave on or about December 2, 1862. Returned to duty on March 1, 1863. Present or accounted for until February 21, 1865; however, he was reported absent sick or absent without leave during most of that period. Retired to the Invalid Corps on February 21, 1865.

BENTHALL, JOHN, Private
Resided in Northampton County and enlisted in Wake County at age 33, July 15, 1862, for the war. Present or accounted for until captured at Petersburg, Virginia, April 3, 1865. Confined at Point Lookout, Maryland, until released on June 24, 1865, after taking the Oath of Allegiance.

BENTHALL, LAWRENCE, Private
Resided in Northampton County and enlisted at age 30, July 15, 1862, for the war. Discharged August 29, 1862, after providing a substitute.

BLAYLOCK, DAVID, Private
Resided in Northampton County and enlisted at age 31, July 15, 1862, for the war. No further records.

BOTTOMS, JOSEPH C., Private
Born in Northampton County where he resided prior to enlisting in Northampton County at age 23, May 23, 1861. Present or accounted for until he died at Margaretsville on or about December 11, 1863, of disease.

BOTTOMS, WILLIAM E., Private
Resided in Northampton County where he enlisted at age 29, May 23, 1861. Present or accounted for until

he died at Richmond, Virginia, October 29, 1862, of "smallpox."

BOWERS, ANDREW B., Private
Resided in Northampton County where he enlisted at age 26, May 23, 1861. Present or accounted for until he died at Danville, Virginia, June 20, 1862, of "diarrhoea chron[ic]."

BOWERS, JOHN, Private
Resided in Northampton County and enlisted at age 25, July 15, 1862, for the war. Present or accounted for until he died on September 1, 1862, of disease. Place of death not reported.

BOYCE, JOHN H., Private
Resided in Northampton County where he enlisted at age 22, May 23, 1861. Company muster rolls dated June 10-August 31, 1861, indicate that he never reported to the company. Dropped from the rolls at an unspecified date.

BOYETTE, ETHELDRED D., Private
Resided in Northampton County and enlisted in Wake County at age 32, July 15, 1862, for the war. Present or accounted for until he died in hospital at Charlotte on May 21, 1864, of "diarrhoea chronica."

BOYKIN, BURGESS B., Corporal
Resided in Northampton County where he enlisted at age 24, May 23, 1861. Mustered in as Private. Present or accounted for until captured at or near Crampton's Pass, Maryland, September 14, 1862. Confined at Fort Delaware, Delaware, until transferred to Aiken's Landing, James River, Virginia, October 2, 1862, for exchange. Declared exchanged at Aiken's Landing on November 10, 1862. Returned to duty prior to January 1, 1863, and was promoted to Corporal on September 1, 1864. Present or accounted for until captured at or near Petersburg, Virginia, on or about April 4, 1865. Died at Newport News, Virginia, June 4, 1865, of "chronic diarrhoea."

BRACY, CHARLES H., Private
Resided in Northampton County where he enlisted at age 25, May 23, 1861. Present or accounted for until captured at or near Crampton's Pass, Maryland, September 14, 1862. Confined at Fort Delaware, Delaware, until transferred to Aiken's Landing, James River, Virginia, October 2, 1862, for exchange. Died in hospital at Richmond, Virginia, October 10, 1862, of "pneumonia."

BRADLEY, WILLIAM K., Private
Resided in Northampton County where he enlisted at age 24, May 23, 1861. Present or accounted for until he died in North Carolina on March 23, 1862, of disease.

BRIDGERS, LEMUEL T., Private
Resided in Northampton County where he enlisted at age 34, May 23, 1861, for one year. Present or accounted for until discharged on August 17, 1862. Reason discharged not reported.

BRITT, THOMAS A., Private
Resided in Northampton County where he enlisted at age 20, May 23, 1861. Mustered in as Private. Present or accounted for until promoted to Quartermaster Sergeant in March-October, 1864, and transferred to the Field and Staff of this regiment.

BRITT, WILLIAM T., Private
Resided in Northampton County where he enlisted at age 38, May 23, 1861. Present or accounted for until discharged on August 17, 1862, by reason of being over age.

BRITTON, ANDREW J., Private
Resided in Northampton County where he enlisted at age 18, May 23, 1861. Present or accounted for until wounded at Fredericksburg, Virginia, December 13, 1862. Returned to duty prior to March 15, 1863, when he was discharged by reason of having provided Private James E. Martin as a substitute.

BRITTON, HENRY T., Private
Resided in Northampton County where he enlisted at age 21, May 23, 1861. Present or accounted for until wounded at Malvern Hill, Virginia, July 1, 1862. Returned to duty prior to January 1, 1863, and present or accounted for until paroled at Appomattox Court House, Virginia, April 9, 1865.

BRITTON, WILLIAM E., Private
Resided in Northampton County where he enlisted at age 25, May 23, 1861. Present or accounted for until reported in hospital at Richmond, Virginia, June 2, 1864, with a gunshot wound; however, place and date wounded not reported. Returned to duty prior to October 31, 1864, and was present or accounted for through that date.

BROWN, JEREMIAH, Private
Resided in Northampton County and enlisted in Wake County at age 22, July 15, 1862, for the war. Present or accounted for until he was reported absent without leave on December 27, 1863. Reported absent without leave through April 30, 1864. No further records.

BROWN, JOHN T., Private
Born in Northampton County where he resided prior to enlisting in Wake County at age 25, July 15, 1862, for the war. Present or accounted for until wounded in the chest at Fredericksburg, Virginia, December 13, 1862. Died in hospital at Richmond, Virginia, December 25, 1862, of wounds.

BURRIS, MURPHEY, Private
Resided in Randolph County. Place and date of enlistment not reported. Took the Oath of Amnesty at or near Richmond, Virginia, on or about June 18, 1865.

CAROON, SAMUEL B., Private
Resided in Northampton County where he enlisted at age 21, May 23, 1861. Present or accounted for until he died in North Carolina in October, 1861, of disease.

CLARK, CHARLES R., Private
Resided in Northampton County where he enlisted at age 20, May 23, 1861. Present or accounted for until wounded at Fredericksburg, Virginia, December 13, 1862. Returned to duty prior to January 1, 1863, and present or accounted for until captured at Hatcher's Run, Virginia, April 2, 1865. Confined at Point Lookout, Maryland, until released on June 26, 1865, after taking the Oath of Allegiance.

CLARK, JAMES A., Private
Resided in Northampton County and enlisted in Wake County at age 21, July 15, 1862, for the war. Present or accounted for until wounded at or near Crampton's

Pass, Maryland, September 14, 1862. Returned to duty prior to January 1, 1863, and present or accounted for through October, 1864.

COGGIN, JAMES A., Private
Resided in Northampton County where he enlisted at age 18, May 23, 1861. Present or accounted for until transferred to the cavalry on November 28, 1864. Unit to which transferred not reported.

COPELAND, RAPHAEL, Musician
Born in Nansemond County, Virginia, and resided in Northampton County where he was by occupation a clerk prior to enlisting in Northampton County at age 16, May 23, 1861. Mustered in as Musician (Drummer). Present or accounted for until discharged on July 15, 1862, by reason of being under age.

COPELAND, VIRGINIUS, Sergeant
Resided in Northampton County where he enlisted at age 19, May 23, 1861. Mustered in as Private and was promoted to Sergeant in September, 1861-December, 1862. Present or accounted for until wounded at or near Crampton's Pass, Maryland, September 14, 1862. Reported absent wounded until transferred to Company H, 19th Regiment N.C. Troops (2nd Regiment N.C. Cavalry), February 2, 1863, by reason of having been declared "not fit for infantry service."

DAUGHTRY, HARRISON R., Private
Resided in Northampton County and enlisted in Wake County at age 32, July 15, 1862, for the war. Present or accounted for until paroled at Appomattox Court House, Virginia, April 9, 1865.

DAVIS, BENJAMIN S., Private
Resided in Northampton County where he enlisted at age 18, May 23, 1861. Present or accounted for until discharged on July 20, 1862, after providing a substitute.

DEBERRY, JOSEPH F., Private
Born in Northampton County where he resided as a student prior to enlisting in Northampton County at age 19, May 23, 1861. Present or accounted for until discharged on December 31, 1861, by reason of "a naturally weak constitution with a strong predisposition to phthisis pulmonalis & in consequence of an attack of typhoid fever. . . ."

DEBERRY, JUNIUS B., Corporal
Resided in Northampton County where he enlisted at age 26, May 23, 1861. Mustered in as Corporal. Present or accounted for until appointed Adjutant and transferred to the North Carolina Militia in March, 1862. Unit to which transferred not reported.

DELOATCH, HENDERSON RANDOLPH, Corporal
Born in Northampton County where he resided prior to enlisting in Northampton County at age 24, May 23, 1861. Mustered in as Private and promoted to Corporal on June 1, 1863. Present or accounted for until wounded in the foot at Bristoe Station, Virginia, October 14, 1863. Transferred to Company H, 19th Regiment N.C. Troops (2nd Regiment N.C. Cavalry), October 29, 1863, in exchange for Private Joseph M. Spivey.

DELOATCH, HENRY T., Private
Resided in Northampton County where he enlisted at age 44, May 23, 1861. Present or accounted for until

discharged on December 1, 1862, by reason of being over age.

DELOATCH, JOHN M., Private
Resided in Northampton County where he enlisted at age 29, May 23, 1861. Present or accounted for until he died "at home" on December 20, 1862, of "consumption."

DELOATCH, MADISON E., Corporal
Born in Northampton County where he resided prior to enlisting in Northampton County at age 24, May 23, 1861. Mustered in as Private and promoted to Corporal on May 2, 1862. Present or accounted for until captured at or near Frederick, Maryland, on or about September 12, 1862. Confined at Fort Delaware, Delaware, until transferred to Aiken's Landing, James River, Virginia, October 2, 1862, for exchange. Declared exchanged at Aiken's Landing on November 10, 1862. Returned to duty in March-April, 1863. Present or accounted for until hospitalized at Richmond, Virginia, June 8, 1864, with a gunshot wound; however, place and date wounded not reported. Died in hospital at Richmond on July 22, 1864. Cause of death not reported.

DELOATCH, MOODY, Private
Born in Northampton County where he resided prior to enlisting in Northampton County at age 23, May 23, 1861. Present or accounted for until wounded in the head at Malvern Hill, Virginia, July 1, 1862. Returned to duty prior to January 1, 1863, and present or accounted for until he died in hospital at Richmond, Virginia, September 22, 1864, of disease.

DELOATCH, NOAH, Private
Born in Northampton County where he resided prior to enlisting in Northampton County at age 32, May 23, 1861. Present or accounted for until he died in hospital at Richmond, Virginia, January 5, 1863, of "variola conf[luen]t."

DELOATCH, WILLIAM C., Private
Resided in Northampton County where he enlisted at age 25, May 23, 1861. Present or accounted for until he died in hospital at Hanover Academy, Virginia, August 28, 1863, of "dysentery."

DRAKE, RICHARD H., Private
Born in Northampton County where he resided prior to enlisting in Northampton County at age 18, May 23, 1861. Present or accounted for until killed at Fredericksburg, Virginia, December 13, 1862.

EARLEY, JESSE T., Private
Resided in Northampton County where he enlisted at age 30, May 23, 1861. Present or accounted for until captured at Amelia Court House, Virginia, April 5, 1865. Confined at Point Lookout, Maryland, until released on June 11, 1865, after taking the Oath of Allegiance.

EDWARDS, HENRY C., Private
Previously served in Company H, 19th Regiment N.C. Troops (2nd Regiment N.C. Cavalry). Transferred to this company on September 5, 1864, in exchange for Private William S. Garriss. Present or accounted for through October, 1864.

EDWARDS, HEZEKIAH D., Private
Previously served in Company H, 19th Regiment N.C.

Troops (2nd Regiment N.C. Cavalry). Transferred to this company on September 5, 1864, in exchange for Sergeant George R. Murfee. Present or accounted for until captured at Petersburg, Virginia, April 3, 1865. Confined at Point Lookout, Maryland, until released on June 11, 1865, after taking the Oath of Allegiance.

EDWARDS, RICHARD H., Private
Born in Northampton County where he resided prior to enlisting in Wake County at age 20, July 15, 1862, for the war. Present or accounted for until he died in hospital at Weldon on January 31, 1863, of "pneumonia typh[oid]."

EDWARDS, WILLIAM C., Private
Born in Northampton County where he resided prior to enlisting in Wake County at age 21, July 15, 1862, for the war. Present or accounted for until killed at Fredericksburg, Virginia, December 13, 1862.

FAISON, JAMES H., Private
Born in Northampton County where he resided as a farmer prior to enlisting in Wake County at age 26, July 15, 1862, for the war. Present or accounted for until discharged on February 8, 1865, by reason of "hypertrophy of the heart."

FUTRELL, DORSEY, Private
Resided in Northampton County where he enlisted on July 15, 1862, for the war. Present or accounted for until he deserted to the enemy at Plymouth on or about March 13, 1864. Took the Oath of Amnesty at Fort Monroe, Virginia, April 4, 1864.

FUTRELL, MATHIAS, Private
Born in Northampton County where he resided as a farmer prior to enlisting at Richmond, Virginia, at age 30, July 15, 1862, for the war. Present or accounted for until discharged at Danville, Virginia, October 28, 1862, by reason of "abscess of lung."

GARRISS, WILLIAM S., Private
Resided in Northampton County where he enlisted at age 25, May 23, 1861. Present or accounted for until reported absent without leave from September 1, 1862, until he was confined at Richmond, Virginia, June 10, 1863. Returned to duty on August 10, 1863, and present or accounted for until transferred to Company H, 19th Regiment N.C. Troops (2nd Regiment N.C. Cavalry), September 5, 1864, in exchange for Private Henry C. Edwards.

GAY, JAMES W., Sergeant
Resided in Northampton County where he enlisted at age 23, May 23, 1861. Mustered in as Private and promoted to Corporal on August 1, 1862. Present or accounted for until captured at or near Crampton's Pass, Maryland, September 14, 1862. Confined at Fort Delaware, Delaware, until transferred to Aiken's Landing, James River, Virginia, October 2, 1862, for exchange. Declared exchanged at Aiken's Landing on November 10, 1862. Returned to duty December 10, 1862, and was promoted to Sergeant on September 1, 1864. Present or accounted for until paroled at Appomattox Court House, Virginia, April 9, 1865.

GAY, SAMUEL C., Private
Resided in Northampton County where he enlisted at age 18, May 23, 1861. Present or accounted for until he died at Seaboard on March 31, 1862, of disease.

GILLIAM, GEORGE W., Private
Resided in Northampton County and enlisted in Wake County at age 28, July 15, 1862, for the war. Present or accounted for until he died in hospital at Richmond, Virginia, November 2, 1863, of "febris typhoides."

GLOVER, JOHN T., Private
Resided in Northampton County where he enlisted at age 30, May 23, 1861. Present or accounted for until transferred to the C.S. Navy on or about April 1, 1864.

GLOVER, ROBERT D., Private
Resided in Northampton County and enlisted in Wake County at age 30, July 15, 1862, for the war. Present or accounted for until he deserted at Suffolk, Virginia, February 15, 1865. North Carolina pension records indicate he was wounded at "Wilderness, Virginia, June 11, 1864." No further records.

GRANT, JORDAN C., Private
Previously served in Mallett's Battalion (Camp Guard). Enlisted in this company on April 7, 1863. Present or accounted for through October, 1864.

GRANT, JOSEPH E., Corporal
Resided in Northampton County where he enlisted at age 19, May 23, 1861. Mustered in as Private. Present or accounted for until wounded at Malvern Hill, Virginia, July 1, 1862. Returned to duty prior to January 1, 1863, and was promoted to Corporal on February 1, 1864. Present or accounted for through October, 1864.

GRANT, JOSHUA T., Private
Resided in Northampton County where he enlisted at age 23, May 23, 1861. Present or accounted for until transferred to Company B, 9th Regiment N.C. State Troops (1st Regiment N.C. Cavalry), February 14, 1864.

HARRISON, GEORGE E., Private
Resided in Brunswick County, Virginia, and enlisted in Northampton County at age 23, May 23, 1861. Present or accounted for until he died "at home" on March 7, 1863, of disease.

HARRISS, EDWIN C., Sergeant
Resided in Northampton County where he enlisted at age 25, May 23, 1861. Mustered in as Private and promoted to Corporal in May-August, 1864. Promoted to Sergeant on September 1, 1864. Present or accounted for until captured at Hatcher's Run, Virginia, April 2, 1865. Confined at Point Lookout, Maryland, until released on June 27, 1865, after taking the Oath of Allegiance.

HOWELL, JAMES B., Private
Resided in Northampton County where he enlisted at age 26, May 23, 1861. Present or accounted for until wounded at Fredericksburg, Virginia, December 13, 1862. Returned to duty prior to January 1, 1863, and present or accounted for through October, 1864.

JOHNSON, ANDREW, Private
Resided in Northampton County and enlisted at age 19, July 15, 1862, for the war. Died in hospital at Lynchburg, Virginia, September 16, 1862, of "dysenteria acute."

JOHNSON, CHRISTOPHER J., Private
Enlisted at Orange Court House, Virginia, March 7, 1864, for the war. Present or accounted for until

wounded on or about May 23, 1864; however, battle in which wounded not reported. Died in hospital at Richmond, Virginia, May 27, 1864, of wounds.

JOHNSON, GEORGE THOMAS, Private

Previously served in Company B, 15th Battalion N.C. Cavalry. Transferred to this company on March 7, 1864. Present or accounted for through October, 1864. North Carolina pension records indicate he was wounded at Wilderness, Virginia, May 5, 1864.

JOHNSON, HENRY C., Private

Resided in Northampton County and enlisted in Wake County at age 18, July 15, 1862, for the war. Present or accounted for until wounded at Sharpsburg, Maryland, September 17, 1862. Never rejoined the company. No further records.

JOHNSON, LEVI, Private

Born in Northampton County where he resided prior to enlisting in Wake County at age 25, July 15, 1862, for the war. Present or accounted for until killed at Fredericksburg, Virginia, December 13, 1862.

JOHNSON, WILLIAM J., Private

Resided in Northampton County and enlisted in Wake County at age 29, July 15, 1862, for the war. Present or accounted for until paroled at Appomattox Court House, Virginia, April 9, 1865.

JONES, ANDREW J., Private

Born in Northampton County where he resided prior to enlisting in Northampton County at age 23, May 23, 1861. Present or accounted for until he died "at home" on or about October 17, 1863, of disease.

JONES, GEORGE A., Private

Enlistment date reported as July 18, 1862; however, he was not listed on the rolls of this company until September-October, 1864. Wounded in an unspecified battle and reported missing on August 21, 1864. No further records.

JONES, PETER M., Private

Enlistment date reported as July 18, 1862; however, he was not listed on the rolls of this company until September-October, 1864. Wounded in an unspecified battle and sent to hospital on August 21, 1864. Reported in hospital at Richmond, Virginia, through August 31, 1864. No further records.

JORDAN, BENJAMIN F., 1st Sergeant

Resided in Northampton County where he enlisted at age 36, May 23, 1861. Mustered in as 1st Sergeant. Present or accounted for until transferred to Company H, 19th Regiment N.C. Troops (2nd Regiment N.C. Cavalry), August 22, 1862.

LANGSTON, DORSEY, Private

Resided in Northampton County and enlisted at age 26, July 15, 1862, for the war. Present or accounted for until he died at Richmond, Virginia, September 3, 1862, of disease.

LASSITER, ABNER, Private

Resided in Northampton County where he enlisted at age 22, May 23, 1861. Present or accounted for until wounded in the thigh at Malvern Hill, Virginia, July 1, 1862. Reported absent wounded until discharged on February 16, 1863. Reason discharged not reported.

LEONARD, DANIEL, _____

North Carolina pension records indicate that he

enlisted on October 15, 1862, and was mortally wounded near Petersburg, Virginia, in February, 1863. Place and exact date of death not reported.

LONG, JAMES K., Corporal

Resided in Northampton County where he enlisted at age 34, May 23, 1861. Mustered in as Private and promoted to Corporal on October 3, 1861. Present or accounted for until he was reported absent sick in North Carolina in May, 1862. No further records.

MARKS, EDWIN G., Private

Resided in Northampton County where he enlisted at age 23, May 23, 1861. Present or accounted for until wounded at Bristoe Station, Virginia, October 14, 1863. Returned to duty prior to May 1, 1864, and present or accounted for until captured at Petersburg, Virginia, or at Farmville, Virginia, April 4-6, 1865. Confined at Newport News, Virginia. Took the Oath of Allegiance at Newport News on June 15, 1865, and was released; however, he was hospitalized at Fort Monroe, Virginia, on or about the same day and died June 23, 1865, of "chronic diarrhoea."

MARKS, HENRY, Private

Born in Northampton County where he resided prior to enlisting in Wake County at age 22, July 15, 1862, for the war. Present or accounted for until wounded in the leg and captured at or near Crampton's Pass, Maryland, September 14, 1862. Confined at Fort McHenry, Maryland, until paroled on November 12, 1862, and transferred to City Point, Virginia, for exchange. Returned to duty in March-April, 1863, and present or accounted for until captured at Bristoe Station, Virginia, October 14, 1863. Confined at Old Capitol Prison, Washington, D.C., until transferred to Point Lookout, Maryland, October 27, 1863. Died in hospital at Point Lookout on January 10, 1864, of "chronic diarrhoea."

MARTIN, JAMES E., Private

Resided in Northampton County where he enlisted at age 17, on or about March 15, 1863, for the war as a substitute for Private Andrew J. Britton. Present or accounted for until captured at Petersburg, Virginia, April 3, 1865. Confined at Point Lookout, Maryland, until released on June 29, 1865, after taking the Oath of Allegiance.

MARTIN, SIMEON P., Private

Resided in Northampton County where he enlisted at age 18, May 23, 1861. Present or accounted for through October, 1864.

MATTHEWS, JOHN R., Private

Born in Hertford or Gates counties and resided in Bertie County where he was by occupation a farmer or planter prior to enlisting at Richmond, Virginia, at age 17, July 6, 1862, for the war as a substitute for Private Junius A. Allen. Present or accounted for until his right arm was "shot off" at or near Crampton's Pass, Maryland, September 14, 1862. Reported absent wounded until he was reported absent without leave from January 1, 1863, through June 30, 1863. Transferred to Company C, 17th Regiment N.C. Troops (2nd Organization), August 18, 1863.

MAYS, JAMES A., Private

Place and date of enlistment not reported. Captured in Burke County on August 28, 1864, and confined at

Camp Chase, Ohio, until transferred to Point Lookout, Maryland, March 26, 1865. Died at Point Lookout on May 26, 1865, of "scurvy."

MILLAR, GEORGE W., Corporal

Resided in Hertford County. Place and date of enlistment not reported. Paroled April 30, 1865. No further records.

MOORE, RICHARD D., Private

Born in Northampton County where he resided as a farmer prior to enlisting in Northampton County at age 22, May 23, 1861. Present or accounted for until discharged on February 8, 1865, by reason of "phthisis pulmonalis."

MOORE, WILLIAM L., Private

Resided in Northampton County where he enlisted at age 37, May 23, 1861. Present or accounted for until discharged on or about May 29, 1862, by reason of "hemoptysis" and/or "rheumatismus."

MULDER, WILLIAM J., Private

Resided in Northampton County and enlisted in Wake County at age 27, July 15, 1862, for the war. Present or accounted for until captured at Hatcher's Run, Virginia, April 2, 1865. Confined at Point Lookout, Maryland, until released on June 29, 1865, after taking the Oath of Allegiance. Records of the Federal Provost Marshal indicate that he was "blind in [the] left eye."

MURFEE, GEORGE R., Sergeant

Resided in Northampton County where he enlisted at age 22, May 23, 1861. Mustered in as Private and promoted to Sergeant on May 2, 1862. Present or accounted for until wounded in the thigh at Malvern Hill, Virginia, July 1, 1862. Returned to duty prior to January 1, 1863, and present or accounted for until transferred to Company H, 19th Regiment N.C. Troops (2nd Regiment N.C. Cavalry) on September 5, 1864, in exchange for Private Hezekiah D. Edwards.

O'BRYAN, JOHN, Private

Resided in Virginia and enlisted at age 27, July 20, 1862, for the war. Deserted the same day.

ODOM, JAMES G., Corporal

Resided in Northampton County where he enlisted at age 20, May 23, 1861. Mustered in as Private and promoted to Corporal on July 10, 1862. Present or accounted for until wounded at Sharpsburg, Maryland, September 17, 1862. Returned to duty on December 10, 1862, and present or accounted for through April, 1863. Company muster roll dated May-June, 1863, indicates he was transferred to the 66th Regiment N.C. Troops; however, records of the 66th Regiment do not indicate that he served therein. No further records.

ODOM, MOORE, Private

Resided in Northampton County and enlisted at age 26, July 15, 1862, for the war. Present or accounted for until he died at Lynchburg, Virginia, on or about September 1, 1862, of disease.

OUTLAND, BENJAMIN T., Private

Resided in Northampton County and enlisted in Wake County at age 25, July 15, 1862, for the war. Present or accounted for until wounded at or near Crampton's Pass, Maryland, September 14, 1862. Reported absent wounded until he was listed as a deserter in

January-February, 1863. Deserted to the enemy on or about June 6, 1863. Confined at Washington, D.C., until released on or about June 24, 1863, after taking the Oath of Allegiance.

PARKER, BENJAMIN FRANKLIN, Private

Born in Northampton County where he resided as a farmer prior to enlisting in Northampton County at age 23, May 23, 1861. Present or accounted for until he died in hospital at Richmond, Virginia, April 21, 1862, of "cont[inued] fever."

PARKER, BENJAMIN P., Private

Resided in Northampton County and enlisted in Wake County at age 20, July 15, 1862, for the war. Present or accounted for until paroled at Keedysville, Maryland, September 20, 1862; however, place and date captured not reported. Paroled again at Winchester, Virginia, October 4, 1862. Rejoined the company prior to January 1, 1863, and present or accounted for until he deserted to the enemy on or about March 27, 1864. Took the Oath of Amnesty at Fort Monroe, Virginia, April 1, 1864.

PARKER, JAMES E., Private

Resided in Northampton County and enlisted in Wake County at age 23, July 15, 1862, for the war. Present or accounted for until paroled at Keedysville, Maryland, September 20, 1862; however, place and date captured not reported. Paroled again at Winchester, Virginia, October 4, 1862. Returned to duty prior to January 1, 1863, and present or accounted for until reported absent without leave from February 8, 1864, through October 31, 1864. Returned to duty prior to April 2, 1865, when he was captured at Hatcher's Run, Virginia. Confined at Point Lookout, Maryland, until released on June 16, 1865, after taking the Oath of Allegiance.

PARKER, JAMES W., Private

Previously served in Company G, 16th Battalion N.C. Cavalry. Transferred to this company on November 28, 1864. No further records.

PARKER, MARCUS L., Private

Resided in Northampton County and enlisted in Rowan County at age 18, May 23, 1861. Present or accounted for until wounded at or near Crampton's Pass, Maryland, September 14, 1862. Returned to duty in January-February, 1863, and present or accounted for until wounded at Bristoe Station, Virginia, October 14, 1863. Returned to duty on October 23, 1863. Present or accounted for until hospitalized at Richmond, Virginia, June 13, 1864, with a gunshot wound of the right leg; however, place and date wounded not reported. Returned to duty on July 11, 1864, and present or accounted for until captured at Hatcher's Run, Virginia, April 2, 1865. Confined at Point Lookout, Maryland, until released on June 16, 1865, after taking the Oath of Allegiance.

PARKER, WILLIAM A., Private

Resided in Northampton County and enlisted in Wake County at age 30, July 15, 1862, for the war. Present or accounted for until he deserted to the enemy on or about March 27, 1864. Released on or about April 1, 1864, after taking the Oath of Amnesty.

PATE, JOHN W., Private

Resided in Northampton County and enlisted in Wake

County at age 28, July 15, 1862, for the war. Present or accounted for until hospitalized at Charlottesville, Virginia, May 10, 1864, with a gunshot wound of the head; however, place and date wounded not reported. Returned to duty on October 6, 1864, and present or accounted for until captured at Hatcher's Run, Virginia, April 2, 1865. Confined at Point Lookout, Maryland, until released on June 16, 1865, after taking the Oath of Allegiance.

PEELE, BENJAMIN E., Private
Resided in Northampton County where he enlisted at age 26, May 23, 1861. Present or accounted for until wounded in the breast at Malvern Hill, Virginia, July 1, 1862. Died in hospital at Richmond, Virginia, July 15, 1862, of wounds.

PEELE, ELBERT J., Private
Resided in Northampton County where he enlisted at age 20, May 23, 1861. Present or accounted for through April, 1864.

PHELPS, ELISHA, Private
Previously served in Company H, 19th Regiment N.C. Troops (2nd Regiment N.C. Cavalry). Transferred to this company on November 1, 1862. Present or accounted for until captured at Old Church, Virginia, or at Totopotomoy Creek, Virginia, June 2, 1864. Confined at Point Lookout, Maryland, until transferred to Elmira, New York, July 12, 1864. Died at Elmira on September 4, 1864, of "chronic diarrhoea and scorbutis."

PHELPS, JOSEPH, Private
Born in Northampton County and resided in Bertie County prior to enlisting in Wake County at age 17, July 15, 1862, for the war. Present or accounted for until wounded at Sharpsburg, Maryland, September 17, 1862. Died at Staunton, Virginia, January 8, 1863, of wounds.

PILAND, BENJAMIN, Private
Resided in Northampton County and enlisted in Wake County at age 20, July 15, 1862, for the war. Present or accounted for until he died in hospital at Danville, Virginia, November 23, 1862, of "pleuritis."

PILAND, JESSE, Private
Resided in Northampton County and enlisted in Wake County at age 30, July 15, 1862, for the war. Present or accounted for until reported absent wounded in September-October, 1864; however, place and date wounded not reported. Reported absent wounded until furloughed for sixty days from hospital at Richmond, Virginia, November 18, 1864.

POWELL, JOHN A., Private
Resided in Northampton County where he enlisted at age 19, May 23, 1861. Present or accounted for until he died near Richmond, Virginia, May 25, 1862, of disease.

POWELL, SOLOMON D., Private
Resided in Northampton County and enlisted at Winchester, Virginia, at age 45, November 1, 1862, for the war. Present or accounted for until paroled at Appomattox Court House, Virginia, April 9, 1865.

PRUDEN, JOHN, Private
Previously served in Company G, 16th Battalion N.C. Cavalry. Transferred to this company on November 28, 1864. No further records.

PRUDEN, NATHANIEL, Private
Resided in Northampton County and enlisted in Wake County at age 33, July 15, 1862, for the war. Present or accounted for through October, 1864.

PRUDEN, SAMUEL T., Private
Resided in Northampton County where he enlisted at age 20, May 23, 1861. Present or accounted for until captured at Hatcher's Run, Virginia, April 2, 1865. Confined at Point Lookout, Maryland, until released on June 17, 1865, after taking the Oath of Allegiance.

RAMSAY, ALLEN D., Private
Resided in Northampton County where he enlisted at age 37, May 23, 1861. Present or accounted for until he died near Yorktown, Virginia, on or about January 15, 1862, of disease.

REESE, WILLIAM H., Private
Resided in Northampton County where he enlisted at age 18, May 23, 1861. Present or accounted for until wounded in the side at Malvern Hill, Virginia, July 1, 1862. Died July 3, 1862, of wounds.

ROGERS, ALBERT, Sergeant
Resided in Northampton County where he enlisted at age 18, May 23, 1861. Mustered in as Corporal and promoted to Sergeant in April, 1862. Present or accounted for until transferred to Company D, 54th Regiment N.C. Troops, July 28, 1862.

ROGERS, JAMES A., Private
Enlisted in Northampton County on May 23, 1861. No further records.

ROSE, GEORGE T., Private
Resided in Northampton County and enlisted in Wake County at age 27, July 15, 1862, for the war. Present or accounted for through October, 1864.

SELDON, JOSEPH N., Private
Enlisted in Rowan County on May 23, 1861. Present or accounted for until paroled at Appomattox Court House, Virginia, April 9, 1865.

SMITH, CHARLES C., Private
Resided in Northampton County where he enlisted at age 33, May 23, 1861. Present or accounted for until transferred to Company H, 19th Regiment N.C. Troops (2nd Regiment N.C. Cavalry), August 20, 1862.

SMITH, JUNIUS B., Private
Born in Northampton County where he resided prior to enlisting in Northampton County at age 22, May 23, 1861. Present or accounted for until "killed by shell" near Petersburg, Virginia, September 21, 1864.

SMITH, SOLOMON, Private
Previously served in Company B, 9th Regiment N.C. State Troops (1st Regiment N.C. Cavalry). Transferred to this company on July 28, 1864. Wounded on or about August 5, 1864; however, battle in which wounded not reported. Reported absent wounded through October, 1864.

SOSBY, JOHN A., Private
Previously served in Mallett's Battalion (Camp Guard). Transferred to this company on April 7, 1863. Present or accounted for until discharged on March 25, 1864, by reason of "amanrosis—dependent upon organic disease of the brain."

SPIVEY, ANDREW B., Corporal

Resided in Northampton County where he enlisted at age 21, May 23, 1861. Mustered in as Private and promoted to Corporal on September 1, 1864. Present or accounted for until captured at Hatcher's Run, Virginia, on or about April 2, 1865. Confined at Point Lookout, Maryland, until released on June 20, 1865, after taking the Oath of Allegiance.

SPIVEY, HENRY T., Private

Born in Northampton County where he resided as a student prior to enlisting in Northampton County at age 22, May 23, 1861. Present or accounted for until he died at Richmond, Virginia, on or about August 5, 1862, of "t[yphoid] fever."

SPIVEY, JESSE T., 1st Sergeant

Born in Northampton County where he resided prior to enlisting in Northampton County at age 24, May 23, 1861. Mustered in as Private and promoted to 1st Sergeant in May, 1862. Present or accounted for until wounded in the head at Malvern Hill, Virginia, July 1, 1862. Returned to duty on May 14, 1863, and present or accounted for until he died "at home" on July 8, 1864, of disease.

SPIVEY, JOHN W., Private

Previously served in Company B, 9th Regiment N.C. State Troops (1st Regiment N.C. Cavalry). Transferred to this company in January-February, 1864, and present or accounted for through October, 1864.

SPIVEY, JOSEPH M., Private

Previously served in Company H, 19th Regiment N.C. Troops (2nd Regiment N.C. Cavalry). Transferred to this company on October 29, 1863, in exchange for Private Henderson Randolph Deloatch. Present or accounted for through October, 1864.

SQUIRES, JUNIUS A., Private

Born in Northampton County where he resided as a student prior to enlisting in Northampton County at age 20, May 23, 1861. Present or accounted for until discharged on June 25, 1862, by reason of disability.

STEPHENSON, AMOS, Jr., Private

Resided in Northampton County where he enlisted at age 29, May 23, 1861. Present or accounted for until paroled at Appomattox Court House, Virginia, April 9, 1865.

STEPHENSON, CHARLES N., Corporal

Born in Northampton County where he resided prior to enlisting in Northampton County at age 24, May 23, 1861. Mustered in as Corporal. Present or accounted for until wounded at Malvern Hill, Virginia, July 1, 1862. Returned to duty prior to September 14, 1862, when he was wounded at or near Crampton's Pass, Maryland. Company muster rolls indicate that he was also captured at Crampton's Pass; however, records of the Federal Provost Marshal do not substantiate that report. Rejoined the company on March 1, 1863, and present or accounted for until he died "at home" on April 9, 1864, of disease.

STEPHENSON, JAMES A., Private

Resided in Northampton County where he enlisted at age 30, May 23, 1861. Present or accounted for until discharged on or about April 27, 1863, after providing a substitute. His substitute was found to be "unlawful" and Private Stephenson was ordered to return to duty;

however, he failed to rejoin the company and was reported absent without leave from September-October, 1863, through October, 1864.

STEPHENSON, JAMES D., Private

Previously served in Company H, 19th Regiment N.C. Troops (2nd Regiment N.C. Cavalry). Transferred to this company on September 1, 1862. Present or accounted for until hospitalized at Richmond, Virginia, September 12, 1862, with a gunshot wound of the breast; however, place and date wounded not reported. Returned to duty prior to January 1, 1863, and present or accounted for until he died "at home" on March 4, 1864, of disease.

STEPHENSON, JOHN T., Private

Resided in Northampton County where he enlisted at age 28, May 23, 1861. Present or accounted for until he died at Yorktown, Virginia, January 4, 1862, of disease.

STEPHENSON, JOSEPH E., Sergeant

Resided in Northampton County where he enlisted at age 24, May 23, 1861. Mustered in as Private. Present or accounted for until wounded at Sharpsburg, Maryland, September 17, 1862. Returned to duty prior to January 1, 1863, and was promoted to Sergeant on September 1, 1864. Present or accounted for until paroled on April 25, 1865.

STEPHENSON, JUNIUS E., Corporal

Resided in Northampton County where he enlisted at age 23, May 23, 1861. Mustered in as Private and promoted to Corporal on September 1, 1864. Present or accounted for until captured in hospital at Richmond, Virginia, April 3, 1865. "Left [the] hosp[ita]l without permission" on April 26, 1865.

STEPHENSON, LORENZO J. W., Sergeant

Resided in Northampton County where he enlisted at age 21, May 23, 1861. Mustered in as Private and promoted to Sergeant on September 20, 1862. Present or accounted for through June 25, 1864.

STEPHENSON, PATRICK H., Sergeant

Resided in Northampton County where he enlisted at age 27, May 23, 1861. Mustered in as Sergeant. Present or accounted for until wounded at Malvern Hill, Virginia, July 1, 1862. Returned to duty on or about December 1, 1862, and present or accounted for through October, 1864.

STEPHENSON, ROBERT P., Private

Resided in Northampton County where he enlisted at age 33, May 23, 1861. Present or accounted for until paroled at Appomattox Court House, Virginia, April 9, 1865.

STEPHENSON, WILLIAM W., Private

Resided in Northampton County where he enlisted at age 29, May 23, 1861. Present or accounted for until discharged on June 13, 1862, by reason of being a railroad agent.

STORK, JOHN J., Private

Place and date of enlistment not reported. Records of the Federal Provost Marshal indicate he was captured at Mine Run, Virginia, May 6, 1864, and confined at Elmira, New York, until paroled on March 2, 1865, and transferred for exchange. No further records.

SUMNER, ISAAC, Private

Resided in Hertford County and enlisted in Wake

County at age 21. Enlistment date reported as July 15, 1862; however, he was not listed on the rolls of this company until May-June, 1863. Present or accounted for until wounded at Bristoe Station, Virginia, October 14, 1863. Returned to duty on November 7, 1863, and present or accounted for through October, 1864. [Company records indicate he served previously in the "12 N.C. Battn" and was transferred to this company on May 11, 1863, in exchange for Corporal James G. Odom; however, records of the 12th Battalion do not indicate that he or Odom served therein.]

SYKES, JOHN FLOYD, Private
Resided in Northampton County where he enlisted at age 21, May 23, 1861. Present or accounted for until discharged on February 28, 1863, by reason of physical disability.

TAYLOR, HENRY E., Private
Resided in Northampton County where he enlisted at age 19, May 23, 1861. Present or accounted for until transferred to Company H, 19th Regiment N.C. Troops (2nd Regiment N.C. Cavalry), November 1, 1862.

TAYLOR, RICHARD M., Private
Born in Virginia and resided in Northampton County where he enlisted at age 19, May 23, 1861. Present or accounted for until he died at Suffolk, Virginia, April 1, 1862, of disease.

VAUGHAN, TIMOTHY, Private
Resided in Northampton County and enlisted in Wake County at age 28, July 15, 1862, for the war. Present or accounted for until wounded at Sharpsburg, Maryland, September 17, 1862. Returned to duty prior to January 1, 1863, and present or accounted for until wounded at Bristoe Station, Virginia, October 14, 1863. Reported absent wounded until he was reported absent without leave on January 18, 1864. Listed as a deserter in March-April, 1864. Deserted to the enemy on February 15, 1865, and took the Oath of Allegiance on or about March 1, 1865.

VINSON, GEORGE B., Private
Resided in Northampton County where he enlisted at age 17, May 23, 1861. Present or accounted for until reported absent without leave on December 1, 1862. Returned to duty on February 20, 1863, and present or accounted for until reported absent without leave on February 11, 1864. Furloughed from an unspecified hospital on June 23, 1864. Transferred to Company G, 16th Battalion N.C. Cavalry, November 28, 1864.

WADE, JAMES C., 1st Sergeant
Resided in Northampton County where he enlisted at age 21, May 23, 1861. Mustered in as Private and promoted to Sergeant on February 4, 1863. Promoted to 1st Sergeant on September 1, 1864. Present or accounted for through October, 1864.

WHEELER, RICHARD THOMAS, Private
Born in Northampton County where he resided. Was a midshipman at the U.S. Naval Academy but resigned when North Carolina seceded from the Union. Enlisted in Northampton County at age 22, May 23, 1861. Present or accounted for until captured at or near Crampton's Pass, Maryland, September 14, 1862. Confined at Fort Delaware, Delaware, until transferred to Aiken's Landing, James River, Virginia,

October 2, 1862, for exchange. Declared exchanged at Aiken's Landing on November 10, 1862. Rejoined the company prior to January 1, 1863. Present or accounted for until hospitalized at Richmond, Virginia, July 30, 1864, with a shell wound of the face; however, place and date wounded not reported. Returned to duty on October 8, 1864, and present or accounted for through October 31, 1864.

WHEELER, SION B., Private
Born in Northampton County where he resided as a farmer prior to enlisting in Northampton County at age 33, May 23, 1861. Present or accounted for until captured at Hatcher's Run, Virginia, April 2, 1865. Confined at Point Lookout, Maryland, until released on June 30, 1865, after taking the Oath of Allegiance.

WOOD, AUGUSTUS M., Private
Resided in Northampton County where he enlisted at age 27, May 23, 1861. Mustered in as Sergeant but was reduced to ranks in September, 1861-May, 1862. Present or accounted for until he was "accidentally shot" at or near Lee's Mill, Virginia, on or about April 16, 1862. Died of wounds prior to May 1, 1862. Place and exact date of death not reported.

COMPANY B

This company, known as the Monroe Light Infantry, was from Union County and enlisted at Monroe on May 3, 1861. It was mustered in and assigned to this regiment as Company B. After joining the regiment the company functioned as a part of the regiment, and its history for the war period is recorded as a part of the regimental history.

The information contained in the following roster of the company was compiled principally from company muster rolls for June 10-August, 1861; November, 1862-April, 1864; and September-October, 1864. No company muster rolls were found for September, 1861-October, 1862; May-August, 1864; or for the period after October, 1864. In addition to the company muster rolls, Roll of Honor records, receipt rolls, hospital records, prisoner of war records, and other primary records, supplemented by state pension applications, United Daughters of the Confederacy records, and postwar rosters and histories, all provided useful information.

OFFICERS

CAPTAINS

MacRAE, WILLIAM
Born in New Hanover County and resided in Union County where he was by occupation a civil engineer prior to enlisting in Union County at age 26. Mustered in as Private and was appointed Captain to rank from May 1, 1861. Present or accounted for until promoted to Lieutenant Colonel on May 2, 1862, and transferred to the Field and Staff of this regiment.

JEROME, ROBERT P.
Resided in Union County where he enlisted at age 21. Appointed 2nd Lieutenant to rank from May 11, 1861, and was elected Captain on May 2, 1862. Present or

accounted for until promoted to Major on November 4, 1864, and transferred to the Field and Staff of this regiment.

LIEUTENANTS

COON, BENJAMIN G., 2nd Lieutenant
Resided in Davie County and enlisted in Union County at age 19, May 3, 1861. Mustered in as Corporal. Present or accounted for until wounded at Lee's Mill, Virginia, April 16, 1862. Returned to duty prior to January 1, 1863, and was promoted to Corporal on March 4, 1863. Promoted to 1st Sergeant on June 4, 1863. Present or accounted for until wounded in the right thigh at Bristoe Station, Virginia, October 14, 1863. Returned to duty on January 26, 1864, and was appointed 2nd Lieutenant on April 2, 1864. Present or accounted for until retired to the Invalid Corps on or about November 29, 1864.

CUTHBERTSON, DAVID GREEN, 3rd Lieutenant
Resided in Union County where he enlisted at age 21, May 3, 1861. Mustered in as Sergeant and promoted to 1st Sergeant on May 2, 1862. Present or accounted for until wounded in the back at or near Crampton's Pass, Maryland, September 14, 1862. Returned to duty in January-February, 1863, and was appointed 3rd Lieutenant on June 4, 1863. Present or accounted for until killed at Bristoe Station, Virginia, October 14, 1863.

HOLMES, LEANDER A., 2nd Lieutenant
Resided in Union County where he enlisted at age 26. Appointed 2nd Lieutenant to rank from May 11, 1861. Present or accounted for until wounded at Lee's Mill, Virginia, April 16, 1862. Defeated for reelection when the regiment was reorganized on May 2, 1862.

HOUSTON, ALEXANDER H., 1st Lieutenant
Resided in Lincoln County. Appointed 1st Lieutenant on or about May 21, 1862. Present or accounted for until wounded at Malvern Hill, Virginia, July 1, 1862. Returned to duty prior to January 1, 1863, and was reported on detail as Acting Adjutant of the regiment from January-February, 1863, through April, 1863. Promoted to Adjutant (1st Lieutenant) on April 30, 1863, to rank from October 1, 1862, and permanently transferred to the Field and Staff of this regiment.

McLARTY, JAMES M., 1st Lieutenant
Resided in Union County where he enlisted at age 21, May 3, 1861. Mustered in as 1st Sergeant and was appointed 2nd Lieutenant to rank from May 2, 1862. Present or accounted for until captured at or near Crampton's Pass, Maryland, on or about September 14, 1862. Confined at Fort Delaware, Delaware, until transferred to Aiken's Landing, James River, Virginia, October 2, 1862, for exchange. Declared exchanged at Aiken's Landing on November 10, 1862. Rejoined the company prior to March 1, 1863, and was promoted to 1st Lieutenant on June 17, 1864. Present or accounted for until paroled at Appomattox Court House, Virginia, April 9, 1865.

MEANS, THEOPHILUS H., 1st Lieutenant
Resided in Mecklenburg County and enlisted in Union County at age 26. Elected 1st Lieutenant on or about May 11, 1861. Present or accounted for until he was defeated for reelection when the regiment was reorganized on May 2, 1862.

ROGERS, FRANKLIN L., 1st Lieutenant
Resided in Union County where he enlisted at age 26, May 3, 1861. Mustered in as Corporal and was appointed 2nd Lieutenant on May 2, 1862. Present or accounted for until wounded in the shoulder and the index finger of the left hand at Malvern Hill, Virginia, July 1, 1862. Returned to duty prior to March 1, 1863, and was promoted to 1st Lieutenant on June 4, 1863. Present or accounted for until wounded in the left arm at Bristoe Station, Virginia, October 14, 1863. Left arm amputated. Reported absent wounded until retired to the Invalid Corps on June 17, 1864.

NONCOMMISSIONED OFFICERS AND PRIVATES

ALBERRON, JAMES, Private
Resided in Caswell County and enlisted on July 15, 1862, for the war. Present or accounted for until mortally wounded at Fredericksburg, Virginia, December 13, 1862. Place and exact date of death not reported.

ALEXANDER, SAMUEL M., Private
Resided in Union County where he enlisted at age 24, May 3, 1861. Present or accounted for until wounded in the ankle at Fredericksburg, Virginia, December 13, 1862. Returned to duty in January-February, 1863, and present or accounted for until paroled at Farmville, Virginia, April 11-21, 1865.

ALEXANDER, WILSON W., Private
Resided in Union County where he enlisted at age 23, May 3, 1861. Present or accounted for until wounded at Malvern Hill, Virginia, July 1, 1862. Returned to duty prior to January 1, 1863, and present or accounted for until paroled at Appomattox Court House, Virginia, April 9, 1865.

ASKEW, JOSEPH, Private
Place and date of enlistment not reported. Died in hospital at Weldon on February 4, 1865, of a gunshot wound. Place and date wounded not reported.

AUSTIN, HARVEY L., Private
Resided in Union County where he enlisted at age 21, May 3, 1861. Present or accounted for until wounded at Malvern Hill, Virginia, July 1, 1862. Returned to duty prior to January 1, 1863, and present or accounted for through October, 1864.

AUSTIN, JAMES E., Private
Resided in Union County where he enlisted at age 23, June 24, 1861. Present or accounted for until transferred to Company I, 48th Regiment N.C. Troops, December 29, 1862.

AUSTIN, JOHN E. W., Private
Resided in Union County where he enlisted on June 18, 1861. Present or accounted for until wounded at Malvern Hill, Virginia, July 1, 1862. Discharged December 31, 1862, after providing Private Henry W. Moser as a substitute.

AUSTIN, JOHN M., Corporal
Resided in Union County where he enlisted at age 24, May 3, 1861. Mustered in as Private. Present or

accounted for until wounded at Bristoe Station, Virginia, October 14, 1863. Returned to duty in November, 1863, and was promoted to Corporal in May-October, 1864. Present or accounted for through October, 1864.

AUSTIN, THOMAS ALLEN, Private
Resided in Union County where he enlisted at age 22, May 3, 1861. Present or accounted for until transferred to Company I, 48th Regiment N.C. Troops, March 1, 1863.

AUSTIN, WADE H., Private
Resided in Union County where he enlisted at age 23, May 3, 1861. Present or accounted for until he died at Fort Grafton on February 25, 1862, of disease.

BAKER, JOHN G., Private
Resided in Union County where he enlisted at age 19, May 3, 1861. Present or accounted for until wounded in the knee at Fredericksburg, Virginia, December 13, 1862. Died in hospital at Richmond, Virginia, February 12, 1863, of wounds.

BARINAU, FREDERICK R., Private
Born at "Williamsburg" and resided in Union County where he was by occupation a farmer prior to enlisting in Union County at age 24, May 3, 1861. Present or accounted for until wounded in the left arm at Lee's Mill, Virginia, April 16, 1862. Reported absent wounded until discharged on or about February 13, 1863, by reason of wounds received at Lee's Mill.

BARKER, GEORGE W., Private
Resided in Union County where he enlisted at age 21, May 3, 1861. Present or accounted for until wounded in the right ankle at Bristoe Station, Virginia, October 14, 1863. Returned to duty in December, 1863, and present or accounted for until captured at or near Hatcher's Run, Virginia, March 31, 1865. Confined at Point Lookout, Maryland, until released on June 23, 1865, after taking the Oath of Allegiance.

BARNES, J. A., Private
Place and date of enlistment not reported. Captured in hospital at Richmond, Virginia, April 3, 1865. No further records.

BECKETT, JAMES S., Private
Resided in Union County where he enlisted at age 26, May 3, 1861. Mustered in as Corporal but was reduced to ranks and detailed as a courier on December 29, 1862. Present or accounted for until paroled at Appomattox Court House, Virginia, April 9, 1865.

BENTON, JAMES W., Private
Born in Union County* where he resided prior to enlisting in Union County at age 21, May 3, 1861. Present or accounted for until wounded at Malvern Hill, Virginia, July 1, 1862. Returned to duty prior to January 1, 1863, and present or accounted for until he died on June 11, 1864, of wounds. Place and date wounded and place of death not reported.

BERMINGHAM, THOMAS, Private
Resided in Union County where he enlisted at age 23, May 3, 1861. Present or accounted for until wounded in the arm and shoulder at Fredericksburg, Virginia, December 13, 1862. Returned to duty prior to January 1, 1863, and present or accounted for until he deserted to the enemy on or about November 30, 1864.

Released on or about December 5, 1864, after taking the Oath of Amnesty.

BIRMINGHAM, JOHN REUBEN, Private
Previously served in Company A, 46th Regiment N.C. Troops. Transferred to this company on May 1, 1863, in exchange for Private Henry W. Moser. Present or accounted for until captured at Bristoe Station, Virginia, October 14, 1863. Confined at Old Capitol Prison, Washington, D.C., until transferred to Point Lookout, Maryland, October 27, 1863. Refused to be exchanged and was last reported at Point Lookout on April 7, 1865. No further records.

BOGAN, I. C., _____
Place and date of enlistment not reported. Wounded and captured at or near Warrenton, Virginia, on or about September 29, 1862. Leg amputated. Paroled September 29, 1862.

BOSWELL, HOWELL, Private
Resided in Caswell County and enlisted in Wake County on July 15, 1862, for the war. Present or accounted for until wounded at or near Crampton's Pass, Maryland, September 14, 1862. Returned to duty on February 28, 1863. Present or accounted for through February 28, 1865; however, he was reported absent on detail as a laborer or as a forage master during most of that period.

BROOKS, CALVIN H., Private
Resided in Union County where he enlisted at age 18, May 3, 1861. Present or accounted for until captured at or near Crampton's Pass, Maryland, September 14, 1862. Confined at Fort Delaware, Delaware, until transferred to Aiken's Landing, James River, Virginia, October 2, 1862, for exchange. Declared exchanged at Aiken's Landing on November 10, 1862. Returned to duty prior to January 1, 1863, and present or accounted for through October, 1864.

BROOKS, CULLIN C., Private
Resided in Union County where he enlisted on July 6, 1861. Present or accounted for until discharged on August 20, 1862, under the provisions of the Conscript Act.

BROOM, ELLERSON L., Private
Resided in Union County where he enlisted at age 19, May 3, 1861. Present or accounted for until wounded in the head at Fredericksburg, Virginia, December 13, 1862. Returned to duty in January-February, 1863, and present or accounted for until transferred to the C.S. Navy on April 1, 1864.

BROOM, LOYD, Private
Resided in Union County where he enlisted at age 19, May 3, 1861. Present or accounted for until wounded in the head at Malvern Hill, Virginia, July 1, 1862. Company records indicate that he died; however, place, date, and cause of death not reported.

BROOM, WILLIAM H., Private
Born in Union County* where he resided as a farmer prior to enlisting in Union County at age 22, May 3, 1861. Present or accounted for until wounded at Malvern Hill, Virginia, July 1, 1862. Died at Fredericksburg, Virginia, December 24, 1862, of disease.

CEHEN, JASON, Private
Born in Union County* where he resided as a miner

prior to enlisting in Union County at age 22, May 3, 1861. Present or accounted for until wounded at Malvern Hill, Virginia, July 1, 1862. Died at Lynchburg, Virginia, on or about December 16, 1862, of "diarrhoea."

CEHEN, WILLIAM, Private
Resided in Union County where he enlisted at age 56, May 3, 1861. Present or accounted for until discharged on August 20, 1862, by reason of being over age.

CHAPMAN, GEORGE, Private
Resided in Union County where he enlisted at age 21, May 3, 1861. Present or accounted for until he died in hospital at Richmond, Virginia, December 16, 1862, of "typhoid fever."

CLARK, AMZI T., Sergeant
Resided in Union County where he enlisted at age 19, May 3, 1861. Mustered in as Corporal and promoted to Sergeant on May 20, 1862. Present or accounted for until wounded at Malvern Hill, Virginia, July 1, 1862. Returned to duty prior to January 1, 1863, and present or accounted for until he died in Union County on or about March 14, 1863, of "pneumonia."

CLONTZ, JEREMIAH, Private
Resided in Union County where he enlisted on June 24, 1861. Present or accounted for until discharged in August, 1862, under the provisions of the Conscript Act.

CONDER, ELIAS C., Private
Resided in Union County where he enlisted at age 23, May 3, 1861. Present or accounted for until he died at Yorktown, Virginia, September 4, 1861, of disease.

CONDER, WILLIAM, Private
Resided in Union County and enlisted at Yorktown, Virginia, December 17, 1861. Present or accounted for until captured at Bristoe Station, Virginia, October 14, 1863. Confined at Old Capitol Prison, Washington, D.C., until transferred to Point Lookout, Maryland, October 27, 1863. Died at Point Lookout on February 19, 1864, of disease.

CONNER, WILLIAM, Private
Name appears on a regimental record dated May, 1862, which states that he enlisted in this company. No further records.

CRAIG, JAMES A., Private
Resided in Union County where he enlisted at age 23, May 3, 1861. Present or accounted for until paroled at Appomattox Court House, Virginia, April 9, 1865.

CRAIGE, JOHN T., Private
Resided in Union County and enlisted at Taylorsville, Virginia, at age 18, August 1, 1863, for the war. Present or accounted for until paroled at Appomattox Court House, Virginia, April 9, 1865.

CUTCHESON, F. Private
Place and date of enlistment not reported. Reported sick in hospital at Williamsburg, Virginia, in April, 1862. No further records.

CUTHBERTSON, WILLIAM F., Private
Resided in Union County and enlisted at Yorktown, Virginia, August 29, 1862, for the war. Present or accounted for until wounded at Lee's Mill, Virginia, April 16, 1862. Returned to duty prior to September 14, 1862, when he was captured at or near Crampton's

Pass, Maryland. Confined at Fort Delaware, Delaware, until transferred to Aiken's Landing, James River, Virginia, October 2, 1862, for exchange. Declared exchanged at Aiken's Landing on November 10, 1862. Reported absent without leave on or about November 8, 1862. Company records do not indicate whether he returned to duty; however, he was transferred to Company I, 48th Regiment N.C. Troops, August 7, 1863.

DANIEL, DRUREY M., Private
Resided in Caswell County and enlisted in Wake County on July 15, 1862, for the war. Present or accounted for until he was "sent to hospital" in August, 1862. Never rejoined the company and was dropped from the rolls on or about September 1, 1863, because he was "supposed to be dead."

DOSTER, JOHN R., Private
Born in Union County* where he resided prior to enlisting in Union County at age 24, May 3, 1861. Present or accounted for until he died in hospital at Staunton, Virginia, May 30, 1864, of wounds. Place and date wounded not reported.

EVANS, HARRISON, Private
Resided in Caswell County and enlisted in Wake County on July 15, 1862, for the war. Present or accounted for until he was "sent to hospital" in August, 1862. Reported absent sick until he was dropped from the rolls on or about September 1, 1863, because he was "supposed to be dead."

FORBIS, HUGH M., Private
Resided in Mecklenburg County. Place and date of enlistment not reported. Captured at or near Burgess' Mill, Virginia, April 2, 1865. Confined at Hart's Island, New York Harbor, until released on June 18, 1865, after taking the Oath of Allegiance.

FORBIS, JOHN H., Corporal
Resided in Union County where he enlisted at age 26, May 3, 1861. Mustered in as Private. Present or accounted for until wounded at Sharpsburg, Maryland, September 17, 1862. Returned to duty in January-February, 1863, and was promoted to Corporal on December 1, 1863. Present or accounted for through April, 1864.

FORBIS, RICHARD C., Private
Resided in Union County where he enlisted at age 23, May 3, 1861. Present or accounted for until wounded in the breast at Fredericksburg, Virginia, December 13, 1862. Returned to duty prior to March 1, 1863, and present or accounted for until paroled at Appomattox Court House, Virginia, April 9, 1865.

FORD, ELMORE, Private
Resided in Union County where he enlisted at age 28, May 3, 1861. Present or accounted for until he died in hospital at Richmond, Virginia, October 29, 1863, of "typhoid fever."

FREEMAN, CHARLES J., Private
Resided in Union County and enlisted at Yorktown, Virginia, October 14, 1861. Present or accounted for until wounded in the head at Fredericksburg, Virginia, December 13, 1862. Returned to duty in March-April, 1863, and present or accounted for until wounded in the right hand on or about May 22, 1863; however, battle in which wounded not reported. Reported

absent wounded or absent on light duty until paroled at Lynchburg, Virginia, April 15, 1865.

FREEMAN, JAMES S., Corporal
Resided in Union County and was by occupation a farmer prior to enlisting in Union County at age 19, May 3, 1861. Mustered in as Private and promoted to Corporal on May 20, 1862. Present or accounted for until wounded in the left thigh and captured at Crampton's Pass, Maryland, September 14, 1862. Hospitalized at Burkittsville, Maryland, until transferred to Fort McHenry, Maryland. Exchanged at City Point, Virginia, on or about November 21, 1862. Reported absent wounded until discharged on or about April 1, 1863, by reason of wounds received at Crampton's Pass.

GORDON, GEORGE N., Sergeant
Resided in Union County where he enlisted at age 25, May 3, 1861. Mustered in as Private and promoted to Sergeant on May 20, 1862. Present or accounted for through October, 1864.

GREEN, JACOB P., Private
Resided in Union County where he enlisted at age 19, May 3, 1861. Present or accounted for until wounded at Malvern Hill, Virginia, July 1, 1862. Transferred to Company I, 48th Regiment N.C. Troops, December 9, 1862.

GRIFFIN, ELISHA W., Private
Resided in Union County where he enlisted at age 18, May 3, 1861. Present or accounted for until wounded at Malvern Hill, Virginia, July 1, 1862. Returned to duty prior to December 13, 1862, when he was wounded in the thigh at Fredericksburg, Virginia. Reported absent wounded until retired to the Invalid Corps on October 19, 1864, by reason of "t[otal] d[isability]."

HAWKINS, JOHN, Private
Resided in Union County and enlisted on July 15, 1862, for the war. Present or accounted for until wounded at or near Crampton's Pass, Maryland, September 14, 1862. Died "at home" on November 5, 1862, of wounds and/or disease.

HELMS, ARCHIBALD B., Sergeant
Resided in Union County where he enlisted at age 23, May 3, 1861. Mustered in as Sergeant. Present or accounted for until wounded at Lee's Mill, Virginia, April 16, 1862. Died May 4, 1862, of wounds. Place of death not reported.

HELMS, CALVIN, Private
Resided in Union County where he enlisted at age 21, May 3, 1861. Present or accounted for until paroled at Appomattox Court House, Virginia, April 9, 1865.

HELMS, GEORGE A., Private
Resided in Union County where he enlisted at age 22, May 3, 1861. Present or accounted for until he died near Yorktown, Virginia, September 6, 1861, of disease.

HELMS, JESSE D., Private
Resided in Union County and was by occupation a farmer prior to enlisting in Union County at age 18, May 3, 1861. Present or accounted for until wounded in the left leg at or near Crampton's Pass, Maryland, September 14, 1862. Company records indicate he was also captured on that date; however, records of the

Federal Provost Marshal do not substantiate that report. Returned to duty in March-April, 1863, and present or accounted for until captured at Bristoe Station, Virginia, October 14, 1863. Confined at Old Capitol Prison, Washington, D.C., until transferred to Point Lookout, Maryland, October 27, 1863. Released on May 15, 1865, after taking the Oath of Allegiance.

HELMS, JOHN A., Private
Resided in Union County where he enlisted at age 22, May 3, 1861. Present or accounted for until wounded at Sharpsburg, Maryland, September 17, 1862. Returned to duty prior to January 1, 1863, and present or accounted for until paroled at Lynchburg, Virginia, April 15, 1865.

HELMS, JOSEPH E., Corporal
Resided in Union County and was by occupation a teacher prior to enlisting in Union County at age 24, May 3, 1861. Mustered in as Private. Present or accounted for until wounded at Malvern Hill, Virginia, July 1, 1862. Returned to duty prior to January 1, 1863, and was promoted to Corporal on April 4, 1863. Present or accounted for until wounded in the thigh at Bristoe Station, Virginia, October 14, 1863. Died in hospital at Richmond, Virginia, November 8, 1863, of wounds.

HEYLAR, W. F., Private
Enlisted near Orange Court House, Virginia, March 4, 186[4]. Died in hospital at Gordonsville, Virginia, April 7, 1864, of disease.

HINKLE, DAVID, Private
Place and date of enlistment not reported. Paroled at Greensboro on or about May 8, 1865.

HINSON, FRANCIS M., Private
Resided in Union County and was by occupation a butcher prior to enlisting in Union County at age 26, May 3, 1861. Present or accounted for until he deserted to the enemy on or about November 30, 1864. Released on or about December 7, 1864, after taking the Oath of Amnesty.

HOUSTON, HUGH W., Private
Resided in Union County where he enlisted on June 18, 1861. Present or accounted for until wounded at Malvern Hill, Virginia, July 1, 1862. Discharged on August 20, 1862, under the provisions of the Conscript Act. Later served in Company C, 10th Battalion N.C. Heavy Artillery.

HOWARD, AMZI, Private
Resided in Union County where he enlisted at age 22, May 3, 1861. Present or accounted for until he was "sent to hospital" on or about October 9, 1863. Never rejoined the company. No further records.

HOWARD, ISAAC N., Private
Resided in Union County where he enlisted at age 25, May 3, 1861. Present or accounted for until wounded at or near Crampton's Pass, Maryland, September 14, 1862. Returned to duty on or about December 19, 1862, and present or accounted for until wounded in the abdomen at Bristoe Station, Virginia, October 14, 1863. Reported absent wounded or absent on light duty through March, 1864.

HOWARD, WILLIAM A., Private
Enlisted in Union County. Enlistment date reported as May 3, 1861; however, he was not listed on the rolls of

this company until January-February, 1864. Present or accounted for until hospitalized at Danville, Virginia, April 3, 1865, with a gunshot wound of the right leg; however, place and date wounded not reported. Furloughed for sixty days on April 9, 1865, and was paroled at Charlotte on May 3, 1865.

IRBY, JULIUS A., Private
Resided in Union County where he enlisted at age 18, May 3, 1861. Present or accounted for until wounded at Bristoe Station, Virginia, October 14, 1863. Returned to duty in January-February, 1864, and present or accounted for until captured at Hatcher's Run, Virginia, April 2, 1865. Confined at Hart's Island, New York Harbor, until released June 19-20, 1865, after taking the Oath of Allegiance.

IRBY, ROBERT G., Private
Resided in Union County where he enlisted at age 20, May 3, 1861. Present or accounted for until captured at Hatcher's Run, Virginia, April 2, 1865. Confined at Hart's Island, New York Harbor, until released June 19-20, 1865, after taking the Oath of Allegiance.

JACKSON, ANDREW, Private
Resided in Union County and enlisted in Wake County on July 15, 1862, for the war. Present or accounted for until captured at Crampton's Pass, Maryland, September 14, 1862. Confined at Fort Delaware, Delaware, until transferred to Aiken's Landing, James River, Virginia, October 2, 1862, for exchange. Furloughed for sixty days on or about October 24, 1862, and was reported absent without leave on December 24, 1862. Never rejoined the company. Died prior to October 5, 1863. Place, cause, and exact date of death not reported.

JEROME, JAMES A., Private
Born in Union County* where he resided as a farmer prior to enlisting in Union County at age 24, May 3, 1861. Present or accounted for until wounded at Malvern Hill, Virginia, July 1, 1862. Returned to duty prior to January 1, 1863, but was discharged on February 1, 1863, by reason of "frequent and aggravated attacks of epilepsy."

KENOUSE, JESSE, Private
Resided in Union County and enlisted in Wake County on July 15, 1862, for the war. Present or accounted for until reported absent without leave on May 4, 1863. Returned to duty in September, 1863, but was discharged "by civil authority" on October 14, 1863. Paroled at Greensboro on May 9, 1865.

KEZIAH, AZER, Private
Resided in Union County where he enlisted at age 22, May 3, 1861. Present or accounted for until he died near Yorktown, Virginia, September 6, 1861, of disease.

KEZIAH, ROBERSON, Private
Resided in Union County where he enlisted at age 21, May 3, 1861. Present or accounted for until killed at Malvern Hill, Virginia, July 1, 1862.

KEZIAH, SAMUEL B., Private
Resided in Union County where he enlisted at age 19, May 3, 1861. Present or accounted for until hospitalized at Richmond, Virginia, May 17, 1864, with a gunshot wound; however, place and date wounded not reported. Returned to duty prior to

November 1, 1864, and present or accounted for until captured at Hatcher's Run, Virginia, April 2, 1865. Confined at Hart's Island, New York Harbor, until released June 19-20, 1865, after taking the Oath of Allegiance.

KING, CHARLES H., Private
Resided in Union County where he enlisted at age 21, May 3, 1861. Present or accounted for until admitted to hospital at Richmond, Virginia, June 4, 1864, with a gunshot wound; however, place and date wounded not reported. Returned to duty prior to October 9, 1864, when he was "sent to hospital." Paroled at Charlotte on May 15, 1865.

KNOTTS, HARRISON B., Private
Resided in Union County where he enlisted at age 20, May 3, 1861. Present or accounted for until wounded in the wrist or left arm at Fredericksburg, Virginia, December 13, 1862. Returned to duty in January-February, 1863, and present or accounted for until paroled at Appomattox Court House, Virginia, April 9, 1865.

LEE, SAMUEL, Private
Enlisted in Wake County on July 15, 1862, for the war. Present or accounted for through October, 1864.

LEMMOND, WILLIAM H., Private
Resided in Union County where he enlisted at age 18, May 3, 1861. Present or accounted for until wounded in September, 1862; however, battle in which wounded not reported. Returned to duty in January-February, 1863. Present or accounted for until hospitalized at Richmond, Virginia, July 11, 1863, with a gunshot wound of the back; however, place and date wounded not reported. Reported absent wounded or absent on detail until he returned to duty in January-February, 1864. Present or accounted for until hospitalized at Danville, Virginia, on or about June 16, 1864, with a gunshot wound of the hand; however, place and date wounded not reported. Reported absent wounded or absent on furlough through October, 1864. Paroled at Charlotte on May 3, 1865.

LEONARD, STEPHEN S., Private
Enlisted in Wake County on July 15, 1862, for the war. Present or accounted for until reported absent without leave on July 1, 1863. Returned to duty in January-February, 1864, and present or accounted for through October, 1864.

LITTLE, JAMES H., Private
Resided in Union County where he enlisted on June 18, 1861. Present or accounted for until hospitalized at Charlotte on June 10, 1864, with a gunshot wound; however, place and date wounded not reported. Returned to duty on August 16, 1864, and present or accounted for through March 2, 1865.

LITTLE, MICHAEL, Private
Resided in Union County where he enlisted at age 50, May 3, 1861. Present or accounted for until discharged on August 20, 1862, by reason of being over age.

LONG, DAVID G., Private
Enlisted in Union County on May 3, 1861. Died June 27, 1861. Place and cause of death not reported.

LONG, ISRAEL B., 1st Sergeant
Resided in Union County where he enlisted at age 23, May 3, 1861. Mustered in as Sergeant. Present or

accounted for until wounded at Bristoe Station, Virginia, October 14, 1863. Returned to duty on March 11, 1864, and was promoted to 1st Sergeant in May-October, 1864. Present or accounted for through October, 1864.

LONG, JOHN C., Private
Resided in Union County where he enlisted on June 24, 1861. Present or accounted for until wounded in the hand at Fredericksburg, Virginia, December 13, 1862. Returned to duty in March-April, 1863, and present or accounted for until transferred to Company K, 27th Regiment N.C. Troops, March 5, 1864.

LONG, JOHN G., Private
Resided in Union County and enlisted on June 18, 1861. Died in hospital at Danville, Virginia, August 11, 1862, of "typhoid fever" or wounds received at the battle of Lee's Mill, Virginia, April 16, 1862.

LONG, REUBEN H., Private
Resided in Union County where he enlisted on June 24, 1861. Present or accounted for until killed at Malvern Hill, Virginia, July 1, 1862.

LONG, WILLIAM GREEN, Corporal
Resided in Union County where he enlisted on June 18, 1861. Mustered in as Private. Present or accounted for until wounded at Malvern Hill, Virginia, July 1, 1862. Returned to duty in January-February, 1863, and was promoted to Corporal in May-October, 1864. Present or accounted for until paroled at Appomattox Court House, Virginia, April 9, 1865.

LUCAS, JAMES A., Private
Resided in Union County where he enlisted at age 25, May 3, 1861. Present or accounted for until he died in Union County on February 28, 1864, of disease.

LYONS, JOSHUA, Private
Resided in Union County where he enlisted at age 35, May 3, 1861. Present or accounted for until discharged on August 20, 1862, by reason of being over age.

McCALL, JAMES C., Private
Resided in Union County where he enlisted at age 21, May 3, 1861. Present or accounted for until wounded in the leg and captured at or near Crampton's Pass, Maryland, September 14, 1862. Hospitalized at Burkittsville, Maryland, where he died on October 14, 1862, of wounds.

McCALL, WILLIAM, Corporal
Resided in Union County where he enlisted at age 21, May 3, 1861. Mustered in as Private and promoted to Corporal in May-October, 1864. Present or accounted for through October, 1864.

McCLELLAN, SANDY R., Private
Resided in Cabarrus County and enlisted in Union County at age 22, May 3, 1861. Present or accounted for until wounded in the head and shoulder at or near Williamsburg, Virginia, on or about May 5, 1862. Returned to duty prior to January 1, 1863. Present or accounted for until hospitalized at Farmville, Virginia, May 6-7, 1864, with a gunshot wound of the ankle; however, place and date wounded not reported. Returned to duty at an unspecified date and was present or accounted for through October, 1864.

McCORKLE, JOHN F., Private
Resided in Union County where he enlisted at age 19,

May 3, 1861. Present or accounted for until hospitalized at Danville, Virginia, on or about June 4, 1864, with a gunshot wound of the hand; however, place and date wounded not reported. Reported absent wounded or absent on detail until paroled at Charlotte on May 3, 1865.

McCORKLE, JOHN H., Private
Resided in Union County where he enlisted at age 17, May 3, 1861. Present or accounted for until he died near Richmond, Virginia, August 25, 1862, of disease.

McCOY, MOSES M., Private
Resided in Union County where he enlisted at age 18, May 3, 1861. Present or accounted for until captured at Hatcher's Run, Virginia, April 2, 1865. Confined at Hart's Island, New York Harbor, until released on June 18, 1865, after taking the Oath of Allegiance.

McCRORY, SAMUEL, Private
Resided in Cabarrus County and enlisted in Union County at age 19, May 3, 1861. Present or accounted for until captured near Boonsboro, Maryland, September 16, 1862. Confined at Fort Delaware, Delaware, until transferred to Aiken's Landing, James River, Virginia, October 2, 1862, for exchange. Declared exchanged at Aiken's Landing on November 10, 1862. Rejoined the company prior to December 13, 1862, when he was killed at Fredericksburg, Virginia.

McDONALD, JOHN, Private
Resided in Cabarrus or Rowan counties and enlisted in Wake County on July 15, 1862, for the war. Present or accounted for through April, 1864. North Carolina pension records indicate he was wounded at Spotsylvania Court House, Virginia, May 15, 1864, and died in hospital "about three days after being wounded"; however, records of the Federal Provost Marshal indicate he was a deserter who took the Oath of Allegiance at Cincinnati, Ohio, October 30, 1864. No further records.

McFARLIN, ZACHARIAH, Private
Enlisted on July 15, 1862, for the war. Present or accounted for until killed at Fredericksburg, Virginia, December 13, 1862.

McLAIN, MATTHEW J., Private
Resided in Union County where he enlisted at age 21, May 3, 1861. Present or accounted for until he left the company without permission on August 25, 1862. Died in hospital at Richmond, Virginia, October 10, 1862, of "diphtheria."

McLAIN, WILLIAM B., Private
Resided in Union County where he enlisted at age 30, May 3, 1861. Present or accounted for until wounded in the right eye and left side at Bristoe Station, Virginia, October 14, 1863. Reported absent wounded until retired to the Invalid Corps on December 8, 1864, by reason of "t[otal] d[isability]." North Carolina pension records indicate that he was "totally blind."

McLARTY, GEORGE C., Sergeant
Resided in Union County where he enlisted at age 18, May 3, 1861. Mustered in as Private. Present or accounted for until wounded in the thigh at Fredericksburg, Virginia, December 13, 1862. Returned to duty prior to January 1, 1863, and was promoted to Corporal on March 4, 1863. Promoted to Sergeant

on June 4, 1863. Present or accounted for until furloughed for sixty days from hospital at Richmond, Virginia, February 20, 1865.

McLELLAN, ROBERT M., Private

Resided in Cabarrus County and enlisted in Union County at age 17, May 3, 1861. Present or accounted for until wounded in the hip at Fredericksburg, Virginia, December 13, 1862. Hospitalized at Richmond, Virginia, where he died December 21, 1862, of wounds.

MALONE, JAMES T., Private

Resided in Caswell County and was by occupation a farmer prior to enlisting in Wake County on July 15, 1862, for the war. Present or accounted for until captured at or near Chapin's Farm, Virginia, on or about October 1, 1864. Confined at Point Lookout, Maryland. Refused to be exchanged in March, 1865. Released at Point Lookout, May 12-14, 1865, after taking the Oath of Allegiance.

MASSEY, AMBROSE M., Private

Born in Union County* where he resided as a farmer prior to enlisting in Union County at age 21, May 3, 1861. Present or accounted for until captured at or near Crampton's Pass, Maryland, September 14, 1862. Confined at Fort Delaware, Delaware, until transferred to Aiken's Landing, James River, Virginia, October 2, 1862, for exchange. Declared exchanged at Aiken's Landing on November 10, 1862. Reported absent on furlough until he was discharged on April 20, 1863, by reason of "tuberculosis."

MEDLIN, De BERRY, Private

Resided in Union County where he enlisted at age 18, May 3, 1861. Present or accounted for until captured at Petersburg, Virginia, April 3, 1865. Confined at Point Lookout, Maryland, until released on June 15, 1865, after taking the Oath of Allegiance.

MILES, BEDFORD B., Private

Resided in Caswell County and enlisted in Wake County on July 15, 1862, for the war. Present or accounted for until captured at or near Crampton's Pass, Maryland, on or about September 14, 1862. Confined at Fort Delaware, Delaware, until transferred to Aiken's Landing, James River, Virginia, October 2, 1862, for exchange. Hospitalized at Richmond, Virginia, October 14, 1862, with syphilis and died December 11, 1862, of "debilitas."

MILLS, THOMAS, Private

Resided in Union County where he enlisted at age 23, May 3, 1861. Present or accounted for until wounded at Lee's Mill, Virginia, April 16, 1862. Died April 17, 1862, of wounds.

MOSER, HENRY W., Private

Resided in Union County where he enlisted at age 17, May 3, 1861. Discharged on August 20, 1862, by reason of being under age. Reenlisted in this company on or about December 31, 1862, as a substitute for Private John E.W. Austin. Transferred to Company A, 46th Regiment N.C. Troops, on May 1, 1863, in exchange for Private John Reuben Birmingham.

MULLIS, ALEXANDER J., Private

Resided in Union County where he enlisted at age 27, May 3, 1861. Present or accounted for until killed at Malvern Hill, Virginia, July 1, 1862.

MUSE, CHARLES B., Private

Resided in Union County where he enlisted at age 24, May 3, 1861. Present or accounted for until wounded in the right leg at Bristoe Station, Virginia, October 14, 1863. Reported absent wounded or absent on light duty through October, 1864.

OSBORNE, ALEXANDER L., Private

Resided in Union County where he enlisted at age 21, May 3, 1861. Present or accounted for until wounded at Sharpsburg, Maryland, September 17, 1862. Returned to duty in March-April, 1863, and present or accounted for until paroled at Lynchburg, Virginia, April 15, 1865.

PINION, JAMES M., Private

Born in Union County* and was by occupation a farmer prior to enlisting in Wake County on May 21, 1861. Present or accounted for until killed at Malvern Hill, Virginia, July 1, 1862. Death records give his age as 33.

PISTOLE, JAMES M., Private

Resided in Union County where he enlisted at age 23, May 3, 1861. Present or accounted for until wounded in the hand and arm at Fredericksburg, Virginia, December 13, 1862. Returned to duty in March-April, 1863, and present or accounted for until captured at Bristoe Station, Virginia, October 14, 1863. Confined at Old Capitol Prison, Washington, D.C., until transferred to Point Lookout, Maryland, October 27, 1863. Paroled and transferred to Aiken's Landing, James River, Virginia, February 24, 1865, for exchange. Returned to duty prior to April 9, 1865, when he was paroled at Appomattox Court House, Virginia.

PORTER, ANDREW J., Private

Resided in Union County where he enlisted on May 3, 1861. Present or accounted for until wounded at Malvern Hill, Virginia, July 1, 1862. Returned to duty prior to January 1, 1863, and present or accounted for until captured at Hatcher's Run, Virginia, April 2, 1865. Confined at Hart's Island, New York Harbor, until released June 17-18, 1865, after taking the Oath of Allegiance.

RAMSEY, JAMES C., Private

Resided in Union County where he enlisted at age 26, May 3, 1861. Present or accounted for until wounded at Malvern Hill, Virginia, July 1, 1862. Deserted from hospital at Danville, Virginia, November 17, 1862, but returned to duty on April 19, 1863. Present or accounted for until captured at Bristoe Station, Virginia, October 14, 1863. Confined at Old Capitol Prison, Washington, D.C., until transferred to Point Lookout, Maryland, February 3, 1864. Paroled and transferred to City Point, Virginia, where he was received April 30, 1864, for exchange. Reported absent without leave on July 4, 1864, but returned to duty on October 30, 1864. No further records.

RAY, THOMAS, Private

Enlisted in Union County on June 24, 1861. Present or accounted for until transferred to Captain Hart's Horse Artillery Company (Washington Artillery), South Carolina Volunteers, June 18, 1862.

RICH, PHILEMON M., Private

Resided in Union County where he enlisted at age 23,

May 3, 1861. Present or accounted for until killed at Fredericksburg, Virginia, December 13, 1862.

RICHARDSON, D. H. W., Private

Born in Union County and enlisted near Orange Court House, Virginia, April 25, 1864, for the war. Died August 4, 1864. Place and cause of death not reported.

RICHARDSON, WILLIAM P., Corporal

Born in Union County* where he resided prior to enlisting in Union County at age 21, May 3, 1861. Mustered in as Private. Present or accounted for until wounded at Malvern Hill, Virginia, July 1, 1862. Returned to duty at an unspecified date. "Fought his way out [when he was] almost entirely surrounded by the enemy" at South Mountain, Maryland, September 14, 1862. Wounded December 13, 1862, at Fredericksburg, Virginia, where "his gallantry elicited the admiration of all who witnessed it." Promoted to Corporal on December 30, 1862, and returned to duty prior to January 1, 1863. Recommended for promotion to 2nd Lieutenant on March 21, 1863, by reason of "his coolness and bravery in every battle in which his Regiment has been engaged"; however, he was not promoted. Present or accounted for until killed in battle on the Petersburg and Weldon Railroad on August 21, 1864.

RINER, WILLIAM C., Private

Resided in Union County where he enlisted at age 25, May 3, 1861. Present or accounted for until reported missing at Sharpsburg, Maryland, September 17, 1862. Dropped from the rolls on or about March 1, 1863, because he was "supposed to be dead."

ROGERS, CYRUS A., Private

Resided in Union County where he enlisted at age 21, May 3, 1861. Present or accounted for until wounded in the liver at Malvern Hill, Virginia, July 1, 1862. Died in hospital at Richmond, Virginia, July 7, 1862, of wounds.

ROGERS, SAMUEL S., Private

Resided in Union County where he enlisted at age 22, May 3, 1861. Present or accounted for until wounded at or near Crampton's Pass, Maryland, September 14, 1862. Returned to duty in January-February, 1863, and present or accounted for until he "fell out on the march" on November 8, 1863. Was captured by Federal forces or deserted to them prior to December 5, 1863, when he was hospitalized at Washington, D.C. Died in hospital at Washington on February 29, 1864, of "variola."

ROSE, DANIEL M., Sergeant

Resided in Union County where he enlisted on May 3, 1861. Mustered in as Private and promoted to Sergeant in September-December, 1861. Present or accounted for until wounded at Malvern Hill, Virginia, July 1, 1862. Returned to duty prior to January 1, 1863, and present or accounted for until captured at Bristoe Station, Virginia, October 14, 1863. Confined at Old Capitol Prison, Washington, D.C., until transferred to Point Lookout, Maryland, October 27, 1863. Released on March 14, 1864, after taking the Oath of Allegiance.

ROYES, WILLIAM, _____

Place and date of enlistment not reported; however, a company muster roll dated June 10-30, 1861, states he was discharged on June 28, 1861, by reason of "physical infirmities."

RYCHE, J. M., Private

Place and date of enlistment not reported. Reported in hospital at Petersburg, Virginia, in April, 1862. No further records.

SCOTT, WILLIAM L., Private

Resided in Caswell County and enlisted in Wake County on July 15, 1862, for the war. Present or accounted for through April, 1864.

SECREST, COLEMAN M., Private

Resided in Union County where he enlisted at age 20, May 3, 1861. Present or accounted for until wounded at Malvern Hill, Virginia, July 1, 1862. Died July 3, 1862, of wounds.

SECREST, JOHN A., Private

Resided in Union County where he enlisted at age 21, May 3, 1861. Present or accounted for until he died near Yorktown, Virginia, September 20, 1861, of disease.

SHELL, WILLIAM F., Private

Enlisted in Union County at age 20, May 3, 1861. Present or accounted for until he died in hospital at Petersburg, Virginia, February 9, 1863, of "phthisis pulmonalis."

SIKES, CORNELIUS BUNYAN, Private

Resided in Union County where he enlisted at age 21, May 3, 1861. Present or accounted for until hospitalized at Charlotte on May 27, 1864, with a gunshot wound; however, place and date wounded not reported. Returned to duty on July 21, 1864, and present or accounted for until captured at Hatcher's Run, Virginia, April 2, 1865. Confined at Hart's Island, New York Harbor, until released June 19-20, 1865, after taking the Oath of Allegiance.

SIKES, JACOB CULPEPPER, Private

Enlisted in Union County at age 21, February 4, 1864, for the war. Present or accounted for until wounded in the hip and foot at Petersburg, Virginia, on or about October 15, 1864. Returned to duty at an unspecified date and present or accounted for until paroled at Appomattox Court House, Virginia, April 9, 1865.

SIKES, JOHN B., Corporal

Born in Union County where he resided as a brickmason prior to enlisting in Union County at age 24, May 3, 1861. Mustered in as Private and promoted to Corporal on June 4, 1863. Present or accounted for until captured at Hatcher's Run, Virginia, April 2, 1865. Confined at Hart's Island, New York Harbor, until released June 17-18, 1865, after taking the Oath of Allegiance.

SOMERS, ROBERT E., Private

Born in Caswell County where he resided prior to enlisting in Wake County on July 15, 1862, for the war. Present or accounted for until he deserted on January 9, 1863. Returned to duty on April 4, 1864, but deserted to the enemy on or about September 2, 1864.

SOPSHIRE, ALEXANDER, Private

Enlisted in Union County at age 21, May 3, 1861. Present or accounted for until he died near Yorktown, Virginia, February 20, 1862, of disease.

STEELE, JOSEPH C., Private

Resided in Union County where he enlisted at age 20, May 3, 1861. Present or accounted for until captured at Bristoe Station, Virginia, October 14, 1863. Confined at Old Capitol Prison, Washington, D.C., until transferred to Point Lookout, Maryland, October 27, 1863. Paroled on May 3, 1864, and transferred to Aiken's Landing, James River, Virginia, for exchange. Returned to duty prior to November 1, 1864. Paroled at Appomattox Court House, Virginia, April 9, 1865.

STEGALL, JOHN B. D., Private

Resided in Union County where he enlisted at age 20, May 3, 1861. Present or accounted for until wounded in the leg at Fredericksburg, Virginia, December 13, 1862. Returned to duty in March-April, 1863, and present or accounted for until wounded in the thigh at Wilderness, Virginia, May 5, 1864. Reported absent wounded through October, 1864, but returned to duty prior to April 2, 1865, when he was captured at Hatcher's Run, Virginia. Confined at Hart's Island, New York Harbor, until released June 17-18, 1865, after taking the Oath of Allegiance.

STERNS, ROBERT, Private

Resided in Union County where he enlisted at age 20, May 3, 1861. Present or accounted for until reported missing at or near Crampton's Pass, Maryland, September 14, 1862. Never rejoined the company and was dropped from the rolls on or about March 1, 1863, because he was "supposed to be dead."

STINSON, DAVID D., Private

Resided in Union County where he enlisted at age 21, May 3, 1861. Present or accounted for until captured at Bristoe Station, Virginia, October 14, 1863. Confined at Old Capitol Prison, Washington, D.C., until transferred to Point Lookout, Maryland, October 27, 1863. Paroled and transferred to Cox's Landing, James River, Virginia, February 13, 1865, for exchange. Reported present with a detachment of paroled and exchanged prisoners at Camp Lee, near Richmond, Virginia, February 17, 1865. Paroled at Appomattox Court House, Virginia, April 9, 1865.

STINSON, GEORGE M., Private

Resided in Union County where he enlisted at age 23, May 3, 1861. Present or accounted for until paroled at Appomattox Court House, Virginia, April 9, 1865.

STINSON, P. C., Private

Enlisted near Orange Court House, Virginia, March 18, 1864, for the war. Present or accounted for until paroled at Charlotte on May 23, 1865.

SUMMERS, JOSEPH, Private

Resided in Caswell County and enlisted in Wake County on July 15, 1862, for the war. Present or accounted for until wounded in the hand at Fredericksburg, Virginia, December 13, 1862. Hospitalized at Farmville, Virginia, where he died December 27, 1862, of wounds and "pneumonia."

TAYLOR, L. S., Private

Place and date of enlistment not reported. Records of the Federal Provost Marshal indicate he was hospitalized at Fort Monroe, Virginia, April 27, 1865, and was released on or about May 31, 1865. Federal hospital records give his age as 16.

TESH, LEVEN, Private

Resided in Caswell County and enlisted in Wake County on July 15, 1862, for the war. Present or accounted for until he was "sent to hospital" in August, 1862. Never rejoined the company and was dropped from the rolls on or about September 1, 1863, because he was "supposed to be dead."

THOMPSON, THOMAS M., Private

Resided in Caswell County and enlisted in Wake County on July 15, 1862, for the war. Present or accounted for until wounded in the right thigh at Fredericksburg, Virginia, December 13, 1862. Returned to duty in March-April, 1863, and present or accounted for until wounded in the right hand at Wilderness, Virginia, May 5, 1864. Returned to duty prior to November 1, 1864, and present or accounted for until captured at Hatcher's Run, Virginia, April 2, 1865. Confined at Hart's Island, New York Harbor, until released June 19-20, 1865, after taking the Oath of Allegiance.

UTLEY, WILLIAM J., Private

Enlisted at Orange Court House, Virginia, in May, 1864, for the war. Present or accounted for through October, 1864.

WATERS, MARION J., Private

Enlisted in Union County at age 19, May 3, 1861. Present or accounted for until wounded at Wilderness, Virginia, May 5, 1864. Reported absent wounded through October, 1864.

WEAVER, HENRY F., Private

Resided in Davidson County and enlisted in Wake County at age 24, July 15, 1862, for the war. Present or accounted for until transferred to Company C of this regiment on September 15, 1863.

WILLIAMSON, ROBERT M., Private

Resided in Union County where he enlisted at age 20, May 3, 1861. Present or accounted for until he died in hospital at Richmond, Virginia, October 22, 1862, of "debility."

WOLFE, WILLIAM C., Sergeant

Resided in Union County where he enlisted at age 26, May 3, 1861. Mustered in as Private. Present or accounted for until wounded at Lee's Mill, Virginia, April 16, 1862. Promoted to Corporal on May 20, 1862, and returned to duty prior to January 1, 1863. Promoted to Sergeant in May-October, 1864. Present or accounted for until paroled at Appomattox Court House, Virginia, April 9, 1865.

WOLFE, WILLIAM T., Private

Resided in Union County where he enlisted at age 18, May 3, 1861. Present or accounted for until paroled at Appomattox Court House, Virginia, April 9, 1865. North Carolina pension records indicate he was wounded in the throat at Fredericksburg, Virginia, December 13, 1862.

YANDELS, WILLIAM C., Private

Resided in Union County where he enlisted at age 21, May 3, 1861. Present or accounted for until killed at Lee's Mill, Virginia, April 16, 1862.

YOUNG, R. H., Private

Place and date of enlistment not reported. Name appears on a regimental return dated April, 1862, which states he was absent in hospital at Petersburg, Virginia. No further records.

COMPANY C

This company, known as the Ellis Guards, was from Cleveland County and enlisted at Shelby on April 27, 1861. It was accepted into state service on May 1 and was ordered to Raleigh on May 15. After arriving at Raleigh on May 23, the company encamped until early June, when it was ordered to Garysburg. There it was assigned to this regiment as Company C. After joining the regiment the company functioned as a part of the regiment, and its history for the war period is recorded as a part of the regimental history.

The information contained in the following roster of the company was compiled principally from company muster rolls for June 2-August, 1861; November-December, 1861; November, 1862-April, 1864; and September-October, 1864. No company muster rolls were found for September-October, 1861; January-October, 1862; May-August, 1864; or for the period after October, 1864. In addition to the company muster rolls, Roll of Honor records, receipt rolls, hospital records, prisoner of war records, and other primary records, supplemented by state pension applications, United Daughters of the Confederacy records, and postwar rosters and histories, all provided useful information.

OFFICERS

CAPTAINS

LOVE, CHRISTOPHER G.
Resided in Cleveland County where he enlisted at age 35. Appointed Captain to rank from May 1, 1861. Present or accounted for until he was defeated for reelection when the company was reorganized on May 2, 1862. Later served as Corporal in Company F, 41st Regiment N.C. Troops (3rd Regiment N.C. Cavalry).

HARDIN, DAVID J.
Resided in Cleveland County where he enlisted at age 24. Appointed 2nd Lieutenant to rank from May 1, 1861, and was elected Captain on May 2, 1862. Present or accounted for until he resigned on March 24, 1865. Reason he resigned not reported.

LIEUTENANTS

BYARS, JOHN S., 2nd Lieutenant
Resided in Cleveland County where he enlisted at age 25. Appointed 2nd Lieutenant on or about April 27, 1861. Present or accounted for until he resigned in October, 1861. Reason he resigned not reported.

HARDIN, WILLIAM K., 2nd Lieutenant
Resided in Cleveland County where he enlisted at age 29, April 27, 1861. Mustered in as Private and promoted to 1st Sergeant in November, 1861. Elected 2nd Lieutenant on May 2, 1862. Present or accounted for through June, 1862. A hospital record datelined Richmond, Virginia, July 16, 1862, states he was suffering from a gunshot wound and returned to duty

on that date; however, place and date wounded not reported. Present or accounted for until wounded at or near Crampton's Pass, Maryland, September 14, 1862. Returned to duty prior to January 1, 1863, and present or accounted for until he resigned on January 17, 1865. Reason he resigned not reported.

JARRETT, JAMES M., 1st Lieutenant
Resided in Cleveland County and was by occupation a mechanic prior to enlisting in Cleveland County at age 24, April 27, 1861. Mustered in as 1st Sergeant and was appointed 2nd Lieutenant to rank from October 30, 1861. Promoted to 1st Lieutenant on May 2, 1862. Present or accounted for until captured at or near Crampton's Pass, Maryland, on or about September 14, 1862. Confined at Fort Delaware, Delaware, until transferred to Aiken's Landing, James River, Virginia, October 2, 1862, for exchange. Declared exchanged at Aiken's Landing on November 10, 1862. Returned to duty prior to March 1, 1863, and present or accounted for until wounded in the left thigh at Bristoe Station, Virginia, October 14, 1863. Reported absent wounded or absent sick through October, 1864.

McBRAYER, ELI W., 2nd Lieutenant
Resided in Cleveland County where he enlisted at age 21, April 27, 1861. Mustered in as Corporal and was promoted to Sergeant in November, 1861. Appointed 2nd Lieutenant on May 2, 1862. Present or accounted for until hospitalized at Richmond, Virginia, September 18, 1864, with a gunshot wound of the side and right arm; however, place and date wounded not reported. Returned to duty at an unspecified date and was paroled at Appomattox Court House, Virginia, April 9, 1865.

NICHOLSON, JOHN N., 1st Lieutenant
Resided in Cleveland County where he enlisted at age 29. Appointed 1st Lieutenant on May 1, 1861. Present or accounted for until he was defeated for reelection when the regiment was reorganized on May 2, 1862.

NONCOMMISSIONED OFFICERS AND PRIVATES

ALLEN, ABNER, Private
Resided in Cleveland County where he enlisted at age 37, April 27, 1861. Present or accounted for until discharged on June 22, 1861. Reason discharged not reported. Died August 7, 1861. Place and cause of death not reported.

ALLEN, LABAN, Private
Resided in Cleveland County where he enlisted at age 30, April 27, 1861. Present or accounted for until transferred to Company H, 34th Regiment N.C. Troops, in September, 1862.

ALLISON, J. H., Private
Resided in Cleveland County where he enlisted at age 43, April 27, 1861. Present or accounted for until discharged on August 19, 1862, by reason of being over age.

AYCOCK, JAMES, Private
Born in Wayne County where he resided as a farmer prior to enlisting in Wake County at age 31, July 15,

1862, for the war. Present or accounted for until wounded in the head at the South Anna River Bridge, near Richmond, Virginia, July 4, 1863. Reported absent wounded until he was reported absent without leave on July 18, 1863. Returned to duty in November-December, 1863, but was reported absent on detail until March 24, 1865, when he was retired from service by reason of wounds and "paralysis of the right arm."

BARRETT, BERRY, Private

Resided in Cleveland County where he enlisted at age 16, April 27, 1861. Present or accounted for until discharged on August 19, 1862, by reason of being under age. Reenlisted in the company on March 1, 1863, and present or accounted for until wounded in the left hand at Wilderness, Virginia, May 5, 1864. Reported absent wounded through October, 1864.

BARRETT, FRANKLIN, Private

Resided in Cleveland County where he enlisted at age 22, April 27, 1861. Present or accounted for until wounded in the right knee and captured at Cold Harbor, Virginia, June 2, 1864. Confined at Point Lookout, Maryland, until transferred to Elmira, New York, July 12, 1864. Paroled at Elmira on March 14, 1865, and transferred to Boulware's Wharf, James River, Virginia, for exchange. Hospitalized at Richmond, Virginia, March 18, 1865, and was furloughed for thirty days on March 23, 1865.

BARRETT, LEVI, Private

Resided in Cleveland County where he enlisted at age 35, March 1, 1863, for the war. Present or accounted for until captured at Bristoe Station, Virginia, October 14, 1863. Confined at Old Capitol Prison, Washington, D.C., where he was hospitalized on November 23, 1863, with "typhoid fever." Died in hospital on November 27, 1863.

BATTIE, C., Private

Enlistment date reported as August 14, 1862; however, he was not listed on the rolls of this company until March-April, 1863. Present or accounted for until wounded at or near Deep Bottom, Virginia, on or about August 6, 1864. Died of wounds in hospital at Richmond, Virginia, "a few days thereafter." [Company records indicate that he served previously in Mallett's Battalion (Camp Guard); however, records of Mallett's Battalion do not indicate that he served therein.]

BIGGERSTAFF, GOVERN M., Private

Enlisted in Cleveland County on February 10, 1864, for the war. Present or accounted for until wounded in the left hand and wrist at Cold Harbor, Virginia, June 2, 1864. Reported absent wounded until retired to the Invalid Corps on December 30, 1864, by reason of "t[otal] d[isability]."

BIGGERSTAFF, HENRY W., Private

Enlisted in Cleveland County on February 10, 1864, for the war. Present or accounted for until paroled at Appomattox Court House, Virginia, April 9, 1865.

BLACK, W. W., Private

Enlisted in Wake County on October 4, 1863, for the war. Present or accounted for until transferred to Company I of this regiment on April 13, 1864.

BLACKWOOD, JOHN F., Private

Enlisted in Cleveland County on July 15, 1864, for the war. Present or accounted for until wounded at Reams' Station, Virginia, August 25, 1864. Reported absent wounded through October, 1864.

BLANTON, DAVID G., Corporal

Resided in Cleveland County where he enlisted at age 21, April 27, 1861. Mustered in as Private and promoted to Corporal on May 2, 1862. Present or accounted for until wounded in the right side at Fredericksburg, Virginia, December 13, 1862. Reported absent without leave in January-February, 1863, but returned to duty in March-April, 1863. Present or accounted for until wounded in the left hand at Wilderness, Virginia, May 5, 1864. Reported absent wounded through October, 1864. Deserted to the enemy on or about February 17, 1865. Released on or about February 21, 1865, after taking the Oath of Allegiance.

BLANTON, EBENEZER J., Private

Resided in Cleveland County where he enlisted at age 20, April 27, 1861. Present or accounted for until wounded at Sharpsburg, Maryland, September 17, 1862. Reported absent wounded until reported absent without leave on March 25, 1863. Returned to duty on September 4, 1863, and present or accounted for until paroled at Appomattox Court House, Virginia, April 9, 1865.

BLANTON, JOSIAH S., Private

Resided in Cleveland County where he enlisted at age 20, December 9, 1861. Present or accounted for until wounded at Malvern Hill, Virginia, July 1, 1862. Returned to duty prior to January 1, 1863, and present or accounted for until transferred to Company H, 28th Regiment N.C. Troops, March 28, 1864.

BLANTON, L. H., Private

Resided in Cleveland County where he enlisted at age 20, April 27, 1861. Mustered in as Private and promoted to Corporal in August, 1863. Reduced to ranks prior to October 14, 1863, when he was killed at Bristoe Station, Virginia.

BLANTON, PINKNEY, Private

Born in Cleveland County where he resided prior to enlisting in Cleveland County at age 18, April 27, 1861. Present or accounted for until he died on July 15, 1862, of disease. Place of death not reported.

BLANTON, ROBERT A., Private

Resided in Cleveland County where he enlisted at age 22, April 27, 1861. Present or accounted for until captured at or near Sharpsburg, Maryland, in September, 1862. Confined at Fort Delaware, Delaware, until transferred to Aiken's Landing, James River, Virginia, October 2, 1862, for exchange. Declared exchanged at Aiken's Landing on November 10, 1862. Returned to duty prior to January 1, 1863, and present or accounted for until wounded in the leg at Bristoe Station, Virginia, October 14, 1863. Reported absent wounded until retired to the Invalid Corps on January 6, 1865. Captured in hospital at Richmond, Virginia, April 3, 1865, and paroled on April 23, 1865.

BLANTON, WILLIAM L., Private

Resided in Cleveland County where he enlisted at age

20, April 27, 1861. Present or accounted for until wounded at Sharpsburg, Maryland, September 17, 1862. Returned to duty in January-February, 1863. Present or accounted for until hospitalized at Richmond, Virginia, May 9, 1864, with a gunshot wound of the left hand; however, place and date wounded not reported. Returned to duty prior to November 1, 1864, and present or accounted for until he deserted to the enemy on or about February 17, 1865. Released on or about February 21, 1865, after taking the Oath of Allegiance.

BLANTON, ZINATHAN, Sergeant
Resided in Cleveland County where he enlisted at age 22, April 27, 1861. Mustered in as Private. Present or accounted for until wounded at Malvern Hill, Virginia, July 1, 1862. Promoted to Sergeant on November 1, 1862, and returned to duty prior to January 1, 1863. Present or accounted for until paroled at Richmond, Virginia, April 24, 1865.

BOGUE, Z. R., Private
Resided in Wayne County and enlisted in Wake County at age 30, July 15, 1862, for the war. Present or accounted for until he died in hospital at Lynchburg, Virginia, November 8, 1863, of "pneumonia."

BORDLY, T. B., Private
Resided in Cleveland County where he enlisted at age 46, April 27, 1861. Present or accounted for until discharged on August 19, 1862, by reason of being over age.

BOWDEN, ANDREW J., Private
Resided in Warren County and enlisted at age 33, July 15, 1862, for the war. Present or accounted for until transferred to Company C, 46th Regiment N.C. Troops, on or about December 1, 1862, in exchange for Private Robert F. Stone.

BOWDON, UPTON T., Private
Resided in Warren County and enlisted at age 20, July 15, 1862, for the war. Present or accounted for until transferred to Company C, 46th Regiment N.C. Troops, December 1, 1862, in exchange for Private Elijah Robinson.

BRACKET, BENJAMIN, Private
Enlisted in Cleveland County in September, 1864, for the war. Present or accounted for through October, 1864.

BRACKETT, ROBERT, Private
Previously served in 2nd Company B, 49th Regiment N.C. Troops. Transferred to this company on January 15, 1863, in exchange for Private William A. Putnam. Present or accounted for through October, 1864.

BRANTON, J. R., Private
Resided in Cleveland County where he enlisted at age 23, April 27, 1861. Present or accounted for until he deserted on June 19, 1862.

BRIMM, J. W., Private
Resided in Cleveland County. Place and date of enlistment not reported. Captured at Sutherland's Station, Virginia, April 2, 1865. Confined at Hart's Island, New York Harbor, until released on June 17, 1865, after taking the Oath of Allegiance.

BRYANT, W. P., Private
Enlisted in Cleveland County on April 27, 1861.

Discharged at Raleigh on June 3, 1861. Reason discharged not reported.

BURNS, M., Private
Resided in Washington, D.C., and enlisted in Wake County at age 30, July 15, 1862, for the war as a substitute. Present or accounted for until wounded in the arm at Fredericksburg, Virginia, December 13, 1862. Returned to duty in January-February, 1863, and present or accounted for until captured at Bristoe Station, Virginia, October 14, 1863. Confined at Old Capitol Prison, Washington, D.C., until released and "sent north" December 13-17, 1863, after taking the Oath of Allegiance.

CHAMPION, JOHN W., Private
Resided in Cleveland County where he enlisted at age 23, April 27, 1861. Present or accounted for until wounded in the right hand at Wilderness, Virginia, May 5, 1864. Returned to duty prior to November 1, 1864, and present or accounted for until paroled at Appomattox Court House, Virginia, April 9, 1865.

COVINGTON, W. J., Private
Resided in Rutherford County where he enlisted at age 23, June 9, 1861. Present or accounted for until discharged on December 4, 1861. Reason discharged not reported. Died in hospital at Richmond, Virginia, January 10, 1862, of disease.

CROWDER, H. D., Private
Resided in Cleveland County where he enlisted at age 15, April 27, 1861. Present or accounted for until he died in Cleveland County on August 27, 1863, of disease.

DAVIS, G. W., Private
Resided in Wayne County and enlisted in Wake County at age 22, July 15, 1862, for the war. Present or accounted for until wounded at Bristoe Station, Virginia, October 14, 1863. Died in hospital at Orange Court House, Virginia, February 29, 1864. Cause of death not reported.

DILLINGER, DANIEL C., Private
Resided in Cleveland County where he enlisted at age 26, April 27, 1861. Present or accounted for until captured at Sharpsburg, Maryland, September 17, 1862. Hospitalized at Baltimore, Maryland, for unspecified reasons. Paroled and transferred to Aiken's Landing, James River, Virginia, where he was received November 5, 1862, for exchange. Declared exchanged at Aiken's Landing on November 10, 1862. Returned to duty prior to January 1, 1863, and present or accounted for until transferred to 2nd Company D of this regiment on April 1, 1863.

DOVER, JAMES, Private
Enlisted in Cleveland County on April 27, 1861. Discharged at Raleigh on June 3, 1861. Reason discharged not reported.

ELLINGTON, A. D., Private
Resided in Warren County and was by occupation a farmer prior to enlisting in Wake County at age 31, July 15, 1862, for the war. Present or accounted for until wounded in the right arm at or near Crampton's Pass, Maryland, September 14, 1862. Returned to duty in January-February, 1863, and present or accounted for until he died at Gordonsville, Virginia, October 3, 1863, of disease.

ELLIS, ANDREW F., Private

Resided in Cleveland County where he enlisted at age 18, March 1, 1863, for the war. Present or accounted for until wounded at Reams' Station, Virginia, August 25, 1864. Reported absent wounded through October, 1864, but returned to duty prior to April 2, 1865, when he was captured at Hatcher's Run, Virginia. Confined at Point Lookout, Maryland, until released on June 12, 1865, after taking the Oath of Allegiance.

ELLIS, ELIJAH R., Private

Enlisted in Cleveland County at age 17, April 1, 1864, for the war. Present or accounted for through October, 1864.

ELLIS, GILBERT, Private

Resided in Wayne County and enlisted in Wake County at age 30, July 15, 1862, for the war. Present or accounted for until reported absent sick on October 17, 1862. Never rejoined the company and died in Wayne County prior to December 5, 1864. Cause and exact date of death not reported.

ELLIS, MARCUS, Private

Resided in Cleveland County where he enlisted at age 35, April 27, 1861. Present or accounted for until discharged on August 19, 1862, by reason of being over age.

ELLIS, ROBERT S., Private

Resided in Cleveland County where he enlisted at age 20, April 27, 1861. Mustered in as Private. Present or accounted for until wounded at Malvern Hill, Virginia, July 1, 1862. Returned to duty prior to January 1, 1863, and was promoted to Corporal on April 1, 1864. Reduced to ranks in May-October, 1864. Present or accounted for until captured at Hatcher's Run, Virginia, April 2, 1865. Confined at Point Lookout, Maryland, until released on June 12, 1865, after taking the Oath of Allegiance.

FALKNER, JOHN R., Private

Resided in Warren County and enlisted in Wake County at age 18, July 15, 1862, for the war. Present or accounted for until he died at Gordonsville, Virginia, October 1, 1863, of disease.

FELZ, ISAAC, Sergeant

Place and date of enlistment not reported. Paroled at Greensboro on May 16, 1865.

FRITTS, H., Private

Resided in Davidson County and enlisted in Wake County at age 32, July 15, 1862, for the war. Present or accounted for until wounded at or near Crampton's Pass, Maryland, September 14, 1862. Captured by Federal forces at an unspecified date and was confined at Fort Delaware, Delaware, until transferred to Aiken's Landing, James River, Virginia, October 2, 1862, for exchange. Declared exchanged at Aiken's Landing on November 10, 1862. Reported absent wounded until discharged on or about February 16, 1863. Reason discharged not reported.

GIBSON, D. D., Private

Resided in Cleveland County where he enlisted at age 25, April 27, 1861. Present or accounted for until he died at Garysburg on June 30, 1861, of disease.

GOBBLE, HUBBARD A., Private

Resided in Davidson County and enlisted in Wake County at age 26, July 15, 1862, for the war. Present or accounted for until he deserted on August 28, 1862. Returned to duty on or about July 31, 1864, and present or accounted for until captured at Hatcher's Run, Virginia, April 2, 1865. Confined at Point Lookout, Maryland, where he died June 15, 1865, of "dia[rrhoea] acute."

GOBBLE, JAMES M., Private

Resided in Davidson County and enlisted in Wake County at age 25, July 15, 1862, for the war. Present or accounted for until he deserted on August 28, 1862. Returned to duty in January-February, 1864, and present or accounted for until captured at Hatcher's Run, Virginia, April 2, 1865. Confined at Point Lookout, Maryland, until released on June 27, 1865, after taking the Oath of Allegiance.

GRAYSON, JOHN, Private

Enlisted in Cleveland County on September 10, 1864, for the war. Present or accounted for through October, 1864.

GRIGG, ELI C., Private

Resided in Cleveland County where he enlisted at age 19, April 27, 1861. Present or accounted for until transferred to Company K, 49th Regiment N.C. Troops, on or about September 1, 1862.

GRUBB, D., Private

Resided in Davidson County and enlisted in Wake County at age 28, July 15, 1862, for the war. Present or accounted for until he deserted in Maryland in September, 1862. Records of the Federal Provost Marshal indicate he was captured at Crampton's Pass, Maryland, September 14, 1862, and paroled. No further records.

GRUBB, H., Private

Resided in Davidson County and enlisted in Wake County at age 30, July 15, 1862, for the war. Present or accounted for until captured at or near Crampton's Pass, Maryland, September 14, 1862. Last reported in a Federal hospital at Philadelphia, Pennsylvania, January 19, 1863. Company records indicate that he was "supposed to have taken the Oath." No further records.

HAM, J. J., Private

Resided in Warren County and enlisted at age 24, July 15, 1862, for the war. Discharged prior to January 1, 1863. Reason discharged not reported.

HAMES, S. A., Private

Enlisted in Wake County on October 14, 1863, for the war. Present or accounted for through October, 1863.

HAMES, W. D., Private

Born in Union County, South Carolina, and resided in Cleveland County where he was by occupation a farmer prior to enlisting in Cleveland County at age 28, April 27, 1861. Present or accounted for until captured at or near Crampton's Pass, Maryland, September 14, 1862. Confined at Fort Delaware, Delaware, until transferred to Aiken's Landing, James River, Virginia, October 2, 1862, for exchange. Declared exchanged at Aiken's Landing on November 10, 1862. Returned to duty prior to December 13, 1862, when he was wounded in the arm and side at Fredericksburg, Virginia. Reported absent wounded until discharged on July 4, 1863, by reason of wounds received at Fredericksburg.

HAMRICK, B. C., Private
Born in Cleveland County* where he resided as a farmer prior to enlisting in Wake County at age 22, August 14, 1862, for the war. Present or accounted for until he died in hospital at Richmond, Virginia, June 25, 1863, of "febris typhoides." [Company records indicate that he served previously in Mallett's Battalion (Camp Guard); however, records of Mallett's Battalion do not indicate that he served therein.]

HAMRICK, B. H., Private
Enlisted in Cleveland County on April 27, 1861. Present or accounted for through June, 1863. No further records.

HAMRICK, DRURY HAMILTON, Private
Born in Cleveland County where he resided as a farmer prior to enlisting in Cleveland County at age 19, June 9, 1861. Present or accounted for until hospitalized at Farmville, Virginia, May 11, 1864, with a gunshot wound of the right foot involving the loss of the second toe; however, place and date wounded not reported. Died in hospital at Richmond, Virginia, August 8, 1864, of wounds.

HAMRICK, J. E., Private
Resided in Cleveland County where he enlisted at age 21, April 27, 1861. Present or accounted for until wounded in the shoulder at Fredericksburg, Virginia, December 13, 1862. Returned to duty in March-April, 1863, and present or accounted for until captured at the Appomattox River, Virginia, April 3, 1865. Confined at Hart's Island, New York Harbor, until released on June 19, 1865, after taking the Oath of Allegiance.

HAMRICK, LARANSY D., Private
Resided in Cleveland County where he enlisted at age 26, April 27, 1861. Mustered in as Corporal and promoted to Sergeant on May 2, 1862. Reduced to ranks in May-December, 1862, "by request." Present or accounted for through October, 1864.

HAMRICK, MILES, Private
Resided in Cleveland County and enlisted in Wake County at age 25. Enlistment date reported as August 14, 1862; however, he was not listed on the rolls of this company until March-April, 1863. Present or accounted for until wounded at Wilderness, Virginia, May 5, 1864. Reported absent wounded through October, 1864. [Company records indicate that he served previously in Mallett's Battalion (Camp Guard); however, records of Mallett's Battalion do not indicate that he served therein.]

HAMRICK, WILLIAM A., Private
Born in Cleveland County* where he resided as a farmer prior to enlisting in Cleveland County at age 24, April 27, 1861. Present or accounted for until captured at Bristoe Station, Virginia, October 14, 1863. Confined at Old Capitol Prison, Washington, D.C., until transferred to Point Lookout, Maryland, February 3, 1864. Paroled on May 3, 1864, and transferred to Aiken's Landing, James River, Virginia, for exchange. Returned to duty prior to August 25, 1864, when he was wounded in the right wrist at Reams' Station, Virginia. Reported absent wounded until retired from service on January 10, 1865, by reason of "loss of the use of the [right] hand."

HARDIN, BENJAMIN H., Private
Resided in Cleveland County where he enlisted at age 20, April 27, 1861. Present or accounted for until reported missing at Wilderness, Virginia, May 5, 1864. No further records.

HARDIN, ELI A., Private
Resided in Cleveland County where he enlisted at age 18, December 9, 1861. Present or accounted for until wounded at Malvern Hill, Virginia, July 1, 1862. Returned to duty prior to January 1, 1863, and present or accounted for until captured at Bristoe Station, Virginia, October 14, 1863. Confined at Old Capitol Prison, Washington, D.C., until transferred to Point Lookout, Maryland, October 27, 1863. Paroled at Point Lookout and transferred to Aiken's Landing, James River, Virginia, February 24, 1865, for exchange. Hospitalized at Richmond, Virginia, February 25, 1865, and was furloughed for thirty days on March 20, 1865.

HARDIN, WALTER R., Private
Resided in Cleveland County and enlisted in Wake County at age 32, July 15, 1862, for the war. Present or accounted for until wounded in the right leg and captured at or near Crampton's Pass, Maryland, September 14, 1862. Right leg amputated. Hospitalized at various Federal hospitals until reported in confinement at Fort McHenry, Maryland, in November, 1862. Paroled and transferred to City Point, Virginia, where he was received December 4, 1862, for exchange. Reported absent wounded through October, 1864.

HARPER, W. H., Private
Resided in Warren County and enlisted in Wake County at age 30, July 15, 1862, for the war. Present or accounted for until killed at or near Crampton's Pass, Maryland, September 14, 1862.

HARRIS, B., Private
Resided in Warren County and enlisted at age 24, July 15, 1862, for the war. Present or accounted for until he died in hospital at Lynchburg, Virginia, September 17, 1862, of "rubeola."

HARRIS, D., Private
Resided in Warren County and enlisted in Wake County at age 18, July 15, 1862, for the war. Present or accounted for until he died in hospital at Richmond, Virginia, September 28, 1862, of "pneumonia."

HARRIS, S. A., Private
Enlisted in Wake County on October 15, 1863, for the war. Present or accounted for until transferred to Company I of this regiment on April 13, 1864.

HEAVENER, HENRY, Private
Resided in Cleveland County where he enlisted at age 19, April 27, 1861. Present or accounted for until he died at Yorktown, Virginia, August 7, 1861, of disease.

HENDRICK, JOHN S., Private
Resided in Warren County and enlisted in Wake County at age 21, July 15, 1862, for the war. Present or accounted for until he "fell out sick on the march" on August 28, 1862. Returned to duty in January-February, 1863, and present or accounted for until captured at Bristoe Station, Virginia, October 14, 1863. Confined at Old Capitol Prison, Washington, D.C., until transferred to Point Lookout, Maryland, October 27, 1863. Paroled at Point Lookout and

transferred for exchange on May 3, 1864. Reported absent on detail until hospitalized at Raleigh on April 1, 1865. Deserted on April 5, 1865.

HIGHT, RICHARD N. O., Private
Resided in Warren or Franklin counties and enlisted in Wake County at age 28, July 15, 1862, for the war. Present or accounted for until wounded at Fredericksburg, Virginia, December 13, 1862. Transferred to Company E of this regiment prior to January 1, 1863.

HOLLOWELL, WILLIE, Private
Resided in Wayne County and enlisted in Wake County at age 33, July 15, 1862, for the war. Present or accounted for until transferred to Company I of this regiment on April 13, 1864.

HOPPER, ROMULUS M. S., 1st Sergeant
Resided in Cleveland County and enlisted at age 19, May 1, 1862, for the war. Mustered in as Private and promoted to 1st Sergeant on May 2, 1862. Present or accounted for until wounded at Malvern Hill, Virginia, July 1, 1862. Transferred to Company H, 34th Regiment N.C. Troops, in October, 1862.

HORD, JAMES YOUNG, Private
Born in Cleveland County* where he resided prior to enlisting in Cleveland County at age 21, April 27, 1861. Present or accounted for until wounded at Malvern Hill, Virginia, July 1, 1862. Returned to duty prior to September 17, 1862, when he was wounded at Sharpsburg, Maryland. Reported absent wounded or absent on duty as a nurse until he deserted from hospital at Staunton, Virginia, in September-October, 1863. Never rejoined the company.

HOWLING, WILLIAM, Private
Resided in Onslow County and enlisted in Wake County at age 17, July 15, 1862, for the war. Present or accounted for until wounded in the right thigh at Bristoe Station, Virginia, October 14, 1863. Reported absent wounded until reported absent without leave on January 17, 1864. Deserted to the enemy on or about March 13, 1864.

HUMPHRIES, E. S., Private
Resided in Cleveland County where he enlisted at age 27, April 27, 1861. Present or accounted for until he died at Yorktown, Virginia, August 7, 1861, of disease.

HUMPHRIES, J. B., Private
Resided in Cleveland County where he enlisted at age 22, June 9, 1861. Present or accounted for until killed at or near Crampton's Pass, Maryland, September 14, 1862.

HUMPHRIES, J. C., Private
Resided in Cleveland County where he enlisted at age 29, June 9, 1861. Present or accounted for through June 26, 1864.

HUMPHRIES, JESSE, Jr., Private
Enlisted in Cleveland County on April 27, 1861. Present or accounted for through August, 1861. Not listed again in the records of this company until January, 1864, when he was reported on duty as a teamster. No further records.

HUMPHRIES, JESSE, Sr., Private
Enlisted in Cleveland County on June 22, 1861. Present or accounted for through August, 1861.

HUMPHRIES, JOHN, Private
Resided in Cleveland County where he enlisted at age 26, April 27, 1861. Present or accounted for until paroled at Appomattox Court House, Virginia, April 9, 1865.

HUMPHRIES, L. L., Private
Resided in Cleveland County where he enlisted at age 40, April 27, 1861. Mustered in as Sergeant but was reduced to ranks in September-December, 1861. Present or accounted for until discharged on August 19, 1862, by reason of being over age.

HUMPHRIES, LAWSON, Private
Resided in Cleveland County where he enlisted at age 18, September 1, 1863, for the war. Present or accounted for until paroled at Appomattox Court House, Virginia, April 9, 1865.

HUMPHRIES, P. G., Jr., Private
Resided in Cleveland County where he enlisted at age 18, March 1, 1863, for the war. Present or accounted for until he died in hospital at Richmond, Virginia, May 4, 1864, of "pneumonia."

HUMPHRIES, PERRY G., Private
Enlistment date reported as September 1, 1861; however, he was not listed on the rolls of this company until March-April, 1864. Present or accounted for until hospitalized at Richmond, Virginia, May 8, 1864, with a gunshot wound of the left knee; however, place and date wounded not reported. Returned to duty prior to November 1, 1864, and present or accounted for until paroled at Appomattox Court House, Virginia, April 9, 1865. [May have served previously in Company H, 28th Regiment N.C. Troops.]

HUMPHRIES, STEPHEN, Private
Resided in Cleveland County where he enlisted at age 28, April 27, 1861. Present or accounted for until reported absent wounded in July-August, 1863; however, battle in which wounded not reported. Returned to duty prior to November 1, 1863, and present or accounted for until captured at Petersburg, Virginia, April 3, 1865. Confined at Point Lookout, Maryland, until released on June 21, 1865, after taking the Oath of Allegiance.

HUMPHRIES, SUMMA, Private
Place and date of enlistment not reported. Paroled at Appomattox Court House, Virginia, April 9, 1865.

HUMPHRIES, THOMAS, Private
Resided in Cleveland County where he enlisted at age 21, April 27, 1861. Present or accounted for until he died in Cleveland County on November 27, 1862, of disease.

HUNT, ELIJAH, Private
Enlisted in Wake County on October 14, 1863, for the war. Present or accounted for until hospitalized at Charlottesville, Virginia, May 7, 1864, with a gunshot wound; however, place and date wounded not reported. Returned to duty prior to November 1, 1864, and present or accounted for until furloughed for sixty days on December 19, 1864.

JACOBS, CARL, Private
Resided in Guilford County and enlisted in Wake County at age 37, July 15, 1862, for the war as a substitute. Present or accounted for through April, 1864. No further records.

JARRELL, ADAM, Private

Enlisted in Wake County on October 14, 1863, for the war. Present or accounted for until transferred to Company I of this regiment on April 13, 1864.

JARRELL, M., Private

Enlisted in Wake County on October 15, 1863, for the war. Present or accounted for until he deserted to the enemy on or about February 17, 1865. Released on or about February 21, 1865, after taking the Oath of Allegiance.

JOHNSON, B. G., Private

Resided in Warren County and enlisted in Wake County at age 18, July 15, 1862, for the war. Present or accounted for until he died in hospital at Richmond, Virginia, November 24, 1862, of "phthisis."

JOLLY, A. H., Private

Resided in Cleveland County where he enlisted at age 34, April 27, 1861. Present or accounted for until discharged on August 19, 1862, by reason of being over age.

JOLLY, B. B., Private

Resided in Cleveland County where he enlisted at age 28, August 1, 1861. Present or accounted for until he died in hospital at Danville, Virginia, June 1, 1862, of "typhoid pneumonia."

JOLLY, C. G., Private

Resided in Cleveland County where he enlisted at age 21, April 27, 1861. Present or accounted for until killed at or near Crampton's Pass, Maryland, September 14, 1862.

JOLLY, H. S., Private

Resided in Cleveland County where he enlisted at age 24, April 27, 1861. Present or accounted for until killed at Malvern Hill, Virginia, July 1, 1862.

JOLLY, M. M., Private

Resided in Cleveland County where he enlisted at age 24, April 27, 1861. Present or accounted for until he died on March 24, 1862, of disease. Place of death not reported.

JOLLY, WASHBURN, Private

Born in Cleveland County* where he resided as a farmer prior to enlisting in Cleveland County at age 22, April 27, 1861. Present or accounted for until discharged on July 11, 1863, by reason of "ascites."

KEETER, FREDERICK, Private

Resided in Rutherford County where he enlisted at age 17, March, 1865, for the war. No further records.

KING, GEORGE W., Private

Transferred to this company from an unspecified unit on August 14, 1862. Present or accounted for until wounded at or near Wilderness, Virginia, on or about May 6, 1864. Returned to duty prior to November 1, 1864. Present or accounted for until hospitalized at Raleigh on December 18, 1864, with a gunshot wound of the left foot; however, place and date wounded not reported. Furloughed for sixty days on December 19, 1864.

LANKFORD, LOVEL E., Private

Resided in Cleveland County where he enlisted at age 19, April 27, 1861. Present or accounted for until wounded in the abdomen and hip at Fredericksburg, Virginia, December 13, 1862.

Reported absent wounded or absent on light duty until he returned to duty in January-February, 1864. Present or accounted for until captured at Farmville, Virginia, April 6, 1865. Confined at Newport News, Virginia, until released on June 30, 1865, after taking the Oath of Allegiance.

LEDBETTER, ELIJAH, Private

Resided in Cleveland County where he enlisted at age 30, April 27, 1861. Present or accounted for until he died at Yorktown, Virginia, September 15, 1861, of "measles."

LOVE, ANDERSON M., Private

Resided in Cleveland County where he enlisted at age 23, April 27, 1861. Mustered in as Sergeant but was reduced to ranks in 1862. Present or accounted for until mortally wounded at Wilderness, Virginia, May 5, 1864. Exact place and date of death not reported.

LOVE, JOHN B., Private

Resided in Cleveland County where he enlisted at age 24, April 17, 1861. Present or accounted for until appointed Ensign on or about April 23, 1864, and transferred to the Field and Staff of this regiment.

LOVE, M. L., _____

Place and date of enlistment not reported. Name appears on a company record dated May 28, 1861. No further records.

McBRAYER, SAMUEL, Private

Resided in Cleveland County where he enlisted at age 30, April 27, 1861. Present or accounted for until he died "at home" on December 6, 1861. Cause of death not reported.

McCRAW, CHESLY, Private

Resided in Cleveland County where he enlisted at age 22, April 27, 1861. Mustered in as Musician but was reduced to ranks in January-February, 1863. Present or accounted for until paroled at Appomattox Court House, Virginia, April 9, 1865.

McCRAW, G. B., Private

Resided in Cleveland County where he enlisted at age 25, April 27, 1861. Present or accounted for until wounded at Bristoe Station, Virginia, October 14, 1863. Died October 17, 1863, of wounds. Place of death not reported.

McCRAW, JOHN C., Private

Enlisted in Cleveland County on February 1, 1864, for the war. Present or accounted for until hospitalized at Richmond, Virginia, May 9, 1864, with a gunshot wound of the breast; however, place and date wounded not reported. Returned to duty prior to November 1, 1864, and was paroled at Appomattox Court House, Virginia, April 9, 1865.

McCRAW, WILLIAM, Private

Resided in Cleveland County where he enlisted at age 30, April 27, 1861. Mustered in as Corporal but was reduced to ranks in September-December, 1861. Present or accounted for until wounded in the thigh and captured at or near Sharpsburg, Maryland, on or about September 28, 1862. Confined at Fort McHenry, Maryland, until paroled and transferred to Aiken's Landing, James River, Virginia, where he was received October 17, 1862, for exchange.

Declared exchanged at Aiken's Landing on November 10, 1862. Died in Cleveland County on December 18, 1862, of wounds.

McENTIRE, JASON J., Private
Resided in Cleveland County where he enlisted at age 19, April 27, 1861. Present or accounted for until wounded and captured at Crampton's Pass, Maryland, September 14, 1862. Hospitalized at Burkittsville, Maryland. Paroled prior to September 22, 1862, when he was hospitalized at Richmond, Virginia. Returned to duty in January-February, 1863, and present or accounted for until captured at Bristoe Station, Virginia, October 14, 1863. Confined at Old Capitol Prison, Washington, D.C., until transferred to Point Lookout, Maryland, October 27, 1863. Paroled and transferred for exchange on March 17, 1864. Returned to duty prior to November 1, 1864, and present or accounted for until captured at Hatcher's Run, Virginia, April 2, 1865. Confined at Point Lookout until released on June 29, 1865, after taking the Oath of Allegiance.

McENTIRE, M. M., Private
Resided in Cleveland County where he enlisted at age 18, April 27, 1861. Present or accounted for until wounded in the thigh and captured at or near Crampton's Pass, Maryland, September 14, 1862. Hospitalized at Burkittsville, Maryland. Paroled and exchanged at an unspecified date and was reported absent wounded or absent on detail from January-February, 1863, through October, 1864. Returned to duty prior to April 2, 1865, when he was captured at Hatcher's Run, Virginia. Confined at Point Lookout, Maryland, until released on June 29, 1865, after taking the Oath of Allegiance.

McGINNIS, G. W., Private
Resided in Rutherford County and enlisted in Cleveland County at age 20, April 27, 1861. Present or accounted for until he died in hospital at Richmond, Virginia, July 17, 1864, of disease.

McGINNIS, JOHN W., Private
Born in Cleveland County* and resided in Rutherford County where he was by occupation a farmer prior to enlisting in Cleveland County at age 22, April 27, 1861. Present or accounted for until discharged on July 2, 1862, by reason of "phthisis pulmonalis."

McSWAIN, J. B., Private
Born in Cleveland County* where he resided as a farmer prior to enlisting in Cleveland County at age 23, April 27, 1861. Present or accounted for until killed at or near Crampton's Pass, Maryland, September 14, 1862.

McSWAIN, J. F., Private
Resided in Cleveland County where he enlisted at age 16, April 27, 1861. Present or accounted for until discharged on August 19, 1862, by reason of being under age.

McSWAIN, THOMAS, Private
Resided in Cleveland County and was by occupation a farmer prior to enlisting in Cleveland County at age 20, June 22, 1861. Present or accounted for until he died on or about July 16, 1862, of disease. Place of death not reported.

MAYHEW, JACOB, Private
Resided in Cleveland County where he enlisted at age 40, May 1, 1863, for the war as a substitute. Present or accounted for until captured at Bristoe Station, Virginia, October 14, 1863. Confined at Old Capitol Prison, Washington, D.C., until transferred to Point Lookout, Maryland, February 3, 1864. Paroled and transferred to Aiken's Landing, James River, Virginia, on or about September 18, 1864, for exchange. Returned to duty at an unspecified date and was captured at or near Petersburg, Virginia, April 2, 1865. Confined at Point Lookout until released on June 29, 1865, after taking the Oath of Allegiance.

MOORE, GENERAL M., Corporal
Resided in Cleveland County where he enlisted at age 23, April 27, 1861. Mustered in as Private and promoted to Corporal on May 2, 1862. Present or accounted for until captured at Sutherland's Station, Virginia, on or about April 3, 1865. Confined at Point Lookout, Maryland, until released on June 29, 1865, after taking the Oath of Allegiance.

MOREHEAD, JOHN R., Private
Born in Cleveland County where he resided as a farmer prior to enlisting in Cleveland County at age 19, April 27, 1861. Present or accounted for until he died at Suffolk, Virginia, on or about March 25, 1862, of disease.

MURPHY, D., Private
Resided in Cleveland County and enlisted in Wake County at age 40, July 15, 1862, for the war as a substitute. Present or accounted for until he deserted on June 24, 1863.

MURPHY, W., Private
Resided in Cleveland County and enlisted in Wake County at age 35, July 15, 1862, for the war as a substitute. Present or accounted for until he deserted on August 5, 1862.

NOWLIN, HARDIN, Private
Resided in Cleveland County where he enlisted at age 59, April 27, 1861. Present or accounted for until discharged on or about May 31, 1862. Reason discharged not reported.

OWENS, ALLEN, Private
Born in Rutherford County where he resided as a farmer prior to enlisting in Cleveland County at age 23, April 27, 1861. Present or accounted for until wounded in the left arm at Sharpsburg, Maryland, September 17, 1862. Reported absent wounded until reported absent without leave on January 1, 1863. Reported absent without leave until discharged on April 2, 1864, by reason of "physical disability" resulting from wounds received at Sharpsburg.

OWENS, THOMAS C., Private
Resided in Cleveland County where he enlisted at age 36, April 1, 1863, for the war. Present or accounted for until he died "in camp" on April 13, 1864, of disease.

PANNEL, COLMAN B., Private
Resided in Rutherford County and enlisted in Wake County at age 31. Enlistment date reported as July 15, 1862; however, he was not listed on the rolls of

this company until March-April, 1863. Present or accounted for until furloughed for sixty days on February 28, 1865. [Company records indicate that he served previously in Mallett's Battalion (Camp Guard); however, records of Mallett's Battalion do not indicate that he served therein.]

PANNELL, ABRAHAM W., Private
Resided in Rutherford County and enlisted in Wake County at age 25, March 8, 1863, for the war. Present or accounted for until wounded in the left foot at Bristoe Station, Virginia, October 14, 1863. Reported absent wounded through October, 1864. [Company records indicate that he enlisted in Mallett's Battalion (Camp Guard) on July 15, 1862, and was transferred to this company on March 8, 1863; however, records of Mallett's Battalion do not indicate that he served therein.]

PARRISH, JORDAN G., Private
Resided in Warren County and enlisted in Wake County at age 31, October 3, 1863, for the war. Present or accounted for until transferred to Company I of this regiment on April 13, 1864.

PARTIAN, W. L., Private
Place and date of enlistment not reported. Paroled at Greensboro on May 9, 1865.

PENDER, WILLIAM, Private
Born in Wayne County where he resided as a farmer prior to enlisting in Wake County at age 27, July 15, 1862, for the war. Present or accounted for until discharged on December 2, 1862, by reason of "chr[onic] rheumatism and anchylosis of the right shoulder joint."

PERKINSON, JAMES R., Private
Resided in Warren County and enlisted in Wake County at age 18, July 15, 1862, for the war. Present or accounted for until wounded at or near Petersburg, Virginia, July 30, 1864. Reported absent wounded through October, 1864. Paroled at Appomattox Court House, Virginia, April 9, 1865.

PHELMET, J. M., Private
Resided in Cleveland County where he enlisted at age 18, April 27, 1861. Present or accounted for until he died at Yorktown, Virginia, July 31, 1861, of disease.

PRICE, D. G., Corporal
Resided in Cleveland County where he enlisted at age 34, April 27, 1861. Mustered in as Private and promoted to Corporal in September-December, 1861. Present or accounted for until discharged on August 19, 1862, by reason of being over age.

PRICHARD, JOSHUA, Private
Enlisted in Cleveland County on November 20, 1863, for the war. Present or accounted for through October, 1864.

PUTNAM, A. C., Private
Previously served in Company K, 49th Regiment N.C. Troops. Transferred to this company in May-September, 1862. Captured at or near Sharpsburg, Maryland, on or about September 17, 1862. Paroled at Keedysville, Maryland, September 20, 1862. Returned to duty prior to December 13, 1862, when he was wounded in the mouth at Fredericks-

burg, Virginia. Died in hospital at Charlottesville, Virginia, January 5, 1863, of wounds.

PUTNAM, A. M., Corporal
Resided in Cleveland County where he enlisted at age 20, April 27, 1861. Mustered in as Private and promoted to Corporal on May 2, 1862. Present or accounted for until wounded at Malvern Hill, Virginia, July 1, 1862. Died July 16, 1862, of disease. Place of death not reported.

PUTNAM, ARTHUR, Corporal
Resided in Cleveland County and enlisted in Wake County at age 34, March 8, 1863, for the war. Mustered in as Private and promoted to Corporal in November, 1864-April, 1865. Present or accounted for until captured at Hatcher's Run, Virginia, April 2, 1865. Confined at Point Lookout, Maryland, where he died May 10, 1865, of "chronic dysentery." [Company records indicate he enlisted in Mallett's Battalion (Camp Guard) on August 14, 1862, and was transferred to this company on March 8, 1863; however, records of Mallett's Battalion do not indicate that he served therein.]

PUTNAM, B. H., Private
Born in Cleveland County where he resided as a farmer prior to enlisting in Cleveland County at age 20, April 27, 1861. Present or accounted for until he died "at home" on January 30, 1862, of disease.

PUTNAM, E. L., Private
Resided in Cleveland County where he enlisted at age 19, December 9, 1861. Present or accounted for until transferred to 2nd Company B, 49th Regiment N.C. Troops, January 15, 1863, in exchange for Private John A. Waters.

PUTNAM, J. G. L., Private
Born in Cleveland County* where he resided as a farmer prior to enlisting in Cleveland County at age 27, April 27, 1861. Mustered in as Corporal but was reduced to ranks in September-December, 1861. Present or accounted for until he died at Yorktown, Virginia, November 4, 1861, of disease.

PUTNAM, J. L., Private
Resided in Cleveland County and enlisted in Wake County at age 33, March 8, 1863, for the war. Present or accounted for until he died at Orange Court House, Virginia, November 20, 1863. Cause of death not reported. [Company records indicate he enlisted in Mallett's Battalion (Camp Guard) on August 14, 1862, and was transferred to this company on March 8, 1863; however, records of Mallett's Battalion do not indicate that he served therein.]

PUTNAM, JAMES T., Private
Born in Cleveland County* where he resided as a farmer prior to enlisting in Cleveland County at age 23, April 27, 1861. Present or accounted for until he died in hospital at Petersburg, Virginia, July 27, 1862, of "pneumonia."

PUTNAM, L. W., Private
Enlisted in Cleveland County on February 10, 1864, for the war. Present or accounted for until he died in hospital at Lynchburg, Virginia, May 12, 1864, of "phthisis pul[monalis]."

PUTNAM, LEONARD M., Corporal
Resided in Cleveland County where he enlisted at age 25, March 1, 1863, for the war. Mustered in as Private and promoted to Corporal in November, 1863. Present or accounted for until paroled at Lynchburg, Virginia, on or about April 13, 1865.

PUTNAM, M. H., Corporal
Born in Cleveland County* where he resided as a mechanic prior to enlisting in Cleveland County at age 23, April 27, 1861. Mustered in as Corporal. Present or accounted for until he died at Goldsboro on February 17, 1863, of disease.

PUTNAM, MARTIN V., Private
Resided in Cleveland County where he enlisted at age 24, July 12, 1861. Mustered in as Private and promoted to Sergeant in October, 1862. Present or accounted for until wounded in the left leg at Bristoe Station, Virginia, October 14, 1863. Returned to duty in January-February, 1864, and present or accounted for until reported absent sick on June 18, 1864. Reduced to ranks in May-October, 1864. Reported absent sick until captured in hospital at Richmond, Virginia, April 3, 1865.

PUTNAM, RUFUS K., Private
Previously served in Company H, 34th Regiment N.C. Troops. Transferred to this company on September 1, 1862. Present or accounted for until captured at Hatcher's Run, Virginia, April 2, 1865. Confined at Point Lookout, Maryland, until released on June 16, 1865, after taking the Oath of Allegiance.

PUTNAM, SIDNEY G., Private
Resided in Cleveland County where he enlisted at age 19, April 27, 1861. Present or accounted for until captured at or near Antietam, Maryland, on or about September 27, 1862. Confined at Fort McHenry, Maryland, where he was paroled on November 12, 1862, and transferred for exchange. Rejoined the company in January-February, 1863, and present or accounted for until captured at Bristoe Station, Virginia, October 14, 1863. Confined at Old Capitol Prison, Washington, D.C., until transferred to Point Lookout, Maryland, October 27, 1863. Paroled on or about February 10, 1865, and transferred to Cox's Landing, James River, Virginia, for exchange. Hospitalized at Richmond, Virginia, February 15, 1865.

PUTNAM, THOMAS J., Sergeant
Resided in Cleveland County where he enlisted at age 20, April 27, 1861. Mustered in as Private and promoted to Sergeant in August, 1862. Present or accounted for until captured at or near Crampton's Pass, Maryland, September 14, 1862. Confined at Fort Delaware, Delaware, until transferred to Aiken's Landing, James River, Virginia, October 2, 1862, for exchange. Declared exchanged at Aiken's Landing on November 10, 1862. Returned to duty prior to January 1, 1863, and present or accounted for until wounded at Bristoe Station, Virginia, October 14, 1863. Returned to duty in January-February, 1864, and present or accounted for until captured at Hatcher's Run, Virginia, April 2, 1865. Confined at Point Lookout, Maryland, until

released on June 16, 1865, after taking the Oath of Allegiance.

PUTNAM, WILLIAM A., Private
Born in Cleveland County where he resided as a farmer prior to enlisting in Cleveland County at age 22, April 27, 1861. Present or accounted for until paroled at Keedysville, Maryland, September 20, 1862; however, place and date captured not reported. Returned to duty prior to January 1, 1863. Present or accounted for until transferred to 2nd Company B, 49th Regiment N.C. Troops, January 15, 1863, in exchange for Private Robert Brackett.

RIPPY, C. G., Private
Resided in Cleveland County and enlisted in Wake County at age 18, March 1, 1863, for the war. Present or accounted for until killed at Bristoe Station, Virginia, October 14, 1863.

RIPPY, SAMUEL H., Sergeant
Resided in Cleveland County where he enlisted at age 26, April 27, 1861. Mustered in as Private and promoted to Corporal in 1862. Reduced to ranks in July-August, 1863, but was promoted to Sergeant in May-October, 1864. Present or accounted for until paroled at Appomattox Court House, Virginia, April 9, 1865.

ROBENSON, G. B., Private
Enlisted in Cleveland County in March, 1864, for the war. Present or accounted for until he died in hospital at Lynchburg, Virginia, May 23, 1864, of "ascites."

ROBINSON, ELIJAH, Private
Previously served in Company C, 46th Regiment N.C. Troops. Transferred to this company on December 1, 1862, in exchange for Private Upton T. Bowdon. Present or accounted for until killed at Fredericksburg, Virginia, December 13, 1862.

ROBINSON, JOSEPH D., Private
Resided in Cleveland County where he enlisted at age 21, April 27, 1861. Present or accounted for until captured at Bristoe Station, Virginia, October 14, 1863. Confined at Old Capitol Prison, Washington, D.C., until transferred to Point Lookout, Maryland, February 3, 1864. Paroled at Point Lookout and transferred to Aiken's Landing, James River, Virginia, September 18, 1864, for exchange. Paroled at Appomattox Court House, Virginia, April 9, 1865, and was paroled again at Newton on or about April 19, 1865.

ROMINGER, FRANKLIN J., Private
Resided in Davidson County and enlisted in Wake County at age 18, July 15, 1862, for the war. Present or accounted for until captured at or near Crampton's Pass, Maryland, September 14, 1862. Confined at Fort Delaware, Delaware, until transferred to Aiken's Landing, James River, Virginia, October 2, 1862, for exchange. Declared exchanged at Aiken's Landing on November 10, 1862. Returned to duty prior to December 13, 1862, when he was wounded at Fredericksburg, Virginia. Returned to duty in March-April, 1863, and present or accounted for until captured at Bristoe Station, Virginia, October 14, 1863. Confined at Old Capitol Prison, Washington, D.C., until transferred to Point

Lookout, Maryland, October 27, 1863. Paroled at Point Lookout on or about February 24, 1865, and transferred to Aiken's Landing for exchange. Received for exchange prior to March 4, 1865.

RUSS, JOHN R., Private
Resided in Cleveland County where he enlisted at age 18, September 1, 1863, for the war. Present or accounted for through April, 1864. No further records.

RUSS, P. R., Private
Born in Cleveland County* where he resided as a farmer prior to enlisting in Cleveland County at age 29, April 27, 1861. Present or accounted for until discharged on December 5, 1861, by reason of "an irreducible scrotal hernia."

SANDERS, ALLEN J., Private
Born in Cleveland County where he resided as a farmer prior to enlisting in Cleveland County at age 16, April 27, 1861. Present or accounted for until discharged on November 29, 1862, by reason of "minority and general bad health." His discharge was declared "illegal" in January-February, 1863, and he returned to duty in March-April, 1863. Present or accounted for until hospitalized at Richmond, Virginia, June 3, 1864, with a gunshot wound of the thumb of the left hand; however, place and date wounded not reported. Returned to duty in September-October, 1864, and present or accounted for through October, 1864.

SANDERS, L. D. S., Private
Enlisted in Cleveland County on February 10, 1864, for the war. Present or accounted for until he died in hospital at Richmond, Virginia, April 28, 1864, of "rubeola."

SARRATT, UGENIS, Sergeant
Resided in Cleveland County where he enlisted at age 21, April 27, 1861. Mustered in as Sergeant. Present or accounted for until wounded at or near Petersburg, Virginia, June 15, 1864. Reported absent wounded until retired to the Invalid Corps on December 15, 1864, by reason of "t[otal] d[isability]."

SHORT, ABNER, Private
Born in Rutherford County and was by occupation a farmer prior to enlisting at Camp Vance on October 15, 1863, for the war. Present or accounted for until discharged on September 5, 1864, by reason of "chronic rheumatism." Discharge records give his age as 37.

SHORT, JOSEPH, Private
Resided in Rutherford County and enlisted in Wake County on October 15, 1863, for the war. Present or accounted for until captured at Hatcher's Run, Virginia, April 2, 1865. Confined at Point Lookout, Maryland, until released on June 20, 1865, after taking the Oath of Allegiance.

SHUFORD, J. M., Sergeant
Born in Buncombe County and resided in Cleveland County where he was by occupation a farmer prior to enlisting in Cleveland County at age 21, April 27, 1861. Mustered in as Private and promoted to Sergeant in August, 1862. Present or accounted for until killed at or near Crampton's Pass, Maryland, September 14, 1862.

SIMPSON, RICHARD, Private
Resided in Union County and enlisted in Wake County at age 30, March 8, 1863, for the war. Present or accounted for until wounded at Wilderness, Virginia, May 5, 1864. Reported absent wounded through October, 1864. [Company records indicate he enlisted in Mallett's Battalion (Camp Guard) on December 15, 1862, and was transferred to this company on March 8, 1863; however, records of Mallett's Battalion do not indicate that he served therein.]

SPAKE, H. E., Private
Resided in Cleveland County where he enlisted at age 35, April 27, 1861. Present or accounted for until discharged on August 19, 1862, by reason of being over age.

SPAKE, P. P., Private
Resided in Cleveland County where he enlisted at age 25, June 6, 1863, for the war. Present or accounted for through April, 1864. No further records.

SPURLIN, ISAAC, Private
Previously served in Company H, 34th Regiment N.C. Troops. Transferred to this company on October 1, 1862. Present or accounted for until captured at Bristoe Station, Virginia, October 14, 1863. Confined at Old Capitol Prison, Washington, D.C., until released on or about December 13, 1863, after taking the Oath of Allegiance.

SPURLIN, J. W., Private
Resided in Rutherford County and enlisted in Wake County at age 34, March 8, 1863, for the war. Present or accounted for until he died in hospital at Gordonsville, Virginia, April 8, 1864, of "pneumonia." [Company records indicate he enlisted in Mallett's Battalion (Camp Guard) on July 15, 1862, and was transferred to this company on March 8, 1863; however, records of Mallett's Battalion do not indicate that he served therein.]

SPURLIN, JOHN JEFFERSON, Private
Born in Cleveland County where he resided as a farmer prior to enlisting in Cleveland County at age 18, September 1, 1863, for the war. Present or accounted for until captured at Hatcher's Run, Virginia, April 2, 1865. Confined at Point Lookout, Maryland, until released on June 20, 1865. North Carolina pension records indicate he was wounded in the "bowels" near Petersburg, Virginia, April 4, 1865.

STEWART, AMOS, Private
Place and date of enlistment not reported. Captured at Hatcher's Run, Virginia, April 2, 1865, and confined at Point Lookout, Maryland, until released on June 20, 1865.

STEWART, MICHAEL M., Private
Resided in Davidson County and enlisted in Wake County at age 23, July 15, 1862, for the war. Present or accounted for until captured at or near Crampton's Pass, Maryland, on or about September 15, 1862. Confined at Fort Delaware, Delaware, until transferred to Aiken's Landing, James River, Virginia, October 2, 1862, for exchange. Declared exchanged at Aiken's Landing on November 10, 1862. Listed as a deserter in November-December, 1862, but returned

to duty prior to March, 1, 1863. Present or accounted for until captured at Hatcher's Run, Virginia, April 2, 1865. Confined at Point Lookout, Maryland, until released on June 20, 1865, after taking the Oath of Allegiance.

STONE, ROBERT F., Private

Previously served in Company C, 46th Regiment N.C. Troops. Transferred to this company on December 1, 1862, in exchange for Private Andrew J. Bowden. Present or accounted for until transferred to Company E of this regiment on April 3, 1863.

SWAIN, MICHAEL, Private

Resided in Davidson County and enlisted in Wake County at age 30, July 15, 1862, for the war. Present or accounted for until captured at or near Crampton's Pass, Maryland, September 14, 1862. Confined at Fort Delaware, Delaware, until transferred to Aiken's Landing, James River, Virginia, October 2, 1862, for exchange. Declared exchanged at Aiken's Landing on November 10, 1862. Deserted at an unspecified date but was apprehended and confined at Castle Thunder Prison, Richmond, Virginia. Died in hospital at Richmond on December 13, 1862, of "typhoid fever."

TATE, KINCHEN T., Private

Resided in Cleveland County where he enlisted at age 20, March 1, 1863, for the war. Present or accounted for until wounded at Bristoe Station, Virginia, October 14, 1863. Returned to duty prior to January 1, 1864, and present or accounted for until he deserted to the enemy on or about April 1, 1865. Released on or about April 6, 1865, after taking the Oath of Allegiance.

TATE, WILLIAM B., Private

Enlisted in Cleveland County on February 10, 1864, for the war. Present or accounted for until he deserted to the enemy on or about April 1, 1865. Released on or about April 6, 1865, after taking the Oath of Allegiance.

TURNER, LEONIDAS, Private

Resided in Cleveland County where he enlisted at age 18, April 27, 1861. Present or accounted for until discharged on August 4, 1862, after providing a substitute.

TURNER, M., _____

Place and date of enlistment not reported. Name appears on a company record dated May 28, 1861. No further records.

TURNER, M. V., Private

Resided in Cleveland County where he enlisted at age 18, April 27, 1861. Present or accounted for until transferred to 2nd Company D of this regiment on April 8, 1863.

TURNER, WILLIAM, Private

Enlisted in Cleveland County on April 27, 1861. Present or accounted for until discharged on June 3, 1861. Reason discharged not reported.

WARREN, A. E., Private

Enlisted in Cleveland County on April 27, 1861. Present or accounted for until discharged on June 3, 1861. Reason discharged not reported.

WATERS, JOHN A., Sergeant

Previously served in 2nd Company B, 49th Regiment N.C. Troops. Transferred to this company on January

15, 1863, in exchange for Private E.L. Putnam. Joined the company with the rank of Private and was promoted to Sergeant in November, 1864-April, 1865. Present or accounted for until wounded in the right thigh and captured at Hatcher's Run, Virginia, April 2, 1865. Right leg amputated. Hospitalized at Washington, D.C., until released on or about June 14, 1865, after taking the Oath of Allegiance.

WEAVER, A., Private

Resided in Davidson County and enlisted in Wake County at age 23, July 15, 1862, for the war. Present or accounted for until wounded at Bristoe Station, Virginia, October 14, 1863. Died October 15, 1863, of wounds. Place of death not reported.

WEAVER, HENRY F., Private

Previously served in Company B of this regiment. Transferred to this company on September 15, 1863. Present or accounted for until captured in hospital at Richmond, Virginia, April 3, 1865. Paroled at Richmond on or about April 18, 1865.

WHISNANT, C., Private

Resided in Cleveland County where he enlisted at age 16, March 1, 1863, for the war. Present or accounted for until discharged on June 5, 1863. Reason discharged not reported.

WHITAKER, MARTIN, Private

Enlisted in Wake County on October 14, 1863, for the war. Present or accounted for until transferred to Company I of this regiment on April 13, 1864.

WHITE, DAVID N., Private

Resided in Cleveland County or in York District, South Carolina, and enlisted in Wake County at age 58, July 15, 1862, for the war as a substitute. Present or accounted for until transferred to 2nd Company D of this regiment on April 8, 1863.

WILEY, WILLIAM G., Private

Resided in Cleveland County where he enlisted at age 23, April 27, 1861. Present or accounted for until wounded at Malvern Hill, Virginia, July 1, 1862. Returned to duty prior to December 13, 1862, when he was wounded in the arm at Fredericksburg, Virginia. Returned to duty prior to January 1, 1863, and present or accounted for until paroled at Appomattox Court House, Virginia, April 9, 1865.

WILIE, R. A., Private

Born in York District, South Carolina, and resided in Cleveland County where he was by occupation a farmer prior to enlisting at age 18, May 4, 1862, for the war. Present or accounted for until wounded in the breast at Malvern Hill, Virginia, July 1, 1862. Hospitalized at Richmond, Virginia, where he died July 12, 1862, of wounds.

WILLIAMS, J. M., Private

Resided in Cleveland County where he enlisted at age 24, March 1, 1863, for the war. Present or accounted for until he died in hospital at Petersburg, Virginia, June 17, 1863, of "febris typhoides."

WILLIAMS, JOHN M., Private

Resided in Cleveland County where he enlisted at age 36, April 27, 1861. Present or accounted for until discharged on June 22, 1861. Reason discharged not reported.

WILLIAMSON, PETER, Private

Resided in Rowan County and enlisted in Wake County at age 56, July 15, 1862, for the war as a substitute. Present or accounted for through October, 1864; however, he was reported absent on detail during most of that period.

WILSON, D. R., Private

Born in Cleveland County* where he resided as a farmer prior to enlisting in Cleveland County at age 23, April 27, 1861. Present or accounted for until killed at Malvern Hill, Virginia, July 1, 1862.

WOOD, GREEN. B. C., Private

Resided in Cleveland County where he enlisted at age 18, October 3, 1863, for the war. Present or accounted for until captured at Hatcher's Run, Virginia, April 2, 1865. Confined at Point Lookout, Maryland, where he died on May 12, 1865. Cause of death not reported.

WOOD, WILLIAM C. S., 1st Sergeant

Resided in Cleveland County where he enlisted at age 20, April 27, 1861. Mustered in as Private and promoted to Sergeant in November, 1861. Promoted to 1st Sergeant in September, 1862. Present or accounted for until wounded and captured at Crampton's Pass, Maryland, September 14, 1862. Paroled at an unspecified date prior to September 26, 1862, and returned to duty prior to March 1, 1863. Present or accounted for until captured at Petersburg, Virginia, April 3, 1865. Confined at Point Lookout, Maryland, until released on June 22, 1865, after taking the Oath of Allegiance.

WRIGHT, JOSEPH J., Private

Resided in Cleveland County and enlisted in Wake County at age 31, March 1, 1863, for the war. Present or accounted for until reported absent wounded on April 17, 1863; however, battle in which wounded not reported. Reported absent without leave from May 25, 1863, through October 31, 1864. Records of the United Daughters of the Confederacy indicate that he died in 1865. Place, cause, and exact date of death not reported.

WYLIE, J. A., Private

Born in York District, South Carolina, and resided in Cleveland County where he enlisted at age 21, April 27, 1861. Present or accounted for until wounded at Malvern Hill, Virginia, July 1, 1862. Returned to duty prior to September 17, 1862, when he was wounded at Sharpsburg, Maryland. Died at "Elias Grove's Farm" on or about September 20, 1862, of wounds.

1st COMPANY D

This company, known as the "Cleveland Mountain Boys," was from Cleveland County and enlisted at Shelby on May 14, 1861. It was mustered in on June 2, 1861, and was assigned to this regiment as Company D. Inasmuch as it was the first of two companies to serve in the regiment as Company D, it was later referred to as 1st Company D. The company served with this regiment until January 9, 1863, when it was transferred to the 49th Regiment N. C. Troops. Because it was the second company to serve as Company B of that regiment, it was

designated 2nd Company B. The following roster covers only the period from the original enlistment date through January 9, 1863. All information after that date will be recorded in the roster of 2nd Company B, 49th Regiment N. C. Troops.

The information contained in the following roster of the company was compiled principally from company muster rolls for June 2-August, 1861, and November-December, 1862. No company muster rolls were found for September, 1861-October, 1862, or for the period after December, 1862. In addition to the company muster rolls, Roll of Honor records, receipt rolls, hospital records, prisoner of war records, and other primary records, supplemented by state pension applications, United Daughters of the Confederacy records, and postwar rosters and histories, all provided useful information.

OFFICERS
CAPTAIN

CORBETT, WILLIAM S.

Resided in Cleveland County where he enlisted at age 26. Appointed Captain to rank from May 14, 1861. Present or accounted for until transferred to 2nd Company B, 49th Regiment N. C. Troops, January 9, 1863.

LIEUTENANTS

CABANISS, HARVEY D., 1st Lieutenant

Resided in Cleveland County where he enlisted at age 36. Appointed 1st Lieutenant on or about May 14, 1861. Appointed Assistant Quartermaster (Captain) on July 19, 1861, and transferred to the Field and Staff of this regiment.

CONLEY, H. CLAY, 2nd Lieutenant

Clark's *Regiments* indicates that he served in this company; however, company records do not substantiate that report. Later served in Company A, 49th Regiment N. C. Troops.

HICKS, F. Y., 3rd Lieutenant

Resided in Cleveland County where he enlisted at age 23, May 14, 1861. Mustered in as Private and promoted to Sergeant at an unspecified date. Appointed 3rd Lieutenant on May 2, 1862. Present or accounted for until captured at or near Crampton's Pass, Maryland, on or about September 14, 1862. Confined at Fort Delaware, Delaware, until transferred to Aiken's Landing, James River, Virginia, October 2, 1862, for exchange. Declared exchanged at Aiken's Landing on November 10, 1862. Present or accounted for until transferred to 2nd Company B, 49th Regiment N. C. Troops, January 9, 1863.

HIGGINS, JAMES MARION, 1st Lieutenant

Clark's *Regiments* indicates that he served in this company; however, company records do not substantiate that report. Later served as Captain of Company A, 49th Regiment N. C. Troops.

HOEY, SAMUEL A., 1st Lieutenant

Previously served as Private in Company F, 5th Regiment South Carolina Infantry. Appointed 1st Lieutenant (Drillmaster) in this company on or about

July 6, 1861. Present or accounted for through August 28, 1861. Appointed Captain of Company H, 34th Regiment N.C. Troops, October 1, 1861.

HORAN, GEORGE P., 3rd Lieutenant
Born in Ireland and was by occupation a painter prior to enlisting in Cleveland County at age 28, March 18, 1862. Mustered in as Corporal and was appointed 3rd Lieutenant on October 7, 1862. Present or accounted for until court-martialed on or about October 28, 1862, under charges that from August 1 until October 5, 1861, he "did bed and cohabit with . . . a free woman of color in an open and notorious manner." Dismissed from service on or about November 22, 1861. Later served as 1st Lieutenant in Company G, 49th Regiment N.C. Troops.

HUNT, ROBERT W., 3rd Lieutenant
Resided in Cleveland County where he enlisted at age 26, May 14, 1861. Mustered in as Sergeant and was appointed 3rd Lieutenant to rank from January 7, 1862. Present or accounted for until he was defeated for reelection when the regiment was reorganized on May 2, 1862.

LATTIMORE, DANIEL D., 2nd Lieutenant
Resided in Cleveland County where he enlisted at age 26. Appointed 2nd Lieutenant to rank from May 14, 1861. Present or accounted for until transferred to 2nd Company B, 49th Regiment N.C. Troops, January 9, 1863.

LYTLE, THOMAS Y., 2nd Lieutenant
Clark's *Regiments* indicates that he served in this company; however, company records do not substantiate that report. Later served as 2nd Lieutenant in Company A, 49th Regiment N.C. Troops.

MAGNESS, JUDSON JORDAN, 1st Lieutenant
Resided in Cleveland County where he enlisted at age 22, May 14, 1861. Mustered in as 1st Sergeant and was appointed 1st Lieutenant on March 13, 1862. Present or accounted for until transferred to 2nd Company B, 49th Regiment N.C. Troops, January 9, 1863.

NONCOMMISSIONED OFFICERS AND PRIVATES

ANTHONY, J. D., Musician
Resided in Cleveland County where he enlisted at age 27, May 14, 1861. Mustered in as Musician. Present or accounted for until transferred to 2nd Company B, 49th Regiment N.C. Troops, January 9, 1863.

BARTEE, G. C., Private
Resided in Cleveland County where he enlisted at age 43, May 14, 1861. Present or accounted for until he died at Danville, Virginia, July 7, 1862, of "pneumonia."

BERRIER, A., Private
Resided in Davidson County and enlisted in Wake County at age 30, July 15, 1862, for the war. Present or accounted for until he deserted on November 30, 1862. Rejoined the company on February 28, 1863, after it was redesignated 2nd Company B, 49th Regiment N.C. Troops.

BOGGS, NOAH ELIAS, Corporal
Resided in Cleveland County where he enlisted at age 21, May 14, 1861. Mustered in as Private. Present or accounted for until captured at or near Crampton's Pass, Maryland, September 14, 1862. Confined at Fort Delaware, Delaware, until transferred to Aiken's Landing, James River, Virginia, October 2, 1862, for exchange. Declared exchanged at Aiken's Landing on November 10, 1862. Promoted to Corporal on December 15, 1862, and was transferred to 2nd Company B, 49th Regiment N.C. Troops, January 9, 1863.

BOGGS, S. M. C., Private
Resided in Cleveland County where he enlisted at age 27, May 14, 1861. Present or accounted for until discharged at Richmond, Virginia, August 19, 1862. Reason discharged not reported.

BRACKETT, J. H., Corporal
Resided in Cleveland County where he enlisted at age 25, May 14, 1861. Mustered in as Corporal. Present or accounted for until he died at Yorktown, Virginia, August 12, 1861, of "fever."

BRACKETT, JOHN, Private
Resided in Cleveland County where he enlisted at age 24, May 14, 1861. Present or accounted for until he died at Yorktown, Virginia, on or about August 12, 1861, of "measles."

BRACKETT, JOSEPH, Corporal
Resided in Cleveland County where he enlisted at age 26, May 14, 1861. Mustered in as Private and promoted to Corporal prior to July 26, 1862. Present or accounted for until transferred to 2nd Company B, 49th Regiment N.C. Troops, January 9, 1863.

BRACKETT, ROBERT, Private
Resided in Cleveland County where he enlisted at age 28, May 14, 1861. Present or accounted for until wounded in the nose at Fredericksburg, Virginia, December 13, 1862. Present or accounted for until transferred to 2nd Company B, 49th Regiment N.C. Troops, January 9, 1863.

BRINKLEY, D., Private
Resided in Davidson County and enlisted in Wake County at age 25, July 15, 1862, for the war. Present or accounted for until he deserted at or near Sharpsburg, Maryland, September 16-17, 1862. Rejoined the company on February 12, 1863, after it had been redesignated 2nd Company B, 49th Regiment N.C. Troops.

BRINKLEY, H., Private
Resided in Davidson County and enlisted in Wake County at age 22, July 15, 1862, for the war. Present or accounted for until he deserted at Hanover Junction, Virginia, August 21, 1862. Reported as a deserter through January 9, 1863, at which time the company was redesignated 2nd Company B, 49th Regiment N.C. Troops.

BRINKLEY, J. H., Private
Resided in Davidson County and enlisted in Wake County at age 23, July 15, 1862, for the war. Present or accounted for until transferred to 2nd Company B, 49th Regiment N.C. Troops, January 9, 1863.

BYERLY, GEORGE LINDSAY, Private
Resided in Davidson County and enlisted in Wake

County at age 17, July 15, 1862, for the war. Present or accounted for until wounded at or near Crampton's Pass, Maryland, September 14, 1862. Returned to duty prior to January 1, 1863, and was transferred to 2nd Company B, 49th Regiment N.C. Troops, January 9, 1863.

BYNUM, BRINKLEY, _____
Negro. North Carolina pension records indicate that he joined this company in February, 1862. No further records.

CABANISS, F. W., Private
Resided in Cleveland County where he enlisted at age 18, May 14, 1861. Mustered in as Corporal but was reduced to ranks in September, 1861-December, 1862. Present or accounted for until transferred to 2nd Company B, 49th Regiment N.C. Troops, January 9, 1863.

CARTER, J. C., Private
Resided in Cleveland County where he enlisted at age 22, May 14, 1861. Present or accounted for until captured at or near Crampton's Pass, Maryland, September 14, 1862. Confined at Fort Delaware, Delaware, until transferred to Aiken's Landing, James River, Virginia, October 2, 1862, for exchange. Declared exchanged at Aiken's Landing on November 10, 1862. Transferred to 2nd Company B, 49th Regiment N.C. Troops, January 9, 1863.

CHARLES, R. F., Private
Resided in Davidson County and enlisted in Wake County at age 30, July 15, 1862, for the war. Present or accounted for until captured at or near Crampton's Pass, Maryland, September 14, 1862. Confined at Fort Delaware, Delaware, until transferred to Aiken's Landing, James River, Virginia, October 2, 1862, for exchange. Declared exchanged at Aiken's Landing on November 10, 1862. Deserted on November 10, 1862, but rejoined the company on February 28, 1863, after it had been redesignated 2nd Company B, 49th Regiment N.C. Troops.

CLODFELTER, GEORGE R., Private
Resided in Davidson County and enlisted in Wake County at age 29, July 15, 1862, for the war. Present or accounted for until he deserted at or near Sharpsburg, Maryland, September 16-17, 1862. Rejoined the company on February 12, 1863, after it had been redesignated 2nd Company B, 49th Regiment N.C. Troops.

CLODFELTER, J., Private
Resided in Davidson County and enlisted in Wake County at age 31, July 15, 1862, for the war. Present or accounted for until transferred to 2nd Company B, 49th Regiment N.C. Troops, January 9, 1863.

CONNER, JOHN, Private
Resided in Catawba County and enlisted in Cleveland County at age 19, May 14, 1861. Present or accounted for until he died at Goldsboro on May 8, 1862, of disease.

CONRAD, L. L., Private
Born in Davidson County where he resided as a farmer prior to enlisting in Wake County on July 15, 1862, for the war. Age variously reported as 25 and 30. Present or accounted for until wounded and captured at or near Crampton's Pass, Maryland, September 14, 1862.

Confined at Fort Delaware, Delaware, until transferred to Aiken's Landing, James River, Virginia, October 2, 1862, for exchange. Declared exchanged at Aiken's Landing on November 10, 1862. Transferred to 2nd Company B, 49th Regiment N.C. Troops, January 9, 1863.

COOK, JAMES MADISON, Private
Resided in Davidson County and enlisted in Wake County at age 18, July 15, 1862, for the war. Present or accounted for until wounded at Sharpsburg, Maryland, September 17, 1862. Reported absent wounded through December, 1862. Transferred to 2nd Company B, 49th Regiment N.C. Troops, January 9, 1863.

CORBETT, _____, Corporal
Place and date of enlistment not reported. Name appears on a regimental record dated May, 1862, which states that he was absent sick at Richmond, Virginia. No further records.

CORNISH, JACOB, Private
Resided in Davidson County and enlisted in Wake County at age 28, July 15, 1862, for the war. Present or accounted for until he deserted at an unspecified date. Returned to duty prior to January 1, 1863, and was transferred to 2nd Company B, 49th Regiment N.C. Troops, January 9, 1863.

CRAVER, F., Private
Resided in Davidson County and enlisted in Wake County at age 30, July 15, 1862, for the war. Present or accounted for until he deserted on August 21, 1862. Rejoined the company on February 15, 1863, after it had been redesignated 2nd Company B, 49th Regiment N.C. Troops.

CRAVER, G. N., Private
Resided in Davidson County and enlisted in Wake County at age 28, July 15, 1862, for the war. Present or accounted for until he deserted on August 21, 1862. Rejoined the company on February 15, 1863, after it had been redesignated 2nd Company B, 49th Regiment N.C. Troops.

CROUCH, JACOB, Private
Resided in Davidson County and enlisted in Wake County at age 28, July 15, 1862, for the war. Present or accounted for until transferred to 2nd Company B, 49th Regiment N.C. Troops, January 9, 1863.

DELAP, JOHN, Private
Resided in Davidson County and enlisted in Wake County on July 15, 1862, for the war. Present or accounted for until wounded in the shoulder and captured at or near Crampton's Pass, Maryland, September 14, 1862. Died in hospital at Burkittsville, Maryland, September 28, 1862, of wounds.

DELAP, V., Private
Resided in Davidson County and enlisted in Wake County at age 27, July 15, 1862, for the war. Present or accounted for until he died at Lynchburg, Virginia, October 1, 1862. Cause of death not reported.

DELLINGER, NOAH H., Private
Resided in Cleveland County where he enlisted at age 26, May 14, 1861. Present or accounted for until transferred to 2nd Company B, 49th Regiment N.C. Troops, January 9, 1863.

DEVINEY, J. M., Private
Resided in Cleveland County where he enlisted at age 21, May 14, 1861. Present or accounted for until he died at Yorktown, Virginia, August 4, 1861, of disease.

DISHER, C., Private
Resided in Davidson County and enlisted in Wake County at age 26, July 15, 1862, for the war. Present or accounted for until hospitalized at Richmond, Virginia, September 16, 1862, with "chronic diarrhoea." Furloughed for thirty days on November 7, 1862, and died in Davidson County on or about November 15, 1862, of disease.

DISHER, H., Private
Resided in Davidson County and enlisted in Wake County at age 32, July 15, 1862, for the war. Present or accounted for until transferred to 2nd Company B, 49th Regiment N.C. Troops, January 9, 1863.

DISHER, THOMAS, Private
Resided in Davidson County and enlisted in Wake County at age 20, July 15, 1862, for the war. Present or accounted for until captured at Crampton's Pass, Maryland, September 14, 1862. Confined at Fort Delaware, Delaware, until transferred to Aiken's Landing, James River, Virginia, October 2, 1862, for exchange. Declared exchanged at Aiken's Landing on November 10, 1862. Transferred to 2nd Company B, 49th Regiment N.C. Troops, January 9, 1863.

DIVINNY, WILLIAM G., Private
Resided in Cleveland County where he enlisted at age 22, May 14, 1861. Present or accounted for until reported absent without leave on October 15, 1862. Reported absent without leave through January 9, 1863, when the company was redesignated 2nd Company B, 49th Regiment N.C. Troops.

DOTY, ISAAC, Private
Resided in Davidson County and enlisted in Wake County at age 30, July 15, 1862, for the war. Present or accounted for until mortally wounded at Sharpsburg, Maryland, September 17, 1862. Exact place and date of death not reported.

DOWNS, JOSEPH, Private
Resided in Cleveland County where he enlisted at age 22, May 14, 1861. Present or accounted for until killed at Lee's Mill, Virginia, April 16, 1862.

ELLER, S. F., Private
Resided in Davidson County and enlisted in Wake County at age 25, July 15, 1862, for the war. Present or accounted for until wounded in the foot at Fredericksburg, Virginia, December 13, 1862. Reported absent wounded through December, 1862. Transferred to 2nd Company B, 49th Regiment N.C. Troops, January 9, 1863.

ELLIOTT, C. B., Corporal
Born in Cleveland County where he resided as a farmer prior to enlisting in Cleveland County at age 18, May 14, 1861. Mustered in as Private and promoted to Corporal on November 10, 1861. Present or accounted for until he died in Cleveland County on January 18, 1862, of disease.

ELLIS, W. H., Private
Resided in Davidson County and enlisted in Wake County at age 27, July 15, 1862, for the war. Present or

accounted for until transferred to 2nd Company B, 49th Regiment N.C. Troops, January 9, 1863.

ESSICK, RANSOM, Private
Resided in Davidson County and enlisted in Wake County at age 28, July 15, 1862, for the war. Present or accounted for until he deserted on August 21, 1862. Rejoined the company on January 28, 1863, after it had been redesignated 2nd Company B, 49th Regiment N.C. Troops.

ESSICK, THOMAS, Private
Resided in Davidson County and enlisted in Wake County at age 25, July 15, 1862, for the war. Present or accounted for until he deserted on August 21, 1862. Rejoined the company on February 15, 1863, after it had been redesignated 2nd Company B, 49th Regiment N.C. Troops.

EVERHART, A., Private
Resided in Davidson County and enlisted in Wake County at age 21, July 15, 1862, for the war. Present or accounted for until wounded in the arm at Fredericksburg, Virginia, December 13, 1862. Returned to duty prior to January 1, 1863, and was transferred to 2nd Company B, 49th Regiment N.C. Troops, January 9, 1863.

EVERHART, BRITTON, Private
Resided in Davidson County and enlisted in Wake County at age 32, July 15, 1862, for the war. Present or accounted for until transferred to 2nd Company B, 49th Regiment N.C. Troops, January 9, 1863.

EVERHART, C., Private
Resided in Davidson County and enlisted in Wake County at age 28, July 15, 1862, for the war. Present or accounted for until wounded at or near Crampton's Pass, Maryland, September 14, 1862. Returned to duty prior to December 13, 1862, when he was wounded in the arm at Fredericksburg, Virginia. Reported absent wounded through December, 1862. Transferred to 2nd Company B, 49th Regiment N.C. Troops, January 9, 1863.

EVERHART, H., Private
Resided in Davidson County and enlisted in Wake County at age 30, July 15, 1862, for the war. Present or accounted for until he deserted at Hanover Junction, Virginia, August 21, 1862. Rejoined the company on August 31, 1864, after it had been redesignated 2nd Company B, 49th Regiment N.C. Troops.

EVERHART, MICHAEL, Private
Resided in Davidson County and enlisted in Wake County at age 29, July 15, 1862, for the war. Present or accounted for until wounded in the hand at Fredericksburg, Virginia, December 13, 1862. Reported absent wounded through December, 1862. Transferred to 2nd Company B, 49th Regiment N.C. Troops, January 9, 1863.

EVERHART, WILLIAM, Private
Resided in Davidson County and enlisted in Wake County at age 33, July 15, 1862, for the war. Present or accounted for until he deserted on October 30, 1862. Rejoined the company on or about February 20, 1864, after it had been redesignated 2nd Company B, 49th Regiment N.C. Troops.

FINCH, WILLIAM M., Private
Resided in Cleveland County where he enlisted at age

26, May 14, 1861. Present or accounted for until killed at Lee's Mill, Virginia, April 16, 1862.

FORBES, JOSEPH T., Private
Resided in Cleveland County where he enlisted at age 21, May 14, 1861. Present or accounted for until transferred to 2nd Company B, 49th Regiment N.C. Troops, January 9, 1863.

FOUTS, A., Private
Resided in Davidson County and enlisted in Wake County at age 31, July 15, 1862, for the war. Present or accounted for until transferred to 2nd Company B, 49th Regiment N.C. Troops, January 9, 1863.

FRITTS, H., Private
Resided in Davidson County and enlisted in Wake County at age 28, July 15, 1862, for the war. Present or accounted for until captured at Crampton's Pass, Maryland, September 14, 1862. Confined at Fort Delaware, Delaware, until transferred to Aiken's Landing, James River, Virginia, October 2, 1862, for exchange. Declared exchanged at Aiken's Landing on November 10, 1862. Present or accounted for until transferred to 2nd Company B, 49th Regiment N.C. Troops, January 9, 1863.

FRONEBARGER, C. M., 1st Sergeant
Resided in Gaston County and enlisted in Cleveland County at age 18, May 14, 1861. Mustered in as Private and promoted to 1st Sergeant on March 13, 1862. Present or accounted for until killed at Malvern Hill, Virginia, July 1, 1862.

FRONEBERGER, J. R., Corporal
Resided in Cleveland County where he enlisted at age 23, May 14, 1861. Mustered in as Private and promoted to Corporal on May 2, 1862. Present or accounted for until killed at Fredericksburg, Virginia, December 13, 1862.

FULTZ, A., Private
Resided in Davidson County and enlisted in Wake County at age 22, July 15, 1862, for the war. Present or accounted for until captured at or near Crampton's Pass, Maryland, September 14, 1862. Confined at an unspecified Federal prison until transferred to Aiken's Landing, James River, Virginia, where he was received October 6, 1862, for exchange. Declared exchanged at Aiken's Landing on November 10, 1862. Returned to duty on December 5, 1862, and was transferred to 2nd Company B, 49th Regiment N.C. Troops, January 9, 1863.

FULTZ, FRANCIS, Private
Resided in Union or Davidson counties and enlisted in Wake County at age 23, July 15, 1862, for the war. Present or accounted for until wounded and captured at or near Crampton's Pass, Maryland, September 14, 1862. Hospitalized at Burkittsville, Maryland, until transferred to Fort Delaware, Delaware, at an unspecified date. Paroled and transferred to Aiken's Landing, James River, Virginia, October 2, 1862, for exchange. Declared exchanged at Aiken's Landing on November 10, 1862. Reported absent wounded until January 9, 1863, when the company was redesignated 2nd Company B, 49th Regiment N.C. Troops.

GLADDEN, W. H., Private
Resided in Cleveland County where he enlisted at age 21, May 14, 1861. Present or accounted for until

hospitalized at Richmond, Virginia, November 7, 1862, with a gunshot wound; however, place and date wounded not reported. Transferred to 2nd Company B, 49th Regiment N.C. Troops, January 9, 1863.

GLENN, J. E., Corporal
Resided in Cleveland County where he enlisted at age 19, May 14, 1861. Mustered in as Private and promoted to Corporal on April 10, 1862. Present or accounted for until wounded in the arm at Malvern Hill, Virginia, July 1, 1862. Died "at home" on July 24, 1862, of wounds.

GOINS, MICHAEL H., Private
Resided in Cleveland County where he enlisted at age 21, May 14, 1861. Present or accounted for until wounded at Sharpsburg, Maryland, September 17, 1862. Returned to duty prior to January 1, 1863, and was transferred to 2nd Company B, 49th Regiment N.C. Troops, January 9, 1863.

GOLD, T. R., Private
Resided in Cleveland County where he enlisted at age 18, May 14, 1861. Present or accounted for until he died at Yorktown, Virginia, December 8, 1861, of disease.

GREEN, S., Private
Resided in Davidson County and enlisted in Wake County at age 25, July 15, 1862, for the war. Present or accounted for until he died in hospital at Winchester, Virginia, on or about October 4, 1862. Cause of death not reported.

GRUBB, R., Private
Resided in Davidson County and enlisted in Wake County at age 20, July 15, 1862, for the war. Present or accounted for until wounded and captured at Sharpsburg, Maryland, September 17, 1862. Paroled and exchanged at an unspecified date. Reported absent wounded through January 9, 1863, when the company was redesignated 2nd Company B, 49th Regiment N.C. Troops.

HARTMAN, J. A., Private
Resided in Davidson County and enlisted in Wake County at age 22, July 15, 1862, for the war. Present or accounted for until transferred to 2nd Company B, 49th Regiment N.C. Troops, January 9, 1863.

HORDE, RICHARD M., Musician
Resided in Cleveland County where he enlisted at age 26, May 14, 1861. Mustered in as Musician. Present or accounted for until captured at or near Crampton's Pass, Maryland, September 14, 1862. Confined at Fort Delaware, Delaware, until transferred to Aiken's Landing, James River, Virginia, October 2, 1862, for exchange. Declared exchanged at Aiken's Landing on November 10, 1862. Transferred to 2nd Company B, 49th Regiment N.C. Troops, January 9, 1863.

HOWARD, ELISHA, _____
Negro. North Carolina pension records indicate that he joined this company on August 1, 1861. No further records.

HOYLE, DANIEL A., Private
Resided in Cleveland County where he enlisted at age 25, May 14, 1861. Present or accounted for until reported absent without leave on October 23, 1862. Reported absent without leave through January 9,

1863, when the company was redesignated 2nd Company B, 49th Regiment N.C. Troops.

HUNT, E., Private

Resided in Cleveland County and enlisted at age 28, August 11, 1861. Present or accounted for until killed at or near Crampton's Pass, Maryland, September 14, 1862.

HUNT, J. P., Private

Resided in Cleveland County where he enlisted at age 22, May 14, 1861. Present or accounted for until he died at Yorktown, Virginia, on or about January 10, 1862, of disease.

HUNT, W. H., Corporal

Resided in Davidson County and enlisted in Cleveland County at age 19, May 14, 1861. Mustered in as Private and promoted to Corporal on July 25, 1862. Present or accounted for until wounded at Fredericksburg, Virginia, December 13, 1862. Reported absent wounded through January 9, 1863, when the company was redesignated 2nd Company B, 49th Regiment N.C. Troops.

IRVIN, A. H., Private

Resided in Cleveland County where he enlisted at age 23, May 14, 1861. Present or accounted for until captured at Crampton's Pass, Maryland, September 14, 1862. Confined at Fort Delaware, Delaware, until transferred to Aiken's Landing, James River, Virginia, October 2, 1862, for exchange. Declared exchanged at Aiken's Landing on November 10, 1862. Returned to duty prior to December 13, 1862, when he was wounded at Fredericksburg, Virginia. Reported absent wounded through December, 1862. Transferred to 2nd Company B, 49th Regiment N.C. Troops, January 9, 1863.

JARRELL, A. B., Private

Resided in Rutherford County and enlisted in Cleveland County at age 20, May 14, 1861. Present or accounted for until wounded in the leg at Malvern Hill, Virginia, July 1, 1862. Returned to duty prior to December 13, 1862, when he was killed at Fredericksburg, Virginia.

JARRELL, MILTON, Private

Resided in Cleveland County where he enlisted at age 27, May 14, 1861. Mustered in as Corporal but was reduced to ranks prior to August 19, 1862, when he was discharged. Reason discharged not reported.

JOHNSON, S. C., Private

Born in Wythe County, Virginia, and resided in Cleveland County where he was by occupation a farmer prior to enlisting at Yorktown, Virginia, at age 24, May 14, 1861. Present or accounted for until he was reportedly transferred to the 29th Regiment Virginia Infantry on June 9, 1862; however, records of that unit do not indicate that he served therein. No further records.

JONES, D. D., Private

Born in Cleveland County* where he resided as a farmer prior to enlisting in Cleveland County at age 31, May 14, 1861. Present or accounted for until discharged on October 28, 1862, by reason of "chronic bronchitis with emphysema and angina pectoris."

LATTIMORE, JOHN L., Corporal

Resided in Cleveland County where he enlisted at age

21, May 14, 1861. Mustered in as Private. Present or accounted for until captured at Crampton's Pass, Maryland, September 14, 1862. Confined at Fort Delaware, Delaware, until transferred to Aiken's Landing, James River, Virginia, October 2, 1862, for exchange. Declared exchanged at Aiken's Landing on November 10, 1862. Promoted to Corporal on December 15, 1862. Transferred to 2nd Company B, 49th Regiment N.C. Troops, January 9, 1863.

LEDFORD, D. A., Private

Resided in Cleveland County where he enlisted at age 19, May 14, 1861. Present or accounted for until he died at Yorktown, Virginia, September 1, 1861, of disease.

LEDFORD, WILLIAM, Private

Resided in Cleveland County where he enlisted at age 27, May 14, 1861. Present or accounted for until August 30, 1862, when he was reported absent without leave. Reported absent without leave through January 9, 1863, when the company was redesignated 2nd Company B, 49th Regiment N.C. Troops.

LEONARD, FELIX W., Private

Resided in Davidson County and enlisted in Wake County at age 21, July 15, 1862, for the war. Present or accounted for until October 20, 1862, when he was reported absent without leave. Reported absent without leave through January 9, 1863, when the company was redesignated 2nd Company B, 49th Regiment N.C. Troops.

LONDON, DAVID, Private

Resided in Cleveland County where he enlisted at age 22, May 14, 1861. Present or accounted for until captured at or near Crampton's Pass, Maryland, September 14, 1862. Confined at Fort Delaware, Delaware, until transferred to Aiken's Landing, James River, Virginia, October 2, 1862, for exchange. Declared exchanged at Aiken's Landing on November 10, 1862. Died in hospital at Richmond, Virginia, January 8, 1863, of "pneumonia."

LONDON, H. S., Private

Resided in Cleveland County where he enlisted at age 21, May 14, 1861. Present or accounted for until wounded in the right thigh and captured at Crampton's Pass, Maryland, September 14, 1862. Died in hospital at Burkittsville, Maryland, January 4, 1863, of wounds.

LONDON, JOHN R., Sergeant

Resided in Cleveland County where he enlisted at age 25, May 14, 1861. Mustered in as Private and promoted to Corporal on May 2, 1862. Promoted to Sergeant on July 2, 1862. Present or accounted for until transferred to 2nd Company B, 49th Regiment N.C. Troops, January 9, 1863.

McENTIRE, S. M., Corporal

Resided in Cleveland County where he enlisted at age 24, May 14, 1861. Mustered in as Corporal. Present or accounted for until he died at Yorktown, Virginia, August 8, 1861, of disease.

McFARLAND, J. W., Private

Resided in Cleveland County where he enlisted at age 20, May 14, 1861. Present or accounted for until killed at Malvern Hill, Virginia, July 1, 1862.

MAGNESS, S. P., Sergeant
Enlisted in Cleveland County on May 14, 1861. Mustered in as Private and promoted to Corporal on May 2, 1862. Promoted to Sergeant on July 2, 1862. Present or accounted for until wounded at or near Crampton's Pass, Maryland, September 14, 1862. Reported absent wounded through December, 1862. Transferred to 2nd Company B, 49th Regiment N.C. Troops, January 9, 1863.

MASON, J. P., Private
Resided in Cleveland County where he enlisted at age 44, May 14, 1861. Present or accounted for until discharged on August 19, 1862. Reason discharged not reported.

MEACHAN, HENRY, Private
Resided in Cleveland County where he enlisted at age 31, May 14, 1861. Present or accounted for until discharged on August 19, 1862. Reason discharged not reported.

MEAD, JOSEPH, Private
Resided in Cleveland County where he enlisted at age 40, May 14, 1861. Present or accounted for until discharged on August 19, 1862. Reason discharged not reported.

MODE, A. F., Private
Resided in Cleveland County where he enlisted at age 18, May 14, 1861. Present or accounted for until transferred to 2nd Company B, 49th Regiment N.C. Troops, January 9, 1863.

MODE, A. H., Private
Resided in Cleveland County where he enlisted at age 24, May 14, 1861. Present or accounted for until he died at Yorktown, Virginia, August 28, 1861, of disease.

MODE, J., Private
Enlisted in Cleveland County on May 14, 1861. Present or accounted for until captured at or near Crampton's Pass, Maryland, September 14, 1862. Confined at Fort Delaware, Delaware, until transferred to Aiken's Landing, James River, Virginia, October 2, 1862, for exchange. Declared exchanged at Aiken's Landing on November 10, 1862. Transferred to 2nd Company B, 49th Regiment N.C. Troops, January 9, 1863.

MODE, SAMUEL, Private
Resided in Cleveland County where he enlisted at age 23, May 14, 1861. Present or accounted for until he died in hospital at Richmond, Virginia, February 23, 1862, of "enteritis."

MODE, WILLIAM, Private
Resided in Cleveland County where he enlisted at age 19, May 14, 1861. Present or accounted for until he died at Yorktown, Virginia, August 29, 1861, of disease.

NOWLIN, M. W., Private
Resided in Cleveland County where he enlisted at age 18, May 14, 1861. Present or accounted for until he died at Yorktown, Virginia, on or about October 2, 1861, of disease.

PARKER, JOSEPH, Private
Resided in Cleveland County where he enlisted at age 17, May 14, 1861. Present or accounted for until wounded and captured at Crampton's Pass, Maryland,

September 14, 1862. Paroled prior to September 22, 1862, when he was hospitalized at Richmond, Virginia. Reported absent wounded through December, 1862. Transferred to 2nd Company B, 49th Regiment N.C. Troops, January 9, 1863.

PETTY, JAMES F., Private
Resided in Cleveland County where he enlisted at age 23, May 14, 1861. Present or accounted for until transferred to 2nd Company B, 49th Regiment N.C. Troops, January 9, 1863.

PHILBECK, A. H., Private
Resided in Cleveland County where he enlisted at age 22, May 14, 1861. Present or accounted for until transferred to 2nd Company B, 49th Regiment N.C. Troops, January 9, 1863.

PHILBECK, JOSIAH, Private
Resided in Cleveland County where he enlisted at age 24, May 14, 1861. Present or accounted for until he died at Yorktown, Virginia, August 20, 1861, of disease.

PHILBECK, P. H., Private
Resided in Cleveland County where he enlisted at age 24, May 14, 1861. Present or accounted for until captured at Crampton's Pass, Maryland, September 14, 1862. Confined at Fort Delaware, Delaware, until transferred to Aiken's Landing, James River, Virginia, October 2, 1862, for exchange. Declared exchanged at Aiken's Landing on November 10, 1862. Returned to duty prior to December 13, 1862, when he was wounded in the thigh at Fredericksburg, Virginia. Reported absent wounded through December, 1862. Transferred to 2nd Company B, 49th Regiment N.C. Troops, January 9, 1863.

PRICE, J. M., Private
Resided in Cleveland County where he enlisted at age 21, May 14, 1861. Present or accounted for until he died at Yorktown, Virginia, August 3, 1861, of disease.

PRICE, J. W., Private
Resided in Cleveland County where he enlisted at age 24, May 14, 1861. Present or accounted for until killed at or near Crampton's Pass, Maryland, September 14, 1862.

PRICE, W. P., Private
Resided in Cleveland County where he enlisted at age 23, May 14, 1861. Present or accounted for until October 30, 1861, when he was reported absent without leave. Reported absent without leave through January 9, 1863, when the company was redesignated 2nd Company B, 49th Regiment N.C. Troops.

PROCTOR, WILLIAM, Private
Resided in Cleveland County and enlisted at age 26, May 14, 1861. Present or accounted for until he died at Goldsboro on March 31, 1862, of disease.

PUTNAM, MARTIN, Private
Born in Cleveland County where he resided as a farmer prior to enlisting in Cleveland County at age 18, May 14, 1861. Present or accounted for until he deserted at Yorktown, Virginia, on or about February 20, 1862.

PUTNAM, SAMUEL, Private
Resided in Cleveland County where he enlisted at age 24, May 14, 1861. Present or accounted for until wounded and captured at Sharpsburg, Maryland,

September 17, 1862. Paroled September 27, 1862. Reported absent wounded through December, 1862. Transferred to 2nd Company B, 49th Regiment N.C. Troops, January 9, 1863.

SHIELDS, R. D., Sergeant
Resided in Cleveland County where he enlisted at age 22, May 14, 1861. Mustered in as Private and promoted to Sergeant on May 2, 1862. Present or accounted for until wounded in the shoulder at Malvern Hill, Virginia, July 1, 1862. Returned to duty prior to January 1, 1863, and was transferred to 2nd Company B, 49th Regiment N.C. Troops, January 9, 1863.

SHORT, ABNER, Private
Resided in Rutherford County and enlisted in Cleveland County at age 37, May 14, 1861. Present or accounted for until discharged on August 19, 1862. Reason discharged not reported.

SHORT, DANIEL, Private
Resided in Rutherford County and enlisted in Cleveland County at age 31, May 14, 1861. Present or accounted for until discharged on August 19, 1862. Reason discharged not reported.

SHORT, J. W., Private
Resided in Cleveland County where he enlisted at age 21, May 14, 1861. Present or accounted for until he died at Goldsboro on April 14, 1862, of disease.

SHORT, JOSEPH, Private
Resided in Rutherford County and enlisted in Cleveland County at age 28, May 14, 1861. Present or accounted for until discharged on August 19, 1862. Reason discharged not reported.

SHORT, WADE H., Private
Born in Rutherford County and resided in Cleveland County where he was by occupation a farmer prior to enlisting in Cleveland County at age 21, May 14, 1861. Present or accounted for until discharged on or about June 6, 1862, by reason of "rheumatism chronic." Later enlisted in 2nd Company B, 49th Regiment N.C. Troops.

SILLS, JOHN, Private
Resided in Rutherford County and enlisted in Cleveland County at age 32, May 14, 1861. Present or accounted for until discharged on August 19, 1862. Reason discharged not reported.

SPECK, J. J., Private
Resided in Rutherford County and enlisted in Cleveland County at age 24, May 14, 1861. Present or accounted for until he died at Williamsburg, Virginia, November 15, 1861, of disease.

SPECK, J. P., Private
Resided in Rutherford County and enlisted in Cleveland County at age 22, May 14, 1861. Present or accounted for until transferred to 2nd Company B, 49th Regiment N.C. Troops, January 9, 1863.

THOMPSON, J., Private
Enlisted in Wake County on July 15, 1862, for the war. Deserted August 21, 1862.

TOWRY, ISAAC, Private
Resided in Cleveland County where he enlisted at age 25, May 14, 1861. Present or accounted for until discharged on or about June 12, 1861. Reason discharged not reported.

TOWRY, JOSEPH, Private
Enlisted in Cleveland County on August 11, 1861. Present or accounted for until killed at Lee's Mill, Virginia, April 16, 1862.

TOWRY, R. P., Private
Enlisted in Cleveland County on May 14, 1861. Present or accounted for through December, 1862.

WATERS, D. W., Private
Resided in Rutherford County and enlisted in Cleveland County at age 23, May 14, 1861. Present or accounted for until he died at Raleigh on September 22, 1862, of "febris typhoides."

WATERS, JOHN A., Private
Resided in Cleveland or Rutherford counties and enlisted in Cleveland County at age 20, May 14, 1861. Mustered in as Sergeant but was reduced to ranks in September, 1861-December, 1862. Present or accounted for until transferred to 2nd Company B, 49th Regiment N.C. Troops, January 9, 1863.

WATERS, JONATHAN, Private
Resided in Rutherford County and enlisted in Cleveland County at age 20, May 14, 1861. Present or accounted for until transferred to 2nd Company B, 49th Regiment N.C. Troops, January 9, 1863.

WHITE, THOMAS, Private
Resided in Rutherford County and enlisted in Cleveland County at age 21, May 14, 1861. Present or accounted for until transferred to 2nd Company B, 49th Regiment N.C. Troops, January 9, 1863.

WHITMORE, _____, Sergeant
Name appears on a regimental record dated May, 1862, which states that he was sick at Richmond, Virginia. No further records.

WIGANS, E. G., Private
Resided in Cleveland County where he enlisted at age 30, May 14, 1861. Present or accounted for until he deserted on August 11, 1862.

WIGANS, F. M., Private
Resided in Cleveland County where he enlisted at age 26, May 14, 1861. Present or accounted for until he died at Yorktown, Virginia, August 14, 1861, of disease.

WIGGINS, R. M., Private
Resided in Cleveland County where he enlisted at age 23, May 14, 1861. Present or accounted for until August 25, 1862, when he was reported absent without leave. Reported absent without leave until January 9, 1863, when the company was redesignated 2nd Company B, 49th Regiment N.C. Troops.

WILLIAMS, ALFRED, Private
Resided in Rutherford County and enlisted in Cleveland County at age 30, May 14, 1861. Present or accounted for until wounded at Malvern Hill, Virginia, July 1, 1862. Died August 6, 1862, of wounds. Place of death not reported.

WILSON, J. A., Private
Resided in Cleveland County where he enlisted at age 24, May 14, 1861. Present or accounted for until he died at Yorktown, Virginia, August 11, 1861, of disease.

WITHROW, J. B., Private

Resided in Rutherford County and enlisted in Cleveland County at age 22, May 14, 1861. Present or accounted for until he died at Yorktown, Virginia, August 4, 1861, of disease.

WITHROW, J. C., Private

Resided in Cleveland County where he enlisted at age 26, May 14, 1861. Mustered in as Sergeant and promoted to 1st Sergeant on July 2, 1862. Reduced to ranks on August 31, 1862. Present or accounted for until wounded at or near Crampton's Pass, Maryland, September 14, 1862. Reported absent wounded through January 9, 1863, when the company was redesignated 2nd Company B, 49th Regiment N.C. Troops.

WITHROW, THOMAS J., Sergeant

Previously served in Company D, 16th Regiment N.C. Troops (6th Regiment N.C. Volunteers). Transferred to this company on June 20, 1861, with the rank of Private. Promoted to Sergeant on May 2, 1862. Present or accounted for until wounded in the leg at Fredericksburg, Virginia, December 13, 1862. Reported absent wounded through January 9, 1863, when the company was redesignated 2nd Company B, 49th Regiment N.C. Troops.

WITHROW, W. P., 1st Sergeant

Resided in Rutherford County and enlisted in Cleveland County at age 24, May 14, 1861. Mustered in as Private and promoted to 1st Sergeant on October 1, 1862. Present or accounted for until wounded in the hand at Fredericksburg, Virginia, December 13, 1862. Reported absent wounded through January 9, 1863, when the company was redesignated 2nd Company B, 49th Regiment N.C. Troops.

2nd COMPANY D

This company was transferred from the 49th Regiment N.C. Troops on January 9, 1863. Inasmuch as it was the first of two companies to serve in that regiment as Company B, it was later referred to as 1st Company B. When the company joined this regiment it was designated Company D. Because it was the second company to serve as Company D, it was officially referred to as 2nd Company D. After joining the regiment the company functioned as a part of the regiment, and its history for the war period is recorded as a part of the regimental history. The following roster covers only the period from the date of transfer to the end of the war. All information prior to the date of transfer will be recorded in the roster of 1st Company B, 49th Regiment N.C. Troops.

The information contained in the following roster of the company was compiled principally from company muster rolls for January, 1863-April, 1864, and September-October, 1864. No company muster rolls were found for May-August, 1864, or for the period after October, 1864. In addition to the company muster rolls, Roll of Honor records, receipt rolls, hospital records, prisoner of war records, and other primary records, supplemented by state pension applications, United Daughters of the Confederacy records, and postwar rosters and histories, all provided useful information.

OFFICERS

CAPTAIN

OLDHAM, YOUNGER A.

Transferred to this company from 1st Company B, 49th Regiment N.C. Troops, January 9, 1863, with the rank of Captain. Present or accounted for until paroled at Appomattox Court House, Virginia, April 9, 1865.

LIEUTENANTS

HORTON, JAMES W., 3rd Lieutenant

Transferred to this company from 1st Company B, 49th Regiment N.C. Troops, January 9, 1863, with the rank of Sergeant. Promoted to 1st Sergeant in March-April, 1863, and was appointed 3rd Lieutenant on September 17, 1863. Present or accounted for until paroled at Appomattox Court House, Virginia, April 9, 1865.

MASSENBURG, ARCHIBALD CARGILL, 2nd Lieutenant

Previously served as Assistant Commissary of Subsistence (Captain) of this regiment. Appointed 2nd Lieutenant of this company on September 13, 1863, after his previous position was abolished. Present or accounted for until wounded in the right ankle at Bristoe Station, Virginia, October 14, 1863. Reported absent wounded until he died "at home" in Franklin County on August 1, 1864, of "chronic diarrhoea."

OLDHAM, WILLIAM E., 1st Lieutenant

Transferred to this company from 1st Company B, 49th Regiment N.C. Troops, January 9, 1863, with the rank of Sergeant. Appointed 3rd Lieutenant on or about January 28, 1863, and was promoted to 1st Lieutenant on September 17, 1863. Present or accounted for until wounded in the left hand at Bristoe Station, Virginia, October 14, 1863. Finger amputated. Returned to duty in January-April, 1864, and present or accounted for until he resigned on July 12, 1864.

NONCOMMISSIONED OFFICERS AND PRIVATES

AUSLEY, JAMES W., Private

Transferred to this company from 1st Company B, 49th Regiment N.C. Troops, January 9, 1863. Present or accounted for through October, 1864.

BENNETT, JAMES G., Private

Transferred to this company from 1st Company B, 49th Regiment N.C. Troops, January 9, 1863. Present or accounted for until captured at or near Hatcher's Run, Virginia, March 31, 1865. Confined at Point Lookout, Maryland, until released on June 24, 1865, after taking the Oath of Allegiance.

BENNETT, WILLIAM B., Private

Transferred to this company from 1st Company B, 49th Regiment N.C. Troops, January 9, 1863, at which time he was absent from the company as a result of wounds received at Fredericksburg, Virginia, December 13, 1862. Reported absent wounded until March

21, 1863, when he was reported absent without leave. Returned to duty on or about December 25, 1863, when he was detailed for light duty as a "bridge guard." Reported absent without leave from February 19, 1864, through April, 1864, and was reported absent sick in September-October, 1864.

BLACK, L. C., Corporal
Resided in Moore County and enlisted at age 30, April 7, 1863, for the war. Mustered in as Private and promoted to Corporal on October 1, 1863. Present or accounted for until he died in hospital at Richmond, Virginia, June 21, 1864, of a gunshot wound; however, place and date wounded not reported. [Company records indicate that he enlisted in Mallett's Battalion (Camp Guard) on July 17, 1862, and transferred to this company on April 7, 1863; however, records of Mallett's Battalion do not indicate that he served therein.]

BREWER, SAMUEL W., Sergeant
Transferred to this company from 1st Company B, 49th Regiment N.C. Troops, January 9, 1863, with the rank of Private. Promoted to Sergeant on June 15, 1863. Present or accounted for until paroled at Appomattox Court House, Virginia, April 9, 1865.

BRIDGES, ANDREW J., Private
Resided in Franklin County. Place and date of enlistment not reported. Present or accounted for until captured at Hatcher's Run, Virginia, April 1, 1865. Confined at Point Lookout, Maryland, until released on June 24, 1865, after taking the Oath of Allegiance.

BROWN, ELISHA B., Private
Transferred to this company from 1st Company B, 49th Regiment N.C. Troops, January 9, 1863. Present or accounted for until captured at Hatcher's Run, Virginia, April 2, 1865. Confined at Hart's Island, New York Harbor, where he died July 21, 1865, of "chronic diarrhoea."

BURGESS, THOMAS H., Private
Resided in Chatham County and enlisted at age 27, April 7, 1863, for the war. Present or accounted for through October, 1864. [Company records indicate he enlisted in Mallett's Battalion (Camp Guard) on July 18, 1862; was wounded at Fredericksburg, Virginia, December 13, 1862; and was transferred to this company on April 7, 1863. However, records of Mallett's Battalion do not indicate that he served therein.]

CALLICUTT, ARCHIBALD, Private
Previously served in Company F, Mallett's Battalion (Camp Guard). Transferred to this company in September, 186[4]. Paroled at Appomattox Court House, Virginia, April 9, 1865.

CARSON, W. L., Private
Resided in Chatham County and enlisted at age 30, April 7, 1863, for the war. Present or accounted for until he died at South Anna, Virginia, September 14, 1863, of "fever." [Company records indicate that he enlisted in Mallett's Battalion (Camp Guard) on July 18, 1862, and was transferred to this company on April 7, 1863; however, records of Mallett's Battalion do not indicate that he served therein.]

CAVINESS, THOMAS, Private
Transferred to this company from 1st Company B,

49th Regiment N.C. Troops, January 9, 1863. Was reported absent without leave from the 49th Regiment at the time of his transfer. Never reported for duty with this company and was dropped from the rolls on or about January 1, 1864.

CLARK, JOSEPH, Private
Resided in Chatham County. Place and date of enlistment not reported. Present or accounted for until captured at or near Hatcher's Run, Virginia, March 31, 1865. Confined at Point Lookout, Maryland, until released on June 26, 1865, after taking the Oath of Allegiance.

CLARK, THOMAS, Private
Transferred to this company from 1st Company B. 49th Regiment N.C. Troops, January 9, 1863. Present or accounted for through October, 1864.

COLE, ELIJAH, Private
Place and date of enlistment not reported. Paroled at Appomattox Court House, Virginia, April 9, 1865.

COLE, GEORGE O., Corporal
Previously served in Company F, Mallett's Battalion (Camp Guard). Date transferred to this company not reported; however, he was first listed on the rolls of this company in September-October, 1864. Promoted from Private to Corporal in November, 1864-April, 1865. Paroled at Appomattox Court House, Virginia, April 9, 1865.

COLE, ISAIAH S., Private
Enlistment date reported as July 18, 1862; however, he was not listed on the rolls of this company until September-October, 1864. Present or accounted for until paroled at Appomattox Court House, Virginia, April 9, 1865.

COLE, JAMES M., Private
Transferred to this company from 1st Company B, 49th Regiment N.C. Troops, January 9, 1863. Present or accounted for until he deserted to the enemy on or about March 22, 1865. Released on or about March 29, 1865, after taking the Oath of Allegiance.

COLE, JOHN, Private
Transferred to this company from 1st Company B, 49th Regiment N.C. Troops, January 9, 1863. Present or accounted for through February, 1863. No further records.

COLE, THOMAS R., Private
Previously served in Company A, Mallett's Battalion (Camp Guard). Date transferred to this company not reported; however, he was first listed on the rolls of this company in August, 1864. Wounded in the left leg at Reams' Station, Virginia, August 25, 1864. Reported absent wounded until retired from service on January 6, 1865, by reason of wounds received at Reams' Station.

COLE, WILLIAM P., Private
Resided in Chatham County where he enlisted at age 16, February 25, 1863, for the war. Present or accounted for until wounded at Bristoe Station, Virginia, October 14, 1863. Returned to duty prior to March 1, 1864, and present or accounted for until paroled at Appomattox Court House, Virginia, April 9, 1865.

CONALY, THOMAS, Private
Place and date of enlistment not reported. Captured at or near Drewry's Bluff, Virginia, on or about May 16, 1864. Confined at Fort Monroe, Virginia, until transferred to Point Lookout, Maryland, on or about May 24, 1864. Paroled and transferred to Aiken's Landing, James River, Virginia, March 14, 1865, for exchange. No further records.

COOK, WILLIAM P., Private
Transferred to this company from 1st Company B, 49th Regiment N.C. Troops, January 9, 1863. Present or accounted for until hospitalized at Richmond, Virginia, February 7, 1865, with a gunshot wound of the "right frontal bone"; however, place and date wounded not reported. Died in hospital at Richmond on February 10, 1865, of wounds.

COOPER, JAMES DANIEL, Private
Transferred to this company from 1st Company B, 49th Regiment N.C. Troops, January 9, 1863. Present or accounted for until paroled on April 24, 1865.

COUNCIL, THOMAS C., Corporal
Resided in Chatham County and enlisted at age 24, April 3, 1863, for the war. Mustered in as Private and promoted to Corporal on October 1, 1863. Present or accounted for until paroled at Appomattox Court House, Virginia, April 9, 1865. [Company records indicate that he enlisted in Mallett's Battalion (Camp Guard) on July 18, 1862, and transferred to this company on April 3, 1863; however, records of Mallett's Battalion do not indicate that he served therein.]

DILLINGER, DANIEL C., Private
Previously served in Company C of this regiment. Transferred to this company on April 1, 1863. Present or accounted for until reported absent without leave on October 15, 1863. Returned to duty in January-February, 1864, and present or accounted for until paroled at Appomattox Court House, Virginia, April 9, 1865.

ELLIS, A. M., Private
Resided in Chatham County. Place and date of enlistment not reported. Captured at Hatcher's Run, Virginia, April 2, 1865, and confined at Hart's Island, New York Harbor, until released on June 18, 1865, after taking the Oath of Allegiance.

EUBANKS, GEORGE W., Private
Resided in Chatham County and enlisted on April 7, 1863, for the war. Present or accounted for until hospitalized at Raleigh on October 6, 1864, with a gunshot wound of the right arm. North Carolina pension records indicate he was wounded "at the Wilderness." Returned to duty on December 11, 1864, and was captured at Hatcher's Run, Virginia, April 2, 1865. Confined at Hart's Island, New York Harbor, until released on June 18, 1865, after taking the Oath of Allegiance. [Company records indicate he enlisted in Mallett's Battalion (Camp Guard) on July 18, 1862, and was transferred to this company on April 7, 1863; however, records of Mallett's Battalion do not indicate that he served therein.]

GOODWIN, JOSEPH M., Private
Place and date of enlistment not reported. Paroled at Appomattox Court House, Virginia, April 9, 1865.

GOODWIN, WILLIAM J., Private
Place and date of enlistment not reported. Captured at or near Amelia Court House, Virginia, April 4, 1865. Confined at Point Lookout, Maryland, until released on June 3, 1865, after taking the Oath of Allegiance.

GOODWIN, WINSHIP, Private
Transferred to this company from 1st Company B, 49th Regiment N.C. Troops, January 9, 1863. Present or accounted for until captured at Bristoe Station, Virginia, October 14, 1863. Confined at Point Lookout, Maryland, until paroled and transferred to Aiken's Landing, James River, Virginia, February 24, 1865, for exchange. Received at Aiken's Landing prior to March 4, 1865.

HACKNEY, ALBERT J., Sergeant
Transferred to this company from 1st Company B, 49th Regiment N.C. Troops, January 9, 1863, with the rank of Sergeant. Died in hospital at Richmond, Virginia, January 24, 1863, of "pneumonia."

HACKNEY, BASIL A., Private
Transferred to this company from 1st Company B, 49th Regiment N.C. Troops, January 9, 1863. Present or accounted for until transferred to Company C, 56th Regiment N.C. Troops, May 28, 1863, in exchange for Private Wright Hathcock.

HACKNEY, BASIL M., Private
Transferred to this company from 1st Company B, 49th Regiment N.C. Troops, January 9, 1863. Present or accounted for until captured at or near Amelia Court House, Virginia, April 3, 1865. Confined at Point Lookout, Maryland, until released on June 27, 1865, after taking the Oath of Allegiance.

HACKNEY, G. G., Private
Resided in Chatham County. Place and date of enlistment not reported. Captured prior to April 7, 1865, when he was confined at Hart's Island, New York Harbor; however, place and date captured not reported. Confined at Hart's Island until released on June 18, 1865, after taking the Oath of Allegiance.

HACKNEY, JESSE E., Private
Transferred to this company from 1st Company B, 49th Regiment N.C. Troops, January 9, 1863. Present or accounted for until paroled at Appomattox Court House, Virginia, April 9, 1865.

HACKNEY, JOSHUA H., Private
Transferred to this company from 1st Company B, 49th Regiment N.C. Troops, January 9, 1863. Present or accounted for until captured at Hatcher's Run, Virginia, April 2, 1865. Confined at Hart's Island, New York Harbor, until released on June 18, 1865, after taking the Oath of Allegiance.

HATHCOCK, WRIGHT, Private
Previously served in Company C, 56th Regiment N.C. Troops. Transferred to this company on May 28, 1863, in exchange for Private Basil A. Hackney. Present or accounted for until wounded in the right knee at Wilderness, Virginia, May 5, 1864. Reported absent wounded until retired from service on December 22, 1864, by reason of wounds received at Wilderness.

HATLEY, JOHN, Private
Previously served in Company C, Mallett's Battalion (Camp Guard). Transferred to this company on or about April 7, 1863. Present or accounted for until he

deserted on July 31, 1863. Returned to duty on February 26, 1864, and present or accounted for until captured at Hatcher's Run, Virginia, April 2, 1865. Confined at Hart's Island, New York Harbor, until released on June 18, 1865, after taking the Oath of Allegiance.

HATLEY, JOSEPH, Private
Previously served in Company C, Mallett's Battalion (Camp Guard). Transferred to this company on or about April 7, 1863. Present or accounted for until he deserted on July 31, 1863. Returned to duty on February 26, 1864, and present or accounted for through April, 1864. No further records.

HATLEY, LAOMI, Private
Resided in Chatham County and enlisted at age 25, April 7, 1863, for the war. Present or accounted for until he deserted on July 31, 1863. Returned to duty on February 26, 1864, and present or accounted for until captured at Hatcher's Run, Virginia, April 2, 1865. Confined at Hart's Island, New York Harbor, until released on June 18, 1865, after taking the Oath of Allegiance. [Company records indicate that he enlisted in Mallett's Battalion (Camp Guard) on July 18, 1862, and was transferred to this company on April 7, 1863; however, records of Mallett's Battalion do not indicate that he served therein.]

HERNDON, SIDNEY LUCIEN, Corporal
Transferred to this company from 1st Company B, 49th Regiment N.C. Troops, January 9, 1863, with the rank of Corporal. Discharged February 15, 1863, by reason of wounds received at Malvern Hill, Virginia, July 1, 1862.

HORTEN, JOHN R., Private
Resided in Chatham County and enlisted at age 22, April 7, 1863, for the war. Mustered in as Private and promoted to Corporal in May-June, 1863. Promoted to Sergeant on October 1, 1863, but was reduced to ranks on October 1, 1864. Present or accounted for through October, 1864. [Company records indicate that he enlisted in Mallett's Battalion (Camp Guard) on July 18, 1862, and was transferred to this company on April 7, 1863; however, records of Mallett's Battalion do not indicate that he served therein.]

HORTON, E., Private
Resided in Chatham County. Place and date of enlistment not reported. Captured at Hatcher's Run, Virginia, April 2, 1865, and confined at Hart's Island, New York Harbor, until released on June 18, 1865, after taking the Oath of Allegiance.

JENKINS, MILTON, Private
Resided in Chatham County and enlisted on April 7, 1863, for the war. Present or accounted for through October, 1864. [Company records indicate that he enlisted in Mallett's Battalion (Camp Guard) on July 18, 1862, and was transferred to this company on April 7, 1863; however, records of Mallett's Battalion do not indicate that he served therein.]

KIRBY, WILEY L., 1st Sergeant
Transferred to this company from 1st Company B, 49th Regiment N.C. Troops, January 9, 1863, with the rank of Private. Promoted to Sergeant on June 17, 1863, and promoted to 1st Sergeant in May-October,

1864. Present or accounted for until paroled at Appomattox Court House, Virginia, April 9, 1865.

LEACH, JAMES A., Private
Enlistment date reported as August 4, 1862; however, he was not listed on the rolls of this company until September-October, 1864. Hospitalized at Richmond, Virginia, February 26, 1865, with "chronic diarrhoea" and died March 18, 1865.

LIVINGSTON, JAMES, Private
Previously served in Company F, Mallett's Battalion (Camp Guard). Date transferred to this company not reported; however, he was first listed on the rolls of this company in September-October, 1864. Captured at Hatcher's Run, Virginia, April 2, 1865, and confined at Hart's Island, New York Harbor, until released June 19-20, 1865, after taking the Oath of Allegiance.

McCOLLUM, MATTHEW, Private
Previously served in Company A, 46th Regiment N.C. Troops. Transferred to this company on May 26, 1863. Deserted on July 3, 1863, but returned to duty in January-February, 1864. Present or accounted for until he died in hospital at Gordonsville, Virginia, May 4, 1864, of "typhoid pneumonia."

MANN, CARNEY C., Private
Transferred to this company from 1st Company B, 49th Regiment N.C. Troops, January 9, 1863. Present or accounted for until paroled at Appomattox Court House, Virginia, April 9, 1865.

MANN, HENRY A., Private
Transferred to this company from 1st Company B, 49th Regiment N.C. Troops, January 9, 1863, with the rank of Private. Promoted to Sergeant on June 17, 1863. Deserted on July 31, 1863, and was reduced to ranks in September-October, 1863. Returned to duty in November-December, 1863. Died in hospital at Richmond, Virginia, June 14, 1864, of a gunshot wound; however, place and date wounded not reported.

MARKS, JAMES A., Private
Transferred to this company from 1st Company B, 49th Regiment N.C. Troops, January 9, 1863. Died in hospital at Goldsboro on February 28, 1863, of disease.

MARKS, THOMAS B., Private
Transferred to this company from 1st Company B, 49th Regiment N.C. Troops, January 9, 1863. Present or accounted for until captured in hospital at Richmond, Virginia, April 3, 1865. Transferred to the Federal Provost Marshal on April 14, 1865.

MARTIN, ELIJAH C., Private
Previously served in Company F, Mallett's Battalion (Camp Guard). Date transferred to this company not reported; however, he was first listed on the rolls of this company in September-October, 1864. Captured at Hatcher's Run, Virginia, April 2, 1865, and confined at Hart's Island, New York Harbor, until released on June 17, 1865, after taking the Oath of Allegiance.

MATTAX, JAMES, Private
Place and date of enlistment not reported. Paroled at Cheraw, South Carolina, March 5, 1865.

MELTON, JAMES, Private
Previously served in Company F, Mallett's Battalion (Camp Guard). Date transferred to this company not

reported; however, he was first listed on the rolls of this company in September-October, 1864. Reported absent wounded on October 8, 1864; however, place and date wounded not reported. Reported absent wounded through October, 1864. No further records.

MELTON, NEILL, Private

Previously served in Company F, Mallett's Battalion (Camp Guard). Date transferred to this company not reported; however, he was first listed on the rolls of this company in September-October, 1864. Present or accounted for until captured at Hatcher's Run, Virginia, April 2, 1865. Confined at Hart's Island, New York Harbor, until released on June 18, 1865, after taking the Oath of Allegiance.

MITCHEL, SIDNEY, Private

Previously served in Company E, 44th Regiment N.C. Troops. Transferred to this company on July 9, 1863. Present or accounted for through October, 1863. No further records.

MITCHELL, CHARLES S., Private

Enlisted at "Riggsbee's Store" on September 24, 1863, for the war. Present or accounted for until paroled at Appomattox Court House, Virginia, April 9, 1865.

MOORE, WILLIAM N., Private

Enlisted at Orange Court House, Virginia, March 6, 1864, for the war. Present or accounted for through October, 1864.

MORGAN, GEORGE T., Private

Previously served in Company F, Mallett's Battalion (Camp Guard). Transferred to this company in June-August, 1864. Present or accounted for until wounded in the head at or near Petersburg, Virginia, on or about August 20, 1864. Reported absent wounded through October, 1864.

NEAL, ELISHA M., Private

Transferred to this company from 1st Company B, 49th Regiment N.C. Troops, January 9, 1863. Present or accounted for until wounded at Wilderness, Virginia, May 5, 1864. Reported absent wounded through October, 1864, but returned to duty prior to April 3, 1865, when he was captured at or near Hatcher's Run, Virginia. Confined at Hart's Island, New York Harbor, until released June 19-20, 1865, after taking the Oath of Allegiance.

NEAL, WILLIAM A., Private

Transferred to this company from 1st Company B, 49th Regiment N.C. Troops, January 9, 1863. Present or accounted for until reported absent wounded in September-October, 1864; however, place and date wounded not reported. Returned to duty prior to April 2, 1865, when he was captured at Hatcher's Run, Virginia. Confined at Hart's Island, New York Harbor, until released June 19-20, 1865, after taking the Oath of Allegiance.

OLDHAM, THOMAS S., Corporal

Transferred to this company from 1st Company B, 49th Regiment N.C. Troops, January 9, 1863, with the rank of Corporal. Present or accounted for until reported absent without leave or absent sick from March 12, 1863, until he returned to duty in January-February, 1864. Present or accounted for until paroled at Appomattox Court House, Virginia, April 9, 1865.

OLIVE, CALVIN, Sergeant

Transferred to this company from 1st Company B, 49th Regiment N.C. Troops, January 9, 1863, with the rank of Corporal. Promoted to Sergeant in May-August, 1864. Present or accounted for until wounded in the left side at Reams' Station, Virginia, August 25, 1864. Died in hospital at Richmond, Virginia, September 24, 1864, of wounds.

PARTIN, BENJAMIN F., Private

Transferred to this company from 1st Company B, 49th Regiment N.C. Troops, January 9, 1863. Present or accounted for until captured at Hatcher's Run, Virginia, April 2, 1865. Confined at Hart's Island, New York Harbor, until released June 17-18, 1865, after taking the Oath of Allegiance.

PARTIN, JOHN A., Private

Resided in Chatham County. Place and date of enlistment not reported. Captured at or near Hatcher's Run, Virginia, March 31, 1865. Confined at Point Lookout, Maryland, until released June 16-17, 1865, after taking the Oath of Allegiance.

PENNINGTON, JACKSON, Private

Transferred to this company from 1st Company B, 49th Regiment N.C. Troops, January 9, 1863. Present or accounted for until he died in hospital at Hardeeville, South Carolina, March 12, 1863, of disease.

PICKARD, ALVIS, Private

Transferred to this company from 1st Company B, 49th Regiment N.C. Troops, January 9, 1863. Never reported for duty and was dropped from the rolls on December 9, 1863.

RAY, FRANCIS, Private

Transferred to this company from 1st Company B, 49th Regiment N.C. Troops, January 9, 1863. Was absent without leave at the time of transfer. Never reported for duty and was reported absent without leave until dropped from the rolls of the company on December 9, 1863.

RHYMER, JOSEPH, Private

Enlisted at Orange Court House, Virginia, March 6, 1864, for the war. Present or accounted for until he died in hospital at Richmond, Virginia, June 1, 1864, of "pneumonia."

RIGGSBEE, ALEXANDER J., Private

Transferred to this company from 1st Company B 49th Regiment N.C. Troops, January 9, 1863. Present or accounted for until captured in hospital at Richmond, Virginia, April 3, 1865.

RIGGSBEE, ELBERT, Sergeant

Transferred to this company from 1st Company B, 49th Regiment N.C. Troops, January 9, 1863, with the rank of Private. Promoted to Corporal on February 5, 1863, and promoted to Sergeant on October 1, 1863. Present or accounted for until hospitalized at Richmond, Virginia, August 27, 1864, with gunshot wounds of both thighs; however, place and date wounded not reported. Reported absent wounded until furloughed for sixty days on September 15, 1864.

RIGGSBEE, FRANCIS M., Private

Enlisted at Camp Holmes on April 15, 1863 for the war. Present or accounted for until furloughed for sixty days on December 24, 1864.

RIGGSBEE, JOHN ALVIS, 1st Sergeant
Transferred to this company from 1st Company B, 49th Regiment N.C. Troops, January 9, 1863, with the rank of 1st Sergeant. Present or accounted for through April, 1864. No further records.

RIGGSBEE, JOHN W., Private
Transferred to this company from 1st Company B, 49th Regiment N.C. Troops, January 9, 1863. Present or accounted for until captured at or near Spotsylvania Court House, Virginia, on or about May 12, 1864. Confined at Point Lookout, Maryland, until transferred to Elmira, New York, August 8, 1864. Died at Elmira on September 16, 1864, of "chronic diarrhoea."

RIGGSBEE, JONES E., Private
Transferred to this company from 1st Company B, 49th Regiment N.C. Troops, January 9, 1863. Present or accounted for until captured at or near Hatcher's Run, Virginia, March 31, 1865. Confined at Point Lookout, Maryland, until released on June 19, 1865, after taking the Oath of Allegiance.

RIGGSBEE, LARKINS J., Private
Transferred to this company from 1st Company B, 49th Regiment N.C. Troops, January 9, 1863. Present or accounted for until captured at or near Petersburg, Virginia, October 1-4, 1864. Confined at Point Lookout, Maryland, until released on June 19, 1865, after taking the Oath of Allegiance.

RIGGSBEE, LUCIAN H., Private
Previously served in Company F, Mallett's Battalion (Camp Guard). Date transferred to this company not reported; however, he was first listed on the rolls of this company in September-October, 1864. Captured at Hatcher's Run, Virginia, April 2, 1865, and confined at Hart's Island, New York Harbor, until released June 19-20, 1865, after taking the Oath of Allegiance.

RIGGSBEE, REVEL, Private
Transferred to this company from 1st Company B, 49th Regiment N.C. Troops, January 9, 1863. Present or accounted for until reported absent without leave from October 28, 1863, through December, 1863. Returned to duty in January-February, 1864, and present or accounted for until paroled at Appomattox Court House, Virginia, April 9, 1865.

ROBERTSON, JOHN L., Private
Previously served in Company F, Mallett's Battalion (Camp Guard). Transferred to this company in September, 186[4]. Present or accounted for until reported absent wounded in September-October, 1864; however, place and date wounded not reported. Paroled at Appomattox Court House, Virginia, April 9, 1865.

STONE, W. F., Private
Resided in Chatham County. Place and date of enlistment not reported. Captured at Hatcher's Run, Virginia, April 2, 1865, and confined at Hart's Island, New York Harbor, until released June 17-18, 1865, after taking the Oath of Allegiance.

SUGGS, THOMAS, Private
Previously served in Company F, Mallett's Battalion (Camp Guard). Date transferred to this company not reported; however, he was first listed on the rolls of this company in September-October, 1864. Present or accounted for until captured at or near Hatcher's Run,

Virginia, March 31, 1865. Confined at Point Lookout, Maryland, until released on June 20, 1865, after taking the Oath of Allegiance.

TURNER, M. V., Private
Previously served in Company C of this regiment. Transferred to this company on April 8, 1863. Present or accounted for until transferred to the C.S. Navy on April 1, 1864.

UPCHURCH, P. B., Private
Resided in Chatham County and enlisted at age 30, April 7, 1863, for the war. Present or accounted for until killed in a skirmish at the South Anna Bridge, on the Richmond and Fredericksburg Railroad, Virginia, July 4, 1863. [Company records indicate that he enlisted in Mallett's Battalion (Camp Guard) on July 15, 1862, and was transferred to this company on April 7, 1863; however, records of Mallett's Battalion do not indicate that he served therein.]

WEBB, SOWEL R., Private
Resided in Johnston County and enlisted in Lenoir County on May 30, 1863, for the war. Present or accounted for through October, 1864.

WHITE, DAVID N., Private
Previously served in Company C of this regiment. Transferred to this company on April 8, 1863. Present or accounted for until he deserted on July 31, 1863. Apprehended prior to July 2, 1864, when he was confined at Castle Thunder Prison, Richmond, Virginia. Reported "absent in arrest" through October, 1864. Captured in hospital at Richmond on April 3, 1865, and confined at Libby Prison, Richmond, until transferred to Newport News, Virginia, on or about April 24, 1865. Released at Newport News on June 15, 1865, after taking the Oath of Allegiance.

WHITFIELD, CANNY L., Private
Transferred to this company from 1st Company B, 49th Regiment N.C. Troops, January 9, 1863. Present or accounted for through October, 1864.

WHITFIELD, WILLIAM T., Private
Transferred to this company from 1st Company B, 49th Regiment N.C. Troops, January 9, 1863. Present or accounted for until hospitalized at Charlottesville, Virginia, January 12, 1864, with "hemiplegia"; however, place and date injured not reported. Reported absent sick through October, 1864.

WICKS, JAMES A., Private
Born in Chatham County where he resided as a farmer prior to enlisting at "Brookses" at age 22. Enlistment date reported as March 1, 1862; however, he was not listed on the rolls of this company until January-February, 1863. Present or accounted for until captured at or near Hatcher's Run, Virginia, March 31, 1865. Confined at Point Lookout, Maryland, until released on June 21, 1865, after taking the Oath of Allegiance.

WILLIAMS, ADDISON J., Private
Transferred to this company from 1st Company B, 49th Regiment N.C. Troops, January 9, 1863. Present or accounted for until he deserted to the enemy on or about March 22, 1865. Released on or about March 29, 1865, after taking the Oath of Allegiance.

WILLIAMS, WILLIAM J., Private
Resided in Chatham County and enlisted at age 28, April 7, 1863, for the war. Present or accounted for until he deserted on July 31, 1863. Died in Chatham County on October 19, 1864, of "consumption." [Company records indicate that he enlisted in Mallett's Battalion (Camp Guard) on July 18, 1862, and was transferred to this company on April 7, 1863; however, records of Mallett's Battalion do not indicate that he served therein.]

WILLIAMSON, CORNELIUS D., Corporal
Previously served in Company F, Mallett's Battalion (Camp Guard). Date transferred to this company not reported; however, he was first listed on the rolls of this company in September-October, 1864. North Carolina pension records indicate he was wounded at Reams' Station, Virginia, "June 15, 1864." Paroled at Appomattox Court House, Virginia, April 9, 1865.

WILLIAMSON, HIRAM, Private
Resided in Moore County and enlisted at age 28, April 7, 1863, for the war. Present or accounted for until he deserted on July 31, 1863. Returned to duty on March 12, 1864. Present or accounted for until paroled at Appomattox Court House, Virginia, April 9, 1865. [Company records indicate that he enlisted in Mallett's Battalion (Camp Guard) on July 18, 1862, and was transferred to this company on April 7, 1863; however, records of Mallett's Battalion do not indicate that he served therein.]

WILLIAMSON, JESSE, Private
Resided in Moore County and enlisted at age 30, April 7, 1863, for the war. Present or accounted for until he deserted on July 31, 1863. Returned to duty on March 5, 1864, and was present or accounted for through October, 1864. [Company records indicate that he enlisted in Mallett's Battalion (Camp Guard) on October 9, 1862, and was transferred to this company on April 7, 1863; however, records of Mallett's Battalion do not indicate that he served therein.]

YOW, ISAAC, Private
Resided in Moore County and enlisted at age 23, April 7, 1863, for the war. Present or accounted for until wounded at Bristoe Station, Virginia, October 14, 1863. Reported absent wounded until reported absent without leave on February 1, 1864. Reported absent without leave through October, 1864. [Company records indicate that he enlisted in Mallett's Battalion (Camp Guard) on July 18, 1862, and was transferred to this company on April 7, 1863; however, records of Mallett's Battalion do not indicate that he served therein.]

YOW, SIMEON J., Corporal
Previously served in Company C, Mallett's Battalion (Camp Guard). Transferred to this company on or about April 7, 1863. Present or accounted for until wounded at Bristoe Station, Virginia, October 14, 1863. Reported absent wounded until he returned to duty on April 4, 1864. Promoted to Corporal in May-August, 1864. Present or accounted for until reported absent without leave on August 24, 1864. Reported absent without leave through October, 1864.

COMPANY E

This company was from Franklin and Granville counties and enlisted at Franklinton on May 16, 1861. It was mustered in and assigned to this regiment as Company E. After joining the regiment the company functioned as a part of the regiment, and its history for the war period is recorded as a part of the regimental history.

The information contained in the following roster of the company was compiled principally from company muster rolls for July-August, 1861; November, 1862-April, 1864; and September-October, 1864. No company muster rolls were found for the period prior to July, 1861; for September, 1861-October, 1862; May-August, 1864; or for the period after October, 1864. In addition to the company muster rolls, Roll of Honor records, receipt rolls, hospital records, prisoner of war records, and other primary records, supplemented by state pension applications, United Daughters of the Confederacy records, and postwar rosters and histories, all provided useful information.

OFFICERS
CAPTAINS

PERRY, WILLIE, Jr.
Resided in Granville County and enlisted in Franklin County at age 35. Appointed Captain to rank from May 16, 1861. Present or accounted for until wounded in the arm at Malvern Hill, Virginia, July 1, 1862. Died July 19, 1862, of wounds. Place of death not reported.

BALLARD, WILLIAM H.
Resided in Franklin County and enlisted at age 20. Appointed 2nd Lieutenant to rank from May 16, 1861, and was promoted to 1st Lieutenant on July 9, 1861. Present or accounted for until wounded in the arm at Malvern Hill, Virginia, July 1, 1862. Promoted to Captain on July 19, 1862. Reported absent wounded until October 31, 1862, when he was reported absent without leave. Reported absent without leave through February, 1863, but returned to duty prior to July 1, 1863. Present or accounted for until captured on the Weldon Railroad, near Petersburg, Virginia, August 21, 1864. Confined at Old Capitol Prison, Washington, D.C., until transferred to Fort Delaware, Delaware, August 27, 1864. Released at Fort Delaware on June 17, 1865, after taking the Oath of Allegiance.

LIEUTENANTS

GREEN, BENJAMIN T., 1st Lieutenant
Resided in Franklin County where he enlisted at age 28. Appointed 1st Lieutenant on May 16, 1861. Promoted to Surgeon on June 1, 1861, and transferred to the Field and Staff of this regiment.

HARRIS, RANSOM S., 2nd Lieutenant
Resided in Franklin County where he enlisted at age 38. Appointed 2nd Lieutenant to rank from May 16, 1861. Present or accounted for until he was defeated for reelection when the regiment was reorganized on May 2, 1862.

KEARNEY, HENRY C., 1st Lieutenant
Born in Franklin County where he resided prior to

enlisting in Franklin County at age 18. Appointed 3rd Lieutenant to rank from May 16, 1861, and was promoted to 2nd Lieutenant on May 2, 1862. Present or accounted for until wounded at Malvern Hill, Virginia, July 1, 1862. Promoted to 1st Lieutenant on July 19, 1862. Returned to duty prior to September 14, 1862, when he was wounded and captured at Crampton's Pass, Maryland. Confined at Fort Delaware, Delaware, until transferred to Aiken's Landing, James River, Virginia, October 2, 1862, for exchange. Declared exchanged at Aiken's Landing on November 10, 1862. Wounded at Fredericksburg, Virginia, December 13, 1862, and was wounded again at White Oak Swamp, Virginia, at an unspecified date. Present or accounted for from January 1, 1864, until he was "wounded in a skirmish near Petersburg while crossing the James River" on or about June 15, 1864. Returned to duty prior to November 1, 1864, and was paroled at Appomattox Court House, Virginia, April 9, 1865.

MORRIS, JOHN A., 2nd Lieutenant
Born in Granville County and resided in Franklin County where he was by occupation a student prior to enlisting in Franklin County at age 18, May 16, 1861. Mustered in as 1st Sergeant and was appointed 2nd Lieutenant on May 2, 1862. Present or accounted for until paroled at Appomattox Court House, Virginia, April 9, 1865.

SHERROD, HENRY H., 3rd Lieutenant
Resided in Franklin County where he enlisted at age 28, May 16, 1861. Mustered in as Sergeant and was promoted to 1st Sergeant on May 2, 1862. Appointed 3rd Lieutenant on July 24, 1862. Present or accounted for until paroled at Appomattox Court House, Virginia, April 9, 1865.

NONCOMMISSIONED OFFICERS AND PRIVATES

ADCOCK, PUMPHREY W., Private
Born in Granville County where he resided as a farmer prior to enlisting in Franklin County at age 18, May 16, 1861. Present or accounted for until he died at Lynchburg, Virginia, or at Staunton, Virginia, February 6-7, 1863, of "phthisis pulmonalis."

ALLEN, DEMARCUS S., Sergeant
Resided in Granville County and enlisted in Franklin County at age 23, May 16, 1861. Mustered in as Private and promoted to Sergeant on July 9, 1861. Present or accounted for until paroled at Appomattox Court House, Virginia, April 9, 1865.

ALLEN, WILLIAM HENRY, Private
Resided in Granville County and was by occupation a farmer prior to enlisting in Franklin County at age 18, May 16, 1861. Present or accounted for until wounded in the breast at Fredericksburg, Virginia, December 13, 1862. Returned to duty prior to January 1, 1863, and present or accounted for through October, 1864.

ANDREWS, G. J., Private
Resided in Franklin County where he enlisted at age 32, March 8, 1862. Present or accounted for until captured at or near Crampton's Pass, Maryland,

September 14, 1862. Confined at Fort Delaware, Delaware, until transferred to Aiken's Landing, James River, Virginia, October 2, 1862, for exchange. Declared exchanged at Aiken's Landing on November 10, 1862. Returned to duty prior to December 13, 1862, when he was wounded in the breast at Fredericksburg, Virginia. Died in hospital at Richmond, Virginia, December 17, 1862, of wounds.

BAILEY, EATON, Private
Resided in Granville County and enlisted in Franklin County at age 18, May 16, 1861. Present or accounted for until he died in hospital at Richmond, Virginia, August 24, 1863, of "typhoid fever."

BAILEY, LEVI J., Private
Born in Granville County where he resided as a farmer prior to enlisting in Franklin County at age 25, May 16, 1861. Present or accounted for through October, 1864.

BEST, HENRY T., Private
Born in Granville County and resided in Franklin County where he was by occupation a farmer prior to enlisting in Franklin County at age 20, May 16, 1861. Present or accounted for until wounded in the buttocks at Fredericksburg, Virginia, December 13, 1862. Returned to duty in January-February, 1863, and present or accounted for until captured at Bristoe Station, Virginia, October 14, 1863. Confined at Old Capitol Prison, Washington, D.C., until transferred to Point Lookout, Maryland, October 27, 1863. Paroled and transferred to Aiken's Landing, James River, Virginia, September 18, 1864, for exchange. Died in hospital at Richmond, Virginia, September 25, 1864, of "ch[ronic] diarrhoea."

BEVER, DANIEL F., Private
Resided in Person County or at South Boston, Virginia, and enlisted in Wake County at age 25, July 15, 1862, for the war. Present or accounted for until wounded in the shoulder at Fredericksburg, Virginia, December 13, 1862. Returned to duty in July-August, 1863, and present or accounted for until wounded in the head and captured at or near Hatcher's Run, Virginia, on or about April 2, 1865. Confined at Old Capitol Prison, Washington, D.C., until transferred to Elmira, New York, May 11, 1865. Released on July 7, 1865, after taking the Oath of Allegiance.

BLACKLEY, BENJAMIN J., Private
Resided in Granville County and enlisted in Franklin County at age 41, May 16, 1861. Present or accounted for until discharged at an unspecified date by reason of being over age.

BLACKLEY, RUFUS H., Private
Resided in Granville County and enlisted in Franklin County at age 21, May 16, 1861. Present or accounted for until wounded in the breast at Fredericksburg, Virginia, December 13, 1862. Died in hospital at Richmond, Virginia, December 21, 1862, of wounds.

BLACKLEY, WILLIAM A., 1st Sergeant
Resided in Granville County and enlisted in Franklin County at age 24, May 16, 1861. Mustered in as Private and promoted to Corporal on September 18, 1861. Promoted to Sergeant on August 1, 1862. Present or accounted for until captured at or near Crampton's Pass, Maryland, September 14, 1862. Confined at Fort Delaware, Delaware, until transferred to Aiken's

Landing, James River, Virginia, October 2, 1862, for exchange. Declared exchanged at Aiken's Landing on November 10, 1862. Returned to duty prior to December 13, 1862, when he was wounded in the hip at Fredericksburg, Virginia. Returned to duty prior to January 1, 1863, and was promoted to 1st Sergeant in May-October, 1864. Present or accounted for until paroled at Appomattox Court House, Virginia, April 9, 1865.

BOWLAND, WILLIAM, Private
Resided in Person County and enlisted in Wake County at age 23, July 15, 1862, for the war. Present or accounted for until transferred to Company E, 35th Regiment N.C. Troops, in June, 1863.

BRAGG, JOHN W., Private
Resided in Granville County and enlisted in Franklin County at age 25, February 24, 1862. Died in hospital at Lynchburg, Virginia, December 24, 1862, of "feb[ris] typhoides."

BRIDGERS, JACKSON, Private
Resided in Franklin County where he enlisted at age 21, May 16, 1861. Present or accounted for through October, 1864; however, he was reported absent sick during much of that period.

BURTON, PAUL W., Private
Resided in Granville County and enlisted in Franklin County at age 28, May 16, 1861. Present or accounted for through February 25, 1865; however, he was reported absent sick or absent on detail during most of that period. Deserted to the enemy on February 26, 1865, and was released on or about March 1, 1865, after taking the Oath of Allegiance.

CARD, DREWY M., Private
Born in Franklin County where he resided as a farmer prior to enlisting in Franklin County at age 23, May 16, 1861. Present or accounted for until he deserted to the enemy on or about March 26, 1865. Released on or about March 1, 1865, after taking the Oath of Allegiance.

CARD, JOHN R., Private
Resided in Franklin County where he enlisted at age 26, March 8, 1862. Present or accounted for until hospitalized at Richmond, Virginia, May 7, 1864, with a gunshot wound of the back; however, place and date wounded not reported. Returned to duty on July 27, 1864, and present or accounted for through October, 1864.

CARSON, JOHN T., Private
Resided in Franklin County where he enlisted at age 32, May 16, 1861. Present or accounted for until he died at Winchester, Virginia, on or about October 4, 1862, of disease.

CARSON, ROBERT, Private
Enlisted in Franklin County on May 16, 1861. Present or accounted for through August, 1861. No further records.

CARSON, WILLIAM R., Private
Resided in Franklin County where he enlisted at age 26, May 16, 1861. Present or accounted for until he deserted to the enemy on or about February 26, 1865. Released on or about March 1, 1865, after taking the Oath of Allegiance.

CARVER, CHESLEY, Private
Resided in Person County and enlisted in Wake County at age 26, July 15, 1862, for the war. Present or accounted for until reported absent without leave on September 12, 1863. Returned to duty on January 6, 1864, and present or accounted for until he deserted to the enemy on or about February 26, 1865. Released on or about March 1, 1865, after taking the Oath of Allegiance.

CARVER, DENNIS, Private
Resided in Person County and enlisted in Wake County at age 26, July 15, 1862, for the war. Present or accounted for until reported absent wounded in May-June, 1863; however, place and date wounded not reported. Returned to duty prior to September 1, 1863. Present or accounted for until hospitalized at Charlottesville, Virginia, May 8, 1864, with a gunshot wound; however, place and date wounded not reported. Reported absent wounded until retired to the Invalid Corps on November 22, 1864.

CARVER, THOMAS JEFFERSON, Private
Resided in Person County and enlisted in Wake County at age 25, July 15, 1862, for the war. Present or accounted for until wounded in the breast at Bristoe Station, Virginia, October 14, 1863. Reported absent wounded until he returned to duty on July 8, 1864. Present or accounted for until he deserted to the enemy on or about February 26, 1865. Released on or about March 1, 1865, after taking the Oath of Allegiance.

CATLETT, BURGESS G., Private
Resided in Granville County and enlisted in Franklin County at age 17, May 16, 1861. Present or accounted for until discharged on August 10, 1862, by reason of being under age. Later served in Company I, 55th Regiment N.C. Troops.

CHANDLER, DAVID R., Private
Resided in Person County and enlisted in Wake County at age 30, July 15, 1862, for the war. Present or accounted for until wounded at or near Crampton's Pass, Maryland, September 14, 1862. Company records indicate that he was also captured at or near Crampton's Pass; however, records of the Federal Provost Marshal do not substantiate that report. Died of wounds received at Crampton's Pass. Place and date of death not reported.

CLAYTON, GREEN J., Private
Resided in Person County and was by occupation a farmer prior to enlisting in Wake County at age 26, July 15, 1862, for the war. Present or accounted for until captured at or near Petersburg, Virginia, October 1, 1864. Confined at Point Lookout, Maryland, until released on May 13, 1865, after taking the Oath of Allegiance.

CLAYTON, JOHN C., Private
Resided in Person County and enlisted in Wake County at age 26, July 15, 1862, for the war. Present or accounted for until he died in hospital at Richmond, Virginia, December 14, 1862, of "phthisis" and/or "pleuritis."

COLLINS, JAMES H., Private
Resided in Franklin County where he enlisted at age 18, May 16, 1861. Present or accounted for until he died at Yorktown, Virginia, August 9, 1861, of disease.

COLLINS, JOHN W., Private

Resided in Franklin County where he enlisted at age 21, May 16, 1861. Present or accounted for until he died in King and Queen County, Virginia, on or about October 10, 1861, of disease.

CONYERS, JAMES M., Private

Resided in Franklin County and enlisted at age 30, February 22, 1862. Present or accounted for until he died at Richmond, Virginia, May 22, 1862, of disease.

COZART, JACOB, Private

Resided in Person County and enlisted in Wake County at age 32, July 15, 1862, for the war. Present or accounted for until captured at or near Crampton's Pass, Maryland, September 14, 1862. Confined at Fort Delaware, Delaware, until transferred to Aiken's Landing, James River, Virginia, October 2, 1862, for exchange. Declared exchanged at Aiken's Landing on November 10, 1862. Reported absent sick or absent on detail until he rejoined the company on February 29, 1864. Present or accounted for through April, 1864.

DAY, JOHN B., Corporal

Resided in Person County and enlisted in Wake County at age 33, July 15, 1862, for the war. Mustered in as Private and promoted to Corporal on December 11, 1863. Present or accounted for until wounded at Wilderness, Virginia, May 5, 1864. Reported absent wounded until furloughed for sixty days from hospital at Richmond, Virginia, February 24, 1865.

DENNY, WILLIAM, Private

Born in Person County where he resided prior to enlisting in Wake County at age 32, July 15, 1862, for the war. Present or accounted for until he died at Montgomery Springs, Virginia, March 3, 1863, of disease.

DICKENS, B. B., Private

Resided in Franklin County where he enlisted at age 18, May 16, 1861. Present or accounted for until he died at Yorktown, Virginia, September 9, 1861, of disease.

DUKE, HENRY C., Private

Born in Franklin County where he resided as a farmer prior to enlisting in Franklin County at age 18, May 16, 1861. Present or accounted for until wounded at Reams' Station, Virginia, August 25, 1864. Reported absent wounded through October, 1864. Deserted to the enemy on or about February 17, 1865, and was released on or about February 21, 1865, after taking the Oath of Allegiance.

DUKE, JAMES B., Private

Born in Granville County where he resided as a farmer prior to enlisting in Franklin County at age 20, May 16, 1861. Present or accounted for until wounded in the head at Malvern Hill, Virginia, July 1, 1862. Returned to duty prior to January 1, 1863, and present or accounted for until captured at Spotsylvania Court House, Virginia, May 12, 1864. Confined at Point Lookout, Maryland, until transferred to Elmira, New York, August 8, 1864. Released on June 19, 1865, after taking the Oath of Allegiance.

ELLINGTON, JUNIUS F., Corporal

Born in Franklin County and resided in Franklin or Chatham counties where he was by occupation a farmer prior to enlisting in Franklin County at age 20, May 16, 1861. Mustered in as Corporal. Present or accounted for until wounded in the shoulder at Fredericksburg, Virginia, December 13, 1862. Returned to duty prior to January 1, 1863, and present or accounted for until transferred to Company E, 44th Regiment N.C. Troops, July 10, 1863.

EVANS, SAMUEL, Private

Resided in Person County and enlisted in Wake County at age 19, July 15, 1862, for the war. Present or accounted for through October, 1864; however, he was reported absent sick or absent on detail during most of that period.

FALKNER, E. B., Private

Resided in Granville County and enlisted at age 28, February 24, 1862. Present or accounted for until he died at Richmond, Virginia, August 12, 1862, of disease.

FALKNER, GEORGE W., Private

Enlisted in Franklin County on February 2, 1864, for the war. Present or accounted for until paroled at Raleigh on May 29, 1865.

FAULKNER, WILLIAM R., Private

Born in Granville County where he resided as a farmer prior to enlisting in Franklin County at age 19, May 16, 1861. Present or accounted for until he died at Richmond, Virginia, August 25, 1862, of disease.

FRAZIER, JOSEPH H., Private

Born in Wake County where he resided as a farmer prior to enlisting in Franklin County at age 18, May 16, 1861. Present or accounted for until wounded in the buttocks at Fredericksburg, Virginia, December 13, 1862. Returned to duty in November-December, 1863, and present or accounted for until wounded at Wilderness, Virginia, May 5, 1864. Reported absent wounded until furloughed for sixty days on December 15, 1864. Captured at Raleigh on or about April 13, 1865.

FULCHIER, L., Private

Resided in Person County and enlisted at age 27, July 15, 1862, for the war. Present or accounted for until killed at or near Crampton's Pass, Maryland, September 14, 1862.

GILL, EZRA T., Corporal

Born in Franklin County where he resided as a farmer prior to enlisting in Franklin County at age 21, May 16, 1861. Mustered in as Private. Present or accounted for until captured at or near Crampton's Pass, Maryland, September 14, 1862. Confined at Fort Delaware, Delaware, until transferred to Aiken's Landing, James River, Virginia, October 2, 1862, for exchange. Declared exchanged at Aiken's Landing on November 10, 1862. Returned to duty prior to January 1, 1863, and was promoted to Corporal on January 1, 1863. Present or accounted for until transferred to the C.S. Navy on or about February 15, 1864.

GOSWICK, WILLIAM H., Private

Resided in Franklin County where he enlisted at age 19, May 16, 1861. Present or accounted for until reported absent wounded in December, 1862; however, place and date wounded not reported. Reported absent without leave on February 21, 1863, but returned to duty in April, 1863. Present or accounted for until hospitalized at Charlottesville, Virginia, May 10, 1864, with a gunshot wound of the breast; however, place and date wounded not reported. Reported absent wounded through October, 1864.

GREEN, ISAAC N., Private
Born in Franklin County where he resided as a farmer prior to enlisting in Franklin County at age 18, May 16, 1861. Present or accounted for until discharged on or about June 21, 1862, by reason of disability.

GRESHAM, JAMES D., Private
Resided in Granville County. Place and date of enlistment not reported. Captured at Hatcher's Run, Virginia, on or about April 3, 1865, and confined at Point Lookout, Maryland, until released on June 27, 1865, after taking the Oath of Allegiance.

HAILEY, G. W., Private
Resided in Granville County and enlisted in Franklin County at age 22, July 22, 1862, for the war. Present or accounted for until mortally wounded at Fredericksburg, Virginia, December 13, 1862. Place and date of death not reported.

HARRIS, CORNELIUS, Private
Resided in Person County and enlisted in Wake County at age 26, July 15, 1862, for the war. Present or accounted for until wounded at or near Jones' Farm, Virginia, on or about October 1, 1864. Reported absent wounded through October 31, 1864. Deserted to the enemy on or about February 26, 1865, and was released on or about March 1, 1865, after taking the Oath of Allegiance.

HARRIS, DOLPHIN, Private
Previously served in Company B, 44th Regiment N.C. Troops. Transferred to this company on July 10, 1863. Present or accounted for until hospitalized at Danville, Virginia, July 26, 1864, with a gunshot wound of the left arm; however, place and date wounded not reported. Returned to duty on September 26, 1864. Deserted to the enemy on or about February 26, 1865, and was released on or about March 1, 1865, after taking the Oath of Allegiance.

HARRIS, JAMES H., Private
Resided in Franklin County where he enlisted at age 24, May 16, 1861. Present or accounted for until captured at or near High Bridge, Virginia, on or about April 6, 1865. Confined at Newport News, Virginia, until released on June 26, 1865, after taking the Oath of Allegiance.

HART, WILLIAM C., Sergeant
Born in Wake County and resided in Franklin County where he was by occupation a farmer prior to enlisting in Franklin County at age 20, May 16, 1861. Mustered in as Private and promoted to Corporal in February-December, 1862. Present or accounted for until captured at or near Crampton's Pass, Maryland, September 14, 1862. Confined at Fort Delaware, Delaware, until transferred to Aiken's Landing, James River, Virginia, October 2, 1862, for exchange. Declared exchanged at Aiken's Landing on November 10, 1862. Returned to duty prior to January 1, 1863, and was promoted to Sergeant on December 11, 1863. Present or accounted for until hospitalized at Charlottesville, Virginia, May 10, 1864, with a gunshot

wound of the breast; however, place and date wounded not reported. Returned to duty on May 11, 1864, and present or accounted for until paroled at Appomattox Court House, Virginia, April 9, 1865.

HAYES, WHITMELL K., Private
Resided in Wake County and enlisted in Franklin County at age 26, May 16, 1861. Present or accounted for until discharged in May, 1863, after providing Private Mason M. White as a substitute.

HICKS, R. R., Private
Resided in Person County and enlisted in Wake County at age 28, July 15, 1862, for the war. Present or accounted for until he died "at home" in Person County on April 30, 1863, of disease.

HIGHT, RICHARD N. O., Private
Previously served in Company C of this regiment. Transferred to this company in December, 1862. Present or accounted for through July 27, 1864.

HOLDEN, RICHARD, Corporal
Resided in Franklin County where he enlisted at age 18, May 16, 1861. Mustered in as Private and promoted to Corporal on July 1, 1863. Present or accounted for until paroled at Appomattox Court House, Virginia, April 9, 1865.

HOLMES, MARCILLUS C., Private
Resided in Franklin County where he enlisted at age 23, May 16, 1861. Present or accounted for until wounded at or near Crampton's Pass, Maryland, September 14, 1862. Captured at Charles Town, Virginia, October 16, 1862, and confined at Fort McHenry, Maryland, until paroled and transferred to Aiken's Landing, James River, Virginia, where he was received October 30, 1862, for exchange. Declared exchanged at Aiken's Landing on November 10, 1862. Returned to duty prior to December 13, 1862, when he was wounded in the foot at Fredericksburg, Virginia. Returned to duty in March-April, 1863, and present or accounted for until wounded in the left arm at Wilderness, Virginia, on or about May 5, 1864. Returned to duty prior to November 1, 1864, and present or accounted for until captured at Hatcher's Run, Virginia, April 2, 1865. Confined at Point Lookout, Maryland, until released on June 13, 1865, after taking the Oath of Allegiance.

HOLSOMBACK, WILLIAM H., Private
Resided in Person County and enlisted in Wake County at age 24, July 15, 1862, for the war. Present or accounted for until reported absent without leave from December 8, 1862, through April, 1863. Reported "absent in hospital" in May-June, 1863, and returned to duty prior to September 1, 1863. Present or accounted for through October, 1864; however, he was reported absent sick during much of that period. Paroled at Appomattox Court House, Virginia, April 9, 1865.

HUFF, JAMES G., Private
Born in Granville County where he resided as a farmer prior to enlisting in Franklin County at age 23, May 16, 1861. Present or accounted for until he deserted to the enemy on or about February 17, 1865. Released on or about February 21, 1865, after taking the Oath of Allegiance. North Carolina pension records indicate he was wounded at Malvern Hill, Virginia, July 1, 1862.

JEFFREYS, S. H., Private

Resided in Nash County and enlisted in Franklin County at age 42, May 16, 1861. Present or accounted for until discharged on August 19, 1862, by reason of being over age.

JENKINS, ARISTARCHUS L., Private

Born in Granville County where he resided as a farmer prior to enlisting in Franklin County at age 22, May 16, 1861. Present or accounted for until wounded at Bristoe Station, Virginia, October 14, 1863. Returned to duty prior to January 1, 1864. Present or accounted for until hospitalized at Richmond, Virginia, on or about May 5, 1864, with a gunshot wound of the shoulder; however, place and date wounded not reported. Returned to duty prior to November 1, 1864. Deserted to the enemy on or about February 17, 1865, and was released on or about February 21, 1865, after taking the Oath of Allegiance.

JENKINS, ELIAS S., Sergeant

Resided in Granville County and enlisted in Franklin County at age 18, May 16, 1861. Mustered in as Sergeant. Present or accounted for until wounded at Reams' Station, Virginia, August 25, 1864. Reported absent wounded through October, 1864.

JENKINS, JONATHAN, Private

Resided in Granville County and enlisted in Franklin County at age 22, February 22, 1862. Present or accounted for until captured at or near High Bridge, Virginia, on or about April 6, 1865. Confined at Newport News, Virginia, until released on June 14, 1865, after taking the Oath of Allegiance.

JENKINS, P. B., Private

Resided in Granville County and enlisted at age 25, February 22, 1862. Present or accounted for until he "drowned in the [Rapidan] River" on August 29, 1862.

KENNEDY, G. G., Private

Resided in Person County and enlisted in Wake County at age 27, July 15, 1862, for the war. Present or accounted for until wounded and captured at or near Crampton's Pass, Maryland, on or about September 14, 1862. Confined at Fort Delaware, Delaware, until transferred to Aiken's Landing, James River, Virginia, October 2, 1862, for exchange. Reported absent without leave from October 11, 1862, through December, 1862. Returned to duty in January-February, 1863, and present or accounted for until he died "at home" on July 28, 1863, of disease.

LENEAVE, JOHN M., Private

Resided in Person County and was by occupation a hatter prior to enlisting in Wake County at age 33, July 15, 1862, for the war. Present or accounted for until captured at Crampton's Pass, Maryland, September 14, 1862. Paroled on or about the same day. Wounded in the hand at Fredericksburg, Virginia, December 13, 1862. Returned to duty in March-April, 1863, and present or accounted for until he was "left as a nurse" at Wilderness, Virginia, May 5, 1864. North Carolina pension records indicate that he was wounded at Wilderness and that he survived the war. No further records.

LONG, JAMES M., Private

Resided in Person County and enlisted in Wake County at age 26, July 15, 1862, for the war. Present or accounted for until captured at Crampton's Pass, Maryland, September 14, 1862. Confined at Fort Delaware, Delaware, until transferred to Aiken's Landing, James River, Virginia, October 2, 1862, for exchange. Declared exchanged at Aiken's Landing on November 10, 1862. Returned to duty prior to March 1, 1863, and present or accounted for until he deserted to the enemy on or about February 26, 1865. Released on or about March 1, 1865, after taking the Oath of Allegiance.

LONG, JESSE J., Private

Resided in Person County and enlisted in Wake County at age 28, July 15, 1862, for the war. Present or accounted for through October, 1864.

LONG, WILLIAM J., Private

Resided in Person County and enlisted in Wake County at age 25, July 15, 1862, for the war. Present or accounted for until wounded at Wilderness, Virginia, May 6, 1864. Died in hospital at Staunton, Virginia, June 11, 1864, of wounds.

LOY, JOHN H., Private

Resided in Person County and enlisted in Wake County at age 30, July 15, 1862, for the war. Present or accounted for until wounded in the arm at Fredericksburg, Virginia, December 13, 1862. Died on or about January 5, 1863, of wounds and disease. Place of death not reported.

LOYD, ANDERSON T., Private

Born in Granville County where he resided as a farmer prior to enlisting in Franklin County at age 22, May 16, 1861. Present or accounted for until he died at Staunton, Virginia, December 16, 1862, of "phthisis pulmonalis."

McCRAW, WILLIAM T., Private

Born in Granville County where he resided as a farmer prior to enlisting in Franklin County at age 25, May 16, 1861. Present or accounted for until he deserted to the enemy on or about February 12, 1865. Released on or about February 17, 1865, after taking the Oath of Allegiance.

MANGUM, GEORGE A., Private

Born in Granville County where he resided as a farmer prior to enlisting in Franklin County at age 36, May 16, 1861. Present or accounted for until he deserted to the enemy on or about February 12, 1865. Released on or about February 17, 1865, after taking the Oath of Allegiance.

MARTIN, WILLIAM H., Private

Resided in Granville County and enlisted in Franklin County at age 35, May 16, 1861. Present or accounted for until he died at Williamsburg, Virginia, on or about December 8, 1861, of disease.

MATHEWS, ELMER, Private

Place and date of enlistment not reported. Died August 6, 1861. Place and cause of death not reported.

MAY, ANTHONY, Private

Resided in Franklin County and was by occupation a farmer prior to enlisting in Franklin County at age 21, May 16, 1861. Present or accounted for until wounded in the right knee at Fredericksburg, Virginia, December 13, 1862. Reported absent wounded until detailed for light duty in September-October, 1863.

Reported absent on detail through October, 1864. Paroled at Appomattox Court House, Virginia, April 9, 1865.

MERRITTE, WILLIAM H., Private
Resided in Franklin County where he enlisted at age 21, March 4, 1862. Present or accounted for until wounded on or about August 10, 1864. Battle in which wounded not reported. Reported absent wounded through October, 1864. Deserted to the enemy on or about February 8, 1865, and was released on or about February 13, 1865, after taking the Oath of Amnesty.

MINNIS, FRANK B., Private
Resided in Granville County and enlisted in Franklin County at age 21, May 16, 1861. Present or accounted for until he died in King and Queen County, Virginia, September 4, 1861, of disease.

MITCHENER, REUBEN S., Private
Previously served in Company A, 1st Regiment N.C. Junior Reserves. Transferred to this company on October 25, 1864. Present or accounted for until paroled at Appomattox Court House, Virginia, April 9, 1865.

MIZE, JAMES P., Private
Born at Danville, Virginia, and resided in Granville County prior to enlisting in Wake County on March 15, 1864, for the war. Present or accounted for until captured at Petersburg, Virginia, April 3, 1865. Confined at Point Lookout, Maryland, until released on June 29, 1865, after taking the Oath of Allegiance. Medical records dated 1864 give his age as 19.

MOORE, ALEXANDER, Private
Born in Granville County where he resided as a farmer prior to enlisting in Franklin County at age 25, May 16, 1861. Present or accounted for until wounded in the leg at Fredericksburg, Virginia, December 13, 1862. Returned to duty in March-April, 1863, and present or accounted for until killed at Bristoe Station, Virginia, October 14, 1863.

MOORE, ALEXANDER S., Corporal
Born in Franklin County where he resided as a farmer prior to enlisting in Franklin County at age 24, May 16, 1861. Mustered in as Private and promoted to Corporal in September, 1861-December, 1862. Present or accounted for until captured at or near Crampton's Pass, Maryland, September 14, 1862. Confined at Fort Delaware, Delaware, until transferred to Aiken's Landing, James River, Virginia, October 2, 1862, for exchange. Declared exchanged at Aiken's Landing on November 10, 1862. Returned to duty prior to January 1, 1863, and present or accounted for until paroled at Appomattox Court House, Virginia, April 9, 1865.

MOORE, H. T., Private
Resided in Granville County and enlisted in Franklin County at age 21, May 16, 1861. Present or accounted for until he died at Yorktown, Virginia, on or about September 9, 1861, of disease.

MOORE, JOSEPH E., Private
Resided in Franklin County where he enlisted at age 17, March 4, 1862, for the war as a substitute for Private W.P. Morris. Present or accounted for through October, 1864.

MOORE, ROBERT G., Private
Resided in Franklin County where he enlisted at age

19, February 25, 1862. Present or accounted for until paroled at Appomattox Court House, Virginia, April 9, 1865.

MOORE, RUFUS R., Private
Enlisted in Wake County on July 15, 1862, for the war. Present or accounted for through April, 1864. No further records.

MOORE, SIMON H., 1st Sergeant
Born in Franklin County where he resided as a farmer prior to enlisting in Franklin County at age 23, May 16, 1861. Mustered in as Private and promoted to Corporal in May, 1862. Present or accounted for until wounded in the head at Malvern Hill, Virginia, July 1, 1862. Promoted to Sergeant in August, 1862, and returned to duty prior to December 13, 1862, when he was wounded in the shoulder and right hand at Fredericksburg, Virginia. Promoted to 1st Sergeant on January 1, 1863, and was reported absent wounded through April, 1863. Detailed for light duty in May-June, 1863, and was reported absent on detail through October, 1864. Paroled at Appomattox Court House, Virginia, April 9, 1865.

MOORE, THOMAS G., Private
Resided in Franklin County where he enlisted at age 29, May 16, 1861. Present or accounted for until wounded in the back and leg at Fredericksburg, Virginia, December 13, 1862. Died in hospital at Richmond, Virginia, January 5, 1863, of "hepatitis" and "excision tibia."

MOOTEN, BENJAMIN G., Private
Born in Granville County and was by occupation a farmer prior to enlisting in Franklin County at age 19, March 29, 1864, for the war. Present or accounted for until wounded in the right shoulder at Davis' Farm, near Petersburg, Virginia, August 29, 1864. Retired from service on or about February 7, 1865, by reason of disability from wounds.

MORRIS, W. P., Private
Resided in Franklin County and enlisted at age 21, March 4, 1862. Present or accounted for until discharged in May, 1862, after providing Private Joseph E. Moore as a substitute.

MORTON, BENJAMIN G., Private
Enlisted in Franklin County on March 30, 1864, for the war. Present or accounted for until wounded in the right shoulder on August 21, 1864; however, battle in which wounded not reported. Reported absent wounded through October, 1864.

MOSS, EDWIN O., Private
Resided in Franklin County where he enlisted at age 32, May 16, 1861. Present or accounted for until he died in Franklin County on or about April 6, 1862, of disease.

MOSS, PETER M., Corporal
Resided in Granville County and enlisted in Franklin County at age 22, May 16, 1861. Mustered in as Corporal. Present or accounted for until promoted to Ordnance Sergeant on May 10, 1862, and transferred to the Field and Staff of this regiment.

MURRY, MOSES G., Private
Resided in Franklin County where he enlisted at age 26, May 16, 1861. Present or accounted for until captured at Hatcher's Run, Virginia, April 2, 1865.

Confined at Point Lookout, Maryland, until released on June 29, 1865, after taking the Oath of Allegiance.

NICHOLSON, JOHN C., Private
Resided in Franklin County and enlisted at age 26. Place and date of enlistment not reported; however, he was first listed in the records of this company in April, 1862. Discharged in July, 1862, after providing Private Thomas Williams as a substitute. Reenlisted in the company on October 21, 1864, and present or accounted for until captured at Hatcher's Run, Virginia, April 2, 1865. Confined at Point Lookout, Maryland, until released on June 15, 1865, after taking the Oath of Allegiance.

OVERTON, JOHN R., Private
Resided in Franklin County where he enlisted at age 21, February 24, 1862, for the war. Present or accounted for until reported absent without leave from October 20, 1862, through December 31, 1862. Returned to duty in January-February, 1863, and present or accounted for until he deserted to the enemy on or about February 17, 1865. Released on or about February 21, 1865, after taking the Oath of Allegiance.

PARHAM, GEORGE KENNON, Sergeant
Resided in Franklin County where he enlisted at age 32, May 16, 1861. Mustered in as Private and promoted to Sergeant in May, 1862. Present or accounted for until wounded in the hand at Malvern Hill, Virginia, July 1, 1862. Returned to duty prior to December 13, 1862, when he was wounded in the side at Fredericksburg, Virginia. Returned to duty prior to January 1, 1863, and present or accounted for until he died in hospital at Charlottesville, Virginia, December 10, 1863, of "diarrh[oea] chro[nic]."

PASCHALL, WILLIAM T., Private
Resided in Franklin County where he enlisted at age 26, May 16, 1861. Present or accounted for until captured at Hatcher's Run, Virginia, April 2, 1865. Confined at Point Lookout, Maryland, until released on June 16, 1865, after taking the Oath of Allegiance.

PEARCE, BENJAMIN W., Sergeant
Resided in Franklin County where he enlisted at age 23, May 16, 1861. Mustered in as Sergeant. Present or accounted for until he died at Petersburg, Virginia, December 3, 1861, of disease.

PEARCE, LEVI E., Private
Born in Franklin County where he resided as a farmer prior to enlisting in Franklin County at age 21, May 16, 1861. Present or accounted for until discharged on December 27, 1861, by reason of "repeated attacks of remittent and intermittent fever."

PEED, G. W., Private
Resided in Person County and enlisted in Wake County at age 28, July 15, 1862, for the war. Present or accounted for until he died in hospital at Richmond, Virginia, October 5, 1862, of "typhoid fever."

PEED, JESSE J., Private
Resided in Person County and enlisted in Wake County at age 25, July 15, 1862, for the war. Present or accounted for until transferred to Company I, 27th Regiment N.C. Troops, April 1, 1864.

PENDLETON, RICHARD, Private
Resided in Franklin County where he enlisted at age

49, March 4, 1862, for the war. Present or accounted for until reported absent without leave since the battle of Crampton's Pass, Maryland, September 14, 1862. No further records.

PERRY, SIDNEY C., Private
Resided in Franklin County where he enlisted at age 18, February 12, 1863, for the war. Present or accounted for until he died in hospital at Gordonsville, Virginia, April 23, 1864, of "bronch[itis] ac[u]t[e] & diarrh[oea]."

POWER, EDWARD, Private
Resided in Franklin County where he enlisted at age 50, February 24, 1862. Present or accounted for through April 7, 1864; however, he was reported absent sick during most of that period. Discharged on April 8, 1864. Reason discharged not reported.

PUCKETT, WILLIAM HENRY,_____
North Carolina pension records indicate he enlisted in January, 1864. No further records.

RICHARDS, GEORGE W., Private
Born in Granville County and resided in Franklin County where he was by occupation a farmer prior to enlisting in Franklin County at age 27, May 16, 1861. Present or accounted for until he died on October 30, 1864, of wounds. Place and date wounded and place of death not reported.

ROBERSON, GEORGE W., Private
Resided in Franklin County where he enlisted at age 17, May 16, 1861. Present or accounted for until he died at Yorktown, Virginia, August 4, 1861, of disease.

RUDD, GUILFORD, Private
Resided in Franklin County where he enlisted at age 31, May 16, 1861. Present or accounted for until he died in June, 1864. Place and cause of death not reported.

SANDLIN, WILLIAM, Private
Born in Granville County where he resided prior to enlisting in Franklin County at age 23, July 1, 1861. Present or accounted for until he died at Thornburg, Virginia, March 4, 1863, of disease.

SHERROD, JOHN M., Private
Resided in Franklin County where he enlisted at age 31, May 16, 1861. Present or accounted for until wounded at Lee's Mill, Virginia, April 16, 1862. Reported absent wounded until discharged on June 2, 1863, by reason of disability.

SIMMS, JAMES, Private
Resided in Granville County and enlisted in Franklin County at age 17, May 16, 1861. Present or accounted for until transferred to Company K, 44th Regiment N.C. Troops, July 10, 1863.

SIMMS, JOHN C., Private
Resided in Granville County and enlisted in Franklin County at age 17, March 4, 1862, for the war. Present or accounted for until paroled at Appomattox Court House, Virginia, April 9, 1865.

SMITH, ABNER, Corporal
Resided in Franklin County where he enlisted at age 23, May 16, 1861. Mustered in as Corporal. Present or accounted for until he died in King and Queen County, Virginia, September 18, 1861, of disease.

SMITH, JOSEPH M., Private
Resided in Franklin County where he enlisted at age 21, May 16, 1861. Present or accounted for until reported "in arrest" at Richmond, Virginia, December 29, 1863. Court-martialed and ordered confined for six months. Reported in confinement through April, 1864, but was reported absent without leave on June 25, 1864. Never rejoined the company.

STANTON, A. F., Private
Resided in Granville County and enlisted in Franklin County at age 20, May 16, 1861. Present or accounted for until reported absent without leave on February 22, 1863. Later enlisted in an unspecified Georgia unit and was wounded in the right arm at Orangeburg Court House, South Carolina, February 11, 1865. Right arm amputated. No further records.

STANTON, J., Private
Resided in Granville County and enlisted in Franklin County at age 23, May 16, 1861. Present or accounted for until he died at Yorktown, Virginia, February 28, 1862, of disease.

STONE, MICHAEL H., Private
Previously served in the Salisbury Prison Guard. Transferred to this company on September 22, 1864. Deserted to the enemy on or about February 17, 1865, and was released on or about February 21, 1865, after taking the Oath of Allegiance.

STONE, ROBERT F., Private
Previously served in Company C of this regiment. Transferred to this company on April 3, 1863. Present or accounted for until transferred to "Captain Cooper's Battery" on July 10, 1863.

STONE, T. D., Private
Resided in Franklin County where he enlisted at age 19, May 16, 1861. Present or accounted for until he died "at home" on March 24, 1862, of disease.

STRICKLAND, AMOS, Private
Resided in Franklin County and enlisted at age 18, March 14, 1862. Present or accounted for until he died in hospital at Danville, Virginia, July 19, 1862, of "pneumonia."

STRICKLAND, GEORGE S., Private
Born in Franklin County where he resided as a farmer prior to enlisting in Franklin County at age 23, May 16, 1861. Present or accounted for until captured at or near Crampton's Pass, Maryland, September 14, 1862. Confined at Fort Delaware, Delaware, until transferred to Aiken's Landing, James River, Virginia, October 2, 1862, for exchange. Declared exchanged at Aiken's Landing on November 10, 1862. Returned to duty in January-February, 1863, and present or accounted for until wounded at Bristoe Station, Virginia, October 14, 1863. Returned to duty in November-December, 1863, and present or accounted for until paroled at Appomattox Court House, Virginia, April 9, 1865.

STRICKLAND, N., Private
Born in Franklin County where he resided as a farmer prior to enlisting in Franklin County at age 19, May 16, 1861. Present or accounted for until captured at or near Crampton's Pass, Maryland, September 14, 1862. Received at Aiken's Landing, James River, Virginia, October 6, 1862, for exchange. Declared exchanged at

Aiken's Landing on November 10, 1862. Returned to duty prior to December 13, 1862, when he was wounded in the buttocks at Fredericksburg, Virginia. Returned to duty prior to January 1, 1863. Present or accounted for through October, 1864; however, he was reported on detail as a butcher during much of that period. Paroled at Appomattox Court House, Virginia, April 9, 1865.

STRICKLAND, WILLIAM S., Private
Resided in Franklin County where he enlisted at age 22, May 16, 1861. Present or accounted for until paroled at Appomattox Court House, Virginia, April 9, 1865.

STROTHER, JOHN P., Private
Resided in Franklin County where he enlisted at age 33, February 21, 1862. Present or accounted for until he was court-martialed "for mutiny" on or about December 31, 1864, and "sentenced to be shot." "Released from arrest" on or about January 28, 1865. Deserted to the enemy on or about February 17, 1865, and was released on or about February 21, 1865, after taking the Oath of Allegiance.

THARINGTON, DAVID C., Private
Resided in Franklin County. Place and date of enlistment not reported. Present or accounted for until captured at Hatcher's Run, Virginia, April 2, 1865. Confined at Point Lookout, Maryland, until released on June 20, 1865, after taking the Oath of Allegiance.

THARRINGTON, MADISON L., Private
Resided in Franklin County where he enlisted at age 32, May 16, 1861. Present or accounted for until wounded in the arm at Malvern Hill, Virginia, July 1, 1862. Discharged on August 19, 1862, under the provisions of the Conscript Act.

THARRINGTON, PRESLEY, Private
Resided in Franklin County and enlisted at age 19, February 21, 1862. Present or accounted for until he died at Richmond, Virginia, June 6, 1862, of disease.

THARRINGTON, SYLVESTER, Private
Born in Franklin County where he resided as a farmer prior to enlisting in Franklin County at age 21, May 16, 1861. Present or accounted for until killed at Malvern Hill, Virginia, July 1, 1862.

THARRINGTON, WILLIS, Private
Resided in Franklin County where he enlisted at age 26, February 21, 1862, for the war. Present or accounted for until wounded in the breast at Fredericksburg, Virginia, December 13, 1862. Returned to duty in March-April, 1863, and present or accounted for until paroled at Appomattox Court House, Virginia, April 9, 1865.

THOMPSON, W. D., Private
Place and date of enlistment not reported. Died in hospital at Richmond, Virginia, May 15, 1864, of wounds. Place and date wounded not reported.

TINGEN, GARRETTE R., Private
Resided in Person County and enlisted in Wake County at age 32, July 15, 1862, for the war. Present or accounted for until captured at Petersburg, Virginia, April 3, 1865. Confined at Point Lookout, Maryland, until released on June 21, 1865, after taking the Oath of Allegiance.

UPCHURCH, ARCHIBALD M. D., Private

Born in Granville County where he resided as a farmer prior to enlisting in Franklin County at age 15, May 16, 1861. Present or accounted for until wounded in the arm at Fredericksburg, Virginia, December 13, 1862. Returned to duty prior to January 1, 1863, and present or accounted for until he died in hospital at Petersburg, Virginia, December 29, 1864, of "febris typhoides."

UPCHURCH, WILLIAM H., Private

Resided in Granville County and enlisted in Franklin County at age 36, May 16, 1861. Present or accounted for until discharged on August 19, 1862, by reason of being over age.

VAN HOOK, ROBERT E., Private

Previously served in Company G of this regiment. Transferred to this company on July 10, 1863. Present or accounted for until he died on April 30, 1864, of "chron[ic] rheumatism." Place of death not reported.

WARD, CHARLES, Private

Resided in Granville County and enlisted in Franklin County at age 22, May 16, 1861. Present or accounted for until he died at Yorktown, Virginia, August 27, 1861, of disease.

WARD, HENRY F., Private

Born in Granville County where he resided as a farmer prior to enlisting in Franklin County at age 16, May 16, 1861. Present or accounted for until he died at Richmond, Virginia, May 25, 1862, of disease.

WARD, RUFUS P., Private

Resided in Granville County and enlisted in Franklin County at age 19, February 22, 1862. Present or accounted for until he died at Charlottesville, Virginia, November 30, 1862, of "pneumonia."

WATKINS, ELMUS, Private

Resided in Granville County and enlisted in Franklin County at age 19, May 16, 1861. Present or accounted for until he died at Yorktown, Virginia, August 6, 1861, of disease.

WEATHERS, JOHN P., Private

Born in Granville County where he resided as an engineer prior to enlisting in Franklin County at age 22, May 16, 1861. Present or accounted for through October, 1864.

WHITE, MASON M., Private

Resided in Granville County and enlisted in Franklin County at age 46, May 19, 1863, for the war as a substitute for Private Whitmell K. Hayes. Present or accounted for until he deserted at Fredericksburg, Virginia, August 23, 1863. Confined at Castle Thunder Prison, Richmond, Virginia, September 7, 1863. Released at an unspecified date and deserted again in November-December, 1863. Reported "in arrest" at Orange Court House, Virginia, February 24, 1864. Died at Orange Court House on March 9, 1864, of disease.

WIER, G. M. C., Private

Born in Franklin County where he resided as a farmer prior to enlisting in Franklin County at age 21, May 16, 1861. Present or accounted for until wounded in the right arm at Fredericksburg, Virginia, December 13, 1862. Reported absent wounded until discharged on May 1, 1864, by reason of disability from wounds.

WILDER, JAMES J., Private

Resided in Franklin County where he enlisted at age 23, May 16, 1861. Mustered in as Corporal but was reduced to ranks in September, 1861-December, 1862. Present or accounted for until wounded in the left arm at Spotsylvania Court House, Virginia, May 10, 1864. May have been wounded also in the side and left hip. Returned to duty at an unspecified date and was paroled at Appomattox Court House, Virginia, April 9, 1865.

WILKINS, JOSEPH, Private

Company records indicate that he served previously in the 36th Regiment N.C. Troops (2nd Regiment N.C. Artillery) and was transferred to this company in May, 1863; however, records of the 36th Regiment do not indicate that he served therein. Present or accounted for until he died in hospital at Richmond, Virginia, November 1, 1863, of "pneumonia."

WILLIAMS, THOMAS, Private

Enlisted at age 20, July, 1862, for the war as a substitute for Private John C. Nicholson. Deserted in July, 1862, but was "caught and brought back." Deserted again in August, 1862, and deserted to the enemy in September, 1862.

WILSON, JAMES W., Private

Resided in Franklin County where he enlisted at age 22, May 16, 1861. Present or accounted for until killed at Fredericksburg, Virginia, December 13, 1862.

WINSTON, DAVID C., Private

Resided in Franklin County where he enlisted at age 24, March 5, 1862, for the war. Present or accounted for until wounded and captured at Bristoe Station, Virginia, October 14, 1863. Died in hospital at Point Lookout, Maryland, January 8, 1864, of "chronic diarrhoea."

WINSTON, G. W., Private

Born in Franklin County where he resided as a farmer prior to enlisting in Franklin County at age 24, May 16, 1861. Present or accounted for until discharged on or about June 25, 1862, by reason of "feb[ris] intermittens."

WINSTON, GERALDUS, Private

Resided in Franklin County where he enlisted at age 19, May 16, 1861. Present or accounted for until wounded in the breast at Fredericksburg, Virginia, December 13, 1862. Died "at home" on June 15, 1863, of wounds and disease.

WINSTON, JAMES MADISON, Private

Born in Franklin County where he resided prior to enlisting in Franklin County at age 21, May 16, 1861. Present or accounted for until captured at Hatcher's Run, Virginia, April 2, 1865. Confined at Point Lookout, Maryland, until released on June 21, 1865, after taking the Oath of Allegiance.

WINSTON, JARRETTE, Private

Resided in Franklin County where he enlisted at age 19, May 16, 1861. Present or accounted for until discharged on or about April 8, 1863, by reason of disability.

WINSTON, NORFLET, Corporal

Resided in Franklin County where he enlisted at age 19, May 16, 1861. Mustered in as Private. Present or accounted for until captured at or near Crampton's

Pass, Maryland, September 14, 1862. Confined at Fort Delaware, Delaware, until transferred to Aiken's Landing, James River, Virginia, October 2, 1862, for exchange. Declared exchanged at Aiken's Landing on November 10, 1862. Returned to duty prior to January 1, 1863, and present or accounted for until wounded in the right knee at Bristoe Station, Virginia, October 14, 1863. Returned to duty in November-December, 1863, and was promoted to Corporal on February 15, 1864. Present or accounted for until paroled at Appomattox Court House, Virginia, April 9, 1865. North Carolina pension records indicate he was wounded at Petersburg, Virginia, at an unspecified date.

WOODLIFF, JOSEPH J., Private
Resided in Franklin County where he enlisted at age 24, February 22, 1862. Present or accounted for until he deserted on or about May 2, 1863. "Shot by the guard" in Franklin County on January 28, 1864.

WOODLIFF, THOMAS D., Private
Resided in Granville County and enlisted in Franklin County at age 38, May 16, 1861. Present or accounted for until discharged on August 19, 1862, by reason of being over age.

WOODLIFF, WILLIAM A., Private
Resided in Franklin or Granville counties and enlisted in Franklin County at age 21, May 16, 1861. Present or accounted for until transferred to Company K, 44th Regiment N.C. Troops, July 10, 1863.

WRENN, WILLIAM D., Private
Resided in Person County and enlisted in Wake County at age 18, July 15, 1862, for the war. Present or accounted for until he died at Richmond, Virginia, June 23, 1863, of "pneumonia."

WYNNE, THOMAS C., Private
Born in Franklin County where he resided as a carpenter prior to enlisting in Franklin County at age 21, May 16, 1861. Present or accounted for until reported "in arrest" from November-December, 1862, through June, 1863. Returned to duty in July-August, 1863, and present or accounted for until wounded at Reams' Station, Virginia, August 25, 1864. Reported absent wounded through October, 1864. Deserted to the enemy on or about February 26, 1865, and was released on or about March 1, 1865, after taking the Oath of Allegiance.

COMPANY F

This company, known as the Harnett Light Infantry, was from Harnett County and enlisted at Summerville on May 18, 1861. It was mustered in and assigned to this regiment as Company F. After joining the regiment the company functioned as a part of the regiment, and its history for the war period is recorded as a part of the regimental history.

The information contained in the following roster of the company was compiled principally from company muster rolls for June 22-August, 1861; November, 1862-February, 1863; March 31, 1863-April, 1864; and September-October, 1864. No company muster rolls were found for September, 1861-October, 1862; March, 1863; May-August, 1864; or for the period after October, 1864.

In addition to the company muster rolls, Roll of Honor records, receipt rolls, hospital records, prisoner of war records, and other primary records, supplemented by state pension applications, United Daughters of the Confederacy records, and postwar rosters and histories all provided useful information.

OFFICERS
CAPTAINS

MURCHISON, KENNETH M.
Resided in Harnett County and enlisted at age 37. Appointed Captain to rank from May 18, 1861. Present or accounted for until he was defeated for reelection when the regiment was reorganized on May 2, 1862. Later served as Captain of Company C, 54th Regiment N.C. Troops, and as Colonel of the same regiment.

McDOUGALD, DANIEL
Resided in Harnett County where he enlisted at age 25. Mustered in as 1st Sergeant and was appointed 1st Lieutenant on December 13, 1861. Promoted to Captain on May 2, 1862. Present or accounted for until wounded at Malvern Hill, Virginia, July 1, 1862. Died at Richmond, Virginia, July 17, 1862, of wounds.

CUTTS, ADDISON D.
Resided in Harnett County where he enlisted at age 22, May 18, 1861. Mustered in as Sergeant. Present or accounted for until wounded at Lee's Mill, Virginia, April 16, 1862. Returned to duty at an unspecified date and was appointed 2nd Lieutenant to rank from May 2, 1862. Promoted to 1st Lieutenant to rank from June 14, 1862, and was promoted to Captain on July 1, 1862. Present or accounted for until captured at or near Crampton's Pass, Maryland, on or about September 13, 1862. Confined at Fort Delaware, Delaware, until transferred to Aiken's Landing, James River, Virginia, October 2, 1862, for exchange. Declared exchanged at Aiken's Landing on November 10, 1862. Returned to duty prior to December 13, 1862, when he was wounded in the forehead at Fredericksburg, Virginia. Returned to duty prior to March 1, 1863, and present or accounted for until he resigned on May 31, 1864.

GREEN, DANIEL E.
Resided in Harnett County where he enlisted at age 22, May 18, 1861. Mustered in as Corporal and was promoted to 1st Sergeant on May 2, 1862. Appointed 2nd Lieutenant on or about June 24, 1862. Wounded at Malvern Hill, Virginia, July 1, 1862. Returned to duty prior to January 1, 1863, and was promoted to 1st Lieutenant on or about September 10, 1863. Promoted to Captain on May 31, 1864. Present or accounted for until paroled at Greensboro on May 1, 1865.

LIEUTENANTS

BARNES, RORY, 1st Lieutenant
Resided in Harnett County and enlisted at Yorktown, Virginia, at age 23, June 28, 1861. Mustered in as Private and was appointed 3rd Lieutenant to rank from August 1, 1862. Present or accounted for until wounded in the right arm at Bristoe Station, Virginia, October 14, 1863. Promoted to 2nd Lieutenant on

December 10, 1863, to rank from September 13, 1863, and returned to duty prior to January 1, 1864. Promoted to 1st Lieutenant on May 31, 1864. Present or accounted for until paroled at Greensboro on May 1, 1865.

HART, BENJAMIN T., 1st Lieutenant

Served in Company I of this regiment; however, he was detailed to command this company on September 15, 1864. Rejoined Company I at an unspecified date subsequent to October 31, 1864.

McLEAN, JOHN T., 1st Lieutenant

Resided in Harnett County and enlisted at Yorktown, Virginia, at age 23, May 18, 1861. Mustered in as Private and was appointed 2nd Lieutenant to rank from January 15, 1862. Promoted to 1st Lieutenant on May 2, 1862. Present or accounted for until he resigned on June 10, 1862, by reason of "bad health."

McNEILL, KENNETH M., 1st Lieutenant

Resided in Harnett County and enlisted at age 26. Appointed 1st Lieutenant on May 18, 1861. Present or accounted for until he resigned on or about December 6, 1861, by reason of disability.

PIPKIN, SAMUEL D., 2nd Lieutenant

Resided in Harnett County and enlisted at age 34. Appointed 2nd Lieutenant to rank from May 18, 1861. Present or accounted for until he resigned on January 10, 1862, by reason of disability. Later served as Private in Company A, 63rd Regiment N.C. Troops (5th Regiment N.C. Cavalry).

SEXTON, DUNCAN McLEAN, 1st Lieutenant

Resided in Harnett County where he enlisted at age 22, May 18, 1861. Mustered in as Corporal and was appointed 2nd Lieutenant to rank from May 2, 1862. Promoted to 1st Lieutenant to rank from July 17, 1862. Present or accounted for until he resigned on August 31, 1863. Later served as Sergeant in Company B, 10th Battalion N.C. Heavy Artillery.

SMITH, ROBERT B., 2nd Lieutenant

Resided in Harnett County and enlisted at age 43. Appointed 2nd Lieutenant to rank from May 18, 1861. Present or accounted for until he was defeated for reelection when the regiment was reorganized on May 2, 1862.

TURNER, P. N., 1st Lieutenant

Appointed 1st Lieutenant on November 9, 1863, but declined the appointment. No further records.

NONCOMMISSIONED OFFICERS AND PRIVATES

ARMSTRONG, JOHN C., Private

Previously served in Company I, 35th Regiment N.C. Troops. Transferred to this company on May 27, 1863, in exchange for Private Haywood Mason. Present or accounted for until he died in hospital at Richmond, Virginia, July 13, 1864, of disease.

ARNOLD, SOLOMON B., Private

Resided in Harnett County where he enlisted at age 26, May 18, 1861. Present or accounted for until paroled at Appomattox Court House, Virginia, April 9, 1865.

ARNOLD, THOMAS H., Private

Resided in Harnett County where he enlisted at age 32, May 18, 1861. Present or accounted for until paroled at Appomattox Court House, Virginia, April 9, 1865.

ATKINS, JAMES W., Private

Resided in Harnett County where he enlisted at age 22, May 18, 1861. Present or accounted for through October, 1864; however, he was reported absent sick or absent on detail during much of that period. Paroled at Appomattox Court House, Virginia, April 9, 1865.

ATKINS, NEILL M., Corporal

Born in Harnett County* where he resided as a farmer prior to enlisting in Harnett County at age 24, May 18, 1861. Mustered in as Private and promoted to Corporal on November 22, 1862. Present or accounted for until wounded in the right arm in a skirmish at Gum Swamp on or about May 22, 1863. Right arm amputated. Discharged on or about December 10, 1863, by reason of disability.

AVERA, CALVIN A., Private

Resided in Harnett County where he enlisted at age 19, May 18, 1861. Present or accounted for until he died on July 7, 1862, of disease. Place of death not reported.

AVERA, LUCIAN A., Private

Born in Harnett County* where he resided prior to enlisting in Harnett County at age 31, May 18, 1861. Present or accounted for until he died at "South Anna Bridge" on July 22, 1863, of disease.

AVERA, WILLIAM A., Private

Born in Harnett County* where he resided prior to enlisting in Harnett County at age 30, May 18, 1861. Present or accounted for until wounded in the head at Lee's Mill, Virginia, April 16, 1862. Returned to duty in March-April, 1863, and present or accounted for until killed "in [the] trenches" at Petersburg, Virginia, August 6, 1864.

BALLARD, ALEXANDER, Private

Resided in Harnett County where he enlisted at age 27, May 18, 1861. Present or accounted for until wounded in the left breast at Bristoe Station, Virginia, October 14, 1863. Reported absent wounded or absent on detail through December, 1864.

BALLARD, JOHN MARSHALL, Private

Resided in Harnett County where he enlisted at age 20, May 18, 1861. Present or accounted for until hospitalized at Richmond, Virginia, July 30, 1864, with a gunshot wound of the right thigh; however, place and date wounded not reported. Reported absent wounded through October, 1864.

BARNES, THOMAS H., 1st Sergeant

Resided in Harnett County where he enlisted at age 20, May 18, 1861. Mustered in as Private. Present or accounted for until hospitalized at Williamsburg, Virginia, April 17, 1862, with a gunshot wound; however, place and date wounded not reported. Returned to duty prior to January 1, 1863. Reported absent on sick furlough from February 7, 1863, until he returned to duty on April 3, 1864. Promoted to 1st Sergeant in November, 1864-April, 1865. Present or accounted for until paroled at Greensboro on May 1, 1865.

BAYLES, JAMES W., Private

Born in Harnett County* where he resided as a farmer prior to enlisting in Harnett County at age 25, May 18, 1861. Present or accounted for until wounded in the right hand at Sharpsburg, Maryland, September 17, 1862. Right forefinger amputated. Returned to duty in January-February, 1863, but was discharged on March 18, 1863, by reason of "numerous abcesses forming on hand and arm, the flexor muscles of the hand have been contracted so as to render his arm & hand permanently disabled."

BAYLES, JOHN J., Private
Resided in Harnett County where he enlisted at age 27, May 18, 1861. Present or accounted for until discharged on September 20, 1861, by reason of disability.

BEASLEY, JASPER J., Private
Previously served in Company C, 31st Regiment N.C. Troops. Transferred to this company on or about March 20, 1863. Present or accounted for until paroled at Lynchburg, Virginia, April 15, 1865.

BISHOP, ARCHIBALD A., Private
Born in Harnett County* where he resided as a cooper prior to enlisting in Harnett County at age 30, May 18, 1861. Present or accounted for until discharged on February 7, 1862, by reason of disability.

BLACK, DANIEL A., Private
Previously served in Company B, 56th Regiment N.C. Troops. Transferred to this company on or about May 27, 1863, in exchange for Private John D. Blizzard. Present or accounted for through October, 1864.

BLACK, DANIEL R., Private
Born in Harnett County* where he resided prior to enlisting in Harnett County at age 18, May 18, 1861. Present or accounted for until killed at Bristoe Station, Virginia, October 14, 1863.

BLACK, DUNCAN, Private
Previously served in Company H, 50th Regiment N.C. Troops. Transferred to this company on May 20, 1863, in exchange for Private James R. Hobbs. Present or accounted for until paroled at Greensboro on May 1, 1865.

BLACK, JOHN A., Private
Previously served in Company B, 56th Regiment N.C. Troops. Transferred to this company on or about May 27, 1863, in exchange for Private Bryant Bowden. Present or accounted for through October, 1864; however, he was reported absent sick or absent without leave during most of that period.

BLIZZARD, DICKSON P., Private
Born in Duplin County and resided in Harnett County where he was by occupation a cooper prior to enlisting in Harnett County at age 37, May 18, 1861. Present or accounted for until discharged on August 14, 1862, by reason of being over age.

BLIZZARD, JOHN D., Private
Resided in Harnett or Cumberland counties and enlisted in Harnett County at age 17, May 18, 1861. Present or accounted for until transferred to Company B, 56th Regiment N.C. Troops, on or about May 27, 1863, in exchange for Private Daniel A. Black.

BOWDEN, BRYANT, Private
Resided in Harnett or Cumberland counties and enlisted in Harnett County at age 30, May 18, 1861. Present or accounted for until he deserted on August 12, 1862. Returned to duty on or about February 7,

1863. Present or accounted for until transferred to Company B, 56th Regiment N.C. Troops, May 27, 1863, in exchange for Private John A. Black.

BRANCH, ISAAC W., Private
Resided in Harnett County where he enlisted at age 46, January 10, 1863, for the war as a substitute for Private Elisha James Pipkin. Present or accounted for until he deserted on May 14, 1863. Returned to duty on August 15, 1864, and present or accounted for through October, 1864.

BROWN, GREENWOOD, Private
Resided in Harnett County where he enlisted at age 18, May 18, 1861. Present or accounted for until wounded at or near Malvern Hill, Virginia, on or about July 2, 1862. Returned to duty prior to January 1, 1863, and present or accounted for through October, 1864.

BYRD, RICHARD D., Private
Born in Harnett County* where he resided as a farmer prior to enlisting in Harnett County at age 30, May 18, 1861. Present or accounted for until wounded at Malvern Hill, Virginia, July 1, 1862. Died at Richmond, Virginia, July 27, 1862, of wounds.

CANADY, CADER A., Corporal
Resided in Harnett County where he enlisted at age 20, May 18, 1861. Mustered in as Private and promoted to Corporal in September, 1861-April, 1862. Died April 11, 1862, of disease. Place of death not reported.

CLEMENTS, ANDERSON, Private
Resided in Harnett County where he enlisted at age 25, May 18, 1861. Present or accounted for until he deserted on July 17, 1864.

COLVILLE, JAMES H., Private
Resided in Harnett County where he enlisted at age 21, May 18, 1861. Present or accounted for until wounded in the right leg at Bristoe Station, Virginia, October 14, 1863. Reported absent wounded until retired to the Invalid Corps on August 18, 1864.

COLVILLE, JOHN R., Private
Born in Harnett County* where he resided prior to enlisting in Harnett County at age 23, May 18, 1861. Present or accounted for until he died in camp near Fredericksburg, Virginia, December 27, 1862, of disease.

COLVILLE, WILLIAM A., Private
Resided in Harnett County where he enlisted at age 27, May 18, 1861. Present or accounted for until wounded in the hip and captured at Crampton's Pass, Maryland, September 14, 1862. Confined at Fort McHenry, Maryland, until paroled and transferred to Aiken's Landing, James River, Virginia, where he was received October 19, 1862, for exchange. Declared exchanged at Aiken's Landing on November 10, 1862. Returned to duty in March-April, 1863, and present or accounted for until wounded in the leg at Bristoe Station, Virginia, October 14, 1863. Returned to duty in November-December, 1863, and present or accounted for through October, 1864.

DOUGLAS, WILLIAM J., Private
Resided in Harnett County where he enlisted at age 21, May 18, 1861. Present or accounted for until killed at or near Jones' Farm, Virginia, on or about October 1, 1864.

DOUGLASS, SILAS J., Sergeant

Born in Harnett County* where he resided prior to enlisting in Harnett County at age 23, May 18, 1861. Mustered in as Private and promoted to Sergeant in November, 1864-April, 1865. Present or accounted for until paroled at Greensboro on or about May 1, 1865.

ELLIS, THOMAS G., Private

Resided in Harnett County and was by occupation a farmer prior to enlisting in Harnett County at age 29, May 18, 1861. Present or accounted for until wounded in the breast and shoulder and captured at Crampton's Pass, Maryland, September 14, 1862. Hospitalized at Baltimore, Maryland, until paroled and transferred to Aiken's Landing, James River, Virginia, where he was received November 5, 1862, for exchange. Declared exchanged at Aiken's Landing on November 10, 1862. Returned to duty in March-April, 1863. Present or accounted for through October, 1864; however, he was reported absent on detail or absent sick during much of that period. Paroled at Appomattox Court House, Virginia, April 9, 1865.

FAULKNER, THOMAS N., Private

Born in Granville County and resided in Harnett County where he was by occupation a farmer prior to enlisting in Harnett County at age 21, May 18, 1861. Present or accounted for until he deserted on August 12, 1862. Returned to duty on April 20, 1863. "Bucked once in front of his regiment and tied up by the thumbs three times at dress parade." Fought at Gum Swamp and Batchelder's Creek, May 22-23, 1863, and was credited with having "killed the notorious house burner and plunderer Colonel [J. Richter] Jones of the Federal Army." Deserted again on June 8, 1863, but was "brought back" on April 7, 1864. Court-martialed and "sentenced to be shot"; however, he was apparently pardoned. Returned to duty prior to November 1, 1864, and present or accounted for until he deserted to the enemy on February 27, 1865. Released on or about March 2, 1865, after taking the Oath of Allegiance.

GASKINS, ALEXANDER, Private

Born in Harnett County* where he resided as a farmer prior to enlisting in Harnett County at age 27, May 18, 1861. Present or accounted for until captured at or near Crampton's Pass, Maryland, September 14, 1862. Confined at Fort Delaware, Delaware, until transferred to Aiken's Landing, James River, Virginia, October 2, 1862, for exchange. Declared exchanged at Aiken's Landing on November 10, 1862. Died on or about January 30, 1863, of disease. Place of death not reported.

GASKINS, IRA, Private

Resided in Harnett County where he enlisted at age 20, May 18, 1861. Present or accounted for until killed at Bristoe Station, Virginia, October 14, 1863.

GASKINS, WILLIAM D., Private

Born in Harnett County* where he resided as a farmer prior to enlisting in Harnett County at age 29, May 18, 1861. Present or accounted for until he died at Yorktown, Virginia, January 5, 1862, of disease.

GILBERT, FRANCIS M., Private

Resided in Harnett County where he enlisted at age 24, May 18, 1861. Present or accounted for until killed at Lee's Mill, Virginia, April 16, 1862.

GILBERT, JOHN QUINCEY, Private

Previously served in Company I, 31st Regiment N.C. Troops. Transferred to this company on or about March 20, 1863. Present or accounted for until he deserted on October 1, 1864.

GRADY, PHINEAS H., Private

Born in Harnett County* where he resided prior to enlisting in Harnett County at age 22, May 18, 1861. Present or accounted for until wounded at Malvern Hill, Virginia, July 1, 1862. Died at Richmond, Virginia, July 9, 1862, of wounds.

GRAHAM, JOHN W., Private

Resided in Harnett County where he enlisted at age 23, May 18, 1861. Present or accounted for until he died on April 13, 1862, of disease. Place of death not reported.

HAM, STEPHEN, Private

Born in Guilford County and resided in Harnett County where he was by occupation a farmer prior to enlisting in Harnett County at age 30, May 18, 1861. Present or accounted for until wounded in the left leg and captured at Crampton's Pass, Maryland, September 14, 1862. Hospitalized at Burkittsville, Maryland, until transferred to Fort McHenry, Maryland, at an unspecified date. Paroled at Fort McHenry on November 12, 1862, and transferred to City Point, Virginia, where he was received November 21, 1862, for exchange. Reported absent wounded until he was retired from service on February 21, 1865, by reason of disability from wounds.

HEARTLEY, WILLIAM H., Private

Resided in Davidson County and enlisted in Wake County at age 18, July 15, 1862, for the war. Present or accounted for until reported absent sick on August 25, 1862. Reported absent sick until he was listed as a deserter on July 1, 1863, and dropped from the rolls.

HOBBS, JAMES R., Private

Resided in Harnett County where he enlisted at age 21, May 18, 1861. Present or accounted for until wounded at Malvern Hill, Virginia, July 1, 1862. Returned to duty prior to March 1, 1863, and present or accounted for until transferred to Company H, 50th Regiment N.C. Troops, May 20, 1863, in exchange for Private Duncan Black.

HOLLAND, ALLISON D., Sergeant

Resided in Harnett County where he enlisted at age 21, May 18, 1861. Mustered in as Private. Present or accounted for until wounded at Malvern Hill, Virginia, July 1, 1862. Promoted to Sergeant on November 22, 1862, and returned to duty prior to January 1, 1863. Present or accounted for until captured at or near Petersburg, Virginia, April 2, 1865. Confined at Point Lookout, Maryland, until released on June 27, 1865, after taking the Oath of Allegiance.

HOLLAND, HENRY B., Corporal

Resided in Harnett County where he enlisted at age 28, May 18, 1861. Mustered in as Corporal. Present or accounted for until he died on October 5, 1861, of disease. Place of death not reported.

HOLMES, WILLIAM H., Private

Born in Harnett County* where he resided as a farmer

prior to enlisting in Harnett County at age 23, May 18, 1861. Present or accounted for until he died on July 30, 1862, of disease. Place of death not reported.

HONRINE, JOHN B., Sergeant
Born in Harnett County* where he resided as a carpenter prior to enlisting in Harnett County at age 26, May 18, 1861. Mustered in as Corporal and promoted to Sergeant on May 2, 1862. Present or accounted for until wounded in the thigh and captured at or near Crampton's Pass, Maryland, September 14, 1862. Hospitalized at Burkittsville, Maryland, until confined at Fort McHenry, Maryland, at an unspecified date. Paroled on or about October 25, 1862, and transferred to Aiken's Landing, James River, Virginia, for exchange. Declared exchanged at Aiken's Landing on November 10, 1862. Returned to duty prior to March 1, 1863, and present or accounted for until wounded in the right shoulder at or near Spotsylvania Court House, Virginia, on or about May 7, 1864. Returned to duty prior to October 31, 1864, and was present or accounted for through that date.

HUST, DURANT C., Private
Born in Wake County and resided in Harnett County prior to enlisting at age 18, May 18, 1861. Present or accounted for until he died on June 4, 1864, of wounds. Place and date wounded and place of death not reported.

HUST, JOHN SPENCER, Private
Resided in Harnett County where he enlisted at age 23, May 18, 1861. Present or accounted for through October, 1864.

HUST, LORENZO D., Private
Resided in Harnett County where he enlisted at age 19, May 18, 1861. Present or accounted for until he died on April 15, 1862, of disease. Place of death not reported.

HUST, WILLIAM H., Private
Born in Wake County and resided in Harnett County where he enlisted at age 23, May 18, 1861. Present or accounted for until he died in hospital at Richmond, Virginia, June 23, 1864, of wounds. Place and date wounded not reported.

JOHNSON, DAVID G., Sergeant
Resided in Harnett County where he enlisted at age 24, May 18, 1861. Mustered in as Sergeant. Present or accounted for until mortally wounded at Malvern Hill, Virginia, July 1, 1862. Died the next day.

JOHNSON, JAMES A., Sergeant
Resided in Harnett County where he enlisted at age 21, May 18, 1861. Mustered in as Private and promoted to Sergeant in May-October, 1864. Present or accounted for until paroled at Appomattox Court House, Virginia, April 9, 1865.

JOHNSON, JOHN A., Private
Born in Harnett County* where he resided as a farmer prior to enlisting in Harnett County at age 24, May 18, 1861. Present or accounted for until he died at Coosawhatchie, South Carolina, April 13, 1863, of disease.

JOHNSON, NEILL A., Private
Born in Harnett County* where he resided prior to enlisting at age 21, May 18, 1861. Present or accounted

for until he died at Orange Court House, Virginia, March 3, 1864, of disease.

JOHNSON, WILLIAM ALEXANDER, Corporal
Resided in Harnett County where he enlisted at age 22, May 18, 1861. Mustered in as Private and promoted to Corporal on December 16, 1863. Present or accounted for through October, 1864.

JOHNSON, WILLIAM ALLEN, Private
Resided in Harnett County where he enlisted at age 19, May 18, 1861. Present or accounted for until transferred to Company C, 31st Regiment N.C. Troops, March 20, 1863.

JONES, JEREMIAH, Private
Resided in Harnett County where he enlisted at age 32, May 18, 1861. Present or accounted for until discharged on December 16, 1861. Reason discharged not reported.

JORDAN, FRANCIS M., Private
Resided in Harnett County where he enlisted at age 22, May 18, 1861. Present or accounted for until wounded in the foot at Malvern Hill, Virginia, July 1, 1862. Reported absent wounded or absent on detail until he returned to duty in January-February, 1864. Present or accounted for until hospitalized at Richmond, Virginia, May 8, 1864, with a gunshot wound of the left arm; however, place and date wounded not reported. Company records do not indicate whether he returned to duty; however, he died in hospital at Richmond, Virginia, December 9-10, 1864, of "typhoid fever."

KELLY, JOHN, Private
Resided in Harnett County where he enlisted at age 26, May 18, 1861. Mustered in as Sergeant but was reduced to ranks in September, 1861-December, 1862. Deserted in May, 1862, and was dropped from the rolls on or about March 1, 1863.

LANIER, JAMES H., Private
Resided in Harnett County where he enlisted at age 22, May 18, 1861. Present or accounted for until transferred to Company I, 31st Regiment N.C. Troops on March 20, 1863.

LEE, CALVIN, Private
Resided in Harnett County where he enlisted at age 21, May 18, 1861. Present or accounted for until he died on September 15, 1861, of disease. Place of death not reported.

LONG, JACOB W., Private
Resided in Davidson County and enlisted in Wake County at age 30, July 15, 1862, for the war. Present or accounted for until captured at La Grange, Georgia, April 20, 1865. Paroled April 21, 1865.

LONG, WILLIAM J., Private
Resided in Davidson County and enlisted in Wake County at age 23, July 15, 1862, for the war. Present or accounted for until he deserted on or about July 1, 1863.

McDONALD, HENRY C., Private
Resided in Harnett County where he enlisted at age 16, May 18, 1861. Present or accounted for until discharged on August 8, 1862, by reason of being under age.

McDONALD, JOHN, Private

Born in Chatham County and resided in Harnett County where he enlisted at age 19, May 18, 1861. Present or accounted for until wounded at Lee's Mill, Virginia, April 16, 1862. Died in hospital at Raleigh on May 31, 1862, of wounds.

McDOUGALD, DANIEL A., Private

Resided in Harnett County where he enlisted at age 26, May 18, 1861. Present or accounted for until wounded in the knee at Fredericksburg, Virginia, December 13, 1862. Returned to duty in January-February, 1863, and present or accounted for until captured at Bristoe Station, Virginia, October 14, 1863. Confined at Old Capitol Prison, Washington, D.C., until transferred to Point Lookout, Maryland, October 27, 1863. Released on January 25, 1864, after taking the Oath of Allegiance and joining the U.S. service. Unit to which assigned not reported.

McDOUGALD, JOHN, Private

Born in Harnett County* where he resided prior to enlisting in Harnett County at age 27, May 18, 1861. Present or accounted for until wounded at Lee's Mill, Virginia, April 16, 1862. Returned to duty in January-February, 1863, and present or accounted for until killed at Reams' Station, Virginia, August 25, 1864.

McLEAN, DANIEL H., Private

Resided in Harnett County and enlisted at Yorktown, Virginia, at age 14, July 6, 1861. Present or accounted for until discharged on August 8, 1862, by reason of being under age.

McLEAN, HECTOR S., Private

Born in Harnett County* where he resided as a teacher prior to enlisting in Harnett County at age 28, May 18, 1861. Present or accounted for until he died at Yorktown, Virginia, September 7, 1861, of disease.

McRARY, JOHN C., Private

Resided in Davidson County and enlisted in Wake County at age 33, July 15, 1862, for the war. Present or accounted for until wounded in the arm at or near Wilderness, Virginia, on or about May 5, 1864. Returned to duty prior to October 31, 1864, and was present or accounted for until that date. Records of the Federal Provost Marshal indicate he was paroled at Appomattox Court House, Virginia, April 9, 1865; however, a North Carolina pension application filed by his widow indicates that he died in April, 186[5], of disease.

McRARY, R., Private

Resided in Davidson County and enlisted at age 23, July 15, 1862, for the war. Present or accounted for until wounded at Sharpsburg, Maryland, September 17, 1862. Died October 3, 1862, of disease. Place of death not reported.

MASON, HAYWOOD, Private

Resided in Harnett or Wayne counties and enlisted in Wake County at age 23, May 18, 1861. Present or accounted for until wounded in the jaw at Fredericksburg, Virginia, December 13, 1862. Returned to duty in March-April, 1863, and was transferred to Company I, 35th Regiment N.C. Troops, May 27, 1863, in exchange for Private John C. Armstrong.

MATTHEWS, ALEXANDER, Private

Resided in Harnett County where he enlisted at age 22, May 18, 1861. Present or accounted for until captured at or near Crampton's Pass, Maryland, September 14, 1862. Confined at Fort Delaware, Delaware, until transferred to Aiken's Landing, James River, Virginia, October 2, 1862, for exchange. Declared exchanged at Aiken's Landing on November 10, 1862. Returned to duty in January-February, 1863, and present or accounted for through October, 1864.

MATTHEWS, DAVID H., Corporal

Resided in Harnett County where he enlisted at age 21, May 18, 1861. Mustered in as Private and promoted to Corporal on November 22, 1862. Present or accounted for until wounded in the right hip at Bristoe Station, Virginia, October 14, 1863. Returned to duty on February 2, 1864, and present or accounted for through October, 1864.

MATTHEWS, FREDERICK J., Private

Born in Harnett County* where he resided as a carpenter prior to enlisting in Harnett County at age 34, May 18, 1861. Present or accounted for until discharged on August 19, 1862, by reason of being over age.

MATTHEWS, JAMES B., Private

Resided in Harnett County where he enlisted at age 36, May 18, 1861. Present or accounted for until discharged on August 8, 1862, by reason of being over age.

MATTHEWS, JOSIAH, Corporal

Resided in Harnett County where he enlisted at age 18, May 18, 1861. Mustered in as Private. Present or accounted for until captured at or near Crampton's Pass, Maryland, September 14, 1862. Confined at Fort Delaware, Delaware, until transferred to Aiken's Landing, James River, Virginia, October 2, 1862, for exchange. Declared exchanged at Aiken's Landing on November 10, 1862. Promoted to Corporal on November 22, 1862, and returned to duty prior to January 1, 1863. Present or accounted for through October, 1864.

MATTHEWS, MARTIN H., Private

Resided in Harnett County where he enlisted at age 19, May 18, 1861. Present or accounted for until captured at Crampton's Pass, Maryland, September 14, 1862. Confined at Fort Delaware, Delaware, until transferred to Aiken's Landing, James River, Virginia, October 2, 1862, for exchange. Declared exchanged at Aiken's Landing on November 10, 1862. Returned to duty in January-February, 1863, and present or accounted for through October, 1864.

MESSER, HENRY, Private

Resided in Davidson County and enlisted in Wake County at age 34, July 15, 1862, for the war. Present or accounted for until discharged on December 3, 1862, by reason of disability.

MILLER, AMOS, Private

Born in Davidson County where he resided prior to enlisting in Wake County at age 26, July 15, 1862, for the war. Present or accounted for until wounded in a skirmish at Gum Swamp on May 22, 1863. Returned to duty prior to July 1, 1863, and present or accounted for until captured at Bristoe Station, Virginia, October

14, 1863. Confined at Old Capitol Prison, Washington, D.C., until transferred to Point Lookout, Maryland, October 27, 1863. Died at Point Lookout on March 13, 1864, of disease.

MILLER, BENJAMIN, Private

Resided in Davidson County and enlisted in Wake County at age 25, July 15, 1862, for the war. Present or accounted for until captured at or near Crampton's Pass, Maryland, on or about September 14, 1862. Confined at Fort Delaware, Delaware, until transferred to Aiken's Landing, James River, Virginia, October 2, 1862, for exchange. Declared exchanged at Aiken's Landing on November 10, 1862. Returned to duty prior to January 1, 1863, and present or accounted for until reported absent without leave on October 16, 1863. Reported absent without leave through October 31, 1864.

MILLER, EDWIN, Private

Born in Davidson County where he resided as a farmer prior to enlisting in Wake County at age 23, July 15, 1862, for the war. Present or accounted for until he died at Liberty, Virginia, October 23, 1862, of disease.

MILLER, JOSIAH, Private

Resided in Davidson County and enlisted in Wake County at age 23, July 15, 1862, for the war. Present or accounted for until wounded in the right arm at Bristoe Station, Virginia, October 14, 1863. Reported absent wounded until reported absent without leave on December 6, 1863. Reported absent without leave through October, 1864.

MOCK, GEORGE, Private

Born in Davidson County where he resided prior to enlisting in Wake County at age 18, July 15, 1862, for the war. Present or accounted for until killed at Reams' Station, Virginia, August 25, 1864.

MOCK, JAMES A., Private

Resided in Davidson County and enlisted in Wake County at age 16, July 15, 1862, for the war as a substitute. Present or accounted for until wounded in the right hand at or near Spotsylvania Court House, Virginia, on or about May 7, 1864. Returned to duty prior to October 31, 1864, and was present or accounted for through that date.

MOCK, LEANDER, Private

Resided in Davidson County and enlisted in Wake County at age 20, July 15, 1862, for the war. Present or accounted for until hospitalized at Richmond, Virginia, May 7, 1864, with a gunshot wound of the right arm and/or left hand. Reported absent wounded until retired to the Invalid Corps on January 6, 1865.

MOCK, PETER W., Private

Resided in Davidson County and enlisted in Wake County at age 32, July 15, 1862, for the war. Present or accounted for until wounded in the right thigh at Bristoe Station, Virginia, October 14, 1863. Returned to duty on January 18, 1864, and present or accounted for through October, 1864.

MOORE, STEPHEN, Private

Resided in Harnett County where he enlisted at age 25, May 18, 1861. Present or accounted for until he deserted on August 12, 1862. Enlisted in Company B, 10th Battalion N.C. Heavy Artillery, February 6, 1863, while a deserter from this company. Arrested and returned to this company on April 27, 1863. Reported "in arrest" until August 11, 1863, when he returned to duty. Present or accounted for until wounded at Bristoe Station, Virginia, October 14, 1863. Died October 16, 1863, of wounds. Place of death not reported.

MORRISON, FRANK, Private

Resided in Harnett County where he enlisted at age 27, May 18, 1861. Present or accounted for until wounded at Lee's Mill, Virginia, April 16, 1862. Discharged September 2, 1862, by reason of "general debility and partial paralysis with extreme emaciation."

MURPHY, WILLIAM, Private

Resided in Harnett County where he enlisted at age 25, May 18, 1861. Present or accounted for until discharged on August 22, 1862, under the provisions of the Conscript Act.

NELSON, R. M., Private

Born in Davidson County where he resided as a farmer prior to enlisting in Wake County at age 19, July 15, 1862, for the war. Present or accounted for until killed at Fredericksburg, Virginia, December 13, 1862.

NORDAN, JAMES A., Private

Resided in Harnett County where he enlisted at age 21, May 18, 1861. Present or accounted for until wounded in the right hand at Bristoe Station, Virginia, October 14, 1863. Returned to duty on January 15, 1864. Present or accounted for until hospitalized at Danville, Virginia, May 18, 1864, with a gunshot wound of the shoulder; however, place and date wounded not reported. Reported absent wounded until he deserted from hospital at Raleigh on or about June 9, 1864.

NORDAN, JOHN A., Private

Resided in Harnett County where he enlisted at age 20, May 18, 1861. Present or accounted for until he died "in camp" on March 18, 1864, of disease.

O'QUIN, DAVID J., Private

Resided in Harnett County where he enlisted at age 23, May 18, 1861. Present or accounted for until he died at or near Petersburg, Virginia, on or about May 2, 1862, of disease.

O'QUIN, EDMUND L., Private

Resided in Harnett County where he enlisted at age 28, May 18, 1861. Present or accounted for until he died at Richmond, Virginia, June 23, 1862, of disease.

O'QUIN, WILEY J., Private

Resided in Harnett County where he enlisted at age 33, May 18, 1861. Present or accounted for until reported absent without leave from July 1, 1862, through December, 1862. Returned to duty in January-February, 1863, and present or accounted for until he died near Kinston on May 24, 1863, of disease.

PARKER, ICA, Private

Resided in Harnett County where he enlisted at age 31, May 18, 1861. Present or accounted for until he died on October 15, 1862, of disease. Place of death not reported.

PARKER, JOSEPH, Private

Born in Hancock County, Georgia, and resided in Harnett County where he was by occupation a farmer prior to enlisting in Harnett County at age 50, May 18,

1861. Present or accounted for until he died at Yorktown, Virginia, August 9, 1861, of disease.

PATTERSON, SHEROD, 1st Sergeant
Resided in Harnett County where he enlisted at age 21, May 18, 1861. Mustered in as Private. Present or accounted for until wounded in the foot at Malvern Hill, Virginia, July 1, 1862. Promoted to 1st Sergeant on August 1, 1862, and returned to duty prior to December 13, 1862, when he was wounded in the neck at Fredericksburg, Virginia. Returned to duty prior to January 1, 1863, and present or accounted for through October, 1864. Served as Acting 2nd Lieutenant from July 10, 1864, through October 31, 1864.

PHILLIPS, WILLIAM A., Private
Born in Harnett County* where he resided prior to enlisting in Harnett County at age 21, May 18, 1861. Present or accounted for until killed at Bristoe Station, Virginia, October 14, 1863.

PICKLE, FRANK, Private
Resided in Davidson County and enlisted in Wake County at age 20, July 15, 1862, for the war. Present or accounted for until captured at Bristoe Station, Virginia, October 14, 1863. Confined at Point Lookout, Maryland, until paroled and transferred to Aiken's Landing, James River, Virginia, February 24, 1865, for exchange. Received for exchange prior to March 4, 1865.

PIPKIN, ARCHELAUS S., Private
Resided in Harnett County where he enlisted at age 23, May 18, 1861. Present or accounted for until he died at or near Richmond, Virginia, in May, 1862, of disease.

PIPKIN, ELISHA JAMES, Private
Resided in Harnett County where he enlisted at age 21, May 18, 1861. Present or accounted for until discharged on January 10, 1863, after providing Private Isaac W. Branch as a substitute.

REARDON, JOHN F., Private
Born in Harnett County* where he resided prior to enlisting in Harnett County at age 23, May 18, 1861. Present or accounted for until he died in hospital at Richmond, Virginia, June 10, 1864, of "dysenteria ch[ronic]."

RISING, JAMES, Private
Born in Harnett County* where he resided prior to enlisting in Harnett County at age 22, May 18, 1861. Present or accounted for until he died at Gordonsville, Virginia, February 1, 1864, of "pneumonia."

ROAMINGER, JACOB E., Private
Resided in Davidson County and enlisted in Wake County at age 19, July 15, 1862, for the war. Present or accounted for until wounded in the right leg at Bristoe Station, Virginia, October 14, 1863. Reported absent wounded until retired to the Invalid Corps on December 22, 1864.

ROBERTS, WILLIAM, Private
Resided in Harnett County where he enlisted at age 22, May 18, 1861. Present or accounted for through October 19, 1863; however, he was reported absent sick during most of that period. Reported absent without leave from October 20, 1863, through October 31, 1864.

ROBERTSON, THOMAS L., Private
Resided in Harnett County and was by occupation a farmer prior to enlisting in Harnett County at age 18, May 18, 1861. Present or accounted for until hospitalized at Richmond, Virginia, August 27, 1864, with a gunshot wound of the left side of the chest; however, place and date wounded not reported. Reported absent wounded until retired to the Invalid Corps on December 22, 1864.

SAINTSING, GEORGE W., Private
Resided in Davidson County and enlisted in Wake County at age 30, July 15, 1862, for the war. Present or accounted for until wounded in the right hip and captured at Sharpsburg, Maryland, September 17, 1862. Confined at Fort McHenry, Maryland, until paroled and transferred to City Point, Virginia, where he was received December 4, 1862, for exchange. Reported absent wounded until detailed as a shoemaker on August 15, 1863. Reported absent on detail through October, 1864. Paroled at Greensboro on May 6, 1865.

SCOTT, ALEX, Private
Resided in Davidson County and enlisted in Wake County at age 32, July 15, 1862, for the war. Present or accounted for until hospitalized at Richmond, Virginia, December 23, 1862, with "typhoid fever." Died the next day.

SEXTON, GREEN, Sergeant
Resided in Harnett County where he enlisted at age 24, May 18, 1861. Mustered in as Private and promoted to Sergeant on October 1, 1862. Present or accounted for until wounded in the right thigh at Wilderness, Virginia, May 5, 1864. Returned to duty prior to October 31, 1864, and was present or accounted for through that date.

SHOAF, HENRY W., Private
Resided in Davidson County and enlisted in Wake County at age 29, July 15, 1862, for the war. Present or accounted for until wounded in the foot at Fredericksburg, Virginia, December 13, 1862. Returned to duty on June 12, 1863, and present or accounted for until wounded in the head at Bristoe Station, Virginia, October 14, 1863. Returned to duty in November-December, 1863, and present or accounted for through October, 1864.

SHOAF, MADISON R., Private
Resided in Davidson County and enlisted in Wake County at age 19, July 15, 1862, for the war. Present or accounted for until he deserted on August 13, 1862. Returned to duty on April 20, 1863. Present or accounted for until hospitalized at Danville, Virginia, June 4, 1864, with a gunshot wound of the leg; however, place and date wounded not reported. Returned to duty at an unspecified date and was present or accounted for through October, 1864.

SHUTT, JAMES C., Private
Resided in Davidson County and enlisted in Wake County at age 17, July 15, 1862, for the war as a substitute. Present or accounted for until captured at or near Crampton's Pass, Maryland, on or about September 14, 1862. Confined at Fort Delaware, Delaware, until transferred to Aiken's Landing, James River, Virginia, October 2, 1862, for exchange. Declared exchanged at Aiken's Landing on November

10, 1862. Reported absent without leave from November 14, 1862, until he returned to duty in March-April, 1863. Present or accounted for until wounded in the leg at Bristoe Station, Virginia, October 14, 1863. Reported absent wounded through April 30, 1864. Returned to duty prior to October 31, 1864, and was present or accounted for through that date.

SINK, G. M., Private
Resided in Davidson County and enlisted in Wake County at age 30, July 15, 1862, for the war as a substitute. Present or accounted for until wounded in the hip at Fredericksburg, Virginia, December 13, 1862. Died in hospital at Richmond, Virginia, December 28, 1862, of wounds.

SINK, JACOB, Private
Resided in Davidson County and enlisted in Wake County at age 21, July 15, 1862, for the war as a substitute. Present or accounted for until wounded in the left leg at Bristoe Station, Virginia, October 14, 1863. Left leg amputated. Died in hospital at Richmond, Virginia, October 28, 1863, of wounds.

SINK, JOHN D., Private
Born in Davidson County where he resided as a farmer prior to enlisting in Wake County at age 24, July 15, 1862, for the war as a substitute. Present or accounted for until hospitalized at Richmond, Virginia, December 11, 1862, with a gunshot wound; however, place and date wounded not reported. Died December 13, 1862, of wounds and/or disease.

SINK, WILLIAM, Private
Resided in Davidson County and enlisted in Wake County at age 34, July 15, 1862, for the war as a substitute. Present or accounted for through October, 1864.

SINK, WILLIAM A., Private
Born in Davidson County where he resided prior to enlisting in Wake County at age 27, July 15, 1862, for the war as a substitute. Present or accounted for until captured at Crampton's Pass, Maryland, September 14, 1862. Paroled on or about September 26, 1862. Returned to duty prior to March 1, 1863, and present or accounted for until captured at Bristoe Station, Virginia, October 14, 1863. Confined at Old Capitol Prison, Washington, D.C., October 16, 1863. Died in hospital at Washington on February 19, 1864, of "chronic diarrhoea."

SMITH, CADER, Private
Born in Harnett County* where he resided as a farmer prior to enlisting in Harnett County at age 22, May 18, 1861. Present or accounted for until he died in hospital at Lynchburg, Virginia, November 15, 1862, of disease.

SMITH, EMANUEL, Private
Resided in Davidson County and enlisted in Wake County at age 24, July 15, 1862, for the war. Present or accounted for until captured at Bristoe Station, Virginia, October 14, 1863. Confined at Old Capitol Prison, Washington, D.C., until transferred to Point Lookout, Maryland, October 27, 1863. Paroled at Point Lookout and transferred to City Point, Virginia, April 27, 1864, for exchange. Returned to duty prior to October 31, 1864, and was present or accounted for through that date.

SMITH, WILLIAM B., Private
Resided in Harnett County where he enlisted at age 24, May 18, 1861. Mustered in as Private and promoted to Corporal in September, 1861-May, 1862. Present or accounted for until wounded in the side and right leg at or near Fredericksburg, Virginia, on or about December 13, 1862. Promoted to Sergeant prior to January 1, 1863, and returned to duty in March-April, 1863. Reduced to ranks in May-October, 1864. Present or accounted for until captured in hospital at Richmond, Virginia, April 3, 1865. Paroled at Richmond on April 23, 1865.

SPAUGH, EMANUEL J., Private
Resided in Davidson County and enlisted in Wake County at age 25, July 15, 1862, for the war. Present or accounted for until reported absent without leave on August 29, 1862. Returned to duty in January-February, 1863, and present or accounted for until wounded in the leg and captured at Bristoe Station, Virginia, October 14, 1863. Confined at Old Capitol Prison, Washington, D.C., until transferred to Point Lookout, Maryland, October 27, 1863. Paroled at Point Lookout on May 3, 1864, and transferred to Aiken's Landing, James River, Virginia, where he was received May 8, 1864, for exchange. Returned to duty prior to October 31, 1864, and was present or accounted for through that date.

SPAUGH, LEWIS, Private
Resided in Davidson County and enlisted in Wake County at age 30, July 15, 1862, for the war. Present or accounted for until killed at or near Crampton's Pass, Maryland, September 14, 1862.

SPAUGH, THEOPHILUS THOMAS, Private
Resided in Davidson County and enlisted in Wake County at age 20, July 15, 1862, for the war. Present or accounted for through June 28, 1863. Reported absent without leave from June 29, 1863, through October 31, 1864.

SPENCE, GEORGE D., Corporal
Resided in Harnett County where he enlisted at age 20, May 18, 1861. Mustered in as Private and promoted to Corporal on November 22, 1862. Present or accounted for through October, 1864.

SPENCE, JOHN A., Private
Resided in Harnett County where he enlisted at age 25, May 18, 1861. Present or accounted for until wounded in the leg at Fredericksburg, Virginia, December 13, 1862. Returned to duty prior to January 1, 1863, and present or accounted for until mortally wounded at Bristoe Station, Virginia, October 14, 1863. Died the same day.

STEWART, JOHN A., Private
Born in Harnett County* where he resided as a farmer prior to enlisting in Harnett County at age 23, May 18, 1861. Present or accounted for until discharged on February 7, 1862, by reason of disability.

WADE, WILLIAM G., Private
Resided in Harnett County where he enlisted at age 24, May 18, 1861. Present or accounted for until reported "in arrest" at Richmond, Virginia, June 13, 1863. "Released from prison" on August 11, 1863, and was present or accounted for through October, 1864.

WADE, WILLIAM H., Musician
Resided in Harnett County where he enlisted at age 23, May 18, 1861. Mustered in as Private and promoted to Musician in January-February, 1863. Present or accounted for until paroled at Appomattox Court House, Virginia, April 9, 1865.

WIGGINS, BRIGHT H., Private
Resided in Harnett County where he enlisted at age 23, May 18, 1861. Present or accounted for until he died at or near Richmond, Virginia, in May, 1862, of disease.

WIGGINS, THOMAS B., Private
Resided in Harnett County where he enlisted at age 25, May 18, 1861. Present or accounted for until he died on November 15, 1861, of disease. Place of death not reported.

WIGGINS, WILLIAM F., Private
Resided in Harnett County where he enlisted at age 22, May 18, 1861. Present or accounted for until wounded at Lee's Mill, Virginia, April 16, 1862. Deserted on August 12, 1862.

WILSON, HENRY W., Private
Born in Stokes County and was by occupation a farmer prior to enlisting at Camp Holmes on July 15, 1862, for the war. Discharged on December 4, 1862, by reason of "epilepsy." Discharge records give his age as 35.

COMPANY G

This company was from Franklin County and enlisted at Louisburg on May 20, 1861. From Louisburg it was ordered to Franklinton and afterwards to Garysburg, where it was mustered in on June 12 and assigned to this regiment as Company G. After joining the regiment the company functioned as a part of the regiment, and its history for the war period is recorded as a part of the regimental history.

The information contained in the following roster of the company was compiled principally from company muster rolls for June 12-August, 1861; November, 1862-April, 1864; and September-October, 1864. No company muster rolls were found for September, 1861-October, 1862; May-August, 1864; or for the period after October, 1864. In addition to the company muster rolls, Roll of Honor records, receipt rolls, hospital records, prisoner of war records, and other primary records, supplemented by state pension applications, United Daughters of the Confederacy records, and postwar rosters and histories, all provided useful information.

OFFICERS

CAPTAINS

JACKSON, JAMES J.
Resided in Franklin County. Appointed Captain to rank from May 20, 1861. Present or accounted for until he was defeated for reelection when the regiment was reorganized on May 2, 1862.

TERRELL, THOMAS T.
Resided in Franklin County where he enlisted at age 24, May 20, 1861. Mustered in as Private and promoted to Sergeant on July 25, 1861. Appointed 2nd Lieutenant on September 19, 1861, and promoted to

1st Lieutenant on October 28, 1861. Promoted to Captain on May 2, 1862. Present or accounted for until captured at or near Crampton's Pass, Maryland, on or about September 14, 1862. Confined at Fort Delaware, Delaware, until transferred to Aiken's Landing, James River, Virginia, October 2, 1862, for exchange. Declared exchanged at Aiken's Landing on November 10, 1862. Returned to duty prior to January 1, 1863, and present or accounted for until he died "at home" in Franklin County on February 21, 1864, of disease.

LIEUTENANTS

BONNER, JAMES M., 2nd Lieutenant
Born in Mississippi and resided in Franklin County prior to enlisting at Yorktown, Virginia, at age 20, August 1, 1861. Mustered in as Private and promoted to Corporal on August 4, 1861. Promoted to Sergeant on November 1, 1861, and was appointed 2nd Lieutenant to rank from May 2, 1862. Present or accounted for until wounded in the heel at Crampton's Pass, Maryland, September 14, 1862. Reported absent wounded until assigned to conscript duty in North Carolina in May-October, 1864. Retired to the Invalid Corps on February 17, 1865. Paroled at Greensboro on May 1, 1865.

BREWER, WILLIAM, 2nd Lieutenant
Resided in Franklin County where he enlisted at age 21, May 20, 1861. Mustered in as Corporal and was appointed 2nd Lieutenant to rank from May 2, 1862. Present or accounted for until wounded at Reams' Station, Virginia, August 25, 1864. Died in hospital at Richmond, Virginia, October 21, 1864, of wounds.

GUPTON, HENRY G., 2nd Lieutenant
Resided in Franklin County where he enlisted. Appointed 2nd Lieutenant on May 20, 1861. Present or accounted for until he resigned on or about July 30, 1861. Reason he resigned not reported.

HIGHT, ALEXANDER C., 2nd Lieutenant
Resided in Franklin County where he enlisted. Appointed 2nd Lieutenant on or about May 20, 1861. Resigned on or about October 1, 1861; however, reason he resigned not reported. Died prior to August 16, 1862. Place, date, and cause of death not reported.

JACKSON, WILLIAM S., 2nd Lieutenant
Resided in Franklin County and enlisted at Yorktown, Virginia, at age 32, October 13, 1861. Mustered in as Private and appointed 2nd Lieutenant to rank from October 30, 1861. Present or accounted for until he resigned on April 4, 1862. Reason he resigned not reported.

MURPHEY, GRAY B., 1st Lieutenant
Resided in Franklin County where he enlisted at age 25, May 20, 1861. Mustered in as Sergeant and was appointed 2nd Lieutenant to rank from October 30, 1861. Promoted to 1st Lieutenant on May 2, 1862. Present or accounted for until wounded in the hip at Sharpsburg, Maryland, September 17, 1862. Returned to duty prior to January 1, 1863, and present or accounted for until paroled at Appomattox Court House, Virginia, April 9, 1865.

STAMPER, M. D., 1st Lieutenant
Resided in Franklin County where he enlisted.

Appointed 1st Lieutenant on May 20, 1861. Present or accounted for until he resigned on September 24, 1861. Reason he resigned not reported.

NONCOMMISSIONED OFFICERS
AND PRIVATES

ALLEN, GEORGE A., Private
Resided in Person County and enlisted in Wake County on July 15, 1862, for the war. Present or accounted for until wounded at Bristoe Station, Virginia, October 14, 1863. Returned to duty in January-February, 1864. Present or accounted for until wounded in the right arm on or about August 6, 1864; however, battle in which wounded not reported. Returned to duty on or about October 22, 1864. Paroled at Greensboro on May 11, 1865.

ALLEN, HENRY, Private
Resided in Person County and enlisted in Wake County on July 15, 1862, for the war. Present or accounted for until wounded at Fredericksburg, Virginia, on or about December 13, 1862. Returned to duty prior to January 1, 1863, and present or accounted for through April, 1864. A North Carolina pension application filed by his widow indicates that he was killed; however, place and date of death not reported.

ALLEN, MONROE S., Private
Transferred to this company from Company A, 50th Regiment N.C. Troops, May 19, 1863, in exchange for Private Ephraim Wheeley. Present or accounted for through October, 1864. Paroled at Greensboro on May 11, 1865.

ANDREWS, GEORGE, Corporal
Resided in Franklin County where he enlisted at age 19, May 20, 1861. Mustered in as Private and promoted to Corporal on May 25, 1862. Present or accounted for until he was reported missing and "supposed to have been killed" at Crampton's Pass, Maryland, September 14, 1862.

AYCOKE, AMBROSE, Private
Resided in Franklin County where he enlisted at age 37, May 20, 1861. Present or accounted for until discharged on August 20, 1862, by reason of being over age.

BARRETT, AARON, Private
Resided in Person County and enlisted in Wake County on July 15, 1862, for the war. Present or accounted for until he died in hospital at Lynchburg, Virginia, January 13, 1863, of "diarrhoea chron[ic]."

BARTHOLOMEW, GEORGE, Private
Resided in Franklin County where he enlisted at age 41, May 20, 1861. Present or accounted for until discharged on August 20, 1862, by reason of being over age.

BARTHOLOMEW, L. E., Private
Resided in Franklin County where he enlisted at age 16, May 20, 1861. Present or accounted for until transferred to Company K, 12th Regiment N.C. Troops (2nd Regiment N.C. Volunteers), June 25, 1862, in exchange for Private Isaac W. Gordon.

BARTHOLOMEW, ONISIMUS G., Private
Resided in Franklin County where he enlisted at age

20, May 20, 1861. Mustered in as Private and promoted to Sergeant on September 19, 1861. Reduced to ranks on May 25, 1862. Present or accounted for through October, 1864. Paroled at Greensboro on May 3, 1865.

BREEDLOVE, HENRY T., Private
Resided in Franklin County where he enlisted at age 20, May 20, 1861. Present or accounted for through October, 1864.

BREEDLOVE, WILLIAM A., Private
Resided in Franklin County where he enlisted at age 22, May 20, 1861. Present or accounted for until wounded in the knee and captured at Crampton's Pass, Maryland, September 14, 1862. Paroled and exchanged at an unspecified date and returned to duty in January-February, 1863. Present or accounted for through October, 1864.

BREWER, JACOB J., Private
Resided in Franklin County where he enlisted at age 19, May 20, 1861. Present or accounted for through October, 1864. Paroled at Greensboro on or about April 29, 1865.

BUNN, C., Private
Place and date of enlistment not reported. First listed on the rolls of this company on November 24, 1864. Paroled at High Point on May 1, 1865. No further records.

BURNETT, JAMES H., Private
Resided in Franklin County where he enlisted at age 22, May 20, 1861. Present or accounted for until wounded in the right arm at Fredericksburg, Virginia, December 13, 1862. Reported absent wounded until retired to the Invalid Corps on April 22, 1864; however, he apparently rejoined the company as he was paroled at Appomattox Court House, Virginia, April 9, 1865.

CARR, ROBERT B., Private
Resided in Franklin County where he enlisted on February 16, 1863, for the war. Present or accounted for until transferred to Company K, 44th Regiment N.C. Troops, on or about July 10, 1863, in exchange for Private John R. Leonard.

CARVER, HENRY, Private
Resided in Person County and enlisted in Wake County on July 15, 1862, for the war. Present or accounted for until wounded at Sharpsburg, Maryland, September 17, 1862. Never rejoined the company and was "supposed to be dead."

CARVER, ISAIAH, Private
Resided in Person County and enlisted in Wake County on July 15, 1862, for the war. Present or accounted for until he died in hospital at Richmond, Virginia, October 8, 1862, of "febris typh[oid]."

CARVER, PAUL, Private
Resided in Person County and enlisted in Wake County on July 15, 1862, for the war. Present or accounted for until he died in camp near Culpeper Court House, Virginia, November 12, 1862, of disease.

CARVER, THOMAS, Private
Resided in Person County and enlisted in Wake County on July 15, 1862, for the war. Present or accounted for until reported absent sick in November-December,

1862. Died prior to March 1, 1864; however, place, date, and cause of death not reported.

COLEY, GRAY J., Private
Resided in Franklin County where he enlisted at age 18, May 20, 1861. Present or accounted for until he died at or near Yorktown, Virginia, on or about September 24, 1861. Cause of death not reported.

COLLIN, J., Private
Resided in Wayne County. Place and date of enlistment not reported. Paroled at Goldsboro on May 9, 1865.

COLVARD, GEORGE W., Private
Resided in Franklin County where he enlisted at age 19, May 20, 1861. Present or accounted for until wounded at Malvern Hill, Virginia, July 1, 1862. Returned to duty prior to December 13, 1862, when he was wounded at Fredericksburg, Virginia. Reported absent wounded until dropped from the rolls on or about November 1, 1863, because he was "supposed to be dead."

COLVARD, WILLIAM T., Private
Resided in Franklin County and enlisted at age 21, May 20, 1861. Present or accounted for until he died at Williamsburg, Virginia, November 10, 1861, of disease.

CUTLER, WILLIAM, Private
Resided in Franklin County where he enlisted at age 53, May 20, 1861. Present or accounted for until discharged on July 16, 1862, by reason of being over age.

DAVIE, THOMAS M., Private
Resided in Person County and enlisted in Wake County on July 15, 1862, for the war. Present or accounted for until "sent to hospital" on October 10, 1863. Reported absent sick through October, 1864.

DAVIS, DOLPHIN B., Private
Resided in Franklin County where he enlisted at age 28, May 20, 1861. Mustered in as 1st Sergeant but was reduced to ranks and transferred to Company L of this regiment in September, 1861-January, 1862.

DEMENT, STEPHEN T., Private
Resided in Franklin County where he enlisted at age 20, May 20, 1861. Present or accounted for until reported absent without leave in January-February, 1863. Returned to duty in May-June, 1863, and present or accounted for until captured at Hatcher's Run, Virginia, April 2, 1865. Confined at Point Lookout, Maryland, until released on June 26, 1865, after taking the Oath of Allegiance. [May have served also in Company G, 47th Regiment N.C. Troops.]

DENTON, LEE J., Sergeant
Resided in Franklin County where he enlisted at age 22, May 20, 1861. Mustered in as Corporal and promoted to Sergeant on May 25, 1862. Present or accounted for until he died in hospital near Richmond, Virginia, August 26, 1862, of disease.

FOOSHEE, HAYWOOD D., Corporal
Resided in Person County and enlisted in Wake County on July 15, 1862, for the war. Mustered in as Private and promoted to Corporal on April 1, 1863. Present or accounted for through October, 1864.

FORD, JOHN, Private
Resided in Person County and enlisted in Wake County on July 15, 1862, for the war. Present or accounted for through October, 1864; however, he was reported absent sick during most of that period.

FOSTER, JAMES H., Private
Resided in Franklin County where he enlisted at age 23, May 20, 1861. Present or accounted for until hospitalized at Richmond, Virginia, July 3, 1862, with a gunshot wound of the left leg; however, place and date wounded not reported. Returned to duty prior to January 1, 1863, and present or accounted for until he died in Franklin County on September 20, 1863, of disease.

FOSTER, JOSEPH J., Private
Resided in Franklin County where he enlisted at age 21, May 20, 1861. Present or accounted for until wounded at Malvern Hill, Virginia, July 1, 1862. Returned to duty prior to January 1, 1863, and present or accounted for through October, 1864. Paroled at Greensboro on May 1, 1865.

FREEMAN, WILLIAM, Private
Resided in Franklin County where he enlisted at age 19, May 20, 1861. Present or accounted for until transferred to Company K, 24th Regiment N.C. Troops (14th Regiment N.C. Volunteers), on or about October 16, 1862.

FULGIUM, JAMES H., Sergeant
Resided in Franklin County where he enlisted at age 21, May 20, 1861. Mustered in as Private and promoted to Sergeant on May 25, 1862. Present or accounted for until he died in hospital at Richmond, Virginia, August 14, 1862, of disease.

GILLIAM, HENRY H., Private
Resided in Franklin County where he enlisted at age 22, May 20, 1861. Mustered in as Musician but was reduced to ranks in March-December, 1862. Present or accounted for until wounded in the hip at Fredericksburg, Virginia, December 13, 1862. Returned to duty in January-February, 1863, and was promoted to Corporal in April, 1863. Reduced to ranks in May-October, 1864. Present or accounted for through October, 1864.

GORDEN, SAMUEL B., Private
Resided in Franklin County where he enlisted at age 21, May 20, 1861. Present or accounted for until wounded at Lee's Mill, Virginia, April 16, 1862. Returned to duty at an unspecified date and was captured at or near Charles Town, Virginia, October 17, 1862. Confined at Fort McHenry, Maryland, until exchanged on or about March 13, 1863. Died in hospital at Petersburg, Virginia, April 1, 1863, of "pneumonia" and/or "feb[ris] typh[oid]."

GORDON, ISAAC W., Private
Previously served in Company K, 12th Regiment N.C. Troops (2nd Regiment N.C. Volunteers). Transferred to this company on June 25, 1862, in exchange for Private L.E. Bartholomew. Present or accounted for until discharged on September 13, 1862, because he was "only 16 years of age" and was "quite feeble from an attack of continued fever."

GOSWICK, GEORGE D., Private
Resided in Franklin County where he enlisted at age

18, May 20, 1861. Present or accounted for through October, 1864.

GOSWICK, J. P., Private
Resided in Franklin County and enlisted in Wake County on April 7, 1863, for the war. Present or accounted for through April, 1864.

GOSWICK, SAMUEL, Private
Resided in Franklin County where he enlisted at age 21, May 20, 1861. Present or accounted for until he died at Yorktown, Virginia, August 9, 1861, of disease.

GUPTON, HENRY S., Private
Previously served in Company K, 44th Regiment N.C. Troops. Transferred to this company on July 10, 1863. Present or accounted for through October, 1864.

GUPTON, JAMES H., Private
Resided in Franklin County where he enlisted at age 25, May 20, 1861. Present or accounted for until he died at Yorktown, Virginia, September 29, 1861, of disease.

GUPTON, JOHN E., Private
Resided in Franklin County where he enlisted at age 45, May 20, 1861. Present or accounted for until discharged on August 20, 1862, by reason of being over age.

GUPTON, LEONDAS C., 1st Sergeant
Born in Franklin County where he resided as a farmer prior to enlisting in Franklin County at age 18, May 20, 1861. Mustered in as Private and promoted to Corporal on May 25, 1862. Promoted to Sergeant on January 1, 1863. Present or accounted for until wounded in the right foot on the Weldon Railroad, near Petersburg, Virginia, August 21, 1864. Promoted to 1st Sergeant on September 1, 1864. Reported absent wounded until discharged on January 6, 1865, by reason of disability from wounds.

GUPTON, WILLIAM B., Private
Resided in Franklin County where he enlisted at age 21, May 20, 1861. Present or accounted for until hospitalized at Yorktown, Virginia, October 10, 1861. Never rejoined the company and was dropped from the rolls on or about March 1, 1863, because he was "supposed to be dead."

GUPTON, WILLIAM C. C., Sergeant
Resided in Franklin County where he enlisted at age 20, May 20, 1861. Mustered in as Private and promoted to Sergeant on October 30, 1861. Reduced to ranks on April 3, 1862, but was promoted to Sergeant on April 1, 1863. Present or accounted for through October, 1864.

GUPTON, WILLIAM H., Private
Resided in Franklin County where he enlisted at age 35, May 20, 1861. Present or accounted for until discharged on August 20, 1862, by reason of being over age.

HADICUM, PATRICK, Private
Resided in Ireland and enlisted in Wake County at age 23, July 15, 1862, for the war as a substitute. Deserted on August 11, 1862.

HAMLET, JESSE B. R., Sergeant
Resided in Franklin County where he enlisted at age 28, May 20, 1861. Mustered in as Sergeant but was reduced to ranks on July 30, 1861. Promoted to

Sergeant in March-December, 1862. Present or accounted for through October, 1864.

HARRIS, JOHN R., Private
Enlisted at Orange Court House, Virginia, April 28, 1864, for the war. Wounded in the arm at Wilderness, Virginia, May 5, 1864. Reported absent wounded or absent on detached service through October, 1864. Paroled at Lynchburg, Virginia, April 14, 1865.

HARRIS, WILLIAM H. A., Private
Resided in Franklin County and enlisted in Wake County. Enlistment date not reported; however, he appears to have enlisted in the spring of 1864. Hospitalized at Richmond, Virginia, May 7, 1864, with a gunshot wound of the right side. May have been wounded also in the head and/or hand. Returned to duty at an unspecified date and was captured at Amelia Court House, Virginia, April 6, 1865. Confined at Point Lookout, Maryland, until released on June 27, 1865, after taking the Oath of Allegiance.

HARRIS, WILLIAM N., Private
Resided in Franklin County where he enlisted at age 23, May 20, 1861. Present or accounted for until wounded at Malvern Hill, Virginia, July 1, 1862. Returned to duty prior to September 14, 1862, when he was wounded at or near Crampton's Pass, Maryland. Returned to duty prior to January 1, 1863, and present or accounted for until wounded in the head at Wilderness, Virginia, May 5, 1864. Reported absent wounded or absent on detached service through October, 1864.

HEDGPETH, JOHN M., Private
Resided in Franklin County where he enlisted at age 19, May 20, 1861. Present or accounted for until he died on March 3, 1862, of disease. Place of death not reported.

HOBGOOD, SIMPSON, Private
Resided in Person County and enlisted in Person or Wake counties on or about April 20, 1863, for the war. Present or accounted for through October, 1864.

HOLSOMBACK, M. R., Private
Born in Person County where he resided as a farmer prior to enlisting in Wake County on July 15, 1862, for the war. Present or accounted for until discharged on April 23, 1863, by reason of "phthisis." Discharge papers give his age as 21.

HOPGOOD, ISAIAH, Private
Resided in Person County and enlisted in Wake County on July 15, 1862, for the war. Present or accounted for until he died in hospital at Gordonsville, Virginia, December 17, 1863, of "febris typhoides."

HUNT, WILLIAM T., Private
Resided in Franklin County where he enlisted at age 37, May 20, 1861. Mustered in as Musician but was reduced to ranks in March, 1862-February, 1863. Present or accounted for until discharged on August 20, 1862, by reason of being over age. Died in Franklin County in June, 1863. Cause of death not reported.

JACKSON, WILLIAM D., Sergeant
Enlistment date reported as July, 1862; however, he was not listed on the rolls of this company until September-October, 1864. Promoted from Private to

Sergeant on September 1, 1864. Paroled at Greensboro on May 1, 1865.

JACOBS, DARBY, Private

Resided in Person County and enlisted in Wake County on July 15, 1862, for the war as a substitute. Present or accounted for until paroled at Appomattox Court House, Virginia, April 9, 1865.

JOHNSON, JAMES SAMUEL, Private

Resided in Franklin County where he enlisted at age 21, May 20, 1861. Present or accounted for until captured at or near Hanover Junction, Virginia, on or about May 24, 1864. Confined at Point Lookout, Maryland, until paroled and transferred to Aiken's Landing, James River, Virginia, September 18, 1864, for exchange. Company records do not indicate whether he returned to duty; however, he deserted to the enemy in April, 1865.

JOHNSTON, GEORGE, Private

Resided in Person County and enlisted in Wake County at age 19, July 15, 1862, for the war as a substitute. Present or accounted for until he deserted on August 11, 1862.

JONES, EDMOND, Corporal

Resided in Franklin County where he enlisted on May 20, 1861. Mustered in as Corporal. Present or accounted for until discharged on June 28, 1861, by reason of disability.

JONES, WILLIAM R., Private

Resided in Person County and enlisted in Wake County on July 15, 1862, for the war. Present or accounted for through October, 1864.

JOYNER, SIDNEY C., Private

Resided in Franklin County where he enlisted at age 17, May 20, 1861. Present or accounted for until wounded at Bristoe Station, Virginia, October 14, 1863. Returned to duty in January-February, 1863, and present or accounted for through October, 1864.

KING, BURWELL, Private

Resided in Franklin County where he enlisted at age 35, May 20, 1861. Present or accounted for until discharged on August 20, 1862, by reason of being over age. Reenlisted in the company on or about August 14, 1863, and present or accounted for until wounded at or near Reams' Station, Virginia, on or about August 25, 1864. Returned to duty prior to November 1, 1864, and was paroled at Appomattox Court House, Virginia, April 9, 1865.

KING, HENRY, Private

Resided in Franklin County where he enlisted at age 19, May 20, 1861. Present or accounted for until paroled at Appomattox Court House, Virginia, April 9, 1865.

LEONARD, JAMES, Jr., Private

Resided in Franklin County where he enlisted at age 23, May 20, 1861. Present or accounted for until killed at Crampton's Pass, Maryland, September 14, 1862.

LEONARD, JAMES M., Sr., Private

Resided in Franklin County where he enlisted at age 20, May 20, 1861. Present or accounted for until wounded at Malvern Hill, Virginia, July 1, 1862 Returned to duty prior to September 17, 1862, when he was wounded at Sharpsburg, Maryland. Returned

to duty prior to January 1, 1863, and present or accounted for until paroled at Appomattox Court House, Virginia, April 9, 1865.

LEONARD, JOHN C., Private

Resided in Franklin County where he enlisted at age 18, May 20, 1861. Present or accounted for until he died "at home" on October 12, 1861, of disease.

LEONARD, JOHN P., Corporal

Resided in Franklin County where he enlisted at age 17, May 20, 1861. Mustered in as Private. Present or accounted for until captured at or near Frederick, Maryland, on or about September 12, 1862. Confined at Fort Delaware, Delaware, until transferred to Aiken's Landing, James River, Virginia, October 2, 1862, for exchange. Declared exchanged at Aiken's Landing on November 10, 1862. Returned to duty prior to January 1, 1863, and was promoted to Corporal on October 1, 1864. Present or accounted for through October, 1864.

LEONARD, JOHN R., Private

Previously served in Company K, 44th Regiment N.C. Troops. Transferred to this company on July 10, 1863, in exchange for Private Robert B. Carr. Present or accounted for until captured at Bristoe Station, Virginia, October 14, 1863. Confined at Old Capitol Prison, Washington, D.C., until transferred to Point Lookout, Maryland, October 27, 1863. Paroled and transferred to City Point, Virginia, where he was received April 30, 1864, for exchange. Company muster roll dated September-October, 1864, states that he was "missing." No further records.

LEONARD, PEYTON R., Corporal

Resided in Franklin County where he enlisted at age 28, May 20, 1861. Mustered in as Private and promoted to Corporal on November 1, 1861. Present or accounted for until he died in hospital near Richmond, Virginia, August 23, 1862, of disease.

LEONARD, ROBERT R., Private

Place and date of enlistment not reported; however, he was first listed in the records of this company on May 1, 1864. Paroled at Appomattox Court House, Virginia, April 9, 1865.

LEONARD, WILLIAM A., Private

Enlisted near Petersburg, Virginia, September 5, 1864, for the war. Present or accounted for through October, 1864.

LEONARD, WILLIAM H., Sergeant

Resided in Franklin County where he enlisted at age 22, May 20, 1861. Mustered in as Private and promoted to Corporal on May 25, 1862. Present or accounted for until captured at or near Crampton's Pass, Maryland, September 14, 1862. Confined at Fort Delaware, Delaware, until transferred to Aiken's Landing, James River, Virginia, October 2, 1862, for exchange. Declared exchanged at Aiken's Landing on November 10, 1862. Returned to duty prior to January 1, 1863, and was promoted to Sergeant on April 1, 1863. Present or accounted for through October, 1864. Medical records indicate that he died in hospital at Richmond, Virginia, January 31, 1865, of "diarrhoea" and "typh[oid] feb[ris]"; however, company records indicate he was paroled at Appomattox Court House, Virginia, April 9, 1865. No further records.

LEONARD, WILLIAM M., Private
Resided in Franklin County where he enlisted at age 20, May 20, 1861. Present or accounted for until he died at Yorktown, Virginia, August 8, 1861, of disease.

LONGMIRE, JAMES Y., Corporal
Resided in Franklin County where he enlisted at age 20, May 20, 1861. Mustered in as Private. Present or accounted for until wounded at Malvern Hill, Virginia, July 1, 1862. Returned to duty prior to December 28, 1862, and promoted to Corporal on April 1, 1863. Present or accounted for through October, 1864.

LOYED, GEORGE, Private
Resided in Franklin County where he enlisted at age 20, May 20, 1861. Present or accounted for until hospitalized at Yorktown, Virginia, March 5, 1862. Reported absent sick through February, 1863. Dropped from the rolls of the company on or about March 1, 1863, because he was "supposed to be dead."

MARION, FRANCIS, Private
Resided in Maryland and enlisted in Wake County at age 20 as a substitute. Enlistment date reported as July 15, 1862; however, medical records indicate he was wounded at Malvern Hill, Virginia, July 1, 1862 Deserted in August, 1862.

MARSHAL, W. R., Private
Resided in Person County and enlisted in Wake County on July 15, 1862, for the war. Present or accounted for until "sent to hospital" in August, 1862. Reported absent sick through October, 1863. Dropped from the rolls of the company on or about January 1, 1864, because he was "supposed to be dead."

MURGISON, WILLIAM, Private
Enlisted in Wake County on July 15, 1862, for the war as a substitute. Deserted on August 11, 1862.

MURPHEY, CHARLES A., Private
Enlisted at Orange Court House, Virginia, March 15, 1864, for the war. Present or accounted for until furloughed for sixty days on March 10, 1865.

MURPHEY, DOCTOR B., Private
Resided in Franklin County where he enlisted at age 20, May 20, 1861. Present or accounted for through October, 1864.

MURPHEY, GRAY B., Private
Resided in Franklin County where he enlisted at age 18, May 20, 1861. Present or accounted for until he died at Yorktown, Virginia, July 31, 1861, of disease.

MURPHEY, PARKER, Private
Enlisted in Wake County on December 9, 1863, for the war. Present or accounted for through October, 1864.

MURPHY, J. G., Private
Resided in Franklin County where he enlisted at age 22, May 20, 1861. Present or accounted for until wounded at Fredericksburg, Virginia, December 13, 1862. Returned to duty in March-April, 1863, and was killed at Bristoe Station, Virginia, October 14, 1863.

MURPHY, JAMES H., Private
Resided in Franklin County where he enlisted at age 23, May 20, 1861. Mustered in as Corporal but was reduced to ranks on June 1, 1861. Present or accounted for until he died at Yorktown, Virginia, August 10, 1861, of disease.

MUSTIAN, WILLOUGHBY, Private
Resided in Franklin County where he enlisted at age 43, May 20, 1861. Present or accounted for until he died in hospital at Yorktown, Virginia, August 4, 1861, of disease.

NEIGHBORS, NELSON, Private
Resided in Person County and enlisted in Wake County on July 15, 1862, for the war. Present or accounted for until wounded and captured at or near Crampton's Pass, Maryland, September 14, 1862. Confined at Fort Delaware, Delaware, until transferred to Aiken's Landing, James River, Virginia, October 2, 1862, for exchange. Declared exchanged at Aiken's Landing on November 10, 1862. Returned to duty prior to January 1, 1863, and present or accounted for through October, 1864. Paroled at Greensboro on May 12, 1865.

NEIGHBORS, SIMEON, Private
Resided in Person County and enlisted in Wake County on July 15, 1862, for the war. Present or accounted for until wounded in the heel and captured at Crampton's Pass, Maryland, September 14, 1862. Hospitalized at or near Burkittsville, Maryland. Exchanged at an unspecified date and returned to duty prior to March 1, 1863. Present or accounted for through October, 1864. Paroled at Greensboro on May 11, 1865.

OAKLEY, HINTON, Private
Resided in Person County and enlisted in Wake County on July 15, 1862, for the war. Present or accounted for until reported absent without leave on August 17, 1864. No further records.

OAKLEY, JERRYMIRE S., Private
Resided in Person County and enlisted in Wake County on July 15, 1862, for the war. Present or accounted for through October, 1864.

OAKLEY, ROBERT H., Private
Resided in Person or Granville counties and enlisted in Wake County on July 15, 1862, for the war. Present or accounted for until transferred to Company E, 46th Regiment N.C. Troops, on or about November 30, 1862.

OAKLEY, W. A., Private
Resided in Person County and enlisted in Wake County on July 15, 1862, for the war. Present or accounted for until mortally wounded at Sharpsburg, Maryland, September 17, 1862. Died the same day.

O'DAY, FRANCIS, Private
Resided in Franklin County where he enlisted at age 36, May 20, 1861. Present or accounted for until discharged on August 20, 1862, by reason of being over age.

PEOPLES, BENJAMIN, Private
Born in Warren County and resided in Franklin County where he was by occupation a farmer prior to enlisting in Franklin County at age 30, May 20, 1861. Present or accounted for until discharged on November 12, 1861, by reason of "chronic bronchitis."

PEOPLES, THOMAS H., Private
Born in Warren County and resided in Franklin County where he was by occupation a farmer prior to enlisting in Franklin County at age 23, May 20, 1861. Present or accounted for until discharged on

November 12, 1861, by reason of "phthisis pulmonalis."

PERRY, NORFLEET, Private

Born in Franklin County where he resided as a farmer prior to enlisting in Franklin County at age 42, May 20, 1861. Present or accounted for until discharged on August 20, 1862, by reason of being over age. Later served in Company A, 3rd Battalion N.C. Senior Reserves.

PERRY, WILLIAM N., Private

Resided in Franklin County where he enlisted at age 20, May 20, 1861. Present or accounted for through October, 1864; however, he was reported absent sick during much of that period. Deserted to the enemy on or about February 17, 1865, and was released on or about February 21, 1865, after taking the Oath of Allegiance.

PLEASANT, W. T., Private

Resided in Franklin County and enlisted at Fredericksburg, Virginia, November 25, 1862, for the war. Present or accounted for through April, 1864. No further records.

PLEASANTS, JOHN W., Corporal

Resided in Franklin County where he enlisted on May 20, 1861. Mustered in as Private. Present or accounted for until captured at or near Crampton's Pass, Maryland, September 14, 1862. Confined at Fort Delaware, Delaware, until transferred to Aiken's Landing, James River, Virginia, October 2, 1862, for exchange. Declared exchanged at Aiken's Landing on November 10, 1862. Returned to duty prior to January 1, 1863, and was promoted to Corporal on April 1, 1863. Present or accounted for through October, 1864. Paroled at Greensboro on May 1, 1865.

PORTERFIELD, W. D., Private

Resided in Person County and enlisted in Wake County on July 15, 1862, for the war. Present or accounted for until he died in hospital at Petersburg, Virginia, January 24, 1863, of "febris typhoides."

RAGAN, EPLURIBUS UNUM, Private

Resided in Person County and enlisted in Wake County on July 15, 1862, for the war. Present or accounted for until "sent to hospital" in November, 1862. Reported absent sick through October, 1864. Paroled May 10, 1865.

RANEY, JAMES R., 1st Sergeant

Resided in Franklin County where he enlisted at age 27, May 20, 1861. Mustered in as Private and promoted to Sergeant on April 3, 1862. Promoted to 1st Sergeant on May 25, 1862. Present or accounted for until captured at Bristoe Station, Virginia, October 14, 1863. Confined at Old Capitol Prison, Washington, D.C., until transferred to Point Lookout, Maryland, October 27, 1863. Died at Point Lookout on or about August 23, 1864, of "acute dysentery."

RUSSELL, J. L., Private

Resided in Person County and enlisted in Wake County on July 15, 1862, for the war. Present or accounted for until wounded in the leg and captured at Crampton's Pass, Maryland, September 14, 1862. Died in hospital at Burkittsville, Maryland, October 4, 1862, of wounds.

SATTIFIELD, GREEN D., Private

Born in Person County where he resided as a farmer prior to enlisting in Wake County on July 15, 1862, for the war. Present or accounted for until discharged on January 3, 1863, by reason of "partial paralysis of the right side." Age given on discharge papers as 31.

SAVAGE, JOHN, Private

Resided in Edgecombe County. Place and date of enlistment not reported. Took the Oath of Allegiance at Fort Delaware, Delaware, on or about May 4, 1865. Place and date captured not reported.

SMITH, JOHN, Private

Resided in Louisiana and enlisted in Wake County at age 24, July 15, 1862, for the war as a substitute. Deserted on or about August 11, 1862.

SMITH, JOHN C., Private

Resided in Person County and enlisted in Wake County on July 15, 1862, for the war. Present or accounted for through October, 1864; however, he was reported absent sick during much of that period. Paroled at Greensboro on May 13, 1865.

SMITH, THOMAS G., Private

Resided in Johnston County and enlisted in Wake County at age 36, July 15, 1862, for the war as a substitute. Present or accounted for until he deserted in August, 1862. Returned to duty on April 6, 1864, and was captured at or near Cold Harbor, Virginia, June 2, 1864. Confined at Point Lookout, Maryland, until transferred to Elmira, New York, July 9, 1864. Released on July 3, 1865, after taking the Oath of Allegiance.

SOLOMON, THOMAS, Private

Resided in Person County and enlisted in Wake County on July 15, 1862, for the war. Present or accounted for until he died in hospital at Winchester, Virginia, October 25, 1862, of disease.

STALLINGS, ADOLPHUS, Private

Resided in Franklin County where he enlisted at age 26, May 20, 1861. Present or accounted for until he died in hospital at Charlottesville, Virginia, December 21, 1863, of "diarrh[oea] chro[nic]."

STALLINGS, GEORGE W., Private

Enlistment date reported as July 10, 1863; however, he was not listed on the rolls of this company until September-October, 1864. Present or accounted for through October, 1864.

STURDIVANT, JESSE W., Private

Enlisted in Wake County on December 9, 1863, for the war. Present or accounted for through March 3, 1865.

STURDIVANT, NICHOLAS, Sergeant

Resided in Franklin County where he enlisted at age 32, May 20, 1861. Mustered in as Private and promoted to Corporal on July 1, 1861. Promoted to Sergeant on May 25, 1862. Present or accounted for until wounded at Sharpsburg, Maryland, September 17, 1862. Died in hospital at Staunton, Virginia, December 12, 1862, of wounds and/or disease.

SUIT, JOHN S., Private

Previously served in Company A, 50th Regiment N.C. Troops. Transferred to this company on December 10, 1863. Present or accounted for until captured at or near Chancellorsville, Virginia, on or about May 6,

1864. Confined at Point Lookout, Maryland, until released on May 21, 1864, after joining the U.S. Army. Unit to which assigned not reported.

SWANSON, MUMFRED E., Private
Resided in Franklin County where he enlisted at age 21, May 20, 1861. Present or accounted for until discharged on or about December 22, 1861, by reason of "general debility."

SWANSON, WILLIAM H., Private
Resided in Franklin County where he enlisted at age 20, May 20, 1861. Present or accounted for through October, 1864. Paroled at Greensboro on May 1, 1865.

THARRANTON, WILLIAM H., Private
Resided in Franklin County where he enlisted at age 41, May 20, 1861. Present or accounted for until discharged on August 20, 1862, by reason of being over age.

TRUE, JOHN HENRY, Private
Resided in Person County and enlisted in Wake County on July 15, 1862, for the war as a substitute. Present or accounted for until wounded in both arms at Bristoe Station, Virginia, October 14, 1863. Both arms amputated. Reported absent wounded through October, 1864. North Carolina pension records indicate that he survived the war.

TUCK, EMLIUS P., Private
Resided in Person County and enlisted in Wake County on July 15, 1862, for the war as a substitute. Present or accounted for through October, 1864.

VAN HOOK, ROBERT E., Private
Resided in Person County and enlisted in Wake County at age 30, July 15, 1862, for the war. Present or accounted for until transferred to Company E of this regiment on July 10, 1863.

WALTER, J., Private
Place and date of enlistment not reported. Name appears on a regimental return dated December, 1862, which states he was missing since July 1, 1862. No further records.

WATSON, CHARLES, Private
Resided in Maryland and enlisted in Wake County at age 29, July 15, 1862, for the war as a substitute. Present or accounted for until he deserted on August 11, 1862.

WATSON, J. C., Private
Resided in Person County and enlisted in Wake County on July 15, 1862, for the war. Present or accounted for until mortally wounded at Sharpsburg, Maryland, September 17, 1862. Place and date of death not reported.

WELCH, EDWARD, Private
Resided in Ireland and enlisted in Wake County at age 37, July 15, 1862, for the war as a substitute. Present or accounted for until he deserted on August 11, 1862.

WESTER, JESSE, Private
Born in Nash County and resided in Franklin County where he was by occupation a farmer prior to enlisting in Franklin County at age 21, May 20, 1861. Present or accounted for until mortally wounded at Malvern Hill, Virginia, July 1, 1862. Place and date of death not reported.

WESTER, SOLOMON, Private
Resided in Franklin County where he enlisted at age 50, May 20, 1861. Present or accounted for until discharged on March 12, 1862, by reason of disability.

WESTER, WILLIAM, Private
Born in Nash County and resided in Franklin County where he was by occupation a farmer prior to enlisting in Franklin County at age 26, May 20, 1861. Present or accounted for until he died in hospital at Richmond, Virginia, June 15, 1862, of "diarrhoea chron[ic]."

WHEELEY, EPHRAIM, Private
Resided in Person County and enlisted in Wake County on July 15, 1862, for the war. Present or accounted for until transferred to Company A, 50th Regiment N.C. Troops, May 19, 1863, in exchange for Private Monroe S. Allen.

WHEELEY, PHILIP, Private
Resided in Person County and enlisted in Wake County on July 15, 1862, for the war. Present or accounted for until he died near Richmond, Virginia, of disease. Date of death not reported; however, he was dropped from the rolls on or about April 1, 1863.

WILKERSON, WILLIAM H., Private
Resided in Person County and enlisted in Wake County on July 15, 1862, for the war. Present or accounted for until he was "left sick on the march" in Virginia in August, 1862. Company records do not indicate that he returned to duty or was wounded; however, North Carolina pension records indicate that he died in Maryland on August 20, 1862, of wounds. Dropped from the rolls of the company on or about November 1, 1863, because he was "reported dead."

WILLIAMS, SAMUEL S., Private
Resided in Franklin County where he enlisted at age 25, May 20, 1861. Present or accounted for through June, 1863; however, he was reported absent sick during much of that period. Discharged on July 20, 1863, by reason of disability.

WILLIARD, ROBERT, Private
Resided in Maryland and enlisted in Wake County at age 18, July 15, 1862, for the war as a substitute. Present or accounted for until he deserted on August 18, 1862.

WILSON, JOHN A., Private
Resided in Franklin County where he enlisted at age 21, May 20, 1861. Present or accounted for until he died at Hobdy's Point, Virginia, September 17, 1861, of disease.

WOOD, LEWIS S., Private
Company records indicate that he served previously in the 12th Regiment N.C. Troops (2nd Regiment N.C. Volunteers) and transferred to this company prior to September, 1862; however, records of the 12th Regiment do not indicate that he served therein. First listed on the rolls of this company in April, 1862. Present or accounted for until December 10, 1862, when he was reported absent without leave. Reported absent without leave through April, 1864. Died in hospital at Richmond, Virginia, August 22, 1864, of disease.

WOOD, WILLIS, Private
Resided in Franklin County where he enlisted at age 25, May 20, 1861. Present or accounted for until

reported absent without leave on April 20, 1864. Returned to duty on October 21, 1864, and present or accounted for through October, 1864.

YARBOROUGH, DAVID, Private
Enlisted in Franklin County on May 20, 1861. A company muster roll dated June 12-30, 1861, indicates that he had "never been sworn in." No further records.

YARBOROUGH, JAMES B., Private
Resided in Franklin County where he enlisted at age 24, May 20, 1861. Present or accounted for until he died "at home" on or about October 20, 1861, of disease.

YARBOROUGH, JOHN, Private
Resided in Franklin County where he enlisted at age 25, May 20, 1861. Present or accounted for until he died at Yorktown, Virginia, August 14, 1861, of disease.

COMPANY H

This company was from Alamance County and enlisted at Graham on May 21, 1861. It was mustered in and assigned to this regiment as Company H. After joining the regiment the company functioned as a part of the regiment, and its history for the war period is recorded as a part of the regimental history.

The information contained in the following roster of the company was compiled principally from company muster rolls for June 17-August, 1861; November-December, 1861; November, 1862-April, 1864; and September-October, 1864. No company muster rolls were found for September-October, 1861; January-October, 1862; May-August, 1864; or for the period after October, 1864. In addition to the company muster rolls, Roll of Honor records, receipt rolls, hospital records, prisoner of war records, and other primary records, supplemented by state pension applications, United Daughters of the Confederacy records, and postwar rosters and histories, all provided useful information.

OFFICERS
CAPTAINS

STOCKARD, JOHN R.
Resided in Alamance County where he enlisted at age 33. Appointed Captain to rank from May 21, 1861. Present or accounted for through March 21, 1862; however, he was reported absent sick during most of that period. "Dropped" on March 22, 1862, by reason of prolonged absence.

THOMPSON, DAVID S.
Resided in Alamance County where he enlisted at age 22. Appointed 1st Lieutenant on or about May 21, 1861, and was promoted to Captain to rank from March 31, 1862. Present or accounted for until he was defeated for reelection when the regiment was reorganized on May 2, 1862. Enlisted as a Private in Company K, 63rd Regiment N.C. Troops (5th Regiment N.C. Cavalry) on November 16, 1862. Transferred back to this company upon appointment

as 1st Lieutenant to rank from August 13, 1863. Present or accounted for until hospitalized at Richmond, Virginia, May 9, 1864, with a gunshot wound of the right shoulder; however, place and date wounded not reported. Returned to duty prior to August 25, 1864, when he was wounded in the left arm at Reams' Station, Virginia. Returned to duty on October 18, 1864. Paroled at Appomattox Court House, Virginia, April 9, 1865.

STONE, WILLIAM J.
Resided in Orange County and enlisted at Yorktown, Virginia, at age 19, July 3, 1861. Mustered in as Private and promoted to Sergeant on July 30, 1861. Appointed 1st Lieutenant on April 2, 1862, and was promoted to Captain on May 2, 1862. Present or accounted for until captured at Crampton's Pass, Maryland, September 14, 1862. Confined at Fort Delaware, Delaware, until transferred to Aiken's Landing, James River, Virginia, October 2, 1862, for exchange. Declared exchanged at Aiken's Landing on November 10, 1862. Returned to duty prior to December 13, 1862, when he was wounded in the head at Fredericksburg, Virginia. Sent by rail to hospital at Richmond, Virginia; however, he was "brought from the Fredericksburg cars dead."

EULISS, ELI S.
Resided in Alamance County where he enlisted at age 23, May 21, 1861. Mustered in as Sergeant and was appointed 1st Lieutenant on May 2, 1862. Promoted to Captain on January 27, 1863. Present or accounted for until paroled at Appomattox Court House, Virginia, April 9, 1865.

LIEUTENANTS

BOOKER, PASCHALL P., 2nd Lieutenant
Resided in Alamance County where he enlisted at age 32, May 21, 1861. Mustered in as Corporal and was appointed 2nd Lieutenant to rank from May 2, 1862. Present or accounted for until wounded at Sharpsburg, Maryland, September 17, 1862. Returned to duty prior to January 1, 1863. Present or accounted for through October, 1864; however, he was reported absent sick during much of that period.

CLENDENIN, GEORGE A., 3rd Lieutenant
Resided in Alamance County where he enlisted at age 24. Appointed 3rd Lieutenant to rank from May 22, 1861. Present or accounted for until he was defeated for reelection when the regiment was reorganized on May 2, 1862. Later served as Private in Company K, 63rd Regiment N.C. Troops (5th Regiment N.C. Cavalry).

CLENDENIN, JOSEPH N. H., 2nd Lieutenant
Resided in Alamance County where he enlisted at age 20. Appointed 2nd Lieutenant to rank from May 21, 1861. Present or accounted for until he was defeated for reelection when the regiment was reorganized on May 2, 1862. Later served as Sergeant in Company K, 63rd Regiment N.C. Troops (5th Regiment N.C. Cavalry).

DAVENPORT, J. A., "Lieutenant"
Place and date of enlistment not reported. Paroled at Farmville, Virginia, April 11-21, 1865.

GOOD, W. C., 2nd Lieutenant

Place and date of enlistment and promotion record not reported. Captured at or near Kinston on June 22, 1864. Confined at Old Capitol Prison, Washington, D:C., until transferred to Fort Delaware, Delaware, July 22, 1864. Transferred to Hilton Head, South Carolina, August 20, 1864, and was confined at Fort Pulaski, Georgia, on or about October 20, 1864. Transferred for exchange on or about December 18, 1864. No further records.

ROBINSON, STEPHEN M., 2nd Lieutenant

Resided in Alamance County where he enlisted at age 21, May 21, 1861. Mustered in as Private and was appointed 2nd Lieutenant to rank from December 6, 1862. Present or accounted for until captured at Bristoe Station, Virginia, October 14, 1863. Confined at Old Capitol Prison, Washington, D.C., until transferred to Johnson's Island, Ohio, November 11, 1863. Released on June 12, 1865, after taking the Oath of Allegiance.

RONEY, JOHN, 2nd Lieutenant

Born in Alamance County* where he resided as a farmer prior to enlisting in Alamance County at age 37, May 21, 1861. Mustered in as Corporal and was appointed 2nd Lieutenant to rank from May 2, 1862. Present or accounted for until he resigned on or about August 8, 1862, by reason of "bad health."

WEBB, WILLIAM R., 1st Lieutenant

Resided in Orange County and enlisted in Alamance County at age 18, May 21, 1861. Mustered in as 1st Sergeant but was reduced to the rank of Sergeant in 1862. Present or accounted for until wounded in the arm at Malvern Hill, Virginia, July 1, 1862. Returned to duty in March-April, 1863, and was appointed 1st Lieutenant on March 17, 1863. Present or accounted for until he resigned on June 27, 1863, by reason of disability.

NONCOMMISSIONED OFFICERS AND PRIVATES

ALBRIGHT, CALVIN H., Private

Resided in Alamance County and enlisted at Yorktown, Virginia, at age 15, November 22, 1861. Present or accounted for until discharged in 1862 by reason of being under age.

BEARD, RICHARD A., Private

Resided in Alamance County where he enlisted at age 33, May 21, 1861. Present or accounted for until he died at Petersburg, Virginia, May 20, 1862, of disease.

BISHOP, IOWA, Private

Resided in Alamance County where he enlisted at age 19, May 21, 1861. Present or accounted for until he died in hospital at Richmond, Virginia, December 17, 1861, of "colica."

BOWMAN, M., Private

Resided in Guilford County. Place and date of enlistment not reported. Captured at Hatcher's Run, Virginia, April 2, 1865, and confined at Hart's Island, New York Harbor, until released on June 14, 1865, after taking the Oath of Allegiance.

BRADSHAW, WILLIAM G. C., Private

Resided in Alamance County where he enlisted at age

18, May 31, 1861. Present or accounted for until wounded at Lee's Mill, Virginia, April 16, 1862. Returned to duty prior to January 1, 1863, and present or accounted for until captured at Sutherland's Station, Virginia, on or about April 3, 1865. Confined at Point Lookout, Maryland, until released on June 23, 1865, after taking the Oath of Allegiance.

BRANSON, ELI B., Jr., Corporal

Resided in Alamance County where he enlisted at age 19, May 21, 1861. Mustered in as Private and promoted to Sergeant on May 2, 1862. Present or accounted for until wounded at South Mountain, Maryland, September 14, 1862. Returned to duty prior to January 1, 1863, and was reduced to ranks at an unspecified date. Promoted to Corporal on June 15, 1863. Present or accounted for until killed at Bristoe Station, Virginia, October 14, 1863.

BRANSON, ELI B., Sr., 1st Sergeant

Resided in Alamance County where he enlisted at age 22, May 21, 1861. Mustered in as Sergeant. Present or accounted for until wounded in the left thigh and captured at or near Crampton's Pass, Maryland, September 14, 1862. Confined at Fort McHenry, Maryland, until paroled and transferred to Aiken's Landing, James River, Virginia, where he was received October 22, 1862, for exchange. Declared exchanged at Aiken's Landing on November 10, 1862. Returned to duty in March-April, 1863, and was promoted to 1st Sergeant in April-October, 1864. Present or accounted for through October, 1864.

BROWN, WILEY D., Private

Resided in Alamance County where he enlisted at age 26, May 21, 1861. Present or accounted for until hospitalized at Richmond, Virginia, June 24, 1864, with a gunshot wound; however, place and date wounded not reported. Returned to duty on September 12, 1864, and present or accounted for until captured at Hatcher's Run, Virginia, April 2, 1865. Confined at Hart's Island, New York Harbor, until released on June 17, 1865, after taking the Oath of Allegiance.

BRYAN, ARCHIBALD P., Private

Born in Alamance County* where he resided as a farmer prior to enlisting in Alamance County at age 20, May 21, 1861. Present or accounted for until paroled at Appomattox Court House, Virginia, April 9, 1865.

BRYAN, JOHN A., Private

Born in Alamance County* where he resided as a farmer prior to enlisting in Alamance County at age 18, May 21, 1861. Present or accounted for until captured at Hatcher's Run, Virginia, April 2, 1865. Confined at Hart's Island, New York Harbor, until released on June 18, 1865, after taking the Oath of Allegiance.

BURNS, JACOB, Private

Resided in Alamance County where he enlisted at age 23, May 21, 1861. Present or accounted for through October, 1864.

BURNS, JOHN, Private

Resided in Alamance County where he enlisted at age 44, May 21, 1861. Present or accounted for until captured at or near Williamsburg, Virginia, May 1-8, 1862. Hospitalized at Williamsburg until transferred to

Washington, D.C., on or about May 16, 1862. Died in hospital at Washington on June 16, 1862, of "diarrhoea chronica."

CAPPS, ANDREW J., Private
Resided in Alamance County where he enlisted at age 19, May 21, 1861. Present or accounted for until captured at Hatcher's Run, Virginia, April 2, 1865. Confined at Hart's Island, New York Harbor, until released on June 18, 1865, after taking the Oath of Allegiance.

CHEEK, CHARLES C., Corporal
Resided in Alamance County and enlisted at Yorktown, Virginia, at age 19, August 3, 1861. Mustered in as Private. Present or accounted for until wounded at Malvern Hill, Virginia, July 1, 1862. Returned to duty on July 15, 1863. Present or accounted for until wounded at Reams' Station, Virginia, August 25, 1864. Returned to duty subsequent to November 1, 1864, and was promoted to Corporal in November, 1864-April, 1865. Present or accounted for until paroled at Appomattox Court House, Virginia, April 9, 1865.

CLENDENIN, HENRY M., Sergeant
Resided in Alamance County where he enlisted at age 20, May 21, 1861. Mustered in as Private and promoted to Sergeant in September, 1861-February, 1862. Present or accounted for until killed at Lee's Mill, Virginia, April 16, 1862.

CLINARD, AHART H., Private
Resided in Davidson County and enlisted in Wake County at age 27, July 15, 1862, for the war. Present or accounted for until wounded at or near Riddell's Shop, Virginia, on or about June 12, 1864. Reported absent wounded through October, 1864.

COBLE, JAMES, Private
Resided in Alamance County where he enlisted at age 18, May 21, 1861. Present or accounted for until transferred to Company K, 44th Regiment N.C. Troops, July 1, 1863, in exchange for Private John Davidson.

COBLE, WILLIS H., Private
Resided in Alamance County where he enlisted at age 20, May 21, 1861. Present or accounted for until wounded at or near Malvern Hill, Virginia, on or about July 1, 1862. Died in hospital at Richmond, Virginia, July 10, 1862, of wounds.

DAVIDSON, CALVIN, Private
Resided in Alamance County where he enlisted at age 27, May 21, 1861. Present or accounted for until he deserted on July 17, 1864.

DAVIDSON, JOHN M., Private
Previously served in Company G, 44th Regiment N.C. Troops. Transferred to this company on July 1, 1863, in exchange for Private James Coble. Present or accounted for until he died in hospital at Richmond, Virginia, July 13, 1864. Cause of death not reported.

EULISS, WILLIAM A., Private
Previously served in Company E, Mallett's Battalion (Camp Guard). Date transferred to this company not reported; however, he was first listed on the rolls of this company in September-October, 1864. Present or accounted for until paroled at Appomattox Court House, Virginia, April 9, 1865.

FALKNER, WILLIAM, Private
Born in Granville County and resided in Alamance County where he was by occupation a farmer prior to enlisting in Alamance County at age 32, May 21, 1861. Present or accounted for until he died in hospital at Richmond, Virginia, May 10, 1862, of disease.

FAUCETT, JOHN, Private
Born in Alamance County* where he resided as a farmer prior to enlisting in Northampton County at age 23, June 12, 1861. Present or accounted for through May 27, 1864. No further records.

FAUST, JAMES W., Private
Resided in Alamance County where he enlisted at age 19, May 21, 1861. Present or accounted for until wounded at Sharpsburg, Maryland, September 17, 1862. Returned to duty on September 10, 1863, and present or accounted for through October, 1864.

GARRETT, DANIEL M., Private
Resided in Alamance County where he enlisted at age 22, May 21, 1861. Present or accounted for until captured at or near Warrenton, Virginia, September 29, 1862. Paroled on or about the same day. Returned to duty in January-February, 1863, and present or accounted for until captured at Hatcher's Run, Virginia, April 2, 1865. Confined at Hart's Island, New York Harbor, until released on June 19, 1865, after taking the Oath of Allegiance.

GORDAY, JOHN, Private
Resided in Davidson County and enlisted in Wake County at age 27, July 15, 1862, for the war. Present or accounted for until wounded at Sharpsburg, Maryland, September 17, 1862. Died in hospital; however, place and date of death not reported.

GRIFFITH, JAMES H., Private
Resided in Virginia and enlisted at Yorktown, Virginia, at age 20, July 3, 1861. Present or accounted for until captured at or near Crampton's Pass, Maryland, September 14, 1862. Confined at Fort Delaware, Delaware, until transferred to Aiken's Landing, James River, Virginia, October 2, 1862, for exchange. Declared exchanged at Aiken's Landing on November 10, 1862. Reported absent without leave until October 25, 1863, when he was returned to the regiment "by a guard." Present or accounted for through October, 1864. Paroled May 9, 1865.

GRIFFITH, TYLER C., Private
Resided in Virginia and enlisted in Alamance County at age 22, May 21, 1861. Present or accounted for until he died at Petersburg, Virginia, in March, 1862, of disease.

GUTHRIE, WILLIAM H., Sergeant
Resided in Alamance County where he enlisted at age 20, May 21, 1861. Mustered in as Private and promoted to Corporal in 1862. Present or accounted for until wounded at Lee's Mill, Virginia, April 16, 1862. Returned to duty prior to September 17, 1862, when he was wounded at Sharpsburg, Maryland. Returned to duty in January-February, 1863, and was promoted to Sergeant on June 15, 1863. Present or accounted for until captured at Bristoe Station, Virginia, October 14, 1863. Confined at Old Capitol Prison, Washington, D.C., until transferred to Point Lookout, Maryland, October 27, 1863. Paroled and

transferred to Aiken's Landing, James River, Virginia, February 24, 1865, for exchange. Hospitalized at Richmond, Virginia, February 25, 1865. Paroled at Greensboro on May 29, 1865.

HARRIS, JOHN W., Private

Born in Alamance County* where he resided prior to enlisting in Alamance County at age 25, May 21, 1861. Present or accounted for until killed at Wilderness, Virginia, May 5, 1864.

HEGE, ELI, Private

Resided in Davidson County and enlisted in Wake County at age 18, July 15, 1862, for the war. Present or accounted for until captured at or near Crampton's Pass, Maryland, September 14, 1862. Confined at Fort Delaware, Delaware, until transferred to Aiken's Landing, James River, Virginia, October 2, 1862, for exchange. Declared exchanged at Aiken's Landing on November 10, 1862. Died at Richmond, Virginia, prior to May 1, 1863, of disease. Exact date of death not reported.

HOPKINS, M. V., Private

Previously served in Company G, 48th Regiment N.C. Troops. Transferred to this company in August, 1862. Present or accounted for until captured at or near Crampton's Pass, Maryland, September 14, 1862. Confined at Fort Delaware, Delaware, until transferred to Aiken's Landing, James River, Virginia, October 2, 1862, for exchange. Declared exchanged at Aiken's Landing on November 10, 1862. Returned to duty prior to January 1, 1863, and present or accounted for until killed at Bristoe Station, Virginia, October 14, 1863.

HUGHES, MARCHELL M., Private

Resided in Alamance County where he enlisted at age 19, May 21, 1861. Present or accounted for until wounded at Bristoe Station, Virginia, October 14, 1863. Returned to duty in January-February, 1864. Present or accounted for until hospitalized at Danville, Virginia, June 16, 1864, with a gunshot wound of the foot; however, place and date wounded not reported. Reported absent wounded through October, 1864. Paroled at Greensboro on May 29, 1865.

INGOLD, ELI, Private

Resided in Guilford County. Place and date of enlistment not reported. Captured at Petersburg, Virginia, April 3, 1865, and confined at Point Lookout, Maryland. Died in hospital at Point Lookout on July 5, 1865, of "scorbutus."

ISLEY, MARTIN V., Sergeant

Resided in Alamance County where he enlisted at age 24, May 21, 1861. Mustered in as Private and promoted to Corporal in September, 1861-December, 1862. Promoted to Sergeant on April 8, 1863. Present or accounted for until wounded at Bristoe Station, Virginia, October 14, 1863. Returned to duty on December 7, 1863, and present or accounted for until paroled at Appomattox Court House, Virginia, April 9, 1865.

JONES, WILLIAM, Private

Resided in Alamance County where he enlisted at age 19, May 21, 1861. Present or accounted for until wounded at or near Crampton's Pass, Maryland, September 14, 1862. Returned to duty in January-

February, 1863, and present or accounted for until captured at Bristoe Station, Virginia, October 14, 1863. Confined at Old Capitol Prison, Washington, D.C., until transferred to Point Lookout, Maryland, October 27, 1863. Transferred to Elmira, New York, August 10, 1864. Paroled on February 20, 1865, and transferred to James River, Virginia, for exchange. Hospitalized at Richmond, Virginia, March 2, 1865, and present or accounted for through March 6, 1865.

KINNY, OLIVER, Private

Resided in Alamance County where he enlisted at age 20, May 21, 1861. Present or accounted for until wounded at Fredericksburg, Virginia, December 13, 1862. Returned to duty on April 30, 1863. Present or accounted for until discharged on April 22, 1864, by reason of disability.

LAMB, ORREN, Private

Born in Alamance County* where he resided as a farmer prior to enlisting in Alamance County at age 19, May 21, 1861. Present or accounted for until killed at Fredericksburg, Virginia, December 13, 1862.

LANKFORD, WILLIAM, Private

Born in Alamance County* where he resided prior to enlisting in Alamance County at age 18, May 21, 1861. Present or accounted for until killed at or near Crampton's Pass, Maryland, September 14, 1862.

LEONARD, ALSON, Private

Resided in Alamance County where he enlisted at age 21, May 21, 1861. Present or accounted for until hospitalized at Richmond, Virginia, September 28, 1862, with a gunshot wound of the leg and right hip; however, place and date wounded not reported. Reported absent wounded or absent sick until he died in hospital at Richmond, Virginia, January 15, 1863, of "variola conf[luen]t."

LININS, ISAAC, Private

Born in Alamance County* where he resided as a farmer prior to enlisting in Alamance County at age 18, May 21, 1861. Present or accounted for until wounded in the left shoulder at Bristoe Station, Virginia, October 14, 1863. Returned to duty in November-December, 1863, and present or accounted for through October, 1864. Paroled at Greensboro on May 18, 1865.

McMURRAY, COLUMBUS C., Private

Born in Alamance County* where he resided as a tinner prior to enlisting in Alamance County at age 21, May 21, 1861. Present or accounted for until wounded in the hip at Lee's Mill, Virginia, April 16, 1862. Reported absent wounded until discharged on September 13, 1862, by reason of disability from wounds.

McRAE, JAMES H., Private

Born in Alamance County* where he resided as a clerk prior to enlisting in Alamance County at age 20, May 21, 1861. Mustered in as Private and promoted to Sergeant in January-December, 1862. Present or accounted for until captured at Charles Town, Virginia, October 16, 1862. Confined at Fort McHenry, Maryland, until paroled and transferred to Aiken's Landing, James River, Virginia, October 30, 1862, for exchange. Declared exchanged at Aiken's Landing on November 10, 1862. Returned to duty in January-February, 1863. Reduced to ranks on June 15,

1863. Present or accounted for until transferred to Company K, 48th Regiment N.C. Troops, June 17, 1863, in exchange for Private Harrison Pitts.

MARSHELL, ASAILS, Private
Previously served in Company G, 48th Regiment N.C. Troops. Transferred to this company on or about July 15, 1862. Present or accounted for until captured at or near Crampton's Pass, Maryland, September 14, 1862. Confined at Fort Delaware, Delaware, until transferred to Aiken's Landing, James River, Virginia, October 2, 1862, for exchange. Declared exchanged at Aiken's Landing on November 10, 1862. Returned to duty in March-April, 1863, and present or accounted for until he died in hospital at Charlottesville, Virginia, December 28, 1863, of "diarr[hoea] chro[nic]."

MAYS, T. R., Private
Place and date of enlistment not reported. Deserted to the enemy on or about March 22, 1865. Released on or about March 29, 1865, after taking the Oath of Allegiance.

MITCHELL, HENRY CLAY, Private
Resided in Alamance County where he enlisted at age 22, May 21, 1861. Present or accounted for until transferred to Company F, 53rd Regiment N.C. Troops, on or about January 12, 1863.

MOIZE, FREDERICK R., Private
Resided in Alamance County where he enlisted at age 22, May 21, 1861. Present or accounted for until wounded at Lee's Mill, Virginia, April 16, 1862. Reported absent wounded until he returned to duty in January-February, 1864. Present or accounted for until wounded in the head at Wilderness, Virginia, May 5, 1864. Returned to duty prior to October 31, 1864, and was present or accounted for through that date.

MORROW, THOMAS A., Corporal
Born in Alamance County* and resided in Orange County where he was by occupation a farmer prior to enlisting in Alamance County at age 20, May 21, 1861. Mustered in as Corporal. Present or accounted for until wounded in the right elbow and captured at Crampton's Pass, Maryland, September 14, 1862. Hospitalized at Burkittsville, Maryland, until transferred to Fort McHenry, Maryland, at an unspecified date. Paroled and transferred to City Point, Virginia, where he was received November 21, 1862, for exchange. Reported absent wounded until discharged on March 4, 1863, by reason of "anchylosis" of the right elbow.

MOSER, JOHN, Private
Resided in Alamance County where he enlisted at age 21, May 21, 1861. Present or accounted for until killed at Fredericksburg, Virginia, December 13, 1862.

MOSLEY, MILTON M., Private
Resided in Banks County, Georgia, and enlisted at Yorktown, Virginia, July 3, 1861. Present or accounted for until transferred to Company B, 3rd Battalion Georgia Sharpshooters on or about August 24, 1861.

NOAH, ALVIN, Private
Resided in Alamance County where he enlisted at age 20, May 21, 1861. Present or accounted for until reported missing at or near Crampton's Pass, Maryland, September 14, 1862. No further records.

PAINTER, HIRAM, Private
Previously served in Company K, 48th Regiment N.C. Troops. Transferred to this company on April 14, 1863. in exchange for Private William E. Payne. Present or accounted for until captured at Bristoe Station, Virginia, October 14, 1863. Confined at Old Capitol Prison, Washington, D.C., until transferred to Point Lookout, Maryland, October 27, 1863. Paroled at Point Lookout and transferred to Aiken's Landing, James River, Virginia, February 24, 1865, for exchange.

PAYNE, WILLIAM E., Private
Resided in Davidson County and enlisted in Wake County at age 19, July 15, 1862, for the war. Present or accounted for until transferred to Company K, 48th Regiment N.C. Troops, April 14, 1863, in exchange for Private Hiram Painter.

PHILLIPS, HARRISON, Private
Resided in Alamance County where he enlisted at age 19, May 21, 1861. Present or accounted for until captured at or near Hatcher's Run, Virginia, March 31, 1865. Confined at Point Lookout, Maryland, until released on June 17, 1865, after taking the Oath of Allegiance.

PICKARD, JOHN F., Private
Born in Orange County and resided in Alamance County where he enlisted at age 18, May 21, 1861. Present or accounted for until killed at Reams' Station, Virginia, August 25, 1864.

PITTS, HARRISON, Private
Previously served in Company K, 48th Regiment N.C. Troops. Transferred to this company on June 17, 1863, in exchange for Private James H. McRae. Present or accounted for until he deserted from hospital at Richmond, Virginia, August 18, 1863.

PROCTOR, ANDREW, Private
Resided in Davidson County and enlisted in Wake County at age 27, July 15, 1862, for the war. Present or accounted for through October, 1864. Paroled at Greensboro on May 4, 1865.

RAY, JOHN, Private
Resided in Alamance County where he enlisted at age 18, May 21, 1861. Present or accounted for until he deserted to the enemy on or about March 29, 1865. Released at an unspecified date after taking the Oath of Allegiance.

RAY, JOHN T., Private
Resided in Alamance County where he enlisted at age 20, May 21, 1861. Present or accounted for until wounded at Lee's Mill, Virginia, April 16, 1862. Reported absent wounded until reported absent without leave on February 1, 1863. Reported absent without leave through October, 1864. Deserted to the enemy on or about March 23, 1865.

RAY, RITTON D., Private
Resided in Alamance County where he enlisted at age 39, May 21, 1861. Present or accounted for until discharged on August 25, 1862, by reason of being over age. [May have served later in Captain Durham's Company, 3rd Battalion N.C. Senior Reserves.]

RAY, WILLIAM, Private
Resided in Alamance County where he enlisted at age 23, May 21, 1861. Present or accounted for until

captured at or near Hatcher's Run, Virginia, March 31, 1865. Confined at Point Lookout, Maryland, until released on June 17, 1865, after taking the Oath of Allegiance.

ROBERSON, MERRITT M., Private

Resided in Alamance County where he enlisted at age 33, May 21, 1861. Present or accounted for until captured at or near Crampton's Pass, Maryland, September 14, 1862. Died at Fort Delaware, Delaware, October 15, 1862. Cause of death not reported.

ROBERSON, WILLIAM G., Private

Resided in Alamance County where he enlisted at age 19, May 21, 1861. Present or accounted for until he died at Yorktown, Virginia, July 20, 1861, of "measles."

ROBERTS, CALVIN, Private

Enlisted in Alamance County on May 21, 1861. Present or accounted for through January, 1862. No further records.

ROBERTS, JAMES C., Private

Resided in Alamance County and enlisted at age 21, May 21, 1861. Present or accounted for until discharged on December 12, 1861, by reason of disability.

ROBERTS, WILLIAM P., Private

Resided in Alamance County where he enlisted at age 20, May 21, 1861. Present or accounted for until reported absent wounded in November-December, 1861; however, place and date wounded not reported. Returned to duty prior to July 1, 1862, when he was wounded at Malvern Hill, Virginia. Returned to duty prior to January 1, 1863. Present or accounted for until hospitalized at Charlottesville, Virginia, May 7, 1864, with a gunshot wound; however, place and date wounded not reported. Returned to duty on October 3, 1864, and was present or accounted for through October, 1864. Paroled at Greensboro on May 22, 1865.

SHARP, ANDERSON M., Private

Resided in Alamance County where he enlisted at age 21, May 21, 1861. Present or accounted for until reported absent wounded in November-December, 1861; however, place and date wounded not reported. Returned to duty prior to July 1, 1862, when he was wounded at Malvern Hill, Virginia. Died July 15, 1862, of wounds. Place of death not reported.

SHARP, MILTON H., Private

Born in Alamance County* where he resided prior to enlisting in Alamance County at age 27, May 21, 1861. Present or accounted for until reported absent wounded in November-December, 1861; however, place and date wounded not reported. Returned to duty prior to July 1, 1862, when he was wounded at Malvern Hill, Virginia. Returned to duty prior to January 1, 1863, and present or accounted for until killed at Reams' Station, Virginia, August 25, 1864.

SHOFFNER, MICHAEL, Private

Born in Alamance County* where he resided prior to enlisting in Alamance County at age 20, May 21, 1861. Present or accounted for until discharged on September 12, 1862, by reason of "periosteal disease of hip with hernia of left side."

SINK, JOHN, Private

Resided in Davidson County and enlisted in Wake County at age 27, July 15, 1862, for the war. Present or accounted for until wounded in the arm at Fredericksburg, Virginia, December 13, 1862. Returned to duty in May-June, 1863, and present or accounted for until he died in hospital at Orange Court House, Virginia, March 20, 1864. Cause of death not reported.

SINK, MATHIAS, Private

Resided in Davidson County and enlisted in Wake County at age 23, July 15, 1862, for the war. Present or accounted for through October, 1864. Paroled at Greensboro on May 8, 1865.

SINK, SOLOMON, Private

Born in Davidson County where he resided as a farmer prior to enlisting in Wake County at age 29, July 15, 1862, for the war. Present or accounted for until he died in hospital at Richmond, Virginia, November 26, 1862, of pneumonia.

SPENCER, D. F., Private

Resided in Davidson County and enlisted in Wake County at age 30, July 15, 1862, for the war. Present or accounted for until killed at Fredericksburg, Virginia, December 13, 1862.

STANFORD, JOHN P., Private

Resided in Alamance County where he enlisted at age 21, May 21, 1861. Present or accounted for until captured at Bristoe Station, Virginia, October 14, 1863. Confined at Old Capitol Prison, Washington, D.C., until transferred to Point Lookout, Maryland, October 27, 1863. Paroled on May 3, 1864, and transferred to Aiken's Landing, James River, Virginia, for exchange. Returned to duty prior to November 1, 1864. Died at or near Richmond, Virginia, February 20, 1865. Cause of death not reported.

STEEL, EMSLEY, Private

Born in Alamance County* where he resided as a farmer prior to enlisting in Alamance County at age 18, May 21, 1861. Present or accounted for until killed at Lee's Mill, Virginia, April 16, 1862.

STEEL, JAMES P., Sergeant

Resided in Alamance County where he enlisted at age 20, May 21, 1861. Mustered in as Sergeant. Present or accounted for until he died at Yorktown, Virginia, July 29, 1861, of "measles."

STEEL, SHADY, Private

Born in Alamance County where he resided as a farmer prior to enlisting in Alamance County at age 23, May 21, 1861. Present or accounted for until captured at or near Crampton's Pass, Maryland, on or about September 14, 1862. Confined at Fort Delaware, Delaware, until transferred to Aiken's Landing, James River, Virginia, October 2, 1862, for exchange. Declared exchanged at Aiken's Landing on November 10, 1862. Died "at home" on January 28, 1863, of disease.

STEPHENS, J. R., Private

Place and date of enlistment not reported. Captured by the enemy in July, 1863. Confined at Point Lookout, Maryland, until paroled on February 18, 1865, and transferred to Boulware's and Cox's Wharf, James River, Virginia, for exchange.

STOCKARD, JOHN WILLIAMSON, Private
Resided in Alamance County where he enlisted at age 23, May 21, 1861. Present or accounted for until hospitalized at Richmond, Virginia, June 24, 1864, with a gunshot wound; however, place and date wounded not reported. Returned to duty on September 30, 1864, and present or accounted for until captured at or near Appomattox, Virginia, April 3, 1865. Confined at Hart's Island, New York Harbor, until released June 19-20, 1865, after taking the Oath of Allegiance.

STOUT, JOEL J., 1st Sergeant
Born in Alamance County* where he resided prior to enlisting in Alamance County at age 21, May 21, 1861. Mustered in as Corporal and promoted to 1st Sergeant on May 2, 1862. Present or accounted for until wounded at Sharpsburg, Maryland, September 17, 1862. Returned to duty in January-February, 1863. Present or accounted for until he died "in camp" on April 3, 1864, of disease.

STRAYHORN, WILLIAM, Private
Born in Alamance County* where he resided as a farmer prior to enlisting in Alamance County at age 19, May 21, 1861. Present or accounted for until captured at Bristoe Station, Virginia, October 14, 1863. Confined at Old Capitol Prison, Washington, D.C., October 15, 1863. Died in hospital at Washington on January 21, 1864, of "diarrhoea chronica."

STROWD, JAHAZA, Private
Resided in Orange County and enlisted at Yorktown, Virginia, at age 18, July 3, 1861. Present or accounted for until he died in hospital at Petersburg, Virginia, December 12, 1861, of disease.

STUART, FRANKLIN, Private
Resided in Davidson County and enlisted at age 25, July 15, 1862, for the war. Transferred to Company G, 48th Regiment N.C. Troops, August 14, 1862.

STUART, H., Private
Resided in Davidson County and enlisted at age 18, July 15, 1862, for the war. Company records indicate he was transferred to Company G, 48th Regiment N.C. Troops; however, records of the 48th Regiment do not indicate that he served therein. Died September 7, 1863, of "dysentery." Place of death not reported.

STUART, H. W., Private
Enlisted in Wake County on July 15, 1862, for the war. Present or accounted for until he died in hospital at Hanover, Virginia, September 5, 1863, of disease.

STUART, M., Private
Resided in Davidson County and enlisted at age 20, July 15, 1862, for the war. Present or accounted for until he reportedly transferred to the 48th Regiment N.C. Troops prior to January 1, 1863; however, records of the 48th Regiment do not indicate that he served therein.

STUART, S. A., Private
Resided in Davidson County and enlisted in Wake County at age 21, July 15, 1862, for the war. Present or accounted for until captured at Bristoe Station, Virginia, October 14, 1863. Confined at Old Capitol Prison, Washington, D.C., until transferred to Point Lookout, Maryland, October 27, 1863. Died at Point Lookout on February 23, 1864. Cause of death not reported.

SUMMER, JAMES B., Private
Born in Alamance County* where he resided as a blacksmith prior to enlisting in Alamance County at age 18, May 21, 1861. Present or accounted for until wounded at Malvern Hill, Virginia, July 1, 1862. Reported absent wounded or absent sick until discharged on February 27, 1863, by reason of "phthisis pulmonalis."

TAYLOR, CHARLES S., Sergeant
Resided in Alamance County where he enlisted at age 31, May 21, 1861. Mustered in as Private and promoted to Corporal in 1862. Promoted to Sergeant in November, 1864-April, 1865. Present or accounted for until captured at or near Hatcher's Run, Virginia, March 31, 1865. Confined at Point Lookout, Maryland, until released on June 20, 1865, after taking the Oath of Allegiance.

TEAGUE, J. M., Private
Resided in Davidson County and enlisted in Wake County at age 19, July 15, 1862, for the war. Present or accounted for until he was reported missing and "supposed dead" at Sharpsburg, Maryland, September 17, 1862.

TESH, GEORGE WILLIAM, Private
Resided in Davidson County and enlisted in Wake County at age 19, July 15, 1862, for the war. Present or accounted for until wounded at Bristoe Station, Virginia, October 14, 1863. Returned to duty in January-February, 1864, and present or accounted for until wounded at Reams' Station, Virginia, August 25, 1864. Reported in hospital at Richmond, Virginia, March 11, 1865, and was paroled at Appomattox Court House, Virginia, April 9, 1865. North Carolina pension records indicate that he received wounds in the right hip, right cheek, and right foot.

TESH, SOLOMON, Corporal
Resided in Davidson County and enlisted in Wake County at age 31, July 15, 1862, for the war. Mustered in as Private. Present or accounted for until wounded at or near Crampton's Pass, Maryland, September 14, 1862. Returned to duty in January-February, 1863, and was promoted to Corporal on April 8, 1863. Present or accounted for until he died in hospital at Richmond, Virginia, December 18, 1864, of "feb[ris] cont[inued]."

THOMAS, JAMES K. P., Private
Resided in Davidson County and enlisted in Wake County at age 18, July 15, 1862, for the war. Present or accounted for until wounded at Reams' Station, Virginia, August 25, 1864. Returned to duty on October 13, 1864. Took the Oath of Allegiance at Point Lookout, Maryland, June 21, 1865; however, place and date captured not reported.

THOMPSON, J. G., Private
Resided in Davidson County and enlisted in Wake County at age 34, July 15, 1862, for the war. Present or accounted for until he died at Lynchburg, Virginia, January 22, 1863, of "apoplexia."

THOMPSON, PHILLIP S., Private
Resided in Davidson County and enlisted in Johnston County at age 18, May 22, 1863, for the war. Present

or accounted for until captured at Bristoe Station, Virginia, October 14, 1863. Confined at Old Capitol Prison, Washington, D.C., until transferred to Fort Delaware, Delaware, June 15, 1864. Paroled and transferred to Venus Point, Savannah River, Georgia, where he was received November 15, 1864, for exchange. Returned to duty at an unspecified date and was captured at or near Bentonville, March 18-22, 1865. Confined at Hart's Island, New York Harbor, until released June 19-20, 1865, after taking the Oath of Allegiance.

TURNER, JAMES A., Private
Resided in Alamance County where he enlisted at age 37, May 21, 1861. Present or accounted for until discharged in or about August, 1862, by reason of being over age.

WAGONER, WILLIAM, Private
Resided in Davidson County and enlisted in Wake County at age 33, July 15, 1862, for the war. Deserted at Hanover Junction, Virginia, August 28, 1862, but returned to duty in January-February, 1863. Present or accounted for until captured at Bristoe Station, Virginia, October 14, 1863. Confined at Old Capitol Prison, Washington, D.C., until transferred to Point Lookout, Maryland, October 27, 1863. Died at Point Lookout on December 24, 1863. Cause of death not reported.

WARNER, BRITTON, Private
Resided in Davidson County and enlisted in Wake County at age 30, July 15, 1862, for the war. Present or accounted for until he deserted to the enemy or was captured at Crampton's Pass, Maryland, September 14, 1862. Died in hospital at Baltimore, Maryland, September 30, 1862, of "chronic diarrhoea."

WEASNER, E. M., Private
Resided in Davidson County and enlisted in Wake County at age 30, July 15, 1862, for the war. Present or accounted for until wounded in the neck at Fredericksburg, Virginia, December 13, 1862. Returned to duty in January-February, 1863, and present or accounted for until captured at Hatcher's Run, Virginia, April 2, 1865. Confined at Hart's Island, New York Harbor, until released on June 18, 1865, after taking the Oath of Allegiance.

WEAVIL, DAVID, Private
Resided in Davidson County and enlisted in Wake County at age 28, July 15, 1862, for the war. Present or accounted for until he died of disease "in camp" near Richmond, Virginia, subsequent to September 1, 1862, but prior to March 1, 1863, when he was dropped from the rolls.

WEEAVIL, HENRY, Private
Born in Davidson County where he resided prior to enlisting in Wake County at age 25, July 15, 1862, for the war. Present or accounted for until he died "at home" on February 22, 1864, of disease.

WEERE, HENRY, Private
Resided in Davidson County and enlisted in Wake County at age 18, July 15, 1862, for the war. Present or accounted for until reported absent sick from September 1, 1862, until May 1, 1863, when he was reported absent without leave.

WEERE, WILEY, "Conscript"
Resided in Davidson County and enlisted at age 22, July 15, 1862, for the war. Died at Lynchburg, Virginia, prior to January 1, 1863, of disease. Exact date of death not reported.

WHITSETT, JOHN H., Private
Born in Alamance County* where he resided as a farmer prior to enlisting in Alamance County at age 24, May 21, 1861. Present or accounted for until wounded in the left leg and captured at Crampton's Pass, Maryland, September 14, 1862. Hospitalized at Burkittsville, Maryland, and was transferred to Fort McHenry, Maryland, April 4, 1863. Paroled and transferred to City Point, Virginia, where he was received April 12, 1863, for exchange. Present or accounted for through October, 1864; however, he was reported absent sick or absent on detail during most of that period.

WHITSETT, WILLIAM W., Private
Resided in Alamance County where he enlisted at age 26, May 21, 1861. Present or accounted for until wounded in the right hand at or near Crampton's Pass, Maryland, September 14, 1862. Returned to duty in March-April, 1863. Present or accounted for through March 11, 1865; however, he was reported absent on detail during much of that period. Paroled at Greensboro on or about April 28, 1865.

WILEY, WILLIAM, Private
Resided in Alamance County and enlisted in Wake County at age 35, May 22, 1863, for the war. Present or accounted for until wounded in the head at Bristoe Station, Virginia, October 14, 1863. Hospitalized at Richmond, Virginia, where he died October 25, 1863, of wounds.

WILKINS, HENRY H., Private
Born in Alamance County* where he resided as a farmer prior to enlisting in Alamance County at age 21, May 21, 1861. Present or accounted for until he died in hospital at Richmond, Virginia, July 15, 1862, of disease.

WILLIAMS, HIRAM F., Private
Resided in Davidson County and enlisted in Wake County at age 19, July 15, 1862, for the war. Present or accounted for until wounded in the right shoulder at Wilderness, Virginia, May 5, 1864. Returned to duty prior to October 31, 1864. Present or accounted for until captured at Hatcher's Run, Virginia, April 2, 1865. Confined at Hart's Island, New York Harbor, until released June 17-18, 1865, after taking the Oath of Allegiance.

WILSON, D., Private
Resided in Davidson County and enlisted in Wake County at age 22, July 15, 1862, for the war. Present or accounted for until captured at or near Crampton's Pass, Maryland, September 14, 1862. Confined at Fort Delaware, Delaware, until transferred to Aiken's Landing, James River, Virginia, October 2, 1862, for exchange. Declared exchanged at Aiken's Landing on November 10, 1862. Died in hospital at Richmond, Virginia, November 11, 1862, of "scurvy."

WILSON, HENRY F., Private
Resided in Davidson County and enlisted in Wake County at age 23, July 15, 1862, for the war. Present or

accounted for until wounded in the face at Wilderness, Virginia, May 5, 1864. Returned to duty on October 22, 1864, and present or accounted for until captured at Hatcher's Run, Virginia, April 2, 1865. Confined at Hart's Island, New York Harbor, until transferred to Davids Island, New York Harbor, July 1, 1865. Released on July 11, 1865, after taking the Oath of Allegiance.

WILSON, LEWIS, Private
Resided in Davidson County and enlisted at age 19, July 15, 1862, for the war. Present or accounted for until captured at Hatcher's Run, Virginia, April 2, 1865. Confined at Hart's Island, New York Harbor, until released June 17-18, 1865, after taking the Oath of Allegiance.

WILSON, M., Private
Resided in Davidson County and enlisted in Wake County at age 33, July 15, 1862, for the war. Present or accounted for through November, 1862. Company muster rolls indicate he was killed at Fredericksburg, Virginia, December 13, 1862; however, medical records indicate he died in hospital at Richmond, Virginia, December 21, 1862, of "febris typhoides."

WIRE, ADAM, Private
Resided in Davidson County and enlisted in Wake County at age 33, July 15, 1862, for the war. Present or accounted for until captured at or near Crampton's Pass, Maryland, September 14, 1862. Confined at Fort Delaware, Delaware, until transferred to Aiken's Landing, James River, Virginia, October 2, 1862, for exchange. Declared exchanged at Aiken's Landing on November 10, 1862. Returned to duty prior to January 1, 1863, and present or accounted for through October, 1864.

WOOD, HANDY SEYMOUR, Private
Resided in Alamance County where he enlisted at age 26, May 21, 1861. Present or accounted for until killed at Lee's Mill, Virginia, April 16, 1862.

WOOD, JASPER N., Sergeant
Resided in Alamance County where he enlisted at age 18, May 21, 1861. Mustered in as Private and promoted to Corporal in March-April, 1863. Promoted to Sergeant in May-October, 1864. Present or accounted for until paroled at Appomattox Court House, Virginia, April 9, 1865.

WOOSLEY, JOHN, Private
Resided in Davidson County and enlisted in Wake County at age 38, July 15, 1862, for the war. Present or accounted for until wounded at Sharpsburg, Maryland, September 17, 1862. Reported absent wounded until November 16, 1862, when he died in hospital at Farmville, Virginia, of "chr[onic] diarrhoea."

YORK, FRANCIS MARION, Corporal
Resided in Alamance County where he enlisted at age 20, May 21, 1861. Mustered in as Private. Present or accounted for until wounded at or near Crampton's Pass, Maryland, September 14, 1862. Returned to duty prior to January 1, 1863, and was promoted to Corporal on December 1, 1863. Present or accounted for until wounded at Reams' Station, Virginia, August 25, 1864. Hospitalized at Washington, D.C., where he was captured on April 3, 1865. Paroled on May 5, 1865.

ZIMMERMAN, JOHN, Private
Resided in Davidson County and enlisted in Wake County at age 19, July 15, 1862, for the war. Present or accounted for until he died in hospital at Richmond, Virginia, September 27, 1862, of "pneumonia."

ZIMMERMEN, D., Private
Resided in Davidson County and enlisted in Wake County at age 22, July 15, 1862, for the war. Present or accounted for until captured at Crampton's Pass, Maryland, September 14, 1862. Paroled prior to September 26, 1862. Returned to duty in March-April, 1863, but was discharged on October 3, 1863. Reason discharged not reported.

COMPANY I

This company, known as the Confederate Guard, was from Edgecombe County and enlisted at Rocky Mount on May 24, 1861. It was accepted into state service and ordered to Garysburg, where it was assigned to this regiment as Company I. After joining the regiment the company functioned as a part of the regiment, and its history for the war period is recorded as a part of the regimental history.

The information contained in the following roster of the company was compiled principally from company muster rolls for May 24-August, 1861; November, 1862-April, 1864; and September-October, 1864. No company muster rolls were found for September, 1861-October, 1862; May-August, 1864; or for the period after October, 1864. In addition to the company muster rolls, Roll of Honor records, receipt rolls, hospital records, prisoner of war records, and other primary records, supplemented by state pension applications, United Daughters of the Confederacy records, and postwar rosters and histories, all provided useful information.

OFFICERS

CAPTAINS

BATTLE, TURNER W.
Resided in Edgecombe County and enlisted at age 34. Appointed Captain to rank from May 22, 1861. Present or accounted for until defeated for reelection when the regiment was reorganized on May 2, 1862.

FOXHALL, EDWIN D.
Resided in Edgecombe County where he enlisted at age 23, May 24, 1861. Mustered in as 1st Sergeant and was appointed Captain to rank from May 2, 1862. Present or accounted for until captured at or near Crampton's Pass, Maryland, on or about September 14, 1862. Confined at Fort Delaware, Delaware, until transferred to Aiken's Landing, James River, Virginia, October 2, 1862, for exchange. Declared exchanged at Aiken's Landing on November 10, 1862. Returned to duty prior to January 1, 1863, and present or accounted for until paroled at Appomattox Court House, Virginia, April 9, 1865.

LIEUTENANTS

BARLOW, DAVID H., 3rd Lieutenant
Resided in Edgecombe County where he enlisted at age 17, May 24, 1861. Mustered in as Private and promoted to Corporal on May 15, 1862. Present or accounted for until captured at Crampton's Pass, Maryland, September 14, 1862. Confined at Fort Delaware, Delaware, until transferred to Aiken's Landing, James River, Virginia, October 2, 1862, for exchange. Promoted to Sergeant on November 1, 1862, and was declared exchanged at Aiken's Landing on November 10, 1862. Returned to duty prior to January 1, 1863, and was promoted to 1st Sergeant on April 1, 1863. Appointed 3rd Lieutenant in January-February, 1864. Present or accounted for until hospitalized at Richmond, Virginia, August 27, 1864, with a gunshot wound of the neck; however, place and date wounded not reported. Returned to duty on October 29, 1864, and present or accounted for until captured at Hatcher's Run, Virginia, April 2, 1865. Confined at Old Capitol Prison, Washington, D.C., until transferred to Johnson's Island, Ohio, April 9, 1865. Released at Johnson's Island on June 18, 1865, after taking the Oath of Allegiance.

DOWD, HENRY A., 1st Lieutenant
Resided in Edgecombe County where he enlisted at age 28. Appointed 1st Lieutenant on May 22, 1861. Present or accounted for until appointed Adjutant on October 7, 1861, and transferred to the Field and Staff of this regiment.

HART, BENJAMIN T., 1st Lieutenant
Resided in Edgecombe County where he enlisted at age 27, May 24, 1861. Mustered in as Private and was appointed 1st Lieutenant to rank from May 2, 1862. Present or accounted for until captured at or near Crampton's Pass, Maryland, on or about September 14, 1862. Confined at Fort Delaware, Delaware, until transferred to Aiken's Landing, James River, Virginia, October 2, 1862, for exchange. Declared exchanged at Aiken's Landing on November 10, 1862. Returned to duty prior to December 13, 1862, when he was wounded in the hand at Fredericksburg, Virginia. Returned to duty prior to January 1, 1863, and present or accounted for until September 15, 1864, when he was detailed to command Company F of this regiment. Reported absent on that detail through October, 1864. Paroled at Greensboro on May 1, 1865.

KNIGHT, EDWARD E., 2nd Lieutenant
Resided in Edgecombe County where he enlisted at age 22, June 19,. 1861. Mustered in as Private and promoted to Corporal in September, 1861-January, 1862. Appointed 2nd Lieutenant to rank from May 2, 1862. Present or accounted for until wounded in the right shoulder and left leg and captured at or near Crampton's Pass, Maryland, September 14, 1862. Confined at various Federal hospitals until transferred to Fort Delaware, Delaware, June 15, 1863. Transferred to Johnson's Island, Ohio, where he arrived July 20, 1863. Transferred to Fort Monroe, Virginia, July 30, 1863, and was transferred to City Point, Virginia, where he was received August 20, 1863, for exchange. Reported absent wounded until he resigned on October 1, 1863, by reason of "complete anchylosis of the right shoulder joint."

PENDER, SOLOMON M., 2nd Lieutenant
Resided in Edgecombe County where he enlisted at age 22, May 24, 1861. Mustered in as Sergeant and was appointed 3rd Lieutenant to rank from May 2, 1862. Present or accounted for until wounded in the hand at Malvern Hill, Virginia, July 1, 1862. Returned to duty prior to December 13, 1862, when he was wounded in the jaw at Fredericksburg, Virginia. Returned to duty prior to January 1, 1863, and was promoted to 2nd Lieutenant on November 2, 1863. Present or accounted for until paroled at Appomattox Court House, Virginia, April 9, 1865.

PHILLIPS, FREDERICK, 2nd Lieutenant
Resided in Edgecombe County where he enlisted at age 23. Appointed 2nd Lieutenant to rank from May 22, 1861. Present or accounted for until he was defeated for reelection when the regiment was reorganized on May 2, 1862. [May have served later as Adjutant and Assistant Quartermaster of the 30th Regiment N.C. Troops.]

SUGG, REDDING S., 2nd Lieutenant
Resided in Edgecombe County where he enlisted at age 26. Appointed 2nd Lieutenant to rank from May 22, 1861. Present or accounted for until he was defeated for reelection when the regiment was reorganized on May 2, 1862.

NONCOMMISSIONED OFFICERS AND PRIVATES

ALLEN, ANDREW J., Private
Born at Norfolk, Virginia, and resided in Edgecombe County prior to enlisting at age 17, February 28, 1863, for the war as a substitute for Private John W. Pippen. Present or accounted for until killed at Bristoe Station, Virginia, October 14, 1863.

ALLEN, JAMES E., Private
Resided in Edgecombe County where he enlisted at age 19, May 24, 1861. Present or accounted for until wounded in the leg at Malvern Hill, Virginia, July 1, 1862. Died July 26, 1862, of wounds. Place of death not reported.

ARCHIBALD, BRINKLEY J., Private
Resided in Edgecombe County where he enlisted at age 21, June 19, 1861. Present or accounted for through October, 1864.

ATKINSON, EDWARD R., Corporal
Born in Edgecombe County where he resided prior to enlisting at Yorktown, Virginia, at age 18, September 30, 1861. Mustered in as Private and was promoted to Corporal on April 1, 1863. Present or accounted for until he died in hospital at Charlottesville, Virginia, October 29, 1863, of "pneumonia."

BARDEN, WILLIAM, Private
Resided in Wayne County and enlisted in Wake County at age 30, July 15, 1862, for the war. Present or accounted for until hospitalized at Charlottesville, Virginia, September 25, 1862, with a gunshot wound; however, place and date wounded not reported. Returned to duty prior to December 13, 1862, when he was wounded at Fredericksburg, Virginia. Returned to duty in January-February, 1863, and present or

accounted for until wounded at Bristoe Station, Virginia, October 14, 1863. Reported absent wounded through October, 1864.

BARNES, M. W., Private
Resided in Wayne County and enlisted at age 34, July 15, 1862, for the war. Present or accounted for until killed at Sharpsburg, Maryland, September 17, 1862.

BARNS, WILLIAM, Private
Enlisted at Camp Holmes on October 18, 1864, for the war. Paroled at Farmville, Virginia, April 11-21, 1865.

BARRON, CHARLES H., Private
Resided in Edgecombe County where he enlisted at age 21, May 24, 1861. Present or accounted for until appointed 1st Lieutenant and transferred to Company C, 8th Regiment N.C. State Troops, June 24, 1861.

BASS, JAMES C., Sergeant
Resided in Halifax County and enlisted in Edgecombe County at age 20, May 27, 1861. Mustered in as Private. Present or accounted for until wounded in the leg at Malvern Hill, Virginia, July 1, 1862. Returned to duty prior to January 1, 1863, when he was promoted to Corporal. Promoted to Sergeant on April 1, 1863. Present or accounted for until reported absent wounded on August 31, 1864; however, battle in which wounded not reported. Reported absent wounded or absent on furlough until he was furloughed for sixty days on December 15, 1864.

BATTEN, A. A., Private
Resided in Wayne County and enlisted in Wake County at age 34, July 15, 1862, for the war. Present or accounted for until wounded in the knee and breast and captured at Crampton's Pass, Maryland, September 14, 1862. Hospitalized at Burkittsville, Maryland, where he died November 3, 1862, of wounds.

BATTLE, GEORGE C., Private
Born in Edgecombe County where he resided as a farmer prior to enlisting in Edgecombe County at age 19, May 27, 1861. Present or accounted for until discharged on January 8, 1862, by reason of "fever," "dysentery," "chronic bronchitis," and "threatened phthisis pulmonalis." Later served in Company K, 10th Regiment N.C. State Troops (1st Regiment N.C. Artillery).

BATTLE, HENRY L., Private
Resided in Edgecombe County where he enlisted at age 28, May 24, 1861. Present or accounted for until he died at Camp Dudley on February 4, 1862, of disease.

BATTLE, MARCUS J., Private
Resided in Edgecombe County where he enlisted at age 23, May 24, 1861. Mustered in as Private and was promoted to Corporal on October 10, 1861. Reduced to ranks on May 5, 1862. Present or accounted for until appointed Hospital Steward on or about October 30, 1863, and assigned to a hospital at Petersburg, Virginia.

BATTS, ISAAC F., Private
Born in Edgecombe County where he resided as a farmer prior to enlisting in Edgecombe County at age 27, May 27, 1861. Present or accounted for until discharged on June 7, 1862, by reason of "organic disease of the heart."

BELLAMY, NAPOLEON B., Private
Born in Edgecombe County where he resided as a farmer prior to enlisting in Edgecombe County at age 27, May 24, 1861. Present or accounted for until discharged on January 6, 1862, by reason of "phthisis pulmonalis."

BILLUPS, LAWRENCE, Corporal
Resided in Edgecombe County where he enlisted at age 22, May 24, 1861. Mustered in as Private. Present or accounted for until wounded in the hip at Fredericksburg, Virginia, December 13, 1862. Returned to duty prior to January 1, 1863, and was promoted to Corporal on February 15, 1864. Present or accounted for until paroled at Appomattox Court House, Virginia, April 9, 1865.

BLACK, W. W., Private
Previously served in Company C of this regiment. Transferred to this company on April 13, 1864. Present or accounted for until captured at Spotsylvania Court House, Virginia, May 12, 1864. Confined at Point Lookout, Maryland, where he died July 21, 1864. Cause of death not reported.

BOGUE, JESSE D., Private
Resided in Wayne County and enlisted in Wake County at age 27, July 15, 1862, for the war. Present or accounted for until he died in hospital at Gordonsville, Virginia, March 17, 1864, of "pneumonia."

BONNER, WILLIAM V., Private
Resided in Beaufort County and enlisted in Edgecombe County at age 31, May 24, 1861. Present or accounted for until appointed Assistant Surgeon on September 26, 1862, to rank from July 30, 1862, and transferred to the Field and Staff of this regiment.

BRADDY, JOSEPHUS, Private
Resided in Edgecombe County and enlisted at Richmond, Virginia, at age 37, August 19, 1862, for the war as a substitute. Present or accounted for until he died in hospital at Gordonsville, Virginia, November 20, 1862, of "pneumonia."

BRADLEY, JOSEPH J., Corporal
Born in Edgecombe County where he resided prior to enlisting at Yorktown, Virginia, at age 24, August 1, 1861. Mustered in as Private. Present or accounted for until captured at Crampton's Pass, Maryland, September 14, 1862. Confined at Fort Delaware, Delaware, until transferred to Aiken's Landing, James River, Virginia, October 2, 1862, for exchange. Declared exchanged at Aiken's Landing on November 10, 1862. Returned to duty prior to December 13, 1862, when he was wounded in the hip at Fredericksburg, Virginia. Returned to duty in March-April, 1863, and was promoted to Corporal on April 1, 1863. Present or accounted for until killed at Bristoe Station, Virginia, October 14, 1863.

BRADLEY, LAWRENCE, Private
Born in Edgecombe County where he resided as a mechanic prior to enlisting in Edgecombe County at age 26, June 4, 1861. Present or accounted for through March 21, 1865; however, he was reported absent sick or absent on light duty during most of that period. Discharged on March 22, 1865, by reason of "hypertrophy of the heart and fistula in ano with general debility."

BRADLEY, SIMON B., Private
Resided in Edgecombe County where he enlisted at age 24, May 24, 1861. Present or accounted for until dropped from the rolls of the company on April 12, 1864. May have been appointed Hospital Steward and transferred for duty at a hospital. No further records.

BROOKSHEER, JAMES, Private
Resided in Georgia and enlisted at Richmond, Virginia, at age 48, August 10, 1862, for the war as a substitute. Present or accounted for until reported absent without leave on December 12, 1863. Reported absent without leave through April, 1864.

BROOM, WILLIAM, Private
Resided in Cleveland County and enlisted at Fredericksburg, Virginia, at age 56, December 21, 1862, for the war as a substitute for Private John A. Davis. Present or accounted for until he died in hospital at Charlotte on March 18, 1864, of "diarrhoea chron[ic]."

BULLOCK, THOMAS O., Private
Resided in Edgecombe County where he enlisted at age 29, May 24, 1861. Present or accounted for until wounded in the head and captured at or near Crampton's Pass, Maryland, September 14, 1862. Died in hospital at Burkittsville, Maryland, prior to November 1, 1862, of wounds.

CHERRY, GEORGE W., Sergeant
Born in Edgecombe County where he resided prior to enlisting in Edgecombe County at age 18, May 27, 1861. Mustered in as Private and promoted to Corporal in September, 1861-December, 1862. Present or accounted for until wounded in the breast at Malvern Hill, Virginia, July 1, 1862. Returned to duty prior to January 1, 1863, and was promoted to Sergeant on January 15, 1863. Present or accounted for until he died in hospital at Gordonsville, Virginia, May 27, 1864, of wounds. Place and date wounded not reported.

CLARK, WILLIAM, Private
Born in Martin County where he resided as a farmer prior to enlisting at Richmond, Virginia, at age 56, August 12, 1862, for the war as a substitute. Present or accounted for until discharged on April 21, 1864, by reason of "old age and general debility."

COBB, BENJAMIN F., Private
Resided in Pitt County and enlisted in Edgecombe County at age 19, June 4, 1861. Present or accounted for until wounded at Malvern Hill, Virginia, July 1, 1862. Returned to duty in July-August, 1863, but was discharged on September 11, 1863, by reason of disability from wounds.

COBB, GRAY, Private
Resided in Pitt County and enlisted in Edgecombe County at age 32, June 4, 1861. Present or accounted for until discharged on August 19, 1862, after providing a substitute.

COBB, JOB, Corporal
Resided in Pitt County and enlisted in Edgecombe County at age 22, May 24, 1861. Mustered in as Private and promoted to Corporal on May 15, 1862. Present or accounted for until killed at Malvern Hill, Virginia, July 1, 1862.

COFFIELD, JOSEPH BRYANT, Sergeant
Resided in Edgecombe County where he enlisted at age 24, May 24, 1861. Mustered in as Corporal and promoted to Sergeant on May 15, 1862. Promoted to Quartermaster Sergeant on December 1, 1862, and transferred to the Field and Staff of this regiment.

COKER, SPIER, Private
Resided in Edgecombe County where he enlisted at age 21, June 4, 1861. Present or accounted for until he died at Yorktown, Virginia, August 5, 1861, of disease.

COLLIER, JOSEPH, Private
Resided in Wayne County and enlisted in Wake County at age 28, July 15, 1862, for the war. Present or accounted for until wounded at or near Spotsylvania Court House, Virginia, on or about May 15, 1864. Reported absent wounded through October, 1864.

COOK, ISAAC W., Private
Resided in Wayne County and enlisted in Wake County at age 29, July 15, 1862, for the war. Present or accounted for through October, 1864. Paroled on or about May 3, 1865.

CROCKER, DAVID, Private
Resided in Wayne County and enlisted in Wake County at age 22, July 15, 1862, for the war. Present or accounted for until captured at or near Crampton's Pass, Maryland, September 14, 1862. Confined at Fort Delaware, Delaware, until transferred to Aiken's Landing, James River, Virginia, October 2, 1862, for exchange. Declared exchanged at Aiken's Landing on November 10, 1862. Reported absent without leave from November 24, 1862, through April, 1864.

CROCKER, JOSIAH, Private
Resided in Wayne County and enlisted in Wake County at age 20, July 15, 1862, for the war. Present or accounted for until he deserted from hospital at Charlottesville, Virginia, November 1, 1862.

CURRY, GEORGE N., Private
Resided in Martin County and was by occupation a merchant prior to enlisting in Edgecombe County at age 30, June 4, 1861. Present or accounted for until he died at Camp Dudley, near Yorktown, Virginia, February 15, 1862, of disease.

DANCY, ROBERT F., Private
Resided in Florida and enlisted in Edgecombe County at age 18, June 19, 1861. Present or accounted for until he was appointed "Cadet C.S.A." on September 21, 1861. No further records.

DAUGHTRY, HENRY H., Private
Resided in Edgecombe County where he enlisted at age 22, May 24, 1861. Present or accounted for until discharged on July 25, 1862, by reason of having provided a substitute.

DAVIS, JO H., Private
Resided in Wayne County and enlisted in Wake County at age 29, July 15, 1862, for the war. Present or accounted for until wounded and captured at or near Crampton's Pass, Maryland, September 14, 1862. Confined at Fort Delaware, Delaware, where he died October 15, 1862, of disease.

DAVIS, JOHN A., Private
Resided in Wayne County and enlisted in Wake County at age 20, July 15, 1862, for the war. Present or

accounted for until captured at or near Old Church, Virginia, June 2, 1864. Confined at Point Lookout, Maryland, until paroled and transferred to Aiken's Landing, James River, Virginia, September 18, 1864, for exchange. Company records do not indicate whether he returned to duty; however, he was paroled at Goldsboro on May 9, 1865.

DAVIS, JOHN A., Private
Resided in Edgecombe County where he enlisted at age 17, May 24, 1861. Present or accounted for until discharged on December 21, 1862, after providing Private William Broom as a substitute. Later served in Company D, 40th Regiment N.C. Troops (3rd Regiment N.C. Artillery).

DAVIS, JOSHUA, Private
Resided in Wayne County and enlisted in Wake County at age 28, July 15, 1862, for the war. Present or accounted for until wounded in the thigh at Fredericksburg, Virginia, December 13, 1862. Returned to duty on January 26, 1863, and present or accounted for through October, 1864.

DAVIS, THOMAS W., Sergeant
Resided in Franklin County and enlisted at age 21, May 24, 1861. Mustered in as Sergeant. Present or accounted for until appointed 2nd Lieutenant on June 24, 1861, and transferred to Company C, 8th Regiment N.C. State Troops.

DAVIS, WHITNEY T., Private
Resided in Wayne County and enlisted in Wake County at age 26, July 15, 1862, for the war. Present or accounted for until wounded in the head at Fredericksburg, Virginia, December 13, 1862. Returned to duty in January-February, 1863, and present or accounted for until wounded in the right shoulder at or near Jones' Farm, Virginia, October 2, 1864. Died in hospital at Farmville, Virginia, November 25, 1864, of wounds.

ECHMONDSON, W., Private
Resided in Wayne County. Place and date of enlistment not reported. Paroled at Goldsboro on May 4, 1865.

EDMONSON, W. R., Private
Resided in Wayne County and enlisted at age 24, July 15, 1862, for the war. Present or accounted for until he died in hospital at Richmond, Virginia, October 19, 1862, of "typhoid fever."

EDWARDS, RANSOM, Private
Born in Wayne County where he resided prior to enlisting in Wake County at age 20, July 15, 1862, for the war. Present or accounted for until wounded at or near Crampton's Pass, Maryland, September 14, 1862. Reported absent wounded until he died in hospital at Raleigh on or about June 23, 1864, of "pneumonia."

ELLINOR, JOSEPH P., Private
Resided in Edgecombe County where he enlisted at age 15, May 24, 1861. Present or accounted for until discharged on August 19, 1862, by reason of being under age.

ETHRIDGE, CALEB, Private
Born in Edgecombe County where he resided as a farmer prior to enlisting in Edgecombe County at age 27, May 24, 1861. Present or accounted for until discharged on August 29, 1861, by reason of

"pulmonary phthisis which has rendered him utterly unfit for duty."

ETHRIDGE, REDDING, Private
Resided in Edgecombe County where he enlisted at age 22, May 24, 1861. Present or accounted for until he died in hospital at Richmond, Virginia, January 2, 1864, of "pneumonia."

FLANNER, BENNETT, Jr., Private
Resided in New Hanover County and enlisted at Yorktown, Virginia, at age 21, August 15, 1861. Present or accounted for until transferred to 1st Company H, 40th Regiment N.C. Troops (3rd Regiment N.C. Artillery), May 23, 1862.

FOLSON, WILLIAM, Private
Resided in Wayne County and enlisted in Wake County at age 20, July 15, 1862, for the war. Present or accounted for until captured at or near Frederick, Maryland, on or about September 12, 1862. Confined at Fort Delaware, Delaware, until transferred to Aiken's Landing, James River, Virginia, October 2, 1862, for exchange. Declared exchanged at Aiken's Landing on November 10, 1862. Returned to duty in January-February, 1863, and present or accounted for until captured at Hatcher's Run, Virginia, April 2, 1865. Confined at Point Lookout, Maryland, until released on June 26, 1865, after taking the Oath of Allegiance.

FOREMAN, WILLIAM, Private
Born in Chowan County and resided in Pitt County where he was by occupation a farmer prior to enlisting in Edgecombe County at age 23, May 24, 1861. Present or accounted for until discharged on May 14, 1862, by reason of "chronic diarrhoea."

FOUNTAIN, COFFIELD, Private
Born in Edgecombe County where he resided as a farmer prior to enlisting in Edgecombe County at age 23, June 4, 1861. Present or accounted for until wounded in the arm at Malvern Hill, Virginia, July 1, 1862. Reported absent wounded until discharged on February 5, 1863, by reason of disability from wounds.

FULLER, JEFFERSON, Private
Resided in Franklin County and enlisted in Edgecombe County at age 22, June 19, 1861. Present or accounted for until reported absent without leave on August 20, 1862. Returned to duty in January-February, 1863, but deserted on May 25, 1863.

GAME, WILLIAM H., Private
Resided in Wayne County and enlisted in Wake County at age 21, July 15, 1862, for the war. Present or accounted for until wounded in the thigh and captured at Crampton's Pass, Maryland, September 14, 1862. Hospitalized at Burkittsville, Maryland, until transferred to Fort McHenry, Maryland. Paroled at Fort McHenry on November 6, 1862, and transferred for exchange. Declared exchanged at Aiken's Landing on November 10, 1862. Returned to duty in July-August, 1863, and present or accounted for until captured at Sutherland's Station, Virginia, on or about April 3, 1865. Confined at Point Lookout, Maryland, until released on June 27, 1865, after taking the Oath of Allegiance.

GARRETT, ISAAC W., Private
Resided in Edgecombe County where he enlisted at age

25, May 24, 1861. Present or accounted for until discharged on December 1, 1861, "by order of [the] Secretary of War."

GORDON, GEORGE L., Private
Resided in Virginia and enlisted in Edgecombe County at age 32, May 24, 1861. Present or accounted for until appointed Adjutant (1st Lieutenant) on June 10, 1862, and transferred to the Field and Staff of this regiment.

GRANTHAM, DAVID J., Private
Resided in Wayne County and enlisted at Camp Holmes at age 34, July 15, 1862, for the war. Discharged on August 2, 1862, after providing a substitute; however, he reenlisted in the company on October 28, 1864. Present or accounted for until paroled at Appomattox Court House, Virginia, April 9, 1865.

GREEN, RICHARD S., Private
Resided in Craven County and enlisted at Yorktown, Virginia, at age 29, August 15, 1861. Present or accounted for until wounded at Lee's Mill, Virginia, April 16, 1862. Transferred to 1st Company H, 40th Regiment N.C. Troops (3rd Regiment N.C. Artillery), May 23, 1862.

GREY, D. T., Private
Resided in Wilson County. Place and date of enlistment not reported. Paroled at Goldsboro on May 11, 1865.

GURLEY, J. T., Private
Born in Wayne County where he resided prior to enlisting in Wake County at age 23, July 15, 1862, for the war. Present or accounted for until captured at Sharpsburg, Maryland, September 17, 1862. Confined at Fort Delaware, Delaware, until transferred to Aiken's Landing, James River, Virginia, October 2, 1862, for exchange. Declared exchanged at Aiken's Landing on November 10, 1862. Returned to duty prior to December 13, 1862, when he was killed at Fredericksburg, Virginia.

HARDY, JOHN, Private
Resided in Edgecombe County and was by occupation a farmer prior to enlisting in Edgecombe County at age 21, May 24, 1861. Present or accounted for until reported absent wounded in September, 1862; however, place and date wounded not reported. Returned to duty in January-February, 1863, and present or accounted for until captured at Hatcher's Run, Virginia, April 2, 1865. Confined at Point Lookout, Maryland, until released on June 27, 1865, after taking the Oath of Allegiance.

HARREL, J. R., Private
Resided in Wayne County and enlisted at age 20, July 15, 1862, for the war. Present or accounted for until discharged on September 12, 1862, by reason of disability.

HARRIS, F., Private
Place and date of enlistment not reported. Paroled at Salisbury on May 22, 1865.

HARRIS, S. A., Private
Previously served in Company C of this regiment. Transferred to this company on April 13, 1864. Present or accounted for until wounded at or near Globe Tavern, Virginia, August 21, 1864. Died in hospital at Richmond, Virginia, September 12, 1864, of wounds.

HART, ALMOND, Private
Resided in Edgecombe County where he enlisted at age 31, May 24, 1861. Present or accounted for until discharged on August 10, 1862, after providing a substitute.

HART, SPENCER L., Corporal
Born in Edgecombe County where he resided as a farmer prior to enlisting in Edgecombe County at age 25, May 24, 1861. Mustered in as Corporal. Present or accounted for until discharged on February 8, 1862, by reason of "a tumor."

HICKS, J. W., Private
Place and date of enlistment not reported. A regimental return dated May, 1862, states he died at Petersburg, Virginia. Date and cause of death not reported.

HOBBIE, JOSEPH W., Private
Resided in Edgecombe County where he enlisted at age 22, May 24, 1861. Present or accounted for until he died at Hobdy's Point, Virginia, September 18, 1861, of disease.

HOLLAND, EXUM H., Private
Born in Wayne County where he resided as a farmer prior to enlisting in Wake County at age 32, July 15, 1862, for the war. Present or accounted for until wounded in the left thigh and captured at Crampton's Pass, Maryland, September 14, 1862. Hospitalized at Burkittsville, Maryland, until transferred to Fort McHenry, Maryland, at an unspecified date. Paroled and transferred to City Point, Virginia, November 12, 1862, for exchange. Reported absent wounded until he was retired from service on December 22, 1864, by reason of disability from wounds.

HOLLAND, U., Private
Resided in Wayne County and enlisted in Wake County at age 34, July 15, 1862, for the war. Present or accounted for until hospitalized at Culpeper, Virginia, September 25, 1862, with a gunshot wound; however, place and date wounded not reported. Returned to duty on or about November 27, 1862, and present or accounted for until reported absent without leave on August 9, 1863. Reported absent without leave until he was dropped from the rolls of the company on April 29, 1864.

HOLLOMAN, G., Private
Enlisted at Coosawhatchie, South Carolina, April 2, 1863, for the war as a substitute. Present or accounted for until sent to hospital at Goldsboro on May 12, 1863. No further records.

HOLLOWELL, WILLIE, Private
Previously served in Company C of this regiment. Transferred to this company on April 13, 1864. Present or accounted for until captured at Hatcher's Run, Virginia, April 2, 1865. Confined at Point Lookout, Maryland, until released on June 27, 1865, after taking the Oath of Allegiance.

HOLT, SAMUEL, Private
Resided in Wayne County and enlisted in Wake County at age 33, July 15, 1862, for the war. Present or accounted for until captured at or near Petersburg, Virginia, April 2, 1865. Confined at Point Lookout,

Maryland, until released on June 27, 1865, after taking the Oath of Allegiance.

HOOKS, W. H., Private

Born in Wayne County where he resided prior to enlisting in Wake County at age 23, July 15, 1862, for the war. Present or accounted for until captured at or near Crampton's Pass, Maryland, September 14, 1862. Confined at Fort Delaware, Delaware, until transferred to Aiken's Landing, James River, Virginia, October 2, 1862, for exchange. Declared exchanged at Aiken's Landing on November 10, 1862. Returned to duty prior to January 1, 1863, and present or accounted for until hospitalized at Richmond, Virginia, June 4, 1864, with a gunshot wound. Place and date wounded not reported. Died in hospital at Richmond on July 17, 1864, of wounds.

HOWELL, JAMES R., Private

Resided in Wayne County and enlisted in Wake County at age 29, July 15, 1862, for the war. Present or accounted for until captured at or near Petersburg, Virginia, April 2, 1865. Confined at Point Lookout, Maryland, until released on June 27, 1865, after taking the Oath of Allegiance.

HUSSEY, MARCELLUS L., Corporal

Resided in Edgecombe County where he enlisted at age 20, May 24, 1861. Mustered in as Private and promoted to Corporal in September, 1861-December, 1862. Reduced to ranks on January 1, 1863, but was promoted to Corporal on October 25, 1864. Present or accounted for until paroled at Appomattox Court House, Virginia, April 9, 1865.

JARRELL, ADAM, Private

Previously served in Company C of this regiment. Transferred to this company on April 13, 1864. Present or accounted for until wounded in the right arm at Wilderness, Virginia, May 5, 1864. Discharged on October 14, 1864, by reason of wounds.

JENKINS, JOSEPH V., Private

Resided in Edgecombe County where he enlisted at age 20, May 27, 1861. Present or accounted for until he died on October 7, 1861, of disease. Place of death not reported.

JOHNSON, GEORGE D. W., Corporal

Born in Edgecombe County where he resided prior to enlisting in Edgecombe County at age 20, May 27, 1861. Mustered in as Private and promoted to Corporal in May-September, 1864. Present or accounted for until wounded "in [the] trenches" near Petersburg, Virginia, September 5, 1864. Died in a field hospital on September 6, 1864.

JOHNSON, JAMES M., 1st Sergeant

Born in Edgecombe County where he resided as a farmer prior to enlisting in Edgecombe County at age 19, July 19, 1861. Mustered in as Private. Present or accounted for until wounded in the breast at Malvern Hill, Virginia, July 1, 1862. Promoted to Sergeant on July 20, 1862. Returned to duty prior to September 14, 1862, when he was wounded in the leg and captured at Crampton's Pass, Maryland. Hospitalized at Burkittsville, Maryland, until transferred to Fort McHenry, Maryland, at an unspecified date. Paroled and transferred to Aiken's Landing, James River, Virginia, November 6, 1862. Declared exchanged at Aiken's

Landing on November 10, 1862. Returned to duty prior to December 13, 1862, when he was wounded in the leg at Fredericksburg, Virginia. Returned to duty prior to December 13, 1862, when he was wounded in the leg at Fredericksburg, Virginia. Returned to duty in July-August, 1863, and was promoted to 1st Sergeant in January-February, 1864. Present or accounted for until paroled at Appomattox Court House, Virginia, April 9, 1865.

JOHNSON, WILLIE, Private

Born in Edgecombe County where he resided prior to enlisting at Petersburg, Virginia, at age 49, January 15, 1863, for the war as a substitute for Sergeant Henry LaFayette Leggett. Present or accounted for until captured at Bristoe Station, Virginia, October 14, 1863. Confined at Old Capitol Prison, Washington, D.C., until transferred to Point Lookout, Maryland, October 27, 1863. Died at Point Lookout on November 15, 1863, of disease.

JORDAN, WILLIAM B., Private

Resided in Edgecombe County where he enlisted at age 24, May 24, 1861. Mustered in as Corporal but was reduced to ranks on December 27, 1861. Present or accounted for until discharged on June 15, 1862. Reason discharged not reported.

KENNEDY, ELIAS J., Private

Resided in Wayne County and enlisted in Wake County at age 29, July 15, 1862, for the war. Present or accounted for until captured at Hatcher's Run, Virginia, April 2, 1865. Confined at Point Lookout, Maryland, until released on June 28, 1865, after taking the Oath of Allegiance.

LANCASTER, JOSHUA, Private

Resided in Wayne County and enlisted in Wake County at age 22, July 15, 1862, for the war. Present or accounted for until transferred to Company D, 8th Battalion N.C. Partisan Rangers, June 7, 1863.

LANCASTER, LEVI, Private

Resided in Wayne County and enlisted in Wake County at age 20, July 15, 1862, for the war. Present or accounted for until transferred to Company D, 8th Battalion N.C. Partisan Rangers, June 7, 1863.

LANDMAN, JAMES, Private

Resided in Edgecombe County and was by occupation a farmer prior to enlisting in Edgecombe County at age 22, June 4, 1861. Present or accounted for until killed at Malvern Hill, Virginia, July 1, 1862.

LANGSTON, DANIEL, Private

Previously served in Company D, 8th Battalion N.C. Partisan Rangers. Transferred to this company on June 5, 1863. Present or accounted for until he deserted to the enemy on or about April 4, 1865. Released on or about April 6, 1865, after taking the Oath of Allegiance.

LANGSTON, WILLIAM, Private

Resided in Wayne County and enlisted in Wake County at age 21, July 15, 1862, for the war. Present or accounted for until wounded in the thigh and captured in Maryland in September-October, 1862. Hospitalized at Burkittsville, Maryland, until transferred to Fort McHenry, Maryland, at an unspecified date. Paroled on November 6, 1862, and transferred for exchange. Declared exchanged at Aiken's Landing,

James River, Virginia, November 10, 1862. Reported absent without leave from December 19, 1862, until he died in camp near Fredericksburg, Virginia, August 21, 1863, of disease.

LATHAM, GEORGE A., Private
Resided in Northampton or Washington counties and enlisted in Edgecombe County at age 26, May 24, 1861. Present or accounted for until transferred to 1st Company H, 40th Regiment N.C. Troops (3rd Regiment N.C. Artillery), May 23, 1862.

LAWRENCE, BENJAMIN J., Private
Resided in Edgecombe County where he enlisted at age 21, May 27, 1861. Present or accounted for until he died on April 28, 1862, of disease. Place of death not reported.

LAWRENCE, NATHAN M., 1st Sergeant
Born in Edgecombe County where he resided prior to enlisting in Edgecombe County at age 20, May 24, 1861. Mustered in as Sergeant and promoted to 1st Sergeant on May 15, 1862. Present or accounted for until wounded in the arm at Malvern Hill, Virginia, July 1, 1862. Returned to duty in November-December, 1862, and present or accounted for until appointed 2nd Lieutenant and transferred to Company C, 8th Regiment N.C. State Troops, March 28, 1863.

LAWRENCE, WILLIAM J., Private
Resided in Edgecombe County where he enlisted at age 27, May 27, 1861. Present or accounted for until he was dropped from the rolls on or about October 30, 1863. Company records indicate that he may have been promoted to Hospital Steward and transferred to hospital duty.

LEGGETT, HENRY LaFAYETTE, Sergeant
Resided in Edgecombe County where he enlisted at age 27, May 27, 1861. Mustered in as Private and promoted to Sergeant in September, 1861-December, 1862. Present or accounted for until wounded in the shoulder at Fredericksburg, Virginia, December 13, 1862. Discharged on January 15, 1863, after providing Private Willie Johnson as a substitute.

LEIGH, WILLIAM R., Private
Resided in Edgecombe County and was by occupation a farmer prior to enlisting in Edgecombe County at age 22, June 4, 1861. Present or accounted for until discharged on September 12, 1862, by reason of disability.

LEWIS, EXUM, Private
Resided in Edgecombe County where he enlisted at age 23, May 24, 1861. Mustered in as Sergeant but was reduced to ranks on May 15, 1862. Present or accounted for until promoted to Sergeant Major on July 6, 1862, and transferred to the Field and Staff of this regiment. Reduced to ranks on January 1, 1863, and transferred back to this company. Present or accounted for until transferred to Company E, 43rd Regiment N.C. Troops, October 29, 1863.

LEWIS, JOEL BATTLE, Private
Resided in Edgecombe County where he enlisted at age 31, May 24, 1861. Detailed as Assistant Surgeon of this regiment from August 29 until December 29, 1861. Present or accounted for until captured at or near Crampton's Pass, Maryland, September 14, 1862.

Confined at Fort Delaware, Delaware, until transferred to Aiken's Landing, James River, Virginia, October 2, 1862, for exchange. Declared exchanged at Aiken's Landing on November 10, 1862. Returned to duty prior to January 1, 1863, and was transferred to the 43rd Regiment N.C. Troops, January 29, 1863, upon appointment as Assistant Surgeon.

LIPSCOMBE, WILLIAM A., Corporal
Resided in Edgecombe County where he enlisted at age 27, May 24, 1861. Mustered in as Private and promoted to Corporal on January 15, 1863. Present or accounted for until hospitalized at Petersburg, Virginia, October 12, 1864, with a gunshot wound of the left arm; however, place and date wounded not reported. Furloughed for sixty days on November 6, 1864. Paroled at Appomattox Court House, Virginia, April 9, 1865.

LITTLE, GEORGE A., Private
Resided in Edgecombe County where he enlisted at age 32, May 27, 1861. Present or accounted for until wounded in the leg at Fredericksburg, Virginia, December 13, 1862. Reported absent wounded until retired to the Invalid Corps on October 25, 1864, by reason of disability from wounds.

LONG, LOVETT, Private
Resided in Edgecombe County and enlisted at Rapidan, Virginia, at age 57, September 1, 1862, for the war as a substitute. Present or accounted for until wounded in the back and captured at Crampton's Pass, Maryland, September 14, 1862. Hospitalized at Burkittsville, Maryland, until transferred to Fort McHenry, Maryland, at an unspecified date. Paroled and transferred to City Point, Virginia, where he was received November 21, 1862, for exchange. Returned to duty in January-February, 1863, and present or accounted for until he died in hospital at Hardeeville, South Carolina, March 16, 1863, of disease.

MAYO, BENJAMIN B., Private
Resided in Edgecombe County where he enlisted at age 25, May 24, 1861. Present or accounted for until killed at Fredericksburg, Virginia, December 13, 1862.

MAYO, BERRY, Private
Resided in Edgecombe County where he enlisted at age 21, May 24, 1861. Present or accounted for until he died at Warwick Court House, Virginia, August 10, 1861, of disease.

MOORE, WILLIAM A., Musician
Resided in Edgecombe County where he enlisted at age 27, May 24, 1861. Mustered in as Musician (Drummer). Present or accounted for through October, 1864; however, he was reported absent sick during much of that period.

MORRIS, HARRY C., Private
Resided in Edgecombe County and enlisted at Yorktown, Virginia, at age 25, September 30, 1861. Present or accounted for until he was dropped from the rolls of the company on October 30, 1863. Company records indicate that he may have been appointed Hospital Steward and transferred to hospital duty.

MYERS, JOSEPH D., Private
Resided in Washington County and enlisted in Edgecombe County at age 26, June 4, 1861. Present or accounted for until discharged on November 19, 1861, by reason of disability.

NEWSOM, JOSIAH, Private
Resided in Wayne County and enlisted in Wake County at age 33, July 15, 1862, for the war. Reported absent sick or absent without leave from November-December, 1862, until he returned to duty on June 8, 1863. Present or accounted for until he died in hospital at Gordonsville, Virginia, March 30, 1864, of "pneumonia."

NEWSOME, BENJAMIN S., Private
Resided in Wayne County and enlisted in Wake County at age 27, July 15, 1862, for the war. Present or accounted for until reported absent without leave on March 1, 1864. Returned to duty on or about November 10, 1864, when he was "sent to hospital." North Carolina pension records indicate that he survived the war.

NICHOLS, D., Private
Born in Pitt County and resided in Wayne County prior to enlisting in Wake County at age 23, July 15, 1862, for the war. Present or accounted for until killed at Fredericksburg, Virginia, December 13, 1862.

OVERMAN, ELIJAH J., Private
Resided in Wayne County and enlisted in Wake County at age 24, July 15, 1862, for the war. Present or accounted for until captured at Crampton's Pass, Maryland, September 14, 1862. Confined at Fort Delaware, Delaware, until transferred to Aiken's Landing, James River, Virginia, October 2, 1862, for exchange. Declared exchanged at Aiken's Landing on November 10, 1862. Returned to duty in January-February, 1863, and present or accounted for until March 2, 1865, when he was furloughed for sixty days.

OVERMAN, WILLIAM T., Private
Previously served in Company D, 8th Battalion N.C. Partisan Rangers. Transferred to this company on June 7, 1863. Present or accounted for until wounded at Bristoe Station, Virginia, October 14, 1863. Died in hospital at Richmond, Virginia, October 21, 1863, of "erysipelas."

PARKER, JAMES H., Private
Resided in Edgecombe County where he enlisted at age 18, June 19, 1861. Present or accounted for until killed at Lee's Mill, Virginia, April 16, 1862.

PARKS, AMAZIAH, Private
Resided in Wayne County and enlisted in Wake County at age 28, July 15, 1862, for the war. Present or accounted for until captured at Crampton's Pass, Maryland, September 14, 1862. Company records do not indicate whether he returned to duty; however, he was transferred to Company K, 27th Regiment N.C. Troops, February 10, 1863, in exchange for Private David Peacock.

PARRISH, JORDAN G., Private
Previously served in Company C of this regiment. Transferred to this company on April 13, 1864. Present or accounted for until he deserted to the enemy on or about February 26, 1865. Released on or about March 1, 1865, after taking the Oath of Allegiance.

PATE, HENRY, Private
Resided in Wayne County and enlisted in Wake County at age 29, July 15, 1862, for the war. Present or accounted for until hospitalized at Charlottesville, Virginia, September 25, 1862, with a gunshot wound;

however, place and date wounded not reported. Returned to duty in January-February, 1863, and present or accounted for until paroled at Appomattox Court House, Virginia, April 9, 1865.

PEACOCK, DAVID, Private
Previously served in Company K, 27th Regiment N.C. Troops. Transferred to this company on or about February 10, 1863, in exchange for Private Amaziah Parks. Present or accounted for until wounded at Bristoe Station, Virginia, October 14, 1863. Returned to duty in March-April, 1864, and present or accounted for until paroled at Appomattox Court House, Virginia, April 9, 1865.

PILKINTON, JAMES H., Private
Resided in Wayne County and enlisted in Wake County at age 25, July 15, 1862, for the war. Present or accounted for until wounded at Reams' Station, Virginia, August 25, 1864. Returned to duty at an unspecified date and was captured at Sutherland's Station, Virginia, on or about April 3, 1865. Confined at Point Lookout, Maryland, until released on June 16, 1865, after taking the Oath of Allegiance.

PIPPIN, JOHN W., Private
Resided in Edgecombe County where he enlisted at age 33, May 24, 1861. Present or accounted for until captured at or near Crampton's Pass, Maryland, September 14, 1862. Confined at Fort Delaware, Delaware, until transferred to Aiken's Landing, James River, Virginia, October 2, 1862, for exchange. Declared exchanged at Aiken's Landing on November 10, 1862. Discharged on February 28, 1863, after providing Private Andrew J. Allen as a substitute.

PITT, MARK BENNETT, Private
Resided in Edgecombe County where he enlisted at age 22, May 24, 1861. Present or accounted for until appointed 2nd Lieutenant and transferred to 2nd Company I, 7th Regiment Confederate Cavalry, September 4, 1862.

PITTMAN, REDDIN G., Private
Resided in Edgecombe County where he enlisted at age 21, May 24, 1861. Present or accounted for until discharged on August 19, 1862, by "the Secretary of War."

PORTER, JOSEPH E., Corporal
Resided in Edgecombe County where he enlisted at age 17, June 19, 1861. Mustered in as Private and promoted to Corporal in September, 1861-December, 1862. Present or accounted for until promoted to Sergeant Major on January 1, 1863, and transferred to the Field and Staff of this regiment.

PRICE, WILLIE, Private
Resided in Edgecombe County where he enlisted at age 22, May 27, 1861. Present or accounted for until reported absent without leave on August 19, 1863. Reported absent without leave until he died in Edgecombe County on February 13, 1864, of disease.

RAPER, JOHN W., Private
Resided in Wayne County and enlisted at Richmond, Virginia, at age 16, August 2, 1862, for the war as a substitute. Present or accounted for until wounded in the foot at or near Petersburg, Virginia, on or about August 19, 1864. Reported absent wounded through November 6, 1864. Reported absent without leave on

March 11, 1865. North Carolina pension records indicate that he "became deaf a year after [the] war from cannon and gun noise."

RICKS, BURTON A., Private
Resided in Edgecombe County where he enlisted at age 34, May 24, 1861. Present or accounted for until discharged on June 6, 1862, by reason of being over age.

RICKS, JAMES W., Private
Resided in Edgecombe County where he enlisted at age 27, May 27, 1861. Present or accounted for until he died in hospital at Richmond, Virginia, April 16, 1862, of "erysipelas."

RICKS, JETHRO D., Private
Born in Edgecombe County where he resided as a farmer prior to enlisting in Edgecombe County at age 22, May 24, 1861. Present or accounted for until discharged on January 29, 1862, by reason of "chronic rheumatism."

RICKS, ROBERT F., Corporal
Resided in Edgecombe County where he enlisted at age 18, May 24, 1861. Mustered in as Private. Present or accounted for until wounded in the breast at Fredericksburg, Virginia, December 13, 1862. Returned to duty prior to January 1, 1863, and was promoted to Corporal on December 15, 1863. Present or accounted for until hospitalized at Charlottesville, Virginia, May 10, 1864, with a gunshot wound of the head; however, place and date wounded not reported. Returned to duty on May 11, 1864, and present or accounted for until wounded at or near Petersburg, Virginia, June 15, 1864. Reported absent wounded through October, 1864. Paroled at Appomattox Court House, Virginia, April 9, 1865.

ROCHESTER, WILLIAM, Private
Resided in Edgecombe County where he enlisted at age 30, May 27, 1861. Present or accounted for until captured at the Appomattox River, Virginia, April 3, 1865. Confined at Point Lookout, Maryland, until released on June 17, 1865, after taking the Oath of Allegiance.

ROSE, TIMOTHY, Private
Resided in Edgecombe County and enlisted at Richmond, Virginia, at age 37, July 29, 1862, for the war as a substitute. Present or accounted for until wounded in the foot at Bristoe Station, Virginia, October 14, 1863. Reported absent wounded until furloughed for sixty days on March 16, 1865.

SESSUMS, WILSON, Private
Resided in Edgecombe County where he enlisted at age 17, May 27, 1861. Present or accounted for until discharged on November 1, 1861, by reason of disability.

SHARPE, EDWARD P., Private
Resided in Edgecombe County where he enlisted at age 19, May 24, 1861. Present or accounted for until discharged on November 27, 1862, after providing Private Owen Sumlin as a substitute.

SMITH, JOHN M., 1st Sergeant
Place and date of enlistment and promotion record not reported. Captured at Jonesboro, Georgia, September 2, 1864, and was sent to Louisville, Kentucky. Transferred to Camp Douglas, Chicago, Illinois, where

he arrived November 26, 1864. Discharged June 17, 1865.

STATON, FERNANDO B., Private
Resided in Edgecombe County where he enlisted at age 22, May 27, 1861. Present or accounted for until discharged on August 10, 1862, after providing a substitute.

STATON, GEORGE H., Private
Resided in Edgecombe County where he enlisted at age 29, May 24, 1861. Present or accounted for until paroled at Appomattox Court House, Virginia, April 9, 1865.

STATON, SIMMONS B., Sergeant
Resided in Edgecombe County where he enlisted at age 20, May 24, 1861. Mustered in as Private. Present or accounted for until captured at or near Crampton's Pass, Maryland, September 14, 1862. Confined at Fort Delaware, Delaware, until transferred to Aiken's Landing, James River, Virginia, October 2, 1862, for exchange. Declared exchanged at Aiken's Landing on November 10, 1862. Returned to duty in January-February, 1863, and was promoted to Corporal on January 1, 1863. Promoted to Sergeant on February 15, 1864. Present or accounted for until paroled at Appomattox Court House, Virginia, April 9, 1865.

SUGG, JOSEPH P., Private
Resided in Edgecombe County where he enlisted at age 19, May 24, 1861. Mustered in as Private. Present or accounted for until appointed Hospital Steward on May 5, 1863, and transferred to the Field and Staff of this regiment.

SUMLIN, OWEN, Private
Resided in Edgecombe County and enlisted at Fredericksburg, Virginia, at age 54, November 27, 1862, for the war as a substitute for Private Edward P. Sharpe. Present or accounted for until wounded in the head at Fredericksburg, Virginia, December 13, 1862. Reported absent wounded until retired to the Invalid Corps on September 22, 1864, because he was "totally disqualified."

TAYLOR, ALLEN F., Private
Resided in Edgecombe County where he enlisted at age 17, May 24, 1861. Present or accounted for until wounded in the breast at Malvern Hill, Virginia, July 1, 1862. Returned to duty prior to December 13, 1862, when he was wounded in the head and/or hand at Fredericksburg, Virginia. Returned to duty in March-April, 1863, and present or accounted for until wounded at Bristoe Station, Virginia, October 14, 1863. Returned to duty in January-February, 1864, and present or accounted for until wounded in the right thigh on September 5, 1864. Battle in which wounded not reported. Reported absent wounded through October, 1864. Captured in hospital at Richmond, Virginia, April 3, 1865, and was paroled on June 6, 1865.

THOMAS, ALEXANDER J., Private
Resided in Edgecombe County where he enlisted at age 27, May 24, 1861. Present or accounted for until he died in hospital at Richmond, Virginia, October 19, 1862, of "valvular disease of heart."

TUNNELL, MARCILLON L., Private
Resided in Edgecombe County where he enlisted at age

18, May 24, 1861. Present or accounted for until discharged on September 1, 1862, after providing a substitute.

WADDELL, ALFRED V., Private
Resided in Wayne County and enlisted in Wake County at age 27, July 15, 1862, for the war. Present or accounted for until captured at Hatcher's Run, Virginia, April 2, 1865. Confined at Point Lookout, Maryland, until released on June 21, 1865, after taking the Oath of Allegiance.

WADDELL, LARRY, Private
Born in Wayne County and resided in Wake County where he enlisted at age 25, July 15, 1862, for the war. Present or accounted for until wounded in the side at Fredericksburg, Virginia, December 13, 1862. Returned to duty prior to January 1, 1863, and present or accounted for until killed at or near Globe Tavern, Virginia, August 21, 1864.

WARD, JOSEPH L., Private
Resided in Edgecombe County where he enlisted at age 22, May 24, 1861. Present or accounted for until discharged on September 4, 1861, by reason of disability.

WEBB, DAVID MONROE, Private
Born in Wayne County where he resided prior to enlisting in Wake County at age 23, July 15, 1862, for the war. Present or accounted for through June, 1864; however, he was reported absent sick during most of that period. Died on July 25, 1864, of disease. Place of death not reported.

WHITAKER, MARTIN, Private
Previously served in Company C of this regiment. Transferred to this company on April 13, 1864. Present or accounted for until captured at Hatcher's Run, Virginia, April 2, 1865. Confined at Point Lookout, Maryland, where he died on June 27, 1865, of "measles."

WHITE, JOHN W., Sergeant
Resided in Halifax County and enlisted in Edgecombe County at age 19, June 4, 1861. Mustered in as Private and promoted to Corporal in September, 1861-December, 1862. Present or accounted for until wounded in the neck at Fredericksburg, Virginia, December 13, 1862. Returned to duty prior to January 1, 1863, and was promoted to Sergeant on April 1, 1863. Present or accounted for through October, 1864. Paroled May 2, 1865.

WIGGS, WILLIAM R., Private
Enlisted at Camp Holmes on October 18, 1864, for the war. Present or accounted for through October, 1864.

WILLIAMS, DONALD, Private
Resided in Edgecombe County where he enlisted at age 24, May 24, 1861. Mustered in as Corporal but was reduced to ranks on October 10, 1861. Present or accounted for until appointed Assistant Surgeon on June 1, 1864, to rank from December 11, 1863, and transferred to the Field and Staff of this regiment.

WILLIAMS, JOHN H., Private
Resided in Edgecombe County and was by occupation a farmer prior to enlisting in Edgecombe County at age 24, May 24, 1861. Present or accounted for until killed at Fredericksburg, Virginia, December 13, 1862.

WILSON, BAKER D., Sergeant
Resided in Edgecombe County where he enlisted at age 17, May 24, 1861. Mustered in as Private and promoted to Corporal on December 15, 1863. Promoted to Sergeant in May-October, 1864. Present or accounted for until captured near Petersburg, Virginia, February 5-6, 1865. Confined at Point Lookout, Maryland, until released on June 3, 1865, after taking the Oath of Allegiance.

WIMBERLY, ROBERT D., Sergeant
Resided in Edgecombe County where he enlisted at age 19, May 24, 1861. Mustered in as Private and promoted to Sergeant in September, 1861-December, 1862. Present or accounted for until wounded and captured at Crampton's Pass, Maryland, September 14, 1862. Died in the hands of the enemy; however, place and date of death not reported.

WOMACK, BENJAMIN, Private
Resided in Edgecombe County where he enlisted at age 15, May 24, 1861. Present or accounted for until discharged on August 19, 1862, by reason of being under age.

WORRELL, WILLIAM, Private
Born in Wayne County where he resided prior to enlisting in Wake County at age 24, July 15, 1862, for the war. Present or accounted for until he died in hospital at Staunton, Virginia, May 19, 1864, of wounds. Place and date wounded not reported.

YELVERTON, IVEY, Private
Resided in Wayne County and enlisted in Wake County at age 34, July 15, 1862, for the war. Present or accounted for until hospitalized at Culpeper, Virginia, September 25, 1862, with a gunshot wound; however, place and date wounded not reported. Returned to duty prior to February 1, 1863, and present or accounted for until wounded in the leg at Bristoe Station, Virginia, October 14, 1863. Died in hospital at Richmond, Virginia, October 30, 1863.

YELVERTON, JACKSON, Private
Resided in Wayne County and enlisted in Wake County at age 32, July 15, 1862, for the war. Present or accounted for until captured at or near Crampton's Pass, Maryland, September 14, 1862. Confined at Fort Delaware, Delaware, until transferred to Aiken's Landing, James River, Virginia, October 2, 1862, for exchange. Declared exchanged at Aiken's Landing on November 10, 1862. Returned to duty in January-February, 1863, and present or accounted for until he died at Hanover Academy, Virginia, August 27, 1863, of "dysentery."

COMPANY K

This company was from Edgecombe County and enlisted at Rocky Mount on April 24, 1861. It was mustered in and assigned to this regiment as Company K. After joining the regiment the company functioned as a part of the regiment, and its history for the war period is recorded as a part of the regimental history.

The information contained in the following roster of the company was compiled principally from company muster rolls for May 13-August, 1861; November, 1862-April, 1864; and September-October, 1864. No company muster rolls were found for September, 1861-October, 1862; May-August, 1864; or for the period after October, 1864. In addition to the company muster rolls, Roll of Honor records, receipt rolls, hospital records, prisoner of war records, and other primary records, supplemented by state pension applications, United Daughters of the Confederacy records, and postwar rosters and histories, all provided useful information.

OFFICERS

CAPTAINS

LEWIS, RICHARD HENRY

Appointed Captain on or about April 16, 1861. Resigned May 20, 1861, following a severe illness which resulted in partial blindness.

HAMMOND, GRAY W.

Born in Franklin County and resided in Edgecombe County where he enlisted at age 31. Appointed 2nd Lieutenant on or about April 24, 1861, and was promoted to Captain to rank from May 24, 1861. Present or accounted for until promoted to Major on February 27, 1863, and transferred to the Field and Staff of this regiment.

WHITE, GEORGE W.

Resided in Edgecombe County and was by occupation a farmer prior to enlisting in Nash County at age 24, June 12, 1861. Mustered in as Private and was appointed 2nd Lieutenant to rank from May 2, 1862. Present or accounted for until wounded at Malvern Hill, Virginia, July 1, 1862. Promoted to 1st Lieutenant on July 16, 1862. Returned to duty prior to December 13, 1862, when he was wounded in the shoulder at Fredericksburg, Virginia. Returned to duty prior to January 1, 1863, and was promoted to Captain on March 20, 1863. Present or accounted for until killed at Bristoe Station, Virginia, October 14, 1863.

CROSS, JAMES P.

Resided in Edgecombe County and was by occupation a clerk prior to enlisting in Gates County at age 27, April 24, 1861. Mustered in as Private and promoted to Corporal in January, 1862. Appointed 2nd Lieutenant to rank from May 2, 1862. Present or accounted for until wounded in the foot at Malvern Hill, Virginia, July 1, 1862. Returned to duty prior to January 1, 1863, and was promoted to 1st Lieutenant on March 14, 1863. Present or accounted for until wounded in the right thigh at Bristoe Station, Virginia, October 14, 1863. Promoted to Captain the same day. Returned to duty prior to January 1, 1864, and present or accounted for until wounded in the left leg at Reams' Station, Virginia, August 25, 1864. Left leg amputated. Died in hospital at Richmond, Virginia, September 20, 1864, of wounds.

BRASWELL, WILLIAM D.

Resided in Edgecombe County where he enlisted at age 23, April 24, 1861. Mustered in as Musician and was appointed 3rd Lieutenant to rank from December 6,

1862. Present or accounted for until wounded in the thigh at Fredericksburg, Virginia, December 16, 1862. Returned to duty prior to January 1, 1863, and was promoted to 2nd Lieutenant in March-April, 1863. Promoted to 1st Lieutenant on October 14, 1863, and was promoted to Captain on September 20, 1864. Present or accounted for through October, 1864.

LIEUTENANTS

GAY, WILLIAM T., 1st Lieutenant

Resided in Edgecombe County where he enlisted at age 28. Appointed 1st Lieutenant on April 16, 1861. Present or accounted for until he resigned on July 16, 1862, by reason of disability.

GRIFFIN, HENRY H., 2nd Lieutenant

Resided in Edgecombe County where he enlisted at age 17, July 1, 1861. Mustered in as Private. Present or accounted for until captured at or near Crampton's Pass, Maryland, September 14, 1862. Confined at Fort Delaware, Delaware, until transferred to Aiken's Landing, James River, Virginia, October 2, 1862, for exchange. Declared exchanged at Aiken's Landing on November 10, 1862. Returned to duty prior to January 1, 1863, and was promoted to Corporal in January-February, 1863. Appointed 3rd Lieutenant on May 6, 1863, and was promoted to 2nd Lieutenant on October 14, 1863. Present or accounted for until wounded in the left arm at Reams' Station, Virginia, August 25, 1864. Reported absent wounded until retired to the Invalid Corps on February 14, 1865, by reason of disability from wounds.

GRIFFIN, THOMAS H., 2nd Lieutenant

Resided in Edgecombe County where he enlisted at age 36. Appointed 2nd Lieutenant to rank from May 31, 1861. Present or accounted for until wounded at Lee's Mill, Virginia, April 16, 1862. Company records do not indicate whether he returned to duty; however, he was defeated for reelection when the regiment was reorganized on May 2, 1862.

REID, JOSEPH J., 2nd Lieutenant

Resided in Edgecombe County where he enlisted at age 23. Appointed 2nd Lieutenant to rank from May 22, 1861. Present or accounted for until wounded at Lee's Mill, Virginia, April 16, 1862. Company records do not indicate whether he returned to duty; however, he was defeated for reelection when the regiment was reorganized on May 2, 1862.

NONCOMMISSIONED OFFICERS AND PRIVATES

ARMSTRONG, BENJAMIN C. C., Private

Resided in Edgecombe County and was by occupation a farmer prior to enlisting in Edgecombe County at age 23, May 5, 1861. Present or accounted for until captured at or near Crampton's Pass, Maryland, September 14, 1862. Confined at Fort Delaware, Delaware, until transferred to Aiken's Landing, James River, Virginia, October 2, 1862, for exchange. Declared exchanged at Aiken's Landing on November 10, 1862. Returned to duty in January-February, 1863, and present or accounted for until paroled at Appomattox Court House, Virginia, April 9, 1865.

ARMSTRONG, JOLLY B., Sergeant

Resided in Edgecombe County and was by occupation a farmer prior to enlisting in Edgecombe County at age 21, April 24, 1861. Mustered in as Sergeant. Present or accounted for until wounded at Lee's Mill, Virginia, April 16, 1862. Returned to duty in January-February, 1863, and present or accounted for until wounded in the left leg at Bristoe Station, Virginia, October 14, 1863. Returned to duty on April 23, 1864, and present or accounted for until captured at the Appomattox River, Virginia, April 3, 1865. Confined at Hart's Island, New York Harbor, until released on June 21, 1865, after taking the Oath of Allegiance.

ARMSTRONG, MICAJAH E., Private

Born in Edgecombe County where he resided as a physician prior to enlisting in Edgecombe County at age 45, May 24, 1861. Present or accounted for until discharged on December 12, 1861, by reason of "general weakness, defective vision, chronic bronchitis, and a chronic papular eruption of the skin."

BARTHOLOMEW, WILLIS, Private

Born in Nash County and resided in Edgecombe County where he enlisted at age 36, February 23, 1863, for the war. Present or accounted for until wounded in the nates and foot at Wilderness, Virginia, May 5, 1864. Died in hospital at Charlottesville, Virginia, June 6, 1864, of "pyaemia."

BOON, WILLIAM, Private

Resided in Edgecombe County where he enlisted at age 39, June 1, 1861. Mustered in as Musician but was reduced to ranks in September-December, 1861. Present or accounted for until killed at Lee's Mill, Virginia, April 16, 1862.

BOWSMAN, JOHN D., Private

Resided in Edgecombe County and was by occupation a farmer prior to enlisting in Edgecombe County at age 21, May 28, 1861. Present or accounted for until paroled at Appomattox Court House, Virginia, April 9, 1865.

BRADLEY, FRANCIS M., Private

Born in Edgecombe County where he resided prior to enlisting in Edgecombe County at age 24, April 24, 1861. Present or accounted for until wounded in the knee at Fredericksburg, Virginia, December 13, 1862. Returned to duty in March-April, 1863. Present or accounted for through February 27, 1865; however, he was reported absent sick during much of that period. Discharged on February 28, 1865, by reason of "erysipelas of the left leg."

BRASWELL, RUFUS H., Private

Resided in Edgecombe County and was by occupation a farmer prior to enlisting in Edgecombe County at age 20, April 24, 1861. Mustered in as Private and promoted to Sergeant in December, 1862. Present or accounted for until wounded in the shoulder at Fredericksburg, Virginia, December 13, 1862. Returned to duty in May-June, 1863, and was reduced to ranks on April 1, 1864. Present or accounted for until paroled at Appomattox Court House, Virginia, April 9, 1865.

BROWN, WILLIAM R., Private

Born in Edgecombe County where he resided as a farmer prior to enlisting in Edgecombe County at age 17, June 1, 1861. Present or accounted for until killed at Wilderness, Virginia, May 5, 1864.

BRYAN, ISAAC R., Private

Resided in Edgecombe County where he enlisted at age 20, April 24, 1861. Present or accounted for until he deserted to the enemy on or about February 28, 1865. Released on or about March 2, 1865, after taking the Oath of Allegiance.

BULLOCK, NED, Private

Resided in Edgecombe County where he enlisted at age 18, April 24, 1861. Present or accounted for until wounded in the head at Fredericksburg, Virginia, December 13, 1862. Discharged January 28, 1863, after providing a substitute.

BULLUCK, JOHN, Private

Resided in Edgecombe County and was by occupation a farmer prior to enlisting in Edgecombe County at age 24, April 24, 1861. Present or accounted for until discharged on or about August 30, 1862, after providing Private John Gill as a substitute.

BUTTS, JOHN W., Private

Resided in Edgecombe County where he enlisted at age 19, March 10, 1862. Present or accounted for until wounded at Lee's Mill, Virginia, April 16, 1862. Returned to duty prior to September 14, 1862, when he was wounded in the hip and captured at or near Crampton's Pass, Maryland. Paroled and transferred for exchange at an unspecified date. Died September 25, 1862, of wounds. Place of death not reported.

CLINARD, RANDAL B., Private

Resided in Davidson County and enlisted in Wake County on July 15, 1862, for the war. Present or accounted for until captured at or near Crampton's Pass, Maryland, September 14, 1862. Confined at Fort Delaware, Delaware, until transferred to Aiken's Landing, James River, Virginia, October 2, 1862, for exchange. Declared exchanged at Aiken's Landing on November 10, 1862. Returned to duty prior to January 1, 1863, and present or accounted for until captured at Hatcher's Run, Virginia, April 2, 1865. Confined at Hart's Island, New York Harbor, until released on June 17, 1865, after taking the Oath of Allegiance.

COGGINS, JOSEPH J., Corporal

Resided in Edgecombe County where he enlisted at age 28, June 12, 1861. Mustered in as Private and promoted to Corporal in May, 1862. Present or accounted for until wounded in the head and thigh at Fredericksburg, Virginia, December 13, 1862. Died in hospital at Richmond, Virginia, December 18, 1862, of wounds.

DAVIS, JOHN S., Private

Resided in Edgecombe County and enlisted at age 18, March 10, 1862. Present or accounted for until discharged on June 11, 1862, by reason of disability.

DAWS, HILLIARD, Private

Resided in Edgecombe County where he enlisted at age 23, April 24, 1861. Present or accounted for until wounded at Lee's Mill, Virginia, April 16, 1862. Returned to duty on May 11, 1863, and present or accounted for through October, 1864.

DAWS, SIAH O., Private

Resided in Edgecombe County where he enlisted at age 19, June 24, 1861. Present or accounted for until wounded in the hips and right arm and captured at or near Crampton's Pass, Maryland, September 14, 1862. Hospitalized at Burkittsville, Maryland, until transferred to Fort McHenry, Maryland, at an unspecified date. Paroled and transferred to City Point, Virginia, where he was received December 4, 1862, for exchange. Returned to duty in March-April, 1863, and present or accounted for until paroled at Appomattox Court House, Virginia, April 9, 1865.

DAWS, WILLIAM, Private
Place and date of enlistment not reported. Paroled at Appomattox Court House, Virginia, April 9, 1865.

DILLIARD, EDWARD, Private
Born in Edgecombe County where he resided prior to enlisting in Edgecombe County at age 19, May 7, 1861. Present or accounted for until paroled at Appomattox Court House, Virginia, April 9, 1865.

DILLIARD, JAMES H., Sergeant
Resided in Edgecombe County and was by occupation a farmer prior to enlisting in Edgecombe County at age 20, May 2, 1861. Mustered in as Private and promoted to Corporal in May, 1862. Promoted to Sergeant in December, 1862. Present or accounted for until paroled at Appomattox Court House, Virginia, April 9, 1865.

DILLIARD, JOHN, Corporal
Born in Edgecombe County where he resided as a farmer prior to enlisting in Edgecombe County at age 26, April 24, 1861. Mustered in as Corporal. Present or accounted for until wounded in the head at Lee's Mill, Virginia, April 16, 1862. Reported absent wounded until discharged on September 12, 1862, by reason of "fracture of the cranium with removal of bone rendering him unable to endure the heat of the sun."

DILLIARD, LEVI, Private
Resided in Edgecombe County and was by occupation a farmer prior to enlisting in Edgecombe County at age 22, April 24, 1861. Present or accounted for until paroled at Appomattox Court House, Virginia, April 9, 1865.

DOUGHTY, W. J., Private
Resided in Edgecombe County and enlisted in Duplin County at age 24, May 1, 1861. Present or accounted for until discharged on September 17, 1861, by reason of disability.

EDWARDS, DORSEY, Private
Resided in Edgecombe County and enlisted at age 18, March 10, 1862. Present or accounted for until he died on August 2, 1862, of disease. Place of death not reported.

EDWARDS, MOSES, Private
Resided in Edgecombe County where he enlisted at age 32, March 10, 1862. Present or accounted for until he died in hospital at Richmond, Virginia, May 11, 1862, of "bronchitis."

ELLIOTT, D. W., Private
Resided in Edgecombe County and enlisted in Guilford County at age 33, June 8, 1861. Present or accounted for until discharged on August 14, 1862, under the provisions of the Conscript Act.

ETHRIDGE, CALVIN, Private
Resided in Edgecombe County and enlisted in Nash County at age 17, May 12, 1861. Present or accounted for until he died on August 12, 1861, of disease. Place of death not reported.

EVERHART, EMANUEL, Private
Resided in Davidson County and enlisted in Wake County at age 37, July 15, 1862, for the war. Present or accounted for until he died at Brandy Station, Virginia, November 1, 1863, of disease.

FISHER, WILLIAM HENRY, Private
Resided in Edgecombe County and enlisted in Nash County at age 22, April 24, 1861. Present or accounted for until wounded at Wilderness, Virginia, May 5, 1864. Reported absent wounded through October, 1864.

FISHER, WILLIS CHRISTOPHER, Sergeant
Resided in Edgecombe County and enlisted in Nash County at age 24, April 24, 1861. Mustered in as Private and promoted to Corporal in May, 1862. Present or accounted for until wounded in the shoulder and head at Sharpsburg, Maryland, September 17, 1862. Returned to duty in January-February, 1863, and was promoted to Sergeant in July, 1863. Present or accounted for until wounded in the left elbow at Wilderness, Virginia, on or about May 5, 1864. Returned to duty prior to November 1, 1864, and was paroled at Appomattox Court House, Virginia, April 9, 1865.

FLANNEGAN, C., Private
Resided in Edgecombe County. Place and date of enlistment not reported. Paroled at Goldsboro on May 18, 1865.

FLOOD, JERRY H., Private
Resided in Edgecombe County where he enlisted at age 17, May 12, 1861. Present or accounted for until he deserted to the enemy or was captured at Petersburg, Virginia, October 1, 1864. Confined at Point Lookout, Maryland, until released on June 26, 1865, after taking the Oath of Allegiance.

FLOOD, JESSE, Private
Born in Edgecombe County where he resided as a farmer prior to enlisting in Edgecombe County at age 29, April 24, 1861. Present or accounted for until wounded at Bristoe Station, Virginia, October 14, 1863. Reported absent wounded until retired to the Invalid Corps on August 11, 1864.

FREEDLE, WILLIAM F., Private
Enlisted in Wake County on December 15, 1863, for the war. Present or accounted for until wounded at Wilderness, Virginia, May 5, 1864. Reported absent wounded through October, 1864. Paroled at Greensboro on May 8, 1865.

FREEMAN, J. H., Private
Resided in Edgecombe County where he enlisted at age 33, July 9, 1861. Present or accounted for until wounded at Lee's Mill, Virginia, April 16, 1862. Company records do not indicate whether he returned to duty; however, he was discharged on August 14, 1862, under the provisions of the Conscript Act.

GARDNER, JAMES W., Private
Resided in Edgecombe County and was by occupation a farmer prior to enlisting in Edgecombe County at age 23, April 24, 1861. Mustered in as Private and promoted to Sergeant in May, 1862. Present or

accounted for until wounded in the right foot and captured at Crampton's Pass, Maryland, September 14, 1862. Hospitalized at Burkittsville, Maryland, and at Baltimore, Maryland, until transferred to Fort McHenry, Maryland, at an unspecified date. Paroled and transferred to City Point, Virginia, where he was received November 21, 1862, for exchange. Reduced to ranks in July-August, 1863, and was reported absent wounded until he was detailed for light duty on October 27, 1863. Reported absent on detail through October, 1864.

GARVEY, WILLIAM F., Private
Resided in Edgecombe County where he enlisted at age 24, March 10, 1862. Present or accounted for until wounded in the arm at Fredericksburg, Virginia, December 13, 1862. Returned to duty in March-April, 1863, and present or accounted for through October, 1864.

GAY, BENNETT, Private
Resided in Edgecombe County where he enlisted at age 41, May 30, 1862, for the war as a substitute. Present or accounted for until captured at or near Crampton's Pass, Maryland, September 14, 1862. Confined at Fort Delaware, Delaware, until transferred to Aiken's Landing, James River, Virginia, October 2, 1862, for exchange. Declared exchanged at Aiken's Landing on November 10, 1862. Returned to duty prior to January 1, 1863, and present or accounted for until captured at Hatcher's Run, Virginia, April 2, 1865. Confined at Hart's Island, New York Harbor, until released on June 17, 1865, after taking the Oath of Allegiance.

GAY, W. H., Private
Resided in Edgecombe County and enlisted in Nash County at age 26, April 24, 1861. Present or accounted for until discharged on July 6, 1861, by reason of disability.

GILL, _____, Private
Enlisted in Edgecombe County on June 30, 1862, for the war. Present or accounted for until wounded at Fredericksburg, Virginia, December 13, 1862. Reported absent wounded or absent sick through April 22, 1863. No further records.

GILL, JOHN, Private
Resided in Edgecombe County and was by occupation a laborer prior to enlisting in Wake County at age 52, on or about July 15, 1862, for the war as a substitute for Private John Bulluck. Present or accounted for until wounded at Fredericksburg, Virginia, December 13, 1862. Discharged on April 23, 1863, by reason of disability from wounds and/or "double hernia."

GILLIAM, JOHN A., Private
Enlisted in Davidson County on July 15, 1862, for the war. Present or accounted for until wounded in the leg and captured at Sharpsburg, Maryland, September 17, 1862. Leg amputated. Hospitalized at Burkittsville, Maryland. "For a few days he seemed to improve under the use of tonics and stimulaters [sic] but soon got worse & died Oct[ober] 12 . . . having been delirious for the last week."

GOBLE, J. ALEXANDER, Private
Resided in Davidson County and enlisted in Wake County on July 15, 1862, for the war. Present or accounted for until captured at or near Crampton's

Pass, Maryland, on or about September 14, 1862. Confined at Fort Delaware, Delaware, until transferred to Aiken's Landing, James River, Virginia, October 2, 1862, for exchange. Declared exchanged at Aiken's Landing on November 10, 1862. Reported absent without leave until he returned to duty on May 29, 1863. Present or accounted for until captured at Bristoe Station, Virginia, October 14, 1863. Confined at Old Capitol Prison, Washington, D.C., until transferred to Point Lookout, Maryland, February 3, 1864. Paroled at Point Lookout on May 3, 1864, and transferred to Aiken's Landing for exchange. Returned to duty prior to November 1, 1864. Captured at Hatcher's Run, Virginia, April 2, 1865, and confined at Hart's Island, New York Harbor, until released on June 19, 1865, after taking the Oath of Allegiance.

GRIFFIN, BENJAMIN W., Private
Resided in Edgecombe County and was by occupation a carpenter prior to enlisting in Edgecombe County at age 21, April 24, 1861. Present or accounted for until wounded in the foot at Malvern Hill, Virginia, July 1, 1862. Returned to duty in March-April, 1863, and present or accounted for until paroled at Appomattox Court House, Virginia, April 9, 1865.

GRIFFIN, JAMES C., Private
Resided in Edgecombe County where he enlisted at age 34, May 1, 1861. Present or accounted for until he died on October 4, 1861, of disease. Place of death not reported.

GRIFFIN, SIMEON H., Sergeant
Born in Edgecombe County where he resided as a farmer or student prior to enlisting in Edgecombe County at age 21, April 24, 1861. Mustered in as Sergeant. Present or accounted for until wounded in the spine and/or left leg at Lee's Mill, Virginia, April 16, 1862. Reported absent wounded until discharged on October 1, 1862, by reason of "partial paralysis of the left leg."

HAINES, CHRISTIAN, Private
Resided in Davidson County and enlisted at age 26, July 15, 1862, for the war. Present or accounted for until he died at Richmond, Virginia, on or about September 5, 1862, of disease.

HARTLEY, DANIEL S., Private
Born in Davidson County where he resided as a farmer prior to enlisting in Wake County at age 26, July 15, 1862, for the war. Present or accounted for until captured at or near Crampton's Pass, Maryland, September 15, 1862. Confined at Fort Delaware, Delaware, until transferred to Aiken's Landing, James River, Virginia, October 2, 1862, for exchange. Declared exchanged at Aiken's Landing on November 10, 1862. Returned to duty prior to January 1, 1863, and present or accounted for until wounded in the left hand on the Weldon Railroad, near Petersburg, Virginia, August 21, 1864. Reported absent wounded until retired from service on March 14, 1865, by reason of disability from wounds.

HARTLEY, HYRAM H., Private
Resided in Davidson County and enlisted in Wake County at age 23, July 15, 1862, for the war. Present or accounted for until captured at or near Crampton's Pass, Maryland, September 15, 1862. Confined at Fort

Delaware, Delaware, until transferred to Aiken's Landing, James River, Virginia, October 2, 1862, for exchange. Declared exchanged at Aiken's Landing on November 10, 1862. Reported absent without leave until he returned to duty on May 29, 1863. Present or accounted for until captured at Spotsylvania Court House, Virginia, May 12, 1864. Confined at Point Lookout, Maryland, until transferred to Elmira, New York, August 8, 1864. Paroled at Elmira on February 13, 1865, and transferred to Boulware's and Cox's Wharf, James River, Virginia, for exchange. Reported present with a detachment of paroled and exchanged prisoners at Camp Lee, near Richmond, Virginia, February 23, 1865.

HEDRICK, ADAM, Private
Resided in Davidson County and enlisted in Wake County at age 25, July 15, 1862, for the war. Present or accounted for until captured at or near Crampton's Pass, Maryland, on or about September 15, 1862. Confined at Fort Delaware, Delaware, until transferred to Aiken's Landing, James River, Virginia, October 2, 1862, for exchange. Declared exchanged at Aiken's Landing on November 10, 1862. Returned to duty in January-February, 1863, and present or accounted for until captured at Bristoe Station, Virginia, October 14, 1863. Confined at Old Capitol Prison, Washington, D.C., until transferred to Point Lookout, Maryland, October 27, 1863. Paroled and transferred to Aiken's Landing on February 24, 1865, for exchange. Returned to duty prior to March 31, 1865, when he was captured at or near Hatcher's Run, Virginia. Confined at Point Lookout until released on June 13, 1865, after taking the Oath of Allegiance.

HEDRICK, DANIEL, Private
Resided in Davidson County and enlisted in Wake County on July 15, 1862, for the war. Present or accounted for until captured at Crampton's Pass, Maryland, September 14, 1862. Confined at Fort Delaware, Delaware, until transferred to Aiken's Landing, James River, Virginia, October 2, 1862, for exchange. Declared exchanged at Aiken's Landing on November 10, 1862. Died in hospital at Richmond, Virginia, February 10, 1863, of "variola conf[luen]t."

HEDRICK, DAVID, Private
Resided in Davidson County and enlisted in Wake County at age 24, July 15, 1862, for the war. Present or accounted for until captured at or near Crampton's Pass, Maryland, on or about September 14, 1862. Confined at Fort McHenry, Maryland, until paroled and transferred to Aiken's Landing, James River, Virginia, October 2, 1862, for exchange. Declared exchanged at Aiken's Landing on or about November 10, 1862. Returned to duty in January-February, 1863, and present or accounted for until captured at or near Hatcher's Run, Virginia, March 31, 1865. Confined at Point Lookout, Maryland, until released on June 27, 1865, after taking the Oath of Allegiance.

HEDRICK, HENRY, Private
Born in Davidson County where he resided as a farmer prior to enlisting in Wake County on July 15, 1862, for the war. Present or accounted for until captured at or near Crampton's Pass, Maryland, on or about September 14, 1862. Confined at Fort Delaware, Delaware, until transferred to Aiken's Landing, James

River, Virginia, October 2, 1862, for exchange. Declared exchanged at Aiken's Landing on November 10, 1862. Listed as a deserter until he was discharged on April 21, 1864, by reason of disability. Discharge papers give his age as 29.

HEGE, ALEXANDER J., Private
Resided in Davidson County and enlisted in Wake County on July 15, 1862, for the war. Present or accounted for until wounded in both eyes and captured at Sharpsburg, Maryland, on or about September 17, 1862. Blinded as a result of his wounds. Confined at Fort McHenry, Maryland, until paroled and transferred to Aiken's Landing, James River, Virginia, where he was received October 17, 1862, for exchange. Declared exchanged at Aiken's Landing on November 10, 1862. Reported absent wounded through October, 1864.

HENDERSON, WALTER S., Private
Resided in Edgecombe County where he enlisted at age 45, April 24, 1861. Present or accounted for until discharged on May 26, 1862, by reason of disability.

HILL, HIRAM, Private
Resided in Davidson County and enlisted in Wake County at age 25, July 15, 1862, for the war. Present or accounted for until captured at Hatcher's Run, Virginia, April 2, 1865. Confined at Hart's Island, New York Harbor, until released on June 18, 1865, after taking the Oath of Allegiance.

HILL, JACKSON, Private
Born in Davidson County where he resided as a farmer prior to enlisting in Wake County at age 20, July 15, 1862, for the war. Present or accounted for until captured at or near Crampton's Pass, Maryland, on or about September 14, 1862. Confined at Fort McHenry, Maryland, until paroled and transferred to City Point, Virginia, where he was received November 21, 1862, for exchange. Reported absent without leave until he returned to duty in March-April, 1863. Present or accounted for until wounded in the shoulder and back at Wilderness, Virginia, May 5, 1864, or near Petersburg, Virginia, August 7, 1864. Reported absent wounded until he was retired from service on February 28, 1865, by reason of disability from wounds.

HILL, JOHN D., Private
Born in Edgecombe County and resided in Davidson County where he was by occupation a farmer prior to enlisting in Edgecombe County at age 22, April 24, 1861. Present or accounted for until he died on January 17, 1863, of disease. Place of death not reported.

HILL, KELAN, Private
Resided in Davidson County and enlisted in Wake County at age 29, July 15, 1862, for the war. Present or accounted for until captured at or near Crampton's Pass, Maryland, September 14, 1862. Confined at Fort McHenry, Maryland, until paroled and transferred to City Point, Virginia, where he was received November 21, 1862, for exchange. Returned to duty in January-February, 1863, and present or accounted for until captured at Hatcher's Run, Virginia, April 2, 1865. Confined at Hart's Island, New York Harbor, until released on June 18, 1865, after taking the Oath of Allegiance.

HILLIARD, SAMUEL RUFFIN, Private
Resided in Davidson County and enlisted in Nash County at age 20, April 24, 1861. Present or accounted for until wounded in the abdomen at Lee's Mill, Virginia, April 16, 1862. Reported absent wounded or absent on detail until he returned to duty in March-April, 1863. Present or accounted for through October, 1864; however, he was reported absent on detail during most of that period. Retired to the Invalid Corps on January 6, 1865.

HINKLE, ALEX, Private
Resided in Davidson County and enlisted in Wake County at age 28, July 15, 1862, for the war. Present or accounted for until he deserted on August 20, 1862.

HINKLE, EMANUEL, Private
Born in Davidson County where he resided as a farmer prior to enlisting in Wake County at age 27, July 15, 1862, for the war. Present or accounted for until discharged on October 5, 1862, by reason of "epileptic fits for 3 weeks every night. . . ."

HINKLE, RANSOM, Private
Resided in Davidson County and enlisted in Wake County at age 25, July 15, 1862, for the war. Present or accounted for until he deserted on August 20, 1862. Returned to duty on March 9, 1863, and present or accounted for until captured at Hatcher's Run, Virginia, April 2, 1865. Confined at Hart's Island, New York Harbor, until released on June 18, 1865, after taking the Oath of Allegiance.

HINKLER, CHRISTIAN, Private
Resided in Davidson County and enlisted in Wake County at age 25, July 15, 1862, for the war. Deserted on August 20, 1862, but returned to duty April 19, 1863. Present or accounted for until captured at Hatcher's Run, Virginia, April 2, 1865. Confined at Hart's Island, New York Harbor, until released on June 18, 1865, after taking the Oath of Allegiance.

HUNEYCUT, AMBROSE, Private
Resided in Davidson County and enlisted in Wake County at age 24, July 15, 1862, for the war. Present or accounted for until wounded in the thigh and captured at Crampton's Pass, Maryland, September 14, 1862. Died in hospital at Burkittsville, Maryland, November 21, 1862.

HUNEYCUT, GEORGE H., Private
Resided in Davidson County and enlisted in Wake County on July 15, 1862, for the war. Present or accounted for until captured at Crampton's Pass, Maryland, September 14, 1862. Confined at Fort Delaware, Delaware, until transferred to Aiken's Landing, James River, Virginia, October 2, 1862, for exchange. Declared exchanged at Aiken's Landing on November 10, 1862. Reported absent without leave until he returned to duty on March 7, 1863. Present or accounted for until captured at Hatcher's Run, Virginia, April 2, 1865. Confined at Hart's Island, New York Harbor, until released on June 18, 1865, after taking the Oath of Allegiance.

HUNTER, MICHAEL, Private
Resided in Edgecombe County and enlisted in Harnett County at age 27, June 2, 1861. Present or accounted for until captured at or near Crampton's Pass, Maryland, September 14, 1862. Confined at Fort Delaware, Delaware, until transferred to Aiken's

Landing, James River, Virginia, October 2, 1862, for exchange. Declared exchanged at Aiken's Landing on November 10, 1862. Reported absent without leave until he was listed as a deserter in March-April, 1863.

HUNTER, RICHARD D., Private
Resided in Edgecombe County and enlisted in Nash County at age 28, April 24, 1861. Present or accounted for until he died April 1, 1862, of disease. Place of death not reported.

HYATT, JOHN A., Private
Resided in Davidson County and enlisted in Wake County at age 26, July 15, 1862, for the war. Present or accounted for until captured at Wilderness, Virginia, May 5, 1864. Confined at Old Capitol Prison, Washington, D.C., May 19, 1864. Died in hospital at Washington on August 11, 1864, of "diarrhoea chronic."

JACKSON, JAMES H., Private
Resided in Edgecombe County and enlisted at age 26, March 10, 1862. Present or accounted for until wounded in the side and thigh at Malvern Hill, Virginia, July 1, 1862. Died in hospital at Richmond, Virginia, July 4, 1862, of wounds.

JAMES, A. J., Private
Resided in Davidson County and enlisted in Wake County at age 18, July 15, 1862, for the war. Present or accounted for until wounded in the shoulder at Fredericksburg, Virginia, December 13, 1862. Died in hospital at Lynchburg, Virginia, January 16, 1863, of "pneumonia."

JARVIS, BRYANT, Private
Born in Davidson County where he resided prior to enlisting in Wake County on July 15, 1862, for the war. Present or accounted for until captured at or near Crampton's Pass, Maryland, September 14, 1862. Confined at Fort Delaware, Delaware, until transferred to Aiken's Landing, James River, Virginia, October 2, 1862, for exchange. Declared exchanged at Aiken's Landing on November 10, 1862. Returned to duty prior to January 1, 1863, and present or accounted for until captured at Bristoe Station, Virginia, on or about October 14, 1863. Confined at Old Capitol Prison, Washington, D.C., until transferred to Point Lookout, Maryland, October 27, 1863. Died at Point Lookout on March 17, 1864. Cause of death not reported.

JOHNSTON, CHARLES, Private
Resided in Edgecombe County where he enlisted at age 19, July 1, 1861. Present or accounted for until he died on August 30, 1861, of disease. Place of death not reported.

JONES, ALLEN, Private
Resided in Edgecombe County and was by occupation a blacksmith prior to enlisting in Nash County at age 23, April 24, 1861. Present or accounted for until hospitalized at Richmond, Virginia, February 7, 1865, with a gunshot wound of the right shoulder; however, place and date wounded not reported. Furloughed for sixty days on February 24, 1865, and was paroled at Goldsboro on May 18, 1865.

JONES, JESSE H., Private
Resided in Edgecombe County and was by occupation a clerk prior to enlisting in Nash County at age 21,

April 24, 1861. Present or accounted for until discharged on November 28, 1861, because he was "suffering from icthyosis or fish skin disease. . . ."

JONES, RICKS, Private
Resided in Edgecombe County and was by occupation a farmer prior to enlisting in Nash County at age 20, May 28, 1861. Present or accounted for until killed at Sharpsburg, Maryland, September 17, 1862.

JORDEN, CORNELIUS H., Private
Resided in Edgecombe County where he enlisted at age 23, May 12, 1861. Present or accounted for until wounded at Malvern Hill, Virginia, July 1, 1862. Returned to duty prior to December 20, 1862, and present or accounted for until captured at or near Hatcher's Run, Virginia, March 31, 1865. Confined at Point Lookout, Maryland, until released on June 28, 1865, after taking the Oath of Allegiance.

JORDEN, JAMES C., Private
Resided in Edgecombe County where he enlisted at age 18, June 27, 1861. Present or accounted for until wounded in the head at Malvern Hill, Virginia, July 1, 1862. Returned to duty prior to January 1, 1863, and present or accounted for until captured at Hatcher's Run, Virginia, on or about March 31, 1865. Confined at Point Lookout, Maryland, until released on June 28, 1865, after taking the Oath of Allegiance.

KEYES, L. S., Private
Resided in Dinwiddie County, Virginia. Place and date of enlistment not reported. Captured at Petersburg, Virginia, April 3, 1865, and confined at Hart's Island, New York Harbor, until released on June 21, 1865, after taking the Oath of Allegiance.

KIMBLE, NOAH, Private
Resided in Davidson County and enlisted at age 19, July 15, 1862, for the war. Present or accounted for until discharged on September 2, 1862, by reason of disability.

KOONTS, ABRAHAM, Private
Resided in Davidson County and enlisted in Wake County on July 15, 1862, for the war. Present or accounted for until wounded and captured at or near Crampton's Pass, Maryland, September 14, 1862. Died September 25, 1862. Place of death not reported.

KOONTS, CASPER, Private
Resided in Davidson County and enlisted in Wake County at age 32, July 15, 1862, for the war. Present or accounted for until he died in hospital at Goldsboro on February 25, 1863, of "typhoid fever."

KOONTS, DAVID, Private
Resided in Davidson County and enlisted in Wake County at age 26, July 15, 1862, for the war. Present or accounted for until reported absent without leave on July 31, 1863. Returned to duty on October 28, 1863, and present or accounted for until captured at Hatcher's Run, Virginia, April 2, 1865. Confined at Hart's Island, New York Harbor, until released June 19-20, 1865, after taking the Oath of Allegiance.

LAMBETH, LORENZO D., Private
Resided in Davidson County and enlisted in Wake County at age 23, July 15, 1862, for the war. Present or accounted for until transferred to Company K, 48th Regiment N.C. Troops, February 3, 1863.

LANDEN, WILLIAM H., Private
Born in Nash County and resided in Edgecombe County where he was by occupation a mason prior to enlisting in Edgecombe County at age 20, April 24, 1861. Present or accounted for until captured at Crampton's Pass, Maryland, September 14, 1862. Confined at Fort Delaware, Delaware, until transferred to Aiken's Landing, James River, Virginia, October 2, 1862, for exchange. Declared exchanged at Aiken's Landing on November 10, 1862. Returned to duty prior to December 13, 1862, when he was wounded in the hand and breast at Fredericksburg, Virginia. Returned to duty in January-February, 1863, and present or accounted for until wounded at Bristoe Station, Virginia, October 14, 1863. Returned to duty on January 8, 1864. Present or accounted for until hospitalized at Danville, Virginia, on or about June 4, 1864, with a gunshot wound of the leg; however, place and date wounded not reported. Reported absent on furlough through October 12, 1864.

LANNING, ROBERT, Private
Born in Davidson County where he resided as a farmer prior to enlisting in Wake County at age 28, July 15, 1862, for the war. Present or accounted for until discharged on November 20, 1862, by reason of "phthisis."

LANNING, WILLIAM, Private
Resided in Davidson County and enlisted in Wake County at age 26, July 15, 1862, for the war. Present or accounted for until he died at Charleston, South Carolina, on or about April 27, 1863, of disease.

LENEAR, EDWARD L., Private
Resided in Davidson County and enlisted in Wake County at age 22, July 15, 1862, for the war. Present or accounted for until wounded at or near Crampton's Pass, Maryland, September 14, 1862. Returned to duty on June 23, 1863, and present or accounted for until captured near Petersburg, Virginia, February 6, 1865. Confined at Point Lookout, Maryland, until released on June 28, 1865, after taking the Oath of Allegiance.

LEONARD, DANIEL, Private
Born in Davidson County* and was by occupation a farmer prior to enlisting in Wake County on December 15, 1863, for the war. Present or accounted for until discharged on January 7, 1865, by reason of "general debility, dropsy, and a gunshot wound of the right leg." Place and date wounded not reported. Discharge papers give his age as 45.

LEONARD, DAVID D., Private
Resided in Davidson County and enlisted in Wake County on July 15, 1862, for the war. Present or accounted for until captured near Petersburg, Virginia, February 6, 1865. Confined at Point Lookout, Maryland, until released on June 28, 1865, after taking the Oath of Allegiance.

LEONARD, VALENTINE, Private
Born in Davidson County where he resided as a farmer prior to enlisting in Wake County on July 15, 1862, for the war. Present or accounted for until discharged on October 5, 1862, by reason of "epilepsy—fits every night." Discharge papers give his age as 22.

LONG, BENNETT, Private
Resided in Edgecombe County and was by occupation

a farmer prior to enlisting in Edgecombe County at age 26, June 1, 1861. Present or accounted for until he died in hospital at Goldsboro on April 6, 1862, of disease.

LONG, JAMES H., Private
Resided in Edgecombe County and was by occupation a farmer prior to enlisting in Edgecombe County at age 20, June 1, 1861. Present or accounted for until he died in hospital at Charlottesville, Virginia, January 28, 1863, of "dropsy ascites."

LONG, JOSEPH, Private
Resided in Edgecombe County where he enlisted at age 18, November 14, 1862, for the war. Present or accounted for until captured at or near Cold Harbor, Virginia, June 2, 1864. Confined at Point Lookout, Maryland, until transferred to Elmira, New York, July 9, 1864. Died at Elmira on March 2, 1865, of "pneumonia."

LONG, RICHARD D., Corporal
Resided in Edgecombe County and was by occupation a farmer prior to enlisting in Edgecombe County at age 24, October 1, 1861. Mustered in as Private and promoted to Corporal in May-December, 1862. Present or accounted for until wounded in the thigh at Fredericksburg, Virginia, December 13, 1862. Returned to duty in March-April, 1863. Present or accounted for until hospitalized at Richmond, Virginia, May 7, 1864, with a gunshot wound of the left hand; however, place and date wounded not reported. Returned to duty prior to November 1, 1864, and was paroled at Appomattox Court House, Virginia, April 9, 1865.

LOOPER, JAMES, Private
Resided in Edgecombe County and was by occupation a farmer prior to enlisting in Edgecombe County at age 39, June 5, 1861. Present or accounted for until transferred to Company C, 8th Regiment N.C. State Troops, February 23, 1863, in exchange for Private Theophilus Moore.

MARTIN, HENRY, Private
Resided in Edgecombe County where he enlisted at age 19, June 7, 1861. Present or accounted for through October, 1864.

MEARES, JAMES B., Corporal
Resided in Edgecombe County and was by occupation a farmer prior to enlisting in Edgecombe County at age 17, April 24, 1861. Mustered in as Private. Present or accounted for until wounded in the leg and ankle at Malvern Hill, Virginia, July 1, 1862. Returned to duty in March-April, 1863, and present or accounted for until wounded at Bristoe Station, Virginia, October 14, 1863. Returned to duty in November-December, 1863, and was promoted to Corporal on April 1, 1864. Present or accounted for until paroled at Appomattox Court House, Virginia, April 9, 1865.

MEARES, R. D., Private
Resided in Edgecombe County where he enlisted at age 41, June 5, 1861. Roll of Honor indicates he was discharged on August 14, 1862, under the provisions of the Conscript Act; however, medical records indicate he was "bruised by [a] shell" and was hospitalized at Richmond, Virginia, August 20, 1862. No further records.

MEARES, STEPHEN B., Private
Previously served in Company E, 2nd Regiment South Carolina Infantry. Transferred to this company on April 30, 1864, and reported for duty on September 22, 1864. Present or accounted for through October, 1864.

MEARS, HIRAM, Private
Resided in Edgecombe County where he enlisted at age 17, June 1, 1861. Present or accounted for until wounded in the side at Malvern Hill, Virginia, July 1, 1862. Died at Richmond, Virginia, July 3, 1862, of wounds.

MEARS, WILLIAM, Private
Resided in Edgecombe County where he enlisted at age 17, January 30, 1863, for the war. Present or accounted for until he died in hospital at Wilmington on May 4, 1863, of "febris typh[oides]."

MEDLEY, JOHN, Private
Resided in Edgecombe County where he enlisted at age 20, May 11, 1861. Present or accounted for until he died on November 5, 1861, of disease. Place of death not reported.

MELTON, JAMES R., Private
Resided in Edgecombe County where he enlisted at age 18, May 30, 1862, for the war. Present or accounted for until he died in hospital at Richmond, Virginia, December 29, 1862, of "chronic dysentery."

MELTON, JOHN W. T., Private
Born in Edgecombe County where he resided as a farmer prior to enlisting in Edgecombe County at age 25, June 1, 1861. Present or accounted for until wounded at Lee's Mill, Virginia, April 16, 1862. Returned to duty prior to December 13, 1862, when he was wounded in the hip at Fredericksburg, Virginia. Returned to duty prior to January 1, 1863. Present or accounted for until hospitalized at Danville, Virginia, on or about May 18, 1864, with a gunshot wound of the head; however, place and date wounded not reported. Reported absent wounded or absent sick until he died "in North Carolina" on October 5, 1864, of wounds and/or disease.

MILLER, CONSTANTINE V., Private
Previously served in Company K, 48th Regiment N.C. Troops. Transferred to this company on February 3, 1863. Present or accounted for until wounded in the right foot at Bristoe Station, Virginia, October 14, 1863. Reported absent wounded until he was reported absent without leave on or about November 1, 1863. Reported as such through February, 1864. Returned to duty at an unspecified date and was discharged on or about May 11, 1864. Reason discharged not reported.

MOORE, DAVID D., Private
Resided in Edgecombe County where he enlisted at age 18, June 7, 1863, for the war. Present or accounted for until he deserted to the enemy on or about February 28, 1865. Released on or about March 2, 1865, after taking the Oath of Allegiance.

MOORE, ELIJAH J., Private
Resided in Edgecombe County and was by occupation a farmer prior to enlisting in Edgecombe County at age 26, April 24, 1861. Present or accounted for through January 6, 1865. North Carolina pension records indicate he was wounded in the left arm at Wilderness, Virginia, and was wounded in the hip near Petersburg, Virginia.

MOORE, JOSHUA L., Private

Resided in Edgecombe County and was by occupation a farmer prior to enlisting in Edgecombe County at age 20, April 24, 1861. Present or accounted for until paroled at Appomattox Court House, Virginia, April 9, 1865.

MOORE, THEOPHILUS, Private

Previously served in Company C, 8th Regiment N.C. State Troops. Transferred to this company on February 23, 1863, in exchange for Private James Looper. Present or accounted for until killed at Bristoe Station, Virginia, October 14, 1863.

MOSELEY, COFFIELD T., Private

Resided in Edgecombe County and enlisted in Nash County at age 20, May 11, 1861. Present or accounted for until paroled at Appomattox Court House, Virginia, April 9, 1865. Paroled again at Goldsboro on May 18, 1865.

NEAL, JAMES D., Private

Resided in Edgecombe County where he enlisted at age 28, April 24, 1861. Mustered in as Sergeant but was reduced to ranks on May 2, 1862. Present or accounted for through October, 1864.

PENDER, JOHN W., Private

Resided in Edgecombe County and enlisted at age 21, March 10, 1862. Present or accounted for until discharged on June 5, 1862, by reason of "phthisis pulmonalis."

PITT, JOHN W., Private

Resided in Nash or Edgecombe counties and was by occupation a farmer prior to enlisting in Nash County at age 25, April 24, 1861. Present or accounted for until transferred to Company I, 30th Regiment N.C. Troops, June 21, 1862.

PITT, MOSES B., 1st Sergeant

Resided in Edgecombe County and was by occupation a farmer prior to enlisting in Nash County at age 24, April 24, 1861. Mustered in as Corporal and was promoted to 1st Sergeant on May 2, 1862. Present or accounted for through October, 1864.

PITT, WILLIAM M., Private

Resided in Nash or Edgecombe counties and enlisted in Nash County at age 22, April 24, 1861. Present or accounted for until transferred to Company I, 30th Regiment N.C. Troops, June 21, 1862.

POLAND, H., Private

Resided in Edgecombe County and enlisted at age 32, March 10, 1861. Present or accounted for until captured at or near Crampton's Pass, Maryland, September 14, 1862. Confined at Fort Delaware, Delaware, until transferred to Aiken's Landing, James River, Virginia, October 2, 1862, for exchange. Died in hospital at Richmond, Virginia, October 22, 1862, of disease.

POWELL, IRVIN, Private

Resided in Edgecombe County where he enlisted at age 29, April 24, 1861. Present or accounted for until he died on August 5, 1861, of disease. Place of death not reported.

PRIVETT, JOHN W., Private

Resided in Edgecombe County and enlisted in Nash County at age 24, June 12, 1861. Present or accounted for until he died on September 25, 1861, of disease. Place of death not reported.

ROBBINS, ISAAC C., Private

Resided in Edgecombe County and was by occupation a farmer prior to enlisting in Edgecombe County at age 25, June 1, 1861. Present or accounted for through October, 1864. North Carolina pension records indicate he was wounded in the right thigh at Reams' Station, Virginia, August 25, 1864.

ROBBINS, STARKEY, Private

Born in Edgecombe County where he resided as a farmer prior to enlisting in Edgecombe County at age 26, June 1, 1861. Present or accounted for until confined at Castle Thunder Prison, Richmond, Virginia, June 12, 1863, for desertion. Returned to duty on August 9, 1863, and present or accounted for until captured at Hatcher's Run, Virginia, April 2, 1865. Confined at Hart's Island, New York Harbor, until released on June 17, 1865, after taking the Oath of Allegiance.

ROGERS, CHARLES W., Private

Born in King William County, Virginia, and resided in Edgecombe County where he was by occupation a harness maker prior to enlisting in Edgecombe County at age 22, April 24, 1861. Present or accounted for until discharged on February 27, 1863, by reason of "chronic rheumatism."

SCATES, THOMAS H., Private

Place and date of enlistment not reported. Hospitalized at Richmond, Virginia, May 28, 1864, with a gunshot wound of the left hand; however, place and date wounded not reported. Returned to duty on July 18, 1864. Deserted to the enemy on or about February 28, 1865, and was released on or about March 2, 1865, after taking the Oath of Allegiance.

SHELTON, JOSEPHUS, Private

Resided in Edgecombe County where he enlisted at age 21, April 24, 1861. Present or accounted for until wounded in the head at Fredericksburg, Virginia, December 13, 1862. Returned to duty in January-February, 1863, and present or accounted for through October, 1864.

SMITH, GEORGE W., Private

Resided in Edgecombe County where he enlisted at age 21, June 9, 1861. Present or accounted for until discharged on September 4, 1861, by reason of "chronic rheumatism."

SPICER, HILLIARD L., Sergeant

Resided in Edgecombe County where he enlisted at age 18, May 30, 1862, for the war. Mustered in as Private. Present or accounted for until wounded at Bristoe Station, Virginia, October 14, 1863. Returned to duty in November-December, 1863, and promoted to Corporal on January 6, 1864. Promoted to Sergeant on April 1, 1864. Present or accounted for until paroled at Appomattox Court House, Virginia, April 9, 1865.

STEWART, JAMES R., Corporal

Resided in Edgecombe County and was by occupation a farmer prior to enlisting in Edgecombe County at age 20, April 24, 1861, for one year. Mustered in as Private and promoted to Corporal in July, 1863. Present or accounted for until paroled at Appomattox Court House, Virginia, April 9, 1865.

SWICEGOOD, HENRY H., Private

Resided in Davidson County and enlisted in Wake County on July 15, 1862, for the war. Present or accounted for until captured at Crampton's Pass, Maryland, September 14, 1862. Confined at Fort Delaware, Delaware, until transferred to Aiken's Landing, James River, Virginia, October 2, 1862, for exchange. Declared exchanged at Aiken's Landing on November 10, 1862. Was listed as a deserter until he returned to duty on June 23, 1863. Present or accounted for until he deserted to the enemy or was captured at Bristoe Station, Virginia, October 14, 1863. Confined at Old Capitol Prison, Washington, D.C., until released on March 15, 1864, after taking the Oath of Amnesty.

THOMAS, GEORGE W., Private

Resided in Edgecombe County where he enlisted at age 20, April 24, 1861. Mustered in as Corporal but was reduced to ranks on May 2, 1862. Present or accounted for through October, 1864; however, he was reported absent sick during much of that period. Paroled at Appomattox Court House, Virginia, April 9, 1865.

THOMAS, REDIN W., 1st Sergeant

Resided in Edgecombe County and was by occupation a farmer prior to enlisting in Edgecombe County at age 21, April 24, 1861. Mustered in as 1st Sergeant. Present or accounted for until wounded in the neck and right shoulder at Lee's Mill, Virginia, April 16, 1862. Discharged on September 2, 1862, by reason of "loss of use of right arm from wound."

THOMAS, ROBERT W., Private

Resided in Edgecombe County where he enlisted at age 22, April 24, 1861. Present or accounted for until he died on October 11, 1862, of disease. Place of death not reported.

THOMPSON, HENRY, Private

Born in Warren County and resided in Edgecombe County prior to enlisting in Warren County at age 24, May 1, 1861. Mustered in as Private and promoted to Corporal in 1862. Present or accounted for until wounded in the foot at Sharpsburg, Maryland, September 17, 1862. Reduced to ranks in January, 1864. Reported absent wounded or absent sick until he died "at home" on January 13, 1864, of "pneumonia" and "consumption."

THOMPSON, WILLIAM, Corporal

Resided in Edgecombe County and enlisted in Warren County at age 21, April 24, 1861. Mustered in as Corporal. Present or accounted for until wounded at Lee's Mill, Virginia, April 16, 1862. Died April 17, 1862, of wounds.

TREVATHAN, WILLIAM H., Private

Resided in Edgecombe County where he enlisted at age 17, May 12, 1861. Present or accounted for until discharged on August 14, 1862, by reason of being under age.

WALKER, FRED, Private

Resided in Edgecombe County where he enlisted at age 30, April 24, 1861. Present or accounted for until killed at Malvern Hill, Virginia, July 1, 1862.

WALKER, ISAAC C., Corporal

Resided in Edgecombe County and was by occupation a farmer prior to enlisting in Edgecombe County at age

16, August 24, 1861. Mustered in as Private. Present or accounted for until wounded at Sharpsburg, Maryland, September 17, 1862. Returned to duty in January-February, 1863, and was promoted to Corporal in May, 1863. Present or accounted for until mortally wounded at Bristoe Station, Virginia, October 14, 1863. Place and date of death not reported.

WHITEHEAD, JAMES H., Private

Born in Edgecombe County where he resided prior to enlisting in Edgecombe County at age 28, May 10, 1862, for the war. Present or accounted for until captured at or near Crampton's Pass, Maryland, September 14, 1862. Confined at Fort Delaware, Delaware, until transferred to Aiken's Landing, James River, Virginia, October 2, 1862, for exchange. Declared exchanged at Aiken's Landing on November 10, 1862. Returned to duty in March-April, 1863, and present or accounted for until he died in hospital at Richmond, Virginia, July 1, 1864, of "diarrhoea."

WHITLEY, JOSEPH, Private

Resided in Edgecombe or Nash counties prior to enlisting in Edgecombe County at age 36, February 23, 1863, for the war. Present or accounted for until wounded in the head and left arm at Wilderness, Virginia, on or about May 5, 1864. Returned to duty at an unspecified date subsequent to September 1, 1864. Captured at Hatcher's Run, Virginia, April 2, 1865, and confined at Hart's Island, New York Harbor, until released on June 17, 1865, after taking the Oath of Allegiance.

WILLIAMS, GRANBERRY, Private

Resided in Edgecombe County where he enlisted at age 18, June 1, 1861. Present or accounted for until captured at Hatcher's Run, Virginia, April 2, 1865. Confined at Hart's Island, New York Harbor, until released on June 17, 1865, after taking the Oath of Allegiance.

WILLIAMS, P. J., Private

Resided in Edgecombe County where he enlisted at age 21, March 1, 1862, for the war. Present or accounted for until transferred to Company E, 10th Regiment N.C. State Troops (1st Regiment N.C. Artillery) in May, 1863.

WILLIAMS, WARREN G., Private

Previously served in Company E, 10th Regiment N.C. State Troops (1st Regiment N.C. Artillery). Transferred to this company in May, 1863. Present or accounted for until wounded at Bristoe Station, Virginia, October 14, 1863. Returned to duty in November-December, 1863, and present or accounted for until captured on the South Side Railroad on April 2, 1865. Confined at Hart's Island, New York Harbor, until released on June 17, 1865, after taking the Oath of Allegiance.

WOMBLE, JAMES R., Corporal

Born in Nash County and resided in Edgecombe County where he was by occupation a farmer prior to enlisting in Edgecombe County at age 19, April 24, 1861. Mustered in as Private. Present or accounted for until wounded in the right hand at Fredericksburg, Virginia, December 13, 1862. Returned to duty in March-April, 1863, and present or accounted for until wounded at Bristoe Station, Virginia, October 14,

1863. Returned to duty in November-December, 1863, and was promoted to Corporal in March-April, 1864. Present or accounted for until hospitalized at Charlottesville, Virginia, May 9, 1864, with a gunshot wound of the right leg; however, place and date wounded not reported. Died in hospital at Charlottesville on June 17, 1864, of wounds.

WOMBLE, W. F., Private
Resided in Edgecombe County and enlisted at age 25, March 10, 1862. Present or accounted for until mortally wounded at Malvern Hill, Virginia, July 1, 1862. Place and date of death not reported.

YOUNG, JAMES A., Private
Resided in Davidson County and enlisted in Wake County on July 15, 1862, for the war. Present or accounted for through April, 1864; however, he was reported absent sick during most of that period. Hospitalized at Danville, Virginia, May 18, 1864, with a gunshot wound of the arm; however, place and date wounded not reported. Reported absent on furlough through October, 1864.

COMPANY L

This company was from Franklin County and enlisted at Louisburg on May 20, 1861. From Louisburg it was ordered to Franklinton and afterwards to Garysburg, where it was mustered in on June 12 and assigned to this regiment as Company L. The company served with this regiment until July 4, 1862, when it was transferred to the 32nd Regiment N.C. Troops. Because it was the second company to serve as Company K of that regiment, it was designated 2nd Company K. The following roster covers only the period from original enlistment through July 4, 1862. All information after that date will be recorded in the roster of 2nd Company K, 32nd Regiment N.C. Troops.

The information contained in the following roster of the company was compiled principally from company muster rolls for June 12-August, 1861, and May-June, 1862. No company muster rolls were found for September, 1861-April, 1862, or for the period after June, 1862. In addition to the company muster rolls, Roll of Honor records, receipt rolls, hospital records, prisoner of war records, and other primary records, supplemented by state pension applications, United Daughters of the Confederacy records, and postwar rosters and histories, all provided useful information.

OFFICERS
CAPTAINS

GREEN, WILLIAM F.
Resided in Franklin County where he enlisted. Appointed Captain on May 20, 1861. Present or accounted for until promoted to Major to rank from June 11, 1861, and transferred to the Field and Staff of this regiment.

PERRY, ALGERNON S.
Resided in Franklin County where he enlisted at age 17. Appointed 2nd Lieutenant on May 20, 1861, and was promoted to Captain to rank from June 15, 1861. Present or accounted for until he was defeated for reelection when the regiment was reorganized on May 2, 1862.

YARBOROUGH, WILLIAM H.
Resided in Franklin County where he enlisted at age 21. Appointed 2nd Lieutenant to rank from May 20, 1861. Promoted to Captain on May 2, 1862, and was promoted to Major and transferred to the Field and Staff of this regiment the same day.

FOSTER, JAMES I.
Resided in Texas or in Franklin County and enlisted in Franklin County at age 21, May 20, 1861. Mustered in as Corporal and was appointed Captain to rank from May 2, 1862. Present or accounted for until transferred to 2nd Company K, 32nd Regiment N.C. Troops, July 4, 1862.

LIEUTENANTS

BALLARD, ROBERT E., 2nd Lieutenant
Resided in Franklin County where he enlisted at age 21, May 20, 1861. Mustered in as Private and was appointed 2nd Lieutenant to rank from May 2, 1862. Present or accounted for until transferred to 2nd Company K, 32nd Regiment N.C. Troops, July 4, 1862.

DAVIS, BARTLETT, 2nd Lieutenant
Resided in Franklin County where he enlisted at age 24, May 20, 1861. Mustered in as Private and was appointed 2nd Lieutenant to rank from May 2, 1862. Present or accounted for until transferred to 2nd Company K, 32nd Regiment N.C. Troops, July 4, 1862.

HARRIS, WILLIAM S., 1st Lieutenant
Resided in Franklin County where he enlisted at age 28. Appointed 3rd Lieutenant on or about May 20, 1861, and was promoted to 1st Lieutenant on June 16, 1861. Medical records indicate he died on April 20, 1862; however, company records indicate that he was defeated for reelection when the regiment was reorganized on May 2, 1862. No further records.

PEARCE, RICKS M., 2nd Lieutenant
Resided in Franklin County where he enlisted at age 22, May 20, 1861. Mustered in as Private and was appointed 2nd Lieutenant to rank from July 17, 1861. Present or accounted for until he was defeated for reelection when the regiment was reorganized on May 2, 1862.

YOUNG, WILLIAM R., 1st Lieutenant
Resided in Franklin County where he enlisted at age 28, May 20, 1861. Mustered in as Private and appointed 1st Lieutenant to rank from May 2, 1862. Present or accounted for until transferred to 2nd Company K, 32nd Regiment N.C. Troops, July 4, 1862.

NONCOMMISSIONED OFFICERS
AND PRIVATES

ALLEN, WILLIAM S., Corporal
Resided in Franklin County where he enlisted at age
19, May 20, 1861. Mustered in as Private and
promoted to Corporal in September, 1861-June, 1862.
Present or accounted for until transferred to 2nd
Company K, 32nd Regiment N.C. Troops, July 4,
1862.

ARRINGTON, BENJAMIN L., Corporal
Resided in Franklin County where he enlisted at age
33, May 20, 1861. Mustered in as Private and
promoted to Corporal in September, 1861-June, 1862.
Present or accounted for until transferred to 2nd
Company K, 32nd Regiment N.C. Troops, July 4,
1862.

ARRINGTON, WILLIAM H., Sergeant
Resided in Franklin County where he enlisted at age
25, May 20, 1861. Mustered in as Sergeant. Present or
accounted for until he was "transferred to [the]
artillery" in June, 1862; however, unit to which
transferred not reported.

AYCOCKE, JOHN C., Private
Born in Brunswick County, Virginia, and resided in
Franklin County where he was by occupation a grocer
prior to enlisting in Franklin County at age 29, May 20,
1861. Present or accounted for until transferred to 2nd
Company K, 32nd Regiment N.C. Troops, July 4,
1862.

BAKER, GEORGE S., Private
Born in Franklin County where he resided as a clerk
prior to enlisting in Franklin County at age 23, May 20,
1861. Present or accounted for until transferred to 2nd
Company K, 32nd Regiment N.C. Troops, July 4,
1862.

BAKER, MARCELLUS C., Private
Resided in Franklin County where he enlisted on May
20, 1861. Present or accounted for until transferred to
2nd Company K, 32nd Regiment N.C. Troops, July 4,
1862.

BAKER, WILLIAM G., Private
Resided in Franklin County where he enlisted at age
25, May 20, 1861. Died June 29, 1861, of disease. Place
of death not reported.

BAKER, WILLIAM M., Private
Born in Franklin County where he resided as a farmer
prior to enlisting in Franklin County at age 24, May 20,
1861. Present or accounted for until transferred to 2nd
Company K, 32nd Regiment N.C. Troops, July 4,
1862.

BARHAM, WILLIAM K., Private
Resided in Franklin County where he enlisted on May
20, 1861. Mustered in as Sergeant but was reduced to
ranks in September, 1861-June, 1862. Present or
accounted for until transferred to 2nd Company K,
32nd Regiment N.C. Troops, July 4, 1862.

BATCHELOR, NEWTON J., Private
Born in Franklin County where he resided as a
mechanic prior to enlisting in Franklin County at age
30, May 20, 1861. Present or accounted for until
transferred to 2nd Company K, 32nd Regiment N.C.
Troops, July 4, 1862.

BOLTON, WILLIAM M., Private
Resided in Mecklenburg County and enlisted in
Franklin County at age 22, May 20, 1861. Mustered in
as Corporal but was reduced to ranks in September,
1861-June, 1862. Present or accounted for until
transferred to 2nd Company K, 32nd Regiment N.C.
Troops, July 4, 1862.

BOWDEN, WILLIAM, Private
Born in Franklin County where he resided as a
mechanic prior to enlisting in Franklin County at age
34, May 20, 1861. Present or accounted for until
transferred to 2nd Company K, 32nd Regiment N.C.
Troops, July 4, 1862.

BOWDEN, WILLIS A., Private
Resided in Franklin County where he enlisted at age
28, May 20, 1861. Present or accounted for until
transferred to 2nd Company K, 32nd Regiment N.C.
Troops, July 4, 1862.

BRANCH, WASHINGTON L., Private
Resided in Franklin County where he enlisted at age
20, May 20, 1861. Present or accounted for until
transferred to 2nd Company K, 32nd Regiment N.C.
Troops, July 4, 1862.

BREEDLOVE, WILLIS M., Private
Resided in Franklin or Granville counties and enlisted
in Franklin County at age 22, May 20, 1861. Present or
accounted for until transferred to 2nd Company K,
32nd Regiment N.C. Troops, July 4, 1862.

BRIDGERS, WILLIAM B., Private
Born in Franklin County where he resided prior to
enlisting in Franklin County at age 17, May 20, 1861.
Present or accounted for until he died at Richmond,
Virginia, May 24, 1862, of disease.

BRODIE, CHARLES E., Private
Resided in Franklin County where he enlisted at age
22, May 20, 1861. Present or accounted for until
wounded at Malvern Hill, Virginia, July 1, 1862.
Transferred to 2nd Company K, 32nd Regiment N.C.
Troops, July 4, 1862.

BUNN, ARCHIBALD C., Private
Resided in Franklin County where he enlisted at age
23, May 20, 1861. Present or accounted for until he
died in August, 1861, of disease. Place of death not
reported.

CAMP, CHARLES A., Private
Born in Warren County and resided in Franklin
County where he was by occupation a student prior to
enlisting in Franklin County at age 18, May 20, 1861.
Present or accounted for until discharged in
December, 1861, by reason of "paralysis of the right
arm [following] an attack of bilious remittent fever."

CLIFTON, JOHN T., _____
Born in Franklin County and was by occupation a
druggist prior to enlisting at age 21, August, 1861.
Present or accounted for until transferred to 2nd
Company K, 32nd Regiment N.C. Troops, July 4,
1862.

COLLINS, THOMAS S., Private
Resided in Franklin County where he enlisted at age
19, May 20, 1861. Present or accounted for until
transferred to 2nd Company K, 32nd Regiment N.C.
Troops, July 4, 1862.

COLLINS, WILLIAM T., Private

Born in Franklin County where he resided as a student prior to enlisting in Franklin County at age 16, May 20, 1861. Present or accounted for until transferred to 2nd Company K, 32nd Regiment N.C. Troops, July 4, 1862.

CONN, DIXON G., 1st Sergeant

Born in Franklin County where he resided as a student prior to enlisting in Franklin County at age 20, May 20, 1861. Mustered in as Private and promoted to 1st Sergeant on May 1, 1862. Present or accounted for until wounded in the left shoulder, left hip, left thigh, and left leg at Malvern Hill, Virginia, July 1, 1862. Transferred to 2nd Company K, 32nd Regiment N.C. Troops, July 4, 1862, while absent wounded.

CONYERS, EPHRAIM G., Private

Resided in Franklin County where he enlisted at age 21, May 20, 1861. Present or accounted for until wounded at Malvern Hill, Virginia, July 1, 1862. Transferred to 2nd Company K, 32nd Regiment N.C. Troops, July 4, 1862.

COOK, JAMES HOPKINS, Private

Resided in Nash County and enlisted in Northampton County at age 22, June 24, 1861. Present or accounted for until transferred to 2nd Company K, 32nd Regiment N.C. Troops, July 4, 1862.

COOKE, JOHN HENRY, Private

Resided in Nash County and enlisted in Franklin County at age 22, May 20, 1861. Present or accounted for until transferred to 2nd Company K, 32nd Regiment N.C. Troops, July 4, 1862.

COTTRELL, DAVID D., Private

Resided in Franklin County where he enlisted at age 45, May 20, 1861. Present or accounted for until transferred to 2nd Company K, 32nd Regiment N.C. Troops, July 4, 1862.

CROWDER, OBEDIAH N., Private

Resided in Franklin County where he enlisted at age 23, May 20, 1861. Present or accounted for until he died on August 7, 1861, of "measles." Place of death not reported.

DAVIS, ARCHIBALD J., Private

Resided in Franklin County where he enlisted at age 22, May 20, 1861. Present or accounted for until transferred to 2nd Company K, 32nd Regiment N.C. Troops, July 4, 1862.

DAVIS, DOLPHIN B., Private

Previously served in Company G of this regiment. Transferred to this company in September, 1861-January, 1862. Present or accounted for until killed "by the falling of [a] tree" at Tree Hill, Alabama, February 1, 1862.

DAVIS, JOHN, Private

Born in Pitt County and resided in Franklin County where he was by occupation a mechanic prior to enlisting in Franklin County at age 28, May 20, 1861. Present or accounted for until discharged on June 9, 1862, by reason of "an attack of . . . bilious fever . . . followed by . . . diarrhoea [and] an incipient disposition [to tuberculosis]."

DAVIS, THOMAS WALTON, Private

Resided in Franklin County where he enlisted at age 20, May 20, 1861. Present or accounted for until killed at Malvern Hill, Virginia, July 1, 1862.

EDWARDS, JOSEPH H., Private

Resided in Franklin County where he enlisted at age 19, May 20, 1861. Present or accounted for until transferred to 2nd Company K, 32nd Regiment N.C. Troops, July 4, 1862.

EGERTON, RUFUS T., Private

Born in Franklin County where he resided as a student prior to enlisting in Franklin County at age 17, May 20, 1861. Present or accounted for until transferred to 2nd Company K, 32nd Regiment N.C. Troops, July 4, 1862.

ENGLE, JULIUS L., Private

Resided in Franklin County where he enlisted at age 21, May 20, 1861. Present or accounted for until transferred to 2nd Company K, 32nd Regiment N.C. Troops, July 4, 1862.

FOSTER, WILLIAM E., Private

Resided in Franklin County where he enlisted at age 18, May 20, 1861. Present or accounted for until transferred to 2nd Company K, 32nd Regiment N.C. Troops, July 4, 1862.

GILL, JAMES H., Private

Resided in Franklin County where he enlisted at age 25, May 20, 1861. Present or accounted for until he died at Petersburg, Virginia, August 10, 1861, of "measles."

GILL, JOHN J., Private

Resided in Franklin County where he enlisted at age 25, May 20, 1861. Present or accounted for until he died in March, 1862, of disease. Place of death not reported.

GREEN, NORFLEET H., Private

Resided in Franklin County where he enlisted at age 26, May 20, 1861. Present or accounted for until he died in hospital at Yorktown, Virginia, on or about October 13, 1861, of disease.

HARPER, GEORGE T., Private

Born in Franklin County where he resided as a mechanic prior to enlisting in Franklin County at age 21, May 20, 1861. Present or accounted for until transferred to 2nd Company K, 32nd Regiment N.C. Troops, July 4, 1862.

HARRIS, A. S., Private

Resided in Franklin County where he enlisted on May 16, 1862, for the war. Present or accounted for until transferred to 2nd Company K, 32nd Regiment N.C. Troops, July 4, 1862.

HARRIS, BENJAMIN F., Private

Resided in Franklin County where he enlisted at age 24, May 20, 1861. Present or accounted for until transferred to 2nd Company K, 32nd Regiment N.C. Troops, July 4, 1862.

HARRIS, EDWARD C., Private

Resided in Franklin County where he enlisted at age 21, May 20, 1861. Present or accounted for until transferred to 2nd Company K, 32nd Regiment N.C. Troops, July 4, 1862.

HARRIS, OLIVER H., Private

Resided in Franklin County where he enlisted at age 23, May 20, 1861. Present or accounted for until

transferred to 2nd Company K, 32nd Regiment N.C. Troops, July 4, 1862.

HARRIS, WILKERSON D., Private

Born in Franklin County where he resided as a farmer prior to enlisting in Franklin County at age 22, May 20, 1861. Present or accounted for until discharged on November 25, 1861, by reason of "complete deafness supervening after repeated attacks of intermittent fever."

HIGHT, JUNIUS W., Private

Resided in Franklin County where he enlisted at age 23, May 20, 1861. Present or accounted for until he died in March, 1862, of disease. Place of death not reported.

HOLLINGSWORTH, DAVID T., Private

Resided in Franklin County where he enlisted at age 21, May 20, 1861. Present or accounted for until transferred 2nd Company K, 32nd Regiment N.C. Troops, July 4, 1862.

HOLT, AUGUSTUS C., Private

Resided in Franklin County where he enlisted at age 22, May 20, 1861. Present or accounted for until wounded at Malvern Hill, Virginia, July 1, 1862. Transferred to 2nd Company K, 32nd Regiment N.C. Troops, July 4, 1862, while absent wounded.

HORTON, GEORGE L., Private

Born in Franklin County and resided in Wake County where he was by occupation a mechanic prior to enlisting in Franklin County at age 26, May 20, 1861. Present or accounted for until transferred to 2nd Company K, 32nd Regiment N.C. Troops, July 4, 1862.

HOWARD, JAMES H., Sergeant

Born in Hyde County and resided in Florida where he was by occupation a student prior to enlisting in Franklin County at age 18, May 20, 1861. Mustered in as Corporal and promoted to Sergeant on May 1, 1862. Present or accounted for until wounded at Malvern Hill, Virginia, July 1, 1862. Transferred to 2nd Company K, 32nd Regiment N.C. Troops, July 4, 1862, while absent wounded.

INSCOE, WILLIAM E., Private

Resided in Franklin County where he enlisted at age 29, May 20, 1861. Present or accounted for until transferred to 2nd Company K, 32nd Regiment N.C. Troops, July 4, 1862.

JACKSON, ALFRED W., Private

Resided in Franklin County where he enlisted at age 21, May 20, 1861. Present or accounted for until transferred to 2nd Company K, 32nd Regiment N.C. Troops, July 4, 1862.

JASPER, HENRY N., Sergeant

Resided in Franklin County where he enlisted at age 25, May 20, 1861. Mustered in as Private and promoted to Sergeant in May, 1862. Present or accounted for until transferred to 2nd Company K, 32nd Regiment N.C. Troops, July 4, 1862.

JOHNSON, WILLIAM J., Private

Born in Franklin County where he resided as a farmer prior to enlisting in Franklin County at age 19, May 20, 1861. Present or accounted for until transferred to 2nd Company K, 32nd Regiment N.C. Troops, July 4, 1862.

JONES, JOSEPH T., Private

Resided in Franklin County where he enlisted at age 28, May 20, 1861. Present or accounted for until transferred to 2nd Company K, 32nd Regiment N.C. Troops, July 4, 1862.

JOYNER, ALGERNON S., Private

Resided in Franklin County where he enlisted at age 22, May 20, 1861. Present or accounted for until transferred to 2nd Company K, 32nd Regiment N.C. Troops, July 4, 1862.

JOYNER, LEWIS W., Private

Resided in Franklin County and enlisted in Northampton County on July 15, 1861. Present or accounted for until transferred to 2nd Company K, 32nd Regiment N.C. Troops, July 4, 1862.

KING, WILLIAM J., Private

Born in Franklin County where he resided as a student prior to enlisting in Franklin County at age 21, May 20, 1861. Present or accounted for until discharged on May 27, 1862, by reason of "permanent impairment of strength of right hand from phlegmonous erysipelas."

LEIGH, THOMAS H., Corporal

Resided in Franklin or Wake counties and enlisted in Franklin County at age 21, May 20, 1861. Mustered in as Private and was promoted to Corporal in July, 1861-June, 1862. Present or accounted for until transferred to 2nd Company K, 32nd Regiment N.C. Troops, July 4, 1862.

LEONARD, WILLIAM E., Private

Resided in Franklin County where he enlisted at age 20, May 20, 1861. Present or accounted for until he died on July 31, 1861, of "measles." Place of death not reported.

LONG, JAMES C., Private

Resided in Franklin County where he enlisted at age 25, June 1, 1861. Present or accounted for until transferred to 2nd Company K, 32nd Regiment N.C. Troops, July 4, 1862.

LONG, MADISON M., Private

Resided in Franklin County where he enlisted at age 23, May 20, 1861. Present or accounted for until transferred to 2nd Company K, 32nd Regiment N.C. Troops, July 4, 1862.

LONG, NICHOLAS G., Private

Resided in Franklin County where he enlisted at age 22, May 20, 1861. Present or accounted for until wounded at Malvern Hill, Virginia, July 1, 1862. Transferred to 2nd Company K, 32nd Regiment N.C. Troops, July 4, 1862.

MACKLIN, WALTER D., Private

Resided in Franklin County where he enlisted at age 21, May 20, 1861. Present or accounted for until transferred to 2nd Company K, 32nd Regiment N.C. Troops, July 4, 1862.

MACON, JOHN A., Private

Resided in Franklin County where he enlisted at age 23, May 20, 1861. Present or accounted for until transferred to 2nd Company K, 32nd Regiment N.C. Troops, July 4, 1862.

MACON, JOSEPH S., Private

Resided in Franklin County where he enlisted at age 18, May 20, 1861. Present or accounted for until

transferred to 2nd Company K, 32nd Regiment N.C. Troops, July 4, 1862.

MARTIN, ROBERT C., Corporal
Resided in Franklin County where he enlisted at age 18, May 20, 1861. Mustered in as Private and promoted to Corporal in September, 1861-June, 1862. Present or accounted for until transferred to 2nd Company K, 32nd Regiment N.C. Troops, July 4, 1862.

MASSENBURG, ARCHIBALD CARGILL, 1st Sergeant
Resided in Franklin County where he enlisted at age 30, May 20, 1861. Mustered in as Private and promoted to 1st Sergeant on July 1, 1861. Present or accounted for until appointed Assistant Commissary of Subsistence (Captain) on November 14, 1861, and transferred to the Field and Staff of this regiment.

MAY, JOSIAH A., Private
Born in Franklin County where he resided as a farmer prior to enlisting in Franklin County at age 21, May 20, 1861. Present or accounted for until discharged on January 7, 1862, by reason of "typhoid fever, repeated attacks of intermittent fever, and chronic bronchitis."

MITCHELL, JOHN A., Corporal
Resided in Franklin County where he enlisted at age 20, May 20, 1861. Mustered in as Private and promoted to Corporal in December, 1861-June, 1862. Present or accounted for until transferred to 2nd Company K, 32nd Regiment N.C. Troops, July 4, 1862.

MONTGOMERY, THOMAS, Private
Resided in Franklin County where he enlisted at age 22, May 20, 1861. Present or accounted for until transferred to 2nd Company K, 32nd Regiment N.C. Troops, July 4, 1862.

MORTON, G. L., _____
Place and date of enlistment not reported. A regimental return dated February, 1862, states he was absent on sick furlough. No further records.

NEILL, T. C., Private
Resided in Franklin County where he enlisted at age 21, May 20, 1861. Present or accounted for until transferred to 2nd Company K, 32nd Regiment N.C. Troops, July 4, 1862.

NEWBY, WILLIAM H., Private
Enlisted in Franklin County on May 20, 1861. Present or accounted for until transferred to 2nd Company K, 32nd Regiment N.C. Troops, July 4, 1862.

NICHOLSON, WILLIAM H., Private
Resided in Franklin County where he enlisted at age 19, May 20, 1861. Present or accounted for until killed at Malvern Hill, Virginia, July 1, 1862.

PARK, BENJAMIN F., Private
Resided in Franklin County where he enlisted at age 22, May 20, 1861. Present or accounted for until transferred to 2nd Company K, 32nd Regiment N.C. Troops, July 4, 1862.

PEARCE, JOHN J., Private
Resided in Franklin County where he enlisted at age 22, May 20, 1861. Mustered in as Sergeant but was reduced to ranks in September, 1861-June, 1862. Present or accounted for until transferred to 2nd

Company K, 32nd Regiment N.C. Troops, July 4, 1862.

PERRY, JAMES R., Private
Resided in Franklin County where he enlisted at age 19, May 20, 1861. Present or accounted for until transferred to 2nd Company K, 32nd Regiment N.C. Troops, July 4, 1862.

PERRY, JEREMIAH, Private
Enlisted in Franklin County on May 20, 1861. Present or accounted for until discharged on or about July 1, 1862, after providing Private John Walson as a substitute.

POWELL, KINSMAN S., Private
Resided in Franklin County where he enlisted at age 27, May 20, 1861. Present or accounted for until transferred to 2nd Company K, 32nd Regiment N.C. Troops, July 4, 1862.

RANSDELL, GEORGE W., Musician
Resided in Franklin County where he enlisted on May 20, 1861. Mustered in as Private and promoted to Musician (Drummer) in September, 1861-June, 1862. Present or accounted for until transferred to 2nd Company K, 32nd Regiment N.C. Troops, July 4, 1862.

RANSDELL, SYLVESTER S., Musician
Resided in Franklin County where he enlisted at age 19, May 20, 1861. Mustered in as Private and promoted to Musician (Drummer) in October, 1861. Present or accounted for until transferred to 2nd Company K, 32nd Regiment N.C. Troops, July 4, 1862.

RAY, WILLIAM E., Private
Born in Warren County and resided in Franklin County where he was by occupation a student prior to enlisting in Franklin County at age 19, May 20, 1861. Present or accounted for until transferred to 2nd Company K, 32nd Regiment N.C. Troops, July 4, 1862.

STALLINGS, CORNELIUS H., Private
Resided in Franklin County where he enlisted at age 26, May 20, 1861. Present or accounted for until he died in September, 1861, of disease. Place of death not reported.

STALLINGS, OLIVER C., Private
Born in Franklin County and was by occupation a schoolboy prior to enlisting in Franklin County at age 16, May 20, 1861. Present or accounted for until discharged on December 4, 1861, by reason of "inability to do military service." Later served in Company B, 13th Battalion N.C. Infantry.

STALLINGS, WILLIAM R., Private
Enlisted in Franklin County on May 20, 1861. Present or accounted for until he was "killed accidentally" on July 23, 1861. Place of death not reported.

STONE, DAVID L., Private
Born in Franklin County where he resided as a physician prior to enlisting in Franklin County at age 21, May 20, 1861. Present or accounted for until discharged on September 1, 1861, by reason of "physical inability to perform military duty."

STROTHER, ALGERNON S., Private
Born in Franklin County where he resided as a

merchant prior to enlisting in Franklin County at age 27, May 20, 1861. Present or accounted for until transferred to 2nd Company K, 32nd Regiment N.C. Troops, July 4, 1862.

SYKES, WILLIAM G., Private

Resided in Franklin County where he enlisted on May 20, 1861. Present or accounted for until he died in March, 1862, of disease. Place of death not reported.

THOMAS, CHARLES H., Private

Resided in Franklin County where he enlisted at age 28, May 20, 1861. Present or accounted for until appointed Assistant Quartermaster (Captain) on March 13, 1862, to rank from March 1, 1862, and transferred to the Field and Staff of this regiment.

THOMAS, HENRY W., Private

Resided in Franklin County where he enlisted on May 20, 1861. Present or accounted for until transferred to 2nd Company K, 32nd Regiment N.C. Troops, July 4, 1862.

TUNSTALL, NATHANIEL R., Private

Resided in Franklin County where he enlisted at age 21, May 20, 1861. Present or accounted for until transferred to 2nd Company K, 32nd Regiment N.C. Troops, July 4, 1862.

WALSON, JOHN, Private

Resided in Russia and enlisted in Franklin County on or about July 1, 1862, for the war as a substitute for Private Jeremiah Perry. Present or accounted for until transferred to 2nd Company K, 32nd Regiment N.C. Troops, July 4, 1862.

WARD, THOMAS J., Corporal

Resided in Franklin County where he enlisted at age 25, May 20, 1861. Mustered in as Corporal. Present or accounted for until he died in hospital at Petersburg, Virginia, March 16, 1862, of "extensive inflammation of the bowels."

WHELESS, JOSEPH W., Sergeant

Resided in Nash County and enlisted in Franklin County at age 19, May 20, 1861. Mustered in as Private and promoted to Sergeant on May 1, 1862. Present or accounted for until wounded in the head at Malvern Hill, Virginia, July 1, 1862. Transferred to 2nd Company K, 32nd Regiment N.C. Troops, July 4, 1862, while absent wounded.

WILHITE, HENRY Y., Private

Resided in Franklin County where he enlisted at age 25, May 20, 1861. Present or accounted for until transferred to 2nd Company K, 32nd Regiment N.C. Troops, July 4, 1862.

WILSON, BENJAMIN W., Private

Born in Franklin County where he resided as a farmer prior to enlisting in Franklin County at age 30, May 20, 1861. Present or accounted for until transferred to 2nd Company K, 32nd Regiment N.C. Troops, July 4, 1862.

WINSTON, PATRICK H., Sergeant

Resided in Franklin County where he enlisted at age 20, May 20, 1861. Mustered in as Private and promoted to Sergeant in September, 1861-June, 1862. Present or accounted for until wounded at Malvern Hill, Virginia, July 1, 1862. Transferred to 2nd Company K, 32nd Regiment N.C. Troops, July 4, 1862.

WYNNE, JAMES C., Private

Resided in Franklin County where he enlisted at age 25, May 20, 1861. Present or accounted for until transferred to 2nd Company K, 32nd Regiment N.C. Troops, July 4, 1862.

YOUNG, LEONARD A., Private

Resided in Franklin County where he enlisted at age 26, May 20, 1861. Present or accounted for until transferred to 2nd Company K, 32nd Regiment N.C. Troops, July 4, 1862.

YOUNG, WILLIAM S., Private

Resided in Franklin County where he enlisted at age 30, May 20, 1861. Mustered in as Sergeant but was reduced to ranks in September, 1861-June, 1862. Present or accounted for until discharged in June, 1862, by reason of having been elected deputy sheriff of Franklin County.

COMPANY M

This company, known as the Chatham Rifles, was from Chatham County and enlisted at Pittsboro on April 15, 1861. It was accepted into state service the same date and was ordered to Raleigh, where it went into camp. On June 4 it was mustered in and ordered to Garysburg, where it was assigned to this regiment as Company M. The company served with this regiment until July 4, 1862, when it was transferred to the 32nd Regiment N.C. Troops. Being the second company to serve as Company I of that regiment, it was designated 2nd Company I. The following roster covers only the period from original enlistment through July 4, 1862. All information after that date will be recorded in the roster of 2nd Company I, 32nd Regiment N.C. Troops.

The information contained in the following roster of the company was compiled principally from company muster rolls for June 4 through August, 1861. No company muster rolls were found for the period prior to June 4, 1861, or for the period after August, 1861. In addition to the company muster rolls, Roll of Honor records, receipt rolls, hospital records, prisoner of war records, and other primary records, supplemented by state pension applications, United Daughters of the Confederacy records, and postwar rosters and histories, all provided useful information.

OFFICERS
CAPTAINS

IHRIE, ROSS R.

Resided in Chatham County and enlisted at age 33. Appointed Captain on April 15, 1861. Present or accounted for until promoted to Lieutenant Colonel on June 11, 1861, and transferred to the Field and Staff of this regiment.

TAYLOR, JOHN W.

Resided in Chatham County where he enlisted at age 30, April 15, 1861. Mustered in as Sergeant and was appointed Captain to rank from June 15, 1861. Present or accounted for until he was defeated for reelection when the regiment was reorganized on May 2, 1862.

LONDON, WILLIAM LORD

Resided in Chatham County where he enlisted at age 24. Appointed 2nd Lieutenant on or about April 15,

1861, and was promoted to 1st Lieutenant on July 9, 1861. Promoted to Captain on May 2, 1862. Present or accounted for until wounded at Malvern Hill, Virginia, July 1, 1862. Present or accounted for until transferred to 2nd Company I, 32nd Regiment N.C. Troops, July 4, 1862.

LIEUTENANTS

MANNING, JOHN, Jr., 1st Lieutenant
Resided in Chatham County where he enlisted at age 30. Appointed 1st Lieutenant on April 15, 1861. Present or accounted for until promoted to Adjutant (1st Lieutenant) on July 9, 1861, and transferred to the Field and Staff of this regiment.

MERRITT, LEONIDAS J., 1st Lieutenant
Resided in Chatham County where he enlisted at age 25, April 15, 1861. Mustered in as Private and was appointed 2nd Lieutenant to rank from October 30, 1861. Present or accounted for until wounded at Lee's Mill, Virginia, April 16, 1862. Promoted to 1st Lieutenant on May 2, 1862. Killed at Malvern Hill, Virginia, July 1, 1862, "while gallantly leading his company."

NEAL, OSCAR M., 2nd Lieutenant
Enlisted in Chatham County. Appointed 2nd Lieutenant on April 15, 1861. Present or accounted for until he was defeated for reelection when the regiment was reorganized on May 2, 1862. [May have served later in Company I, 41st Regiment N.C. Troops (3rd Regiment N.C. Cavalry).]

POE, CLARENCE C., 3rd Lieutenant
Resided in Chatham County where he enlisted at age 23, April 15, 1861. Mustered in as Corporal and was appointed 3rd Lieutenant on July 9, 1861. Present or accounted for until he died at Yorktown, Virginia, August 7, 1861, of "typhoid fever."

ROGERS, JAMES T., 2nd Lieutenant
Resided in Chatham County where he enlisted at age 31, April 15, 1861. Mustered in as Private and promoted to Corporal on July 9, 1861. Promoted to Sergeant in December, 1861. Present or accounted for until wounded at Lee's Mill, Virginia, April 16, 1862. Appointed 2nd Lieutenant to rank from May 2, 1862. Returned to duty prior to July 1, 1862, when he was wounded in the ankle at Malvern Hill, Virginia. Transferred to 2nd Company I, 32nd Regiment N.C. Troops, July 4, 1862, while absent wounded.

TYSON, WILLIAM H. H., 2nd Lieutenant
Resided in Chatham County where he enlisted at age 30, April 15, 1861. Mustered in as Private and was appointed 2nd Lieutenant to rank from May 2, 1862. Present or accounted for until wounded at Malvern Hill, Virginia, July 1, 1862. Transferred to 2nd Company I, 32nd Regiment N.C. Troops, July 4, 1862.

NONCOMMISSIONED OFFICERS AND PRIVATES

ALSTON, CHARLES W., Private
Resided in Chatham County where he enlisted at age 22, April 15, 1861. Present or accounted for until he died in Chatham County on or about April 23, 1862, of "consumption and chronic dysentery."

ALSTON, JOHN J., Private
Born in Chatham County where he resided as a farmer prior to enlisting in Northampton County at age 30, June 29, 1861. Present or accounted for until discharged on December 5, 1861, by reason of "chronic nephritis [and] enlarged prostate gland."

ALSTON, N. M., Private
Resided in Chatham County where he enlisted at age 25, April 15, 1861. Present or accounted for until transferred to 2nd Company I, 32nd Regiment N.C. Troops, July 4, 1862.

ATCHISON, WILLIAM A., Private
Resided in Chatham County where he enlisted at age 25, April 15, 1861. Present or accounted for until transferred to 2nd Company I, 32nd Regiment N.C. Troops, July 4, 1862.

BAKER, WILLIAM J., Private
Resided in Chatham County where he enlisted at age 27, April 15, 1861. Present or accounted for until killed at Malvern Hill, Virginia, July 1, 1862. "A faithful soldier."

BARRY, NED, Private
Resided in Chatham County where he enlisted at age 32, April 15, 1861. Present or accounted for until wounded in the head and hip at Malvern Hill, Virginia, July 1, 1862. Transferred to 2nd Company I, 32nd Regiment N.C. Troops, July 4, 1862, while absent wounded.

BENNETT, M. H., Private
Resided in Chatham County and enlisted at Yorktown, Virginia, at age 22, July 2, 1861. Present or accounted for until killed by "a rifle ball through the neck" at Lee's Mill, Virginia, April 16, 1862.

BERRY, WILLIAM F., Private
Resided in Chatham County where he enlisted at age 35, April 15, 1861. Present or accounted for until wounded at Malvern Hill, Virginia, July 1, 1862. Transferred to 2nd Company I, 32nd Regiment N.C. Troops, July 4, 1862.

BLAND, WILLIAM G., Private
Born in Chatham County where he resided as a farmer prior to enlisting in Chatham County at age 27, April 15, 1861. Present or accounted for until transferred to 2nd Company I, 32nd Regiment N.C. Troops, July 4, 1862.

BOLTON, H. H., Musician
Resided in Chatham County where he enlisted at age 30, April 15, 1861. Mustered in as Musician. Present or accounted for until transferred to 2nd Company I, 32nd Regiment N.C. Troops, July 4, 1862.

BROOKS, ROBERT D., Private
Resided in Chatham County where he enlisted at age 18, April 15, 1861. Present or accounted for until transferred to 2nd Company I, 32nd Regiment N.C. Troops, July 4, 1862.

BROWN, L. M., Private
Resided in Chatham County where he enlisted at age 28, April 15, 1861. Present or accounted for until he was "sent home for mental derangement" on July 17, 1861. Reported "insane in Chatham Co[unty]"

through December, 1861. Transferred to 2nd Company I, 32nd Regiment N.C. Troops, July 4, 1862.

BROWN, LUCIAN, Private
Resided in Chatham County where he enlisted at age 26, April 15, 1861. Present or accounted for until transferred to 2nd Company I, 32nd Regiment N.C. Troops, July 4, 1862.

BUDD, ABRAM V., Private
Resided in Chatham County where he enlisted at age 34, April 15, 1861. Present or accounted for until transferred to 2nd Company I, 32nd Regiment N.C. Troops, July 4, 1862.

BURKE, JAMES E., Private
Resided in Chatham County where he enlisted at age 22, April 15, 1861. Present or accounted for until transferred to 2nd Company I, 32nd Regiment N.C. Troops, July 4, 1862.

BYNUM, ALVIS J., Private
Resided in Chatham County where he enlisted at age 22, April 15, 1861. Present or accounted for until transferred to 2nd Company I, 32nd Regiment N.C. Troops, July 4, 1862.

CAUDLE, JOHN D., Private
Resided in Chatham County where he enlisted at age 22, April 15, 1861. Present or accounted for until transferred to 2nd Company I, 32nd Regiment N.C. Troops, July 4, 1862.

CLARK, A. J., Private
Place and date of enlistment not reported. A regimental return dated February, 1862, states he was absent sick in North Carolina. No further records.

CLARK, T. L., Private
Resided in Chatham County where he enlisted at age 23, April 15, 1861. Present or accounted for until transferred to 2nd Company I, 32nd Regiment N.C. Troops, July 4, 1862.

CLEGG, BENJAMIN F., Private
Resided in Chatham County where he enlisted at age 24, April 15, 1861. Present or accounted for until transferred to 2nd Company I, 32nd Regiment N.C. Troops, July 4, 1862.

CLEGG, R., Private
Place and date of enlistment not reported. A regimental return dated April, 1862, states he was absent sick at Petersburg, Virginia. No further records.

CLEGG, THOMAS A., Private
Resided in Chatham County where he enlisted at age 18, April 15, 1861. Present or accounted for until he died in King and Queen County, Virginia, October 11, 1861, of "typhoid fever."

CLEGG, THOMAS D., Private
Resided in Chatham County where he enlisted at age 23, April 15, 1861. Present or accounted for until wounded at Malvern Hill, Virginia, July 1, 1862. Transferred to 2nd Company I, 32nd Regiment N.C. Troops, July 4, 1862.

CLEGG, WILLIAM BAXTER, Private
Resided in Chatham County where he enlisted at age 24, April 15, 1861. Present or accounted for until transferred to 2nd Company I, 32nd Regiment N.C. Troops, July 4, 1862.

COTTON, RICHARD C., Private
Born in Chatham County where he resided as a farmer prior to enlisting in Chatham County at age 31, April 15, 1861. Mustered in as Private and was promoted to Sergeant in September, 1861-January, 1862. Reduced to ranks at an unspecified date. Present or accounted for until discharged on March 15, 1862, by reason of "chronic disease of the heart & liver."

COUNCIL, T. A., Private
Resided in Chatham County and enlisted at Yorktown, Virginia, at age 25, July 2, 1861. Present or accounted for until wounded at Malvern Hill, Virginia, July 1, 1862, where he suffered a broken arm. Transferred to 2nd Company I, 32nd Regiment N.C. Troops, July 4, 1862.

CRUMP, JOHN J., Private
Born in Chatham County where he resided prior to enlisting in Chatham County at age 24, April 15, 1861. Present or accounted for until appointed 2nd Lieutenant and transferred to Company E, 44th Regiment N.C. Troops, on or about April 15, 1862.

CRUTCHFIELD, E. B., Private
Place and date of enlistment not reported. A regimental return dated February, 1862, states he was absent sick in North Carolina. No further records.

CRUTCHFIELD, HUGH, Private
Resided in Chatham County where he enlisted at age 18, April 15, 1861. Present or accounted for until discharged on December 31, 1861, by reason of disability.

DEZERNE, LEWIS, Private
Resided in Chatham County where he enlisted at age 22, April 15, 1861. Present or accounted for until wounded at Malvern Hill, Virginia, July 1, 1862. Transferred to 2nd Company I, 32nd Regiment N.C. Troops, July 4, 1862.

EDWARDS, JOHN M., Private
Born in Chatham County and was by occupation a farmer prior to enlisting in Chatham County on April 15, 1861. Present or accounted for until wounded in the arm at Malvern Hill, Virginia, July 1, 1862. Transferred to 2nd Company I, 32nd Regiment N.C. Troops, July 4, 1862.

ELLINGTON, JAMES B., Private
Resided in Chatham County where he enlisted at age 25, April 15, 1861. Present or accounted for until transferred to 2nd Company I, 32nd Regiment N.C. Troops, July 4, 1862.

ELLINGTON, SAMUEL J., Private
Resided in Chatham County where he enlisted at age 27, April 15, 1861. Present or accounted for until transferred to 2nd Company I, 32nd Regiment N.C. Troops, July 4, 1862.

ELLIS, ALFRED M., Private
Resided in Chatham County where he enlisted at age 18, April 15, 1861. Present or accounted for until discharged on June 12, 1861, by reason of disability.

EUBANKS, JOHN T., Sergeant
Resided in Chatham County where he enlisted at age 29, April 15, 1861. Mustered in as Sergeant. Present or accounted for until transferred to 2nd Company I, 32nd Regiment N.C. Troops, July 4, 1862.

EUBANKS, WILLIAM G., Private
Resided in Chatham County where he enlisted at age 22, April 15, 1861. Present or accounted for until transferred to 2nd Company I, 32nd Regiment N.C. Troops, July 4, 1862.

FANN, JAMES, Private
Resided in Wake County and enlisted in Chatham County at age 20, April 15, 1861. Present or accounted for until transferred to 2nd Company I, 32nd Regiment N.C. Troops, July 4, 1862.

FOOSHEE, JOHN R., Private
Born in Chatham County where he resided as a farmer prior to enlisting in Chatham County at age 26, April 15, 1861. Present or accounted for until transferred to 2nd Company I, 32nd Regiment N.C. Troops, July 4, 1862.

FOOSHEE, SAMUEL, Private
Resided in Chatham County where he enlisted at age 19, April 15, 1861. Present or accounted for until killed at Lee's Mill, Virginia, April 16, 1862.

FOWLER, FERRINGTON, Private
Resided in Chatham or Wake counties and enlisted in Chatham County at age 20, April 15, 1861. Present or accounted for until transferred to 2nd Company I, 32nd Regiment N.C. Troops, July 4, 1862.

FOX, JOHN M., Private
Resided in Chatham or Alamance counties and enlisted in Chatham County at age 22, April 15, 1861. Present or accounted for until transferred to 2nd Company I, 32nd Regiment N.C. Troops, July 4, 1862.

GARRETT, W. L., Private
Resided in Chatham County where he enlisted at age 22, April 15, 1861. Present or accounted for until transferred to 2nd Company I, 32nd Regiment N.C. Troops, July 4, 1862.

GILMORE, JOSEPH, Private
Resided in Chatham County where he enlisted at age 36, April 15, 1861. Present or accounted for until wounded at Malvern Hill, Virginia, July 1, 1862. Transferred to 2nd Company I, 32nd Regiment N.C. Troops, July 4, 1862.

GOUGH, ARTHUR, Private
Resided in Chatham County where he enlisted at age 31, April 15, 1861. Present or accounted for until wounded at Malvern Hill, Virginia, July 1, 1862. Transferred to 2nd Company I, 32nd Regiment N.C. Troops, July 4, 1862.

GUNTER, BENJAMIN, Private
Resided in Chatham County where he enlisted at age 22, April 15, 1861. Present or accounted for until wounded in the hand at Malvern Hill, Virginia, July 1, 1862. Transferred to 2nd Company I, 32nd Regiment N.C. Troops, July 4, 1862.

GUTHRIE, WILLIAM H., Private
Resided in Chatham County where he enlisted at age 25, April 15, 1861. Present or accounted for until transferred to 2nd Company I, 32nd Regiment N.C. Troops, July 4, 1862.

HACKNEY, J. A., Private
Resided in Chatham County and enlisted at Yorktown, Virginia, at age 19, July 2, 1861. Present or accounted

for until transferred to 2nd Company I, 32nd Regiment N.C. Troops, July 4, 1862.

HANKS, LUCIAN A., Private
Resided in Chatham County and was by occupation a medical student prior to enlisting in Chatham County at age 22, April 15, 1861. Present or accounted for until transferred to 2nd Company I, 32nd Regiment N.C. Troops, July 4, 1862.

HARMAN, H. H., Private
Resided in Chatham County where he enlisted at age 21, April 15, 1861. Present or accounted for until transferred to 2nd Company I, 32nd Regiment N.C. Troops, July 4, 1862.

HARRIS, D. C., Corporal
Resided in Chatham County where he enlisted at age 25, April 15, 1861. Mustered in as Private and promoted to Corporal on July 9, 1861. Present or accounted for until transferred to 2nd Company I, 32nd Regiment N.C. Troops, July 4, 1862.

HARRIS, THOMAS W., Sergeant
Resided in Chatham County where he enlisted at age 22, April 15, 1861. Mustered in as Sergeant. Present or accounted for until transferred to 2nd Company I, 32nd Regiment N.C. Troops, July 4, 1862.

HART, WILLIAM, Private
Resided in Chatham County where he enlisted at age 19, April 15, 1861. Present or accounted for until transferred to 2nd Company I, 32nd Regiment N.C. Troops, July 4, 1862.

HATCH, JAMES M., Private
Resided in Chatham County where he enlisted at age 20, April 15, 1861. Present or accounted for until discharged on August 27, 1861. Reason discharged not reported.

HOLT, SAMUEL M., Private
Resided in Chatham or Wake counties and enlisted in Chatham County at age 24, April 15, 1861. Present or accounted for until transferred to 2nd Company I, 32nd Regiment N.C. Troops, July 4, 1862.

HORTON, HORACE C., Private
Resided in Chatham County where he enlisted at age 30, April 15, 1861. Present or accounted for until discharged on September 17, 1861, by reason of disability.

JOHNSON, MINTER G., Private
Resided in Chatham County where he enlisted at age 23, April 15, 1861. Present or accounted for until wounded in the leg at Malvern Hill, Virginia, July 1, 1862. Transferred to 2nd Company I, 32nd Regiment N.C. Troops, July 4, 1862.

JORDAN, JOHN A., Private
Resided in Chatham County where he enlisted at age 26, April 15, 1861. Present or accounted for until transferred to 2nd Company I, 32nd Regiment N.C. Troops, July 4, 1862.

KNIGHT, JOHN J., Private
Resided in Chatham County where he enlisted at age 25, April 15, 1861. Present or accounted for until transferred to 2nd Company I, 32nd Regiment N.C. Troops, July 4, 1862.

LASSITER, THOMAS B., Private
Resided in Chatham County where he enlisted at age

28, April 15, 1861. Present or accounted for until transferred to 2nd Company I, 32nd Regiment N.C. Troops, July 4, 1862.

LEACH, GEORGE T., Private
Born in Johnston County and resided in Chatham County where he was by occupation a "soldier" prior to enlisting in Chatham County at age 24, April 15, 1861. Present or accounted for until appointed 2nd Lieutenant in May, 1862, and transferred to Company C, 53rd Regiment N.C. Troops.

LINDLEY, GEORGE W., Private
Resided in Chatham County where he enlisted at age 22, April 15, 1861. Present or accounted for until he died in hospital at Petersburg, Virginia, April 4, 1862, of "typhoid fever."

LONG, EDWIN, Private
Resided in Chatham County where he enlisted at age 20, April 15, 1861. Present or accounted for until transferred to 2nd Company I, 32nd Regiment N.C. Troops, July 4, 1862.

LONG, JOHN H., Private
Resided in Chatham County and enlisted at Yorktown, Virginia, at age 20, July 2, 1861. Present or accounted for until transferred to 2nd Company I, 32nd Regiment N.C. Troops, July 4, 1862.

LOYD, ANDREW J., Private
Resided in Chatham County where he enlisted at age 18, April 15, 1861. Present or accounted for until wounded at Malvern Hill, Virginia, July 1, 1862. Transferred to 2nd Company I, 32nd Regiment N.C. Troops, July 4, 1862.

McCLENAHAN, J. B., Private
Resided in Chatham County where he enlisted at age 25, April 15, 1861. Present or accounted for until transferred to 2nd Company I, 32nd Regiment N.C. Troops, July 4, 1862.

McCLENAHAN, J. T., 1st Sergeant
Born in Chatham County where he resided as a lawyer prior to enlisting in Chatham County at age 30, April 15, 1861. Mustered in as Corporal and promoted to Sergeant on June 15, 1861. Promoted to 1st Sergeant on February 1, 1862. Present or accounted for until wounded at Malvern Hill, Virginia, July 1, 1862. Died July 2, 1862, of wounds.

McCLENAHAN, WILLIAM, Private
Resided in Chatham County where he enlisted at age 23, April 15, 1861. Present or accounted for until transferred to 2nd Company I, 32nd Regiment N.C. Troops, July 4, 1862.

McIVER, DUNCAN R., Corporal
Resided in Chatham County where he enlisted at age 31, April 15, 1861. Mustered in as Corporal. Present or accounted for until he died at Yorktown, Virginia, August 9, 1861, of "fever."

MALLORY, JAMES R., Commissary Sergeant
Born in Granville County and resided in Chatham County where he was by occupation a merchant prior to enlisting in Chatham County at age 26, April 15, 1861. Mustered in as Private and promoted to Commissary Sergeant on July 1, 1861. Present or accounted for until discharged on December 2, 1861, by reason of "frequent attacks of . . . fever terminating in chronic hepatitis & enlargement of the spleen."

MALLORY, JOHN T., Chief Musician
Born in Granville County and resided in Chatham County where he was by occupation a painter prior to enlisting in Chatham County at age 24, April 15, 1861. Mustered in as Musician and was promoted to Chief Musician (Drum Major) prior to September 1, 1861. Present or accounted for until transferred to 2nd Company I, 32nd Regiment N.C. Troops, July 4, 1862.

MEACHAM, JAMES A., Private
Resided in Chatham County where he enlisted at age 22, April 15, 1861. Present or accounted for until transferred to 2nd Company I, 32nd Regiment N.C. Troops, July 4, 1862.

MORRIS, WILLIAM J., Private
Resided in Chatham County where he enlisted at age 20, April 15, 1861. Present or accounted for until he died at Yorktown, Virginia, September 23, 1861. Cause of death not reported.

PEARSON, STANFORD, Private
Resided in Chatham County where he enlisted at age 20, April 15, 1861. Present or accounted for until transferred to 2nd Company I, 32nd Regiment N.C. Troops, July 4, 1862.

PERRY, ABNER B., Private
Resided in Chatham County where he enlisted at age 22, April 15, 1861. Present or accounted for until transferred to 2nd Company I, 32nd Regiment N.C. Troops, July 4, 1862.

PETTY, JOSEPH E., Musician
Resided in Chatham County where he enlisted at age 37, April 15, 1861, for the war as a substitute. Mustered in as Private and promoted to Musician prior to September 1, 1861. Present or accounted for until transferred to 2nd Company I, 32nd Regiment N.C. Troops, July 4, 1862.

PETTY, NATHANIEL, Private
Born in Chatham County where he resided as a farmer prior to enlisting in Chatham County on April 15, 1861. Present or accounted for through May, 1862. Name appears on a discharge certificate dated June 10, 1862, which gives his age as 24; however, it appears he was not discharged. Transferred to 2nd Company I, 32nd Regiment N.C. Troops, July 4, 1862.

PETTY, T. D., Private
Place and date of enlistment not reported. Name appears on a regimental return dated April, 1862, which states he was absent sick in hospital at Petersburg, Virginia. No further records.

POE, WILLIAM, Private
Resided in Chatham County where he enlisted at age 43, April 15, 1861. Present or accounted for until transferred to 2nd Company I, 32nd Regiment N.C. Troops, July 4, 1862.

RAMSEY, EDWARD B., Private
Resided in Chatham County where he enlisted at age 23, April 15, 1861. Present or accounted for until transferred to 2nd Company I, 32nd Regiment N.C. Troops, July 4, 1862.

RAMSEY, NATHAN ALEXANDER, Sergeant
Born in Chatham County where he resided as a merchant prior to enlisting in Chatham County at age 33, April 15, 1861. Mustered in as Sergeant. Present or

accounted for until appointed Captain of Company D, 61st Regiment N.C. Troops, March 21, 1862.

RAMSEY, WILLIAM S., Private
Born in Chatham County where he resided as an apothecary prior to enlisting in Chatham County at age 25, in November, 1861. Present or accounted for until transferred to Company D, 61st Regiment N.C. Troops, on or about June 13, 1862, upon appointment as 1st Lieutenant.

REASON, S., Private
Place and date of enlistment not reported. A regimental return dated February, 1862, states he was on duty as a nurse in the regimental hospital. No further records.

RICH, JOHN MORRIS, Corporal
Resided in Chatham County where he enlisted at age 23, April 15, 1861. Mustered in as Corporal. Reported "in arrest" for desertion from June 20, 1861, through February, 1862. Reported absent sick in May, 1862. Transferred to 2nd Company I, 32nd Regiment N.C. Troops, July 4, 1862.

RIGGSBEE, A. G., Private
Resided in Chatham County and enlisted at Yorktown, Virginia, at age 19, July 2, 1861. Present or accounted for until he died in hospital at Richmond, Virginia, May 2, 1862, of "typhoid fever."

RIGGSBEE, S. M., Private
Resided in Chatham County and enlisted at Yorktown, Virginia, at age 18, July 2, 1861. Present or accounted for until wounded at Lee's Mill, Virginia, April 16, 1862. Transferred to 2nd Company I, 32nd Regiment N.C. Troops, July 4, 1862.

RIGLAND, _____, Private
Place and date of enlistment not reported. A regimental return dated April, 1862, states he was absent sick in hospital at Petersburg, Virginia. No further records.

ROBERTS, JOHN H., Private
Resided in Chatham County where he enlisted at age 18, April 15, 1861. Present or accounted for until transferred to 2nd Company I, 32nd Regiment N.C. Troops, July 4, 1862.

ROGERS, LEVI, Private
Resided in Chatham County where he enlisted at age 28, April 15, 1861. Present or accounted for until transferred to 2nd Company I, 32nd Regiment N.C. Troops, July 4, 1862.

SAUNDERS, J. M., Private
Resided in Chatham County where he enlisted at age 20, April 15, 1861. Present or accounted for until killed at Malvern Hill, Virginia, July 1, 1862, "while charging the enemy's battery."

SEYMOUR, MATTHEW, Private
Resided in Chatham County where he enlisted at age 19, April 15, 1861. Present or accounted for until wounded in the arm at Malvern Hill, Virginia, July 1, 1862. Transferred to 2nd Company I, 32nd Regiment N.C. Troops, July 4, 1862, while absent wounded.

STEDMAN, JOHN R., Private
Resided in Chatham County where he enlisted at age 20, April 15, 1861. Present or accounted for until killed at Malvern Hill, Virginia, July 1, 1862.

STRAUGHAN, T. B., Private
Resided in Chatham or Wake counties and enlisted in Chatham County at age 23, April 15, 1861. Present or accounted for until transferred to 2nd Company I, 32nd Regiment N.C. Troops, July 4, 1862.

STRAUGHN, THOMAS J., Private
Resided in Chatham County where he enlisted at age 20, April 15, 1861. Present or accounted for until he died at Yorktown, Virginia, in September, 1861. Cause of death not reported.

TAYLOR, JAMES P., Private
Resided in Chatham County where he enlisted at age 24, April 15, 1861. Present or accounted for until transferred to 2nd Company I, 32nd Regiment N.C. Troops, July 4, 1862.

TORRENCE, RICHMOND P., Private
Born in Moore County and resided in Chatham County where he was by occupation a student prior to enlisting in Chatham County at age 26, April 15, 1861. Present or accounted for until transferred to 2nd Company I, 32nd Regiment N.C. Troops, July 4, 1862.

TURNER, JOEL A., Private
Resided in Chatham County where he enlisted at age 23, April 15, 1861. Present or accounted for until transferred to 2nd Company I, 32nd Regiment N.C. Troops, July 4, 1862.

TYSON, GEORGE W., Private
Resided in Chatham County where he enlisted at age 21, April 15, 1861. Present or accounted for until transferred to 2nd Company I, 32nd Regiment N.C. Troops, July 4, 1862.

TYSOR, JOSEPH C., Corporal
Resided in Chatham County where he enlisted at age 25, April 15, 1861. Mustered in as Private and promoted to Corporal on June 15, 1861. Present or accounted for until wounded in the head at Malvern Hill, Virginia, July 1, 1862. Transferred to 2nd Company I, 32nd Regiment N.C. Troops, July 4, 1862.

TYSOR, THOMAS B., Private
Resided in Chatham County where he enlisted at age 24, April 15, 1861. Present or accounted for until transferred to 2nd Company I, 32nd Regiment N.C. Troops, July 4, 1862.

WARD, JOSHUA H., Private
Resided in Chatham County where he enlisted at age 26, April 15, 1861. Present or accounted for until transferred to 2nd Company I, 32nd Regiment N.C. Troops, July 4, 1862.

WEBSTER, JAMES GALLATIN, Private
Resided in Chatham County where he enlisted at age 24, April 15, 1861. Present or accounted for until he died in hospital at Yorktown, Virginia, January 10, 1862, of disease.

WILSON, WILLIAM R., Private
Born in Hall County, Georgia, and resided in Chatham County where he was by occupation a laborer prior to enlisting in Chatham County at age 30, April 15, 1861. Present or accounted for until discharged on February 24, 1862, by reason of "chronic rheumatism."

WOMBLE, CORNELIUS H., Private
Resided in Chatham County where he enlisted at age 21, April 15, 1861. Present or accounted for until

wounded at Malvern Hill, Virginia, July 1, 1862. Transferred to 2nd Company I, 32nd Regiment N.C. Troops, July 4, 1862, while absent wounded.

WOMBLE, WILLIAM, Private

Resided in Wake or Chatham counties and enlisted in Chatham County at age 20, April 15, 1861. Present or accounted for until transferred to 2nd Company I, 32nd Regiment N.C. Troops, July 4, 1862.

WORKMAN, GEORGE, Private

Resided in Chatham County where he enlisted at age 19, April 15, 1861. Present or accounted for until transferred to 2nd Company I, 32nd Regiment N.C. Troops, July 4, 1862.

MISCELLANEOUS

The following list of names was compiled from primary records which indicate that these men served in the 15th Regiment N.C. Troops but do not specify the company to which they belonged.

BRAILEY, HUGH, Private

Place and date of enlistment not reported. Records of the Federal Provost Marshal dated April 28, 1865, indicate that he was a deserter. No further records.

CHRISTMAN, JOHN, _____

North Carolina pension records indicate he enlisted on August 13, 1864, and was "shot through the head" and killed in Virginia in September, 1864.

KIMBROUGH, I. A., 1st Lieutenant

Place and date of enlistment not reported. A record of the Federal Provost Marshal dated April 24, 1865, states that he was paroled. No further records.

LANNING, WILLIAM, Private

Place and date of enlistment not reported. Deserted to the enemy on or about February 27, 1865. Released on or about March 2, 1865, after taking the Oath of Allegiance.

LEWIS, W. H., Private

Place and date of enlistment not reported. A record of the Federal Provost Marshal dated April 27, 1865, states that he was paroled. No further records.

MORGAN, W. H., Sergeant

Place and date of enlistment not reported. Records of the Federal Provost Marshal dated April 24, 1865, state that he was paroled. No further records.

MOSS, A. G., _____

Resided in Cleveland County. Place and date of enlistment not reported. Deserted to the enemy or was captured at the Great Cacapon River, West Virginia, October 25, 1864. Released on October 26, 1864, after taking the Oath of Allegiance.

PUTMAN, WILLIAM, Sergeant

Place and date of enlistment not reported. Records of the Federal Provost Marshal indicate he was paroled in April, 1865. No further records.

SMULLEN, JOHN, Private

Resided in Cleveland County. Place and date of enlistment not reported. Records of the Federal Provost Marshal indicate that he took the Oath of Allegiance and was released at Point Lookout, Maryland, June 20, 1865.

INDEX

This index contains citations for individuals listed in the foregoing unit rosters and for all persons and places mentioned in the unit histories. Except in instances where a signature or family information was available, personal names are spelled as they were recorded in Confederate records. Corrupted spellings of some names are included with cross-references to the spelling under which the name appears.

Blue Ridge Mountains, 4, 108, 110, 278, 281, 388, 391, 498
Blum, Henry, 415
Blum, Peter, 484
Blunt. *See* Blount
Bobbitt, Burge B., 396
Bobbitt, Gideon C., 397
Bobbitt, Harvey, 148
Bobbitt, J. R., 226
Bobbitt, James M., 187
Bobbitt, Plummer A., 187
Bobbitt, Stephen E., 397
Bobbitt, William H., Jr., 187
Bobbitt, William Henry, Sr., 187
Bodeker, Ferdinand W., 484
Bogan, I. C., 515
Boggan, Walter J., 414
Boggan, William H., 415
Boggs. *See also* Biggs
Boggs, Noah Elias, 536
Boggs, S. M. C., 536
Boggs, William B., 328
Bogue, Jesse, 59
Bogue, Jesse D., 586
Bogue, Z. R., 525
Boiles. *See* Boyles
Bolch. *See also* Belch, Bolick
Bolch, Jacob, 148
Bolch, Salathiel A., 119
Boles. *See also* Boyles
Boles, James D., 338
Bolick. *See also* Bolch, Bulloch, Bullock, Bulluck
Bolick, B. Sidney, 86
Bolick, Noah, 426
Bolick, S. B., 197
Bolton. *See also* Belton
Bolton, H. H., 611
Bolton, John, 397
Bolton, William M., 606
Boman. *See* Bowman
Bond, William R., 197
Bonds, Newton, 426
Bond's Saw Mill, Virginia, 391
Bonner, James M., 568
Bonner, William V., 503, 586
Booe, George W., 338
Booker. *See also* Baker
Booker, George W., 356
Booker, J. C., 66
Booker, Paschall P., 576
Bookout, David H., 426
Boon. *See also* Boone
Boon, James H., 66
Boon, Pinkney, 259
Boon, Sampson, 158
Boon, Stephen, 158
Boon, Thomas, 397
Boon, William, 596
Boone. *See also* Boon
Boone, A. N., 197
Boone, G. A., 197
Boonsboro, Maryland, 107, 277, 387
Booth, Nash, 248

Borcha. *See* Boscha
Bordeker. *See* Bodeker
Borders, James A., 426
Borders, Michael, 426
Borders, William, 426
Bordly, T. B., 525
Borland, Andrew J., 248
Boscha, Giovanni, 484
Boseman. *See also* Bowman, Bowsman, Bozeman
Boseman, James H., 348
Boshamer, Henry R., 319
Bosler, John, 356
Bost. *See also* Bess, Best
Bost, Elias G., 119
Bost, Harvey, 119
Bost, Noah A., 119
Bost, Robert A., 119
Bostick, Daniel J., 265
Bostick, David R., 141, 265
Bostick, Thomas J., 141
Bostick, W. H., 175
Boston. *See* Poston
Boswell, George W., 288
Boswell, Howell, 515
Boswell, James T., 265
Boswell, John A., 266
Boswell, Joseph, 219
Boswell, Peter, 397
Bosworth, Bedford A., 288
Bottom, James A., 187
Bottoms, Joseph C., 505
Bottoms, Richard, 207
Bottoms, William E., 505
Bougue. *See* Bogue
Bounds. *See* Pounds
Bow. *See* Booe
Bowden. *See also* Bowdon
Bowden, Andrew J., 525
Bowden, Bryant, 561
Bowden, J. W., 254
Bowden, John A., 254
Bowden, Louis T., 105
Bowden, Moses B., 254
Bowden, Robert T. D., 254
Bowden, Samuel D., 300
Bowden, William, 606
Bowden, William B., 141, 254
Bowden, William H., 148
Bowden, Willis A., 606
Bowdon. *See also* Bowden
Bowdon, Upton T., 525
Bowen. *See* Bowin
Bower. *See also* Bauer, Bowers, Brower, Power
Bower, Charles, 328
Bowers. *See also* Bower, Powers
Bowers, _____, 288
Bowers, Andrew B., 506
Bowers, David, 475
Bowers, J. A., 33
Bowers, John, 506
Bowers, Lorenzo W., 475
Bowers, Robert D., 197

Bowie. *See* Buie
Bowin, William, 248
Bowland, William, 551
Bowles. *See* Boles, Boyles
Bowlin, Jeremiah, 288
Bowling Green, Virginia, 388
Bowman. *See also* Boseman, Bowsman, Bozeman
Bowman, Cornelius C., 415
Bowman, Elkana L., 119
Bowman, George R., 376
Bowman, J. A., 119
Bowman, Jacob, 21
Bowman, John, 415
Bowman, Lanson, 119
Bowman, M., 577
Bowman, Noah, 119
Bowman, Polycarp C., 119
Bowman, Q. E., 119
Bowman, Samuel, 22
Bowman, Thomas P. 376
Bowman, William, 119
Bowman, Wilson, 119
Bowsman. *See also* Boseman, Bowman, Bozeman
Bowsman, John D., 596
Boxley. *See* Baxley
Boyce, Charles B., 76
Boyce, Hugh, 77
Boyce, John H., 506
Boyce, Kenny, 59
Boyd, B. S., 415
Boyd, Benjamin F., 96
Boyd, David, 77
Boyd, J. J., 77
Boyd, James E., 328
Boyd, James S., 338
Boyd, James T., 300
Boyd, Jesse A., 77, 300
Boyd, John, 300
Boyd, Robert J., 197
Boydton Plank Road, Virginia, 6, 283, 501
Boyers. *See* Bowers
Boyett, Jonas, 141
Boyette, Etheldred D., 506
Boyette, James W., 259
Boykin, Burgess B., 506
Boykin, James M., 436
Boykin, Littleberry W., 504
Boyle, Francis A., 234
Boyles. *See also* Bailes, Bayles, Boles
Boyles, Alexander, 86
Boyles, David A., 376
Boyles, Frank J., 86
Boyles, John, 86
Boyles, John W., 376
Boyles, Joseph, 86
Boyles, William S., 86
Bozeman. *See also* Boseman, Bowman, Bowsman
Bozeman, Isaac, 348
Brabble, Edmund C., 233
Bracey. *See* Bracy

Britt, Alexander, Jr., 158
Britt, Alexander, Sr., 158
Britt, Alva G., 158
Britt, Arick, 158
Britt, Frank J., 406
Britt, Henry L., 158
Britt, James E., 158
Britt, John G., 158
Britt, Thomas A., 504, 506
Britt, W., 455
Britt, William T., 506
Brittain. *See also* Bratten, Britten, Britton, Bruton
Brittain, J. H.,445
Brittain, J. T., 41
Brittain, James, 445
Brittain, Jesse J., 415
Brittain, Joseph McCord, 445
Brittain, O. J., 41
Brittain, Samuel, 41
Brittain, William T., 98
Britten. *See also* Bratten, Brittain, Britton, Bruton
Britten, M., 455
Brittingham, John W., 475
Britton. *See also* Bratten, Brittain, Britten, Bruton
Britton, Andrew J., 506
Britton, Daniel W., 33
Britton, Henry T., 506
Britton, John W., 244
Britton, William E., 506
Broach, Vincent, 319
Broadstreet, Joseph R., 446
Broadway, William Henry, 475
Broadwell, Ruffin, 226
Brocius, William K., 165
Brock. *See also* Brake
Brock, David, 266
Brock, Henry N., 175
Brock, John J., 259
Brockenbrough, J. M., 2-3
Brockwell, A. J., 66
Brockwell, Anderson, 66
Brockwell, George W., 248
Brockwell, James, 248
Brodie. *See also* Braddy, Bradley, Brady
Brodie, Charles E., 606
Brodie, E. G., 165
Brodway. *See* Broadway
Brogden, Benjamin H., 266
Brogden, William G., 33
Brookes, David M., 175
Brooks, Calvin H., 515
Brooks, Cullin C., 515
Brooks, John T., 310
Brooks, Robert D., 611
Brooks, Silas, 187
Brooks, Thomas B., 446
Brooksheer, James, 587
Broom. *See also* Brame
Broom, Ellerson L., 515
Broom, Loyd, 515

Broom, William, 587
Broom, William H., 515
Brosius. *See* Brocius
Broughton. *See* Roughton
Brower. *See also* Bauer, Bower
Brower, A. M., 77
Brower, John A., 416
Brower, William H., 416
Brown. *See also* Bran, Brann
Brown, Bryant, 141
Brown, C., 464
Brown, Calvin N., 120
Brown, Calvin S., 40
Brown, Charles Z., 187
Brown, Columbus W., 300
Brown, Elisha B., 544
Brown, Franklin, 259
Brown, G. J., 349
Brown, G. W., 117
Brown, George, 484
Brown, Greenwood, 561
Brown, Grey L., 346
Brown, Hezekiah, 141
Brown, Isaac, 141
Brown, Jacob, 356
Brown, James, 120, 165
Brown, James M., 118
Brown, James W., 237, 377
Brown, James William, 77, 286, 300
Brown, Jeremiah, 506
Brown, Jesse, 259
Brown, John, 207
Brown, John A., 86
Brown, John T., 506
Brown, John W., 141
Brown, Joseph, 455
Brown, Joshua B., 244
Brown, L. M., 611
Brown, Lucian, 612
Brown, Mike, 141
Brown, Richard, 266
Brown, Robert G., 175
Brown, Rufus E., 300
Brown, Samuel, 120
Brown, Samuel S., 445
Brown, Thomas Kivel, 98
Brown, Thompson, 377
Brown, Wiley D., 577
Brown, William, 215, 377, 397
Brown, William C., 394, 446
Brown, William E., 397
Brown, William J., 11
Brown, William R., 596
Browning, Gastin, 248
Browning, James H., 248
Browning, Jefferson, 248
Browning, John W., 248
Browning, Moses, 248
Browning, Sidney, 248
Browning, William, 248
Brownsville, Maryland, 497
Broyles. *See* Boyles
Bruce, G. W., 475
Bruner, Joseph J., 416

Bruton. *See also* Brittain, Britten, Britton, Burton
Bruton, D. Alexander, 436
Bryan. *See also* Bran, Brann, Bryant, O'Brien, O'Bryan
Bryan, Archibald P., 577
Bryan, Dempsey T., 207
Bryan, Isaac R., 596
Bryan, John A., 577
Bryan, John S., 482
Bryan, Robert H., 259·
Bryan, Thomas K., 141
Bryant. *See also* Bryan
Bryant, Augustus M., 244
Bryant, Benjamin W., 244
Bryant, Cornelius, 475
Bryant, John Quint, 484
Bryant, Robert C., 266
Bryant, Sidney A., 77
Bryant, Thomas, 407
Bryant, W. P., 525
Bryce. *See* Boyce
Bryson, J. M., 207
Buchanan, Frederick A., 416
Buchannon, Micajah T., 132
Buckland, Virginia, 281
Bucknell. *See* Brockwell, Bushnell
Budd, Abram V., 612
Bugg, William P., 148
Buie, John A., 407
Bullard. *See also* Ballard
Bullard, B. A., 158
Bullard, Elseph, 158
Bulloch. *See also* Bolick, Bullock, Bulluck
Bulloch, Robert, 237
Bullock. *See also* Bolick, Bulloch, Bulluck
Bullock, Alex, 158
Bullock, Atlas, 159
Bullock, Charles Baker, 159
Bullock, George Burns, 132
Bullock, Joseph H., 159
Bullock, Ned, 596
Bullock, Richard A., 117, 132
Bullock, Thomas O., 587
Bullock, William A., 159
Bullock, William P. 159
Bulluck. *See also* Bolick, Bulloch, Bullock
Bulluck, John, 596
Bumganer, William C., 310
Bumgarner, T. H., 120
Bunker Hill, West Virginia, 4
Bunn, Archibald C., 606
Bunn, C., 569
Bunn, David, 254
Bunn, Elias, 115, 207
Bunn, William H., 205
Bunting, C. H. C., 254
Bunting, James V., 253
Bunting, T. B., 254
Burch. *See also* Burge
Burch, Angus J., 310

Clarke. *See also* Clark
Clarke, Alexander A., 301
Clarke, B. B., 23
Clarke, Charles D., 484
Clarke, George C., 149
Clarke, Maborn, 357
Clarke, Patrick H., 149
Clarke, William H., 446
Clarke, William P., 465
Clauntz. *See also* Clontz
Clauntz, Jones, 23
Clay, J. M., 42
Clay, James Hervey, 42
Clayton. *See also* Cayton
Clayton, Green J., 551
Clayton, John C., 551
Clayton, William L., 98
Clear. *See* Cler
Clegg, Benjamin F., 612
Clegg, R., 612
Clegg, Thomas A., 612
Clegg, Thomas D., 612
Clegg, William Baxter, 612
Clement. *See also* Clements, Clemmens
Clement, Wiley A., 337
Clements. *See also* Clement, Clemmens
Clements, Amos Gooch, 165
Clements, Anderson, 561
Clements, George R., 67
Clements, James H., 67
Clements, Jesse A., 336
Clements, John R., 67
Clements, William E., 398
Clements, William G., 68
Clemmens. *See also* Clement, Clements
Clemmens, Robert R., 51
Clendenin, George A., 576
Clendenin, Henry M., 578
Clendenin, Joseph N. H., 576
Clendenin, Robert J., 329
Clendenin, William, 329
Cler. *See also* Ceherr, Coier
Cler, Anthony, 357
Clerk. *See* Clark, Clarke
Click. *See also* Clack
Click, Daniel W., 338
Clifton, James Beverly, 503
Clifton, John T., 606
Clinard, Ahart H., 578
Clinard, Randal B., 596
Cline, Ambrose, 175
Cline, Eli P. R., 120
Cline, Henry L., 120
Cline, Jonathan, 120
Cline, Labin Wilson, 175
Cline, Perry R., 120
Cline, William A., 8, 87
Cline, William H., 120
Clingman, Thomas L., 499
Clinton. *See* Clanton
Clock. *See* Clack, Click
Clodfelter, Adam E., 475
Clodfelter, David C., 475
Clodfelter, George R., 537

Clodfelter, Henry, 465
Clodfelter, J., 537
Clodfelter, Jacob H., 465
Cloninger, Alonzo, 338
Cloninger, Elcanah, 120
Clontz. *See also* Clauntz
Clontz, Jeremiah, 516
Clubb, W. J., 357
Clutts. *See* Cutts
Coach. *See* Couch
Cobb, Andrew J., 367
Cobb, Archibald, 378
Cobb, Benjamin F., 587
Cobb, C. R., 78
Cobb, Charles E., 78
Cobb, G. W., 349
Cobb, Gray, 587
Cobb, Howell, 494-497
Cobb, Job, 587
Cobb, Needham Bryan, 395
Cobb, R. C., 426
Cobb, T. R. R., 498
Cobbett. *See* Corbett
Cobble. *See also* Cable, Cauble, Coble, Cobler, Gobble
Cobble, B., 133
Coble. *See also* Cable, Cauble, Cobble, Cobler, Gobble
Coble, Alfred M., 329
Coble, Daniel O., 329
Coble, James, 578
Coble, Willis H., 578
Cobler. *See also* Cobble, Coble
Cobler, Elijah, 368
Cobler, Harvey, 368
Cobler, Robert, 368
Cochrane, John F., 12
Coddington. *See* Covington
Cody, Absalom G., 87
Cody, James, 87
Cody, John, 87
Cody, W. A., 42
Coffey, A., 120
Coffey, Benjamin Morrow, 78
Coffey, John C., 23
Coffield, Joseph Bryant, 504, 587
Cogdill. *See also* Coghill
Cogdill, John, 436
Coggin. *See also* Coggins, Cogins, Scoggin
Coggin, Daniel C., 207
Coggin, James A., 507
Coggin, John J., 215
Coggin, Willie, 215
Coggin, Willis, 215
Coggins. *See also* Coggin, Cogins
Coggins, Joseph J., 596
Coggins, M. L., 198
Coghill. *See also* Cogdill
Coghill, George, 378
Cogins. *See also* Coggin, Coggins
Cogins, Thomas, 349
Cohen. *See* Cehen
Coier. *See also* Ceherr, Cler

Coier, John C., 416
Coke. *See also* Cope
Coke, George H., 116
Coker. *See also* Crocker
Coker, Joseph W., 240
Coker, Spier, 587
Coker, Windsor C., 266
Colberson. *See* Culberson
Cold Harbor, Virginia, 5, 106, 112, 276, 282, 387, 392, 501
Coldwell. *See* Caldwell
Cole. *See also* Cale
Cole, Elijah, 544
Cole, Elisha, 105
Cole, George, 68
Cole, George O., 544
Cole, Isaiah S., 544
Cole, James M., 544
Cole, John, 544
Cole, R. L., 165
Cole, Robert N., 142
Cole, Thomas R., 544
Cole, William David, 249
Cole, William P., 544
Coleman, Abner G., 320
Coleman, Bartlett Y., 368
Coleman, C. A., 23
Coleman, H. G., 78
Coleman, Henry Eaton, 114, 130
Coleman, Milton, 368
Coleman, Nathaniel R., 117
Coleman, Robert L., 96
Coley, Gray J., 570
Coley, Isham, 465
Coley, J. C., 227
Coley, John, 227
Collett, William J., 407
Collier, Joseph, 587
Collin, J., 570
Collins, A. J., 254
Collins, B. F., 198
Collins, Benjamin M., 115, 147
Collins, G. W., 254
Collins, James H., 551
Collins, James S., 149
Collins, Jesse M., 133
Collins, John M., 176
Collins, John W., 552
Collins, Jones, 207, 215
Collins, Joseph, 254
Collins, Lewis C., 378
Collins, Michael, 187
Collins, Peter H., 426
Collins, Peyton C., 207
Collins, Randall P., 159
Collins, Robert, 378
Collins, S. A., 219
Collins, Thomas S., 606
Collins, William T., 607
Colly. *See* Coley
Colquitt, Alfred H., 107, 277
Colston, Raleigh E., 108, 275-276, 386
Colston, William G., 234
Colter, Davidson M., 198

James River, Virginia, 5, 113, 275, 282, 386, 392, 501
Jamison, Emory A., 303
Jamison, James W., 53
Jamison, Jones W., 53
Jamison, Thomas J., 53
Janes. *See* James
Jarrald, Addison, 399
Jarratt's Station, Virginia, 501
Jarrell, A. B., 540
Jarrell, Adam, 529, 590
Jarrell, James M., 261
Jarrell, M., 529
Jarrell, Milton, 540
Jarrell, R. T., 360
Jarrell, W. A., 385
Jarrett. *See also* Garratt, Garrett
Jarrett, James M., 523
Jarrett, M. W., 180, 200
Jarrold. *See* Jarrald, Jarrell
Jarvis, Bryant, 600
Jasper, Henry N., 608
Jaynes. *See* James
Jefferson, James T., 360
Jeffreys. *See also* Jeffries
Jeffreys, Benton, 250
Jeffreys, James Henry, 457
Jeffreys, John G., 292
Jeffreys, S. H., 554
Jeffries. *See also* Jeffreys
Jeffries, James H., 385
Jeffries, Lea, 292
Jemison. *See* Jamison
Jenkins, Aristarchus L., 554
Jenkins, Bennett P., 347
Jenkins, Bradford S., 399
Jenkins, Cornelius, 160
Jenkins, David, 15
Jenkins, Doctrine, 36
Jenkins, Elias S., 554
Jenkins, George F., 399
Jenkins, Hiram, 44
Jenkins, Jacob, 15
Jenkins, Jefferson, 245
Jenkins, Jesse, 173
Jenkins, John F., 400
Jenkins, Jonathan, 554
Jenkins, Joseph, 261
Jenkins, Joseph P., 214
Jenkins, Joseph V., 590
Jenkins, Micah, 498
Jenkins, Milton, 546
Jenkins, Newsom Edward, 395, 400
Jenkins, P. B., 554
Jenkins, Robert Alexander, 135
Jenkins, Robert T., 400
Jenkins, Thomas G., 487
Jenkins, William C., 400
Jenkins, William F., 400
Jenkins, Wilson T., 396
Jennett. *See* Jinnett
Jennings, Isaac, 477
Jennings, James R., 65
Jericho Mills, Virginia, 282

Jernigan, George W., 143
Jernigan, Samuel, 36
Jerome, James A., 518
Jerome, Robert P., 502, 513
Jerrald. *See* Jarrald, Jarrell
Jerregon. *See* Jernigan
Jervis. *See* Jarvis
Jetton, Taylor B., 91
Jetton, William H., 91
Jinnett, John G., 269
Johns. *See also* Jones
Johns, Anthony Benning, Jr., 355
Johnson. *See also* Johnston
Johnson, Addison, 487
Johnson, Andrew, 408, 508
Johnson, B. G., 529
Johnson, Carey, 418
Johnson, Christopher J., 508
Johnson, Daniel L., 44
Johnson, David, 26
Johnson, David G., 563
Johnson, Durrell, 251
Johnson, Edward, 108-109, 111-112, 388, 390-392
Johnson, Elbridge A., 487
Johnson, Eli, 91
Johnson, Eli W., 477
Johnson, Elias, 216
Johnson, Elias J., 245
Johnson, George D. W., 590
Johnson, George Thomas, 509
Johnson, Hardy, 269
Johnson, Harvey M., 91
Johnson, Haywood, 229
Johnson, Henry C., 509
Johnson, J. A., 313
Johnson, J. W., 44, 81
Johnson, James, 115, 135, 322
Johnson, James A., 563
Johnson, James H., 245
Johnson, James M., 590
Johnson, James Samuel, 572
Johnson, John, 26, 457
Johnson, John A., 563
Johnson, John J., 292
Johnson, John R., 229
Johnson, John W., 269, 487
Johnson, Leonidas, 91
Johnson, Levi, 509
Johnson, Marcus R., 245
Johnson, Mathew T., 269
Johnson, Minter G., 613
Johnson, Neill A., 563
Johnson, Robert, 91, 313
Johnson, Robert N., 44
Johnson, S. C., 540
Johnson, Samuel M., 313
Johnson, Solomon, 26
Johnson, Thomas Neal, 16
Johnson, Tobias, 292
Johnson, W. Gaston, 200
Johnson, W. T., 261
Johnson, William, 216
Johnson, William Alexander, 563

Johnson, William Allen, 563
Johnson, William E., 186
Johnson, William J., 509, 608
Johnson, William W., 292
Johnson, Willie, 590
Johnston. *See also* Johnson
Johnston, Alfred, 16
Johnston, Anthony M., 400
Johnston, Charles, 600
Johnston, Francis M., 400
Johnston, George, 572
Johnston, Henry F., 303
Johnston, J. W., 53
Johnston, James C., 53
Johnston, James H., 287, 292
Johnston, James T., 400
Johnston, John Franklin, 100
Johnston, John P., 222
Johnston, John S., 454
Johnston, Joseph E., 275-276, 386, 495
Johnston, Joseph Forney, 118
Johnston, Richard, 457
Johnston, Robert B., 394
Johnston, Robert D., 109-114
Johnston, Thomas Dillard, 445
Johnston, Thomas M., 400
Johnston, Whitmel A., 400
Johnston, William, 322
Johnston, William A., 388, 394, 396
Johnston, Willis R., 400
Joiner. *See* Joyner
Jolie. *See also* Jolley, Jolly
Jolie, D. I., 467
Jolley. *See also* Jolie, Jolly
Jolley, Crawford D. D., 180
Jolley, Stanford W., 180
Jolly. *See also* Jolie, Jolley
Jolly, A. H., 529
Jolly, B. B., 529
Jolly, C. G., 529
Jolly, H. S., 529
Jolly, Johnson J., 487
Jolly, M. M., 529
Jolly, Thomas J., 487
Jolly, Washburn, 529
Jolly, William, 70
Jones. *See also* Johns
Jones, A. T., 448
Jones, Addison, 488
Jones, Alby, 408
Jones, Alexander, 261
Jones, Allen, 600
Jones, Anderson W., 341
Jones, Andrew J., 509
Jones, Anon H., 448
Jones, Asbury N., 180
Jones, B. F., 191
Jones, Craven S., 269
Jones, Cyrus P., 405
Jones, D. D., 540
Jones, D. W., 210
Jones, Daniel, 370
Jones, David C., 379
Jones, David H., 341

Kennan. *See* Kenan
Kennedy. *See also* Canady, Cannaday, Cannady
Kennedy, David R., 488
Kennedy, Elias J., 590
Kennedy, G. G., 554
Kennedy, William, 16, 235
Kennerly. *See* Quinerly
Kenney. *See* Kinney, Kinny
Kennon, William G., 292
Kenouse, Jesse, 518
Kent, David, 342
Kepley, Andrew, 477
Keply, Mathias, 477
Kerns, John Dixon, 16
Kerns, Thomas J., 16
Kernstown, Virginia, 113, 392
Kerr. *See also* Carr, Kehr
Kerr, John B., 303
Kerr, John T., 287, 303
Kerr, Nathaniel R., 292
Kerr, Rufus D., 81
Kerr, William J., 49
Kersey, Lorenzo D., 314
Kershaw, Joseph B., 392
Kesler. *See also* Kestler, Kistler
Kesler, Robert, 477
Kestler. *See also* Kesler, Kistler
Kestler, Alfred, 477
Keuister. *See* Kuester
Key. *See also* Kee, McKee
Key, Abel, 81
Key, G., 152
Keyes, L. S., 601
Keziah, Azer, 518
Keziah, Roberson, 518
Keziah, Samuel B., 518
Kick. *See* Keck
Kiersey. *See* Kersey
Kiles. *See* Kyles
Killian, William S., 123
Kilpatrick. *See also* Kirkpatrick
Kilpatrick, Warren L., 261
Kilpatrick, William F., 81
Kimball, Bartholomew, 152
Kimble, Noah, 601
Kimbrell, James L., 304
Kimbro. *See also* Kimbrough
Kimbro, James W., 292
Kimbro, John T., 292
Kimbro, Rufus, 292
Kimbrough. *See also* Kimbro
Kimbrough, Alexander, 293
Kimbrough, I. A., 616
Kincaid, Cephas G., 91
Kincaid, George W., 40
Kincaid, J. W., 44
Kincaid, Robert, 26
Kincaid, W. J., 40
Kincaid, W. W., 44
Kincaid, William, 26
Kindall. *See* Kendall
Kindley. *See* Kinley
Kindrick. *See* Kendrick

King, A., 191
King, Anthony C., 152
King, Arguile, 53
King, Baxter, 70
King, Bellfield, 70
King, Burwell, 572
King, Campbell C., 16
King, Charles H., 518
King, E., 191
King, Francis M., 143
King, George W., 529
King, H., 53
King, Henry, 572
King, Henry D., 152
King, James, 70
King, James A., 269
King, John, 70
King, John A., 16
King, Joseph, 36
King, M. E., 222
King, Nathaniel E., 400
King, Richard M., 400
King, Rufus, 70
King, T., 191
King, Thomas E., 400
King, W. D., 70
King, Whitfield, 71
King, William C., 251
King, William E., 332
King, William H., 71
King, William J., 608
King, Willis, 71
King and Queen Court House, Virginia, 242
King's Landing, Virginia, 275
King's School House, Virginia, 106, 276
Kingsbury, Charles F., 167
Kinlaw, Pinkney J., 160
Kinley, William, 200
Kinney. *See also* Kinny, McKinney
Kinney, A. D., 44, 430
Kinney, B. R., 430
Kinney, Benjamin, 16
Kinney, Mebane, 332
Kinny. *See also* Kinney, McKinney
Kinny, Oliver, 579
Kinston, M., 26
Kinston, North Carolina, 1-2, 499
Kirby. *See also* Irby
Kirby, Wiley L., 546
Kirby, William H., 418
Kirk, James F., 468
Kirkendall, Newton, 449
Kirkland, John, 251
Kirkland, W. W., 4-5, 281, 499-501
Kirkman, A. C., 430
Kirkman, Lafayette, 261
Kirkpatrick. *See also* Kilpatrick
Kirkpatrick, James F., 304
Kirksey. *See* Kersey
Kiser, Henry, 91
Kiser, Hiram Abram, 91
Kiser, Jacob, 91

Kiser, John A., 92
Kisort. *See also* Casort, Cozart
Kisort, Willie, 314
Kistler. *See also* Kesler, Kestler
Kistler, Paul H., 53
Kitchin, William Hodge, 167, 200, 218
Kittrell, Egbert P., 167
Kittrell, Henry Clay, 136
Kline. *See* Cline
Knapp. *See also* Knott
Knapp, Theodore Judson, 7, 58
Knight. *See also* McKnight
Knight, Edward E., 585
Knight, George W., 245
Knight, John J., 613
Knight, Thomas W., 235
Knight, William M., 439
Knipper, Thomas, 16
Knott. *See also* Knapp, Knotts
Knott, Beverly F., 136
Knott, George F., 136
Knott, James W., 136
Knott, John H., 379
Knott, John Henry, 136
Knott, William H., 136
Knotts. *See also* Knott
Knotts, Harrison B., 518
Knotts, Wilson, 418
Knowles, David J., 269
Knowles, Stephen, 269
Knox. *See also* Knoy
Knox, James F., 304
Knox, John D., 304
Knox, John H., 76
Knox, John N., 304
Knox, Joseph M., 304
Knox, Thomas N., 304
Knox, William H., 81
Knoy. *See also* Knox
Knoy, William, 408
Koonts. *See also* Cutts
Koonts, Abraham, 601
Koonts, Casper, 601
Koonts, David, 601
Koonts, Ezekiel, 477
Koonts, William F., 478
Kreiger, Charles, 396, 488
Kuester, Ferdinand, 488
Kurfees, Caleb W., 342
Kurfees, Franklin J., 342
Kurfees, Zedock C., 342
Kuter. *See also* Keeter
Kuter, James L., 36
Kyle. *See* Cale, Kale, Kyles
Kyles. *See also* Cale, Kale
Kyles, Fielding, 53
Kyles, James, 100
Kyles, John, 53
Kyles, William, 53

L

Lacey's Springs, Virginia, 113
Lackey, Dixon, 430

Massenburg, Archibald Cargill, 503, 543, 609
Massey. *See also* Masi, Massie
Massey, Ambrose M., 520
Massey, Burwell G., 270
Massey, Daniel F., 270
Massey, John J., 270
Massey, Rainey C., 293
Massey, West, Jr., 270
Massey, William, 270
Massey, William C., 270
Massie. *See also* Masi, Massey
Massie, James W., 242
Massinburg. *See* Massenburg
Mastello. *See* Mosteller
Matheson, John S., 55
Mathews. *See also* Mathis, Matthews
Mathews, Calvin, 351
Mathews, Elmer, 554
Mathews, James, 222
Mathews, John H., 242
Mathews, John R., 401
Mathews, Noel, 270
Mathews, T. H., 222
Mathis. *See also* Mathews, Matthews
Mathis, James M., 333
Mathis, John, 124
Mathis, Kedar L., 144
Mathis, Noel, 270
Mathis, Richard, 270
Mathis, Wells, 270
Matlock, William, 323
Mattaponi River, Virginia, 388
Mattax. *See also* Maddox
Mattax, James, 546
Matthews. *See also* Mathews, Mathis
Matthews, Alexander, 564
Matthews, David H., 564
Matthews, Frederick J., 564
Matthews, George E., 256
Matthews, James, 256
Matthews, James B., 564
Matthews, John R., 509
Matthews, Josiah, 564
Matthews, Martin H., 564
Matthews, William, 136
Matthis. *See* Mathis
Maulden. *See also* Mulder
Maulden, N. M., 469
Mauncy. *See* Mooney
Maxwell, Robert A., 380
May. *See also* Mayes, Mays
May, Anthony, 554
May, B. F., 256
May, Caleb E., 333
May, Henderson, 333
May, J. D., 261
May, James S., 261
May, John S., 256
May, Joshua B., 410
May, Josiah A., 609
May, S. K., 256
May, Theophilus Celkert, 256
May, Urban C., 343

Mayberry. *See* Mabery, Mabry
Mayes. *See also* Mace, May, Mays, Mize, Muse
Mayes, William S., 251
Mayfield, James, 431
Mayfield, James H., 153
Mayfield, John W., 147
Mayhan, William F., 251
Mayhew, Jacob, 530
Maynard, Henry C., 293
Maynard, Richard L., 333
Mayo, Benjamin B., 591
Mayo, Berry, 591
Mayo, James R., 351
Mays. *See also* Mace, May, Mayes, Mize, Muse
Mays, J. C., 458
Mays, James A., 509
Mays, T. R., 580
Meacham. *See also* Meachan, Meachum, Micham
Meacham, James A., 614
Meachan. *See also* Meacham, Meachum, Micham
Meachan, Henry, 541
Meachum. *See also* Meacham, Meachan, Micham
Meachum, William Gaston, 414
Mead. *See also* Meade, Mode
Mead, Joseph, 541
Meade. *See also* Mead, Mode
Meade, George, 4, 281, 499-500
Meador, William W., 371
Meadows, Gideon, 216
Meadows, John D., 410
Meadows, John Steven, 168
Meadows, L. P., 168
Meadows, Thomas P., 169
Meadows, William, 216
Means, John S., 55
Means, Theophilus H., 514
Means, William N. M., 49
Meares. *See also* Mears, Myers
Meares, James B., 602
Meares, R. D., 602
Meares, Stephen B., 602
Mears. *See also* Meares, Myers
Mears, Dwight H., 161
Mears, Hiram, 602
Mears, Joel, 440
Mears, John C., 161
Mears, William, 602
Mebane. *See also* McBane
Mebane, William N., 286, 361
Mecham. *See* Meacham, Meachum
Mechanicsville, Virginia, 106, 276, 386-387, 495
Medford, James R., 351
Medley, Benjamin Frank, 420
Medley, John, 602
Medlin, De Berry, 520
Medow. *See* Meador
Meekins, Frederic, 235

Megee. *See also* McGee, McGehee, McGhee
Megee, Jonas M., 124
Meggs, Joseph, 238
Meggs, William, 238
Mehegan, Robert N., 352
Melchor, C. G., 469
Melchor, Leonard E., 470
Melchor, William H., 470
Melton, Atlas D., 470
Melton, E. A., 45
Melton, Green, 470
Melton, Henry H., 361
Melton, Isaac, 489
Melton, J. C., 449
Melton, J. M., 449
Melton, James, 546
Melton, James R., 602
Melton, John W. T., 602
Melton, Joseph, 470
Melton, Neill, 547
Melton, W. H. A., 45
Memms. *See* Munds
Mercer. *See also* Messer
Mercer, John P., 161
Meridith, J. M., 371
Merrett. *See* Merritt, Merritte
Merrill, Benjamin W., 449
Merrimon, Augustus P., 449
Merrimon, Branch A., 449
Merrimon, Emory H., 449
Merritt. *See also* Merritte
Merritt, Asa, 235
Merritt, George, 235
Merritt, George B., 201
Merritt, James Y., 71
Merritt, Leonidas J., 611
Merritt, Louis S., 270
Merritt, Robert Hooks, 270
Merritt, Samuel N., 82
Merritt, Solomon, 294
Merritte. *See also* Merritt
Merritte, William H., 555
Messer. *See also* Mercer
Messer, Alexander, 440
Messer, Henry, 564
Meyers. *See* Myers
Michael. *See also* Mitchel, Mitchell
Michael, Henry, 124, 352
Michael, Peter, 124
Micham. *See also* Meacham, Meachan, Meachum
Micham, Hugh C., 431
Michaux, John P., 27
Michell. *See* Mitchel, Mitchell
Micrary. *See also* McCrary, McRary
Micrary, William, 352
Middleton, Isaac J., 144
Miers. *See* Myers
Miles. *See also* Mills
Miles, Bedford B., 520
Miles, James W., 201
Miles, Lawson H., 361
Millar. *See also* Miller

Pritchard, Jeremiah O., 202
Pritchard, Joseph J., 38
Pritchet. See also Fitchett, Pritchard, Pritchett, Privett
Pritchet, T. H., 381
Pritchett. See also Fitchett, Pritchard, Pritchet, Privett
Pritchett, B. Y., 459
Pritchett, Bartlett Y., 381
Privett. See also Pritchard, Pritchet, Pritchett
Privett, E. B., 471
Privett, John W., 603
Privett, Joseph Bryant, 257
Privett, William R., 264
Privett, Zachariah F., 211
Probst. See Propst
Proctor, Andrew, 580
Proctor, Herbert, 251
Proctor, John A., 251
Proctor, John R., 63
Proctor, William, 541
Proctor, William H., 353
Proffit, Luther C., 362
Propst, J. H., 170
Propst, John, 154
Propst, L. H., 102
Propst, Noah L., 125
Pruden, John, 511
Pruden, Nathaniel, 511
Pruden, Samuel T., 511
Pruett. See also Pruitt, Prutt, Puett
Pruett, Ransom, 46
Pruitt. See also Pruett, Prutt, Puett
Pruitt, Squire, 324
Prutt. See also Pruett, Pruitt, Puett
Prutt, H., 479
Pryor, Thomas A., 402
Pucket. See also Pickett, Puckett
Pucket, E. W., 29
Puckett. See also Pickett, Pucket
Puckett, Julius J., 56
Puckett, William C., 56
Puckett, William Henry, 556
Puett. See also Pruett, Pruitt, Prutt
Puett, John Wesley, 29
Pugh, William J., 397
Pullen, W. P., 223
Pulliam, James N., 372
Pulman. See Putman
Purcell. See also Pernell
Purcell, James T., 372
Purcell, William W., 372
Purser, Hugh, 471
Purtle. See Pirtle
Putman. See also Pitman, Pittman, Putnam
Putman, Devany, 182
Putman, William, 616
Putnam. See also Pitman, Pittman, Putman, Putney
Putnam, A. C., 531
Putnam, A. M., 531
Putnam, Arthur, 531

Putnam, B. H., 531
Putnam, E. L., 531
Putnam, J. G. L., 531
Putnam, J. L., 531
Putnam, James T., 531
Putnam, L. W., 531
Putnam, Leonard M., 532
Putnam, M. H., 532
Putnam, Martin, 541
Putnam, Martin V., 532
Putnam, Rufus K., 532
Putnam, Samuel, 541
Putnam, Sidney G., 532
Putnam, Thomas J., 532
Putnam, William A., 532
Putney. See also Putnam
Putney, William H., Jr., 489
Puttick, James A., 490
Pyle, Andrew J., 334

Q

Qualls, Henry S., 193
Qualls, James, 193
Query, R. L., 18
Query, S. F., 18
Quick, James E., 235
Quickel, Levi H., 93
Quin. See also Cain, O'Quin, Quinn
Quin, William F., 144
Quincey, George R., 154
Quinerly, James E., 262
Quinerly, John P., 262
Quinerly, Lewis B., 262
Quinerly, Stephen S., 258
Quinn. See also Cain, O'Quin, Quin
Quinn, Anonymous W., 182
Quinn, Robert S., 262

R

Rabb. See Robb
Raben. See also Raborn, Raiban
Raben, Samuel W., 344
Raborn. See also Raben, Raiban
Raborn, M. D., 18
Raccoon Ford, Virginia, 111, 391
Rachford. See Ratchford
Rackley, Joseph R., 271
Rackley, Joshua A., 271
Rackley, L. D., 211
Radford, James E., 239
Radford, Theodore, 231
Ragan, Epluribus Unum, 574
Ragged Island, Virginia, 275
Ragle, Selita, 295
Ragsdale, Daniel, 421
Raiban. See also Raben, Raborn
Raiban, Arman, 162
Raines. See Rains
Rainey. See also Raney
Rainey, John P., Jr., 309
Rainey, Josiah N., 316
Rainey, William W., 309
Rains, G. J., 494

Rains, James, 324
Raker. See also Raper
Raker, David, 411
Raleigh. See Rawley
Raleigh, North Carolina, 1, 287, 297, 309, 318, 396, 404, 413, 424, 434, 444, 453, 463, 482, 523, 610
Raleigh & Gaston Railroad, 253
Ralston. See Alston
Ramsay. See also Ramsey
Ramsay, Allen D., 511
Ramsay, John, 362
Ramsay, Walter Jones, 490
Ramseur, David P., 395
Ramseur, John F., 93
Ramseur, John M., 93
Ramseur, Oliver A., 85
Ramseur, Stephen D., 108, 110, 112-113, 388-393
Ramseur, Theodore J., 93
Ramseur, Walter G., 93
Ramsey. See also Ramsay
Ramsey, Edward B., 614
Ramsey, James C., 520
Ramsey, John, 381
Ramsey, Jonas, 46
Ramsey, Nathan Alexander, 614
Ramsey, R. Nelson, 93
Ramsey, Richard, 381
Ramsey, William S., 615
Ranaleburg, North Carolina, 297
Randal. See also Randall, Randle
Randal, Joseph W., 451
Randall. See also Randal, Randle
Randall, J. A., 432
Randall, J. P., 432
Randall, John C., 432
Randle. See also Randal, Randall
Randle, Edmund D., 471
Randolph, James B., 504
Raney. See also Rainey
Raney, C. W., 170
Raney, George, 170
Raney, James R., 574
Ranford, William, 262
Ransdell, George W., 609
Ransdell, Sylvester S., 609
Ransom, Robert, 498-499
Raper. See also Draper, Raker
Raper, John W., 592
Rapidan River, Virginia, 4, 110-111, 281, 391, 499-500
Rapidan Station, Virginia, 391
Rappahannock River, Virginia, 2, 4, 108-109, 111, 278-279, 281, 388-389, 391, 498-500
Rash, J. C., 316
Ratchford, E. C., 18
Ratliff, James C., 362
Ratliff, W. T., 471
Rawles. See Rawls
Rawley, Hugh S., 459
Rawley, J. W., 459
Rawley, Taylor L., 376, 459